D1297579

GRADE 7 | TEACHER'S EDITION

myPerspectives®

ENGLISH LANGUAGE ARTS

SAVVAS
LEARNING COMPANY

Savvas Learning Company LLC, 15 East Midland Avenue, Paramus, NJ 07652

Photo locators denoted as follows: Top (T), Center (C), Bottom (B), Left (L), Right (R), Background (Bkgd)

Cover: © vikka/Shutterstock; T3: londoneye/Getty Images; T4: Artishok/Shutterstock; T5B: PathDoc/Shutterstock; T5B: Franck Boston/Shutterstock; T19: Victoria Kisel/Shutterstock; T20: karandaev/fotolia; T23: Jojje/Shutterstock; T25: Nikada/Getty Images; T26B: Creativa Images/Shutterstock; T32: Monkey Business Images/Shutterstock; T33B: Hocus Focus Studio/Getty Images; T34: artagent/Fotolia; T5B: Derek Latta/E+/Getty Images; T5B: OJO Images Ltd/Alamy

ISBN-13: 978-1-418-37103-6
ISBN-10: 1-418-37103-3
3 21

Welcome!

myPerspectives is a student-centered English Language Arts program that embraces culturally responsive learning through diverse representation of literature, authors, characters, cultures, and themes. The program uniquely provides many opportunities for students to use their voices as they share their lived experiences, allows them to make choices in their learning, and gives them the opportunity to ask critical questions of the texts, the teacher, and each other. *myPerspectives* is built on the foundation of culturally responsive instruction in that the program focuses on what we do with students and how they interact with and learn from each other.

Ernest Morrell, Ph.D., helped inform the development of *myPerspectives* to ensure the program fosters a polyvocal classroom that encourages students to talk with each other, learn from each other, and more importantly, bring knowledge from their different backgrounds and cultures to enrich critical literacy in the classroom. The texts, Essential Questions, and learning tasks encourage discussions that allow students to draw upon their prior experiences, diverse identities, varied experiences, and the richness of their cultural backgrounds. This active learning environment brings students together as they develop intercultural competence, learn from each other, and gain the confidence that allows them to be agents of change.

myPerspectives honors student choice and voice as students respond to activities using their own experiences, perform research in response to a prompt or task that they choose, and complete project-based tasks in a format of their choosing. Allowing students to make decisions in their learning and apply their experiences affirms cultural identities, fosters positive outcomes, and encourages growth and achievement through critical thinking and application.

We hope your students enjoy using this program as they develop their own perspectives and learn from each other.

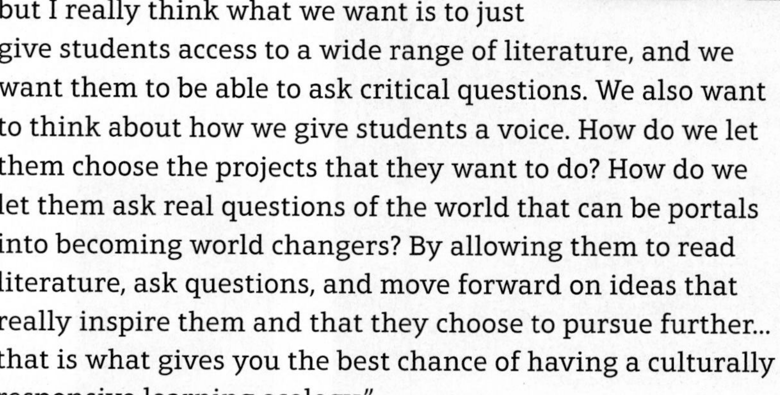

"When I think of culturally responsive instruction, I think of three pillars: there's representation, there's intercultural understanding, and there's voice. The representation in terms of multicultural literature is a key component, but I really think what we want is to just give students access to a wide range of literature, and we want them to be able to ask critical questions. We also want to think about how we give students a voice. How do we let them choose the projects that they want to do? How do we let them ask real questions of the world that can be portals into becoming world changers? By allowing them to read literature, ask questions, and move forward on ideas that really inspire them and that they choose to pursue further... that is what gives you the best chance of having a culturally responsive learning ecology."

—Dr. Ernest Morrell

Experts' Perspectives

myPerspectives is informed by a team of respected experts whose experiences working with students and study of instructional best practices have positively impacted education. From their views on the evolving role of the teacher to how students learn in a digital age, our authors bring new ideas, innovations, and strategies that transform teaching and learning in today's competitive and interconnected world.

Ernest Morrell, Ph.D.

is the Coyle Professor of Literacy Education and the Inaugural Director of the Center for Literacy Education at the University of Notre Dame. He was formerly Macy Professor of English Education and Director of the Institute for Urban and Minority Education at Teachers College, Columbia University. Dr. Morrell is also past-president of the National Council of Teachers of English, a Fellow of the American Educational Research Association (AERA), and an appointed member of International Literacy Association's Literacy Research Panel.

Dr. Morrell works with schools, districts, and families across the country to infuse social and emotional learning, digital media, culturally responsive instruction, and multicultural literature into literacy practices aimed at developing powerful readers and writers among all students. Dr. Morrell has influenced the development of *myPerspectives* in Assessment, Writing & Research, Student Engagement, and Collaborative Learning.

Elfrieda Hiebert, Ph.D.

is President and CEO of TextProject, a nonprofit that provides resources to support higher reading levels. She is also a research associate at the University of California, Santa Cruz. Dr. Hiebert has worked in the field of literacy, language, and culture for almost 50 years, first as a teacher's aide and teacher in California's San Joaquin Valley and, subsequently, as a teacher and researcher. Her research addresses how fluency, vocabulary, and knowledge can be fostered through appropriate texts. Dr. Hiebert has influenced the development of *myPerspectives* in Vocabulary, Text Complexity, and Assessment.

Kelly Gallagher, M.Ed.

has been a high school English teacher for 35 years. Twenty-five years ago, he was a founding member of the first Puente Project site in Orange County, a program which has helped numerous underrepresented students make it into universities and colleges. He is the former co-director of the South Basin Writing Project at California State University, Long Beach, and the former president of the Secondary Reading Group for the International Literacy Association. Gallagher, who has worked with teachers throughout the United States as well as internationally, is the author of several books on adolescent literacy, most notably *Readicide: How Schools Are Killing Reading and What You Can Do About It* and *Write Like This*. His latest book, co-written with Penny Kittle, is *180 Days: Two Teachers and the Quest to Engage and Empower Adolescents*. Gallagher has influenced the development of *myPerspectives* in Writing, Close Reading, and the Role of Teachers.

Jim Cummins, Ph.D.

is a Professor Emeritus in the Department of Curriculum, Teaching, and Learning at the University of Toronto. His research focuses on literacy development in school contexts characterized by cultural and linguistic diversity. In recent years, he has been working with teachers to identify ways in which they can connect the curriculum to students' lives and increase students' active engagement with literacy. Dr. Cummins has influenced the development of *myPerspectives* in English Language Learner and English Language Development support.

Contents

myPerspectives
ENGLISH LANGUAGE ARTS

Each unit focuses on an engaging topic related to the Essential Question.

UNIT 1 Generations

UNIT INTRODUCTION

WHOLE-CLASS LEARNING

SMALL-GROUP LEARNING

ESSENTIAL QUESTION: What can one generation learn from another?

An Essential Question frames all unit activities and discussions.

 INDEPENDENT LEARNING

These selections can be accessed via the Interactive Student Edition.

 PERFORMANCE-BASED ASSESSMENT PREP

 PERFORMANCE-BASED ASSESSMENT

UNIT REFLECTION

DIGITAL PERSPECTIVES

- Unit Introduction Videos
- Media Selections
- Modeling Videos
- Selection Audio Recordings

Additional digital resources can be found in:

- Interactive Student Edition
- *my*Perspectives+

All unit activities are backwards-designed to the Performance-Based Assessment.

Grades 6–8 are intentionally designed with five units allowing students ample opportunity to learn the routines of the program. Doing so allows students to develop skills in preparation for the rigor and expectations of high school, which is critical at these grades.

The Launch Text introduces a perspective on the unit topic.

Teachers lead the shared reading experience, providing modeling and support, as students begin exploring perspectives on the unit topic.

Students encounter diverse perspectives on the unit topic, working in collaborative teams.

UNIT 2 A Starry Home

UNIT INTRODUCTION

WHOLE-CLASS LEARNING

SMALL-GROUP LEARNING

Students self-select a text to explore an aspect of the unit topic and share their learning with the class.

INDEPENDENT LEARNING

POETRY
Science-Fiction Cradlesong
C. S. Lewis

WEB ARTICLE
UFO Sightings and News
Benjamin Radford

PERSUASIVE ESSAY
from Packing for Mars
Mary Roach

SCIENCE ARTICLE
Trip to Mars Could Damage Astronauts' Brains
Laura Sanders

These selections can be accessed via the Interactive Student Edition.

PERFORMANCE-BASED ASSESSMENT PREP

PERFORMANCE-BASED ASSESSMENT

UNIT REFLECTION

DIGITAL PERSPECTIVES

- Unit Introduction Videos
- Media Selections
- Modeling Videos
- Selection Audio Recordings

Additional digital resources can be found in:

- Interactive Student Edition
- *my*Perspectives+

The Launch Text models the mode of writing that will be at the core of the Performance-Based Assessment.

Performance Tasks build toward and prepare students for the Unit Performance-Based Assessment.

UNIT  Turning Points

UNIT INTRODUCTION

 WHOLE-CLASS LEARNING

 SMALL-GROUP LEARNING

ESSENTIAL QUESTION: What can cause a sudden change in someone's life?

INDEPENDENT LEARNING

REFLECTIVE ESSAY
Little Things Are Big
Jesús Colón

NEWS ARTICLE
Profile: Malala Yousafzai
BBC

BIOGRAPHY
Noor Inayat Khan
from Women Heroes of WWII
Kathryn J. Atwood

SHORT STORY
A Retrieved Reformation
O. Henry

These selections can be accessed via the Interactive Student Edition.

PERFORMANCE-BASED ASSESSMENT PREP

PERFORMANCE-BASED ASSESSMENT

UNIT REFLECTION

DIGITAL PERSPECTIVES

- Unit Introduction Videos
- Media Selections
- Modeling Videos
- Selection Audio Recordings

Additional digital resources can be found in:

- Interactive Student Edition
- *my*Perspectives+

Students pull together their notes, evidence, completed activities, and Performance Tasks to prepare for the Performance-Based Assessment.

UNIT 4 People and the Planet

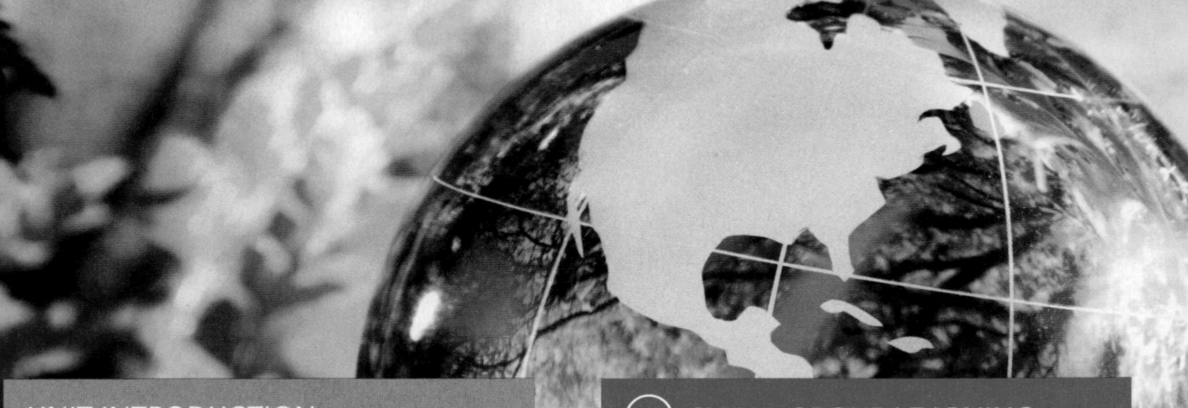

Comparing a text and media version of classic literature deepens the learning experience and develops critical skills.

A rich array of media selections engage students in multi-modal learning.

UNIT INTRODUCTION

WHOLE-CLASS LEARNING

SMALL-GROUP LEARNING

INDEPENDENT LEARNING

These selections can be accessed via the Interactive Student Edition.

PERFORMANCE-BASED ASSESSMENT PREP

PERFORMANCE-BASED ASSESSMENT

UNIT REFLECTION

DIGITAL PERSPECTIVES

- Unit Introduction Videos
- Media Selections
- Modeling Videos
- Selection Audio Recordings

Additional digital resources can be found in:

- Interactive Student Edition
- *my*Perspectives+

Digital resources, including editable worksheets, can be found in *my*Perspectives+.

UNIT 5 Facing Adversity

UNIT INTRODUCTION

WHOLE-CLASS LEARNING

SMALL-GROUP LEARNING

ESSENTIAL QUESTION: How do we overcome obstacles?

INDEPENDENT LEARNING

These selections can be accessed via the Interactive Student Edition.

PERFORMANCE-BASED ASSESSMENT

UNIT REFLECTION

Unit Reflection allows students to revisit learning goals and review skills and content learned.

DIGITAL PERSPECTIVES

- Unit Introduction Videos
- Media Selections
- Modeling Videos
- Selection Audio Recordings

Additional digital resources can be found in:

- Interactive Student Edition
- *my*Perspectives+

myPerspectives Components

myPerspectives is perfect for **distance learning**—whether your students are in class, working remotely, or a combination of the two—because all program resources are online. What's more, Savvas Realize integrates with multiple platforms so you can access content easily.

VIDEO LIBRARY

Skills, background, TED Talks, Crash Course Literature, and multimodal selections

NOVELS

Recommended texts and Study Guides for student choice

DIGITAL TEXTS

Interactive reading selections and lessons

STUDENT RESOURCES

Digital Interactive & PDF Student Edition
Consumable Interactive Student Edition
Digital Novels Library
Collaboration Center Modeling Videos
Writing Gallery Videos & Tutorials
Skills Reinforcement Videos
EssayScorer
Plagiarism Checker
Graphic Organizers
Writing Rubrics and Models
Interactive Lessons (Writing, Grammar, Research, Speaking & Listening, Vocabulary)

DIFFERENTIATED INSTRUCTION

Leveled Texts
Spanish Translations
English & Spanish Audio Summaries
Reteach & Practice Activities
High-Interest Readings
Multilingual Glossary

CURRENT EVENTS

Daily podcasts powered by Listenwise

DISCUSSION BOARD

Anytime online discussion forum

LEVELED TEXTS

Varied reading levels to reach all students

TEACHER RESOURCES

Digital Teacher's Edition with hyperlinked resources
Print & PDF Teacher's Edition
Distance Learning Implementation Videos
Distance Learning Lesson Planning Guide
Customizable Lesson Plans
Live Chat, 24/7 Tutorials, Webinars
Professional Development Videos
myPerspectives+ Digital Resources
Lessons Plans for Novels
Wiriting Worksheets (English & Spanish)
Grammar Practice Worksheets (English & Spanish)
Hook & Inspire Texts

ASSESSMENT & REPORTING

Selection Tests
Extension Selection Tests
Beginning-of, Mid-, & End-of-Year Tests
Extension Beginning-of, Mid-, End-of-Year Tests
Performance-Based Assessments
Unit Tests with Auto-Assigned Remediation
ExamView® Installer with Customizable Test Banks
Student/Class/District Reporting
High Stakes Test Prep Banks

Reach ALL Students Through the Unit Design

The *myPerspectives* unit allows students to share their voices as they explore different perspectives on an Essential Question. As students discuss the texts and the Essential Questions, they will develop their own perspectives and become aware of those of their classmates. During this process, they will draw on their diverse backgrounds, develop a deeper respect for others' differences, and enhance their sense of empathy.

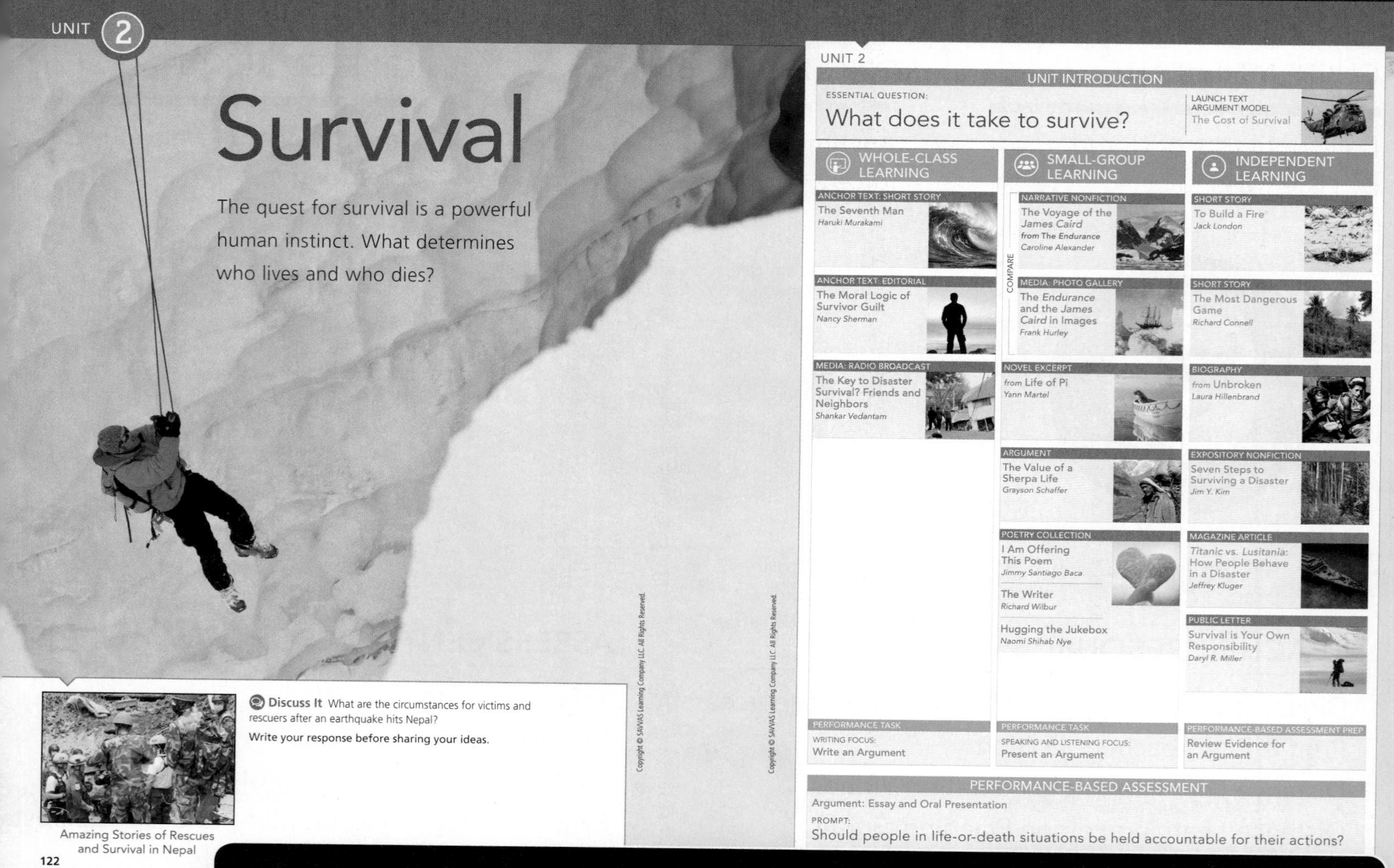

UNIT 2

Survival

The quest for survival is a powerful human instinct. What determines who lives and who dies?

Amazing Stories of Rescues and Survival in Nepal

Discuss It What are the circumstances for victims and rescuers after an earthquake hits Nepal?

Write your response before sharing your ideas.

UNIT 2

UNIT INTRODUCTION

ESSENTIAL QUESTION:

What does it take to survive?

LAUNCH TEXT ARGUMENT MODEL
The Cost of Survival

WHOLE-CLASS LEARNING	SMALL-GROUP LEARNING	INDEPENDENT LEARNING
ANCHOR TEXT: SHORT STORY The Seventh Man *Haruki Murakami*	NARRATIVE NONFICTION The Voyage of the *James Caird* *from The Endurance* *Caroline Alexander*	SHORT STORY To Build a Fire *Jack London*
ANCHOR TEXT: EDITORIAL The Moral Logic of Survivor Guilt *Nancy Sherman*	COMPARE MEDIA: PHOTO GALLERY The *Endurance* and the *James Caird* in Images *Frank Hurley*	SHORT STORY The Most Dangerous Game *Richard Connell*
MEDIA: RADIO BROADCAST The Key to Disaster Survival? Friends and Neighbors *Shankar Vedantam*	NOVEL EXCERPT from Life of Pi *Yann Martel*	BIOGRAPHY from Unbroken *Laura Hillenbrand*
	ARGUMENT The Value of a Sherpa Life *Grayson Schaffer*	EXPOSITORY NONFICTION Seven Steps to Surviving a Disaster *Jim Y. Kim*
	POETRY COLLECTION I Am Offering This Poem *Jimmy Santiago Baca* The Writer *Richard Wilbur* Hugging the Jukebox *Naomi Shihab Nye*	MAGAZINE ARTICLE *Titanic* vs. *Lusitania*: How People Behave in a Disaster *Jeffrey Kluger*
		PUBLIC LETTER Survival is Your Own Responsibility *Daryl R. Miller*
PERFORMANCE TASK WRITING FOCUS: Write an Argument	PERFORMANCE TASK SPEAKING AND LISTENING FOCUS: Present an Argument	PERFORMANCE-BASED ASSESSMENT PREP Review Evidence for an Argument

PERFORMANCE-BASED ASSESSMENT

Argument: Essay and Oral Presentation

PROMPT:

Should people in life-or-death situations be held accountable for their actions?

SOCIAL AND EMOTIONAL LEARNING

Whether working together or alone, students will develop real-world skills, such as:

- Setting Goals
- Building Relationships
- Responsible Behavior
- Problem Solving
- Making Decisions
- Self-Motivation
- Reflecting

UNIT INTRODUCTION

- The **Essential Question** draws ALL students in as they **share** their **ideas, backgrounds,** and **lived experiences** to set the stage for learning.
- The unit opener video and discussion prompt **spark students' interests** as they begin to **build knowledge** on the unit theme or topic.
- An accessible **Launch Text** provides a model for the unit's writing mode.
- Students **set goals** and high expectations for themselves as they develop **responsibility for their learning.**

WHOLE-CLASS LEARNING

- Teachers **model** how to **close read** and **analyze complex texts** with anchor texts.
- Teachers **lead discussions** and model important behaviors as students **ask questions** of each other and the teacher.

PERFORMANCE TASK

- Students are guided through the **writing process** as they write, use feedback to revise, and **produce high-quality** work through a Writing Performance Task.

SMALL-GROUP LEARNING

- Students work **collaboratively** as they read texts and complete projects, **holding each other accountable** in supportive ways.
- As a group, **students choose** how to **deliver projects,** leveraging the **diverse learning** styles, **unique backgrounds,** and **interests** of individuals in the group.

PERFORMANCE TASK

- Students **collaboratively** share their ideas and learning as they **develop formal presentations, mock trials, debates,** or other activities through a Speaking & Listening Performance Task.

INDEPENDENT LEARNING

- Students **choose** a text to **read and analyze independently.**
- Teachers **advise** and **encourage** students as they implement **close-reading** strategies.

SHARE INDEPENDENT LEARNING

- Students **reflect** on, **evaluate,** and **share** the information they gain from independently reading a **self-selected text.**

PERFORMANCE-BASED ASSESSMENT

- Students **push themselves academically** as they gather their notes and learning from the unit to write and present a **Performance-Based Assessment.**

UNIT REFLECTION

- Students **reflect on their goals,** the texts they read, and what they **learned from their peers,** as they assess **personal growth** and **development.**

Hook & Inspire Your Students

The Hook & Inspire features include suggestions for connecting classic texts with students' interests, knowledge, and culture through the use of videos, move clips, music, and other digital content. Pair these resources with *myPerspectives* to help your students make connections between the classics and their lives today!

HOOK& INSPIRE

Inspired by the *myPerspectives* program authors!

Kelly Gallagher, M.Ed.
Ernest Morrell, Ph.D.

Provides teachers with ideas for engaging students' interest, Into, Through, and Beyond the core instruction.

Hooks

Engage your students' imaginations and connect them to the text with these suggested "hooks." Use any or all of them throughout the lesson.

Into
Choose from among these ideas to launch students into the story.

- **"Crazy," Song by Gnarls Barkley**
  Play the official video of this hit song to get students thinking about questions of sanity and madness.
- **A Brief History of Goths (myPerspectives Video Library)**
  Share this video essay about the roots of Gothic literature—of which this story is a prime example—and "Goth" culture.
- **Opera Production Photos**
  Show students these photos of the San Francisco Opera's adaptation of Poe's tale and invite them to make predictions about the story's characters and plot.

Through
Sustain student interest by using any or all of these ideas.

- **Scene from the Short Film "The Fall of the House of Usher"**
  After students have read paragraphs 1 and 2, in which the narrator describes his

Includes short passages aligned to the skills being taught in the core selection.

Includes ideas to extend learning through writing and text analysis.

Recommended titles can be used for book clubs or class discussions.

Teaching Inspirations

Enhance your curriculum with the following ideas.

Passage Study
Zoom in on skills with these recommended passages and related selections.

Focus Passage and Skill	Related Text or Media
Paragraphs 1 and 11 Literary Element: Diction and Syntax	Scene from the Film *Roxanne*
Paragraph 28 Literary Element: Mood	**Option 1: *The Simpsons* Present "The Raven"**

Extension Activities
Choose from among these project ideas to deepen and extend student learning.

Parody Have students write a parody of the story.

Tourist Brochure Have students collaborate to create a tourist brochure for the Usher mansion as a haunted attraction.

Movie Trailer Invite students to create a movie trailer for a new film adaptation of the story.

Casting Call Have students collaborate on casting current actors to play the parts of Usher, Madeline, and the narrator. Students should present their choices and explain their reasoning, drawing on story details.

Dear Narrator Have students write Roderick Usher's letter to the narrator—the one he sends before the story begins. Students' letters should reflect details from paragraphs 2 and 3 of the story.

Book Talk Titles
Consider using these high-interest titles for informal book clubs, as student choice for independent reading, or to prompt rich conversations.

Edgar Allan Poe: Complete Tales and Poems, Edgar Allan Poe

To My Beloved Heart: The Last Journey of Edgar Allan Poe, James Marchiori

The Raven's Tale, Cat Winters

Clockwork Angel, Cassandra Clare

ake Literature Relevant

media resources allow students to interact with the text as they tate and ask questions, express their opinions, engage in discussions, espond to their peers.

KGROUND, AUTHOR, and STANDARDS
ction-specific information builds kground knowledge and sets a purpose eading.

SELECTION AUDIO
Professionally recorded audio provides students with enhanced reading and listening support.

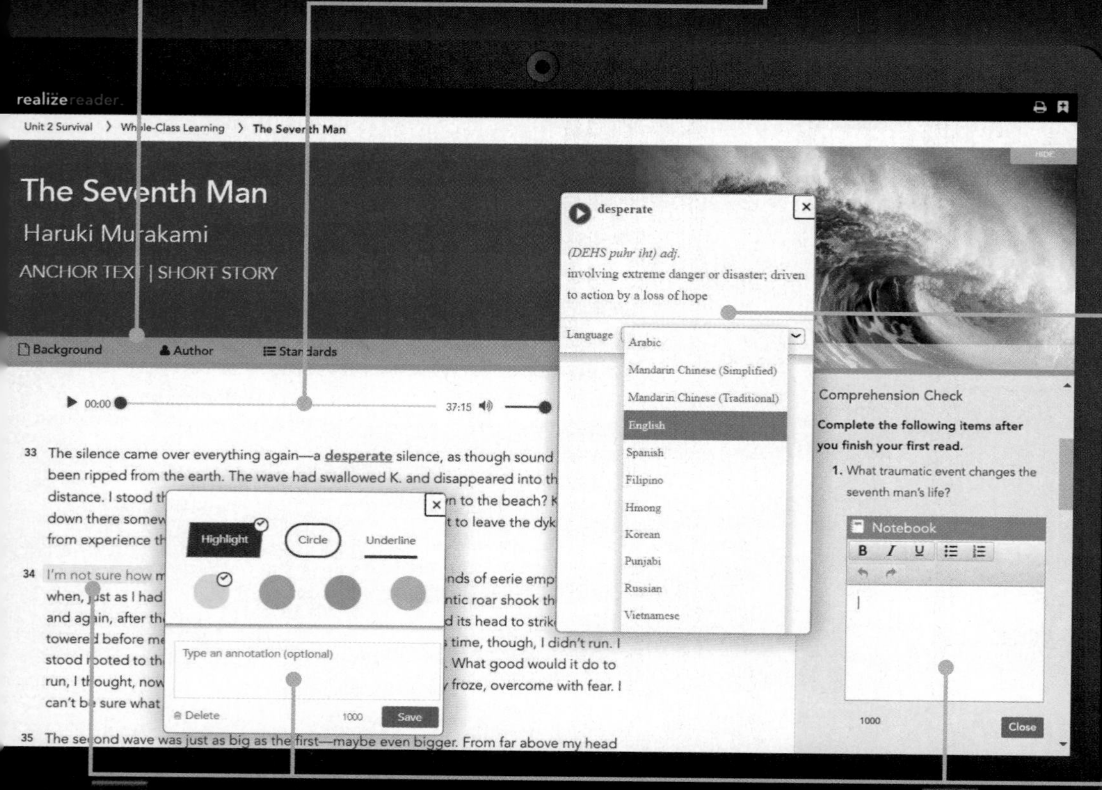

VOCABULARY
Glossary terms are defined with audio support and translations in multiple languages.

INTERACTIVES, NOTEBOOK, ANNOTATION
Capture and organize annotations with integrated tools.

> "The *myPerspectives* classroom is dynamic. The teacher inspires, models, instructs, facilitates, and advises students as they evolve and grow. When teachers guide students through meaningful learning tasks and then pass them ownership of their own learning, students become engaged and work harder. This is how we make a difference in student achievement—by putting students at the center of their learning and giving them the opportunities to choose, explore, collaborate, and work independently."
>
> —Kelly Gallagher

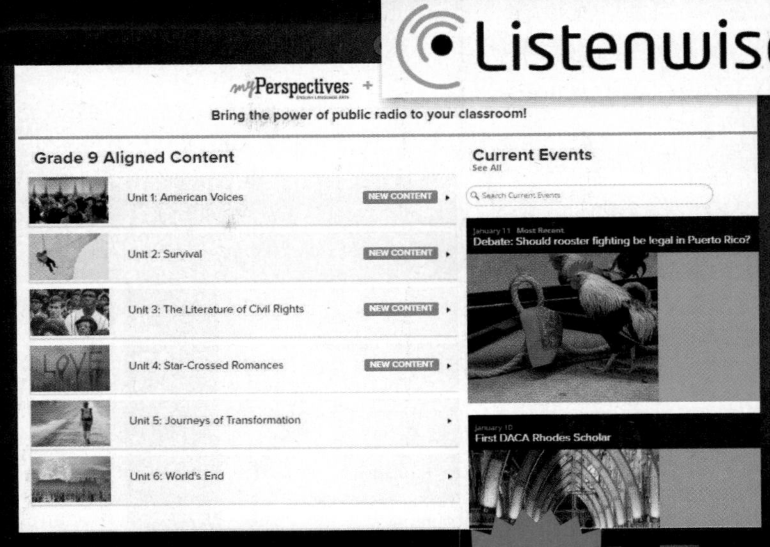

CURRENT EVENTS

Connect students to what's happening in the world and what they're learning in class.

VIDEO LIBRARY

Customize your lessons with compelling videos that have been curated for classrooms!

Videos include news footage, instructional clips, TED Talks, and tutorials from popular sources, such as:

- YouTube EDU channels
- Crash Course Literature
- TED
- Sky News
- PBS NewsHour
- Bloomberg News
- Reuters
- Associated Press

REALIZE DISCUSSION BOARD

Use the Realize Discussion Board to create a lively classroom!

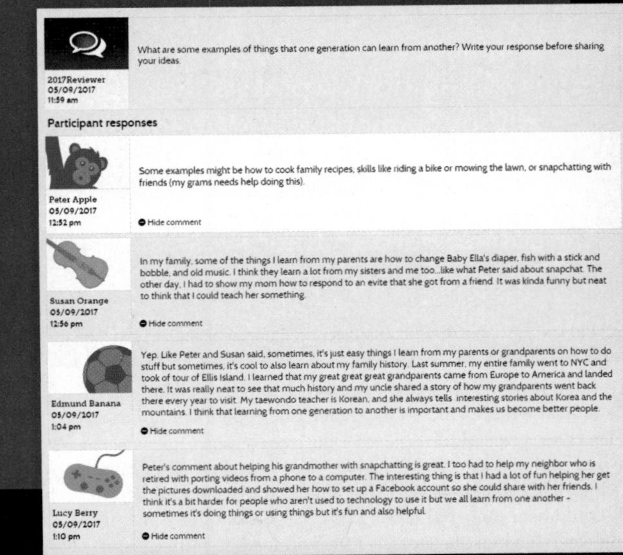

Making Meaning of Complex Texts

Students analyze complex texts, study their academic language and author's craft, and apply close-reading strategies. Following the reading, students respond to rigorous questions and complete tasks to ensure they comprehend the text.

First Read FICTION

Apply these strategies as you conduct your first read. You will have an opportunity to complete the close-read notes after your first read.

NOTICE *whom* the story is about, *what* happens, *where* and *when* it happens, and *why* those involved react as they do.

ANNOTATE by marking vocabulary and key passages you want to revisit.

First Read

CONNECT ideas within the selection to what you already know and what you have already read.

RESPOND by completing the Comprehension Check and by writing a brief summary of the selection.

Students apply first-read routines as they ask questions of the text and annotate. Questions may include: Who is the author? Where is the author coming from? When did he/she write the text? Students are invited to make connections to their lives as they ask these questions.

CLOSER LOOK

Analyze Character

Students may have marked paragraph 10 during their first read. Use this paragraph to help students understand the seventh man's relationship with K. Encourage them to talk about the annotations that they marked. You may want to model a close read with the class based on the highlights shown in the text.

ANNOTATE: Have students mark details in paragraph 10 that describe K.'s appearance and personality, or have students participate while you highlight them.

QUESTION: Guide students to consider what these details might tell them. Ask what a reader can infer from these descriptions about K.'s character, and accept student responses.

Possible response: K. is an artistic, sensitive boy who is often bullied because he is weak and has a speech impediment. Most people think that there is something wrong with him.

CONCLUDE: Help students to formulate conclusions about the importance of these details in the text. Ask students why the author might have included these details.

Possible responses: The descriptions explain why K. might need protection. They also explain why the seventh man likes and admires K. By adding these details, the author gives reasons why the seventh man makes himself responsible for K.'s safety.

Remind students that there are two types of characterization. In **direct characterization,** the author directly states a character's traits. In **indirect characterization,** an author provides clues about a character by describing the character's appearance, actions, and feelings, as well as how other characters react to him or her. With indirect characterization, the reader has to add up the details to draw conclusions about the character's personality.

Closer Look notes, found only in the Teacher's Edition, provide additional close-reading opportunities.

"A huge wave nearly swept me away," said the seventh man, almost whispering. "It happened one September afternoon when I was ten years old."

The man was the last one to tell his story that night. The hands of the clock had moved past ten. The small group that huddled in a circle could hear the wind tearing through the darkness outside, heading west. It shook the trees, set the windows to rattling, and moved past the house with one final whistle.

"It was the biggest wave I had ever seen in my life," he said. "A strange wave. An absolute giant."

He paused.

"It just barely missed me, but in my place it swallowed everything that mattered most to me and swept it off to another world. I took years to find it again and to recover from the experience—precious years that can never be replaced."

NOTES

CLOSE READ

ANNOTATE: Mark details in paragraph 2 that describe where the action takes place.

QUESTION: What can you tell about the story's setting?

What details about the setting are left unclear?

CONCLUDE: Describe the **mood**, or feeling, that the annotated details create.

Close Read notes enable students to study structures, diction, and other elements of author's craft.

Comprehension Check

Complete the following items after you finish your first read.

1. What traumatic event changes the seventh man's life?
2. Why does the seventh man's father allow him to go outside during the storm?
3. At the beach, why doesn't K. respond when his friend calls out to him?
4. What does the seventh man see inside the second wave?
5. What does the seventh man do when he returns to his hometown that shows he has finally recovered from his traumatic experience?
6. Notebook To confirm your understanding, write a summary of "The Seventh Man."

RESEARCH

Research to Clarify Choose at least one unfamiliar detail from the text. Briefly research that detail. In what way does the information you learned shed light on an aspect of the story?

Research to Explore Choose something from the text that interested you and formulate a research question.

DIGITAL PERSPECTIVES

Comprehension Check

Possible responses:

1. The seventh man's life is changed when he does not try to rescue his best friend K. from a giant wave. As a result, K. drowns.
2. The seventh man's father allows him to go outside during the storm because it is during the eye of the storm and everything is calm.
3. K. doesn't respond when the seventh man calls out to him because K. was likely absorbed in something that interested him, or the seventh man's voice did not reach him.
4. Inside the second wave, the seventh man sees K. grinning and reaching out to him.
5. When he returns to his hometown, the seventh man goes into the ocean, an act that shows he has finally recovered from his traumatic experience.
6. Summaries will vary; however, students should include a description of the storm, K.'s death, the narrator's years of guilt, and the narrator's recovery in the end.

Research to Clarify If students struggle to come up with a detail to research, you may want to suggest that they focus on one of the following topics: typhoons, Nagano Province, watercolors.

Research to Explore If students aren't sure how to go about formulating a research question, suggest that they use their findings from Research to Clarify as a starting point. For example, if students researched what watercolor painting is, they might formulate a question such as *What is the history of watercolor painting?*

Students respond to questions with text evidence to determine comprehension of the first read.

Students choose a research activity to learn more.

TEACHING

Jump Start

CLOSE READ Have students close read the title "The Seventh Man." Ask students what they know about the number seven. Explain that the number seven is considered a lucky number in Japanese culture. Knowing this, one might wonder if the author intended the reader to infer that the seventh man is really "The Lucky Man." Ask students if they think the seventh man is truly lucky.

Close Read the Text

Walk students through the annotation model on the student page. Encourage them to complete items 2 and 3 on their own. Review and discuss the sections students have marked. If needed, continue to model close reading by using the Annotation Highlights in the Interactive Teacher's Edition.

Analyze the Text

Possible responses:

1. To the seventh man, the wave symbolizes the loss of his childhood innocence and joy. Paragraph 65 DOK 2
2. (a) After he rediscovers K.'s watercolors, the seventh man looks at one for hours every day when he gets home from work. DOK 1 (b) To the seventh man, K.'s paintings symbolize the rediscovery of who he was before K. was killed. Paragraph 52 DOK 2
3. (a) Ignoring your fear will destroy your life. You must face your fear in order to overcome it. DOK 2 (b) I agree, because if the seventh man hadn't ignored his fear, he could have forgiven himself much earlier and lived a happier life. DOK 3
4. Most students will observe that the seventh man suffered terribly after the wave took K.'s life.

MAKING MEANING

THE SEVENTH MAN

Close Read the Text

1. The model, from paragraph 5 of the story, shows two sample annotations, along with questions and conclusions. Close read the passage, and find another detail to annotate. Then, write a question and your conclusion.

ANNOTATE: This phrase describes the wave in almost human terms.
QUESTION: What effect does this word choice create?
CONCLUDE: This description makes the wave seem alive and evil.

"It just barely missed me, but in my place it swallowed everything that mattered most to me and swept it off to another world. I took years to find it again and to recover from the experience—precious years that can never be replaced."

ANNOTATE: This word is repeated.
QUESTION: Why does the author repeat the word *years*?
CONCLUDE: The repetition emphasizes how long it takes the man to recover from the experience.

Tool Kit
Close-Read Guide and Model Annotation

2. For more practice, go back into the story and complete the close-read notes.
3. Revisit a section of the text you found important during your first read. Read this section closely, and **annotate** what you notice. Ask yourself **questions** such as "Why did the author make this choice?" What can you **conclude**?

Analyze the Text

CITE TEXTUAL EVIDENCE to support your answers.

Notebook Respond to these questions.

1. **Interpret** What does the wave **symbolize**, or represent, to the seventh man?
2. (a) After he rediscovers K.'s watercolors, what does the seventh man do with them? (b) **Interpret** What do K.'s watercolors symbolize to him?
3. (a) **Paraphrase** When you **paraphrase**, you restate a text in your own words. Paraphrase the seventh man's comments about fear in the story's final paragraph. (b) **Make a Judgment** Do you agree or disagree with the seventh man's comments? Explain.
4. **Evaluate** Although the seventh man did not die, did he truly escape the wave? Explain your position, citing story details.
5. **Essential Question:** *What does it take to survive?* What have you learned about the nature of survival by reading this story?

An annotated passage models for students how to close read the text.

Questions are aligned to DOKs.

Students continue to build insight as they tackle an array of questions that build in complexity and cognitive demand.

FIRST READ EXTENSION QUESTIONS
The Seventh Man

Name: Date:

The Seventh Man
Haruki Murakami

SHORT-RESPONSE QUESTIONS

DIRECTIONS: Complete the following items after you have read the text.

RL.9-10.2 Determine a theme or central idea of a text and analyze in detail its development over the course of the text, including how it emerges and is shaped and refined by specific details; provide an objective summary of the text.

1. **(a) Determine a theme or central idea of a text and analyze in detail its development over the course of a text, including how it emerges and is shaped and refined by specific details.**
Identify a theme, or message, of "The Seventh Man." How does the author introduce the theme, and how does he develop it over the course of the text?

(b) Provide an objective summary of the text.
Write a summary of "The Seventh Man" that includes key events and details but not personal opinions or judgments.

RL.9-10.3 Analyze how complex characters (e.g., those with multiple or conflicting motivations) develop over the course of a text, interact with other characters, and advance the plot or develop the theme.

Standards-based critical-thinking questions allow for even deeper analysis of the text.

Integrated Reading, Writing, Speaking and Listening

Reading, writing, speaking, and listening are integrated within *myPerspectives*. Students analyze texts through the eyes of a reader and writer, create their own compositions, and complete the Performance-Based Assessment—all while exploring the Essential Question.

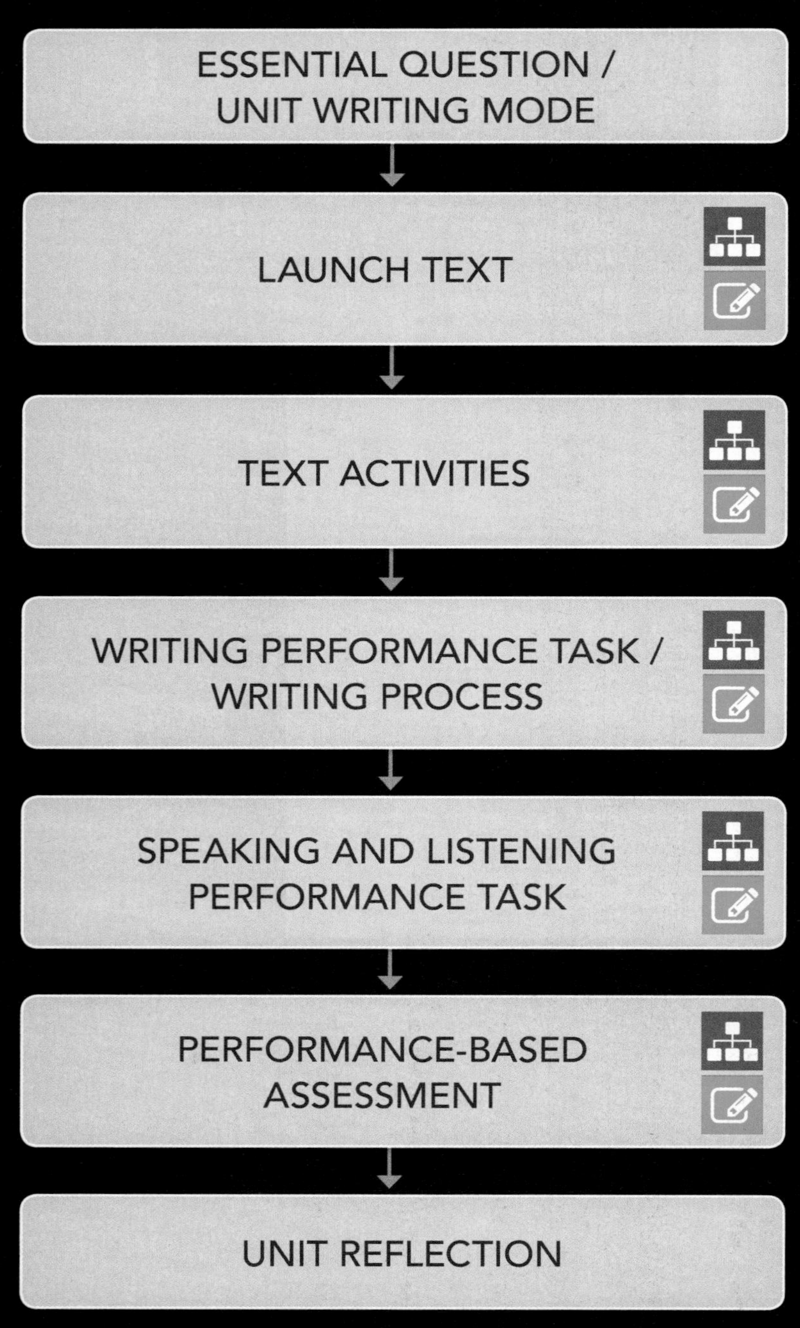

WORD NETWORK

Students gather academic vocabulary as they read, creating a network of words for clear communication in their discussions and writing.

EVIDENCE LOG

Students' perspectives evolve as they write to sources and collect text evidence throughout the unit.

Students revisit the Launch Text, Evidence Log, and Word Network to complete the Performance-Based Assessment.

ESSENTIAL QUESTION / UNIT WRITING MODE

Each unit focuses on a writing mode—Informative/Explanatory, Narrative, Argument—and on an Essential Question.

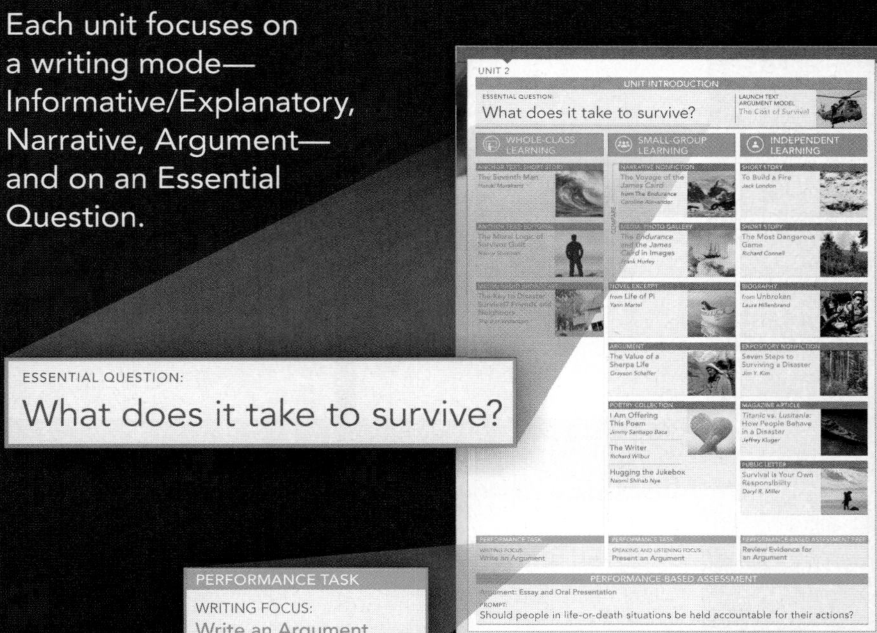

UNIT 2

UNIT INTRODUCTION

ESSENTIAL QUESTION: What does it take to survive?

LAUNCH TEXT ARGUMENT MODEL: The Cost of Survival

WHOLE-CLASS LEARNING | SMALL-GROUP LEARNING | INDEPENDENT LEARNING

PERFORMANCE-BASED ASSESSMENT

Argument: Essay and Oral Presentation

PROMPT: Should people in life-or-death situations be held accountable for their actions?

123

ESSENTIAL QUESTION:
What does it take to survive?

PERFORMANCE TASK
WRITING FOCUS:
Write an Argument

LAUNCH TEXT

The Launch Text models the unit's writing mode. Students complete a summary to check their comprehension and then participate in a QuickWrite to start engaging with the unit theme.

UNIT 2 INTRODUCTION

LAUNCH TEXT | ARGUMENT MODEL

This selection is an example of an argumentative text, a type of writing in which an author states and defends a position on a topic. This is the type of writing you will develop in the Performance-Based Assessment at the end of the unit.

As you read, look at the way the writer builds a case. Mark the text to help you answer this question: What is the writer's position and what evidence supports it?

The Cost of Survival

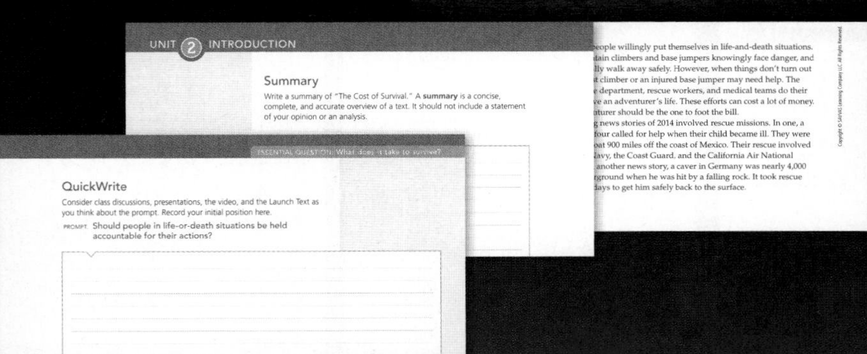

UNIT 2 INTRODUCTION

Summary

Write a summary of "The Cost of Survival." A summary is a concise, complete, and accurate overview of a text. It should not include a statement of your opinion or an analysis.

ESSENTIAL QUESTION: What does it take to survive?

QuickWrite

Consider class discussions, presentations, the video, and the Launch Text as you think about the prompt. Record your initial position here.

PROMPT: Should people in life-or-death situations be held accountable for their actions?

WRITING TO SOURCES

Short writing opportunities allow students to develop their skills, using the texts as models and sources.

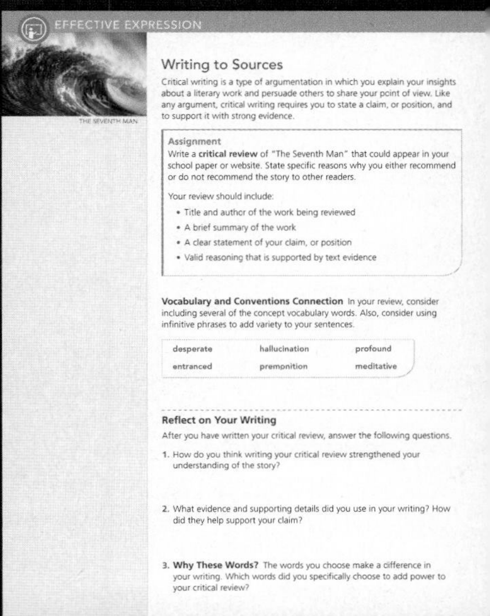

EFFECTIVE EXPRESSION

THE SEVENTH MAN

Writing to Sources

Critical writing is a type of argumentation in which you explain your insights about a literary work and persuade others to share your point of view. Like any argument, critical writing requires you to state a claim, or position, and to support it with strong evidence.

Assignment

Write a **critical review** of "The Seventh Man" that could appear in your school paper or website. State specific reasons why you either recommend or do not recommend the story to other readers.

Your review should include:

- Title and author of the work being reviewed
- A brief summary of the work
- A clear statement of your claim, or position
- Valid reasoning that is supported by text evidence

Vocabulary and Conventions Connection In your review, consider including several of the concept vocabulary words. Also, consider using infinitive phrases to add variety to your sentences.

desperate	hallucination	profound
entranced	premonition	meditative

Reflect on Your Writing

After you have written your critical review, answer the following questions.

1. How do you think writing your critical review strengthened your understanding of the story?
2. What evidence and supporting details did you use in your writing? How did they help support your claim?
3. **Why These Words?** The words you choose make a difference in your writing. Which words did you specifically choose to add power to your critical review?

SPEAKING AND LISTENING

Students share their thinking through media and presentations.

ESSENTIAL QUESTION: What does it take to survive?

Speaking and Listening

Assignment

With a partner, prepare a **retelling** of "The Seventh Man" from another point of view. For example, you may choose to retell the story from K.'s parents' point of view, or from that of a hidden onlooker. Refresh your memory by rereading the selection. Then, follow these steps to complete the assignment.

1. **Identify Your Character** Choose your character and determine how he or she fits into the original story. Decide what important information you will need to tell your audience to clarify the character's background and motivations.
2. **Plan Your Retelling** Once you've identified your character, think about his or her perspective on the events in the story. As you plan your retelling, keep the following in mind:
   - How does your character see the story differently from the seventh man? What fresh perspective does he or she offer?
   - Make a list of the story events, as experienced by your character. Then, weave those events into a coherent retelling.
   - Choose language that is appropriate to the character you chose. For example, a child would choose simple words and sentences and may not fully understand what is he or she is observing.
3. **Prepare Your Delivery** Practice your retelling with your partner. Include the following performance techniques to help you achieve the desired effect.
   - Vary your intonation to reflect the emotions of your character. Avoid speaking in a flat, monotone style.
   - As you speak, use facial expressions and gestures that help convey your character's personality.
   - Make eye contact with your audience to engage them in the story.
4. **Evaluate Retellings** As your classmates deliver their retellings, listen attentively. Use an evaluation guide like the one shown to analyze their delivery.

EVALUATION GUIDE

Rate each statement on a scale of 1 (not demonstrated) to 4 (demonstrated).

- The character was clearly identified.
- The speaker communicated clearly and expressively.
- The speaker used a variety of speaking tones and pitches.
- The speaker used effective gestures and other body language.

EVIDENCE LOG

Before moving on to a new selection, go to your Evidence Log and record what you learned from "The Seventh Man."

Integrated Reading, Writing, Speaking and Listening

WRITING PERFORMANCE TASK

In Whole-Class Learning, students write, revise, and edit to produce a high-quality writing piece in the unit's focus mode of writing.

The Launch Text is used as a model to guide students through the writing process.

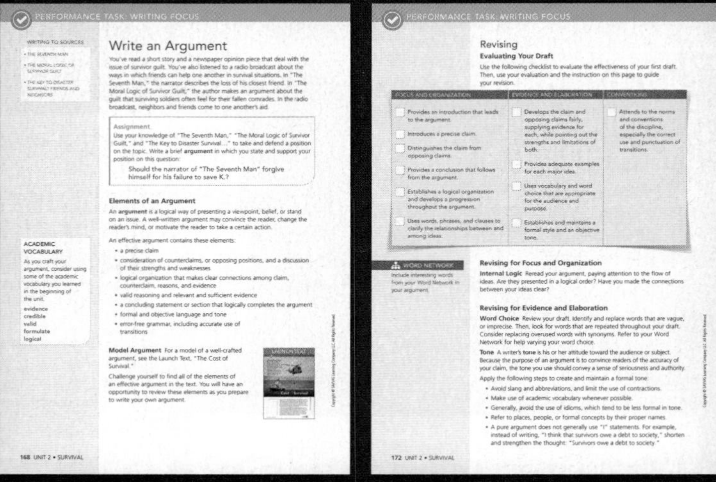

SPEAKING AND LISTENING PERFORMANCE TASK

In Small-Group Learning, students apply their diverse learning styles and interests to collaboratively complete a Speaking and Listening project.

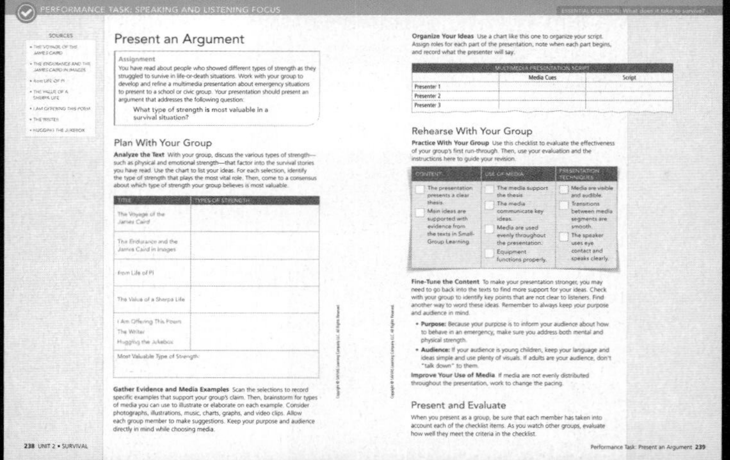

PERFORMANCE-BASED ASSESSMENT

Reflecting on their Evidence Log, learning from their peers, personal growth, and perspectives on the Essential Question, students craft both written and oral responses to complete a two-part assessment.

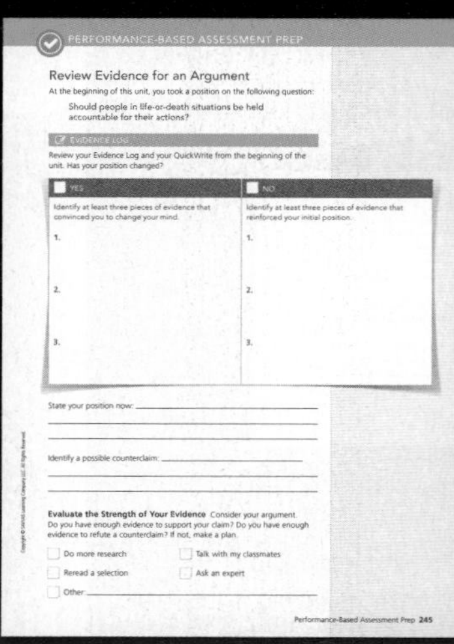

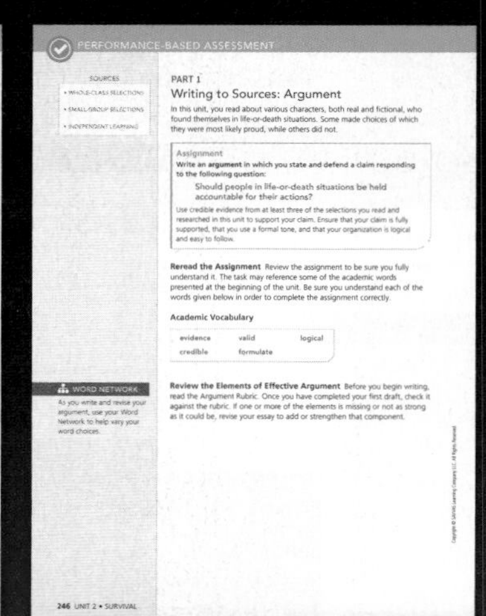

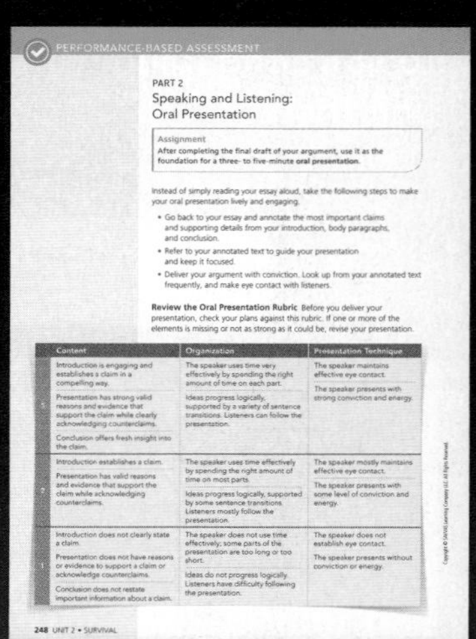

INTERACTIVE LESSONS

Students can take ownership of their learning to improve their skills with Interactive Writing and Speaking & Listening Lessons.

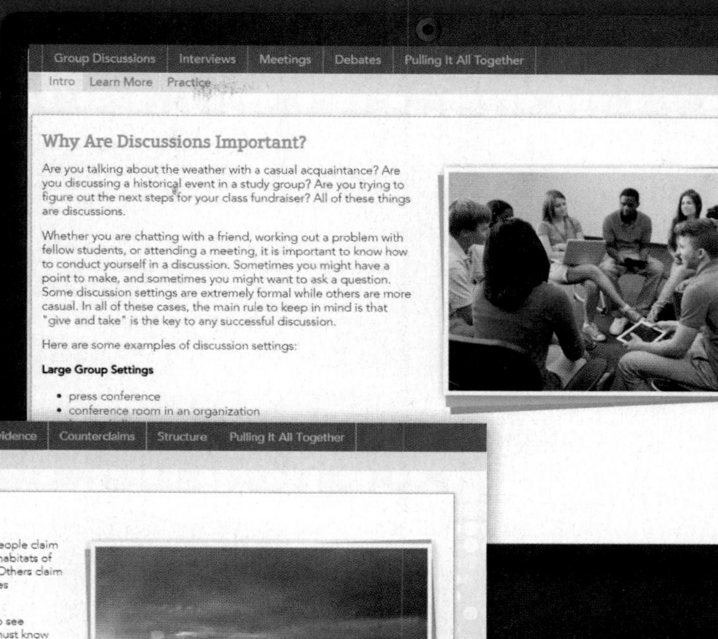

WRITING MODELS AND RUBRICS

Rubrics and writing models are available for students to reference.

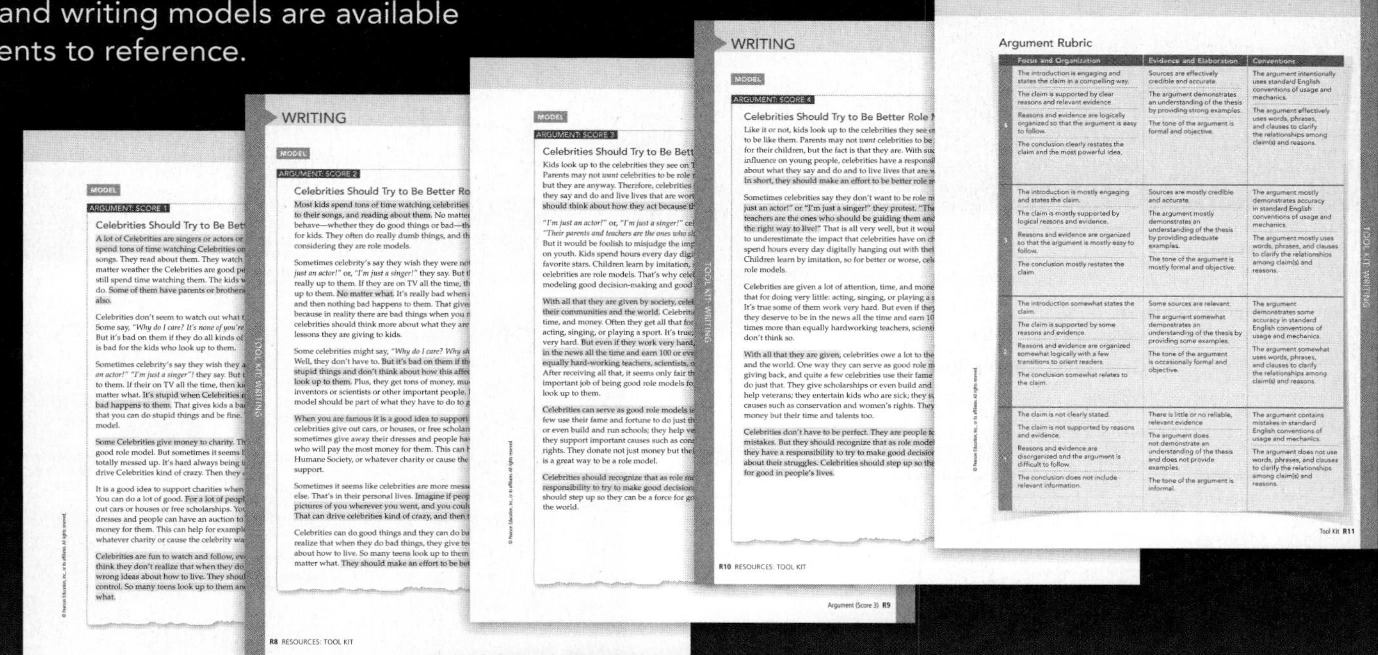

Integrated Reading, Writing, Speaking and Listening

CONVENTIONS

Conventions instruction and practice is taught at point of use, but sometimes you want to assign more!

INTERACTIVE MINI-LESSONS

Student-facing Interactive Mini-Lessons provide additional instruction and practice. Students can choose lessons to complete independently.

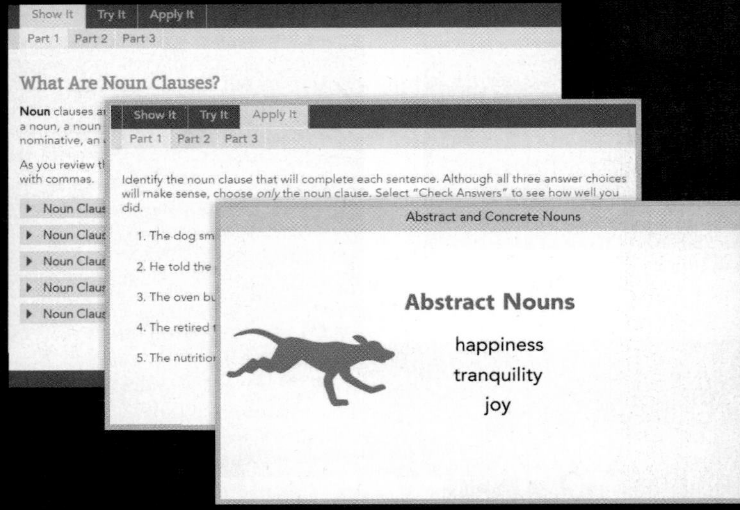

WORKSHEETS

Assign worksheets for extra practice. Worksheets are customizable and available in Spanish!

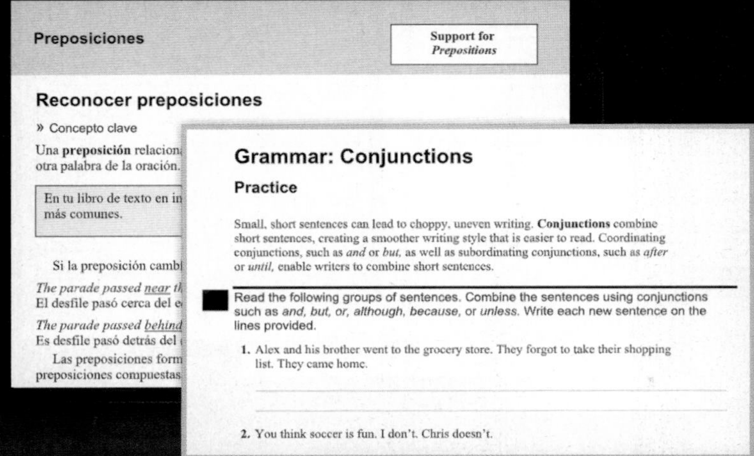

SKILLS VIDEOS

Engaging tutorial videos teach and reinforce important skills concepts.

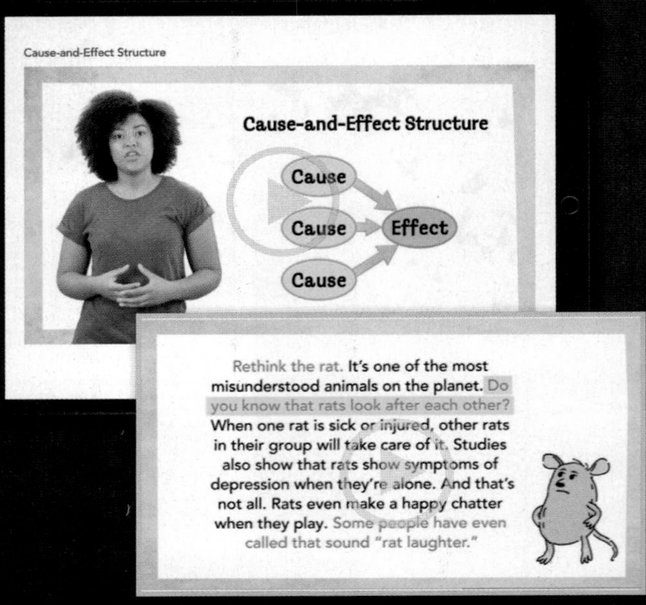

COLLABORATION CENTER

Real-life videos model for students how to participate in groups, how to give positive feedback, how to build on the ideas of others, how to listen actively and respond appropriately, and how to communicate to resolve conflict.

RESEARCH

Interactive Mini-Lessons help students learn important aspects of the research process including how to cite sources, choose a topic, find evidence, and how to integrate quotations and images.

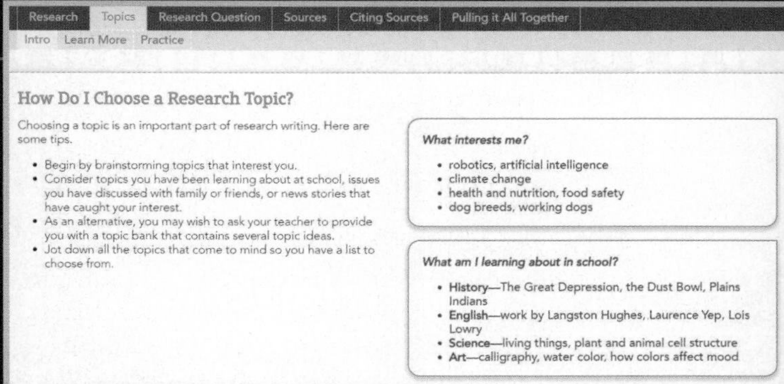

PLAGIARISM CHECKER

A plagiarism checker looks for multiple forms of plagiarism to teach students the value of academic integrity, proper attribution, and authentic writing. Color-coding, filters, and source comparison make it easy to interpret results.

ESSAYSCORER

EssayScorer offers automatic feedback for students as they work to improve their writing. Prompts include the Writing Performance Task as well as prompts for agnostic practice.

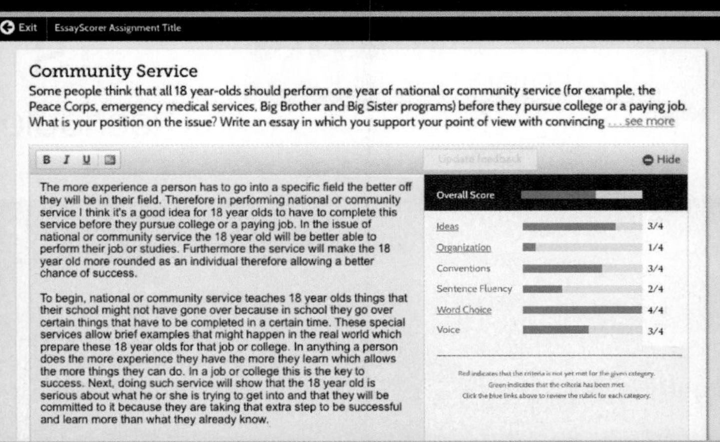

igital Dashboard

ize is your online destination for digital urces, assessments, and data. Digital s give you freedom and control to omize the program.

LOCATION IS EVERYTHING!

World-class interoperability lets you connect Realize to your digital content with any IMS certified platform—nothing could be easier!

Partner
Google for Education

IMS GLOBAL®
CERTIFIED

SAFARI MONTAGE

Learn more on the Savvas Realize YouTube Channel!

GETTING STARTED

Helpful implementation resources including correlations, planning guides, and How-To Use videos.

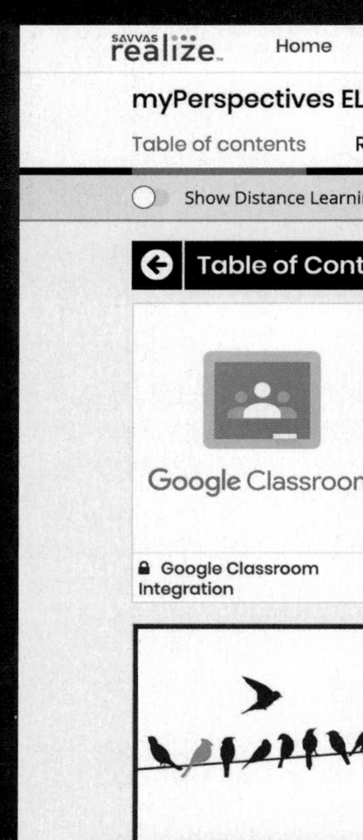

OPEN EDUCATIONAL RESOURCES

Take the guesswork out of searching for vetted, online educational resources. Easily search for resource types across all disciplines through our partnership with Mosaic™ by ACT® Digital Learning Library.

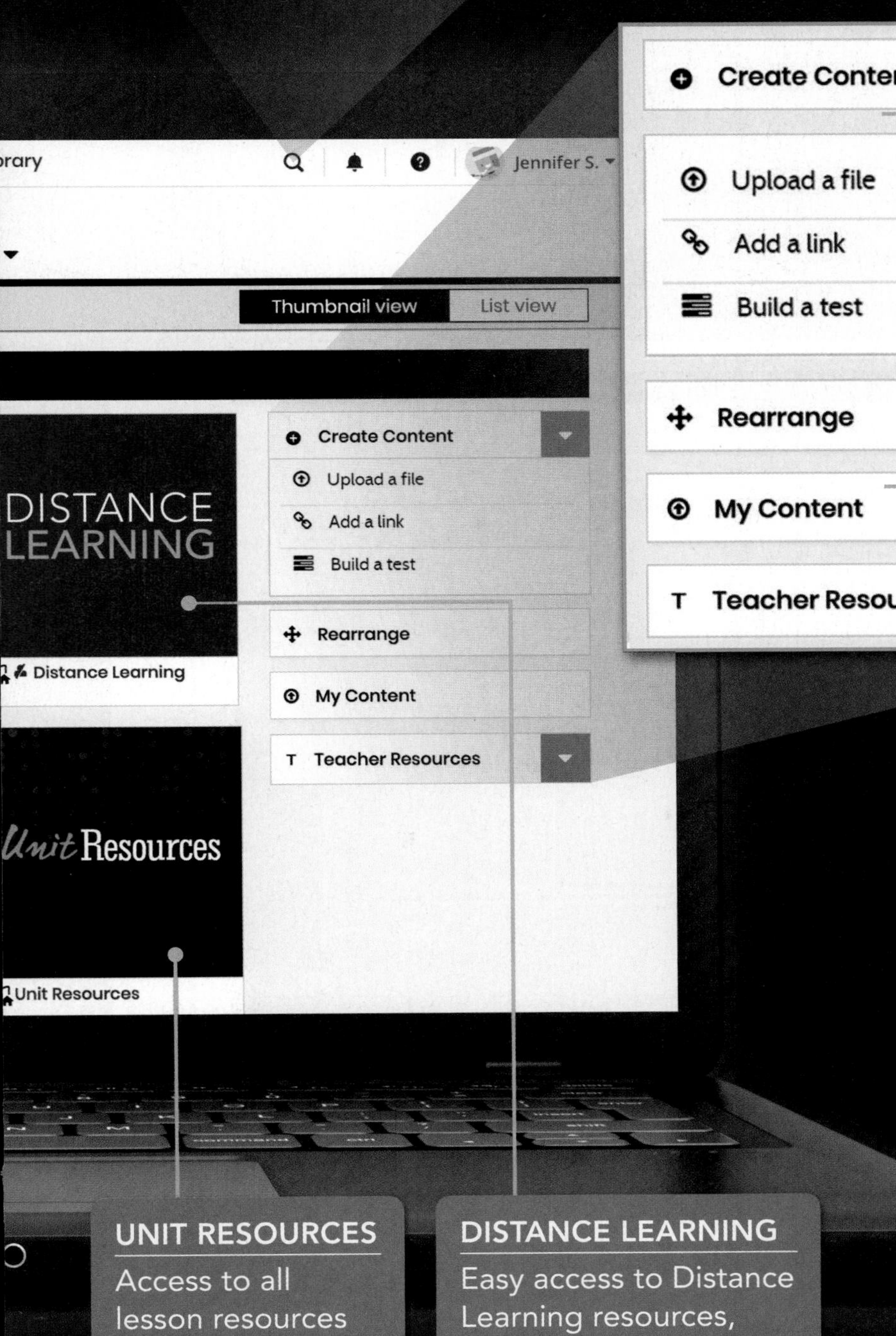

REARRANGE & CUSTOMIZE

Customize the program by rearranging the Table of Contents, creating your own tests, and uploading your own resources.

CREATE YOUR OWN PLAYLIST

Choose selections and resources to create your own units and lessons.

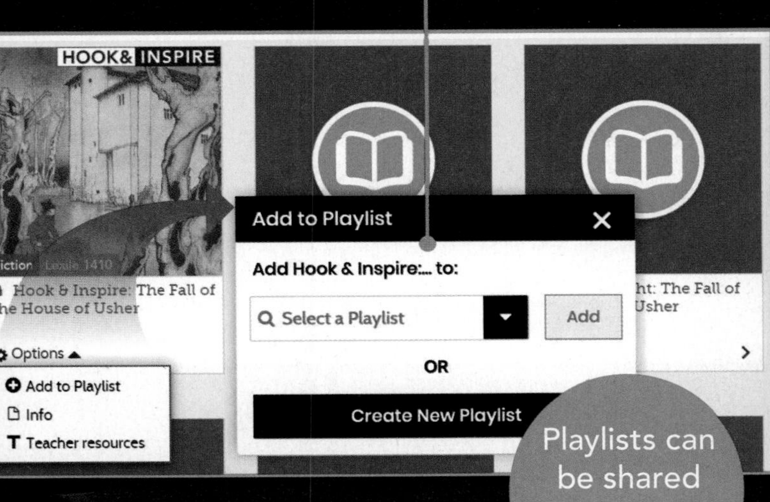

Playlists can be shared among teachers!

UNIT RESOURCES

Access to all lesson resources makes assigning resources easy.

DISTANCE LEARNING

Easy access to Distance Learning resources, including guidance videos for teachers.

Flexible and Customizable: Lesson Planning

Whether you follow the program as intended, pick and choose units or selections, or want to integrate novels, you will find the tools you need to guide your planning. What's more, you can customize the program within Realize!

PACING
Daily pacing is recommended and can be modified based on classroom needs.

LEXILE LEVEL
Lexile levels help you plan to meet student needs.

UNIT AT A GLANCE
Includes standards, skills, and other data to help teachers plan.

UNIT PLANNING

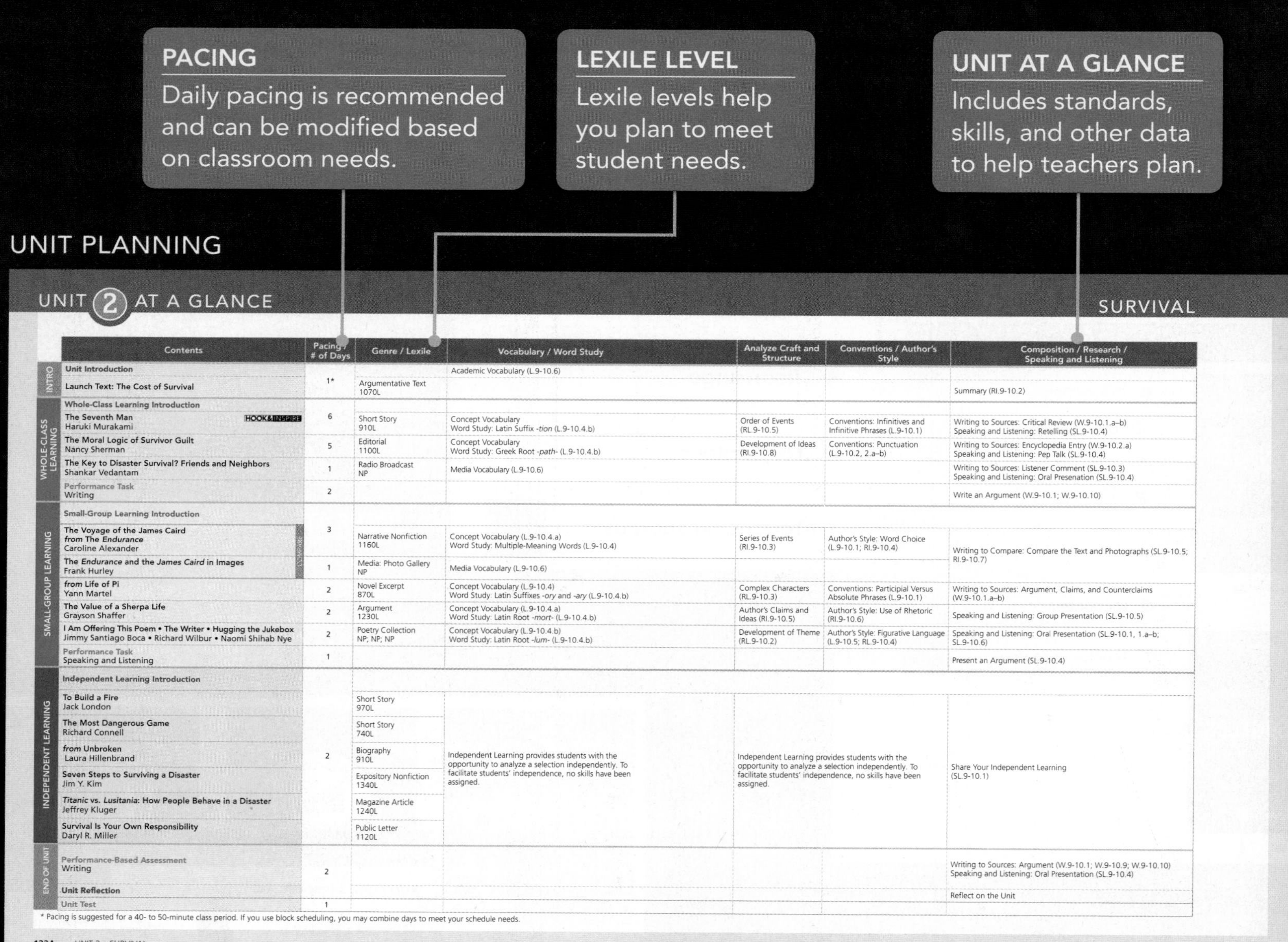

UNIT 2 AT A GLANCE — SURVIVAL

	Contents	Pacing / # of Days	Genre / Lexile	Vocabulary / Word Study	Analyze Craft and Structure	Conventions / Author's Style	Composition / Research / Speaking and Listening
INTRO	**Unit Introduction**	1*		Academic Vocabulary (L.9-10.6)			
INTRO	**Launch Text: The Cost of Survival**		Argumentative Text 1070L				Summary (RI.9-10.2)
WHOLE-CLASS LEARNING	**Whole-Class Learning Introduction**						
WHOLE-CLASS LEARNING	**The Seventh Man** Haruki Murakami (HOOK & INSPIRE)	6	Short Story 910L	Concept Vocabulary Word Study: Latin Suffix *-tion* (L.9-10.4.b)	Order of Events (RL.9-10.5)	Conventions: Infinitives and Infinitive Phrases (L.9-10.1)	Writing to Sources: Critical Review (W.9-10.1.a–b) Speaking and Listening: Retelling (SL.9-10.4)
WHOLE-CLASS LEARNING	**The Moral Logic of Survivor Guilt** Nancy Sherman	5	Editorial 1100L	Concept Vocabulary Word Study: Greek Root *-path-* (L.9-10.4.b)	Development of Ideas (RI.9-10.8)	Conventions: Punctuation (L.9-10.2, 2.a–b)	Writing to Sources: Encyclopedia Entry (W.9-10.2.a) Speaking and Listening: Pep Talk (SL.9-10.4)
WHOLE-CLASS LEARNING	**The Key to Disaster Survival? Friends and Neighbors** Shankar Vedantam	1	Radio Broadcast NP	Media Vocabulary (L.9-10.6)			Writing to Sources: Listener Comment (SL.9-10.3) Speaking and Listening: Oral Presenation (SL.9-10.4)
WHOLE-CLASS LEARNING	Performance Task Writing	2					Write an Argument (W.9-10.1; W.9-10.10)
SMALL-GROUP LEARNING	**Small-Group Learning Introduction**						
SMALL-GROUP LEARNING	**The Voyage of the James Caird *from The Endurance*** Caroline Alexander (COMPARE)	3	Narrative Nonfiction 1160L	Concept Vocabulary (L.9-10.4.a) Word Study: Multiple-Meaning Words (L.9-10.4)	Series of Events (RI.9-10.3)	Author's Style: Word Choice (L.9-10.1; RI.9-10.4)	Writing to Compare: Compare the Text and Photographs (SL.9-10.5; RI.9-10.7)
SMALL-GROUP LEARNING	**The *Endurance* and the *James Caird* in Images** Frank Hurley (COMPARE)	1	Media: Photo Gallery NP	Media Vocabulary (L.9-10.6)			
SMALL-GROUP LEARNING	***from* Life of Pi** Yann Martel	2	Novel Excerpt 870L	Concept Vocabulary (L.9-10.4) Word Study: Latin Suffixes *-ory* and *-ary* (L.9-10.4.b)	Complex Characters (RL.9-10.3)	Conventions: Participial Versus Absolute Phrases (L.9-10.1)	Writing to Sources: Argument, Claims, and Counterclaims (W.9-10.1.a–b)
SMALL-GROUP LEARNING	**The Value of a Sherpa Life** Grayson Shaffer	2	Argument 1230L	Concept Vocabulary (L.9-10.4.a) Word Study: Latin Root *-mort-* (L.9-10.4.b)	Author's Claims and Ideas (RI.9-10.5)	Author's Style: Use of Rhetoric (RI.9-10.6)	Speaking and Listening: Group Presentation (SL.9-10.5)
SMALL-GROUP LEARNING	**I Am Offering This Poem • The Writer • Hugging the Jukebox** Jimmy Santiago Boca • Richard Wilbur • Naomi Shihab Nye	2	Poetry Collection NP; NP; NP	Concept Vocabulary (L.9-10.4.b) Word Study: Latin Root *-lum-* (L.9-10.4.b)	Development of Theme (RL.9-10.2)	Author's Style: Figurative Language (L.9-10.5; RL.9-10.4)	Speaking and Listening: Oral Presentation (SL.9-10.1, 1.a–b; SL.9-10.6)
SMALL-GROUP LEARNING	Performance Task Speaking and Listening	1					Present an Argument (SL.9-10.4)
INDEPENDENT LEARNING	**Independent Learning Introduction**						
INDEPENDENT LEARNING	**To Build a Fire** Jack London		Short Story 970L	Independent Learning provides students with the opportunity to analyze a selection independently. To facilitate students' independence, no skills have been assigned.	Independent Learning provides students with the opportunity to analyze a selection independently. To facilitate students' independence, no skills have been assigned.		Share Your Independent Learning (SL.9-10.1)
INDEPENDENT LEARNING	**The Most Dangerous Game** Richard Connell		Short Story 740L				
INDEPENDENT LEARNING	***from* Unbroken** Laura Hillenbrand	2	Biography 910L				
INDEPENDENT LEARNING	**Seven Steps to Surviving a Disaster** Jim Y. Kim		Expository Nonfiction 1340L				
INDEPENDENT LEARNING	***Titanic* vs. *Lusitania*: How People Behave in a Disaster** Jeffrey Kluger		Magazine Article 1240L				
INDEPENDENT LEARNING	**Survival Is Your Own Responsibility** Daryl R. Miller		Public Letter 1120L				
END OF UNIT	Performance-Based Assessment Writing	2					Writing to Sources: Argument (W.9-10.1; W.9-10.9; W.9-10.10) Speaking and Listening: Oral Presentation (SL.9-10.4)
END OF UNIT	**Unit Reflection**						Reflect on the Unit
END OF UNIT	Unit Test	1					

* Pacing is suggested for a 40- to 50-minute class period. If you use block scheduling, you may combine days to meet your schedule needs.

122A UNIT 2 • SURVIVAL

UNIT 2 • AT A GLANCE 122B

Unit at a Glance is a valuable resource to use with your school or district curriculum. You can easily map the standards and skills in *myPerspectives* to your own curriculum.

DIGITAL PERSPECTIVES

Audio

Video

Document

Annotation Highlights

Online Assessment

STANDARDS
Standards are aligned to lesson activities.

HOOK & INSPIRE
Hook & Inspire texts are identified.

DIGITAL RESOURCES
Lesson resources are identified with digital icons.

LESSON PLANNING

PLANNING WHOLE-CLASS LEARNING • THE SEVENTH MAN

The Seventh Man

AUDIO SUMMARIES
Audio summaries of "The Seventh Man" are available online in both English and Spanish in the Interactive Teacher's Edition or Unit Resources. Assigning these summaries prior to reading the selection may help students build additional background knowledge and set a context for their first read.

Summary

In Haruki Murakami's "The Seventh Man," seven people tell stories on a stormy night. The seventh man tells the story of a great wave that devastated his life. He explains that as a child, he lived by the ocean in Japan. When he was ten years old, a typhoon hit his town. People stayed safely inside, but during the calm at the center of the storm, he and his best friend K. walked to the beach. As they looked around, he saw a great wave approaching. He called to K., but K. didn't hear. The seventh man ran for safety; K. was drowned. He could have reached K.—but could he have saved him, or would they both have died? For forty years, the seventh man is haunted by guilt and uncertainty—but then something makes him reconsider what he did, or failed to do, that day.

Insight

The choices survivors make are not always easy or clear. Reading "The Seventh Man" will help students begin their reflections on how complicated survival can be. Although a survivor may have escaped with his or her life, that life may never be the same.

Some students may find "The Seventh Man" disturbing. The realization that a childhood decision might color someone's whole life is sobering and may require support.

ESSENTIAL QUESTION:
What does it take to survive?

Connection to Essential Question

"The Seventh Man" provides an unusual perspective on the Essential Question, "What does it take to survive?" The main character physically survives a giant wave by reacting almost instinctively: Fear causes him to run away from the beach. However, the guilt that he feels about having left his best friend behind persists for years. The seventh man only truly begins to survive emotionally when he faces and overcomes his guilt.

WHOLE-CLASS LEARNING PERFORMANCE TASK
Should the seventh man forgive himself for his failure to save K.?

UNIT PERFORMANCE-BASED ASSESSMENT
Should people in life-or-death situations be held accountable for their actions?

Connection to Performance Tasks

Whole-Class Learning Performance Task In this Performance Task, students will consider the concept of survivor's guilt. "The Seventh Man" provides a literary perspective on the price survivors pay. Students will be combining this perspective with facts about survivor's guilt that they glean from further reading.

Unit Performance-Based Assessment This selection provides an interesting insight into the question students will respond to on the Performance-Based Assessment. Students should consider whether the seventh man should be held accountable for his actions.

132A UNIT 2 • SURVIVAL

HOOK& INSPIRE

DIGITAL PERSPECTIVES Audio Video Document Annotation Highlights Online Assessment

LESSON RESOURCES

	Making Meaning	Language Development	Effective Expression
Lesson	**First Read** **First Read Questions** **Close Read** **Analyze the Text** **Analyze Craft and Structure**	**Concept Vocabulary** **Word Study** **Conventions**	**Writing to Sources** **Speaking and Listening**
Instructional Standards	**RL.9-10.10** By the end of grade 9, read and comprehend literature . . . **RL.9-10.5** Analyze how an author's choices concerning how to structure a text, order events within it . . .	**L.9-10.1** Demonstrate command of the conventions of standard English . . . **L.9-10.4.b** Identify and correctly use patterns of word changes . . . **L.9-10.5** Demonstrate understanding of figurative language word relationships, and nuances . . .	**W.9-10.1.a** Introduce precise claim(s) . . . **W.9-10.1.b** Develop claim(s) and counterclaims fairly . . . **SL.9-10.4** Present information, findings, and supporting evidence . . .
STUDENT RESOURCES			
Available online in the Interactive Student Edition or Unit Resources	Selection Audio First-Read Guide: Fiction Close-Read Guide: Fiction	Word Network	Evidence Log
	Close-Read Guide: Fiction		
TEACHER RESOURCES			
Selection Resources Available online in the Interactive Teacher's Edition or Unit Resources	Audio Summaries Annotation Highlights EL Highlights Analyze Craft and Structure: Order of Events English Language Support Lesson: Order of Events	Concept Vocabulary and Word Study Conventions: Infinitives and Infinitive Phrases	Writing to Sources: Critical Review Speaking and Listening: Retelling
Reteach/Practice (RP) Available online in the Interactive Teacher's Edition or Unit Resources	Analyze Craft and Structure: Order of Events (RP)	Word Study: Latin Suffix *–tion* (RP) Conventions: Infinitives and Infinitive Phrases (RP)	Writing to Sources: Critical Review (RP) Speaking and Listening: Retelling (RP)
Assessment Available online in Assessments	Selection Test		
My Resources	A Unit 2 Answer Key is available online and in the Interactive Teacher's Edition		

Whole-Class Learning 132B

CUSTOMIZABLE RESOURCES
Lesson resources and assessments are editable.

ASSESSMENTS
Assessments are aligned to where they should be implemented in the lesson.

A customizable version of the Lesson Planning chart is available online!

ble and Customizable: *myPerspectives+*

ves+ includes hundreds of additional resources you can use to customize including interactive lessons, grammar tutorials, skills videos, digital novels, esources are student-facing to allow students to work independently.

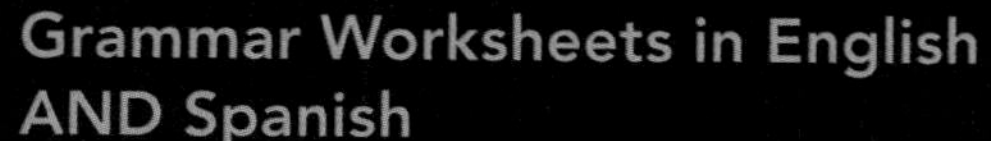

Grammar Worksheets in English AND Spanish

Grammar Tutorials

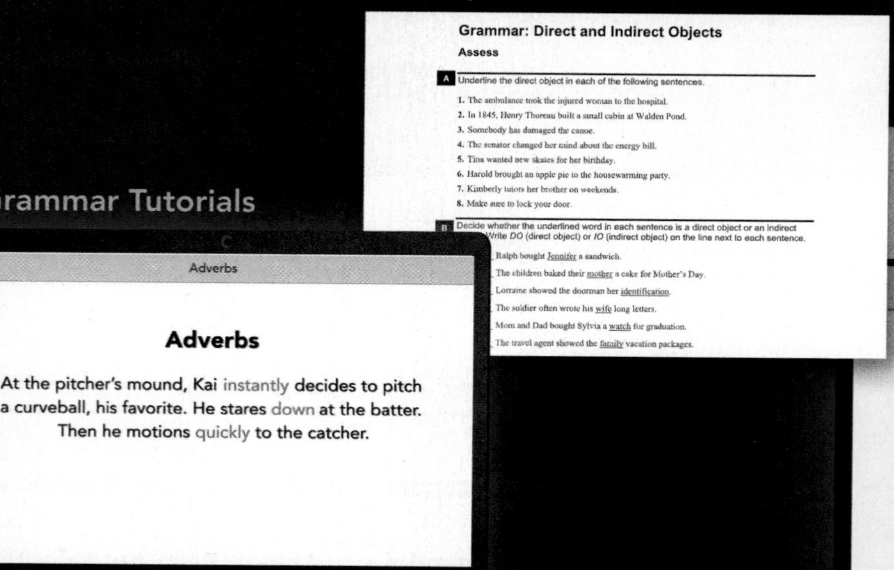

Grammar: Direct and Indirect Objects

Assess

A Underline the direct object in each of the following sentences.

1. The ambulance took the injured woman to the hospital.
2. In 1845, Henry Thoreau built a small cabin at Walden Pond.
3. Somebody has damaged the canoe.
4. The senator changed her mind about the energy bill.
5. Tina wanted new skates for her birthday.
6. Harold brought an apple pie to the housewarming party.
7. Kimberly tutors her brother on weekends.
8. Make sure to lock your door.

B Decide whether the underlined word in each sentence is a direct object or an indirect Write *DO* (direct object) or *IO* (indirect object) on the line next to each sentence.

Ralph bought Jennifer a sandwich.
The children baked their mother a cake for Mother's Day.
Lorraine showed the doorman her identification.
The soldier often wrote his wife long letters.
Mom and Dad bought Sylvia a watch for graduation.
The travel agent showed the family vacation packages.

SAVVAS realize. Home Browse Classes

myPerspectives ELA National Grade 9

Table of contents Resources Standards

Show Distance Learning Resources

Table of Contents

Digital Library

Trade Book Lesson Pla

PDF Tool

can annotate with a r or freeform draw ents can even use ol to respond to and to complete ganizers!

can assign a program-PDF OR they can even eir OWN PDFs!

o need to download es—all work can eted and submitted Savvas Realize!

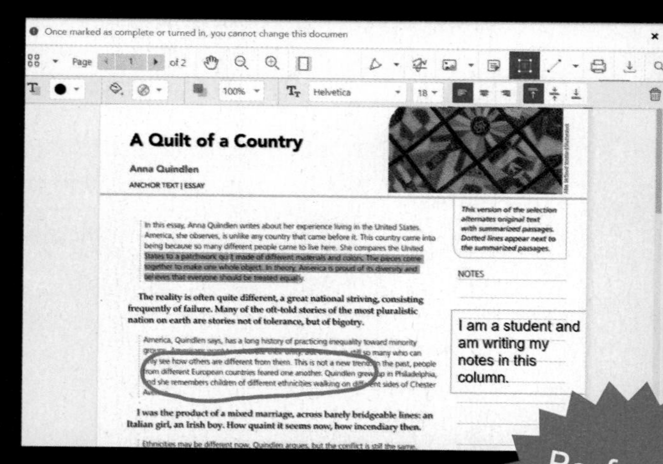

Perfect for Distance Learning!

Anchor Charts

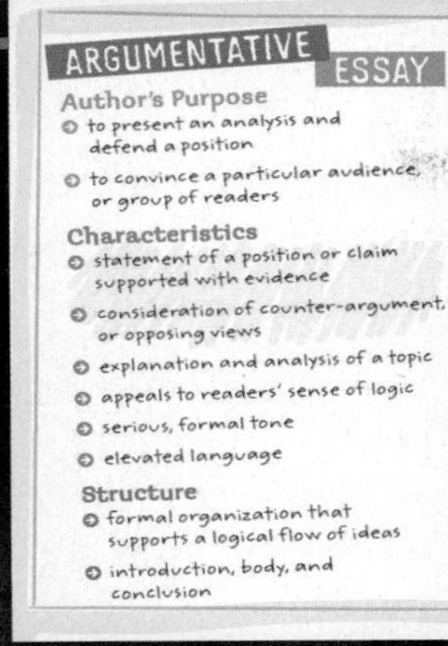

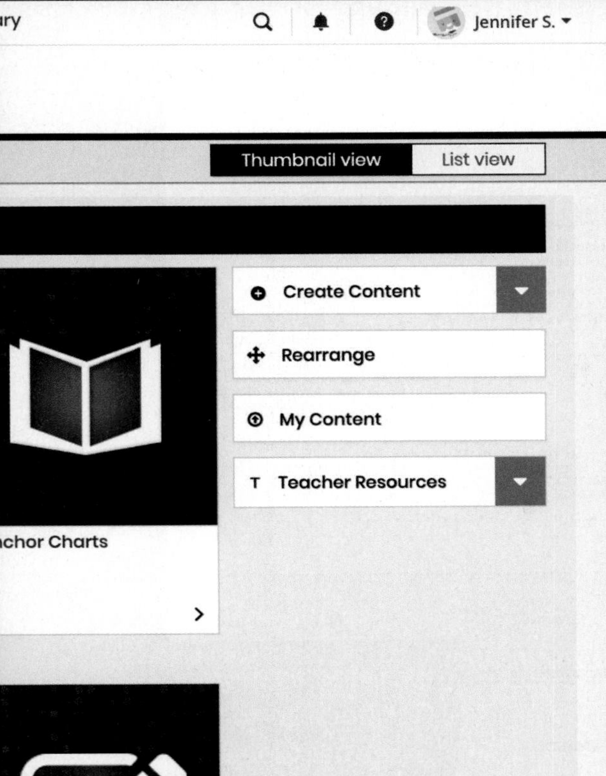

Collaboration Center Peer Modeling Videos

Skills Videos

Writing Gallery Videos

CONTENTS

Chapter I: Down The Rabbit-Hole

Alice was beginning to get very tired of sitting by her sister on the bank, and of having nothing to do: once or twice she had peeped into the book her sister was reading, but it had no pictures or conversations in it, 'and what is the use of a book,' thought Alice 'without pictures or conversation?'

So she was considering in her own mind (as well as she could, for the hot day made her feel very sleepy and stupid), whether the pleasure of making a daisy-chain would be worth the trouble of getting up

5

140+ Digital Novels

Flexible and Customizable: Novels

Whether you want to replace a unit, integrate novels within a unit, allow student choice, or expand your classroom library, *myPerspectives* gives you options. The novels offered will allow your students to expand their world as they read about and experience other cultures, backgrounds, and characters.

TEACHING WITH TRADE BOOKS

Each unit includes suggested novels that align to the unit theme. Teaching support includes suggested pacing and a Lesson Plan with student-facing activities.

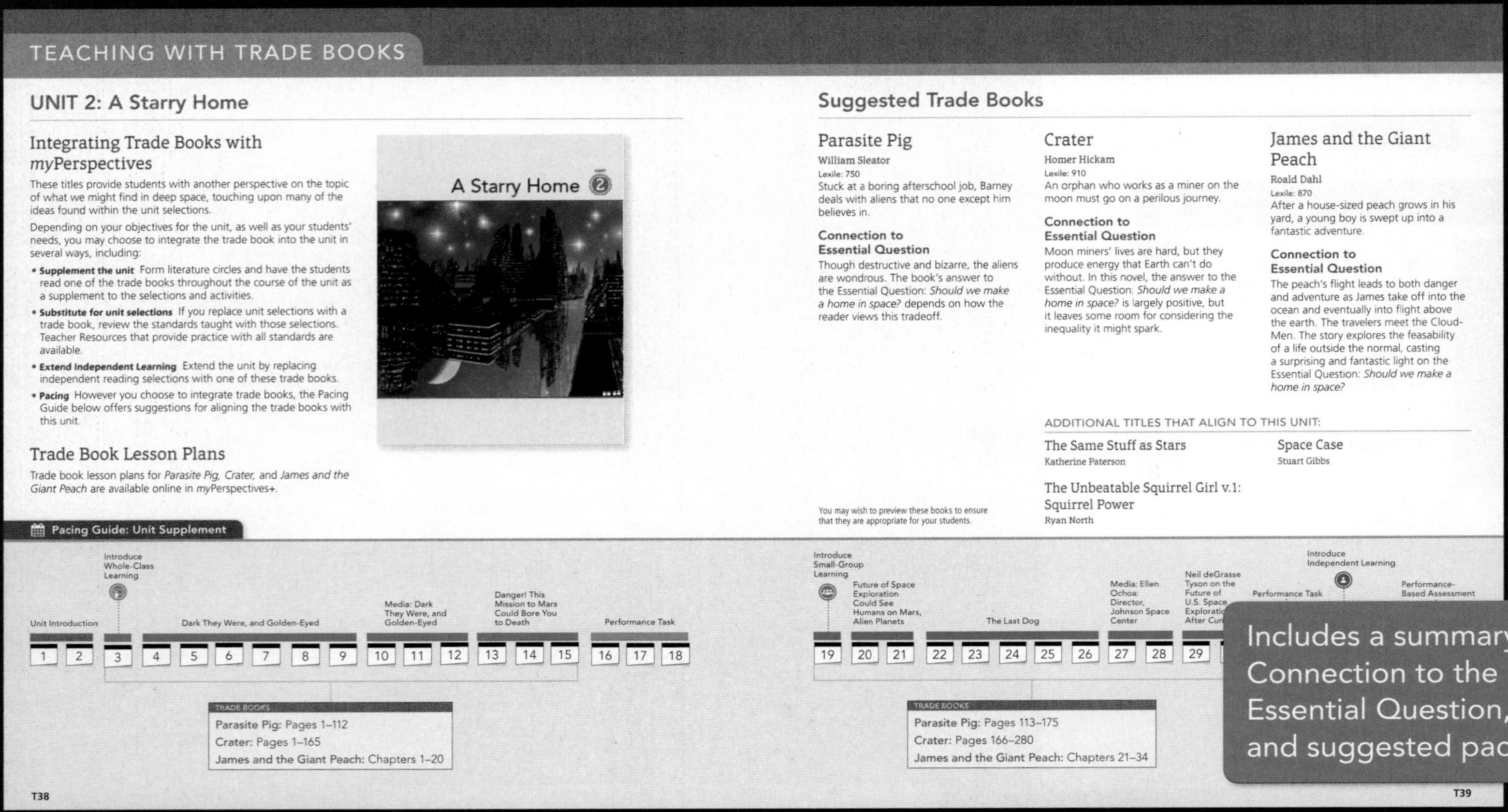

TEACHING WITH TRADE BOOKS

UNIT 2: A Starry Home

Integrating Trade Books with *my*Perspectives

These titles provide students with another perspective on the topic of what we might find in deep space, touching upon many of the ideas found within the unit selections.

Depending on your objectives for the unit, as well as your students' needs, you may choose to integrate the trade book into the unit in several ways, including:

- **Supplement the unit** Form literature circles and have the students read one of the trade books throughout the course of the unit as a supplement to the selections and activities.
- **Substitute for unit selections** If you replace unit selections with a trade book, review the standards taught with those selections. Teacher Resources that provide practice with all standards are available.
- **Extend Independent Learning** Extend the unit by replacing independent reading selections with one of these trade books.
- **Pacing** However you choose to integrate trade books, the Pacing Guide below offers suggestions for aligning the trade books with this unit.

A Starry Home 2

Trade Book Lesson Plans

Trade book lesson plans for *Parasite Pig, Crater,* and *James and the Giant Peach* are available online in *my*Perspectives+.

Suggested Trade Books

Parasite Pig

William Sleator

Lexile: 750

Stuck at a boring afterschool job, Barney deals with aliens that no one except him believes in.

Connection to Essential Question

Though destructive and bizarre, the aliens are wondrous. The book's answer to the Essential Question: *Should we make a home in space?* depends on how the reader views this tradeoff.

Crater

Homer Hickam

Lexile: 910

An orphan who works as a miner on the moon must go on a perilous journey.

Connection to Essential Question

Moon miners' lives are hard, but they produce energy that Earth can't do without. In this novel, the answer to the Essential Question: *Should we make a home in space?* is largely positive, but it leaves some room for considering the inequality it might spark.

James and the Giant Peach

Roald Dahl

Lexile: 870

After a house-sized peach grows in his yard, a young boy is swept up into a fantastic adventure.

Connection to Essential Question

The peach's flight leads to both danger and adventure as James take off into the ocean and eventually into flight above the earth. The travelers meet the Cloud-Men. The story explores the feasability of a life outside the normal, casting a surprising and fantastic light on the Essential Question: *Should we make a home in space?*

ADDITIONAL TITLES THAT ALIGN TO THIS UNIT:

The Same Stuff as Stars
Katherine Paterson

Space Case
Stuart Gibbs

The Unbeatable Squirrel Girl v.1: Squirrel Power
Ryan North

You may wish to preview these books to ensure that they are appropriate for your students.

Pacing Guide: Unit Supplement

Lesson	Days
Unit Introduction	1, 2
Introduce Whole-Class Learning	3
Dark They Were, and Golden-Eyed	4, 5, 6, 7, 8, 9
Media: Dark They Were, and Golden-Eyed	10, 11, 12
Danger! This Mission to Mars Could Bore You to Death	13, 14, 15
Performance Task	16, 17, 18
Introduce Small-Group Learning	19
Future of Space Exploration Could See Humans on Mars, Alien Planets	20, 21
The Last Dog	22, 23, 24, 25, 26
Media: Ellen Ochoa: Director, Johnson Space Center	27, 28
Neil deGrasse Tyson on the Future of U.S. Space Exploratio[n] After Cur[...]	29
Performance Task	
Introduce Independent Learning	
Performance-Based Assessment	

TRADE BOOKS (Days 3–15)
Parasite Pig: Pages 1–112
Crater: Pages 1–165
James and the Giant Peach: Chapters 1–20

TRADE BOOKS (Days 19–29)
Parasite Pig: Pages 113–175
Crater: Pages 166–280
James and the Giant Peach: Chapters 21–34

T38

T39

Includes a summary, Connection to the Essential Question, and suggested pacing.

Choose from 1400+ contemporary and classic titles to add to your classroom library.

Spanish Titles Available

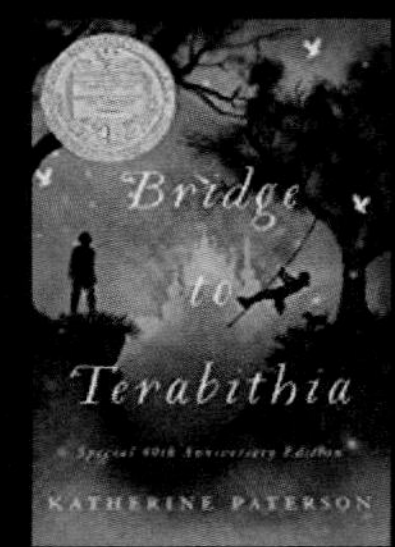

DIGITAL NOVELS

Digital novels in *myPerspectives+* are assignable or available for independent reading.

The Book of Dragons

by Edith Nesbit

When the people in the town saw the Dragon and the Hippogriff fly off after the King, they all came out of their houses to look, and when they saw them disappear they made up their minds to the worst, and began to think what they would wear for Court mourning.

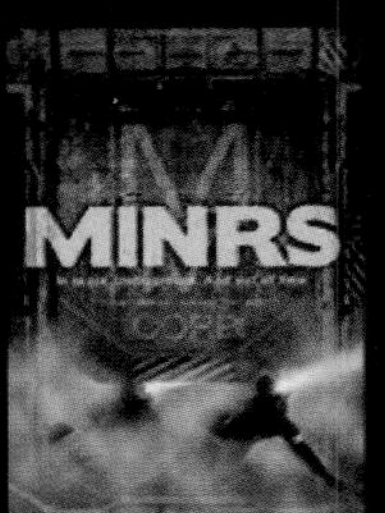

Differentiated Instruction

Planning resources, talking points, and instructional strategies provide teachers with suggestions to adapt lessons to diverse learning styles.

TEXT COMPLEXITY

Text Complexity Rubrics provide quantitative and qualitative information that help teachers plan for making texts accessible for all students.

LEVELED SUPPORT

Practical and easy-to-implement differentiation suggestions related to the Text Complexity Rubric are available before the lesson.

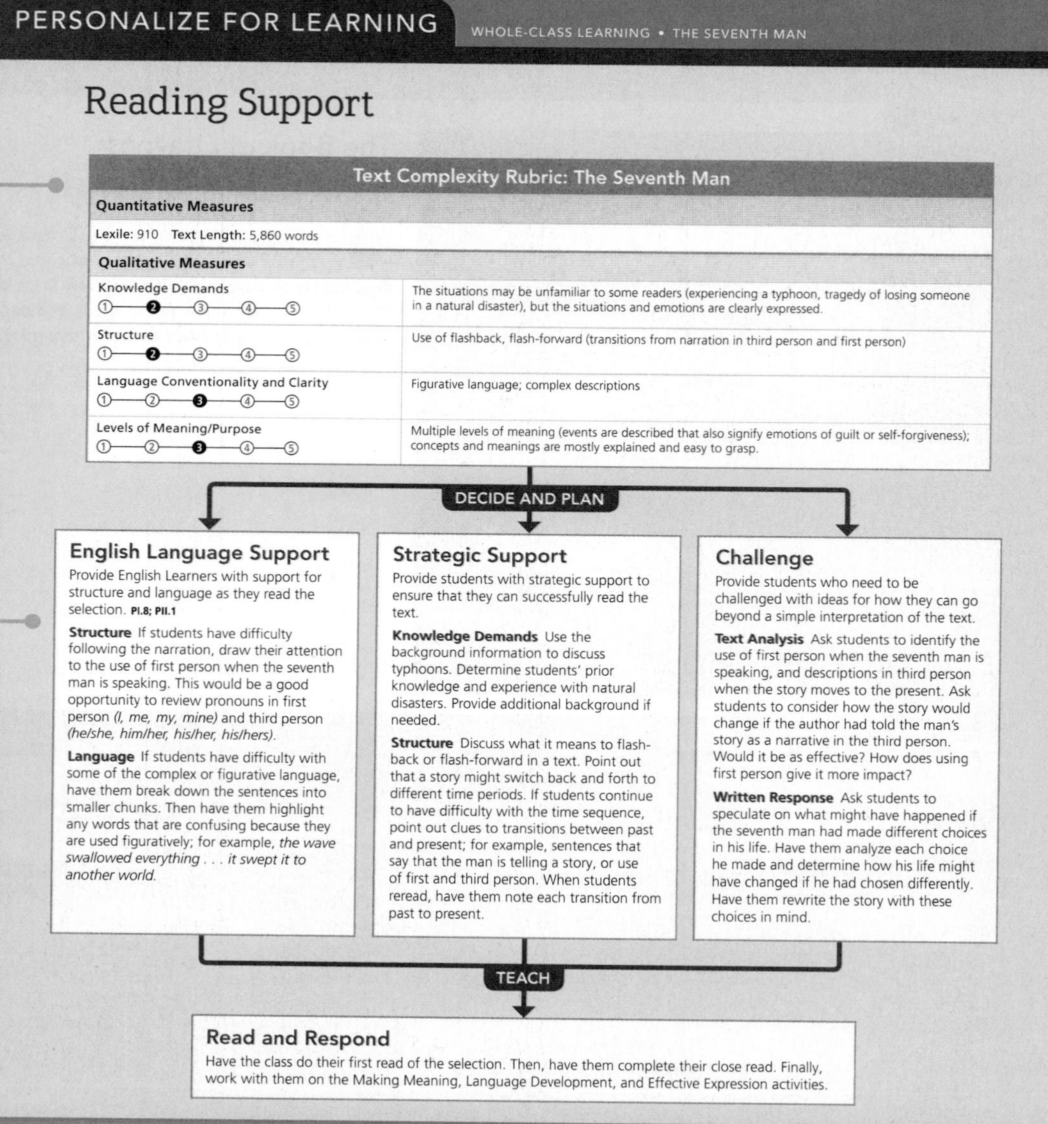

PERSONALIZE FOR LEARNING WHOLE-CLASS LEARNING • THE SEVENTH MAN

Reading Support

Text Complexity Rubric: The Seventh Man	
Quantitative Measures	
Lexile: 910 Text Length: 5,860 words	
Qualitative Measures	
Knowledge Demands ①—❷—③—④—⑤	The situations may be unfamiliar to some readers (experiencing a typhoon, tragedy of losing someone in a natural disaster), but the situations and emotions are clearly expressed.
Structure ①—❷—③—④—⑤	Use of flashback, flash-forward (transitions from narration in third person and first person)
Language Conventionality and Clarity ①—②—❸—④—⑤	Figurative language; complex descriptions
Levels of Meaning/Purpose ①—②—❸—④—⑤	Multiple levels of meaning (events are described that also signify emotions of guilt or self-forgiveness); concepts and meanings are mostly explained and easy to grasp.

DECIDE AND PLAN

English Language Support

Provide English Learners with support for structure and language as they read the selection. **PI.8; PII.1**

Structure If students have difficulty following the narration, draw their attention to the use of first person when the seventh man is speaking. This would be a good opportunity to review pronouns in first person *(I, me, my, mine)* and third person *(he/she, him/her, his/her, his/hers)*.

Language If students have difficulty with some of the complex or figurative language, have them break down the sentences into smaller chunks. Then have them highlight any words that are confusing because they are used figuratively; for example, *the wave swallowed everything . . . it swept it to another world.*

Strategic Support

Provide students with strategic support to ensure that they can successfully read the text.

Knowledge Demands Use the background information to discuss typhoons. Determine students' prior knowledge and experience with natural disasters. Provide additional background if needed.

Structure Discuss what it means to flash-back or flash-forward in a text. Point out that a story might switch back and forth to different time periods. If students continue to have difficulty with the time sequence, point out clues to transitions between past and present; for example, sentences that say that the man is telling a story, or use of first and third person. When students reread, have them note each transition from past to present.

Challenge

Provide students who need to be challenged with ideas for how they can go beyond a simple interpretation of the text.

Text Analysis Ask students to identify the use of first person when the seventh man is speaking, and descriptions in third person when the story moves to the present. Ask students to consider how the story would change if the author had told the man's story as a narrative in the third person. Would it be as effective? How does using first person give it more impact?

Written Response Ask students to speculate on what might have happened if the seventh man had made different choices in his life. Have them analyze each choice he made and determine how his life might have changed if he had chosen differently. Have them rewrite the story with these choices in mind.

TEACH

Read and Respond

Have the class do their first read of the selection. Then, have them complete their close read. Finally, work with them on the Making Meaning, Language Development, and Effective Expression activities.

EVERY TEACHER'S ELL TOOLKIT

Includes mini-lessons grouped by skill areas: Newcomers, Vocabulary, Grammar and Spelling, Listening and Speaking, Reading, Writing, and Critical Thinking Skills.

Each mini-lesson supports language and content-area objectives and also presents learning strategies, such as using prior knowledge.

TEACHER-FACING NOTES

Teacher-facing notes allow you to help all learners access the instruction no matter students' learner levels. Notes can be used as talking points, remediation, and/or extension activities.

Notes include:

- Language Support
- Strategic Support
- Challenge
- English Language Support
- Author's Perspective Notes
- Vocabulary Development
- Digital Perspectives
- Cross-Curricular Perspectives
- WriteNow
- How Language Works

PERSONALIZE FOR LEARNING

Language Support

Multiple-Meaning Words Explain to students that the word *stuff* in paragraph 72 has several different meanings. As it's used in this part of the story, it's a noun that means "something consumed or introduced into the body." As a noun, it can also mean personal property ("I can't keep track of all my stuff."); a matter to be considered ("The ideas in this book are serious stuff."); a group or scattering of objects or articles ("Pick up all that stuff on the floor."); or subject matter ("Yo... also be a ve... a box.").

PERSONALIZE FOR LEARNING

Strategic Support

Personification Remind students that personification is the technique of giving human qualities to nonhumans. Point out the following example of personification in paragraph 41: This was the moment Mars had waited for. Now it would eat them. Encourage students to look for more examples of personification as they continue reading. What effect does personification create in the reader?

Personalize for Learning notes offer strategies for all learner levels.

PERSONALIZE FOR LEARNING

English Language Support

Character Motivation Support English Learners in their understanding of character motivation.

Present a small group of students with a newspaper story about an individual who has done something philanthropic. Read the article with students. Once they understand the content, ask students to collaborate in writing one or two sentences describing why this person might have done what they did. **EMERGING**

Give students a newspaper story about an individual who has done something philanthropic. Ask students to write a paragraph describing the person's possible motives for what he or she did. **EXPANDING**

Give students two articles: one about a person who has done something philanthropic and one about a person who is seeking elected office. Ask students to write a paragraph that compares and contrasts what the motives of these two people might be. **BRIDGING**

AUTHOR'S PERSPECTIVE Kelly Gallagher, M.Ed.

The Best Writer in the Room Intensive modeling is one of the most effective ways to improve writing instruction. When teachers model at every stage of the writing process, they stop *assigning* writing and start *teaching* it. While you are teaching writing through this Performance Task, show your students how you attack these parts of the assignment:

Prewriting Brainstorm counterclaims and ask students to add their own ideas to your list. List types of evidence you could use.

Drafting Outline the argument and draft alongside students.

Revising Use your model or a student model as an example.

Do this work in front of students each time. While it may seem more efficient to follow the same steps with each class or show a perfectly polished essay, don't take this path. If you authentically model the work of writing, students may be more open to the work of writing. It is important for the students to see the teacher struggle a bit with the work.

Author's Perspective notes provide mini Professional Development strategies.

VOCABULARY DEVELOPMENT

Concept Vocabulary Reinforcement Discuss the word *atmosphere* in paragraph 175, pointing out that it has several meanings. The meaning used in the story is "the gaseous envelope of a celestial body (for example, a planet); the whole mass of air surrounding the earth." It also has other meanings, including "a surrounding influence or environment" (for example, an atmosphere of hostility) and "an intriguing or singular tone, effect, or appeal" (for example, a park with a friendly atmosphere).

CROSS-CURRICULAR PERSPECTIVES

Science Have students research Mars, focusing on its natural features and atmospheric conditions, and write short reports on the challenges people from Earth would face if they lived on Mars. How might these challenges be overcome? Are these challenges addressed in the story? How?

> "It's critical to give students the opportunity to read a wide range of highly engaging texts and to immerse themselves in exploring powerful ideas and how these ideas are expressed. In *myPerspectives,* we focus on building up students' awareness of how academic language works, which is especially important for English language learners."
>
> —Jim Cummins

Reach All Learners

The goal is for ALL students to be reading grade-level texts, yet some students struggle and need support. The leveled texts in *myPerspectives* are intended to help students build comprehension and background knowledge, allowing them to be able to participate in class activities and discussions of the texts.

LEVELED TEXTS

The Last Dog

Katherine Paterson

On-Level

The Last Dog

Katherine Paterson

SHORT STORY

This version of the selection alternates original text with summarized passages. Dotted lines appear next to the summarized passages.

NOTES

Brock approached the customs gate. Although he did not reach for the scanner, a feeling it might have labeled "excitement" made him tremble. His fingers shook as he punched in his number on the inquiry board. "This is highly irregular, Brock 095670038," the disembodied voice said. "What is your reason for external travel?"

Brock took a deep breath. "Scientific research," he replied. He didn't need to be told that his behavior was "irregular." He'd never heard of anyone doing research outside the dome—actual rather than virtual research. "I—I've been cleared by my podmaster and the Research Team. ..."

The machine continues to question him. It asks when Brock plans to return, if he has the proper equipment, and if he understands that the water supply is limited.

Why weren't they questioning him further? Were they eager for him to go? Ever since he'd said out loud in group speak that he wanted to go outside the dome, people had treated him strangely—that session with the podmaster and then the interview with the representative from Research. Did they think he was a deviant?[1] Deviants sometimes disappeared. The word was passed around that they had "gone outside," but no one really knew. No deviant had ever returned.

The gate opens and Brock steps outside the dome. Even though he wears a screened helmet, his eyes are sensitive to the sunlight. He has learned everything he knows about the sun—and about the mountains he sees in the distance—from his virtual lessons.

It was, he pulled the scanner from his outside pouch and checked it, "hot." Oh, that was what he was feeling. Hot. He remembered "hot" from a virtual lesson he'd had once on deserts.

Brock knows from other lessons not to take off his protective suit. He adjusts the controls on the suit instead, and soon he is cooler.

Brock can't believe he's the only one who is curious about the outside world. Other people laugh at him when he tries to talk about it. But Brock is different in other ways too. While the people from his pod play virtual games, he likes to visit the "ancient fictions." The stories, and the people in them, make Brock feel both afraid and eager. He returns to the ancient fictions often.

Within a short distance from the dome, the land was clear and barren, but after he had been walking for an hour or so he began to pass rusting

1. **deviant** (DEE vee uhnt) *n.* strange, irregular person.

GRADE 7 • UNIT 2 • Accessible Leveled Text • The Last Dog 1

Leveled

Summarized and Authentic Text is chunked

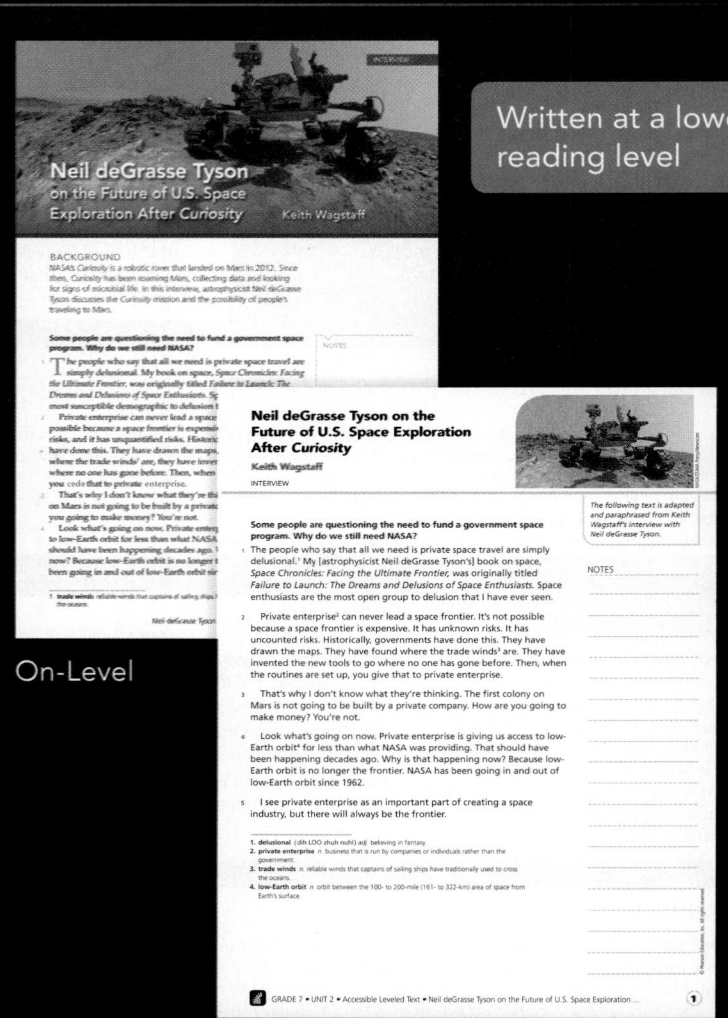

Neil deGrasse Tyson on the Future of U.S. Space Exploration After *Curiosity*

Keith Wagstaff

On-Level

Neil deGrasse Tyson on the Future of U.S. Space Exploration After *Curiosity*

Keith Wagstaff

INTERVIEW

The following text is adapted and paraphrased from Keith Wagstaff's interview with Neil deGrasse Tyson.

NOTES

Some people are questioning the need to fund a government space program. Why do we still need NASA?

1 The people who say that all we need is private space travel are simply delusional.[1] My [astrophysicist Neil deGrasse Tyson's] book on space, *Space Chronicles: Facing the Ultimate Frontier,* was originally titled *Failure to Launch: The Dreams and Delusions of Space Enthusiasts.* Space enthusiasts are the most open group to delusion that I have ever seen.

2 Private enterprise[2] can never lead a space frontier. It's not possible because a space frontier is expensive. It has unknown risks. It has uncounted risks. Historically, governments have done this. They have drawn the maps. They have found where the trade winds[3] are. They have invented the new tools to go where no one has gone before. Then, when the routines are set up, you give that to private enterprise.

3 That's why I don't know what they're thinking. The first colony on Mars is not going to be built by a private company. How are you going to make money? You're not.

4 Look what's going on now. Private enterprise is giving us access to low-Earth orbit[4] for less than what NASA was providing. That should have been happening decades ago. Why is that happening now? Because low-Earth orbit is no longer the frontier. NASA has been going in and out of low-Earth orbit since 1962.

5 I see private enterprise as an important part of creating a space industry, but there will always be the frontier.

1. **delusional** (dih LOO zhuh nuhl) *adj.* believing in fantasy.
2. **private enterprise** *n.* business that is run by companies or individuals rather than the government.
3. **trade winds** *n.* reliable winds that captains of sailing ships have traditionally used to cross the oceans.
4. **low-Earth orbit** *n.* orbit between the 100- to 200-mile (161- to 322-km) area of space from Earth's surface.

GRADE 7 • UNIT 2 • Accessible Leveled Text • Neil deGrasse Tyson on the Future of U.S. Space Exploration ... 1

Leveled

Written at a lower reading level

LITERARY TEXTS

Leveled Literary Texts allow students to read portions of the authentic literature, with summarized paragraphs, to aid in comprehension.

INFORMATIONAL TEXTS

Leveled Informational Texts are written with simplified vocabulary and varied sentence structure, making the text more accessible through a lower reading level.

Spanish Resources

SPANISH TRANSLATIONS

Spanish Translations of text selections, including media selections and unit opener videos, are available.

Cuento corto realista

El príncipe Francis

Roddy Doyle

CONTEXTO

Este cuento está incluido en la antología de cuentos cortos para jóvenes *Free? Stories About Human Rights*, que celebra la Declaración Universal de los Derechos Humanos. Cada uno de los cuentos se enfoca en un artículo de este importante documento de las Naciones Unidas. En este relato, un niño que ha tenido que dejar su hogar en África espera hacer nuevos amigos en Irlanda, donde vive actualmente.

1 Era realmente emocionante. Toda la clase iba a ser entrevistada, como si estuvieran en la televisión. De hecho, estaban en la televisión.

2 La cámara estaba en posición, al fondo de la clase, en la parte más alta. Daragh era el camarógrafo.

3 Francis envidiaba a Daragh. A él le hubiera gustado ser el camarógrafo. Había levantado la mano: "¡Señor! ¡Señor! ¡Señor, yo!", pero Señor había elegido a Daragh.

4 No había problema. A Francis, en realidad, no le importaba. Se llevaba bien con Daragh.

5 —*Ciúnas* —dijo Señor.

6 Francis sabía que *ciúnas* significaba "silencio" en irlandés. Sabía, también, algunas otras palabras irlandesas. *Buachaill* quería decir "niño", y *leithreas* significaba "baño".

7 —Estamos listos —dijo Señor—. ¿Quién será nuestra primera estrella?

8 Los estudiantes rieron e intercambiaron miradas. Esto iba a ser divertido.

9 Una de las niñas, Alicia, era la entrevistadora. Llevaba un vestido negro que había pertenecido a su abuela, y usaba en los ojos una sombra negra que la hacía parpadear. Tenía una tabla sujetapapeles sobre el regazo con las preguntas que iba a hacer.

10 —Kevin —dijo Señor—. Serás el primero.

El príncipe Francis 1

MULTILINGUAL GLOSSARY

Vocabulary words are defined, with audio, in English and Spanish.

AUDIO SUPPORT

Full Selection Audio and Selection Summaries in English and Spanish, recorded with authentic narrators, support multimodal learners.

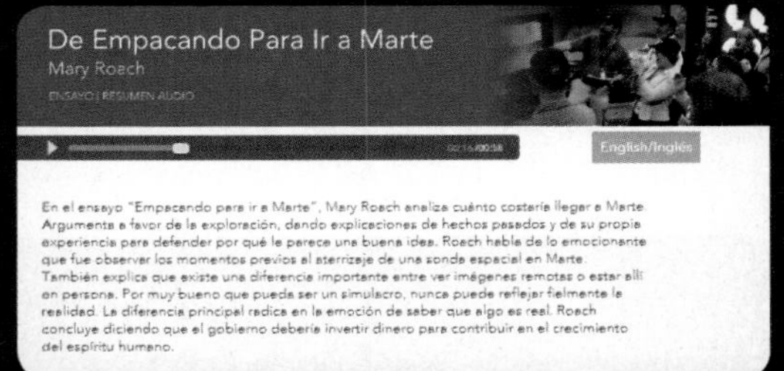

STUDENT REFERENCE MATERIALS

The Student Edition Toolkit includes Academic and Concept Vocabulary and a Literary Handbook in English and Spanish.

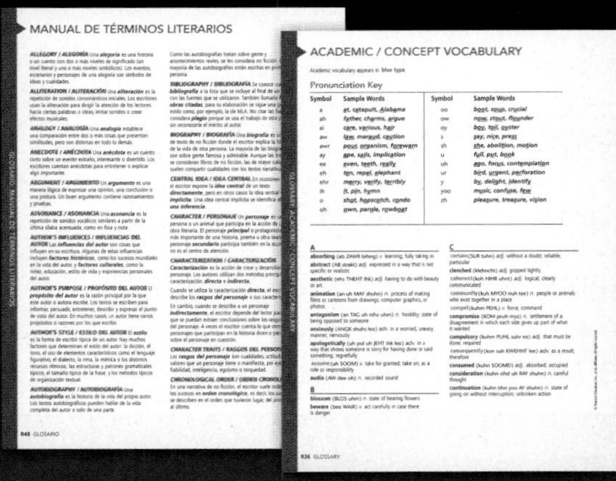

Assessment Overview

WHAT YOU NEED TO...

INFORM INSTRUCTION
Formative and Performance-Based Assessments

POINT-OF-USE OPPORTUNITIES

Gather comprehensive data to inform instructional pathways using embedded routines:

- If / Then Teacher Notes
- Reteach and Practice
- First Read Questions
- First Read Extension Questions
- Analyze the Text Questions
- Selection Instructional Activities

PERFORMANCE-BASED ASSESSMENTS

Monitor student critical thinking and synthesis of the unit themes, Essential Questions, and skills knowledge through:

- Writing Performance Tasks
- Speaking and Listening Performance Tasks
- End-of-Unit Performance-Based Assessments

SELECTION TESTS

Monitor student understanding of texts read in each unit.

DELIVERED HOW YOU NEED IT...

	print	digital	customizable
Point-of-Use Opportunities	•	•	
Performance-Based Assessments	•	•	
Beginning, Mid, End-of-Year Tests		•	•
Extension Beginning, Mid, End-of-Year Tests		•	•
Selection Tests		•	•
Extension Selection Tests		•	•
Unit Test		•	•
High Stakes Test Prep Banks		•	•

All items aligned to Standards and DOKs

DATA AND REPORTING

Teachers and districts can gather and track student, class, and district growth. Data can be exported and shared with your school's learning management system.

Reports include:

- Class Mastery by Standards
- Student Mastery
- Average Mastery
- Standards Item Analysis
- Progress by Student
- Usage by Student

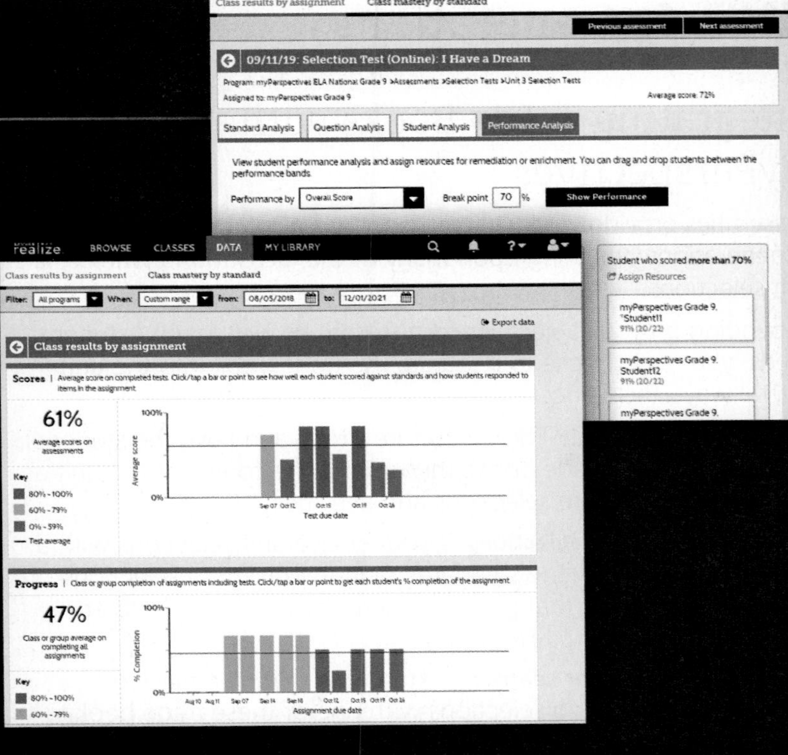

PRIORITY STANDARDS

A correlation to the Priority Standards (identified by Student Achievement Partners) can be found in the Distance Learning folder. You can search for instructional assets by Priority Standard on Realize to help focus your instruction.

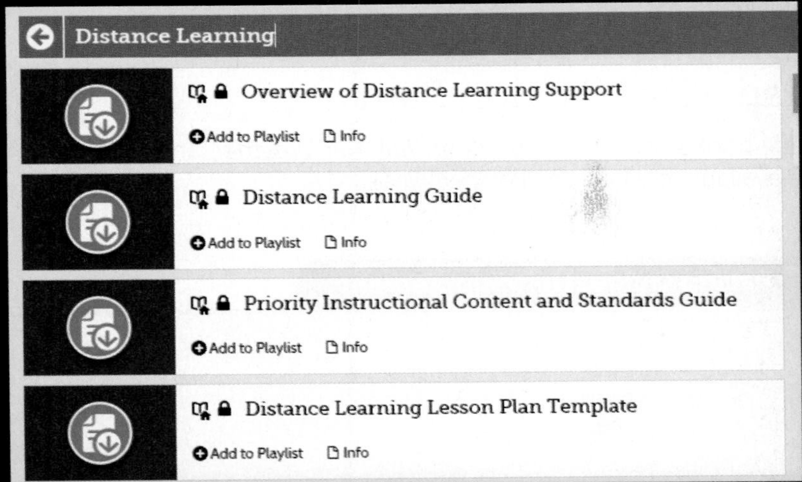

realize™
Online Assessment

Customizable Digital Assessments and Editable Word Documents allow teachers to edit, add, or delete questions or to build a test from scratch.

Data and Reports allow teachers and districts to gather and track student, class, and district growth on grade-level knowledge and skills.

UNIT 1: Generations

Integrating Trade Books with *my*Perspectives

These titles provide students with another perspective on the topic of generations, touching upon many of the ideas found within the unit selections.

Depending on your objectives for the unit, as well as your students' needs, you may choose to integrate the trade book into the unit in several ways, including:

- **Supplement the unit** Form literature circles and have the students read one of the trade books throughout the course of the unit as a supplement to the selections and activities.
- **Substitute for unit selections** If you replace unit selections with a trade book, review the standards taught with those selections. Teacher Resources that provide practice with all standards are available.
- **Extend Independent Learning** Extend the unit by replacing independent reading selections with one of these trade books.
- **Pacing** However you choose to integrate trade books, the Pacing Guide below offers suggestions for aligning the trade books with this unit.

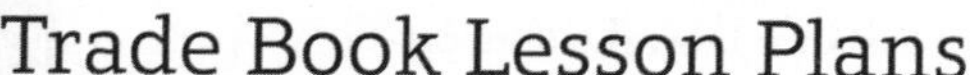

Trade Book Lesson Plans

Trade book lesson plans for *Stand Tall, Fair Weather,* and *Ribbons* are available online in *my*Perspectives+.

Pacing Guide: Unit Supplement

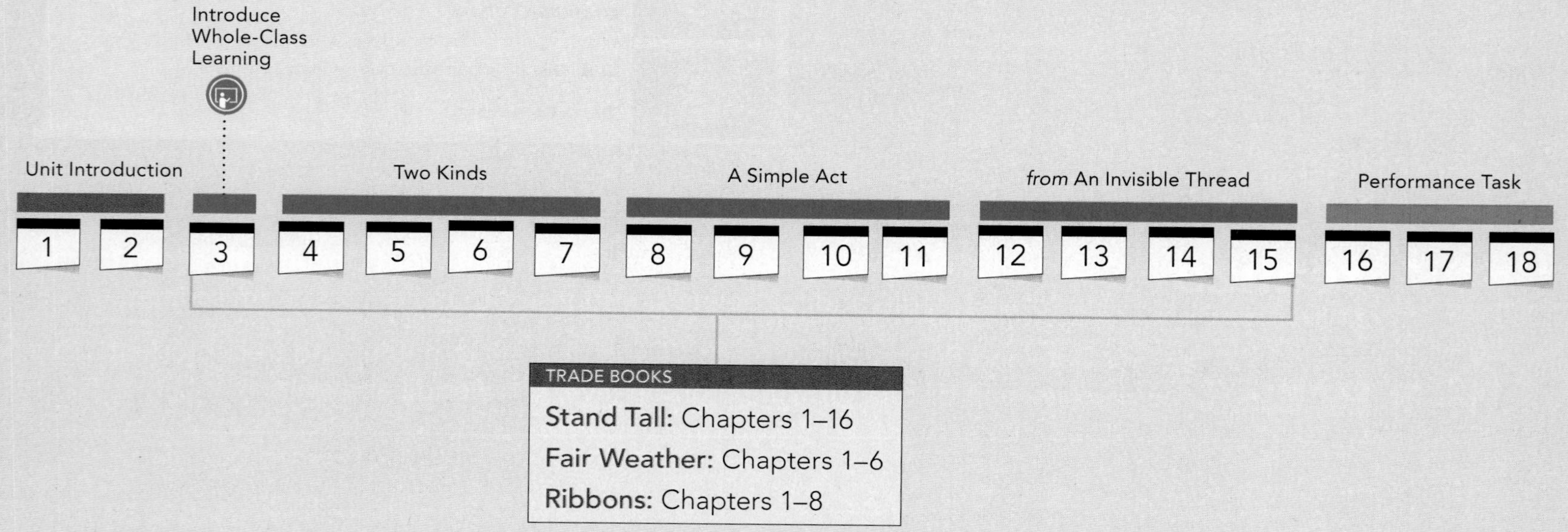

Suggested Trade Books

Stand Tall

Joan Bauer

Lexile: 520

Tree is the tallest kid in school, and he doesn't fit in. After his parents' divorce, he doesn't feel at home even in his own house. But Tree finds others who don't fit in —his disabled grandfather, and the new girl Sophie. By helping others, he makes a place to belong.

Connection to Essential Question

Despite his age, Tree's grandfather is going through his own transition. He recently lost his leg. He and Tree teach each other adapt to the new difficulties in their lives, a clear illustration of the Essential Question: *What can one generation learn from another?*

Fair Weather

Richard Peck

Lexile: 670

After a surprise invitation, Rosie and her family travel from their small farm to the big city for the 1893 World's Fair. The event opens their eyes to how fast the world and each of their lives is changing, and the trip helps them change for the better.

Connection to Essential Question

Through the relationship between Rosie and her aunt, this novel provides insight into the Essential Question: *What can one generation learn from another?* Rosie's Aunt Euterpe exposes her to the sophistication of city life, while Rosie's perspective helps Aunt Euterpe reconcile with the tragedies of her past.

Ribbons

Laurence Yep

Lexile: 710

Robin Lee loves ballet. But after her grandmother comes from Hong Kong to live with the family, the cost of taking care of her means they can no longer afford Robin's ballet lessons. Neither Robin nor her grandmother care about each other at first, but they come to understand how much they have in common.

Connection to Essential Question

Robin grows to appreciate her family's culture through learning about her grandmother's experiences. At the same time, her determination to dance despite injured feet parallels her grandmother's difficulty walking after foot-binding. Shared physical experience draws them into shared cultural experience, revealing a powerful answer to the Essential Question: *What can one generation learn from another?*

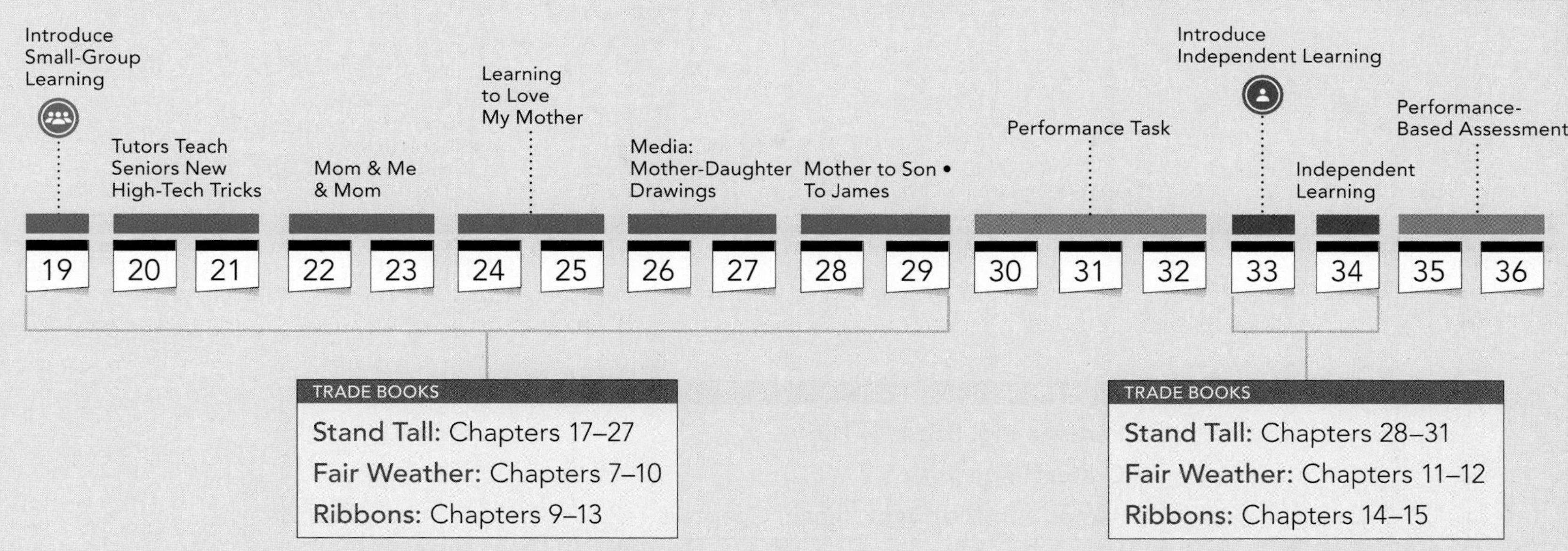

UNIT 2: A Starry Home

Integrating Trade Books with *my*Perspectives

These titles provide students with another perspective on the topic of what we might find in deep space, touching upon many of the ideas found within the unit selections.

Depending on your objectives for the unit, as well as your students' needs, you may choose to integrate the trade book into the unit in several ways, including:

- **Supplement the unit** Form literature circles and have the students read one of the trade books throughout the course of the unit as a supplement to the selections and activities.
- **Substitute for unit selections** If you replace unit selections with a trade book, review the standards taught with those selections. Teacher Resources that provide practice with all standards are available.
- **Extend Independent Learning** Extend the unit by replacing independent reading selections with one of these trade books.
- **Pacing** However you choose to integrate trade books, the Pacing Guide below offers suggestions for aligning the trade books with this unit.

Trade Book Lesson Plans

Trade book lesson plans for *Parasite Pig, Crater,* and *James and the Giant Peach* are available online in *my*Perspectives+.

Pacing Guide: Unit Supplement

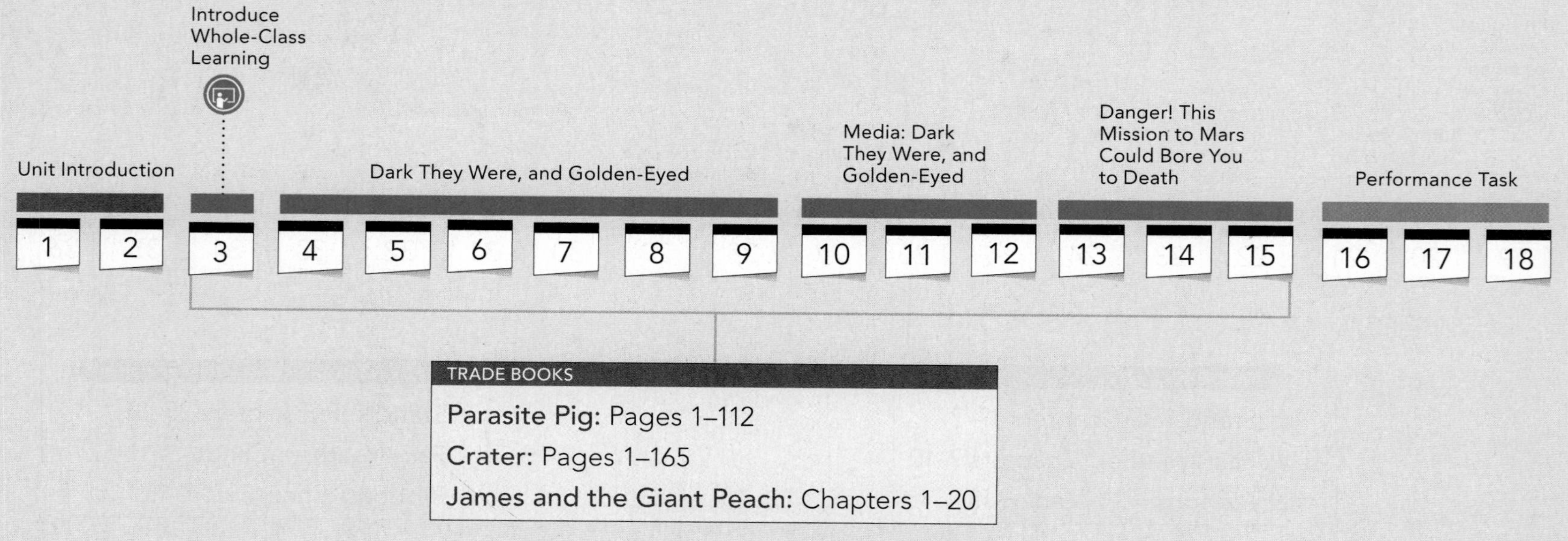

Suggested Trade Books

Parasite Pig

William Sleator

Lexile: 750

Stuck at a boring afterschool job, Barney deals with aliens that no one except him believes in.

Connection to Essential Question

Though destructive and bizarre, the aliens are wondrous. The book's answer to the Essential Question: *Should we make a home in space?* depends on how the reader views this tradeoff.

Crater

Homer Hickam

Lexile: 910

An orphan who works as a miner on the moon must go on a perilous journey.

Connection to Essential Question

Moon miners' lives are hard, but they produce energy that Earth can't do without. In this novel, the answer to the Essential Question: *Should we make a home in space?* is largely positive, but it leaves some room for considering the inequality it might spark.

James and the Giant Peach

Roald Dahl

Lexile: 870

After a house-sized peach grows in his yard, a young boy is swept up into a fantastic adventure.

Connection to Essential Question

The peach's flight leads to both danger and adventure as James take off into the ocean and eventually into flight above the earth. The travelers meet the Cloud-Men. The story explores the feasability of a life outside the normal, casting a surprising and fantastic light on the Essential Question: *Should we make a home in space?*

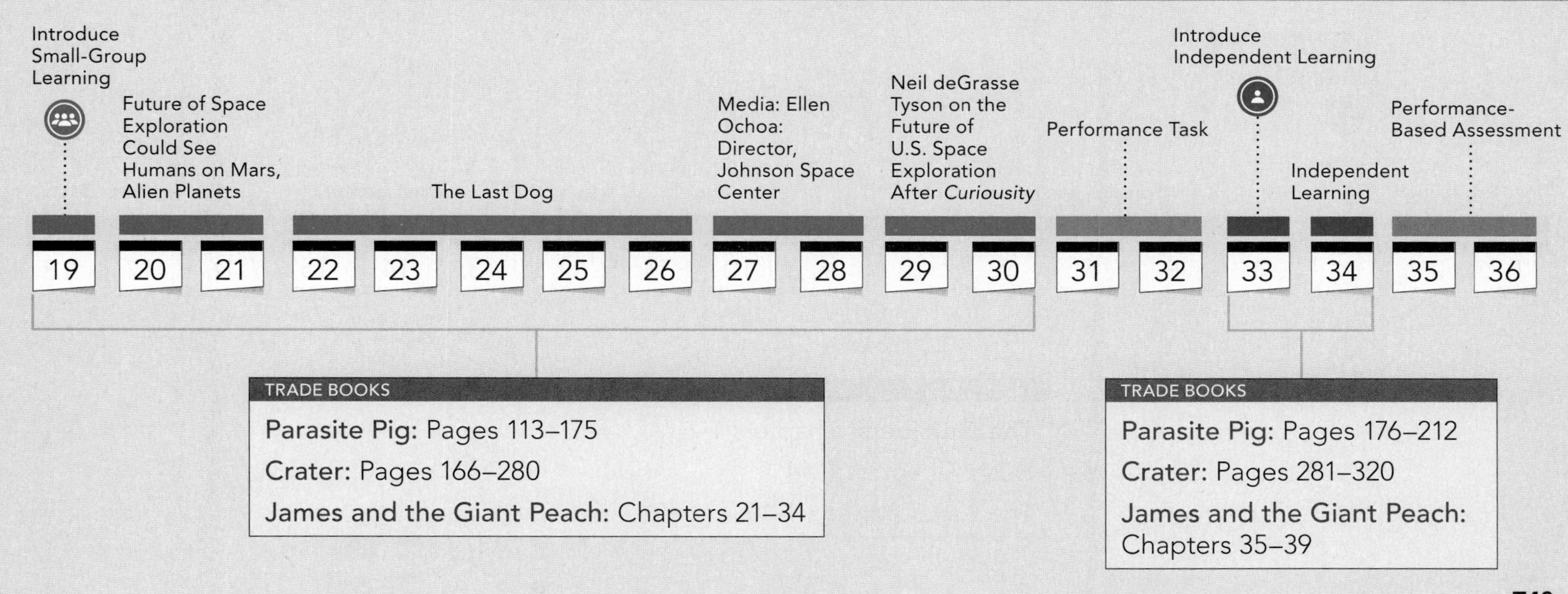

UNIT 3: Turning Points

Integrating Trade Books with *my*Perspectives

These titles provide students with another perspective on the topic of turning points, touching upon many of the ideas found within the unit selections.

Depending on your objectives for the unit, as well as your students' needs, you may choose to integrate the trade book into the unit in several ways, including:

- **Supplement the unit** Form literature circles and have the students read one of the trade books throughout the course of the unit as a supplement to the selections and activities.
- **Substitute for unit selections** If you replace unit selections with a trade book, review the standards taught with those selections. Teacher Resources that provide practice with all standards are available.
- **Extend Independent Learning** Extend the unit by replacing independent reading selections with one of these trade books.
- **Pacing** However you choose to integrate trade books, the Pacing Guide below offers suggestions for aligning the trade books with this unit.

Trade Book Lesson Plans

Trade book lesson plans for *The Outsiders, Hush,* and *The Cay* are available online in *my*Perspectives+.

Pacing Guide: Unit Supplement

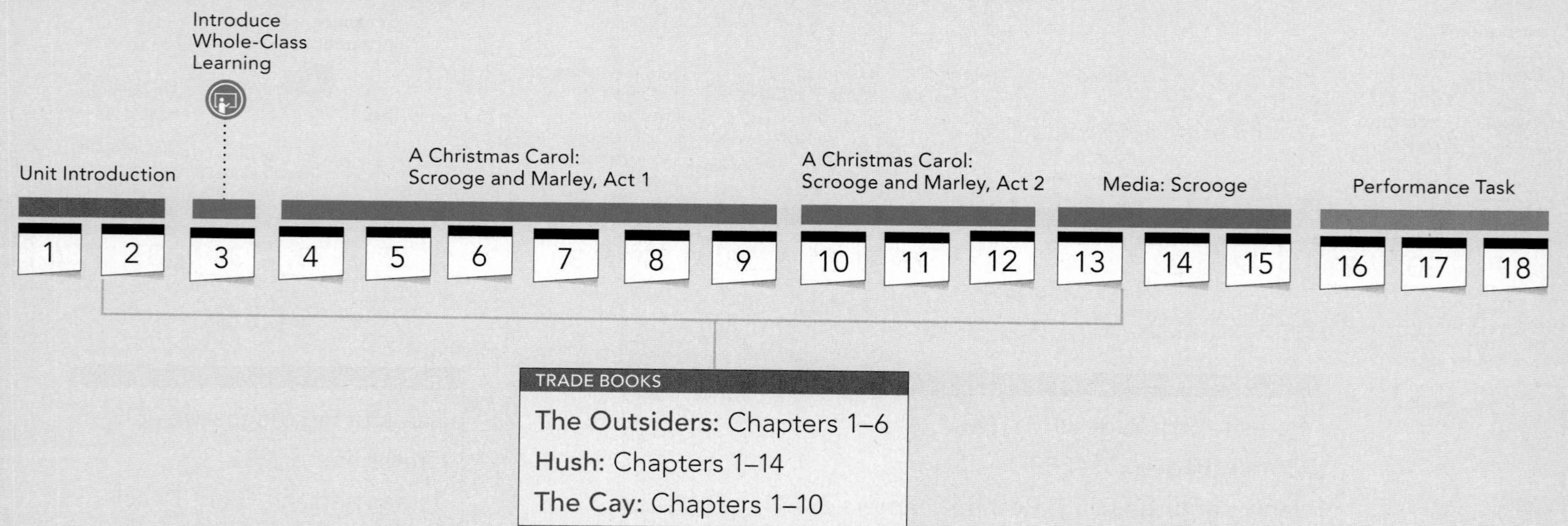

Suggested Trade Books

The Outsiders

S.E. Hinton

Lexile: 750

Fourteen-year-old Ponyboy Curtis struggles with right and wrong in a society where he feels like an outsider.

Connection to Essential Question

Violence and an ensuing cycle of revenge nearly destroy Pony Boy's life. This novel is a clear exploration of the Essential Question: *What can cause a sudden change in someone's life?* Fortunately, Pony Boy finds a second chance.

Hush

Jacqueline Woodson

Lexile: 640

Toswiah must move to a new city after her father gets in trouble for reporting a crime that fellow police committed.

Connection to Essential Question

Toswiah's life is upended because someone close to her chose to do the just thing regardless of how this would make people view him. Her father's action shows readers one perspective on the Essential Question: *What can cause a sudden change in someone's life?*

The Cay

Theodore Taylor

Lexile: 860

A blind boy and an old man struggle to survive after a shipwreck.

Connection to Essential Question

The other novels in this unit answer the Essential Question: *What can cause a sudden change in someone's life?* with social events; here there is a more physical turning point. The accident that takes away Phillip's sight also changes what he considers important and how he views the world.

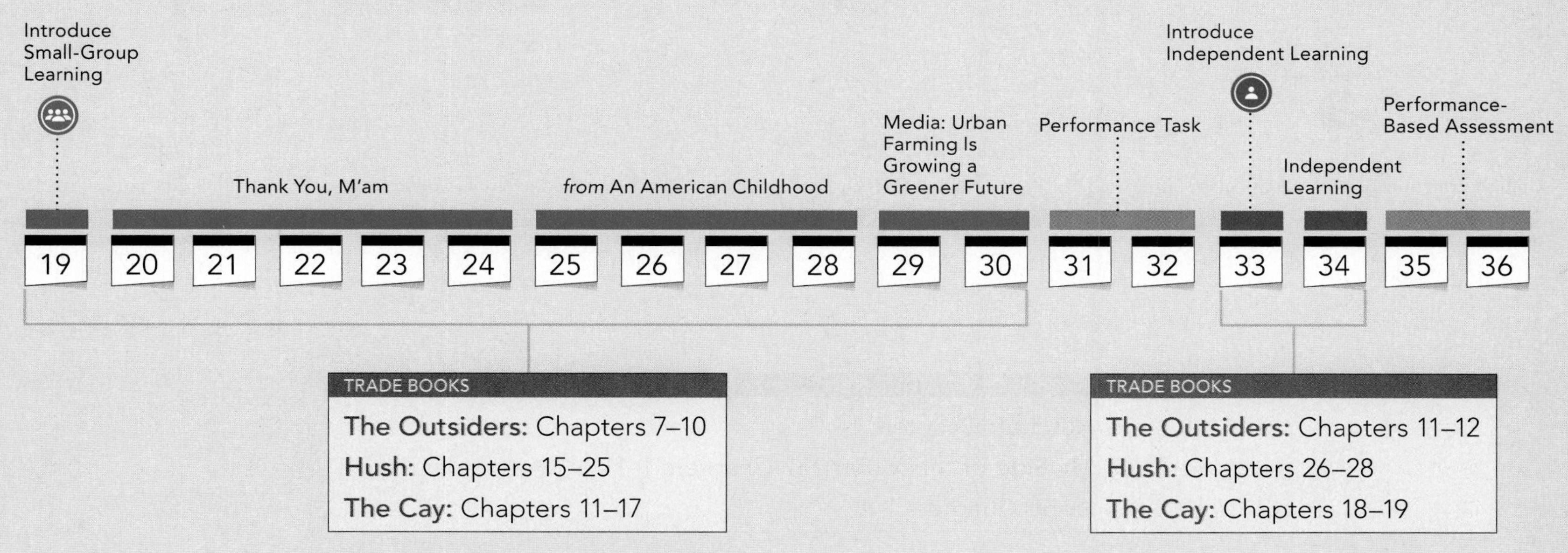

UNIT 4: People and the Planet

Integrating Trade Books with *my*Perspectives

These titles provide students with another perspective on the topic of the people's effect on the planet, touching upon many of the ideas found within the unit selections.

Depending on your objectives for the unit, as well as your students' needs, you may choose to integrate the trade book into the unit in several ways, including:

- **Supplement the unit** Form literature circles and have the students read one of the trade books throughout the course of the unit as a supplement to the selections and activities.
- **Substitute for unit selections** If you replace unit selections with a trade book, review the standards taught with those selections. Teacher Resources that provide practice with all standards are available.
- **Extend Independent Learning** Extend the unit by replacing independent reading selections with one of these trade books.
- **Pacing** However you choose to integrate trade books, the Pacing Guide below offers suggestions for aligning the trade books with this unit.

Trade Book Lesson Plans

Trade book lesson plans for *Hatchet, My Side of the Mountain,* and *Hoot* are available online in *my*Perspectives+.

Pacing Guide: Unit Supplement

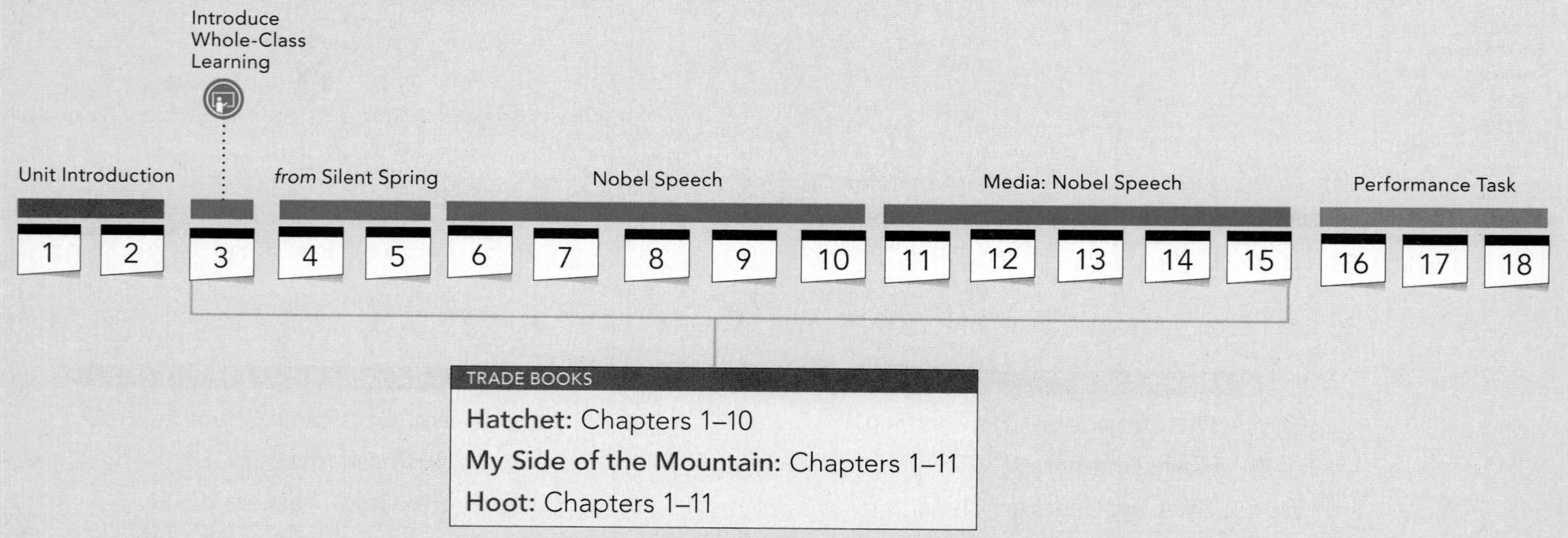

Suggested Trade Books

Hatchet

Gary Paulsen

Lexile: 1020

Brian's plane crashes in the woods, and he must survive with nothing but a gift his mother gave him.

Connection to Essential Question

Brian's father works in the oil fields, and Brian himself alters the woods around him to make survival easier. The novel helps readers see both large-scale and personal answers to the Essential Question: *What effects do people have on the environment?*

My Side of the Mountain

Jean Craighead George

Lexile: 810

Sam runs away from home and is caught between wanting to fend for himself and wanting to be with the people he loves.

Connection to Essential Question

Sam tames animals and nearly accidentally starts a forest fire. He finds the corpses of several deer killed by poachers. This novel provides both hopeful and alarming insights into the Essential Question: *What effects do people have on the environment?*

Hoot

Carl Hiaasen

Lexile: 760

Friends team up to prevent a developer from destroying animals' homes.

Connection to Essential Question

The construction of a new restaurant would kill many burrowing owls and perhaps destabilize the local ecosystem. Tempered by the successful prevention of the developer's plans, Hiaasen provides an otherwise pessimistic answer to the Essential Question: *What effects do people have on the environment?*

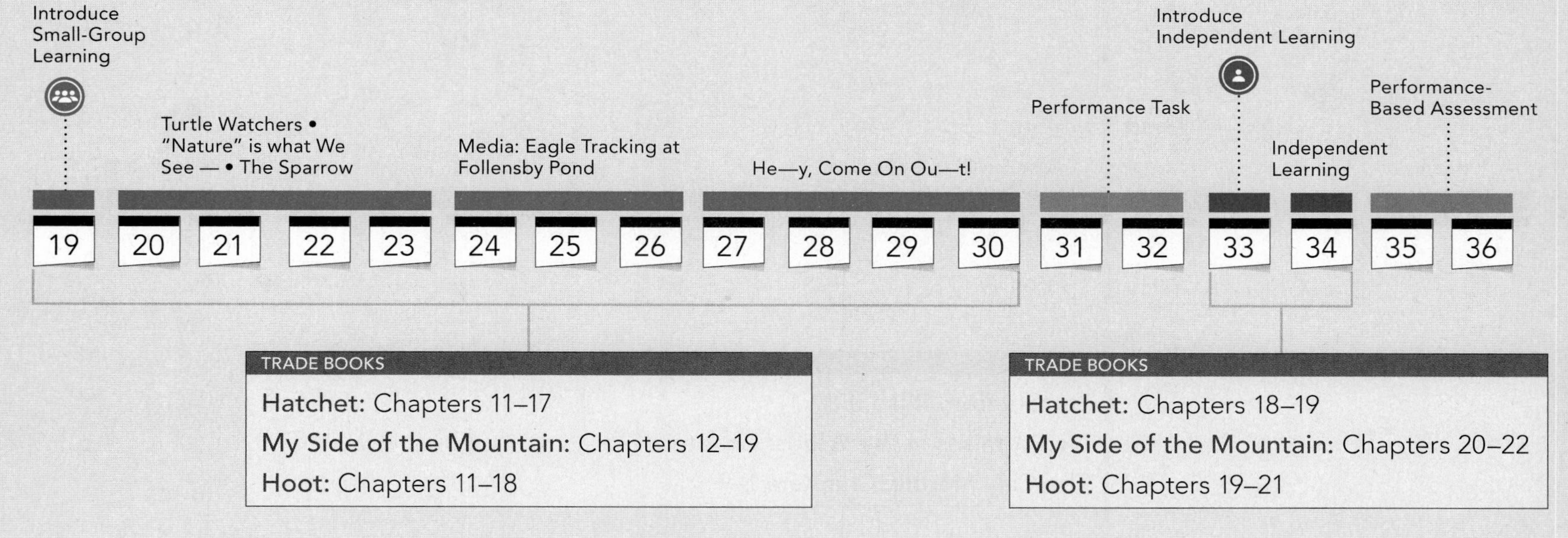

UNIT 5: Facing Adversity

Integrating Trade Books with *my*Perspectives

These titles provide students with another perspective on the topic of facing adversity, touching upon many of the ideas found within the unit selections.

Depending on your objectives for the unit, as well as your students' needs, you may choose to integrate the trade book into the unit in several ways, including:

- **Supplement the unit** Form literature circles and have the students read one of the trade books throughout the course of the unit as a supplement to the selections and activities.
- **Substitute for unit selections** If you replace unit selections with a trade book, review the standards taught with those selections. Teacher Resources that provide practice with all standards are available.
- **Extend Independent Learning** Extend the unit by replacing independent reading selections with one of these trade books.
- **Pacing** However you choose to integrate trade books, the Pacing Guide below offers suggestions for aligning the trade books with this unit.

Trade Book Lesson Plans

Trade book lesson plans for *Letters from Rifka, No Promises in the Wind, The Clay Marble* are available online in *my*Perspectives+.

Pacing Guide: Unit Supplement

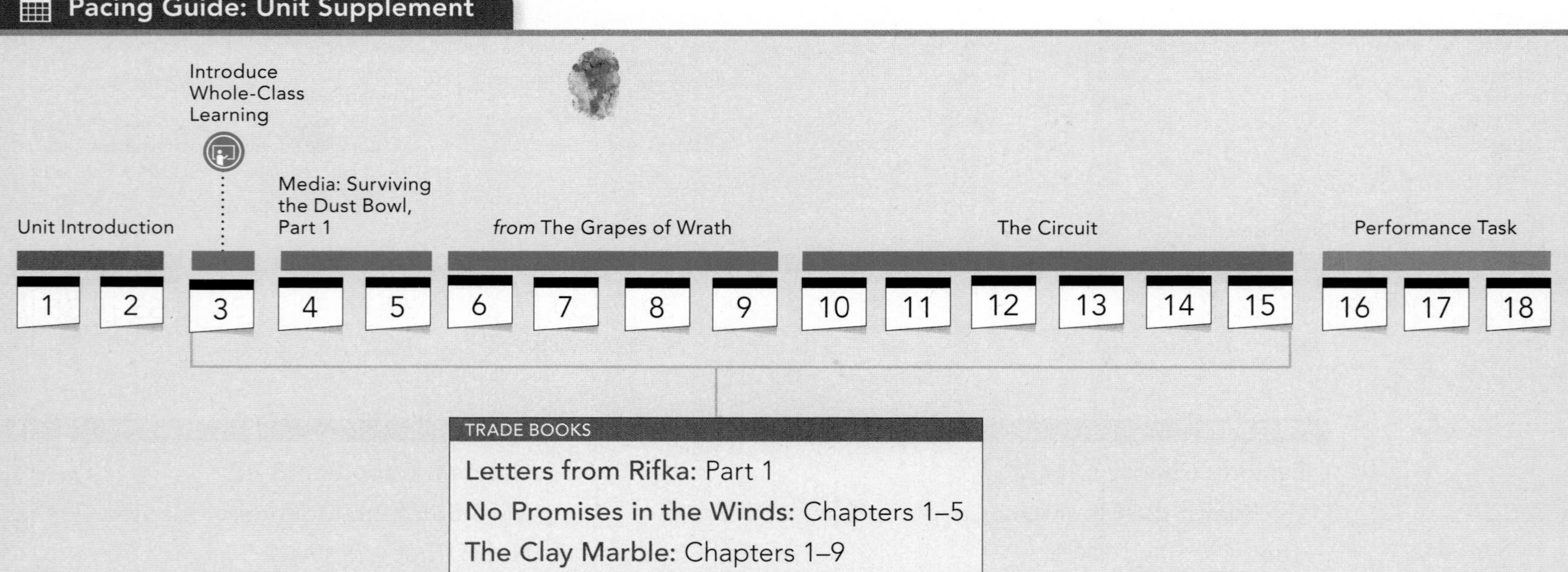

Suggested Trade Books

Letters from Rifka

Karen Hesse

Lexile: 660

Rifka flees the Russian Civil War for America, and discovers her strength and passions.

Connection to Essential Question

Bravery, wits, and kindness all help Rifka make her way despite illness, hunger, separation from family, and the cruelness of others. The novel provides insight into the Essential Question: *How do we overcome obstacles?*

No Promises in the Wind

Irene Hunt

Lexile: 930

During the Great Depression, a trio of kids set out from home and try to make a living.

Connection to Essential Question

Josh and his friends face key challenges to survival by begging and trade. But when Josh is at his lowest, reaching out to a friend saves his life. His experiences help us consider the Essential Question: *How do we overcome obstacles?*

The Clay Marble

Minfong Ho

Lexile: 860

Dara, a young refugee, finds the courage to survive in war-torn Cambodia.

Connection to Essential Question

Dara is brave not just physically, but mentally; she stands up against her older brother when he wants to leave their family and fight. Her struggle through a long ordeal helps us consider the Essential Question: *How do we overcome obstacles?*

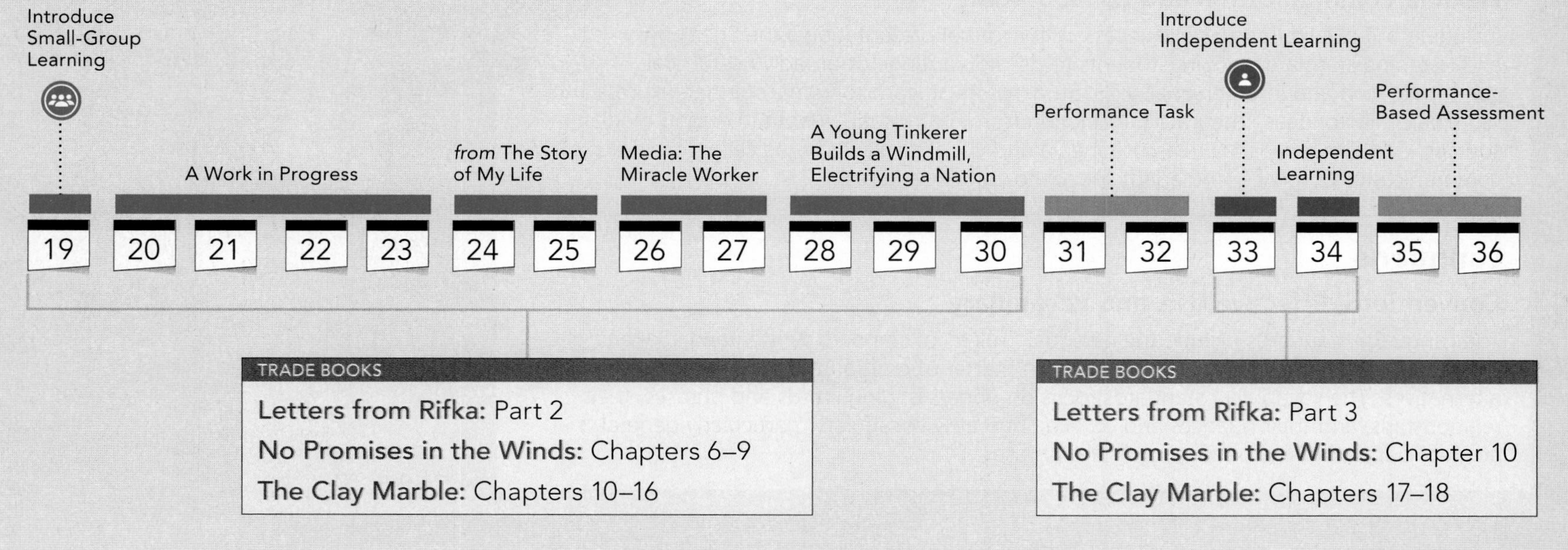

Standards Correlation

Key Features of the Standards

Reading

Text Complexity and the Growth of Comprehension

The Reading standards place equal emphasis on the sophistication of what students read and the skill with which they read. Standard 10 defines a grade-by-grade "staircase" of increasing text complexity that rises from beginning reading to the college and career readiness level. Whatever they are reading, students must also show a steadily growing ability to discern more from and make fuller use of text. This process should include making an increasing number of connections among ideas and between texts, considering a wider range of textual evidence, and becoming more sensitive to inconsistencies, ambiguities, and poor reasoning in texts.

Writing

Text Types, Responding to Reading, and Research

The Standards acknowledge the fact that whereas some writing skills, such as the ability to plan, revise, edit, and publish, are applicable to many types of writing, other skills are more properly defined in terms of specific writing types: arguments, informative/explanatory texts, and narratives. Standard 9 stresses the importance of the writing-reading connection by requiring students to draw upon and write about evidence from literary and informational texts. Because of the centrality of writing to most forms of inquiry, research standards are prominently included in this strand, though skills important to research are infused throughout the document.

Speaking and Listening

Flexible Communication and Collaboration

Including but not limited to skills necessary for formal presentations, the Speaking and Listening standards require students to develop a range of broadly useful oral communication and interpersonal skills. Students must learn to work together, express and listen carefully to ideas, integrate information from oral, visual, quantitative, and media sources, evaluate what they hear, use media and visual displays strategically to help achieve communicative purposes, and adapt speech to context and task.

Language

Conventions, Effective Use, and Vocabulary

The Language standards include the essential "rules" of standard written and spoken English, but they also approach language as a matter of craft and informed choice among alternatives. The vocabulary standards focus on understanding words and phrases, their relationships, and their nuances and on acquiring new vocabulary, particularly general academic and domain-specific words and phrases.

Correlation to *myPerspectives® English Language Arts*

The following correlation shows points at which focused standards instruction is provided in the Student Edition. The Teacher's Edition provides further opportunity to address standards through Personalize for Learning notes and additional resources available only in the Interactive Teacher's Edition.

Standards for Reading

College and Career Readiness Anchor Standards for Reading

Key Ideas and Details

1. Read closely to determine what the text says explicitly and to make logical inferences from it; cite specific textual evidence when writing or speaking to support conclusions drawn from the text.
2. Determine central ideas or themes of a text and analyze their development; summarize the key supporting details and ideas.
3. Analyze how and why individuals, events, and ideas develop and interact over the course of a text.

Craft and Structure

4. Interpret words and phrases as they are used in a text, including determining technical, connotative, and figurative meanings, and analyze how specific word choices shape meaning or tone.
5. Analyze the structure of texts, including how specific sentences, paragraphs, and larger portions of the text (e.g., a section, chapter, scene, or stanza) relate to each other and the whole.
6. Assess how point of view or purpose shapes the content and style of a text.

Integration of Knowledge and Ideas

7. Integrate and evaluate content presented in diverse formats and media, including visually and quantitatively, as well as in words.
8. Delineate and evaluate the argument and specific claims in a text, including the validity of the reasoning as well as the relevance and sufficiency of the evidence.
9. Analyze how two or more texts address similar themes or topics in order to build knowledge or to compare the approaches the authors take.

Range of Reading and Level of Text Complexity

10. Read and comprehend complex literary and informational texts independently and proficiently.

Standards Correlation

Grade 7 Reading Standards for Literature		
STANDARD CODE	Standard	Print and Interactive Editions
Key Ideas and Details		
RL.7.1	Cite several pieces of textual evidence to support analysis of what the text says explicitly as well as inferences drawn from the text.	**SE/TE:** "Two Kinds," 26; "Mother to Son" / "To James," 100; *A Christmas Carol: Scrooge and Marley, Act II,* 292; *Scrooge:* 301; "Thank You, M'am," 321; "Turtle Watchers" / "'Nature' is what We see—" / "The Sparrow," 410; "He—y, Come On Ou—t!" 427; "The Circuit," 476; Students will address this standard in Analyze the Text features which appear with every literature selection.
RL.7.2	Determine a theme or central idea of a text and analyze its development over the course of the text; provide an objective summary of the text.	**SE/TE:** "Mother to Son" / "To James," 100; "Turtle Watchers" / "'Nature' is what We see—" / "The Sparrow," 410; "He—y, Come On Ou—t!" 427; *The Grapes of Wrath,* 462; "The Circuit," 476, 480
RL.7.3	Analyze how particular elements of a story or drama interact (e.g., how setting shapes the characters or plot).	**SE/TE:** "The Last Dog," 197; *A Christmas Carol: Scrooge and Marley,* Act I, 260; *A Christmas Carol: Scrooge and Marley,* Act II, 292; "Thank You, M'am," 321; "He—y, Come On Ou—t!" 427; *The Grapes of Wrath,* 462
Craft and Structure		
RL.7.4	Determine the meaning of words and phrases as they are used in a text, including figurative and connotative meanings; analyze the impact of rhymes and other repetitions of sounds (e.g., alliteration) on a specific verse or stanza of a poem or section of a story or drama.	**SE/TE:** "Mother to Son" / "To James," 100, 102; "Dark They Were, and Golden-Eyed," 142; "Turtle Watchers" / "'Nature' is what We see—" / "The Sparrow," 410
RL.7.5	Analyze how a drama's or poem's form or structure (e.g., soliloquy, sonnet) contributes to its meaning.	**SE/TE:** *A Christmas Carol: Scrooge and Marley,* Act I, 260; *A Christmas Carol: Scrooge and Marley,* Act II, 292; "Turtle Watchers" / "'Nature' is what We see—" / "The Sparrow," 408
RL.7.6	Analyze how an author develops and contrasts the points of view of different characters or narrators in a text.	**SE/TE:** "Two Kinds," 26, 30; "Turtle Watchers" / "'Nature' is what We see—" / "The Sparrow," 409
Integration of Knowledge and Ideas		
RL.7.7	Compare and contrast a written story, drama, or poem to its audio, filmed, staged, or multimedia version, analyzing the effects of techniques unique to each medium (e.g., lighting, sound, color, or camera focus and angles in a film).	**SE/TE:** "Dark They Were, and Golden-Eyed" (short story) / "Dark They Were, and Golden-Eyed" (radio play), 150; *A Christmas Carol / Scrooge,* 302–303
RL.7.8	(Not applicable to literature)	
RL.7.9	Compare and contrast a fictional portrayal of a time, place, or character and a historical account of the same period as a means of understanding how authors of fiction use or alter history.	**SE/TE** *The Grapes of Wrath,* 463; "Surviving the Dust Bowl" / *The Grapes of Wrath,* 466–467
Range of Reading and Level of Text Complexity		
RL.7.10	By the end of the year, read and comprehend literature, including stories, dramas, and poems, in the grades 6–8 text complexity band proficiently, with scaffolding as needed at the high end of the range.	**SE/TE:** "Two Kinds," 12; "Mother to Son" / "To James," 94; First-Read Guide, Unit 1: 108, Unit 2: 216, Unit 3: 344, Unit 4: 434, Unit 5: 532; Close-Read Guide, Unit 1: 109, Unit 2: 217, Unit 3: 345, Unit 4: 435, Unit 5: 533; "Dark They Were, and Golden-Eyed," 126; "Dark They Were, and Golden-Eyed" (radio play), 146; "The Last Dog," 182; *A Christmas Carol: Scrooge and Marley,* Act I, 234; *A Christmas Carol: Scrooge and Marley,* Act II, 264; *Scrooge,* 298; "Thank You, M'am," 314; "Turtle Watchers" / "'Nature' is what We see—" / "The Sparrow," 402; "He—y, Come On Ou—t!" 420; *The Grapes of Wrath,* 456; "The Circuit," 468

STANDARD CODE	Standard	Print and Interactive Editions
Key Ideas and Details		
RI.7.1	Cite several pieces of textual evidence to support analysis of what the text says explicitly as well as inferences drawn from the text.	**SE/TE:** "A Simple Act," 38; "Tutors Teach Seniors New High-Tech Tricks,"66; *Mom & Me & Mom,* 78; *An American Childhood,* 329; *Silent Spring,* 366; "A Young Tinkerer Builds a Windmill, Electrifying a Nation," 524; Students will address this standard in *Analyze the Text* features which appear with every informational text selection.
RI.7.2	Determine two or more central ideas in a text and analyze their development over the course of the text; provide an objective summary of the text.	**SE/TE:** "Tutors Teach Seniors New High-Tech Trick," 66; *An American Childhood,* 329; *Silent Spring,* 366
RI.7.3	Analyze the interactions between individuals, events, and ideas in a text (e.g., how ideas influence individuals or events, or how individuals influence ideas or events).	**SE/TE:** *Mom & Me & Mom,* 78; *An American Childhood,* 329; "A Work in Progress," 500; "A Young Tinkerer Builds a Windmill, Electrifying a Nation," 524
Craft and Structure		
RI.7.4	Determine the meaning of words and phrases as they are used in a text, including figurative, connotative, and technical meanings; analyze the impact of a specific word choice on meaning and tone.	**SE/TE:** "Neil deGrasse Tyson on the Future of U.S. Space Exploration After *Curiosity,"* 209; *Silent Spring,* 366; "A Work in Progress," 500; *The Story of My Life,"* 509–510
RI.7.5	Analyze the structure an author uses to organize a text, including how the major sections contribute to the whole and to the development of the ideas.	**SE/TE:** "Tutors Teach Seniors New High-Tech Tricks," 67; "Danger! This Mission to Mars Could Bore You to Death!," 158-159; "Future of Space Exploration Could See Humans on Mars, Alien Planets," 179; "A Young Tinkerer Builds a Windmill, Electrifying a Nation," 524
RI.7.6	Determine an author's point of view or purpose in a text and analyze how the author distinguishes his or her position from that of others.	**SE/TE:** "A Simple Act," 38; *An Invisible Thread,* 46; "Neil deGrasse Tyson on the Future of U.S. Space Exploration After *Curiosity,"* 209; "A Work in Progress," 500; *The Story of My Life,* 510
Integration of Knowledge and Ideas		
RI.7.7	Compare and contrast a text to an audio, video, or multimedia version of the text, analyzing each medium's portrayal of the subject (e.g., how the delivery of a speech affects the impact of the words).	**SE/TE:** *Mom & Me & Mom* / "Learning to Love My Mother," 84-85; *Nobel Speech* (text) / *Nobel Speech* (video), 390-391; *The Story of My Life* / "How Helen Keller Learned to Talk," 516
RI.7.8	Trace and evaluate the argument and specific claims in a text, assessing whether the reasoning is sound and the evidence is relevant and sufficient to support the claims.	**SE/TE:** "Leaving Main Street," 123; "Neil deGrasse Tyson on the Future of U.S. Space Exploration After *Curiosity,"* 209; "Rethinking the Wild," 359; *Nobel Speech,* 382
RI.7.9	Analyze how two or more authors writing about the same topic shape their presentations of key information by emphasizing different evidence or advancing different interpretations of facts.	**SE/TE:** "A Simple Act" / An Invisible Thread, 50; Whole-Class Performance Task, Unit 4: 392; *The Story of My Life* / "How Helen Keller Learned to Talk," 516–517
Range of Reading and Level of Text Complexity		
RI.7.10	By the end of the year, read and comprehend literary nonfiction in the grades 6–8 text complexity band proficiently, with scaffolding as needed at the high end of the range.	**SE/TE:** "A Simple Act," 32; *An Invisible Thread,* 42; "Tutors Teach Seniors New High-Tech Tricks," 62; *Mom & Me & Mom,* 70; "Learning to Love My Mother," 80; "Mother-Daughter Drawings," 86; First-Read Guid, Unit 1: 108, Unit 2: 216, Unit 3: 344, Unit 4: 434, Unit 5: 532; Close-Read Guide, Unit 1: 109, Unit 2: 217, Unit 3: 344, Unit 4: 435, Unit 5: 533; "Danger! This Mission to Mars Could Bore You to Death!" 152; "Future of Space Exploration Could See Humans on Mars, Alien Planets," 174; "Ellen Ochoa: Director, Johnson Space Center," 200; "Neil deGrasse Tyson on the Future of U.S. Space Exploration After *Curiosity,"* 204; *An American Childhood,* 324; "Urban Farming Is Growing a Greener Future," 332; *Silent Spring,* 362; *Nobel Speech,* 372; *Nobel Speech* (video), 386; "Eagle Tracking at Follensby Pond," 412; "Surviving the Dust Bowl," 452; "A Work in Progress," 492; *The Story of My Life,* 504; "How Helen Keller Learned to Talk," 512; "A Young Tinkerer Builds a Windmill, Electrifying a Nation," 518

Standards Correlation

Standards for Writing

College and Career Readiness Anchor Standards for Writing

Text Types and Purposes

1. Write arguments to support claims in an analysis of substantive topics or texts using valid reasoning and relevant and sufficient evidence.
2. Write informative/explanatory texts to examine and convey complex ideas and information clearly and accurately through the effective selection, organization, and analysis of content.
3. Write narratives to develop real or imagined experiences or events using effective technique, well-chosen details and well-structured event sequences.

Production and Distribution of Writing

4. Produce clear and coherent writing in which the development, organization, and style are appropriate to task, purpose, and audience.
5. Develop and strengthen writing as needed by planning, revising, editing, rewriting, or trying a new approach.
6. Use technology, including the Internet, to produce and publish writing and to interact and collaborate with others.

Research to Build and Present Knowledge

7. Conduct short as well as more sustained research projects based on focused questions, demonstrating understanding of the subject under investigation.
8. Gather relevant information from multiple print and digital sources, assess the credibility and accuracy of each source, and integrate the information while avoiding plagiarism.
9. Draw evidence from literary or informational texts to support analysis, reflection, and research.

Range of Writing

10. Write routinely over extended time frames (time for research, reflection, and revision) and shorter time frames (a single sitting or a day or two) for a range of tasks, purposes, and audiences.

Grade 7 Writing Standards		
STANDARD CODE	**Standard**	**Print and Interactive Editions**
Text Types and Purposes		
W.7.1	Write arguments to support claims with clear reasons and relevant evidence.	**SE/TE:** "Danger! This Mission to Mars Could Bore You to Death!" 162; Whole-Class Performance Task, Unit 2, 164–166, 168–169, Unit 4: 392, 394; Performance-Based Assessment, Unit 2: 219–220, Unit 4: 437–438; *Silent Spring,* 370; *Nobel Speech* (text), / *Nobel Speech* (video), 390–391; "Surviving the Dust Bowl" / *The Grapes of Wrath,* 466
W.7.1.a	Introduce claim(s), acknowledge alternate or opposing claims, and organize the reasons and evidence logically.	**SE/TE:** "Danger! This Mission to Mars Could Bore You to Death!" 162; Whole-Class Performance Task, Unit 2: 165–166, 168, Unit 4: 393, 396; Performance-Based Assessment, Unit 2: 219, Unit 4: 437; *Silent Spring,* 370; *Nobel Speech* (text) / *Nobel Speech* (video), 391; "Surviving the Dust Bowl" / *The Grapes of Wrath,* 466
W.7.1.b	Support claim(s) with logical reasoning and relevant evidence, using accurate, credible sources and demonstrating an understanding of the topic or text.	**SE/TE:** "Danger! This Mission to Mars Could Bore You to Death!" 162; Whole-Class Performance Task, Unit 2: 165, Unit 4: 393; Performance-Based Assessment, Unit 2: 219, Unit 4: 437; Silent Spring, 370; *Nobel Speech* (text) / *Nobel Speech* (video), 390–391; "Surviving the Dust Bowl" / *The Grapes of Wrath,* 466–467
W.7.1.c	Use words, phrases, and clauses to create cohesion and clarify the relationships among claim(s), reasons, and evidence.	**SE/TE:** Whole-Class Performance Task, Unit 2: 166, 169, Unit 4: 396; *Silent Spring,* 370; *Nobel Speech* (text) / *Nobel Speech* (video), 391; "Surviving the Dust Bowl" / *The Grapes of Wrath,* 467
W.7.1.d	Establish and maintain a formal style.	**SE/TE:** "Danger! This Mission to Mars Could Bore You to Death!" 162; Whole-Class Performance Task, Unit 2: 168–169, Unit 4: 394; Silent Spring, 370
W.7.1.e	Provide a concluding statement or section that follows from and supports the argument presented.	**SE/TE:** "Danger! This Mission to Mars Could Bore You to Death!" 162; Whole-Class Performance Task, Unit 2: 166, Unit 4: 396
W.7.2	Write informative/explanatory texts to examine a topic and convey ideas, concepts, and information through the selection, organization, and analysis of relevant content.	**SE/TE:** *An Invisible Thread,* 51; "Learning to Love My Mother," 85; "Dark They Were, and Golden-Eyed," 150–151; "Neil deGrasse Tyson on the Future of U.S. Space Exploration After *Curiosity,*" 211; *A Christmas Carol: Scrooge and Marley,* Act II, 296; *Scrooge,* 302–303; Whole-Class Performance Task, Unit 3: 304-309, Unit 5: 482-483, 486; Small-Group Performance Task, Unit 3: 340, Unit 5: 528; Performance-Based Assessment, Unit 3: 347–348, Unit 5: 535–536; "Eagle Tracking at Follensby Pond," 419; "The Circuit," 480; *The Story of My Life* / "How Helen Keller Learned to Talk," 517
W.7.2.a	Introduce a topic clearly, previewing what is to follow; organize ideas, concepts, and information, using strategies such as definition, classification, comparison/contrast, and cause/effect; include formatting (e.g., headings), graphics (e.g., charts, tables), and multimedia when useful to aiding comprehension.	**SE/TE:** "Learning to Love My Mother," 85; "Dark They Were, and Golden-Eyed," 151; *A Christmas Carol: Scrooge and Marley,* Act II, 296; Whole-Class Performance Task, Unit 3: 305–306, Unit 5: 483–484, 486; Performance-Based Assessment, Unit 3: 347, Unit 5: 535; "Eagle Tracking at Follensby Pond," 419; *The Story of My Life* / "How Helen Keller Learned to Talk," 517; "A Young Tinkerer Builds a Windmill, Electrifying a Nation," 527
W.7.2.b	Develop the topic with relevant facts, definitions, concrete details, quotations, or other information and examples.	**SE/TE:** *An Invisible Thread,* 51; "Learning to Love My Mother," 85; "Dark They Were, and Golden-Eyed," 151; *A Christmas Carol: Scrooge and Marley,* Act II, 296; *Scrooge,* 302; Whole-Class Performance Task, Unit 3: 305, Unit 5: 483–484, 486; Performance-Based Assessment, Unit 3: 347, Unit 5: 535; "Eagle Tracking at Follensby Pond," 419; "The Circuit," 480; *The Story of My Life* / "How Helen Keller Learned to Talk," 517; "A Young Tinkerer Builds a Windmill, Electrifying a Nation," 527
W.7.2.c	Use appropriate transitions to create cohesion and clarify the relationships among ideas and concepts.	**SE/TE:** *An Invisible Thread,* 51; "Learning to Love My Mother," 85; Whole-Class Performance Task, Unit 3: 306, Unit 5: 483
W.7.2.d	Use precise language and domain-specific vocabulary to inform about or explain the topic.	**SE/TE:** "Dark They Were, and Golden-Eyed," 151; *A Christmas Carol: Scrooge and Marley,* Act II 296; *Scrooge,* 303; Whole-Class Performance Task, Unit 3: 307–308, Unit 5: 486
W.7.2.e	Establish and maintain a formal style.	**SE/TE:** *A Christmas Carol: Scrooge and Marley,* Act II, 296; Whole-Class Performance Task, Unit 3: 309, Unit 5: 486
W.7.2.f	Provide a concluding statement or section that follows from and supports the information or explanation presented.	**SE/TE:** "Dark They Were, and Golden-Eyed," 151; *A Christmas Carol: Scrooge and Marley,* Act II, 296; *Scrooge,* 303; Whole-Class Performance Task, Unit 3: 308; Unit 5: 484

Standards Correlation

Grade 7 Writing Standards (continued)		
STANDARD CODE	Standard	Print and Interactive Editions
W.7.3	Write narratives to develop real or imagined experiences or events using effective technique, relevant descriptive details, and well-structured event sequences.	**SE/TE:** "Two Kinds," 30; Whole-Class Performance Task, Unit 1: 52-53, 55-56; "Mother to Son" / "To James," 103; Performance-Based Assessment, 111-112; "The Last Dog," 199; "Thank You, M'am," 323; "He—y, Come On Ou—t!" 429
W.7.3.a	Engage and orient the reader by establishing a context and point of view and introducing a narrator and/or characters; organize an event sequence that unfolds naturally and logically.	**SE/TE:** "Two Kinds," 30; Whole-Class Performance Task, Unit 1: 54, 56; "Mother to Son" / "To James," 103; Performance-Based Assessment, 111; "Thank You, M'am," 323
W.7.3.b	Use narrative techniques, such as dialogue, pacing, and description, to develop experiences, events, and/or characters.	**SE/TE:** "Two Kinds," 30; Whole-Class Performance Task, Unit 1: 53; "Mother to Son" / "To James," 103; "The Last Dog," 199; "He—y, Come On Ou—t!" 429
W.7.3.c	Use a variety of transition words, phrases, and clauses to convey sequence and signal shifts from one time frame or setting to another.	**SE/TE:** Whole-Class Performance Task, Unit 1: 54; "Thank You, M'am," 323
W.7.3.d	Use precise words and phrases, relevant descriptive details, and sensory language to capture the action and convey experiences and events.	**SE/TE:** "Two Kinds," 30; Whole-Class Performance Task, Unit 1: 55, 56; "Mother to Son" / "To James," 103; "Thank You, M'am," 323; "He—y, Come On Ou—t!" 429
W.7.3.e	Provide a conclusion that follows from and reflects on the narrated experiences or events.	**SE/TE:** Whole-Class Performance Task, Unit 1: 56; "The Last Dog," 199; "He—y, Come On Ou—t!," 429
Production and Distribution of Writing		
W.7.4	Produce clear and coherent writing in which the development, organization, and style are appropriate to task, purpose, and audience.	**SE/TE:** *Scrooge,* 303; Whole-Class Performance Task, Unit 1, Unit 2, Unit 3, Unit 4, Unit 5; Performance-Based Assessment, Unit 3: 348, Unit 4: 438, Unit 5: 536
W.7.5	With some guidance and support from peers and adults, develop and strengthen writing as needed by planning, revising, editing, rewriting, or trying a new approach, focusing on how well purpose and audience have been addressed.	**SE/TE:** "Mother to Son" / "To James," 103; "He—y, Come On Ou—t!" 429; Whole-Class Performance Task, Unit 1, Unit 2, Unit 3, Unit 4, Unit 5
W.7.6	Use technology, including the Internet, to produce and publish writing and link to and cite sources as well as to interact and collaborate with others, including linking to and citing sources.	**SE/TE:** "Learning to Love My Mother," 85; Whole-Class Performance Task, Unit 3: 309, Unit 4: 392, 397; "Urban Farming Is Growing a Greener Future," 338; Performance-Based Assessment, Unit 5: 538
Research to Build and Present Knowledge		
W.7.7	Conduct short research projects to answer a question, drawing on several sources and generating additional related, focused questions for further research and investigation.	**SE/TE:** "Tutors Teach Seniors New High-Tech Tricks," 69; "Danger! This Mission to Mars Could Bore You to Death!" 162; "Future of Space Exploration Could See Humans on Mars, Alien Planets," 181; "Neil deGrasse Tyson on the Future of U.S. Space Exploration After *Curiosity,*" 211; *A Christmas Carol: Scrooge and Marley,* Act II, 297; "Urban Farming Is Growing a Greener Future," 338; *Silent Spring,* 371; "Eagle Tracking at Follensby Pond," 419; "The Circuit," 481; "A Young Tinkerer Builds a Windmill, Electrifying a Nation," 527
W.7.8	Gather relevant information from multiple print and digital sources, using search terms effectively; assess the credibility and accuracy of each source; and quote or paraphrase the data and conclusions of others while avoiding plagiarism and following a standard format for citation.	**SE/TE:** "Future of Space Exploration Could See Humans on Mars, Alien Planets," 181; "Neil deGrasse Tyson on the Future of U.S. Space Exploration After *Curiosity,*" 211; "Urban Farming Is Growing a Greener Future," 338; *Silent Spring,* 371; Whole-Class Performance Task, Unit 4: 397; "Eagle Tracking at Follensby Pond," 419; "A Young Tinkerer Builds a Windmill, Electrifying a Nation," 527
W.7.9	Draw evidence from literary or informational texts to support analysis, reflection, and research.	**SE/TE:** *An Invisible Thread* 50; "Learning to Love My Mother," 84; "Mother to Son" / "To James," 103; Performance-Based Assessment, Unit 1: 111–112, Unit 3: 348, Unit 5: 536; *A Christmas Carol: Scrooge and Marley,* Act II, 296; *Scrooge,* 302; "Surviving the Dust Bowl" / *The Grapes of Wrath,* 467; "The Circuit," 480; *The Story of My Life* / "How Helen Keller Learned to Talk," 517; Small-Group Performance Task, Unit 5: 528

Grade 7 Writing Standards (continued)		
STANDARD CODE	Standard	Print and Interactive Editions
W.7.9.a	Apply *grade 7 Reading standards* to literature (e.g., "Compare and contrast a fictional portrayal of a time, place, or character and a historical account of the same period as a means of understanding how authors of fiction use or alter history").	**SE/TE:** "Mother to Son" / "To James," 103; "Dark They Were, and Golden-Eyed," 150; *A Christmas Carol: Scrooge and Marley,* Act II, 296; *Scrooge,* 302; "Surviving the Dust Bowl" / *The Grapes of Wrath,* 467; "The Circuit," 480
W.7.9.b	Apply *grade 7 Reading standards* to literary nonfiction (e.g. "Trace and evaluate the argument and specific claims in a text, assessing whether the reasoning is sound and the evidence is relevant and sufficient to support the claims").	**SE/TE:** "Learning to Love My Mother," 84; "Neil deGrasse Tyson on the Future of U.S. Space Exploration After *Curiosity*" 209; *Nobel Speech,* 383; *The Story of My Life* / "How Helen Keller Learned to Talk," 517
Range of Writing		
W.7.10	Write routinely over extended time frames (time for research, reflection, and revision) and shorter time frames (a single sitting or a day or two) for a range of discipline-specific tasks, purposes, and audiences.	**SE/TE:** Whole-Class Performance Task, Unit 1: 52, Unit 2: 164, Unit 3: 304, Unit 4: 392, Unit 5: 482; Performance-Based Assessment, Unit 1: 112, Unit 2: 220, Unit 3: 348, Unit 4: 438, Unit 5: 536; "The Last Dog," 199

Standards Correlation

Standards for Speaking and Listening

College and Career Readiness Anchor Standards for Speaking and Listening

Comprehension and Collaboration

1. Prepare for and participate effectively in a range of conversations and collaborations with diverse partners, building on others' ideas and expressing their own clearly and persuasively.
2. Integrate and evaluate information presented in diverse media and formats, including visually, quantitatively, and orally.
3. Evaluate a speaker's point of view, reasoning, and use of evidence and rhetoric.

Presentation of Knowledge and Ideas

4. Present information, findings, and supporting evidence such that listeners can follow the line of reasoning and the organization, development, and style are appropriate to task, purpose, and audience.
5. Make strategic use of digital media and visual displays of data to express information and enhance understanding of presentations.
6. Adapt speech to a variety of contexts and communicative tasks, demonstrating command of formal English when indicated or appropriate.

Grade 7 Speaking and Listening Standards

STANDARD CODE	Standard	Print and Interactive Editions
Comprehension and Collaboration		
SL.7.1	Engage effectively in a range of collaborative discussions (one-on-one, in groups, and teacher-led) with diverse partners on *grade 7 topics, texts, and issues,* building on others' ideas and expressing their own clearly.	**SE/TE:** "Tutors Teach Seniors New High-Tech Tricks," 69; *Mom & Me & Mom,* 77; "Mother-Daughter Drawings," 93; Small-Group Performance Task, Unit 1: 104, Unit 3: 341, Unit 4: 430, Unit 5: 529; "Future of Space Exploration Could See Humans on Mars, Alien Planets," 178; "Ellen Ochoa: Director, Johnson Space Center," 203; Share Your Independent Learning, Unit 2: 218, Unit 4: 436, Unit 5: 534; "Thank You, M'am," 323; *An American Childhood,* 331; "He—y, Come On Ou—t!" 426; "The Circuit," 481; "A Work in Progress," 502; *The Story of My Life* / "How Helen Keller Learned to Talk," 517
SL.7.1.a	Come to discussions prepared, having read or researched material under study; explicitly draw on that preparation by referring to evidence on the topic, text, or issue to probe and reflect on ideas under discussion.	**SE/TE:** "Mother-Daughter Drawings," 93; Small-Group Performance Task, Unit 1: 104, Unit 4: 430, Unit 5: 529; "Ellen Ochoa: Director, Johnson Space Center," 203; *An American Childhood,* 331; "The Circuit," 481; "A Work in Progress," 502
SL.7.1.b	Follow rules for collegial discussions, track progress toward specific goals and deadlines, and define individual roles as needed.	**SE/TE:** "Tutors Teach Seniors New High-Tech Tricks," 69; Small-Group Performance Task, Unit 1: 104, Unit 4: 430; "Ellen Ochoa: Director, Johnson Space Center," 203; "Thank You, M'am," 323; *An American Childhood,* 331; "A Work in Progress," 502; *The Story of My Life* / "How Helen Keller Learned to Talk," 517; Students will address this standard in *Working as a Team* features which appear in the Small Group Learning Overview lessons.
SL.7.1.c	Pose questions that elicit elaboration and respond to others' questions and comments with relevant observations and ideas that bring the discussion back on topic as needed.	**SE/TE:** "Tutors Teach Seniors New High Tech Tricks," 69; "Ellen Ochoa: Director, Johnson Space Center," 203; from *An American Childhood:* 331; "The Circuit," 481; "A Work in Progress," 502; Students will address this standard in *Launch Activity* features which appear in the Unit Introduction and in *Working as a Team* features which appear in the Small Group Learning Overview lessons.
SL.7.1.d	Acknowledge new information expressed by others and, when warranted, modify their own views.	**SE/TE:** "Tutors Teach Seniors New High-Tech Tricks," 69; "Ellen Ochoa: Director, Johnson Space Center," 203; "Thank You, M'am," 323; *An American Childhood,* 331; "He—y, Come On Ou—t!" 426; Students will address this standard in *Launch Activity* features which appear in the Unit Introduction, in *Working as a Team features* which appear in the Small Group Learning Overview lessons, and *Group Discussion Tips* which appear throughout the program.
SL.7.2	Analyze the main ideas and supporting details presented in diverse media and formats (e.g., visually, quantitatively, orally) and explain how the ideas clarify a topic, text, or issue under study.	**SE/TE:** "Learning to Love My Mother," 83; "Mother-Daughter Drawings," 92; Small-Group Performance Task, Unit 1: 104, Unit 3: 341, Unit 4: 430; "Dark They Were, and Golden-Eyed" (radio play), 149; *Scrooge,* 302; "Urban Farming Is Growing a Greener Future," 338; "Eagle Tracking at Follensby Pond," 418; *The Story of My Life* / "How Helen Keller Learned to Talk," 517
SL.7.3	Delineate a speaker's argument and specific claims, evaluating the soundness of the reasoning and the relevance and sufficiency of the evidence.	**SE/TE:** *Nobel Speech* (video), 389; *Nobel Speech* (text) / *Nobel Speech* (video), 390; Small-Group Performance Task, Unit 4: 431
Presentation of Knowledge and Ideas		
SL.7.4	Present claims and findings, emphasizing salient points in a focused, coherent manner with pertinent descriptions, facts, details, and examples; use appropriate eye contact, adequate volume, and clear pronunciation.	**SE/TE:** "Two Kinds," 30; "Tutors Teach Seniors New High-Tech Tricks," 69; Small-Group Performance Task, Unit 1: 105, Unit 2: 213, Unit 3: 341, Unit 4: 431, Unit 5: 529; Performance-Based Assessment, Unit 1: 114, Unit 2: 222, Unit 3: 350, Unit 4: 440, Unit 5: 538; "Danger! This Mission to Mars Could Bore You to Death!" 162; *A Christmas Carol: Scrooge and Marley,* Act II, 297; *Silent Spring,* 371; "Turtle Watchers" / "'Nature' is what We see—" / "The Sparrow," 411; "The Circuit," 481
SL.7.5	Include multimedia components and visual displays in presentations to clarify claims and findings and emphasize salient points.	**SE/TE:** "Tutors Teach Seniors New High-Tech Tricks," 69; "Mother-Daughter Drawings," 93; Performance-Based Assessment, Unit 1: 114, Unit 2: 222, Unit 3: 350, Unit 4: 440, Unit 5: 538; "Danger! This Mission to Mars Could Bore You to Death!" 162; "Future of Space Exploration Could See Humans on Mars, Alien Planets," 181; Small-Group Performance Task, Unit 2: 213, Unit 3: 341, Unit 4: 431, Unit 5: 529; *A Christmas Carol: Scrooge and Marley,* Act II, 297; "Urban Farming Is Growing a Greener Future," 338; *Silent Spring,* 371; "Turtle Watchers" / "'Nature' is what We see—" / "The Sparrow," 411; *The Story of My Life* / "How Helen Keller Learned to Talk," 517
SL.7.6	Adapt speech to a variety of contexts and tasks, demonstrating command of formal English when indicated or appropriate.	**SE/TE:** Small-Group Performance Task, Unit 1: 105, Unit 3: 341, Unit 4: 431; Performance-Based Assessment, Unit 2: 222, Unit 4: 440; "Turtle Watchers" / "'Nature' is what We see—" / "The Sparrow," 411

Standards Correlation

Standards for Language

College and Career Readiness Anchor Standards for Language
Conventions of Standard English **1.** Demonstrate command of the conventions of standard English grammar and usage when writing or speaking. **2.** Demonstrate command of the conventions of standard English capitalization, punctuation, and spelling when writing.
Knowledge of Language **3.** Apply knowledge of language to understand how language functions in different contexts, to make effective choices for meaning or style, and to comprehend more fully when reading or listening.
Vocabulary Acquisition and Use **4.** Determine or clarify the meaning of unknown and multiple-meaning words and phrases by using context clues, analyzing meaningful word parts, and consulting general and specialized reference materials, as appropriate. **5.** Demonstrate understanding of figurative language, word relationships, and nuances in word meanings. **6.** Acquire and use accurately a range of general academic and domain-specific words and phrases sufficient for reading, writing, speaking, and listening at the college and career readiness level; demonstrate independence in gathering vocabulary knowledge when considering a word or phrase important to comprehension or expression.

Grade 7 Language Standards

STANDARD CODE	Standard	Print and Interactive Editions
Conventions of Standard English		
L.7.1	Demonstrate command of the conventions of standard English grammar and usage when writing or speaking.	**SE/TE:** "A Simple Act," 40; "Tutors Teach Seniors New High-Tech Tricks," 68; *Mom & Me & Mom,* 79;"Dark They Were, and Golden-Eyed," 145; "Danger! This Mission to Mars Could Bore You to Death!" 160; Whole-Class Performance Task, Unit 2: 167, Unit 3: 307, Unit 4: 395; "Future of Space Exploration Could See Humans on Mars, Alien Planets," 180; "The Last Dog,"198; "Neil deGrasse Tyson on the Future of U.S. Space Exploration After *Curiosity,*" 210; *A Christmas Carol: Scrooge and Marley,* Act I, 263; "Thank You, M'am," 322; *Silent Spring,* 368; *Nobel Speech,* 384; "A Work in Progress," 502
L.7.1.a	Explain the function of phrases and clauses in general and their function in specific sentences.	**SE/TE:** *Mom & Me & Mom,* 79; "Thank You, M'am," 322; *An American Childhood,* 330; *Nobel Speech,* 384
L.7.1.b	Choose among simple, compound, complex, and compound-complex sentences to signal differing relationships among ideas.	**SE/TE:** *A Christmas Carol: Scrooge and Marley,* Act II, 295; Whole-Class Performance Task, Unit 3: 307
L.7.1.c	Place phrases and clauses within a sentence, recognizing and correcting misplaced and dangling modifiers.	**SE/TE:** *An American Childhood,* 330; Whole-Class Performance Task, 395–396; *The Story of My Life,* 511
L.7.2	Demonstrate command of the conventions of standard English capitalization, punctuation, and spelling when writing.	**SE/TE:** "Two Kinds," 28; *An Invisible Thread,* 48, 51; Whole-Class Performance Task, Unit 2: 167, Unit 4: 397, Unit 5: 485, 487; "Neil deGrasse Tyson on the Future of U.S. Space Exploration After *Curiosity,*" 210; *An American Childhood,* 330; "He—y, Come On Ou—t!" 428; "The Circuit," 479; "A Work in Progress," 502; "A Young Tinkerer Builds a Windmill, Electrifying a Nation," 526
L.7.2.a	Use a comma to separate coordinate adjectives (e.g., *It was a fascinating, enjoyable movie* but not *He wore an old[,] green shirt*).	**SE/TE:** *An Invisible Thread,* 48; "The Circuit," 479; Whole-Class Performance Task, Unit 5: 485, 487
L.7.2.b	Spell correctly.	**SE/TE:** *An Invisible Thread,* 51; "Learning to Love My Mother," 85; "Dark They Were, and Golden-Eyed," 151; *Scrooge,* 303; Whole-Class Performance Task, Unit 1: 57, Unit 2: 169, Unit 3: 309, Unit 4: 397, Unit 5: 487
Knowledge of Language		
L.7.3	Use knowledge of language and its conventions when writing, speaking, reading, or listening.	**SE/TE:** "Tutors Teach Seniors New High-Tech Tricks," 68; Whole-Class Performance Task, Unit 2: 167, Unit 3: 307, Unit 4: 395; "The Last Dog," 198; *Silent Spring,* 368
L.7.3.a	Choose language that expresses ideas precisely and concisely, recognizing and eliminating wordiness and redundancy.	**SE/TE:** "Tutors Teach Seniors New High-Tech Tricks," 68; Whole-Class Performance Task, Unit 2: 167, Unit 3: 307, Unit 4: 395; "The Last Dog," 198

Standards Correlation

Grade 7 Language Standards (continued)		
STANDARD CODE	Standard	Print and Interactive Editions
Vocabulary Acquisition and Use		
L.7.4	Determine or clarify the meaning of unknown and multiple-meaning words and phrases based on *grade 7 reading and content,* choosing flexibly from a range of strategies.	**SE/TE:** "Two Kinds," 28; "A Simple Act,"40; *An Invisible Thread,* 48; "Tutors Teach Seniors New High-Tech Tricks," 62, 66; *Mom & Me & Mom,* 70, 77; "Mother to Son" / "To James," 94; "Dark They Were, and Golden-Eyed," 144; "Danger! This Mission to Mars Could Bore You to Death!" 160; "Future of Space Exploration Could See Humans on Mars, Alien Planets," 174, 178; "The Last Dog," 182, 196; "Neil deGrasse Tyson on the Future of U.S. Space Exploration After *Curiosity,* " 204, 208; *A Christmas Carol: Scrooge and Marley,* Act I, *262; A Christmas Carol: Scrooge and Marley,* Act II, 294; "Thank You, M'am," 320; *An American Childhood,* 328; *Silent Spring,* 368; *Nobel Speech,* 384; *Nobel Speech* (video), 389; "Turtle Watchers" / "'Nature' is what We see—" / "The Sparrow," 402, 408; "He—y, Come On Ou—t!" 420, 426; *The Grapes of Wrath,* 464; "The Circuit," 478; "A Work in Progress," 492, 500; *The Story of My Life,* 504, 509; "A Young Tinkerer Builds a Windmill, Electrifying a Nation," 518, 524
L.7.4.a	Use context (e.g., the overall meaning of a sentence or paragraph; a word's position or function in a sentence) as a clue to the meaning of a word or phrase.	**SE/TE:** "Tutors Teach Seniors New High-Tech Tricks," 62; "Mother to Son" / "To James": 94; "Future of Space Exploration Could See Humans on Mars, Alien Planets," 174; "The Last Dog," 182, 196; "Thank You, M'am," 314; "He—y, Come On Ou—t!," 420; "The Circuit," 478; "A Work in Progress," 492; *The Story of My Life:* 504; "A Young Tinkerer Builds a Windmill, Electrifying a Nation," 518
L.7.4.b	Use common, grade-appropriate Greek or Latin affixes and roots as clues to the meaning of a word (e.g., *belligerent, bellicose, rebel*).	**SE/TE:** "Two Kinds," 28; *An Invisible Thread,* 48; *Mom & Me & Mom, 77;* "Danger! This Mission to Mars Could Bore You to Death!" 160; "Future of Space Exploration Could See Humans on Mars, Alien Planets," 178; *A Christmas Carol: Scrooge and Marley,* Act I, 262; *A Christmas Carol: Scrooge and Marley,* Act II, 294; *Nobel Speech,* 384; "Turtle Watchers" / "'Nature' is what We see—" / "The Sparrow," 408; "He—y, Come On Ou—t!" 426; *The Grapes of Wrath,* 464; "The Circuit," 478; "A Work in Progress," 500 *The Story of My Life,* 509; "A Young Tinkerer Builds a Windmill, Electrifying a Nation," 524
L.7.4.c	Consult general and specialized reference materials (e.g., dictionaries, glossaries, thesauruses), both print and digital, to find the pronunciation of a word or determine or clarify its precise meaning or its part of speech.	**SE/TE:** "Tutors Teach Seniors New High-Tech Tricks," 66; "Neil deGrasse Tyson on the Future of U.S. Space Exploration After *Curiosity,*" 208; *A Christmas Carol: Scrooge and Marley,* Act I, 262; *A Christmas Carol: Scrooge and Marley,* Act II, 294; "Thank You, M'am," 320; Whole-Class Performance Task, Unit 4: 397; "Turtle Watchers" / "'Nature' is what We see—" / "The Sparrow," 402; "He—y, Come On Ou—t!" 426
L.7.4.d	Verify the preliminary determination of the meaning of a word or phrase (e.g., by checking the inferred meaning in context or in a dictionary).	**SE/TE:** *Mom & Me & Mom,* 77; "Future of Space Exploration Could See Humans on Mars, Alien Planets," 178; *A Christmas Carol: Scrooge and Marley,* Act II, 294; "Thank You, M'am," 320; *An American Childhood,* 328

Grade 7 Language Standards (continued)		
STANDARD CODE	Standard	Print and Interactive Editions
Vocabulary Acquisition and Use (continued)		
L.7.5	Demonstrate understanding of figurative language, word relationships, and nuances in word meanings.	**SE/TE:** *An Invisible Thread,* 48; "Mother to Son" / "To James," 100, 102; "Dark They Were, and Golden-Eyed," 142, 144; "The Last Dog," 196; *A Christmas Carol: Scrooge and Marley,* Act II, 294; *An American Childhood,* 328
L.7.5.a	Interpret figures of speech (e.g., literary, biblical, and mythological allusions) in context.	**SE/TE:** "Dark They Were, and Golden-Eyed," 142; "The Last Dog,"196; *The Story of My Life,* 507
L.7.5.b	Use the relationship between particular words (e.g., synonym/antonym, analogy) to better understand each of the words.	**SE/TE:** *An Invisible Thread,* 48; *A Christmas Carol: Scrooge and Marley,* Act II, 294; *An American Childhood,* 324, 328; *Silent Spring,* 368
L.7.5.c	Distinguish among the connotations (associations) of words with similar denotations (definitions) (e.g., *refined, respectful, polite, diplomatic, condescending*).	**SE/TE:** "A Simple Act," 39; *An Invisible Thread,* 48; "Mother to Son" / "To James," 100; "Dark They Were, and Golden-Eyed," 144; *Silent Spring,* 366-367
L.7.6	Acquire and use accurately grade-appropriate general academic and domain-specific words and phrases; gather vocabulary knowledge when considering a word or phrase important to comprehension or expression.	**SE/TE:** Unit Goals, Unit 1: 4, Unit 2: 118, Unit 3: 226, Unit 4: 354, Unit 5: 444; "Learning to Love My Mother," 80, 83; "Mother-Daughter Drawings," 86, 92–93; "Dark They Were, and Golden-Eyed" (radio play), 146; "Ellen Ochoa: Director, Johnson Space Center," 200; *Scrooge,* 298, 301; "Urban Farming Is Growing a Greener Future," 332; "Eagle Tracking at Follensby Pond," 412, 418; "Surviving the Dust Bowl," 455; *The Grapes of Wrath,* 464; "How Helen Keller Learned to Talk," 512, 515

UNIT 1 AT A GLANCE

	Contents	Pacing / # of Days	Genre / Lexile	Vocabulary / Word Study
INTRO	**Unit Introduction**	2*		Academic Vocabulary (L.7.6)
	Launch Text: Grounded		Nonfiction Narrative 640L	
WHOLE-CLASS LEARNING	**Whole-Class Learning Introduction**			
	Two Kinds Amy Tan — HOOK&INSPIRE	5	Novel Excerpt 870L	Concept Vocabulary Word Study: Latin Prefix *in-* (L.7.4, b)
	A Simple Act Tyler Jackson — COMPARE	4	News Blog 930L	Concept Vocabulary Word Study: Multiple-Meaning Words (L.7.4)
	***from* An Invisible Thread** Laura Schroff and Alex Tresnioski	4	Memoir 890L	Concept Vocabulary Word Study: Latin Suffix: *-ity* (L.7.4, b)
	Performance Task Writing	3		
SMALL-GROUP LEARNING	**Small-Group Learning Introduction**			
	Tutors Teach Seniors New High-Tech Tricks Jennifer Ludden	3	News Article 1020L	Concept Vocabulary (L.7.4, a) Word Study: Suffix *-ment* (L.7.4, c)
	***from* Mom & Me & Mom** Maya Angelou — COMPARE	2	Memoir 610L	Concept Vocabulary (L.7.4) Word Study: Latin Prefix: *super-* (L.7.4.b, d)
	Learning to Love My Mother Maya Angelou with Michael Maher	2	Media: Video NP	Media Vocabulary (L.7.6)
	Mother-Daughter Drawings Mica and Myla Hendricks	3	Media: Image Gallery NP	Media Vocabulary (L.7.6)
	Mother to Son • To James Langston Hughes • Frank Horne	2	Poetry NP; NP	Concept Vocabulary (L.7.4.a) Word Study: Connotations and Denotations (L.7.5.c)
	Performance Task Speaking and Listening	3		
INDEPENDENT LEARNING	**Independent Learning Introduction**	2		
	Lineage • Family Margaret Walker • Grace Paley		Poetry NP; NP	Independent Learning provides students with the opportuni to analyze a selection independently. To facilitate students' independence, no skills have been assigned.
	"Gotcha Day" Isn't a Cause for Celebration Sophie Johnson		Opinion Piece 1090L	
	The Grandfather and His Little Grandson Leo Tolstoy		Short Story 870L	
	Bridging the Generational Divide Between a Football Father and a Soccer Son • John McCormick		Blog Post 1120L	
	Water Names Lan Samantha Chang		Short Story 900L	
	An Hour With Abuelo Judith Ortiz Cofer		Short Story 840L	
END OF UNIT	**Performance-Based Assessment** Writing	2		
	Unit Reflection			
	Unit Test	1		

* Pacing is suggested for a 40- to 50-minute class period. If you use block scheduling, you may combine days to meet your schedule needs.
NP: Nonprose selection

Analyze Craft and Structure	Conventions / Author's Style	Composition / Research / Speaking and Listening
		Summary (RI.7.2)
Character and Point of View (RL.7.1; RL.7.6)	Conventions: Nouns and Pronouns (L.7.2)	Writing to Sources: Retelling a Scene (W.7.3, a, b, d) Speaking and Listening: Monologue (SL.7.4)
Author's Point of View (RI.7.1; RI.7.6)	Conventions: Adverbs (L.7.1)	Writing to Compare: Explanatory Essay (RI.7.9; W.7.2, b, c; W.7.9; L.7.2)
Narrative Point of View (RI.7.6)	Conventions: Adjectives (L.7.2, a)	
		Write a Nonfiction Narrative (W.7.3, a–e; W.7.4; W.7.5; W.7.10)
Development of Central Ideas (RI.7.1; RI.7.2)	Conventions: Conjunctions (L.7.1; L.7.3, a)	Speaking and Listening: Multimedia Presentation (SL.7.1, b–d; SL.7.4; SL.7.5; W.7.7)
Characterization (RI.7.1; RI.7.3)	Conventions: Independent and Dependent Clauses (L.7.1, a)	Writing to Compare: Comparison-and-Contrast Essay (RI.7.7; W.7.2, a–c; W.7.6; W.7.9.b)
		Speaking and Listening: Multimedia Slideshow (SL.7.1, a; SL.7.5)
Figurative Language: Symbolism (RL.7.1; RL.7.2; RL.7.4)	Author's Style: Rhythm and Repetition (RL.7.4; L.7.5)	Writing to Sources: Narrative Poem (W.7.3, a, b, d; W.7.5; W.7.9.a)
		Present a Nonfiction Narrative (SL.7.1, a–b; SL.7.2; SL.7.4; SL.7.6)
Independent Learning provides students with the opportunity to analyze a selection independently. To facilitate students' independence, no skills have been assigned.		Share Your Independent Learning (SL.7.1)
		Writing to Sources: Nonfiction Narrative (W.7.3; W.7.9; W.7.10) Speaking and Listening: Multimedia Presentation (SL.7.4; SL.7.5)
		Reflect on the Unit

INTRODUCTION

Jump Start

Engage students in discussion based on the following questions:

"What have you learned from people who are more than 20 years older than you? Were these lessons valuable? In 20 years, will you be teaching a teenager the same things? Why or why not?"

Have students write three things they have learned from someone 20 years older than themselves. Then poll the class to determine the three most popular lessons learned. Discuss how relevant these lessons will be 20 years from now.

Generations

Ask students what the word *generations* suggests to them. Point out that as they work through this unit, they will read many examples about how people of different generations interact and learn from one another.

Video

Project the introduction video in class or ask students to open the video in their interactive textbooks.

Discuss It If you want to make this a digital activity, go online and navigate to the Discussion Board. Alternatively, students can share their responses in a class discussion.

Block Scheduling

Each day in this Pacing Plan represents a 40–50 minute class period. Teachers using block scheduling may combine days to reflect their class schedule. In addition, teachers may revise pacing to differentiate and support core instruction by integrating components and resources as students require.

UNIT 1

Generations

Young people often learn from older people, but sometimes it works the other way around.

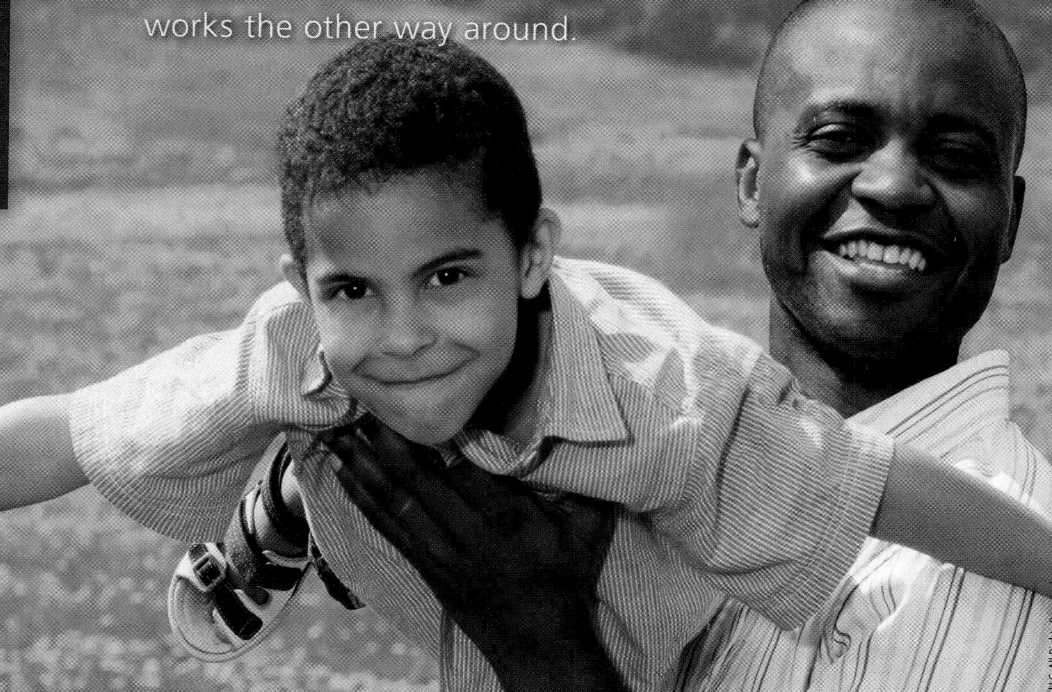

Grizzly Bear Teaches Her Cubs

Discuss It What are some examples of things that one generation can learn from another?

Write your response before sharing your ideas.

2

Pacing Plan

Introduce Whole-Class Learning

Unit Introduction		Introduce Whole-Class Learning	Two Kinds				A Simple Act				*from* An Invisible Thread				Performance Task		
1	2	3	4	5	6	7	8	9	10	11	12	13	14	15	16	17	18

DIGITAL PERSPECTIVES

Audio

Video

Document

Annotation Highlights

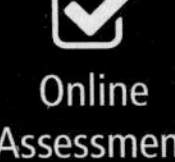
EL Highlights

Online Assessment

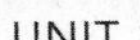

UNIT 1

UNIT INTRODUCTION

ESSENTIAL QUESTION: What can one generation learn from another?

LAUNCH TEXT NONFICTION NARRATIVE MODEL
Grounded

WHOLE-CLASS LEARNING

NOVEL EXCERPT
Two Kinds
from The Joy Luck Club
Amy Tan

COMPARE

NEWS BLOG
A Simple Act
Tyler Jackson

MEMOIR
from An Invisible Thread
Laura Schroff and Alex Tresniowski

▸ MEDIA CONNECTION: Maurice's Toast

PERFORMANCE TASK
WRITING FOCUS:
Write a Nonfiction Narrative

SMALL-GROUP LEARNING

NEWS ARTICLE
Tutors Teach Seniors New High-Tech Tricks
Jennifer Ludden

▸ MEDIA CONNECTION: Cyber-Seniors

COMPARE

MEMOIR
from Mom & Me & Mom
Maya Angelou

MEDIA: VIDEO
Learning to Love My Mother
Maya Angelou with Michael Maher

MEDIA: IMAGE GALLERY
Mother-Daughter Drawings
Mica and Myla Hendricks

POETRY COLLECTION 1
Mother to Son
Langston Hughes

To James
Frank Horne

PERFORMANCE TASK
SPEAKING AND LISTENING FOCUS:
Present a Nonfiction Narrative

INDEPENDENT LEARNING

POETRY COLLECTION 2
Lineage
Margaret Walker

Family
Grace Paley

OPINION PIECE
"Gotcha Day" Isn't a Cause for Celebration
Sophie Johnson

SHORT STORY
The Grandfather and His Little Grandson
Leo Tolstoy

BLOG POST
Bridging the Generational Divide Between a Football Father and a Soccer Son
John McCormick

SHORT STORY
Water Names
Lan Samantha Chang

SHORT STORY
An Hour With Abuelo
Judith Ortiz Cofer

PERFORMANCE-BASED ASSESSMENT PREP
Review Evidence for a Nonfiction Narrative

PERFORMANCE-BASED ASSESSMENT

Narration: Nonfiction Narrative and Multimedia Presentation

PROMPT: In what situations can one generation learn from another?

What can one generation learn from another?

Introduce the Essential Question and point out that students will respond to related prompts.

- **Whole-Class Learning** *What unexpected event shows how a person can influence someone from another generation?*
- **Small-Group Learning** *What new knowledge or skills can you learn from someone of a different generation?*
- **Performance-Based Assessment** *In what situations can one generation learn from another?*

Using Trade Books

Refer to the Teaching with Trade Books section for suggestions on how to incorporate the following thematically related titles into this unit:

- *Stand Tall* by Joan Bauer
- *Fair Weather* by Richard Peck
- *Ribbons* by Laurence Yep

Current Perspectives

To increase student engagement, search online for stories about how people of different generations learn from one another. Always preview content before sharing it with your class.

- **News Story: "Why Should We Listen to Old People? A Very Good Question" (*Huffington Post*)** We can learn valuable lessons from our elders.
- **Video: "Bridging the Years . . . Teens and Seniors Mix It Up!" (*PBS*)** Teens and seniors come together to talk and create art.

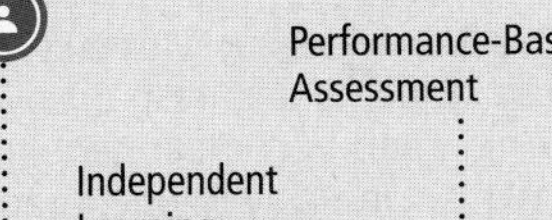

Day	Activity
19	Introduce Small-Group Learning
20–21	Tutors Teach Seniors New High-Tech Tricks
22–23	*from* Mom & Me & Mom
24–25	Learning to Love My Mother
26–27	Mother-Daughter Drawings
28–29	• Mother to Son • To James
30–32	Performance Task
33	Introduce Independent Learning
34	Independent Learning
35–36	Performance-Based Assessment

About the Unit Goals

These unit goals were backward designed from the Performance-Based Assessment at the end of the unit and the Whole-Class and Small-Group Performance Tasks. Students will practice and become proficient in many more standards over the course of this unit.

Unit Goals

Review the goals with students and explain that as they read and discuss the selections in this unit, they will improve their skills in reading, writing, research, language, and speaking and listening.

- Have students watch the video on Goal Setting.
- A video on this topic is available online in the Professional Development Center.

Reading Goals Tell students they will read and evaluate nonfiction narratives. They will also read a variety of genres to better understand the ways writers express ideas.

Writing and Research Goals Tell students that they will learn elements of nonfiction narrative writing. They will write their own nonfiction narrative. They will also write for a variety of reasons, including organizing and sharing ideas. They will conduct research to explore ideas.

Language Goal Tell students that they will develop a deeper understanding of voice, or style of writing, with word choice and sentence structure to convey meaning and add variety to their writing.

Speaking and Listening Goals Explain to students that they will work together to build on one another's ideas, develop consensus, and communicate with one another. They will also learn to incorporate audio, visuals, and text in presentations.

HOME Connection

A Home Connection letter to students' parents or guardians is available in *myPerspectives+*. The letter explains what students will be learning in this unit and how they will be assessed.

Unit Goals

Throughout this unit you will deepen your perspective about different generations by reading, writing, speaking, listening, and presenting. These goals will help you succeed on the Unit Performance-Based Assessment.

Rate how well you meet these goals right now. You will revisit your ratings later when you reflect on your growth during this unit.

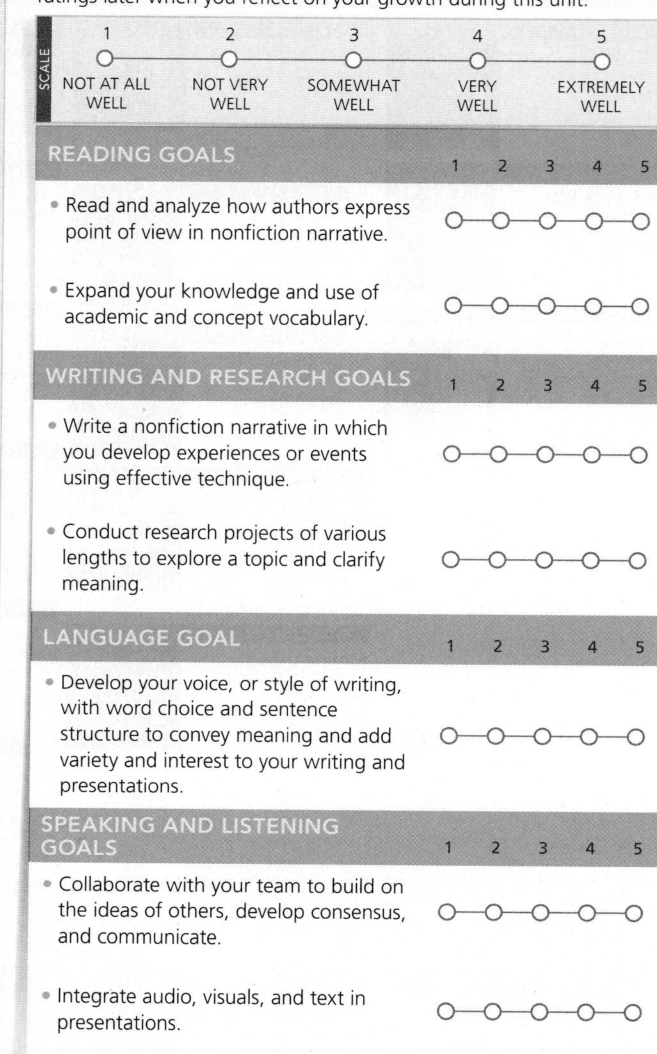

SCALE

1	2	3	4	5
NOT AT ALL WELL	NOT VERY WELL	SOMEWHAT WELL	VERY WELL	EXTREMELY WELL

READING GOALS	1	2	3	4	5
• Read and analyze how authors express point of view in nonfiction narrative.	O	O	O	O	O
• Expand your knowledge and use of academic and concept vocabulary.	O	O	O	O	O

WRITING AND RESEARCH GOALS	1	2	3	4	5
• Write a nonfiction narrative in which you develop experiences or events using effective technique.	O	O	O	O	O
• Conduct research projects of various lengths to explore a topic and clarify meaning.	O	O	O	O	O

LANGUAGE GOAL	1	2	3	4	5
• Develop your voice, or style of writing, with word choice and sentence structure to convey meaning and add variety and interest to your writing and presentations.	O	O	O	O	O

SPEAKING AND LISTENING GOALS	1	2	3	4	5
• Collaborate with your team to build on the ideas of others, develop consensus, and communicate.	O	O	O	O	O
• Integrate audio, visuals, and text in presentations.	O	O	O	O	O

STANDARDS

Language

Acquire and use accurately grade-appropriate general academic and domain-specific words and phrases; gather vocabulary knowledge when considering a word or phrase important to comprehension or expression.

AUTHOR'S PERSPECTIVE Ernest Morrell, Ph.D.

Why Goal Setting Matters Establishing goals helps students take responsibility for their own learning and become independent scholars and thinkers. One way to encourage students to set, follow, and achieve goals is to have them write their goals down. Students can use the following process for crafting well-defined and measurable goals:

- **Decide What You Want:** Have students skim the Unit 1 Table of Contents and decide what they most want to learn from the unit. Guide students to set specific, realistic goals, such as "learn and correctly use five new concept words from the unit."
- **Write the Goals Down:** Have students draft the goals in clear, precise language. Students should also include a way to measure results so they can assess their progress.
- **Set a Time Frame:** Have students include a realistic schedule for completion, using the length of the selections in Unit 1 as a guide. As necessary, have students break large goals into smaller ones to make the goal more likely to be completed.

When students take more responsibility for their learning, they may learn to rely more on themselves and take more interest in their success.

Academic Vocabulary: Nonfiction Narrative

Understanding and using academic terms can help you read, write, and speak with precision and clarity. Here are five academic words that will be useful in this unit as you analyze and write narrative texts.

Complete the chart.

1. Review each word, its root, and the mentor sentences.
2. Use the information and your own knowledge to predict the meaning of each word.
3. For each word, list at least two related words.
4. Refer to the dictionary or other resources if needed.

FOLLOW THROUGH
Study the words in this chart, and mark them or their forms wherever they appear in the unit.

WORD	SENTENCES	PREDICT MEANING	RELATED WORDS
dialogue ROOT: ***-log-*** "word"	1. The television show was known for its well-written *dialogue* between characters. 2. The confusion between Dina and Janet started a *dialogue* that cleared the air.		monologue; logical
consequence ROOT: ***-sequ-*** "follow"	1. A *consequence* of oversleeping is being late for school. 2. Earning an A on my math test was a positive *consequence* of studying all week.		
perspective ROOT: ***-spec-*** "look"	1. It's important to keep *perspective* when facing a challenging situation. 2. The personal essay was written from the author's *perspective*.		
notable ROOT: ***-not-*** "mark"	1. Every *notable* person in the city was invited to the mayor's fund-raising gala. 2. It had been a long week, and nothing particularly *notable* had happened.		
contradict ROOT: ***-dict-*** "speak" or "assert"	1. The facts of the case remain unclear because the witnesses' statements *contradict* each other. 2. The new test results *contradict* what we once thought to be true about the product.		

DIGITAL PERSPECTIVES

Academic Vocabulary: Nonfiction Narrative

Introduce the blue academic vocabulary words in the chart on the student page. Point out that the root of each word provides a clue to its meaning. Discuss the mentor sentences to ensure students understand each word's usage. Students should also use the mentor sentences as context to help them predict the meaning of each word. Check that students are able to fill in the chart correctly. Complete pronunciations, parts of speech, and definitions are provided for you. Students are only expected to provide the definitions.

Possible responses:

dialogue *n.* (DY uh lawg)
Meaning: conversation
Related words: dialogues
Additional words related to the root *-log-*: prologue, monologue, logical

consequence *n.* (KON suh kwehns)
Meaning: the effect or result
Related words: consequences, consequential
Additional words related to the root *-sequ-*: sequence, sequel

perspective *n.* (pur SPEHK tihv)
Meaning: a particular way of looking at something; a point of view
Related words: perspectives, perspectively
Additional words related to the root *-spec-*: speculate, spectacle, respect, retrospective

notable *adj.* (NOH tuh buhl)
Meaning: outstanding; remarkable
Additional words related to the root *-not-*: notary, annotation, connotation, denotation

contradict *v.* (kon truh DIHKT)
Meaning: to state the contrary or opposite; to deny
Related words: contradicted, contradictory
Additional words related to the root *-dic-*: dictate, verdict, diction

PERSONALIZE FOR LEARNING

English Language Support

Cognates Many of the academic vocabulary words have Spanish cognates. Use these cognates with students whose home language is Spanish. **ALL LEVELS**

notable—notable
perspective—perspectiva
dialogue—diálogo
consequence—consecuencia

Purpose of the Launch Text

The Launch Text provides students with a common starting point to address the unit topic. After reading the Launch Text, all students will be able to participate in discussions about generations.

Lexile: 640 The easier reading level of this selection makes it perfect to assign for homework. Students will need little or no support to understand it.

Additionally, "Grounded" provides a writing model for the Performance-Based Assessment students will complete at the end of the unit.

Launch Text: Nonfiction Narrative Model

Remind students to determine the main idea of the nonfiction narrative and how the author conveys that idea.

Have students pay attention to how the narrator and her grandmother communicate with each other. How does the narrator relate to her grandmother's situation? Students should note that the narrator feels her parents are "in the middle, dragging us toward the center, where we did not want to be." Have students think about the scene where the grandmother stops the car. What kind of communication occurs then?

Encourage students to read this text on their own and annotate unfamiliar words and sections of text they think are particularly important.

AUDIO SUMMARIES

Audio summaries of "Grounded" are available online in both English and Spanish in the Interactive Teacher's Edition or Unit Resources. Assigning these summaries before students read the Launch Text may help them build additional background knowledge and set a context for their reading.

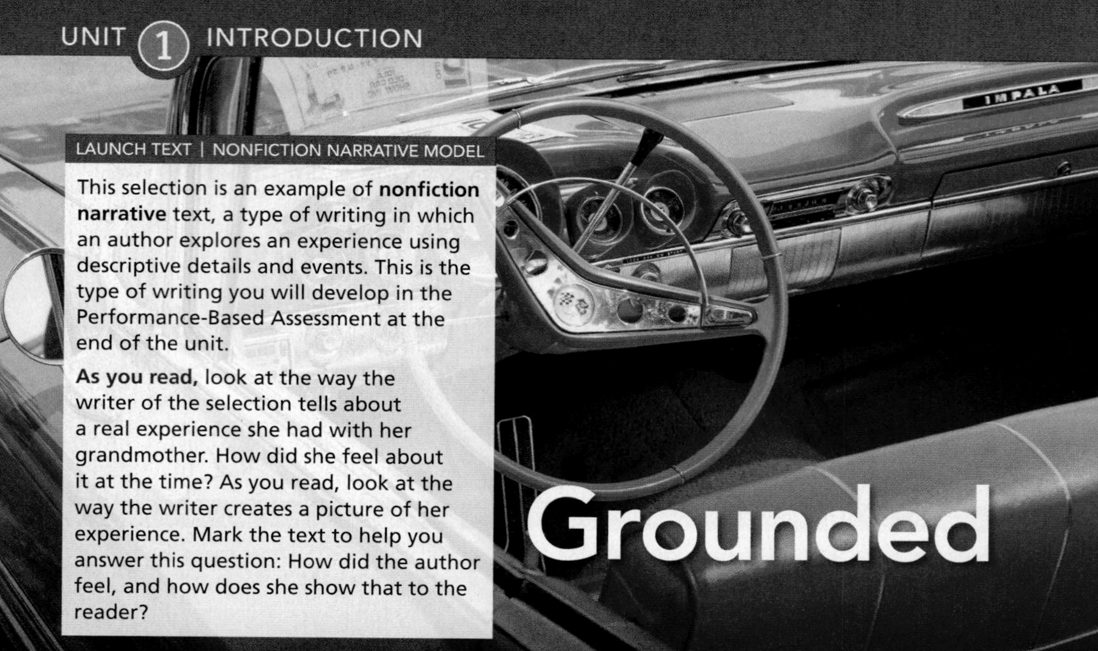

LAUNCH TEXT | NONFICTION NARRATIVE MODEL

This selection is an example of **nonfiction narrative** text, a type of writing in which an author explores an experience using descriptive details and events. This is the type of writing you will develop in the Performance-Based Assessment at the end of the unit.

As you read, look at the way the writer of the selection tells about a real experience she had with her grandmother. How did she feel about it at the time? As you read, look at the way the writer creates a picture of her experience. Mark the text to help you answer this question: How did the author feel, and how does she show that to the reader?

Grounded

1 Growing up I really didn't know my grandmother. She was a private person, and didn't talk about her past much, but I know she had one. She once told me that before she got married she was a backup singer in a band that I had actually heard of. But that's all she would say about it, no matter how often I prodded.

2 "El pasado es el pasado," she told me. *The past is the past.*

3 To me, she talked in Spanish. I talked back in English. We understood each other.

4 The thing I remember most about Grandma Sofia was how much she loved driving, especially since she came to live with us. She had a 1960s red Chevy Impala convertible that was all her own, a remnant of her band days. She loved driving with the top down, the radio blasting, singing at the top of her lungs when a good song came on. Driving was her independence, her freedom.

5 My parents, however, were concerned that she was getting too old to drive around by herself. One night, I overheard them:

6 "She's okay for now, but how long before she can't manage?"

7 "I'll speak to her tomorrow."

8 I felt sick at the thought of Grandma giving up her car. I knew what driving meant to her. I knew that without her wheels she'd feel ordinary—just another grandma, hovering and wise.

9 Sometimes it felt like Grandma and I were on the sidelines and my parents were in the middle, dragging us toward the center, where we did not want to be. I was often grounded for the smallest things. I didn't really mind, under normal circumstances.

CROSS-CURRICULAR PERSPECTIVES

Music Ask students to think about the music they hear in movies. Discuss how music is used to set a tone or create a mood. Then ask them to propose music that could be used as background for "Grounded." Encourage them to be prepared to justify their choices by pointing out the changing moods of the narrative and how their music choices support each mood.

DIGITAL PERSPECTIVES

10 One time—the time I'm writing about—circumstances were not normal. My parents had grounded me for the weekend of Luisa's party, easily the social event of the season. No way was I going to miss it. But my parents weren't even going to be home! They were going to my Aunt Leticia's. It would just be me and Grandma. Me and Grandma and a 1966 red Chevy Impala convertible . . .

11 Saturday night arrived and I was itching to go to the party, so I did the unthinkable: I asked Grandma to drive me to Luisa's. I figured she didn't know about me being grounded. She looked at me quizzically and said she would. I got dressed and ran out to the car. She was waiting for me. I got in.

12 The sky was just beginning to darken, blue clouds against a darker blue sky. Soon it would be nighttime. Grandma looked a little uncomfortable. At first I thought it was because she knew about me being grounded. But then I wondered if maybe she didn't want to drive at night and didn't want to tell me.

13 At that moment I wouldn't have minded getting out and going back home. I felt bad about Grandma. I felt bad about disobeying my parents. But how could I say any of this?

14 We took off. She drove slowly, maybe too slowly. But we didn't get very far. Suddenly she pulled over and stopped the car.

15 We must have been sitting in that car for five minutes, which is a long time if you're sitting in a car not talking. I couldn't ask her if she stopped because she was nervous about driving. And I couldn't ask if she stopped because she knew I was grounded.

16 Finally she turned to me. "Regresamos?" *Shall we turn back?*

17 "Sure," I replied. I was so relieved I could have cried.

18 "Bueno," she said, with a nod. She started the car and turned on the radio. It was a song we both knew by heart. But it was clear that Grandma and I could still learn a lot from each other. ❧

NOTES

WORD NETWORK FOR GENERATIONS

Vocabulary A Word Network is a collection of words related to a topic. As you read the selections in this unit, identify interesting words related to the idea of generations and add them to your Word Network. For example, you might begin by adding words from the Launch Text, such as *concerned, disobeying,* and *independence*. Continue to add words as you complete this unit.

Tool Kit Word Network Model

GENERATIONS
- concerned
- disobeying
- independence

Word Network for Generations

Tell students that they can fill in the Word Network as they read the texts in the unit, or they can jot down the words elsewhere and add them later. Point out to students that people may have personal associations with some words. A word that one student thinks is related to the concept of generations might not be a word another student would pick. However, students should feel free to add any relevant words to their Word Network. Each person's Word Network will be unique. If you choose to print the Word Network, distribute it to students at this point so they can use it throughout the rest of the unit.

AUTHOR'S PERSPECTIVE Elfrieda Hiebert, Ph.D.

Generative Vocabulary Rare words are the words that typically account for only 10 percent of all the words in a text, compared with more common vocabulary words that students know better. Generative vocabulary strategies can help students build their rare vocabulary.

Generative refers to the way students can apply knowledge of how words work—morphologically and conceptually—when encountering new words. Building off a big idea like this unit's *generations,* words can be taught as networks of ideas rather than as single, unrelated but grade-appropriate words. Studying words in conceptual groupings enables students to learn more words while reading.

Although some "generations" words may be unfamiliar to students, the concept of connections over time among relatives or people of different age groups should be familiar to them. Word networks help students build vocabulary by showing them that a wide variety of words can relate to one concept.

Summary

Have students read the introductory paragraph. Provide them with tips for writing a summary:

- Write in the present tense.
- Make sure to include the title of the work.
- Be concise: a summary should not be equal in length to the original text.
- If you need to quote the words of the author, use quotation marks.
- Don't put your own opinions, ideas, or interpretations into the summary. The purpose of writing a summary is to accurately represent what the author says, not to provide a critique.

See possible summary on the student page.

Launch Activity

Explain to students that as they work on this unit, they will have many opportunities to discuss the topic of generations. Point out that everybody has unique relationships with people in older generations. Each of these relationships comes with different kinds—or levels—of communication. Then have students put themselves in the shoes of a person from an older generation. How does the communication with a younger person look from that perspective?

Summary

Write a summary of "Grounded." A **summary** is a concise, complete, and accurate overview of a text. It should not include a statement of your opinion or an analysis.

Possible response: The narrative "Grounded" focuses on the narrator's relationship with her grandmother. The grandmother used to sing in a band and likes to drive her red convertible and sing, a throwback to her youth. However, the narrator's parents are concerned that it is no longer safe for Grandma to keep driving at her age. The narrator worries about this because she knows how much driving means to her grandmother. She feels a parallel between herself and her grandmother, wanting to go their own ways but being dragged back by her parents. Finally, she tells the suspenseful story of a time she was grounded but tried to get around it by having her grandmother drive her to a party.

Launch Activity

Conduct a Discussion Consider this statement: **Senior citizens can learn a lot from younger people.** Decide your position, and rate your response using this scale.

☐ Strongly Agree ☐ Agree ☐ Disagree ☐ Strongly Disagree

Discuss your ratings with classmates and then participate in a whole-class discussion:

- Give examples from stories you have heard or read in which seniors learn from younger people.
- Exchange ideas and comments about the examples that were discussed.
- As a class, come to consensus about the statement.

QuickWrite

Consider class discussions, the video, and the launch text as you think about the prompt. Record your first thoughts here.

PROMPT: **In what situations can one generation learn from another?**

Possible response: In "Grounded," the narrator and her grandmother learn from each other even though they are from different generations. Grandma Sofia seems to teach the narrator an important lesson about her parents: They have her best interests in mind, so they must have grounded her for a reason. Likewise, Grandma Sofia learns from the narrator. If the narrator is grounded for good reason, her parents' reluctance to allow Grandma Sofia to drive is likely rooted in concern for her well-being.

The text shows that people shouldn't judge each other based on age. If we keep an open mind, we can learn—regardless of age. What's important is to not get caught up in the belief that we can't learn anything from older or younger people.

EVIDENCE LOG FOR GENERATIONS

Review your QuickWrite. Summarize your initial position in one sentence to record in your Evidence Log. Then, record evidence from "Grounded" that supports your initial position.

After each selection you will continue to use your Evidence Log to record the evidence you gather and the connections you make.

Tool Kit
Evidence Log Model

Title of Text: ________ Date: ________

CONNECTION TO PROMPT	TEXT EVIDENCE/DETAILS	ADDITIONAL NOTES/IDEAS

How does this text change or add to my thinking? Date: ________

DIGITAL PERSPECTIVES

QuickWrite

In this QuickWrite, students should present their own answer to the question based on the material in the Unit Opener. This initial response will help inform their work when they complete the Performance-Based Assessment at the end of the unit. Students should make sure they provide a good example and support it with accurate details.

See possible QuickWrite on the student page.

Evidence Log for Generations

Students should record their initial thinking in their Evidence Logs. Then, they should record evidence from "Grounded" that supports their initial thinking.

If you choose to print the Evidence Log, distribute it to students at this point so they can use it throughout the rest of the unit.

Performance-Based Assessment: Refining Your Thinking

- Have students watch the video on Refining Your Thinking.
- A video on this topic is available online in the Professional Development Center.

WriteNow Express and Reflect

Description The narrator's description of Grandma Sofia makes their relationship come alive. Have students write a one-page description of someone close to them, reflecting on what that person means to them. Remind students to include details about their friend or relative that reveal the person's personality, not just his or her appearance. Point out that in "Grounded," the narrator's description of her grandmother's love of driving and singing, her type of car, and her history as a backup singer in a band reveal a lot about her personality.

OVERVIEW

WHOLE-CLASS LEARNING

What can one generation learn from another?

Engage students in a conversation about how people from different generations can learn from one another. Point out that older people can teach younger people how to do certain things. Young people can also teach older people how to think about matters from a different perspective. For example, a teenager might give her grandfather a fresh insight on the benefits of recycling and reusing materials. During Whole-Class Learning, students will read three selections about how people of different generations learn from one another.

Whole-Class Learning Strategies

Review the Learning Strategies with students and explain that as they work through Whole-Class Learning they will develop strategies to work in large-group environments.

- Have students watch the video on Whole-Class Learning Strategies.
- A video on this topic is available online in the Professional Development Center.

You may wish to discuss some action items to add to the chart as a class before students complete it on their own. For example, for "Listen actively," you might solicit the following actions from students:

- If you don't understand someone's point, ask for further clarification.
- Take notes to help you retain information.

Block Scheduling

Each day in this Pacing Plan represents a 40–50 minute class period. Teachers using block scheduling may combine days to reflect their class schedule. In addition, teachers may revise pacing to differentiate and support core instruction by integrating components and resources as students require.

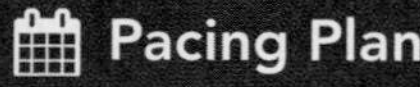

Pacing Plan

Introduce Whole-Class Learning

Unit Introduction — Two Kinds — A Simple Act — *from* An Invisible Thread — Performance Task

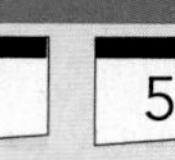

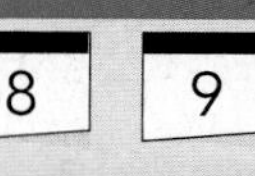

1 2 3 4 5 6 7 8 9 10 11 12 13 14 15 16 17 18

WHOLE-CLASS LEARNING

OVERVIEW: WHOLE-CLASS LEARNING

ESSENTIAL QUESTION:

What can one generation learn from another?

The famous Indian leader Mahatma Gandhi said, "Learn as if you were to live forever." You are always learning, from peers as well as from teachers, parents, and relatives. You will work with your whole class to explore ways in which generations can learn from each other.

Whole-Class Learning Strategies

Throughout your life, in school, in your community, and in your career, you will continue to learn and work in large-group environments.

Review these strategies and the actions you can take to practice them as you work with your whole class. Add ideas of your own to each step. Get ready to use these strategies during Whole-Class Learning.

STRATEGY	ACTION PLAN
Listen actively	• Eliminate distractions. For example, put your cell phone away. • Keep your eyes on the speaker. •
Clarify by asking questions	• If you're confused, other people probably are, too. Ask a question to help your whole class. • If you see that you are guessing, ask a question instead. •
Monitor understanding	• Notice what information you already know and be ready to build on it. • Ask for help if you are struggling. •
Interact and share ideas	• Share your ideas and answer questions, even if you are unsure. • Build on the ideas of others by adding details or making a connection. •

CONTENTS

The Whole-Class readings illustrate the influence of one generation on another. After reading, you will write a nonfiction narrative about an event in which a person from one generation influenced a person from a different generation.

DIGITAL PERSPECTIVES

Contents

Anchor Texts Preview the anchor texts with students to generate interest. Encourage students to discuss other texts they have read or movies or television shows they have seen that deal with the issues of how people of different generations influence and learn from one another.

You might wish to conduct a poll to determine which selection students think looks most interesting and discuss the reasons for their preference. Students can return to this poll after they have read the selections to see if their preference changed.

Performance Task

Write a Nonfiction Narrative Explain to students that after they have finished reading the selections, they will write a nonfiction narrative about the influence someone from a different generation has had on them or someone they know. To help them prepare, encourage students to think about the topic as they progress through the selections and as they participate in the Whole-Class Learning experience.

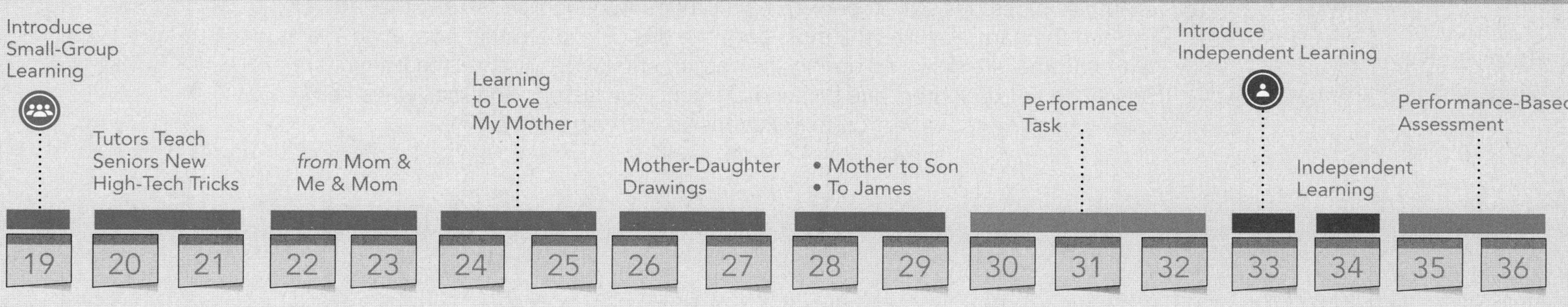

Two Kinds

AUDIO SUMMARIES
Audio summaries of "Two Kinds" are available online in both English and Spanish in the Interactive Teacher's Edition or Unit Resources. Assigning these summaries prior to reading the selection may help students build additional background knowledge and set a context for their first read.

Summary

In Amy Tan's excerpt, "Two Kinds," nine-year-old Jing-mei faces pressure to be great from her immigrant mother. Mrs. Woo watches child "geniuses" perform feats that make them famous. She wants Jing-mei to become famous, too. At first Jing-mei shares her mother's hopes, but soon she realizes she may never be the talented child of her mother's dreams. She begins to resent her mother's efforts. However, when Mrs. Woo watches a Chinese child pianist on television, she thinks she has found the perfect activity for Jing-mei. As the story continues, Jing-mei and her mother both learn to understand each other's point of view.

Insight

The differences between generations are often a source of tension. Reading "Two Kinds" will help students see that when members of the older generation project all of their hopes and dreams onto the younger generation, the pressure to live up to those dreams can be too much. Often, the younger generation must reject the ways of the older generation before they can claim their own identity.

ESSENTIAL QUESTION:
What can one generation learn from another?

Connection to Essential Question

"Two Kinds" will help students answer the Essential Question—*What can one generation learn from another?*—through the realization that Jing-mei has at the end of the story. As a child, Jing-mei does not want to learn anything from her mother. She rejects all of Mrs. Woo's plans and expectations for who Jing-mei should be and asserts her independence from Mrs. Woo in the most hurtful way she can. As an adult, however, Jing-mei discovers that the song she played at the talent show, "Pleading Child," has a companion piece titled "Perfectly Contented." The pairing of these titles represents Jing-mei's rejection of her mother's dreams for her and her eventual understanding that her mother's lessons in obedience were meant to give Jing-mei a better life than she had.

WHOLE-CLASS LEARNING PERFORMANCE TASK
What unexpected event shows how a person can influence someone from a different generation?

UNIT PERFORMANCE-BASED ASSESSMENT
In what situations can one generation learn from another?

Connection to Performance Tasks

Whole-Class Learning Performance Task In this Performance Task, students will write personal narratives about the way someone from a different generation has influenced them or someone they know. Students will have the opportunity to compare their own experiences with the relationship in "Two Kinds," which shows how a mother with ambition tries to teach her daughter about obedience.

Unit Performance-Based Assessment This selection provides students with examples of lessons shared between a mother and daughter; lessons that are learned the hard way. For the most part, the bits of wisdom that Mrs. Woo shares with Jing-mei are delivered during their arguments, when she yells that there are only obedient daughters and willful daughters. The lessons Jing-mei learns come later, when she can reflect on her relationship with her mother.

HOOK& INSPIRE

DIGITAL PERSPECTIVES  Audio  Video  Document  Annotation Highlights  Online Assessment

LESSON RESOURCES

	Making Meaning	Language Development	Effective Expression
Lesson	**First Read** **Close Read** **Analyze the Text** **Analyze Craft and Structure**	**Concept Vocabulary** **Word Study** **Conventions**	**Writing to Sources** **Speaking and Listening**
Instructional Standards	**RL.7.10** By the end of the year, read and comprehend literature . . . **RL.7.1** Cite several pieces of textual evidence to support . . . **RL.7.6** Analyze how an author develops and contrasts the points of view . . .	**L.7.4** Determine or clarify the meaning of unknown and multiple-meaning words . . . **L.7.4.b** Use common, grade-appropriate Greek or Latin affixes and roots as clues . . . **L.7.2** Demonstrate command of the conventions of standard English . . .	**W.7.3** Write narratives . . . **W.7.3.a** Engage and orient the reader . . . **W.7.3.b** Use narrative techniques . . . **W.7.3.d** Use precise words and phrases . . . **SL.7.4** Present claims and findings . . .
STUDENT RESOURCES			
Available online in the Interactive Student Edition or Unit Resources	Selection Audio First-Read Guide: Fiction Close-Read Guide: Fiction	Word Network	Evidence Log
TEACHER RESOURCES			
Selection Resources Available online in the Interactive Teacher's Edition or Unit Resources	Audio Summaries: English and Spanish Annotation Highlights Accessible Leveled Text First Read Extension Questions Analyze Craft and Structure: Character and Point of View	Concept Vocabulary and Word Study Conventions: Nouns and Pronouns	Writing to Sources: Retelling a Scene Speaking and Listening: Monologue
Reteach/Practice (RP) Available online in the Interactive Teacher's Edition or Unit Resources	Analyze Craft and Structure: Character and Point of View (RP)	Word Study: Latin Prefix *in-* (RP) Conventions: Nouns and Pronouns (RP)	Writing to Sources: Retelling a Scene (RP) Speaking and Listening: Monologue (RP)
Assessment Available online in Assessments	Selection Test: English Selection Test: Spanish Extension Selection Test		
My Resources	A Unit 1 Answer Key is available online and in the Interactive Teacher's Edition		

Reading Support

Text Complexity Rubric: Two Kinds	
Quantitative Measures	
Lexile: 870 **Text Length:** 4,592 words	
Qualitative Measures	
Knowledge Demands ①—②—❸—④—⑤	The Chinese immigrant experience may be unfamiliar to most students. The concept of a *child prodigy* is central, as are the pressures or high expectations for talent and success. References are made to Shirley Temple.
Structure ①—②—❸—④—⑤	Narrative is mostly told in sequence, but spans many years. Some background information/ history told by narrator is mixed with events in story. Use of dialogue helps to break up narrative.
Language Conventionality and Clarity ①—②—❸—④—⑤	Intentional grammatical errors are used for mother's speech to show that she is learning English. Daughter's speech is correct English; some figurative language and above level vocabulary is used.
Levels of Meaning/Purpose ①—②—③—❹—⑤	At times meaning needs to be inferred from the way characters speak to one another or from their actions. Some metaphorical ideas used, especially in ending.

DECIDE AND PLAN

English Language Support

Provide English Learners with support for knowledge demands and language as they read the selection.

Knowledge Demands Display the words *prodigy, genius, talent,* and *expectations.* Talk about the meaning of each word. Ask students to find and read the sentences containing those words. Ask students to practice using these words in their own sentences.

Language Ask students to write some of the sentences that the mother says. Discuss phrases that need correction, for example, *you can be prodigy; because you not trying.* Ask students if they can correct the phrases. Use the sentences to discuss correct use of the articles *a* and *the: (You can be a prodigy)* and verbs *(you're not trying).*

Strategic Support

Provide students with strategic support to ensure that they can successfully read the text.

Knowledge Demands Determine students' understanding of the term *child prodigy.* Before students read, discuss what a child prodigy is and what pressures could come with trying to have a special talent. At different points in the reading, draw attention to ideas related to the concept of high expectations; for example, *I would soon become perfect* (paragraph 10).

Meaning As students read, pause to ask about the characters' words, thoughts, or behaviors and what they indicate about how the characters feel. For example, first Jing-mei is excited and imagines a ballerina or Cinderella. Later she is impatient and frustrated (paragraph 9).

Challenge

Provide students who need to be challenged with ideas for how they can go beyond a simple interpretation of the text.

Text Analysis Pair students. Ask them to discuss the metaphorical meaning of the final sentence. Prompt by asking *How do the two parts of music reflect the character's experience?* Ask each pair to write a response together and then present it to the class.

Written Response Ask students to write their thoughts on what the mother in the story could have done to motivate her daughter without creating so much pressure. Ask them to give their ideas about what parents and teachers can do to prevent stress and pressure while still motivating students to do their best.

TEACH

Read and Respond

Have the class do their first read of the selection. Then have them complete the close read. Finally, work with them on the Making Meaning, Language Development, and Effective Expression activities.

Standards Support Through Teaching and Learning Cycle

IDENTIFY NEEDS

Analyze results of the Beginning-of-Year Assessment, focusing on the items relating to Unit 1. Also take into consideration student performance to this point and your observations of where particular students struggle.

DECIDE AND PLAN

- If students have performed poorly on items matching these standards, then provide selection scaffolds before assigning them the on-level lesson provided in the Student Edition.
- If students have done well on the Beginning-of-Year Assessment, then challenge them to keep progressing and learning by giving them opportunities to practice the skills in depth.
- Use the Selection Resources listed on the Planning pages for "Two Kinds" to help students continually improve their ability to master the standards.

Instructional Standards: Two Kinds

	Catching Up	This Year	Looking Forward
Reading	You may wish to administer the **Analyze Craft and Structure: Character and Point of View (RP)** worksheet to help students understand that the thoughts and feelings of a narrator influence how the reader experiences the story events.	**RL.6** Analyze how an author develops and contrasts the points of view of different characters or narrators in a text.	Ask students to find a sentence or passage from the story that shows how moments of humor are connected to the thoughts, feelings and personality of the narrator from whose point of view the story is told.
Writing	You may wish to administer the **Writing to Sources: Retelling a Scene (RP)** worksheet to help students understand how to convey character traits through what a character says, does, thinks, or feels.	**W.3.b** Use narrative techniques, such as dialogue, pacing, and description, to develop experiences, events, and/or characters.	Encourage students to write a letter that the narrator's mother would have written to a friend about her daughter. In the letter, have the mother convey events, in order, and use dialogue and description to convey her experience of her daughter's personality and abilities.
Speaking and Listening	You may wish to administer the **Speaking and Listening: Monologue (RP)** worksheet to help students understand how to orally present a claim effectively through its delivery, clarity, and strong points.	**SL.4** Present claims and findings, emphasizing salient points in a focused, coherent manner with pertinent descriptions, facts, details, and examples; use appropriate eye contact, adequate volume, and clear pronunciation.	Challenge students to imagine that they are giving an award to Amy Tan for her story. Orally, have students effectively present a claim that supports the reasons for their choice.
Language	You may wish to administer the **Word Study: Latin Prefix *in-* (RP)** worksheet to help students understand that knowing the meaning of the prefix *in-* contributes to the overall meaning of the word, as in the word *indignity*.	**L.4.b** Use common, grade-appropriate Greek or Latin affixes and roots as clues to the meaning of a word.	Have students identify two or three words in the selection that include a prefix. One word may include the prefix *in-*, but students should also select a word with a different prefix. Students should use a print or online dictionary to learn the meaning of each prefix, the base word, and the meaning of each full word they studied.

ANALYZE AND REVISE

- Analyze student work for evidence of student learning.
- Identify whether or not students have met the expectations in the standards.
- Identify implications for future instruction.

TEACH

Implement the planned lesson, and gather evidence of student learning.

Jump Start

FIRST READ Prior to students' first read, ask them to talk about parents or guardians and what they wish for their children. What happens when children disagree with the dreams that their parents or guardians have for them? Help students make connections between the text and their own experiences.

Two Kinds

Who is the narrator? How does her story connect to the concept of generations? How does the expectation of being a prodigy affect her relationship with her mother? Modeling questions such as these will help students connect to "Two Kinds" and to the Performance Task assignment. Selection audio and print capability for the selection are available in the Interactive Teacher's Edition.

Concept Vocabulary

Support students as they rank the words. Ask if they've ever heard, read, or used them. Reassure them that the definitions for these words are listed in the selection.

FIRST READ

As they read, students should perform the steps of the first read:

NOTICE: Encourage students to notice who the narrator is and what events develop the conflict of the narrative.

ANNOTATE: Remind students to mark key passages, such as the ones that illuminate the rising tension between the narrator and her mother. Students may want to revisit these passages in their close read.

CONNECT: Encourage students to go beyond the text to think about how the text connects with their own experiences. What would they do if they were pressured to follow someone else's dream?

RESPOND: Students will answer questions and write a summary to demonstrate understanding.

Point out to students that while they will always complete the Respond step at the end of the first read, the other steps will probably happen somewhat concurrently. You may wish to print copies of the **First-Read Guide: Fiction** for students to use.

Remind students that during their first read, they should not answer the close-read questions that appear in the selection.

About the Author

If her mother had gotten her way, **Amy Tan** (b. 1952) would have two professions—doctor and concert pianist. Although Tan showed early promise in music, at 37 she became a successful fiction writer instead. Tan has written many books—most for adults, and some for children. Writing is sometimes tough, Tan admits, but she keeps this in mind: "A story should be a gift." That thought propels Tan to keep creating memorable characters and events.

Tool Kit
First-Read Guide and Model Annotation

Two Kinds

Concept Vocabulary

You will encounter the following words as you read "Two Kinds."

Before reading, note how familiar you are with each word. Then, rank the words in order from most familiar (1) to least familiar (6).

WORD	YOUR RANKING
lamented	
indignity	
reproach	
discordant	
squabbling	
devastated	

After completing your first read, come back to the concept vocabulary and review your rankings. Mark changes to your original rankings as needed.

First Read FICTION

Apply these strategies as you conduct your first read. You will have an opportunity to complete the close-read notes after your first read.

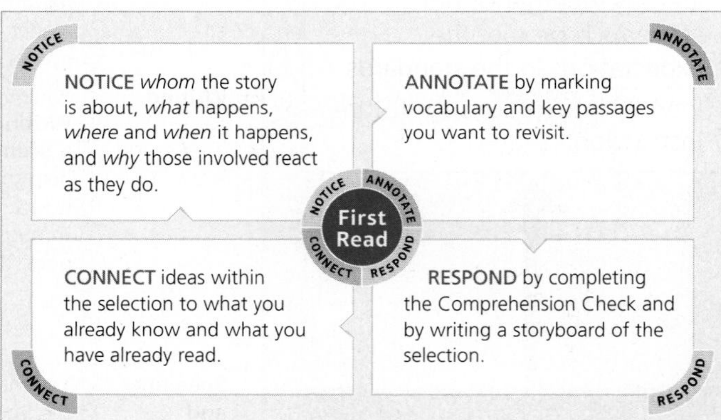

STANDARDS
Reading Literature
By the end of the year, read and comprehend literature, including stories, dramas, and poems, in the grades 6–8 text complexity band proficiently, with scaffolding as needed at the high end of the range.

Two Kinds

from The Joy Luck Club

Amy Tan

BACKGROUND

In 1949, following years of civil war, the Communist Party seized control of China. A number of Chinese who feared Communists—like the mother in "Two Kinds"—fled to the United States. Many lost everything except their hopes for a better future. They placed these hopes on the shoulders of their children born in the new land.

1 My mother believed you could be anything you wanted to be in America. You could open a restaurant. You could work for the government and get good retirement. You could buy a house with almost no money down. You could become rich. You could become instantly famous.

2 "Of course, you can be prodigy,[1] too," my mother told me when I was nine. "You can be best anything. What does Auntie Lindo know? Her daughter, she is only best tricky."

3 America was where all my mother's hopes lay. She had come here in 1949 after losing everything in China: her mother and father, her family home, her first husband, and two daughters, twin baby girls. But she never looked back with regret. There were so many ways for things to get better.

* * *

NOTES

1. **prodigy** (PROD uh jee) *n.* child of unusually high talent.

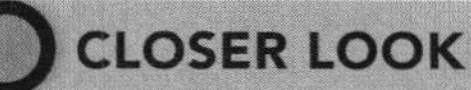

Analyze Character 

Students may have marked paragraphs 1–3 during their first read. Use these paragraphs to help students understand the mother's character. Encourage them to talk about the annotations that they marked. You may want to model a close read with the class based on the highlights shown in the text.

ANNOTATE: Have students mark details in these paragraphs that suggest how the mother's past experiences might have influenced her feelings about life in America, or have students participate while you highlight them.

QUESTION: Guide students to consider what these details might tell them. Ask what a reader can infer from what was annotated, and accept student responses.

Possible response: The mother has come to America after experiencing great personal loss in China. It seems that these losses may have fueled grand expectations for her and her daughter.

CONCLUDE: Help students to formulate conclusions about the importance of these details in the text. Ask students why the author might have included these details

Possible response: The mother has developed some irrational beliefs and unproven expectations about her daughter's potential. By adding these details, the author sets the scene for disappointment, and for conflict between mother and daughter.

Remind students that the **characters** in a short story are the people who are involved in the action. Their beliefs, statements, and actions can set up the conflict, or problem in the story.

AUTHOR'S PERSPECTIVE **Kelly Gallagher, M.Ed.**

Teacher as the Best Reader in the Class

Rather than being the wizard behind the curtain, use modeling to do the work of reading in front of students. When students see that even good readers wrestle with difficult text, they gain confidence. Use these methods:

- **Using think-alouds.** Choose a passage from this unit and model read-alouds/think-alouds to show students what effective readers do when they are confused. The *Annotate Question Conclude* feature and the Teacher's Edition support the importance of this work.
- **Marking the text.** If students say they don't understand, have them use a yellow highlighter (or sticky notes) for parts they understand and a pink highlighter for those they don't.
- **Using sentence starters.** To identify where students are having comprehension problems, have them complete this sentence starter: "I don't understand…" Then, as a class, work to resolve the issues. Use these additional sentence starters: *I noticed…; I wonder…; I think…; I'm surprised that…; I realized…; I'm not sure…*

It is also important for students to know that applying tools like these doesn't always work: sometimes, readers decide to live with ambiguity.

CLOSE READ

Remind students to focus on the italicized words as they read paragraphs 4 and 5. Explain that authors use italics for different reasons, including to add emphasis or to indicate a non-English word. You may wish to model the Close Read using the following think-aloud format. Possible responses to questions on the student page are included. You may also want to print copies of the **Close-Read Guide: Fiction** for students to use.

ANNOTATE: As I read paragraphs 4 and 5, I notice and mark the word that appears in italics.

QUESTION: *Ni kan* is a Chinese term, which the narrator's mother uses several times when she wants her daughter to pay attention to something.

CONCLUDE: The author's decision to include the Chinese term creates tension. The narrator's mother is putting a lot of pressure on her daughter to succeed as an American by having her act like someone whom she thinks epitomizes what it means to be American: Shirley Temple. The fact that the mother's urging is in Chinese is significant because it reminds readers that she is a Chinese immigrant—one who wants to achieve success in America through her daughter.

NOTES

CLOSE READ

ANNOTATE: Mark the italicized words in paragraphs 4 and 5.

QUESTION: What is different or unusual about these words?

CONCLUDE: What effect is created by the author's use of these words?

lamented (luh MEHNT ihd) *v.* expressed regret

indignity (ihn DIHG nuh tee) *n.* feeling that one has been disrespected

reproach (rih PROHCH) *n.* criticism or disapproval

4 We didn't immediately pick the right kind of prodigy. At first my mother thought I could be a Chinese Shirley Temple.[2] We'd watch Shirley's old movies on TV as though they were training films. My mother would poke my arm and say, *"Ni kan"*—You watch. And I would see Shirley tapping her feet, or singing a sailor song, or pursing her lips into a very round O while saying, "Oh my goodness."

5 *"Ni kan,"* said my mother as Shirley's eyes flooded with tears. "You already know how. Don't need talent for crying!"

6 Soon after my mother got this idea about Shirley Temple, she took me to a beauty training school in the Mission district and put me in the hands of a student who could barely hold the scissors without shaking. Instead of getting big fat curls, I emerged with an uneven mass of crinkly black fuzz. My mother dragged me off to the bathroom and tried to wet down my hair.

7 "You look like Negro Chinese," she **lamented**, as if I had done this on purpose.

8 The instructor of the beauty training school had to lop off these soggy clumps to make my hair even again. "Peter Pan is very popular these days," the instructor assured my mother. I now had hair the length of a boy's, with straight-across bangs that hung at a slant two inches above my eyebrows. I liked the haircut and it made me actually look forward to my future fame.

9 In fact, in the beginning, I was just as excited as my mother, maybe even more so. I pictured this prodigy part of me as many different images, trying each one on for size. I was a dainty ballerina girl standing by the curtains, waiting to hear the right music that would send me floating on my tiptoes. I was like the Christ child lifted out of the straw manger, crying with holy **indignity**. I was Cinderella stepping from her pumpkin carriage with sparkly cartoon music filling the air.

10 In all of my imaginings, I was filled with a sense that I would soon become *perfect*. My mother and father would adore me. I would be beyond **reproach**. I would never feel the need to sulk for anything.

11 But sometimes the prodigy in me became impatient. "If you don't hurry up and get me out of here, I'm disappearing for good," it warned. "And then you'll always be nothing."

* * *

12 Every night after dinner, my mother and I would sit at the Formica kitchen table. She would present new tests, taking her examples from stories of amazing children that she read in *Ripley's Believe It or Not*, or *Good Housekeeping*, *Reader's Digest*, and a dozen

2. **Shirley Temple** American child star of the 1930s. She started in her first movie at age three and won an Academy Award at age six.

PERSONALIZE FOR LEARNING

Strategic Support

Prodigies For students to understand paragraphs 4–11, they will need to know the word *prodigy* and what it represents. Have students look the word up in a dictionary and research modern or historical prodigies. Lead a class discussion about these prodigies, encouraging students to draw conclusions about the phenomenon. What experiences do prodigies have in common? What challenges do they face?

other magazines she kept in a pile in our bathroom. My mother got these magazines from people whose houses she cleaned. And since she cleaned many houses each week, we had a great assortment. She would look through them all, searching for stories about remarkable children.

13 The first night she brought out a story about a three-year-old boy who knew the capitals of all the states and even most of the European countries. A teacher was quoted as saying the little boy could also pronounce the names of the foreign cities correctly.

14 "What's the capital of Finland?" My mother asked me, looking at the magazine story.

15 All I knew was the capital of California, because Sacramento was the name of the street we lived on in Chinatown. "Nairobi!" I guessed, saying the most foreign word I could think of. She checked to see if that was possibly one way to pronounce "Helsinki" before showing me the answer.

16 The tests got harder—multiplying numbers in my head, finding the queen of hearts in a deck of cards, trying to stand on my head without using my hands, predicting the daily temperatures in Los Angeles, New York, and London.

17 One night I had to look at a page from the Bible for three minutes and then report everything I could remember. "Now Jehoshaphat had riches and honor in abundance and . . . that's all I remember, Ma," I said.

18 And after seeing my mother's disappointed face once again, something inside of me began to die. I hated the tests, the raised hopes and failed expectations. Before going to bed that night, I looked in the mirror above the bathroom sink and when I saw only my face staring back—and that it would always be this ordinary face—I began to cry. Such a sad, ugly girl! I made high-pitched noises like a crazed animal, trying to scratch out the face in the mirror.

19 And then I saw what seemed to be the prodigy side of me—because I had never seen that face before. I looked at my reflection, blinking so I could see more clearly. The girl staring back at me was angry, powerful. This girl and I were the same. I had new thoughts, willful thoughts, or rather thoughts filled with lots of won'ts. I won't let her change me, I promised myself. I won't be what I'm not.

20 So now on nights when my mother presented her tests, I performed listlessly, my head propped on one arm. I pretended to be bored. And I was. I got so bored I started counting the bellows of the foghorns out on the bay while my mother drilled me in other areas. The sound was comforting and reminded me of the cow jumping over the moon. And the next day, I played a game with myself, seeing if my mother would give up on me before

NOTES

CLOSE READ

ANNOTATE: Mark words or phrases in paragraphs 18 and 19 that reveal the narrator's feelings.

QUESTION: Why might the author have chosen to reveal the contrasting emotions of the narrator?

CONCLUDE: What effect does this choice have on the reader?

DIGITAL PERSPECTIVES 

CLOSE READ

Remind students to focus on words and phrases that indicate the narrator's feelings. You may wish to model the Close Read of paragraphs 18 and 19 using the following think-aloud format. Possible responses to questions on the student page are included.

ANNOTATE: As I read paragraphs 18 and 19, I notice and mark words and phrases that indicate the narrator's feelings. I look for descriptions of how the narrator views herself or how her recent experiences make her feel.

QUESTION: The author may have chosen to reveal the contrasting emotions so that readers understand the narrator better. In paragraph 18, the narrator still believes she has let her mother down—despite the fact that her mother's expectations are impossibly high. In paragraph 19, the narrator is seeing a new side of herself—and her self-confidence is growing.

CONCLUDE: The choice to include the shifting emotions allows the reader to understand that the narrator has undergone a change and is maturing as an individual. The narrator begins to believe in herself and is defiant—she's no longer the person who will try so hard to please her mother.

WriteNow Express and Reflect

Interior Monologue In paragraphs 18 and 19, the narrator's interaction with her reflection in the mirror creates a vivid picture of conflicting parts of her personality. Have students write a short interior monologue that illustrates how different parts of a person's personality can be in conflict. The monologue can be about themselves or invented characters. Encourage them to write details that reveal the conflict rather than explain it. Then have students reflect on how such interior conflicts make us who we are.

NOTES

eight bellows. After a while I usually counted only one, maybe two bellows at most. At last she was beginning to give up hope.

21 Two or three months had gone by without any mention of my being a prodigy again. And then one day my mother was watching *The Ed Sullivan Show*[3] on TV. The TV was old and the sound kept shorting out. Every time my mother got halfway up from the sofa to adjust the set, the sound would go back on and Ed would be talking. As soon as she sat down, Ed would go silent again. She got up, the TV broke into loud piano music. She sat down. Silence. Up and down, back and forth, quiet and loud. It was like a stiff embraceless dance between her and the TV set. Finally, she stood by the set with her hand on the sound dial.

22 She seemed entranced by the music, a little frenzied piano piece with this mesmerizing quality, sort of quick passages and then teasing lilting ones before it returned to the quick playful parts.

23 *"Ni kan,"* my mother said, calling me over with hurried hand gestures. "Look here."

24 I could see why my mother was fascinated by the music. It was being pounded out by a little Chinese girl, about nine years old, with a Peter Pan haircut. The girl had the sauciness of a Shirley Temple. She was proudly modest like a proper Chinese child. And

3. ***The Ed Sullivan Show*** popular television variety show that ran from 1948 to 1971.

DIGITAL PERSPECTIVES

Enriching the Text The 1993 feature film *The Joy Luck Club* contains scenes based on this excerpt from the novel. After students complete their close read, show these clips from the movie and have students compare them with the written text. How do the movie scenes add to students' understanding of the narrative? Preview all videos before showing them in class. **(Research to Clarify)**

she also did this fancy sweep of a curtsy, so that the fluffy skirt of her white dress cascaded slowly to the floor like the petals of a large carnation.

25 In spite of these warning signs, I wasn't worried. Our family had no piano and we couldn't afford to buy one, let alone reams of sheet music and piano lessons. So I could be generous in my comments when my mother bad-mouthed the little girl on TV.

26 "Play note right, but doesn't sound good! No singing sound," complained my mother.

27 "What are you picking on her for?" I said carelessly. "She's pretty good. Maybe she's not the best, but she's trying hard." I knew almost immediately that I would be sorry I said that.

28 "Just like you," she said. "Not the best. Because you not trying." She gave a little huff as she let go of the sound dial and sat down on the sofa.

29 The little Chinese girl sat down also to play an encore of "Anitra's Dance" by Grieg.[4] I remember the song, because later on I had to learn how to play it.

30 Three days after watching *The Ed Sullivan Show,* my mother told me what my schedule would be for piano lessons and piano practice. She had talked to Mr. Chong, who lived on the first floor of our apartment building. Mr. Chong was a retired piano teacher and my mother had traded housecleaning services for weekly lessons and a piano for me to practice on every day, two hours a day, from four until six.

31 When my mother told me this, I felt as though I had been sent to hell. I whined and then kicked my foot a little when I couldn't stand it anymore.

32 "Why don't you like me the way I am? I'm *not* a genius! I can't play the piano. And even if I could, I wouldn't go on TV if you paid me a million dollars!" I cried.

33 My mother slapped me. "Who ask you be genius?" she shouted. "Only ask you be your best. For you sake. You think I want you be genius? Hnnh! What for! Who ask you!"

34 "So ungrateful," I heard her mutter in Chinese, "If she had as much talent as she has temper, she would be famous now."

35 Mr. Chong, whom I secretly nicknamed Old Chong, was very strange, always tapping his fingers to the silent music of an invisible orchestra. He looked ancient in my eyes. He had lost most of the hair on top of his head and he wore thick glasses and had eyes that always looked tired and sleepy. But he must have been younger than I thought, since he lived with his mother and was not yet married.

36 I met Old Lady Chong once and that was enough. She had this peculiar smell like a baby that had done something in its pants.

4. **Grieg** (greeg) Edvard Grieg (1843–1907), Norwegian composer.

NOTES

CLOSE READ

ANNOTATE: Mark the punctuation in paragraphs 32 and 33 that reveals how the mother and daughter communicate.

QUESTION: What does the punctuation suggest about the tone of the conversation?

CONCLUDE: How does the punctuation in these paragraphs help you to better understand the conflict between the mother and the daughter?

DIGITAL 
PERSPECTIVES

CLOSE READ

Remind students that the punctuation of sentences in dialogue tells us something about how the words are spoken. You may wish to model the close read of paragraphs 32 and 33 using the following think-aloud format. Possible responses to questions on the student page are included.

ANNOTATE: As I read paragraphs 32 and 33, I notice and mark punctuation that tells me something about how the narrator and her mother are communicating.

QUESTION: Exclamation points are used by authors to suggest strong emotion. The tone of the conversation is therefore emotional, heated, and tense.

CONCLUDE: The punctuation in these paragraphs underscores the divide between the strong-willed mother and her equally strong-willed daughter. Both are firmly set in their beliefs and positions, and they are emotional about them to the point of shouting.

NOTES

And her fingers felt like a dead person's, like an old peach I once found in the back of the refrigerator; the skin just slid off the meat when I picked it up.

37 I soon found out why Old Chong had retired from teaching piano. He was deaf. "Like Beethoven!"[5] he shouted to me. "We're both listening only in our head!" And he would start to conduct his frantic silent sonatas.

38 Our lessons went like this. He would open the book and point to different things, explaining their purpose: "Key! Treble! Bass! No sharps or flats! So this is C major! Listen now and play after me!"

39 And then he would play the C scale a few times, a simple chord, and then, as if inspired by an old, unreachable itch, he gradually added more notes and running trills and a pounding bass until the music was really something quite grand.

40 I would play after him, the simple scale, the simple chord, and then I just played some nonsense that sounded like a cat running up and down on top of garbage cans. Old Chong smiled and applauded and then said, "Very good! But now you must learn to keep time!"

41 So that's how I discovered that Old Chong's eyes were too slow to keep up with the wrong notes I was playing. He went through the motions in half-time. To help me keep rhythm, he stood behind me, pushing down on my right shoulder for every beat. He balanced pennies on top of my wrists so I would keep them still as I slowly played scales and arpeggios.[6] He had me curve my hand around an apple and keep that shape when playing chords. He marched stiffly to show me how to make each finger dance up and down, staccato[7] like an obedient little soldier.

42 He taught me all these things, and that was how I also learned I could be lazy and get away with mistakes, lots of mistakes. If I hit the wrong notes because I hadn't practiced enough, I never corrected myself. I just kept playing in rhythm. And Old Chong kept conducting his own private reverie.

43 So maybe I never really gave myself a fair chance. I did pick up the basics pretty quickly, and I might have become a good pianist at that young age. But I was so determined not to try, not to be anybody different that I learned to play only the most ear-splitting preludes, the most **discordant** hymns.

discordant (dihs KAWRD uhnt) *adj.* lacking harmony

44 Over the next year, I practiced like this, dutifully in my own way. And then one day I heard my mother and her friend Lindo Jong both talking in a loud bragging tone of voice so others could hear. It was after church, and I was leaning against the

5. **Beethoven** (BAY toh vuhn) Ludwig van Beethoven (1770–1827), German composer. Some of his greatest pieces were written when he was completely deaf.
6. **arpeggios** (ahr PEHJ ee ohz) *n.* notes in a chord played separately in quick succession.
7. **staccato** (stuh KAHT oh) *adv.* played crisply, with clear breaks between notes.

CROSS-CURRICULAR PERSPECTIVES

Music In paragraph 43, the narrator describes the *discordant* music she plays. Have the class make some *discordant* music. You can be the conductor. Divide the class into at least three groups and give each group a different rhythm and exercise—handclapping, pencil tapping, and foot stomping. Encourage students to also whistle, blow horns, and hum. As conductor, give a signal to start and stop the groups. Conduct your classroom orchestra and join in with your own discordant notes. Finally, ask students to comment on the experience of listening to this music and discuss why the narrator might have decided to play only discordant tunes. **(Research to Clarify)**

brick wall wearing a dress with stiff white petticoats. Auntie Lindo's daughter, Waverly, who was about my age, was standing farther down the wall about five feet away. We had grown up together and shared all the closeness of two sisters **squabbling** over crayons and dolls. In other words, for the most part, we hated each other. I thought she was snotty. Waverly Jong had gained a certain amount of fame as "Chinatown's Littlest Chinese Chess Champion."

45 "She bring home too many trophy," lamented Auntie Lindo that Sunday. "All day she play chess. All day I have no time do nothing but dust off her winnings." She threw a scolding look at Waverly, who pretended not to see her.

46 "You lucky you don't have this problem," said Auntie Lindo with a sigh to my mother.

47 And my mother squared her shoulders and bragged: "Our problem worser than yours. If we ask Jing-mei wash dish, she hear nothing but music. It's like you can't stop this natural talent."

48 And right then, I was determined to put a stop to her foolish pride.

* * *

49 A few weeks later, Old Chong and my mother conspired to have me play in a talent show which would be held in the church hall. By then, my parents had saved up enough to buy me a secondhand piano, a black Wurlitzer spinet with a scarred bench. It was the showpiece of our living room.

50 For the talent show, I was to play a piece called "Pleading Child" from Schumann's[8] *Scenes from Childhood*. It was a simple, moody piece that sounded more difficult than it was. I was supposed to memorize the whole thing, playing the repeat parts twice to make the piece sound longer. But I dawdled over it, playing a few bars and then cheating, looking up to see what notes followed. I never really listened to what I was playing. I daydreamed about being somewhere else, about being someone else.

51 The part I liked to practice best was the fancy curtsy: right foot out, touch the rose on the carpet with a pointed foot, sweep to the side, left leg bends, look up and smile.

52 My parents invited all the couples from the Joy Luck Club to witness my debut. Auntie Lindo and Uncle Tin were there. Waverly and her two older brothers had also come. The first two rows were filled with children both younger and older than I was. The littlest ones got to go first. They recited simple nursery rhymes, squawked out tunes on miniature violins, twirled Hula

NOTES

squabbling (SKWAHB blihng) *v.* fighting noisily over small matters

8. **Schumann** (SHOO mahn) Robert Alexander Schumann (1810–1856), German composer.

PERSONALIZE FOR LEARNING

Challenge

Research In paragraph 50, the narrator explains that she was supposed to practice a piece by Schumann. Have students research the German composer Robert Schumann. Ask them to write a brief biography of the man, outlining his professional career, including the creation of *Scenes from Childhood.* What do the names of the pieces in *Scenes from Childhood* tell us about Schumann? Have students listen to the fourth piece, "Pleading Child," and, if possible, play a recording of it for the class.

TEACHING

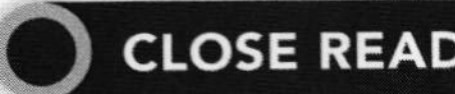 

CLOSE READ

Remind students to focus on descriptive words. You may wish to model the Close Read of paragraph 54 using the following think-aloud format. Possible responses to questions on the student page are included.

ANNOTATE: As I read paragraph 54, I mark descriptive words and take note of what these words describe.

QUESTION: The author uses positive descriptions to highlight the narrator's excitement about the recital as it begins. She uses negative descriptions to indicate when and why the narrator's feelings change.

CONCLUDE: The descriptions relate a change that occurs over the course of the recital. As the recital begins, the narrator is captivated by the moment and feels positive. But then things change as her performance falters, and by the end, she is aware of her failure. The author shows the change by using descriptive words at key points.

NOTES

CLOSE READ

ANNOTATE: In paragraph 54, mark descriptive words, and note what they describe.

QUESTION: Why does the author use positive and negative descriptions?

CONCLUDE: What effect do these descriptions have over the course of the paragraph?

Hoops, pranced in pink ballet tutus, and when they bowed or curtsied, the audience would sigh in unison, "Awww," and then clap enthusiastically.

53 When my turn came, I was very confident. I remember my childish excitement. It was as if I knew, without a doubt, that the prodigy side of me really did exist. I had no fear whatsoever, no nervousness. I remember thinking to myself, This is it! This is it! I looked out over the audience, at my mother's blank face, my father's yawn, Auntie Lindo's stiff-lipped smile, Waverly's sulky expression. I had on a white dress, layered with sheets of lace, and a pink bow in my Peter Pan haircut. As I sat down, I envisioned people jumping to their feet and Ed Sullivan rushing up to introduce me to everyone on TV.

54 And I started to play. It was so beautiful. I was so caught up in how lovely I looked that at first I didn't worry how I would sound. So it was a surprise to me when I hit the first wrong note and I realized something didn't sound quite right. And then I hit another and another followed that. A chill started at the top of my head and began to trickle down. Yet I couldn't stop playing, as though my hands were bewitched. I kept thinking my fingers would adjust themselves back, like a train switching to the right track. I played this strange jumble through two repeats, the sour notes staying with me all the way to the end.

55 When I stood up, I discovered my legs were shaking. Maybe I had just been nervous and the audience, like Old Chong, had seen me go through the right motions and had not heard anything wrong at all. I swept my right foot out, went down on my knee, looked up and smiled. The room was quiet, except for Old Chong, who was beaming and shouting "Bravo! Bravo! Well done!" But then I saw my mother's face, her stricken face. The audience clapped weakly, and as I walked back to my chair, with my whole face quivering as I tried not to cry, I heard a little boy whisper loudly to his mother, "That was awful," and the mother whispered back, "Well, she certainly tried."

56 And now I realized how many people were in the audience, the whole world it seemed. I was aware of eyes burning into my back. I felt the shame of my mother and father as they sat stiffly throughout the rest of the show.

57 We could have escaped during intermission. Pride and some strange sense of honor must have anchored my parents to their chairs. And so we watched it all: the eighteen-year-old boy with a fake moustache who did a magic show and juggled flaming hoops while riding a unicycle. The breasted girl with white makeup who sang from *Madama Butterfly* and got honorable mention. And the eleven-year-old boy who won first prize playing a tricky violin song that sounded like a busy bee.

58 After the show, the Hsus, the Jongs, and the St. Clairs from the Joy Luck Club came up to my mother and father.

59 "Lots of talented kids," Auntie Lindo said vaguely, smiling broadly.

60 "That was somethin' else," said my father, and I wondered if he was referring to me in a humorous way, or whether he even remembered what I had done.

61 Waverly looked at me and shrugged her shoulders. "You aren't a genius like me," she said matter-of-factly. And if I hadn't felt so bad, I would have pulled her braids and punched her stomach.

62 But my mother's expression was what **devastated** me: a quiet, blank look that said she had lost everything. I felt the same way, and it seemed as if everybody were now coming up, like gawkers at the scene of an accident, to see what parts were actually missing. When we got on the bus to go home, my father was humming the busy-bee tune and my mother was silent. I kept thinking she wanted to wait until we got home before shouting at me. But when my father unlocked the door to our apartment, my mother walked in and then went to the back, into the bedroom. No accusations. No blame. And in a way, I felt disappointed. I had been waiting for her to start shouting, so I could shout back and cry and blame her for all my misery.

* * *

63 I assumed my talent-show fiasco meant I never had to play the piano again. But two days later, after school, my mother came out of the kitchen and saw me watching TV.

64 "Four clock," she reminded me as if it were any other day. I was stunned, as though she were asking me to go through the talent-show torture again. I wedged myself more tightly in front of the TV.

65 "Turn off TV," she called from the kitchen five minutes later.

66 I didn't budge. And then I decided. I didn't have to do what my mother said anymore. I wasn't her slave. This wasn't China. I had listened to her before and look what happened. She was the stupid one.

67 She came out from the kitchen and stood in the arched entryway of the living room. "Four clock," she said once again, louder.

68 "I'm not going to play anymore," I said nonchalantly. "Why should I? I'm not a genius."

69 She walked over and stood in front of the TV. I saw her chest was heaving up and down in an angry way.

NOTES

devastated (DEH vuh stay tihd) *v.* destroyed; completely upset

VOCABULARY DEVELOPMENT

Word Forms Support student understanding of the word *devastated* in paragraph 62. Model other forms of the word in sentences.

A *devastating* earthquake struck the region at 4:06 A.M.

After the storm passed, our farm was a picture of *devastation*.

Samantha is a skilled debater; she will *devastate* you with her rhetoric.

Word	Part of Speech	Meaning
devastating	adjective	terrible, destructive
devastation	noun	ruin, destruction
devastate	verb	to bring to ruin, to overwhelm

NOTES

70 "No!" I said, and I now felt stronger, as if my true self had finally emerged. So this was what had been inside me all along.

71 "No! I won't!" I screamed.

72 She yanked me by the arm, pulled me off the floor, snapped off the TV. She was frighteningly strong, half pulling, half carrying me toward the piano as I kicked the throw rugs under my feet. She lifted me up and onto the hard bench. I was sobbing by now, looking at her bitterly. Her chest was heaving even more and her mouth was open, smiling crazily as if she were pleased I was crying.

73 "You want me to be someone that I'm not!" I sobbed. "I'll never be the kind of daughter you want me to be!"

74 "Only two kinds of daughters," she shouted in Chinese. "Those who are obedient and those who follow their own mind! Only one kind of daughter can live in this house. Obedient daughter!"

75 "Then I wish I wasn't your daughter. I wish you weren't my mother," I shouted. As I said these things I got scared. It felt like worms and toads and slimy things crawling out of my chest, but it also felt good, as if this awful side of me had surfaced, at last.

76 "Too late change this," said my mother shrilly.

77 And I could sense her anger rising to its breaking point. I wanted to see it spill over. And that's when I remembered the babies she had lost in China, the ones we never talked about. "Then I wish I'd never been born!" I shouted. "I wish I were dead! Like them."

78 It was as if I had said the magic words. Alakazam!—and her face went blank, her mouth closed, her arms went slack, and she backed out of the room, stunned, as if she were blowing away like a small brown leaf, thin, brittle, lifeless.

79 It was not the only disappointment my mother felt in me. In the years that followed, I failed her so many times, each time asserting my own will, my right to fall short of expectations. I didn't get straight A's. I didn't become class president. I didn't get into Stanford. I dropped out of college.

80 For unlike my mother, I did not believe I could be anything I wanted to be. I could only be me.

81 And for all those years, we never talked about the disaster at the recital or my terrible accusations afterward at the piano bench. All that remained unchecked, like a betrayal that was now unspeakable. So I never found a way to ask her why she had hoped for something so large that failure was inevitable.

82 And even worse, I never asked her what frightened me the most: Why had she given up hope?

83 For after our struggle at the piano, she never mentioned my playing again. The lessons stopped. The lid to the piano was closed, shutting out the dust, my misery, and her dreams.

PERSONALIZE FOR LEARNING

English Language Support

Idioms Idioms can be confusing to English Learners. The expressions *breaking point* in paragraph 77 and *to fall short* in paragraph 79 are idiomatic. Help students use context clues, such as *rising,* to understand the meaning of *breaking point*—the moment of greatest strain, when something reaches its limit and "breaks." Then help them use context clues, such as *disappointed* and *failed her so many times,* to figure out the meaning of *to fall short*—to not quite achieve one's goals or desires. **ALL LEVELS**

84 So she surprised me. A few years ago, she offered to give me the piano, for my thirtieth birthday. I had not played in all those years. I saw the offer as a sign of forgiveness, a tremendous burden removed.

85 "Are you sure?" I asked shyly. "I mean, won't you and Dad miss it?"

86 "No, this your piano," she said firmly. "Always your piano. You only one can play."

87 "Well, I probably can't play anymore," I said. "It's been years."

88 "You pick up fast," said my mother, as if she knew this was certain. "You have natural talent. You could been genius if you want to."

89 "No I couldn't."

90 "You just not trying," said my mother. And she was neither angry nor sad. She said it as if to announce a fact that could never be disproved. "Take it," she said.

91 But I didn't at first. It was enough that she had offered it to me. And after that, every time I saw it in my parents' living room, standing in front of the bay windows, it made me feel proud, as if it were a shiny trophy I had won back.

* * *

NOTES

CLOSER LOOK

Analyze Symbols

Students may have marked paragraphs 94 and 95 during their first read. Use these paragraphs to help students understand how to think about symbols. Encourage them to talk about the annotations that they marked. You may want to model a close read with the class based on the highlights shown in the text.

ANNOTATE: Have students mark details in the paragraphs that show how the narrator compares "Pleading Child" with "Perfectly Contented," or have students participate while you highlight them.

QUESTION: Guide students to consider what these details might tell them. Ask what a reader can infer from these annotations, and accept student responses.

Possible response: She says it was quite easy to play "Perfectly Contented," which has a lighter melody than "Pleading Child," and she notices that "Perfectly Contented" is longer, faster, and easier than "Pleading Child."

CONCLUDE: Help students to formulate conclusions about the importance of these details in the text. Ask students why the author might have included these details

Possible response: The author intended these two pieces to symbolize different stages in the narrator's development. They form a single song—a single person. By adding these details, the author intends to show that the narrator has come to a peaceful resolution with her mother.

Review symbols and symbolism with students. A **symbol** is something—an object, a person, an animal, a place, or an image—that represents something else. It stands for something larger than itself, usually an abstract idea. **Symbolism**—the use of symbols—plays an important role in many literary genres.

NOTES

92 Last week I sent a tuner over to my parents' apartment and had the piano reconditioned, for purely sentimental reasons. My mother had died a few months before and I had been getting things in order for my father, a little bit at a time. I put the jewelry in special silk pouches. The sweaters she had knitted in yellow, pink, bright orange— all the colors I hated—I put those in moth-proof boxes. I found some old Chinese silk dresses, the kind with little slits up the sides. I rubbed the old silk against my skin, then wrapped them in tissue and decided to take them home with me.

93 After I had the piano tuned, I opened the lid and touched the keys. It sounded even richer than I remembered. Really, it was a very good piano. Inside the bench were the same exercise notes with handwritten scales, the same secondhand music books with their covers held together with yellow tape.

94 I opened up the Schumann book to the dark little piece I had played at the recital. It was on the left-hand side of the page, "Pleading Child." It looked more difficult than I remembered. I played a few bars, surprised at how easily the notes came back to me.

95 And for the first time, or so it seemed, I noticed the piece on the right-hand side. It was called "Perfectly Contented." I tried to play this one as well. It had a lighter melody but the same flowing rhythm and turned out to be quite easy. "Pleading Child" was shorter but slower; "Perfectly Contented" was longer, but faster. And after I played them both a few times, I realized they were two halves of the same song. ❧

WriteNow Analyze and Interpret

Analysis Throughout "Two Kinds," the narrator describes her relationship with her mother. Have students write a one-page analysis of that relationship. Remind students to include details about these characters' dreams, how they express themselves, and the conflicts they experience. How does the relationship change over the course of the narrative?

Comprehension Check

Complete the following items after you finish your first read.

1. In what ways does the mother pressure her daughter to change?

2. How does the mother arrange for her daughter to take piano lessons?

3. How does the narrator prepare for the talent show?

4. What happens when the narrator performs at the talent show?

5. What happens to the piano at the end of the story?

Notebook Draw a storyboard of key events in "Two Kinds" to confirm your understanding of the story.

RESEARCH

Research to Clarify Choose at least one unfamiliar detail from the text. Briefly research that detail. In what way does the information you learned shed light on an aspect of the story?

Research to Explore Choose something that interested you from the text and formulate a research question.

CROSS-CURRICULAR PERSPECTIVES

Social Studies Have students research and write a short report about life in China in 1949. They should include information about the political system and its effects on Chinese citizens. What kinds of jobs were available? Where and how did people live? How did ordinary citizens respond to the political turmoil of the era?

DIGITAL PERSPECTIVES 

Comprehension Check

Possible responses:

1. She pressures her daughter to become a child prodigy. First she pressures the daughter to become an actress. Next, she pressures her to learn facts in order to appear on television. Then, she pressures her to become an accomplished pianist.
2. The mother exchanges housecleaning services for piano lessons from Mr. Chong, a retired piano teacher who lives in their apartment building.
3. The narrator practices as little as she can for the talent show. She purposely makes no effort, and because Mr. Chong is deaf and cannot hear how well she is playing, he does not notice.
4. The narrator's piano performance at the recital is terrible, and no one applauds except for Mr. Chong. The daughter expects her mother to be angry because she was so poorly prepared. Instead, the mother shows only *a quiet, blank look that said she had lost everything.*
5. The mother gives the daughter the old piano. The daughter has it tuned and plays the same song that she played at the talent show.

Answers will vary. Storyboards should include these events: In China, the mother's twin daughters die. She comes to America. She pressures her daughter to become a prodigy (first an actress, then a whiz kid, then a pianist). She exchanges housecleaning for piano lessons. The daughter resists her mother's pressure. At a talent show, the daughter plays a piece badly because she did not rehearse enough. The mother and daughter have a fight about their expectations. The daughter disappoints her mother in other ways. The mother gives the piano to the daughter once she becomes an adult.

Research

Research to Clarify If students struggle to come up with a detail to research, suggest that they focus on one of the following topics: Shirley Temple, *The Ed Sullivan Show,* Chinatown in San Francisco, or composer Robert Schumann.

Research to Explore If students have a difficult time formulating a research question, suggest that they look back through the story for inspiration.

Jump Start

CLOSE READ Have students close read "Two Kinds." Remind them that the mother said there are only two kinds of daughters: *Those who are obedient and those who follow their own mind!* With this in mind, ask students to discuss why the author titled the narrative "Two Kinds."

Close Read the Text

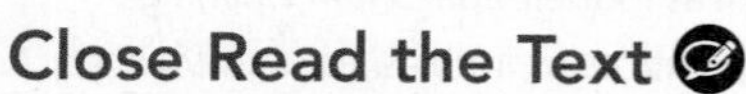

Walk students through the Annotation Model on the student page. Then have them use the models as they annotate another detail. Encourage them to complete items 2 and 3 on their own. Review and discuss the sections students have marked. If needed, continue to model close reading by using the Annotation Highlights in the Interactive Teacher's Edition.

Analyze the Text

Possible responses:

1. (a) Both mother and daughter are strong-willed. The mother is more idealistic, believing that all things are possible. The daughter is more realistic, believing that one must accept restrictions in real life. **DOK 2** (b) The daughter believes she can never meet her mother's expectations, and the mother is angry because the daughter refuses to try. **DOK 2**
2. Some students may respond that no one wins. The mother never achieves the life she wants for her daughter, and the daughter doesn't develop the self-esteem she might have had if she had followed her mother obediently. **DOK 3**
3. The mother pushed her daughter too hard. The mother's efforts backfired. Her daughter believed she would never be good enough and stopped trying. **DOK 3**
4. Students might point out that the story shows that people of different generations can learn from the ways that each other acts under pressure and tries to influence each other. **DOK 3**

TWO KINDS

Close Read the Text

1. This model, from paragraph 10 of the text, shows two sample annotations, along with questions and conclusions. Close read the passage, and find another detail to annotate. Then, write a question and conclusion.

ANNOTATE: The author uses italics to emphasize a specific word.

QUESTION: Why is the word *perfect* emphasized?

CONCLUDE: The narrator believes that the only way her parents will be satisfied with her is if she is without fault.

In all of my imaginings, I was filled with a sense that I **would** soon become *perfect*. My mother and father **would** adore me. I **would** be beyond reproach. I **would** never feel the need to sulk for anything.

ANNOTATE: The word *would* is repeated several times.

QUESTION: What idea is stressed by the repetition of *would*?

CONCLUDE: The repetition shows the narrator's hopes for the future. It also shows that she does not feel that her parents adore her, she often feels criticized, and she likely sulks a lot.

2. For more practice, go back into the text and complete the close-read notes.
3. Revisit a section of the text you found important. Read this section and **annotate** what you notice. Ask yourself **questions** such as "Why did the author make this choice?" What can you **conclude**?

Tool Kit
Close-Read Guide and Model Annotation

Analyze the Text

CITE TEXTUAL EVIDENCE to support your answers.

Notebook Respond to these questions.

1. (a) **Compare and Contrast** How are the mother and her daughter similar and different? (b) **Analyze Cause and Effect** How does the difference in their attitudes cause problems?
2. **Draw Conclusions** In this story, **conflict,** or a struggle between the characters, results when a mother pushes her daughter to succeed. Is there a winner in this conflict? Explain.
3. **Make a Judgment** Should the narrator's mother have pushed the daughter as she did? Explain.
4. **Essential Question** ***What can one generation learn from another?*** What have you learned about how people of different generations interact from reading this story?

STANDARDS

Reading Literature

- Cite several pieces of textual evidence to support analysis of what the text says explicitly as well as inferences drawn from the text.
- Analyze how an author develops and contrasts the points of view of different characters or narrators in a text.

FORMATIVE ASSESSMENT

Analyze the Text

- **If** students fail to cite evidence, **then** remind them to support their ideas with specific information from the text.
- **If** students struggle to compare and contrast the personalities of the mother and daughter, **then** discuss the process of comparing and contrasting and illustrate with examples.

VOCABULARY DEVELOPMENT

Graphic Organizer Have students fill out a word map for the word *reproach*.

Definition in your own words	Synonyms
Reproach	
Use it in a sentence.	Antonyms

Analyze Craft and Structure

Character and Point of View A **character** is a person or an animal in a literary work.

- **Character traits** are the individual qualities that make each character unique. You can identify character traits by **making inferences**, or educated guesses, about a character based on how he or she thinks, acts, and speaks.
- A **character's motives** are the emotions or goals that drive him or her to act in a certain way.
- A **character's perspective** is how he or she views events based on his or her experiences and emotions.

Point of view is the perspective from which the story is told.

- When a story is told from the **first-person point of view,** the narrator is a character who participates in the action and uses first-person pronouns such as *I* and *me* to refer to himself or herself.
- When a story is told from the **third-person point of view,** the narrator is not a character in the story. The narrator uses third-person pronouns such as *he* and *she* to refer to the characters.

Practice

CITE TEXTUAL EVIDENCE to support your answers.

Notebook Respond to these questions.

1. Use the diagram to list the daughter's character traits.

THE DAUGHTER

2. Reread paragraphs 24–28 of the text. What does this passage show about the difference between the mother's motives and the daughter's motives?
3. How do the different perspectives of the mother and daughter create challenges for each character?
4. (a) From what point of view is the story told? (b) What details in the text enabled you to identify the point of view?
5. How might the story be different if it were told from the mother's point of view?

DIGITAL PERSPECTIVES

Analyze Craft and Structure

Character and Point of View Discuss with students why an author might choose to use first-person point of view when writing a story. Have them identify whether the selection "Two Kinds" is written in first-person or third-person point of view, citing a few words from the text that led them to their conclusion. Then have them think about how the story would have been different if it had been told from a different point of view (in this case, third-person point of view). For more support, see **Analyze Craft and Structure: Character and Point of View**.

Practice

Possible responses:

1. Answers will vary. Students might describe the daughter as *rebellious, insecure, proud, arrogant, funny, undisciplined*.
2. The mother wants to inspire her daughter to be the best while the daughter wants her mother to accept less.
3. The mother's high expectations make disappointment inevitable; the daughter's perspective leads to feelings of guilt and resentment.
4. (a) The story is told from the daughter's first-person point of view. (b) She uses first-person pronouns—*I, me, my*—and describes her own thoughts and feelings about the events in the story.
5. If the mother were the narrator, the story would focus on her thoughts and feelings instead of the daughter's.

FORMATIVE ASSESSMENT

Analyze Craft and Structure

If students fail to identify the narrative's point of view, **then** have them look for clues that indicate the point of view. For example, the person narrating the story might be directly involved in the story itself.

If students are unable to identify character traits, **then** remind them to pay close attention to how each character reacts to events and conflicts. For Reteach and Practice, see **Analyze Craft and Structure: Character and Point of View (RP).**

PERSONALIZE FOR LEARNING

English Language Support

Character Motivation Support English Learners in their understanding of character motivation.

Present a small group of students with a newspaper story about an individual who has done something philanthropic. Read the article with students. Once they understand the content, ask students to collaborate in writing one or two sentences describing why this person might have done what they did. **EMERGING**

Give students a newspaper story about an individual who has done something philanthropic. Ask students to write a paragraph describing the person's possible motives for what he or she did. **EXPANDING**

Give students two articles: one about a person who has done something philanthropic and one about a person who is seeking elected office. Ask students to write a paragraph that compares and contrasts what the motives of these two people might be. **BRIDGING**

An expanded **English Language Support Lesson** on Motives is available in the Interactive Teacher's Edition.

TEACHING

Concept Vocabulary

Why These Words? Discuss with students the differences between using words such as *glad* and *overjoyed*. Even though the words are synonymous, they have different degrees of intensity. Then have students think about why an author might choose to use one word over the other to describe a character.

Possible responses:

1. The narrator thinks that her mother *lamented* her bad haircut. The word *discordant* describes the type of hymns the narrator learns to play. *Devastated* describes how the narrator feels when she sees her mother's expression after her performance.
2. *willful* (paragraph 19), *whined* (paragraph 31), *foolish* (48)

Practice

Possible responses:

1. A person who experiences *indignity* feels humiliation, shame, or embarrassment. These feelings often lead to anger.
2. A celebrity chef is someone who has received a great deal of approval for his or her cooking. This can lead her or him to feel beyond *reproach*.
3. The neighbors might complain about loud, *discordant* music because it could interfere with their ability to sleep.
4. To help people avoid *squabbling*, I would encourage them to take turns listening to each other.
5. If a student *lamented* after taking a test, the test probably did not go well at all.
6. A tornado might have *devastated*, or destroyed, an apple orchard.

Word Network

Possible words: *retirement, prodigy, disappointed, expectations, ungrateful*

Word Study

For more support, see **Concept Vocabulary and Word Study**.

Possible responses:

1. *Indignity* means something that hurts a person's dignity.
2. *Incorrect* means not correct, or wrong. *Inactive* means not active or not working. *Incomplete* means not complete or unfinished.

FORMATIVE ASSESSMENT

Concept Vocabulary

If students fail to see the connection between the words, **then** have them use each word in a sentence and think about what is similar about the sentences.

Word Study

If students struggle to define *indignity*, **then** have them describe embarrassing situations that would hurt a person's dignity. For Reteach and Practice, see **Word Study: Latin Prefix *in-* (RP).**

LANGUAGE DEVELOPMENT

TWO KINDS

Concept Vocabulary

lamented	reproach	squabbling
indignity	discordant	devastated

Why These Words? These concept vocabulary words relate to the idea of conflict. For example, the narrator fantasizes that she might one day be beyond *reproach*. The word *reproach* describes the heavy criticism that she feels as a result of her mother's actions.

1. Select three of the concept vocabulary words, and explain how each word helps the reader better understand the conflict between the mother and the daughter.
2. What other words in the selection connect to the concept of conflict, or struggle?

Practice

Notebook The concept vocabulary words appear in "Two Kinds." Answer the questions, using the vocabulary words to show your understanding.

1. Why might a person who experiences *indignity* feel upset or angry?
2. Why might a famous chef feel that his or her cooking is beyond *reproach?*
3. Why might someone's neighbors complain about *discordant* music coming from a stereo?
4. What advice can you give people to help them avoid *squabbling* with each other?
5. If a student *lamented* after taking a test, how did the student do?
6. What kind of weather might have *devastated* an apple orchard?

WORD NETWORK

Look in the text for words related to the topic of generations, and add them to your Word Network.

Word Study

Latin Prefix: *in-* The prefix *in-* means "not." When this prefix is added to a base word, the new word takes on the opposite meaning from the original word. Practice your knowledge of this prefix by completing the following activities.

1. When people have *dignity*, they are worthy of honor and respect. Write a definition of the word *indignity* based on your knowledge of the prefix *in-*.
2. Define these words that contain the prefix *in-*: *incorrect, inactive, incomplete.*

STANDARDS

Language

- Determine or clarify the meaning of unknown and multiple-meaning words and phrases based on *grade 7 reading and content*, choosing flexibly from a range of strategies.
  - b. Use common, grade-appropriate Greek or Latin affixes and roots as clues to the meaning of a word.
- Demonstrate command of the conventions of standard English capitalization, punctuation, and spelling when writing.

AUTHOR'S PERSPECTIVE Elfrieda Hiebert, Ph.D.

Author's Word Choice When the theme is left unstated, readers can find clues in the text to infer the author's overarching message. Among the most useful clues are the author's choice of words, and understanding how vocabulary functions in this way can help students identify the selection's theme.

Teachers can convey the power of vocabulary to convey theme by selecting a narrative from Unit 1 and guiding students to find words and phrases that are part of a network. Model for students how to choose words that belong in a network. For example, if the passage describes cooking, students can select words from the passage such as *warm, clean, fragrant,* and *sweetness*. Be sure the list is focused and that students can explain the relationship among the words. Then have students explore the effect of the words and explain how they convey the author's theme and make the story richer.

Conventions

Nouns and Pronouns A **common noun** names a person, place, thing, or idea. A **proper noun** names a specific person, place, or thing. A **possessive noun** shows ownership.

COMMON NOUNS	PROPER NOUNS	POSSESSIVE NOUNS
mother, daughter, country, street	Mr. Chong, China, Main Street	the audience's reaction Lucas's piano the musicians' bows the children's concert

A **personal pronoun** takes the place of a noun or several nouns named elsewhere in the text, referring to a specific person or thing. A **possessive pronoun** shows possession or ownership.

Personal Pronouns	I, me, we, us, you, he, him, she, her, it, they, them
Possessive Pronouns	my, mine, our, ours, your, yours, his, hers, its, their, theirs

TIP

CLARIFICATION
Proper nouns are always capitalized. Examples of proper nouns include *Abraham Lincoln, London,* and *Selena.*

Read It

Reread paragraph 29 of "Two Kinds." Mark the nouns. Then, classify each noun as common or proper. Finally, identify the possessive noun in the paragraph.

Write It

Revise the sentences. Replace nouns with appropriate pronouns.

1. When the daughter performed, the daughter's playing was sloppy.
2. My father listened patiently, although my father did not want to be there.
3. The youngest children played first. Most of the youngest children were prepared.

Notebook Write three sentences about an important scene between the mother and daughter in the selection. Include at least one of each type of noun and pronoun in your sentences.

HOW LANGUAGE WORKS

Pronoun-Antecedent Agreement Explain to students that pronouns usually refer to someone or something that was already mentioned in a sentence (or in a previous sentence). Using pronouns avoids repetition—the same nouns do not have to be used over and over again. When a pronoun replaces a noun, the word being replaced is called an antecedent. A pronoun must agree with its antecedent in number (singular or plural) and gender (male or female).

Sally brought *her* guinea pig to show the class.

The children thought *they* deserved a treat.

Have students write sentences with pronouns. Then have them draw an arrow from each pronoun to its antecedent. Do their pronouns agree with the antecedents?

DIGITAL PERSPECTIVES

Conventions

Nouns and Pronouns Discuss the definitions of common nouns, proper nouns, personal pronouns, and possessive pronouns with students. Have students practice using the different kinds of nouns in sentences. As you review the examples of possessive nouns, consider explaining the rules for apostrophes.

Singular nouns: Add *'s*.
the woman's hat, the cat's tail, Tess's favorite song

Plural nouns: Add *'s* unless the noun ends in *s*. Then just add an apostrophe.
women's restroom, mice's feet, four carpenters' tools, three bears' den

For more support, see **Conventions: Nouns and Pronouns.**

Read It

Proper nouns: "Anitra's Dance" and Grieg; common nouns: girl, encore, and song; possessive noun: Anitra's

MAKE IT INTERACTIVE
Have students rewrite the paragraph, using a different color pencil or marker to write each kind of noun (common, proper, possessive).

Write It

Possible responses:

1. When the daughter performed, her playing was sloppy.
2. My father listened patiently, although he did not want to be there.
3. The youngest children played first. Most of them were prepared.

Awhile after the recital, Jing-mei (proper) tells her (possessive pronoun) mother that she (personal pronoun) wishes she hadn't been born. The mother's (possessive) face goes blank. Then the mother backs out of the room (common.)

FORMATIVE ASSESSMENT

Conventions

- **If** students can't identify nouns, **then** remind them to look for the person, place, or thing doing the action.
- **If** students can't replace nouns with appropriate pronouns, **then** have them think about whether the noun refers to a male or female and whether it is singular or plural.

For Reteach and Practice, see **Conventions: Nouns and Pronouns (RP).**

TEACHING

Writing to Sources

Review point of view and perspective with students, making sure they understand that "Two Kinds" is written from the first-person point of view. Briefly discuss the character traits and actions of both the mother and daughter. Encourage students to choose a scene that is emotionally charged.

Two people can experience the same event but come away with very different impressions about what took place, including basic facts, such as what was said, and the way something made the person feel. Tell students to keep this in mind as they write. For more support, see **Writing to Sources: Retelling a Scene**.

Reflect on Your Writing

1. If students need support, encourage them to consider the daughter's actions and words from the mother's perspective. What insights does this point of view give them?
2. Encourage students to give examples of dialogue, description, and vivid words that they used. Have them discuss which techniques worked best, and why.
3. **Why These Words?** Responses will vary. Have students list specific examples of words they have chosen that bring the mother's point of view to life.

EFFECTIVE EXPRESSION

TWO KINDS

Writing to Sources

Writing an effective narrative, whether fiction or nonfiction, requires creativity and imagination. When developing a narrative, consider the points of view of all the characters, because each one has unique experiences and perspectives. By doing so, you will gain a deeper understanding of how point of view shapes your writing.

Assignment

Choose a scene from the story, and write a **retelling** of the scene from the mother's point of view.

- Review the story, and note important details that can help you identify the mother's character traits and motives. Use these details to ensure that you accurately portray the mother's character.
- Present a clear sequence of events for the scene that you chose.
- Use narrative techniques, such as dialogue and description, to convey the mother's thoughts and feelings.

Vocabulary and Conventions Connection Think about including several of the concept vocabulary words in your retelling. Be sure to correctly use nouns and pronouns to establish a clear point of view and clarify the relationships between characters.

lamented	reproach	squabbling
indignity	discordant	devastated

Reflect on Your Writing

After you have written your retelling, answer the following questions.

1. How did writing from the mother's point of view help you to better understand her perspective?
2. What narrative techniques did you use in your writing? Which narrative technique do you think was most effective in portraying the mother's character?
3. **Why These Words?** The words you choose make a difference in your writing. Which words did you specifically choose to bring the mother's point of view to life?

STANDARDS

Writing

- Write narratives to develop real or imagined experiences or events using effective technique, relevant descriptive details, and well-structured event sequences.
  - a. Engage and orient the reader by establishing a context and point of view and introducing a narrator and/or characters; organize an event sequence that unfolds naturally and logically.
  - b. Use narrative techniques, such as dialogue, pacing, and description, to develop experiences, events, and/or characters.
  - d. Use precise words and phrases, relevant descriptive details, and sensory language to capture the action and convey experiences and events.

Speaking and Listening

Present claims and findings, emphasizing salient points in a focused, coherent manner with pertinent descriptions, facts, details, and examples; use appropriate eye contact, adequate volume, and clear pronunciation.

FORMATIVE ASSESSMENT

Writing

If students are struggling to identify a scene from the story to retell, **then** have them choose the scene that they remember as the most interesting. For Reteach and Practice, see **Writing to Sources: Retelling a Scene (RP).**

PERSONALIZE FOR LEARNING

English Language Support

Point of View "Two Kinds" is written from the daughter's perspective. Pair students with a partner to imagine and write a conversation between the mother and the father the day after the talent show. Make sure they write this conversation from the mother's point of view. Have partners perform their conversations for the class. **ALL LEVELS**

Speaking and Listening

A **monologue** is a dramatic speech presented by a single character. The character speaks from the first-person point of view and relates his or her thoughts and feelings about an event.

Assignment

Choose one of the passages listed, and develop a **dramatic monologue** in which the daughter expresses aloud her thoughts and feelings in this moment of the story.

- paragraphs 18–20
- paragraphs 54–56
- paragraphs 84–91

1. **Organize Your Monologue** Use the following questions to gather ideas and prepare notes.

What happened earlier in the story?	Think about how these events influence the daughter's feelings.
How will your monologue begin?	Choose a strong statement to grab your audience's interest.
What happens during the monologue?	Show how the daughter's thoughts and feelings change during the monologue.
How will your monologue end?	Conclude your monologue with a thought-provoking statement that ends the scene.

2. **Prepare Your Delivery** Using your notes, practice your monologue.
   - Maintain eye contact with members of your audience as you speak.
   - Vary the volume of your voice and your pacing to reflect emotion.

3. **Evaluate Monologues** Use a presentation evaluation guide like the one shown to analyze your classmates' monologues.

PRESENTATION EVALUATION GUIDE

Rate each statement on a scale of 1 (not demonstrated) to 5 (demonstrated).

☐ The speaker communicated events from the daughter's point of view.

☐ The speaker provided details to demonstrate shifts in feeling.

☐ The speaker maintained eye contact with audience members.

☐ The monologue was clear and easy to follow.

EVIDENCE LOG

Before moving on to a new selection, go to your Evidence Log and record what you learned from "Two Kinds."

DIGITAL PERSPECTIVES

Illuminating the Text Find, preview, and show video clips from *The Ed Sullivan Show*. This will help students understand the influence of popular culture during the period in which "Two Kinds" takes place. Then have students create a Venn diagram in which they note similarities and differences between this show and current variety or talent shows. Do the current shows have the same kind of impact on society that *The Ed Sullivan Show* had?

DIGITAL PERSPECTIVES

Speaking and Listening

1. **Organize Your Monologue** You may wish to review the following elements of a successful monologue with students.
   - **Confidence** The confidence of the speaker of a monologue inspires believability in the character and the character's words.
   - **Character** A well-rounded character is more engaging to the audience than one that shows no depth or personality.
   - **Movement** Using gestures and movement brings life to the words and ideas of the speaker.
2. **Prepare Your Delivery** Pair students and have them present their monologues to each other. Then, instruct students to use the Presentation Evaluation Guide to provide feedback to their partners prior to presenting to the class.
3. **Evaluate Monologues** Encourage students to give constructive criticism about their classmates' monologues and to make supportive comments.

For more support, see **Speaking and Listening: Monologue.**

Evidence Log Support students in completing their Evidence Log. This paced activity will help prepare them for the Performance-Based Assessment at the end of the unit.

FORMATIVE ASSESSMENT

Speaking and Listening

If students struggle writing their monologues, **then** remind them to focus on the thoughts and feelings of the character. For Reteach and Practice, see **Speaking and Listening: Monologue (RP).**

Selection Test

Administer the "Two Kinds" Selection Test, which is available in both print and digital formats online in Assessments.

A Simple Act

AUDIO SUMMARIES
Audio summaries of "A Simple Act" are available online in both English and Spanish in the Interactive Teacher's Edition or Unit Resources. Assigning these summaries prior to reading the selection may help students build additional background knowledge and set a context for their first read.

Summary

Tyler Jackson's article "A Simple Act" begins with a boy asking a stranger for money to buy food. The stranger walks away, but she's drawn back by what she calls an "invisible thread." She takes the boy to lunch, and they become friends. The woman is Laura Schroff, a successful advertising executive. The boy is eleven-year-old Maurice Mazyck, who lives in a welfare hotel. Through Laura, Maurice gets to know a different life. Through Maurice, Laura experiences the love of a child. The article describes how Maurice loves Laura's sister's big dining room table because the whole family can sit around it. He wants one just like it when he grows up. Now that Maurice is grown, the article describes what became of his dream of having a big table of his own and a family to sit around it.

Insight

Frequently, there are unexpected benefits to giving to others. Reading "A Simple Act" will help students reflect on the give-and-take that often occurs with an act of kindness. When one person selflessly gives to another, the rewards that come back can be life altering.

ESSENTIAL QUESTION:
What can one generation learn from another?

Connection to Essential Question

"A Simple Act" will help students answer the Essential Question—*What can one generation learn from another?*—when they consider the lessons that Laura Schroff and Maurice Mazyck learned from each other. Laura, as part of an older generation, teaches Maurice about the possibilities in life by exposing him to opportunities and experiences he would otherwise not have had. Maurice, as part of a younger generation, teaches Laura that children crave connection and a feeling of belonging more than they crave material things.

WHOLE-CLASS LEARNING PERFORMANCE TASK
What unexpected event shows how a person can influence someone from a different generation?

UNIT PERFORMANCE-BASED ASSESSMENT
In what situations can one generation learn from another?

Connection to Performance Tasks

Whole-Class Learning Performance Task In this Performance Task, students will write personal narratives about an unexpected event that reveals how someone from a different generation has influenced them or someone they know. Students will have the opportunity to compare their experiences with the relationship in "A Simple Act," which shows how two strangers from different generations came into each other's lives by chance and changed the course of both their lives.

Unit Performance-Based Assessment This selection shows students that the younger generation can teach the older generation about what is important to children, and that the older generation can help to guide the younger generation and expose them to important new experiences.

DIGITAL PERSPECTIVES

 Audio  Video 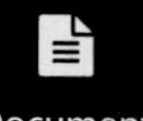 Document  Annotation Highlights Online Assessment

LESSON RESOURCES

	Making Meaning	Language Development
Lesson	**First Read** **Close Read** **Analyze the Text** **Analyze Craft and Structure**	**Concept Vocabulary** **Word Study** **Conventions**
Instructional Standards	**RI.7.10** By the end of the year, read and comprehend literary nonfiction . . . **RI.7.1** Analyze what a text says explicitly . . . **RI.7.6** Determine an author's point of view or purpose in a text . . .	**L.7.1** Demonstrate command of the conventions of standard English grammar and usage . . . **L.7.4** Determine or clarify the meaning of unknown and multiple-meaning words and phrases . . .
STUDENT RESOURCES		
Available online in the Interactive Student Edition or Unit Resources	Selection Audio First-Read Guide: Nonfiction Close-Read Guide: Nonfiction	Word Network
TEACHER RESOURCES		
Selection Resources Available online in the Interactive Teacher's Edition or Unit Resources	Audio Summaries: English and Spanish Annotation Highlights Accessible Leveled Text First Read Extension Questions Analyze Craft and Structure: Author's Point of View	Concept Vocabulary and Word Study Conventions: Adverbs
Reteach/Practice (RP) Available online in the Interactive Teacher's Edition or Unit Resources	Analyze Craft and Structure: Author's Point of View (RP)	Word Study: Multiple-Meaning Words (RP) Conventions: Adverbs (RP)
Assessment Available online in Assessments	Selection Test: English Selection Test: Spanish Extension Selection Test	
My Resources	A Unit 1 Answer Key is available online and in the Interactive Teacher's Edition	

Reading Support

Text Complexity Rubric: A Simple Act	
Quantitative Measures	
Lexile: 930 **Text Length:** 794 words	
Qualitative Measures	
Knowledge Demands ①—②—❸—④—⑤	Students need knowledge of homelessness in cities in order to understand references (asking for change, panhandlers, welfare hotel, lack of food) and to understand the relationship between the people in the article.
Structure ①—❷—③—④—⑤	The account is told sequentially, starting in 1986 and going to present day.
Language Conventionality and Clarity ①—②—❸—④—⑤	Sentences are mostly average length or short, with syntax that is easy to understand. Vocabulary is mostly on-level. Some figures of speech used *(invisible thread; might as well have been another planet).*
Levels of Meaning/Purpose ①—❷—③—④—⑤	Meaning and concepts are straightforward, with one level of meaning. The figurative phrase *invisible thread,* central to the meaning, is explained.

DECIDE AND PLAN

English Language Support

Provide English Learners with support for knowledge demands and language as they read the selection.

Knowledge Demands In order to ensure that students understand the situation of the people in the selection, make sure they understand the meaning of these words and phrases they will see as they read: *scruffy clothes, panhandlers, welfare hotel*. If necessary, explain Maurice's situation and why he is asking for food.

Language Discuss figurative language such as *invisible thread, another planet*. First ask about the literal meaning to make sure students understand the words. For example, *What is* thread? *What does* invisible *mean?* Then discuss the figurative meaning.

Strategic Support

Provide students with strategic support to ensure that they can successfully read the text.

Knowledge Demands Discuss what students know about the need for welfare hotels or shelters for people who don't have homes or enough food. Make sure students understand that Maurice is living in a welfare hotel with his family and begging for food when he meets Laura. As they read, ask them to think about how the two different situations impact the friendship.

Meaning Ask questions that help students focus on the meaning of figurative language. For example, *What does it mean that the welfare hotel "might as well have been a different planet?"* (It was completely different from Laura's home.)

Challenge

Provide students who need to be challenged with ideas for how they can go beyond a simple interpretation of the text.

Text Analysis Ask students to discuss the questions that Laura asks herself (paragraph 4) and the emotions associated with each one. Have them explore the meaning of each question. For example, what would it mean to help someone just as a way to help yourself?

Written Response Ask students to write what might have happened to Maurice if Laura had not decided to turn back to go talk to him. Encourage them to include details about what Laura and Maurice might do and how they would feel.

TEACH

Read and Respond

Have the class do their first read of the selection. Then have them complete their close read. Finally, work with them on the Making Meaning and Language Development activities.

Standards Support Through Teaching and Learning Cycle

IDENTIFY NEEDS

Analyze results of the Beginning-of-Year Assessment, focusing on the items relating to Unit 1. Also take into consideration student performance to this point and your observations of where particular students struggle.

DECIDE AND PLAN

- If students have performed poorly on items matching these standards, then provide selection scaffolds before assigning them the on-level lesson provided in the Student Edition.
- If students have done well on the Beginning-of-Year Assessment, then challenge them to keep progressing and learning by giving them opportunities to practice the skills in depth.
- Use the Selection Resources listed on the Planning pages for "A Simple Act" to help students continually improve their ability to master the standards.

Instructional Standards: A Simple Act

	Catching Up	This Year	Looking Forward
Reading	You may wish to administer the **Analyze Craft and Structure: Author's Point of View (RP)** worksheet to help students see that a point of view can help you understand a scene from a different perspective.	**RI.6** Determine an author's point of view or purpose in a text and analyze how the author distinguishes his or her position from that of others.	Have students identify the conflicting viewpoints that might arise if the selection were told from another point of view.
Language	Use the **Word Study: Multiple-Meaning Words (RP)** worksheet to help students understand that many English words have more than one meaning.	**L.4** Determine or clarify the meaning of unknown and multiple-meaning words and phrases based on *grade 7 reading and content*, choosing flexibly from a range of strategies.	Have students work in pairs to identify three sentences in the text that include a multiple-meaning word. Students should use a print or online dictionary to find the multiple meanings for each word and name the part of speech. Then have partners take turns explaining how context clues in each sentence help them to know which meaning to apply to the multiple-meaning word.

TEACH

Implement the planned lesson, and gather evidence of student learning.

ANALYZE AND REVISE

- Analyze student work for evidence of student learning.
- Identify whether students have met the expectations in the standards.
- Identify implications for future instruction.

TEACHING

Jump Start

FIRST READ Before students' first read, ask them to talk about chance encounters with people and how those encounters sometimes lead to important, lasting friendships. *How did students meet their closest friends? In what ways have those friends influenced their lives?*

A Simple Act

How do Laura and Maurice meet? What is the "invisible thread"? What lessons do they learn from one another? Modeling questions such as these will help students connect to "A Simple Act" and to the Performance Task assignment. Selection audio and print capability for the selection are available in the Interactive Teacher's Edition.

Concept Vocabulary

Support students as they rate the words. Ask if they've ever heard, read, or used them. Reassure them that the definitions for these words are listed in the selection.

FIRST READ

As they read, students should perform the steps of the first read:

NOTICE: Encourage students to notice the key events in Laura and Maurice's friendship.

ANNOTATE: Remind students to mark passages that describe how the two friends learn from and help each other.

CONNECT: Ask students to make connections by thinking about friendships they have with people from older generations. Students can also consider relationships in movies or texts they know.

RESPOND: Students will answer questions and write a summary to demonstrate understanding.

Point out to students that while they will always complete the Respond step at the end of the first read, the other steps will probably happen somewhat concurrently. You may wish to print copies of the **First-Read Guide: Nonfiction** for students to use.

Remind students that during their first read they should not answer the close-read questions that appear in the selection.

MAKING MEANING

A SIMPLE ACT

Comparing Texts

In this lesson, you will read and compare "A Simple Act" and an excerpt from *An Invisible Thread.* First you will complete the first-read and close-read activities for "A Simple Act."

from AN INVISIBLE THREAD

About the Author

Tyler Jackson (b. 1981) was raised in England but has traveled extensively, writing about many of the places he has lived. Jackson has survived a hurricane in North Carolina and a flood in Texas, and says, "People pull together in a disaster, but it's remarkable to see the small acts of kindness that usually go unreported."

A Simple Act

Concept Vocabulary

You will encounter the following words as you read "A Simple Act."

Before reading, rate how familiar you are with each word. Indicate how well you know it on a scale of 1 (do not know it) to 5 (know it very well).

WORD	YOUR RANKING
connects	
influence	
encouraged	
bond	

After completing your first read, come back to the concept vocabulary and review your rankings. Mark changes to your original rankings as needed.

First Read NONFICTION

Apply these strategies as you conduct your first read. You will have an opportunity to complete the close-read notes after your first read.

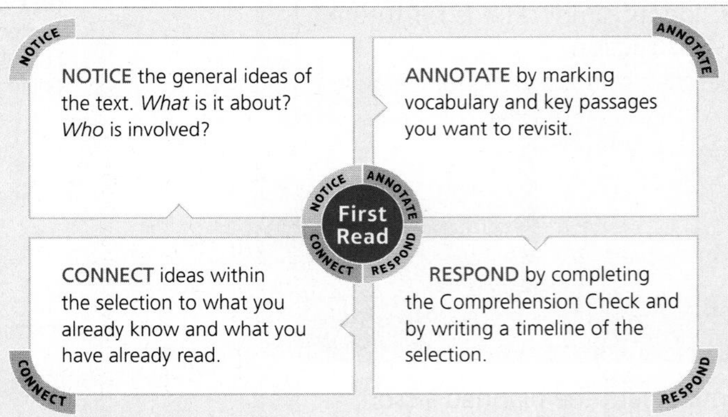

STANDARDS

Reading Informational Text
By the end of the year, read and comprehend literary nonfiction in the grades 6–8 text complexity band proficiently, with scaffolding as needed at the high end of the range.

PERSONALIZE FOR LEARNING

English Language Support

Using Concept Vocabulary

Contextualize Support students with scaffolding to help them learn the concept vocabulary. Complete each sentence with a word from the list.

connects influence encouraged bond

1. My older brothers and sisters were a big ____________ on my life.
2. The George Washington Bridge ________ Manhattan, New York and New Jersey.
3. A ________ between two people is a strong connection between them.
4. My math teacher ________ me to go to college to study accounting.

Then ask volunteers to create a sentence of their own using a concept vocabulary word and write it on the board. **ALL LEVELS**

A Simple Act

Tyler Jackson

BACKGROUND

In a big city like New York, thousands of strangers from many different backgrounds cross paths every day. But they rarely stop on the street to get to know each other. When people from very different places make the effort to connect, unexpected friendships can form.

1 It was the first day of September in 1986, and the morning rain had given way to bright sunshine. A successful advertising executive made her way across 56th street toward Broadway, on the west side of Manhattan. A young boy—all of eleven years old and dressed in scruffy clothes—asked for some change for something to eat. Laura Schroff lowered her head and walked on; Manhattan was full of panhandlers, and she hardly even noticed them any more.

NOTES

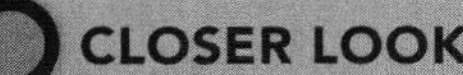

Analyze Relationships 

Students may have marked paragraph 1 during their first read. Use this paragraph to help students understand the two main characters. Encourage them to talk about the annotations that they marked. You may want to model a close read with the class based on the highlights shown in the text.

ANNOTATE: Have students mark details in the paragraph that describe the characters, or have students participate while you highlight them.

QUESTION: Guide students to consider what these details might tell them. Ask what a reader can infer from these details, and accept student responses.

Possible response: Laura and the young man come from very different socioeconomic backgrounds. While Laura is a successful businesswoman, Maurice is a scruffy eleven-year-old beggar.

CONCLUDE: Help students to formulate conclusions about the importance of these details in the text. Ask students why the author might have included these details.

Possible response: The descriptions show that their friendship is unusual for at least two reasons. Laura and Maurice are from different generations, and they come from very different backgrounds. By including these details, the author emphasizes the unlikelihood of any friendship developing between these two characters.

Remind students that the **relationships** between people are key to many nonfiction narratives. Instead of explaining the similarities and differences, a good author will simply present them and allow readers to draw their own conclusions.

CLOSE READ

In paragraph 4, have students pay attention to the author's writing style. You may wish to model the close read using the following think-aloud format. Possible responses to questions on the student page are included. You may also want to print copies of the **Close-Read Guide: Nonfiction** for students to use.

ANNOTATE: As I read paragraph 4, I notice a series of questions in the narrative.

QUESTION: These questions help me understand the kinds of issues that Laura is facing as she considers her own motivations for getting involved in Maurice's life.

CONCLUDE: In paragraph 4, Laura and Maurice are still forming their friendship. In paragraph 5, the friendship is more established. The questions help Laura focus on the potential problems that might arise and they help her decide whether to commit to this friendship. The change in the way Maurice is referred to reflects their changed relationship.

Additional **English Language Support** is available in the Interactive Teacher's Edition.

NOTES

connects (kuh NEHKTS) *v.* joins together

influence (IHN floo uhns) *v.* affect someone in an important way

encouraged (ehn KUR ihjd) *v.* inspired; offered support to

bond (BAHND) *n.* uniting connection; link

CLOSE READ

ANNOTATE: Mark the questions included in paragraph 4.

QUESTION: Why might the author have included these questions?

CONCLUDE: What effect do these questions have on Laura?

2 But something drew Laura back to the boy. She still doesn't know what it was, but she calls it an "invisible thread." There's an old Chinese proverb that says that an invisible thread **connects** two people who are destined to meet and **influence** each other. Laura believes she felt that thread. She turned back from the middle of the street and took the boy to lunch.

3 The boy lived in a single room in a welfare hotel with his mother and numerous other relatives. It was only two blocks away from Laura's home, but it might as well have been a different planet. As they talked over their lunch, Laura learned about the boy's life. She herself had not had an easy childhood, but what she heard shocked her, and before she left, she told him to phone her if he was ever hungry. When she didn't hear from him after several days, she returned to the spot they had met—and there he was, in the same clothes and too-tight sneakers. They arranged to meet again the next Monday.

4 Every Monday, Laura Schroff and Maurice Mazyck had dinner together. Some Mondays they ate at Laura's home, and Maurice discovered a life he had only seen on television. Gradually, Laura became the young boy's first role model. She **encouraged** him to have dreams about his future, and got involved in his education. Maurice's teacher was perhaps the only other person who believed in him, and she made Laura take a long hard look at what she was doing. Was she helping Maurice just as a way of helping herself? Could she commit to being there for Maurice even when she didn't feel like it? What kind of damage might it cause Maurice if she were to abandon him after becoming so important to him? Laura thought it through, and came to a decision.

5 The two continued sharing dinner every Monday, and a close **bond** formed between them. Laura introduced Maurice to new places, new ideas, and new possibilities. And Maurice became almost like the child Laura had always wanted. One day, she offered to make lunch for Maurice and leave it with her doorman for him to pick up on his way to school. He asked her if she could put the lunch in a brown paper bag, because then the other kids would know that someone cared about him.

6 Maurice had never left the city until Laura took him to visit her sister's family on Long Island. Her memory of their trip is a favorite one. She had expected Maurice to be amazed by the huge

VOCABULARY DEVELOPMENT

Multiple Meanings Tell students that the word *drew,* which appears in the first sentence of paragraph 2, is the past tense of *draw* and has multiple meanings. Discuss the following sentences with the students.

1. He drew a picture. (Made an image by making lines on a surface.)
2. The performer drew the crowd's attention. (Caused something to be directed toward something else.)
3. The shooters drew their weapons. (Took out a sword, pistol, or other weapon.)
4. The teacher drew the winning name from a hat. (Selected randomly.)

Have students reread the following sentence in paragraph 2, *But something drew Laura back to the boy.* Guide them to identify which meaning is used in the sentence. Discuss how to use context clues to define a word with multiple meanings.

front lawn and even larger backyard. But what amazed him the most was the large dining room table where they all sat down and talked and ate together. He declared that he wanted a table like that when he had a family of his own. Only months earlier, Maurice had seriously doubted that he would live to be an adult.

NOTES

7 Laura and Maurice's relationship lasted, and in 1997 a magazine published an article, less than one page long, about it. Laura's friends suggested that she write a book telling the whole story. It was 10 years before she began writing—and another three years before she found a co-writer and started seriously getting down to business. The result of their work, *An Invisible Thread,* reached number one on the *New York Times* best sellers list.

8 Today, Maurice works in construction. He is the first person in his family to earn a paycheck. He has a family of his own, and his children are all very fond of their "Aunt Laurie." If you were to visit the family's apartment, you might notice that there is no couch in the living room. But there is a huge dining room table.

9 The writer Ernest Hemingway said, "The best way to find out if you can trust somebody is to trust them." Over the years, Laura discovered the truth of that statement. She feels that Maurice has given her one of the greatest gifts she has ever had. He repaid her trust by giving her life more meaning than her success at work ever did. He taught her to be grateful for what she has, and for the chance to share it. ❧

PERSONALIZE FOR LEARNING

Challenge

Conclusions Review paragraph 9 with the class. Ask students about the impact of the last paragraph of the narrative. Point out that the last paragraph of a narrative often includes a conclusion or "take-away." Reread the last paragraph of the selection, pausing after the quote by Ernest Hemingway. Ask students to consider other final paragraphs that have had meaning for them. Have students write a short essay comparing and contrasting the final paragraphs of several articles, stories, or books they have read. What do these final paragraphs have in common? How are they different?

Comprehension Check

Possible responses:

1. Laura and Maurice met when Maurice stopped Laura on the street and asked her for some change. Laura kept walking, but then she turned around and went back to Maurice. After talking, Laura took Maurice out to lunch.
2. An old Chinese proverb says that an "invisible thread" connects people who are destined to meet and influence each other.
3. After their first meeting, Laura and Maurice began eating dinner together every Monday.
4. Maurice's favorite part of the visit to Laura's sister's home was the large dining room table where everyone talked and ate together.
5. As an adult, Maurice works in construction and has a wife and children. He also has a large dining room table in his living room.

Comprehension Check

Complete the following items after you finish your first read.

1. How did Laura Schroff and Maurice Mazyck meet?

2. What does the old Chinese proverb say connects two people who are destined to meet and influence each other?

3. What weekly ritual do Laura and Maurice begin after their first meeting?

4. What was Maurice's favorite part of the visit to Laura's sister?

5. Describe Maurice's adult life, professionally and personally.

PERSONALIZE FOR LEARNING

Challenge

Proverbs Have students write a short report about the Chinese proverb about the invisible thread connecting people that was mentioned in the narrative. Encourage them to research the proverb (and other Chinese proverbs) to put it in social and historical context. Ask them to analyze and interpret the proverb from two perspectives—that of a citizen in ancient China and that of a student in contemporary America.

Comprehension Check

6. How did Laura share the story of her relationship with Maurice with an audience?

7. Notebook Write a timeline of key events in "A Simple Act."

RESEARCH

Research to Clarify Choose at least one unfamiliar detail from the text. Briefly research that detail. In what way does the information you learned shed light on an aspect of the story?

Research to Explore Choose something that interested you from the text and formulate a research question about it.

Comprehension Check

6. Laura shared the story of her relationship with Maurice with an audience by writing a book, which became a *New York Times* best-seller.
7. Timelines will vary but should include the following events:

   September 1986 – Laura and Maurice meet.
   1997 – A magazine publishes a short article about Laura and Maurice's friendship.
   2007 – Laura begins writing the story of their relationship.
   2010 – Laura finds a co-writer and begins writing her book more seriously.

Research

Research to Clarify If students have difficulty finding a detail to research, suggest the following options: welfare hotels in New York City, advertising as an occupation.

Research to Explore If students have trouble formulating a research question, suggest the following options: What was life like for Maurice when he and his family lived in a welfare hotel? What was life like for Laura as a successful advertising executive? How does the magazine article portray Laura and Maurice's friendship?

TEACHING

Jump Start

CLOSE READ Before students start their close read, have them discuss the different ways, large and small, that people can help each other. Ask students to share their personal experiences with helping others—or being helped by others. Encourage them to explore the benefits to both parties.

Close Read the Text

Walk students through the Annotation Model on the student page. Then have them use the models as they annotate another detail. Encourage them to complete items 2 and 3 on their own. Review and discuss the sections students have marked. If needed, continue to model close reading by using the Annotation Highlights in the Interactive Teacher's Edition.

Analyze the Text

Possible responses:

1. (a) Laura expects Maurice to be impressed by the large front and back yards, but he's most excited by the large dining room table where everyone talks and eats together. **DOK 1** (b) Readers learn that Maurice is most impressed by connections between loved ones. **DOK 3**
2. Maurice gains food and a friendship, as well as exposure to "new places, new ideas, and new possibilities" (paragraph 5). Laura gains a child to care for—*Maurice became almost like the child she'd always wanted* (paragraph 5). **DOK 3**
3. Answers will vary. Students might point out that the friendship is both unusual and inspirational. It is unusual because Laura and Maurice come from such different backgrounds, and it is inspirational because they help each other. **DOK 3**
4. Answers will vary. Students might point out that the article shows how people of different generations, and classes, can come together, build strong friendships, and take the time to listen to one another. **DOK 3**

FORMATIVE ASSESSMENT

Analyze the Text

- **If** students fail to cite evidence, **then** remind them to support their ideas with specific information**.**
- **If** students struggle to recall details of the trip to Laura's sister's house, **then** suggest they reread paragraph 6.

MAKING MEANING

A SIMPLE ACT

Close Read the Text

1. The model, from paragraph 6 of the essay, shows two sample annotations, along with questions and conclusions. Close read the passage and find another detail to annotate. Then, write a question and your conclusion.

ANNOTATE: This passage describes what most impressed Maurice.

QUESTION: Why does the writer include this information in the text?

CONCLUDE: The writer shows that Maurice yearns for a close family, which he doesn't currently have.

She had expected Maurice to be amazed by the huge front lawn and even larger backyard. But what amazed him the most was the large dining room table where they all sat down and talked and ate together. He declared that he wanted a table like that when he had a family of his own.

ANNOTATE: The word *amazed* is repeated.

QUESTION: Why does the author repeat this word?

CONCLUDE: The author wants to emphasize that Maurice has a stronger interest in how the family spends time together than in property size.

2. For more practice, go back into the text and complete the close-read notes.
3. Revisit a section of the text you found important during your first read. Read this section closely and **annotate** what you notice. Ask **questions** such as "Why did the author make this choice?" What can you **conclude**?

Analyze the Text

CITE TEXTUAL EVIDENCE to support your answers.

Notebook Respond to these questions.

1. (a) **Analyze** How does Maurice surprise Laura when he explains in paragraph 6 what he liked most about visiting Laura's sister? (b) **Infer** What do readers learn about Maurice's values?
2. **Draw Conclusions** How do both Laura and Maurice benefit from their relationship?
3. **Evaluate** In paragraph 7 the author mentions that a book about Laura and Maurice's friendship became a best-seller. Why do you think people became so interested in this friendship?
4. **Essential Question** ***What can one generation learn from another?*** What have you learned about how people of different generations learn from each other?

STANDARDS

Reading Informational Text

- Cite several pieces of textual evidence to support analysis of what the text says explicitly as well as inferences drawn from the text.
- Determine an author's point of view or purpose in a text and analyze how the author distinguishes his or her position from that of others.

PERSONALIZE FOR LEARNING

English Language Support

Express Attitudes and/or Opinions Put students in small groups to discuss "A Simple Act," the story of the unusual friendship between a business executive, Laura, and a young "panhandler" she met on the street in Manhattan.

Give each group a question to answer.

1. Would you have stopped to get to know Maurice the way Laura did? Explain why or why not.
2. Do you think it was safe for Laura to get closer to Maurice, even inviting him to her house? Explain your point of view.
3. Would you have brought Maurice to visit your sister on Long Island? Explain your answer.
4. Do you think Maurice and Laura had a true friendship, or was she just taking care of him? Explain your answer.

Analyze Craft and Structure

Author's Point of View The attitudes and approach that an author takes in an informational text show the **author's point of view.** In some informational texts, authors take an objective approach, avoiding opinions and other biases. These texts are based almost entirely on factual information.

In other informational texts, authors are more subjective—mixing facts with their own commentary and interpretation. The commentary may take the form of direct opinions, or it may involve using **weighted words**—words that have strong emotional associations beyond their basic meanings.

- In "A Simple Act," the phrase "all of eleven years old" in paragraph 1 shows that the author is concerned that the boy was too young to be begging for money on the streets.
- In paragraph 4, the author writes that Maurice's teacher "made Laura take a long hard look at what she was doing" to show that the teacher took Maurice's situation very seriously.

In these paragraphs, the author uses weighted words to create sympathy for Maurice in the reader's mind.

Practice

CITE TEXTUAL EVIDENCE to support your answers.

Notebook Respond to these questions.

1. Reread paragraph 3, and use the chart to analyze the author's use of weighted words and phrases, and the effect these word choices have on readers.

WORD OR PHRASE	PRECISE MEANING	EFFECT
a. See possible responses in the Teacher's Edition.	b.	c.

2. Explain how the weighted words in paragraph 3 affect the reader's understanding of the differences between Maurice's life and Laura's life.
3. Find an additional example of weighted words in paragraphs 5–9, and explain why the author might have chosen such language.
4. How would the reader's understanding of the article differ if the author had avoided using weighted words and used more objective language?

DIGITAL PERSPECTIVES

Analyze Craft and Structure

Author's Point of View Explain to students that an author's point of view in an informational text is his or her beliefs and opinions about the subject. For instance, an author may admire the subject, be critical of the subject, or find the subject amusing. Remind students that an author's point of view is often revealed through his or her word choice, including the use of weighted words and phrases. Have students discuss Tyler Jackson's point of view with respect to the relationship between Laura Schroff and Maurice Mazyck. Ask them to support their responses with specific examples of word choice from the text. For more support, see **Analyze Craft and Structure: Author's Point of View.**

Practice

Possible responses:

1. a. "too-tight sneakers" b. Maurice's sneakers are too small for him. c. The phrase has the effect of creating sympathy for Maurice because his family can't afford to purchase shoes that fit him properly.
2. The weighted words in paragraph 3 show that Laura had a much more comfortable life than Maurice did.
3. In paragraph 6, the author says that Maurice "had seriously doubted that he would live to be an adult." The author is trying to show that Maurice had little hope for his future before he met Laura.
4. More objective language would probably result in the reader's having less sympathy for Maurice and less appreciation of what Laura did for him.

FORMATIVE ASSESSMENT

Analyze Craft and Structure

If students have trouble identifying other examples of weighted words or phrases, **then** ask them to focus on the last sentence of paragraph 1.

For Reteach and Practice, see **Analyze Craft and Structure: Author's Point of View (RP).**

TEACHING

Concept Vocabulary

Why These Words? Discuss with students the different ways the words can be used. Someone can influence a friend in a positive, helpful way. But a bully can influence his classmates, too. Remind students to pay attention to context clues.

Possible responses:

1. The concept vocabulary is clear and descriptive, so it lets readers feel what Maurice and Laura felt.
2. *involved, felt, learned, sharing, "Aunt Laurie"*

Practice

Possible responses:

1. My best friend and I share a special bond that connects us through good times and bad. I know that I can trust her to be a positive influence in my life. I've always encouraged her to do her best and she's always encouraged me as well.
2. friendship, family, secure, supportive, stable, romantic

Word Network

Possible words: *camaraderie, fellowship, linked, familial*

Word Study

For more support, see **Concept Vocabulary and Word Study**.

Possible responses:

Bond in paragraph 5 means "an experience of feeling shared between two people that forms a connection between them."
Two more definitions of *bond* are (1) an agreement with legal force and (2) physical restraints, especially ropes or chains.

FORMATIVE ASSESSMENT

Concept Vocabulary

- **If** students fail to see that the concept vocabulary words relate to Laura and Maurice's relationship, **then** have them use one or more of the words in sentences that tell about Laura and Maurice.

Word Study

- **If** students struggle to find words with multiple meanings, **then** suggest *bright* and *change* in paragraph 1.

For Reteach and Practice, see **Word Study: Multiple-Meaning Words (RP).**

LANGUAGE DEVELOPMENT

A SIMPLE ACT

Concept Vocabulary

connects	encouraged
influence	bond

Why These Words? The concept vocabulary words help to show relationships between people. For example, the old Chinese proverb says that an invisible thread *connects*, or joins together, two people who are destined to meet. In turn, these two people will *influence* each other, or affect each other in an important way. Notice that both words relate to the relationship between Laura and Maurice.

1. How does the concept vocabulary sharpen the reader's understanding of the relationship between Laura and Maurice?

2. Identify two other words in the selection that are related to this concept, and explain how they are related.

WORD NETWORK

Look in the text for words related to the topic of generations, and add them to your Word Network.

Practice

Notebook The concept words appear in "A Simple Act."

1. Use each concept word in a sentence that shows your understanding of each word's meaning.
2. Work with a partner, and take turns trying to list as many words as you can about interpersonal relationships.

Word Study

Multiple-Meaning Words A multiple-meaning word is a word with more than one definition. Sometimes the definitions of multiple-meaning words are similar, but in other cases they may be completely unrelated. For example, the word *bond*, which appears in "A Simple Act," has several different meanings. Write the meaning of *bond* as it is used in the fifth paragraph. Then, use a dictionary to find two more definitions of the word *bond*.

STANDARDS

Language

- Demonstrate command of the conventions of standard English grammar and usage when writing or speaking.
- Determine or clarify the meaning of unknown and multiple-meaning words and phrases based on *grade 7 reading and content*, choosing flexibly from a range of strategies.

Conventions

Adverbs An **adverb** is a word that modifies or describes a verb, adjective, or another adverb. These words provide information by answering the question *How? When? Where? How often?* or *To what extent?* Many adverbs end in the suffix *-ly*. This chart shows examples:

How?	Maurice asked politely for change.
When?	Laura said no, but soon changed her mind.
Where?	They went inside for a meal.
How often?	They usually met for dinner on Monday night.
To what extent?	Today, Maurice and Laura are extremely good friends.

Read It

1. Identify the adverb or adverbs in each sentence. Then, identify the word each adverb modifies or describes.

a. Maurice and Laura shared meals regularly and enthusiastically.

b. They often exchanged opinions and frequently agreed.

c. Later, Laura befriended Maurice's children, too.

d. Laura's book was very popular and deeply affected many readers.

2. Reread paragraphs 4–7 of the text. Mark the adverbs, identify the verbs they modify, and tell how these words clarify information.

Write It

Notebook The sample sentence here was revised by adding an adverb that addresses the question in parentheses. Add adverbs to the sentences provided, based on the questions in parentheses.

EXAMPLE

Laura was glad she went back to meet Maurice. (To what extent was she glad?)

Laura was **extremely** glad she went back to meet Maurice.

1. Maurice and Laura became good friends. (When did they become friends?)

2. Maurice confided in his new friend. (How did he confide?)

3. They pushed each other to try new things. (How often did they push each other?)

PERSONALIZE FOR LEARNING

English Language Support

Adverbs Support English Learners in developing their understanding of adverbs.

Ask pairs of students to choose adverbs that describe the following verbs: *jump, eat, play,* and *draw*. Have students act out the adverbs they have chosen. **EMERGING**

List the following verbs on the board: *jump, eat, play,* and *draw*. Ask students to write sentences with these verbs and adverbs that describe each verb. **EXPANDING**

Ask students to write a paragraph about how Laura changed Maurice's life. Have them include adverbs to describe the verbs that they use. **BRIDGING**

DIGITAL PERSPECTIVES 

Conventions

Adverbs Discuss the definition of adverbs with students, emphasizing the questions that adverbs answer. Review the examples in the chart with students, reading the sentences with and without the adverbs to show students how each word functions in the sentence. For more support, see **Conventions: Adverbs.**

Read It

MAKE IT INTERACTIVE

Write the sentences on the board. Have students underline the adverbs, then have other students draw arrows from the adverbs to the words they modify or describe.

Possible responses:

1. (a) *Regularly* and *enthusiastically* modify *shared.*

(b) *Often* modifies *exchanged,* and *frequently* modifies *agreed.*

(c) *Later* modifies *befriended.*

(d) *Very* modifies *popular,* and *deeply* modifies *affected.*

2. Paragraph 4: *Gradually* modifies *became* (how?). Paragraph 5: *Always* modifies *wanted* (when?). Paragraph 6: *Never* modifies *left* (how often?), *seriously* modifies *doubted* (to what extent?). Paragraph 7: *Seriously* modifies *getting* ***down to*** (how?).

Write It

Possible responses:

1. Laura and Maurice soon became good friends.
2. Maurice openly confided in his new friend.
3. They frequently pushed each other to try new things.

FORMATIVE ASSESSMENT

Conventions

- **If** students struggle to locate adverbs, **then** tell them many adverbs end in *ly*.
- **If** students can't identify what an adverb modifies, **then** ask them to list all the verbs and adjectives in the sentence. The adverb must modify one of them.

For Reteach and Practice, see **Conventions: Adverbs (RP).**

Selection Test

Administer the "A Simple Act" Selection Test, which is available in both print and digital formats online in Assessments.

from An Invisible Thread

AUDIO SUMMARIES
Audio summaries of "An Invisible Thread" are available online in both English and Spanish in the Interactive Teacher's Edition or Unit Resources. Assigning these summaries prior to reading the selection may help students build additional background knowledge and set a context for their first read.

Summary

An Invisible Thread is Laura Schroff's account of her friendship with Maurice Mazyck. Her co-writer Alex Tresniowski helped her tell the story, and the book was published in 2008. In this excerpt, Maurice gives a speech at Laura's fiftieth birthday celebration. He recalls their meeting on a New York street 15 years earlier. He was a hungry boy, and he asked her for money to buy food. Laura walked on—but something made her come back. Maurice thanks her for helping him become the man he is today. Laura writes that she corrects people when they say how lucky Maurice is to have met her, and she lists the reasons that she's the lucky one.

Insight

Reading this excerpt from *An Invisible Thread* will help students reflect on the chain reaction that can occur when people of two different generations influence one another. The impact—in this case a positive one—upon one generation is often passed down to the next and the one after that.

ESSENTIAL QUESTION:
What can one generation learn from another?

Connection to Essential Question

The excerpt from *An Invisible Thread* will help students answer the Essential Question—*What can one generation learn from another?*—when they consider the lessons that Laura Schroff and Maurice Mazyck learned from each other. Laura, as part of the older generation, teaches Maurice about the possibilities in life by exposing him to opportunities and people he would otherwise not have had or met. Maurice, as part of the younger generation, teaches Laura that children crave connection and a feeling of belonging more than they crave material things.

WHOLE-CLASS LEARNING PERFORMANCE TASK
What unexpected event shows how a person can influence someone from a different generation?

UNIT PERFORMANCE-BASED ASSESSMENT
In what situations can one generation learn from another?

Connection to Performance Tasks

Whole-Class Learning Performance Task In this Performance Task, students will write personal narratives about how an unexpected event shows how someone from a different generation has influenced them or someone they know. Students will have the opportunity to compare their own experiences with the relationship in *An Invisible Thread*, which shows how two strangers from different generations came into each other's lives by chance and changed the course of both their lives.

Unit Performance-Based Assessment This selection shows students that the younger generation can teach the older generation about what is important to children, and that the older generation can help guide the younger generation and expose them to important new experiences.

DIGITAL PERSPECTIVES

 Audio  Video  Document  Annotation Highlights Online Assessment

LESSON RESOURCES

	Making Meaning	Language Development	Effective Expression
Lesson	**First Read** **Close Read** **Analyze the Text** **Analyze Craft and Structure**	**Concept Vocabulary** **Word Study** **Conventions**	**Writing to Compare**
Instructional Standards	**RI.7.10** By the end of the year, read and comprehend literary nonfiction . . . **RI.7.6** Determine an author's point of view or purpose . . .	**L.7.2.a** Use a comma to separate coordinate adjectives. **L.7.4.b** Use common, grade-appropriate Greek or Latin affixes and roots . . . **L.7.5** Demonstrate understanding of figurative language, word relationships . . . **L.7.5.b** Use the relationship between particular words to better understand . . .	**RI.7.9** Analyze how two or more authors . . . **W.7.9** Draw evidence from literary or informational texts to support . . . **W.7.2** Write informative/explanatory texts . . . **W.7.2.b** Develop the topic . . . **W.7.2.c** Use appropriate transitions . . . **L.7.2.b** Spell correctly.
STUDENT RESOURCES			
Available online in the Interactive Student Edition or Unit Resources	Selection Audio First-Read Guide: Nonfiction Close-Read Guide: Nonfiction	Word Network	Evidence Log
TEACHER RESOURCES			
Selection Resources Available online in the Interactive Teacher's Edition or Unit Resources	Audio Summaries: English and Spanish Annotation Highlights Accessible Leveled Text First Read Extension Questions Analyze Craft and Structure: Narrative Point of View	Concept Vocabulary and Word Study Conventions: Adjectives	Writing to Compare: Explanatory Essay
Reteach/Practice (RP) Available online in the Interactive Teacher's Edition or Unit Resources	Analyze Craft and Structure: Narrative Point of View (RP)	Word Study: Latin Suffix *–ity* (RP) Conventions: Adjectives (RP)	
Assessment Available online in Assessments	Selection Test: English Selection Test: Spanish Extension Selection Test		
My Resources	A Unit 1 Answer Key is available online and in the Interactive Teacher's Edition		

Reading Support

Text Complexity Rubric: An Invisible Thread	
Quantitative Measures	
Lexile: 890 **Text Length:** 519 words	
Qualitative Measures	
Knowledge Demands ①—②—❸—④—⑤	Students need some knowledge of homelessness in cities in order to understand references to begging, shelters, and lack of food, and to understand the relationship between Maurice and Laura.
Structure ①—①—❸—④—⑤	The account is told from the present looking back to the past. Reader needs to recognize that some quotations are spoken by adults about their memories of the past, and others are words they said in the past.
Language Conventionality and Clarity ①—❷—③—④—⑤	Sentences are mostly average length or short, with syntax that is easy to understand. Vocabulary is mostly on-level.
Levels of Meaning/Purpose ①—❷—③—④—⑤	Meaning and concepts are straightforward, without multiple levels of meaning. The one figurative phrase used (invisible thread) is explained.

DECIDE AND PLAN

English Language Support

Provide English Learners with support for knowledge demands and structure as they read the selection.

Knowledge Demands In order to ensure that students understand the situation of the two people in the selection, make sure they understand the meaning of these words and phrases they will see as they read: *begged, shelter, spare change, fend for himself.* If necessary, explain Maurice's situation and why he asked for food, thereby starting the friendship with Laura.

Structure To help students follow the structure of the narrative, point out that most of the quotations are from the present but refer to past events. The exceptions are paragraphs 2 and 15, which include quotations of things Maurice said in the past.

Strategic Support

Provide students with strategic support to ensure that they can successfully read the text.

Knowledge Demands Discuss with students the challenges that people face when they face financial hardships. Ask them to think about the basic needs that people in these situations might need assistance with. As they read, ask them to think about how someone might feel when they get help from a stranger.

Structure As students read, check that they are understanding the sequence of the narrative. If students have trouble determining whether quotations are spoken in the past (paragraphs 2 and 15) or the present, have them look for clues in the surrounding sentences. Then have them reread the quotations.

Challenge

Provide students who need to be challenged with ideas for how they can go beyond a simple interpretation of the text.

Text Analysis Ask students to discuss what it means to have a "guardian angel." Have them think about the times in their lives or in the life of someone they know when a stranger has stepped in and offered assistance with a difficult problem or situation.

Written Response Ask students to investigate ways in which they can assist people in their community who are in need. Have students prepare a brief presentation for the class that outlines these opportunities.

TEACH

Read and Respond

Have the class do their first read of the selection. Then have them complete their close read. Finally, work with them on the Making Meaning, Language Development, and Effective Expression activities.

Standards Support Through Teaching and Learning Cycle

IDENTIFY NEEDS

Analyze results of the Beginning-of-Year Assessment, focusing on the items relating to Unit 1. Also take into consideration student performance to this point and your observations of where particular students struggle.

DECIDE AND PLAN

- If students have performed poorly on items matching these standards, then provide selection scaffolds before assigning them the on-level lesson provided in the Student Edition.
- If students have done well on the Beginning-of-Year Assessment, then challenge them to keep progressing and learning by giving them opportunities to practice the skills in depth.
- Use the Selection Resources listed on the Planning Pages for *An Invisible Thread* to help students continually improve their ability to master the standards.

Instructional Standards: An Invisible Thread

	Catching Up	This Year	Looking Forward
Reading	You may wish to administer the **Analyze Craft and Structure: Narrative Point of View (RP)** worksheet to help students understand a scene from a different perspective.	**RI.6** Determine an author's point of view or purpose in a text and analyze how the author distinguishes his or her position from that of others.	Have students identify the conflicting viewpoints that might arise if the selection were told from another point of view.
Language	You may wish to administer the **Conventions: Adjectives (RP)** worksheet to help students understand that commas separate coordinate adjectives, or two adjectives that modify the same noun.	**L.2.a** Use a comma to separate coordinate adjectives.	Have students say or write a sentence about *An Invisible Thread* that includes two coordinating adjectives separated by a comma. Ask students to read their sentence, using the punctuation as a cue for when to pause as they read.

ANALYZE AND REVISE

- Analyze student work for evidence of student learning.
- Identify whether students have met the expectations in the standards.
- Identify implications for future instruction.

TEACH

Implement the planned lesson, and gather evidence of student learning.

TEACHING

Jump Start

FIRST READ Prior to students' first read, ask them to think about their circles of friends. Did any of them meet a friend in an unusual way? This discussion will help them make connections between the text and their own experiences.

An Invisible Thread 

Why does Maurice consider Laura to be so special? Why did she do what she did? Modeling questions such as these will help students connect to the excerpt from *An Invisible Thread* and to the Performance Task assignment. Selection audio and print capability for the selection are available in the Interactive Teacher's Edition.

Concept Vocabulary

Support students as they rank their words. Ask if they've ever heard, read, or used them. Reassure them that the definitions for these words are listed in the selection.

FIRST READ

As they read, students should perform the steps of the first read:

NOTICE: Have students notice the point of view of the narrative by thinking about who is telling the story.

ANNOTATE: Students should mark passages they find memorable as well as those they find difficult.

CONNECT: Encourage students to think about their own friendships with people from older generations. How will they view such friendships when they are older?

RESPOND: Students will answer questions and write a summary to demonstrate understanding.

Point out to students that while they will always complete the Respond step at the end of the first read, the others steps will probably happen somewhat concurrently. You may wish to print copies of the **First-Read Guide: Nonfiction** for students to use.

Remind students that during their first read, they should not answer the close-read questions that appear in the selection.

MAKING MEANING

A SIMPLE ACT

Comparing Texts

You will now read an excerpt from *An Invisible Thread*. First, complete the first-read and close-read activities. Then, compare the point of view of "A Simple Act" with the point of view of *An Invisible Thread*.

from AN INVISIBLE THREAD

About the Authors

Laura Schroff had a career in advertising sales for more than 30 years and helped launch *USA Today* and several other highly successful publications. She is now a motivational speaker and encourages people to make a difference in the lives of others.

Alex Tresniowski is a writer based in New York City. He has been a senior writer for *People* magazine, writing human-interest, crime, and sports articles, and he is the co-author of several books, including *An Invisible Thread* and *The Vendetta*.

from *An Invisible Thread*

Concept Vocabulary

You will encounter the following words as you read an excerpt from *An Invisible Thread*.

Before reading, note how familiar you are with each word. Then, rank the words in order from most familiar (1) to least familiar (3).

WORD	YOUR RANKING
resilience	
perseverance	
generosity	

After completing the first read, come back to the concept vocabulary and review your rankings. Mark changes to your original rankings as needed.

First Read NONFICTION

Apply these strategies as you conduct your first read. You will have an opportunity to complete the close-read notes after your first read.

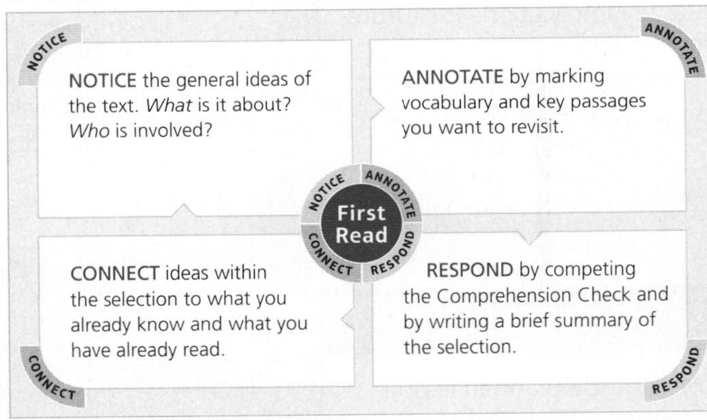

STANDARDS

Reading Informational Text

By the end of the year, read and comprehend literary nonfiction in the grades 6–8 text complexity band proficiently, with scaffolding as needed at the high end of the range.

DIGITAL PERSPECTIVES

Enriching the Text To give students a better understanding of how Laura and Maurice's relationship developed, show their interview on the *Today* show to the class. Be sure to preview the video before sharing it with the class.

What special names does Maurice use to refer to Laura? Ask the students how they feel about the pictures shown and what the pictures reflect about Laura and Maurice's relationship.

Point out the reactions of the hosts while they are learning more about Laura and Maurice's story. Might you, the viewers, have had a similar reaction? How does emotion encourage people to promote a cause?

Discuss how Laura and Maurice's relationship has motivated them to spread awareness about child hunger and work to help hungry children.

from An Invisible Thread

Laura Schroff and Alex Tresniowski

DIGITAL PERSPECTIVES   

BACKGROUND

Laura Schroff and Maurice Mazyck had been friends for 15 years when he gave the final toast at the celebration of her 50th birthday. Maurice's words, and Laura's reaction to them, reveal what each had gained from their long friendship.

1 Then came the final toast. The speaker was in a sharp black tuxedo with spectacular black-and-white shoes, and his wife was in a stunning navy blue gown, her hair swept up. Nearly everyone in the room had met him or at least knew his story, and so everyone was excited to see him and hear him speak. He kissed his wife, walked up and took the microphone, and began his toast.

2 "Laurie, where can I start," Maurice began. "We met . . . the way we met was so special to me. I was a young boy on the street with barely nothing, and I was very hungry that day and I asked this lady, 'Miss, can you spare some change?' And she walked away. And then she stopped. She was in the middle of the street—she almost got hit—and she looked and came back and took me to McDonald's. We ate and then walked around Central Park; she took me to Haagen-Dazs and then we played some games.

3 "You know, at that moment she saved my life. 'Cause I was going down the wrong road, the wrong hill, and, you know, my mother—bless her soul, my mother died—and the Lord sent me an angel. And my angel was Laurie.

4 "Without you," Maurice said, raising his glass, "I could not be the man I am today."

5 I was so incredibly moved when I heard Maurice say I saved his life. Heck, I nearly lost it throughout his whole darn toast. Whenever I hear someone tell me how lucky Maurice is to have

NOTES

CLOSE READ

ANNOTATE: In paragraphs 3 and 4, mark the punctuation.

QUESTION: Why do you think the author uses this type of punctuation in transcribing Maurice's words?

CONCLUDE: Would this passage have the same effect if it had just summarized what Maurice said? Explain.

CLOSE READ 

Remind students that while the direct quotations in paragraphs 3 and 4 show the words that Maurice said, the punctuation gives an idea of how he said it. You may wish to model the close read using the following think-aloud format. Possible responses to questions on the student page are included. You may also want to print copies of the **Close-Read Guide: Nonfiction** for students to use.

ANNOTATE: As I read paragraphs 3 and 4, I first notice and mark the dashes. When used in pairs like this, dashes set off a separate thought that is inserted in the middle of a sentence. But I also mark the apostrophe that appears with the word "Cause."

QUESTION: Rather than simply giving a flat, lifeless transcription of Maurice's toast, the author uses this punctuation to give readers a sense of what it was like to be in the audience and hear Maurice give his toast on that day. We get a feel for Maurice's personality—he seems like a real person. As a result, the toast comes to life and has meaning.

CONCLUDE: If the passage just summarized what Maurice said, it would not have the same effect. Maurice's words and the way he speaks them convey that it's an emotional moment—he's honoring someone who means a lot to him and he's talking about his mother's passing. The author's use of punctuation reflects this emotion.

PERSONALIZE FOR LEARNING

English Language Support

Idioms In paragraph 3, Maurice tells the audience that he was *going down the wrong road*. He further specifies that his road was *the wrong hill*. Explain to students that *going down the wrong road* is an idiom, or an expression that means something more or different from the meaning of the words that make it up; the words are not meant literally. Point out that one strategy a reader might use to understand idioms is to look for context clues about the meaning of *down the wrong road*.

A clue that comes before the idiom is that Maurice says Laura saved his life. Clues that come after the idiom are that Maurice's mother was a drug addict and he considers Laura an angel.

Discuss why Maurice would then say that it was down the *wrong hill*. You may wish to point out that *going down the wrong hill* is not a common idiom but may be a combination of the idioms *going down the wrong road* and *going downhill*. Ask students to picture what the exact meaning of *going down the wrong hill* would look like. Then have them think about what that would mean when applied to someone's life.

CLOSER LOOK

Draw Conclusions

Students may have marked paragraph 6 during their first read. Encourage them to talk about the annotations that they marked.

ANNOTATE: Have students mark details that show what Maurice gave to Laura.

QUESTION: Guide students to consider what these details might tell them. Ask what a reader can infer from these details, and accept student responses.

Possible response: Laura learned from Maurice that a paper-bag lunch showed his classmates that someone loved him.

CONCLUDE: Help students to formulate conclusions about the importance of these details in the text. Ask students why the author might have included these details.

Possible response: Laura learned from and grew in her relationship with Maurice. The help she gave him benefited her as well. By including these details, the author helps the reader draw the conclusion that he taught her the value of things that she used to take for granted, and that she grew to love him.

Remind students that authors make careful choices in deciding which details to include in a story. The details included should help readers **draw conclusions** about a story's underlying message, and about subtleties of characterization.

MEDIA CONNECTION

Project the Media Connection video in class or ask students to open the video in their interactive textbooks.

Discuss It

Possible responses: Viewers may feel that seeing and hearing Maurice shows how he emphasizes certain words, giving the words more depth. Viewers may feel that his words "come alive," helping them connect the words to their own experience.

NOTES

resilience (rih ZIHL yuhns) *n.* ability to recover quickly

perseverance (pur suh VIHR uhns) *n.* continued, patient effort

generosity (jehn uhr AHS uh tee) *n.* willingness to give or share

met me, I have to stop them and correct them. The truth is that the lucky one is me.

6 Maurice taught me so many things; I can't possibly list them all. He taught me how to live. He taught me one of the most important lessons a person can hope to learn—he taught me to be grateful for what I have. He taught me about **resilience**, courage, **perseverance**, and about the special strength that comes from overcoming adversity. He taught me the true value of money, the real meaning of lunch in a brown paper bag, the importance of a silly ritual like baking cookies. He taught me, more than I ever taught him, what it means to be a friend.

7 Everything I ever gave to Maurice, he gave back to me tenfold. Every meal, every shirt, every bike or toothbrush, was matched by Maurice with a more genuine appreciation than I have ever known. Every hand I ever lent him was returned with a hug; every kindness was paid back with an impossibly optimistic smile. If love is the greatest gift of all—and I believe it is—then the greatest privilege of all is to be able to love someone. Maurice appeared out of nowhere and allowed me to love him, and for that, I simply can never thank him enough. His **generosity** of spirit continues to astound me, and to this day my relationship with him is the relationship I am most proud of in my life. ❧

MEDIA CONNECTION

Maurice's Toast

Discuss It In what way does this video of Maurice's toast deepen your understanding of and appreciation for the text?

Write your response before sharing your ideas.

VOCABULARY DEVELOPMENT

Suffix *-fold* Call students' attention to the word *tenfold* in the first sentence of paragraph 7. Remind students that when they encounter an unfamiliar word in their reading, they can try different strategies to help them figure out the word's meaning. One strategy is to look for word parts. Students know the meaning of the word *ten*, and from the context clues, ten doesn't seem like a very high number. Encourage them to guess the meaning of *tenfold*. Then, explain that the suffix *-fold* means "multiplied by," and it can be used with other words, such as *twofold, fivefold*, and so on.

Comprehension Check

Complete the following items after you finish your first read.

1. At what stage of his life does Maurice give a toast explaining how he and Laura met?

2. What statement does Maurice make that makes Laura "nearly lose it"?

3. How does Laura respond when people say that Maurice was lucky to meet her?

4. What does Laura say she learned from knowing Maurice?

5. According to Laura, what are the greatest gift and greatest privilege of all?

6. **Notebook** Write a summary of the excerpt from *An Invisible Thread* to confirm your understanding of the selection.

RESEARCH

Research to Clarify Choose at least one unfamiliar detail from the text. Briefly research that detail. In what way does the information you learned shed light on an aspect of the story?

Research to Explore Choose something that interests you from the text and formulate a research question.

DIGITAL PERSPECTIVES

Comprehension Check

Possible responses:

1. Maurice gives the toast as an adult, when he is already married.
2. Maurice says that Laura saved his life and that without her, he would "not be the man" he is today.
3. Laura insists that she was the lucky one because she received as much from Maurice as he received from her.
4. She learned about "resilience, courage, perseverance," and "overcoming adversity." She learned "the true value of money" and the importance of seemingly unimportant rituals, "like baking cookies." Most importantly, she learned about friendship.
5. The greatest gift of all is love, and the greatest privilege is "to be able to love someone."
6. Summaries will vary. **Sample response:** At a formal event, Maurice gives a toast in which he says that Laura's friendship saved his life and prevented him from making poor life choices. Laura responds by saying that she gained even more from Maurice. She learned the true value of friendship.

Research

Research to Clarify If students struggle to choose a detail to research, suggest they look for unusual friendships or success stories.

Research to Explore If students have trouble choosing a subject for their research question, suggest they start with the detail they researched in Research to Clarify. They might want to research the definition of friendship or what spurs people to succeed.

PERSONALIZE FOR LEARNING

Challenge

Illuminating the Text To help students understand Maurice's life, have them research child poverty in the United States. Review statistics on the extent of child poverty, as well as on the life expectancy, incarceration rate, and cycle of poverty later in life for poor children. Find graphical representations of the issue to help students conceptualize the statistics.

Remind students of the part of Maurice's toast in which he states that Laura saved his life because he was going down the wrong road. Discuss whether he meant that metaphorically, literally, or both. Ask students to consider how the changes in Maurice's life are likely to impact his children.

Jump Start

CLOSE READ Have students close read the excerpt from *An Invisible Thread*. Ask them to recall the meaning of the phrase *an invisible thread* from their reading of "A Simple Act." Discuss the influence their meeting had on Laura and Maurice.

Close Read the Text 

Walk students through the Annotation Model on the student page. Then have them use the models as they annotate another detail. Encourage them to complete items 2 and 3 on their own. Review and discuss the sections students have marked. If needed, continue to model close reading by using the Annotation Highlights in the Interactive Teacher's Edition.

Analyze the Text

Possible responses:

1. The words "sharp" and "spectacular" contribute most to the positive tone. **DOK 2**
2. She may have turned around because she realized she could help him and wanted to try. **DOK 3**
3. Laura's statement suggests that although she gave some material things to Maurice, he returned those gifts with equally or more valuable emotional rewards. **DOK 3**
4. Maurice may have been invited to give the final toast at Laura's fiftieth birthday celebration because of how close they have become. **DOK 3**
5. Answers will vary. Students might point out that people of different generations can teach by acting as role models, demonstrating important values through their actions. **DOK 3**

FORMATIVE ASSESSMENT

Analyze the Text

- **If** students fail to cite evidence, **then** remind them to support their ideas with specific information.
- **If** students have trouble selecting words that give a positive impression of Maurice, **then** suggest they look at the adjectives in the first paragraph.

from AN INVISIBLE THREAD

Close Read the Text

1. The model, from paragraph 1 of the essay, shows two sample annotations, along with questions and conclusions. Close read the passage, and find another detail to annotate. Then, write a question and your conclusion.

ANNOTATE: This phrase has unusual word order.

QUESTION: Why did the author choose to put the verb before the noun?

CONCLUDE: Using this word order makes the sentence seem more formal, which suits the setting of the scene.

Then came the final toast. The speaker was in a sharp black tuxedo with spectacular black-and-white shoes, and his wife was in a stunning navy blue gown, her hair swept up.

ANNOTATE: The author uses vivid language here.

QUESTION: Why does the author provide so much detail about the speaker and his wife?

CONCLUDE: These details emphasize that Maurice has become successful.

2. For more practice, go back into the text and complete the close-read notes.
3. Revisit a section of the text you found important and **annotate** what you notice. Ask **questions** such as "Why did the author make this choice?" What can you **conclude**?

Analyze the Text

CITE TEXTUAL EVIDENCE to support your answers.

Notebook Respond to these questions.

1. **Analyze** In the first paragraph of the excerpt from her memoir, Laura Schroff gives the reader a positive impression of Maurice. Which of her word choices contribute most to this positive tone?
2. **Draw Conclusions** In his toast, Maurice says that when he asked Laura for spare change, at first she walked past him. Then, she stopped in the middle of the street, almost got hit by a car, and then walked back to him. Why do you think Laura turned around?
3. **Interpret** In paragraph 7, Laura says, "Everything I ever gave to Maurice, he gave back to me tenfold." What does this statement suggest about her friendship with Maurice?
4. **Make Inferences** Why do you think Maurice gave the final toast?
5. **Essential Question:** ***What can one generation learn from another?*** How did reading this excerpt affect your understanding of how people from different generations can learn from one another?

STANDARDS

Reading Informational Text
Determine an author's point of view or purpose in a text and analyze how the author distinguishes his or her position from that of others.

PERSONALIZE FOR LEARNING

Strategic Support

Description Lead students in reviewing the description of Maurice's clothes and shoes from "A Simple Act," found in paragraph 1 and paragraph 3. As a class, reread the description of Maurice's clothes and shoes in paragraph 1 of the excerpt from *An Invisible Thread* to contrast the two descriptions. Discuss how these descriptions give the reader important details about the drastic changes in Maurice's lifestyle as a result of his relationship with Laura. Ask students how such a stark contrast in Maurice's outer appearance helps them form these opinions.

Analyze Craft and Structure

Narrative Point of View *An Invisible Thread* is a memoir written from the **first-person point of view.** You can tell a work of nonfiction is written from the first-person point of view by looking for the following clues.

- The author uses the pronoun *I* to refer to himself or herself.
- The author is involved in the events being described.
- Authors often use **direct quotations,** or a person's exact words, to reflect the views of other people involved in the narrative.

Memoirs are usually written from the first-person point of view. Authors of memoirs use the first-person point of view because they are describing events and experiences in their *own* lives—both what happened as well as personal reactions and emotions.

Practice

CITE TEXTUAL EVIDENCE to support your answers.

Notebook Respond to these questions.

1. Record two examples of first-person point of view in paragraphs 5–7 of the text. Rewrite each example to change the point of view to third person by using the pronoun *she*. An example is shown.

   Example: "**I** was so incredibly moved when **I** heard Maurice say **I** saved his life." **She** was so incredibly moved when **she** heard Maurice say **she** saved his life.

ORIGINAL PASSAGE	REWRITTEN PASSAGE
"Heck, I nearly lost it throughout his whole darn toast."	Heck, she nearly lost it throughout his whole darn toast.
"He taught me how to live."	He taught her how to live.

2. (a) When the text begins, the point of view is unclear. At what point in the text is it evident that it is written in the first-person point of view? (b) What clues in the text helped you to recognize point of view?
3. (a) What strategy do the writers of *An Invisible Thread* use to present Maurice's point of view? (b) Do you think this strategy is effective? Why or why not?
4. How do the ideas expressed by the first-person narrator in *An Invisible Thread* deepen your understanding of relationship between Laura and Maurice?

WriteNow Express and Reflect

Write a Speech Ask students to reflect on someone who has been influential in their lives, such as a coach, a family member, a best friend, or a teacher. As a class, review the elements of Maurice's speech in paragraphs 2–4 of this excerpt from *An Invisible Thread*: the way that they met, his impression of Laura, the details about some of the important things they did together, and the impact they had on his life. Instruct students to write a toast honoring a person who influenced them. The toast should describe the person's actions, as well as the impact those actions have had on the student's life. Encourage students to use Maurice's toast as inspiration.

DIGITAL PERSPECTIVES 

Analyze Craft and Structure

Narrative Point of View Ask students how reading a first-person narrative makes them feel. Do they feel more connected to the text and the experiences of the narrator? Discuss how the use of first-person narrative helps readers understand the events from Laura's perspective. For more support, see **Analyze Craft and Structure: Narrative Point of View.**

MAKE IT INTERACTIVE

Project the digital version of the excerpt from *An Invisible Thread* and read paragraph 5. To help students understand what they have to do to complete the chart correctly, model how to locate pronouns that reflect the first-person point of view.

Practice

Possible responses:

1. See possible response in chart on student page.
2. (a) Paragraph 5 is the first indication that Laura is the narrator. (b) Clues include the use of the pronoun I and the other details in paragraph 5 which reveal her feelings about Maurice's speech.
3. (a) The writers include direct quotations from Maurice to show how he feels. (b) Answers will vary. Students may feel that the strategy helps readers to "hear" Maurice's voice, as in the quotation: "'Cause I was going down the wrong road, the wrong hill, and, you know, my mother—bless her soul, my mother died—and the Lord sent me an angel."
4. Reading Laura's first-person narration in the excerpt from *An Invisible Thread* helps readers understand the "impact on each other's lives" described in the article. The first-person point of view makes Laura's thoughts and feelings clear.

FORMATIVE ASSESSMENT

Analyze Craft and Structure

If students have trouble identifying the first-person point of view, **then** help them write a sentence in the third-person point of view and change it to first person. For Reteach and Practice, see **Analyze Craft and Structure: Narrative Point of View (RP).**

TEACHING

Concept Vocabulary

Why These Words? Point out that all three of the words describe positive qualities a person might have. Laura says that Maurice has those qualities and that she has learned them from him.

Possible responses:

1. Laura learned those qualities from Maurice, but it's possible that Maurice wouldn't have developed them without the support he got from Laura.
2. Choices include *moved, grateful, courage, strength, appreciation, kindness, spirit, proud*.

Practice

Possible responses:

1. My mother showed her *resilience* by bouncing back from any problem, no matter how difficult. His *perseverance* helped him pass the math test, even though he finds the subject confusing. My brother's *generosity* is evident in the way he loves to help younger members of his track team.
2. **resilience** synonyms: *grit, tolerance, flexibility;* antonyms: *brittle, unyielding*
   perseverance synonyms: *persistence, tenacity;* antonyms: *apathy, weakness, laziness*
   generosity synonyms: *unselfishness, goodness, benevolence;* antonyms: *meanness, selfishness*

Word Network

Possible words: *ritual, lessons, privilege, relationship*

Word Study

For more support, see **Concept Vocabulary and Word Study**.

Possible responses:

1. The adjective *generous* means "unselfish" and "free in giving." Adding the suffix *-ity* forms the noun *generosity*, which means "the quality of being unselfish and free in giving."
2. The word *adversity* combines the base word *adverse* with the suffix *-ity*. *Adverse* is an adjective meaning "preventing success." Adding the suffix *-ity* forms a noun that means "the state of having success prevented."

FORMATIVE ASSESSMENT

Concept Vocabulary

If students have trouble seeing that the words all reflect positive attributes, **then** challenge them to use each word in a sentence that is critical of someone.

Word Study

If students are unable to define the words, **then** check to be sure they know the meaning of the root words. For Reteach and Practice, see **Word Study: Latin Suffix *-ity* (RP).**

LANGUAGE DEVELOPMENT

from AN INVISIBLE THREAD

Concept Vocabulary

resilience	perseverance	generosity

Why These Words? These concept vocabulary words show positive qualities or personality traits. Maurice and Laura demonstrate these qualities in their relationship with each other. For example, the way Maurice overcomes adversity teaches Laura about *resilience* and *perseverance*. Notice that both of these words show positive aspects of Maurice's personality.

1. How does the concept vocabulary sharpen your understanding of how both Laura and Maurice benefited from their relationship?

2. What other words in the selection connect to the concept of positive personality traits?

WORD NETWORK

Add words related to generations from the text to your Word Network.

Practice

Notebook The concept vocabulary words appear in the excerpt from *An Invisible Thread*.

1. Use each word in a sentence that demonstrates your understanding of the word's meaning.
2. Work with a partner, and take turns coming up with as many **synonyms,** or words with similar meanings, and **antonyms,** or words with opposite meanings, as you can for each concept vocabulary word.

Word Study

Latin Suffix: *-ity* The Latin suffix *-ity* means the "state, quality, or condition of." In the selection, the author refers to Maurice's "*generosity* of spirit."

1. Explain how the suffix *-ity* contributes to the meaning of the concept vocabulary word *generosity*.

2. Look at paragraph 6, and find another word that uses the suffix *-ity*. Identify the base word that was combined with the suffix. Write a definition for that word.

STANDARDS

Language

- Demonstrate command of the conventions of standard English capitalization, punctuation, and spelling when writing.
  a. Use a comma to separate coordinate adjectives.
- Determine or clarify the meaning of unknown and multiple-meaning words and phrases based on grade 7 reading and content, choosing flexibly from a range of strategies.
  b. Use common, grade-appropriate Greek or Latin affixes and roots as clues to the meaning of a word.
- Demonstrate understanding of figurative language, word relationships, and nuances in word meanings.
  b. Use the relationship between particular words to better understand each of the words.

DIGITAL PERSPECTIVES

Illuminating the Text As a class, read the Five Take-Aways on Breaking the Cycle of Poverty on the San Francisco Foundation website. Lead a class discussion of each of the items on the list. Ask students to relate what they've read with the description of Maurice's life as a child. Discuss the ways that Maurice's relationship with Laura helped him to break the cycle of poverty.

Discuss the likelihood of other impoverished children finding a champion like Laura. Ask students to brainstorm other ways that people might help break the cycle of poverty.

Conventions

Adjectives An **adjective** is a word that modifies or describes a noun or pronoun. Adjectives may answer the question *What kind? How many? Which one?* or *Whose?* Possessive nouns and pronouns are used as adjectives to answer the question *Whose?*

What kind?	The young boy had a genuine smile.	Which one?	Have you read that book?
How many?	They talked for fifty minutes.	Whose?	I greatly admired Maurice's speech.

Two or More Adjectives Coordinate adjectives are two or more adjectives that modify the same noun and are separated by a comma. You can tell whether adjectives are coordinate if the word *and* could be used in place of the comma and you could reverse the adjectives. **Cumulative adjectives** also modify the same noun, but they are not separated by a comma. Cumulative adjectives cannot be reversed.

COORDINATE ADJECTIVES	CUMULATIVE ADJECTIVES
They became lifelong, devoted friends. You could say: *They became devoted and lifelong friends.*	She wore a light blue sweater. (*She wore a blue light sweater* does not mean the same thing.)

Read It

Identify the adjectives in each sentence, and name the nouns they modify. Then tell whether the adjectives are coordinate or cumulative and explain why.

1. Maurice gave an emotional, heartfelt speech.
2. His warm good nature inspired many listeners.
3. The book teaches many valuable life lessons.

Write It

The original sentence in the example below was revised by adding two adjectives. Review the example, and then add two adjectives to each practice sentence. Separate the adjectives with commas if needed.

EXAMPLE
Original: Laura wrote a memoir.
Revision: Laura wrote an *unforgettable personal* memoir.

1. Maurice shared a story with the audience.

2. Laura wore a dress.

Notebook Write a paragraph describing Laura and Maurice's relationship. Include at least one pair of coordinate and one pair of cumulative adjectives.

PERSONALIZE FOR LEARNING

English Language Support

Adjective Placement In English, adjectives are almost always placed in front of the nouns they modify. In Spanish, adjectives can be placed either in front of or after the noun. In some cases, the placement of the adjective in Spanish does not affect the meaning; however, in other cases, the meaning will change. Students may need a reminder that in English, they should place the adjective in front of the noun. **ALL LEVELS**

DIGITAL PERSPECTIVES 

Conventions

Adjectives Discuss the definition of adjectives with students. Review the examples from the text; then, as a class, compile a list of adjectives that answer the questions *What kind? How many? Which one?* and *Whose?*

Two or More Adjectives Provide the following models to explain the difference between coordinate and cumulative adjectives.

Coordinate	Can be reversed	Take a comma
It came in a square heavy box. She played a slow sad song.	It came in a heavy square box. She played a sad slow song.	It came in a square, heavy box. She played a slow, sad song.
Cumulative	**Cannot be reversed**	**Do not take a comma**
She wore a thick wool sweater. She played a familiar country song.	She wore a wool thick sweater. She played a country familiar song.	She wore a thick wool sweater. She played a familiar country song.

For more support, see **Conventions: Adjectives.** 

Read It

1. *Emotional* and *heartfelt* are coordinate adjectives that modify *speech*. Can be reversed, can take a comma.
2. *Warm* and *good* are cumulative adjectives that modify *nature*. Cannot be reversed.
3. *Many, valuable,* and *life* are cumulative adjectives that modify *lessons*. Cannot be reversed.

Write It

Possible responses:

1. Maurice shared a funny true story with the audience.
2. Laura wore a long red dress.

Maurice and Laura were important, lifelong friends. Laura contributed financial support to Maurice, while he contributed valuable emotional support to her.

FORMATIVE ASSESSMENT

Conventions

If students have difficulty differentiating between coordinate and cumulative adjectives, **then** suggest they insert the word *and* between the two adjectives. If the sentence makes sense and doesn't change its meaning, they need to use a comma when they write the sentence. For Reteach and Practice, see **Conventions: Adjectives (RP).**

TEACHING

Writing to Compare

As students prepare to compare the two selections, they will consider the benefits of friendship for Laura and Maurice and how those benefits are presented in each selection.

Analyze the Texts

Gather Evidence Encourage students to review each selection to consider how each presents Laura and Maurice's friendship.

a. food, support, caring, help with education, awareness of new possibilities.

b. He became like a son, taught her gratitude, helped give life meaning.

c. food, got help in choosing a better life path, friendship.

d. Learned resilience, courage, perseverance; made a close friend, and was allowed to love.

1. **Possible response:** "A Simple Act" presents the friendship and its benefits from the time it began to the present. It uses the third-person point of view. The excerpt from *An Invisible Thread* presents the friendship through Laura's first-person point of view. It begins with Maurice making a toast as an adult, in which he tells the story of how they met.
2. **Possible response:** Both texts include information about how the two people met.
3. The excerpt from *An Invisible Thread* includes more information about the value of the friendship to each person. It is a more emotional description.

EFFECTIVE EXPRESSION

A SIMPLE ACT

from AN INVISIBLE THREAD

Writing to Compare

You have read two selections about the friendship between Laura Stroff and Maurice Mazyck: the news blog "A Simple Act" and the excerpt from the memoir *An Invisible Thread.* Now, deepen your analysis and express your observations in writing.

Assignment

The news blog and the memoir tell about how Laura and Maurice's friendship helped them both. To prepare for your assignment, consider the following:

- How the friendship started and grew
- Why the friendship lasted so long

Write an **explanatory essay** in which you analyze ways in which the authors of the two pieces present information about the same topic: the friendship between Laura and Maurice.

Analyze the Texts

Gather Evidence Reread both "A Simple Act" and the excerpt from *An Invisible Thread* to examine the key information that the two authors provide when describing their friendship. Use the chart to record your notes.

As you gather evidence, ask yourself the following questions:

- What descriptive details do the two texts provide?
- What quotations, if any, are used?
- Does the text focus on a series of events or more on the quality of the friendship?

	Types of Details Used	Overall Effect of the Text
A Simple Act	a. See possible responses in Teacher's Edition.	b.
from An Invisible Thread	c.	d.

STANDARDS

Reading Informational Text
Analyze how two or more authors writing about the same topic shape their presentations of key information by emphasizing different evidence or advancing different interpretations of facts.

Writing
Draw evidence from literary or informational texts to support analysis, reflection, and research.

Notebook Respond to these questions.

1. How do the two texts differ in their presentation of the benefits of friendship?
2. What key information is the same across the two texts?
3. In which text is the emphasis on friendship more apparent? Explain your response.

Planning and Prewriting

Determine Your Central Idea In one sentence, write the central idea, or thesis, you will develop in your essay:

Central Idea/Thesis:______________________________________

____

Create an Outline To help you structure your essay, create an outline to organize your ideas.

Outline

I. Types of Details Used
   A. "A Simple Act"
   B. excerpt from *An Invisible Thread*

II. Overall Effect of the Text
   A. "A Simple Act"
   B. excerpt from *An Invisible Thread*

Drafting

Write a First Draft Use your completed outline to write your first draft. Develop your essay with details from the texts and present a smooth and logical explanation of your ideas. Use clear language and transitions to connect your ideas.

Use Transition Words Using transition words can help you present your ideas in a logical sequence and you make your essay flow more smoothly. There are several types of transitional words and phrases.

- Words and phrases that show **similarities:** *also, in addition, likewise*
- Words and phrases that show **differences:** *but, however, yet*
- Words and phrases that show **sequence:** *first, next, then, finally*
- Words and phrases that show **examples:** *for example, for instance*

Review and Revise

Once you are done writing, critically review your essay. Make sure you have given specific examples to support your ideas. Then, check to be sure you have used transitions to link those ideas. Finally, proofread your work to ensure it is free from errors in grammar, spelling, and punctuation.

EVIDENCE LOG

Before moving on to a new selection, go to your Evidence Log and record what you learned from these selections.

STANDARDS

Writing
Write informative/explanatory texts to examine a topic and convey ideas, concepts, and information through the selection, organization, and analysis of relevant content.
b. Develop the topic with relevant facts, definitions, concrete details, quotations, or other information and examples.
c. Use appropriate transitions to create cohesion and clarify the relationships among ideas and concepts.

Language
Demonstrate command of the conventions of standard English capitalization, punctuation, and spelling when writing.
b. Spell correctly.

PERSONALIZE FOR LEARNING

Challenge

Research Have students research another person who managed to break the cycle of poverty, either with help from someone outside their community, as Maurice did, with help from someone within their community, or entirely on their own. Possible subjects include George Soros, Michael Oher, and Oprah Winfrey. Students should report back with a brief biography and an explanation of what they believe made it possible for their subject to succeed.

DIGITAL PERSPECTIVES

Planning and Prewriting

Determine Your Central Idea Remind students that the central idea, or thesis, is not just a main topic. It is the central argument for the essay. The evidence that students use in the essay should support this central idea.

Create an Outline As students create outlines, they should identify several direct quotations from the text to support their claims. Remind students that the material does not have to appear in the same order that it did in each selection.

Drafting

Use Transition Words You may wish to have students first draft their essays and then add transitions to connect ideas. Remind students that the transition words will help readers follow the important claims in their essays.

Review and Revise

Be sure students also check basics such as spelling, punctuation, and grammar as they revise. Students may want to share their essays with partners. Are the partners convinced? Do they find each other's theses persuasive? For more support, see **Writing to Compare: Explanatory Essay.**

Evidence Log Support students in completing their Evidence Log. This paced activity will help prepare them for the Performance-Based Assessment at the end of the unit.

FORMATIVE ASSESSMENT

Writing to Compare

If students have difficulty coming up with a thesis, **then** have them imagine they are telling a friend about the point of view in the two texts.

Selection Test

Administer the *An Invisible Thread* Selection Test, which is available in both print and digital formats online in Assessments.

Jump Start

What is the moral of the story?

Students are undoubtedly familiar with parables and fairy tales that contain a moral, or lesson to be learned. Poll students about favorite stories that teach a lesson or communicate a time-tested truism. Remind students a well-written narrative communicates that in a way that allows the reader to make connections to what is being said.

Write a Nonfiction Narrative

Make sure students understand what they are being asked to do in the assignment. Explain that they will be using their own personal experiences with generational influence to make connections to the selections in Whole-Class Learning.

Students should complete the assignment using word processing software to take advantage of editing tools and features.

Elements of a Nonfiction Narrative

Remind students that an effective nonfiction narrative, such as "Grounded," contains all of the listed required elements, is organized in a logical manner, and uses vivid, descriptive details and powerful sensory language to create an engaging and interesting text.

MAKE IT INTERACTIVE

Project "Grounded" from the Interactive Teacher's Edition and have students identify the elements of a nonfiction narrative, such as characters, problem or conflict, and a conclusion or resolution.

Academic Vocabulary

Provide students with one or two sample sentences in which you use an academic vocabulary word. Then, ask volunteers to offer additional sample sentences using academic vocabulary words, and, as a class, discuss how the words might be applied to the writing topic.

PERFORMANCE TASK: WRITING FOCUS

WRITING TO SOURCES

- TWO KINDS
- A SIMPLE ACT
- *from* AN INVISIBLE THREAD

Tool Kit
Student Model of a Nonfiction Narrative

ACADEMIC VOCABULARY

As you craft your argument, consider using some of the academic vocabulary you learned in the beginning of the unit.

dialogue
consequence
perspective
notable
contradict

Write a Nonfiction Narrative

You have just read texts in which people of different generations have an influence on each other's lives. In "Two Kinds," an ambitious mother ends up teaching her child unexpected but valuable lessons. "A Simple Act" and the excerpt from *An Invisible Thread* present the story of two friends whose chance meeting enriched both of their lives. Now you will use your knowledge of these texts to write a nonfiction narrative about the ways in which people of different generations can influence each other.

Assignment

Write a **nonfiction narrative** about the influence someone from a different generation has had on you or someone you know. In your narrative, draw on the texts you have read in this section. Your narrative should answer this question:

> **What unexpected event shows how a person can influence someone from a different generation?**

Elements of a Nonfiction Narrative

A **nonfiction narrative** is a story of something that actually happened. In a personal narrative, the writer uses the first-person point of view (employing pronouns *I* and *me*) to tell the true story of something that he or she has experienced. Other nonfiction narratives, such as biography, are written from the third-person point of view.

An engaging nonfiction narrative contains these elements:

- well-developed major and minor characters as well as a narrator, who is you, the writer
- a problem or conflict
- a clear sequence of events that unfolds naturally and logically
- narrative techniques such as dialogue, description, and pacing
- a variety of transitional words, phrases, and clauses to convey sequence and signal shifts from one setting or time frame to another
- precise words, well-chosen quotations, vivid descriptive details, and powerful sensory language
- a conclusion that follows from and reflects on the experiences in the narrative

Model Nonfiction Narrative For a model of a well-crafted nonfiction narrative, see the Launch Text, "Grounded."

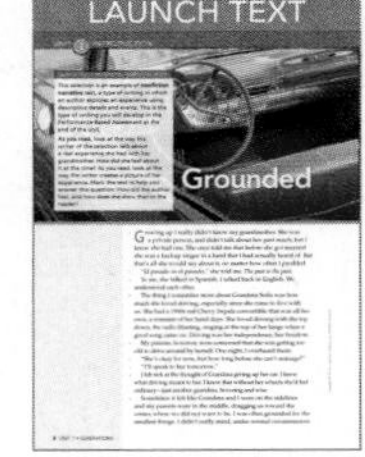

Challenge yourself to find all of the elements of an effective nonfiction narrative in the text. You will have an opportunity to review these elements as you prepare to write your own nonfiction narrative.

STANDARDS

Writing

- Write narratives to develop real or imagined experiences or events using effective technique, relevant descriptive details, and well- structured event sequences.
- Write routinely over extended time frames and shorter time frames for a range of discipline-specific tasks, purposes, and audiences.

AUTHOR'S PERSPECTIVE Kelly Gallagher, M.Ed.

Pump Up the Volume of Writing Spend some time talking to kids about why they should write—not just how. Students should write more than the teacher can grade. To help students get the most from their writing, teachers can use techniques such as these:

- **Confer** Teachers can achieve more in a two-minute conference than they can by spending five to seven minutes writing comments on a paper. Developing writers need face time with the most experienced writer in the class—the teacher.
- **Model** Teachers can model how they write by frequently writing in front of students. Show students that effective writing extends far past correctness. Teachers can do this in short bursts, and model authentic writing, whether brainstorming a topic, working to add details, or revising to find the right word. Note: other times the teacher can bring a model to class that has already been written for the students to study.
- **Share models of excellent writing** Show students models from professional writers and from other students. As they study mentor texts, students begin to see the moves a writer has made, and they can work to emulate those moves.
- **Use a Rubric** Experiment with changing the rubric. Encourage students to help you build it. This creates buy-in when the students see that each rubric is personalized to some degree to their needs.

Prewriting / Planning

Focus Your Topic Reread the assignment. Consider the person and event you would like to highlight in your narrative. State your main idea in a sentence:

______________________ helped to influence ______________________
(person from generation 1) (person from generation 2)

by ____.
(action that influenced person from generation 2)

Develop Characters Realistic, engaging characters make a narrative come alive. Think about each character you will include in your narrative. List traits and descriptive details that make him or her unique and interesting. Consider the ways in which dialogue between the characters will help propel the action in your narrative. Don't forget to include yourself as the narrator!

CHARACTERS	TRAITS	DETAILS/DIALOGUE

Gather Details Details for a nonfiction narrative come mainly from your own memories and experiences. A photo album or a conversation with a relative may stimulate your memory and help you find a topic.

There are many different types of details you can use to craft your nonfiction narrative:

- **anecdotes:** brief stories that illustrate a point or key idea
- **dialogue/quotations:** statements from personal interviews or conversations with the people who are featured in your narrative
- **examples:** facts, ideas, and events that support an idea or insight

Study the Launch Text to identify ways in which the writer uses various types of details to develop characters and ideas.

EVIDENCE LOG

Review your Evidence Log and identify types of details you may want to cite in your nonfiction narrative.

STANDARDS

Writing

Write narratives to develop real or imagined experiences or events using effective technique, relevant descriptive details, and well-structured event sequences.

b. Use narrative techniques, such as dialogue, pacing, and description, to develop experiences, events, and/or characters.

DIGITAL PERSPECTIVES

Prewriting/Planning

Focus Your Topic Remind students that the first step in writing their narrative is to identify the characters and the influence someone from one generation had on someone from another generation. Encourage students who struggle to brainstorm for several topics and then choose the idea they find most interesting.

Develop Characters Explain that well-developed characters are both realistic and relatable to the reader. Remind students that a character's traits, both positive and negative, provide depth to the text and help build a reader's interest in the story. You may choose to model your own thinking as you complete a graphic organizer like the one shown. This will help your students get a better sense of the activity.

Gather Details Have students review their Evidence Log to find possible support for their narrative. Remind them that if they don't have sufficient key details in their Evidence Log, they may want to go back and review the selections to identify additional or stronger details for their narrative. Students should also consider using other sources to support their message and should make a plan for identifying and citing details from these sources.

PERSONALIZE FOR LEARNING

English Language Support

Characters Support English Learners as they develop characters for their nonfiction narrative.

Have students create a T-chart for one of their characters, with columns for the character's actions, thoughts, and feelings. **EMERGING**

Have students write three complete sentences in which they describe a character's actions, what the character is thinking, and what the character is feeling. **EXPANDING**

Have students write a short paragraph in which they describe a character's actions, thoughts, and feelings. **BRIDGING**

TEACHING

Drafting

Organize a Sequence of Events Explain to students that creating a sequence of events is essential to developing a well-written narrative. When one event follows another in an organized fashion, it makes it easier for the reader to follow the story. Remind students that a timeline is an outline that can be used to organize their writing.

Use Transitions Emphasize that transitions are essential to developing a strong narrative because they add clarity and cohesion. You may want to ask students to find examples of transitional words in the Launch Text.

Write a First Draft As students write their first draft, they should focus on getting their ideas on paper, incorporating all of the elements of nonfiction narrative writing. Students should remember to include sufficient details to ensure that a reader with no knowledge of their characters or the story can understand what is being said.

Encourage students to grab the reader's attention in the introduction by including an anecdote or pertinent quotation from one of the selections.

PERFORMANCE TASK: WRITING FOCUS

Drafting

Organize a Sequence of Events In a nonfiction narrative, the writer often sequences events in **chronological order**, so that one event proceeds to the next in the order in which they actually happened.

Use a timeline to organize your narrative so that it flows in chronological order. Then, add details to elaborate on the action. The timeline here shows key events in the Launch Text. Use it as a model to construct a timeline of your own narrative.

LAUNCH TEXT

MODEL: "Grounded" Timeline

INTRODUCTION
Narrator, Grandma, and their relationship are described.

1. Parents talk about Grandma's driving.
2. Narrator is grounded.
3. Narrator asks Grandma for a ride to a party.
4. Narrator and Grandma feel bad on the ride.
5. Grandma asks to turn back; narrator agrees.

CONCLUSION
Grandma and narrator have learned from each other and share an understanding.

Nonfiction Narrative Timeline

INTRODUCTION

1.
2.
3.
4.
5.

CONCLUSION

STANDARDS
Writing
• Engage and orient the reader by establishing a context and point of view and introducing a narrator and/or characters; organize an event sequence that unfolds naturally and logically.
• Use a variety of transition words, phrases, and clauses to convey sequence and signal shifts from one time frame or setting to another.

Use Transitions To make the sequence of events in your narrative clear to readers, use transition words, such as *first, then, next, later,* and *finally,* to establish a clear chronological order. Use the numbered events in your timeline to help you determine which transition words to use and where in your writing to use them.

Write a First Draft Refer to your timeline as you write your first draft. As you draft your narrative, refer to the elements of nonfiction narrative writing as well as your Prewriting/Planning notes.

AUTHOR'S PERSPECTIVE **Jim Cummins, Ph.D.**

Writing to Enhance Student Identity Writing is an expression of oneself, and writing projects that self into the new social spheres. However, students learning English are often defined by what they are missing rather than by what they possess. While teaching writing through the Performance Tasks in *myPerspectives*, you may want to supplement the writing instruction and practice for English learners by using *identity texts*. These texts allow students to invest their identities into their writing. The results hold a mirror up to students and reflect their identities in a positive light. Teachers can use this process:

1. Encourage students to have a hand in picking the topic to ensure they are writing about something that reflects themselves or their identities. Have students write their drafts in English, illustrate them, and work with various sources, such as parents and older students fluent in their home language, to translate the drafts into their home language.
2. Publish these texts. Help students share identity texts with multiple audiences including peers,

LANGUAGE DEVELOPMENT

Develop Technique: Finding Your Voice

Voice A writer's distinctive style is referred to as **voice**, and it can be influenced by word choice, **sentence structure** (the way the author constructs a sentence), and **tone**—the writer's attitude toward his or her subject. Developing a unique voice can take time. These tips and activities will help get you started.

Read It

This chart shows examples from the Launch Text that contribute to the author's voice.

Word Choice	*singing at the top of her lungs; just beginning to darken with blue clouds against a darker blue sky*
Varied Sentence Structure and Dialogue	*We took off. She drove slowly, maybe too slowly. "Bueno," she said, with a nod.*
Reflective, Genuine Tone	*But how could I say any of this? I was so relieved I could have cried.*

Write It

As you draft your nonfiction narrative, think of ways in which you can develop your voice. To do so, ask yourself questions such as: *What should the tone of my narrative be? What emotions do I want the audience to experience?* and *How can I make my personality as narrator more authentic?*

Also pay close attention to your sentence structures, and strive to mimic real speech patterns. When writing from the first-person point of view, you might be inclined to begin many of your sentences with the pronoun *I*, which will create a repetitive, dull pattern. This chart provides strategies to help you avoid repetitive sentence beginnings and create variety.

STANDARDS

Writing

Write narratives to develop real or imagined experiences or events using effective technique, relevant descriptive details, and well-structured event sequences.

d. Use precise words and phrases, relevant descriptive details, and sensory language to capture the action and convey experiences and events.

ORIGINAL	STRATEGY TO ADD VARIETY	REVISION
I was surprised to see my sister on the stage.	*Start your sentence with a word that describes your emotion or mood.*	Startled, I noticed the familiar figure of my sister on the stage.
I rushed to congratulate her after the play ended.	*Move another part of the sentence to the beginning.*	After the play ended, I rushed to congratulate her.
I said her portrayal of the character was so realistic I forgot she was my sister.	*Start with a real quotation instead of writing that someone said something.*	"Great job!" I exclaimed. "You really made me believe you were Alice."

teachers, parents, grandparents, sister classes, and the media. It is critical that students share their writing with broad audiences to build this positive experience. Students are likely to receive positive feedback and affirmation of self by providing true audiences with which to share their work.

Writing and publishing identity texts helps ELL students take active control and ownership of the learning process and invest their identities in their drafts.

DIGITAL PERSPECTIVES

Develop Technique: Finding Your Voice

Voice

Explain to students that they will learn more about creating an effective voice through the reading and writing activities that follow.

Read It

Emphasize that word choice, sentence structure, and tone are essential to developing a well-written nonfiction narrative because these elements of writing help communicate the writer's attitude toward the subject.

MAKE IT INTERACTIVE

Use the Interactive Teacher's Edition to project "Grounded" and ask students to identify additional examples of powerful word choice:

- *without her wheels she'd feel ordinary* (paragraph 8)
- *I was itching to go to the party* (paragraph 11)
- *She drove slowly, maybe too slowly.* (paragraph 14)

Write It

Support student analysis of voice with questions like these: Does the tone of their writing invite the reader to engage with the story and the characters? Do their word choices provide a level of detail that helps the reader envision the action in the narrative?

Consider asking students to share a sentence from their narrative with the class, and guide them through the process of adding variety to their writing.

Revising

Evaluating Your Draft

Ask students to review the prompt as part of their revision work. Before students begin revising their writing, they should first evaluate their draft to make sure it contains all of the required elements, is organized in a logical manner, and adheres to the norms and conventions of nonfiction narrative writing.

Revising for Focus and Organization

Provide a Clear Conclusion Students should ensure that they provide a clear conclusion that resolves any conflicts or questions that arise in the narrative. Remind students that making personal connections to the resolution in their writing helps personalize the narrative and improves the richness of their writing.

Revising for Evidence and Elaboration

Use Precise Language Remind students as they revise their narratives that using precise language is an important part of narrative writing. Explain that the purpose of a narrative is to communicate a clear message and that the more specific they are in their word choice, the easier a reader will understand what they are trying to say.

Adjust Pacing Remind students that telling a story well involves knowing what to include. Encourage students to take a critical look at their narratives to find any sections that could be cut or that could be improved through thorough editing.

PERFORMANCE TASK: WRITING FOCUS

Revising

Evaluating Your Draft

Use the following checklist to evaluate the effectiveness of your first draft. Then, use your evaluation and the instruction on this page to guide your revision.

FOCUS AND ORGANIZATION	EVIDENCE AND ELABORATION	CONVENTIONS
☐ Provides an introduction that establishes a clear context and point of view. ☐ Presents a clear chronological sequence of events that are linked by clarifying transitions. ☐ Provides a conclusion that follows from and reflects on the events and experiences in the narrative.	☐ Effectively uses narrative techniques, such as dialogue, pacing, and description. ☐ Uses descriptive details, sensory language, and precise words and phrases. ☐ Establishes voice through word choice, sentence structure, and tone.	☐ Attends to the norms and conventions of the discipline.

WORD NETWORK

Include interesting words from your Word Network in your personal narrative.

STANDARDS

Writing

- Write narratives to develop real or imagined experiences or events using effective technique, relevant descriptive details, and well-structured event sequences.
  - a. Engage and orient the reader by establishing a context and point of view and introducing a narrator and/or characters; organize an event sequence that unfolds naturally and logically.
  - d. Use precise words and phrases, relevant descriptive details, and sensory language to capture the action and convey experiences and events.
  - e. Provide a conclusion that follows from and reflects on the narrated experiences or events.
- Produce clear and coherent writing in which the development, organization, and style are appropriate to task, purpose, and audience.

Revising for Focus and Organization

Provide a Clear Conclusion The conclusion of a nonfiction narrative clarifies the overall message and provides readers with a sense of **resolution**, or completion. It resolves any conflicts or questions presented in the narrative. To increase the clarity of your conclusion, check to be sure that it follows logically from the body of your essay. Then, consider whether your conclusion provides a fresh insight on your topic.

Revising for Evidence and Elaboration

Use Precise Language In order to craft a lively narrative that engages readers, avoid words and language that leave the reader with questions such as *What kind? How? In what way? How often?* and *To what extent?* As you review your draft, identify vague words that do not provide specific answers to questions such as those in the previous sentence. As you revise, replace these vague words with specific, precise words that convey your ideas more vividly and accurately. Here are some examples:

vague noun: *stuff* *use* *souvenirs, gifts, photos*
vague verb: *said* *use* *exclaimed, whispered, declared*
vague adjective: *pretty* *use* *attractive, exquisite, adorable*
vague adverb: *greatly* *use* *enormously, incredibly, remarkably*

Adjust Pacing Read through your draft. If part of your story seems to lag or feel boring, try one of the following: Cut unneeded plot events; put dialogue in place of description; or shorten the sentences so that events seem to happen more rapidly.

HOW LANGUAGE WORKS

Adjectives Reinforce the concept that if two or more adjectives modify the same noun and are separated by a comma, they're coordinate. Students can tell if adjectives are coordinate if the word *and* can be used in place of the comma and the order of the adjectives can be reversed without changing the meaning of the sentence. Cumulative adjectives also modify the same noun, but they aren't separated by a comma, and they can't be reversed without changing the meaning of the sentence.

As students revise their nonfiction narratives, they should check to see if they've used coordinate and cumulative adjectives correctly. First, they should identify if they've used these types of adjectives, looking for sentences in which more than one adjective modifies the same noun. Next, they should determine if the adjectives are coordinate or cumulative and, based on their findings, whether a comma is needed.

If students haven't used coordinate and cumulative adjectives in their writing, encourage them to do so, explaining that it will add richness and variety to their descriptions. If students struggle to generate coordinate and cumulative adjectives, have them brainstorm for new descriptive words to add to existing adjectives or combine descriptions of the same noun that appear in different sentences.

PEER REVIEW

Exchange narratives with a classmate. Use the checklist to evaluate your classmate's narrative, and provide supportive feedback.

1. Is the point of view clear, and are the characters well developed?
   ☐ yes ☐ no If no, suggest how the writer might improve them.
2. Is there a clear sequence of events that unfolds chronologically and is clarified by transitions?
   ☐ yes ☐ no If no, explain what confused you.
3. Does the narrative end with a conclusion that connects to and reflects on the events and experiences presented?
   ☐ yes ☐ no If no, tell what you think might be missing.
4. What is the strongest part of your classmate's narrative? Why?

Editing and Proofreading

Edit for Conventions Reread your draft for accuracy and consistency. Correct errors in grammar and word usage. Be sure you have included a variety of sentence structures and word choices that reflect your unique voice.

Proofread for Accuracy Read your draft carefully, looking for errors in spelling and punctuation. As you proofread, make sure that any **dialogue**—the actual words spoken by a character—is enclosed in quotation marks. A split dialogue is a quotation that is interrupted by the inclusion of additional information, such as the identification of the speaker. Refer to the Launch Text for examples of each type of dialogue.

Publishing and Presenting

Create a final version of your narrative. Share it with a small group so that your classmates can read it and make comments. In turn, review and comment on your classmates' work. As a group, discuss what your narratives have in common and the ways in which they are different.

Reflecting

Reflect on what you learned as you wrote your narrative. In what ways did writing about past experiences and events help to heighten your understanding of them? What was the most challenging aspect of composing your narrative? Did you learn something from reviewing the work of others and discussing your narrative that might inform your narrative writing process in the future?

STANDARDS

Writing

With some guidance and support from peers and adults, develop and strengthen writing as needed by planning, revising, editing, rewriting, or trying a new approach, focusing on how well purpose and audience have been addressed.

PERSONALIZE FOR LEARNING

English Language Support

Subject-Verb Agreement English Learners often struggle with subject-verb agreement when writing. Remind students that the subject and the verb in a sentence need to agree. For example, singular subjects need a singular verb (The boy runs.), and plural subjects need a plural verb (The girls run.). Suggest that students review their narrative for subject-verb agreement as part of their editing process. **ALL LEVELS**

DIGITAL PERSPECTIVES

Peer Review

Remind students before they begin their peer review that they are reviewing for clarity and completeness. Suggest that students note any questions they have as they review their partner's narrative. Students should then revise their narratives to ensure that their message is clearly communicated and does not leave the reader wondering about something that happened in the story.

Editing and Proofreading

As students proofread, they should check for grammar, spelling, and punctuation errors. Remind them that although many software programs catch grammar and spelling mistakes, they are not foolproof. Students should still manually review their work.

Publishing and Presenting

As students read several of their classmates' papers to look for similarities, encourage them to respond to each narrative respectfully. After groups work together, lead a discussion to ask students to share what they learned from each other.

Reflecting

Students should reflect not only on their narrative and process of writing it, but also on the comments received from their peers.

OVERVIEW

SMALL-GROUP LEARNING

What can one generation learn from another?

Explain that it's not just the younger generation that can learn from its elders. Often, especially in today's fast-paced, technology-driven world, younger generations have much to teach their older relatives, friends, and community members. During Small-Group Learning, students will read selections that reveal the ways in which generations interact and learn from one another.

Small-Group Learning Strategies

Review the Learning Strategies with students and explain that as they work through Small-Group Learning they will develop strategies to work in small-group environments.

- Have students watch the video on Small-Group Learning Strategies.
- A video on this topic is available online in the Professional Development Center.

You may wish to discuss some action items to add to the chart as a class before students complete it on their own. For example, for "Support others," you may solicit the following actions from students:

- Ask constructive questions about others' opinions.
- Be patient when others are struggling.

Block Scheduling

Each day in this Pacing Plan represents a 40–50 minute class period. Teachers using block scheduling may combine days to reflect their class schedule. In addition, teachers may revise pacing to differentiate and support core instruction by integrating components and resources as students require.

OVERVIEW: SMALL-GROUP LEARNING

ESSENTIAL QUESTION:

What can one generation learn from another?

What people value can change from one generation to the next, but there are always some common threads despite these differences. You can gain new insight and knowledge when you understand the values and challenges facing other generations. You will work in a group to continue your exploration of the relationship between generations.

Small-Group Learning Strategies

Throughout your life, you'll continue to develop strategies that make you a better learner. In school, in your community, in college, and in your career, you will continue to learn and work in teams.

Look at these strategies and the actions you can take to practice them. Add ideas of your own for each step. Get ready to use these strategies during Small-Group Learning.

STRATEGY	ACTION PLAN
Prepare	• Complete your assignments so that you are prepared for group work. • Organize your thinking so you can contribute to your group's discussions. •
Participate fully	• Make eye contact to signal that you are listening and taking in what is being said. • Use text evidence when making a point. •
Support others	• Build off ideas from others in your group. • Invite others who have not yet spoken to do so. •
Clarify	• Paraphrase the ideas of others to ensure that your understanding is correct. • Ask follow-up questions. •

Pacing Plan

Introduce Whole-Class Learning

Unit Introduction: 1, 2, 3
Two Kinds: 4, 5, 6, 7
A Simple Act: 8, 9, 10, 11
from An Invisible Thread: 12, 13, 14, 15
Performance Task: 16, 17, 18

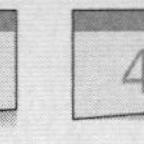

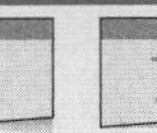

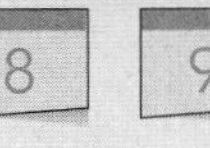

CONTENTS

NEWS ARTICLE

Tutors Teach Seniors New High-Tech Tricks

Jennifer Ludden

It's never too late to learn something new.

▸ MEDIA CONNECTION: Cyber-Seniors

COMPARE

MEMOIR

from Mom & Me & Mom

Maya Angelou

A young girl is reunited with the mother who once abandoned her.

MEDIA: VIDEO

Learning to Love My Mother

Maya Angelou with Michael Maher

Maya Angelou talks about her complicated relationship with her mother.

MEDIA: IMAGE GALLERY

Mother-Daughter Drawings

Mica and Myla Hendricks

An artist collaborates with her four-year-old child.

POETRY COLLECTION 1

Mother to Son

Langston Hughes

To James

Frank Horne

Two parents pass on some hard-earned wisdom.

PERFORMANCE TASK

SPEAKING AND LISTENING FOCUS

Present a Nonfiction Narrative

The Small-Group readings explore the insights that people of different generations share with each other. After reading, your group will plan and deliver a multimedia presentation about a lesson one generation can learn from another.

DIGITAL PERSPECTIVES

Contents

Selections Circulate among the groups as they preview the selections. You might encourage groups to discuss any knowledge they already have about any of the selections or the situations and settings shown in the photographs. Students may wish to take a poll within their group to determine which selections look most interesting.

Remind students that communicating and collaborating in groups is an important skill that they will use throughout their lives—in school, in their careers, and in their community.

Performance Task

Present a Nonfiction Narrative Give groups time to read about and briefly discuss the multimedia presentation they will create after reading. Encourage students to do some preliminary thinking about the types of media they might want to use. This may help focus their subsequent reading and group discussion.

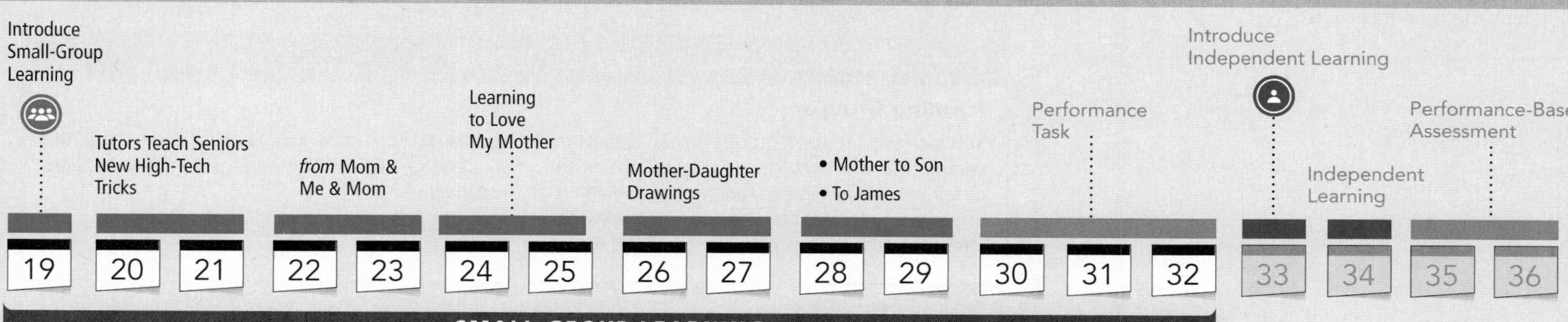

SMALL-GROUP LEARNING

Working as a Team

1. **Discuss the Topic** Remind groups to let all members share their responses. You may wish to set a time limit for this discussion.
2. **List Your Rules** You may want to have groups share their lists of rules and consolidate them into a master list to be displayed and followed by all groups.
3. **Apply the Rules** As you circulate among the groups, ensure that students are staying on task. Consider a short time limit for this step.
4. **Name Your Group** This task can be creative and fun. If students have trouble coming up with a name, suggest that they think of something related to generations. Encourage groups to share their names with the class.
5. **Create a Communication Plan** Encourage groups to agree upon times during the day to share ideas. They should also devise a method for recording and saving their communications.

Accountable Talk

Remind students that groups should communicate politely. You can post these Accountable Talk suggestions and encourage students to add their own. Students should:

Remember to . . .
Ask questions when you are confused.

Which sounds like . . .
Can you say that again?
Can you give me an example?

Remember to . . .
Make connections.

Which sounds like . . .
This reminds me of _____.
How does that relate to the point made by ____?

Remember to . . .
Explain your thinking . . .

Which sounds like . . .
I think this is right because _____.

OVERVIEW: SMALL-GROUP LEARNING

Working as a Team

1. **Discuss the Topic** In your group, discuss the following question:

   What kinds of ideas and experiences can young people and adults share?

   As you take turns sharing your thoughts, be sure to provide examples for your response. After all group members have shared, discuss the similarities and differences among your responses.

2. **List Your Rules** As a group, decide on the rules that you will follow as you work together. Two samples are provided. Add two more of your own. You may add or revise rules based on your experience together.
   - Everyone should participate in group discussions.
   - People should not interrupt.
   - ______________________________
   - ______________________________

3. **Apply the Rules** Before you engage in group discussions or activities, review the rules and adapt them as needed based on your group's experience.

4. **Name Your Group** Choose a name that reflects the unit topic.

   Our group's name: ______________________________

5. **Create a Communication Plan** Decide how you want to communicate with one another. For example, you might use online collaboration tools, email, or instant messaging.

   Our group's decision: ______________________________

FACILITATING SMALL-GROUP LEARNING

Forming Groups

You may wish to form groups for Small-Group Learning so that each consists of students with different abilities. Some students may be adept at organizing information whereas others may have strengths related to generating or synthesizing information. A good mix of abilities can make the experience of Small-Group Learning dynamic and productive.

Making a Schedule

First, find out the due dates for the small-group activities. Then, preview the texts and activities with your group and make a schedule for completing the tasks.

SELECTION	ACTIVITIES	DUE DATE
Tutors Teach Seniors New High-Tech Tricks		
from Mom & Me & Mom Learning to Love My Mother		
Mother-Daughter Drawings		
Mother to Son To James		

Working on Group Projects

Different projects require different roles. As your group works together, you'll find it more effective if each person has a specific role. Before beginning a project, decide among yourselves on each group member's role. Here are some possible roles; add your own ideas.

Project Manager: monitors the schedule and keeps everyone on task

Researcher: organizes research activities

Recorder: takes notes during group meetings

____

____

____

____

____

DIGITAL PERSPECTIVES

Making a Schedule

Encourage groups to preview the reading selections and to consider how long it will take them to complete the activities accompanying each selection. Point out that they can adjust the due dates for particular selections as needed as they work on their small-group projects. However, they must complete all assigned tasks before the group Performance Task is due. Encourage groups to review their schedules upon completing the activities for each selection to make sure they are on track to meet the final due date.

Working on Group Projects

Point out to groups that the roles they assign can also be changed later. Students might have to make changes based on who is best at doing what.

Also, you should review the roles each group assigns to its members. Based on your understanding of students' individual strengths, you might find it necessary to suggest some changes.

AUTHOR'S PERSPECTIVE **Kelly Gallagher, M.Ed.**

Meaningful Talk Instead of asking teacher-directed questions that lead students to see specific elements, give the power back to the students. Help them find their own big ideas and support them by building in talk opportunities. Use these two strategies to help students achieve deeper comprehension.

- **See the Relevance in Reading:** Teachers have students read great works of literature to give students an opportunity to think deeply about issues that will affect their lives. Asking students "What is worth talking about here?" helps them find themes and interpretations and get to the heart of the unit theme.
- **One Question; One Comment Strategy:** To get students to revisit a chapter or passage they find particularly challenging and generate an in-depth discussion of the text, teachers can ask students to come to class with one question and one comment generated from their reading assignment. During the class discussion, have the first student share one comment or question. The next student can answer the question, respond to the comment, or build on the discussion with his or her own question or comment. Continue the process until everyone in class has participated.

Using these strategies will lessen student dependence on the teacher and so help to build independence.

Tutors Teach Seniors New High-Tech Tricks

AUDIO SUMMARIES
Audio summaries of "Tutors Teach Seniors New High-Tech Tricks" are available in both English and Spanish in the Interactive Teacher's Edition or Unit Resources. Assigning these summaries prior to reading the selection may help students build additional background knowledge and set a context for their first read.

Summary

When Pamela Norr, of Bend, Oregon, found herself struggling to help her parents with a tech problem, she asked herself whom she turned to with her own tech difficulties. "My teenage kids," she says. In her news article "Tutors Teach Seniors New High-Tech Tricks," Jennifer Ludden reports that many high school students in Oregon have signed up to help seniors with digital cameras, smartphones, and social networking, and explains how the program promotes mutual respect between generations. Jean Coppola, of Pace University, New York, has set up a similar program. Coppola describes some of the extraordinary things tutors do to improve their understanding of deafness, visual impairment, arthritis, and other conditions that senior citizens have.

Insight

Knowledge isn't always handed down from generation to generation—sometimes it is handed up. Reading "Tutors Teach Seniors New High-Tech Tricks" will help students see that it is not always incumbent on the older generation to teach the younger generation. Reversing the flow of knowledge changes the dynamic between the generations and may result in a narrowing of the generation gap.

ESSENTIAL QUESTION:
What can one generation learn from another?

Connection to Essential Question

"Tutors Teach Seniors New High-Tech Tricks" will help students answer the Essential Question—*What can one generation learn from another?*—by providing the real-world example of teens and young adults teaching senior citizens to participate in the digital world. After closely reading the selection, students should also be able to understand that by engaging with one another in this way, the younger generation can learn a new appreciation for, and empathy with, the older generation.

SMALL-GROUP LEARNING PERFORMANCE TASK
What new knowledge or skills can you learn from someone of a different generation?

UNIT PERFORMANCE-BASED ASSESSMENT
In what situations can one generation learn from another?

Connection to Performance Tasks

Small-Group Learning Performance Task In this Performance Task, students will present a nonfiction narrative about what knowledge or skills they can learn from someone of a different generation. "Tutors Teach Seniors New High-Tech Tricks" offers students two presentation topic perspectives: the tech lessons that the elderly learned from their young tutors, and the newfound empathy that the young tutors learned from teaching the elderly.

Unit Performance-Based Assessment This selection provides students with practical examples of lessons shared between two generations, such as how to send an email or how to create a Facebook account. It also provides more abstract insights, such as how it feels to have age-related physical limitations. Students may refer to these examples in their narratives.

DIGITAL PERSPECTIVES

 Audio  Video 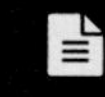 Document  Annotation Highlights 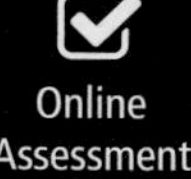 Online Assessment

LESSON RESOURCES

	Making Meaning	Language Development	Effective Expression
Lesson	**First Read** **Close Read** **Analyze the Text** **Analyze Craft and Structure**	**Conventions** **Concept Vocabulary** **Word Study**	**Speaking and Listening**
Instructional Standards	**RI.7.10** By the end of the year, read and comprehend literary nonfiction . . . **L.7.4** Determine or clarify the meaning of unknown and multiple-meaning words and phrases . . . **L.7.4.a** Use context as a clue . . . **RI.7.1** Cite several pieces of textual evidence to support . . . **RI.7.2** Determine two or more central ideas . . .	**L.7.4** Determine or clarify the meaning of unknown and multiple-meaning words and phrases . . . **L.7.4.c** Consult general and specialized reference materials . . . **L.7.1** Demonstrate command of the conventions of standard English . . . **L.7.3.a** Choose language that expresses ideas precisely . . .	**SL.7.1** Engage effectively in a range of collaborative discussions . . . **SL.7.4** Present claims and findings, emphasizing salient points . . . **SL.7.5** Include multimedia components and visual displays in presentations . . . **W.7.7** Conduct short research projects . . .
STUDENT RESOURCES			
Available online in the Interactive Student Edition or Unit Resources	Selection Audio First-Read Guide: Nonfiction Close-Read Guide: Nonfiction	Word Network	Evidence Log
TEACHER RESOURCES			
Selection Resources Available online in the Interactive Teacher's Edition or Unit Resources	Audio Summaries: English and Spanish Annotation Highlights Accessible Leveled Text Text Questions First Read Extension Questions Analyze Craft and Structure: Central Ideas	Conventions: Conjunctions Concept Vocabulary and Word Study	Speaking and Listening: Multimedia Presentation
Reteach/Practice (RP) Available online in the Interactive Teacher's Edition or Unit Resources	Analyze Craft and Structure: Central Ideas (RP)	Conventions: Conjunctions (RP) Word Study: Suffix *-ment* (RP)	Speaking and Listening: Multimedia Presentation (RP)
Assessment Available online in Assessments	Selection Test: English Selection Test: Spanish Extension Selection Test		
My Resources	A Unit 1 Answer Key is available online and in the Interactive Teacher's Edition		

Reading Support

Text Complexity Rubric: Tutors Teach Seniors New High-Tech Tricks	
Quantitative Measures	
Lexile: 1020 **Text Length:** 668 words	
Qualitative Measures	
Knowledge Demands ① ② **❸** ④ ⑤	Text relies on practical knowledge and is based on situation students may be able to relate to (older people having trouble with technology).
Structure ① **❷** ③ ④ ⑤	Text is organized logically and broken up with subheadings and quotations that make it easy to follow ideas.
Language Conventionality and Clarity ① ② **❸** ④ ⑤	Text contains explicit, literal language, familiar vocabulary; some sentences are lengthy but with familiar syntax; selection contains some idioms and figurative language.
Levels of Meaning/Purpose ① ② **❸** ④ ⑤	Selection has explicitly stated concepts with only one level of meaning; some of the supporting details are not explicitly explained (section on sensitivity training).

DECIDE AND PLAN

English Language Support

Provide English Learners with support for language and meaning as they read the selection.

Language Ask students to highlight figurative phrases in the selection. Discuss each one, drawing from students' experience: *usher older adults into the digital age* (paragraph 1); discuss *ushers* in the theater who *usher,* or guide, people to their seats; *the light bulb went off* paragraph 2)—discuss that the light bulb is a symbol for an idea.

Meaning Make sure students understand the sensitivity training described in the selection. Have students read and list the methods mentioned (wearing special glasses, taping two fingers together, wearing cotton balls in ears). Discuss each one before having them reread the paragraph.

Strategic Support

Provide students with strategic support to ensure that they can successfully read the text.

Knowledge Demands Use the background information to begin discussion about the use of technology by seniors. Discuss the experience students have had with grandparents or other older people who are not as comfortable with technology.

Meaning As students read, have them summarize key points by listing ideas from each section. If students have trouble doing this, suggest specific tasks, for example listing three methods of sensitivity training cited in paragraphs 12–17. Discuss each method. Then have students reread those paragraphs to think about the methods in context.

Challenge

Provide students who need to be challenged with ideas for how they can go beyond a simple interpretation of the text.

Text Analysis Discuss the section on sensitivity training. Ask students to describe or write about why sensitivity training is important and effective. Encourage them to use details from the selection about the different methods of sensitivity training.

Written Response Ask students to use a computer to go to a typical website they use. Then have them write a short analysis of what aspects of the site might pose difficulties for an elderly person. For example, how easy is it to navigate and find information? Are there many distractions? Would the text size have to be increased?

TEACH

Read and Respond

Have groups read the selection and complete the Making Meaning, Language Development, and Effective Expression activities.

Standards Support Through Teaching and Learning Cycle

IDENTIFY NEEDS

Analyze results of the Beginning-of-Year Assessment, focusing on the items relating to Unit 1. Also take into consideration student performance to this point and your observations of where particular students struggle.

DECIDE AND PLAN

- If students have performed poorly on items matching these standards, then provide selection scaffolds before assigning them the on-level lesson provided in the Student Edition.
- If students have done well on the Beginning-of-Year Assessment, then challenge them to keep progressing and learning by giving them opportunities to practice the skills in depth.
- Use the Selection Resources listed on the Planning pages for "Tutors Teach Seniors New High-Tech Tricks" to help students continually improve their ability to master the standards.

Instructional Standards: Tutors Teach Seniors New High-Tech Tricks

	Catching Up	This Year	Looking Forward
Reading	You may wish to administer the **Analyze Craft and Structure: Central Ideas (RP)** worksheet to help students understand how to identify the central idea of a text.	**RI.2** Determine two or more central ideas in a text and analyze their development over the course of the text; provide an objective summary of the text.	Working in small groups, challenge students to identify two or more ideas in the selection related to the concept of "changing perspectives." Students and group members should identify details in the text that support each idea.
Speaking and Listening	You may wish to administer the **Speaking and Listening: Multimedia Presentation (RP)** worksheet to help students understand that visuals and/or multimedia components enhance and clarify oral explanations or reports.	**SL.5** Include multimedia components and visual displays in presentations to clarify claims and findings and emphasize salient points.	Have students choose a selection from the unit and explain how they would enhance an oral summary of the selection by including visuals and/or multimedia components in the presentation. Also challenge students to name the visuals or multimedia components they would include, and why.
Language	You may wish to administer the **Conventions: Conjunctions (RP)** worksheet to help students understand how authors use conjunctions to combine related ideas into one sentence.	**L.1** Demonstrate command of conventions of standard English grammar and usage when writing or speaking.	Encourage students to find sentences that include conjunctions in this selection. Using those sentences as models, have students say a sentence of their own that expresses something (or some things) they liked about the selection and includes a conjunction.

TEACH

Implement the planned lesson, and gather evidence of student learning.

ANALYZE AND REVISE

- Analyze student work for evidence of student learning.
- Identify whether students have met the expectations in the standards.
- Identify implications for future instruction.

FACILITATING

Jump Start

FIRST READ Ask students to imagine themselves transformed into senior citizens. Have them imagine how their needs and abilities during that life stage might affect their capacity for learning new skills.

Groups should discuss strategies for teaching seniors and identify activities that might present difficulties for people in that age group.

Tutors Teach Seniors New High-Tech Tricks

What are some challenges seniors face in their daily lives? Why might seniors find new technology difficult to use and even reject it? Modeling questions such as these will help students connect to "Tutors Teach Seniors New High-Tech Tricks" and to the Small-Group Performance Task assignment. Selection audio and print capability for the selection are available in the Interactive Teacher's Edition.

Concept Vocabulary

Encourage groups to discuss the three concept vocabulary words and share their familiarity or knowledge of each one. Then, ask groups to study the modeling of context clues. Encourage students to discuss words surrounding the unknown word that help them clarify meaning, especially when the unknown words have multiple meanings, including one that is a technical meaning.

FIRST READ

Have students perform the steps of the first read independently:

NOTICE: Encourage students to notice what prompts people in the selection to come together, as well as what happens for individuals as a result of those meetings.

ANNOTATE: Remind students to focus on passages of key importance or of particular interest.

CONNECT: Encourage students to make connections between ideas in the selection and ideas they may have encountered in their own reading or in their own lives.

RESPOND: Students will answer questions and write a summary to demonstrate their understanding.

Point out to students that while they will always complete the Respond step at the end of the first read, the other steps will probably happen somewhat concurrently. You may wish to print copies of the **First-Read Guide: Nonfiction** for students to use.

MAKING MEANING

About the Author

Jennifer Ludden (b. 1967) is a correspondent for National Public Radio (NPR). Ludden has won and shared in several awards for her work as a foreign reporter covering the Middle East, Europe, and West and Central Africa. She graduated from Syracuse University in 1988.

Tutors Teach Seniors New High-Tech Tricks

Concept Vocabulary

You will encounter the following words as you read "Tutors Teach Seniors New High-Tech Tricks."

struggling	impairments	frustrated

Context Clues To find the meaning of unfamiliar words, look for clues in the context, which is made up of the surrounding words and phrases.

Example: To edit the photo on her laptop, Sigrid had to **download** a new program.

Context clue: To get a new program on your computer, you need to **download** it.

Possible meaning: To **download** means "to transfer data to your computer."

Example: My computer is infected with a nasty **worm**.

Context clues: The word *nasty* means "unpleasant," and it describes the worm that has *infected a computer*.

Possible meaning: A **worm** means "a computer bug" or "problem."

Apply your knowledge of context clues and other vocabulary strategies to determine the meanings of unfamiliar words you encounter during your first read.

First Read NONFICTION

Apply these strategies as you conduct your first read. You will have an opportunity to complete a close read after your first read.

NOTICE the general ideas of the text. *What* is it about? *Who* is it about?

ANNOTATE by marking vocabulary and key passages you want to revisit.

CONNECT ideas within the selection to what you already know and what you have already read.

RESPOND by completing the Comprehension Check and by writing a brief summary of the selection.

STANDARDS

Reading Informational Text
By the end of the year, read and comprehend literary nonfiction in the grades 6–8 text complexity band proficiently, with scaffolding as needed at the high end of the range.

Language
Determine or clarify the meaning of unknown and multiple-meaning words and phrases based on *grade 7 reading and content*, choosing flexibly from a range of strategies.

a. Use context as a clue to the meaning of a word or phrase.

AUTHOR'S PERSPECTIVE **Jim Cummins, Ph.D.**

Literacy Engagement Academic language is found primarily in printed text rather than in everyday conversation. Thus, when students have abundant access to printed texts and engage actively with these texts, they have far greater opportunities to broaden their vocabulary knowledge and develop strong reading comprehension skills. Students' engagement will be enhanced when they discuss in small groups the texts they have read in *myPerspectives* as well as other selections of their choice. Teachers can help make texts more meaningful to students in the following ways:

- **Scaffold Meaning:** Visuals such as illustrations and graphic organizers in the text enhance students' understanding. Students who are learning English can also use electronic translators and bilingual dictionaries to gain access to the meaning of words or phrases.

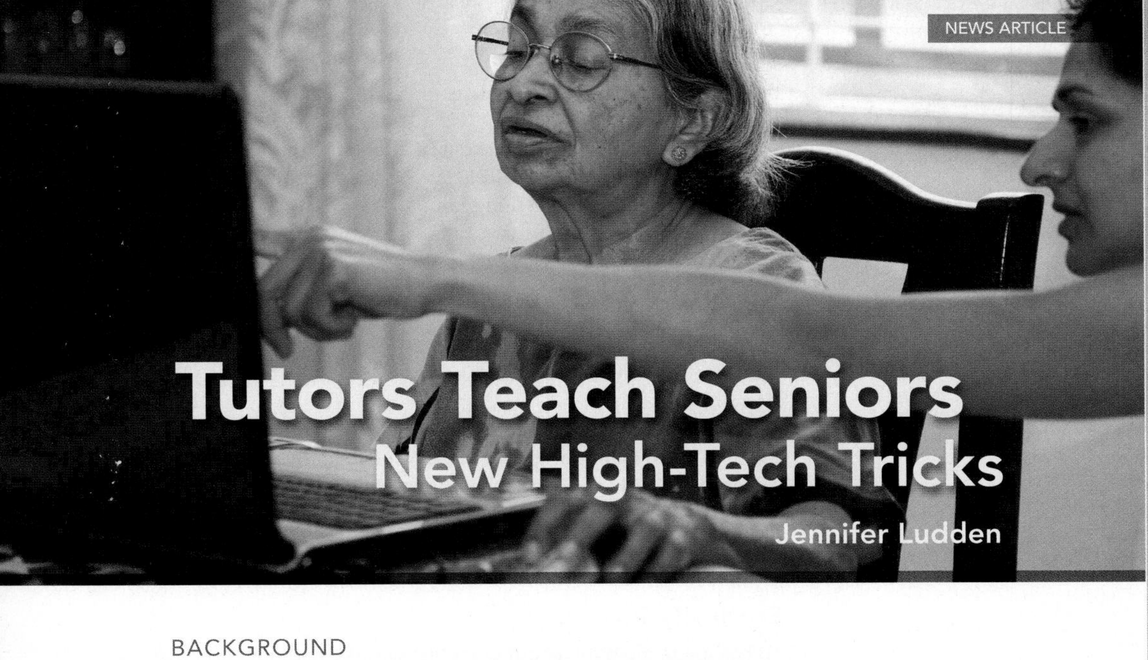

Tutors Teach Seniors New High-Tech Tricks

Jennifer Ludden

DIGITAL PERSPECTIVES 

BACKGROUND

Modern technology allows us to easily connect with one another. People can instantaneously share photographs and have face-to-face conversations with friends and family both down the street and on the other side of the world. However, technology changes so quickly that senior citizens are often left behind.

1 A week after Christmas, many Americans are no doubt trying to figure out how to use the high-tech gadgets they got as gifts. This can be especially challenging for seniors. But a number of programs across the country are finding just the right experts to help usher older adults into the digital age.

2 For Pamela Norr, of Bend, Ore., the light bulb went off as she, yet again, was trying to help her own elder parents with a tech problem. To whom did she turn?

3 "My teenage kids," she says.

4 Norr happens to head the Central Oregon Council on Aging, and thus was born TECH—Teenager Elder Computer Help.

5 "I thought if my parents need it, probably other seniors need it, too," she says.

6 High school students studying computer tech or involved with the National Honor Society sign up to teach local senior citizens about Facebook, Skype, smartphones, even something as seemingly simple as a camera. Norr discovered that many seniors had been given digital cameras by their children.

7 "They were going around town taking all these great pictures that they wanted to send to their family members," she says. But

NOTES

CLOSER LOOK

Analyze Author's Tone

Circulate among groups as students conduct their close read. Suggest that groups close read paragraphs 2–5. Encourage them to talk about the annotations that they mark. If needed, provide the following support.

ANNOTATE: Have students mark details in these paragraphs that demonstrate the way the author seems to feel about her subject or work with small groups to have students participate while you highlight them together.

QUESTION: Guide students to consider what these details might tell them. Ask what a reader can infer from what was annotated, and accept student responses.

Possible response: The author is warm and friendly toward her readers and determined to make a potentially difficult subject as easy as possible. She adopts a chatty, personal tone as she tells Pamela Norr's story.

CONCLUDE: Help students to formulate conclusions about the importance of these details in the text. Ask students why the author might have included these details.

Possible response: The author personalizes the problem that she is addressing, so that in these paragraphs we are reading "Pamela Norr's story." Phrases like "the light bulb went off," and "yet again" involve the reader with Norr. By including such details, the author is helping readers relate to Norr's problem. It is probable that most of her readers know seniors with these problems, or are themselves seniors.

Remind students that the **author's tone** is the writer's attitude toward the subject and the readers. In informative text, a good author addresses readers in a tone that helps them to understand the subject.

- **Connect to Students' Lives:** It is important to activate students' pre-existing knowledge so that they can relate new information to what they already know. English Learners can use their first language as a resource to help them extend their English academic skills (e.g., by brainstorming in groups, writing in their first language as a stepping stone to writing in English, and carrying out Internet research in their first language).
- **Extend Language:** Teachers can extend students' academic language skills by consistently and explicitly drawing attention to new words, unusual syntax, and other textual features that are not found in everyday conversation.

FACILITATING

Concept Vocabulary

Struggling If groups are having difficulty trying to define *struggling* in paragraph 8, point out how surrounding words or phrases refer to Sigrid Scully's attempts to stay connected with family. These include "not returning calls" and "don't write letters." These details should lead students to infer that *struggling* means "trying hard and having difficulty doing something."
Possible response: *Struggling* must mean "making attempts to do something."

Impairments If groups are having difficulty trying to define *impairment* in paragraph 15, point out that the paragraph includes a quotation about students who "get to feel what it's like to be 70, 80, 90 years old" and who wear specially prepared glasses. These details should lead students to infer that *impairments* are specific physical problems or limitations.
Possible responses: *Impairments* must mean "specific physical weaknesses."

Concept Vocabulary

Frustrated If groups are struggling to define *frustrated* in paragraph 16, point out how the paragraph includes discussion of students taping fingers together to understand what it feels like to have arthritis or other physical limitations. As a result, students are *not* frustrated when they go to work with the elderly. These details should lead students to infer that *frustrated* means "irritated."
Possible responses: *Frustrated* must mean "bothered or irritated."

NOTES

Mark context clues or indicate another strategy you used that helped you determine meaning.

struggling (STRUHG lihng) *v.*

MEANING:

Mark context clues or indicate another strategy you used that helped you determine meaning.

impairments (ihm PAIR muhnts) *n.*

MEANING:

Mark context clues or indicate another strategy you used that helped you determine meaning.

frustrated (FRUHS trayt ehd) *adj.*

MEANING:

they "couldn't figure out how to connect to the USB port[1] or take out the SIM card.[2]"

8 Many elders have moved to central Oregon to retire. Sigrid Scully, 84, signed up for a TECH class because she was **struggling** to stay connected with far-flung family.

9 "My kids were not returning calls," she says. "They don't write letters. They are so knowledgeable about texting and email, and so I needed to get to know how to do that."

10 Scully worried she'd never catch on. She'd read a computer manual once, but didn't understand words like "icon" or "cookies." She says her teen tutor was personable and used plain language.

11 "So many teenagers think that seniors are just old people that don't know anything," she says. "And actually, the camaraderie and knowledge that we can transmit to one another is so wonderful and so helpful. I had that feeling with this class."

Sensitivity Training

12 "It has made me think about what life was like without Facebook and the Internet," says 15-year-old Tucker Rampton, who's helped train about a dozen Oregon seniors. He's been surprised to have to explain email, something he thought everyone had mastered. Then again, a lot of seniors ask him about Twitter, which Rampton admits he knows nothing about. He says teaching tech to seniors has changed his perspective.

13 "I think it's a very good idea to work on your patience," he says, "and be more understanding when it comes to what's going on in their minds."

14 At Pace University in New York, college students who tutor seniors in local retirement homes are prepped with sensitivity training.

15 "They get to feel what it's like to be 70, 80, 90 years old," says associate professor Jean Coppola, who directs the program. "They wear specially prepared glasses that give them different visual **impairments**."

16 Coppola also has students do things like tape two fingers together—to simulate the effects of arthritis or a stroke—then try to navigate a mouse. By the time they're at the computer with an elder, she says, they're not **frustrated** at all.

17 "They'll say something a hundred times because they've worn cotton balls or earplugs in their ear," she says. "They understand that they have to speak up, articulate their words."

1. **USB port** *n.* computer hardware for connecting other devices to computers.
2. **SIM card** *n.* smart card used in cell phones to store identification information.

DIGITAL PERSPECTIVES

Illuminating the Text Have students find a video on the Internet that demonstrates clearly and reliably how to make a USB connection to operate a camera through a computer. Have them take notes throughout the demonstration. Students should use those notes to create three key concepts that they believe will enable seniors to form a practical understanding of this example of modern technology. Have students explain their concepts to their groups and discuss them with fellow group members. **(Research to Clarify)**

18 Coppola says the whole thing is a bonding experience for both generations. Applause often breaks out the first time a senior receives an email. Some have been able to see new grandchildren for the first time through emailed photos.

19 Pamela Norr, in Oregon, says young trainers also gain new confidence. They see that the seniors are "not criticizing me for the way I dress," she says, "or clucking their tongue. They're actually respecting me for the knowledge base that I have."

20 Perhaps most unexpected, some teen trainers and seniors have even become friends. They keep in touch long after class ends—through Facebook, of course. ❧

NOTES

MEDIA CONNECTION

Cyber-Seniors

Discuss It What benefits do young people get when they teach seniors about technology and the Internet?

Write your response before sharing your ideas.

Comprehension Check

Notebook **Complete the following items after you finish your first read. Review and clarify details with your group.**

1. What situation led Pamela Norr to start TECH—Teenager Elder Computer Help?
2. What kinds of things do seniors want to do with computers and other tech devices?
3. In the Pace University program, how did teenagers experience what it is like to be an older person?
4. Write a summary of the selection that answers *Who, What, Where, When, Why,* and *How?*

RESEARCH

Research to Clarify Briefly research at least one unfamiliar detail from the selection. In what way does the information shed light on an aspect of the article?

PERSONALIZE FOR LEARNING

Strategic Support

Order of Events To help students organize events sequentially, have pairs of students work together. One student can interview the other, asking about a few important facts in this nonfiction narrative. For example, they might ask what happened first, next, and so on. The interviewer should take notes. Then, using these notes, students can build a timeline that contains the basic information about the narrative, organizing the events sequentially.

DIGITAL PERSPECTIVES

EXTENSION QUESTIONS

The Comprehension Check tests students' comprehension of the reading. If your students would benefit from more rigorous critical-thinking questions, assign the **First Read Extension Questions**, found on Realize.

Comprehension Check

Possible responses:

1. Norr turned to her teenage children for help with her own computer problems.
2. Seniors want to be able to use email and social media and operate smartphones and other electronic devices.
3. They could take photos but could not send them electronically.
4. Teenagers used various devices to simulate sensory and physical impairments.

Possible responses for summary:

Who: Pamela Norr, Head of the Council on Aging; Sigrid Scully, senior; Tucker Rampton, teen; Jean Coppola, Professor; and many other teens and seniors

What: TECH (Teenager Elder Computer Help) and other programs have teens helping seniors solve computer problem

Where: Central Oregon; New York

When: Ongoing

Why: Seniors are often confused by modern technology and require help.
Teens are often technologically adept and require no special training to help seniors.

How: Teens meet with seniors and find hands-on, on-site solutions to their problems with technology.

Research

Research to Clarify
If groups struggle to come up with a research topic, you may want to suggest that they focus on one of the following topics: How does Skype work? What does USB stand for, and what does it enable? What function does a SIM card perform in a smartphone?

Research to Explore
If groups struggle to come up with a research topic, you may want to suggest that they focus on one of the following topics: a new texting app or a social media platform, such as Facebook or Twitter.

FACILITATING

Jump Start

CLOSE READ Ask students to think about how technology has changed in their lifetime. What were cell phones like when they were younger? How do they think the Internet has changed?

As students discuss these questions in their groups, ask them to project into the future. What new technologies do they think might be available in 20 years? 50 years?

Close Read the Text

If needed, model close reading by using the Annotation Highlights in the Interactive Teacher's Edition. Remind groups to use Accountable Talk in their discussions and to support one another as they complete the close read.

Analyze the Text

1. **Responses will vary by group.** Students should note that Tucker was forced to think about life before the Internet, which helped him to be more patient and understanding.
2. **Passages will vary by group.** Remind students to explain why they chose the passage they presented to group members.
3. **Responses will vary by group.**

Concept Vocabulary

Why These Words? The words are associated with feelings and issues one might need to overcome when learning something new. Another word that fits the category is *problems*.

Practice

Possible responses:

- The children were struggling to finish a timed quiz online.
- She overcame hearing impairments with a hearing aid.
- The man grew frustrated when he could not send photos electronically.

Word Network

Possible words: *seniors, elders, teenagers*

Word Study

Possible responses:

advertisement: an announcement that calls attention to something; *amusement:* something that amuses; *settlement:* a place where people have settled. In each case, *-ment* creates the noun form. For more support, see **Concept Vocabulary and Word Study.**

MAKING MEANING

TUTORS TEACH SENIORS NEW HIGH-TECH TRICKS

Close Read the Text

With your group, revisit sections of the text you marked during your first read. **Annotate** details that you notice. What **questions** do you have? What can you **conclude**?

Analyze the Text

CITE TEXTUAL EVIDENCE to support your answers.

Notebook Complete the activities.

1. **Review and Clarify** With your group, reread paragraphs 12–13 of the selection. Discuss how helping seniors with tech problems has changed the perspective of Tucker Rampton. In what way has reading this selection changed your own perspective?
2. **Present and Discuss** Share with your group the passages from the selection that you found especially important. Take turns presenting your passages. Discuss what you noticed in the selection, what questions you asked, and what conclusions you reached.
3. **Essential Question: *What can one generation learn from another?*** What has this article taught you about how different generations can learn from one another? Discuss with your group.

TIP

GROUP DISCUSSION
If you do not fully understand a classmate's comment, don't hesitate to ask for clarification. Use a friendly and respectful tone when you ask.

WORD NETWORK
Look in the text for words related to the topic of generations, and add them to your Word Network.

STANDARDS

Reading Informational Text
- Cite several pieces of textual evidence to support analysis of what the text says explicitly as well as inferences drawn from the text.
- Determine two or more central ideas in a text and analyze their development over the course of the text; provide an objective summary of the text.

Language
Determine or clarify the meaning of unknown and multiple-meaning words and phrases based on *grade 7 reading and content*, choosing flexibly from a range of strategies.
c. Consult general and specialized reference materials, both print and digital, to find the pronunciation of a word or determine or clarify its precise meaning or its part of speech.

LANGUAGE DEVELOPMENT

Concept Vocabulary

struggling	impairments	frustrated

Why These Words? The concept vocabulary words from the text are related. With your group, determine what the words have in common. Write your ideas and add another word that fits the category.

Practice

Notebook Confirm your understanding of the concept vocabulary words by using each word in a sentence that demonstrates your understanding of the word.

Word Study

Notebook **Suffix: *-ment*** The suffix *-ment* means "the result of an action." When added to a verb (the action), the suffix creates a noun. Use a dictionary to find the meaning of the following words that contain the suffix *-ment: advertisement, amusement, settlement.* Explain how the suffix *-ment* contributes to the meaning of each word.

FORMATIVE ASSESSMENT

Analyze the Text

If students struggle to close read the text, **then** provide the **Tutors Teach Seniors New High-Tech Tricks: Text Questions** available online in the Interactive Teacher's Edition or Unit Resources. Answers and DOK levels are also available.

Concept Vocabulary

If students struggle to identify the concept, **then** have them look online for the meanings of these words.

Word Study

If students fail to identify other words that end in *-ment*, **then** have them review verbs such as *encourage* that turn into nouns with the ending. For Reteach and Practice, see **Word Study: Suffix *-ment* (RP).**

Analyze Craft and Structure

Development of Central Ideas The **central idea,** or **main idea,** is the most important point in a text. Sometimes the writer directly states the central idea of a text. More often, the central idea is unstated, or implied. When a central idea is implied, readers must **make inferences,** or educated guesses, from the details included in the text in order to determine the central idea.

When you read nonfiction, adjust your reading rate to help you recognize the central idea.

- **Skim,** or look over the text quickly, to get a sense of important ideas before you begin reading.
- **Read closely** to learn what the central ideas are.
- **Scan,** or run your eyes over the text, to find answers to questions, to clarify, or to find supporting details.

Practice

CITE TEXTUAL EVIDENCE to support your answers.

Notebook Respond to these questions.

1. What details does the article provide to support the central idea that teens are well-suited to help seniors with technology?
2. (a) Complete the chart below to help you analyze the development of central ideas in the article. Identify the needs of each group, what group members provided for each other, and how they benefited from each other.

	WHAT THEY NEED	WHAT THEY PROVIDE	HOW GROUP BENEFITS
Seniors	Seniors have difficulty with high-tech gadgets.	Seniors give respect to their teen teachers.	Seniors master new technology skills.
Teens	Teens need appreciation and approval.	Teens share technology expertise.	Teens gain confidence.

   (b) Review your chart entries. How well do the needs of each group match what the other group is able to provide? Explain.

3. How does the author's use of quotations from program participants contribute to the development of central ideas?
4. At the end of the article, the author describes how seniors and teens continue to maintain their friendships through Facebook. In what way does this detail connect with the central idea of the text?

Analyze Craft and Structure

Development of Central Ideas Explain to students that although authors often put their central ideas at the beginning of articles, they sometimes don't reveal the central ideas until the conclusion. For more support, see **Analyze Craft and Structure: Central Ideas.**

Practice

Possible responses:

1. The article indicates that teens are frequent users of social media and the Internet. Some are studying computer science and many understand technology that is confusing to seniors.
2. a. See possible responses in the chart on the student page.
   b. The seniors lack technical expertise, and the teens don't feel like they get the respect they deserve. Their needs match up well because the tech tutoring gives each group what it needs.
3. The quotations make the participants immediate, real, and convincing. Hearing actual people speak helps illustrate the central ideas and gives the ideas more weight.
4. This detail connects with the central idea that seniors and teens can develop bonds when teens teach seniors new skills. The Facebook friendships are examples of those bonds.

PERSONALIZE FOR LEARNING

English Language Support

Central Ideas Present students with a short informational text that includes text features and photographs. Have students list three sources of information or three features that can help them find the central idea. Then ask them to discuss how this information affects their reading of the text. **EMERGING**

Have students read a brief informational text and ask them to write a few sentences summarizing it and stating the central idea. Have students discuss how summarizing the text helps them focus on the most important information. **EXPANDING**

Have students read a brief informational text and ask them to write a paragraph stating the central idea and three details that support it. Ask students to have a small group discussion about how they located the central idea. **BRIDGING**

An expanded **English Language Support Lesson** on Development of Central Ideas is available in the Interactive Teacher's Edition. 

FORMATIVE ASSESSMENT

Analyze Craft and Structure

If students struggle to identify the central idea, **then** have them reread the article with one question in mind, *What is the author's main point, or argument?* For Reteach and Practice, see **Analyze Craft and Structure: Central Ideas (RP).**

FACILITATING

Conventions

Conjunctions Use the chart to remind students how conjunctions operate. As you assist them in reviewing conjunctions, ask for their help with constructing sentences that illustrate how coordinating and subordinating conjunctions work. Use these sentences to model the difference between each type of conjunction.

Emily likes fruit, *so* she bought an apple at the market. (coordinating)

Caleb went to the park *before* Ella got home from school. (subordinating)

For more support, see **Conventions: Conjunctions.**

Read It

1. because—subordinating
2. or—coordinating

Write It

Possible responses:

1. When Edward's tech class ended, he enrolled in additional computer classes.
2. Marsha mumbled, but Steve understood every word she said.

FORMATIVE ASSESSMENT

Conventions

If students fail to identify coordinating and subordinating conjunctions, **then** help them review the definitions of each type of conjunction and practice using the conjunctions in sentences. Later, work to identify the functions of each word. For Reteach and Practice, see **Conventions: Conjunctions (RP).** 

LANGUAGE DEVELOPMENT

TUTORS TEACH SENIORS NEW HIGH-TECH TRICKS

Conventions

Conjunctions connect parts of a sentence. Coordinating and subordinating conjunctions both clarify relationships between ideas. **Coordinating conjunctions** connect words, phrases, and clauses of equal importance. **Subordinating conjunctions** connect a less important clause to a more important clause.

TYPE OF CONJUNCTION	CONJUNCTIONS	EXAMPLES
coordinating	*and, but, for, nor, or, so, yet*	**Original:** Tommy was tired. He watched the movie anyway. **Revised:** *Tommy was tired but watched the movie anyway.*
subordinating	*after, although, as, as if, as long as, because, before, even though, how, if, in order that, since, so that, than, that, though, till, unless, until, when, whenever, where, whereas, wherever, whether, while, why*	**Original:** Gabby made her bed. It was evening. **Revised:** *Gabby made her bed even though it was evening.*

Read It

Identify the conjunction in each sentence. Label each conjunction as coordinating or subordinating.

1. Sigrid joined the program because she had no idea how to send email.
2. Today, Omar will teach seniors how to email or how to use a digital camera.

Write It

Notebook Sometimes, too many short sentences in a row can seem choppy and unclear. Using conjunctions can create a smoother writing style. To fix short and choppy sentences, rewrite them by following these steps. First, identify whether the ideas in the sentences are of equal importance or unequal importance. Then, combine the sentences using either coordinating or subordinating conjunctions. Look at the example, and then revise the sentences provided.

EXAMPLE

Original: Pamela couldn't download an app. She asked her teenaged son for help.

Revised: *Pamela couldn't download an app until she asked her teenaged son for help.*

1. Edward's tech class ended. He enrolled in additional computer classes.
2. Marsha mumbled. Steve understood every word she said.

STANDARDS

Language

- Demonstrate command of the conventions of standard English grammar and usage when writing or speaking.
- Use knowledge of language and its conventions when writing, speaking, reading, or listening.
  a. Choose language that expresses ideas precisely and concisely, recognizing and eliminating wordiness and redundancy.

PERSONALIZE FOR LEARNING

English Language Support

Cognates Many academic vocabulary words have Spanish cognates. Use the following cognates to help students whose first language is Spanish.

conjunction – conjunción
subordinating conjunction – conjunción subordinada (*because = porque, since = pues que, as, since = como*)

coordinating conjunction – conjunción de coordinación (*and = y, and = e, neither/nor = ni*)

ALL LEVELS

EFFECTIVE EXPRESSION

Speaking and Listening

Assignment

Work with your group to create a **multimedia presentation** in which you incorporate text, charts, images, videos, music, or other media that help you to convey your ideas effectively. Choose from the following topics:

- ☐ an **instructional brochure** in which you explain to seniors how to use a technology application
- ☐ a **program proposal** in which you present an idea for a program that would connect teens and seniors in new ways

Project Plan Make a list of tasks that your group will need to carry out. Assign individual group members to carry out each task. Determine how you will obtain or create multimedia items for your presentation. Use this chart to organize your plans.

TASK	WHO	QUESTIONS TO ANSWER

Organize and Practice Organize your project plan by making a script that includes speakers' lines and indicates media cues. Then, practice your presentation before you present it to your class. Use the following techniques:

- Record each speaker and then play the recording to ensure all are speaking clearly and with adequate volume.
- Work on transitions between speakers and various media to ensure the presentation flows smoothly.
- Time your presentation to ensure that it is paced appropriately. Slow down when necessary so that your audience can understand what you are saying.

Present and Evaluate Present your work to the class, and invite questions when you are finished. Listen to the presentations of other groups, and ask questions if anything is unclear. Note presentation techniques and creative ideas in other groups' presentations that you found interesting.

EVIDENCE LOG

Before moving on to a new selection, go to your log and record what you learned from "Tutors Teach Seniors New High-Tech Tricks."

STANDARDS

Speaking and Listening

• Engage effectively in a range of collaborative discussions with diverse partners on *grade 7 topics, texts, and issues,* building on others' ideas and expressing their own clearly.

b. Follow rules for collegial discussions, track progress toward specific goals and deadlines, and define individual roles as needed.

c. Pose questions that elicit elaboration and respond to others' questions and comments with relevant observations and ideas that bring the discussion back on topic as needed.

d. Acknowledge new information expressed by others and, when warranted, modify their own views.

• Present claims and findings, emphasizing salient points in a focused, coherent manner with pertinent descriptions, facts, details, and examples; use appropriate eye contact, adequate volume, and clear pronunciation.

• Include multimedia components and visual displays in presentations to clarify claims and findings and emphasize salient points.

Writing

Conduct short research projects to answer a question, drawing on several sources and generating additional related, focused questions for further research and investigation.

DIGITAL PERSPECTIVES

Speaking and Listening

Students may struggle to select which modes of media to include in their presentation. Have group members discuss their greatest strengths, as a group and as individuals. Encourage them to decide which option allows them to demonstrate their greatest strengths best. If, for example, the group represents a broad range of musical interests and contains at least one proficient musician, members might use text and music in a program proposal. If members know how to use video editing software and have access to a camera or phone with video capabilities, they might decide to make a short film.

Project Plan Remind groups to make sure everyone is assigned a specific task as they create their Project Plan. Check the Project Plan to ensure that each group member bears a responsibility for the group's progress and has the resources and support to fulfill that responsibility.

Organize and Practice The bullet points in this section will help students/groups organize their presentations and think through the essential ingredients of an effective presentation. Encourage groups to practice in front of mirrors or to film their rehearsals so they can see how their presentation flows.

Present and Evaluate After each group presents, discuss how each presentation addressed the topic.

For more support, see **Speaking and Listening: Multimedia Presentation.**

Evidence Log Support students in completing their Evidence Log. This paced activity will help prepare them for the Performance-Based Assessment at the end of the unit.

WriteNow Express and Reflect

Description Prompt students to brainstorm for ideas to help them get started with their multimedia presentation. Ask students questions such as: *What will be the theme? What will be the aim of the presentation? What resources will you use?* Have students develop a one-page plan explaining their goals and objectives and the actions they will take to achieve them.

Remind students that people learn in all kinds of ways, and that's why they should aim to create a project that everybody will have good reasons to enjoy.

FORMATIVE ASSESSMENT

Speaking and Listening

If students struggle with creating a multimedia presentation, **then** have them find and study examples of multimedia presentations online. For Reteach and Practice, see **Speaking and Listening: Multimedia Presentation (RP).**

Selection Test

Administer the "Tutors Teach Seniors New High-Tech Tricks" Selection Test, which is available in both print and digital formats online in Assessments.

from Mom & Me & Mom

AUDIO SUMMARIES
Audio summaries of the excerpt from *Mom & Me & Mom* are available online in English and Spanish in the Interactive Teacher's Edition or Unit Resources. Assigning these summaries prior to reading the selection may help students build additional background knowledge and set a context for their first read.

Summary

In this excerpt from her memoir *Mom & Me & Mom*, a nervous thirteen-year-old Maya Angelou travels to San Francisco with her grandmother. She has come to live with the mother she has never known. Maya has lived her whole life with her grandmother in rural Arkansas. Her mother loves jazz and looks like a movie star. Maya finds it impossible to call her "Mother," and calls her "Lady" instead.

When Maya's brother, Bailey, arrives, he seems to forget that their mother abandoned them. He greets her at the railroad station as if he were her long-lost son. Maya feels betrayed and alone, and wants to go back to Arkansas. In the car to her mother's house, however, a childish gesture of affection from Bailey seems to promise that life in California might work out after all.

Insight

Reading this excerpt from *Mom & Me & Mom* will help students begin to reflect on the complicated nature of relationships among different generations, and how the interplay between multiple generations can ease tensions. It may be difficult to bridge the gap between two close generations, but the space between more distant generations may actually help.

ESSENTIAL QUESTION:
What can one generation learn from another?

Connection to Essential Question

This excerpt from *Mom & Me & Mom* will help students answer the Essential Question—*What can one generation learn from another?*—through its depiction of the complex relationships between thirteen-year-old Maya Angelou, the grandmother she calls "Momma," and her mother. When Maya's mother presses Maya to give her a smile and then cries tears of happiness, young Maya learns the power of being charitable—a lesson that carries on into her adult life. The more subtle lesson that young Maya learns, though, is found in her grandmother's actions. Grandmother demonstrates acceptance of Vivian and her differences, thus serving as a model for forgiveness, and a discouragement for Maya to act on her resentment toward her mother.

SMALL-GROUP LEARNING PERFORMANCE TASK
What new knowledge or skills can you learn from someone of a different generation?

UNIT PERFORMANCE-BASED ASSESSMENT
In what situations can one generation learn from another?

Connection to Performance Tasks

Small-Group Learning Performance Task In this Performance Task, students will present a personal narrative about their own experience or observation of a lesson between generations that is depicted in one of this Module's selections. This excerpt from *Mom & Me & Mom* gives students the choice of presenting the lesson about being charitable that is handed down from Vivian to Maya, or the lessons of tolerance and acceptance that Maya's grandmother teaches, leading by example.

Unit Performance-Based Assessment This selection provides students with an explicit example of a lesson shared between two generations, when Maya's mother teaches Maya the power of being charitable. It also provides more subtle insights, such as what it looks like to accept human beings for who they are. Students may refer to these examples in their personal narratives.

DIGITAL PERSPECTIVES

Audio

Video

Document

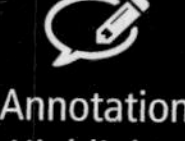
Annotation Highlights

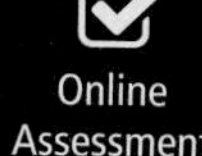
Online Assessment

LESSON RESOURCES

	Making Meaning	Language Development
Lesson	**First Read** **Close Read** **Analyze the Text** **Analyze Craft and Structure**	**Concept Vocabulary** **Word Study** **Conventions**
Instructional Standards	**RI.7.10** By the end of the year, read and comprehend literary nonfiction . . . **L.7.4** Determine or clarify the meaning of unknown and multiple-meaning words and phrases . . . **SL.7.1** Engage effectively in a range of collaborative discussions . . . **RI.7.1** Cite several pieces of textual evidence to support . . . **RI.7.3** Analyze the interactions between individuals, events, and ideas . . .	**L.7.4** Determine or clarify the meaning of unknown and multiple-meaning words and phrases . . . **L.7.4.b** Use common, grade-appropriate Greek or Latin affixes and roots . . . **L.7.4.d** Verify preliminary determination of the meaning . . . **L.7.1.a** Explain the function of phrases and clauses . . .
STUDENT RESOURCES		
Available online in the Interactive Student Edition or Unit Resources	Selection Audio First-Read Guide: Nonfiction Close-Read Guide: Nonfiction	Word Network Evidence Log
TEACHER RESOURCES		
Selection Resources Available online in the Interactive Teacher's Edition or Unit Resources	Audio Summaries: English and Spanish Annotation Highlights Accessible Leveled Text Spanish Translation Text Questions First Read Extension Questions Analyze Craft and Structure: Characterization	Concept Vocabulary and Word Study Conventions: Independent and Dependent Clauses
Reteach/Practice (RP) Available online in the Interactive Teacher's Edition or Unit Resources	Analyze Craft and Structure: Characterization (RP)	Word Study: Latin Prefix *super-* (RP) Conventions: Independent and Dependent Clauses (RP)
Assessment Available online in Assessments	Selection Test: English Selection Test: Spanish Extension Selection Test	
My Resources	A Unit 1 Answer Key is available online and in the Interactive Teacher's Edition	

Reading Support

Text Complexity Rubric: *from* Mom & Me & Mom	
Quantitative Measures	
Lexile: 610 **Text Length:** 1,825 words	
Qualitative Measures	
Knowledge Demands ①—②—❸—④—⑤	Selection explores ideas that may be common to some readers and unfamiliar to others: separation from parents, divorce, difficulty of reuniting with unfamiliar family members.
Structure ①—❷—③—④—⑤	Selection follows narrative structure that is chronological. Dialogue is included and makes it easier to follow structure.
Language Conventionality and Clarity ①—❷—③—④—⑤	Literal language is easy to understand, mainly simple sentences with conversational language.
Levels of Meaning/Purpose ①—②—❸—④—⑤	There are multiple levels of meaning; reader must infer characters' feelings from actions. Theme is clear but conveyed with some subtlety.

DECIDE AND PLAN

English Language Support

Provide English Learners with support for knowledge demands and meaning as they read the selection.

Knowledge Demands Before students read the selection, review the background information. Ask questions to encourage students to restate the background information. For example, *Who is the story about? How old were they when their parents divorced? How old were they when they moved? Whom did they live with in Arkansas? and in San Francisco?*

Levels of Meaning Point out certain phrases and guide students to describe their understanding of the plot and of the feelings of the two characters. For example, *against my will, I smiled* (paragraph 17). Ask *What does* against my will *mean? Does she feel like smiling?*

Strategic Support

Provide students with strategic support to ensure that they can successfully read the text.

Knowledge Demands Use the background information to review the characters and information necessary to understand the excerpt. Ask students to discuss the possible reactions a thirteen-year-old might have to meeting his or her mother for the first time.

Meaning/Purpose As students read, encourage them to consider the characters' feelings that may be behind their actions. If students have trouble, ask questions to help them identify emotions. For example, refer to paragraph 49 and ask *Why does she refer to the mother and brother as new lovers? What is she feeling at that moment?* After defining emotions, have students reread that paragraph.

Challenge

Provide students who need to be challenged with ideas for how they can go beyond a simple interpretation of the text.

Text Analysis Ask students to describe some of the mixed feelings that Maya has on meeting her mother and what she feels when her brother arrives. Ask if they think her feelings will change after he squeezes her hand.

Read and Discuss Suggest that students read more sections of the book, the entire book, or other works by Maya Angelou. Have students write discussion questions for their partners in order to start a discussion in small groups about aspects of the book or other selection.

TEACH

Read and Respond

Have the groups read the selection and complete the Making Meaning and Language Development activities.

Standards Support Through Teaching and Learning Cycle

IDENTIFY NEEDS

Analyze results of the Beginning-of-Year Assessment, focusing on the items relating to Unit 1. Also take into consideration student performance to this point and your observations of where particular students struggle.

DECIDE AND PLAN

- If students have performed poorly on items matching these standards, then provide selection scaffolds before assigning them the on-level lesson provided in the Student Edition.
- If students have done well on the Beginning-of-Year Assessment, then challenge them to keep progressing and learning by giving them opportunities to practice the skills in depth.
- Use the Selection Resources listed on the Planning Pages for from *Mom & Me & Mom* to help students continually improve their ability to master the standards.

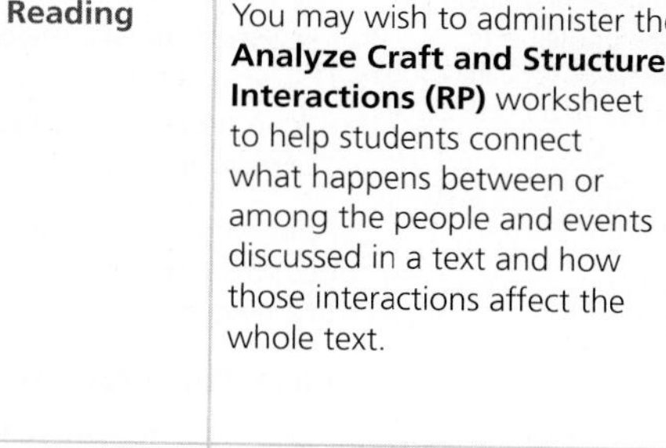

Instructional Standards: *from* Mom & Me & Mom

	Catching Up	This Year	Looking Forward
Reading	You may wish to administer the **Analyze Craft and Structure: Interactions (RP)** worksheet to help students connect what happens between or among the people and events discussed in a text and how those interactions affect the whole text.	**RI.3** Analyze the interactions between individuals, events, and ideas in a text.	Suggest that students choose another nonfiction selection they have read in this or a previous unit and compare and contrast how two people (or groups of people) discussed in the text respond to the same event. Challenge students to explain how the interaction affects the meaning of the complete text.
Language	You may wish to administer the **Word Study: Latin Prefix *super-* (RP)** worksheet to help students understand that knowing the meaning of the Latin prefix *super-* contributes to the overall meaning of a word, as in the word *supervision*. You may wish to administer the **Conventions: Clauses (RP)** worksheet to help students understand the differences between a dependent and an independent clause.	**L.4.b** Use common, grade-appropriate Greek or Latin affixes and roots as clues to the meaning of a word. **L.1** Demonstrate command of the conventions of standard English grammar and usage when writing or speaking.	Have students work in groups and use a print or online dictionary to list other words that include the Latin prefix *super-*. Group members can take turns saying the meaning of one of the listed words and explaining how the meaning of the Latin prefix contributes to the meaning of the full word. Have students choose a paragraph of the selection and identify both the dependent and independent clauses used by the author.

ANALYZE AND REVISE

- Analyze student work for evidence of student learning.
- Identify whether or not students have met the expectations in the standards.
- Identify implications for future instruction.

TEACH

Implement the planned lesson, and gather evidence of student learning.

Jump Start

FIRST READ *What makes a family? How many different kinds of families do you know?*

Engaging students in a discussion about different kinds of families sets the context for reading the excerpt from *Mom & Me & Mom*. As students share their thoughts, have them focus on factors that might contribute to different family structures.

from Mom & Me & Mom 

How would a thirteen year-old feel about meeting her mother for the first time? What would her mother say to her? Modeling questions such as these will help students connect to the excerpt from *Mom & Me & Mom* and to the Small-Group Performance Task assignment. Selection audio and print capability for the selection are available in the Interactive Teacher's Edition.

Concept Vocabulary

Discuss how identifying base words can help clarify the meaning of the concept vocabulary words. Encourage groups to think of how they could apply this strategy to other unfamiliar words in the text.

FIRST READ

Have students perform the steps of the first read independently:

NOTICE: Students should keep track of the words spoken and actions taken by each of the four main individuals.

ANNOTATE: If students have trouble following a section of the story, they should mark it to revisit.

CONNECT: Connecting events in the text to times when they felt frightened or apprehensive will help students understand Maya's actions.

RESPOND: Students will complete the Comprehension Check and write a brief summary of the selection.

Point out to students that while they will always complete the Respond step at the end of the first read, the other steps will probably happen somewhat concurrently. You may wish to print copies of the **First-Read Guide: Nonfiction** for students to use.

MAKING MEANING

from MOM & ME & MOM

Comparing Text to Media

In this lesson, you will read an excerpt from Maya Angelou's memoir *Mom & Me & Mom*. Then, you will watch a video in which Angelou discusses her relationship with her mother. The work your group does on this selection will prepare you to compare it with the video.

LEARNING TO LOVE MY MOTHER

About the Author

Born Marguerite Johnson, **Maya Angelou** (1928–2014) struggled with racism, poverty, and ill treatment early in her life. Across her long career she was a dancer, actress, singer, teacher, and writer. Angelou became one of the best-known African American authors in the world, and she was an activist for women and for the African American community.

from Mom & Me & Mom

Concept Vocabulary

As you perform your first read of the excerpt from *Mom & Me & Mom*, you will encounter these words.

supervision	charitable	philanthropist

Base Words Use your knowledge of the "inside," or base, word along with context to determine the meaning of an unfamiliar word. Here is an example of how to apply the strategy.

Unfamiliar Word *artisan*

Familiar "Inside" Word *art*, which means "something made through skill and creativity."

Context The beautiful ceramic jug was created by an **artisan** in the town next to ours.

Conclusion The jug was a beautiful ceramic piece made by someone. *Artisan* must mean "someone who creates a type of art."

Apply your knowledge of base words and other vocabulary strategies to determine the meanings of unfamiliar words you encounter during your first read.

First Read NONFICTION

Apply these strategies as you conduct your first read. You will have an opportunity to complete a close read after your first read.

NOTICE the general ideas of the text. *What* is it about? *Who* is involved?

ANNOTATE by marking vocabulary and key passages you want to revisit.

CONNECT ideas within the selection to other knowledge and other selections you have read.

RESPOND by completing the Comprehension Check and by writing a brief summary of the selection.

First Read: NOTICE, ANNOTATE, CONNECT, RESPOND

STANDARDS

Reading Informational Text
By the end of the year, read and comprehend literary nonfiction in the grades 6–8 text complexity band proficiently, with scaffolding as needed at the high end of the range.

Language
Determine or clarify the meaning of unknown and multiple-meaning words and phrases based on *grade 7 reading and content*, choosing flexibly from a range of strategies.

VOCABULARY DEVELOPMENT

Concept Vocabulary Reinforcement To increase familiarity with the concept vocabulary, ask students to use each of the words in a sentence. Encourage students to include context clues in their own sentences to demonstrate their knowledge of the word. If students are still struggling with the words, encourage them to identify the base word in each term, look up the base word in the dictionary, and then use the definition to come up with the meaning of the concept vocabulary word.

from Mom & Me & Mom

Maya Angelou

BACKGROUND
When Maya Angelou was 3 years old and her brother Bailey was 5, her parents divorced and sent the children off to live with their grandmother in Stamps, Arkansas. When Maya was 13, she and Bailey were sent back to San Francisco to live with their mother, Vivian Baxter.

Chapter 3

1 My grandmother made arrangements with two Pullman car[1] porters and a dining car waiter for tickets for herself, my brother, and me. She said she and I would go to California first and Bailey would follow a month later. She said she didn't want to leave me without adult **supervision**, because I was a thirteen-year-old girl. Bailey would be safe with Uncle Willie. Bailey thought he was looking after Uncle Willie, but the truth was, Uncle Willie was looking after him.

2 By the time the train reached California, I had become too frightened to accept the idea that I was going to meet my mother at last.

3 My grandmother took my hands. "Sister, there is nothing to be scared for. She is your mother, that's all. We are not surprising her.

NOTES

Mark base words or indicate another strategy you used that helped you determine meaning.

supervision
(soo pehr VIH zhun) *n.*
MEANING:

1. **Pullman car** *n.* type of railroad sleeping car built by the Pullman Company.

Concept Vocabulary

SUPERVISION If groups are struggling to define the word *supervision* in paragraph 1, point out that the base word, *vision*, has to do with looking or seeing. Encourage students to use their knowledge of this "inside word" to determine the meaning of *supervision*. Context clues will also help students understand the word. Students should then be able to infer that *supervision* means "overseeing something or watching over someone." Since Maya is a child, she needs an adult to look after her.

Possible response: *Supervision* means "looking after someone or something."

FACILITATING SMALL-GROUP CLOSE READING

CLOSE READ: Memoir As groups perform the close read, circulate and offer support as needed.

- Remind students that a memoir is a narrative that expresses the author's feelings about events in his or her life.
- Encourage students to look for details that tell them about the writer's beliefs and perspective.
- Challenge students to find information that helps them understand why the writer chose to focus on a specific incident or idea.

CLOSER LOOK

Analyze Characters

Circulate among groups as students conduct their close read. Suggest that groups close read paragraph 9. Encourage them to talk about the annotations that they mark. If needed, provide the following support.

ANNOTATE: Have students mark details in the paragraph that contrast the different ways that the two generations of women in Maya's life express affection, or work with small groups to have students participate while you highlight them together.

QUESTION: Guide students to consider what these details might tell them. Ask what a reader can infer from what was annotated, and accept student responses.

Possible response: Her grandmother has never kissed her and does not show much affection but is proud of her, while her mother is very open about showing affection.

CONCLUDE: Help students to formulate conclusions about the importance of these details in the text. Ask students why the author might have included these details.

Possible response: Vivian seems to be a free spirit. Grandmother is much more reserved. It may be that Vivian is demonstrating affection to stop Maya from remembering that she abandoned her. It may be that the grandmother has been careful not to show affection because she does not want to alienate Maya's affection from her mother. The author includes these details to show Maya's confusion and to demonstrate that different people have different ways of showing their love and different reasons for showing, or not showing, affection.

Remind students that a good author can reveal subtleties and conflict in **character** through sympathetic descriptions of their behavior toward family members.

NOTES

When she received my letter explaining how Junior was growing up, she invited us to come to California."

4 Grandmother rocked me in her arms and hummed. I calmed down. When we descended the train steps, I looked for someone who could be my mother. When I heard my grandmother's voice call out, I followed the voice and I knew she had made a mistake, but the pretty little woman with red lips and high heels came running to my grandmother.

5 "Mother Annie! Mother Annie!"

6 Grandmother opened her arms and embraced the woman. When Momma's arms fell, the woman asked, "Where is my baby?"

7 She looked around and saw me. I wanted to sink into the ground. I wasn't pretty or even cute. That woman who looked like a movie star deserved a better-looking daughter than me. I knew it and was sure she would know it as soon as she saw me.

8 "Maya, Marguerite, my baby." Suddenly I was wrapped in her arms and in her perfume. She pushed away and looked at me. "Oh baby, you're beautiful and so tall. You look like your daddy and me. I'm so glad to see you."

9 She kissed me. I had not received one kiss in all the years in Arkansas. Often my grandmother would call me and show me off to her visitors. "This is my grandbaby." She would stroke me and smile. That was the closest I had come to being kissed. Now Vivian Baxter was kissing my cheeks and my lips and my hands. Since I didn't know what to do, I did nothing.

10 Her home, which was a boardinghouse,[2] was filled with heavy and very uncomfortable furniture. She showed me a room and said it was mine. I told her I wanted to sleep with Momma. Vivian said, "I suppose you slept with your grandmother in Stamps, but she will be going home soon and you need to get used to sleeping in your own room."

11 My grandmother stayed in California, watching me and everything that happened around me. And when she decided that everything was all right, she was happy. I was not. She began to talk about going home, and wondering aloud how her crippled son was getting along. I was afraid to let her leave me, but she said, "You are with your mother now and your brother will be coming soon. Trust me, but more than that trust the Lord. He will look after you."

12 Grandmother smiled when my mother played jazz and blues very loudly on her record player. Sometimes she would dance just because she felt like it, alone, by herself, in the middle of the floor. While Grandmother accepted behavior so different, I just couldn't get used to it.

2. **boardinghouse** *n.* house where people rent one or more rooms for either short or long periods of time.

PERSONALIZE FOR LEARNING

English Language Support

Figurative Language English language learners may struggle with the figurative language often present in everyday speech. Ask students to look at paragraph 8. The narrator uses "wrapped in" for both her mother's arms and her mother's perfume. The first use is conventional and suggests that she was smothered rather than simply held. The second use smartly reinforces that suggestion and implies that the perfume was very strong.

13 My mother watched me without saying much for about two weeks. Then we had what was to become familiar as "a sit-down talk-to."

14 She said, "Maya, you disapprove of me because I am not like your grandmother. That's true. I am not. But I am your mother and I am working some part of my anatomy[3] off to pay for this roof over your head. When you go to school, the teacher will smile at you and you will smile back. Students you don't even know will smile and you will smile. But on the other hand, I am your mother. If you can force one smile on your face for strangers, do it for me. I promise you I will appreciate it."

15 She put her hand on my cheek and smiled. "Come on, baby, smile for Mother. Come on. Be **charitable**."

16 She made a funny face and against my will, I smiled. She kissed me on my lips and started to cry. "That's the first time I have seen you smile. It is a beautiful smile. Mother's beautiful daughter can smile."

17 I was not used to being called beautiful.

18 That day, I learned that I could be a giver simply by bringing a smile to another person. The ensuing[4] years have taught me that a kind word or a vote of support can be a charitable gift. I can move over and make another place for another to sit. I can turn my music up if it pleases, or down if it is annoying.

19 I may never be known as a **philanthropist**, but I certainly want to be known as charitable.

* * *

20 I was beginning to appreciate her. I liked to hear her laugh because I noticed that she never laughed at anyone. After a few weeks it became clear that I was not using any title when I spoke to her. In fact, I rarely started conversations. Most often, I simply responded when I was spoken to.

21 She asked me into her room. She sat on her bed and didn't invite me to join her.

22 "Maya, I am your mother. Despite the fact that I left you for years, I am your mother. You know that, don't you?"

23 I said, "Yes, ma'am." I had been answering her briefly with a few words since my arrival in California.

24 "You don't have to say 'ma'am' to me. You're not in Arkansas."

25 "No, ma'am. I mean no."

26 "You don't want to call me 'Mother,' do you?"

27 I remained silent.

3. **anatomy** (uh NAT uh mee) *n.* the structure of the body.
4. **ensuing** *adj.* following.

NOTES

Mark base words or indicate another strategy you used that helped you determine meaning.

charitable (CHAIR ih tuh buhl) *adj.*

MEANING:

philanthropist (fih LAN thruh pihst) *n.*

MEANING:

Concept Vocabulary

CHARITABLE If groups are having trouble defining the word *charitable,* explain that one of the meanings of the base word, *charity*, is "affection or good will toward others." Remind students that the suffix *–able* means "capable of." Then ask students to define the word.

Possible response: *Charitable* must mean "capable of showing affection or good will to others."

PHILANTHROPIST If groups are having trouble defining the word *philanthropist*, it may be because it has two roots: *phil*, which means "having a strong affinity or love for," and *anthrop*, which means "human." Explain the two roots, then ask students to define the word.

Possible response: A *philanthropist* is "someone who has a strong affinity or love for humanity." The word is most often used for someone who donates large sums of money to charities.

VOCABULARY DEVELOPMENT

Word Forms Explain that the words *charitable* (paragraph 15) and *philanthropist* (paragraph 19) often appear in other, related forms.

charitably	adverb	add "y" to express relationship of manner, degree, etc.
philanthropic	adjective	add suffix *-ic* to mean "related to"

Model sentences using these other forms of the concept vocabulary words.

After she learned of my dire situation, she treated me more charitably.

The wealthy Smith family wanted to start a philanthropic foundation.

CLOSER LOOK

Infer Author's Attitude

Circulate among groups as students conduct their close read. Suggest that groups close read paragraphs 42 and 43. Encourage them to talk about the annotations that they mark. If needed, provide the following support.

ANNOTATE: Have students mark details in the paragraphs that show the author's attitude to the past as she remembers and reports this conversation with her grandmother, or work with small groups to have students participate while you highlight them together.

QUESTION: Guide students to consider what these details might tell them. Ask what a reader can infer from what was annotated, and accept student responses.

The author reports that as a child she inferred from her grandmother's wish to discuss this topic that her mother must have spoken to her. The author reports the conversation as direct speech, without commenting on the way she felt about it at the time or how she feels about it now.

Possible response: Grandmother does not approve because she feels that Vivian loves Maya and deserves respect as her mother.

CONCLUDE: Help students to formulate conclusions about the importance of these details in the text. Ask students why the author might have included these details.

Possible response: The author wants her memory to speak for itself, without comment. She reports the details of the conversation in direct speech to preserve it as it happened and to pass it on precisely to the reader. She does not comment, for instance, on the fact that her grandmother addresses her as "sister." By including these details, the author allows the characters' voices to be heard by the reader, without being prejudged.

Remind students that, particularly in a memoir, an **author's attitude** to the truth can appear as an absence of the kind of commentary and description that we usually associate with attitude. In this memoir, the narrator is a younger version of the author. The ways the author grew and changed sometimes contribute to the theme of the memoir.

NOTES

28 "You have to call me something. We can't go through life without you addressing me. What would you like to call me?"

29 I had been thinking of that since I first saw her. I said, "Lady."

30 "What?"

31 "Lady."

32 "Why?"

33 "Because you are beautiful, and you don't look like a mother."

34 "Is Lady a person you like?"

35 I didn't answer.

36 "Is Lady a person you might learn to like?"

37 She waited as I thought about it.

38 I said, "Yes."

39 "Well, that's it. I am Lady, and still your mother."

40 "Yes, ma'am. I mean yes."

41 "At the right time I will introduce my new name."

42 She left me, turned up the player, and sang loudly with the music. The next day I realized she must have spoken to my grandmother.

43 Grandmother came into my bedroom. "Sister, she is your mother and she does care for you."

44 I said, "I'll wait until Bailey gets here. He will know what to do, and whether we should call her Lady."

DIGITAL PERSPECTIVES

Enriching the Text To help students understand one way people traveled in past generations, show a film about the revival of the Pullman Sleeping Car Company. This can be found in the Media section of the Pullman Rail Journeys site. Encourage students to consider whether the video gives an accurate portrayal of Maya's 1941 trip from Arkansas to California, described in paragraphs 1–4.

You might want to note that segregation on interstate transportation was not ended until 1956 and that the state of Arkansas did not formally repeal the law that required segregated railway cars until 1973.

Chapter 4

NOTES

45 Mother, Grandmother, and I waited at the railway station. Bailey descended from the train and saw me first. The smile that took over his face made me forget all the discomfort I had felt since coming to California.

46 His eyes found Grandmother and his smile changed to a grin, and he waved to her. Then he saw Mother and his response broke my heart. Suddenly he was a lost little boy who had been found at last. He saw his mother, his home, and then all his lonely birthdays were gone. His nights when scary things made noise under the bed were forgotten. He went to her as if hypnotized. She opened her arms and she clasped him into her embrace. I felt as if I had stopped breathing. My brother was gone, and he would never come back.

47 He had forgotten everything, but I remembered how we felt on the few occasions when she sent us toys. I poked the eyes out of each doll, and Bailey took huge rocks and smashed to bits the trucks or trains that came wrapped up in fancy paper.

48 Grandmother put her arm around me and we walked ahead of the others back to the car. She opened the door and sat in the backseat. She looked at me and patted the seat beside her. We left the front seat for the new lovers.

49 The plan was that Grandmother would return to Arkansas two days after Bailey arrived. Before Lady and Bailey Jr. reached the car I said to Grandmother, "I want to go back home with you, Momma."

50 She asked, "Why?"

51 I said, "I don't want to think of you on that train all alone. You will need me."

52 "When did you make that decision?" I didn't want to answer.

53 She said, "When you saw the reunion of your brother and his mother?" That she should have such understanding, being an old woman and country, too: I thought it was amazing. It was just as well that I had no answer, because Bailey and his mother had already reached the car.

54 Vivian said to Grandmother, "Mother Annie, I didn't look for you two. I knew you would go to the car." Bailey didn't turn to look at me. His eyes were glued to his mother's face. "One thing about you that cannot be denied, you are a true sensible woman."

55 Grandmother said, "Thank you, Vivian. Junior?"

56 She had to call twice to get his attention, "Junior, how was the train? Did somebody make food for your trip? How did you leave Willie?"

57 Suddenly he remembered there was someone else in the world. He grinned for Grandmother. "Yes, ma'am, but none of them can cook like you."

FACILITATING

Comprehension Check

Possible responses:

1. Maya was frightened by the idea of meeting her mother, whom she had not seen in years.
2. Maya did not think of herself as "pretty or even cute," so she did not expect her mother to look like a movie star, so "beautiful and tall."
3. Maya learns that being kind and charitable brings joy to both the giver and the receiver.
4. Summaries will vary; however, students should include the following points in their summary:
   - Maya was going to live with her mother, who she had not seen in years.
   - Maya struggled with how to feel about and treat her mother.

NOTES

58 He turned to me and asked, "What's happening, My? Has California got your tongue? You haven't said a word since I got in the car."

59 I made my voice as cold as possible. I said, "You haven't given me a chance."

60 In a second he said, "What's the matter, My?"

61 I had hurt him and I was glad. I said, "I may go back to Stamps with Momma." I wanted to break his heart.

62 "No, ma'am, you will not." My grandmother's voice was unusually hard.

63 My mother asked, "Why would you leave now? You said all you were waiting on was your brother. Well, here he is." She started the car and pulled out into traffic.

64 Bailey turned back to her. He added, "Yep, I'm in California."

65 Grandmother held my hand and patted it. I bit the inside of my mouth to keep from crying.

66 No one spoke until we reached our house. Bailey dropped his hand over the back of the front seat. When he wiggled his fingers, I grabbed them. He squeezed my fingers and let them go and drew his hand back to the front seat. The exchange did not escape Grandmother's notice, but she said nothing. ❧

* * *

Comprehension Check

Complete the following items after you finish your first read. Review and clarify details with your group.

1. What was Angelou frightened of at the beginning of the story?

2. Why did Angelou think her grandmother had been mistaken in identifying the woman on the train platform as her mother?

3. What lesson does Angelou learn from her mother when she finally smiles for her?

4. **Notebook** Write a summary of the excerpt from *Mom & Me & Mom* to confirm your understanding of the memoir.

WriteNow Express and Reflect

Description After being apart for so long, Maya and her mother have gotten off to a rocky start, to say the least. Have students write a brief essay about someone with whom they did not initially get along but later became friends with. Students should describe some differences in their personalities and reflect on what keeps them close even though they don't always agree.

Close Read the Text

With your group, revisit sections of the text you marked during your first read. **Annotate** details that you notice. What **questions** do you have? What can you **conclude**?

from MOM & ME & MOM

Analyze the Text

CITE TEXTUAL EVIDENCE to support your answers.

Notebook Complete the activities.

1. **Review and Clarify** With your group, reread paragraphs 45–48 of the excerpt. How does Angelou describe her brother Bailey's reunion with their mother? What was Angelou's response to seeing their reunion? Why might she have responded this way?
2. **Present and Discuss** Now, work with your group to share passages from the memoir that you found especially important. Take turns presenting your passages. Discuss what you noticed in the text, what questions you asked, and what conclusions you reached.
3. **Essential Question:** ***What can one generation learn from another?*** What has this excerpt taught you about the ways in which people of different generations can learn from each other?

TIP

GROUP DISCUSSION
Be sure to identify specific events or passages so your classmates can follow your thinking. Use precise words and specific details to express your thoughts.

LANGUAGE DEVELOPMENT

Concept Vocabulary

charitable | philanthropist | supervision

Why These Words? The three concept words from the text are related. With your group, determine what the words have in common. Write your ideas and add another word that fits the category.

Practice

Notebook Confirm your understanding of the concept vocabulary words from the text by using them in sentences. Be sure to use context clues that signal the meaning of the words.

Word Study

Latin Prefix: *super-* The Latin prefix *super-* means "above," "over," or "beyond." Angelou's grandmother did not want Maya to leave without adult *supervision;* she wanted an adult to be watching *over* Maya. Using your knowledge of the prefix *super-,* determine the meanings of the following words: *superhuman, superstructure, supersonic.* Then, use a dictionary to find the precise meaning of each word.

WORD NETWORK
Identify words from the memoir that relate to generations. Add these words to your Word Network.

STANDARDS

Speaking and Listening
Engage effectively in a range of collaborative discussions (one-on-one, in groups, and teacher-led) with diverse partners on grade 7 topics, texts, and issues, building on others' ideas and expressing their own clearly.

Language
Determine or clarify the meaning of unknown and multiple-meaning words and phrases based on *grade 7 reading and content,* choosing flexibly from a range of strategies.
b. Use common, grade-appropriate Greek or Latin affixes and roots as clues to the meaning of a word.
d. Verify the preliminary determination of the meaning of a word or phrase.

FORMATIVE ASSESSMENT

Analyze the Text
If students struggle to close read the text, **then** provide the *from* Mom & Me & Mom: Text Questions available online in the Interactive Teacher's Edition or Unit Resources. Answers and DOK levels are also available.

Concept Vocabulary
If students struggle to identify the concept, **then** have them use each word in a sentence and think about what is similar about the sentences.

Word Study
If students fail to identify other words, **then** suggest that they refer to a dictionary to browse words that have the prefix *super-*. For Reteach and Practice, See **Word Study: Latin Prefix *super-* (RP).**

DIGITAL PERSPECTIVES

Jump Start

CLOSE READ Ask groups to consider the following prompt: What are some of the benefits and drawbacks when three or more generations live together in the same home? As students discuss in their groups, ask them to consider some of the conditions that would be helpful for different generations to live happily together.

Close Read the Text

If needed, model close reading by using the Annotation Highlights in the Interactive Teacher's Edition. Remind groups to use Accountable Talk in their discussions and to support one another as they complete the close read.

Analyze the Text

Possible responses:

1. She describes him going to their mother "as if hypnotized" (paragraph 46). Angelou feels betrayed by Bailey's behavior toward their mother because they both experienced her neglect. Seeing her brother and mother act so lovingly toward each other makes Angelou feel even more alone.
2. Responses will vary. Remind students to explain why they chose each passage they presented.
3. Responses will vary by group.

Concept Vocabulary

Why These Words?
Possible response: Each word involves someone giving to fill the need of someone else. Another word that fits the category is *volunteer.*

Practice
Possible responses:
Emma took a cooking class, but calling her a chef would be *charitable*.

Being a *philanthropist* is the opposite of being stingy.

The children needed *supervision* in the swimming pool so that they would not drown.

Word Network
Possible words: *grandmother, mother, daddy, grandbaby*

Word Study
Possible responses:
Superhuman means "beyond human ability." *Superstructure* means "the part of a building above its base." *Supersonic* refers to speed beyond the speed of sound. For more support, see **Concept Vocabulary and Word Study.**

FACILITATING

Analyze Craft and Structure

Narrative Nonfiction: Characterization Discuss with students the elements of a nonfiction narrative, or storytelling based on true events. Though artfully written, the story must be true in order to be classified as nonfiction. Since they are often autobiographical, nonfiction narratives are usually written as first-person narratives; that is, the author is telling his or her own story as a personal essay, a diary, or, in Maya Angelou's case, a memoir. Have students consider how this influences the portrayal of characters. Note that authors reveal information about characters through the words and actions that they choose to include, and that readers' ideas about characters may change as they continue to read. For more support, see **Analyze Craft and Structure: Characterization.**

Possible responses:

a. I wanted to sink into the ground. I wasn't pretty or even cute. That woman who looked like a movie star deserved a better-looking daughter than me. I knew it and was sure she would know it as soon as she saw me.
b. insecure
c. "Maya, Marguerite, my baby." Suddenly I was wrapped in her arms and in her perfume. She pushed away and looked at me.
"Oh baby, you're beautiful and so tall. You look like your daddy and me. I'm so glad to see you."
d. affectionate

FORMATIVE ASSESSMENT

Analyze Craft and Structure

If students are unable to identify key character traits for Maya, her mother, and her grandmother, **then** have them reread paragraphs 1–9, and point out the details that reveal character. For Reteach and Practice, see **Analyze Craft and Structure: Characterization (RP).**

MAKING MEANING

from MOM & ME & MOM

TIP

CLOSE READING

When analyzing characterization, pay attention to the words the author uses to describe *how* the characters speak.

STANDARDS

Reading Informational Text

- Cite several pieces of textual evidence to support analysis of what the text says explicitly as well as inferences drawn from the text.
- Analyze the interactions between individuals, events, and ideas in a text.

Analyze Craft and Structure

Narrative Nonfiction: Characterization Authors of nonfiction use descriptions and details to help a reader understand the people about whom they are writing. These descriptions help reveal **character traits,** the qualities that make people unique. For example, a person may have the character traits of intelligence and friendliness.

Characterization is the process that writers use to develop their descriptions of people. For instance, in describing a person, a writer might focus on one type of character trait early in a piece of writing and switch to another character trait later in the piece to further develop the portrayal. There are two types of characterization:

- **Direct characterization:** The writer directly describes a person's character traits.
- **Indirect characterization:** The writer reveals a person's character traits through the person's own words and actions and from the words and actions of other people. Readers must **make inferences,** or educated guesses, to determine character traits from indirect characterization.

Practice

CITE TEXTUAL EVIDENCE to support your answers.

Use the chart to analyze indirect characterization in *Mom & Me & Mom.* First, write down some of the person's words and actions that are revealed in the text. Then, make an inference about a character trait of the person, based on these words and actions. The first row has been done for you.

PERSON	WORDS AND ACTIONS IN TEXT	INFERENCE ABOUT CHARACTER TRAIT
Grandmother	*My grandmother took my hands. "Sister, there is nothing to be scared for. She is your mother, that's all. We are not surprising her."* (paragraph 3)	nurturing
Maya	a. See possible responses in Teacher's Edition.	b.
Mother	c.	d.

WriteNow Analyze and Interpret

Description People of different generations often express themselves differently, and we usually think of the younger generation as being less inhibited. This was not the case with Maya and her mother, however. Have students write a short paper that describes how they express themselves differently than people of older generations do. Suggest that students focus on patterns of speech, body language, or even style. Then have them discuss why those differences might exist.

LANGUAGE DEVELOPMENT

Conventions

Independent and Dependent Clauses A **clause** is a group of words that has both a subject and a verb. An **independent clause** has a subject and a verb, and it can stand by itself as a sentence. A **dependent,** or **subordinate, clause** has a subject and a verb, but it cannot stand alone as a complete sentence.

TYPE OF CLAUSE	EXAMPLES
Independent Clause	• My grandmother took my hands • Grandmother rocked me in her arms and hummed • She asked me into her room • Mother, Grandmother, and I waited at the railway station
Dependent Clause	• Because I was a thirteen-year-old girl • Since I didn't know what to do • While Grandmother accepted behavior so different • When he wiggled his fingers

Read It

1. Identify each group of words as an independent clause or a dependent clause.

   a. I had not received one kiss in all the years in Arkansas

   b. That woman who looked like a movie star

   c. I was beginning to appreciate her

   d. Before Lady and Bailey Jr. reached the car

2. Reread paragraph 20 of *Mom & Me & Mom*. Mark and then label one example of an independent clause and one example of a dependent clause.

Write It

Notebook Write a brief paragraph that describes how Maya's interactions with her mother changed before Bailey's arrival. Include two independent clauses and two dependent clauses in your writing. Then label these types of clauses in your finished paragraph.

EVIDENCE LOG

Before moving on to a new selection, go to your Evidence Log and record what you learned from the excerpt from *Mom & Me & Mom*.

STANDARDS

Language

Demonstrate command of the conventions of standard English grammar and usage when writing or speaking.

a. Explain the function of phrases and clauses in general and their function in specific sentences.

PERSONALIZE FOR LEARNING

English Language Support

Independent and Dependent Clauses Ask pairs of students to write complete sentences that describe the grandmother in the story. Remind students that sentences require a subject and a verb. **EMERGING**

Ask students to write three complete sentences that describe how Maya feels about her brother, Bailey, in the story. Ask students to use a combination of nouns and pronouns for their subjects. **EXPANDING**

Ask students to write a brief opinion on how they think Maya and her brother will fare once they settle in to live with their mother again. Encourage students to use nouns and pronouns as their subjects and action words, as well as forms of *to be* for their verbs. **BRIDGING**

An expanded **English Language Support Lesson** on Independent and Dependent Clauses is available in the Interactive Teacher's Edition. 

DIGITAL PERSPECTIVES

Conventions

Independent and Dependent Clauses Discuss the definitions of independent and dependent clauses with students. As you review the examples with students, remind them of the following terms:

subject: The subject of a sentence or clause is the person, place, or thing that is doing something or being something.

verb: Verbs express physical and mental action or a state of being. Every sentence must have a verb.

For more support, see **Conventions: Independent and Dependent Clauses.**

Read It

MAKE IT INTERACTIVE

Bring two paper bags to class. On the front of each bag, use a marker to write a dependent clause.

Next, pass out two slips of blank paper to each student. Have students write a phrase that will complete each of the dependent clauses on the paper bags, forming sentences. Then, have students deposit their slips in the appropriate bags.

Finally, have students take turns drawing slips from the bags and reading them aloud—with the dependent clause written on the bag—to form complete sentences.

1. a. independent; b. dependent; c. independent; d. dependent
2. independent – *I liked to hear her laugh*: dependent – *because I noticed that she never laughed at anyone*

Write It

Paragraphs will vary, but make sure students identify independent and dependent clauses correctly.

Evidence Log Support students in completing their evidence log. This paced activity will help prepare them for the Performance-Based Assessment at the end of the unit.

FORMATIVE ASSESSMENT

Conventions

- **If** students cannot identify independent clauses, **then** remind them that an independent clause can stand alone as a sentence.
- **If** students cannot identify an independent or a dependent clause, **then** remind them that each needs a subject and a verb.

For Reteach and Practice, see **Conventions: Independent and Dependent Clauses (RP).**

Selection Test

Administer the "*from* Mom & Me & Mom (*with* Learning to Love My Mother)" Selection Test, which is available in both print and digital formats online in Assessments.

Learning to Love My Mother

AUDIO SUMMARIES
Audio summaries of "Learning to Love My Mother" are available online in both English and Spanish in the Interactive Teacher's Edition or Unit Resources. Assigning these summaries prior to reviewing the selection may help students build additional background knowledge and set a context for their first review.

Summary

In Michael Maher's BBC TV interview with Maya Angelou, the writer talks about her relationship with her mother. After her parents' divorce, Angelou found herself abandoned by her mother at the age of three. She didn't see her mother again until she went to live with her in San Francisco ten years later. Their relationship had many problems, but Angelou was able to forgive her mother for the simple reason that her mother loved her. Angelou says that her relationship with her mother taught her that love heals. Angelou reads an excerpt from her book, *Mom & Me & Mom*, and Maher asks her what lessons she hopes readers will learn. Angelou's answer demonstrates great kindness and a profound insight into the essential bond between mothers and daughters.

Insight

Watching "Learning to Love My Mother" will help students reflect on the complex relationships between people of different generations and the transforming power of love to simplify and heal those relationships.

ESSENTIAL QUESTION:
What can one generation learn from another?

Connection to Essential Question

"Learning to Love My Mother" provides an autobiographical connection to the Essential Question, *What can one generation learn from another?* Maya Angelou learns from her relationship with her mother that love heals. The wounds that her mother inflicted on Angelou are healed by the simple fact of her mother's love. The patience that Angelou preaches, though, seems to have been taught to her by her grandmother, whom Angelou describes as patient and kind.

SMALL-GROUP LEARNING PERFORMANCE TASK
What new knowledge or skills can you learn from someone of a different generation?

UNIT PERFORMANCE-BASED ASSESSMENT
In what situations can one generation learn from another?

Connection to Performance Tasks

Small-Group Learning Performance Task In this Performance Task, students will present a multimedia presentation about the lessons found in the Small-Group Learning selections in this unit. Students may look to "Learning to Love My Mother" as a selection that teaches that love has the power to heal, even when the wounds are inflicted by the person one loves.

Unit Performance-Based Assessment This selection provides students with the lesson that love heals, which Maya Angelou learns from her mother. In addition, Angelou seems to be sharing a lesson she may have learned from her grandmother—to be patient with children.

DIGITAL PERSPECTIVES

 Audio  Video  Document  Annotation Highlights 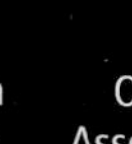 Online Assessment

LESSON RESOURCES

	Making Meaning		Effective Expression
Lesson	**First Review** **Close Review** **Analyze the Media**	**Language Development** **Media Vocabulary**	**Writing to Compare**
Instructional Standards	**RI.7.10** By the end of the year, read and comprehend literary nonfiction . . . **L.7.6** Acquire and use accurately grade-appropriate general academic and domain-specific words . . . **SL.7.2** Analyze the main ideas and supporting details presented in diverse media . . .	**L.7.6** Acquire and use accurately grade-appropriate general academic and domain-specific words . . .	**RI.7.7** Compare and contrast a text... **W.7.9.b** Apply *grade 7 Reading standards* . . . **W.7.2** Write informative/explanatory texts . . . **W.7.2.a** Introduce a topic . . . **W.7.2.b** Develop the topic . . . **W.7.2.c** Use appropriate transitions . . . **W.7.6** Use technology . . .
STUDENT RESOURCES			
Available online in the Interactive Student Edition or Unit Resources	Selection Video First-Review Guide: Media-Video Close-Review Guide: Media-Video		Evidence Log
TEACHER RESOURCES			
Selection Resources Available online in the Interactive Teacher's Edition or Unit Resources	Audio Summaries: English and Spanish Spanish Translation Media Questions First Review Extension Questions	Media Vocabulary	Writing to Compare: Comparison-and-Contrast Essay
My Resources	A Unit 1 Answer Key is available online and in the Interactive Teacher's Edition		

Media Complexity Rubric: Learning to Love My Mother

Quantitative Measures	
Format/Length: video of 3 min, 8 sec	
Qualitative Measures	
Knowledge Demands 1—2—3—**4**—5	To understand video, students will need background information, as none is given in the video. Reference is made to Maya Angelou's book (*Mom & Me & Mom*) that students will read in this unit.
Structure 1—2—3—**4**—5	Most of the video shows Angelou and the interviewer speaking. Only some contextual visual support is given: photos (Angelou, her mother, cover of book) and clips of events (President Obama giving award).
Language Conventionality and Clarity 1—2—**3**—4—5	Language is generally conversational and easy to understand. Speech may be hard to understand in some places due to accents and lack of vocal clarity of speakers.
Levels of Meaning/Purpose 1—2—**3**—4—5	Meaning and purpose is explicitly stated, but understanding meaning depends on understanding content that may be unfamiliar to many students.

FACILITATING

Jump Start

FIRST REVIEW Is love for one's mother or grandmother automatic?

Engage students in a discussion about the bonds, and sometimes the divide, between generations.

Learning to Love My Mother

Does the title of this selection seem strange? What might be the outcome when adults reflect on their life experiences through the eyes of a child? Modeling questions such as these will help students connect to "Learning to Love My Mother" and to the Small-Group Performance Task assignment. Selection audio for the selection is available in the Interactive Teacher's Edition.

Media Vocabulary

Encourage groups to discuss the media vocabulary. Have they seen the words in texts before? Do they use any of the words in their speech or writing?

Ask groups to look closely at the three terms to see what they have in common. Students will notice that two of the words are applicable to fiction as well.

FIRST REVIEW

Have students perform the steps of the first review independently:

WATCH: Encourage students to watch how the interviewer and the subject interact with one another.

NOTE: Remind students to write down those exchanges in the interview that they find interesting and wish to revisit during their close review.

CONNECT: Students should connect Angelou's relationship with her mother to those of people they know and of characters they've read about and seen on TV and in movies.

RESPOND: Students will answer questions to demonstrate understanding.

Point out to students that, while they will always complete the Respond step at the end of the first review, the other steps will probably happen somewhat concurrently. You may wish to print copies of the **First-Review Guide: Media-Video** for students to use.

MAKING MEANING

from MOM & ME & MOM

Comparing Text to Media

The video interview you will watch features Maya Angelou, the author of *Mom & Me & Mom,* describing some of the experiences she wrote about in her memoir. While watching this video, think about ways in which both written text and spoken words can tell a story.

LEARNING TO LOVE MY MOTHER

About the Interviewer

Michael Maher has produced and filmed numerous videos, including many for *BBC News Magazine*. In most of his work—even when he is the interviewer—he is not very visible, and the focus of the video doesn't stray from the subject.

Learning to Love My Mother

Media Vocabulary

The following words or concepts will be useful to you as you analyze, discuss, and write about video interviews.

set: where the interview takes place	• The set of an interview is usually free of noise and other distractions. • The set may be in a location that suits the subject matter of the interview.
questions: what the interviewer chooses to ask an interviewee to elicit specific information	• The questions may ask for factual responses or encourage the subject to reflect on a particular topic or experience. • "Leading" questions suggest the particular answer an interviewer wants to hear.
tone: the attitude of an interviewer or interviewee toward the subject matter or audience	• The overall tone of an interview may vary depending on the topic and interviewer's purpose. • Word choice, vocal qualities, and facial expressions set the tone of the interview.

First Review MEDIA: VIDEO

Apply these strategies as you watch the video interview. Be sure to note time codes so you can more easily revisit specific sections of the video.

WATCH *who* speaks, *what* they say, and *how* they say it.

NOTE elements that you find interesting and want to revisit.

First Review

CONNECT details in the interview to other texts you've read or images you've seen.

RESPOND by completing the Comprehension Check at the end.

STANDARDS

Reading Informational Text
By the end of the year, read and comprehend literary nonfiction in the grades 6–8 text complexity band proficiently, with scaffolding as needed at the high end of the range.

Language
Acquire and use accurately grade-appropriate general academic and domain-specific words and phrases; gather vocabulary knowledge when considering a word or phrase important to comprehension or expression.

MEDIA: VIDEO

Learning to Love My Mother

Maya Angelou with Michael Maher

BACKGROUND

When Maya Angelou was three years old, she and her brother were sent to live with their grandmother. Their mother, Vivian Baxter, was not ready to be tied down with a family. Ten years later, the two children returned to live with their mother. More than 70 years later, Angelou wrote about this transition in her memoir *Mom & Me & Mom*. In this interview, she tells Michael Maher some of the lessons she learned from her experiences.

NOTES

PERSONALIZE FOR LEARNING

English Language Support

View Actively Support students as they watch "Learning to Love My Mother." Form groups and have them watch the video in 30-second increments. Students should take notes on key ideas and details given in each segment. After listening for 30 seconds, have group members compare their notes. Repeat the process until students have watched the entire video. **ALL LEVELS**

DIGITAL PERSPECTIVES

CLOSER REVIEW

Supporting Claims

Circulate among groups as students conduct their close review. Suggest that groups close review 0:40 to 1:31 in the video. Encourage them to talk about what they note. If needed, provide the following support.

NOTE: Have students note details in the video that support Angelou's claim that "Love heals—not sentimentality, but love," or have students participate while you note them together.

QUESTION: Guide students to consider what these details might tell them. Ask what a viewer can infer from what was noted, and accept student responses.

Possible response: When Maya Angelou first lived with her mother at the age of thirteen, it was love that helped her overcome her initial feelings of abandonment. She learned to love her mother after the kindness that her mother exhibited. Angelou feels that her mother's love healed her and helped her get over all the terrible feelings she experienced during her childhood.

CONCLUDE: Help students to formulate conclusions about the importance of these details in the video. Ask students why the interviewer might have included these details.

Possible response: The interview shows that Angelou knew and accepted her mother for who she was, not what she'd like her to have been (which would have shown sentimentality). There was no sentimentality in her attitude at the time to a mother who had abandoned her as a baby, nor has she developed any sentimentality toward her over the years. Her answer to Maher's question about how she got past her feelings of abandonment is spontaneous and clearly true: "She loved me" (0:55)—love healed her of her anger. Her mother had no sentimentality either: she accepted her daughter's refusal to call her "mother." Maher included these details to help the viewer understand how Angelou grew to love her mother.

Explain to students that a good interviewer will look for clarification and evidence to **support claims** made by the interviewee.

Comprehension Check

Possible responses:

1. Maya Angelou's grandmother spoke slowly, was patient, and was kind. Vivian Baxter "spoke fast," "wore lipstick," "wiggled," and "always had records on."
2. Vivian Baxter accepted that her daughter referred to her as "Lady."
3. According to Angelou, Vivian Baxter would have thought that, were there to be an African American president, "it should have been her."
4. Angelou feels two lessons people should learn are that, first, they should "exercise patience with themselves so they can forgive themselves for all of the dumb things that they do," and secondly, they should exercise patience with their children and "learn to be a little kinder."
5. One reason Maya Angelou forgives her mother is that she sensed her mother's love for her.
6. She learned to look past her mother's shortcomings and found that she was actually a very kind person. She reiterated that "love" helped her form a strong relationship with her mother. Her advice to others is to exercise patience with themselves first, then learn to exercise it with others.

Comprehension Check

Compete the following items after you finish your first review. Review and clarify details with your group.

1. What are some of the ways in which Vivian Baxter was unlike Maya Angelou's grandmother?
2. How did Vivian Baxter react to her daughter's calling her *Lady*?
3. According to Angelou, what would Vivian Baxter have thought about there being an African American president?
4. What are two life lessons Angelou thinks people should learn?
5. What is one reason Angelou forgives her mother for abandoning her?
6. Explain how Maya Angelou overcame her problems with her mother, and describe how she based her advice to others on her own experience.

MAKING MEANING

Close Review

Watch the interview again. Write down any new observations that seem important. What **questions** do you have? What can you **conclude**?

LEARNING TO LOVE MY MOTHER

Analyze the Media

Notebook **Complete the activities.**

1. **Present and Discuss** Choose a section of the interview that you find most interesting and powerful. Share your choice with your group and discuss why you chose it. Explain what you noticed in the section, what questions it raised for you, and what conclusions you reached about it.

2. **Review and Synthesize** With your group, review the video. What impact do the old photographs of Angelou and her family create? How do they affect your understanding of Angelou and her experiences? Discuss with your group.

3. **Essential Question:** ***What can one generation learn from another?*** What did Maya Angelou learn from her mother and grandmother? What does Angelou hope future generations will take away from her story? Discuss your response with the group.

LANGUAGE DEVELOPMENT

Media Vocabulary

Use these words in your responses to the questions.

set	questions	tone

1. If you were conducting this interview, what location would you have chosen?

2. Would you have asked Maya Angelou anything that the interviewer did not?

3. How did the interviewer relate to Maya Angelou on a personal level? How does the tone of both speakers affect your viewing of the interview?

STANDARDS

Speaking and Listening
Analyze the main ideas and supporting details presented in diverse media and formats and explain how the ideas clarify a topic, text, or issue under study.

Language
Acquire and use accurately grade-appropriate general academic and domain-specific words and phrases; gather vocabulary knowledge when considering a word or phrase important to comprehension or expression.

DIGITAL PERSPECTIVES

Jump Start

CLOSE REVIEW Ask groups to consider the following prompt: *What did Maya Angelou learn when she visited her mother?* As students discuss the prompt in their groups, have them support their ideas using evidence from the memoir.

Close Review

If needed, model close reviewing by using the Closer Review notes in the Interactive Teacher's Edition.

Remind groups to use Accountable Talk in their discussions and to support one another as they complete the close read.

Media Vocabulary

Remind students to use the media vocabulary words while discussing and writing about the video interview. For example:

- Angelou's own home formed the *set* of the interview.
- The interviewer's *questions* were probing, but respectful.
- The *tone* of the interview was courteous, but frank.

For more support, see **Media Vocabulary**. 

Analyze the Media

Possible responses:

1. Answers will vary. Remind students to explain why they chose the section they presented to the group.
2. The family photographs show the warmth between Angelou and her mother and help viewers understand their relationship.
3. Maya Angelou learned the importance of patience and kindness from her mother and grandmother. She hopes that others will notice the importance of patience with themselves and with children.

FORMATIVE ASSESSMENT

Analyze the Media

If students struggle to the video, **then** provide the Maya Angelou: Learning to Love My Mother: Media Questions available online in the Interactive Teacher's Edition or Unit Resources. Answers and DOK levels are also available.

Media Vocabulary

If students struggle to identify the *tone* and the *set* of the interview, **then** have them review the definitions of both words and look for examples of them in other video interviews.

FACILITATING

Writing to Compare

As students prepare to compare the text and the video, they will consider the relationship between the mother and daughter, and how that relationship is shown in each selection.

Prewriting and Planning

Compare the Text and Video Discuss with students factors to consider as they locate similarities and differences between the video interview and the text. For example, while watching the video, students should consider the set, tone, and the interviewer's questions. In the text, students should consider the topic or subject, main idea, word choice, dialogue, and plot.

a. She is pretty. She looks like a movie star, not like her grandmother. She likes to kiss Maya.

b. "I didn't understand her." She spoke fast and giggled all the time.

c. Her physical and characteristic descriptions of her mother remain the same.

d. She says it is because she is beautiful; she doesn't look like a mother.

e. She states it was because she didn't understand her.

f. The text explains specifically; the video provides an abstract response.

g. She learned to appreciate her after a few weeks. Once Bailey arrives, her initial feelings return.

h. Love healed their relationship.

i. At the end of the selection, she is still unsure about living with her mother. The video takes the relationship timeline further.

Possible responses:

1. The video gives more information about how Maya Angelou's mother behaved and how Maya felt about her.
2. The text provides a scene that shows Maya Angelou's reasons for calling her mother "Lady."

EFFECTIVE EXPRESSION

from MOM & ME & MOM

LEARNING TO LOVE MY MOTHER

Writing to Compare

Both *Mom & Me & Mom* and the interview with Maya Angelou, "Learning to Love My Mother," discuss Angelou's relationship with her mother. Review the selections and consider how the medium in which information is provided—text and audiovisual—affects what you learn about the subject.

Assignment

Write a **comparison-and-contrast essay** in which you analyze the similarities and differences in the way each medium portrays Maya Angelou and her relationship with her mother.

Prewriting and Planning

You will complete the Prewriting and Planning sections as a group, and work individually to write your essay. After you finish your first draft, you will work with your group to revise your essay before handing it in.

Compare the Text and Video With your group, compare the ways in which the text and the video provide information. Use the chart to record your findings.

ANGELOU'S EXPERIENCES	WHAT I LEARNED FROM *MOM & ME & MOM*	WHAT I LEARNED FROM "LEARNING TO LOVE MY MOTHER"	HOW THE TEXT COMPARES WITH THE VIDEO INTERVIEW
Maya's first impressions of her mother	a. See possible responses in Teacher's Edition.	b.	c.
Why Maya calls her mother *Lady*	d.	e.	f.
How Maya's feelings about her mother change	g.	h.	i.

Notebook Respond to these questions.

1. Does the video reveal aspects of the mother-daughter relationship that the text does not?
2. Does the text provide information not found in the video?

STANDARDS

Reading Informational Text
Compare and contrast a text to an audio, video, or multimedia version of the text, analyzing each medium's portrayal of the subject.

Writing
Draw evidence from literary or informational texts to support analysis, reflection, and research.

b. Apply *grade 7 Reading standards* to literary nonfiction.

PERSONALIZE FOR LEARNING

Strategic Support

Comparison Group members may have difficulty seeing how both sources work together to convey more information about when Angelou reunited with her mother. To help them learn more about the emotions that Angelou felt, have students skim the excerpt from *Mom & Me & Mom*. Ask them to suggest where the video could be placed in the memoir to clarify, reinforce, and illustrate the text. Have students discuss their choices.

Assign Tasks Make a list of tasks that members of your group will need to complete for your project. Assign each task to a different group member.

Organize Your Essay Before you begin drafting, decide how you will organize information for your comparison-and-contrast essay. Choose the method that will best suit your purpose.

- **Block Method:** Present all details about one of your subjects. Then, present all details about your next subject. This method emphasizes the subjects being discussed, since each gets its own treatment.
- **Point-by-Point Method:** Discuss one aspect of both subjects, then another aspect of both subjects, and so on. This method emphasizes the points of comparison rather than the subjects being compared.

Regardless of the method you choose, be sure that each of your main points is stated clearly and supported by evidence from the selections.

Drafting

Using Transitions Once you have gathered details and decided on an organizing structure, draft the essay. As you draft, use words and phrases to show the relationships between ideas in your essay. Transition words and phrases can emphasize points of comparison and of contrast.

	TRANSITION WORDS AND PHRASES
Comparisons	*similarly, also, in addition, furthermore*
Contrasts	*although, however, but, on the other hand*

Review, Revise, and Edit

Work with your group to critically review and then revise and edit your essay. If the answer to any of these questions is no, edit your work before submitting a final draft.

- Are the main points of the essay clearly stated? Is each point supported with evidence in the text?
- Is the essay clearly organized using either the block method or the point-by-point method?
- Are the relationships between ideas clarified by transition words and phrases?
- Is your essay free from errors in grammar, spelling, and punctuation?

EVIDENCE LOG

Before moving on to a new selection, go to your Evidence Log and record what you learned from *Mom & Me & Mom* and "Learning to Love My Mother."

STANDARDS

Reading Informational Text
Compare and contrast a text to an audio, video, or multimedia version of the text, analyzing each medium's portrayal of the subject.

Writing
- Write informative/explanatory texts to examine a topic and convey ideas, concepts, and information through the selection, organization, and analysis of relevant content.
  a. Introduce a topic clearly, previewing what is to follow; organize ideas, concepts, and information, using strategies such as definition, classification, comparison/contrast, and cause/effect; include formatting, graphics, and multimedia when useful to aiding comprehension.
  b. Develop the topic with relevant facts, definitions, concrete details, quotations, or other information and examples.
  c. Use appropriate transitions to create cohesion and clarify the relationships among ideas and concepts.
- Use technology, including the Internet, to produce and publish writing and link to and cite sources as well as to interact and collaborate with others, including linking to and citing sources.

DIGITAL PERSPECTIVES 

Assign Tasks Keep in mind individual group members' strengths and talents as you assign tasks.

Organize Your Essay Support groups as they decide on an organizational method for their essay, making sure they understand the block method and the point-by-point method before they make their choice.

Drafting

Using Transitions Encourage students to pay special attention to transition words as they draft their essays. Remind them that transition words help readers understand a writer's analysis.

Review, Revise, and Edit

After students have edited their essays based on feedback from the group, encourage them to reread the essay so that they can fix any remaining spelling or grammar errors.

For more support, see **Writing to Compare: Comparison-and-Contrast Essay.**

Evidence Log Support students in completing their Evidence Log. This paced activity will help prepare them for the Performance-Based Assessment at the end of the unit.

WriteNow Analyze and Inform

Theme That love is a path to the relief of forgiveness emerges as a major theme that runs through the excerpt from *Mom & Me & Mom* by Maya Angelou. A young Maya is hesitant to forgive her mother when she arrives in California to live with her. She even has a problem with calling her mother "Mom" and would prefer to call her "Lady." Yet, upon her brother's arrival in California, he forgives their mother at once and feels love toward her almost immediately. In the video interview, "Learning to Love My Mother," Maya Angelou discusses how love finally broke down the negative feelings that she held for her mother.

Have students find other themes in the excerpt from *Mom & Me & Mom* that may be more subtle and write about them. Have them share their ideas with their group.

FORMATIVE ASSESSMENT

Writing to Compare

If students struggle to find quotes for their writing, **then** have them think about the important details in the narrative or video.

Mother-Daughter Drawings

AUDIO SUMMARIES
Audio summaries of "Mother-Daughter Drawings" are available online in both English and Spanish in the Interactive Teacher's Edition or Unit Resources. Assigning these summaries prior to viewing the selection may help students build additional background knowledge and set a context for their first viewing.

Summary

The "Mother-Daughter Drawings" shown in the Image Gallery were created by artist Mica Angela Hendricks and her four-year-old daughter, Myla. The photograph that introduces this collection of images shows Myla's paint-spattered hand resting in her mother's larger hand. Mica is proudly presenting Myla as an artist and is protective of Myla as her daughter. Working from old photographs, Mica made a series of color drawings of women's faces. Myla added the bodies, first drawing them and then coloring them with acrylic paints. They suggest woodland creatures, insects, and shellfish. Together, the images and the accompanying text form a narrative of creative collaboration between the generations—mother and daughter inspire each other and learn from each other.

Insight

Viewing "Mother-Daughter Drawings" will provide students with the visual proof that people from different generations can maintain their own vision while working together. Collaboration between two different generations does not have to mean that the older generation calls all of the shots. In fact, allowing the younger generation to contribute in its own way may result in the creation of something unexpected and delightful.

ESSENTIAL QUESTION:
What can one generation learn from another?

Connection to Essential Question

"Mother-Daughter Drawings" provides an artistic connection to the Essential Question, *What can one generation learn from another?* When trying to teach her daughter, Myla, about sharing, Mica Angela Hendricks was forced to practice what she preached. She learned from her daughter that letting go of control and trusting her daughter could lead to a wealth of creativity.

SMALL-GROUP LEARNING PERFORMANCE TASK
What new knowledge or skills can you learn from someone of a different generation?

UNIT PERFORMANCE-BASED ASSESSMENT
In what situations can one generation learn from another?

Connection to Performance Tasks

Small-Group Learning Performance Task In this Performance Task, students will present a multimedia presentation about the lessons found in the Small-Group selections. "Mother-Daughter Drawings" exposes students to the lesson that parents must set an example for their children, and that true collaboration means giving a partner the freedom to contribute as he or she wants.

Unit Performance-Based Assessment An example of a lesson one generation can learn from another that students may identify in this selection is the lesson that Hendricks learns from working with her daughter. She learns that she must practice what she preaches, and that the best work that she and her daughter produce comes when she stops trying to control her daughter.

DIGITAL PERSPECTIVES

Audio

Video

Print on Demand

Interactive Activity

Online Assessment

LESSON RESOURCES

	Making Meaning	Language Development	Effective Expression
Lesson	**First Review** **Close Review** **Analyze the Media**	**Media Vocabulary**	**Speaking and Listening**
Instructional Standards	**RI.7.10** By the end of the year, read and comprehend literary nonfiction . . . **L.7.6** Acquire and use accurately grade-appropriate general academic and domain-specific words and phrases . . . **SL.7.2** Analyze the main ideas and supporting details presented in diverse media . . .	**L.7.6** Acquire and use accurately grade-appropriate general academic and domain-specific words and phrases . . .	**SL.7.1.a** Come to discussions prepared . . . **SL.7.5** Include multimedia components and visual displays . . . **L.7.6** Acquire and use accurately grade-appropriate general academic and domain-specific words and phrases . . .
STUDENT RESOURCES			
Available online in the Interactive Student Edition or Unit Resources	Selection Video First-Review Guide: Media Art/ Photography Close-Review Guide: Media Art/ Photography		Evidence Log
TEACHER RESOURCES			
Selection Resources Available online in the Interactive Teacher's Edition or Unit Resources	Audio Summaries: English and Spanish Spanish Translation Media Questions First Read Extension Questions	Media Vocabulary	Speaking and Listening: Multimedia Slideshow

Media Complexity Rubric: Mother-Daughter Drawings

Quantitative Measures	
Format / Length 5 images with captions	
Qualitative Measures	
Knowledge Demands ① ② **❸** ④ ⑤	In order to fully appreciate how the art was made, students need to understand the background information.
Structure ① **❷** ③ ④ ⑤	Information is presented in background information and in captions corresponding to particular art pieces. Explanation of the process is sequential from caption to caption.
Language Conventionality and Clarity ① **❷** ③ ④ ⑤	Language used in background information and captions is clear and explicit. Sentences mostly contain simple constructions, with some long sentences.
Levels of Meaning/Purpose ① **❷** ③ ④ ⑤	Purpose is clear and explicit in the background information and captions. Correspondence of photos and captions makes purpose easy to understand.

FACILITATING

Jump Start

FIRST REVIEW *Can a four-year-old make true art? Who can be an artist?*

Engaging students in a discussion about art and artists will help set the context for students as they view the collaborative drawings of Mica and Myla Hendricks. As students discuss these questions, have them focus on the subjective nature of art.

Mother-Daughter Drawings

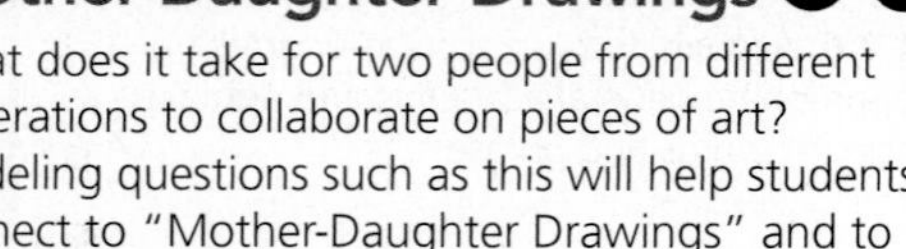

What does it take for two people from different generations to collaborate on pieces of art? Modeling questions such as this will help students connect to "Mother-Daughter Drawings" and to the Small-Group Performance Task assignment. Selection audio and print capability for the selection are available in the Interactive Teacher's Edition.

Media Vocabulary

Encourage groups to discuss the media vocabulary. Have they seen the terms in texts before? Do they use any of the words in their speech or writing?

Ask groups to look at the three terms and discuss what they have in common. Students should notice that the terms describe physical aspects of painting and drawing—and how those aspects affect the viewing experience. Encourage students to identify examples of the three terms in classroom drawings or paintings.

FIRST REVIEW

Have students perform the steps of the first review independently:

LOOK: Encourage students to look at each image and read the accompanying caption.

NOTE: Students should note the drawings that capture their attention.

CONNECT: Encourage students to connect the drawings with drawings they made as young children.

RESPOND: Students will answer questions and write a description to demonstrate their understanding.

Point out to students that while they will always complete the Respond step at the end of the first review, the other steps will probably happen somewhat concurrently. You may wish to print copies of the **First-Review Guide: Media Art/Photography** for students to use.

MAKING MEANING

About the Artist

Mica Angela Hendricks was born into a military family and traveled to many countries. As a child, she would carry a sketchbook everywhere she went. People who didn't know her well would simply call her "that girl that draws." Hendricks is now an illustrator and has collaborated with her four-year-old daughter, Myla, on the sketchbook "Share With Me."

Mother-Daughter Drawings

Media Vocabulary

These words will be useful to you as you analyze, discuss, and write about drawings.

composition: arrangement of elements in a drawing	• The elements of a drawing's composition include color, line, shape, space, form, and texture. • The way an artist arranges the elements may create emphasis on one part of the drawing over others.
light and shadow: techniques that add depth to a drawing and make it more realistic	• Light and shadow can turn a two-dimensional shape, such as a circle, into a three-dimensional form, such as a sphere. • Light and shadow help create perspective and mood
perspective: technique used to create the illusion of a three-dimensional world on a two-dimensional surface, such as a piece of paper	• Correct proportion helps a drawing look realistic, taking into account how close or far objects in it are meant to be. • Smaller objects in a drawing appear to be farther way, and larger ones closer.

First Review MEDIA: ART AND PHOTOGRAPHY

Apply these strategies as you study each drawing.

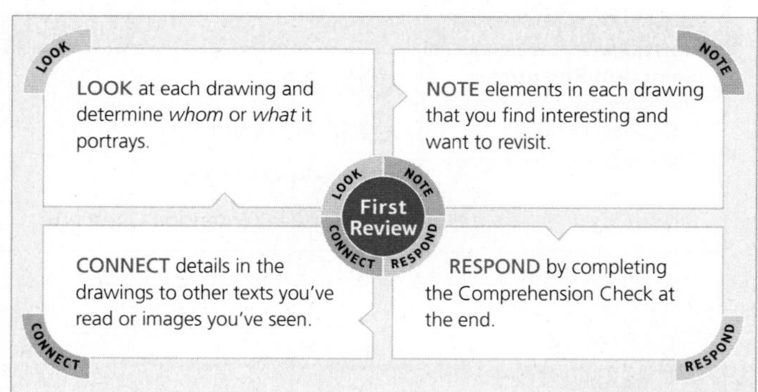

STANDARDS

Reading Informational Text
By the end of the year, read and comprehend literary nonfiction in the grades 6–8 text complexity band proficiently, with scaffolding as needed at the high end of the range.

Language
Acquire and use accurately grade-appropriate general academic and domain-specific words and phrases; gather vocabulary knowledge when considering a word or phrase important to comprehension or expression.

86 UNIT 1 • GENERATIONS

PERSONALIZE FOR LEARNING

Strategic Support

Students with Visual Impairments Help students who are visually impaired by showing enlarged images of the Hendricks' artwork on a class screen. If possible, zoom in on the photos showing how the mother and daughter work together, and then focus on the details of their artwork. Encourage students to discuss the elements of composition, the colors, and the unusual proportions in this collaborative art.

MEDIA: IMAGE GALLERY

Mother-Daughter Drawings

Mica and Myla Hendricks

BACKGROUND

Artist Mica Angela Hendricks had always tried to teach her four-year-old daughter Myla the importance of sharing. But it's easier to talk about sharing than to do it. Mica found that out when Myla noticed her mother drawing in a sketchbook and asked if she could draw in it too. Mica was afraid Myla would ruin her drawings, but decided she had to set a good example by practicing what she preached, especially after Myla quoted her words back to her: "If you can't share, we might have to take it away."

DIGITAL PERSPECTIVES

CLOSER REVIEW

Analyze Composition

Circulate among groups as students conduct their close review. Suggest that groups close review the photo on this page. Encourage them to talk about what they note. If needed, provide the following support.

NOTE: Have students note details in the photo that emphasize the placement of the items in the photograph—or work with small groups to have students participate while you note them together.

QUESTION: Guide students to consider what these details might tell them. Ask what a viewer can infer from what was notated, and accept student responses.

Possible response: The child's hand has several different colors of paint on it, suggesting that the child has some responsibility for the creation of the art. The mother's hand is open, displaying but also protecting the child's hand.

CONCLUDE: Help students to formulate conclusions about the importance of these details in the photo. Ask students why the photographer might have included these details against the art in the background.

Possible response: The paint on the child's hand clearly relates to the art in the background, and the two hands are in full contact. The photographer included these details in the composition to show that their collaboration is fundamental to their art.

Remind students that **composition** is the arrangement of objects in a piece of art. It allows the artist to stress one part of an artwork.

PERSONALIZE FOR LEARNING

English Language Support

Pronouns Remind English Learners that authors often use pronouns to make a text more cohesive. Pronouns are words that refer back to nouns. They allow an author to avoid unnecessary repetition and make a text easier to read. Ask: *In the third sentence, the author writes "Mica found that out…" What does the word* that *refer to?* (It is easier to talk about sharing than do it.) *Which word in the third sentence refers to the sketchbook?* (it) *Who asked to draw in the sketchbook, too?* (Myla) *What pronoun is used to refer to Myla?* (she) *In the fourth sentence, who is afraid of her drawings being ruined?* (Mica) Suggest that students read the sentences again, this time replacing the pronouns with the nouns that they stand for. **ALL LEVELS**

CLOSER REVIEW

Analyze Composition

Circulate among groups as students conduct their close review. Suggest that groups close review Image 1 on this page. Encourage them to talk about what they note. If needed, provide the following support.

NOTE: Have students note the relative sizes of different elements within the composition, or work with small groups to have students participate while you note them together.

QUESTION: Guide students to consider what these details might tell them. Ask what a viewer can infer from the proportions in this composition and accept student responses.

Possible response: The woman's head appears to be much too large for her body. This is, however, not a woman but an imaginary creature, so who but the artists can decide? In terms of the picture itself, the composition of the head, body, and tail harmonize to form an "S" shape in the center. This creates movement—it turns clockwise in opposition to the anti-clockwise movement of the landscape around her.

CONCLUDE: Help students to formulate conclusions about the importance of these details in the picture. Ask students why the artists might have included these details.

Possible response: Other features appear to be out of proportion with each other—but only the artists know how big the tree trunk and the mushrooms "should" be. The artist includes these details to express something other than relative size of elements in a landscape.

Remind students that **composition** is the arrangement of elements in a drawing. Artists work with perspective to make some objects or individuals appear closer than others. This may emphasize certain objects over others.

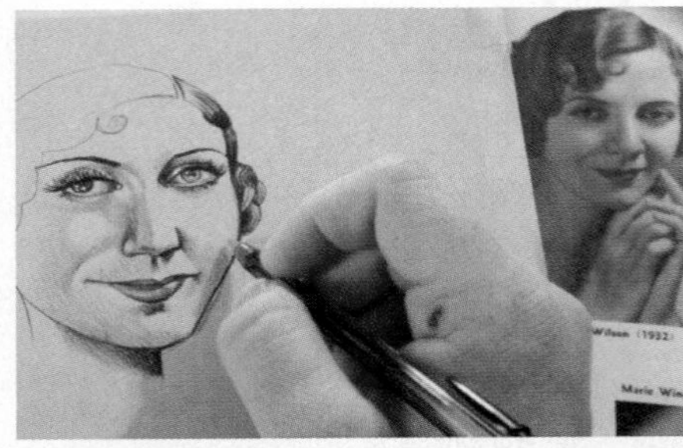

IMAGE 1: Mica had just drawn a woman's face from an old photograph. She let Myla draw the woman's body and then used acrylic paint to add color, highlights, and texture to the entire piece.

NOTES

DIGITAL PERSPECTIVES

IMAGE 2: Mica was impressed that her collaboration with her daughter turned out so well and wanted to try it again.

NOTES

IMAGE 3: Mica began filling her sketchbook with drawings of heads and letting Myla draw the bodies.

NOTES

FACILITATING SMALL-GROUP CLOSE LEARNING

Close Review: Image Gallery As groups perform the close review, circulate among them and offer support as needed.

- Emphasize that these are unusual pieces of art because they are the result of two people's collaboration—and one of the artists is a young girl. What are the advantages and disadvantages of such a collaboration?
- Remind students to think about the drawings' composition, light and shadow, and perspective. How do these concepts give students the tools they need to analyze and appreciate the drawings?

IMAGE 4: At first, Mica tried telling Myla what kind of bodies to draw. She soon realized the drawings turned out better when Myla did what she wanted. "In most instances, kids' imaginations *way* outweigh a grown-up's," Mica says.

NOTES

IMAGE 5: Working with her daughter taught Mica that giving up control is not just fun, but necessary. "Those things you hold so dear cannot change and grow and expand unless you loosen your grip on them a little," she says.

NOTES

PERSONALIZE FOR LEARNING

Challenge

Perspective Have students make their own drawings of a person on a beach (or elsewhere) using Image 5 as inspiration. First, have them draw the person with realistic perspective. Then have them redraw the person, altering the perspective. Have students share their drawings with members of their group and discuss how altering the perspective changes the viewers' experience.

Comprehension Check

The image gallery uses both words and images to tell a story. Use the chart below to note specific details about each image, then describe how each image relates to the text that accompanies it. Share your responses with your group.

IMAGE	WHAT THE IMAGE SHOWS	HOW THE IMAGE RELATES TO THE TEXT
IMAGE 1 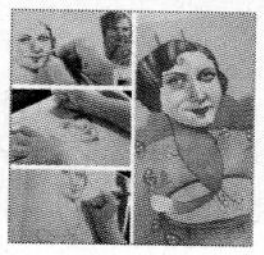	The image is a composite of four images showing how Mica and Myla draw a woman's face with a body that appears to look like that of a fox.	The text explains the steps in the process of creating the image.
IMAGE 2 	The image shows a woman's face attached to the body of a fish. The fish appears to be flying in rainy weather.	The text says that Mica was impressed by her daughter's collaboration, and so they continued, presumably with this or a similar image.
IMAGE 3 	The image shows Myla drawing bodies on faces that Mica had drawn in her sketchbook.	The text explains what the image shows—that Myla is working on faces in Mica's sketchbook.
IMAGE 4 	The image shows Mica watching Myla, who is drawing.	The text explains that at first Mica tried to direct what Myla drew, but soon learned to let Myla follow her own imagination.
IMAGE 5 	The image shows a woman's face with what looks like the body of a sea creature, near the water's edge at a beach.	The text explains that Mica gained an important insight while working with Myla: "giving up control" is not only fun, but necessary. The image shows the result.

NOTES

DIGITAL PERSPECTIVES

Comprehension Check

See possible responses in the chart on the student page.

FACILITATING

Jump Start

CLOSE REVIEW Ask groups to consider the following prompt: *What did Mica learn when she began to create art with her daughter?* As students talk in their groups, ask them to consider Mica's attitudes about sharing and control before and after she began collaborating with her four-year-old daughter.

Close Review

If needed, model close reviewing by using the Closer Review notes in the Interactive Teacher's Edition.

Remind groups to use Accountable Talk in their discussions and to support one another as they complete the close review.

Analyze the Media

1. **Responses will vary by group.** Each student should draw a definite conclusion about the image he or she chose.
2. **Possible response:** The images reveal that intriguing art is created when artists are open to collaboration and are willing to let go of control.
3. **Notebook: Responses will vary by group.** Each student should make an argument and support it with evidence from the images.

Media Vocabulary

Possible responses:

1. The four separate photographs show the step-by-step process that was used to create each **composition.**
2. Image 4 conveys a mood of warmth and tenderness. It is created through Mica's closeness to Myla and through the sunlight in the background.
3. In image 5, the primary focus is on the woman's face and the animal body. The background is the ocean.

For more support, see **Media Vocabulary**.

Word Network

Possible words: *daughter, kids, grown-up*

MAKING MEANING

MOTHER-DAUGHTER DRAWINGS

Close Review

With your group, revisit the images and your first-review notes. Record any new observations that seem important. What **questions** do you have? What can you **conclude**?

Analyze the Media

Notebook Complete the activities.

1. **Present and Discuss** Choose the image you find most interesting or powerful. Share your choice with the group and discuss why you chose it. Explain what you noticed in the image, what questions it raised for you, and what conclusions you reached about it.
2. **Review and Synthesize** With your group, review all the images. What does Mica Hendricks's experience drawing with her daughter reveal about how art is created?
3. **Notebook Essential Question:** ***What can one generation learn from another?*** What do you think the mother and daughter might have learned from each other by drawing together? What has learning about the Hendricks' process taught you about the ways in which one generation can learn from another?

WORD NETWORK

Look in the image gallery for words related to the topic of generations, and add them to your Word Network.

STANDARDS

Speaking and Listening
Analyze the main ideas and supporting details presented in diverse media and formats and explain how the ideas clarify a topic, text, or issue under study.

Language
Acquire and use accurately grade-appropriate general academic and domain-specific words and phrases; gather vocabulary knowledge when considering a word or phrase important to comprehension or expression.

LANGUAGE DEVELOPMENT

Media Vocabulary

composition **light and shadow** **perspective**

Use the concept vocabulary words in your responses to the following questions.

1. Why might Image 1 be made up of four separate photographs?
2. What mood is suggested by Image 4? How is that mood created?
3. In Image 5, what is the primary focus and what constitutes the background?

FORMATIVE ASSESSMENT

Analyze the Text Media

If students struggle to close review the drawings, **then** provide the **Mother-Daughter Drawings: Media Questions** available online in the Interactive Teacher's Edition or Unit Resources. Answers and DOK levels are also available.

Media Vocabulary

If students struggle to use the vocabulary words, **then** have them review the definitions and try to answer the questions again.

EFFECTIVE EXPRESSION

Speaking and Listening

Assignment

Sharing her sketchbook with her four-year-old daughter taught Mica Angela Hendricks that giving up control can help people grow. Write a brief narrative of an event that taught you a lesson about life, and share it with your group. Then, work together to create a **multimedia slideshow.** Choose one description on which to focus and combine it with at least four images, such as photos, illustrations, or other types of visual multimedia.

Choose Your Images As your group researches images for your slideshow, consider what you have learned about the ways in which **composition, perspective,** and **light and shadow** affect an image. Discuss these questions with your group:

- What mood or feeling do you want your images to convey?
- Which images should be photographs, which should be illustrations, and which should be a combination of both?
- What materials, props, and locations do you need to create your images?

Plan the Project Once you have considered these questions, make a storyboard. Decide which part of the narrative each image will represent. Arrange the images in a logical sequence.

STORYBOARD TEMPLATE

Draft and Rehearse Work with your group to finalize the narrative and slideshow. Assign roles for presenting, and rehearse to ensure that speakers are prepared and that the media is integrated smoothly.

Present and Discuss Read the narrative for the class and then present the slideshow. Discuss which aspects of the narrative are best told in words and which are best told in pictures.

Reflect With Your Group In the caption that accompanies the last image of the gallery, Mica Hendricks says, "Those things you hold so dear cannot change and grow and expand unless you loosen your grip on them a little." How did the process of working with your group to develop the slideshow influence your ideas about this quote? Did you find that it was difficult to "loosen your grip" and work collaboratively? What did you learn from the experience?

TIP

GROUP DISCUSSION

Think about the relationship between your images with your group. Should they have a similar look, or should they contrast with each other? Why?

EVIDENCE LOG

Before moving on to a new selection, go to your Evidence Log and record what you learned from "Mother-Daughter Drawings."

STANDARDS

Speaking and Listening

- Engage effectively in a range of collaborative discussions with diverse partners on *grade 7 topics, texts, and issues,* building on others' ideas and expressing their own clearly.
  a. Come to discussions prepared, having read or researched material under study; explicitly draw on that preparation by referring to evidence on the topic, text, or issue to probe and reflect on ideas under discussion.
- Include multimedia components and visual displays in presentations to clarify claims and findings and emphasize salient points.

Language

Acquire and use accurately grade-appropriate general academic and domain-specific words and phrases; gather vocabulary knowledge when considering a word or phrase important to comprehension or expression.

DIGITAL PERSPECTIVES

Speaking and Listening

If groups have trouble choosing a narrative, encourage them to consider which idea would best lend itself to visual storytelling.

Choose Your Images Have each group brainstorm two ideas for photographs and/or illustrations for each narrative. Then, have group members think about which images are the most effective or the most interesting. After all the group members have given their opinions, have them pick the strongest ideas for images to use in their slideshow.

Plan the Project Remind groups to consult the schedule for Small-Group Activities as they plan their project. Check to make sure each group has made assignments and that the work is divided evenly among group members.

Draft and Rehearse Encourage students to rehearse in front of others before doing the final presentation of their slideshow.

Present and Discuss As students discuss the different slideshows, remind them to follow the rules for collegial discussions. For more support, see **Speaking and Listening: Multimedia Slideshow.**

MAKE IT INTERACTIVE

Using the Interactive Teacher's Edition, project Image 1 from "Mother-Daughter Drawings." Ask students to consider what a reader might expect the story to be about if the set of photographs had one of these captions instead.

- A woman who is an artist teaches her young daughter how to draw.
- A mother becomes concerned when her daughter draws in the mother's sketchbook.
- Creating a painting from start to finish involves a series of steps.

Then have students briefly discuss how text can complement an image, and vice versa.

Evidence Log Support students in completing their Evidence Log. This paced activity will help prepare them for the Performance-Based Assessment at the end of the unit.

VOCABULARY DEVELOPMENT

Media Vocabulary Reinforcement Reinforce students' comprehension of media vocabulary with "show-you-know" sentences. The first part of the sentence uses the vocabulary word in an appropriate context. The second part—the "show-you-know" part—clarifies the first. Model the strategy with this example.

We loved the painting's *composition*, with horses in the foreground and meadows stretching to the horizon.

Then give students these sentence prompts and coach them to create the clarification parts.

1. It was a photo of dark, jutting *shadows* that showed ____.
2. She worked hard to draw the elephant's *proportions* right, but ____.
3. The old man's sketch had remarkable *perspective*; with just a few charcoal lines, he ____.

FORMATIVE ASSESSMENT

Speaking and Listening

If students struggle with locating images, **then** have them refine their search terms to more accurately describe the images they want—or have them create some of their own images.

Mother to Son • To James

AUDIO SUMMARIES
Audio summaries of "Mother to Son" and "To James" are available online in both English and Spanish in the Interactive Teacher's Edition or Unit Resources. Assigning these summaries prior to reading the selection may help students build additional background knowledge and set a context for their first read.

Summary

In Langston Hughes's poem "Mother to Son," the poet adopts the voice of an African American mother giving advice to her son. She tells him her life has not been a crystal staircase. Her staircase has tacks, splinters, torn-up boards, and no carpet. However, that hasn't stopped her from climbing the staircase, even in the dark. She tells him she's still climbing, and he must do the same, even though it's hard.

In the poem "To James" by Frank Horne, a father addresses his son. He takes pride in the boy's prowess on the running track and advises him that life itself is a short sprint. He tells his son to start out strong and run hard. He urges him to focus on the finish line and hold nothing back. He wants his son to experience the supreme joy of victory.

Insight

It is the job of the earlier generations to share the life lessons they have learned, so later generations can achieve happiness and fulfillment. Reading "Mother to Son" and "To James" will help students see how one generation paves the way for the next generation. One generation may sacrifice comforts or struggle through difficult times or fight against injustice just so the following generation will have an easier time. An earlier generation may pass down everything it knows so that the next generation can succeed.

ESSENTIAL QUESTION:
What can one generation learn from another?

Connection to Essential Question

The poems "Mother to Son" and "To James" provide a clear connection to the Essential Question, *What can one generation learn from another?* The speaker in "Mother to Son" warns her son against letting the difficulties of life stop him from continuing on. When she says that her son shouldn't give up just because he finds life "kinder hard," she is suggesting that he has encountered his own difficulties and she wants him to learn from her experience that he must not stop trying. The speaker of "To James" gives direct advice to James in the second stanza, telling the boy that to succeed in life, he must treat it like a race and give it everything he's got.

SMALL-GROUP LEARNING PERFORMANCE TASK
What new knowledge or skills can you learn from someone of a different generation?

UNIT PERFORMANCE-BASED ASSESSMENT
In what situations can one generation learn from another?

Connection to Performance Tasks

Small-Group Learning Performance Task "Mother to Son" gives students the choice of presenting the lesson that the mother teaches her son—that life is hard but you must not give up. "To James" gives students the choice of presenting the lesson that the speaker teaches James—that to succeed in life, you must try your hardest and maintain your focus on your goals.

Unit Performance-Based Assessment This selection provides students with strong examples of the types of lessons that one generation may share with another. Both poems have parental speakers who directly advise children on how to survive and succeed in life.

DIGITAL PERSPECTIVES

 Audio  Video 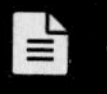 Document 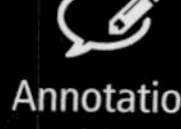 Annotation Highlights 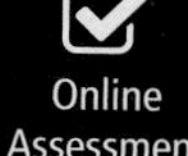 Online Assessment

LESSON RESOURCES

	Making Meaning	Language Development	Effective Expression
Lesson	**First Read** **Close Read** **Analyze Craft and Structure**	**Author's Style** **Concept Vocabulary** **Word Study**	**Writing to Sources**
Instructional Standards	**RL.7.10** By the end of the year, read and comprehend literature . . . **L.7.4** Determine or clarify the meaning of unknown and multiple-meaning words and phrases . . . **L.7.4.a** Use context as a clue . . . **RL.7.1** Cite several pieces of textual evidence to support analysis . . . **RL.7.2** Determine a theme or central idea of a text . . . **RL.7.4** Determine the meaning of words and phrases as they are used in a text . . .	**L.7.5** Demonstrate understanding of figurative language . . . **L.7.5.c** Distinguish among the connotations of words with similar denotations . . . **RL.7.4** Determine the meaning of words and phrases as they are used in a text . . .	**W.7.3** Write narratives . . . **W.7.3.a** Engage and orient the reader by establishing a context . . . **W.7.3.b** Use narrative techniques . . . **W.7.3.d** Use precise words and phrases, relevant descriptive details . . . **W.7.5** With some guidance and support from peers and adults, develop and strengthen writing . . . **W.7.9** Draw evidence from literary or informational texts . . . **W.7.9.a** Apply *grade 7 Reading standards* to literature . . .
STUDENT RESOURCES			
Available online in the Interactive Student Edition or Unit Resources	Selection Audio First-Read Guide: Poetry Close-Read Guide: Poetry	Word Network	Evidence Log
TEACHER RESOURCES			
Selection Resources Available online in the Interactive Teacher's Edition or Unit Resources	Audio Summaries: English and Spanish Annotation Highlights Text Questions First Read Extension Questions Analyze Craft and Structure: Symbolism	Author's Style: Rhythm and Repetition Concept Vocabulary and Word Study	Writing to Sources: Narrative Poem
Reteach/Practice (RP) Available online in the Interactive Teacher's Edition or Unit Resources	Analyze Craft and Structure: Figurative Language: Symbolism (RP)	Author's Style: Rhythm and Repetition (RP) Word Study: Connotations and Denotations (RP)	Writing to Sources: Narrative Poem (RP)
Assessment Available online in Assessments	Selection Test: English Selection Test: Spanish Extension Selection Test		
My Resources	A Unit 1 Answer Key is available online and in the Interactive Teacher's Edition		

Reading Support

Text Complexity Rubric: Mother to Son • To James	
Quantitative Measures	
Lexile: NP; NP **Text Length:** 20 lines; 51 lines	
Qualitative Measures	
Knowledge Demands ①—②—❸—④—⑤	To understand the poems, it is helpful to have an understanding of African American culture during the Harlem Renaissance. An understanding of running will help facilitate understanding of "To James."
Structure ①—❷—③—④—⑤	Both poems are written with free verse structure, in conversational style.
Language Conventionality and Clarity ①—②—❸—④—⑤	Vernacular language is used (pattern of speech and diction of conversation); "Mother to Son" contains speech patterns common among African Americans during the early twentieth century.
Levels of Meaning/Purpose ①—②—❸—④—⑤	Meaning requires understanding of metaphorical language (the crystal stair and wooden stair as metaphors for life). The metaphor has multiple possible meanings (glamor, beauty, social class).

DECIDE AND PLAN

English Language Support

Provide English Learners with support for language and meaning as they read the selections.

Language Students learning English may have difficulty with patterns of speech they don't normally see in modern English, for example: *there ain't been no light,* and *I'se still climbin'*. Ask them to highlight unfamiliar phrases. Point out that *ain't* is used to mean *not, isn't, hasn't,* or *haven't,* that *I'se* means *I've* or *I'm.*

Meaning Have students highlight words that are part of the symbol of the race. Ask them to think about how each part of the race relates to life's journey.

Strategic Support

Provide students with strategic support to ensure that they can successfully read the text.

Knowledge Demands Ask students to visualize a running race. Have them think about the actions a runner takes each step of the race.

Levels of Meaning Ask students to describe what a crystal stair would look like and then describe one with boards, tacks, splinters, and no carpet. What would the stairs be made of? What would they look like? Discuss the images as metaphors for life by asking students to describe the difference between life as a crystal stair (easy, rich, etc.) and as an old, wooden stair (difficult, poor, etc.).

Challenge

Provide students who need to be challenged with ideas for how they can go beyond a simple interpretation of the text.

Text Analysis Ask students to discuss the possible meanings of a crystal stair and what someone's socioeconomic class may be if they have a life represented by a crystal stair as opposed to a broken wooden stair.

Written Response Have students research Langston Hughes or Frank Horne to find out more about their lives or their reasons for writing the poems. Students may also read other poems by these authors and write an analysis of a favorite poem.

TEACH

Read and Respond

Have the groups read the selections and complete the Making Meaning, Language Development, and Effective Expression activities.

Standards Support Through Teaching and Learning Cycle

IDENTIFY NEEDS

Analyze results of the Beginning-of-Year Assessment, focusing on the items relating to Unit 1. Also take into consideration student performance to this point and your observations of where particular students struggle.

DECIDE AND PLAN

- If students have performed poorly on items matching these standards, then provide selection scaffolds before assigning them the on-level lesson provided in the Student Edition.
- If students have done well on the Beginning-of-Year Assessment, then challenge them to keep progressing and learning by giving them opportunities to practice the skills in depth.
- Use the Selection Resources listed on the Planning pages for "Mother to Son" and "To James" to help students continually improve their ability to master the standards.

Instructional Standards: Mother to Son • To James

	Catching Up	This Year	Looking Forward
Reading	You may wish to administer the **Author's Style: Rhythm and Repetition (RP)** worksheet to help students understand that repeating the same sounds at the beginning of words (or repeating the same words) in a poem adds meaning and power to the poem.	**RL.4** Determine the meaning of words and phrases as they are used in a text, including figurative and connotative meanings; analyze the impact of a specific word choice on meaning and tone.	Have partners find lines in "To James" that have words that repeat or begin with the same sound (alliteration). Have partners take turns reading those lines and discussing how the repeated sounds or word(s) emphasize an idea in the poem. Encourage student pairs to share their findings with the class.
Writing	You may wish to administer the **Writing to Sources: Narrative Poem (RP)** worksheet to help students connect words or phrases that describe the senses (sight, sound, feel, taste, smell) with vivid descriptions of events or experiences.	**W.3.d** Use precise words and phrases, relevant descriptive details, and sensory language to capture the action and convey experiences and events.	Ask students to write a poem in response to a previous selection they read in this or an earlier unit. Encourage and challenge them to include sensory words and phrases to make their poems vivid and clear.
Language	You may wish to administer the **Analyze Craft and Structure: Symbols (RP)** worksheet to help students understand that complex symbols can suggest layers of meaning.	**L.5** Demonstrate understanding of figurative language, word relationships, and nuances in word meanings.	Ask students to find another poem that uses complex symbols to suggest layers of meaning and write one paragraph about the author's use of symbolism and how it influences the meaning of the poem.

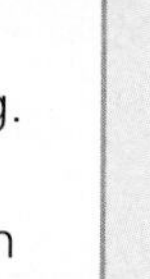

ANALYZE AND REVISE

- Analyze student work for evidence of student learning.
- Identify whether students have met the expectations in the standards.
- Identify implications for future instruction.

TEACH

Implement the planned lesson, and gather evidence of student learning.

FACILITATING

Jump Start

FIRST READ Engage students with this prompt: *Imagine you are going to write a letter that will be read by your children sometime in the future. What advice would you give? What is the most important thing to share with them before they enter school? Before they become teenagers?* Engage students in a discussion about giving advice to their children to set the context for reading "Mother to Son" and "To James."

Concept Vocabulary

Encourage groups to discuss the three concept vocabulary words. Have they seen the words in texts before? Do they use any of the words in their speech or writing? Do they recognize any word parts, such as a base word, a prefix, or a suffix?

Have groups look closely at the two types of context clues—familiar situations and familiar base words—and discuss how these types of clues can help determine meaning. Encourage groups to think of one other type of context clue they might encounter in a text. Possibilities include synonyms, antonyms, and restatements of an idea.

FIRST READ

Have students perform the steps of the first read independently.

NOTICE: Students should focus on the basic elements of each poem to ensure that they can identify the speaker and what the text describes.

ANNOTATE: Have students mark passages they would like to revisit in order to enhance comprehension or to increase their aesthetic appreciation.

CONNECT: Students should compare the feelings expressed in the poems with those of parents and sons they have heard or read about.

RESPOND: Students will demonstrate their understanding of the poems by answering questions.

Point out to students that while they will always complete the Respond step at the end of the first read, the other steps will probably happen somewhat concurrently. You may wish to print copies of the **First-Read Guide: Poetry** for students to use.

MAKING MEANING

POETRY COLLECTION 1

Mother to Son

To James

Concept Vocabulary

As you perform your first read of these two poems, you will encounter the following words.

flung	catapulted	lurched

Context Clues If these words are unfamiliar to you, try using **context clues**—other words and phrases that appear in a text—to help you determine their meanings. There are various types of context clues that you might encounter as you read.

Restatement of Idea: As they fought to get past the finish line, one runner **hurled** himself forward, throwing his body over the line.

Synonym: At the beginning of the race, he **launched,** or propelled, himself over the start line.

Contrast of Idea: The winners of the race glided across the finish line, while the remaining competitors **stumbled** behind them.

Apply your knowledge of context clues and other vocabulary strategies to determine the meanings of unfamiliar words you encounter during your first read of the two poems.

First Read POETRY

Refer to these strategies as you conduct your first read. You will have an opportunity to complete a close read after your first read.

NOTICE *who* or *what* is "speaking" the poem and whether the poem tells a story or describes a single incident.

ANNOTATE by marking vocabulary and key passages you want to revisit.

CONNECT ideas within the selection to what you already know and you have already read.

RESPOND by completing the Comprehension Check.

STANDARDS

Reading Literature
By the end of the year, read and comprehend literature, including stories, dramas, and poems, in the grades 6–8 text complexity band proficiently, with scaffolding as needed at the high end of the range.

Language
Determine or clarify the meaning of unknown and multiple-meaning words and phrases based on *grade 7 reading and content,* choosing flexibly from a range of strategies.

a. Use context as a clue to the meaning of a word or phrase.

About the Poets

Langston Hughes (1902–1967) was an African American writer known for jazz-inspired poems that portrayed African American life in America. His work was controversial. Some critics worried that it played into racial stereotypes. Others praised Hughes for reaching everyday people by using language and themes "familiar to anyone who had the ability simply to read."

Frank Horne (1899–1974) was an African American writer and activist. As a director at the U.S. Housing Authority, he fought to end segregated housing. As a poet, he fought discrimination with poems that conveyed dignity and pride.

Backgrounds

Mother to Son

Even after the abolition of slavery, life was very hard for most African Americans. Poetry, music, and the other arts were creative outlets that allowed them to express the hardships of their lives and to find inspiration.

To James

From 1914 through 1937, Harlem, a neighborhood in New York City, was the setting for an awakening of African American culture that came to be known as the Harlem Renaissance. During this period, African American writers such as Langston Hughes and Frank Horne searched for the truest way to express their experiences. Each developed a unique style that ultimately helped shape not just African American culture but also world culture.

FACILITATING SMALL-GROUP CLOSE READING

CLOSE READ: Poems As students work together, monitor their discussions and offer support as needed.

- Lead a brief discussion on the differences between poetry and prose.
- Help students see that the sounds made by the combination of words is more important in poetry than in prose.
- Explain that poems tend to be shorter and therefore must make their point more directly.
- Literary devices such as simile and metaphor are more common in poetry than in prose.

Encourage groups to find and interpret examples of figurative language.

DIGITAL PERSPECTIVES

Mother to Son
To James

What kind of life do parents want their children to have? What can a parent do to help make that life possible?

Modeling questions such as these will help students connect to "Mother to Son" and "To James" and to the Small-Group Performance Task assignment. Selection audio and print capability for the selection are available in the Interactive Teacher's Edition.

FACILITATING

CLOSER LOOK

Analyze Symbolism

Circulate among groups as students conduct their close read. Suggest that groups read the entire poem without interruption. Encourage them to talk about the annotations that they mark. If needed, provide the following support.

ANNOTATE: Have students mark details in lines 3–6 of the poem that describe the staircase, or work with small groups to have students participate while you highlight them together.

QUESTION: Guide students to consider what these details might tell them. Ask what a reader can infer from what was annotated, and accept student responses.

Possible response: These details very effectively create an impression of a dingy and dangerous staircase.

CONCLUDE: Help students to formulate conclusions about the importance of these details in the text. Ask students why the poet might have included these details.

Possible response: The dingy staircase is the reality of life for this mother, and the poet transforms it into a symbol of noble human endeavor and purpose.

Remind students that, in order to work successfully, a **symbol** should operate on two levels: it should have a functional, literal meaning, and it should be able to bear the weight of a much greater significance.

POETRY

Mother to Son

Langston Hughes

NOTES

Well, son, I'll tell you:
Life for me ain't been no crystal stair.
It's had tacks in it,
And splinters,
And boards torn up,
And places with no carpet on the floor—
Bare.
But all the time
I'se been a-climbin' on,
And reachin' landin's,
And turnin' corners,
And sometimes goin' in the dark
Where there ain't been no light.
So boy, don't you turn back.
Don't you set down on the steps
'Cause you finds it's kinder hard.
Don't you fall now—
For I'se still goin', honey,
I'se still climbin',
And life for me ain't been no crystal stair.

PERSONALIZE FOR LEARNING

English Language Support

Figurative Language English Learners may struggle with the figurative language in poetry. Point out that students can use context clues to determine the meaning of confusing phrases or ideas. Read lines 2 through 5 of the poem: *Life for me ain't been no crystal stair./It's had tacks in it,/And splinters./And boards torn up.* Ask: *What is the speaker in this poem talking about in these lines?* (life) *What words does the speaker use to help you understand how she feels?* (tacks, splinters, torn) *What is the speaker saying about her subject in these lines?* (Her life has been difficult.) *How do you know?* (She is explaining something rough and hard to navigate.) Guide students to use context clues to determine the meaning of other figurative language in "Mother to Son" and "To James." **ALL LEVELS**

To James

Frank Horne

Do you remember
How you won
That last race . . . ?
How you **flung** your body
At the start . . .
How your spikes
Ripped the cinders[1]
In the stretch . . .
How you **catapulted**
Through the tape . . .
Do you remember . . . ?
Don't you think
I **lurched** with you
Out of those starting holes . . . ?
Don't you think
My sinews[2] tightened
At those first
Few strides . . .
And when you flew into the stretch

1. **cinders** *n.* ashes.
2. **sinews** *n.* strong tissue that connects muscle to bone.

NOTES

Mark context clues or indicate another strategy you used that helped you determine meaning.

flung (FLUHNG) *v.*
MEANING:

catapulted (KA tuh puhl tihd) *v.*
MEANING:

lurched (LURCHT) *v.*
MEANING:

DIGITAL PERSPECTIVES

Concept Vocabulary

FLUNG If groups are struggling to define the word *flung* in line 4, suggest that they use context clues to determine the meaning. These clues indicate that the writer is describing the start of a race, and students can imagine what a competitor does at the start of a race. Have students use these context clues to define the word.

Possible response: *Flung* means "threw."

CATAPULTED If groups are struggling to define the word *catapulted* in line 9, point out that the base word is *catapult*. Tell students to think about what a catapult does, and then to define the word.
Possible response: *Catapulted* means "hurled or launched with great force."

LURCHED If groups are struggling to define the word *lurched* in line 13, suggest that they use context clues to determine its meaning. One of the clues should prompt them to think about how a person would move if the sinews of his or her legs had tightened. Have students use these context clues to define the word. Remind students to look at the footnote if they aren't sure what *sinews* means.
Possible response: *Lurched* means "moved jerkily."

VOCABULARY DEVELOPMENT

Verb Tenses Ask students what all three vocabulary words in lines 4, 9, and 13 have in common. (All are verbs, all are related to motion, and all are in the past tense.) Point out that two of the past-tense verbs are formed in the usual way, but one is irregular.

Copy this chart onto the board and challenge students to complete it.

Infinitive	Past	Present	Future
to fling	flung	*fling*	*will fling*
to catapult	catapulted	*catapult*	*will catapult*
to lurch	lurched	*lurch*	*will lurch*

CLOSER LOOK

Analyze Tone

Circulate among groups as students conduct their close read. Suggest that groups close read the whole poem, without interruption. Encourage them to talk about the annotations that they mark. If needed, provide the following support.

ANNOTATE: Have students mark details in the poem that signify a change in the way the speaker seems to sound, starting at line 29 and concentrating on the verbs, or work with small groups to have students participate while you highlight them together.

QUESTION: Guide students to consider what these details might tell them. Ask what a reader can infer from the tone of the verbs, and accept student responses.

Possible response: The verbs are all imperatives. The speaker is giving James instructions.

CONCLUDE: Help students to formulate conclusions about the importance of these details in the text. Ask students why the poet might have included these details.

Possible response: The speaker is encouraging James to win. The poet included these details of tone to contrast with the questions that dominate the first 28 lines, and to make it possible for the speaker to suggest that there is a much greater race to win.

Remind students that **tone** expresses the poet's attitude to the subject and to the reader—and the speaker's attitude to the person he or she is addressing. Tone is often most easily established by the mood of the verbs. Here, lines 1–28 are interrogative; 29–51 are imperative.

NOTES

Was not all my thrill
Of a thousand races
In your blood . . . ?
At your final drive
Through the finish line
Did not my shout
Tell of the
Triumphant ecstasy
Of victory . . . ?
Live
As I have taught you
To run, Boy—
It's a short dash
Dig your starting holes
Deep and firm
Lurch out of them
Into the straightaway
With all the power
That is in you
Look straight ahead
To the finish line
Think only of the goal
Run straight
Run high
Run hard
Save nothing
And finish
With an ecstatic burst
That carries you
Hurtling
Through the tape
To victory. . . .

WriteNow Analyze and Interpret

Response In lines 14–17 of "Mother to Son" and in lines 19–51 of "To James," a parent is giving a child advice about life and the best way to live it. Have students write a brief poem in response to one of these parents. Students should imagine that they are the child being addressed in the original poem. How do they feel about getting advice? Do they agree or disagree with the advice? What would they want to say to the parent in response?

After students have completed their poems, you may choose to have volunteers read their work aloud to the class.

Comprehension Check

Complete the following items after you finish your first read. Review and clarify details with your group.

MOTHER TO SON

1. Identify three words or phrases from the poem that describe the staircase.

2. What does the speaker tell her son NOT to do?

TO JAMES

1. What event does the speaker refer to at the poem's start?

2. What goal does the speaker of the poem identify?

3. Which actions repeat throughout the poem?

RESEARCH

Research to Explore These poems may spark your curiosity to learn more. Briefly research a topic related to one of the poems. Then, share what you have learned with your group.

DIGITAL PERSPECTIVES 

Comprehension Check

MOTHER TO SON
Possible responses:

1. boards torn up, bare, dark
2. She tells her son not to give up when things get difficult.

TO JAMES
Possible responses:

1. The speaker refers to "you" winning a race.
2. The speaker identifies victory as the goal.
3. Running and racing repeat throughout the poem.

Research

Research to Explore If students have trouble selecting a research topic, suggest that they consider researching other poems by Langston Hughes, such as "Still Here," "I, Too," or "Dream Deferred."

DIGITAL PERSPECTIVES

Enriching the Text Both Langston Hughes and Frank Horne are closely associated with the Harlem Renaissance. To help students understand the culture these poets were writing in, and the relationship between generations in that culture, go online to find images of people from different generations living in Harlem and other urban neighborhoods in the 1920s and 30s. Display the images after students have finished reading both poems. Then have groups share with the class how the images provide insight into the poems. Encourage them to consider how—or whether—their views of interactions between generations changed based on the images.

Jump Start

CLOSE READ Engage students in a discussion about what makes poetry a unique way of exploring the interactions between generations. What is different about the way poetry affects the reader?

Close Read the Text

If needed, model close reading by using the Annotation Highlights in the Interactive Teacher's Edition. Remind groups to use Accountable Talk in their discussions and to support one another as they complete the close read.

Analyze the Text

1. **Possible response:** The mother demonstrates persistence and strength. She needs these qualities to get through the difficulties she has faces.
2. **Responses will vary by group** but be sure that students explain why they choose the lines they shared with the group.
3. **Responses will vary.**

Concept Vocabulary

Why These Words? Possible response: These words express fast, forceful, or sudden movement and create an overall sense of momentum that carries through the entire poem. Another word that fits the category is *lunged.*

Practice

Sample responses: She **flung** the javelin past the trees; The pole vaulter **catapulted** to new heights; The exhausted runner **lurched** to the finish line.

Word Network

Possible words: *son, boy, blood, taught*

Word Study

Connotations and Denotations

Possible responses:

flung: the denotative meaning is "threw forcefully." The connotation is that the action is made with passion, or without fear of the consequences. Two words that share the denotation of *flung* are *toss* and *heave*. The connotation of *toss* is that the action is casual. The connotation of *heave* is that the action is made with great effort.

For more support, see **Concept Vocabulary and Word Study.**

MAKING MEANING

POETRY COLLECTION 1

Close Read the Text

With your group, revisit sections of the text that you marked during your first read. **Annotate** details that you notice. What **questions** do you have? What can you **conclude**?

Analyze the Text

CITE TEXTUAL EVIDENCE to support your answers.

Notebook Complete the activities.

1. **Review and Clarify** With your group, reread "Mother to Son." What qualities does the mother demonstrate through her words and actions? Why does the mother need these qualities?
2. **Present and Discuss** Now, work with your group to share lines from the poems that you found especially important. Take turns presenting your lines. Discuss what you noticed in the lines, what questions you asked, and what conclusions you reached.
3. **Essential Question:** *What can one generation learn from another?* What have these poems revealed about what one generation teaches another? Discuss your ideas with the group.

WORD NETWORK

Look in the text for words related to the topic of generations, and add them to your Word Network.

STANDARDS

Reading Literature

- Cite several pieces of textual evidence to support analysis of what the text says explicitly as well as inferences drawn from the text.
- Determine a theme or central idea of a text and analyze its development over the course of the text; provide an objective summary of the text.
- Determine the meaning of words and phrases as they are used in a text, including figurative and connotative meanings; analyze the impact of rhymes and other repetitions of sounds on a specific verse or stanza of a poem or section of a story or drama.

Language

Demonstrate understanding of figurative language, word relationships, and nuances in word meanings.

c. Distinguish among the connotations of words with similar denotations.

LANGUAGE DEVELOPMENT

Concept Vocabulary

flung	catapulted	lurched

Why These Words? The concept vocabulary words from the poems are related. With your group, determine what the words have in common. Write your ideas and add another word that fits the category.

Practice

Notebook To gain a better understanding of the concept vocabulary words, write a sentence for each word that demonstrates your understanding of the word's meaning.

Word Study

Connotations and Denotations A **connotation** is an association or feeling that a word suggests in addition to its literal dictionary definition, or **denotation**. Two words can have similar denotations but different connotations. For example, the words *mother* and *matriarch* have the same basic denotation. However, *mother* has positive connotations of warmth and security, whereas *matriarch* suggests a feeling of distance and formality.

Find two synonyms in a thesaurus for the concept vocabulary word *flung*. Write an explanation of how the connotations of the three words differ.

FORMATIVE ASSESSMENT

Analyze the Text

If students struggle to close read the text, **then** provide the **Poetry Collection 1: Text Questions** available online in the Interactive Teacher's Edition or Unit Resources. Answers and DOK levels are also available.

Concept Vocabulary

If students struggle to identify the concept, **then** discuss the words in more detail, emphasizing the actions these words represent.

Word Study

If students fail to identify connotations for the concept vocabulary, **then** ask them to say the word aloud and write down the first thing that comes to mind. For Reteach and Practice, see **Word Study: Connotations and Denotations (RP).**

Analyze Craft and Structure

Figurative Language: Symbolism A **symbol** is anything—an object, person, animal, place, or situation—that represents something else. A symbol has its own meaning, but it also stands for something larger than itself, usually an abstract idea. For example, a dove is a type of bird that symbolizes peace.

In poetry, an author's use of symbolism can often reveal the **theme**, or insight about life, of a poem. To determine the theme of a poem that incorporates symbolism, **make inferences**, or educated guesses, as to what the symbol might represent based on the details in the poem. Then, consider the meaning of the symbol and how it suggests the theme.

Practice

CITE TEXTUAL EVIDENCE to support your answers.

Gather your notes in this chart and share with your group.

	MOTHER TO SON	TO JAMES
How is symbolism used in the poem? What is the symbol?	a. See possible responses in the Teacher's Edition.	b.
What impression of life does this symbol create? What details from the poem suggest this impression?	c.	d.
What does this symbol suggest about how people should live their lives?	e.	f.
What is the theme of the poem? What details from your analysis of the author's use of symbolism support this inference?	g.	h.

PERSONALIZE FOR LEARNING

Challenge

Symbolism Every generation has symbols that have come to represent its experiences, culture, and important moments in its youth. For example, the peace symbol is often associated with the youth of the late 1960s, whereas emoticons are more closely associated with today's youth.

Have students interview family and friends from different generations about the symbols of their youth. Students should then create a brief digital slide show of images of those symbols. As you project each student's slides, have the class try to guess which generation the symbols belong to.

DIGITAL PERSPECTIVES  

Analyze Craft and Structure

Figurative Language: Symbolism Engage students in a discussion about symbolism in their lives. Discuss how symbols can convey very deep sentiments quickly, without using a lot of words. What makes symbolism so important to poetry? How is it different from the use of symbolism in prose? For more support, see **Analyze Craft and Structure: Symbols.**

MAKE IT INTERACTIVE

Choose a digital image that is easily recognizable as a symbol of something of importance to your students and project it for the class. Ask students to take a minute to write down what the symbol means to them. Then, ask students to discuss in their groups similarities or differences in their interpretation of the symbol.

Possible responses:

a. A staircase symbolizes life.

b. A race symbolizes life.

c. Life is a hard, constant, winding uphill climb; life is sometimes rough, confusing and painful. Details such as "had tacks in it/And splinters" suggest the difficulty of life.

d. Life is an exciting competition; life can be a straight path with a goal at the end. Details such as "flew into the stretch" and "through the finish line" help create the impression.

e. The symbol suggests that people should keep going, even when times are hard. They shouldn't expect life to ever be easy, but they should never give up.

f. The symbol suggests that people should have a goal and just go for it with all of their strength and concentration.

g. The theme is that it is necessary to persevere even when life is difficult. The details that suggest that it's necessary to persevere include "I'se still climbin."

h. The theme is that one should try hard to succeed in life. The details that suggest that theme include "Run straight/Run high/Run hard," and "Through the tape/To victory. . . ."

FORMATIVE ASSESSMENT

Analyze Craft and Structure

If students are unable to identify what the symbols represent, **then** have them think about the people, places, or things that the symbols are identified with. For Reteach and Practice, see **Analyze Craft and Structure: Symbols (RP).**

FACILITATING

Author's Style

Rhythm and Repetition Students may automatically associate poetry with rhyme (the repetition of sounds at the ends of words). Explain to students that not all poems include rhyme. Free verse poetry, such as "To James" or "Mother to Son," does not employ rhyme, and often follows the rhythm of natural speech. For more support, see **Author's Style: Rhythm and Repetition.**

Read It

Possible responses:

Mother to Son

- *and*; lines 4, 5, 6, 10, 11, 12, and 20
- *I'se . . . climbin'*: lines 9 and 19

To James

- *Do you*: lines 1 and 11
- *Don't you think*: lines 12 and 15
- *Run . . .*: lines 42, 43, and 44
- *. . .?*: lines 3, 11, 14, 22, and 28

Write It

Responses will vary but students should identify uses of rhythm and repetition in their chosen poem. Ask them to explain why particular rhythms and repetitions are appropriate to the poem or to particular parts of the poem.

FORMATIVE ASSESSMENT

Author's Style

If students struggle to identify repetition in the poems, **then** have them read aloud the first and last words of each line, looking and listening for words or phrases that repeat. For Reteach and Practice, see **Author's Style: Rhythm and Repetition (RP).**

LANGUAGE DEVELOPMENT

POETRY COLLECTION 1

TIP

GROUP DISCUSSION
Take turns presenting portions of each poem aloud. Discuss how listening to a poem read aloud helps you to hear rhythm, rhyme, and other sound devices. Discuss the connection between the sound of a poem and its meaning.

Author's Style

Rhythm and Repetition **Rhythm** is the pattern of strong and weak beats in spoken or written language.

In free verse poems such as "To James" by Frank Horne and "Mother to Son" by Langston Hughes, the structural pattern can be irregular and closer to the natural rising and falling of spoken language. The term "free verse" refers to poetry that has no standard pattern of rhyme or rhythm.

Repetition is the repeated use of any element of language. Poets can repeat a sound, a word, a phrase, a sentence, a rhyme, a rhythm, or all of these elements to emphasize ideas and create musical effects. Here are some examples:

- *The sun sank in the sea.*
- *We didn't look, we didn't listen, we only were.*
- *I gallop'd, Dirck gallop'd, we gallop'd all three;*

Notice that in these examples, both words and sounds are repeated.

Read It

Test your understanding of repetition with a game. Working individually, make a list of the repeated elements in "To James" and "Mother to Son." Identify as many examples as you can; then rejoin your group and compare lists.

Write It

Choose one poem from the collection and write a paragraph describing how the poet uses rhythm and repetition to emphasize certain ideas.

STANDARDS

Reading Literature
Determine the meaning of words and phrases as they are used in a text, including figurative and connotative meanings; analyze the impact of rhymes and other repetitions of sounds on a specific verse or stanza of a poem or section of a story or drama.

Language
Demonstrate understanding of figurative language, word relationships, and nuances in word meanings.

PERSONALIZE FOR LEARNING

English Language Support

Rhythm in Poetry Explain to students that when reading poetry aloud, it is important to find the rhythm of the words.

Have pairs of students work together to discuss rhythm. Have one student read "To James" softly to him or herself and have one student read "Mother to Son" to him or herself. Then have each student explain to the other how free verse, or the absence of a regular rhythm, affects each poem. **EMERGING**

Have pairs of students read "To James" and "Mother to Son" out loud and discuss the effect that free verse, or the absence of a regular rhythm, has on how a poem sounds. Ask them to discuss if they prefer free verse or a poem with a regular rhythm and why. **EXPANDING**

Ask students to read "To James" and "Mother to Son" and discuss the effect that free verse, or the absence of a regular rhythm, has on how a poem sounds. Ask them to write a brief paragraph about whether they prefer free verse or a poem with a regular rhythm and why. **BRIDGING**

An expanded **English Language Support Lesson** on Rhythm is available in the Interactive Teacher's Edition.

Writing to Sources

Assignment

Write a **narrative poem** in which the speaker shares with readers a lesson learned through personal experience. Include at least one symbol in your poem.

You will work individually to craft your poem. After you have completed your poems, you will revise and discuss them as a group.

Analyze Sources for Inspiration As you brainstorm ideas for your poem, review the poems by Hughes and Horne. Note the ways in which the poets use symbols to convey the experience of the speaker and to develop the theme of the poem. Also, note other techniques, such as description, that the poets use to capture the experiences of the speaker and the subjects. Studying the ways poets effectively use symbols and narrative techniques can help you better apply them to your own writing.

Organize Your Ideas Consider the following questions to organize your thoughts and add interest to your poem:

- What experience will my poem describe? What symbol will I use to convey this experience?
- Who is the speaker of my poem? Whom will the speaker be addressing, and what is their relationship?
- What is the setting of my poem? What specific details describe the setting?
- How can I use **sensory language,** or language that appeals to one or more of the five senses, to vividly describe my speaker, subjects, setting, and experience?
- What is the theme of my poem? What lesson is the experience in my poem meant to convey?

Draft Your Poem Once you have planned your poem, write it down. Try not to self-edit at this point; strive to get it written in one sitting so that you can maintain your flow of ideas.

Revise and Evaluate Exchange the first draft of your poem with a group member. See if you can determine the subject, symbol, and theme of your classmate's poem. Also, consider your classmate's use of sensory language and descriptive details: *Is any sensory language confusing or inaccurate? Are there places where descriptive details would make the poem more interesting?* Provide feedback to your classmate politely and respectfully.

Discuss as a Group Read the final version of your poem to your group. After all members have recited their poems, discuss the similarities and differences between them. Discuss the process of writing a poem and creating a symbol: *How was this challenging? How did the process increase your understanding of the ways in which symbols can be effective in poetry?*

EVIDENCE LOG

Before moving on to a new selection, go to your log and record what you learned from "Mother to Son" and "To James."

STANDARDS

Writing

- Write narratives to develop real or imagined experiences or events using effective technique, relevant descriptive details, and well-structured event sequences.
  - a. Engage and orient the reader by establishing a context and point of view and introducing a narrator and/or characters; organize an event sequence that unfolds naturally and logically.
  - b. Use narrative techniques, such as dialogue, pacing and description, to develop experiences, events, and/or characters.
  - d. Use precise words and phrases, relevant descriptive details, and sensory language to capture the action and convey experiences and events.
- With some guidance and support from peers and adults, develop and strengthen writing as needed by planning, revising, editing, rewriting, or trying a new approach, focusing on how well purpose and audience have been addressed.
- Draw evidence from literary or informational texts to support analysis, reflection, and research.
  - a. Apply *grade 7 Reading standards* to literature.

DIGITAL PERSPECTIVES

Writing to Sources

Ensure that all group members have an opportunity to think about how they would share a lesson they learned through personal experience.

Analyze Sources for Inspiration Remind students to think about how the poets use symbols to convey their insights, as well as how the speakers in the poems share advice.

Organize Your Ideas Encourage students to take notes as they consider each question. Point out that they may change their minds about various details as they begin drafting the poem.

Draft Your Poem Have students work independently to draft their poems. Encourage them to use the ideas they have noted but point out that they should be open to new ideas in their writing process.

Revise and Evaluate Students may not immediately recognize symbols or themes in poetry. It will be valuable for students to be able to name the symbol, theme, and descriptive language of their own poems, as well as the poems of others. Encourage them to discuss the strengths and weaknesses of each other's poems while keeping a collegial tone.

Discuss as a Group Students should reflect on the process of using symbols and descriptive language to convey an insight in poetry. For more support, see **Writing to Sources: Narrative Poem.**

Evidence Log Support students in completing their Evidence Log. This paced activity will help prepare them for the Performance-Based Assessment at the end of the unit.

FORMATIVE ASSESSMENT

Writing to Sources

If groups struggle to combine and revise their poem, **then** suggest they think about what the group members' individual drafts have in common and how they complement one another. For Reteach and Practice, see **Writing to Sources: Narrative Poem (RP).**

Selection Test

Administer the "Mother to Son; To James" Selection Test, which is available in both print and digital formats online in Assessments.

Present a Nonfiction Narrative

Remind groups to consult the schedule for Small-Group Learning to guide their work during the Performance Task.

Students should complete the assignment using presentation software to take advantage of text, graphics, and sound features.

Plan With Your Group

Analyze the Texts Students should understand that each text may contain more than one lesson, and the same lesson may have been taught in more than one text.

Assign Roles Have students try to accommodate individual group members' wishes to act as the speaker or narrator for a given text, especially if a person feels he or she has special insight. Remind students that all group members will have an important role to play in the discussion.

SOURCES

- TUTORS TEACH SENIORS NEW HIGH-TECH TRICKS
- *from* MOM & ME & MOM
- LEARNING TO LOVE MY MOTHER
- MOTHER TO SON
- TO JAMES

Present a Nonfiction Narrative

Assignment

Work with your group to present a **panel discussion** in which you tell stories and give examples that relate to the following question.

What new knowledge or skills can you learn from someone of a different generation?

Plan With Your Group

Analyze the Texts With your group, identify a key lesson about life taught in each text listed. Summarize your ideas on this chart.

TITLE	LESSON TAUGHT / SUPPORTING DETAILS
Tutors Teach Seniors New High-Tech Tricks	
from Mom & Me & Mom	
Learning to Love My Mother	
Mother to Son	
To James	

Assign Roles When the chart is complete, review with your group. Then, identify one group member to act as moderator and the other group members to represent one narrator or one speaker in the panel discussion.

STANDARDS

Speaking and Listening

- Engage effectively in a range of collaborative discussions with diverse partners on *grade 7 topics, texts, and issues,* building on others' ideas and expressing their own clearly.
  - a. Come to discussions prepared, having read or researched material under study; explicitly draw on that preparation by referring to evidence on the topic, text, or issue to probe and reflect on ideas under discussion.
  - b. Follow rules for collegial discussions, track progress toward specific goals and deadlines, and define individual roles as needed.
- Analyze the main ideas and supporting details presented in diverse media and formats and explain how the ideas clarify a topic, text, or issue under study.

AUTHOR'S PERSPECTIVE **Ernest Morrell, Ph.D.**

How to Package a Speech/Oral Presentation The Small-Group speaking and listening activity will help students learn how to engage an audience during a presentation. This is important for students as they prepare for careers, public service, and higher education. Help students learn to become better speakers by reminding them to ask themselves these questions as they practice and rehearse their speeches and oral presentation:

- **Posture:** Does my posture convey authority and ease? Do I look relaxed and comfortable as I'm presenting?
- **Body language:** How do I connect physically with my audience? For instance, do I make eye contact, lean forward at key points to show emphasis, and use appropriate gestures?
- **Voice:** Am I changing my voice by varying my pitch and volume to show emotion and convey meaning? Does my voice project to the back rows?
- **Humor:** How do I add humor when it suits my audience and purpose? Do I tell jokes or anecdotes, for instance?
- **Tone:** Do I speak with passion to engage my audience?

Remind students that the way they present their information is often just as important as what they are saying.

Plan Your Panel Discussion Allow time for the moderator to prepare questions for the discussion about life lessons that are passed on between generations. Other group members should use this time to become expert on the speaker or narrator of a given text. Keep the following in mind:

- The moderator's questions should lead responders to relate **anecdotes,** or short, true-life stories, about their experiences.
- Panel members should be prepared to respond to the moderator's questions with stories about what they learned from another generation.

Rehearse With Your Group

Review Requirements As you practice your panel discussion, use this checklist to evaluate the effectiveness of your first run-through. Then, use your evaluation and these instructions to guide any changes you make to the format of the panel discussion.

CONTENT	PRESENTATION TECHNIQUES
☐ The questions posed are meaningful and answerable. ☐ The responses should be in the form of a narrative.	☐ Speakers make eye contact and speak clearly. ☐ Speakers adjust volume and pacing as appropriate. ☐ Speakers use their tone of voice to emphasize main points.

Fine-Tune the Content If the connection between the moderator's questions and the panel members' responses are not yet clear, work as a group to make the connections stronger. You may need to perform further analysis of the source texts to strengthen the content.

Brush Up on Your Presentation Techniques Practice making eye contact with the moderator and with other panel members as they speak. Avoid multitasking during the discussion so that the focus remains on the person speaking.

Present and Evaluate

Remember that you must use teamwork to make this presentation effective. As you listen to other groups present, take notes and be ready to ask questions and provide feedback at the conclusion of their discussion.

STANDARDS

Speaking and Listening

- Present claims and findings, emphasizing salient points in a focused, coherent manner with pertinent descriptions, facts, details, and examples; use appropriate eye contact, adequate volume, and clear pronunciation.
- Adapt speech to a variety of contexts and tasks, demonstrating command of formal English when indicated or appropriate.

DIGITAL PERSPECTIVES

Plan Your Panel Discussion Students may choose to work together to plan questions that the moderator may ask. Encourage students to think about the answers to those questions from the point of view of the speaker or narrator each is representing.

Rehearse With Your Group

Review Requirements After the first run-through, have students discuss whether the questions were meaningful and whether the answers were stories told from the point of view of the speakers and narrators of the texts.

Fine-Tune the Content If students are having difficulty in asking or answering questions based on the texts, encourage them to share their own ideas about the texts, so that the narratives presented can be stronger.

Brush Up on Your Presentation Techniques Remind students that when taking part in the panel discussion, they may need to speak at a volume that is somewhat louder than they are accustomed to so that their voice projects to the entire presentation space.

MAKE IT INTERACTIVE

Suggest that groups video record their rehearsal and watch it together as a strategy for refining their panel discussion.

Present and Evaluate

Before beginning the panel discussions, set the expectations for the audience. You may wish to have students consider these questions as groups present.

- What are the main lessons addressed in the presentation?
- How does each panelist address lessons about life through narratives related to the texts you have read?
- What presentation skills did the group excel at?

As students provide feedback to the presenting group, remind them that compliments are just as valuable as constructive criticism.

PERSONALIZE FOR LEARNING

Challenge

Building Understanding Have groups discuss how the genres and/or media of the selections in the Small-Group Learning section affected students' understandings of and receptiveness to the lessons presented throughout the unit. Encourage students to share which genre or medium they found most understandable or thought-provoking Remind students that there is no one genre that is better than another, and that a genre or format they find easy to understand may be challenging for another student.

OVERVIEW

INDEPENDENT LEARNING

What can one generation learn from another?

Encourage students to think carefully about what they have already learned and what more they want to know about the unit topic of generations. This is a key first step to previewing and selecting the text they will read in Independent Learning.

Independent Learning Strategies

Review the Learning Strategies with students and explain that as they work through Independent Learning they will develop strategies to work on their own.

- Have students watch the video on Independent Learning Strategies.
- A video on this topic is available online in the Professional Development Center.

Students should include any favorite strategies that they might have devised on their own during Whole-Class and Small-Group Learning. For example, for the strategy "Take notes," students might include:

- Organize notes in a chart.
- Highlight most important notes so they are easy to find.

Block Scheduling

Each day in this Pacing Plan represents a 40–50 minute class period. Teachers using block scheduling may combine days to reflect their class schedule. In addition, teachers may revise pacing to differentiate and support core instruction by integrating components and resources as students require.

OVERVIEW: INDEPENDENT LEARNING

ESSENTIAL QUESTION:

What can one generation learn from another?

People from different generations sometimes have very different ways of looking at the world. For your final reading selection in this unit, you will choose one additional text about generations. Follow these steps to help you choose.

Look Back Think about the selections you have already read. What more do you want to know about the topic of generations?

Look Ahead Preview the selections by reading the descriptions. Which one seems most interesting and appealing to you?

Look Inside Take a few minutes to scan through the text you chose. Make another selection if this text doesn't meet your needs.

Independent Learning Strategies

Throughout your life, in school, in your community, and in your career, you will need to rely on yourself to learn and work on your own. Review these strategies and the actions you can take to practice them during Independent Learning. Add ideas of your own for each category.

STRATEGY	ACTION PLAN
Create a schedule	• Make a plan for what to do each day. • Understand your goals and deadlines. •
Practice what you've learned	• Use first-read and close-read strategies to deepen your understanding. • Evaluate the usefulness of the evidence to help you understand the topic. • Consider the quality and reliability of the source. •
Take notes	• Record important ideas and information. • Review notes before preparing to share with a group. •

Pacing Plan

Introduce Whole-Class Learning

Unit Introduction			Two Kinds				A Simple Act				*from* An Invisible Thread				Performance Task		
1	2	3	4	5	6	7	8	9	10	11	12	13	14	15	16	17	18

CONTENTS

Choose one selection. Selections are available online only.

DIGITAL PERSPECTIVES

Contents

Selections Encourage students to scan and preview the selections before choosing the one they would like to read. Suggest that they consider the genre and subject matter of each one before making their decision. You can use the information on the following Planning pages to advise students in making their choice.

> Remind students that the selections for Independent Learning are only available in the Interactive Student Edition. Allow students who do not have digital access at home to preview the selections using classroom or computer lab technology. Then either have students print the selection they choose or provide a printout for them.

Performance-Based Assessment Prep

Review Evidence for a Nonfiction Narrative

Point out to students that collecting evidence during Independent Learning is the last step in completing their Evidence Log. After they finish their independent reading, they will synthesize all the evidence they have compiled in the unit.

The evidence students collect will serve as the primary source of information they will use to complete the writing and oral presentation for the Performance-Based Assessment at the end of the unit.

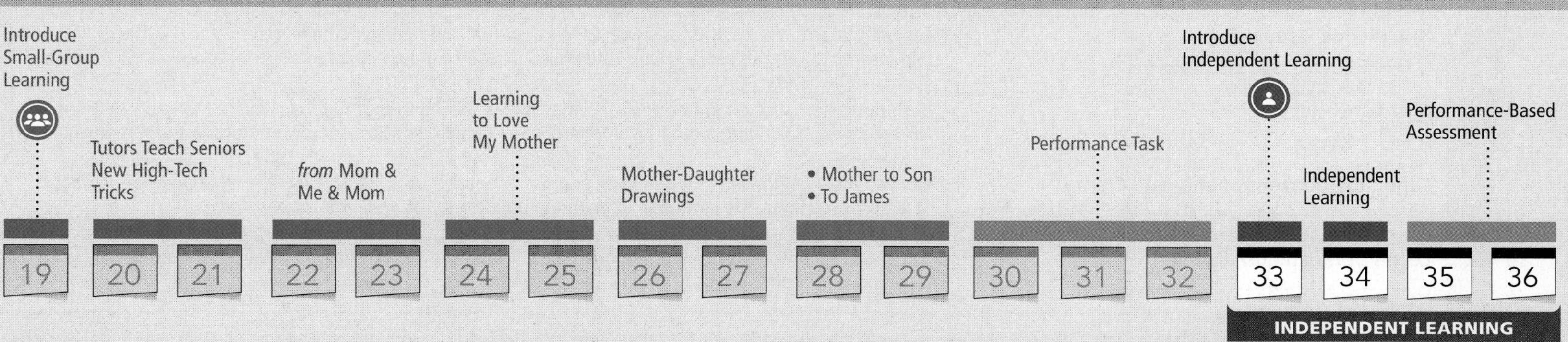

SELECTION RESOURCES

- First-Read Guide: Poetry
- Close-Read Guide: Poetry
- Poetry Collection 2: Text Questions
- Audio Summaries
- Selection Audio
- Selection Test

Lineage • Family

Summaries

Margaret Walker's poem "Lineage" is composed of two six-line stanzas, the first in the past tense, the second in the present. Both stanzas describe the speaker's grandmothers. In the first, they are working the land and singing. In the second, they tell stories of the past, and they smell of cooking and cleanliness. The speaker wants to ask them a question, but they suddenly disappear into the past, and they will never reply.

In Grace Paley's autobiographical poem "Family," the poet lists groups of adjectives and phrases that she heard as a child. They were used among her family to describe various family members. To Paley as a child, they seemed mysterious and dramatic. In time, some of them came to describe her, too, but others never did, because she is American.

Insight

Reading "Lineage" and "Family" will help students reflect on how different experiences and external forces shape each generation. When one generation is defined by trials and hardships, the people of later generations may compare themselves with those ancestors and either come up short or appreciate the opportunities they've been given.

Connection to Essential Question

These poems provide reflective perspectives on the Essential Question—*What can one generation learn from another?* In "Lineage," the speaker's reflections on her grandmothers' strength makes her wonder why she herself is not strong. In "Family," the speaker reflects on her family members and finds that, because she never had to endure the hardships they faced in their home country and as immigrants in America, she has escaped some of their negative traits.

Connection to Performance Task

Unit Performance-Based Assessment This selection shows students that it is important for younger generations to acknowledge the hard work of older generations that made life better for those who followed. Students should consider this in light of the question they will answer in the Performance-Based Assessment: *What is an example of a lesson one generation can learn from another?*

Text Complexity Rubric: Poetry: Lineage • Family	
Quantitative Measures	
Lexile: NP; NP **Text Length:** 12 lines; 9 lines	
Qualitative Measures	
Knowledge Demands ①—②—❸—④—⑤	For both poems it is helpful for students to know that the family members referred to may be immigrants to the U.S., so activities referenced in poems may have been in other countries.
Structure ①—❷—③—④—⑤	Both poems are written in free verse, so they follow the rhythm of natural speech. Many of the lines are full sentences, following a repetitive pattern (for example, multiple sentences starting the same way).
Language Conventionality and Clarity ①—②—❸—④—⑤	Conventional language is used in both poems. "Lineage" uses literal language, evoking strong images. "Family" uses figurative language (*fell among adjectives… buried with opportunity.*)
Levels of Meaning/Purpose ①—②—❸—④—⑤	"Lineage" is very straightforward in meaning; "Family" is mostly straightforward but ends with meaning that is ambiguous and must be interpreted.

DIGITAL PERSPECTIVES

Audio Video Document Annotation Highlights EL Highlights Online Assessment

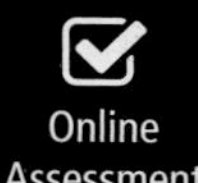

SELECTION RESOURCES

- First-Read Guide: Nonfiction
- Close-Read Guide: Nonfiction
- "Gotcha Day" Isn't a Cause for Celebration: Text Questions
- Audio Summaries
- Selection Audio
- Selection Test

"Gotcha Day" Isn't a Cause for Celebration

Summary

Families with an adopted child like to make an annual celebration of the date their new son or daughter joined the family. Some families call this anniversary "Gotcha Day." In her opinion piece "'Gotcha Day' Isn't a Cause for Celebration," Sophie Johnson explains why she finds the name inappropriate. Sophie is an adopted child herself, and very happy—her adoptive parents came to China when she was five and took her with them back to America. Adoption is something to celebrate, but Sophie points out that every adopted child was once lost, abandoned, or rejected. For every adoptive family, there was once a biological mother and father. Sophie and her family have abandoned "Gotcha Day" and adopted a different name for their annual celebration.

Insight

Sometimes it takes the clear eyes of a new generation to point out the mistakes of the past. Reading "'Gotcha Day' Isn't a Cause for Celebration" will help students understand that the traditions of past generations, such as celebrating "Gotcha Day," may not be welcomed by the current generation. Those traditions that no longer have meaning or are hurtful need to change to accommodate the sensibilities of a new generation.

Connection to Essential Question

"'Gotcha Day' Isn't a Cause for Celebration" relates to the Essential Question—*What can one generation learn from another?*—in that Sophie Johnson is a teenager who teaches her parents to be more mindful of the loss surrounding adoption. Drawing on her personal experience, Sophie points out to her adoptive parents that the flip side of their happiness is someone else's grief.

Connection to Performance Task

Unit Performance-Based Assessment This selection shows students that a younger generation can provide a new perspective on an idea that has gone unquestioned for generations. Students should consider this as they prepare to answer the question in the Performance-Based Assessment: *What is an example of a lesson one generation can learn from another?*

Text Complexity Rubric: "Gotcha Day" Isn't a Cause for Celebration

Quantitative Measures	
Lexile: 1090 **Text Length:** 658 words	
Qualitative Measures	
Knowledge Demands (1–2–**3**–4–5)	The selection is about a topic that might not be familiar to all students (conflicting feelings about adoption), but the situations and feelings are clearly explained.
Structure (1–**2**–3–4–5)	The structure is a straightforward account of facts and feelings. Connection between ideas is clear.
Language Conventionality and Clarity (1–2–**3**–4–5)	Account is written in conversational language. Some sentences are lengthy, with multiple clauses.
Levels of Meaning/Purpose (1–2–**3**–4–5)	Concepts are clearly explained. Understanding the meaning of the selection requires being able to see two sides of an issue (why "Gotcha Day" can be a "mixed bag").

SELECTION RESOURCES

- First-Read Guide: Fiction
- Close-Read Guide: Fiction
- The Grandfather and His Little Grandson: Text Questions
- Audio Summaries
- Selection Audio
- Selection Test

The Grandfather and His Little Grandson

Summary

In his short story "The Grandfather and His Little Grandson," Leo Tolstoy tells a tale of three generations living under the same roof. The grandfather is so old and weak that his food sometimes falls from his lips as he eats. His son and daughter-in-law make him eat near the stove, instead of at the table with them. When he breaks a bowl, his daughter-in-law tells him she's going to give him his food in a wooden bowl from now on. One day, his little grandson, Misha, is on the floor making something from wood. His parents ask him what he's making, and Misha's reply makes them ashamed of themselves.

Insight

Reading "The Grandfather and His Little Grandson" will help students reflect on the responsibilities that one generation has for another. The parents in the story have a responsibility to take care of the older generation, but they also have a responsibility to lead the younger generation by example.

Connection to Essential Question

"The Grandfather and His Little Grandson" provides a fable-like perspective on the Essential Question—*What can one generation learn from another?* The young child in the story innocently delivers the moral "What goes around comes around." He assumes that his parents' treatment of his grandfather is the right way to behave, so he plans to treat them the same way. They are treating the old man cruelly, and, if the child follows their example, their own son would in turn be treating them cruelly. Learning their lesson, they treat the old man the way they themselves would like to be treated.

Connection to Performance Task

Unit Performance-Based Assessment This selection illustrates for students that someone from a younger generation can show people of an older generation how to be better people, simply by reflecting back to them their questionable behavior. The child in the story is a mirror in which the parents are forced to see themselves. Students should consider lessons older generations can learn from younger generations as they prepare to answer the question in the Performance-Based Assessment: *What is an example of a lesson one generation can learn from another?*

Text Complexity Rubric: The Grandfather and His Little Grandson	
Quantitative Measures	
Lexile: 870 **Text Length:** 239 words	
Qualitative Measures	
Knowledge Demands 1 —**2**— 3 — 4 — 5	The theme of family life and interactions are mostly common and familiar. Some references will not be as familiar because of the folk origin (peasant couple, living in a hut, playing with bits of wood, wooden bucket).
Structure 1 —**2**— 3 — 4 — 5	Story is told chronologically and is easy to predict. There is a small amount of dialogue.
Language Conventionality and Clarity 1 —**2**— 3 — 4 — 5	Selection has mainly simple sentences. The longer sentences are compound sentences that can be easily broken down to understand.
Levels of Meaning/Purpose 1 — 2 —**3**— 4 — 5	The meaning of the story is presented with some subtlety (students must infer meaning from child's behavior and words), but conclusion of story is clearly stated.

DIGITAL PERSPECTIVES — Audio | Video | Document | Annotation Highlights | EL Highlights | Online Assessment

Bridging the Generational Divide Between a Football Father and a Soccer Son

Summary

John McCormick loves football. His son Will loves soccer. This difference in sporting loyalties causes endless argument between father and son. McCormick tells the story of how peace was restored in his blog post, "Bridging the Generational Divide Between a Football Father and a Soccer Son." One day, when Will refers to soccer as "a sport whose time has come," McCormick remembers that he used the same argument to defend football when his own father tried to tell him baseball was the best sport. McCormick sees a pattern here and decides to bring this intergenerational dispute to an end.

Insight

The more things change, the more they stay the same. Reading "Bridging the Generational Divide Between a Football Father and a Soccer Son" will help students understand that the generations are more alike than different. The younger generation may feel that it knows better than the prior generation, but the prior generation very likely felt the same way when it was the younger generation.

SELECTION RESOURCES

- First-Read Guide: Nonfiction
- Close-Read Guide: Nonfiction
- Bridging the Generational Divide: Text Questions
- Audio Summaries
- Selection Audio
- Selection Test

Connection to Essential Question

"Bridging the Generational Divide Between a Football Father and a Soccer Son" looks at the Essential Question—*What can one generation learn from another?*—from the perspective of family traditions. As the author argues with his son about the best sport, he realizes that despite their differences, they are very much the same. The father and son prefer different sports because they are the products of different generations, but their support for a sport "whose time has come" is almost a family trait, passed down from one generation to the next.

Connection to Performance Task

Unit Performance-Based Assessment This selection illustrates for students that a child can help a parent gain a new perspective. The son in this selection, by arguing for soccer, forces his father to reconsider his lifelong belief that football is "the beautiful sport," and inadvertently uncovers a common thread between the generations. Students should consider different generations' viewpoints when answering the Performance-Based Assessment question: *What is an example of a lesson one generation can learn from another?*

Text Complexity Rubric: Bridging the Generational Divide . . .

Quantitative Measures	
Lexile: 1120 **Text Length:** 683 words	
Qualitative Measures	
Knowledge Demands: 1 — **2** — 3 — 4 — 5	Subject matter relies on common practical language with some discipline-specific content knowledge (sports: soccer and football).
Structure: 1 — 2 — **3** — 4 — 5	Connection between ideas is mostly explicit. Arguments laid out in dialogue in pairs of contrasting ideas can enhance understanding.
Language Conventionality and Clarity: 1 — 2 — **3** — 4 — 5	Selection contains some complex sentences and figurative language; most language is easy to understand, with some occasions for more complex meaning.
Levels of Meaning/Purpose: 1 — 2 — **3** — 4 — 5	Purpose is explicitly stated. Some double meanings are implied but easy to identify based on the context.

SELECTION RESOURCES

- First-Read Guide: Fiction
- Close-Read Guide: Fiction
- Water Names: Text Questions
- Audio Summaries
- Selection Audio
- Selection Test

Water Names

Summary

In "Water Names," a short story by Lan Samantha Chang, the narrator remembers an old Chinese story her grandmother told her. She often told stories in Chinese because she wanted her grandchildren to honor their heritage. This story was about one of their ancestors, Wen Zhiqing, who lived 1,200 years ago and loved to go fishing with his daughter on the Yangtze River. One day they caught a very big fish and found a pearl ring in its stomach. The daughter believed that it was a gift from a young man who had drowned many years ago. She believed he now ruled an underwater kingdom, and he wanted her to join him. Wen was afraid and forbade her to go near the river. The following spring there was a great flood. The daughter was nowhere to be found.

Insight

Cultural history bridges the gaps between generations. Reading "Water Names" will help students consider the bond between generations when ancestral ties are not forgotten. The city girls in the story forge a link with their cultural past by imagining the river they've never seen and the beauty of their grandmother as a young woman they never knew.

Connection to Essential Question

"Water Names" looks at the Essential Question—*What can one generation learn from another?*—from the perspective of ancestry. Waipuo may be teaching her granddaughters a lesson about controlling their passions or teaching them to follow their passions, but she most certainly is teaching them not to ignore their ancestry. Wen Zhiqing's daughter either fulfills her dream of living a magical life with her water husband or she drowns in the flood. Either way, the river seals her fate, and the river symbolizes the girls' Chinese ancestry.

Connection to Performance Task

Unit Performance-Based Assessment This selection provides students with the cultural lessons that Waipuo teaches her granddaughters, helping them connect to their ancestry even though they live American lives. Students should think about how meaning in older generations' storytelling can help them answer the Performance-Based Assessment question: *What is an example of a lesson one generation can learn from another?*

Text Complexity Rubric: Water Names	
Quantitative Measures	
Lexile: 900 **Text Length:** 1,335 words	
Qualitative Measures	
Knowledge Demands 1—2—3—**4**—5	Selection contains stories told by a grandmother with themes that are unfamiliar to most readers (China long ago and Chinese folklore).
Structure 1—2—3—**4**—5	Selection contains two storylines and time shifts from present to ancient times.
Language Conventionality and Clarity 1—2—3—**4**—5	Story has dense and complex language, with abundant use of figurative language, similes and metaphors, and vivid imagery.
Levels of Meaning/Purpose 1—2—3—**4**—5	Multiple levels of meaning that may be difficult to identify; theme is subtle and is revealed over the entirety of the text.

DIGITAL PERSPECTIVES

Audio | Video | Document | Annotation Highlights | EL Highlights | Online Assessment

SELECTION RESOURCES

- First-Read Guide: Fiction
- Close-Read Guide: Fiction
- An Hour with Abuelo: Text Questions
- Audio Summaries
- Selection Audio
- Selection Test

An Hour with Abuelo

Summary

Judith Ortiz Cofer's short story "An Hour with Abuelo" begins when Arturo finally agrees to visit his grandfather for just one hour. His grandfather, or abuelo, is writing when Arturo arrives. After checking the time, Arturo asks Abuelo to read his story. It is called "That's the Way Life Is."

Abuelo always loved words and books. He went to high school and later got a teaching job he loved. Then the war came and he had to join up. He wanted to teach young soldiers, but his sergeant said no. After the war, he couldn't get his teaching job back. He gave up and became a farmer. Arturo wants to tell Abuelo he should have fought for his dream. Abuelo has to go, though. He's off to a poetry reading. Arturo wants to come, but his hour is up.

Insight

Reading "An Hour With Abuelo" will help students reflect on the mistake that people of one generation make when they underestimate or disregard the people of a different generation.

Connection to Essential Question

"An Hour with Abuelo" provides an interesting perspective on the Essential Question, *What can one generation learn from another?* Arturo is very concerned with time: how much he has left to finish his reading, how long he has to spend with his abuelo, and the time remaining in his visit. His grandfather pointedly remarks that Arturo has plenty of time to hear his life story, and then just as pointedly remarks that Arturo has run out of time and cannot stay to hear the poetry reading. In this way, Arturo's abuelo teaches Arturo that time—in this case "one hour"—can change what you think you know about someone else.

Connection to Performance Task

Unit Performance-Based Assessment This selection shows students that it is possible, with time, to reach across the gap between the generations. Students should think about how Arturo's meeting with his abuelo can help them to answer the Performance-Based Assessment Question: *What is an example of a lesson one generation can learn from another?*

Text Complexity Rubric: An Hour with Abuelo	
Quantitative Measures	
Lexile: 840 **Text Length:** 1,893 words	
Qualitative Measures	
Knowledge Demands (1 **2** 3 4 5)	The story focuses on the relationships among family members. The situations presented will be familiar to most students and are clearly explained.
Structure (1 2 **3** 4 5)	The selection is a narrative in the first person (from the grandson's perspective). It also has flashbacks that provide background about the characters, and a story told by the grandfather, also in first person.
Language Conventionality and Clarity (1 2 **3** 4 5)	Clear, conversational, modern language is used. Style of speech changes between characters. Tense also changes to accommodate narration and flashbacks.
Levels of Meaning/Purpose (1 2 3 **4** 5)	The selection contains multiple levels of meaning. It addresses what happens between the two characters, and it presents feelings and attitudes that must be inferred from actions or words.

ADVISING

You may wish to direct students to use the generic **First-Read** and **Close-Read Guides** in the Print Student Edition. Alternatively, you may wish to print copies of the genre-specific **First-Read** and **Close-Read Guides** for students. These are available online in the Interactive Student Edition or Unit Resources.

FIRST READ

Students should perform the steps of the first read independently:

NOTICE: Students should focus on the basic elements of the text to ensure they understand what is happening.

ANNOTATE: Students should mark any passages they wish to revisit during their close read.

CONNECT: Students should increase their understanding by connecting what they've read to other texts or personal experiences.

RESPOND: Students will write a summary to demonstrate their understanding.

Point out to students that while they will always complete the Respond step at the end of the first read, the other steps will probably happen somewhat concurrently. Remind students that they will revisit their first-read annotations during the close read.

After students have completed the First-Read Guide, you may wish to assign the Text Questions for the selection that are available in the Interactive Teacher's Edition.

Anchor Standards

In the first two sections of the unit, students worked with the whole class and in small groups to gain topical knowledge and greater understanding of the skills required by the anchor standards. In this section, they are asked to work independently, applying what they have learned and demonstrating increased readiness for college and career.

INDEPENDENT LEARNING

First-Read Guide

Tool Kit
First-Read Guide and Model Annotation

Use this page to record your first-read ideas.

Selection Title: ______________________________

NOTICE

NOTICE new information or ideas you learn about the unit topic as you first read this text.

ANNOTATE

ANNOTATE by marking vocabulary and key passages you want to revisit.

NOTICE ANNOTATE First Read CONNECT RESPOND

CONNECT

CONNECT ideas within the selection to other knowledge and the selections you have read.

RESPOND

RESPOND by writing a brief summary of the selection.

STANDARD

Reading Read and comprehend complex literary and informational texts independently and proficiently.

PERSONALIZE FOR LEARNING

English Language Support

Skim, Predict, and Use KWL Chart Use the Text Complexity Rubrics to help individual students select a text appropriate for their English proficiency level.

Help students identify the genre of the selection they chose: poem, short story, or opinion piece. Then have them skim the selection to notice text features, such as headings or visuals. They can also look for quotation marks and words that stand out to them. Explain to students that when they skim, they should focus on understanding the general idea and should not stop to figure out unfamiliar words.

Next, have students work with a partner to predict what their selection will be about. Instruct them to ask and answer *Wh-* questions. Provide sample question frames, such as *What ____? Who ____? How ____?*

Finally, help partners complete a KWL chart to note what they already know about the topic and what they want to learn, and then after their first read, what they learned:

Know	Want to Know	Learned

ALL LEVELS

Close-Read Guide

Tool Kit
Close-Read Guide and Model Annotation

Use this page to record your close-read ideas.

Selection Title: ______________________________

Textual Evidence

Annotate • Question • Conclude
Revisit sections of the text you marked during your first read. Read the sections closely and annotate what you notice. Ask yourself questions about the text. What can you conclude? Write your ideas.

Focus on Big Ideas

Think about the author's choice of patterns, structure, techniques, and ideas included in the text. Select one and record your thoughts about what this choice conveys.

QuickWrite

Pick a paragraph from the text that grabbed your interest. Explain the power of this passage.

STANDARD
Reading Read and comprehend complex literary and informational texts independently and proficiently.

CLOSE READ

Students should begin their close read by revisiting the annotations they made during their first read. Then, students should analyze one of the author's choices regarding the following elements:

- **patterns,** such as repetition or parallelism
- **structure,** such as cause-and-effect or problem-solution
- **techniques,** such as description or dialogue
- **ideas,** such as the author's main idea or claim

MAKE IT INTERACTIVE
Group students according to the selection they have chosen. Then, have students meet to discuss the selection in depth. Their discussions should be guided by their insights and questions.

PERSONALIZE FOR LEARNING

English Language Support

Read Aloud and Confirm Predictions Pair students or put them in groups so they can take turns reading aloud to one another. Each student can read one paragraph, or you can split up the text in any other way that makes sense. For example, for a short story, you may wish to assign different characters and the role of narrator to individual students to take turns reading aloud.

Have students make predictions as they listen, and then have partners or groups discuss, compare, and confirm the predictions they made. Ask: *Did anything surprise you? Were any predictions correct? Which ones?* Finally, have partners or groups work together to add more details about what they learned on their Close-Read Guide. **ALL LEVELS**

ADVISING

Share Your Independent Learning

Prepare to Share

Explain to students that sharing what they learned from their Independent Learning selection provides classmates who did not read the same selection with an opportunity to consider the text as a source of evidence during the Performance-Based Assessment. As students prepare to share, remind them to highlight how their selection contributed to their knowledge of the concept of generations as well as how the selection connects to the question *What can one generation learn from another?*

Learn From Your Classmates

As students discuss the Independent Learning selections, direct them to take particular note of how their classmates' chosen selections align with their current position on the Performance-Based Assessment question.

Reflect

Students may want to add their reflection to their Evidence Log, particularly if their insight relates to a specific selection from the unit.

MAKE IT INTERACTIVE

Divide a board or large piece of paper at the front of the classroom into a chart or table with sections for each independent learning selection. Have each student write his or her insight on a sentence strip and attach it to the section of the chart that corresponds to his or her selection. As a class, discuss any patterns that emerge between the student insights. For example, did some students have the same insight even though they read different selections? Did students who chose the same selection tend to have the same insights?

Evidence Log Support students in completing their Evidence Log. This paced activity will help prepare them for the Performance-Based Assessment at the end of the unit.

INDEPENDENT LEARNING

EVIDENCE LOG

Go to your Evidence Log and record what you learned from the text you read.

Share Your Independent Learning

Prepare to Share

What can one generation learn from another?

When you read something independently, you can continue to grow by sharing what you have learned with others. Reflect on the text you explored independently, and write notes about its connection to the unit. In your notes, consider why this text belongs in this unit.

Learn From Your Classmates

Discuss It Share your ideas about the text you explored on your own. As you talk with your classmates, jot down ideas that you learn from them.

Reflect

Review your notes, and mark the most important insight you gained from these writing and discussion activities. Explain how this idea adds to your understanding of the topic of generations.

AUTHOR'S PERSPECTIVE **Ernest Morrell, Ph.D.**

Learning From Others Independent learning helps students build vocabulary, background knowledge, and fluency. Teach students how to learn from each other by modeling how to ask clarifying questions when other students are sharing their experiences. Questions like these can guide the discussion:

- Why did you choose this text? For example, did the topic interest you? Have you heard of the author or read anything else by the author?
- For narrative text: What is the problem in the story? When and where does the story take place? Why?
- For nonfiction text: How is the information organized? What is the most interesting thing you've learned so far?
- What parts of the text do you think were most important? Why?
- Did the text meet your expectations? Why or why not? Would you recommend this text to a classmate? Explain your answer.
- How does the text relate to other texts you have read on this subject? How does it relate to your life?

PERFORMANCE-BASED ASSESSMENT PREP

Review Evidence for a Nonfiction Narrative

At the beginning of the unit, you expressed your own ideas in response to the following question:

In what situations can one generation learn from another?

EVIDENCE LOG

Review your Evidence Log and your QuickWrite from the beginning of the unit. Did you learn anything new?

NOTES

Identify at least three pieces of evidence that interested you about the relationships between generations.

1.

2.

3.

Identify a real-life experience that illustrates one of your current ideas about the ways in which people of different generations can learn from each other.

____

To develop your thoughts into a topic for your nonfiction narrative, complete this sentence starter:

I learned a great deal about the ways in which people from different generations can learn from each other when

____

____

Evaluate Your Evidence Consider your original ideas and thoughts on the subject. How did the selections you read and watched impact your ideas and opinions?

STANDARDS

Writing

- Write narratives to develop real or imagined experiences or events using effective technique, relevant descriptive details, and well-structured event sequences.
  - a. Engage and orient the reader by establishing a context and point of view and introducing a narrator and/or characters; organize an event sequence that unfolds naturally and logically.
- Draw evidence from literary or informational texts to support analysis, reflection, and research.

DIGITAL PERSPECTIVES

Review Evidence for a Nonfiction Narrative

Evidence Log Students should understand that their ideas about an issue could evolve as they learn more about the subject and are exposed to additional points of view. Point out that just because they expressed ideas in response to the question *In what situations can one generation learn from another?* doesn't mean that the ideas can't change after careful consideration of their learning and evidence.

Evaluate Your Evidence Remind students that there are many different types of evidence they can use to support their ideas, including:

- nonfiction texts and media
- fiction texts and media
- anecdotes
- personal experiences

In addition to supporting their writing with evidence, students should understand the factors that led them to their ideas and opinions. Point out that these ideas and opinions should be:

- based on objective evidence while incorporating subjective experience
- flexible and open to other points of view

PERSONALIZE FOR LEARNING

Strategic Support

Identify Insights If a student struggles to identify a real-life experience about knowledge or skills passed between generations, it may be helpful for the student to create a chart that organizes individuals in his or her personal life into two or more columns representing different generations. In the different columns, the student can list interactions he or she has had with, or witnessed between, individuals of different generations. The student can then select the interaction that best represents his or her point of view.

Writing to Sources: Nonfiction Narrative

Students should complete the Performance-Based Assessment independently, with little to no input or feedback during the process. Students should use word processing software to take advantage of editing tools and features.

Prior to beginning the Assessment, ask students to think about times when they either learned something from or taught something to an individual of a different generation.

Review the Elements of Effective Nonfiction Narrative Students can review the work they did earlier in the unit as they complete the Performance-Based Assessment. They may also consult other resources, such as:

- the elements of a nonfiction narrative, including people, sequence, dialogue, and point of view, available in Whole-Class Learning
- their Evidence Log
- their Word Network

Although students will use evidence from the unit selections for their nonfiction narrative, they may need to collect additional evidence, including anecdotes and personal experiences.

Connect to the Selections Encourage students to include references to specific selections from the unit in their narratives, in order to help them convey the ideas they want to express. Point out that they need not try to include a reference to every selection, but only to the ones that will help them better communicate their ideas.

PERFORMANCE-BASED ASSESSMENT

SOURCES

- WHOLE-CLASS SELECTIONS
- SMALL-GROUP SELECTIONS
- INDEPENDENT-LEARNING SELECTION

PART 1

Writing to Sources: Nonfiction Narrative

In this unit, you read about a variety of characters who influenced one another across generations. Often, the insight went both ways, as older people learned from younger people, just as children learned from adults.

Assignment

Write a nonfiction narrative in which you use dialogue, description, and precise words to develop and convey experiences and events. Your narrative should respond to the following prompt:

In what situations can one generation learn from another?

Your narrative might be about an experience that you had with an older relative or another person from a different generation. As an alternative, you could write about an experience one of your friends or family members had with someone from a different generation. Conclude your narrative by reflecting on the ways in which the selections in this unit and the process of writing this narrative have deepened your understanding of the relationships between people of different generations.

WORD NETWORK

As you write and revise your nonfiction narrative, use your Word Network to help vary your word choices.

Reread the Assignment Review the assignment to be sure you fully understand it. The assignment may reference some of the academic words presented at the beginning of the unit. Be sure you understand each of the words here in order to complete the assignment correctly.

Academic Vocabulary

dialogue	consequence	perspective
notable	contradict	

Review the Elements of a Nonfiction Narrative Before you begin writing, read the Nonfiction Narrative Rubric. Once you have completed your first draft, check it against the rubric. If one or more of the elements is missing or not as strong as it could be, revise your narrative to add or strengthen that component.

Connect to the Selections In your narrative, make connections to the selections in this unit by including details and examples that clarify the ideas in your narrative. Review the literary techniques, such as description and dialogue, that the authors use in the selections to engage readers. You may use the authors' examples as a model to develop the use of literary techniques in your own narrative.

STANDARDS

Writing

- Write narratives to develop real or imagined experiences or events using effective technique, relevant descriptive details, and well-structured event sequences.
- Draw evidence from literary or informational texts to support analysis, reflection, and research.
- Write routinely over extended time frames and shorter time frames for a range of discipline-specific tasks, purposes, and audiences.

AUTHOR'S PERSPECTIVE **Kelly Gallagher, M. Ed.**

Building a Writing Portfolio with Students Teachers can create a portfolio that enables students to demonstrate the variety of writing they complete over the year. There are three elements of keeping a portfolio—collection of all the writing a student has done, selection of the best pieces, and reflection to evaluate growth.

Teachers can set the criteria using such categories as *Best Argument, Best Narrative Piece, Best Informative Piece, Best On-Demand Writing, Best Poetry, Best Blended Genre, Best Writing from Another Class, Best Model of Revision,* and *Best Single Line You Wrote This Year.* Students should also include a reflective letter at the end of the year.

To help them learn to reflect, use questions like these throughout the year.

- Where does your writing still need improvement? How will you improve?
- Reflect on a struggle you faced during this unit. How did you overcome it?

Nonfiction Narrative Rubric

	Focus and Organization	Evidence and Elaboration	Language Conventions
4	The introduction is engaging and introduces the characters and situation in a way that appeals to readers. Events in the narrative progress in logical order and are linked by clear transitions. The conclusion follows the events in the narrative and provides insightful reflection on the related experiences in the narrative.	Narrative techniques, such as dialogue, pacing, and description, are used to add interest to the narrative and to develop the characters and events. Precise, vivid words and sensory language are frequently used to convey the experiences in the narrative and to help the reader imagine the characters and scenes.	The narrative intentionally uses standard English conventions of usage and mechanics.
3	The introduction is engaging and clearly introduces the characters and situation. Events in the narrative progress logically, and transition words are used frequently. The conclusion follows the rest of the narrative and provides some reflection on the experiences related in the narrative.	Narrative techniques, such as dialogue, pacing, and description, are often used to add interest to the narrative and to develop experiences and events. Precise, vivid words and sensory language are usually used to convey the experiences in the narrative and to describe the characters and events.	The narrative demonstrates accuracy in standard English conventions of usage and mechanics.
2	The introduction introduces the characters. Events in the narrative progress somewhat logically, and some transition words are used. The conclusion adds little to the narrative and does not provide reflection on the experiences in the narrative.	Narrative techniques, such as dialogue and description, are sometimes used in the narrative. Precise, vivid words and sensory language are sometimes used to convey experiences.	The narrative demonstrates some accuracy in standard English conventions of usage and mechanics.
1	The introduction does not introduce the characters and situation, or there is no introduction. Events in the narrative do not progress logically. The ideas seem disconnected and are not linked by transitional words and phrases. The conclusion does not connect to the narrative, or there is no conclusion.	Few, if any, narrative techniques are used in the narrative. The narrative fails to incorporate sensory language and precise words to convey experiences and to develop characters.	The narrative contains mistakes in standard English conventions of usage and mechanics.

DIGITAL PERSPECTIVES

Nonfiction Narrative Rubric

As you review the Nonfiction Narrative Rubric with students, remind them that the rubric is a resource that can guide their revisions. Students should pay particular attention to the differences between a nonfiction narrative that contains all of the required elements (a score of 3) and one that is engaging, insightful, and progresses in a logical and thoughtful manner (a score of 4).

- Discuss a specific writing strategy you used and how it worked for you.
- What strengths have you developed as a writer? Where are those strengths found in this portfolio?
- Where can you demonstrate in this portfolio that you have improved as a reader and as a writer?

At the end of the year, students can review these pieces to see their growth as writers.

ASSESSING

Speaking and Listening: Multimedia Presentation

Students should annotate their nonfiction narrative in preparation for the multimedia presentation, marking the important elements (characters, situation) as well as critical anecdotes or examples.

Remind students that the effectiveness of a multimedia presentation relies on how the speaker establishes credibility with his or her audience. If a speaker comes across as confident and authoritative, it will be easier for the audience to give credence to the speaker's presentation.

Review the Rubric As you review the Rubric with students, remind them that it's a valuable tool that can help them plan their presentation. They should strive to include all of the criteria required to achieve a score of 3. Draw their attention to some of the subtle differences between scores of 2 and 3.

PERFORMANCE-BASED ASSESSMENT

PART 2

Speaking and Listening: Multimedia Presentation

Assignment

After completing the final draft of your nonfiction narrative, use it as the foundation for a **multimedia presentation**.

Do not simply read your narrative aloud. Take the following steps to make your multimedia presentation lively and engaging.

- Review your narrative, and concentrate your presentation on the parts of your narrative that provide reflection on the events and experiences presented.
- Include different types of media that will help emphasize the main points of your presentation.
- Use appropriate eye contact, adequate volume, and clear pronunciation.

STANDARDS

Speaking and Listening

- Present claims and findings, emphasizing salient points in a focused, coherent manner with pertinent descriptions, facts, details, and examples; use appropriate eye contact, adequate volume, and clear pronunciation.
- Include multimedia components and visual displays in presentations to clarify claims and findings and emphasize salient points.

Review the Rubric Before you deliver your presentation, check your plans against this rubric. If one or more of the elements is missing or not as strong as it could be, revise your presentation.

	Content	Use of Media	Presentation Technique
3	The narrative effectively establishes a point of view and follows a logical sequence. The speaker effectively uses narrative techniques and a variety of transitions for cohesion and clarity. The speaker includes relevant descriptive details.	The media connect to all parts of the narrative. The media enhance and add interest to the narrative. The timing of the media matches the timing of the narrative.	The speaker makes eye contact and speaks clearly. The speaker adjusts volume and pacing effectively.
2	The narrative establishes a point of view and generally follows a logical sequence. The speaker uses some narrative techniques and some transitions. The speaker includes some descriptive details.	The media connect to some parts of the narrative. The media add interest to the narrative. The timing of the media sometimes matches the timing of the narrative.	The speaker sometimes makes eye contact and speaks clearly. The speaker somtimes adjusts volume and pacing.
1	The narrative does not establish a point of view and does not follow a logical sequence. The speaker does not use narrative techniques and transitions. The speaker does not include descriptive details.	The media do not connect to the narrative. The media do not add interest to the narrative. The timing of the media does not match the timing of the narrative.	The speaker does not make eye contact and does not speak clearly. The speaker does not adjust volume and pacing.

DIGITAL PERSPECTIVES

Preparing for the Assignment To help students understand what an effective multimedia presentation looks and sounds like, find examples on the Internet of students or adults incorporating multimedia as they tell nonfiction narratives. Project the examples for the class (after previewing them yourself), and have students note the techniques that make each speaker successful (that is, gestures, pacing, tone, use of media, and so on). Suggest that students record themselves presenting their narratives prior to presenting to the class so that they can practice incorporating some of the elements in the examples you showed them.

Reflect on the Unit

Now that you've completed the unit, take a few moments to reflect on your learning.

Reflect on the Unit Goals

Look back at the goals at the beginning of the unit. Use a different-colored pen to rate yourself again. Then, think about readings and activities that contributed the most to the growth of your understanding. Record your thoughts.

Reflect on the Learning Strategies

Discuss It Write a reflection on whether you were able to improve your learning based on your Action Plans. Think about what worked, what didn't, and what you might do to keep working on these strategies. Record your ideas before a class discussion.

Reflect on the Text

Choose a selection that you found challenging, and explain what made it difficult.

Describe something that surprised you about a text in the unit.

Which activity taught you the most about generations? What did you learn?

DIGITAL PERSPECTIVES

Reflect on the Unit

- Have students watch the video on Reflecting on Your Learning.
- A video on this topic is available online in the Professional Development Center.

Reflect on the Unit Goals

Students should re-evaluate how well they met the unit goals now that they have completed the unit. You might ask them to provide a written commentary on the goal they made the most progress with, as well as the goal they feel warrants continued focus.

Reflect on the Learning Strategies

Discuss It If you want to make this a digital activity, go online and navigate to the Discussion Board. Alternatively, students can share their learning strategies reflections in a class discussion.

Reflect on the Text

Consider having students share their text reflections with one another.

MAKE IT INTERACTIVE

Have students prepare one slide using presentation software that summarizes their reflection.

Collate student slides into a presentation that can be viewed by the class. Students should be prepared to give a 30-second oral summary for their slide.

Unit Test and Remediation 

After students have completed the Performance-Based Assessment, administer the Unit Test. Based on students' performance on the test, assign the resources as indicated on the Interpretation Guide to remediate. Students who take the test online will be automatically assigned remediation, as warranted by test results.

UNIT 2 AT A GLANCE

Section	Contents	Pacing / # of Days	Genre / Lexile	Vocabulary / Word Study
INTRO	**Unit Introduction**	2*		Academic Vocabulary (L.7.6)
INTRO	**Launch Text: Leaving Main Street**		Argumentative Text 1060L	
WHOLE-CLASS LEARNING	**Whole-Class Learning Introduction**	7		
WHOLE-CLASS LEARNING	**Dark They Were, and Golden-Eyed** Ray Bradbury (HOOK&INSPIRE; COMPARE)		Short Story 490L	Concept Vocabulary Word Study: Synonyms and Nuance (L.7.5)
WHOLE-CLASS LEARNING	**Dark They Were, and Golden-Eyed** Ray Bradbury, and Michael McDonough (producer) (COMPARE)	3	Media: Radio Play NP	Media Vocabulary (L.7.6)
WHOLE-CLASS LEARNING	**Danger! This Mission to Mars Could Bore You to Death!** Maggie Koerth-Baker	3	News Article 1290L	Concept Vocabulary Word Study: Latin Prefix *sub-* (L.7.4.b)
WHOLE-CLASS LEARNING	**Performance Task** Writing	3		
SMALL-GROUP LEARNING	**Small-Group Learning Introduction**	3		
SMALL-GROUP LEARNING	**Future of Space Exploration Could See Humans on Mars, Alien Planets** Nola Taylor Redd		News Article 1250L	Concept Vocabulary (L.7.4.a) Word Study: Latin Suffix *-ary* (L.7.4.b)
SMALL-GROUP LEARNING	**The Last Dog** Katherine Paterson	5	Short Story 820L	Concept Vocabulary (L.7.4.a) Word Study: Latin Suffix *-tion* (L.7.4.b)
SMALL-GROUP LEARNING	**Ellen Ochoa: Director, Johnson Space Center** Ellen Ochoa	2	Media: Video NP	Technical Vocabulary (L.7.6)
SMALL-GROUP LEARNING	**Neil deGrasse Tyson on the Future of U.S. Space Exploration After *Curiosity*** Keith Wagstaff	2	Interview 930L	Concept Vocabulary (L.7.4) Multiple-Meaning Words (L.7.4.c)
SMALL-GROUP LEARNING	**Performance Task** Speaking and Listening	2		
INDEPENDENT LEARNING	**Independent Learning Introduction**	2		
INDEPENDENT LEARNING	**Science-Fiction Cradlesong** C. S. Lewis		Poetry NP	Independent Learning provides students with the opportunity to analyze a selection independently. To facilitate students' independence, no skills have been assigned.
INDEPENDENT LEARNING	**UFO Sightings and News** Benjamin Radford		Web Article 1420L	
INDEPENDENT LEARNING	***from* Packing for Mars** Mary Roach		Persuasive Essay 1020L	
INDEPENDENT LEARNING	**Trip to Mars Could Damage Astronauts' Brains** Laura Sanders		Science Article 870L	
END OF UNIT	**Performance-Based Assessment** Writing	2		
END OF UNIT	**Unit Reflection**			
END OF UNIT	**Unit Test**	1		

* Pacing is suggested for a 40- to 50-minute class period. If you use block scheduling, you may combine days to meet your schedule needs.

Analyze Craft and Structure	Conventions / Author's Style	Composition / Research / Speaking and Listening
		Summary (RI.7.2)
Metaphor and Simile (RL.7.4; L.7.5.a)	Conventions: Comparisons Using Adjectives and Adverbs (L.7.1)	Writing to Compare: Argument (RL.7.7; W.7.2, a, b, d, f; W.7.9.a)
Text Structure: Informative Writing (RI.7.5)	Conventions: Action Verbs and Linking Verbs (L.7.1)	Writing to Sources: Blog Post (W.7.1, a, b, d, e; W.7.7) Speaking and Listening: Visual Presentation (W.7.7; SL.7.4; SL.7.5)
		Write an Argument: Editorial (W.7.1, a–e; W.7.5; W.7.10; L.7.1; L.7.2; L.7.3, a)
Development of Ideas: Text Structure (RI.7.5)	Conventions: The Principal Parts of Verbs (L.7.1)	Speaking and Listening: Multimedia Presentation (W.7.7; W.7.8; SL.7.5)
Conflict and Resolution (RL.7.3)	Conventions: Simple and Compound Subjects and Predicates (L.7.3.a)	Writing to Sources: Revised Ending (W.7.3, b, e)
		Speaking and Listening: Biography: Group Discussion (SL.7.1, a–d)
Evaluate Argument and Claims (RI.7.4; RI.7.6; RI.7.8)	Conventions: Sentence Functions and End Marks (L.7.1; L.7.2)	Research: Informational Report (W.7.2; W.7.7; W.7.8)
		Present an Argument (SL.7.4; SL.7.5)
Independent Learning provides students with the opportunity to analyze a selection independently. To facilitate students' independence, no skills have been assigned.		Share Your Independent Learning (SL.7.1)
		Writing to Sources: Argument (W.7.1, a–b; W.7.10) Speaking and Listening: Oral Presentation (SL.7.4)
		Reflect on the Unit

Jump Start

Ask students what they think fascinates people about the sky—especially a starry sky. Why do humans seem driven to explore space? How important to the future do they think space exploration is?

A Starry Home

Ask students what the phrase *A Starry Home* suggests to them. Point out that as they work through this unit, they will read many examples about space exploration and the future of human voyages to worlds beyond Earth.

Video

Project the introduction video in class or ask students to open the video in their interactive textbooks.

Discuss It If you want to make this a digital activity, go online and navigate to the Discussion Board. Alternatively, students can share their responses in a class discussion.

Block Scheduling

Each day in this pacing calendar represents a 40–50-minute class period. Teachers using block scheduling may combine days to reflect their class schedule. In addition, teachers may revise pacing to differentiate and support core instruction by integrating components and resources as students require.

UNIT 2

A Starry Home

Are there worlds beyond our galaxy? Should we find out?

Earth Views

Discuss It Why are people curious about our galaxy and what lies beyond?

Write your response before sharing your ideas.

116

Pacing Plan

Introduce Whole-Class Learning

Unit Introduction		Introduce Whole-Class Learning	Dark They Were, and Golden-Eyed						Media: Dark They Were, and Golden-Eyed			Danger! This Mission to Mars Could Bore You to Death!			Performance Task		
1	2	3	4	5	6	7	8	9	10	11	12	13	14	15	16	17	18

DIGITAL PERSPECTIVES

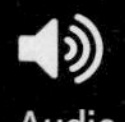
Audio

Video

Document

Annotation Highlights

EL Highlights

Online Assessment
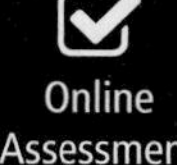

UNIT 2

UNIT INTRODUCTION

ESSENTIAL QUESTION:

Should we make a home in space?

LAUNCH TEXT
ARGUMENT MODEL
Leaving Main Street

WHOLE-CLASS LEARNING

COMPARE

ANCHOR TEXT: SHORT STORY
Dark They Were, and Golden-Eyed
Ray Bradbury

MEDIA: RADIO PLAY
Dark They Were, and Golden-Eyed
Ray Bradbury, and Michael McDonough (producer)

ANCHOR TEXT: NEWS ARTICLE
Danger! This Mission to Mars Could Bore You to Death!
Maggie Koerth-Baker

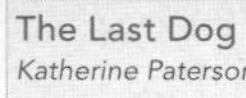

PERFORMANCE TASK
WRITING FOCUS:
Write an Argument

SMALL-GROUP LEARNING

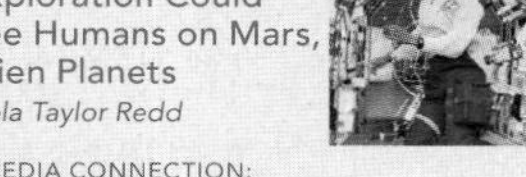

NEWS ARTICLE
Future of Space Exploration Could See Humans on Mars, Alien Planets
Nola Taylor Redd

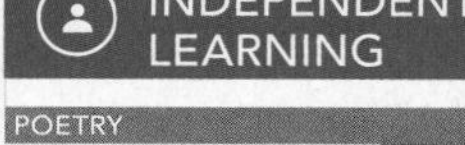

MEDIA CONNECTION:
Starship

SHORT STORY
The Last Dog
Katherine Paterson

MEDIA: VIDEO
Ellen Ochoa: Director, Johnson Space Center
Ellen Ochoa

INTERVIEW
Neil deGrasse Tyson on the Future of U.S. Space Exploration After *Curiosity*
Keith Wagstaff

PERFORMANCE TASK
SPEAKING AND LISTENING FOCUS:
Present an Argument

INDEPENDENT LEARNING

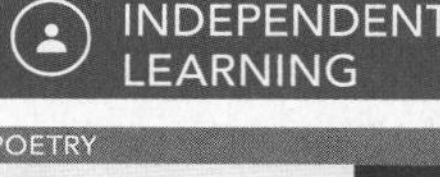

POETRY
Science-Fiction Cradlesong
C. S. Lewis

WEB ARTICLE
UFO Sightings and News
Benjamin Radford

PERSUASIVE ESSAY
from Packing for Mars
Mary Roach

SCIENCE ARTICLE
Trip to Mars Could Damage Astronauts' Brains
Laura Sanders

PERFORMANCE-BASED ASSESSMENT PREP
Review Evidence for an Argument

PERFORMANCE-BASED ASSESSMENT

Argument: Essay and Oral Presentation

PROMPT:
Should we spend valuable resources on space exploration?

117

Should we make a home in space?

Introduce the Essential Question and point out that students will respond to related prompts.

- **Whole-Class Learning** *Do the benefits of exploring Mars outweigh the risks?*
- **Small-Group Learning** *Should space exploration be a priority for our country?*
- **Performance-Based Assessment** *Should we spend valuable resources on space exploration?*

Using Trade Books

Refer to the Teaching with Trade Books section in this book or online in the Interactive Teacher's Edition for suggestions on how to incorporate the following thematically related novels into this unit:

- *Robot Dreams* by Isaac Asimov
- *Crater* by Homer Hickam
- *James and the Giant Peach* by Roald Dahl

Current Perspectives

To increase student engagement, search online for stories about space exploration, and invite your students to recommend stories they find. Always preview content before sharing it with your class.

- **Article: NASA's Next Horizon in Space** An article by Michael Roston ***(The New York Times)*** features the opinions of several experts concerning the next place in the solar system that humans should explore.
- **Video: Bill Nye Talks Aliens on Mars** Bill Nye ***(HuffPost Live)*** discusses the possibility of establishing a human colony on Mars.

Introduce Small-Group Learning — 19
Future of Space Exploration Could See Humans on Mars, Alien Planets — 20, 21
The Last Dog — 22, 23, 24, 25, 26
Media: Ellen Ochoa: Director, Johnson Space Center — 27, 28
Neil deGrasse Tyson on the Future of U.S. Space Exploration After *Curiosity* — 29, 30
Performance Task — 31, 32
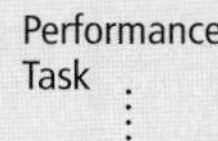
Introduce Independent Learning — 33
Independent Learning — 34

Performance-Based Assessment — 35, 36

About the Unit Goals

These unit goals were backward designed from the Performance-Based Assessment at the end of the unit and the Whole-Class and Small-Group Performance Tasks. Students will practice and become proficient in many more standards over the course of this unit.

Unit Goals

Review the goals with students and explain that as they read the selections in this unit, they will improve their skills in reading, writing, research, language, and speaking and listening.

Reading Goals Tell students they will read and evaluate arguments. They will also read nonfiction narratives and explanatory essays to better understand the ways writers express ideas.

Writing and Research Goals Tell students that they will learn the elements of writing arguments. Students will write for a number of reasons, sharing ideas, reflecting on experiences, and gathering evidence. They will conduct research to clarify and explore ideas.

Language Goal Tell students that they will develop understanding of the proper use of verb tenses. They will then practice demonstrating those verb tenses in their own writing.

Speaking and Listening Explain to students that they will work together to build on one another's ideas and communicate with one another. They will also learn to incorporate audio, visuals, and text in presentations.

HOME Connection

A Home Connection letter to students' parents or guardians is available in the Interactive Teacher's Edition. The letter explains what students will be learning in this unit and how they will be assessed.

Unit Goals

Throughout this unit you will deepen your perspective about space exploration by reading, writing, speaking, listening, and presenting. These goals will help you succeed on the Unit Performance-Based Assessment.

Rate how well you meet these goals right now. You will revisit your ratings later, when you reflect on your growth during this unit.

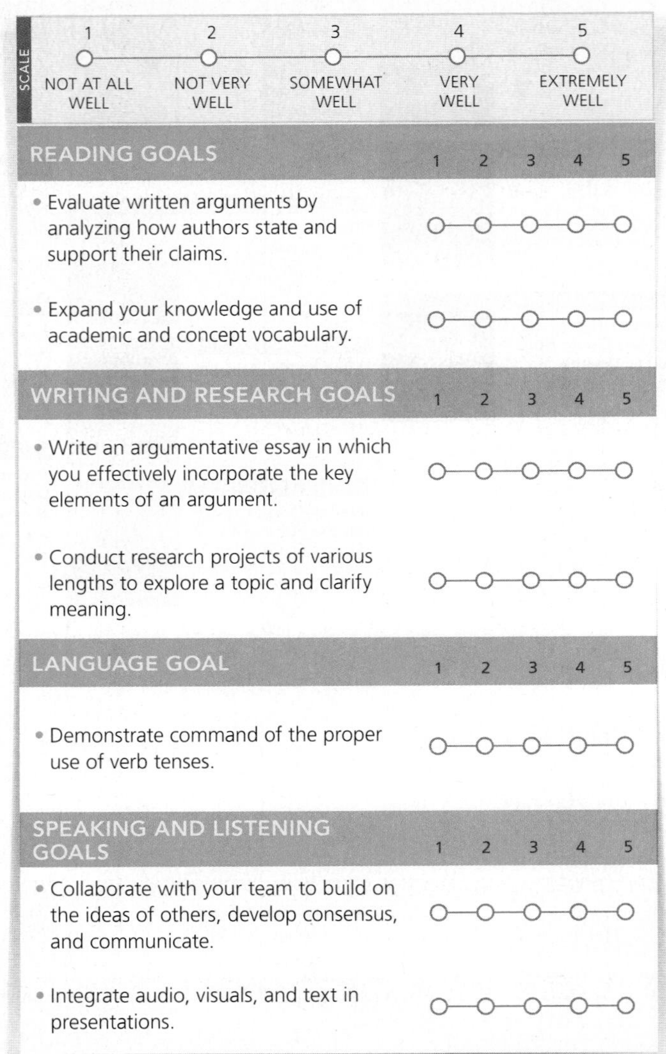

SCALE	1	2	3	4	5
	NOT AT ALL WELL	NOT VERY WELL	SOMEWHAT WELL	VERY WELL	EXTREMELY WELL

READING GOALS	1	2	3	4	5
• Evaluate written arguments by analyzing how authors state and support their claims.	O	O	O	O	O
• Expand your knowledge and use of academic and concept vocabulary.	O	O	O	O	O
WRITING AND RESEARCH GOALS	**1**	**2**	**3**	**4**	**5**
• Write an argumentative essay in which you effectively incorporate the key elements of an argument.	O	O	O	O	O
• Conduct research projects of various lengths to explore a topic and clarify meaning.	O	O	O	O	O
LANGUAGE GOAL	**1**	**2**	**3**	**4**	**5**
• Demonstrate command of the proper use of verb tenses.	O	O	O	O	O
SPEAKING AND LISTENING GOALS	**1**	**2**	**3**	**4**	**5**
• Collaborate with your team to build on the ideas of others, develop consensus, and communicate.	O	O	O	O	O
• Integrate audio, visuals, and text in presentations.	O	O	O	O	O

STANDARDS

Language
Acquire and use accurately grade appropriate general academic and domain-specific words and phrases; gather vocabulary knowledge when considering a word or phrase important to comprehension or expression.

AUTHOR'S PERSPECTIVE Ernest Morrell, Ph.D.

Self-Assessing Progress The Unit Goals will help students share responsibility for their learning. This is an important ownership for students as they prepare for life in higher education, in their professional career, and as leaders in their families and communities. One way to encourage students to practice monitoring their own learning is to give them guiding questions like these to help them assess their progress as they work through the unit. Remind students to ask themselves such questions as they complete each selection or activity in the unit so they can track their progress.

- Do I have a better understanding of the parts of an argument and how to recognize them when reading and using them when writing?
- Do I have a better understanding of the differences between academic and concept vocabulary?
- Am I recognizing different types of verbs?
- Am I effective when I collaborate with others?

DIGITAL PERSPECTIVES 

Academic Vocabulary: Argument

Academic terms appear in all subjects and can help you read, write, and discuss with more precision. Here are five academic words that will be useful to you in this unit as you analyze and write arguments.

Complete the chart.

1. Review each word, its root, and the mentor sentences.
2. Use the information and your own knowledge to predict the meaning of each word.
3. For each word, list at least two related words.
4. Refer to the dictionary or other resources if needed.

TIP

FOLLOW THROUGH

Study the words in this chart, and mark them or their forms wherever they appear in the unit.

WORD	MENTOR SENTENCES	PREDICT MEANING	RELATED WORDS
justify ROOT: ***-jus-*** "law"; "right"	1. Raymond had to *justify* his position on a controversial subject during the debate. 2. Lucy decided to *justify* her lateness by saying she was stuck in traffic.		justice; justification
alternative ROOT: ***-alt-*** "other"	1. The guest speaker presented an *alternative* point of view. 2. Tania developed an *alternative* way to study for math tests.		
certainty ROOT: ***-cert-*** "sure"	1. Winning a scholarship seemed to be a *certainty* for the valedictorian. 2. The astronomers knew with *certainty* that the comet would return again in ten years.		
discredit ROOT: ***-cred-*** "believe"	1. The scientist had to *discredit* his partner's work because the correct procedure was not followed. 2. The lawyer used facts to *discredit* the testimony of the star witness.		
assumption ROOT: ***-sum-*** "take up"	1. The scientist made an *assumption* about life on Mars based on his experiments. 2. It is not a good idea to make an *assumption* if you do not have all the facts and research.		

Academic Vocabulary: Argument

Introduce the blue academic vocabulary words in the chart on the student page. Point out that the root of each word provides a clue to its meaning. Discuss the mentor sentences to ensure students understand each word's usage. Students should also use the mentor sentences as context to help them predict the meaning of each word. Check that students are able to fill in the chart correctly. Complete pronunciations, parts of speech, and definitions are provided for you. Students are only expected to provide the definition.

Possible responses:

justify *v.* (JUHS tuh fy)
Meaning: to give a reason for something
Related words: justified, justifying
Additional words related to the root *-jus-*: adjust, judge, juror, jury

alternative *adj.* (awl TUR nuh tihv)
Meaning: representing a different option
Related words: alternate, alternatively
Additional words related to the root *-alt-*: altruistic, altercation

certainty *n.* (SUR tuhn tee)
Meaning: a state of being free from doubt
Related words: certain, certainly
Additional words related to the root *-cert-*: ascertain, certify, certificate

discredit *v.* (dihs KREHD iht)
Meaning: to debunk something, or destroy the credibility of someone or something
Related words: discredited, discredits
Additional words related to the root *-cred-*: credo, incredible, credulous, credence, creed

assumption *n.* (uh SUHMP shuhn)
Meaning: something that is accepted as true, without proof or evidence
Related words: assume, assumed
Additional words related to the root *-sum-*: consume, resume, subsume, presume

PERSONALIZE FOR LEARNING

English Language Support

Cognates Many of the academic words have Spanish cognates. Use these cognates with students whose home language is Spanish.

justify – justificar
discredit – desacreditado
alternative – alternativa
assumption – asunción
certainty – certeza

Not all English learners will recognize and use these cognates automatically. Help students build their cognate awareness by pointing out that these cognates share the same root in both English and Spanish. **ALL LEVELS**

Purpose of the Launch Text

The Launch Text provides students with a common starting point to address the unit topic. After reading the Launch Text, all students will be able to participate in discussions about a starry home.

Lexile: 1060 The easier reading level of this selection makes it perfect to assign for homework. Students will need little or no support to understand it.

Additionally, "Leaving Main Street" provides a writing model for the Performance-Based Assessment students complete at the end of the unit.

Launch Text: Argument Model

Remind students to determine the main point of the argument and how the author supports that point.

Have students pay attention to the structure of the text. They should note that the author doesn't state a position immediately. Instead the article begins with information about a particular space mission and then presents different sides of the issue. Students should note that the author doesn't begin to state a position until the seventh paragraph—"Humans explore space because it's in our genes"—and that the following paragraphs provide details supporting that position. The concluding paragraph restates the author's position.

Encourage students to read this text on their own and annotate unfamiliar words and sections of text they think are particularly important.

AUDIO SUMMARIES

Audio summaries of "Leaving Main Street" are available in both English and Spanish in the Interactive Teacher's Edition or Unit Resources. Assigning these summaries before students read the Launch Text may help them build additional background knowledge and set a context for their reading.

LAUNCH TEXT | ARGUMENT

This selection is an example of an **argumentative text**, a type of writing in which an author states and defends a position on a topic. This is the type of writing you will develop in the Performance-Based Assessment at the end of the Unit.

As you read, look at the way the writer presents the argument that people are born to explore the unknown.

Leaving Main Street

NOTES

1 In July, 2015, the world watched in awe as close-up photographs of Pluto streamed back to Earth from three billion miles away. The spacecraft *New Horizons* had traveled nine years to study the dwarf planet at the edge of our solar system.

2 As a result of the mission, scientists discovered that Pluto is not just a giant ball of ice. It has a molten core, tectonic plates, and volcanic activity, just as Earth does. It may even support some form of life. The *New Horizons* mission has been hailed as a triumph of human ingenuity, and a huge leap forward for the future of space exploration.

3 Yet it almost didn't happen. The mission had to overcome some serious challenges before it could get underway—such as repeated threats to defund it.

4 There have always been naysayers who've questioned the need for space exploration. The argument goes that the United States has more important things to spend its money on, such as ending hunger and poverty.

5 Others argue that a successful space program adds to our national prestige, helps the economy, creates jobs, and improves national security. It inspires students to pursue innovative projects and careers in science and technology. At a cost of six-tenths of a percent of the federal budget, it's well worth the price: The cost of exploration is vastly outweighed by the idea of extending humankind's sphere of influence to outer space.

6 But these are not the real reasons for continuing the space program, says Michael Griffin in *Air & Space Magazine*. Griffin makes the point that people go to space for reasons that are not necessarily logical. In other words, money doesn't have much

CROSS-CURRICULAR PERSPECTIVES

Science "Leaving Main Street" discusses the *New Horizons* space mission, which, in 2015, led to groundbreaking new information about Pluto. This, of course, is only one of many space missions. Have students conduct research about other space missions and address the following questions:

- When did the mission take place?
- What was the purpose of the mission?
- What did the mission accomplish?
- Were there any problems with the mission?

Have volunteers share their responses with the class.

to do with it. "When we contemplate committing large sums of money to a project, we tend to dismiss reasons that are emotional or value-driven," Griffin says. He goes on to say that Americans need the prospect of exploring space.

7 Humans explore space because it's in our genes. We're hardwired with certain built-in features that compel us in that direction. Here's how it breaks down:

8 First, there is something about the human condition that strives to be the best, or the first, at something. Our ancestors survived by outperforming others.

9 Second, humans are by nature curious about exploring new places. Everyone remembers being a kid and wanting to see what's "over there." Humans will not tolerate boundaries; their dream is to explore what's beyond.

10 Third, humans have always created monuments to commemorate their great achievements, so that the next generation will remember who they are and how they spent their time here. What we want to be remembered for is finding life on other worlds, maybe even for landing on Mars.

11 Finally, NASA's space program inspires competition and innovation. The Hubble Space Telescope and the robotic missions to the planets have been shining examples of what can be achieved when a project is based on goals set by scientists rather than by politicians.

12 If we stop exploring space, soon society will have forgotten what it's like to be human. It's human to wonder about things we can't see, to look for what's over the horizon. And how can we be so narrow-minded as to think we're the only ones out there? ❧

NOTES

WORD NETWORK FOR A STARRY HOME

Vocabulary A Word Network is a collection of words related to a topic. As you read the selections in this unit, identify interesting words related to the idea of space exploration and add them to your Word Network. For example, you might begin by adding words from the Launch Text, such as *mission, exploration,* and *curious.* Continue to add words as you complete this unit.

Tool Kit Word Network Model

SPACE EXPLORATION

mission

exploration

curious

Word Network for A Starry Home

Tell students that they can fill in the Word Network as they read the texts in the unit, or they can jot down the words elsewhere and add them later. Point out to students that people may have personal associations with some words. A word that one student thinks is related to the concept of a starry home might not be a word another student would pick. However, students should feel free to add any relevant words to their Word Network. Each person's Word Network will be unique. If you choose to print the Word Network, distribute it to students at this point so they can use it throughout the rest of the unit.

AUTHOR'S PERSPECTIVE **Elfrieda Hiebert, Ph.D.**

Generative Vocabulary Rare words are the words that typically account for only 10 percent of all the words in a text, compared to the more common vocabulary words that students know better. Generative vocabulary strategies can help students build their rare vocabulary.

"Generative" refers to the way students can apply knowledge of how words work—morphologically and conceptually—when encountering new words. Building off of a big idea like this unit's starry home, words can be taught as networks of ideas rather than as single, unrelated but grade-appropriate words. Studying words in conceptual groupings enables students to learn more words while reading.

Although some "starry home" words may be unfamiliar to students, the overarching concept will not be. Students may not know every word related to the idea of a "starry home," but the concept of connections between life on Earth and space travel should be familiar to them. Word Networks help students build vocabulary as they see that a wide variety of words can relate to one concept.

Summary

Have students read the introductory paragraph. Provide them with tips for writing a summary:

- Write in the present tense.
- Make sure to include the title of the work.
- Be concise: a summary should not be equal in length to the original text.
- If you need to quote the words of the author, use quotation marks.
- Don't put your own opinions, ideas, or interpretations into the summary. The purpose of writing a summary is to accurately represent what the author says, not to provide a critique.

See possible summary on the student page.

Launch Activity

Explain to students that as they work on this unit, they will have many opportunities to discuss the topic of a starry home. Remind them that there is no right or wrong position, but they should be able to support their positions with evidence from the material they've viewed, read, and analyzed as well as their prior knowledge.

Encourage students to keep an open mind and really listen to their classmates.

Summary

Write a summary of "Leaving Main Street." A **summary** is a concise, complete, and accurate overview of a text. It should not include a statement of your opinion or an analysis.

Possible response: This argumentative text makes the case that we should explore space. It begins by discussing a recent mission that found out a lot about Pluto. There were many threats to defund this mission beforehand. The author contends that we should explore space because of moral values, and that cost shouldn't even factor into the question. According to the author, human nature drives us to explore, to be curious, and to try to compete for great achievements. Thus, without space exploration we will "forget what it's like to be human."

Launch Activity

Launch a Four-Corner Debate Consider this statement: **We should stop exploring space because the money spent on space missions could be put to better use here on Earth.**

- Record your position on the statement and explain your thinking.

  ☐ Strongly Agree ☐ Agree ☐ Disagree ☐ Strongly Disagree

- Form a group with like-minded students in one corner of the classroom.
- Discuss questions such as "What examples from the text or your own prior knowledge led you to take this position?"
- After your discussion, have a representative from each group present a brief two- or three-minute summary of the group's position.
- After all the groups have presented their views, move into the four corners again. If you change your corner, be ready to explain why.

QuickWrite

Consider class discussions, presentations, the video, and the Launch Text as you think about the prompt. Record your first thoughts here.

PROMPT: **Should we spend valuable resources on space exploration?**

Possible response: Space exploration is possibly the most important thing we can spend resources on. It will be dangerous and have little payoff at first. But we should remember that the European colonization of the Americas initially cost a great deal of money and lives, with little return. And since space is *actually* uninhabited, unlike the Americas in 1492, creating new infrastructure in space won't destroy cultures the way European colonization of the Americas did. One might argue that we should save resources for deprived people on Earth. But settling space will greatly expand the resources available to humanity—after its initial starting costs. Space exploration will make it possible for everyone to have enough.

EVIDENCE LOG FOR A STARRY HOME

Review your QuickWrite and summarize your point of view to record in your Evidence Log. Then, record evidence from "Leaving Main Street" that supports your point of view.

After each selection, you will continue to use your Evidence Log to record the evidence you gather and the connections you make. This graphic shows what your Evidence Log looks like.

Tool Kit Evidence Log Model

Title of Text: ____________ Date: ______

CONNECTION TO PROMPT	TEXT EVIDENCE/DETAILS	ADDITIONAL NOTES/IDEAS

How does this text change or add to my thinking? Date: ______

DIGITAL PERSPECTIVES

QuickWrite

In this QuickWrite, students should present their own answer to the question based on the material in the Unit Opener. This initial response will help inform their work when they complete the Performance-Based Assessment at the end of the unit. Students should make sure they state a clear position and support it with logical reasoning.

See possible QuickWrite on the student page.

Evidence Log for A Starry Home

Students should record their initial response in their Evidence Logs. Then, they should record evidence from "Leaving Main Street" that supports their initial response.

If you choose to print the Evidence Log, distribute it to students at this point so they can use it throughout the rest of the unit.

Performance-Based Assessment: Refining Your Thinking

- Have students watch the video on Refining Your Thinking.
- A video on this topic is available online in the Professional Development Center.

WHOLE-CLASS LEARNING

Should we make a home in space?

Lead students in a discussion of why humans have long dreamed of living in space. Ask students to think about what it means to make a home in space and whether humans are close to realizing that dream. During Whole-Class Learning, students will read selections about the human thirst to keep exploring, learning, and knowing about what it could be like to live in space.

Whole-Class Learning Strategies

Review the Learning Strategies with students and explain that as they work through Whole-Class Learning they will develop strategies to work in large-group environments.

- Have students watch the video on Whole-Class Learning Strategies.
- A video on this topic is available online in the Professional Development Center.

You may wish to discuss some action items to add to the chart as a class before students complete it on their own. For example, for "Listen actively," you might solicit the following from students:

- Discuss and compare notes with classmates.
- When you are unclear about something, ask questions afterwards.

Block Scheduling

Each day in this Pacing Plan represents a 40- to 50-minute class period. Teachers using block scheduling may combine days to reflect their class schedule. In addition, teachers may revise pacing to differentiate and support core instruction by integrating components and resources as students require.

OVERVIEW: WHOLE-CLASS LEARNING

ESSENTIAL QUESTION:

Should we make a home in space?

Some people gaze up at a starry sky and think it is beautiful. Some people look up at the same sky and want to find out who or what is up there. You will work with your whole class to explore the pros and cons of space exploration.

Whole-Class Learning Strategies

Throughout your life, in school, in your community, and in your career, you will continue to learn and work in large-group environments.

Review these strategies and the actions you can take to practice them as you work with your whole class. Add ideas of your own for each category for each step. Get ready to use these strategies during Whole-Class Learning.

STRATEGY	ACTION PLAN
Listen actively	• Eliminate distractions. For example, put your cellphone away. • Keep your eyes on the speaker. •
Clarify by asking questions	• If you're confused, other people probably are, too. Ask a question to help your whole class. • If you see that you are guessing, ask a question instead. •
Monitor understanding	• Notice what information you already know and be ready to build on it. • Ask for help if you are struggling. •
Interact and share ideas	• Share your ideas and answer questions, even if you are unsure. • Build on the ideas of others by adding details or making a connection. •

Pacing Plan

Unit Introduction		Introduce Whole-Class Learning	Dark They Were, and Golden-Eyed						Media: Dark They Were, and Golden-Eyed			Danger! This Mission to Mars Could Bore You to Death!			Performance Task		
1	2	3	4	5	6	7	8	9	10	11	12	13	14	15	16	17	18

WHOLE-CLASS LEARNING

CONTENTS

COMPARE

ANCHOR TEXT: SHORT STORY

Dark They Were, and Golden-Eyed

Ray Bradbury

Something strange is happening to these settlers on Mars.

MEDIA: RADIO PLAY

Dark They Were, and Golden-Eyed

Ray Bradbury, and Michael McDonough (producer)

Experience this Ray Bradbury story as a radio play.

ANCHOR TEXT: NEWS ARTICLE

Danger! This Mission to Mars Could Bore You to Death!

Maggie Koerth-Baker

Could space travel actually be boring?

PERFORMANCE TASK

WRITING FOCUS

Write an Argument

The Whole-Class readings represent different attitudes toward space travel and the experience of actually living on another planet. After reading and listening, you will write an argument about the advantages or disadvantages of exploring outer space.

DIGITAL PERSPECTIVES

Contents

Anchor Texts To preview the anchor texts and media with students, first ask them to offer ideas as to what the titles and illustrations make them think of. Extend the discussion to other texts they may have read or movies or television shows they may have seen that deal with issues of exploring space.

Suggest students take a vote on the selection that looks most interesting, along with the reasons for their preferences. Students can return to voting numbers after they have read the selections to see if any preferences changed.

Performance Task

Write an Argument Explain to students that after they have finished reading the selections, they will write an argument about the advantages and disadvantages of exploring space. To help them prepare, encourage students to think about the topic as they progress through the selections and as they participate in the Whole-Class Learning experience.

Introduce Small-Group Learning

Future of Space Exploration Could See Humans on Mars, Alien Planets

The Last Dog

Media: Ellen Ochoa: Director, Johnson Space Center

Neil deGrasse Tyson on the Future of U.S. Space Exploration After *Curiosity*

Performance Task

Introduce Independent Learning

Independent Learning

Performance-Based Assessment

19 20 21 22 23 24 25 26 27 28 29 30 31 32 33 34 35 36

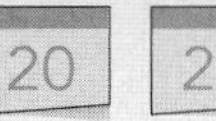

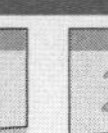

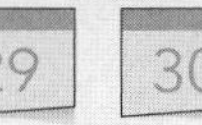

Dark They Were, and Golden-Eyed

AUDIO SUMMARIES
Audio summaries of "Dark They Were, and Golden-Eyed" are available online in both English and Spanish in the Interactive Teacher's Edition or Unit Resources. Assigning these summaries prior to reading the selection may help students build additional background knowledge and set a context for their first read.

Summary

Ray Bradbury's short story "Dark They Were, and Golden-Eyed" takes place on Mars. A family arrives from Earth as colonists. Harry, the father, is uneasy from the beginning. Shortly after the family's arrival they get news that nuclear war has broken out on Earth; they are stranded on Mars. Soon, the plants they brought with them from Earth seem to be changing in small ways, and Harry fears that the seemingly extinct Martian natives might still exist somewhere on the planet. He becomes terribly afraid of contamination, of some infection or influence that will change everything the family cares about.

Insight

At the end of the story, survivors from Earth arrive to find that the colony is deserted; all the colonists now live as native Martians. The story reflects on cultural change and assimilation. Within a few years, the visitors have adapted to their new planet so thoroughly that no one realizes they came from Earth.

ESSENTIAL QUESTION:
Should we make a home in space?

Connection to Essential Question

"Dark They Were, and Golden-Eyed" provides a fictional scenario about living life on another planet. Although it is a fictional account of life on Mars, it connects directly to the Essential Question as to whether people should make their homes in space by addressing a series of issues concerning the ability of humans to adapt to the unknown conditions of another planet.

WHOLE-CLASS LEARNING PERFORMANCE TASK
Do the benefits of exploring Mars outweigh the risks?

UNIT PERFORMANCE-BASED ASSESSMENT
Should we spend valuable resources on space exploration?

Connection to Performance Tasks

Whole-Class Learning Performance Task This selection provides strong support for the point of view that the risks of exploring Mars far outweigh the benefits, as the Bittering family is slowly changed from human to Martian by their new environment.

Unit Performance-Based Assessment This selection initially presents strong evidence in favor of using valuable resources to explore space. The Bitterings arrive to find an entire civilization abandoned, but in the end it is all for naught, as the humans sent to rescue those who have landed on Mars find nothing but Martians—there are no humans to be found.

DIGITAL PERSPECTIVES

Audio

Video

Document

Annotation Highlights

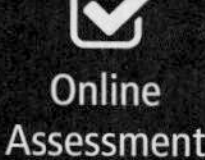
Online Assessment

LESSON RESOURCES

	Making Meaning	Language Development
Lesson	**First Read** **Close Read** **Analyze the Text** **Analyze Craft and Structure**	**Concept Vocabulary** **Word Study** **Conventions**
Instructional Standards	**RL.7.10** By the end of the year, read and comprehend literature . . . **RL.7.4** Determine the meaning of words and phrases . . . **L.7.5** Demonstrate understanding of figurative language . . . **L.7.5.a** Interpret figures of speech in context.	**L.7.4** Determine or clarify the meaning of unknown and multiple-meaning words and phrases . . . **L.7.5** Demonstrate understanding of figurative language . . . **L.7.1** Demonstrate command of the conventions of standard English . . .
STUDENT RESOURCES		
Available online in the Interactive Student Edition or Unit Resources	Selection Audio First-Review Guide: Fiction Close-Review Guide: Fiction	Evidence Log
TEACHER RESOURCES		
Selection Resources Available online in the Interactive Teacher's Edition or Unit Resources	Audio Summaries: English and Spanish Annotation Highlights Accessible Leveled Text First Read Extension Questions Analyze Craft and Structure: Metaphor and Simile	Concept Vocabulary and Word Study Conventions: Comparison of Adjectives and Adverbs English Language Support Lesson: Comparatives and Superlatives
Reteach and Practice (RP)	Analyze Craft and Structure: Metaphor and Simile (RP)	Word Study: Synonyms and Nuance (RP) Conventions: Comparison of Adjectives and Adverbs (RP)
Assessment Available online in Assessments	Selection Test: English Selection Test: Spanish Extension Selection Test	
My Resources	A Unit 2 Answer Key is available online and in the Interactive Teacher's Edition.	

Reading Support

Text Complexity Rubric: Dark They Were, and Golden-Eyed	
Quantitative Measures	
Lexile: 490 **Text Length:** 4,701 words	
Qualitative Measures	
Knowledge Demands (1 2 3 **4** 5)	Explores sophisticated themes including cultural adaptation, fear of changing identity, and colonization. Story was written in 1949 and has references to atom bomb, Rockefeller, Ford, etc.
Structure (1 2 **3** 4 5)	Story is mostly chronological, but plot elements are not revealed immediately. Plot events are intertwined with internal reflection of main character; use of dialogue makes story easy to follow.
Language Conventionality and Clarity (1 2 **3** 4 5)	Language does not sound contemporary; mostly short sentences with simple construction, some more complex sentences with descriptive or figurative phrases.
Levels of Meaning/Purpose (1 2 3 **4** 5)	Multiple levels of meaning are complex and subtle (plot events as well as commentary on culture, colonization, and changing identity); meaning is revealed as story develops.

DECIDE AND PLAN

English Language Support

Provide English Learners with support for knowledge demands and meaning as they read the selection.

Knowledge Demands Write 1949, the year the story was written, on the board. Then list some of the situations that students will find in the story: *space exploration, war and atomic bombs, family adjusting to Mars, people from Earth renaming land.* Point out that paragraph 48 lists names that Earth people in the story gave when they came to Mars. Explain that the names (Ford, Roosevelt, etc.) are names of U.S. presidents and other historical figures.

Meaning After reading the story once through, have students reread sections. As a group, write sentences summarizing the events and characters' feelings in each section.

Strategic Support

Provide students with strategic support to ensure that they can successfully read the text.

Knowledge Demands Discuss some of the story themes that are related to the time the story was written (1949). For example, the first atomic bombing occurred in 1945, and WWII had just ended. How might these major events have shaped the story's themes?

Meaning Ask questions to determine if students understand the different levels of meaning. For example, *Why can't the family return to Earth? Who renamed the Martian mountains?* Then discuss the meaning that is implied. Have students reread paragraphs 43 and 48. Ask *How does Bittering feel about Earthmen changing Martian names? (He does not think they should have changed names).*

Challenge

Provide students who need to be challenged with ideas for how they can go beyond a simple interpretation of the text.

Text Analysis Ask students to reread paragraphs 43 and 48. Discuss Bittering's thoughts about renaming the Martian landscape. Ask students to describe his opinion about the name change. Then ask why they think the author compares the name changes on Mars to the names American settlers used for Indian territories.

Written Response Ask students to imagine they are a new character in the story—a son or daughter. Have them think about how the character reacts to being on Mars. Ask them to write a short dialogue between the father and this character. They may include narration detailing characters' actions or feelings.

TEACH

Read and Respond

Have the class do their first read of the selection. Then, have the students complete their close read. Finally, work with them on the Making Meaning and Language Development activities.

Standards Support Through Teaching and Learning Cycle

IDENTIFY NEEDS

Analyze results of the Beginning-of-Year Assessment, focusing on the items relating to Unit 2. Also take into consideration student performance to this point and your observations of where particular students struggle.

DECIDE AND PLAN

- If students have performed poorly on items matching these standards, then provide selection scaffolds before assigning them the on-level lesson provided in the Student Edition.
- If students have done well on the Beginning-of-Year Assessment, then challenge them to keep progressing and learning by giving them opportunities to practice the skills in depth.
- Use the Selection Resources listed on the Planning pages for "Dark They Were, and Golden-Eyed" to help students continually improve their ability to master the standards.

Instructional Standards: Dark They Were, and Golden-Eyed

	Catching Up	This Year	Looking Forward
Reading	You may wish to administer the **Analyze Craft and Structure: Metaphor and Simile (RP)** worksheet to help students understand how figurative language is used in a text.	**L.5** Demonstrate understanding of figurative language, word relationships, and nuances in word meanings.	Encourage students to find the metaphors and similes in the selection and discuss the impact that they have on the text.
Language	You may wish to administer the **Conventions: Comparison of Adjectives and Adverbs (RP)** worksheet to help students understand how adjectives and adverbs are used. You may wish to administer the **Word Study: Synonyms and Nuance (RP)** worksheet to help students understand that nuances add subtle differences to words.	**L.1** Demonstrate command of the conventions of standard English grammar and usage when writing or speaking. **L.4** Determine or clarify the meaning of unknown and multiple-meaning words and phrases based on *grade 7 reading and content,* choosing flexibly from a range of strategies.	Challenge students to use more and varied adjectives and adverbs in their writing. You may wish to challenge students to look at a list of common words and, after finding synonyms, find related words that add nuance.

ANALYZE AND REVISE

- Analyze student work for evidence of student learning.
- Identify whether students have met the expectations in the standards.
- Identify implications for future instruction.

TEACH

Implement the planned lesson, and gather evidence of student learning.

Jump Start

FIRST READ *Would you like to live on another planet? Why or why not?* Prior to students' first read, have them discuss what they think it would be like to live on another planet to help them make connections between the text and their own ideas and experiences.

Dark They Were, and Golden-Eyed

Will people from Earth someday live on other planets? If they do, what challenges might they face? What benefits might they get? Modeling questions such as these will help students connect to "Dark They Were, and Golden-Eyed" and to the Whole-Class Performance Task assignment. Selection audio and print capability for the selection are available in the Interactive Teacher's Edition.

Concept Vocabulary

Support students as they rank the words. Ask if they've ever heard, read, or used them. Reassure them that the definitions for these words are listed in the selection.

FIRST READ

As they read, students should perform the steps of the first read:

NOTICE: You may want to encourage students to notice how the characters change as the story goes on.

ANNOTATE: Remind students to mark passages that include characterization, figurative language, and other descriptive language.

CONNECT: Encourage students to make connections beyond the text. If they cannot make connections to their own lives or other texts, have them consider movies and TV shows.

RESPOND: Students will answer questions and write a summary to demonstrate understanding.

Point out to students that while they will always complete the Respond step at the end of the first read, the other steps will probably happen somewhat concurrently. You may wish to print copies of the **First-Read Guide: Fiction** for students to use.

Remind students that during their first read, they should not answer the close-read questions that appear in the selection.

MAKING MEANING

Comparing Text to Media

DARK THEY WERE, AND GOLDEN-EYED (short story)

In this lesson, you will read the short story "Dark They Were, and Golden-Eyed" and listen to a radio play performance of it. You will then compare the text to the radio play.

DARK THEY WERE, AND GOLDEN-EYED (radio play)

About the Author

As a boy, **Ray Bradbury** (1920–2012) loved magicians, circuses, and science fiction stories. He began writing at the age of 12 and went on to become one of the most celebrated writers of science fiction and fantasy. *The Martian Chronicles,* a collection of Bradbury's stories about Earth's colonization of Mars, was published in 1950 and is considered a classic today.

Dark They Were, and Golden-Eyed

Concept Vocabulary

You will encounter the following words as you read the short story. Before reading, note how familiar you are with each word. Then, rank the words in order from most familiar (1) to least familiar (6).

WORD	YOUR RANKING
submerged	
forlorn	
canals	
immense	
atmosphere	
mosaic	

After completing your first read, come back to the concept vocabulary and review your rankings. Mark changes to your rankings as needed.

First Read FICTION

Apply these strategies during your first read. You will have an opportunity to complete the close-read notes after your first read.

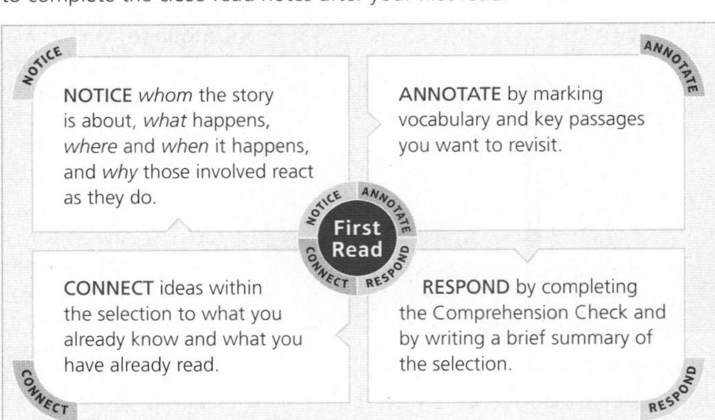

Tool Kit
First-Read Guide and Model Annotation

STANDARDS
Reading Literature
By the end of the year, read and comprehend literature, including stories, dramas, and poems, in the grades 6–8 text complexity band proficiently, with scaffolding as needed at the high end of the range.

AUTHOR'S PERSPECTIVE Kelly Gallagher, M.Ed.

First Read Strategies As students encounter unfamiliar and challenging text for the first time, some may hit a frustration point early. Students often think that if they don't understand something on the first try that they will never understand. Comprehension when reading is not an all-or-nothing situation. Share these strategies for getting through the gray areas:

- ***Read on with Uncertainty*** Students who are "a little bit lost" may be able to read a little further to resolve confusion. Model this mindset with the opening paragraphs of a novel or long work. Read the text, and show students what questions you already have. Demonstrate that many questions arise at the beginning as readers place themselves in the

ANCHOR TEXT | SHORT STORY

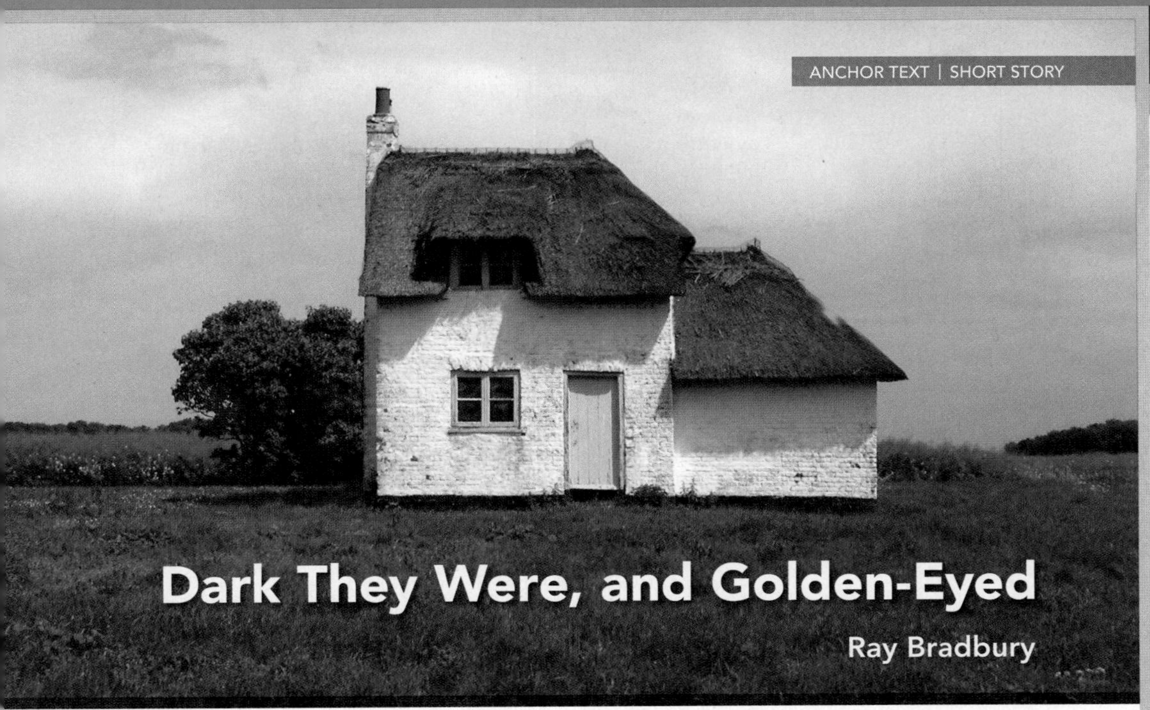

Dark They Were, and Golden-Eyed

Ray Bradbury

BACKGROUND

The astronomer Carl Sagan once wrote, "Mars has become a kind of mythic arena onto which we have projected our earthly hopes and fears." People have always been fascinated by the possibility of alien life on Mars. In this story, author Ray Bradbury does away with hard science, choosing instead to explore the aura of mystery that has always surrounded the Red Planet.

1 The rocket metal cooled in the meadow winds. Its lid gave a bulging *pop*. From its clock interior stepped a man, a woman, and three children. The other passengers whispered away across the Martian meadow, leaving the man alone among his family.

2 The man felt his hair flutter and the tissues of his body draw tight as if he were standing at the center of a vacuum. His wife, before him, seemed almost to whirl away in smoke. The children, small seeds, might at any instant be sown to all the Martian climes.

3 The children looked up at him, as people look to the sun to tell what time of their life it is. His face was cold.

4 "What's wrong?" asked his wife.

5 "Let's get back on the rocket."

6 "Go back to Earth?"

7 "Yes! Listen!"

8 The wind blew as if to flake away their identities. At any moment the Martian air might draw his soul from him, as marrow

NOTES

CLOSE READ

ANNOTATE: In paragraph 2, mark the things that are being compared.

QUESTION: What is unusual about these comparisons?

CONCLUDE: What mood or overall impression has Bradbury created with these comparisons?

DIGITAL PERSPECTIVES  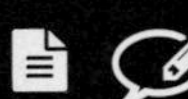 

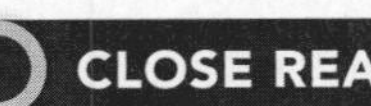

CLOSE READ

As students look for a simile and a metaphor, review that, while these examples of figurative language take slightly different forms, they both compare things that are essentially unlike in order to describe a certain quality of one of them. You may wish to model the close read using the following think-aloud format. Possible responses to questions on the student page are included. You may also want to print copies of the **Close-Read Guide: Fiction** for students to use.

ANNOTATE: As I read paragraph 2, I notice a comparison between his body tissues and the inside of a vacuum; his wife and smoke; and his children and seeds.

QUESTION: I notice the comparison is unusual because it compares people to the effects of wind.

CONCLUDE: When I think about the mood created by these comparisons, I see that they suggest that the family is not entirely safe. I think the author is suggesting that Earth people are vulnerable on Mars.

world the writer has created. Good readers can live with this confusion because within a few paragraphs or pages, key ideas often become more clear.

- ***Monitor Comprehension*** To make their comprehension more concrete for students, have them use two different colors to mark the text: one color for text they understand, and another color to highlight the text that is challenging to them. This will help pinpoint areas of confusion and show how much of the text they understand.
- ***Apply Fix-It Strategies*** Students who are struggling with comprehension may use fix-it strategies to start by rereading at the word level and decoding words they don't know. They can then move to the sentence level to make sure that they are following the text.

When students have the tools to monitor their comprehension, they may feel more empowered to get through their first read. Once they can get past the literal interpretation of text, they can then move toward uncovering deeper meaning.

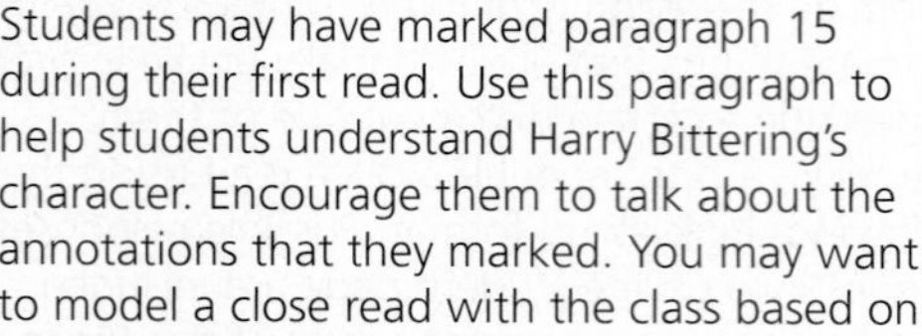

CLOSER LOOK

Analyze Character

Students may have marked paragraph 15 during their first read. Use this paragraph to help students understand Harry Bittering's character. Encourage them to talk about the annotations that they marked. You may want to model a close read with the class based on the highlights shown in the text.

ANNOTATE: Have students mark details in this paragraph that reveal how Harry feels about being on Mars, or have students participate while you highlight them.

QUESTION: Guide students to consider what these details might tell them. Ask what a reader can infer from these details and accept student responses.

Possible response: Harry is unhappy about being on Mars.

CONCLUDE: Help students to formulate conclusions about the importance of these details in the text. Ask students why the author might have included these details at this point in the story.

Possible response: The author might have included these details at this point in the story to create tension.

Point out that in this part of the story the author is using **indirect characterization** (showing a character's traits through dialogue or actions rather than narration). The character is expressing his feelings about not belonging on Mars instead of the narrator telling us about those feelings. Also point out Bradbury's use of a simile to describe Harry's feelings: "I feel like a salt crystal in a mountain stream."

NOTES

submerged (suhb MURJD) *adj.* completely covered with a liquid

comes from a white bone. He felt **submerged** in a chemical that could dissolve his intellect and burn away his past.

9 They looked at Martian hills that time had worn with a crushing pressure of years. They saw the old cities, lost in their meadows, lying like children's delicate bones among the blowing lakes of grass.

10 "Chin up, Harry," said his wife. "It's too late. We've come over sixty million miles."

11 The children with their yellow hair hollered at the deep dome of Martian sky. There was no answer but the racing hiss of wind through the stiff grass.

12 He picked up the luggage in his cold hands. "Here we go," he said—a man standing on the edge of a sea, ready to wade in and be drowned.

13 They walked into town.

14 Their name was Bittering. Harry and his wife Cora; Dan, Laura, and David. They built a small white cottage and ate good breakfasts there, but the fear was never gone. It lay with Mr. Bittering and Mrs. Bittering, a third unbidden partner at every midnight talk, at every dawn awakening.

15 "I feel like a salt crystal," he said, "in a mountain stream, being washed away. We don't belong here. We're Earth people. This is Mars. It was meant for Martians. For heaven's sake, Cora, let's buy tickets for home!"

16 But she only shook her head. "One day the atom bomb will fix Earth. Then we'll be safe here."

17 "Safe and insane!"

18 *Tick-tock, seven o'clock* sang the voice-clock; *time to get up*. And they did.

19 Something made him check everything each morning—warm hearth, potted blood-geraniums—precisely as if he expected something to be amiss. The morning paper was toast-warm from the 6 A.M. Earth rocket. He broke its seal and tilted it at his breakfast place. He forced himself to be convivial.[1]

20 "Colonial days all over again," he declared. "Why, in ten years there'll be a million Earthmen on Mars. Big cities, everything! They said we'd fail. Said the Martians would resent our invasion. But did we find any Martians? Not a living soul! Oh, we found their empty cities, but no one in them. Right?"

21 A river of wind submerged the house. When the windows ceased rattling Mr. Bittering swallowed and looked at the children.

22 "I don't know," said David. "Maybe there're Martians around we don't see. Sometimes nights I think I hear 'em. I hear the wind. The sand hits my window. I get scared. And I see those towns way

1. **convivial** (kuhn VIHV ee uhl) *adj.* social and friendly.

CROSS-CURRICULAR PERSPECTIVES

Social Studies Review paragraph 20. Harry remarks, "Colonial days all over again." Have students research and write short reports on colonialism. They should include information about where and when their examples of colonialism took place, and what happened as a result. How do these examples of colonialism relate to the story?

up in the mountains where the Martians lived a long time ago. And I think I see things moving around those towns, Papa. And I wonder if those Martians *mind* us living here. I wonder if they won't do something to us for coming here."

23 "Nonsense!" Mr. Bittering looked out the windows. "We're clean, decent people." He looked at his children. "All dead cities have some kind of ghosts in them. Memories, I mean." He stared at the hills. "You see a staircase and you wonder what Martians looked like climbing it. You see Martian paintings and you wonder what the painter was like. You make a little ghost in your mind, a memory. It's quite natural. Imagination." He stopped. "You haven't been prowling up in those ruins, have you?"

24 "No, Papa." David looked at his shoes.

25 "See that you stay away from them. Pass the jam."

26 "Just the same," said little David, "I bet something happens."

27 Something happened that afternoon.

28 Laura stumbled through the settlement, crying. She dashed blindly onto the porch.

29 "Mother, Father—the war, Earth!" she sobbed. "A radio flash just came. Atom bombs hit New York! All the space rockets blown up. No more rockets to Mars, ever!"

30 "Oh, Harry!" The mother held onto her husband and daughter.

31 "Are you sure, Laura?" asked the father quietly.

32 Laura wept. "We're stranded on Mars, forever and ever!"

33 For a long time there was only the sound of the wind in the late afternoon.

34 Alone, thought Bittering. Only a thousand of us here. No way back. No way. No way. Sweat poured from his face and his hands and his body; he was drenched in the hotness of his fear. He wanted to strike Laura, cry, "No, you're lying! The rockets will come back!" Instead, he stroked Laura's head against him and said, "The rockets will get through someday."

35 "Father, what will we do?"

36 "Go about our business, of course. Raise crops and children. Wait. Keep things going until the war ends and the rockets come again."

37 The two boys stepped out onto the porch.

38 "Children," he said, sitting there, looking beyond them, "I've something to tell you."

39 "We know," they said.

40 In the following days, Bittering wandered often through the garden to stand alone in his fear. As long as the rockets had spun a silver web across space, he had been able to accept Mars. For he had always told himself: Tomorrow, if I want, I can buy a ticket and go back to Earth.

NOTES

CLOSE READ

ANNOTATE: Mark details in the beginning of paragraph 34 that describe Bittering's inner thoughts.

QUESTION: Why are these thoughts expressed in incomplete sentences, with a lot of repetition?

CONCLUDE: What does this use of language help reveal about Bittering's emotional state?

DIGITAL PERSPECTIVES

CLOSE READ

Remind students that a character's inner thoughts might not be set off with quotation marks. You may wish to model the close read using the following think-aloud format. Possible responses to questions on the student page are included.

ANNOTATE: As I read paragraph 34, I notice that Bittering is conflicted. He is afraid, but he is also trying to reassure his daughter.

QUESTION: I think the fragments and repetition speed the action and add to the tension.

CONCLUDE: The language shows two purposes: it shows his panic, and using "No" several times shows his inner conflict.

CLOSE READ

As students look for examples of descriptive language, remind them to be aware of strong adjectives and verbs. You may wish to model the close read using the following think-aloud format. Possible responses to questions on the student page are included.

ANNOTATE: As I read paragraph 41, I notice and highlight text that appeals to the senses and paints pictures with words.

QUESTION: For me, the second image suggests the strange beauty and intense climate of Mars.

CONCLUDE: The passage builds suspense because it emphasizes the destruction that has taken place on Earth and how cut off from Earth the people on Mars are.

NOTES

CLOSE READ

ANNOTATE: Mark examples of descriptive language in paragraph 41.

QUESTION: What idea about Mars does this use of language suggest?

CONCLUDE: How does this passage build suspense?

41 But now: The web gone, the rockets lying in jigsaw heaps of molten girder and unsnaked wire. Earth people left to the strangeness of Mars, the cinnamon dusts and wine airs, to be baked like gingerbread shapes in Martian summers, put into harvested storage by Martian winters. What would happen to him, the others? This was the moment Mars had waited for. Now it would eat them.

42 He got down on his knees in the flower bed, a spade in his nervous hands. Work, he thought, work and forget.

43 He glanced up from the garden to the Martian mountains. He thought of the proud old Martian names that had once been on those peaks. Earthmen, dropping from the sky, had gazed upon hills, rivers, Martian seats left nameless in spite of names. Once Martians had built cities, named cities; climbed mountains, named mountains; sailed seas, named seas. Mountains melted, seas drained, cities tumbled. In spite of this, the Earthmen had felt a silent guilt at putting new names to these ancient hills and valleys.

44 Nevertheless, man lives by symbol and label. The names were given.

45 Mr. Bittering felt very alone in his garden under the Martian sun, anachronism[2] bent here, planting Earth flowers in a wild soil.

46 Think. Keep thinking. Different things. Keep your mind free of Earth, the atom war, the lost rockets.

47 He perspired. He glanced about. No one watching. He removed his tie. Pretty bold, he thought. First your coat off, now your tie. He hung it neatly on a peach tree he had imported as a sapling from Massachusetts.

48 He returned to his philosophy of names and mountains. The Earthmen had changed names. Now there were Hormel Valleys, Roosevelt Seas, Ford Hills, Vanderbilt Plateaus, Rockefeller Rivers,[3] on Mars. It wasn't right. The American settlers had shown wisdom, using old Indian prairie names: Wisconsin, Minnesota, Idaho, Ohio, Utah, Milwaukee, Waukegan, Osseo. The old names, the old meanings.

49 Staring at the mountains wildly, he thought: Are you up there? All the dead ones, you Martians? Well, here we are, alone, cut off! Come down, move us out! We're helpless!

50 The wind blew a shower of peach blossoms.

51 He put out his sun-browned hand and gave a small cry. He touched the blossoms and picked them up. He turned them, he touched them again and again. Then he shouted for his wife.

52 "Cora!"

53 She appeared at a window. He ran to her.

2. **anachronism** (uh NA kruh nih zuhm) *n.* something that seems to belong to the past instead of the present.
3. **Hormel Valleys . . . Rockefeller Rivers** the colonists have named places on Mars after well-known families from mid-twentieth-century America.

PERSONALIZE FOR LEARNING

Strategic Support

Personification Remind students that personification is the technique of giving human qualities to nonhumans. Point out the following example of personification in paragraph 41: This was the moment Mars had waited for. Now it would eat them. Encourage students to look for more examples of personification as they continue reading. What effect does personification create in the reader?

54 "Cora, these blossoms!"

55 She handled them.

56 "Do you see? They're different. They've changed! They're not peach blossoms any more!"

57 "Look all right to me," she said.

58 "They're not. They're wrong! I can't tell how. An extra petal, a leaf, something, the color, the smell!"

59 The children ran out in time to see their father hurrying about the garden, pulling up radishes, onions, and carrots from their beds.

60 "Cora, come look!"

61 They handled the onions, the radishes, the carrots among them.

62 "Do they look like carrots?"

63 "Yes . . . no." She hesitated. "I don't know."

64 "They're changed."

65 "Perhaps."

66 "You know they have! Onions but not onions, carrots but not carrots. Taste: the same but different. Smell: not like it used to be." He felt his heart pounding, and he was afraid. He dug his fingers into the earth. "Cora, what's happening? What is it? We've got to get away from this." He ran across the garden. Each tree felt his touch. "The roses. The roses. They're turning green!"

67 And they stood looking at the green roses.

68 And two days later Dan came running. "Come see the cow. I was milking her and I saw it. Come on!"

69 They stood in the shed and looked at their one cow.

70 It was growing a third horn.

NOTES

DIGITAL PERSPECTIVES 

CLOSER LOOK

Analyze Character

Students may have marked paragraphs 54–58 during their first read. Use these paragraphs to help students understand the changes that are starting to happen and how different characters are reacting to them. Encourage students to talk about the annotations that they marked. You may want to model a close read with the class based on the highlights shown in the text.

ANNOTATE: Have students mark details in these paragraphs that describe the changes and how different characters are reacting to them.

QUESTION: Guide students to consider what these details might tell them. Ask what a reader can infer from these details and accept student responses.

Possible response: The plants are beginning to change. This upsets Harry but doesn't seem to bother Cora at all.

CONCLUDE: Help students to formulate conclusions about the importance of these details in the text. Ask students what this change suggests might happen to Harry and Cora as the story goes on.

Possible response: Harry will find it difficult to accept other changes, while Cora may not be bothered by them.

Point out that how **characters** respond to situations and events reveals something about them. Explain that characters reacting to the same event or situation differently can create tension in a story.

PERSONALIZE FOR LEARNING

Challenge

Speculate Review the changes that are described in paragraphs 61–70. Ask students to speculate on the changes that are occurring. Have them write their own original descriptions of an onion that isn't an onion; a carrot that isn't a carrot; a rose that isn't a rose; a cow that isn't a cow.

CLOSE READ

Remind students to look at the dialogue as well as the narrative part of the text. You may wish to model the close read using the following think-aloud format. Possible responses to questions on the student page are included.

ANNOTATE: As I read paragraphs 83–85, I notice that Harry is alarmed by the news, but the others do not take it seriously.

QUESTION: I see that the dialogue makes the action move quickly.

CONCLUDE: I think description might have slowed down the action and made the difference between Harry and the others seem less intense.

NOTES

71 And the lawn in front of their house very quietly and slowly was coloring itself like spring violets. Seed from Earth but growing up a soft purple.

72 "We must get away," said Bittering. "We'll eat this stuff and then we'll change—who knows to what? I can't let it happen. There's only one thing to do. Burn this food!"

73 "It's not poisoned."

74 "But it is. Subtly, very subtly. A little bit. A very little bit. We mustn't touch it."

75 He looked with dismay at their house. "Even the house. The wind's done something to it. The air's burned it. The fog at night. The boards, all warped out of shape. It's not an Earthman's house any more."

76 "Oh, your imagination!"

77 He put on his coat and tie. "I'm going into town. We've got to do something now. I'll be back."

78 "Wait, Harry!" his wife cried.

79 But he was gone.

80 In town, on the shadowy step of the grocery store, the men sat with their hands on their knees, conversing with great leisure and ease.

81 Mr. Bittering wanted to fire a pistol in the air.

82 What are you doing, you fools! he thought. Sitting here! You've heard the news—we're stranded on this planet. Well, move! Aren't you frightened? Aren't you afraid? What are you going to do?

83 "Hello, Harry," said everyone.

84 "Look," he said to them. "You did hear the news, the other day, didn't you?"

85 They nodded and laughed. "Sure. Sure, Harry."

86 "What are you going to do about it?"

87 "Do, Harry, do? What *can* we do?"

88 "Build a rocket, that's what!"

89 "A rocket, Harry? To go back to all that trouble? Oh, Harry!"

90 "But you *must* want to go back. Have you noticed the peach blossoms, the onions, the grass?"

91 "Why, yes, Harry, seems we did," said one of the men.

92 "Doesn't it scare you?"

93 "Can't recall that it did much, Harry."

94 "Idiots!"

95 "Now, Harry."

96 Bittering wanted to cry. "You've got to work with me. If we stay here, we'll all change. The air. Don't you smell it? Something in the air. A Martian virus, maybe; some seed, or a pollen. Listen to me!"

97 They stared at him.

CLOSE READ

ANNOTATE: Mark details in paragraphs 83–85 that indicate disagreement between Bittering and the other men.

QUESTION: Why might Bradbury have chosen to build conflict through the use of dialogue?

CONCLUDE: Would this passage be as effective if it had been written as description rather than dialogue? Explain.

PERSONALIZE FOR LEARNING

English Language Support

Multiple-Meaning Words Explain to students that the word *stuff* in paragraph 72 has several different meanings. As it's used in this part of the story, it's a noun that means "something consumed or introduced into the body." As a noun, it can also mean personal property ("I can't keep track of all my stuff."); a matter to be considered ("The ideas in this book are serious stuff."); a group or scattering of objects or articles ("Pick up all that stuff on the floor."); or subject matter ("You really know your stuff."). Stuff can also be a verb ("Just stuff everything into a box.").

NOTES

98 "Sam," he said to one of them.

99 "Yes, Harry?"

100 "Will you help me build a rocket?"

101 "Harry, I got a whole load of metal and some blueprints. You want to work in my metal shop on a rocket, you're welcome. I'll sell you that metal for five hundred dollars. You should be able to construct a right pretty rocket, if you work alone, in about thirty years."

102 Everyone laughed.

103 "Don't laugh."

104 Sam looked at him with quiet good humor.

105 "Sam," Bittering said. "Your eyes—"

106 "What about them, Harry?"

107 "Didn't they used to be gray?"

108 "Well now, I don't remember."

109 "They were, weren't they?"

110 "Why do you ask, Harry?"

111 "Because now they're kind of yellow-colored."

112 "Is that so, Harry?" Sam said, casually.

113 "And you're taller and thinner—"

114 "You might be right, Harry."

115 "Sam, you shouldn't have yellow eyes."

116 "Harry, what color eyes have *you* got?" Sam said.

117 "My eyes? They're blue, of course."

118 "Here you are, Harry." Sam handed him a pocket mirror. "Take a look at yourself."

119 Mr. Bittering hesitated, and then raised the mirror to his face.

120 There were little, very dim flecks of new gold captured in the blue of his eyes.

121 "Now look what you've done," said Sam a moment later. "You've broken my mirror."

122 Harry Bittering moved into the metal shop and began to build the rocket. Men stood in the open door and talked and joked without raising their voices. Once in a while they gave him a hand on lifting something. But mostly they just idled and watched him with their yellowing eyes.

123 "It's suppertime, Harry," they said.

124 His wife appeared with his supper in a wicker basket.

125 "I won't touch it," he said. "I'll eat only food from our Deepfreeze. Food that came from Earth. Nothing from our garden."

126 His wife stood watching him. "You can't build a rocket."

127 "I worked in a shop once, when I was twenty. I know metal. Once I get it started, the others will help," he said, not looking at her, laying out the blueprints.

PERSONALIZE FOR LEARNING

Challenge

Dialogue Review paragraphs 81–121 and point out that a good portion of this part of the story is dialogue. Using little narrative, Bradbury advances the story mainly through the words his characters speak. Have students continue this part of the story, writing dialogue that picks up after paragraph 121 and creating several more exchanges between Harry and the men.

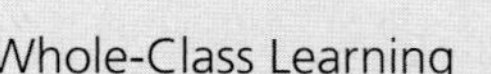

TEACHING

CLOSE READ

Remind students that the word they're looking for isn't English and that italics are used to offset specific words. You may wish to model the close read using the following think-aloud format. Possible responses to questions on the student page are included.

ANNOTATE: As I read paragraph 135, I notice and highlight text that isn't English.

QUESTION: *Iorrt* is an old Martian word for "Earth," but Harry Bittering says he knows no Martian words. I think the author wants to show Harry's character is changing.

CONCLUDE: I can infer that the change in Harry's speech is significant to the story because it marks a new change and a big change: Harry is beginning to speak Martian.

NOTES

forlorn (fawr LAWRN) *adj.* abandoned or deserted

CLOSE READ

ANNOTATE: Mark the Martian word Mr. Bittering says in paragraph 135.

QUESTION: Why does the author have Bittering speak Martian at this point in the story?

CONCLUDE: In what way is this event significant?

128 "Harry, Harry," she said, helplessly.

129 "We've got to get away, Cora. We've *got* to!"

130 The nights were full of wind that blew down the empty moonlit sea meadows past the little white chess cities lying for their twelve-thousandth year in the shallows. In the Earthmen's settlement, the Bittering house shook with a feeling of change.

131 Lying abed, Mr. Bittering felt his bones shifted, shaped, melted like gold. His wife, lying beside him, was dark from many sunny afternoons. Dark she was, and golden-eyed, burnt almost black by the sun, sleeping, and the children metallic in their beds, and the wind roaring **forlorn** and changing through the old peach trees, the violet grass, shaking out green rose petals.

132 The fear would not be stopped. It had his throat and heart. It dripped in a wetness of the arm and the temple and the trembling palm.

133 A green star rose in the east.

134 A strange word emerged from Mr. Bittering's lips.

135 "*Iorrt. Iorrt.*" He repeated it.

136 It was a Martian word. He knew no Martian.

137 In the middle of the night he arose and dialed a call through to Simpson, the archaeologist.

138 "Simpson, what does the word *Iorrt* mean?"

139 "Why that's the old Martian word for our planet Earth. Why?"

140 "No special reason."

141 The telephone slipped from his hand.

142 "Hello, hello, hello, hello," it kept saying while he sat gazing out at the green star. "Bittering? Harry, are you there?"

143 The days were full of metal sound. He laid the frame of the rocket with the reluctant help of three indifferent men. He grew very tired in an hour or so and had to sit down.

144 "The altitude," laughed a man.

145 "Are you *eating*, Harry?" asked another.

146 "I'm eating," he said, angrily.

147 "From your Deepfreeze?"

148 "Yes!"

149 "You're getting thinner, Harry."

150 "I'm not."

151 "And taller."

152 "Liar!"

153 His wife took him aside a few days later. "Harry, I've used up all the food in the Deepfreeze. There's nothing left. I'll have to make sandwiches using food grown on Mars."

154 He sat down heavily.

155 "You must eat," she said. "You're weak."

156 "Yes," he said.

PERSONALIZE FOR LEARNING

English Language Support

Words That Sound Alike Point out the word *metal* in paragraph 143 and explain to students that it means "a substance that is a good conductor of electricity." Then, point out, pronounce, and define the following words: *medal* ("a piece of metal often resembling a coin and having a stamped design that is issued to commemorate a person or event or awarded for excellence or achievement"); *meddle* ("to interest oneself in what is not one's concern"); and *mettle* ("vigor and strength of spirit or temperament"). **ALL LEVELS**

DIGITAL PERSPECTIVES

157 He took a sandwich, opened it, looked at it, and began to nibble at it.

158 "And take the rest of the day off," she said. "It's hot. The children want to swim in the **canals** and hike. Please come along."

159 "I can't waste time. This is a crisis!"

160 "Just for an hour," she urged. "A swim'll do you good."

161 He rose, sweating. "All right, all right. Leave me alone. I'll come."

162 "Good for you, Harry."

163 The sun was hot, the day quiet. There was only an **immense** staring burn upon the land. They moved along the canal, the father, the mother, the racing children in their swimsuits. They stopped and ate meat sandwiches. He saw their skin baking brown. And he saw the yellow eyes of his wife and his children, their eyes that were never yellow before. A few tremblings shook him, but were carried off in waves of pleasant heat as he lay in the sun. He was too tired to be afraid.

164 "Cora, how long have your eyes been yellow?"

165 She was bewildered. "Always, I guess."

166 "They didn't change from brown in the last three months?"

167 She bit her lips. "No. Why do you ask?"

NOTES

canals (kuh NALZ) *n.* artificial waterways for transportation or irrigation

immense (ih MEHNS) *adj.* very large

PERSONALIZE FOR LEARNING

Strategic Support

Comparison Review paragraphs 158–159. Lead a class discussion about the differences between Harry and Cora at this point in the story. Use these questions to prompt discussion: *What is Harry focused on? What is Cora's response? What's the main difference between them?* Then have students write a paragraph about what this difference suggests and what might happen regarding Harry and Cora as the story goes on.

CLOSER LOOK

Analyze Plot

Students may have marked paragraphs 179–181 during their first read. Use these paragraphs to help students understand the changes that are now taking place and to appreciate this turning point in the story. Encourage students to talk about the annotations that they marked. You may want to model a close read with the class based on the highlights shown in the text.

ANNOTATE: Have students mark details in these paragraphs that show changes that indicate a turning point in the plot.

QUESTION: Guide students to consider what these details might tell them. Ask what a reader can infer from these details and accept student responses.

Possible response: Harry's son is now beginning to use Martian words.

CONCLUDE: Help students to formulate conclusions about the importance of these details in the text. Ask students why it's a turning point in the story.

Possible response: This suggests that Harry's son will now start speaking Martian. It's a turning point in the story because it suggests that Harry's son is starting to become Martian and that more changes are on the way.

Remind students that the **plot** is the series of events in a story. Point out that a well-constructed plot keeps moving forward, developing characters and the story as it progresses. Until now, the story centered mainly on Harry and his responses to the changes. Now the changes are affecting Harry's son who, unlike Harry isn't bothered by what's happening. This development suggests the story is about to go in a new direction.

NOTES

atmosphere (AT muhs fihr) *n.* the gas surrounding the earth; the air

168 "Never mind."

169 They sat there.

170 "The children's eyes," he said. "They're yellow, too."

171 "Sometimes growing children's eyes change color."

172 "Maybe *we're* children, too. At least to Mars. That's a thought." He laughed. "Think I'll swim."

173 They leaped into the canal water, and he let himself sink down and down to the bottom like a golden statue and lie there in green silence. All was water-quiet and deep, all was peace. He felt the steady, slow current drift him easily.

174 If I lie here long enough, he thought, the water will work and eat away my flesh until the bones show like coral. Just my skeleton left. And then the water can build on that skeleton—green things, deep water things, red things, yellow things. Change. Change. Slow, deep, silent change. And isn't that what it is up *there*?

175 He saw the sky submerged above him, the sun made Martian by **atmosphere** and time and space.

176 Up there, a big river, he thought, a Martian river; all of us lying deep in it, in our pebble houses, in our sunken boulder houses, like crayfish hidden, and the water washing away our old bodies and lengthening the bones and—

177 He let himself drift up through the soft light.

178 Dan sat on the edge of the canal, regarding his father seriously.

179 "*Utha,*" he said.

180 "What?" asked his father.

181 The boy smiled. "You know. *Utha's* the Martian word for 'father.'"

182 "Where did you learn it?"

183 "I don't know. Around. *Utha!*"

184 "What do you want?"

185 The boy hesitated. "I—I want to change my name."

186 "Change it?"

187 "Yes."

188 His mother swam over. "What's wrong with Dan for a name?"

189 Dan fidgeted. "The other day you called Dan, Dan, Dan. I didn't even hear. I said to myself, That's not my name. I've a new name I want to use."

190 Mr. Bittering held to the side of the canal, his body cold and his heart pounding slowly. "What is this new name?"

191 "Linnl. Isn't that a good name? Can I use it? Can't I, please?"

192 Mr. Bittering put his hand to his head. He thought of the silly rocket, himself working alone, himself alone even among his family, so alone.

193 He heard his wife say, "Why not?"

194 He heard himself say, "Yes, you can use it."

VOCABULARY DEVELOPMENT

Concept Vocabulary Reinforcement Discuss the word *atmosphere* in paragraph 175, pointing out that it has several meanings. The meaning used in the story is "the gaseous envelope of a celestial body (for example, a planet); the whole mass of air surrounding the earth." It also has other meanings, including "a surrounding influence or environment" (for example, an atmosphere of hostility) and "an intriguing or singular tone, effect, or appeal" (for example, a park with a friendly atmosphere).

136 UNIT 2 • A STARRY HOME

195 "Yaaa!" screamed the boy. "I'm Linnl, Linnl!"

196 Racing down the meadowlands, he danced and shouted.

197 Mr. Bittering looked at his wife. "Why did we do that?"

198 "I don't know," she said. "It just seemed like a good idea."

199 They walked into the hills. They strolled on old **mosaic** paths, beside still pumping fountains. The paths were covered with a thin film of cool water all summer long. You kept your bare feet cool all the day, splashing as in a creek, wading.

200 They came to a small deserted Martian villa with a good view of the valley. It was on top of a hill. Blue marble halls, large murals, a swimming pool. It was refreshing in this hot summertime. The Martians hadn't believed in large cities.

201 "How nice," said Mrs. Bittering, "if we could move up here to this villa for the summer."

202 "Come on," he said. "We're going back to town. There's work to be done on the rocket."

203 But as he worked that night, the thought of the cool blue marble villa entered his mind. As the hours passed, the rocket seemed less important.

204 In the flow of days and weeks, the rocket receded and dwindled. The old fever was gone. It frightened him to think he had let it slip this way. But somehow the heat, the air, the working conditions—

205 He heard the men murmuring on the porch of his metal shop.

206 "Everyone's going. You heard?"

207 "All going. That's right."

208 Bittering came out. "Going where?" He saw a couple of trucks, loaded with children and furniture, drive down the dusty street.

209 "Up to the villas," said the man.

210 "Yeah, Harry. I'm going. So is Sam. Aren't you Sam?"

211 "That's right, Harry. What about you?"

212 "I've got work to do here. "

213 "Work! You can finish that rocket in the autumn, when it's cooler."

214 He took a breath. "I got the frame all set up."

215 "In the autumn is better." Their voices were lazy in the heat.

216 "Got to work," he said.

217 "Autumn," they reasoned. And they sounded so sensible, so right.

218 "Autumn would be best," he thought. "Plenty of time, then."

219 No! cried part of himself, deep down, put away, locked tight, suffocating. No! No!

220 "In the autumn," he said.

221 "Come on, Harry," they all said.

222 "Yes," he said, feeling his flesh melt in the hot liquid air. "Yes, in the autumn. I'll begin work again then."

NOTES

mosaic (moh ZAY ihk) *adj.* made of many small pieces of colored glass or stone

CLOSE READ

ANNOTATE: Mark the words or ideas that are repeated in paragraphs 212–222.

QUESTION: Why are these words or ideas repeated so often? What is happening to Bittering as the discussion progresses?

CONCLUDE: What important change has occurred as Bittering echoes the words of others?

DIGITAL PERSPECTIVES 

CLOSE READ

Point out to students that authors may use repetition to emphasize a particular idea or achieve a particular affect. You may wish to model the close read using the following think-aloud format. Possible responses to questions on the student page are included.

ANNOTATE: As I read paragraphs 213–222, I notice the repeated words "work" and "autumn."

QUESTION: To me, the repeated words suggest that Bittering is going through a conflict about the urgency of his work on the rocket. As the discussion goes on, he feels less and less committed to this "work" and more and more enticed by the idea of putting it off until "autumn."

CONCLUDE: For me, the change shows Bittering is becoming more like the other men.

PERSONALIZE FOR LEARNING

English Language Support

Multiple-Meaning Words Explain to students that the word *film* in paragraph 199 has different meanings. As it's used in this part of the story, it's a noun that means "a thin covering or coating." It can also mean "a motion picture." (That was an exciting film.) *Film* can also be a verb meaning "to make a motion picture." (Today we are going to film a car chase.) **ALL LEVELS**

NOTES

223 "I got a villa near the Tirra Canal," said someone.

224 "You mean the Roosevelt Canal, don't you?"

225 "Tirra. The old Martian name."

226 "But on the map—"

227 "Forget the map. It's Tirra now. Now I found a place in the Pillan Mountains—"

228 "You mean the Rockefeller Range," said Bittering.

229 "I mean the Pillan Mountains," said Sam.

230 "Yes," said Bittering, buried in the hot, swarming air. "The Pillan Mountains."

231 Everyone worked at loading the truck in the hot, still afternoon of the next day.

232 Laura, Dan, and David carried packages. Or, as they preferred to be known, Ttil, Linnl, and Werr carried packages.

233 The furniture was abandoned in the little white cottage.

234 "It looked just fine in Boston," said the mother. "And here in the cottage. But up at the villa? No. We'll get it when we come back in the autumn."

235 Bittering himself was quiet.

236 "I've some ideas on furniture for the villa," he said after a time. "Big, lazy furniture."

237 "What about your encyclopedia? You're taking it along, surely?"

238 Mr. Bittering glanced away. "I'll come and get it next week."

239 They turned to their daughter. "What about your New York dresses?"

240 The bewildered girl stared. "Why, I don't want them any more."

241 They shut off the gas, the water, they locked the doors and walked away. Father peered into the truck.

242 "Gosh, we're not taking much," he said. "Considering all we brought to Mars, this is only a handful!"

243 He started the truck.

244 Looking at the small white cottage for a long moment, he was filled with a desire to rush to it, touch it, say good-bye to it, for he felt as if he were going away on a long journey, leaving something to which he could never quite return, never understand again.

245 Just then Sam and his family drove by in another truck.

246 "Hi, Bittering! Here we go!"

247 The truck swung down the ancient highway out of town. There were sixty others traveling in the same direction. The town filled with a silent, heavy dust from their passage. The canal waters lay blue in the sun, and a quiet wind moved in the strange trees.

248 "Good-bye, town!" said Mr. Bittering.

249 "Good-bye, good-bye," said the family, waving to it.

250 They did not look back again.

PERSONALIZE FOR LEARNING

Strategic Support

Names Review paragraphs 223–233. Help students understand the significance of the changes in names of geographical formations and people. Discuss why geological formations such as mountains and canals are getting new names. Why are people choosing new names? What does this represent in the story?

DIGITAL 
PERSPECTIVES

251 Summer burned the canals dry. Summer moved like flame upon the meadows. In the empty Earth settlement, the painted houses flaked and peeled. Rubber tires upon which children had swung in back yards hung suspended like stopped clock pendulums in the blazing air.

252 At the metal shop, the rocket frame began to rust.

253 In the quiet autumn Mr. Bittering stood, very dark now, very golden-eyed, upon the slope above his villa, looking at the valley.

254 "It's time to go back," said Cora.

255 "Yes, but we're not going," he said quietly. "There's nothing there any more."

256 "Your books," she said. "Your fine clothes.

257 "Your *Illes* and your fine *ior uele rre*," she said.

258 "The town's empty. No one's going back," he said. "There's no reason to, none at all."

259 The daughter wove tapestries and the sons played songs on ancient flutes and pipes, their laughter echoing in the marble villa.

260 Mr. Bittering gazed at the Earth settlement far away in the low valley. "Such odd, such ridiculous houses the Earth people built."

261 "They didn't know any better," his wife mused. "Such ugly people. I'm glad they've gone."

262 They both looked at each other, startled by all they had just finished saying. They laughed.

263 "Where did they go?" he wondered. He glanced at his wife. She was golden and slender as his daughter. She looked at him, and he seemed almost as young as their eldest son.

264 "I don't know," she said.

265 "We'll go back to town maybe next year, or the year after, or the year after that," he said, calmly. "Now—I'm warm. How about taking a swim?"

266 They turned their backs to the valley. Arm in arm they walked silently down a path of clear-running spring water.

* * *

267 Five years later a rocket fell out of the sky. It lay steaming in the valley. Men leaped out of it, shouting.

268 "We won the war on Earth! We're here to rescue you! Hey!"

269 But the American-built town of cottages, peach trees, and theaters was silent. They found a flimsy rocket frame rusting in an empty shop.

270 The rocket men searched the hills. The captain established headquarters in an abandoned bar. His lieutenant came back to report.

271 "The town's empty, but we found native life in the hills, sir. Dark people. Yellow eyes. Martians. Very friendly. We talked a bit,

NOTES

CLOSE READ

ANNOTATE: Mark details in paragraphs 269–278 that reveal the findings of the rescue mission from Earth.

QUESTION: Why has Bradbury chosen to include this scene? What clues to the colonists' fate are hinted at?

CONCLUDE: Does this lingering mystery improve or weaken the story? Explain.

Point out to students that they should consider the entire story as they look for the answer. You may wish to model the close read using the following think-aloud format. Possible responses to questions on the student page are included.

ANNOTATE: As I read paragraphs 269–278, I realize that those on the mission are finding positive things to say about the Martians.

QUESTION: I think Bradbury has chosen to include this scene to hint that the colonists may end up changing in some way.

CONCLUDE: This lingering mystery adds to the story by creating drama. It also suggests that the Martians might remember they were once Earth people but they are not sharing this information with the new arrivals from Earth.

CLOSER LOOK

Analyze Plot

Students may have marked paragraphs 281–283 during their first read. Use these paragraphs to help students understand the ending of the story. Encourage students to talk about the annotations that they marked. You may want to model a close read with the class based on the highlights shown in the text.

ANNOTATE: Have students mark details in these paragraphs that indicate what Bradbury is suggesting at the end of the story.

QUESTION: Guide students to consider what these details might tell them. Ask what a reader can infer from these details and accept student responses.

Possible response: The lieutenant's attention is elsewhere as the captain talks. He seems captivated by the Martian landscape.

CONCLUDE: Help students to formulate conclusions about the importance of these details in the text. Ask students what this ending suggests.

Possible response: It suggests that, like Harry and the others, these new arrivals will slowly become Martians, too.

Point out that this is suggested, not directly stated. The lieutenant's focus on "the blue color and the quiet mist of the hills far beyond the town" hints that he is already being consumed and taken over by Mars, just as Harry and the others were.

NOTES

not much. They learn English fast. I'm sure our relations will be most friendly with them, sir."

272 "Dark, eh?" mused the captain. "How many?"

273 "Six, eight hundred, I'd say, living in those marble ruins in the hills, sir. Tall, healthy. Beautiful women."

274 "Did they tell you what became of the men and women who built this Earth settlement, Lieutenant?"

275 "They hadn't the foggiest notion of what happened to this town or its people."

276 "Strange. You think those Martians killed them?"

277 "They look surprisingly peaceful. Chances are a plague did this town in, sir."

278 "Perhaps. I suppose this is one of those mysteries we'll never solve. One of those mysteries you read about."

279 The captain looked at the room, the dusty windows, the blue mountains rising beyond, the canals moving in the light, and he heard the soft wind in the air. He shivered. Then, recovering, he tapped a large fresh map he had thumbtacked to the top of an empty table.

280 "Lots to be done, Lieutenant." His voice droned on and quietly on as the sun sank behind the blue hills. "New settlements. Mining sites, minerals to be looked for. Bacteriological specimens taken. The work, all the work. And the old records were lost. We'll have a job of remapping to do, renaming the mountains and rivers and such. Calls for a little imagination.

281 "What do you think of naming those mountains the Lincoln Mountains, this canal the Washington Canal, those hills—we can name those hills for you, Lieutenant. Diplomacy. And you, for a favor, might name a town for me. Polishing the apple. And why not make this the Einstein Valley, and farther over . . . are you *listening*, Lieutenant?"

282 The lieutenant snapped his gaze from the blue color and the quiet mist of the hills far beyond the town.

283 "What? Oh, *yes*, sir!" ❧

Comprehension Check

Complete the following items after you finish your first read.

1. What is the story's setting?

2. What causes the people from Earth to become stranded on Mars?

3. What change does Harry first notice in the world around him?

4. What does the rescue crew find when they arrive on Mars after five years?

5. **Notebook** Write a summary of "Dark They Were, and Golden-Eyed."

RESEARCH

Research to Clarify Choose at least one unfamiliar detail from the text. Briefly research that detail. In what way does the information you learned shed light on an aspect of the story?

DIGITAL PERSPECTIVES

Comprehension Check

Possible responses:

1. The setting is Mars, during a time when people have fled Earth to avoid war.
2. There is an atomic war on Earth.
3. The peach blossoms are changing.
4. Everyone from Earth has become Martian.

Summaries will vary; however, students should include: Harry Bittering, his wife, and their three children arrive from Earth to live on Mars; Harry is immediately anxious and fearful and wants to return to Earth; Cora wants to stay because she thinks there will be an atomic war on Earth; the war happens and people from Earth are stranded on Mars; Harry's plants and animals start changing; Harry believes there will be more changes and starts building a rocket so they can leave Mars; bit by bit, Harry and his family slowly become Martians; five years later, when a rocket from Earth arrives on Mars, there are no more Earth people; Harry and everyone else have become Martians.

Research

Research to Clarify If students struggle to identify an unfamiliar detail, have them reread key parts of the story and look for an idea or concept that might be new to them, such as ruins or villas.

PERSONALIZE FOR LEARNING

Challenge

Extend Ask students to consider what they think will happen next. Have them write 1–4 paragraphs extending the story several years after it ends. What will happen regarding the Martians? What will happen regarding the new arrivals from Earth? Remind them there is no right or wrong answer but that their responses should be based on what they've read.

Jump Start

CLOSE READ Have students close read the story "Dark They Were, and Golden-Eyed." Ask students what they think the title means. *Who are "They"? Why did Bradbury decide to pick this title for this story?* Ask students if they think this is a good title for the story. Why, or why not?

Close Read the Text

Walk students through the Annotation Model on the student page. Encourage them to complete items 2 and 3 on their own. Review and discuss the sections students have marked. If needed, continue to model close reading by using the Annotation Highlights in the Interactive Teacher's Edition.

Analyze the Text

Possible responses:

1. The constantly blowing wind represents the power of Mars, blowing against the people from Earth. **DOK 3**
2. They start to speak Martian, their eye color changes, and they start to view Earth houses as odd and Earth people as ugly. **DOK 1**
3. Perhaps the rescue team will also be influenced by being on Mars and become distracted from their original mission. This possibility is suggested when the lieutenant says, "What? Oh, yes, sir!" at the end of the story. **DOK 2**
4. Responses will vary. Students may conclude that if we move away from Earth, our home, we may begin to lose what makes us human. **DOK 3**

FORMATIVE ASSESSMENT

Analyze the Text

- **If** students fail to cite evidence, **then** remind them to support their ideas with specific information.
- **If** students struggle to identify what the wind represents, **then** discuss the concept of one thing representing another (symbolism), and illustrate with examples.

MAKING MEANING

DARK THEY WERE, AND GOLDEN-EYED

Close Read the Text

1. This model, from paragraph 251 of the text, shows two sample annotations, along with questions and conclusions. Close read the passage, and find another detail to annotate. Then, write a question and your conclusion.

Close Read: ANNOTATE · QUESTION · CONCLUDE

ANNOTATE: I notice that many words contain the letter *m*.

QUESTION: What effect does this repetition create?

CONCLUDE: The repeated sound creates a drowsy mood.

Summer burned the canals dry. Summer moved like flame upon the meadows. In the empty Earth settlement, the painted houses flaked and peeled. Rubber tires upon which children had swung in back yards hung suspended like stopped clock pendulums in the blazing air.

ANNOTATE: I notice that an unusual comparison is made.

QUESTION: What effect is created with this simile?

CONCLUDE: It emphasizes the heat and desolation of the setting.

2. For more practice, go back into the text and complete the close-read notes.
3. Revisit a section of the text you found important during your first read. Read this section closely and **annotate** what you notice. Ask yourself **questions** such as "Why did the author make this choice?" What can you **conclude**?

Tool Kit
Close-Read Guide and Model Annotation

Analyze the Text

CITE TEXTUAL EVIDENCE to support your answers.

Notebook Respond to these questions.

1. **Analyze** What might the constantly blowing wind represent?
2. **Analyze** In what ways does the author indicate that the Bittering family has begun to change significantly?
3. **Speculate** The fate of the original colonists is not specifically described. What do you think will become of the rescue team? What story details support your idea?
4. **Essential Question:** *Should we make a home in space?* What idea about living in space is suggested by this story?

STANDARDS

Reading Literature
Determine the meaning of words and phrases as they are used in a text, including figurative and connotative meanings; analyze the impact of rhymes and other repetitions of sounds on a specific verse or stanza of a poem or section of a story or drama.

Language
Demonstrate understanding of figurative language, word relationships, and nuances in word meaning.
a. Interpret figures of speech in context.

CROSS-CURRICULAR PERSPECTIVES

Science Have students research Mars, focusing on its natural features and atmospheric conditions, and write short reports on the challenges people from Earth would face if they lived on Mars. How might these challenges be overcome? Are these challenges addressed in the story? How?

Analyze Craft and Structure

Figurative Language: Metaphor and Simile **Figurative language** is writing or speech that is not meant to be taken literally. The use of figurative language creates layers of meaning and helps readers see things in new ways.

- A **simile** compares two apparently unlike things using the words *like* or *as*: *The rocket was like a speeding bullet that tore through the sky.*
- A **metaphor** compares two apparently unlike things by saying that one thing *is* another: *The rocket was a speeding bullet that tore through the sky.*
- **Personification** is a comparison in which a nonhuman subject is given human characteristics: *The rocket gently enfolded its passengers as it tore through the sky.*

Practice

CITE TEXTUAL EVIDENCE to support your answers.

Notebook Respond to these questions.

1. Read each passage from the story shown in the chart. Identify each as an example of simile, metaphor, or personification. Some passages may contain more than one type of figurative language. In the final column of the chart, give reasons for your answers.

TEXT PASSAGE	TYPE(S) OF FIGURATIVE LANGUAGE	EXPLANATION
The children, small seeds, might at any instant be sown to all the Martian climes. (paragraph 2)	metaphor	The children are compared to seeds without using *like* or *as*.
They saw the old cities, . . . lying like children's delicate bones among the blowing lakes of grass. (paragraph 9)	personification and simile	Cities are described as bones; the language compares cities' posture to bones using *like*
This was the moment Mars had waited for. Now it would eat them. (paragraph 41)	personification	Mars is portrayed as a monster, capable of eating humans.

2. Rewrite a simile you identified in the chart as a metaphor.

3. Write a sentence in which you personify the blowing wind that is described throughout the story.

DIGITAL PERSPECTIVES

Analyze Craft and Structure

Figurative Language: Metaphor and Simile Discuss with students why an author might choose to use metaphors and similes. What might be some advantages to using figurative language? Also have students think about what makes a particularly strong metaphor or simile. For more support, see **Analyze Craft and Structure: Metaphor and Simile.**

MAKE IT INTERACTIVE

Have students create two strong similes and two strong metaphors of their own. Ask volunteers to share their work with the class.

Practice

Possible responses:

1. For possible responses, see the chart on the student page.
2. The old cities were delicate children's bones.
3. The wind was a ghost that glided across their lives, turning their souls to brittle clay.

FORMATIVE ASSESSMENT

Analyze Craft and Structure

- **If** students are unable to identify similes, **then** discuss common similes, pointing out the use of *like* or *as*, and showing the comparison.
- **If** students are unable to identify metaphors, **then** discuss common metaphors, pointing out the absence of *like* or *as*, and showing the comparison.

For Reteach and Practice, see **Analyze Craft and Structure: Metaphor and Simile (RP).**

WriteNow Express and Reflect

Figurative Language Have students think of a recent event and write a paragraph describing it using figurative language. Encourage students to use both similes and metaphors.

TEACHING

Concept Vocabulary

Why These Words?

Possible responses:

1. The concept vocabulary gives the reader a sense of what people from Earth are seeing, feeling, and experiencing on Mars.
2. *empty* (paragraph 20); *peaks* (paragraph 43); *ancient* (paragraph 43)

Practice

1. Responses will vary but should reflect the proper meaning of each vocabulary word.
2. Responses will vary.

Word Network

Possible words: *rocket, vacuum, million, empty, scared, steaming, silent*

Word Study

For more support, see **Concept Vocabulary and Word Study.**

Answers will vary.

FORMATIVE ASSESSMENT

Concept Vocabulary

If students fail to see the connection between the words, **then** have them use each word in a sentence relating to the story and think about what is similar about the sentences.

Word Study

If students have trouble finding appropriate synonyms for *forlorn*, encourage them to use the words in sentences and say the sentences aloud to explore their meaning. For Reteach and Practice, see **Word Study: Synonyms and Nuance (RP).**

LANGUAGE DEVELOPMENT

DARK THEY WERE, AND GOLDEN-EYED

Concept Vocabulary

submerged	canals	atmosphere
forlorn	immense	mosaic

Why These Words? The concept vocabulary words from the text describe Bradbury's vision of Mars. For example, the Bitterings' house is *submerged* by a river of wind, which also roars "*forlorn* and changing through the old peach tree."

1. How does the concept vocabulary sharpen the reader's understanding of what it is like for the Bitterings to live on Mars?
2. What other words in the selection connect to the concept of describing an alien world?

Practice

Notebook The concept vocabulary words appear in "Dark They Were, and Golden-Eyed."

1. Use each concept word in a sentence that demonstrates your understanding of the word's meaning.
2. Challenge yourself to replace each concept word with one or two synonyms. How does the word change affect the meaning of your sentence? For example, which sentence is stronger? Which has a more positive meaning?

WORD NETWORK

Add interesting words related to space exploration from the text to your Word Network.

Word Study

Synonyms and Nuance Words that have the same basic meaning are called **synonyms.** Often, however, there are subtle shades of meaning, or **nuances,** between synonyms. For example, the basic meaning of *forlorn* is "sad," but its nuances indicate that it is a type of sadness caused by abandonment or loneliness.

1. Identify the basic meaning of these synonyms, and then describe their differences in nuance: *immense / colossal.*
2. Using a thesaurus, find two other words related to *forlorn*. Record a definition for each synonym, and then use each word in a sentence that reflects its nuances, or shades of meaning.

STANDARDS

Language

- Determine or clarify the meaning of unknown and multiple-meaning words and phrases based on *grade 7 reading and content,* choosing flexibly from a range of strategies.
- Demonstrate understanding of figurative language, word relationships, and nuances in word meanings.

AUTHOR'S PERSPECTIVE **Elfrieda Hiebert, Ph.D.**

Collecting Sentences To help students become more adept with words, give them the experience of working with them. By studying sentences that use new vocabulary well, students can build their vocabulary strength. Encourage students to collect model sentences using two strategies:

- **Find sentences in the text.** Help students locate sentences that use new vocabulary, or have students identify sentences where word choice truly packs power into the text. Discuss how the words are used, and have students emulate the writer by writing similar sentences.
- **Find sentences in online vocabulary resources.** When students are learning new words, it is useful to see the word used correctly in a variety of contexts. Many online dictionaries provide contemporary and cross-curricular examples to help learners see the words in action.

There are several benefits of this approach. First, a study of words and the way they are used can help students appreciate and understand writers. Second, looking closely at vocabulary and the spectrum of related words can help students improve their own writing.

Conventions

Comparisons Using Adjectives and Adverbs **Adjectives** modify, or describe, nouns or pronouns. **Adverbs** modify verbs, adjectives, and other adverbs. Most adjectives and adverbs have three degrees of comparison.

- The **positive degree** is used when no comparison is made. For example: "Jackson Avenue is a *long* street." "We progressed *quickly*."
- The **comparative degree** is used when two things are being compared. The comparative degree of most one- or two-syllable modifiers ends with *-er*. The word *more* is used to form the comparative degree of most longer modifiers or adverbs that end with *-ly*. For example: "Washington Avenue is *longer* than Jackson Avenue." "We progressed *more quickly* than they did."
- The **superlative degree** is used when three or more things are being compared. The superlative degree of most one- or two-syllable modifers ends with *-est*. The word *most* is used to form the superlative degree of most longer modifiers or adverbs that end with *-ly*. For example: "Lincoln Avenue is the *longest* street in town." "We progressed the *most quickly* of all."

Read It

1. Mark the adjectives and adverbs in these sentences. Label each one *positive*, *comparative*, or *superlative*.
   a. They were determined to build the strongest rocket that they possibly could.
   b. It was a cold, dreary night on the quiet, red planet.
   c. Everybody thought it was odd that Harry's eyes turned gold more quickly than Cora's eyes did.
2. Reread paragraph 275 of "Dark They Were, and Golden-Eyed." Identify the superlative adjective.

Write It

Respond to these items.

1. Rewrite each sentence below twice. Replace each positive, comparative, or superlative adjective or adverb with the forms of the other two degrees of comparison for that word—whichever two forms are not used in the original sentence.
   a. James drew a funny picture.
   b. This room has been repainted with a darker shade of green.
   c. It rained heavily through the night.
2. **Notebook** Write a brief paragraph that includes at least one positive, one comparative, and one superlative adjective or adverb.

TIP

FOLLOW THROUGH
Refer to the Grammar Handbook to learn more about adjectives and adverbs.

EVIDENCE LOG

Before moving on to a new selection, go your Evidence Log and record what you've learned from "Dark They Were, and Golden-Eyed."

STANDARDS

Language
Demonstrate command of the conventions of standard English grammar and usage when writing or speaking.

PERSONALIZE FOR LEARNING

English Language Support

Using Comparatives and Superlatives Ask students to list two adjectives and two adverbs that describe the selection "Dark They Were, and Golden-Eyed" and then write down their comparative and superlative forms. **EMERGING**

Have students write a few sentences that explain their reaction to the selection "Dark They Were, and Golden-Eyed." Encourage students to use comparative and superlative adjectives and adverbs whenever possible in their sentences. **EXPANDING**

Have students write a paragraph that discusses the use of imagery in the selection "Dark They Were, and Golden-Eyed." Encourage students to use comparative and superlative adjectives and adverbs whenever possible in their paragraph. **BRIDGING**

An expanded **English Language Support Lesson** on Comparatives and Superlatives is available in the Interactive Teacher's Edition.

DIGITAL PERSPECTIVES

Conventions

Comparison of Adjectives and Adverbs Explain that when an adjective or adverb has three or more syllables, we don't use the *-er* or *-est* form of the word. In these cases, *more* is used for a comparative adjective or adverb, and *most* is used for a superlative adjective or adverb. Also point out that *more* and *most* are used with some two-syllable adjectives and adverbs (for example: *vivid; precise*) For more support, see **Conventions: Comparison of Adjectives and Adverbs.**

MAKE IT INTERACTIVE
Have pairs of students work together to write sentences for the comparative form of *tall* and the superlative form of *intelligent*. Challenge students to write creative or amusing sentences.

Read It

Possible responses:

1. (a) determined *(positive)*, strongest *(superlative)*, possibly *(positive)*; (b) cold *(positive)*, dreary *(positive)*, quiet *(positive)*, red *(positive)*; (c) odd *(positive)*, gold *(positive)*, more quickly *(comparative)*
2. *foggiest*

Write It

Possible responses:

1. a. James drew a funnier picture than Luke. James drew the funniest picture in the class.
   b. Last year, this room was a different shade of dark green. Three years ago, it had the darkest shade of green we had ever seen.
   c. It rained more heavily this year than last year. It rained most heavily during the month of October.
2. Answers will vary but should include at least one example of a positive, a comparative, and a superlative adjective or adverb.

FORMATIVE ASSESSMENT

Conventions

- **If** students can't identify or form comparative adjective or adverbs, **then** review the comparative form and have students practice with the following words: *short; funny; understanding*.

For Reteach and Practice, see **Conventions: Comparison of Adjectives and Adverbs (RP).**

Selection Test

Administer the "Dark They Were, and Golden-Eyed" Selection Test, which is available in both print and digital formats online in Assessments.

Dark They Were, and Golden-Eyed (Audio)

AUDIO SUMMARIES
Audio summaries of "Dark They Were, and Golden-Eyed" are available online in both English and Spanish in the Interactive Teacher's Edition or Unit Resources. Assigning these summaries prior to listening to the selection may help students build additional background knowledge and set a context for their first review.

Summary

This radio play opens as a family of colonists land on Mars. The wind is constant and one of the children thinks he can hear Martians' voices in it. However, there does not appear to be any evidence of living Martians, though there are remains of Martian cities in the hills.

A nuclear war on Earth makes it impossible for more rockets to come to Mars. The family father fears that Mars' original inhabitants will come and attack them; but something more subtle happens. The planet itself seems to be changing them and the things they brought with them. They are becoming Martian.

Insight

This radio play vividly gets across the emotion of the story, and sound effects make the details come to life. It suggests that moving to a new place necessarily forces people to adapt, making them fit better in the new place.

ESSENTIAL QUESTION:
Should we make a home in space?

Connection to Essential Question

"Dark They Were, and Golden-Eyed" speaks to the Essential Question, "Should we make a home in space?" This story shows people assimilating into a new home in space, until they no longer consider themselves "Earth people." They also seem to have developed a new definition of *home*.

WHOLE-CLASS LEARNING PERFORMANCE TASK
Do the benefits of exploring Mars outweigh the risks?

UNIT PERFORMANCE-BASED ASSESSMENT
Should we spend valuable resources on space exploration?

Connection to Performance Tasks

Whole-Class Learning Performance Task In this story, there is no physical danger in exploring Mars, but it does *change* the people who land there in unusual ways. Students can use details from the radio play and their thinking about these details in the editorial they write in response to the question, "Do the benefits of exploring Mars outweigh the risks?"

Unit Performance-Based Assessment Students may discover that they can use their thinking about the issues brought up in this radio play to support the argument they write for the Performance-Based Assessment. In that argument, students will take a position on the following question: Should we spend valuable resources on space exploration?

LESSON RESOURCES

	Making Meaning	Language Development	Effective Expression
Lesson	**First Review** **Close Review** **Analyze the Media**	**Media Vocabulary**	**Writing to Compare**
Instructional Standards	**RL.7.10** By the end of the year, read and comprehend literature . . . **SL.7.2** Analyze the main ideas and supporting details presented in diverse media and formats . . .	**L.7.6** Acquire and use accurately grade-appropriate general academic and domain-specific words and phrases . . .	**RL.7.7** Compare and contrast a written story . . . **W.7.9.a** Apply *grade 7 Reading standards* to literature . . . **W.7.2** Write informative/explanatory texts . . . **W.7.2.a** Introduce a topic clearly . . . **W.7.2.b** Develop the topic . . . **W.7.2.d** Use precise language . . . **W.7.2.f** Provide a concluding statement . . .
STUDENT RESOURCES			
Available online in the Interactive Teacher's Edition or Unit Resources	Selection Audio First-Review Guide: Media-Audio Close-Review Guide: Media-Audio		Evidence Log
TEACHER RESOURCES			
Selection Resources Available online in the Interactive Teacher's Edition or Unit Resources	Audio Summaries: English and Spanish First Review Extension Questions	Media Vocabulary	Writing to Compare: Argument
My Resources	A Unit 2 Answer Key is available online and in the Interactive Teacher's Edition.		

Media Complexity Rubric: Dark They Were, and Golden Eyed (Audio)

Quantitative Measures	
Format and Length : Audio, 27 min, 30 sec	
Qualitative Measures	
Knowledge Demands ① ② ③ **❹** ⑤	Explores sophisticated themes including cultural adaptation, fear of changing identity, and colonization. Audio is based on a story written in 1949, with references to atom bomb, names *Rockefeller, Ford,* etc.
Structure ① ② **❸** ④ ⑤	Dramatic reading is easy to follow, with clear and slow speech in dialogue with multiple voices and sound effects. No narration is used, so audience must follow events through dialogue.
Language Conventionality and Clarity ① **❷** ③ ④ ⑤	Language in dialogue is all conversational and familiar; sentences and vocabulary are not complex; style of speech sometimes does not sound contemporary, as it is typical style of 1950s.
Levels of Meaning/Purpose ① ② ③ **❹** ⑤	Multiple levels of meaning are revealed over the course of the story; audience must follow plot events through dialogue at the same time as interpreting implicit meaning.

TEACHING

Jump Start

FIRST REVIEW Have any students heard a radio play? Engage students in a discussion about how reading a story and listening to a radio play of that same story might be different. What might the radio play have that the text would not?

Dark They Were, and Golden-Eyed

Do the differences between a radio play and a text version of the same story make one better or more enjoyable than the other? Why, or why not? Modeling questions such as these will help students connect to "Dark They Were, and Golden-Eyed" and to the Whole-Class Performance Task assignment. Selection audio is available in the Interactive Teacher's Edition.

Media Vocabulary

Encourage students to discuss the media vocabulary. Have they seen or used these terms before? Do they use any of them in their speech or writing? Have students brainstorm three examples of sound effects and share with the class. For more support, see **Media Vocabulary**

FIRST REVIEW

Have students perform the steps of the first review independently:

LISTEN: Encourage students to notice things they hear, such as sound effects, actors' voices, and music.

NOTE: Remind students to focus on how the actors speak their dialogue and to think about whether this changes their ideas about the story.

CONNECT: Encourage students to make connections beyond the radio and the story. If they cannot make connections to their own lives, have them consider films or TV shows they may have seen.

RESPOND: Students will answer questions to demonstrate understanding. Point out to students that while they will always complete the Respond step at the end of the first review, the other steps will probably happen concurrently. You may wish to print copies of the **First-Review Guide: Media: Audio** for students to use.

MAKING MEANING

DARK THEY WERE, AND GOLDEN-EYED (short story)

Comparing Text to Media

In this lesson, you will listen to a radio play of "Dark They Were, and Golden-Eyed." You will then compare the story and the performance of the radio play.

DARK THEY WERE, AND GOLDEN-EYED (radio play)

About the Producer

Michael McDonough is a professional sound designer and the producer of the *Bradbury 13* series. For *Bradbury 13*, McDonough wrote all the scripts and created spectacular original sound effects. McDonough first learned sound design as a student at Brigham Young University and went on to work on dozens of films and television shows.

Dark They Were, and Golden-Eyed

Media Vocabulary

These words will be useful to you as you analyze, discuss, and write about the radio play.

sound effects: sounds produced artificially for a radio production	• Sound effects indicate settings and actions (city noises; the dropping of a book). • Certain sound effects also help create mood and atmosphere (a rusty door; the screech of an owl).
human voice: the central conveyor of events and interactions in a radio play	• Voices in a radio play need to be distinct so listeners know which character is speaking. • A speaker's pitch, volume, and pacing take on even more importance in a radio play.
silence: the absence of sound	• Silence after rapid dialogue can heighten suspense. • Silence or near silence can focus listeners' attention on characters' probable inner thoughts or on something ominous, such as the over-loud ticking of a clock.

First Review MEDIA: AUDIO

Study the radio play using these strategies. Take note of time codes as you listen so that you can go back and analyze sections you find interesting.

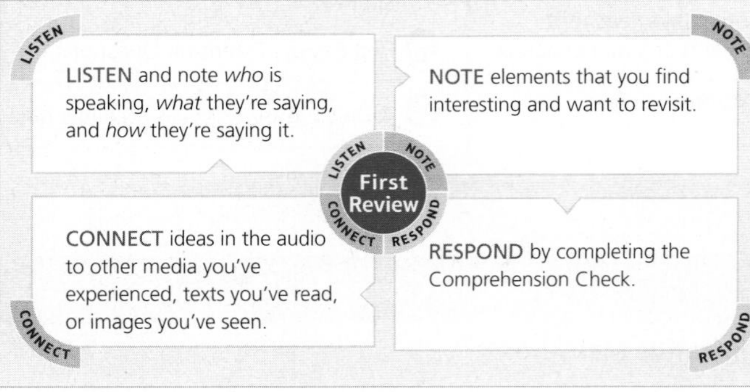

STANDARDS

Reading Literature
By the end of the year, read and comprehend literature, including stories, dramas, and poems, in the grades 6–8 text complexity band proficiently, with scaffolding as needed at the high end of the range.

Language
Acquire and use accurately grade-appropriate general academic and domain-specific words and phrases; gather vocabulary knowledge when considering a word or phrase important to comprehension or expression.

146 UNIT 2 • A STARRY HOME

PERSONALIZE FOR LEARNING

English Language Support

Similar Words Help students understand the difference between *effect* and *affect*. Explain that *effect* is most often used as a noun that means "the result of something," and *affect* is most often used as a verb that means "to produce a result." (When extreme cold *affects* a city, the *effect* might be snow.) Explain that *sound effects* are sounds used in radio shows and other productions that make the show more real. Ask students to identify one or two sound effects they heard when they listened to the radio play. **ALL LEVELS**

MEDIA | RADIO PLAY

Dark They Were, and Golden-Eyed

Michael McDonough, Producer

BACKGROUND

During the 1930s and 1940s, radio plays were a highly popular form of entertainment. However, with the rise of television, radio plays all but disappeared. In 1984, National Public Radio aired *Bradbury 13*, a series of radio adaptations of Ray Bradbury's works that re-create the feel of classic radio drama.

NOTES

CLOSER REVIEW

Radio Plays

Students may have noted the section of the play from 2:21 to 3:49 during their first review. Use this segment to help students understand how listening to the radio play is different from reading the story. Encourage students to talk about what they noted. You may want to model a closer review with the class based on the notes below.

NOTE: Have students note details in the radio play that present the story differently from the text version of the story.

Possible response: In the radio play, the listener hears the rocket landing on Mars, hears other people arrive with the Bitterings, and hears the wind blowing. Also, there is music.

QUESTION: Guide students to consider how this affects the experience of hearing the radio play, and accept student responses.

Possible response: The sound effects help make the radio play more realistic. The music adds drama to the play.

CONCLUDE: Help students to formulate conclusions about these differences.

Possible response: Some people might prefer the radio play to the text version because the sound effects and music make the radio play more realistic and more fun.

Remind students that **radio plays** develop a story's world using sound only. Have students look for and note other details in the radio play that make it different from the text version of the story.

DIGITAL PERSPECTIVES

Illuminating the Selection To help students understand how Mars and Martians were viewed during the 1950s (the time period of the story), use search terms such as "Martians in the 1950s" to find video footage online showing this mindset. Be sure to preview any video before showing it to students. Have students discuss the video and how it helps them understand the story or the radio play. Then, have students write a paragraph discussing how the video was similar to or different from "Dark They Were, and Golden-Eyed."

Comprehension Check

Possible responses:

1. Ray Bradbury and an unnamed announcer who introduces the radio play begin the broadcast.
2. We learn that nuclear bombs were focused on New York and that they destroyed the launch pads for rockets to Mars.
3. Responses will vary.

Research

Research to Clarify If students struggle to choose an element, ask them to name the first thing about the radio play that comes to mind and have them research that.

Comprehension Check

Complete the following items after you finish your first review.

1. What two speakers that are not in the original text begin the radio broadcast?

2. What additional details about the bombs on Earth are revealed in the radio play?

3. The Bitterings relocate to the villa toward the end of the story. In what way does the restructuring of description and dialogue from the original text to the radio play aid in your understanding of the characters' changing attitudes?

RESEARCH

Research to Explore Choose one of the following to research: the story's author, the series called *Bradbury 13,* or the history of radio plays in general. How does this new knowledge help deepen your appreciation of this selection?

PERSONALIZE FOR LEARNING

Challenge

Sound Effects Have students listen to the radio play again and make a list of sound effects that they would want to add to the recording. Have students note the section of the play, describe what is happening, identify the sound effect they would add, and explain why it would make a good addition to the play.

MAKING MEANING

Close Review

Listen again to the radio play. Write any new observations that seem important. What **questions** do you have? What can you **conclude**?

DARK THEY WERE, AND GOLDEN-EYED (radio play)

Analyze the Media

Notebook Respond to these questions.

1. **Compare and Contrast** **(a)** In what way is the opening scene of the radio play similar to the story's opening scene? **(b)** In what way does the opening scene differ from the story?
2. **Evaluate** Which version of the story did you enjoy more, the text or the audio? Give reasons for your response.
3. **Connect** If you were to cast the radio play, what actor would you choose to play each part? Explain your choices.
4. **Essential Question:** ***Should we make a home in space?*** What have you learned about living in space by listening to this radio play?

POINT OF COMPARISON

The text and the audio version of "Dark They Were, and Golden-Eyed" tell the same story. Pay attention to how experiencing the story is different when you read it and when you listen to it.

LANGUAGE DEVELOPMENT

Media Vocabulary

Use media vocabulary words in your responses to the following:

sound effects **human voice** **silence**

1. In what way has the Martian atmosphere been brought to life in the radio play?
2. Do the characters sound the way you thought they would sound, based on your reading of the story?
3. How are changes of scene indicated in the radio play?

STANDARDS

Speaking and Listening
Analyze the main ideas and supporting details presented in diverse media and formats and explain how the ideas clarify a topic, text, or issue under study.

PERSONALIZE FOR LEARNING

Strategic Support

Actors Help students understand and appreciate what an actor's performance can add to a story. Have students write a paragraph discussing how hearing the actors added to their understanding or appreciation of the story. Did the actors' performances change their ideas about the story? Why or why not? Did the performances help them better understand or better appreciate a detail or part of the story? How?

DIGITAL PERSPECTIVES

Close Review

Discuss with students how hearing the dialogue spoken by actors affected their experience of hearing the story performed. Ask them how listening to the play, rather than reading it themselves, changes their perspective on the events of the story. Does it raise questions or answer them, or both?
If needed, model close reviewing by using the Closer Review notes in the Interactive Teacher's Edition.

Analyze the Media

Possible responses:

1. (a) The same events occur: The family arrives on Mars. (b) The radio play contains only dialogue, and sound effects enhance the mood.
2. Responses will vary.
3. Responses will vary. Students should include all three media vocabulary terms in their answers and say how each helped show what living in space was like for the characters.
4. Responses will vary.

Media Vocabulary

For more support, see **Media Vocabulary** 

Possible Responses:

1. Responses will vary. Students should identify how the Martian atmosphere is brought to life in the radio play.
2. Responses will vary. Students should include or reference specific examples of human vocal sounds and explain how and why they helped them envision the characters.
3. Changes of scene are indicated by music.

FORMATIVE ASSESSMENT

Analyze the Media

- **If** students struggle with comparing and contrasting the opening scenes, **then** have them reread the beginning of the short story and relisten to the beginning of the radio play, one right after the other.

Media Vocabulary

- **If** students struggle to use the media vocabulary correctly in their responses, **then** review relevant parts of the radio play and point out the use of the terms.

Writing to Compare

Students will compare two presentations of the same story to determine how the each medium affects the way the narrative is conveyed.

Students' responses will vary but should indicate comparison and contrast and emphasize their understanding of the techniques used in both formats.

Prewriting

Analyze Author's Purpose Students' responses will vary but should reflect plausible interpretations of Bradbury's and McDonough's goals, based on an understanding of the two different formats.

Compare Elements Students' responses will vary but should demonstrate their knowledge of the plot, characters, and mood of each format.

EFFECTIVE EXPRESSION

DARK THEY WERE, AND GOLDEN-EYED (short story)

DARK THEY WERE, AND GOLDEN-EYED (radio play)

STANDARDS

Reading Literature
Compare and contrast a written story, drama, or poem to its audio, filmed, staged, or multimedia version, analyzing the effects of techniques unique to each medium.

Writing
- Write informative/explanatory texts to examine a topic and convey ideas, concepts, and information through the selection, organization, and analysis of relevant content.
- Draw evidence from literary or informational texts to support analysis, reflection, and research.
  a. Apply *grade 7 Reading standards* to literature.

Writing to Compare

You have read Ray Bradbury's science fiction tale "Dark They Were, and Golden-Eyed" and listened to a radio play adaptation of the story. Now, deepen your analysis and express your observations in writing.

Assignment

Both the story and the radio play describe the experiences of the Bittering family and other people from Earth living in a colony on Mars. To prepare for your assignment, consider the following:

- How are the story and radio play similar?
- What are the most important differences between the two?

Write a **comparison-and-contrast essay** in which you analyze the techniques each version uses to bring this tale to life. Conclude with an evaluation that tells which version is more effective.

Prewriting

Notebook **Analyze Author's Purpose** Skim Bradbury's story. Consider what his goals might have been when he was writing it in 1949. Then, think about the goals of Michael McDonough, the producer of the radio play. How might his goals have differed? Write your thoughts below.

Bradbury's goals	
McDonough's goals	

Compare Elements Both versions tell the same story, but they use techniques specific to their mediums. A short story uses language to develop plot, characters, and mood. A radio play uses voices, sound effects, and music to develop the same elements. Use a chart like this one to compare.

DARK THEY WERE, AND GOLDEN-EYED		
	SHORT STORY	RADIO PLAY
Plot How are events presented?		
Characters Who are the main characters, and how are they depicted?		
Mood What is the atmosphere of the work? What creates this mood?		

PERSONALIZE FOR LEARNING

English Language Support

Word Forms Review with students the different word forms for *narration*. *Narration* is a noun that means "the act or process or an instance of telling a story." *Narrate* is a verb that means "to tell a story or to provide spoken commentary for a movie or television show." *Narrative* is a noun that means "something that is told, such as a story." **ALL LEVELS**

Notebook Respond to these questions.

1. Which narrative elements are stronger in Bradbury's short story?
2. Which elements have a greater impact in the radio play?
3. Which version of the tale is more effective? Why?

Drafting

Draft a strong introduction, body, and conclusion for your comparison-and-contrast essay. Follow an outline that includes details you collected. Write one paragraph for each numbered section in your outline.

Introduction	
I. Opening	Describe the narrative and mediums you are comparing.
Body	
II. Plot	Explain how the plot is developed in each version.
III. Characters	Tell how characters are presented in each version.
IV. Mood	Identify the mood created by each version.
Conclusion	
V. Evaluation	State which version is more effective.

Use Transitions Clearly identify which version of the tale you are writing about in each sentence. Transitions such as the following can help to distinguish versions and identify comparisons and contrasts:

In Bradbury's story . . .	*However,* in the radio play . . .
The language of the story . . .	*On the other hand,* the radio play . . .
The story's characters . . .	*Similarly,* the settlers in the radio play . . .

Where the story uses _____, the radio play employs _____.

Whereas the radio play takes advantage of _____, the story benefits from _____.

Support Your Conclusion Cite specific evidence from both versions of "Dark They Were, and Golden-Eyed" to support the evaluation in your conclusion. You may wish to describe the strengths of both versions, but emphasize why one version has a greater overall impact.

Review, Revise, and Edit

When you are done drafting, review and revise your essay. Make sure your essay presents information in a logical way. Make sure the points of comparison and contrast are clearly identified, and a concluding evaluation is supported by effective evidence. Proofread your draft for spelling and grammar errors. Finally, work with a partner to have a peer review of each other's essays.

EVIDENCE LOG

Before moving on to a new selection, go to your Evidence Log and record what you've learned from the text and audio versions of "Dark They Were, and Golden-Eyed."

STANDARDS

Writing

Write informative/explanatory texts to examine a topic and convey ideas, concepts, and information through the selection, organization, and analysis of relevant content.

a. Introduce a topic clearly, previewing what is to follow; organize ideas, concepts, and information, using strategies such as definition, classification, comparison/contrast, and cause/effect; include formatting, graphics, and multimedia when useful to aiding comprehension.

b. Develop the topic with relevant facts, definitions, concrete details, quotations, or other information and examples.

d. Use precise language and domain-specific vocabulary to inform about or explain the topic.

f. Provide a concluding statement or section that follows from and supports the information or explanation presented.

DIGITAL PERSPECTIVES 

1. Students' responses will vary but should be supported by evidence from the story.
2. Students' responses will vary but should be supported with evidence from the radio play.
3. Students' responses will vary but should be supported with evidence from both formats.

Drafting

Use Transitions Remind students that transitions such as the ones listed will help readers understand the comparisons being made. These transitions help readers keep track of the versions being addressed.

Support Your Conclusion Remind students that the conclusion is their opportunity to offer their own opinions about which version is more effective. Emphasize that their opinions should be supported by specific evidence from both versions.

Review, Revise, and Edit

Remind students that evidence should be specific, relevant, and logical. If they are presenting evidence to support a claim about the radio play, the evidence should mention a relevant detail in the radio play. If they are presenting evidence to support a claim about the story, the evidence should mention a relevant detail in the story. For more support, see **Writing to Compare: Comparison-and-Contrast Essay.**

Evidence Log Support students in completing their Evidence Log. This paced activity will help prepare them for the Performance-Based Assessment at the end of the unit.

Danger! This Mission to Mars Could Bore You to Death!

AUDIO SUMMARIES
Audio summaries of "Danger! This Mission to Mars Could Bore You to Death!" are available online in both English and Spanish in the Interactive Teacher's Edition or Unit Resources. Assigning these summaries prior to reading the selection may help students build additional background knowledge and set a context for their first read.

Summary

"Danger! This Mission to Mars Could Bore You to Death!" is a newspaper article by Maggie Koerth-Baker that describes an experiment NASA set up to investigate what will happen to people who spend a long time traveling through space. With current technology, scientists know it will take nearly eight months to reach Mars, and boredom could be a serious threat to the mission. Researchers are now studying the effects of such isolation and boredom. As part of that research, they have learned that people who work in Antarctica schedule most of their days to avoid boredom. People who are bored can take dangerous risks, forget how to do their jobs, and potentially risk their lives. People's minds, not just their bodies, need something to do to stay fit.

Insight

This article emphasizes the often-neglected psychological side of exploration. It can help students see the value of mental stimulus and understand how boredom can cause people to make mistakes. People living in long-term isolation devise activities that short-circuit boredom—like inventing holidays to celebrate—as ways to give them something to anticipate.

ESSENTIAL QUESTION:
Should we make a home in space?

Connection to the Essential Question

The information in this article will help students consider the Essential Question—Should we make a home in space? Like life in Antarctic research stations, the early days of life in space would mix peril with extreme boredom. Very few people would want to live forever in desolate, remote places on Earth. Life in space would be at least as hard as life in the Antarctic.

WHOLE-CLASS LEARNING PERFORMANCE TASK
Do the benefits of exploring Mars outweigh the risks?

UNIT PERFORMANCE-BASED ASSESSMENT
Should we spend valuable resources on space exploration?

Connection to the Performance Tasks

Whole-Class Learning Performance Task As they consider the Whole-Class Learning Performance Task prompt, students will see that getting to Mars will not only be dangerous, it will be hard on the minds of those who go. Students may question whether it is worth the risk.

Unit Performance-Based Assessment Students may find evidence in this article that questions the wisdom of space exploration. The significant expense of preparatory work like that described in Koerth-Baker's article would add enormously to the cost of exploring space. Such funding could otherwise be spent on things like education, hunger relief, and other important activities on Earth.

DIGITAL PERSPECTIVES

 Audio  Video  Document Annotation Highlights Online Assessment

LESSON RESOURCES

	Making Meaning	Language Development	Effective Expression
Lesson	**First Read** **Close Read** **Analyze the Text** **Analyze Craft and Structure**	**Concept Vocabulary** **Word Study** **Conventions**	**Writing to Sources** **Speaking and Listening**
Instructional Standards	**RI.7.10** By the end of the year, read and comprehend literary nonfiction . . . **RI.7.5** Analyze the structure an author uses to organize a text . . .	**L.7.1** Demonstrate command of the conventions of standard English . . . **L.7.4** Determine or clarify the meaning of unknown and multiple-meaning words and phrases . . . **L.7.4.b** Use common, grade-appropriate Greek or Latin affixes and roots . . .	**W.7.1** Write arguments . . . **W.7.1.a** Introduce claim(s) . . . **W.7.1.b** Support claim(s) . . . **W.7.1.d** Establish and maintain . . . **W.7.1.e** Provide a concluding statement . . . **W.7.7** Conduct short research projects . . . **SL.7.4** Present claims and findings . . . **SL.7.5** Include multimedia components and visual displays . . .
STUDENT RESOURCES			
Available online in the Interactive Student Edition or Unit Resources	Selection Audio First-Read Guide: Nonfiction Close-Read Guide: Nonfiction	Word Network	Evidence Log
TEACHER RESOURCES			
Selection Resources Available online in the Interactive Teacher's Edition or Unit Resources	Audio Summaries: English and Spanish Annotation Highlights Accessible Leveled Text First Read Extension Questions Analyze Craft and Structure: Informative Writing	Concept Vocabulary and Word Study Conventions: Action Verbs and Linking Verbs	Writing to Sources: Blog Post English Language Support Lesson: Blog Post Speaking and Listening: Visual Presentation
Reteach/Practice (RP) Available online in the Interactive Teacher's Edition or Unit Resources	Analyze Craft and Structure: Informative Writing (RP)	Word Study: Latin Prefix *sub-* (RP) Conventions: Action Verbs and Linking Verbs (RP)	Writing to Sources: Blog Post (RP) Speaking and Listening: Visual Presentation (RP)
Assessment Available online in Assessments	Selection Test: English Selection Test: Spanish Extension Selection Test		
My Resources	A Unit 2 Answer Key is available online and in the Interactive Teacher's Edition.		

Reading Support

Text Complexity Rubric: Danger! This Mission to Mars Could Bore You to Death!	
Quantitative Measures	
Lexile: 1290 **Text Length:** 1,199 words	
Qualitative Measures	
Knowledge Demands ①—②—❸—④—⑤	Selection relies partly on practical knowledge but also contains discipline-specific content about NASA, research on the brain, stimulus and response, sensory stimulation, and psychology.
Structure ①—❷—③—④—⑤	Connections between ideas are mostly explicit and clear; main ideas are explained with multiple detailed examples.
Language Conventionality and Clarity ①—②—③—❹—⑤	Language is dense and complex but concrete and literal; selection contains some academic vocabulary; some sentences are complex with multiple clauses.
Levels of Meaning/Purpose ①—②—❸—④—⑤	Purpose is explicitly stated and concrete; some concepts are complex; main concepts are mostly explained with supporting details.

DECIDE AND PLAN

English Language Support

Provide English Learners with support for knowledge demands and language as they read the selection.

Knowledge Demands Explain that NASA stands for National Aeronautics and Space Administration. If necessary, explain that NASA is responsible for our space program and research about space. Tell students that the article is about the way people's brains react to being in space. Have students list unfamiliar words about the brain and the research described in the article.

Language Write the word *bore* from the title, and list related words with students' help (*boring, bored, boredom*). Have students look for these words in the selection. Point out that *bore* is a verb, *boredom* a noun, and *bored* an adjective. Have students read the sentences and write their own sentences with the words.

Strategic Support

Provide students with strategic support to ensure that they can successfully read the text.

Knowledge Demands Find out what students know about NASA and review that this organization is charged with directing our space programs. Discuss some of the terms that students will find related to brain research, such as *cognitive neuroscience, sensory stimulation, mental stimulus,* and *brain activity patterns.*

Meaning After students read the article once through, break it down into paragraphs and have students reread. As a group, help them to summarize the main points of each paragraph. List these main ideas. Then reread the list, asking students to find examples in the reading about each point.

Challenge

Provide students who need to be challenged with ideas for how they can go beyond a simple interpretation of the text.

Text Analysis Pair students. Ask them to reread paragraphs 4, 5, 6, 8, and 9. Assign each pair one or two of those paragraphs. Ask the partners to talk about the examples given to illustrate the main points. Then ask them to come up with additional examples. Ask pairs to share their examples with the class.

Written Response Ask students to reread the article to locate strategies for fighting boredom in space. Then, ask them to write their ideas for what they would do to prevent boredom. Have them include details about how these strategies would work in space or what problems they might encounter.

TEACH

Read and Respond

Have the class do their first read of the selection. Then have students complete their close read. Finally, work with them on the Making Meaning, Language Development, and Effective Expression activities.

Standards Support Through Teaching and Learning Cycle

IDENTIFY NEEDS

Analyze results of the Beginning-of-Year Assessment, focusing on the items relating to Unit 2. Also take into consideration student performance to this point and your observations of where particular students struggle.

DECIDE AND PLAN

- If students have performed poorly on items matching these standards, then provide selection scaffolds before assigning them the on-level lesson provided in the Student Edition.
- If students have done well on the Beginning-of-Year Assessment, then challenge them to keep progressing and learning by giving them opportunities to practice the skills in depth.
- Use the Selection Resources listed on the Planning pages for "Danger! This Mission to Mars Could Bore You to Death!" to help students continuously improve their ability to master the standards.

Instructional Standards: Danger! This Mission to Mars Could Bore You to Death!

	Catching Up	This Year	Looking Forward
Reading	You may wish to administer the **Analyze Craft and Structure: Informative Writing (RP)** worksheet to help students understand the purpose of writing this type of essay and how its structure contributes to the development of ideas.	**RI.5** Analyze the structure an author uses to organize a text, including how the major sections contribute to the whole and to the development of the ideas.	Challenge students to read an informative essay and then write an outline for the essay. Have them pay close attention to how each idea builds on the last and how examples and details are used to support ideas.
Writing	You may wish to administer the **Writing to Sources: Blog Post (RP)** worksheet to help students understand how to write a blog post in a formal voice that states and supports claims and identifies counterclaims.	**W.1** Write arguments to support claims with clear reasons and relevant evidence. **W.1.d** Establish and maintain a formal style.	Challenge students to write comments in response to the blog post they have written. Comments should address both the claim and counterclaims and feature evidence and reasons for the stated point of view.
Speaking and Listening	You may wish to administer the **Speaking and Listening: Visual Presentation (RP)** worksheet to help students understand how to conduct research and then present their findings using multimedia components.	**SL.5** Include multimedia components and visual displays in presentations to clarify claims and findings and emphasize salient points.	Challenge students to create a plan for a piece of investigative journalism having to do with the space program.
Language	You may wish to administer the **Conventions: Action Verbs and Linking Verbs (RP)** worksheet to help students understand the difference between and uses for action verbs and linking verbs. You may wish to administer the **Word Study: Latin Prefix *sub-* (RP)** worksheet to help students understand that prefixes can be used as clues to determine the meaning of unfamiliar words.	**L.1** Demonstrate command of the conventions of standard English grammar and usage when writing or speaking. **L.4** Determine or clarify the meaning of unknown and multiple-meaning words and phrases based on *grade 7 reading and content,* choosing flexibly from a range of strategies.	Challenge students to use a variety of action and linking verbs in their writing. Have students find words with Latin prefixes in their reading. Challenge them to determine the meaning of the words using the meaning of the prefixes as clues.

ANALYZE AND REVISE

- Analyze student work for evidence of student learning.
- Identify whether students have met the expectations in the standards.
- Identify implications for future instruction.

TEACH

Implement the planned lesson, and gather evidence of student learning.

Jump Start

FIRST READ Prior to students' first read, engage them in a discussion about boredom to help them make connections between the text and their own experiences. *In what situations do they get bored? What happens when they get bored? What do they do to deal with boredom?*

Danger! This Mission to Mars Could Bore You to Death!

Can people get bored even if they're doing something exciting or dangerous? What might happen if someone gets bored while doing something complicated or risky? Modeling questions such as these will help students connect to "Danger! This Mission to Mars Could Bore You to Death!" and to the Performance Task assignment. Selection audio and print capability for the selection are available in the Interactive Teacher's Edition.

Concept Vocabulary

Support students as they rank their words. Ask if they've ever heard, read, or used these words. Reassure them that the definitions for these words are listed in the selection.

FIRST READ

As they read, students should perform the steps of the first read:

NOTICE: You may want to encourage students to notice the author's main point and the details she uses to support it.

ANNOTATE: Remind students to mark passages they feel are particularly important or worthy of analysis in their close read. For example, students may want to focus on passages that discuss causes and effects of boredom.

CONNECT: Encourage students to go beyond the text and make connections to their experiences or other texts. If they cannot make connections to their own lives or other texts, have them consider movies and TV shows.

RESPOND: Students will answer questions and write a summary to demonstrate understanding.

Point out to students that while they will always complete the Respond step at the end of the first read, the other steps will probably happen somewhat concurrently. You may wish to print copies of the **First-Read Guide: Nonfiction** for students to use.

Remind students that during their first read, they should not answer the close-read questions that appear in the selection.

About the Author

Maggie Koerth-Baker (b. 1981) is an American science journalist and author. She is the science editor at *BoingBoing*, a general-interest blog, and has contributed articles to the *New York Times Magazine*. Koerth-Baker writes about the relationship between science, culture, and human behavior.

Danger! This Mission to Mars Could Bore You to Death!

Concept Vocabulary

You will encounter the following words as you read "Danger! This Mission to Mars Could Bore You to Death!" Before reading, note how familiar you are with each word. Then, rank the words in order from most familiar (1) to least familiar (6).

WORD	YOUR RANKING
chronic	
stimulus	
subconsciously	
excruciatingly	
monotony	
catastrophic	

After completing the first read, come back to the concept vocabulary and review your rankings. Mark changes to your original rankings as needed.

First Read NONFICTION

Apply these strategies as you conduct your first read. You will have an opportunity to complete the close-read notes after your first read.

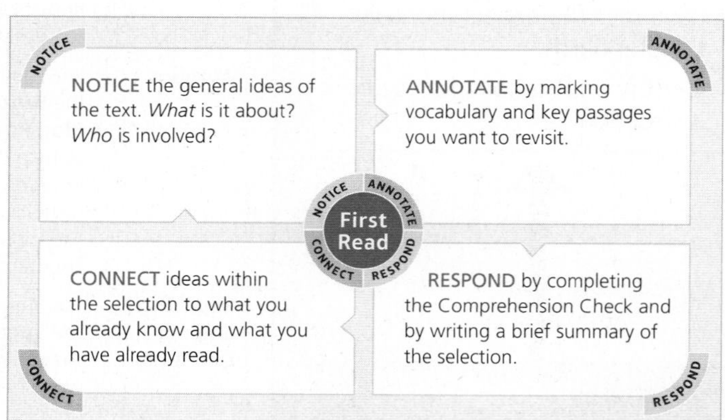

STANDARDS
Reading Informational Text
By the end of the year, read and comprehend literary nonfiction in the grades 6–8 text complexity band proficiently, with scaffolding as needed at the high end of the range.

VOCABULARY DEVELOPMENT

Concept Vocabulary Reinforcement Students will benefit from additional examples and practice with the concept vocabulary. Reinforce their comprehension with "show-you-know" sentences. The first part of the sentence uses the vocabulary word in an appropriate context. The second part of the sentence—the show-you-know part—clarifies the first. Model the strategy with this example for *chronic*:

Tyrel had a *chronic* (paragraph 3) cough; it lasted for a long time.

Then, give students these sentence prompts, and coach them in creating the clarification part:

1. He *subconsciously* (paragraph 8) envied his brother's red hair; ______.

   Possible response: without being aware of it, he wished he had red hair, too.

2. The landslide was *catastrophic*; (paragraph 13) ______.

   Possible response: it completely destroyed the entire village.

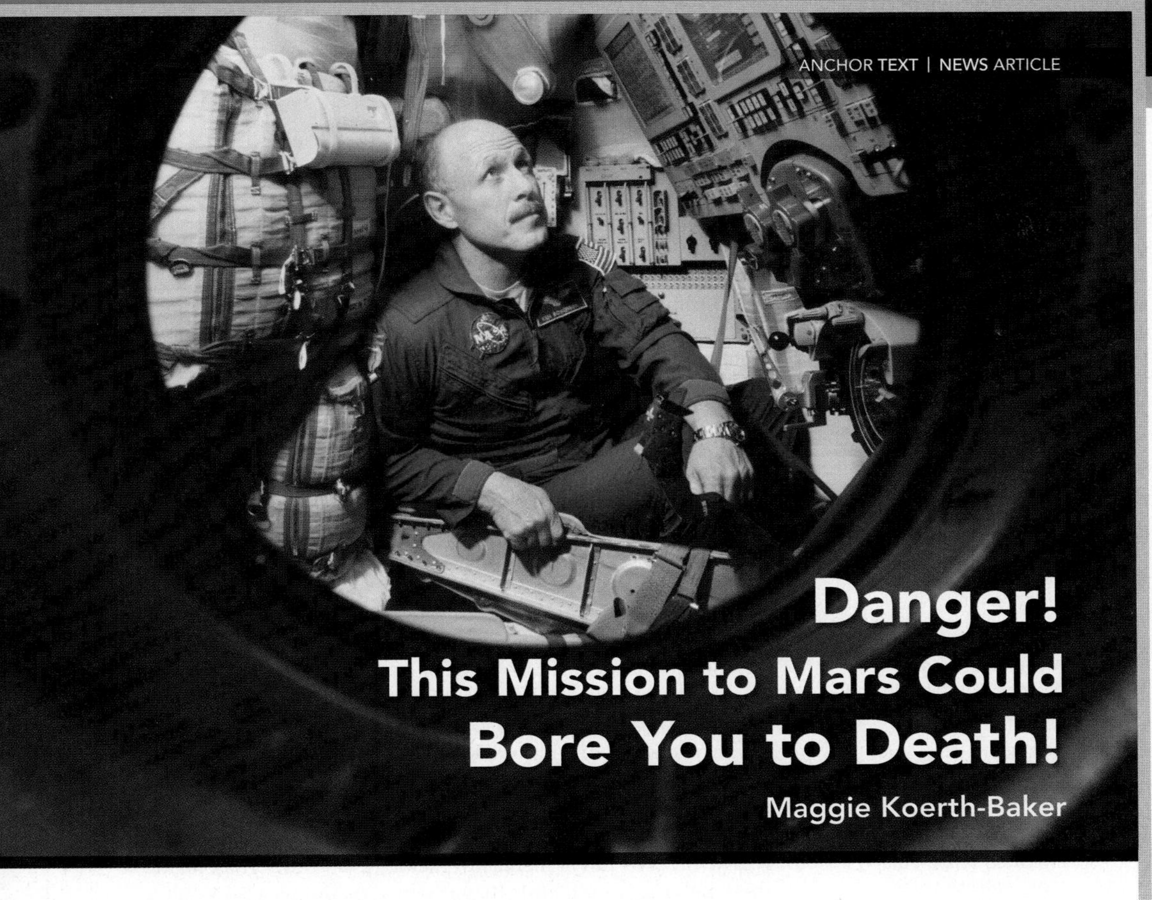

ANCHOR TEXT | NEWS ARTICLE

Danger! This Mission to Mars Could Bore You to Death!

Maggie Koerth-Baker

DIGITAL PERSPECTIVES

BACKGROUND

This article mentions Ernest Shackleton, who led several expeditions to the South Pole in the early 1900s. While these icy voyages took a huge toll on the crew's bodies, crew members also struggled with the mental stress of being isolated from society for months on end. On a mission to Mars, astronauts would also have to endure long periods of isolation and boredom.

1 Right now, six people are living in a nearly windowless, white geodesic dome[1] on the slopes of Hawaii's Mauna Loa volcano. They sleep in tiny rooms, use no more than eight minutes of shower time a week and subsist on a diet of freeze-dried, canned or preserved food. When they go outside, they exit through a mock air lock, clad head to toe in simulated spacesuits. The dome's occupants are playing a serious version of the game of pretend—what if we lived on Mars?

NOTES

1. **geodesic dome** round building that is inexpensive to build and is known for its structural strength, efficiency, and durability.

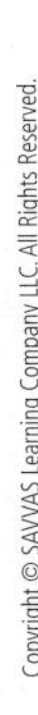

PERSONALIZE FOR LEARNING

Strategic Support

Making Connections to Self Have students imagine what it might be like to live under the conditions described in paragraph 1, and have them write a paragraph describing life in this situation. Students should include one or two thoughts that a person living like this might have.

CLOSE READ

You may wish to model the Close Read using the following think-aloud format. Possible responses to questions on the student page are included. You may also want to print copies of the **Close-Read Guide: Nonfiction** for students to use.

ANNOTATE: As I read paragraph 4, I notice and highlight text that indicates the behavior of living things.

QUESTION: I think the writer uses these examples to show that even the most basic creatures—amoebas—need sensory stimulation.

CONCLUDE: The details support the topic sentence by showing that people aren't the only iving things negatively affected by boredom.

Additional **English Language Support** is available in the Interactive Teacher's Edition.

NOTES

2 Research at the Hawaii Space Exploration Analog and Simulation (HI-SEAS) project, funded in part by NASA, is a continuation of a long history of attempts to understand what will happen to people who travel through outer space for long periods of time. It's more than a technical problem. Besides multistage rockets to propel a spacecraft out of Earth's atmosphere, years of planning and precise calculations and massive amounts of fuel, traveling the tens of millions of miles to Mars will take a tremendous amount of time. With current technology, the journey takes more than eight months each way.

3 Which means that astronauts will get bored. In fact, a number of scientists say that—of all things—boredom is one of the biggest threats to a manned Mars mission, despite the thrill inherent in visiting another planet. And so, attention is being paid to the effects of boredom at HI-SEAS, and on the International Space Station. But because of the causes of **chronic** boredom, scientists say, research facilities in Antarctica might actually provide a better simulation of the stress of a journey to Mars.

chronic (KRON ihk) *adj.* lasting a long time or recurring often

CLOSE READ

ANNOTATE: Mark descriptive details you find in paragraph 4.

QUESTION: What point is the author making by listing such details?

CONCLUDE: Do the details effectively support the topic sentence of the paragraph?

4 Most living things constantly seek out sensory stimulation—new smells, tastes, sights, sounds or experiences. Even single-celled amoebas will move to investigate new sources of light or heat, says Sheryl Bishop, who studies human performance in extreme environments at the University of Texas Medical Branch. Animals deprived of naturalistic environments and the mental stimulation that comes with them can fall into repetitive, harmful patterns of behavior. Anybody of a certain age will remember zoos full of manically pacing tigers, bears gnawing on their metal cages and birds that groomed themselves bald—all a result, we now know, of their rather unstimulating lifestyles.

5 Human boredom isn't quite as well understood, says James Danckert, a professor of cognitive neuroscience at the University of Waterloo. He's currently working on what he says may be the first study of how our brain activity changes when we're bored. Danckert is hoping to find out whether boredom is connected to a phenomenon called the "default network"—a background hum of brain activity that seems to remain on even when you aren't directly focused on something. There's a lot of observable activity in the brains of people who are staring at a blank screen—way more than anybody expected, Danckert says. The default network maps closely to the brain-activity patterns scientists see when someone's mind is wandering. It suggests that what we call a restless mind is just that—a mind desperate for something to amuse it, searching frantically for **stimulus**.

stimulus (STIHM yuh luhs) *n.* something that causes action or reaction

6 Boredom, it turns out, is a form of stress. Psychologically, it's the mirror image of having too much work to do, says Jason Kring, president of the Society of Human Performance in Extreme

CROSS-CURRICULAR PERSPECTIVES

Science The article details studies of human brain activity. Have students conduct research and report on one other study of human brain activity. Students might use the search terms "studies on brain activity." Reports should answer the following questions:

- When did the study take place?
- What was the purpose of the study?
- What was learned?
- Does this study relate to the content of the article? If it does, in what way?

Have volunteers share their responses with the class. **(Research to Clarify)**

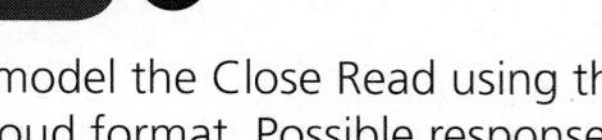

DIGITAL PERSPECTIVES

Environments, an organization that studies how people live and work in space, underwater, on mountaintops and other high-risk places. If your brain does not receive sufficient stimulus, it might find something else to do—it daydreams, it wanders, it thinks about itself. If this goes on too long, it can affect your mind's normal functioning. Chronic boredom correlates with depression and attention deficits.

7 Astronaut candidates go through two years of training before they're even approved to fly. And before they are chosen to be candidates, they have to compete against thousands of other applicants. The 2013 class, for instance, had more than 6,000 applicants and only 8 were chosen. Astronauts are rigorously tested for psychological as well as physical fitness. But no mission in NASA's history has raised the specter of chronic boredom to the degree that a Mars mission does, because none have involved such a long journey through nothingness.

8 What if, millions of miles from home, a chronically bored astronaut forgets a certain safety procedure? What if he gets befuddled while reading an oxygen gauge? More important, Danckert and Kring say, bored people are also prone to taking risks, **subconsciously** seeking out stimulation when their environment bores them.

9 The cognitive and social psychologist Peter Suedfeld says that people will sometimes do reckless, stupid things when they suffer from chronic boredom. In Antarctica, where winter can cut scientists and crew off from the rest of the world for as long as nine months, the isolation can lead to strange behavior. Suedfeld told me he has heard about Antarctic researchers venturing outside in 40-below weather without proper clothing and without telling anyone else they were going out.

10 The diaries of early polar explorers are full of tales of extreme boredom, depression and desperate attempts at entertainment reminiscent of prisoners' stories from solitary confinement. An important lesson that Antarctica can impart on a Mars expedition is this: even scientists on important missions can get **excruciatingly** bored.

11 One effective way astronauts combat boredom is by staying busy with work. That's a strategy at HI-SEAS, where the crew member Kate Greene told me that her schedule is packed—every hour planned and accounted for, from the time she wakes up to the time she goes to bed at night. Life on the International Space Station is similar. (In fact, historically, NASA's problem has been overworking people: in 1973, the exhausted crew of Skylab 4[2] actually staged a relaxation rebellion and took an unscheduled day off.) But Antarctica is different from HI-SEAS or the

2. **Skylab 4** mission aboard United States space station Skylab.

NOTES

CLOSE READ

ANNOTATE: Mark facts in paragraph 7 that show the challenges with which astronauts are faced.

QUESTION: Why did the author include these facts?

CONCLUDE: How do these facts help you to better understand the reason that chronic boredom is especially problematic for a Mars mission?

subconsciously (suhb KON shuhs lee) *adv.* occurring in the mind without one's full awareness

excruciatingly (ehk SKROO shee ay tihng lee) *adv.* painfully; miserably

CLOSE READ

You may wish to model the Close Read using the following think-aloud format. Possible responses to questions on the student page are included.

ANNOTATE: As I read paragraph 7, I notice details about problems with boredom.

QUESTION: I think the author included these facts to emphasize the seriousness of the problem.

CONCLUDE: The phrase "a long journey through nothingness" strongly conveys the challenges of traveling to Mars.

DIGITAL PERSPECTIVES

Illuminating the Text Review paragraph 7 and discuss the goals of astronaut training. To help students understand the rigors of astronaut training, use search terms such as "astronaut training" to find video footage online showing how astronauts train. Be sure to preview any video before showing it to students. Have students discuss how seeing this video helps illuminate the process or helps them understand the article.

NOTES

monotony (muh NOT uh nee) *n.* sameness; boredom

catastrophic (kat uh STROF ihk) *adj.* disastrous

International Space Station. Communications are limited. There's nobody outside the base directing your day. Spectacular views vanish in a haze of white. It's just you, the people you came in with, no way out and little to break up the **monotony**.

12 And so some researchers there have learned to actively fend off boredom by creating what you might call a unique office culture. They celebrate a ridiculous number of holidays, both traditional and invented. You need something to look forward to, Suedfeld says, and planning the events helps change the routine. Even Ernest Shackleton's Antarctic crew found ways to put on skits and concerts. On one expedition, Shackleton brought a small printing press. At McMurdo Station,[3] the 1983 winter crew created costumes, learned lines and acted out scenes from the movie *Escape From New York*. It's possible that we may, someday, watch recordings of Mars-bound astronauts acting out other John Carpenter films. (It's not so far-fetched. Chris Hadfield, a Canadian astronaut, made a tribute to David Bowie's "Space Oddity" that racked up more than 16 million views on YouTube.)

13 It might sound absurd, but many scientists say strategies like this are necessary because, without proper mental stimulus, we risk making a physically and technologically challenging endeavor into a psychologically grueling one. It would be **catastrophic** if humanity's greatest voyage were brought low by the mind's tendency to wander when left to its own devices. ❧

3. **McMurdo Station** Antarctic research station.

PERSONALIZE FOR LEARNING

English Language Support

Idioms Students might struggle with some of the idioms and expressions in paragraph 12. Point out and explain the following: *fend off* (defend against); *look forward to* (be excited about or be eager to do); *far-fetched* (unlikely to be true); and *racked up* (gained, achieved, accumulated). **ALL LEVELS**

Comprehension Check

Complete the following items after you finish your first read.

1. Why are six people living in a geodesic dome on the slopes of a volcano in Hawaii?

2. With our current technology, how long will a journey to Mars take?

3. According to scientists, what is one of the biggest threats to a manned Mars mission?

4. Notebook Write a brief summary of "Danger! This Mission to Mars Could Bore You to Death!"

RESEARCH

Research to Clarify Choose at least one unfamiliar detail from the news article. Briefly research that detail. In what way does the information you learned shed light on an aspect of the article?

DIGITAL PERSPECTIVES

Comprehension Check

Possible responses:

1. They are living as if they were on Mars. They are testing the effects of extreme boredom.
2. A journey to Mars will take about eight months each way.
3. One of the biggest threats to a manned Mars mission is boredom.

Summaries will vary. Students should include most of the following: Scientists are studying boredom because it is one of the biggest threats to a manned Mars mission as well as other long journeys through space; when most living things get bored, they look for sensory stimulation; boredom is not well understood in people, but it seems the human brain is always active; people who are bored experience a form of stress; on a long space journey, if bored people make a mistake there could be a disaster; living in Antarctica is similar to living in space, and Antarctic explorers have done disastrous things because of boredom; to combat boredom, scientists working in Antarctica invent ways to entertain themselves, and astronauts are kept constantly busy on space missions; if we are going to successfully travel to distant planets, we must find ways to deal with boredom.

Research

Research to Clarify If students struggle to identify an unfamiliar detail, have them reread the article and consider an idea or a concept that might be new to them, such as geodesic domes or subconscious behavior.

PERSONALIZE FOR LEARNING

Challenge

Research Encourage students to conduct research and write brief reports about expeditions to or scientific work being done in Antarctica and the Arctic Circle. When possible, students should read and report on diaries kept by people on these expeditions who are doing this work. Discuss how this material and information relates to the content of the article.

Jump Start

CLOSE READ Have students consider the title "Danger! This Mission to Mars Could Bore You to Death!" Ask students why they think the author chose this title. Also ask why this is a particularly good title for this article. Ask students to suggest other titles for the article. Are they as good as this title? Why, or why not?

Close Read the Text

Walk students through the Annotation Model on the student page. Encourage them to complete items 2 and 3 on their own. Review and discuss the sections students have marked. If needed, continue to model close reading by using the Annotation Highlights in the Interactive Teacher's Edition.

Analyze the Text

Possible responses:

1. Lack of stimulation can affect the mind's normal functioning. Long-term boredom can be like depression. **DOK 2**
2. Responses to (a) and (b) will vary but should be supported by evidence from the text. **DOK 2**
3. Responses will vary. Students might say a benefit of space travel is it demands that people perform at their best. A drawback to space travel is that people might face the challenge of chronic boredom. **DOK 4**

MAKING MEANING

DANGER! THIS MISSION TO MARS COULD BORE YOU TO DEATH!

Close Read the Text

1. This model, from paragraph 8 of the text, shows two sample annotations, along with questions and conclusions. Close read the passage, and find another detail to annotate. Then, write a question and conclusion.

Close Read: ANNOTATE · QUESTION · CONCLUDE

ANNOTATE: The author begins this paragraph with two questions that introduce possible situations.

QUESTION: Why does the author ask two questions without providing answers to them?

CONCLUDE: The author is showing that there are many other potential risks resulting from astronaut boredom.

What if, millions of miles from home, a chronically bored astronaut forgets a certain safety procedure? What if he gets befuddled while reading an oxygen gauge? More important, Danckert and Kring say, bored people are also prone to taking risks, subconsciously seeking out stimulation when their environment bores them.

ANNOTATE: The author includes information from subject-matter experts.

QUESTION: Why does the author include this information?

CONCLUDE: Expert information supports and strengthens the author's explanation.

2. For more practice, go back into the text and complete the close-read notes.
3. Revisit a section of the text you found important during your first read. Read this section closely and **annotate** what you notice. Ask yourself **questions** such as "Why did the author make this choice?" What can you **conclude**?

Tool Kit
Close-Read Guide and Model Annotation

Analyze the Text

CITE TEXTUAL EVIDENCE to support your answers.

Notebook Respond to these questions.

1. **Connect** How is chronic boredom a form of stress?
2. **Classify** (a) Which details about the dangers of boredom were most convincing? (b) Which details were least convincing?
3. **Essential Question** ***Should we make a home in space?*** What have you learned about the benefits and drawbacks of space travel from reading this article?

STANDARDS
Reading Informational Text
Analyze the structure an author uses to organize a text, including how the major sections contribute to the whole and to the development of the ideas.

FORMATIVE ASSESSMENT

Analyze the Text

- **If** students fail to cite relevant or logical evidence, **then** ask them questions that test the relevance or logic of their evidence and suggest they find new evidence.
- **If** students fail to understand the concept that boredom is a serious challenge, **then** have them review the parts of the article that address this issue.

PERSONALIZE FOR LEARNING

English Language Support

Words Used in Comparisons Review and clarify words and phrases used in comparisons. Show students the following: *benefits and drawbacks, pros and cons, different and alike,* and *unlike or similar.*

Have students create a two-column alike-different chart and write each word in the appropriate column, identifying whether it refers to a similarity or a difference.

Encourage students to use these words as they discuss the article.
ALL LEVELS

Analyze Craft and Structure

Text Structure: Informative Writing Any kind of writing that teaches, informs, or explains is called **informative writing.** Effective informative texts present numerous aspects of a topic in a way that is easy to follow and understand.

- The topic of the text is introduced and then developed in related sections or paragraphs. These sections or paragraphs build on one another to present a clear picture of the topic.
- The author provides support for his or her ideas with facts, statistics, and other details that describe and elaborate on the topic; the support may also include quotations from experts on the topic.
- Transition words and phrases, such as *finally, since,* and *in fact,* are often used to show how ideas are connected.

Practice

CITE TEXTUAL EVIDENCE to support your answers.

Notebook Respond to these questions.

1. Use the chart to identify key information provided in the article.

What details are provided in the introduction?	Chronic boredom is boredom that lasts for a very long time.
What aspects of the topic are explored in the body paragraphs?	Chronic boredom is a major challenge for astronauts on space missions as well as for other people living in extreme, isolated situations for a long period of time.
What key idea is reinforced in the conclusion?	Chronic boredom can lead to disastrous mistakes on space missions and can lead people to engage in risky behavior.

2. (a) Identify three transition words or phrases in paragraph 3 of the article. (b) How do these words and phrases link the ideas in this paragraph together?

3. How effectively has the author introduced ideas and supported them? Cite details to support your response.

DIGITAL PERSPECTIVES

Analyze Craft and Structure

Discuss with students the tone an author uses in informative writing. Because the author's purpose is to explain or inform, an expository article or essay usually has a formal tone. Writing in a formal tone encourages readers to take the writing seriously and to really consider what the author is saying. For more support, see **Analyze Craft and Structure: Informative Writing.**

MAKE IT INTERACTIVE

Have students list three possible topics for an expository article or essay. Ask volunteers to share their responses with the class.

Practice

Possible responses:

1. (a) For possible responses, see the chart on the student page. (b) Students' responses will vary, but they should provide examples and evidence from the text to support their viewpoint.
2. (a) *In fact; and so; but* (b) *In fact* is used for emphasis, *and so* is used to show cause and effect, and *but* is used to show a contradictory shift in thought.
3. Like scientists at HI-SEAS and astronauts on the International Space Station, people on expeditions to Antarctica are living in extreme, isolated conditions and face chronic boredom.

FORMATIVE ASSESSMENT

Analyze Craft and Structure

- **If** students are unable to understand the ideas related to chronic boredom, **then** review the parts of the article that discuss these ideas.
- **If** students are unable to identify transition words and phrases, **then** review common transitions and discuss what each one indicates.

For Reteach and Practice, see **Analyze Craft and Structure: Informative Writing (RP).**

PERSONALIZE FOR LEARNING

Strategic Support

Informative Writing If students struggle with the structure of informative writing, have a partner conduct a think aloud to explain the thought process as he or she works through the key parts of exposition. Ask the partners to locate the introduction, body, and conclusion of the text. Next, students can isolate key details that show how the author of this article supports her ideas with facts, statistics, details, and information from experts.

TEACHING

Concept Vocabulary

Why These Words?

Possible responses:

1. Responses will vary. Students might say the concept vocabulary gives them a better sense of how serious and intense boredom can be.
2. *windowless* (paragraph 1); *repetitive* (paragraph 4); *harmful* (paragraph 4)

Practice

Possible responses:

1. A patient's *chronic* cough might signal a more serious condition.
2. One *stimulus* a person might seek if he or she were sleepy could be exercising.
3. If someone were *subconsciously* nervous about speaking in front of people, he or she might make a lot of mistakes.
4. An *excruciatingly* painful headache might feel like there was a loud drum pounding in your head.
5. People might find *monotony* in household chores because these tasks are usually repetitive.
6. In a *catastrophic* oceanic event, a ship might sink.

Word Network

Possible words: *threats, effects, stress, suffer, isolation*

Word Study

For more support, see **Concept Vocabulary and Word Study**.

Possible responses:

1. Because he felt *subconsciously* guilty about lying to Lydia, Peter was unable to look at her.
2. *submarine*: a vessel that travels under water. A modern *submarine* can travel around the world underwater. *subzero*: below zero. It is dangerous to go out in *subzero* temperatures without protective clothing. *subaudible*: below the range of hearing. People cannot hear *subaudible* sounds.

FORMATIVE ASSESSMENT

Concept Vocabulary

If students fail to see the connection between the words, **then** have them use each word in a sentence relating to the article and tell you what the sentences have in common.

Word Study

If students have trouble finding appropriate words, **then** show them different words to which *sub-* can be added (*station, committee, basement, contract*) and discuss each word.

For Reteach and Practice, see **Word Study: Latin Prefix *sub-* (RP).**

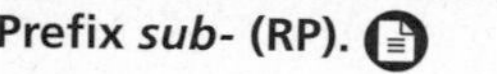

LANGUAGE DEVELOPMENT

DANGER! THIS MISSION TO MARS COULD BORE YOU TO DEATH!

Concept Vocabulary

chronic	subconsciously	monotony
stimulus	excruciatingly	catastrophic

Why These Words? The concept vocabulary words from the text are related to boredom. For example, when we are bored, we might *subconsciously* seek some sort of *stimulus*.

1. How does the concept vocabulary sharpen your understanding of how people respond to boredom?
2. What other words in the selection connect to the condition of boredom or the potential risks it poses?

WORD NETWORK

Add interesting words related to space exploration from the text to your Word Network.

Practice

Notebook Respond to these questions.

1. Why might a doctor be concerned if a patient had a *chronic* cough?
2. What sort of *stimulus* might a person seek if he or she were sleepy?
3. What might happen if someone were *subconsciously* nervous about speaking in front of people?
4. What might it feel like to have an *excruciatingly* painful headache?
5. Why might many people find *monotony* in household chores?
6. What might happen to a ship in a *catastrophic* disaster at sea?

Word Study

Latin Prefix: *sub-* The Latin prefix *sub-* means "under" or "below." The word *subconsciously* means "in a way that is below consciousness"; that is, it refers to a thought or action that occurs in a way in which a person is not directly aware of having the thought or performing the action. In the article, the author says that when people become bored, they *subconsciously* seek out stimulation, or they look for things to stimulate them without even being aware that they are doing so.

1. Write a sentence that correctly uses the word *subconsciously*.
2. Using a dictionary or thesaurus, find three other words that have the prefix *sub-*. Record the definition for each word, and write a sentence that correctly uses each word.

STANDARDS

Language

- Demonstrate command of the conventions of standard English grammar and usage when writing or speaking.
- Determine or clarify the meaning of unknown and multiple-meaning words and phrases based on *grade 7 reading and content*, choosing flexibly from a range of strategies.
  - b. Use common, grade-appropriate Greek or Latin affixes and roots as clues to the meaning of a word.

VOCABULARY DEVELOPMENT

Word Analysis Remind students that when they come across an unfamiliar word, they might be able to figure out its meaning from a prefix or suffix. For example, the Latin prefix *circum-* means "around, on all sides." Discuss the following words:

- *circumvent* (to make a circuit around; to get around especially by ingenuity)
- *circumference* (the external boundary of a circle)
- *circumnavigate* (to go completely around [as the earth] especially by water; to go around instead of through; to bypass)

Conventions

Action Verbs and Linking Verbs A **verb** is a word that expresses an action or a state of being. A complete sentence must have at least one verb.

- An **action verb** tells what action someone or something is doing.
- A **linking verb** joins the subject of a sentence with a word or phrase that describes or renames the subject. The most common linking verbs are forms of *be,* such as *am, is, are, was, were, has been,* and *will be.* Other linking verbs include *seem, become, stay,* and *feel.*

Several verbs can be used either as action verbs or as linking verbs. The examples in this chart will help you tell the difference between action and linking verbs.

ACTION VERBS	LINKING VERBS
Manny *tastes* the apple. *(The subject,* Manny, *is eating an apple.)*	The apple *tastes* sour. *(The adjective,* sour, *describes the subject,* apple.*)*
The farmer *grows* corn. *(The subject, the* farmer, *is raising corn.)*	The corn *grows* tall. *(The adjective,* tall, *describes the subject,* corn.*)*
Jeri *felt* the turtle's shell. *(The subject,* Jeri, *was touching the shell.)*	The turtle's shell *felt* hard. (Hard *describes the subject, the turtle's* shell.*)*

Read It

Mark the verbs in these excerpts from the news article, and label each as an action verb or a linking verb.

1. When they go outside, they exit through a mock air lock. . . .
2. The diaries of early polar explorers are full of tales of extreme boredom, depression and desperate attempts at entertainment reminiscent of prisoners' stories from solitary confinement.
3. . . . astronauts will get bored.

Write It

Notebook Write a sentence for each item, using the subject indicated and the action or linking verb in parentheses. If a verb can be either action or linking, choose which form to use, and label it next to your sentence.

1. astronaut (look)
2. scientists (research)
3. boredom (stimulate)
4. International Space Station (will be)

DIGITAL PERSPECTIVES

Conventions

Action Verbs and Linking Verbs Review action verbs and linking verbs. Remind students that a sentence without a verb is a fragment that must be corrected by adding a verb. For more support, see **Conventions: Action Verbs and Linking Verbs.**

MAKE IT INTERACTIVE

Have students write two sentences that have action verbs and two sentences that have linking verbs.

Possible responses:

Janice left a note on the table. (action)
This is a beautiful day. (linking)
Mike was late, as usual. (linking)
Harper smiles a lot. (action)

Read It

Possible responses:

1. go (action); exit (action)
2. are (linking)
3. will get (linking)

Write It

Possible responses:

1. An astronaut looks almost like a creature when he or she is dressed in gear.
2. Scientists research topics that we want to learn more about.
3. Boredom can lead people to stimulate themselves in unusual or creative ways.
4. In the future, the International Space Station will be a starting point for space missions.

HOW LANGUAGE WORKS

Action Verbs and Linking Verbs If students struggle to understand the difference between action verbs and linking verbs or have trouble identifying them, have them read the following sentences and identify the action or linking verbs in each.

1. Boredom is a big problem on long space missions.
2. Scientists study the human brain to learn how it responds to boredom.
3. People who live in isolated conditions are likely to face boredom.
4. Boredom will be a serious problem if a person who is bored behaves dangerously.

FORMATIVE ASSESSMENT

Conventions

- **If** students can't identify or work with action verbs, **then** review common action verbs and discuss how they demonstrate action.
- **If** students can't identify or work with linking verbs, **then** review linking verbs and discuss how they function in a sentence.

For Reteach and Practice, see **Conventions: Action Verbs and Linking Verbs (RP).**

TEACHING

Writing to Sources

Discuss with students the importance of stating a position clearly so readers know what position the blog will defend. Also remind students that it's important to use credible sources to support their argument and to address counterclaims to their position. For more support, see **Writing to Sources: Blog Post.**

Reflect on Your Writing

Possible responses:

1. Responses will vary. If students need support, ask them to consider the insights they gained from writing their blog post.
2. Responses will vary. Encourage students to be specific in their responses and to give a reason for why something was surprising.
3. **Why These Words?** Responses will vary. Have students list specific words they chose that add power to their narrative.

FORMATIVE ASSESSMENT

Writing to Sources

If students have trouble articulating a position, **then** ask them to tell you how they feel and give you reasons for why they feel as they do. Then, have students write their ideas in a two-column chart with the heads *Position* and *Reason*. For Reteach and Practice, see **Writing to Sources: Blog Post (RP).**

EFFECTIVE EXPRESSION

DANGER! THIS MISSION TO MARS COULD BORE YOU TO DEATH!

Writing to Sources

A **blog post** is a piece of writing added to an online journal called a **blog,** in which someone provides information about or expresses his or her thoughts on various subjects.

Assignment

Write an argument in the form of a **blog post** in response to "Danger! This Mission to Mars Could Bore You to Death!" In your post, state your position on the topic of combating astronauts' boredom while traveling to Mars. Is the effort to combat boredom worth the expense? Briefly research different perspectives on the topic, and then make and support your claim in your blog post.

- Identify your claim, and decide on a research plan.
- Conduct research—using accurate, credible sources—to compile evidence to support your argument.
- Organize the information you will use in your blog post so that your reasons and evidence are clearly connected and flow logically.
- Acknowledge and address alternative or opposing claims.
- Provide a concluding statement that follows from and supports your argument.

Vocabulary and Conventions Connection Think about including several of the concept vocabulary words in your writing. You may also want to be aware of your use of action and linking verbs. Using too many linking verbs may make your writing dull.

chronic	subconsciously	monotony
stimulus	excruciatingly	catastrophic

Reflect on Your Writing

After you have written your blog post, answer these questions.

1. Was it easy or difficult to support your claim?
2. What is the most surprising thing you learned during your research?
3. **Why These Words?** The words you choose make a difference in your writing. Which words did you specifically choose to strengthen your argument?

STANDARDS

Writing

- Write arguments to support claims with clear reasons and relevant evidence.
  - a. Introduce claim(s), acknowledge alternate or opposing claims, and organize the reasons and evidence logically.
  - b. Support claim(s) with logical reasoning and relevant evidence, using accurate, credible sources and demonstrating an understanding of the topic or text.
  - d. Establish and maintain a formal style.
  - e. Provide a concluding statement or section that follows from and supports the argument presented.
- Conduct short research projects to answer a question, drawing on several sources and generating additional related, focused questions for further research and investigation.

Speaking and Listening

- Present claims and findings, emphasizing salient points in a focused, coherent manner with pertinent descriptions, facts, details, and examples; use appropriate eye contact, adequate volume, and clear pronunciation.
- Include multimedia components and visual displays in presentations to clarify claims and findings and emphasize salient points.

PERSONALIZE FOR LEARNING

English Language Support

Evaluating a Blog Post Give students a blog post to read. Ask pairs of students to point out the characteristics of the blog. Tell them to discuss whether the blog draws them in and is easy to read. **EMERGING**

Give students a blog post to read. Have them write their impression of the opening paragraph, what the author's tone is, and whether the blog is easy to read. **EXPANDING**

Give students a blog post and a newspaper article to read. Have students write a brief paragraph explaining how the two are different, based on what they have learned. **BRIDGING**

An expanded **English Language Support Lesson** on Blog Posts is available in the Interactive Teacher's Edition.

Speaking and Listening

A **visual presentation** is a way of conveying information through the use of visual aids such as charts, diagrams, illustrations, photos, or video clips.

Assignment

Briefly research activities that are designed to combat boredom. Use these ideas, as well as those in the article, to create an activity that could help astronauts combat boredom during an eight-month journey to Mars. Share your idea with the class in a **visual presentation**. Be sure to clearly explain why your activity will effectively combat the boredom that astronauts will face.

1. **Plan Your Presentation**
   - Consult several print and digital sources to gather information.
   - Gather or create a variety of visual aids.
2. **Organize Your Presentation**
   - Create a script that flows logically. Indicate in the script the point at which you will show visuals.
   - Arrange the visuals in the order in which you will show them.
   - Rehearse your presentation. You may want to work with a peer and get feedback.
3. **Deliver Your Presentation**
   - Maintain appropriate eye contact with your audience.
   - Speak clearly and at an appropriate volume.
   - Ensure that your classmates can clearly see and examine the visuals you display.
4. **Evaluate Presentations** Use a presentation evaluation guide like the one shown to evaluate your own as well as your classmates' presentations.

PRESENTATION EVALUATION GUIDE

Rate each statement on a scale of 1 (not demonstrated) to 5 (demonstrated).

- ☐ The idea for an activity was creative and original.
- ☐ The speaker supported his or her ideas with details, descriptions, and examples.
- ☐ The presentation was well organized and easy to follow.
- ☐ The presentation included a variety of visual aids.
- ☐ The speaker maintained eye contact with the audience.
- ☐ The speaker spoke clearly and at an appropriate volume.

EVIDENCE LOG

Before moving on to a new selection, go to your Evidence Log and record what you've learned from "Danger! This Mission to Mars Could Bore You to Death!"

PERSONALIZE FOR LEARNING

Strategic Support

If students have difficulty thinking of an activity, suggest that they think about times when they're bored and what they do to deal with boredom. As an alternative, suggest that students imagine themselves in a small space with very little to do. What might they do for stimulation? Remind students that their idea for this assignment can be playful, as long as it makes sense. Encourage students to be creative.

DIGITAL PERSPECTIVES

Speaking and Listening

1. **Plan Your Presentation** You may wish to guide students in choosing their digital sources of information. Encourage students to use information only from .gov or .edu sites. These are often the most reliable.
2. **Organize Your Presentation** Suggest to students that they rehearse their presentation several times so they are comfortable with the logic and organization. Emphasize practicing any words or phrases that they might be having trouble saying.
3. **Deliver Your Presentation** Remind students to take their time when they give their presentations. Tell students that when they present calmly and without rushing, they will appear more confident and project more authority.
4. **Evaluate Presentations** Encourage students to make one supportive comment about each presentation. For more support, see **Speaking and Listening: Visual Presentation.**

Evidence Log Support students in completing their Evidence Log. This paced activity will help prepare them for the Performance-Based Assessment at the end of the unit.

FORMATIVE ASSESSMENT

Speaking and Listening

- **If** students have trouble finding information, **then** suggest sources they can use.
- **If** students have trouble delivering their presentation to the class, **then** have them simply tell their information to one classmate they are comfortable with. For Reteach and Practice, see **Speaking and Listening: Visual Presentation (RP).**

Selection Test

Administer the "Warning! This Mission to Mars Could Bore You to Death!" Selection Test, which is available in both print and digital formats online in Assessments.

Jump Start

Ask students to write two things they have learned about exploring space and other worlds as a result of reading and listening to "Dark They Were, and Golden-Eyed" and reading "Danger! This Mission to Mars Could Bore You to Death!" You might guide them with questions such as "What are some good things about exploring space and other worlds? What are some bad things or potentially bad things?" As students share, ask them to cite specific examples from the texts or radio play to support their ideas.

Write an Argument

Make sure students understand what they are being asked to do in the assignment. Explain that they are being asked to take a position on this question because the selections they've read and listened to relate to exploring Mars.

Students should complete the assignment using word processing software to take advantage of editing tools and features.

Elements of an Argument

Remind students that an effective argument clearly states a position, supports that position with logical, relevant evidence, and addresses counterarguments. It is also written in a formal tone and clearly shows the relationships among its ideas. Remind students that they'll find the elements of an effective argument in "Leaving Main Street."

MAKE IT INTERACTIVE

Project "Leaving Main Street" from the Interactive Teacher's Edition and have students identify the elements of an argument, such as the claim, counterclaims, reasons, evidence, and concluding statement.

Academic Vocabulary

Ask students for examples of how they might use the academic vocabulary in their arguments.

PERFORMANCE TASK: WRITING FOCUS

WRITING TO SOURCES

- LEAVING MAIN STREET
- DARK THEY WERE, AND GOLDEN-EYED (short story)
- DARK THEY WERE, AND GOLDEN-EYED (radio play)
- DANGER! THIS MISSION TO MARS COULD BORE YOU TO DEATH!

Write an Argument

The texts and radio play in this section all relate to the exploration of Mars. In "Dark They Were, and Golden-Eyed," a family faces enormous changes on Mars. "Danger! This Mission to Mars Could Bore You to Death!" examines the challenges that chronic boredom poses to astronauts on very long space missions. Now, you will use your knowledge of these texts to write an argument about space exploration, in the form of an editorial.

Assignment

Based on the texts and audio you've encountered in this unit, as well as outside reading and prior knowledge, write an **editorial** in which you respond to the following question:

Do the benefits of exploring Mars outweigh the risks?

Tool Kit

Student Model of an Argument

Elements of an Argument

An **editorial** is a type of argument that typically appears in a newspaper and takes a position on a specific topic or issue. In an argument, the writer states and supports a **claim**, or position, based on factual evidence and logical reasoning. Editorials usually include the writer's opinions as well, revealing personal viewpoints.

An effective argument contains these elements:

- a clear statement of your claim on an issue that has more than one side
- information about the issue
- persuasive evidence and logical reasoning that support the claim
- statements that acknowledge opposing views and offer counterarguments to these views
- a clear organizational structure
- words, phrases, and clauses that show the relationships among claims, reasons, and evidence
- a formal style

ACADEMIC VOCABULARY

As you craft your argument, consider using some of the academic vocabulary you learned in the beginning of the unit.

justify
alternative
certainty
discredit
assumption

Model Argument For a model of a well-crafted argument, see the Launch Text, "Leaving Main Street."

Challenge yourself to find all of the elements of an effective argument in the text. You will have an opportunity to review these elements as you prepare to write your own argument.

LAUNCH TEXT

STANDARDS

Writing

- Write arguments to support claims with clear reasons and relevant evidence.
- Write routinely over extended time frames and shorter time frames for a range of discipline-specific tasks, purposes, and audiences.

AUTHOR'S PERSPECTIVE **Kelly Gallagher, M.Ed.**

The Best Writer in the Room Intensive modeling is one of the most effective ways to improve writing instruction. When teachers model at every stage of the writing process, they stop *assigning* writing and start *teaching* it. While you are teaching writing through this Performance Task, show your students how you attack these parts of the assignment:

Prewriting Brainstorm counterclaims and ask students to add their own ideas to your list. List types of evidence you could use.

Drafting Outline the argument and draft alongside students.

Revising Use your model or a student model as an example.

Do this work in front of students each time. While it may seem more efficient to follow the same steps with each class or show a perfectly polished essay, don't take this path. If you authentically model the work of writing, students may be more open to the work of writing. It is important for the students to see the teacher struggle a bit with the work.

Prewriting / Planning

Develop a Claim To determine the claim you will make in your editorial, begin by reviewing the texts to evaluate the benefits and risks of exploring Mars. Make a two-column list in which you write benefits in one column and risks in the other. Then, decide which position you will defend in your editorial.

Write a Claim To make your position clear to readers, review your notes and develop a **thesis statement**—one strong sentence that states your claim. Include this sentence in your introduction.

Consider Possible Counterclaims In order to effectively make your claim, you must consider all sides of an issue. This means that you must identify **counterclaims,** or views that oppose your position, and explain why these views are flawed. Addressing counterclaims to your argument will make your claim more persuasive and powerful. To anticipate counterclaims to your argument, complete these sentences:

Another reader might say that ______________________.

The reason he or she might think this is because ______________________.

The evidence that supports this alternative position is ______________________.

However, my position is stronger because ______________________.

Gather Evidence Reread the texts to find evidence that supports your ideas. Supporting evidence includes facts, statistics, quotations, examples, and other details. For example, the author of the Launch Text uses the following example as evidence to support a claim:

> *. . . there is something about the human condition that strives to be the best, or the first, at something. Our ancestors survived by outperforming others.*
>
> —from "Leaving Main Street"

Connect Across Texts To effectively present and support your argument with evidence from the Anchor Texts, review the texts and note key ideas. You can **paraphrase**, or restate in your own words, ideas and insights from the texts. You can also use **direct quotations**, or an author's exact words. If you quote an author, be sure you put the words in quotation marks and name the author and work from which you are quoting.

Note how the author of the Launch Text presents and supports an argument. Ask questions such as:

- How does the author state and support a claim?
- How does the author connect the claims, evidence, and reasons in the argument?

EVIDENCE LOG

Review your Evidence Log and identify key details you may want to include in your argument.

STANDARDS

Writing
Write arguments to support claims with clear reasons and relevant evidence.
a. Introduce claim(s), acknowledge alternate or opposing claims, and organize the reasons and evidence logically.
b. Support claim(s) with logical reasoning and relevant evidence, using accurate, credible sources and demonstrating an understanding of the topic or text.

DIGITAL PERSPECTIVES

Prewriting/Planning

Develop a Claim Suggest that students think about how they will be able to support their claims.

Write a Claim Encourage students to make their claims clear and strong.

Consider Possible Counterclaims Remind students to include counterclaims in their argument. Explain that including and addressing counterclaims makes an argument stronger because it shows that the writer is fully considering the topic. Also remind students that when they address counterclaims, their evidence should be relevant and their reasoning should be logical.

Gather Evidence Have students review their Evidence Log to find possible support for their claim. Remind them that if they don't have sufficient information in their Evidence Log, they can review the selections to identify additional or stronger evidence for their argument. Remind students that they can also use other sources to support their claim.

Connect Across Texts Remind students to try to use as many of the selections as they can. "Dark They Were, and Golden-Eyed" is fiction; "Leaving Main Street" and "Danger! This Mission to Mars Could Bore You to Death!" are nonfiction. Remind students to be aware of this difference as they connect ideas from different selections. Information in the nonfiction selections is supported by facts and evidence. Ideas in fiction come from the author's imagination; they might or might not be supported by actual facts. Even so, students can still use Bradbury's story to support their argument.

PERSONALIZE FOR LEARNING

Strategic Support

Argument Point out to students that "Leaving Main Street" presents an argument in favor of exploring space. "Danger! This Mission to Mars Could Bore You to Death!" doesn't present an argument for or against exploring space or going to Mars, but it does discuss an issue that could be used to support an argument against traveling to Mars. "Dark they Were, and Golden-Eyed" doesn't present an argument; it's one writer's vision of what could happen if humans did to go Mars. Tell students they can make any argument they want to in their essay. After they decide on their position, they should look at the selections for information and ideas that support their stance. If they can't find sufficient evidence in the selections, they should look for other sources.

Drafting

Organize Your Argument Encourage students to make a second outline for their argument. This one will include their claim, evidence that supports their claim, counterarguments, and answers to counterarguments. Point out that if they complete both outlines, their argument is already half-written. All they have to do next is "fill in the blanks."

Clearly Connect Your Ideas Tell students that in addition to using transitional words and phrases to connect their ideas, they can use introductory sentences when they present evidence. For example, instead of simply citing a study, they can first include a sentence such as "Many studies have demonstrated this fact." Or instead of going right to a quotation from an expert, they can first include a sentence such as "Dr. Michael Smith is one of many experts who agree." Introductory sentences such as these will make their writing flow better.

Write a Strong Conclusion Remind students of the importance of a strong conclusion. A good conclusion sums up and restates (in different words) the position taken in the essay and leaves readers with a powerful impression. Tell students to keep in mind that it's the last thing the reader sees.

Write a First Draft Tell students that their first draft does not have to be perfect. When writing a first draft, they should focus on expressing their ideas and including all the elements of an argument. Once everything is on paper, they can focus on improving the support for their argument when they edit. If they try to write a perfect argument in their first draft, they might slow their writing process or perhaps make it more stressful.

PERFORMANCE TASK: WRITING FOCUS

Drafting

Organize Your Argument Most arguments are composed of three parts:

- the **introduction**, in which you state your claim
- the **body**, in which you provide analysis, supporting reasons, and evidence
- the **conclusion**, in which you summarize or restate your claim

Each part of your argument should build on the part that came before, and every point should connect directly to your main claim. This outline shows the key sections of the Launch Text. Notice that each paragraph fulfills a specific purpose.

LAUNCH TEXT

MODEL: "Leaving Main Street"

INTRODUCTION AND CLAIM

Author presents first set of arguments and supporting details

Author addresses counterarguments

Author presents strongest argument

Author concludes the argument

My Argument

INTRODUCTION

BODY

CONCLUSION

Clearly Connect Your Ideas In order for an argument to be effective, it must show clear connections between claims, counterclaims, reasoning, and evidence. Some transitional words and phrases show the connections between similar ideas, whereas others show the connections between opposing ideas. Refer to the examples as you draft. First, determine the relationship between two ideas. Then, choose an appropriate word that will clarify this relationship.

Similar Ideas: *because, in addition, also, likewise, moreover, as well as, similarly, furthermore*
Opposing Ideas: *although, but, in contrast, even though, despite, whereas, regardless, however*

Write a Strong Conclusion You should conclude your editorial with a powerful conclusion that follows the logic of your reasoning and supports the position you defined in your thesis statement. Do not introduce new ideas or information in your conclusion. Because your conclusion is your last chance to make your case to your audience, it should be clear and persuasive.

Write a First Draft As you draft your editorial, review the elements of an argument, as well as the information you gathered in the Prewriting/Planning section of this Performance Task.

STANDARDS

Writing

Write arguments to support claims with clear reasons and relevant evidence.

a. Introduce claim(s), acknowledge alternate or opposing claims, and organize the reasons and evidence logically.

c. Use words, phrases, and clauses to create cohesion and clarify the relationships among claim(s), reasons, and evidence.

e. Provide a concluding statement or section that follows from and supports the argument presented.

AUTHOR'S PERSPECTIVE **Jim Cummins, Ph.D.**

Sentence Frames Students learning English may be challenged by a blank page. Support them with scaffolding to help them organize their arguments and flesh out their outlines. They may benefit from using sentence frames like the following to help them map out their writing.

Introduction: I believe the benefits of exploring Mars outweigh/do not outweigh the risks because ________.
Evidence from the text: My point of view is supported by the fact that ________.

Counterclaim: Others may/may not say that the benefits of exploring Mars outweigh/do not outweigh the risks because ________, but I disagree because ________.

Remind students that the writing process is recursive, and they will be able to refine their outlines and sentence frames as they draft. These are simply tools to help them organize their thoughts before they begin writing.

LANGUAGE DEVELOPMENT: CONVENTIONS

Revising for Correct Verb Tense

A **verb** expresses an action or a state of being. Verbs have **tenses,** or different forms, that tell when something happens or exists.

Present tense indicates an action that happens regularly or indicates a general truth.

Past tense indicates an action that has already happened.

Future tense indicates an action that will happen.

Present perfect tense indicates an action that happened sometime in the past or an action that happened in the past and is still happening now.

Past perfect tense indicates an action that was completed before another action in the past.

Future perfect tense indicates an action that will have been completed before another.

Read It

These sentences from the Launch Text show different verb tenses.

- *It has a molten core, tectonic plates, and volcanic activity. . . .* (present tense)
- *Our ancestors survived by outperforming others.* (past tense)
- *Humans will not tolerate boundaries. . . .* (future tense)
- *Humans have always created monuments to commemorate achievements. . . .* (present perfect)
- *The spacecraft* New Horizons *had traveled nine years to study the dwarf planet at the edge of our solar system.* (past perfect)
- *If we stop exploring space, soon society will have forgotten what it's like to be human.* (future perfect)

TIP

PUNCTUATION
Use periods or semicolons to separate complete sentences or ideas. Semicolons are appropriate if two complete ideas are closely related.

Write It

To fix an incorrect form of a verb, first identify any questionable verbs in your editorial. Then, verify the correct form using one of the following methods:

1. **Review the basic forms of the six tenses.** First, identify the time—present, past, or future—in which the action occurs. Then, review the examples in Read It to determine which verb form corresponds with that time. Avoid shifting from one tense to another unnecessarily.
2. **Rewrite the sentence.** Consider which verb tense will make your ideas as precise as possible. Then, revise the sentence using that tense.

STANDARDS
Language
- Demonstrate command of the conventions of standard English grammar and usage when writing or speaking.
- Demonstrate command of the conventions of standard English capitalization, punctuation, and spelling when writing.
- Use knowledge of language and its conventions when writing, speaking, reading, or listening.
  a. Choose language that expresses ideas precisely and concisely, recognizing and eliminating wordiness and redundancy.

DIGITAL PERSPECTIVES

Revising for Correct Verb Tense

Read It

Emphasize that correct verb tenses, and consistent verb tenses, are important for effectively communicating a writer's ideas. Incorrect or inconsistent verb tenses can confuse readers and can pull them out of the writing while they try to figure out what the author means.

MAKE IT INTERACTIVE

Project these sentences from "Leaving Main Street" from the Interactive Teacher's Edition and ask students to identify the tenses of the verbs.

- It **inspires** (present) students to pursue innovative projects and careers in science and technology.
- Third, humans **have** always **created** (present perfect) monuments to commemorate their great achievements, so that the next generation **will remember** (future) who they **are** (present) and how they **spent** (past) their time here.

Write It

As students revise their drafts, remind them to look for incorrect or inconsistent verb tenses.

PERSONALIZE FOR LEARNING

English Language Support

Verb Tenses Review the present, past, and future verb tenses and how to form them. Provide the following sentence frames and have students rewrite them in all three tenses.

Victor ______ his new computer. (use)

Jeanine ______ her bike. (ride)

Kim ______ lunch. (eat)

Hal ______ fast. (run)

ALL LEVELS

Revising

Evaluating Your Draft Remind students to use the chart to evaluate their draft to make sure it contains all the required elements of a well-constructed, well-organized, and effective argument.

Highlight Your Main Points Help students identify their main points by suggesting that they express each important idea in one clear, simple sentence. Then have them reread their essay to see if they have expressed it as clearly in their writing.

Choose Precise Words Remind students that precise words help make an argument stronger. Suggest that they read their essay again, this time looking only at their word choice. Have they always picked the most precise or most vivid word for each idea or sentence?

PERFORMANCE TASK: WRITING FOCUS

Revising

Evaluating Your Draft

Use the following checklist to evaluate the effectiveness of your first draft. Then, use your evaluation and the instruction on this page to guide your revision.

FOCUS AND ORGANIZATION	EVIDENCE AND ELABORATION	CONVENTIONS
☐ Provides a clearly stated claim and context surrounding the issue. ☐ Establishes a clear organizational structure. ☐ Uses words, phrases, and clauses that help tie together ideas and make the relationships among ideas clear. ☐ Acknowledges opposing claims and offers counterarguments. ☐ Provides a conclusion that follows from and supports the argument.	☐ Supports claims with logical reasoning and persuasive evidence from credible sources.	☐ Uses a formal style. ☐ Attends to the norms and conventions of the discipline.

WORD NETWORK

Include appropriate words from your Word Network in your argument.

Highlight Your Main Points To be sure that your editorial is organized clearly, use the following strategies as you revise your writing.

- If a reader needs to know one main point to understand a second one, make sure the first main point comes *before* the second.
- If one main point is essentially the same as another, combine these points or combine the paragraphs in which they appear.
- If one main point is stronger than the others, move it to the end of the body of your editorial. This will ensure that your editorial progresses logically, with your strongest point preceding your conclusion.

Tone

- Make use of academic vocabulary whenever possible.
- A pure argument is not written in the "I" form. Instead of writing "I think that humans explore space because it's in our genes," shorten and strengthen the thought: "Humans explore space because it's in our genes."

Choose Precise Words When you evaluate your draft, check to see that you have used precise language. Precise language helps convey your point and builds support for your position. Create an authoritative voice by using precise, lively words that will appeal to readers' sense of reason.

Vague: a *good* mission

Precise: a *life-changing* mission

STANDARDS

Writing

Write arguments to support claims with clear reasons and relevant evidence.

a. Introduce claim(s), acknowledge alternate or opposing claims, and organize the reasons and evidence logically.

d. Establish and maintain a formal style.

HOW LANGUAGE WORKS

Verb Tenses Review the **present perfect** (indicates an action that happened sometime in the past or an action that happened in the past and is still happening now); the **past perfect** (indicates an action that was completed before another action in the past) and the **future perfect** (indicates an action that will have been completed before another).

Use these sentences, pointing out the verb tense in each:

We **have painted** this house twice this year. (present perfect)

We **had painted** that house before we installed the windows. (past perfect)

We **will have painted** the house before its new owners see it. (future perfect)

PEER REVIEW

Exchange editorials with a classmate. Use the checklist to evaluate your classmate's editorial and provide supportive feedback.

1. Is there a clearly stated claim?
   ☐ yes ☐ no If no, suggest ways in which the writer might clarify it.
2. Is there support for the claim based on logical reasoning and relevant evidence from accurate, credible sources?
   ☐ yes ☐ no If no, point out where the writer should provide support.
3. Is there a concluding statement that follows from and supports the argument?
   ☐ yes ☐ no If no, suggest that the writer include one.
4. What is the strongest part of your classmate's editorial? Why?

Editing and Proofreading

Edit for Conventions Reread your draft for accuracy and consistency. Correct errors in grammar and word usage. Make sure you have maintained a formal style—free of contractions, slang, and other casual language—throughout your writing. Be sure you have included a variety of transition words and phrases that connect your ideas. Also check to ensure your verb tenses are consistent.

Proofread for Accuracy Read your draft carefully, correcting errors in spelling and punctuation. Pay particular attention to end-sentence and mid-sentence punctuation. Reading your draft aloud will help you see where sentences end, which is where you need appropriate end-sentence punctuation.

Publishing and Presenting

Create a final version of your editorial. Share it with your class or a small group of classmates, so they can read it and make comments. In turn, review and comment on your classmates' work. As a group, discuss what your editorials have in common and the ways in which they are different. Always maintain a polite and respectful tone when commenting on someone else's work.

Reflecting

Think about what you learned by writing your editorial. What could you do differently the next time you write an argument to make the writing experience easier and to make your argument stronger?

STANDARDS

Writing

- Write arguments to support claims with clear reasons and relevant evidence.
  - c. Use words, phrases, and clauses to create cohesion and clarify the relationships among claim(s), reasons, and evidence.
  - d. Establish and maintain a formal style.
- With some guidance and support from peers and adults, develop and strengthen writing as needed by planning, revising, editing, rewriting, or trying a new approach, focusing on how well purpose and audience have been addressed.

DIGITAL PERSPECTIVES

Peer Review

Before students begin their peer review, remind them that they are reviewing for clarity and completeness, not whether they agree or disagree with the author's ideas. Their position on the question might be different, but they should not comment on whether the author is "right" or "wrong." They can, however, make helpful suggestions if they see something in the editorial that could be better.

Editing and Proofreading

As students proofread, they should check for grammar, spelling, and punctuation errors. Remind them to check for the proper formatting of quotations. The exact words being quoted should be inside quotation marks. The punctuation that ends the quotation should also be inside the quotation marks. Also, remind students to check for correct and consistent verb tenses.

Publishing and Presenting

Before students review their classmates' arguments, remind them to:

- Be honest, but maintain a respectful tone in their comments.
- Use formal rather than informal language.
- Move the discussion forward by building on the ideas of others.
- Disagree courteously. Different opinions are fine, but they should be expressed politely.
- Support their position with evidence if they disagree.

Reflecting

Encourage students to reflect not only on their argument and the process of writing it, but also on the comments they received.

PERSONALIZE FOR LEARNING

English Language Support

Word Forms Review these word forms for *argument*.

- *argument*: a noun meaning "a presentation of ideas intended to persuade."

  Jack's argument persuaded us all to agree with him.
- *argue*: a verb meaning "to give reasons for or against something."

  I am going to argue with you because I think you are wrong.
- *argumentative*: an adjective meaning "given to argue."

  Robert is argumentative, always disagreeing with everyone. **ALL LEVELS**

OVERVIEW

SMALL-GROUP LEARNING

Should we make a home in space?

Space exploration is dangerous and expensive, and yet we are driven by our innate curiosity to venture further out into the unknown. Is it worth the risk for humans to try to make a new home beyond Earth? During Small-Group Learning, students will read selections that detail the risks—both realistic and fantastic. Yet, humans know that there is a potential for huge rewards in exploring the universe and attempting to live in a new and unfamiliar world.

Small-Group Learning Strategies

Review the Learning Strategies with students and explain that as they work through Small-Group Learning they will develop strategies to work in small-group environments.

- Have students watch the video on Small-Group Learning Strategies.
- A video on this topic is available online in the Professional Development Center.

You may wish to discuss some action items to add to the chart as a class before students complete it on their own. For example, for "Participate fully," you might solicit the following from students:

- Compare and discuss one another's notes with classmates.
- Ask questions and make a list of a few of the most important ones.

Block Scheduling

Each day in this Pacing Plan represents a 40–50-minute class period. Teachers using block scheduling may combine days to reflect their class schedule. In addition, teachers may revise pacing to differentiate and support core instruction by integrating components and resources as students require.

OVERVIEW: SMALL-GROUP LEARNING

ESSENTIAL QUESTION:

Should we make a home in space?

Some people think that space exploration is the biggest thrill of all. Others think it is a big waste of time and money. You will read selections that examine different aspects of this subject. Work in a small group to continue your investigation into the concept of space travel.

Small-Group Learning Strategies

Throughout your life, in school, in your community, and in your career, you will continue to learn and work with others.

Look at these strategies and the actions you can take to practice them as you work in teams. Add ideas of your own for each step. Use these strategies during Small-Group Learning.

STRATEGY	ACTION PLAN
Prepare	• Complete your assignments so that you are prepared for group work. • Organize your thinking so you can contribute to your group's discussions. •
Participate fully	• Make eye contact to signal that you are listening and taking in what is being said. • Use text evidence when making a point. •
Support others	• Build off ideas from others in your group. • Invite others who have not yet spoken to do so. •
Clarify	• Paraphrase the ideas of others to ensure that your understanding is correct. • Ask follow-up questions. •

170 UNIT 2 • A STARRY HOME

Pacing Plan

Unit Introduction: 1, 2
Introduce Whole-Class Learning: 3
Dark They Were, and Golden-Eyed: 4, 5, 6, 7, 8, 9
Media: Dark They Were, and Golden-Eyed: 10, 11, 12
Danger! This Mission to Mars Could Bore You to Death!: 13, 14, 15
Performance Task: 16, 17, 18

DIGITAL PERSPECTIVES

CONTENTS

Contents

Selections Circulate among groups as they preview the selections. Suggest groups discuss any knowledge they already have about any of the selections or the situations and settings shown in the photographs. Ask students to select the title that looks most interesting and state the reason. List the suggestions so that later students can determine which selections turned out to be the most interesting.

Remind students that communicating and collaborating in groups is an important skill that they will use throughout their lives—in school, in their careers, and in their community.

Performance Task

Present an Argument Give groups time to read about and briefly discuss the multimedia presentation they will create after reading. Encourage students to do some preliminary thinking about the types of media they may want to use. This preparation may help focus their subsequent reading and group discussion.

Introduce Small-Group Learning — 19

Future of Space Exploration Could See Humans on Mars, Alien Planets — 20, 21

The Last Dog — 22, 23, 24, 25, 26

Media: Ellen Ochoa: Director, Johnson Space Center — 27, 28

Neil deGrasse Tyson on the Future of U.S. Space Exploration After *Curiosity* — 29, 30

Performance Task — 31, 32

Introduce Independent Learning — 33

Independent Learning — 34

Performance-Based Assessment — 35, 36

SMALL-GROUP LEARNING

OVERVIEW

SMALL-GROUP LEARNING

Working as a Team

1. **Take a Position** Remind groups to let all members share their responses. You may suggest students write down privately the position each decides to take; after the readings, ask them to check if they have changed their minds on their positions.
2. **List Your Rules** You may want to have groups discuss first why rules can help a discussion. Ask volunteers to consolidate the rules into a master list to be displayed and followed by all groups.
3. **Apply the Rules** As you circulate among the groups, ensure that students are staying on task. Consider a short time limit for this step.
4. **Name Your Group** This task can be creative and fun. If students have trouble coming up with a name, suggest that they think of something related to the unit topic or something that a selection title suggests. Encourage groups to share their names with the class.
5. **Create a Communication Plan** Encourage groups to include in their plans agreed-upon times during the day to share ideas. They should also devise a method for recording and saving their communications.

Accountable Talk

Remind students that groups should communicate politely. You can post these Accountable Talk suggestions and encourage students to add their own. Students should:

Remember to... Ask clarifying questions.

Which sounds like...

Can you please repeat what you said?

Would you give me an example?

I think you said ______. Did I understand you correctly?

Remember to... Explain your thinking.

Which sounds like...

I believe ______ is true because ______.

I feel ______ because ______.

Remember to... Build on the ideas of others.

Which sounds like...

When ______ said ______, it made me think of ______.

OVERVIEW: SMALL-GROUP LEARNING

Working as a Team

1. **Take a Position** In your group, discuss the following question:

   Would you rather stay here on Earth or experience life on another planet?

   As you take turns sharing your positions, be sure to provide examples for your choice. After all group members have shared, discuss the challenges you might encounter if you were living on another planet.

2. **List Your Rules** As a group, decide on the rules that you will follow as you work together. Two samples are provided. Add two more of your own. You may add or revise rules based on your experience together.
   - Everyone should participate in group discussions.
   - People should not interrupt.
   - ______________________________
   - ______________________________

3. **Apply the Rules** Practice working as a group. Share what you have learned about living in space. Make sure each person in the group contributes. Take notes and be prepared to share with the class one thing that you heard from another member of your group.

4. **Name Your Group** Choose a name that reflects the unit topic.

   Our group's name: ______________________________

5. **Create a Communication Plan** Decide how you want to communicate with one another. For example, you might use online collaboration tools, email, or instant messaging.

   Our group's decision: ______________________________

FACILITATING SMALL-GROUP LEARNING

Forming Groups You may wish to form groups for Small-Group Learning so that each consists of students with different learning abilities. Some students may be adept at organizing information, whereas others may have strengths related to generating or synthesizing information—especially about space exploration. A good mix of abilities can make the experience of Small-Group Learning dynamic and productive.

Making a Schedule

First, find out the due dates for the small-group activities. Then, preview the texts and activities with your group and make a schedule for completing the tasks.

SELECTION	ACTIVITIES	DUE DATE
Future of Space Exploration Could See Humans on Mars, Alien Planets		
The Last Dog		
Ellen Ochoa: Director, Johnson Space Center		
Neil deGrasse Tyson on the Future of U.S. Space Exploration After *Curiosity*		

Working on Group Projects

As your group works together, you'll find it more effective if each person has a specific role. Different projects require different roles. Before beginning a project, discuss the necessary roles and choose one for each group member. Some possible roles are listed here. Add your own ideas to the list.

Project Manager: monitors the schedule and keeps everyone on task

Researcher: organizes research activities

Recorder: takes notes during group meetings

____

____

____

____

____

DIGITAL PERSPECTIVES

Making a Schedule

Encourage groups to preview the reading selections and to consider how long it will take them to complete the activities accompanying each selection. Point out that they can adjust the due dates for particular selections as needed as they work on their small-group projects. However, they must complete all assigned tasks before the group Performance Task is due. Encourage groups to review their schedules upon completing the activities for each selection to make sure they are on track to meet the final due date.

Working on Group Projects

Point out to groups that the roles they assign can also be changed later. Students might have to make changes based on who is best at doing what. Try to make sure that there is no favoritism, cliquishness, or stereotyping by gender or other means in the assignment of roles.

Also, you should review the roles each group assigns to its members. Based on your understanding of students' individual strengths, you might find it necessary to suggest some changes.

AUTHOR'S PERSPECTIVE **Ernest Morrell, Ph.D.**

Supporting Small-Group Learning
Because the dominant mode of discourse in classrooms has historically been teacher-led, many students may not be immediately comfortable discussing and collaborating in groups. The first few times students meet in their groups, you may need to provide additional support by setting expectations for collaborative behavior and discussions.

Remind students that it is important for all group members to contribute to discussions, but that no one member of the group should monopolize discussion. Whether students are speaking or listening, they should be active participants. Visit groups to explain that even when students aren't speaking, they should be listening to other group members and noting important points that they would like to build upon when it is their turn to speak.

Future of Space Exploration Could See Humans on Mars, Alien Planets

AUDIO SUMMARIES
Audio summaries of "Future of Space Exploration Could See Humans on Mars, Alien Planets" are available in both English and Spanish in the Interactive Teacher's Edition or Unit Resources. Assigning these summaries prior to reading the selection may help students build additional background knowledge and set a context for their first read.

Summary

"Future of Space Exploration Could See Humans on Mars, Alien Planets" discusses the 100-Year Starship project, which is dedicated to developing the technology necessary to travel to another planetary system within the next 100 years. Mae Jemison, project lead and America's first African-American female in space, points out two key challenges to the project: public enthusiasm and funding. Creating enthusiasm requires bringing in people from a variety of backgrounds, including engineers and astrophysicists, as well as artists and writers. To adequately fund this project, people need to understand that space exploration can bring about innovations that will improve life on Earth. Jemison emphasizes that for the project to succeed, everyone must work toward the same goal.

Insight

This selection illustrates that social challenges—such as convincing people to work for a goal—are often greater obstacles than engineering challenges. The twist later on is that a trip to another star would take longer than any human society has lasted. Space travel might require great social advancement, not just technological advancement.

ESSENTIAL QUESTION:
Should we make a home in space?

Connection to Essential Question

Colonizing remote parts of our solar system would be hard; colonizing a different solar system entirely would magnify the difficulties many times over. Would it be worth trying?

SMALL-GROUP LEARNING PERFORMANCE TASK
Should space exploration be a priority for our country?

UNIT PERFORMANCE-BASED ASSESSMENT
Should we spend valuable resources on space exploration?

Connection to Performance Tasks

Small-Group Learning Performance Task Jemison argues that the main obstacle to space exploration is not developing the technology, but rather creating public interest. This raises the question, *Should* people in our country be more interested in space exploration than other issues?

Unit Performance-Based Assessment Jemison's project is called the "100-Year Starship," indicating that space exploration is no short-term project. Colonizing another solar system would take abundant resources, and those resources would never return home. Is it worth investing the time and resources in a project such as this when there are so many more pressing needs here on Earth?

DIGITAL PERSPECTIVES

 Audio  Video  Document  Annotation Highlights 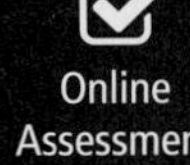 Online Assessment

LESSON RESOURCES

	Making Meaning	Language Development	Effective Expression
Lesson	**First Read** **Close Read** **Analyze the Text** **Analyze Craft and Structure**	**Concept Vocabulary** **Word Study** **Conventions**	**Speaking and Listening**
Instructional Standards	**RI.7.10** By the end of the year, read and comprehend literary nonfiction . . . **L.7.4** Determine or clarify the meaning of unknown and multiple-meaning words and phrases . . . **L.7.4.a** Use context as a clue to the meaning of a word or phrase. **SL.7.1** Engage effectively in a range of collaborative discussions . . . **RI.7.5** Analyze the structure an author uses to organize . . .	**L.7.4** Determine or clarify the meaning of unknown and multiple-meaning words and phrases . . . **L.7.4.b** Use common, grade-appropriate Greek or Latin affixes and roots . . . **L.7.4.d** Verify the preliminary determination of the meaning of a word . . . **L.7.1** Demonstrate command of the conventions of standard English . . .	**W.7.7** Conduct short research projects . . . **W.7.8** Gather relevant information from multiple print and digital sources . . . **SL.7.5** Include multimedia components and visual displays . . .
STUDENT RESOURCES			
Available online in the Interactive Student Edition or Unit Resources	Selection Audio First-Read Guide: Nonfiction Close-Read Guide: Nonfiction	Word Network	Evidence Log
TEACHER RESOURCES			
Selection Resources Available online in the Interactive Teacher's Edition or Unit Resources	Audio Summaries: English and Spanish Annotation Highlights Accessible Leveled Text Spanish Translation Text Questions First Read Extension Questions Analyze Craft and Structure: Text Structure	Concept Vocabulary and Word Study Conventions: Principal Parts of Verbs	Speaking and Listening: Multimedia Presentation
Reteach/Practice (RP) Available online in the Interactive Teacher's Edition or Unit Resources	Analyze Craft and Structure: Text Structure (RP)	Word Study: Latin Suffix *-ary* (RP) Conventions: Principal Parts of Verbs (RP)	Speaking and Listening: Multimedia Presentation (RP)
Assessment Available online in Assessments	Selection Test: English Selection Test: Spanish Extension Selection Test		
My Resources	A Unit 2 Answer Key is available online and in the Interactive Teacher's Edition.		

Reading Support

Text Complexity Rubric: Future of Space Exploration Could See Humans on Mars, Alien Planets	
Quantitative Measures	
Lexile: 1250 **Text Length:** 381 words	
Qualitative Measures	
Knowledge Demands ① ② ❸ ④ ⑤	Selection relies mostly on common knowledge but also has references to NASA and spacecraft *Voyager 1.*
Structure ① ❷ ③ ④ ⑤	Organization is clear, logical, and explicit. Quotations from several sources are included, which breaks up information and makes text more accessible.
Language Conventionality and Clarity ① ② ❸ ④ ⑤	Language is contemporary and familiar; there is some difficult vocabulary, and many sentences are complex, with multiple clauses.
Levels of Meaning/Purpose ① ❷ ③ ④ ⑤	Purpose of text is narrowly focused and explicitly stated; many concepts are explained and then restated in other ways by use of quotations.

DECIDE AND PLAN

English Language Support

Provide English learners with support for knowledge demands and language as they read the selection.

Knowledge Demands Ask students to recall what they know about NASA from reading other selections. Write *100-Year Starship project* on the board. Have students read paragraph 2 to determine what the project aims to do.

Language Ask students to make lists of words that are unfamiliar. Pair students and ask them to read the lists aloud and to see if they can help each other with any of the words. Then discuss the words as a group. Break lengthy and complex sentences into clauses. Ask questions to clarify meaning, for example (paragraph 6): *What makes an impact on programs? (innovation and unexpected technology)*

Strategic Support

Provide students with strategic support to ensure that they can successfully read the text.

Knowledge Demands Ask students to recall what they know about NASA. Ask a volunteer to read paragraph 2 aloud. Have students highlight or copy the name of the program (*100-Year Starship project*) and key words or phrases that explain the main idea *(fly a spaceship to another planetary system, innovation and enthusiasm for interstellar travel)*

Meaning For each paragraph of the text, ask volunteers to restate in their own words the information that was in that paragraph. List this information on the board. Then have another volunteer read the list. As a group, discuss the purpose of the article.

Challenge

Provide students who need to be challenged with ideas for how they can go beyond a simple interpretation of the text.

Text Analysis Ask students to reread paragraph 6. Discuss the first line, which suggests that there are people who object to funding space programs when there are humanitarian needs on Earth. Ask students to give their opinions on whether it is important to fund space programs, and why.

Written Response Ask students to look up the 100-Year Starship project and read other articles that they find about it. Ask them to write what they learned and then write a list of questions that they may still have about the program. Have students read their written work and their questions to the class.

TEACH

Read and Respond

Have the groups read the selection and complete the Making Meaning, Language Development, and Effective Expression activities.

Standards Support Through Teaching and Learning Cycle

IDENTIFY NEEDS

Analyze results of the Beginning-of-Year Assessment, focusing on the items relating to Unit 2. Also take into consideration student performance to this point and your observations of where particular students struggle.

DECIDE AND PLAN

- If students have performed poorly on items matching these standards, then provide selection scaffolds before assigning them the on-level lesson provided in the Student Edition.
- If students have done well on the Beginning-of-Year Assessment, then challenge them to keep progressing and learning by giving them opportunities to practice the skills in depth.
- Use the Selection Resources listed on the Planning pages for "Future of Space Exploration Could See Human on Mars, Alien Planets" to help students continually improve their ability to master the standards.

Instructional Standards: Future of Space Exploration Could See Humans on Mars . . .

	Catching Up	This Year	Looking Forward
Reading	You may wish to administer the **Analyze Craft and Structure: Text Structure (RP)** worksheet to help students understand how authors select and organize details to convey information.	**RI.5** Analyze the structure an author uses to organize a text, including how the major sections contribute to the whole and to the development of the ideas.	Challenge students to determine and analyze the author's purpose for an informational text that they have read. Have them discuss how the author made his or her position known.
Speaking and Listening	You may wish to administer the **Speaking and Listening: Multimedia Presentation (RP)** worksheet to help students understand how to present their findings, using multimedia components, in a focused and vivid manner.	**SL.5** Include multimedia components and visual displays in presentations to clarify claims and findings and emphasize salient points.	You may wish to challenge students to create their own artwork to accompany their presentations.
Language	You may wish to administer the **Conventions: Principal Parts of Verbs (RP)** worksheet to help students understand the four forms of the verb. You may wish to administer the **Word Study: Latin Suffix *-ary* (RP)** worksheet to help students understand that suffixes can be used as clues to determine the meaning of unfamiliar words.	**L.1** Demonstrate command of the conventions of standard English grammar and usage when writing or speaking. **L.4.b** Use common, grade-appropriate Greek or Latin affixes and roots as clues to the meaning of a word.	Challenge students to write four sentences, each with a different principal part of a verb. Sentences should all use the same verb. You may wish to challenge students to look at a list of Latin suffixes and their meanings and then use new words with those suffixes in their writing.

ANALYZE AND REVISE

- Analyze student work for evidence of student learning.
- Identify whether students have met the expectations in the standards.
- Identify implications for future instruction.

TEACH

Implement the planned lesson, and gather evidence of student learning.

Jump Start

FIRST READ Engage students in a discussion about the importance of space exploration by asking if they have seen TV shows or movies that depict the colonization of other planets. Point out that some say that the future of the human race depends upon space exploration. Ask students if they agree. Why or why not? Have students identify specific reasons for their opinions.

Future of Space Exploration Could See Humans on Mars, Alien Planets

Why is space exploration important? What are obstacles to further exploration of space and how can they be overcome? Modeling the questions readers might ask as they read "Future of Space Exploration Could See Humans on Mars, Alien Planets" for the first time brings the text alive for students and connects it to the Small-Group Performance Task assignment. Selection audio and print capability for the selection are available in the Interactive Teacher's Edition.

Concept Vocabulary

Ask groups to look closely at the three types of context clues and discuss how these types of clues can clarify meaning. Encourage groups to think of one other type of context clue they might encounter in a text. Possibilities include examples, antonyms, and definitions.

FIRST READ

As they read, students should perform the steps of the first read:

NOTICE: You may want to encourage students to notice the goals of the 100-Year Starship project.

ANNOTATE: Remind students to mark passages that include reasons to support space exploration.

CONNECT: Encourage students to consider explorations that they have undertaken, such as to visit a new place or to meet new people.

RESPOND: Students will answer questions and write a summary to demonstrate understanding.

Point out to students that while they will always complete the Respond step at the end of the first read, the other steps will probably happen somewhat concurrently. You may wish to print copies of the **First-Read Guide: Nonfiction** for students to use.

MAKING MEANING

About the Author

Nola Taylor Redd is a science and astronomy writer. Redd's work has been featured in *Scientific American*, *Astronomy Magazine*, and *Sky & Telescope Magazine*, as well as on Space.com.

Future of Space Exploration Could See Humans on Mars, Alien Planets

Concept Vocabulary

As you perform your first read of "Future of Space Exploration Could See Humans on Mars, Alien Planets," you will encounter these words.

colonize | planetary | interstellar

Context Clues If these words are unfamiliar to you, try using **context clues**—other words and phrases that appear near the unfamiliar words—to help you determine their meanings. There are various types of context clues that you may encounter as you read.

Synonyms: If the satellite is knocked out of **orbit**, scientists will have to recalculate its path.

Restatement of an Idea: The rocket **boost** gave the ship the extra power it needed to launch.

Contrast of Ideas: We knew the **blackout** had ended because we regained radio communication with our team.

Apply your knowledge of context clues and other vocabulary strategies to determine the meanings of unfamiliar words you encounter during your first read.

First Read NONFICTION

Apply these strategies as you conduct your first read. You will have an opportunity to complete a close read after your first read.

NOTICE the general ideas of the text. *What* is it about? *Who* is involved?

ANNOTATE by marking vocabulary and key passages you want to revisit.

CONNECT ideas within the selection to what you already know and what you have already read.

RESPOND by completing the Comprehension Check and by writing a brief summary of the selection.

First Read: NOTICE, ANNOTATE, CONNECT, RESPOND

STANDARDS

Reading Informational Text
By the end of the year, read and comprehend literary nonfiction in the grades 6–8 text complexity band proficiently, with scaffolding as needed at the high end of the range.

Language
Determine or clarify the meaning of unknown and multiple-meaning words and phrases based on *grade 7 reading and content*, choosing flexibly from a range of strategies.

a. Use context as a clue to the meaning of a word or phrase.

AUTHOR'S PERSPECTIVE **Jim Cummins, Ph.D.**

Importance of Background Knowledge
It is important for all students, and especially for English learners, to learn to tap into their background knowledge when they read a text. Teachers can help students access this knowledge and integrate it with new textual information. One way to do this is to encourage groups to share what they know about the topic of the text before they begin reading. For example, on a superficial level, some students may have prior knowledge about recent space missions, which can help scaffold understanding of "Future of Space Exploration." On a deeper level, more students may be able to relate to the idea of the extraordinary distances—and effort—involved in space travel. After students have completed their first read, have them discuss how their background knowledge helped them understand the text.

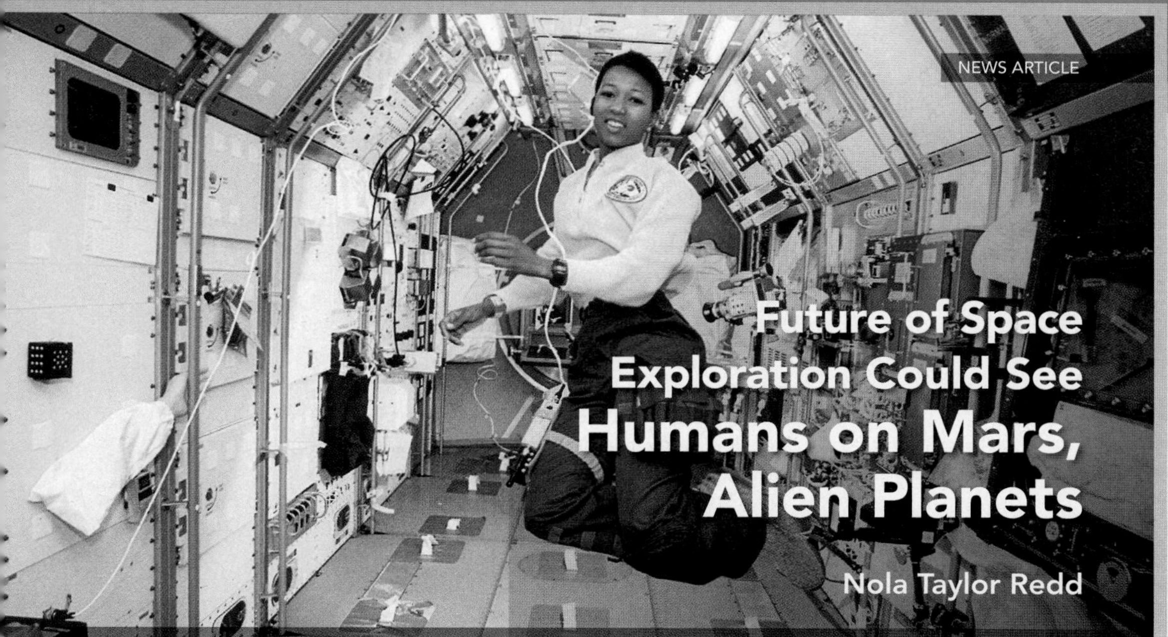

BACKGROUND

In 1969, Neil Armstrong became the first astronaut to walk on Earth's moon. The next big step in space exploration is to put a person on another planet, such as Mars. In this article, former astronaut Mae Jemison and NASA engineer Adam Steltzner discuss the future of space exploration and what is needed to make it possible.

"An inclusive journey"

1 Mars may be one of the closest planets humans want to **colonize**, but it certainly isn't the only one. Mae Jemison described the 100-Year Starship project to an interested audience.

2 Funded by NASA's Ames Research Center and the Defense Advanced Research Projects Agency (DARPA), the 100-Year Starship project aims to develop the tools and technology necessary to build and fly a spaceship to another **planetary** system within the next 100 years. The program isn't necessarily concerned with building the ship itself as much as it seeks to foster innovation and enthusiasm for **interstellar** travel.

3 "The reason we're not on the moon has nothing to do with technology and everything to do with public will and commitment," Jemison said.

4 As a result, the project, which Jemison heads, seeks to increase public enthusiasm for space as well. The 100-Year Starship

NOTES

Mark context clues or indicate another strategy you used that helped you determine meaning.

colonize (KOL uh nyz) *v.*
MEANING:

planetary (PLAN uh tehr ee) *adj.*
MEANING:

interstellar (ihn tuhr STEHL uhr) *adj.*
MEANING:

DIGITAL PERSPECTIVES

Concept Vocabulary

COLONIZE If groups are struggling to define the word *colonize* in paragraph 1, point out that they should look for context clues. Point out that paragraph 2 describes people flying a spaceship to another planetary system, so colonizing must involve visiting another planet. Students can also use their prior knowledge about the related word *colonists* to help them define the word.

Possible response: *Colonize* means "to settle and to establish control over."

PLANETARY If groups are struggling to define the word *planetary* in paragraph 2, have them look for context clues to help them determine its meaning. Suggest that students also call on their knowledge of word parts. For instance, they probably know the base word *planet*.

Possible response: The adjective *planetary* means "having to do with planets."

INTERSTELLAR If groups are struggling to define the word *interstellar* in paragraph 2, encourage them to look for context clues. Students can also use their knowledge of word parts. For instance, they may know the base word *stellar* means "star-like" or "related to stars."

Possible response: *Interstellar* means "among or between stars."

DIGITAL PERSPECTIVES

Enriching the Text Before reading paragraph 1, show students a video clip of Neil Armstrong walking on the moon. Then ask students if they think people living a century before the first moon landing would have thought it was possible for a person to walk on the moon. By extension, what might be possible in the future of space exploration that seems unlikely today? Have students write a paragraph predicting what could happen in space exploration in the next 100 years.

FACILITATING

Media Connection

Project the Media Connection video in class or ask students to open the video in their interactive textbooks.

Discuss It

Possible response: Practical skills like engineering and mechanics would benefit the space program. However, imaginative skills like being innovative and creative would also be beneficial, because you could think of solutions that might not occur to other people.

NOTES

program not only includes engineers and astrophysicists,[1] but also artists and science fiction writers.

5 "It has to be an inclusive journey," she said.

6 Though many people object to funding the space program when there are humanitarian needs that have to be met on Earth, Jemison points out that such exploration often leads to innovation and unexpected technology that make an impact on Earth-based programs.

7 "I believe that pursuing an extraordinary tomorrow will create a better world today," she said.

8 Traveling to another star takes far more time than just developing the necessary technology. Jemison compares the distance to Proxima Centauri, the nearest star, to that between New York City and Los Angeles. If NASA's *Voyager 1* spacecraft, which launched in 1977, was en route, it would have traveled only 1 mile in the past four decades.

9 At that rate, it would take 70,000 years to reach Proxima Centauri.

10 Speaking to the long time frames of space travel, Steltzner said, "I can't really think of a country that's been stable for 1,000 years."

11 Without the development of a method to warp or shrink space-time, or a new propulsion system[2]—both ideas that the 100-Year Starship program is exploring—humanity would need to find a way to overcome some of its instability problems.

12 To get there, Jemison emphasized that everyone must be involved in the process.

13 "The public did not leave space," she said while discussing the reduced enthusiasm. "The public was left out of space." ❧

1. **astrophysicists** scientists who study how objects in space behave.
2. **propulsion system** parts of a rocket that push it through air and space.

MEDIA CONNECTION

Starship

Discuss It What skills and talents would benefit the space program?

Write your response before sharing your ideas.

CROSS-CURRICULAR PERSPECTIVES

Science Review paragraphs 9–13. Have groups research one of the two ways Jemison suggests scientists could enable a spaceship to reach another planet in the next 100 years—warping or shrinking space-time, or developing a new propulsion system. Each group should choose one of these topics, conduct research, and report their findings to the class.

Comprehension Check

Complete the following items after you finish your first read. Review and clarify details with your group.

1. What is the goal of the 100-Year Starship project?

2. What does Jemison mean when she says that the project must be inclusive?

3. What is one of the challenges faced by the project?

4. **Notebook** Confirm your understanding of the news article by writing a brief summary of its main points.

RESEARCH

Research to Clarify Choose at least one unfamiliar scientific detail in the text, such as Proxima Centauri or possible methods to warp space-time. Briefly research that detail. In what way does this information deepen your understanding of the news article? Share your findings with your group.

DIGITAL PERSPECTIVES

Comprehension Check

Possible responses:

1. The goal of the project is to develop tools and technology to build and fly a spaceship to another planetary system in the next 100 years.
2. Jemison means that it must include not only scientists but also artists and writers.
3. A big challenge is the incredible distance involved.

Summaries will vary but should include information about Mae Jemison, her role with the 100-Year Starship project, and a description of the project.

Research

Research to Clarify If groups struggle to find a research topic, suggest one of the following: Ames Research Center, DARPA, interstellar travel, or *Voyager 1*.

PERSONALIZE FOR LEARNING

Challenge

Social Studies In paragraph 10, Jemison notes: "I can't really think of a country that's been stable for 1,000 years." In their small groups, have students discuss the implications of this statement. What do they think Jemison means? How is the inability of nations to remain stable related to space exploration? How can humanity overcome its "instability problems"? Challenge each group to explain Jemison's statement, tell how it relates to space exploration, and suggest at least one possible solution. Groups should present the results of their discussions to the class.

Jump Start

CLOSE READ Ask students to consider the following prompt: Imagine you are asked to go on a mission to Mars or another far-away planet, knowing that you would probably never again return to Earth. You would be undertaking a historic journey and seeing things that nobody has ever seen before. Would you do it? Have students discuss these questions in their groups.

Close Read the Text

If needed, model close reading by using the Annotation Highlights in the Interactive Teacher's Edition.

Remind students to use Accountable Talk in their discussions and to support one another as they complete the close read.

Analyze the Text

Possible responses:

1. Jemison hopes to revive public interest in, and commitment to, space exploration. Without public support, funding will not be available for space travel. She also hopes the project will lead to inventions that can help people today. She wants to involve all kinds of people in the project.
2. Students should support their ideas with evidence from the text.
3. Responses will vary, but students should present a reasoned response to the question that is well supported with text evidence.

Concept Vocabulary

Why These Words? Possible response: The words all relate to space exploration and travel.

Word Network

Possible words: *astrophysicist, warp, space-time*

Word Study

For more support, see **Concept Vocabulary and Word Study.**

Possible responses: *customary*—belonging to a custom
honorary—related to honor
revolutionary—related to a revolution

Dictionary meanings:

customary—according to usual tradition(s) given as a symbol, *honorary*—given as a symbol, without the usual requirements, *revolutionary*—engaged in or promoting change

MAKING MEANING

FUTURE OF SPACE EXPLORATION COULD SEE HUMANS ON MARS, ALIEN PLANETS

Close Read the Text

With your group, revisit sections of the text you marked during your first read. **Annotate** what you notice. What **questions** do you have? What can you **conclude**?

TIP

GROUP DISCUSSION
Come to group discussions prepared to contribute. Be sure you have read and understood the selection in advance, verifying the meanings of any unfamiliar words.

Analyze the Text

CITE TEXTUAL EVIDENCE to support your answers.

1. **Review and Clarify** With your group, review the article. Discuss Jemison's goals. Why do you think she believes it is important for the public to be enthusiastic about space travel?
2. **Present and Discuss** Now, work with your group to share passages from the article that you found especially important. Take turns presenting your passages. Discuss what you noticed in the text, the questions you asked, and the conclusions you reached.
3. **Essential Question:** ***Should we make a home in space?*** What has this selection taught you about the possibility of making a home in space? Discuss with your group.

LANGUAGE DEVELOPMENT

Concept Vocabulary

colonize	planetary	interstellar

Why These Words? The concept vocabulary words from the text are related. With your group, determine what the words have in common. Write your ideas and add another word that fits the category.

WORD NETWORK
Add interesting words related to space exploration from the text to your Word Network.

Practice

Use the concept vocabulary words in a group discussion of this question: *What would it take to convince people to participate in a space mission to another planet?*

STANDARDS

Speaking and Listening
Engage effectively in a range of collaborative discussions with diverse partners on *grade 7 topics, texts, and issues,* building on others' ideas and expressing their own clearly.

Language
Determine or clarify the meaning of unknown and multiple-meaning words and phrases based on *grade 7 reading and content*, choosing flexibly from a range of strategies.
b. Use common, grade-appropriate Greek or Latin affixes and roots as clues to the meaning of a word.
d. Verify the preliminary determination of the meaning of a word or phrase.

Word Study

Notebook **Latin Suffix**: ***-ary*** According to the article, the 100-Year Starship project wants to fly a spaceship to another planetary system. The word *planetary* ends with the Latin suffix *-ary*, meaning "belonging to" or "relating to." Using your knowledge of the suffix *-ary*, determine the meanings of the following words: *customary, honorary, revolutionary*. Then, use a dictionary to find the precise meaning of each word.

FORMATIVE ASSESSMENT

Analyze the Text

If students struggle to close read the text, **then** provide the **Future of Space Exploration: Text Questions** available online in the Interactive Teacher's Edition or Unit Resources. Answers and DOK levels are also available.

Concept Vocabulary

If students cannot see the connection between the words, **then** have them use each word in a sentence and consider what is similar about the sentences.

Word Study

If students cannot think of another word that contains the suffix *-ary*, **then** suggest that they think about levels of schools (*elementary, primary, secondary*). For Reteach and Practice, see **Word Study: Latin Suffix *-ary* (RP).**

Analyze Craft and Structure

Development of Ideas: Text Structure Authors not only consider what they want to write about, but also the best way to present that information. In "Future of Space Exploration Could See Humans on Mars, Alien Planets," Nola Taylor Redd has organized details from an interview she conducted with Mae Jemison and Adam Steltzner into a cohesive text.

To develop the ideas in her article Redd:

- Sets the context and background for the interview
- Arranges the details from the interview into a logical order
- Uses transitions to link ideas
- Concludes with a strong quotation from an interview subject

STANDARDS

Reading Informational Text
Analyze the structure an author uses to organize a text, including how the major section contribute to the whole and to the development of the ideas.

Practice

CITE TEXTUAL EVIDENCE to support your answers.

1. Work with your group to identify various types of details used in the article. Reread sections of the text as necessary, and record your findings in this chart.

Topic: ______________________________

	TEXT EXAMPLE(S)	NOTES
Context and Background		
Use of Quotations		
Use of Paraphrases From Interview		
Use of Transitions to Link Ideas		
Concluding Idea		

2. When you have completed the chart, discuss with your group the overarching central idea that Redd conveys. Provide support for your responses.
3. Then, working alone, rate the effectiveness of the overall structure of the article using this scale. A "1" is least effective; a "5" is most effective. Then, compare your ratings with the group and discuss.

1	2	3	4	5

DIGITAL PERSPECTIVES

Analyze Craft and Stucture

Text Structure Remind students that there are different structures for writing. Nola Taylor Redd uses a problem-solution structure to persuade her audience. Ask students to mention other examples they know of that demonstrate the use of expert sources to strengthen authors' writing. For more support, see **Analyze Craft and Structure: Text Structure.**

Practice

Students' responses will vary but should be clearly supported with text examples.

FORMATIVE ASSESSMENT

Analyze Craft and Structure

If students are unable to determine the author's purpose, **then** have them skim the selection and summarize each paragraph. For Reteach and Practice, see **Analyze Craft and Structure: Text Structure (RP).**

WriteNow Inform and Explain

Author's Purpose Have students consider the purpose of their speech during any one hour of their day. It could be the hour after they wake, an hour at school, or an hour after school. Suggest that they use this time to think about how they have structured their speech to achieve their purpose. Are they entertaining those around them, informing others, or trying to persuade? Have students write a paragraph analyzing their purpose.

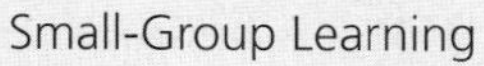

FACILITATING

Conventions

The Principal Parts of Verbs Point out to students that the principal parts of verbs are used to form different verb tenses. **Verb tenses** show the time of the action or state of being. You might also want to remind students that a regular verb is one that forms its past and past participle by adding *-ed* or *-d* to the present form. For instance, *jump, play,* and *work* are all regular verbs whose past and past participles are formed by adding *-ed*: *jumped, played, worked*.

For more support, see **Conventions: Principal Parts of Verbs.**

Read It

Possible responses:

1. *is,* present tense
2. *have imagined,* past participle
3. *planned,* past
4. *are working,* present participle

Write It

Possible responses:

Paragraphs will vary, but make sure that students use each of the principal parts of verbs.

FORMATIVE ASSESSMENT

Conventions

If students are unable to identify the principles parts of verbs, **then** provide additional examples of each. For Reteach and Practice, see **Conventions: Principal Parts of Verbs (RP).**

LANGUAGE DEVELOPMENT

FUTURE OF SPACE EXPLORATION COULD SEE HUMANS ON MARS, ALIEN PLANETS

Conventions

The Principal Parts of Verbs A verb has four **principal parts: present, present participle, past,** and **past participle.**

The chart shows the four principal parts of the regular verb *walk*. It also includes the principal parts of some commonly misused irregular verbs. Notice that present and past participles are used with helping verbs such as *has, have, had, am, is, are,* and *were*. A verb together with its helping verb or verbs is called a **verb phrase.**

PRESENT	PRESENT PARTICIPLE	PAST	PAST PARTICIPLE
walk	(is) walking	walked	(has) walked
am, is, are	(is) being	was, were	(has) been
go	(is) going	went	(has) gone
begin	(is) beginning	began	(has) begun

Read It

Identify the verb or verb phrase in each sentence. Label each as either *present, present participle, past,* or *past participle.*

1. Jemison is an astronaut.
2. People have imagined trips to other planets.
3. Hillary planned the construction of a spaceship.
4. Scientists are working constantly on the problem.

Write It

Notebook Should we spend money to send a spaceship to another planetary system, or should we use that money to solve problems closer to home? Write a paragraph in which you persuade readers either to fund or not to fund the 100-Year Starship project. Include an example of each of the four principal parts of verbs in your paragraph.

STANDARDS

Language
Demonstrate command of the conventions of standard English grammar and usage when writing or speaking.

PERSONALIZE FOR LEARNING

English Language Support

Using Participles Ask student pairs to have a discussion addressing the point raised in the selection about funding the space program when there are needs to be met on Earth. Encourage students to use and identify participles in their discussion. **EMERGING**

Ask students to use and identify present participles in a paragraph addressing the point raised in the selection about funding the space program when there are needs to be met on Earth. **EXPANDING**

Ask students to use and identify present participles in a paragraph addressing the point raised in the selection about funding the space program when there are needs to be met on Earth. Encourage students to use present participles as a part of a verb, as adjectives, and as nouns. **BRIDGING**

An expanded **English Language Support Lesson** on Present Participles is available in the Interactive Teacher's Edition.

EFFECTIVE EXPRESSION

Speaking and Listening

Assignment

Create a **multimedia presentation** in which you incorporate text and images to explain a topic. Choose from the following topics:

- ☐ An **illustrated biography** about Mae Jemison that includes the highlights of her career and her interest in the 100-Year Starship project
- ☐ An **informational brochure** in which you explain the requirements necessary for achieving the goals of the 100-Year Starship project, including various spaceship designs that would allow people to "warp" time in space

Project Plan Assign a role for each member of your group. Roles can include text researcher, multimedia researcher, note taker, and presenter.

Here are some questions to consider as you plan your presentation.

- What reliable print and digital sources will I use in addition to the selection?
- What information will be better conveyed with text?
- What information will be better conveyed with multimedia?
- What materials and equipment will the group need for the presentation?

Once you have completed your research and considered these questions, work collaboratively to make a plan, or storyboard, for your visual presentation.

Credit Sources It is important to properly credit the research sources you used for your presentation. Ask your teacher what method of citation you should use, and be sure to include accurate citations for all of your sources to avoid **plagiarism,** or presenting someone else's ideas as if they were your own. When you deliver your presentation, credit sources by using phrases such as "According to . . ." or "In the article by. . . ."

Rehearse and Present Decide on the presentation roles for your group, and set aside time to rehearse.

- Make sure that any equipment is working properly before you begin your presentation.
- Speak clearly and with enough volume so that everyone in the audience can hear.
- Make sure audience members can see images clearly.

EVIDENCE LOG

Before moving on to a new selection, go to your log and record what you learned from "Future of Space Exploration Could See Humans on Mars, Alien Planets."

STANDARDS

Writing

- Conduct short research projects to answer a question, drawing on several sources and generating additional related, focused questions for further research and investigation.
- Gather relevant information from multiple print and digital sources, using search terms effectively; assess the credibility and accuracy of each source; and quote or paraphrase the data and conclusions of others while avoiding plagiarism and following a standard format for citation.

Speaking and Listening

Include multimedia components and visual displays in presentations to clarify claims and findings and emphasize salient points.

PERSONALIZE FOR LEARNING

Strategic Support

Research If students are doing their research on the Internet, discuss the importance of search terms. What is the specific information they need to complete the assignment? For instance, searching "spaceship" may yield too many results. Have students try adding another term to their search, such as "spaceship design."

DIGITAL PERSPECTIVES

Speaking and Listening

Discuss with students the criteria for an effective informational visual presentation. Criteria may include:

- a clear main idea or focus
- accurate, specific information about the topic
- informative, engaging visuals, such as charts, graphs, diagrams, photographs, and video directly related to the topic
- effective speaking techniques, such as eye contact, pauses for emphasis, and adequate volume

Project Plan Encourage groups to discuss their sources and how they determined the reliability of each source. Remind groups to consult the schedule for Small-Group Activities as they create their project plans. You may wish to check that each group has made assignments and that the assignments more or less match students' skills and interests. For more support, see **Speaking and Listening: Multimedia Presentation**.

Present Encourage students to practice their presentations so they can feel comfortable.

Evidence Log Support students in completing the Evidence Log. This paced activity will help prepare them for the Performance-Based Assessment at the end of the unit.

FORMATIVE ASSESSMENT

Speaking and Listening: Visual Presentation

If groups have difficulty finding information and visual elements for their reports, **then** make suggestions about websites and other places they can search. For Reteach and Practice, see **Speaking and Listening: Multimedia Presentation (RP)**.

Selection Test

Administer the "Future of Space Exploration Could See Humans on Mars, Alien Planets" Selection Test, which is available in both print and digital formats online in Assessments.

The Last Dog

AUDIO SUMMARIES
Audio summaries of "The Last Dog" are available in both English and Spanish in the Interactive Teacher's Edition or Unit Resources. Assigning these summaries prior to reading the selection may help students build additional background knowledge and set a context for their first read.

Summary

In the selection "The Last Dog," by Katherine Paterson, a boy lives in what seems to be the last city on Earth. Everyone lives in an airtight dome, with only occasional exploration out; they believe that the rest of the world is lifeless and poisoned. But on a research trip out, the protagonist—Brock—finds a living puppy. He saves the dog, feeds it, and quickly becomes deeply attached to it. And then he begins to realize the full implications of what he found. Unlike what he's been told, dogs aren't extinct. What if everything else he's been told about the world is wrong, too?

Insight

This story emphasizes the importance of empathy and connection with other living things. It also puts value on exploration and finding things out for oneself.

ESSENTIAL QUESTION:
Should we make a home in space?

Connection to Essential Question

While this story takes place on Earth, we can see it as a reflection on space travel from two different directions. The first is that life in space might be like the cramped, depersonalized life in the dome. The second is to see the dome as a metaphor for Earth itself—a small place that we can expand from out into a much wider universe.

SMALL-GROUP LEARNING PERFORMANCE TASK
Should space exploration be a priority for our country?

UNIT PERFORMANCE-BASED ASSESSMENT
Should we spend valuable resources on space exploration?

Connection to Performance Tasks

Small-Group Learning Performance Task In this story, the main character takes the risk of exploring outside the safety of his known world. Knowing there are risks in space exploration, should that be a priority for our country?

Unit Performance-Based Assessment By exploring outside the dome, Brock finds something that points to great opportunities. Could exploring outside Earth do that for us?

DIGITAL PERSPECTIVES

 Audio  Video  Document  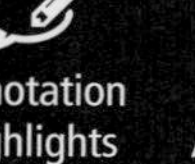 Annotation Highlights 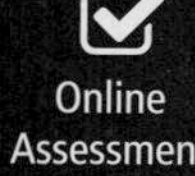 Online Assessment

LESSON RESOURCES

	Making Meaning	Language Development	Effective Expression
Lesson	**First Read** **Close Read** **Analyze the Text** **Analyze Craft and Structure**	**Concept Vocabulary** **Word Study** **Conventions**	**Writing to Sources**
Instructional Standards	**RL.7.10** By the end of the year, read and comprehend literature . . . **L.7.4** Determine or clarify the meaning of unknown and multiple-meaning words and phrases . . . **L.7.4.a** Use context as a clue to the meaning of a word or phrase. **L.7.5.a** Interpret figures of speech in context. **RL.7.3** Analyze how particular elements of a story or drama interact.	**L.7.4** Determine or clarify the meaning of unknown and multiple-meaning words and phrases . . . **L.7.4.b** Use common, grade-appropriate Greek or Latin affixes and roots . . . **L.7.1** Demonstrate command of the conventions of standard English . . . **L.7.3** Use knowledge of language and its conventions . . . **L.7.3.a** Choose language that expresses ideas precisely . . .	**W.7.3** Write narratives . . . **W.7.3.b** Use narrative techniques . . . **W.7.3.e** Provide a conclusion. . . **W.7.10** Write routinely over extended time frames . . .
STUDENT RESOURCES			
Available online in the Interactive Student Edition or Unit Resources	Selection Audio First-Read Guide: Fiction Close-Read Guide: Fiction	Word Network	Evidence Log
TEACHER RESOURCES			
Selection Resources Available online in the Interactive Teacher's Edition or Unit Resources	Audio Summaries: English and Spanish Annotation Highlights Accessible Leveled Text Spanish Translation Text Questions First Read Extension Questions Analyze Craft and Structure: Conflict and Resolution	Concept Vocabulary and Word Study Conventions: Simple and Compound Subjects and Predicates	Writing to Sources: Revised Ending
Reteach/Practice (RP) Available online in the Interactive Teacher's Edition or Unit Resources	Analyze Craft and Structure: Conflict and Resolution (RP)	Word Study: Latin Suffix *-tion* (RP) Conventions: Simple and Compound Subjects andPredicates (RP)	Writing to Sources: Revised Ending (RP)
Assessment Available online in Assessments	Selection Test: English Selection Test: Spanish Extension Selection Test		
My Resources	A Unit 2 Answer Key is available online and in the Interactive Teacher's Edition.		

Reading Support

Text Complexity Rubric: The Last Dog	
Quantitative Measures	
Lexile: 820 **Text Length:** 4,971 words	
Qualitative Measures	
Knowledge Demands 1—2—3—**4**—5	Selection explores multiple themes of varying complexity, including dangers of modern society becoming impersonal, companionship and relationships, self-knowledge and emotions, and courage.
Structure 1—2—**3**—4—5	Story is mostly told chronologically, but with flashbacks to previous events, including dialogue that reader needs to distinguish between current dialogue and past dialogue.
Language Conventionality and Clarity 1—2—**3**—4—5	Vocabulary and syntax are on-level.
Levels of Meaning/Purpose 1—2—3—**4**—5	Reader must infer multiple levels of meaning, including how current environmental changes could impact life in the future.

DECIDE AND PLAN

English Language Support

Provide English Learners with support for structure and language as they read the selection.

Structure Have students look at the dialogue in the beginning of the story and then at paragraphs 20–23. Point out that the dialogue in these later paragraphs is a flashback. A clue that this is not in the present is the use of the word *had: The podmaster had looked;... the representative had asked.* In paragraph 24 the story continues in the present.

Language Point out some of the language that is meant to show that the story takes place in the future and shows how people relate to one another. For example, at the customs gate, Brock is called by name and number.

Strategic Support

Provide students with strategic support to ensure that they can successfully read the text.

Knowledge Demands Guide students to understand some of the themes in the story. (See Knowledge Demands in the rubric above.) Suggest a word such as *courage* and ask volunteers to say how it is shown in the story. Write their ideas for each theme. Then have them reread the story.

Meaning After reading, have volunteers take turns reading several lines aloud. Have students help you list details that show life in the future. For example, paragraphs 2 and 10 tell us people live inside a dome. Prompt students to think about meanings; for example, *How do people in the story know their emotions? (by checking a scanner).*

Challenge

Provide students who need to be challenged with ideas for how they can go beyond a simple interpretation of the text.

Text Analysis Write a list of some themes of the story, asking students to contribute their ideas. (See Knowledge Demands in the rubric above.) Have students work in pairs. Ask them to choose two themes from the list and to write a paragraph about each, explaining how that theme is expressed in the story. Have pairs share their paragraphs with the class.

Written Response Ask students to write a continuation of the story, describing what happens to Brock and the puppy on the first day after leaving the dome. Have them include details about what happens and what Brock says to the puppy at different moments.

TEACH

Read and Respond

Have the groups read the selection and complete the Making Meaning, Language Development, and Effective Expression activities.

Standards Support Through Teaching and Learning Cycle

IDENTIFY NEEDS

Analyze results of the Beginning-of-Year Assessment, focusing on the items relating to Unit 2. Also take into consideration student performance to this point and your observations of where particular students struggle.

DECIDE AND PLAN

- If students have performed poorly on items matching these standards, then provide selection scaffolds before assigning them the on-level lesson provided in the Student Edition.
- If students have done well on the Beginning-of-Year Assessment, then challenge them to keep progressing and learning by giving them opportunities to practice the skills in depth.
- Use the Selection Resources listed on the Planning pages for "The Last Dog" to help students continually improve their ability to master the standards.

Instructional Standards: The Last Dog

	Catching Up	This Year	Looking Forward
Reading	You may wish to administer the **Analyze Craft and Structure: Conflict and Resolution (RP)** worksheet to help students understand how authors use elements of a story or drama to create a conflict and then set events in motion toward resolution.	**RL.3** Analyze how particular elements of a story or drama interact.	Ask students to reframe the story with a different conflict and resolution and then analyze the steps they had to take to make the changes.
Writing	You may wish to administer the **Writing to Sources: Revised Ending (RP)** worksheet to help students understand that there is more than one way for a narrative to conclude.	**W.3.e** Provide a conclusion that follows from and reflects on the narrated experiences or events.	Work with students to discuss how their new ending follows from and reflects the narrated events in the story.
Language	You may wish to administer the **Conventions: Simple and Compound Subjects and Predicates (RP)** worksheet to help students understand how to form compound subjects and verbs. You may wish to administer the **Word Study: Latin Suffix *-tion* (RP)** worksheet to help students understand that the suffix *–tion* turns a verb into a noun.	**L.1** Demonstrate command of the conventions of standard English grammar and usage when writing or speaking. **L.4** Determine or clarify the meaning of unknown and multiple-meaning words and phrases based on *grade 7 reading and content,* choosing flexibly from a range of strategies.	Challenge students to use increasingly complex subjects and predicates in their writing. Encourage students to use a variety of words that have Latin suffixes in their speaking and writing.

ANALYZE AND REVISE

- Analyze student work for evidence of student learning.
- Identify whether students have met the expectations in the standards.
- Identify implications for future instruction.

TEACH

Implement the planned lesson, and gather evidence of student learning.

FACILITATING

Jump Start

FIRST READ Engage students in a discussion about the possibility of environmental degradation so profound that humans would need to live on another planet. Ask students to consider these questions: *If humans were forced to leave Earth and colonize another planet, what would be important to take with us? Why?* Have students identify specific reasons for their opinions.

The Last Dog

What if it were too dangerous to go outside? What if all animals were extinct? What if life as we know it were over? Modeling questions such as these will help students connect to "The Last Dog" and to the Small-Group Performance Task assignment. Selection audio and print capability for the selection are available in the Interactive Teacher's Edition.

Concept Vocabulary

Ask groups to look closely at the examples of context clues and discuss how these types of clues can clarify meaning. Encourage groups to think of one other type of context clue they might encounter in a text. Possibilities include examples, synonyms, antonyms, comparisons, and definitions.

FIRST READ

As they read, students should perform the steps of the first read:

NOTICE: You may want to encourage students to notice details that describe the setting of the story.

ANNOTATE: Remind students to mark passages that reveal what life is like inside the dome and what motivates Brock.

CONNECT: Encourage students to consider any "domes" they might have constructed for themselves. Ask: Have you ever ventured outside your comfort zone and been pleasantly surprised?

RESPOND: Students will answer questions and write a summary to demonstrate understanding.

Point out to students that while they will always complete the Respond step at the end of the first read, the other steps will probably happen somewhat concurrently. You may wish to print copies of the **First-Read Guide: Fiction** for students to use.

MAKING MEANING

About the Author

The daughter of two American missionaries, **Katherine Paterson** (b. 1932) was born in China and lived there during her early childhood years. Paterson became a renowned writer of children's novels. She has twice won the Newbery Medal and National Book Award.

The Last Dog

Concept Vocabulary

As you perform your first read of "The Last Dog," you will encounter these words.

threatening	extinct	mutation

Context Clues To find the meaning of unfamiliar words, look for clues in the context, which is made up of the words, punctuation, and images that surround the unknown word.

Example: The **inquisitive** dog searched the unknown surroundings.

Context Clue: The dog is described as *inquisitive* and is searching unknown areas.

Possible Meaning: *Inquisitive* means "curious."

Example: The **deviant** robot was taken out of service for its strange behavior.

Context Clue: A robot described as *deviant* is taken out of service because of its strange behavior.

Possible Meaning: *Deviant* means "considered strange by others."

Apply your knowledge of context clues and other vocabulary strategies to determine the meanings of unfamiliar words you encounter during your first read of "The Last Dog."

First Read FICTION

Apply these strategies as you conduct your first read. You will have an opportunity to complete a close read after your first read.

NOTICE *whom* the story is about, *what* happens, *where* and *when* it happens, and *why* those involved react as they do.

ANNOTATE by marking vocabulary and key passages you want to revisit.

CONNECT ideas within the selection to what you already know and what you have already read.

RESPOND by completing the Comprehension Check and by writing a brief summary of the selection.

First Read

STANDARDS

Reading Literature
By the end of the year, read and comprehend literature, including stories, dramas, and poems, in the grades 6–8 text complexity band proficiently, with scaffolding as needed at the high end of the range.

Language
Determine or clarify the meaning of unknown and multiple-meaning words and phrases based on *grade 7 reading and content*, choosing flexibly from a range of strategies.
a. Use context as a clue to the meaning of a word or phrase.

PERSONALIZE FOR LEARNING

Strategic Support
First Read If group members struggle to comprehend the text during the first read, have another group member conduct a think-aloud to explain the thought process as he or she works through the NOTICE, ANNOTATE, CONNECT, and RESPOND steps. For instance, the students might note that when they read the first paragraph, they read that the setting is futuristic and that people are assigned numbers rather than last names.

The Last Dog

Katherine Paterson

DIGITAL PERSPECTIVES

CLOSER LOOK

Analyze Setting

Circulate among groups as students conduct their close read. Suggest that groups read paragraphs 1–7. Encourage them to talk about the annotations that they mark. If needed, provide the following support.

ANNOTATE: Have students mark details in these paragraphs that provide clues about the setting, or have students participate while you highlight them.

QUESTION: Guide students to consider what these details might tell them. Ask what a reader can infer from these details about life inside the sealed dome, and accept student responses.

Possible responses: It is regimented, futuristic, and sterile.

CONCLUDE: Help students formulate conclusions about the importance of these details in the text. Ask students why the author might have included these details.

Possible responses: Details suggest that life inside the dome is directed or controlled by computers and is similar to being inside a spaceship, where astronauts eat freeze-dried food and must put on a space suit to leave the ship. Readers might infer that the story is set in the distant future.

Remind students that writers often use specific details to establish the **setting,** or time and place, of a story.

BACKGROUND

In this science fiction story, the author imagines a future in which people live in a sealed dome and believe that the outside world is unsafe and in ruins. The story's main character discovers something that everyone thinks can't exist—and it changes everything.

1 Brock approached the customs gate. Although he did not reach for the scanner, a feeling it might have labeled "excitement" made him tremble. His fingers shook as he punched in his number on the inquiry board. "This is highly irregular, Brock 095670038," the disembodied voice said. "What is your reason for external travel?"

2 Brock took a deep breath. "Scientific research," he replied. He didn't need to be told that his behavior was "irregular." He'd never heard of anyone doing research outside the dome—actual rather than virtual research. "I—I've been cleared by my podmaster and the Research Team. . . ."

3 "Estimated time of return?" So, he wasn't to be questioned further.

4 "Uh, 1800 hours."

5 "Are you wearing the prescribed dry suit with helmet and gloves?"

6 "Affirmative."

7 "You should be equipped with seven hundred fifty milliliters of liquid and food tablets for one day travel."

8 "Affirmative." Brock patted the sides of the dry suit to be sure.

9 "Remember to drink sparingly. Water supply is limited." Brock nodded. He tried to lick his parched lips, but his whole mouth felt dry. "Is that understood?"

NOTES

FACILITATING SMALL-GROUP CLOSE READING

CLOSE READ: Short Story As groups perform the close read of this story, circulate and offer support as needed.

- Remind groups that when they read a narrative, they should be sure to identify the main characters and the setting.
- If a group is confused about the setting, have them think about science fiction movies they have seen.
- Challenge groups to predict what the conflict in the story will be.

FACILITATING

Concept Vocabulary

THREATENING If groups are struggling to define the word *threatening* in paragraph 14, point out that they should consider what type of environment would discourage people from entering it—even with protective equipment. Ask: What do context clues in the sentence tell you about the meaning of *threatening*. Tell students to consider the word *threat*. Ask: What is a threat?

Possible response: *Threatening* means "having a frightening quality."

Additional **English Language Support** is available in the Interactive Teacher's Edition.

NOTES

10 "Affirmative." Was he hoping customs would stop him? If he was, they didn't seem to be helping him. Well, this was what he wanted, wasn't it? To go outside the dome.

11 "Turn on the universal locator, Brock 095670038, and proceed to gate."

12 Why weren't they questioning him further? Were they eager for him to go? Ever since he'd said out loud in group speak that he wanted to go outside the dome, people had treated him strangely—that session with the podmaster and then the interview with the representative from Research. Did they think he was a deviant?[1] Deviants sometimes disappeared. The word was passed around that they had "gone outside," but no one really knew. No deviant had ever returned.

13 The gate slid open. Before he was quite ready for it, Brock found himself outside the protection of the dome. He blinked. The sun—at least it was what was called "the sun" in virtual lessons—was too bright for his eyes even inside the tinted helmet. He took a deep breath, one last backward look at the dome, which, with the alien sun gleaming on it, was even harder to look at than the distant star, and started across an expanse of brown soil [was it?] to what he recognized from holograms as a line of purplish mountains in the distance.

14 It was, he pulled the scanner from his outside pouch and checked it, "hot." Oh, that was what he was feeling. Hot. He remembered "hot" from a virtual lesson he'd had once on deserts. He wanted to take off the dry suit, but he had been told since he could remember that naked skin would suffer irreparable burning outside the protection of the dome. He adjusted the control as he walked so that the unfamiliar perspiration would evaporate. He fumbled a bit before he found the temperature adjustment function. He put it on twenty degrees centigrade and immediately felt more comfortable. No one he really knew had ever left the dome (stories of deviants exiting the dome being hard to verify), but there was all this equipment in case someone decided to venture out. He tried to ask the clerk who outfitted him, but the woman was evasive. The equipment was old, she said. People used to go out, but the outside environment was **threatening**, so hardly anyone (she looked at him carefully now), hardly anyone ever used it now.

Mark context clues or indicate another strategy you used that helped you determine meaning.

threatening (THREHT uhn ihng) *adj.*

MEANING:

15 Was Brock, then, the only normal person still curious about the outside? Or had all those who had dared to venture out perished, discouraging further forays? Perhaps he *was* a deviant for wanting to see the mountains for himself. When he'd mentioned it to others, they had laughed, but there was a hollow sound to the laughter.

1. **deviant** (DEE vee uhnt) *n.* strange, irregular person.

DIGITAL PERSPECTIVES

Enriching the Text Review paragraph 13 and discuss the challenges of being "outside the dome." Show students images of spacesuits. Include images of real spacesuits worn by astronauts and cosmonauts and also images of spacesuits from popular culture. Then have students make labeled diagrams of the spacesuit described in the story. Students can use details in the story as well as their imaginations and the images of spacesuits they have seen to create their drawings. Display the drawings in the classroom.

16 If he never returned, he'd have no one to blame but himself. He knew that. While his podfellows played virtual games, he'd wandered into a subsection of the historical virtuals called "ancient fictions." Things happened in these fictions more—well, more densely than they did in the virtuals. The people he met there—it was hard to describe—but somehow they were more *actual* than dome dwellers. They had strange names like Huck Finn and M. C. Higgins the Great. They were even a little scary. It was their insides. Their insides were very loud. But even though the people in the ancient fictions frightened him a bit, he couldn't get enough of them. When no one was paying attention, he went back again and again to visit them. They had made him wonder about that other world—that world outside the dome.

17 Perhaps, once he had realized the danger the ancient fictions posed, he should have left them alone, but he couldn't help himself. They had made him feel hollow, hungry for something no food pellet or even virtual experience could satisfy. And now he was in that world they spoke of and the mountains of it were in plain view.

18 He headed for the purple curves. Within a short distance from the dome, the land was clear and barren, but after he had been walking for an hour or so he began to pass rusting hulks and occasional ruins of what might have been the dwellings of ancient peoples that no one in later years had cleared away for recycling or vaporization.

19 He checked the emotional scanner for an unfamiliar sensation. "Loneliness," it registered. He rather liked having names for these new sensations. It made him feel a bit "proud," was it? The scanner was rather interesting. He wondered when people had stopped using them. He hadn't known they existed until, in that pod meeting, he had voiced his desire to go outside.

20 The podmaster had looked at him with a raised eyebrow and a sniff. "Next thing you'll be asking for a scanner," he said.

21 "What's a scanner?" Brock asked.

22 The podmaster requisitioned one from storage, but at the same time, he must have alerted Research, because it was the representative from Research who had brought him the scanner and questioned him about his expressed desired for an Actual Adventure—a journey outside the dome.

23 "What has prompted this, uh—unusual ambition?" the representative had asked, his eyes not on Brock but on the scanner in his hand. Brock had hesitated, distracted by the man's fidgeting with the strange instrument. "I—I'm interested in scientific research," Brock said at last.

24 So here he was out of the pod, alone for the first time in his life. Perhaps, though, he should have asked one of his podfellows to

NOTES

DIGITAL PERSPECTIVES

CLOSER LOOK

Analyze Conflict

Circulate among groups as students conduct their close read. Suggest that groups read paragraphs 16–19. Encourage them to talk about the annotations that they mark. If needed, provide the following support.

ANNOTATE: Have students mark details in these paragraphs that describe the internal conflict—the struggle going on within Brock. Then have students mark details that describe the external conflict—the struggle between Brock and outside forces. Alternatively, you could have students participate while you highlight them.

QUESTION: Guide students to consider what these details tell them about the conflicts developing in this story. Ask what a reader can infer from these details about Brock's struggles with himself and with outside forces. What things are at war within him? What outside forces must he confront? Accept student responses.

Possible responses: Details suggest that Brock's internal conflict is that he struggles with feeling different from others and the loneliness that results. Details suggest that the external conflict involves his adventure in the outside world and whether he will survive.

CONCLUDE: Help students formulate conclusions about the internal and external conflicts.

Possible responses: In "The Last Dog," both the internal and the external conflict are related to Brock's desire for adventure. The internal conflict causes Brock to leave the dome, which initiates the external conflict that is beginning to unfold.

Remind students that the **conflict** is the story's problem. Conflicts drive the plot action and are usually resolved by the end of the story.

PERSONALIZE FOR LEARNING

English Language Support

Coined Terms Review paragraph 22 and explain to students that the author of this story has coined, or made up, many terms that might be confusing for English learners. For instance, *ancient fictions* (paragraph 16), *podmaster* (paragraph 22), and *Actual Adventure* (paragraph 22) are all terms coined by the author in this story. Have students mark these unfamiliar terms and then assign a peer partner to assist in deciphering them. Partners can work together to use context clues to figure out the meanings of coined words and phrases. You might ask students to create dictionaries of such terms for future students to use. **ALL LEVELS**

FACILITATING

Concept Vocabulary

EXTINCT If groups are struggling to define the word *extinct* in paragraph 26, point out that context clues in sentences at the beginning of paragraph 26 show that Brock is surprised to see trees, which suggests that he does not expect to see them. Then, point out that context clues in the sentence indicate that trees have been considered "extinct" for hundreds of years. Tell students to combine what they know about plants with this information and make an educated guess about the meaning of *extinct*.

Possible response: *Extinct* means "no longer in existence."

NOTES

Mark context clues or indicate another strategy you used that helped you determine meaning.

extinct (ehk STIHNGKT) *adj.*

MEANING:

come along. Or even the pod robopet. But the other fellows all laughed when he spoke of going outside, their eyes darting back and forth. Nothing on the outside, they said, could equal the newest Virtual Adventure. He suddenly realized that ever since he started interfacing with the ancient fictions, his fellows had given him that look. They did think he was odd—not quite the same as a regular podfellow. Brock didn't really vibe with the pod robopet. It was one of the more modern ones, and when they'd programmed its artificial intelligence they'd somehow made it too smart. The robopet in the children's pod last year was older, stupider, and more "fun" to have around.

25 He'd badly underestimated the distance to the mountains. The time was well past noon, and he had at least three kilometers to go. Should he signal late return or turn about now? He didn't have much more than one day's scant supply of water and food tablets. But he was closer to the hills than to the dome. He felt a thrill ["excitement"] and pressed on.

26 There were actual trees growing on the first hill. Not the great giants of virtual history lessons, more scrubby and bent. But they were trees, he was sure of it. The podmaster had said that trees had been **extinct** for hundreds of years. Brock reached up and pulled off a leaf. It was green and had veins. In some ways it looked like his own hand. He put the leaf in his pack to study later. He didn't want anyone accusing him of losing his scientific objectivity.[2] Only deviants did that. Farther up the hill he heard an unfamiliar burbling sound. No, he knew that sound. It was water running. He'd heard it once when the liquid dispenser had malfunctioned. There'd been a near panic in the dome over it. He checked the scanner. There was no caution signal, so he hurried toward the sound.

27 It was a—a "brook"—he was sure of it! Virtual lessons had taught that there were such things outside in the past but that they had long ago grown poisonous, then in the warming climate had dried up. But here was a running brook, not even a four-hour journey from his dome. His first impulse was to take off his protective glove and dip a finger in it, but he drew back. He had been well conditioned to avoid danger. He sat down clumsily on the bank. Yes, this must be grass. There were even some tiny flowers mixed in the grass. Would the atmosphere poison him if he unscrewed his helmet to take a sniff? He punched the scanner to read conditions, but the characters on the scanner panel danced about uncertainly until, at length, the disembodied voice said "conditions unreadable." He'd better not risk it.

28 He pushed the buttons now for liquid and pellets. A tube appeared in his mouth. It dropped a pellet on his tongue. From

2. **objectivity** (ob jehk TIHV uh tee) *n.* perspective based on facts, not feelings or opinions.

the tube he sucked liquid enough to swallow his meal. What was it they called outside nourishment in the history virtuals? *Pecnec*? Something like that. He was having a *pecnec* in the *woods* by a *brook*. A hasty consulting of the scanner revealed that what he was feeling was "pleasure." He was very glad he hadn't come with an anxious podfellow or, worse, an advanced robopet that would, no doubt, be yanking at his suit already, urging him back toward the dome.

NOTES

29 It was then, in the middle of the post-*pecnec* satisfaction, that he heard the new sound. Like that programmed into a robopet, yet different. He struggled to his feet. The dry suit from storage was certainly awkward when you wanted to stand up or sit down. Nothing on the scanner indicated danger, so he went into the scrubby woods toward the sound. And stopped abruptly.

30 Something was lying under the shadow of a tree. Something about a meter long. It was furred and quite still. The sound was not coming from it. And then he saw the small dog—the puppy. He was sure it was a puppy, nosing the stiff body of what must once have been its mother, making the little crying sounds that he'd heard from the brook. Later, much later, he realized that he should have been wary. If the older dog had died of some extradomal[3] disease, the puppy might have been a carrier. But at the time, all he could think of was the puppy, a small creature who had lost its mother.

31 He'd found out about mothers from the Virtuals. Mothers were extinct in the dome. Children were conceived and born in the lab and raised in units of twelve in the pods, presided over by a bank of computers and the podmaster. Nuclear families,[4] as everyone knew, had been wasteful of time, energy, and space. There was an old proverb: The key to survival is efficiency. So though Brock could guess the puppy was "sad" (like that fictions person, Jo, whose podmate expired), he didn't know what missing a mother would feel like. And who would whimper for a test tube?

32 Brock had never seen a dog, of course, but he'd seen plenty of dog breed descriptions on the science/history virtuals. Dogs had been abundant once. They filled the ancient fictions. They even had names there—Lassie, Toto, Sounder. But now dogs were extinct, gone during the dark ages when the atmosphere had become warm and poisonous. The savages who had not had the intelligence or wealth to join the foresighted dome crafters had killed all animals wild or domesticated for food before they had eventually died out themselves. It was all in one of the very first virtual lessons. He had seen that one many times. He never confessed to anyone how, well, sad it made him feel.

3. **extradomal** *adj.* from outside the dome.
4. **nuclear families** groups consisting of parents and their children.

CROSS-CURRICULAR PERSPECTIVES

Science Review paragraph 31 and discuss the futuristic way children are born in the dome. Have students do brief research reports on cloning and other scientific techniques that allow animals to be conceived in laboratories. What are the ethical implications of these techniques? Should scientists be allowed to use such techniques to clone or otherwise reproduce humans? Challenge students to conclude their reports by discussing the ethical issues involved.

NOTES

33 But obviously, dogs were not quite extinct. Cautiously, he moved toward the small one.

34 "Alert. Alert. Scanning unknown object."

35 Brock pushed the off button. "Are you sure you want to turn off scanner?"

36 "Affirmative." He stuck the scanner into his pouch.

37 The puppy had lifted its head at the sound of his voice. It looked at him, head cocked, as though deciding whether to run or stay.

38 "It's all right, dog," Brock said soothingly. "I won't hurt you." He stayed still. He didn't want to frighten the little beast. If it ran, he wasn't sure he'd be able to catch it in his clumsy dry suit.

39 Slowly he extended his gloved hand. The dog backed away anxiously, but when Brock kept the hand extended, the puppy slowly crept toward him and sniffed, making whimpering sounds. It wasn't old enough to be truly afraid, it seemed. The pup licked his glove tentatively, then backed away again. It was looking for food, and plasticine gloves weren't going to satisfy.

40 Brock looked first at the dead mother, whose source of nourishment must have long dried up, then around the landscape. What would a dog eat? A puppy on its own? He took off his glove and reached through his pouch into the inside pocket that held his pellet supply. Making every move slow and deliberate so as not to startle the dog, he held out a pellet. The dog came to his hand, licked it, then the pellet. It wrinkled its nose. Brock laughed. He didn't need the scanner now to tell him that what he felt was "pleasure." He loved the feel of the rough tongue on his palm and the little furred face, questioning him.

41 "It's all right, fellow. You can eat it."

42 As though understanding, the pup gulped down the pellet. Then looked around for more, not realizing that it had just bolted

HOW LANGUAGE WORKS

Sentence Structure Review paragraphs 34–39 and ask students to notice the sentence structure here. Explain to students that authors craft sentences carefully to reflect meaning and tone. By using different sentence structures, authors can convey a change in tone. Direct students' attention to paragraphs 34–39, and have them identify the different sentence structures the author uses (short declarative sentences and longer compound and complex sentences). Ask: What is the effect of these different sentence structures on the tone of the story?

Possible responses: The short, declarative sentences, such as "Alert." and "Affirmative." give the story a cold and official tone. The longer sentences that describe the interaction between Brock and the dog provide a warmer and more human tone.

down a whole meal. When the dog saw there was no more coming, it ran over to the brook. Brock watched in horror as it put its head right down into the poisonous stream and lapped noisily.

43 "Don't!" Brock cried.

44 The puppy turned momentarily at the sound, then went back to drinking, as though it was the most normal thing in the world. Well, it was, for the dog. Where else would a creature in the wild get liquid? If the streams were not all dried up, they must have learned to tolerate the water. But then, it was breathing the poisoned atmosphere, wasn't it? Why hadn't it hit Brock before? This was a fully organic creature on the outside *without any life support system*. What could that mean? Some amazing **mutation** must have occurred, making it possible for at least some creatures to breathe the outside atmosphere and drink its poisoned water. Those who couldn't died, those who could survived and got stronger. Even the ancient scientist Darwin[5] knew that. And Brock had come upon one of these magnificent mutants!

45 The puppy whimpered and looked up at Brock with large, trusting eyes. How could he think of it as a mutant specimen? It was a puppy. One who had lost its mother. What would it eat? There was no sign of food for a carnivore. Perhaps way back in the mountains some small mammals had also survived, keeping the food chain going, but the puppy would not live long enough to find its way there, much less know how to hunt with its mother gone. For the first time in his life something deep inside Brock reached out toward another creature. The thought of the puppy languishing here by the side of its dead parent until it, too . . .

46 "Your name is Brog, all right?" The ancient astronomers had named stars after themselves. He had discovered something just as wonderful. Didn't he have the right to name it sort of after himself while preserving the puppy's uniqueness? "Don't worry, Brog. I won't let you starve."

47 Which is why Brock appeared at the customs portal after dark, the front of his dry suit stained, carrying a wriggling *Canis familiaris*[6] of uncertain breed.

48 If there had been any way to smuggle the dog in, Brock would have. But he couldn't for the life of him figure out how. As it was, every alarm in the area went off when he stepped into the transitional cubicle. The disembodied voice of the monitor queried him.

49 "Welcome back, Brock 095670038. You're late."

50 "Affirmative."

51 "And you are carrying contraband."

52 "I pulled a leaf."

5. **Darwin** Charles Darwin (1809–1882); scientist who first formulated the theory of evolution.
6. ***Canis familiaris*** (KAY nihs fuh mihl ee AR ihs) scientific name for a dog.

NOTES

Mark context clues or indicate another strategy you used that helped you determine meaning.

mutation (myoo TAY shuhn) *n.*

MEANING:

DIGITAL PERSPECTIVES

Concept Vocabulary

MUTATION If groups are struggling to define the word *mutation* in paragraph 44, point out the context clues in the paragraph. For instance, the sentence in which the word occurs says that the mutation is "amazing" and that it made some creatures able to do impossible things. Consequently, the reader can infer that a mutation is something that causes significant, dramatic changes in creatures.

Possible response: A *mutation* is "a change in hereditary material."

NOTES

53 "Deposit same in quarantine bins."

54 "Affirmative."

55 "Sensors denote warm-blooded presence not on official roster."

56 "I found a dog," Brock mumbled.

57 "Repeat."

58 "A dog."

59 "*Canis familiaris* is extinct."

60 "Well, maybe it's just a robopet that got out somehow."

61 "Correction. Robopets are bloodless. Leave dry suit for sterilization and proceed to quarantine inspection."

62 The officials in quarantine inspection, who rarely had anything to inspect, were at first nervous and then, as they watched the puppy happily licking Brock's face, interested despite themselves. An actual dog! None of them had ever seen one, of course, and Brock's dog was so much, well, more vital than a robopet. And although, on later reflection, they knew they should have terminated or expelled it, they couldn't quite bring themselves to do so that night.

63 "It will have to go to Research," the chief inspector finally declared.

64 "Permission requested to hand carry the dog known as Brog to Research," Brock said. There was a bit of an argument about that. Several inspectors sought the honor, but the chief declared that Brock, having shed his dry suit and being already contaminated, should be placed with the dog in a hermetically sealed air car and transported to Research.

65 The scientists in Research were predictably amazed to see a live *Canis familiaris*. But being scientists and more objective than the lower-grade quarantine inspectors, they kept a safe distance both physically and psychically from the creature. Only the oldest scientist, dressed in proper protective clothing, came into the laboratory with Brock and the dog. He scanned and poked and prodded the poor little fellow until it began to whimper in protest.

66 "Brog needs to rest," said Brock, interrupting the scientist in the midst of his inspection. "She's (for by this time gender had been indisputably established) had a hard day. And if there's some actual food available—she's not used to pellets."

67 "Of course, of course," said one of the researchers through the speaker in the observation booth. "How thoughtless. Send someone out for a McLike burger without sauce. She may regard it as meat. Anyhow, it will seem more like food to her than a pellet, affirmative, Brock?"

68 The scientists, Brock soon realized, were looking to him for advice. He was, after all, the discoverer of the last dog. It gave him sudden scientific status. Brock had sense enough to take advantage of this. After Brog had swallowed the McLike burger in three quick gulps, Brock insisted that he be allowed to stay

PERSONALIZE FOR LEARNING

Challenge

Research Review paragraph 65 and discuss the scientists' reaction to the dog. Have groups research animals that have become extinct during the past 100 years. Students should identify the animal's Latin name and describe its appearance, former habitat, and reason for extinction. Then, have students research an animal on the Endangered Species list and find out what action they can take to help save it from extinction. Groups should present their findings to the class.

DIGITAL PERSPECTIVES

with Brog, so that he might interact and sleep with her. "She's not like us," he explained. "She's used to tumbling about and curling up with other warm bodies. In the old myths," he added, "puppies separated from their litters cried all night long. She will need constant interaction with another warm-blooded creature or she might well die of," he loved using his new vocabulary, "loneliness."

69 The scientists agreed. After all, research was rather like quarantine, and since Brock had touched the dog ungloved and unprotected, he might well have picked up some germ from her. It was better to keep them both isolated in the research lab where proper precautions would be taken.

70 For nearly a week, Brock lived with Brog in the research center, eating McLike burgers, playing "fetch," teaching Brog to "sit," "heel," "come"—all the commands he could cull from the ancient texts. The dog quickly learned to obey Brock's commands, but it wasn't the automatic response of a robopet. Brog delighted in obedience. She wanted to please Brock, and those few times when she was too busy nosing about the lab and failed to obey instantly, those times when Brock's voice took on a sharp tone of reproof, the poor little thing put her tail between her legs, looked up at him with sorrowful eyes, begging to be forgiven. Brock was tempted to speak sharply to her even when there was no need, for the sight of her drooping ears and tail, her mournful eyes, was so dear to him that he did what Travis Coates had done to Old Yeller. He hugged her. There was no other way to explain it. He simply put his arms around her and held her to his chest while she beat at him with her tail and licked his face raw. Out of the corner of his eye he was aware that one of the scientists was watching. Well, let him watch. Nothing was as wonderful as feeling this warmth toward another creature.

71 For the first week, the researchers seemed quite content to observe dog and boy from their glass-paneled observation booth and speak copious notes into their computers. Only the oldest of them would come into the lab and actually touch the alien creature, and he always wore a sterile protective suit with gloves. The others claimed it would interfere with objectivity if they got close to the dog, but they all seemed to behave positively toward Brog. No mention was made to Brock of his own less than-objective behavior. So Brock was astounded to awake in the middle of the night to the sounds of an argument. Someone had forgotten to turn off the communication system.

72 "Cloning—it's the only thing to do. If she's the last, we owe it to posterity to keep the line going."

73 "And how are we going to raise a pack of dogs in a dome? One is nearly eating and drinking us out of test tube and petri dish. We can't go on this way. As drastic as it may seem, we have

NOTES

CLOSER LOOK

Analyze Conflict 

Circulate among groups as students conduct their close read. Suggest that groups read paragraph 70. Encourage them to talk about the annotations that they mark. If needed, provide the following support.

ANNOTATE: Have students mark passages in this paragraph that relate to Brock's feelings and state of mind, or you could have students participate while you highlight them.

QUESTION: Guide students to consider what these passages tell them about Brock's internal conflict. Ask what a reader can infer from these details about Brock's struggles with loneliness. Accept student responses.

Possible responses: Details about Brog's desire to please Brock and Brock's feelings toward her and the fact that he hugged her suggest that Brock's internal conflict with loneliness is in the process of being resolved.

CONCLUDE: Help students formulate conclusions about the internal conflict in this story.

Possible responses: In "The Last Dog," the internal conflict of Brock's loneliness is at least partially resolved through his love for the dog, Brog.

Remind students that this short story, like many others, has more than one **conflict**. Ask what students predict about the external conflict in the story.

NOTES

to be realistic. Besides, no one has had the chance to do actual experiments since the dark ages. Haven't you ever, just once, yearned to compare virtual research with actual?"

74 "What about the boy? He won't agree. Interfacing daily with the dog, he's become crippled by primal urges."

75 "Can you think what chaos might ensue if a flood of primordial[7] emotions were to surface in a controlled environment such as ours?" another asked. "Apparently, emotions are easily triggered by interactions with primitive beasts, like dogs."

76 "Shh. Not now. The speaker is—" The system clicked off.

77 But Brock had already heard. He knew he had lost anything resembling scientific objectivity. He was no longer sure objectivity was a desirable trait. He rather enjoyed being flooded by "primordial emotions." But he was more worried for Brog than for himself. It wasn't hard to figure out what the scientists meant by "actual experiments." Cloning would be bad enough. Ten dogs who looked just like Brog so no one would know how special, how truly unique Brog was. But experiments! They'd cut her open and examine her internal organs, the way scientists had in the dark ages. They'd prod her with electric impulses and put chips in her brain. They'd try to change her personality or modify her behavior. They'd certainly try to make her eat and drink less!

78 In the dark, he put his arm around Brog and drew her close. He loved the terrible smell of her breath and the way she snored when she slept. They'd probably fix that, too.

79 The next day he played sick. Brog, faithful dog that she was, hung around him whimpering, licking his face. The scientists showed no particular concern. They were too busy plotting what they might do with Brog.

80 Brock crept to the nearest terminal[8] in the lab. It was already logged in. The scientists had been doing nothing but research on *Canis familiaris*. COMMON CANINE DISEASES. Brock scrolled down the list with descriptions. No, *distemper* wouldn't do. The first symptom was loss of appetite. He couldn't make Brog fake that. On and on it went—no, *heartworms* wouldn't do. What he needed was a disease that might affect *Homo sapiens* as well as *Canis familiaris*. Here it was! "Rabies: A viral disease occurring in animals and humans, especially in dogs and wolves. Transmitted by bite or scratch. The early stages of the disease are most dangerous, for an otherwise healthy and friendly appearing animal will suddenly bite without provocation."

81 Rabies was it! Somehow he would have to make Brog bite him. There was no antirabies serum in the dome, he felt sure. There were no animals in the dome. Why would they use precious space

7. **primordial** (pry MAWR dee uhl) *adj.* very ancient and basic.
8. **terminal** *n.* computer.

PERSONALIZE FOR LEARNING

Strategic Support

Scientific Names Review paragraph 80 and call student attention to the scientific language in the text. Tell students that *Canis familiaris* is the scientific term for domesticated dogs and *Homo sapiens* is the scientific name for humans. Explain that scientists around the world use a common system for naming organisms. In this system, two words are used to name each animal, plant, or organism. The first word identifies the genus and the second is the specific name. Have students research and share the scientific names of their favorite animals.

to store an unneeded medication? So they'd have to expel him as well as Brog for fear of spreading the disease. He shivered, then shook himself. No matter what lay on the outside, he could not stand to go back to the life he had lived in the dome before he met Brog.

82 He crept back to bed, pulling the covers over Brog. When one of the scientists came into the observation booth, Brock pinched Brog's neck as hard as he could. Nothing. He pinched again, harder. Brog just snuggled closer, slobbering on his arm.

83 Disgusted, Brock got out of bed. Brog hopped down as well, rubbing against his leg. Pinching obviously was not going to do it. While the scientist on duty in the booth was bending over a computer terminal, Brock brought his foot down on Brog's paw. A tiny *yip* was all he got from that cruel effort—not enough sound even to make the man look up.

84 "Feeling better, Brock 095670038?" The oldest researcher had come into the lab.

85 "Affirmative," Brock answered.

86 "And how are you, puppy-wuppy?" The old man tickled Brog under her chin with his gloved hand. *If I were a dog, I'd bite someone like that*, thought Brock, but Brog, of course, simply licked the researcher's glove and wagged her tail.

87 That was when he got his great idea. He waited to execute it until the proper moment. For the first time, all the scientists had gathered in the lab, all of them in protective garb, some of them twitching nervously in their chairs. They were sitting in a circle around Brock and Brog, explaining what must be done.

88 "It has to be done for the sake of science," they began. Then they went on to, "For the sake of the dome community, which is always, as you well know, short on food, and particularly short on water." Brock listened to their arguments, nodding solemnly, pretending to agree. "It won't be as if she'll really be gone, you know. We've made virtuals of her—a special series just for you to keep. You can virtually play with her whenever you like."

89 That was the cue. Brock turned and bit Brog on the tail so hard that the blood started. Brog, surprised and enraged, spun around and bit Brock on the nose.

90 There was a shocked silence. Every scientist leaned backward, body pressed hard against his or her chair back. Every eye was on the two of them.

91 "I—I don't know what got into me," Brock said. "I've been feeling very weird." The scientists continued to stare. "I was checking the historical records. . . ."

92 All of the scientists fled the room. Someone ran to a computer terminal. When Brock offered to take Brog out of the dome and let her loose in the mountains, no one argued. Neither did they

NOTES

CLOSER LOOK

Analyze Plot 

Circulate among groups as students conduct their close read. Suggest that groups read paragraphs 82–90. Encourage them to talk about the annotations that they mark. If needed, provide the following support.

ANNOTATE: Have students mark events in these paragraphs that help develop the plot, or you could have students participate while you highlight them.

QUESTION: Guide students to consider how these events heighten the tension and move the conflict toward its climax. Accept student responses.

Possible responses: Each time that Brock tried to get Brog to bite him, it heightens the suspense about what will happen and complicates the plot.

CONCLUDE: Help students formulate conclusions about the rising action in this story.

Possible responses: The complications in paragraphs 82–90 create rising action that gains momentum as the plot reaches a climax.

Remind students that the **plot** is the series of events that unfold in a story. After the climax, the conflict lessens in intensity until the last stage of the plot when the conflict is resolved.

NOTES

say, "Hurry back," or even, "Take care." No one came close as he loaded his pouch with water and food pellets. The customs gate monitor asked no questions.

93 Out of sight of the dome, Brog was delirious with joy, jumping and running about in circles around Brock's boots. Why wasn't the atmosphere choking Brog if it was as poisonous as the dome dwellers claimed? His heart beating rapidly, Brock unscrewed his helmet just enough to let in a little of the outside atmosphere. Nothing happened. In fact, he seemed to be breathing perfectly normally. He took off the helmet entirely. He was still breathing freely. But his heart was beating so hard, he couldn't be sure. He waited for the choking sensation he had been warned of. It didn't occur. Could they be wrong? Could the outside world have healed itself? Perhaps—perhaps the reason the scanner had so much trouble reading the outside atmosphere was because it wasn't within the range of computerized expectations.

94 Could it be? Could it be that fear had kept the dome dwellers prisoner many years longer than a poisoned environment would have?

95 He unfastened the dry suit and slowly stepped out of it into the sunlight.

96 It was wonderful how much faster he could walk without the clumsy suit. "Who knows?" Brock said to a frisking Brog. "Who knows, maybe out here you aren't the last dog. Your mother had to come from somewhere."

97 Brog barked happily in reply.

98 "And maybe, just maybe, where there are dogs, there are humans as well."

99 They stopped at the brook where they'd met, and both of them had a long drink. Brock no longer carried a scanner, but he knew what he felt was excitement. The water was delicious. ❧

VOCABULARY DEVELOPMENT

Concept Vocabulary Reinforcement Students will benefit from additional examples and practice with the concept vocabulary. Reinforce their comprehension with "show-you-know" sentences. The first part of the sentence uses the vocabulary word in an appropriate context. The second part of the sentence—the show-you-know part—clarifies the first. Model the strategy with this example for *extinct* (paragraph 26): Brock hoped that perhaps dogs were not *extinct* and that they would not only find dogs living outside the dome but also humans.

Then, give students these sentence prompts, and coach them in creating the clarification part:

1. The *mutation* (paragraph 44) gave him a superpower; ______________.

   Possible response: he could make people hiccup at will

2. It looked *threatening* (paragraph 14) outside, ______________.

   Possible response: with dark clouds gathering on the horizon

Comprehension Check

Complete the following items after you finish your first read. Review and clarify details with your group.

1. Where does Brock live?

2. What do people believe about the world outside the dome?

3. What does Brock discover about the world outside the dome?

4. **Notebook** Confirm your understanding of the text by writing a brief plot summary. Your summary should include only the most important events in the story.

RESEARCH

Research to Clarify Choose at least one unfamiliar detail from the story. Briefly research that detail. In what way does the information you learned shed light on an aspect of the story?

Research to Explore Research Biosphere 2, a scientific research facility in Arizona. Formulate two research questions about it. For instance, questions could include: What is the purpose of Biosphere 2? What was its first mission? What challenges has it faced? Briefly research the answer to your question and share your findings with your group.

DIGITAL PERSPECTIVES

Comprehension Check

Possible responses:

1. Inside "the dome," a manufactured world
2. People believe it is uninhabitable.
3. It contains living things like trees, grass, and a dog. It is not uninhabitable.

Possible summary: The main character, Brock, lives inside a dome because the earth is believed to be uninhabitable. However, Brock wants to leave the dome and explore the outside world. When he does so, he discovers plant and animal life. He finds a puppy, which he brings back to the dome. Scientists plan to experiment on the puppy. To save it, Brock leaves the dome with the puppy and discovers that the outside world is not uninhabitable after all.

Research

Research to Clarify If students struggle to choose details, ask each student to submit a detail on a slip of paper. Put the slips of paper in a bag and then have each group choose one. Groups can research the details they picked.

Research to Explore If students struggle to formulate research questions, have them pretend they are reporters researching a story about Biosphere 2. What would be the first two questions they would want to ask the scientists of Biosphere 2?

PERSONALIZE FOR LEARNING

Challenge

Discussion Direct students' attention to this sentence from paragraph 94: "Could it be that fear had kept the dome dwellers prisoner many years longer than a poisoned environment would have?" What fears keep us prisoner, as individuals and as a society? Have students discuss this question in their small groups. Challenge each group to summarize its discussion in a brief presentation to the class.

Jump Start

CLOSE READ Ask students to compare living in the dome in "The Last Dog" to living on another planet. How are they similar? How are they different? If Earth's environment became poisonous, would you rather live inside such a dome or on another planet? Why? Have students discuss these questions in their groups.

Close Read the Text

If needed, model close reading by using the Annotation Highlights in the Interactive Teacher's Edition.

Remind students to use Accountable Talk in their discussions and to support one another as they complete the close read.

Analyze the Text

Teams' responses will vary but should include reasons that the allusions to the characters were chosen and how they enhance understanding.

Concept Vocabulary

Why These Words? Possible response: The words all relate to life outside the dome.

Word Network

Possible words: *evaporate, scanner, venture, barren*

Practice

Sample responses:

1. The *threatening* clouds brought an end to the picnic.
2. Mastodons used to roam this region, but are now *extinct*.
3. The third horn on the goat's head is a *mutation*.

Word Study

For more support, see **Concept Vocabulary and Word Study.**

Possible response:

A mutation is a change. *Mutation* is a noun.

MAKING MEANING

THE LAST DOG

Close Read the Text

With your group, revisit sections of the text you marked during your first read. **Annotate** what you notice. What **questions** do you have? What can you **conclude**?

Analyze the Text

CITE TEXTUAL EVIDENCE to support your answers.

Notebook Complete the activities.

1. **Review and Clarify** With your group, reread paragraph 16 of the story. Then, identify the author's use of **allusion,** or references to well-known people, events, or literary works. Discuss the ways in which the use of allusion improves or weakens the story.
2. **Present and Discuss** Now, work with your group to share the passages from the text that you found especially important. Discuss what you noticed in the text, the questions you asked, and the conclusions you reached.
3. **Essential Question:** *Should we make a home in space?* What has this selection taught you about the problems of making a home in space?

TIP

GROUP DISCUSSION

When you work in your group to answer the Analyze the Text questions, be sure to support your opinions and ideas with evidence from the text.

LANGUAGE DEVELOPMENT

Concept Vocabulary

threatening	extinct	mutation

Why These Words? The concept vocabulary words from the text are related. With your group, determine what the words have in common. Write your ideas and add another word that fits the category.

Practice

Notebook Confirm your understanding of these words by using them in sentences. Include context clues that hint at each word's meaning.

Word Study

Latin Suffix: *-tion* In the story, Brock thinks that the puppy is the product of a *mutation* that enables her to survive in the outside world. The word *mutation* is built from the verb *mutate*, meaning "to change," and the Latin suffix *-tion,* which turns a verb into a noun. Based on that information, identify the meaning and part of speech of *mutation*.

WORD NETWORK

Add interesting words related to space exploration from the text to your Word Network.

STANDARDS

Language

- Determine or clarify the meaning of unknown and multiple-meaning words and phrases based on *grade 7 reading and content*, choosing flexibly from a range of strategies.
  - a. Use context as a clue to the meaning of a word or phrase.
- Demonstrate understanding of figurative language, word relationships, and nuances in word meanings.
  - a. Interpret figures of speech in context.

FORMATIVE ASSESSMENT

Analyze the Text

If students struggle to close read the text, **then** provide **The Last Dog: Text Questions** available online in the Interactive Teacher's Edition or Unit Resources. Answers and DOK levels are also available.

Concept Vocabulary

If students cannot see the connection among the words, **then** have them use each word in a sentence about the story's setting. Have them consider similarities in the sentences.

Word Study

If students cannot identify the meaning and part of speech of *mutation*, **then** have them consult a dictionary. For Reteach and Practice, see **Word Study: Latin Suffix *-tion* (RP).**

Analyze Craft and Structure

Elements of a Short Story: Conflict and Resolution In most stories, the plot centers on a **conflict**, or struggle between opposing forces. There are two types of conflict.

- **External conflict** is a struggle between a character and an outside force, such as another character or nature.
- **Internal conflict** is a struggle within a character as he or she wrestles with opposing feelings, beliefs, needs, or desires.

A story often has more than one conflict and may include both an external and an internal conflict. In most stories, a series of small conflicts contribute to the main conflict. The **resolution**, or outcome, often comes toward the end of the story when the conflicts, or problems, are settled in some way.

STANDARDS
Reading Literature
Analyze how particular elements of a story or drama interact.

Practice

CITE TEXTUAL EVIDENCE to support your answers.

Use this graphic organizer to analyze the conflicts and resolution in "The Last Dog." Work individually to complete the graphic organizer.

CONFLICT AND RESOLUTION IN "THE LAST DOG"	
Conflict(s): What does the main character struggle with? What other conflicts exist?	The main character struggles with feelings of loneliness and isolation. He also struggles to save the last dog from the experimentation of the scientists.
Type(s) of Conflict: External or internal?	both
Resolution: How are the conflicts settled, or resolved?	The main character's internal struggle with loneliness is resolved by his relationship with the dog. His struggle with the scientists is resolved when he figures out a way to get them to throw him and the dog out of the dome.

When you have finished, share your completed chart with your group and discuss the following questions:

- Is there a main conflict that stands out in the story? Explain.
- How are the external conflicts and the internal conflicts related?
- Did the resolution settle the conflicts in the story? Did you find the resolution satisfying?

DIGITAL PERSPECTIVES

Analyze Craft and Stucture

Conflict and Resolution Discuss with students the differences between internal and external conflicts, providing examples of various conflicts. Remind them that both types of conflicts escalate until they reach a climax. After the climax, the conflict lessens in intensity and moves toward the resolution. This last stage of the plot resolves the conflict, ties up all the plot's loose ends, and often conveys a general insight or change on the part of the protagonist. For more support, see **Analyze Craft and Structure: Conflict and Resolution.**

Practice

See possible responses in the chart on the student page.

FORMATIVE ASSESSMENT

Analyze Craft and Structure

If students are unable to identify the conflict and resolution, **then** have them summarize events in the story. Guide them to see how these events are part of the story's plot. For Reteach and Practice, see **Analyze Craft and Structure: Conflict and Resolution (RP).**

PERSONALIZE FOR LEARNING

English Language Support

Understanding Conflict and Resolution Have pairs of students work together to choose a familiar story that features a conflict between a character and nature (man *vs.* nature). Then have them write a few sentences explaining the nature of the conflict. **EMERGING**

Have students think of a familiar story that features a character's inner conflict. Then have them write a paragraph explaining the nature of the conflict. **EXPANDING**

Have students think of two stories they know that feature a conflict between a character and an outside group and a character's inner conflict. Then have them write a paragraph comparing and contrasting the nature of these conflicts. **BRIDGING**

An expanded **English Language Support Lesson** on Conflict and Resolution is available in the Interactive Teacher's Edition.

FACILITATING

Conventions

Simple and Compound Subjects and Predicates Point out to students that they can make their writing more coherent and interesting by combining sentences. Two simple sentences can be combined to form a sentence with a compound subject or a compound predicate. Point out to students that a compound subject joined by *and* requires a plural verb.

Zach loves to wrestle. and *Huck loves to wrestle.* can be combined to form *Zach and Huck love to wrestle.*

Mari loves to swim. and *Mari loves to play.* can be combined to form *Mari loves to swim and play.*

For more support, see **Conventions: Simple and Compound Subjects and Predicates.**

Read It

Possible responses:

Simple Subject: Brock took a deep breath.

Compound Predicate: He took a deep breath, one last backward look at the dome, which, with the alien sun gleaming on it, was even harder to look at than the distant star, and started across an expanse of brown soil [was it?] to what he recognized from holograms as a line of purplish mountains in the distance.

Write It

Possible response:

My sister and I take care of our dogs. My sister and I feed them, walk them, and give them water. We sometimes brush their coats. Taking care of dogs is a lot of work!

FORMATIVE ASSESSMENT

Conventions

If students are unable to revise the passage, **then** have them work with a partner to do so. For Reteach and Practice, see **Conventions: Simple and Compound Subjects and Predicates (RP).**

LANGUAGE DEVELOPMENT

THE LAST DOG

Conventions

Simple and Compound Subjects and Predicates Every sentence has a subject and a predicate and expresses a complete thought. The **subject** tells whom or what the sentence is about. The **predicate** tells what the subject is, does, or has done to it.

PART OF SENTENCE	EXAMPLE
A **simple subject** is a single main noun or pronoun.	Brog drinks water from the brook.
A **compound subject** is two or more nouns or pronouns that share the same verb. The subjects are joined by a conjunction such as *and* or *or.*	Brock and Brog drink water from the brook.
A **simple predicate** is a single main verb or verb phrase.	Brog **drinks** water from the brook.
A **compound predicate** contains two or more main verbs that share the same subject. The verbs are joined by a conjunction such as *and* or *or.*	Brog **drinks** and **laps** water from the brook.

Read It

Work with your group to identify an example of a simple subject and an example of a compound predicate in "The Last Dog." Write your examples in the chart.

PART OF SENTENCE	EXAMPLE
Simple Subject	
Compound Predicate	

Write It

Notebook Sometimes too many short, simple sentences in a row can make your writing choppy and repetitive. Try adding sentence variety by combining simple subjects and predicates into compound subjects and predicates. Revise the following passage so that it includes at least one more compound predicate and one more compound subject.

My sister and I take care of our dogs. I feed them. My sister feeds them. I also walk them. I give them water. My sister also walks them and gives them water. My sister sometimes brushes their coats. I also sometimes brush their coats. Taking care of dogs is a lot of work!

STANDARDS

Language

- Demonstrate command of the conventions of standard English grammar and usage when writing or speaking.
- Use knowledge of language and its conventions when writing, speaking, reading, or listening.
  a. Choose language that expresses ideas precisely and concisely, recognizing and eliminating wordiness and redundancy.

PERSONALIZE FOR LEARNING

English Language Support

Subjects and Predicates Have students work in pairs to write sentences with simple and compound subjects and predicates. Pairs should put their names into the following sentence starters. For the third sentence, students will also need to add a second verb to the sentence.

Simple sentence: ______ is writing a sentence.

Compound subject: ______ and ______ are learning.

Compound subject and predicate: ______ and ______ are writing a sentence and ______.

ALL LEVELS

EFFECTIVE EXPRESSION

Writing to Sources

A fictional narrative uses a combination of narrative strategies to tell a story and engage readers. These strategies include characterization, description, dialogue, figurative language, and imagery.

Assignment

Use your imagination to write your own version of the last seven paragraphs of this story. Begin your **revised ending** with the words "Out of sight of the dome, . . ." For your revision, choose one of the following options:

- ☐ Change the narrator, and write from the perspective of the puppy, Brog, giving her a human voice.
- ☐ Add a character to the story, who influences the story's resolution.

Develop Your Story Choose an option for your revision of the end of the story. How will it be similar to or different from the author's resolution to the story?

Think carefully about how your choice will affect the resolution of the narrative. For example, how would writing from the puppy's perspective affect the end of the story? How might introducing a new character change the story's ending?

Carefully choose words and descriptive details that engage the reader and bring your revised ending to life. Take notes in a chart like the one shown, and then draft your revised ending.

	NOTES FOR MY VERSION
Narrator	
Plot Events	
Resolution	

Reflect on Your Writing When your draft is completed, share it with others in your group. Then, as a group, discuss the following questions.

- What purpose does the narrator's perspective serve in a story?
- What effects do different resolutions have on a story?
- What type of resolution do you find most satisfying?

EVIDENCE LOG

Before moving on to a new selection, go to your Evidence Log and record what you learned from "The Last Dog."

STANDARDS

Writing

- Write narratives to develop real or imagined experiences or events using effective technique, relevant descriptive details, and well-structured event sequences.
  - b. Use narrative techniques, such as dialogue, pacing, and description, to develop experiences, events, and/or characters.
  - e. Provide a conclusion that follows from and reflects on the narrated experiences or events.
- Write routinely over extended time frames and shorter time frames for a range of discipline-specific tasks, purposes, and audiences.

DIGITAL PERSPECTIVES

Writing to Sources

Explain to students that regardless of which revised ending they choose to write, their ending will be much more effective if they remember to include a clear main idea, or focus.

- **Include Sensory Details.** If they are telling the story from the point of view of the puppy, they should keep in mind the sorts of sensory details a dog would notice. For instance, dogs have a very keen sense of smell.
- **Tie Up Loose Ends.** Create a satisfying ending for readers by tying up loose ends. Remember, however, that doesn't mean you have to say whether Brock and Brog find companions.
- **Show Readers How the Main Character Has Changed Since the Beginning of the Story.** What has Brock learned about himself or the world around him, or both?

Develop Your Story Encourage students to choose an ending that makes sense, given the narrative that precedes it. The ending can leave some questions unanswered, however.

Reflect on Your Writing Encourage groups to also discuss how listening to the story endings written by others affected their understanding of the story. Were they surprised by any of the endings? For fun, you might also ask students to decide who they would cast in a movie version of the story and how a film version might be different. For more support, see **Writing to Sources: Revised Ending.**

Evidence Log Support students in completing their Evidence Log. This paced activity will help prepare them for the Performance-Based Assessment at the end of the unit.

FORMATIVE ASSESSMENT

Writing to Sources

If groups have difficulty writing a revised ending, **then** suggest they work with a partner to revise the ending. For Reteach and Practice, see **Writing to Sources: Revised Ending (RP).**

Selection Test

Administer the "The Last Dog" Selection Test, which is available in both print and digital formats online in Assessments.

Ellen Ochoa: Director, Johnson Space Center

AUDIO SUMMARIES
Audio summaries of "Ellen Ochoa: Director, Johnson Space Center" are available in both English and Spanish in the Interactive Teacher's Edition or Unit Resources. Assigning these summaries prior to reading the selection may help students build additional background knowledge and set a context for their first read.

Summary

Ellen Ochoa is not only the head of the Johnson Space Center, but she is also the first Hispanic woman in space. In this video interview, Ochoa discusses how she became interested in space and decided to study engineering. She worked both as an astronaut and in Mission Control. While at Mission Control, Ochoa contributed to the recovery from one of NASA's worst disasters—the loss of the Space Shuttle *Columbia*. Now, as director of the Johnson Space Center, Ochoa has bright plans for the future.

Insight

This interview is a candid look at how a person grows into and achieves such an impressive career. It also emphasizes recovery from tragedy, and the new growth possibilities in its wake.

ESSENTIAL QUESTION:
Should we make a home in space?

Connection to Essential Question

"Ellen Ochoa: Director, Johnson Space Center" provides a clear-cut connection to the Essential Question, "Should We Make a Home in Space?" As director of the Johnson Space Center, part of Dr. Ochoa's job is focused on exploring better ways to keep people in space.

SMALL-GROUP LEARNING PERFORMANCE TASK
Should space exploration be a priority for our country?

UNIT PERFORMANCE-BASED ASSESSMENT
Should we spend valuable resources on space exploration?

Connection to Performance Tasks

Small-Group Learning Performance Task In this Performance Task, students will develop a multimedia presentation that addresses the Essential Question. This video provides students with information on the importance of space exploration from a former astronaut and the direction of the Johnson Space Center.

Unit Performance-Based Assessment Ochoa vividly describes the dangers of space shuttle trips—which are as routine and safe as any space travel has been. Is space exploration worth the expense and the potential risks?

DIGITAL PERSPECTIVES

 Audio  Video  Document  Annotation Highlights 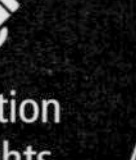 Online Assessment

LESSON RESOURCES

	Making Meaning	Language Development	Effective Expression
Lesson	**First Review** **Close Review** **Analyze the Media**	**Technical Vocabulary**	**Speaking and Listening**
Instructional Standards	**RI.7.10** By the end of the year, read and comprehend literary nonfiction . . . **SL.7.1** Engage effectively in a range of collaborative discussions . . .	**L.7.6** Acquire and use accurately grade-appropriate general academic and domain-specific words and phrases . . .	**SL.7.1.a** Come to discussions prepared . . . **SL.7.1.b** Follow rules for collegial discussions . . . **SL.7.1.c** Pose questions . . . **SL.7.1.d** Acknowledge new information . . .
STUDENT RESOURCES			
Available online in the Interactive Student Edition or Unit Resources	Selection Audio First-Review Guide: Media: Video Close-Review Guide: Media: Video	Word Network	Evidence Log
TEACHER RESOURCES			
Selection Resources Available online in the Interactive Teacher's Edition or Unit Resources	Audio Summaries: English and Spanish Spanish Translation Media Questions First Review Extension Questions	Technical Vocabulary	Speaking and Listening: Biography: Group Discussion
My Resources	A Unit 2 Answer Key is available online and in the Interactive Teacher's Edition.		

Media Complexity Rubric: Ellen Ochoa: Director, Johnson Space Center

Quantitative Measures	
Length and Format: Video, 2 minutes, 5 seconds	
Qualitative Measures	
Knowledge Demands ① — ② — ❸ — ④ — ⑤	Video relies on some discipline-specific knowledge (*Apollo 11* moon landing, space shuttle *Columbia*, and the fact that it was not common for women to be astronauts).
Structure ① — ❷ — ③ — ④ — ⑤	Video has high correspondence of audio and images (Ochoa in spoken interview, and images of her experiences). Video also includes screens with only text, detailing events chronologically.
Language Conventionality and Clarity ① — ② — ❸ — ④ — ⑤	Spoken language is clear and easy to understand, with contemporary and familiar vocabulary; screens of text explanations are clearly written with simple sentences.
Levels of Meaning/Purpose ① — ❷ — ③ — ④ — ⑤	Purpose of video is explicit, clear, concrete, and narrowly focused. Ochoa talks about her experience as the first Hispanic woman astronaut.

Jump Start

FIRST REVIEW Ask students to consider the following prompt: *What image comes to mind when you think of an astronaut?* Engage students in a discussion of the stereotypes they have about the kinds of people who become astronauts.

Ellen Ochoa: Director, Johnson Space Center

What makes one person more suited to become an astronaut than another? What qualities would a person need to travel into space? Modeling the questions readers might ask as they review "Ellen Ochoa: Director, Johnson Space Center" brings the video alive for students and connects it to the Small-Group Performance Task assignment. Selection audio is available in the Interactive Teacher's Edition.

Technical Vocabulary

Encourage students to discuss the technical vocabulary. Have they seen or used these terms before? Do they use any of them in their speech or writing? Have students brainstorm three examples of aptitudes and share with the class.

FIRST REVIEW

As they review, students should perform the steps of the first review:

WATCH: Encourage students to notice sound effects, people's voices, and music.

NOTE: Remind students to focus on what Ellen Ochoa says about becoming an astronaut.

CONNECT: Encourage students to make connections beyond the video. If they cannot make connections to their own lives, have them consider films or TV shows they may have seen or selections they have read in this unit.

RESPOND: Students will answer questions to demonstrate understanding. Point out to students that while they will always complete the Respond step at the end of the first review, the other steps will probably happen concurrently. You may wish to print copies of the **First-Review Guide: Media: Video** for students to use.

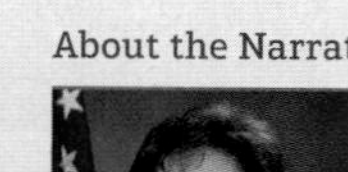

MAKING MEANING

About the Narrator

Ellen Ochoa, Ph.D, (b. 1958) was born in Los Angeles, California. She became the first Latina astronaut to go to space, as a crewmember aboard the space shuttle *Discovery*. In 2012, Dr. Ochoa was named Director of NASA's Johnson Space Center. "Don't be afraid to reach for the stars," Dr. Ochoa says. "I believe a good education can take you anywhere on Earth and beyond."

Ellen Ochoa: Director, Johnson Space Center

Technical Vocabulary

These words will be useful to you as you analyze, discuss, and write about the video. Context sentences are provided to the right of each word.

aptitude: natural ability or talent	• Carla's math teacher encouraged her to do extra credit work because of Carla's aptitude for math.
calculus: math used to study change	• Carla thinks that studying calculus is challenging but fascinating.
mission control: a command center for the control, monitoring, and support of activities connected with manned space flight	• Carla is hoping to visit mission control one day in order to see the technology of manned space flight at work.

First Review MEDIA: VIDEO

Study the video using these strategies.

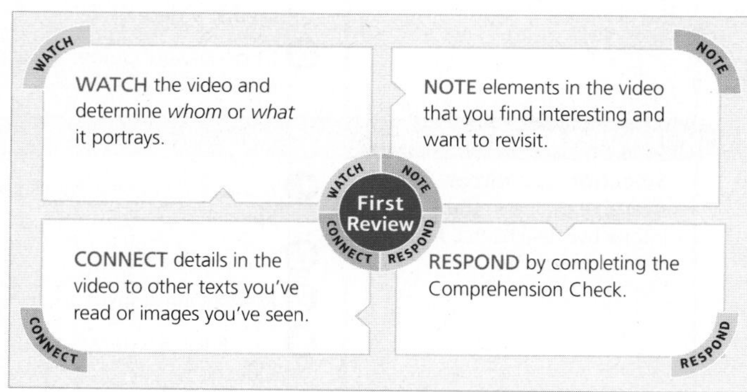

STANDARDS

Reading Informational Text
By the end of the year, read and comprehend literary nonfiction in the grades 6–8 text complexity band proficiently, with scaffolding as needed at the high end of the range.

Language
Acquire and use accurately grade-appropriate general academic and domain-specific words and phrases; gather vocabulary knowledge when considering a word or phrase important to comprehension or expression.

PERSONALIZE FOR LEARNING

English Language Support

Technical Vocabulary: Domain-Specific Words Help students understand the technical vocabulary by providing concrete examples. For instance, point out to each student his or her own aptitudes, such as an aptitude for drawing, sports, or learning languages. Then, provide an example of a calculus equation and show students pictures of mission control. Making things as concrete as possible will help students understand and learn these words. **ALL LEVELS**

MEDIA | VIDEO

Ellen Ochoa: Director, Johnson Space Center

BACKGROUND

In this interview, Johnson Space Center Director Dr. Ellen Ochoa talks about how she came to be an astronaut with NASA. She mentions Sally Ride as one of her influences. In 1983, Ride became the first woman from the United States to launch into outer space when she joined the team aboard the space shuttle *Challenger*. Since then, more than 50 women scientists have joined Ride in making the journey to space.

NOTES

DIGITAL PERSPECTIVES

CLOSER REVIEW

Analyze Anecdotes

Circulate among groups as students conduct their first review. Suggest that groups review the section of the video from 00:00 to 00:45. Encourage them to talk about the notes they make. If needed, provide the following support.

NOTE: Have students note details at the beginning of the video about the effect Ms. Ochoa's voice and body language have as she tells the stories, or work with small groups to have students participate while you note them together.

Possible response: In the video, the viewer can hear the warmth and humor in Ochoa's voice and see her facial expressions as she tells the short anecdotes from her life. This helps the viewer connect with her.

QUESTION: Guide students to consider how hearing Ochoa tell these stories affects the experience of watching the rest of the video, and accept student responses.

Possible response: The anecdotes help viewers feel connected to Ochoa, and they make students more interested in the rest of the video.

CONCLUDE: Help students formulate conclusions about the importance of anecdotes like these in a biographical video.

Possible response: Personal stories are important in a video like this one because they engage the viewer and make the person in the biographical video more relatable.

Remind students that an **anecdote** is a brief story about an interesting, amusing, or strange event, told to entertain or to make a point.

CROSS-CURRICULAR PERSPECTIVES

Science Have students work in their small groups to research the qualifications for becoming an astronaut. What talents and aptitudes are helpful? What educational background is necessary? Are there any physical requirements involved? What other qualities does NASA look for in its astronauts? When groups have finished their research, have them use a resume template to create a resume for an imaginary person who wants to become an astronaut.

FACILITATING

Comprehension Check

Possible responses:

1. The moon landing; Sally Ride
2. By becoming the first Hispanic female astronaut
3. Sally Ride showed Ochoa that it was possible for a woman to become an astronaut.

Jump Start

CLOSE REVIEW Have groups discuss the following prompt: *Would you like to work in space exploration? What would be your biggest obstacle to a career in space?* As students discuss in their groups, have them consider ways to overcome any obstacles.

Close Review

Remind students to clarify anything they did not understand during their first review. You may wish to print the **Close-Review Guide: Media: Video** for students to use.

Analyze the Media

Possible responses:

1. Students' impressions will vary. Make sure students choose words that accurately and vividly describe Ellen Ochoa or another compelling aspect of the video.
2. Students' opinions will vary. Remind them to support their opinions with specific evidence from the video.
3. Students' opinions will vary. Remind them to support their opinions with specific evidence from the video.

Technical Vocabulary

For more support, see **Technical Vocabulary.**

Word Network

Possible words: *astronauts, planet, moon*

FORMATIVE ASSESSMENT

Analyze the Text 

If students struggle to close review the video, **then** provide the **Ellen Ochoa: Director, Johnson Space Center: Media Questions** available online in the Interactive Teacher's Edition or Unit Resources. Answers and DOK levels are also available.

Technical Vocabulary

If students struggle to use the words in their writing**, then** have them practice using the words in sentences within their groups.

MAKING MEANING

Comprehension Check

Complete the following items after you finish your first review. Review and clarify details with your group.

1. Identify at least one thing that inspired Ochoa to become an astronaut.
2. How did Ochoa make history?
3. How did Sally Ride influence Ochoa?

TECHNICAL VOCABULARY

Use these words as you discuss and write about the video.

aptitude
calculus
mission control

WORD NETWORK

Add interesting words related to space exploration from the video to your Word Network.

Close Review

Watch the video again. Write any new observations that seem important. What **questions** do you have? What can you **conclude**?

Analyze the Media

CITE TEXTUAL EVIDENCE to support your answers.

Notebook Complete the activities.

1. **Present and Discuss** Choose the section of the video you find most interesting or powerful. Share your choice with the group and discuss why you chose it. Explain what you noticed in that part of the video, the questions it raised for you, and the conclusions you reached.
2. **Review and Synthesize** With your group, review the video. How is Ochoa's experience as an astronaut similar to and different from what you might expect? Explain.
3. **Essential Question: *Should we make a home in space?*** What has this video taught you about space exploration by humans? Discuss with your group.

EFFECTIVE EXPRESSION

Speaking and Listening

ELLEN OCHOA: DIRECTOR, JOHNSON SPACE CENTER

Assignment

Work as a group to write and present a short **biography** of Ochoa's life. Watch the video again and have each member of the group take notes. Then, briefly research Ellen Ochoa's career. Afterward, hold a group discussion to decide which details from the video and from your research to include in the biography.

Define Individual Roles Before viewing, writing, and discussing, assign tasks to group members. These might include:

- leading the planning discussion
- integrating research into the draft
- typing the final draft
- presenting the biography to the class

Analyze and Discuss Use these tips to guide your note-taking, discussion, and presentation:

- Watch the video several times in order to catch and note important details about Ochoa's life and her motivations for becoming an astronaut. Pause the video as needed.
- Don't write down everything you hear. Focus on specific dates and facts. Fill in details in later viewings. Use a chart like the one shown.

VIDEO TIME CODE	DETAILS FROM VIDEO
Additional Details From Research	

Plan Once you have gathered details, discuss with your group each item to include in the biography. Work collaboratively to determine a logical order in which to present your information. You may want to create a timeline to accompany your presentation.

Present Rehearse and then present your finished biography to the class. Invite questions and feedback from the class after your presentation.

EVIDENCE LOG

Before moving on to a new selection, go to your Evidence Log and record what you learned from the video.

STANDARDS

Speaking and Listening
Engage effectively in a range of collaborative discussions (one-on-one, in groups, and teacher-led) with diverse partners *on grade 7 topics, texts, and issues,* building on others' ideas and expressing their own clearly.

a. Come to discussions prepared, having read or researched material under study; explicitly draw on that preparation by referring to evidence on the topic, text, or issue to probe and reflect on ideas under discussion.
b. Follow rules for collegial discussions, track progress toward specific goals and deadlines, and define individual roles as needed.
c. Pose questions that elicit elaboration and respond to others' questions and comments with relevant observations and ideas that bring the discussion back on topic as needed.
d. Acknowledge new information expressed by others and, when warranted, modify their own views.

DIGITAL PERSPECTIVES

Speaking and Listening

Define Individual Roles Remind students that roles ensure students share responsibility and help keep discussion focused. For this discussion, each group will need a moderator, a note taker, and a timekeeper.

Analyze and Discuss Remind students to set time limits for speakers and to avoid getting sidetracked from answering the questions and working together to fill in the chart.

Plan Help students to organize the information they present in the biography. For example, they may choose to include information chronologically or by order of importance.

For more support, see **Speaking and Listening: Biography: Group Discussion.**

Evidence Log Support students in completing their Evidence Log. This paced activity will help prepare them for the Performance-Based Assessment at the end of the unit.

FORMATIVE ASSESSMENT

Speaking and Listening

If students struggle to analyze different elements of the video, **then** have them choose one scene and describe its visuals and sounds.

PERSONALIZE FOR LEARNING

English Language Support

Holding a Group Discussion Ask small groups of students to choose a topic for a group discussion and write a list of sample open-ended questions that could be asked during the discussion. **EMERGING**

Ask small groups of students to choose a topic for a group discussion, write a list of open-ended questions that could be asked, and then have a discussion. **EXPANDING**

Have two small groups work together to critique each other's group discussion. Ask each small group to choose a topic for a group discussion, write a list of questions that could be asked, and then have a discussion while the other group observes. Then the groups trade places and share feedback with each other. **BRIDGING**

Neil deGrasse Tyson on the Future of U.S. Space Exploration After *Curiosity*

AUDIO SUMMARIES
Audio summaries of "Neil deGrasse Tyson on the Future of U.S. Space Exploration After *Curiosity*" are available in both English and Spanish in the Interactive Teacher's Edition or Unit Resources. Assigning these summaries prior to reading the selection may help students build additional background knowledge and set a context for their first read.

Summary

In this interview, Keith Wagstaff asks Neil deGrasse Tyson, the famous astronomer, about his work with the *Curiosity* Rover. The *Curiosity* mission used a robot to explore much of Mars with great success. Here, Tyson argues passionately for the continued importance of government-funded space travel, like the *Curiosity* mission. Private space companies have become increasingly prominent, but it is very hard to make space exploration profitable and reliable. As Tyson makes clear, the United States needs government-funded missions to go first, and private companies to follow.

Insight

Tyson provides an optimistic but realistic view of the challenges facing space exploration. He sees both advantages and drawbacks in both government and private enterprise.

ESSENTIAL QUESTION:
Should we make a home in space?

Connection to Essential Question

This interview directly addresses the Essential Question. Tyson believes that space exploration is a good idea. He is more concerned with the process of funding the space program than with arguing for why we should do it. He does, though, suggest that landing on Mars would give a whole generation a lasting, positive memory.

SMALL-GROUP LEARNING PERFORMANCE TASK
Should space exploration be a priority for our country?

UNIT PERFORMANCE-BASED ASSESSMENT
Should we spend valuable resources on space exploration?

Connection to Performance Tasks

Small-Group Learning Task This selection speaks to whether the government should fund space exploration rather than private corporations, who do not depend on taxpayers for their budgets. As for the priority, students may suggest that the question should be whether we, as Americans, should prioritize it over taking care of matters on Earth. Some students may question whether it is possible to do both.

Unit Performance-Based Assessment Tyson argues that the government should fund space exploration, and that ultimately comes from tax money. Students may suggest that this interview focuses on the need for the government's interaction, and as a result reinforces the idea that citizens are the ones who bear the risk of paying for space exploration.

DIGITAL PERSPECTIVES

 Audio

 Video

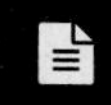 Document

 Annotation Highlights

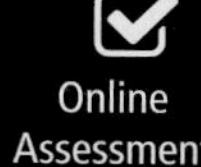 Online Assessment

LESSON RESOURCES

	Making Meaning	Language Development	Effective Expression
Lesson	**First Read** **Close Read** **Analyze the Text** **Analyze Craft and Structure**	**Concept Vocabulary** **Word Study** **Conventions**	**Research**
Instructional Standards	**RI.7.10** By the end of the year, read and comprehend literary nonfiction . . . **L.7.4** Determine or clarify the meaning of unknown and multiple-meaning words and phrases . . . **RI.7.4** Determine the meaning of words and phrases as they are used in a text . . . **RI.7.6** Determine an author's point of view or purpose . . . **RI.7.8** Trace and evaluate the argument . . .	**L.7.4** Determine or clarify the meaning of unknown and multiple-meaning words and phrases . . . **L.7.4.c** Consult general and specialized reference materials . . . **L.7.1** Demonstrate command of the conventions . . . **L.7.2** Demonstrate command of the conventions . . .	**W.7.2** Write informative/ explanatory texts . . . **W.7.7** Conduct short research projects . . . **W.7.8** Gather relevant information from multiple print and digital sources . . .
STUDENT RESOURCES			
Available online in the Interactive Student Edition or Unit Resources	Selection Audio First-Read Guide: Nonfiction Close-Read Guide: Nonfiction	Word Network	Evidence Log
TEACHER RESOURCES			
Selection Resources Available online in the Interactive Teacher's Edition or Unit Resources	Audio Summaries: English and Spanish Annotation Highlights Accessible Leveled Text Spanish Translation Text Questions First Read Extension Questions Analyze Craft and Structure: Evaluate Argument and Claims	Concept Vocabulary and Word Study Conventions: Sentence Functions and End Marks	Research: Research Project
Reteach/Practice (RP) Available online in the Interactive Teacher's Edition or Unit Resources	Analyze Craft and Structure: Evaluate Argument and Claims (RP)	Word Study: Multiple-Meaning Words (RP) Conventions: Sentence Functions and End Marks (RP)	Research: Research Project (RP)
Assessment Available online in Assessments	Selection Test: English Selection Test: Spanish Extension Selection Test		
My Resources	A Unit 2 Answer Key is available online and in the Interactive Teacher's Edition.		

Reading Support

Text Complexity Rubric: Neil deGrasse Tyson on the Future . . .	
Quantitative Measures	
Lexile: 930 **Text Length:** 908 words	
Qualitative Measures	
Knowledge Demands ①—②—❸—④—⑤	Selection contains discipline-specific references, including NASA, Mars missions, *Curiosity* mission, Hubble Telescope, International Space Station, and Neil Armstrong.
Structure ①—②—❸—④—⑤	Interview format with questions clearly marked makes structure easy to follow. Some answers have a range of ideas and organization that is not entirely evident.
Language Conventionality and Clarity ①—②—③—❹—⑤	As the transcript of a spoken interview, the style is casual and conversational. Some sentences have unclear referents, unfamiliar vocabulary and usage, or figures of speech.
Levels of Meaning/Purpose ①—②—③—❹—⑤	Main topics are explicitly stated in questions. Answers contain details and examples that are mostly clear, but organization and language at times make meaning harder to understand.

DECIDE AND PLAN

English Language Support

Provide English Learners with support for language and meaning as they read the selection.

Language Point out figurative or exaggerated language. For example, in paragraph 1, *delusional* is an exaggeration of people who are not being realistic. In paragraph 8, a *flywheel of innovation* increases momentum. Clarify the referents for pronouns. For example, in the last paragraph, *that* refers to innovation.

Meaning You may want to clarify the meaning of the questions. For example, for question 1, explain that NASA is government-funded. The question is about government vs. private funding. Restate ideas and guide students as necessary. For example, *He says private enterprise cannot lead a space program* (paragraph 2). Guide students to see that as a result, NASA is important.

Strategic Support

Provide students with strategic support to ensure that they can successfully read the text.

Knowledge Demands Make a list of names of people, programs, and organizations students will find in the reading: NASA, *Curiosity* mission, Neil deGrasse Tyson, Neil Armstrong, Hubble Telescope, International Space station. Find out what students know about them. Clarify what or who they are if necessary.

Meaning Discuss each of the interview questions. For each question, ask student volunteers to tell their understanding of the answers. List ideas. For example, for the first question, ask for reasons we need NASA instead of private funding. Students may say that the space frontier is expensive and has unknown risks, and the government is better at inventing tools and setting up routines.

Challenge

Provide students who need to be challenged with ideas for how they can go beyond a simple interpretation of the text.

Text Analysis Discuss the second question, on inspiring people to go into STEM fields. Ask students what would inspire them or other young people to go into these fields. Find out if they agree that the *Curiosity* mission alone is not sufficient to inspire study in these fields.

Written Response Have students find Neil deGrasse Tyson's blogs and articles on the Hayden Planetarium website. Or, have them look up information about Mars missions on the NASA site. For either site, ask students to read one or more articles to write an essay about what they read, what they found interesting, and what they would like to know more about.

TEACH

Read and Respond

Have the groups read the selection and complete the Making Meaning, Language Development, and Effective Expression activities.

Standards Support Through Teaching and Learning Cycle

IDENTIFY NEEDS

Analyze results of the Beginning-of-Year Assessment, focusing on the items relating to Unit 2. Also take into consideration student performance to this point and your observations of where particular students struggle.

ANALYZE AND REVISE

- Analyze student work for evidence of student learning.
- Identify whether students have met the expectations in the standards.
- Identify implications for future instruction.

TEACH

Implement the planned lesson, and gather evidence of student learning.

DECIDE AND PLAN

- If students have performed poorly on items matching these standards, then provide selection scaffolds before assigning them the on-level lesson provided in the Student Edition.
- If students have done well on the Beginning-of-Year Assessment, then challenge them to keep progressing and learning by giving them opportunities to practice the skills in depth.
- Use the Selection Resources listed on the Planning pages for "Neil deGrasse Tyson on the Future of U.S. Space Exploration After *Curiosity*" to help students continually improve their ability to master the standards.

Instructional Standards: Neil deGrasse Tyson on the Future . . .

	Catching Up	This Year	Looking Forward
Reading	You may wish to administer the **Analyze Craft and Structure: Evaluate Argument and Claims (RP)** worksheet to help students understand how to develop a claim, identify opposing claims, and support their reasons with evidence.	**RI.6** Determine an author's point of view or purpose in a text and analyze how the author distinguishes his or her position from that of others. **RI.8** Trace and evaluate the argument and specific claims in a text, assessing whether the reasoning is sound and the evidence is relevant and sufficient to support the claims.	Challenge students to develop an argument that uses as its claim one of the counterclaims from their original argument.
Language	You may wish to administer the **Conventions: Sentence Functions and End Marks (RP)** worksheet to help students understand how to end a sentence correctly. You may wish to administer the **Word Study: Multiple-Meaning Words (RP)** worksheet to help students understand that they can determine the meaning of unfamiliar words based on content and context.	**L.2** Demonstrate command of the conventions of standard English capitalization, punctuation, and spelling when writing. **L.4** Determine or clarify the meaning of unknown and multiple-meaning words and phrases based on *grade 7 reading and content,* choosing flexibly from a range of strategies.	Ask pairs of students to work together. Each student will write down five sentences from the text without end marks. Students will then trade and add end marks to their sentences. Ask students to discuss how they knew what kind of mark to use. Have students identify multiple-meaning words in their reading. Ask them to write definitions for the words based on the context in which the words are used.

FACILITATING

Jump Start

FIRST READ What inspires people to do something that they've never done before? Engage students in a discussion about people who have taken a chance and done something new that was a challenge. Encourage students to discuss the motivations for the decision, the challenges, as well as the positive and negative aspects of the decision and its outcome.

Neil deGrasse Tyson on the Future of U.S. Space Exploration After *Curiosity*

What intrigues people about making a home in space? How does this interest impact space exploration? Modeling questions such as these will help students connect to "Neil deGrasse Tyson on the Future of U.S. Space Exploration After *Curiosity*" and to the Small-Group Performance Task assignment. Selection audio and print capability for the selection are available in the Interactive Teacher's Edition.

Concept Vocabulary

Ask groups to look closely at the "inside" word in the example and discuss how looking at the familiar word helps to determine the meaning of the unfamiliar word. Encourage groups to discuss other vocabulary strategies they could use if they are unfamiliar with the base word.

FIRST READ

As they read, students should perform the steps of the first read:

NOTICE: You may want to encourage students to notice how strong the claims made in the interview are regarding the topic.

ANNOTATE: Remind students to mark passages that may support the argument.

CONNECT: Encourage students to discuss news stories that they remember regarding space exploration.

RESPOND: Students will answer questions and write a summary to demonstrate understanding.

Point out to students that while they will always complete the Respond step at the end of the first read, the other steps will probably happen somewhat concurrently. You may wish to print copies of the **First-Read Guide: Nonfiction** for students to use.

MAKING MEANING

About the Author

Keith Wagstaff is a science and technology journalist. He has written for *Time* magazine, *NBC News*, and other outlets.

Neil deGrasse Tyson on the Future of U.S. Space Exploration After *Curiosity*

Concept Vocabulary

As you perform your first read, you will encounter these words.

cede	enterprise	capitalistic

Base Words If these words are unfamiliar to you, analyze each one to see whether it contains a **base word** you know. Then, use your knowledge of the "inside" word, along with context, to determine the meaning of the concept word. Here is an example of how to apply the strategy.

Unfamiliar Word: *investment*

Familiar "Inside" Word: *invest*, meaning "to spend money in hopes of earning more back"

Context: "It's an investment, not a handout."

Conclusion: The item being discussed is not given out freely; a return is expected. *Investment* might mean "something bought with the expectation of making money or getting something out of it."

Apply your knowledge of base words and other vocabulary strategies to determine the meanings of unfamiliar words you encounter during your first read.

First Read NONFICTION

Apply these strategies as you conduct your first read. You will have an opportunity to complete a close read after your first read.

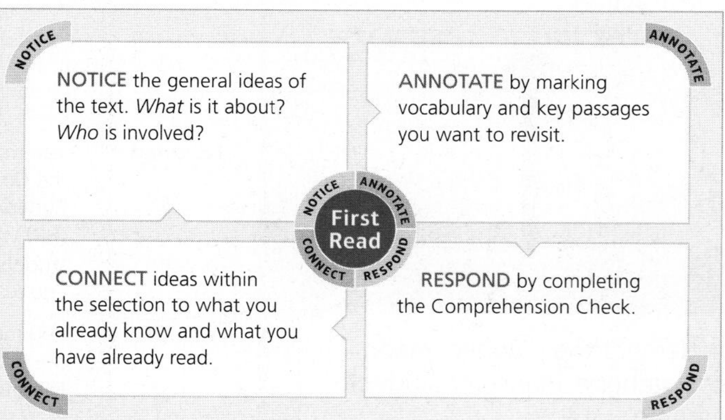

STANDARDS

Reading Informational Text
By the end of the year, read and comprehend literary nonfiction in the grades 6–8 text complexity band proficiently, with scaffolding as needed at the high end of the range.

Language
Determine or clarify the meaning of unknown and multiple-meaning words and phrases based on *grade 7 reading and content*, choosing flexibly from a range of strategies.

FACILITATING SMALL-GROUP CLOSE READING

CLOSE READ: Interview As groups perform the close read, circulate and offer support as needed.

- Remind students to carefully read each question posed in the interview.
- Encourage groups to discuss their opinions to each question.
- Remind students to find the claim in the response and cite evidence from the text to support the claim.
- Challenge the groups to compare and contrast their ideas with those expressed in the interview.

Neil deGrasse Tyson on the Future of U.S. Space Exploration After *Curiosity*

Keith Wagstaff

BACKGROUND

NASA's *Curiosity* is a robotic rover that landed on Mars in 2012. Since then, *Curiosity* has been roaming Mars, collecting data and looking for signs of microbial life. In this interview, astrophysicist Neil deGrasse Tyson discusses the *Curiosity* mission and the possibility of people's traveling to Mars.

Some people are questioning the need to fund a government space program. Why do we still need NASA?

1 The people who say that all we need is private space travel are simply delusional. My book on space, *Space Chronicles: Facing the Ultimate Frontier,* was originally titled *Failure to Launch: The Dreams and Delusions of Space Enthusiasts.* Space enthusiasts are the most susceptible demographic to delusion that I have ever seen.

2 Private enterprise can never lead a space frontier. It's not possible because a space frontier is expensive, it has unknown risks, and it has unquantified risks. Historically, governments have done this. They have drawn the maps, they have found where the trade winds[1] are, they have invented the new tools to go where no one has gone before. Then, when the routines are set up, you **cede** that to private **enterprise**.

3 That's why I don't know what they're thinking. The first colony on Mars is not going to be built by a private company. How are you going to make money? You're not.

4 Look what's going on now. Private enterprise is giving us access to low-Earth orbit for less than what NASA was providing. That should have been happening decades ago. Why is that happening now? Because low-Earth orbit is no longer the frontier. NASA has been going in and out of low-Earth orbit since 1962.

NOTES

Mark base words or indicate another strategy you used that helped you determine meaning.

cede (seed) *v.*

MEANING:

enterprise (EHN tuhr pryz) *n.*

MEANING:

1. **trade winds** reliable winds that captains of sailing ships have traditionally used to cross the oceans.

DIGITAL PERSPECTIVES

Concept Vocabulary

CEDE If groups are struggling to define the word *cede* in paragraph 2, point out that *cede* is a base word, and they may want to consider familiar words that have *cede* as the base word. Encourage students to list some words such as *concede, recede,* or *secede* to provide context clues. If they are still unsure of the meaning, have them consider context clues. What is government *ceding* to private enterprise?

Possible response: The word *cede* means "to yield control."

ENTERPRISE If groups are struggling to define the word *enterprise* in paragraph 2, draw their attention to the context clues in the previous sentences. Point out that these prior sentences are an example of contrast, which can be helpful in identifying the meaning. What is being contrasted with government?

Possible response: In this context, *enterprise* means "business or industry."

DIGITAL PERSPECTIVES

Enriching the Text To help groups better understand the type of missions referred to in paragraph 2, use the search terms "Curiosity robotic rover" to find video footage online showing the mission of the rover *Curiosity*.

Preview videos before sharing them with students. Have groups discuss how seeing and hearing these images and interviews helps provide a deeper understanding of the types of missions that NASA leads and why these missions are too costly for private enterprise.

Then, have students write a sentence or two explaining how the video footage helps clarify the NASA mission. If necessary, provide a sample sentence, such as, Curiosity *is the largest mission of its kind, and scientists hope to continue to learn from its findings for many years to come.*

FACILITATING

CLOSER LOOK

Analyze Argument

Circulate among groups as students conduct their close read. Suggest that groups close read paragraphs 6 and 7. Encourage them to talk about the annotations they mark. If needed, provide the following support.

ANNOTATE: Have students mark details in paragraphs 6 and 7 that identify the speaker's claim, or work with small groups as you highlight them together.

QUESTION: Guide students to consider what these details might tell them. Ask what a reader can infer from these claims and the reasons used to support the claims, and accept student responses.

Possible response: Based on examples from past missions, NASA's actions create interest among students. However, he doesn't feel that interest will be enough to fund a mission to Mars.

CONCLUDE: Help students to formulate conclusions about the importance of these details in the text. Ask students why the author might have included these details.

Possible response: The details help us to understand the speaker's argument. The claims and reasons in paragraphs 6 and 7 show that the speaker supports NASA's efforts and believes that they will help inspire young people but will not be enough to encourage building homes on Mars.

Remind groups that an **argument** includes the **claim** that a writer or speaker presents, as well as supporting reasons and **evidence**. To evaluate a writer's argument, decide whether the claim is clearly presented and strongly supported by logical reasons and relevant evidence.

Additional **English Language Support** is available in the Interactive Teacher's Edition.

NOTES

5 I see private enterprise as a fundamental part of creating a space industry, but there will always be the frontier.

When *Curiosity* touches down,[2] will that be enough to inspire young people to go into the STEM fields (science, technology, engineering, and mathematics) and to get the American people behind a manned mission to Mars?

6 Anything NASA does in space that has never been done before drums up interest in science. Images from the Hubble Telescope, the *Spirit* and *Opportunity* rovers, broadcasts from the International Space Station—anything NASA does accomplishes this.

7 Whether that's enough to get humans on Mars, I don't think so. *Curiosity* is cheap compared to sending humans out of low-Earth orbit. A different kind of understanding of the value of sending humans into space needs to be had before that happens. I don't think *Curiosity* is a stepping stone to that.

Are the barriers to sending humans to Mars political?

8 No. It's an understanding—that the public does not yet have—of the role of NASA as a flywheel[3] of innovation, influencing not only direct spin-offs but also the culture itself. When you feel that you are part of an innovation nation, you think innovatively, no matter your field.

9 You start thinking that the science fiction story you just read or movie you just saw is maybe in reach. Maybe it's possible. For example, in the movie *Prometheus*, they have these flying spheres that go up and down caves and use laser tomography to map their structure. We don't have that, but that's really cool and I can imagine having that.

10 That idea might inspire me to try and create it instead of just sitting back and saying, "Oh, that's the future and it will probably never happen. Now let me go back and watch Snooki."[4]

11 I am certain that once that flywheel is set into motion and the discoveries of NASA become writ large in the newspapers, that people will come to understand that innovations in science and technology—brought to you by the force of nature we call NASA—are the engines of 21st Century economies. It's an investment, not a handout.

What is it going to mean to the human race if we land on Mars?

12 Here's the problem. I don't know how old you are, but I'm guessing you were born after we landed on the Moon. Now, given that fact, I'm guessing that there is no single event in your life that is positive where you say, "I remember where I was at that moment." Is there?

No.

2. **When *Curiosity* touches down** This interview took place four days before *Curiosity* was scheduled to land on Mars.
3. **flywheel** *n.* wheel that controls a machine's speed and power.
4. **Snooki** star of a reality television show.

PERSONALIZE FOR LEARNING

English Language Support

Evaluating an Argument Review the question and answer in paragraphs 8–11. Groups may struggle to identify the claims and reasons within each question of the interview. Support groups as they identify the overarching argument of this interview. Call students' attention to these sentences in the text:

- Paragraph 2: *Private enterprise can never lead a space frontier.*
- Paragraph 16: *All of that is possible when you have a healthy NASA exploring the cosmos.*

Have groups review the definition of argument and discuss the argument that the speaker is making. Encourage them to identify and write the argument in a complete sentence. **ALL LEVELS**

13 I have the benefit of being able to say I know where I was when Neil Armstrong walked on the Moon. You don't have it. You don't have that moment. We have bred multiple generations of people who have not experienced knowing where you are the moment a news story broke, with that news story being great and grand and something that elevates society instead of diminishes it. If we land on Mars, you'll know where you were the day that happened. Landing on Mars expands the space frontier and that makes headlines.

14 Boldly going where hundreds have gone before does not make headlines. If you make the headlines, that's what stimulates STEM interest. You won't need a program to excite people to get into the sciences. You won't need tariffs[5] to keep your factories stateside, because you'll be innovating at a pace where you're making products the rest of the world hasn't figured out how to make yet.

15 When an industry matures, it means it's not advancing and of course the jobs go overseas. That's the obligation of the multi-national corporation, to put the factory where it can make the widget as cheap as possible. Don't get angry when a corporation does that, we've all bought into this concept. We live in a **capitalistic** society. That's how it works.

16 You don't complain. You say "Let's innovate so we can make things that [other countries] can't." All of that is possible when you have a healthy NASA exploring the cosmos. All of that. ❧

NOTES

Mark base words or indicate another strategy you used that helped you determine meaning.

capitalistic (kap uh tuh LIHS tihk) *adj.*

MEANING:

5. **tariffs** (TAIR ihfs) *n.* taxes on goods imported from other countries.

Comprehension Check

Complete the following items after you finish your first read. Review and clarify details with your group.

1. In Neil deGrasse Tyson's opinion, who can best lead the exploration of frontiers?

2. What role does deGrasse Tyson see for private companies?

RESEARCH

Research to Clarify Choose at least one unfamiliar detail in the selection. Briefly research that detail. In what way does the information you learned shed light on the selection?

DIGITAL PERSPECTIVES

Concept Vocabulary

CAPITALISTIC If groups are struggling to define the word *capitalistic* in paragraph 15, point out the base word *capital*. Also draw their attention to other words and phrases in paragraph 15, such as *industry*, *corporation*, and "make the widget as cheap as possible," which are context clues that can help provide a definition for the word.

Possible response: In this context, *capitalistic* describes "an economic system in which businesses strive to make profits."

Comprehension Check

Possible responses:

1. Governments
2. Private enterprise can help to create a space industry that fuels the economy.

Research

Research to Clarify If students struggle to choose a detail, suggest one of the following: history of NASA, *Curiosity*, low-Earth orbit, or *Prometheus*.

PERSONALIZE FOR LEARNING

Challenge

Your Own Video In paragraph 13, the speaker states, "We have bred multiple generations of people who have not experienced knowing where you are the moment a news story broke, with that news story being great and grand and something that elevates society instead of diminishes it." While many students can imagine events that involved war, or danger, challenge them to think of the type of event that Tyson describes—one that is positive. Encourage interested students to create a brief video in which they imagine that they are a news crew interviewing people who are sharing their reaction to such an event from history. What questions should students ask? What would the people say? Students can write scripts upon which to base their interviews and then use mobile devices to film the interviews.

Jump Start

CLOSE READ Ask groups to consider the following prompt: *Have you ever considered living in outer space? What things would you miss most and want to make a part of life in your new home?* As students discuss in their groups, ask them to consider the argument in the interview surrounding sending humans to Mars.

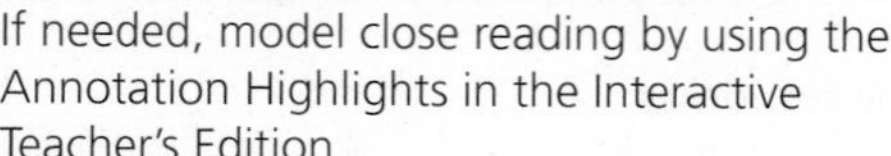

Close Read the Text

If needed, model close reading by using the Annotation Highlights in the Interactive Teacher's Edition.

Remind students to use Accountable Talk in their discussions and to support one another as they complete the close read.

Analyze the Text

Possible responses:

1. They are not accepting the reality that first there has to be exploration, which is too expensive to be funded privately.
2. Remind students to explain why they chose the passages they presented to group members.
3. Responses will vary.

Concept Vocabulary

Why These Words? Possible response: All of these words have to do with business ventures. Other words that fit the category could be *market* or *economy*.

Practice

Responses will vary. Groups should support their claim with reasons and include concept vocabulary.

Word Network

Possible words: *orbit, frontier, rovers, science*

Word Study

For more support, see **Concept Vocabulary and Word Study.**

Possible response:

In this interview, *enterprise* (paragraph 2) means "a business venture" because the next sentence describes expenses and risks, and businesses avoid excessive unknown expenses and risks.

MAKING MEANING

NEIL DEGRASSE TYSON ON THE FUTURE OF U.S. SPACE EXPLORATION AFTER *CURIOSITY*

Close Read the Text

With your group, revisit sections of the text you marked during your first read. **Annotate** details that you notice. What **questions** do you have? What can you **conclude**?

Analyze the Text

CITE TEXTUAL EVIDENCE to support your answers.

Notebook Complete the activities.

1. **Review and Clarify** With your group, review paragraphs 1–5 of the interview. According to deGrasse Tyson, why are people who say that we only need private space travel "simply delusional"?
2. **Present and Discuss** Now, work with your group to share the passages from the selection that you found especially important. Take turns presenting your passages. Discuss what you noticed in the selection, the questions you asked, and the conclusions you reached.
3. **Essential Question: *Should we make a home in space?*** What has this selection taught you about humans making a home in space? Discuss with your group.

TIP

GROUP DISCUSSION
If you disagree with a group member's opinion, do so respectfully. Be prepared to support your own opinion with details from the selection.

WORD NETWORK

Add interesting words related to space exploration from the text to your Word Network.

LANGUAGE DEVELOPMENT

Concept Vocabulary

cede   enterprise   capitalistic

Why These Words? The concept vocabulary words from the text are related. With your group, determine what the words have in common. Write your ideas and add another word that fits the category.

Practice

Notebook Confirm your understanding of the concept vocabulary words by using them in a discussion of the role of money in space exploration. Should the government play the leading role in funding space travel, or should space travel be handled by private companies?

Word Study

Multiple-Meaning Words In the interview, deGrasse Tyson discusses the role of private enterprise in exploring space. The word *enterprise* has several meanings. Use a dictionary to find all of the definitions of *enterprise*. Then, determine which meaning is the correct meaning for *enterprise* as it is used in the interview.

STANDARDS

Language
Determine or clarify the meaning of unknown and multiple-meaning words and phrases based on *grade 7 reading and content*, choosing flexibly from a range of strategies.

c. Consult general and specialized reference materials, both print and digital, to find the pronunciation of a word or determine or clarify its precise meaning or its part of speech.

FORMATIVE ASSESSMENT

Analyze the Text

If students struggle to close read the text, **then** provide the **Neil deGrasse Tyson on the Future: Text Questions** available online in the Interactive Teacher's Edition or Unit Resources. Answers and DOK levels are also available.

Concept Vocabulary

If students fail to see a connection between the words, **then** have them use each word in a sentence and think about what is similar about the sentences.

Word Study

If students struggle to identify the correct meaning of *enterprise*, **then** have them write a sentence using meaning 1 and meaning 3. For Reteach and Practice, see **Word Study: Multiple-Meaning Words (RP).**

Analyze Craft and Structure

Evaluate Argument and Claims An **argument** is a logical way of presenting a specific belief, conclusion, or perspective on an issue or action. A good argument provides logical reasons and relevant evidence in support of a **claim,** or position on the topic or action at hand.

- **relevant evidence: facts,** or statements that can be proved true, from credible sources that are current
- **logical reasons:** conclusions that are reached based on an analysis of the relevant evidence

Word choice, or the words, phrases, and expressions an author uses, can strengthen an argument. Most arguments are characterized by precise, formal language that clearly shows the connections between claims, reasons, and evidence. However, an author may use **figurative language,** or language that is not meant literally, to appeal to his or her audience or to simplify a complex idea.

STANDARDS

Reading Informational Text

- Determine the meaning of words and phrases as they are used in a text, including figurative, connotative, and technical meanings; analyze the impact of a specific word choice on meaning and tone.
- Determine an author's point of view or purpose in a text and analyze how the author distinguishes his or her position from that of others.
- Trace and evaluate the argument and specific claims in a text, assessing whether the reasoning is sound and the evidence is relevant and sufficient to support the claims.

Practice

CITE TEXTUAL EVIDENCE to support your answers.

Notebook Work with your group to analyze Neil deGrasse Tyson's argument. Use a chart such as the one shown to record your notes. Then, answer the questions that follow.

CLAIM	EVIDENCE	REASONS
Government must drive the funding of the space program.	Historically, governments have had this role.	Space exploration is too expensive and risky for private companies.
Private companies are focused on making money.	*Curiosity* will stimulate student interest in STEM subjects.	Space exploration and moon walking are important.

1. (a) What is deGrasse Tyson's main claim? (b) What evidence and reasons support his argument?

2. A **metaphor** is a type of figurative language that compares two unlike things by saying that one thing is another. (a) What is the metaphor deGrasse Tyson uses in paragraphs 8–11? (b) How does the use of this metaphor affect his argument?

3. Based on your analysis, is deGrasse Tyson's argument effective and convincing? Why or why not?

DIGITAL PERSPECTIVES

Analyze Craft and Stucture

Evaluate Argument and Claims Discuss with groups the difference between a *claim* and the *reasons* or *evidence* that support that claim. Remind students that they should exclude their personal opinions when identifying a speaker's claim or supporting reasons. For more support, see **Analyze Craft and Structure: Evaluate Argument and Claims.**

Possible responses:

See chart on student page for possible responses to Notebook activity.

1. (a) Tyson claims that it is necessary to fund a government space program. (b) Tyson argues that private companies cannot be expected to explore the frontiers of space because their goal is to make money and exploration is too expensive and risky. He also argues that such exploration is necessary for innovation and scientific and economic progress. Tyson points out that historically governments have been responsible for exploration. To support the idea that sparking the imagination is important for innovation, he provides an example from a movie. He also elaborates on the importance of momentous events like walking on the moon.
2. (a) Tyson calls NASA "a flywheel of innovation." (b) He strengthens his argument by using an image that portrays NASA as a powerful tool for invention.
3. Opinions will vary. Students should support their opinions with evidence from the text.

FORMATIVE ASSESSMENT

Analyze Craft and Structure

If students struggle to identify Tyson's claim, **then** have them analyze each interview question and identify the main idea being discussed to better evaluate the claim. Allow them to find the answer to the main question and then skim the response to find the claim if needed. For Reteach and Practice, see **Analyze Craft and Structure: Evaluate Argument and Claims (RP).**

PERSONALIZE FOR LEARNING

Strategic Support

Clarifying Elements of an Argument If students struggle to comprehend the elements of an argument in "Neil deGrasse Tyson on the Future of the U.S. Space Exploration After *Curiosity,*" suggest that they track their comprehension with two-color highlighting. Ask them to use one color to mark the sentences and paragraphs that they understand and another color for the text that is challenging. When students identify a passage that is confusing or overwhelming, have a group member summarize the text in his or her own words to unlock the meaning.

FACILITATING

Conventions

Sentence Functions and End Marks As you review sentence functions and end marks with students, consider providing additional examples to reinforce their understanding of the concepts. You might also ask volunteers to share examples. For more support, see **Conventions: Sentence Functions and End Marks**.

Read It

See possible responses in the chart on the student page.

Write It

Responses will vary but should include at least one example of each sentence type with the appropriate end mark.

FORMATIVE ASSESSMENT

Conventions

If students can't identify imperative or exclamatory sentences in the selection, **then** have them select a sentence from paragraphs 15 and 16 and work together to identify sentence type and function. For Reteach and Practice, see **Conventions: Sentence Functions and End Marks (RP).**

LANGUAGE DEVELOPMENT

NEIL DEGRASSE TYSON ON THE FUTURE OF U.S. SPACE EXPLORATION AFTER *CURIOSITY*

Conventions

Sentence Functions and End Marks There are four types of sentences, which can be classified according to how they function. End marks vary according to the function of the sentence.

TYPE OF SENTENCE	FUNCTION	END MARK	EXAMPLE
Declarative	To make statements	period (.)	I have no desire to ride in a spaceship.
Interrogative	To ask questions	question mark (?)	Would you want to travel to another planet?
Imperative	To give commands or directions	exclamation point (!) or period (.)	Put on your seatbelt. Sit down, now!
Exclamatory	To call out or exclaim	exclamation point (!)	What a thrill!

Read It

Work with your group to fill in the chart with an example from the selection of each type of sentence. If you cannot find an example, write a sentence of your own.

TYPE OF SENTENCE	EXAMPLE
Declarative	Private enterprise can never lead a space frontier.
Interrogative	Why do we still need NASA?
Imperative	Look what's going on now.
Exclamatory	What a great idea!

Write It

Notebook Using different types of sentences can make your writing more interesting to read. Write a paragraph about space exploration in which you use each type of sentence and end mark at least once. Share your paragraph with your group.

STANDARDS

Language
- Demonstrate command of the conventions of standard English grammar and usage when writing or speaking.
- Demonstrate command of the conventions of standard English capitalization, punctuation, and spelling when writing.

210 UNIT 2 • A STARRY HOME

PERSONALIZE FOR LEARNING

English Language Support

Using Sentence Types Ask pairs of students to collaborate on four sentences that model each of the sentence types. Students should write sentences that relate to their daily activities. **EMERGING**

Have students work independently to write one sentence for each of the sentence types. The sentences should relate to the students' daily activities. **EXPANDING**

Have students write a short paragraph describing their day. Encourage them tfo use all four sentence types and express a range of emotions. **BRIDGING**

An expanded **English Language Support Lesson** on Sentence Function is available in the Interactive Teacher's Edition.

EFFECTIVE EXPRESSION

Research

Assignment

Work with your group to conduct research and write a short **informational report** on one of the following topics:

- ☐ the life and work of Neil deGrasse Tyson
- ☐ the planet Mars
- ☐ the robotic rover *Curiosity*

Your group should formulate a research question; gather information from multiple, reliable sources; and present the information in a clear, organized way.

Project Plan With your group, choose a topic and then formulate your research plan. Use this chart to help gather details.

Topic and Research Plan: ______________________________

SOURCE (TITLE, AUTHOR, AND DATE)	WHAT I LEARNED

Organize and Draft Share your research findings with the group, and decide which details to use in your group report. Organize the details logically, and create a first draft. Be sure to cite the sources you used.

Reflect on Your Research Project After you have presented your project, reflect on the experience by asking yourself these questions.

- What did I learn?
- Was it challenging to work in a group on a written project?
- What parts of the group's process worked well?
- What might I do differently when working on group projects?

EVIDENCE LOG

Before moving on to a new selection, go to your Evidence Log and record what you learned from "Neil deGrasse Tyson on the Future of U.S. Space Exploration After *Curiosity*."

STANDARDS

Writing

- Write informative/explanatory texts to examine a topic and convey ideas, concepts, and information through the selection, organization, and analysis of relevant content.
- Conduct short research projects to answer a question, drawing on several sources and generating additional related, focused questions for further research and investigation.
- Gather relevant information from multiple print and digital sources, using search terms effectively; assess the credibility and accuracy of each source; and quote or paraphrase the data and conclusions of others while avoiding plagiarism and following a standard format for citation.

DIGITAL PERSPECTIVES

Research

If groups have trouble deciding which topic to choose, encourage them to consider which option best plays to their group's interests and strengths. If the group is comprised of concrete thinkers, they may wish to choose the straightforward research project on the life and work of Neil deGrasse Tyson. Those interested in science or exploration may prefer researching the planet Mars or *Curiosity*. Remind them, however, that all options will require multiple reliable sources and will be presented in a clear and organized way.

Project Plan Remind groups to consult the schedule for Small-Group Activities as they create their topic and research plan. Remind them to divide the tasks equally among members.

Reflect on Your Research Project Encourage students to make supportive comments about each speaker's presentation, mode, words, ideas, sources, and conclusions. For more support, see **Research: Research Project.**

Evidence Log Support students in completing their Evidence Log. This paced activity will help prepare them for the Performance-Based Assessment at the end of the unit.

FORMATIVE ASSESSMENT

Research

If groups struggle to find credible sources, **then** help them refine their search terms to more accurately describe their topic. For Reteach and Practice, see **Research: Research Project (RP).**

Selection Test

Administer the "Neil deGrasse Tyson on the Future of U.S. Space Exploration After *Curiosity*" Selection Test, which is available in both print and digital formats online in Assessments.

PERSONALIZE FOR LEARNING

Strategic Support

Formulate Research Questions Students may struggle when formulating the research question to guide their project. Encourage groups to create open-ended questions to help guide their research. From these open-ended questions, they can develop their key word search and organize their time and presentation appropriately. They may also use the open-ended question as their first search and refine the key word search from there.

Closed Question	Open-Ended Research Question
Are private enterprises involved in space exploration?	What is the role of private businesses in space exploration?

Present an Argument

Before groups begin work on their projects, have them clearly differentiate the role each group member will play. Remind groups to consult the schedule for Small-Group Learning to guide their work during the Performance Task.

Students should complete the assignment using presentation software to take advantage of text, graphics, and sound features.

Plan With Your Group

Analyze the Text Remind students that they should be able to find benefits and drawbacks to space exploration in each of the texts they have read. Even if a text seems to embrace only the benefits, for example, students can infer the drawbacks. Later, if students have trouble reacting to the opposing viewpoint, they can look back at these inferences.

Also, let students know that they can use their own ideas about benefits and drawbacks, as long as they can find a reliable source to back up those ideas. Students should add these additional ideas to the bottom of the chart. Tell students that examples of reliable sources include government websites, reports from national newspapers and magazines, and encyclopedias.

Gather Evidence and Media Examples In addition to citing text and media examples that support their claim, remind students that they also need to cite the opposing viewpoint and think about how they plan to counter that viewpoint.

Suggest that students add a column to the right side of the charts that they used to analyze the texts. In this column, they can jot down the specific quotation or page number that they plan to cite in their presentations.

PERFORMANCE TASK: SPEAKING AND LISTENING FOCUS

SOURCES

- FUTURE OF SPACE EXPLORATION COULD SEE HUMANS ON MARS, ALIEN PLANETS
- THE LAST DOG
- ELLEN OCHOA: DIRECTOR, JOHNSON SPACE CENTER
- NEIL DEGRASSE TYSON ON THE FUTURE OF U.S. SPACE EXPLORATION AFTER *CURIOSITY*

Present an Argument

Assignment

You have read different selections that address the benefits and drawbacks of space exploration. With your group, develop and deliver a **multimedia presentation** that addresses this question:

Should space exploration be a priority for our country?

Plan With Your Group

Analyze the Text With your group, discuss the various ideas and opinions about space exploration that are presented in the texts you have read. Use the chart to list your ideas. For each selection, identify benefits and drawbacks of space exploration. Then, come to a consensus, or agreement, about whether the benefits of space exploration by our country outweigh the drawbacks.

TITLE	SPACE EXPLORATION BENEFITS AND DRAWBACKS
Future of Space Exploration Could See Humans on Mars, Alien Planets	
The Last Dog	
Ellen Ochoa: Director, Johnson Space Center	
Neil deGrasse Tyson on the Future of U.S. Space Exploration After *Curiosity*	

Gather Evidence and Media Examples Review the selections and note specific examples that support your group's claim. Once the chart is complete, do some additional research to learn more about current NASA programs and to find relevant media to include in the group presentation. Consider photographs, illustrations, music, charts, graphs, and video clips. Allow each group member to make suggestions.

AUTHOR'S PERSPECTIVE **Ernest Morrell, Ph.D.**

Strategic Use of Media Media is becoming more important as a communication tool, but teachers need to guide students to understand media's value. As groups plan their presentation, remind them that it is important to use media and visuals strategically so that they support the presentation but don't dominate it. Share these suggestions:

- Students should ensure that each piece of media has a specific purpose and is not mere "filler."
- Encourage students to let the content of their arguments drive their decisions about which media support to include rather than finding appealing media and trying to force-fit the media into a presentation where it might not work.
- Remind groups that although media and visuals can enhance a presentation, the content of what students say during the presentation is what is most important.

Ultimately, the presentation should be able to stand alone without media support and still make sense.

Organize Your Ideas Use a script outline, such as the one shown, to organize your presentation. Assign roles for each part of the presentation, note when each part begins, and record what each presenter will say.

MULTIMEDIA PRESENTATION SCRIPT		
	Media Cues	Script
Presenter 1		
Presenter 2		
Presenter 3		

Rehearse With Your Group

Practice With Your Group As you practice delivering your portion of the presentation, use this checklist to evaluate the effectiveness of your group's rehearsal. Then, use your evaluation and the instruction here to guide revisions to your presentation.

CONTENT	USE OF MEDIA	PRESENTATION TECHNIQUES
☐ The claims of the presentation are clear. ☐ The claims are supported with evidence from the texts in this section.	☐ The media support the claim. ☐ The media communicate key ideas. ☐ The media are sequenced effectively. ☐ The equipment functions properly.	☐ The media are visible and audible. ☐ The transitions between the media segments are smooth. ☐ The speaker uses eye contact and speaks clearly.

Fine-Tune the Content To make your argument strong, you may need to go back into the texts and your research sources to find more support for your claims. Work with your group to identify any points that are confusing and need clarification.

Improve Your Use of Media Double-check that media equipment is in working order, and make a backup plan in case your equipment fails. If the media are not well distributed through the presentation, work to change the pacing.

Brush Up on Your Presentation Techniques Practice delivering your presentation several times as a group until you are comfortable. Give each other feedback and encouragement to improve and polish your presentation.

Present and Evaluate

When you present as a group, be sure that each member has taken into account each of the checklist items. As you watch other groups, evaluate how well they meet the checklist criteria.

STANDARDS

Speaking and Listening

- Present claims and findings, emphasizing salient points in a focused, coherent manner with pertinent descriptions, facts, details, and examples; use appropriate eye contact, adequate volume, and clear pronunciation.
- Include multimedia components and visual displays in presentations to clarify claims and findings and emphasize salient points.

PERSONALIZE FOR LEARNING

Strategic Support

Presenting Evidence Remind students that just as they do in written reports, they must give credit in their presentations to their sources of evidence. In speaking, they can do this by referring to the name of the text's title and author as they introduce a piece of evidence. Suggest the following templates for presenting evidence in presentation:

- In "Neil deGrasse Tyson on the Future of U.S. Space Exploration After *Curiosity*," Tyson says, "...."
- Here is Elena Ochoa in a video interview explaining . . .

Tell students that quotations that are both brief and memorable can make effective supporting visual media.

DIGITAL PERSPECTIVES

Organize Your Ideas Unless you require a written copy of the presentation, give presenters a choice of what they want to include in their individual scripts. Some presenters may simply need a bulleted list of the key points and evidence they plan to present, while others may feel more comfortable having every word they plan to say written down.

Rehearse With Your Group

Practice With Your Group As one student is delivering a part of the presentation, another student may be required to run the presentation software. Remind students to be sure to practice handing off the control of the software ahead of time so that the transitions go smoothly.

Fine-Tune the Content Remind group members to pay attention to transitions between sections of the presentation. Suggest that each follow-up speaker begin by referring to the previous speaker's key point and then explain how the information they are about to present supports the group's claim. Such a transition might be phrased as, "Maria just explained how the scientific advances around space exploration benefit everybody. The next reason that space exploration should be a priority for our country is that . . ."

Improve Your Use of Media Help students who are less technologically adept practice using media so they feel confident that it works.

Brush Up on Your Presentation Techniques Check in with groups as they rehearse and observe the presentation's flow. If a presenter stumbles over words or uses too many filler words, suggest reading through the script a couple of times until it sounds more polished. On the other hand, if a presenter fails to make eye contact, suggest memorizing more of the script rather than relying on it continually throughout the presentation.

Present and Evaluate

Before the presentations, set the expectations for the audience. You may wish to have students consider these questions as groups present:

- What was the presenting group's claim?
- What were some of their supporting ideas?
- Did the group address the opposing argument successfully?
- Did the media examples support the group's argument?
- What presentation skills did this group excel at?

As students provide feedback to the presenting group, remind them to identify where and how each group succeeded as well as pointing out areas that need improvement.

OVERVIEW

INDEPENDENT LEARNING

Should we make a home in space?

Encourage students to think carefully about what they have already learned and what more they want to know about the unit topic of A Starry Home. This is a key first step to previewing and selecting the text they will read in Independent Learning.

Independent Learning Strategies

Review the Learning Strategies with students and explain that as they work through Independent Learning they will develop strategies to work on their own.

- Have students watch the video on Independent Learning Strategies.
- A video on this topic is available online in the Professional Development Center.

Students should include any favorite strategies that they might have devised on their own during Whole-Class and Small-Group Learning. For example, for the strategy "Take notes," students might include:

- Write down any questions you might have, so you can ask later.
- Compare notes with your classmates.

Block Scheduling

Each day in this Pacing Plan represents a 40- to 50-minute class period. Teachers using block scheduling may combine days to reflect their class schedule. In addition, teachers may revise pacing to differentiate and support core instruction by integrating components and resources as students require.

OVERVIEW: INDEPENDENT LEARNING

ESSENTIAL QUESTION:

Should we make a home in space?

There is much we don't know about the universe. Some people are eager to support further space exploration, whereas others would prefer to devote time and money to improving conidtions on our own planet. In this section, you will choose one additional selection about outer space for your final reading experience in this unit. Follow these steps to help you choose.

Look Back Think about the selections you have already read. What more do you want to know about outer space?

Look Ahead Preview the selections by reading the descriptions. Which one seems most interesting and appealing to you?

Look Inside Take a few minutes to scan through the text you chose. Make another selection if this text doesn't meet your needs.

Independent Learning Strategies

Throughout your life, in school, in your community, and in your career, you will need to rely on yourself to learn and work on your own. Review these strategies and the actions you can take to practice them during Independent Learning. Add ideas of your own for each category.

STRATEGY	ACTION PLAN
Create a schedule	• Understand your goals and deadlines. • Make a plan for what to do each day. •
Take notes	• Record important ideas and information. • Review your notes before preparing to share with a group. •
Practice what you've learned	• Use first-read and close-read strategies to deepen your understanding. • After you read, evaluate the usefulness of the evidence to help you understand the topic. • Consider the quality and reliability of the source. •

Pacing Plan

Unit Introduction: 1, 2
Introduce Whole-Class Learning: 3
Dark They Were, and Golden-Eyed: 4, 5, 6, 7, 8, 9
Media: Dark They Were, and Golden-Eyed: 10, 11, 12
Danger! This Mission to Mars Could Bore You to Death!: 13, 14, 15
Performance Task: 16, 17, 18

CONTENTS

Choose one selection. Selections are available online only.

POETRY

Science-Fiction Cradlesong

C. S. Lewis

Where we end up might be the same as where we began.

WEB ARTICLE

UFO Sightings and News

Benjamin Radford

Don't believe your eyes.

PERSUASIVE ESSAY

from Packing for Mars

Mary Roach

If it's out there, we should try to reach it.

SCIENCE ARTICLE

Trip to Mars Could Damage Astronauts' Brains

Laura Sanders

Great adventures involve great risks.

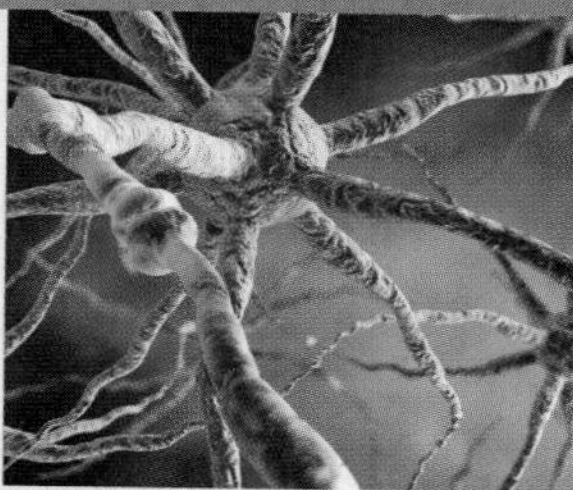

PERFORMANCE-BASED ASSESSMENT PREP

Review Evidence for an Argument

Complete your Evidence Log for the unit by evaluating what you've learned and synthesizing the information you've recorded.

DIGITAL PERSPECTIVES

Contents

Selections Encourage students to scan and preview the selections before choosing the one they would like to read. Suggest that they consider the genre and subject matter of each one before making their decision. You can use the information on the following Planning pages to advise students in making their choice.

Remind students that the selections for Independent Learning are only available in the Interactive Student Edition. Allow students who do not have digital access at home to preview the selections using classroom or computer lab technology. Then either have students print the selection they choose or provide a printout for them.

Performance Based-Assessment Prep

Review Evidence for an Argument Point out to students that collecting evidence during Independent Learning is the last step in completing their Evidence Log. After they finish their independent reading, they will synthesize all the evidence they have compiled in the unit.

The evidence students collect will serve as the primary source of information they will use to complete the writing and oral presentation for the Performance-Based Assessment at the end of the unit.

SELECTION RESOURCES

- First-Read Guide: Poetry
- Close-Read Guide: Poetry
- Science-Fiction Cradlesong: Text Questions
- Audio Summaries
- Selection Audio
- Selection Test

Science-Fiction Cradlesong

Summary

In C.S. Lewis's poem "Science-Fiction Cradlesong," the speaker says that people are always trying to get into outer space and that people are trapped on Earth looking at the sky and stars. The speaker reminds readers that once in space, people are trapped in rockets, still gazing at the sky and stars. Stars and the vast space between them look the same from both earth and space. The speaker determines that outer space is just a concept, not a place.

Insight

This poem takes a much more negative view of space exploration than one usually sees. Lewis's perspective that space exploration cannot take us away from our problems is commonly held but rarely written down.

Connection to Essential Question

The essential question for this unit is "Should we make a home in space?" Lewis takes a jaded view of life in space, seeing it as a futile attempt to escape problems that are best addressed in other ways.

Connection to Performance-Based Assessment

The Performance-Based Assessment prompt asks, "Should we spend valuable resources on space exploration?" Lewis sees space exploration as useless—it serves as a distraction from more important or more personal struggles. Students may decide to include his perspective in their response.

Text Complexity Rubric: Science-Fiction Cradlesong	
Quantitative Measures	
Lexile: NP **Text Length:** 24 lines	
Qualitative Measures	
Knowledge Demands ① ② ③ ❹ ⑤	Poem explores themes of varying level of complexity and abstraction including a fascination with exploring space and searching beyond our experience.
Structure ① ❷ ③ ④ ⑤	Poem has a predictable structure of four stanzas, each with rhyming scheme and some repetition of phrasing.
Language Conventionality and Clarity ① ② ❸ ④ ⑤	Language is explicit and easy to understand. It is mostly concrete; vocabulary is familiar and contemporary; poem has both simple sentences and phrases.
Levels of Meaning/Purpose ① ② ③ ❹ ⑤	Poem has multiple levels of meaning. While it seems simple, it provides a commentary on space travel and human's quest to find answers.

DIGITAL PERSPECTIVES

Audio | Video | Document | Annotation Highlights | EL Highlights | Online Assessment

SELECTION RESOURCES

- First-Read Guide: Nonfiction
- Close-Read Guide: Nonfiction
- UFO Sightings and News: Text Questions
- Audio Summaries
- Selection Audio
- Selection Test

UFO Sightings and News

Summary

The news article "UFO Sightings and News," by Benjamin Radford, discusses the phenomenon of unidentified flying objects. This seemingly neutral term is usually linked to the idea of alien spaceships or visitors from other planets. The writer explains how people came to think that strange lights are aliens. There have been a number of famous cases in the last 50 years where people believed they saw—or were abducted by—aliens. The article includes information about the reasons that people believe they see UFOs. He says that seeing objects in the dark can be difficult. Often, people who see something that they can't identify assume that the object is a UFO.

Insight

This article shows students how an idea that seems to have evidence may actually lack evidence. Some mistakes are easy to make, and different people will make the same mistake many times.

Connection to Essential Question

Considering whether life exists in space is a key part of answering the Essential Question, "Should we make a home in space?" Students may be interested in learning how the idea of alien visitors is relatively new in history. Do we need to make our own space colonies so we can compete with them?

Connection to Performance-Based Assessment

The Performance-Based Assessment prompt asks "Should we spend valuable resources on space exploration?" A great deal of money has gone into investigating UFOs, and this article provides context to explain why people believe they see them. It has come up with no real evidence that any of them are alien.

Text Complexity Rubric: UFO Sightings and News

Quantitative Measures	
Lexile: 1420 **Text Length:** 1,369 words	
Qualitative Measures	
Knowledge Demands (1 2 **3** 4 5)	Selection content involves information about the history of UFO sightings. Students may have limited prior knowledge of this topic, but information is clearly presented and explained.
Structure (1 **2** 3 4 5)	Selection contains a mix of reported events and analysis; organization is clear, logical, and evident; subheadings and chronological listing of UFO sightings make text easier to navigate.
Language Conventionality and Clarity (1 2 **3** 4 5)	Language is explicit, literal, and straightforward; some sentences are simple or compound, many others are more complex with multiple clauses; vocabulary is mostly on-level.
Levels of Meaning/Purpose (1 **2** 3 4 5)	Article focuses on exploring the history and psychology of UFOs. Purpose is concrete, explicitly stated, and narrowly focused. Examples and details back up main ideas.

from Packing for Mars

Summary

In the essay "Packing for Mars," Mary Roach examines how much it would cost to get to Mars. She argues for going, giving accounts from the past and from her own experience to explain why it's a good idea. Roach discusses how exciting it was to watch the buildup to a Mars probe landing. She also argues that there is a very important difference between looking at remote images and being there in person. No matter how good a simulation is, it can't fully capture reality. The difference comes in the emotion of knowing that something is real. Roach closes by saying the government should spend money to continue to grow the human spirit.

Insight

This essay argues for the value of space exploration. Its ending twist is an interesting rebuttal to many arguments against space exploration: yes, the money *could* be spent on high priorities on Earth, but it probably *wouldn't* be.

SELECTION RESOURCES

- First-Read: Nonfiction
- Close-Read Guide: Nonfiction
- From Packing for Mars: Text Questions
- Audio Summaries
- Selection Audio
- Selection Test

Connection to Essential Question

Roach argues that a physical, human presence somewhere is essentially different from sending a probe and looking at a simulation. This helps answer the question "Should we make a home in space?"

Connection to Performance-Based Assessment

The Performance-Based Assessment prompt asks "Should we spend valuable resources on space exploration?" Roach directly argues that we should pursue this direction because it is exciting and potentially rewarding.

Text Complexity Rubric: *from* Packing for Mars

Quantitative Measures	
Lexile: 1020 **Text Length:** 841 words	
Qualitative Measures	
Knowledge Demands ①—②—③—❹—⑤	Selection relies on knowledge of topics and situations that are discipline-specific, including space and the challenges of simulation versus live experience.
Structure ①—②—❸—④—⑤	Organization of opinion piece is generally clear; connections between all ideas are not always immediately apparent but are revealed through the entirety of the text.
Language Conventionality and Clarity ①—②—❸—④—⑤	Language is fairly complex, with some theoretical concepts and figurative language; vocabulary is subject-specific; some sentences are complex with multiple clauses.
Levels of Meaning/Purpose ①—②—❸—④—⑤	Purpose is explicitly stated, and some examples and anecdotes may make the content more accessible to students.

DIGITAL PERSPECTIVES

 Audio
 Video
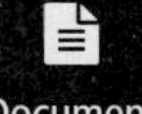 Document
 Annotation Highlights
EL Highlights
Online Assessment

SELECTION RESOURCES

- First-Read Guide: Nonfiction
- Close-Read Guide: Nonfiction
- Trip to Mars Could Damage Astronaut's Brains: Text Questions
- Audio Summaries
- Selection Audio
- Selection Test

Trip to Mars Could Damage Astronauts' Brains

Summary

"Trip to Mars Could Damage Astronauts' Brains" is a science article by Laura Sanders. The writer describes a problem with space exploration that is not yet well understood. Radioactive bursts called cosmic rays are common in space, emitted by exploding stars. Cosmic rays don't cause much trouble on Earth, because Earth's magnetic field blocks most of them. To test the effect of cosmic rays, researchers exposed mice to radiation similar to cosmic rays. They found that this caused the mice to have trouble with remembering old knowledge and forming new memories. This discovery is troubling, because it implies that prolonged space travel might damage astronauts' brains.

Insight

This selection gives readers more insight into the unexpected risks of exploration. The ending suggests a solution—adding shielding to the spacecraft—but notes that this would make the launch even more expensive.

Connection to Essential Question

The essential question for this unit is "Should we make a home in space?" This selection describes a surprising risk that increases the danger or expense of doing so.

Connection to Performance-Based Assessment

The Performance-Based Assessment prompt asks "Should we spend valuable resources on space exploration?" Students may conclude that in addition to deciding whether we should pay at all, we must decide how much we're willing to trade safety for cost.

Text Complexity Rubric: Trip to Mars Could Damage Astronauts' Brains

Quantitative Measures	
Lexile: 870 **Text Length:** 484 words	
Qualitative Measures	
Knowledge Demands (1)—(2)—(**3**)—(4)—(5)	Selection contains content about space travel and brain research that is discipline-specific and may be unfamiliar. However, concepts are not complicated, are explained clearly, and are easy to grasp.
Structure (1)—(**2**)—(3)—(4)—(5)	Journalistic structure is easy to follow with subheadings dividing some ideas; organization is clear, logical, and sequential; connections between ideas are explicit.
Language Conventionality and Clarity (1)—(2)—(**3**)—(4)—(5)	Language is clear and concrete; sentence structure is mostly simple, but there is a lot of academic, scientific vocabulary related to brain research and space particles.
Levels of Meaning/Purpose (1)—(2)—(**3**)—(4)—(5)	Overall purpose and main idea is explicitly stated, clear, concrete, and narrowly focused. However, the supporting details and explanations require reader to understand scientific concepts.

ADVISING

FIRST READ 

Students should perform the steps of the first read independently.

NOTICE: Students should focus on the basic elements of the text to ensure they understand what is happening.

ANNOTATE: Students should mark any passages they wish to revisit during their close read.

CONNECT: Students should increase their understanding by connecting what they've read to other texts or personal experiences.

RESPOND: Students will write a summary to demonstrate their understanding.

Point out to students that while they will always complete the Respond step at the end of the first read, the other steps will probably happen somewhat concurrently. Remind students that they will revisit their first-read annotations during the close read. You may wish to print copies of the First-Read Guide for students to use.

After students have completed the First-Read Guide, you may wish to assign the Text questions for the selection that are available in the Interactive Teacher's Edition.

Anchor Standards

In the first two sections of the unit, students worked with the whole class and in small groups to gain topical knowledge and greater understanding of the skills required by the anchor standards. In this section, they are asked to work independently, applying what they have learned and demonstrating increased readiness for college and career.

INDEPENDENT LEARNING

First-Read Guide

 **Tool Kit**
First-Read Guide and Model Annotation

Use this page to record your first-read ideas.

Selection Title: ______________________________

NOTICE

NOTICE new information or ideas you learn about the unit topic as you first read this text.

ANNOTATE

ANNOTATE by marking vocabulary and key passages you want to revisit.

First Read: NOTICE, ANNOTATE, CONNECT, RESPOND

CONNECT ideas within the selection to other knowledge and the selections you have read.

CONNECT

RESPOND by writing a brief summary of the selection.

RESPOND

STANDARD

Reading Read and comprehend complex literary and informational texts independently and proficiently.

PERSONALIZE FOR LEARNING

Strategic Support

Text Preview Remind students who struggle with independent reading to preview the text by looking at the title along with visuals, captions, and headings. Ask them to track their ideas about the topic or genre of the text, along with their thoughts about the author's purpose for writing. Encourage students to consider what they already know about the topic or genre they think they will encounter.

During the First Read, students should annotate words that are unfamiliar or stand out to them as possible clues to the meaning of the text.

When First- and Close-Read Guide entries are completed by students independently, and students learn the meaning of all their annotated words, encourage students to compile the vocabulary words into a class dictionary that everyone can consult.

Close-Read Guide

Tool Kit
Close-Read Guide and Model Annotation

Use this page to record your close-read ideas.

Selection Title: ______

Close Read the Text

Revisit sections of the text you marked during your first read. Read these sections closely and **annotate** what you notice. Ask yourself **questions** about the text. What can you **conclude**? Write down your ideas.

Analyze the Text

Think about the author's choices of patterns, structure, techniques, and ideas included in the text. Select one and record your thoughts about what this choice conveys.

QuickWrite

Pick a paragraph from the text that grabbed your interest. Explain the power of this passage.

STANDARD
Reading Read and comprehend complex literary and informational texts independently and proficiently.

DIGITAL PERSPECTIVES

CLOSE READ

Students should begin their close read by revisiting the annotations they made during their first read. Then, students should analyze one of the author's choices regarding the following:

- **patterns,** such as repetition or parallelism
- **structure,** such as cause-and-effect or problem-solution
- **techniques,** such as description or dialogue
- **ideas,** such as the author's main idea or claim

You may wish to print copies of the Close-Read Guide for students to use.

MAKE IT INTERACTIVE
Group students according to the selection they have chosen. Then, have students meet to discuss the selection in depth. Their discussions should be guided by their insights and questions.

PERSONALIZE FOR LEARNING

Strategic Support
Annotations Reinforce the strategies of close reading for students who struggle with its benefits. After they complete the Close-Read Guide, review the experience. Have students choose a First-Read annotation that helped them understand the text more deeply during the close read. Discuss the following questions with students:

- How did a revisit of the first-read annotation help you better understand the text during your close read?
- What did you learn about that passage during the close read? What strategies did you use to study the passage you marked?
- What can you conclude about the text, based on the passage you selected?

Ask for student volunteers to discuss how using the First-Read and Close-Read Guides helped them understand the text better.

Share Your Independent Learning

Prepare to Share

Explain to students that sharing what they learned from their Independent Learning selection provides classmates who read a different selection with an opportunity to consider the text as a source of evidence during the Performance-Based Assessment. As students prepare to share, remind them to highlight how their selection contributed to their knowledge of the concept of survival as well as how the selection connects to the question *Should we make a home in space?*

Learn from Your Classmates

As students discuss the Independent Learning selections, direct them to take particular note of how their classmates' chosen selections align with their current position on the Performance-Based Assessment question.

Reflect

Students may want to add their reflection to their Evidence Log, particularly if their insight relates to a specific selection from the unit.

Evidence Log Support students in completing their Evidence Log. This paced activity will help prepare them for the Performance-Based Assessment at the end of the unit.

INDEPENDENT LEARNING

EVIDENCE LOG

Go to your Evidence Log and record what you learned from the text you read.

Share Your Independent Learning

Prepare to Share

Should we make a home in space?

Even when you read something independently, your understanding continues to grow when you share what you have learned with others. What did you learn about making a home in space? Reflect on the text you explored independently and write notes about its connection to the unit. In your notes, consider why this text belongs in this unit.

Learn From Your Classmates

Discuss It Share your ideas about the text you explored on your own. As you talk with others in your class, jot down a few ideas that you learned from them.

Reflect

Review your notes, and mark the most important insight you gained from these writing and discussion activities. Explain how this idea adds to your understanding of space exploration.

STANDARDS

Speaking and Listening

Engage effectively in a range of collaborative discussions with diverse partners on *grade 7 topics, texts, and issues,* building on others' ideas and expressing their own clearly.

AUTHOR'S PERSPECTIVE **Ernest Morrell, Ph.D.**

Active Listening and Learning It's important to support students as they learn and develop the skills of participating in small-group discussions. As students discuss their Independent Learning selection with classmates, remind them that it is important to be an active, but not dominant, participant. Explain that an active participant is one who speaks confidently but also listens carefully to others, while a dominant participant is one who takes over and does not allow others to contribute. Remind students that being an active listener involves these strategies:

- Taking notes: Students who take useful notes capture the speaker's main points and note ideas to contribute once the speaker is done talking.
- Restating others' ideas to show understanding: Encourage students to use such language as "This is what I heard you saying . . ." and "I think this is what you meant when you said . . ."

PERFORMANCE-BASED ASSESSMENT PREP

Review Evidence for an Argument

At the beginning of this unit, you took a position on the following question:

Should we spend valuable resources on space exploration?

EVIDENCE LOG

Review your Evidence Log and your QuickWrite from the beginning of the unit. Did your opinion change?

☐ YES	☐ NO
Identify at least three pieces of evidence that convinced you to change your mind.	Identify at least three pieces of evidence that reinforced your initial position.
1.	1.
2.	2.
3.	3.

State your position now:

____

____

Identify a possible counterclaim:

____

____

Evaluate the Strength of Your Evidence Consider your point of view. How did the texts you read impact your point of view?

- ☐ Do more research
- ☐ Talk with my classmates
- ☐ Reread a selection
- ☐ Ask an expert
- ☐ Other: _______________

STANDARDS

Writing

Write arguments to support claims with clear reasons and relevant evidence.

a. Introduce claim(s), acknowledge alternate or opposing claims, and organize the reasons and evidence logically.

b. Support claim(s) with logical reasoning and relevant evidence, using accurate, credible sources and demonstrating an understanding of the topic or text.

DIGITAL PERSPECTIVES

Review Evidence for an Argument

Evidence Log Students should understand that their position on an issue could evolve as they learn more about the subject and are exposed to additional points of view. Point out that just because they took an initial position on the question *Should we spend valuable resources on space exploration?* doesn't mean that their position can't change after careful consideration of their learning and evidence.

Evaluate the Strength of Your Evidence Remind students that there are many different types of evidence they can use to support their argument, including:

- facts
- statistics
- anecdotes
- quotations from authorities
- examples

In addition to ensuring they have sufficient evidence to support their claim and address counterclaims, students should evaluate the reliability of their evidence. Discuss the characteristics that make evidence credible:

- reliable sources, including government, educational, and professional organizations
- degree to which experts have reviewed the evidence for accuracy
- credibility of references and confirmation provided by the source of the evidence

Asking clarifying questions: When they don't understand, or if they want to move the conversation forward, students might ask peers questions like, "Could you explain what you meant when you said . . ."

Writing to Sources: Argument

Students should complete the Performance-Based Assessment independently, with little to no input or feedback during the process. Students should use word processing software to take advantage of editing tools and features.

Prior to beginning the assessment, have students think about the time and the types of resources that are spent on space exploration.

Reread the Assignment Suggest that students take a little extra time to make sure they fully understand the task.

Review the Elements of Effective Argument Students can review the work they did earlier in the unit as they complete the Performance-Based Assessment. They may also consult other resources such as:

- the elements of an argument, including a clear statement of the claim, logical reasoning and persuasive evidence that support the claim, and attention to opposing arguments, available in Whole-Class Learning
- their Evidence Log
- their Word Network

Although students will use evidence from unit selections for their argument, they may need to collect additional evidence, including facts, statistics, anecdotes, quotations from authorities, or examples.

PERFORMANCE-BASED ASSESSMENT

SOURCES

- WHOLE-CLASS SELECTIONS
- SMALL-GROUP SELECTIONS
- INDEPENDENT-LEARNING SELECTION

PART 1

Writing to Sources: Argument

In this unit you read about space exploration, real and imagined, from various perspectives. Some authors argued in favor of continued or increased exploration of the frontiers of space. Other authors warned of the dangers that may come as a result of it.

Assignment

Write an argument in which you state and defend a claim in response to the following question:

> **Should we spend valuable resources on space exploration?**

Use credible evidence from the selections that you read and researched in this unit to justify your claim. Support your claim with logical reasoning and relevant evidence, and organize your ideas effectively so that your argument is easy to follow. Remember to address counterclaims, or alternative viewpoints, to your position. Use a formal tone in your writing.

WORD NETWORK

As you write and revise your argument, use your Word Network to help vary your word choices.

Reread the Assignment Review the assignment to be sure you fully understand it. The assignment may reference some of the academic words presented at the beginning of the unit. Be sure you understand each of the words given below to complete the assignment correctly.

Academic Vocabulary

justify	alternative	certainty
discredit	assumption	

Review the Elements of Effective Argument Before you begin writing, read the Argument Rubric. Once you have completed your first draft, check it against the rubric. If one or more of the elements is missing or not as strong as it could be, revise your essay to add or strengthen that component.

STANDARDS

Writing

- Write arguments to support claims with clear reasons and relevant evidence.
- Write routinely over extended time frames and shorter time frames for a range of discipline-specific tasks, purposes, and audiences.

Argument Rubric

	Focus and Organization	Evidence and Elaboration	Conventions
4	The introduction is engaging and states the claim in a persuasive way. The claim is supported by logical reasons and relevant evidence, and opposing claims are addressed. Reasons and evidence are logically organized so that the argument is easy to follow. Words, phrases, and clauses create cohesion and clearly show the relationships between claims, reasons, and evidence. The conclusion supports the argument and offers a fresh insight into the topic.	Each claim and reason is clearly and logically supported by evidence from the texts. The tone of the argument is formal and objective. Words are carefully chosen and suited to purpose and audience.	The argument intentionally uses standard English conventions of usage and mechanics.
3	The introduction is somewhat engaging and states the claim clearly. The claim is supported by reasons and evidence, and opposing claims are acknowledged. Reasons and evidence are organized so that the argument is easy to follow. Words, phrases, and clauses clearly show the relationships between claims, reasons, and evidence. The conclusion supports the argument.	Each claim and reason is supported by evidence from the texts. The tone of the argument is mostly formal and objective. Words are generally suited to purpose and audience.	The argument demonstrates accuracy in standard English conventions of usage and mechanics.
2	The introduction states the claim. The claim is supported by some reasons and evidence, and opposing claims may be briefly acknowledged. Reasons and evidence are organized somewhat logically with a few words and phrases that create cohesion. The conclusion relates to the claim.	Most claims and reasons are supported by evidence from the texts. The tone of the argument is occasionally formal and objective. Words are somewhat suited to purpose and audience.	The argument demonstrates some accuracy in standard English conventions of usage and mechanics.
1	The claim is not clearly stated. The claim is not supported by reasons and evidence, and opposing claims are not acknowledged. Reasons and evidence are disorganized and the argument is difficult to follow. The conclusion does not relate to the argument or is missing entirely.	Claims and reasons are not supported by evidence from the texts. The tone is informal. Words are not suited to purpose and audience.	The argument contains mistakes in standard English conventions of usage and mechanics.

DIGITAL PERSPECTIVES

Argument Rubric

As you review the Argument Rubric with students, remind them that the rubric is a resource that can guide their revisions. Students should pay particular attention to the differences between claims that are supported by reasons and evidence (a score of 3) and claims that are supported by logical reasons and relevant evidence (a score of 4).

PERSONALIZE FOR LEARNING

English Language Support

Writing a Claim Support students as they write a claim for their argument. Have students review the definition of argument. Encourage them to write their claim in a short, complete sentence. **EMERGING**

Have students review the definition of argument. Encourage them to write their claim in a complete sentence, paying attention to how their statement is organized. **EXPANDING**

Ask students to keep in mind that they are writing an argument. Encourage them to write their claim and offer supporting reasons. **BRIDGING**

Speaking and Listening: Oral Presentation

Students should annotate their written argument in preparation for the oral presentation, marking the important elements such as reasons and evidence, transitions between ideas, and the conclusion, as well as facts, statistics, and quotations from experts.

Remind students that the effectiveness of an oral argument relies on how the speaker establishes credibility with his or her audience. If a speaker comes across as confident and authoritative, it will be easier for the audience to give credence to the speaker's presentation.

Review the Rubric As you review the Oral Presentation Rubric with students, remind them that it is a valuable tool that can help them plan their presentation. They should strive to include all of the criteria required to achieve a score of 3. Draw their attention to some of the subtle differences between scores of 2 and 3.

PERFORMANCE-BASED ASSESSMENT

PART 2

Speaking and Listening: Oral Presentation

Assignment

After completing the final draft of your argument, use it as the foundation for a brief **oral presentation**. Do not simply read your argument aloud. Take the following steps to make your presentation lively and engaging.

- Review your argument, and mark key reasons and evidence that support your claim. Use these annotations as a guide for your presentation script.
- Choose visuals that add interest to your presentation.
- Prepare a final draft of your presentation, and deliver to the class.

STANDARDS

Speaking and Listening

- Present claims and findings, emphasizing salient points in a focused, coherent manner with pertinent descriptions, facts, details, and examples; use appropriate eye contact, adequate volume, and clear pronunciation.
- Include multimedia components and visual displays in presentations to clarify claims and findings and emphasize salient points.
- Adapt speech to a variety of contexts and tasks, demonstrating command of formal English when indicated or appropriate.

Review the Rubric Before you deliver your presentation, check your plans against this rubric.

	Content	Organization	Presentation Techniques
3	The introduction is engaging and establishes the claim in a persuasive way. The presentation includes strong, valid reasons and evidence to support the claim and address counterclaims. Conclusion offers fresh insight into the claim.	The speaker uses time effectively, spending the right amount on each part. Ideas progress logically, with clear transitions among ideas so the argument is easy for listeners to follow. The sequence of the visuals matches the timing of the speaker.	The speaker maintains eye contact and speaks clearly and with adequate volume. The speaker presents the argument with energy and strong conviction.
2	The introduction establishes a claim. The presentation includes some reasons and evidence to support the claim and vaguely acknowledges counterclaims. The conclusion offers some insight and restates important information.	The speaker uses time somewhat effectively, spending the right amount of time on most parts. Ideas progress logically with some transitions among ideas. The sequence of visuals sometimes matches the timing of the speaker.	The speaker sometimes maintains eye contact and speaks somewhat clearly and with adequate volume. The speaker presents with some energy and conviction.
1	The introduction does not clearly state a claim. The presentation does not include reasons or evidence to support a claim or acknowledge counterclaims. The conclusion does not restate important information about a claim.	The speaker does not use time effectively and focuses too much time on some parts and too little on others. Ideas do not progress logically. The sequence of visuals does not match the timing of the speaker.	The speaker does not maintain eye contact or speak clearly with adequate volume. The speaker's argument lacks energy or conviction.

DIGITAL PERSPECTIVES

Preparing for the Assignment To help students understand what an effective argument looks like, find examples on the Internet of speakers presenting editorial commentary or other types of arguments. Project the examples for the class, and have students note the elements that make each presentation successful (that is, an engaging introduction with a clear statement of the claim, appropriate pacing and gestures to emphasize main reasons and evidence, and an effective speaking style). Suggest that students record themselves presenting their arguments before they present them to the class so that they can practice incorporating some of the elements from the examples they have seen.

Reflect on the Unit

Now that you've completed the unit, take a few moments to reflect on your learning.

Reflect on the Unit Goals

Look back at the goals at the beginning of the unit. Use a different-colored pen to rate yourself again. Think about readings and activities that contributed the most to the growth of your understanding. Record your thoughts.

Reflect on the Learning Strategies

Discuss It Write a reflection on whether you were able to improve your learning based on your Action Plans. Think about what worked, what didn't, and what you might do to keep working on these strategies. Record your ideas before joining in a class discussion.

Reflect on the Text

Choose a selection that you found challenging and explain what made it difficult.

Explain something that surprised you about a text in the unit.

Which activity taught you the most about making a home in outer space? What did you learn?

DIGITAL PERSPECTIVES

Reflect on the Unit

- Have students watch the video on Reflecting on Your Learning.
- A video on this topic is available online in the Professional Development Center.

Reflect on the Unit Goals

Students should reevaluate how well they met the unit goals now that they have completed the unit. You might ask them to provide a written commentary on the goal they made the most progress with as well as the goal they feel warrants continued focus.

Reflect on the Learning Strategies

Discuss It If you want to make this a digital activity, go online and navigate to the Discussion Board. Alternatively, students can share their learning strategies reflections in a class discussion.

Reflect on the Text

Consider having students share their text reflections with one another.

MAKE IT INTERACTIVE

Have students prepare one slide using presentation software that summarizes their reflection.

Collate student slides into a presentation that can be viewed by the class. Students should be prepared to give a 30-second oral summary for their slide.

Unit Test and Remediation 

After students have completed the Performance-Based Assessment, administer the Unit Test. Based on students' performance on the test, assign the resources as indicated on the Interpretation Guide to remediate. Students who take the test online will be automatically assigned remediation, as warranted by test results.

UNIT 3 AT A GLANCE

	Contents	Pacing / # of Days	Genre / Lexile	Vocabulary / Word Study
INTRO	**Unit Introduction**	2*		Academic Vocabulary (L.7.6)
	Launch Text: At the Crossroads		Explanatory Text 930L	
WHOLE-CLASS LEARNING	**Whole-Class Learning Introduction**	7		
	A Christmas Carol: Scrooge and Marley, Act I HOOK&INSPIRE Israel Horovitz (COMPARE)		Drama NP	Concept Vocabulary Word Study: Latin Prefix *mal-* (L.7.4.b)
	A Christmas Carol: Scrooge and Marley, Act II Israel Horovitz (COMPARE)	3	Drama NP	Concept Vocabulary Word Study: Greek Prefix *para-* (L.7.4.b)
	***from* Scrooge** directed by Henry Edwards (COMPARE)	3	Media: Film NP	Media Vocabulary (L.7.6)
	Performance Task Writing	3		
SMALL-GROUP LEARNING	**Small-Group Learning Introduction**	6		
	Thank You, M'am HOOK&INSPIRE Langston Hughes		Short Story 800L	Concept Vocabulary (L.7.5.b; L.7.4.d) Word Study: Multiple-Meaning Words (L.7.4; L.7.5)
	***from* An American Childhood** Annie Dillard	4	Memoir 1050L	Technical Vocabulary (L.7.4, d) Word Study: Prefix *-en* (L.7.5, b)
	Urban Farming Is Growing a Greener Future Hillary Schwei	2	Media: Photo Gallery NP	Media Vocabulary (L.7.6)
	Performance Task Speaking and Listening	2		
INDEPENDENT LEARNING	**Independent Learning Introduction**	2		
	Little Things Are Big Jesús Colón		Reflective Essay 1150L	Independent Learning provides students with the opportunity to analyze a selection independently. To facilitate students' independence, no skills have been assigned.
	Profile: Malala Yousafzai BBC		News Article 1330L	
	Noor Inayat Khan ***from* Women Heroes of WWII** Kathryn J. Atwood		Biography 1170L	
	A Retrieved Reformation O. Henry		Short Story 850L	
END OF UNIT	Performance-Based Assessment Writing	2		
	Unit Reflection			
	Unit Test	1		

* Pacing is suggested for a 40- to 50-minute class period. If you use block scheduling, you may combine days to meet your schedule needs.

Analyze Craft and Structure	Conventions / Author's Style	Composition / Research / Speaking and Listening
		Summary (RI.7.2)
Dialogue in Drama (RL.7.3; RL.7.5)	Conventions: Subject-Verb Agreement (L.7.1)	Writing to Sources: Explanatory Essay (W.7.2, a–b, d–f; W.7.9, a) Speaking and Listening: Costume Plan (W.7.7; SL.7.4; SL.7.5)
Stage Directions (RL.7.3; RL.7.5)	Conventions: Sentence Structures (L.7.1.b)	
		Writing to Compare: Essay (RL.7.7; W.7.2, b, d, f; W.7.9, a; SL.7.2; SL.7.4)
		Explanatory Essay (W.7.2, a–f; W.7.5; W.7.6; W.7.10; L.7.1, b; L.7.3, a)
Plot (RL.7.1; RL.7.3)	Conventions: Prepositions and Prepositional Phrases (L.7.1, a)	Writing to Sources: Journal Entry (W.7.3, a, c–d; SL.7.1, b, d)
Reflective Writing (RI.7.1; RI.7.2; RI.7.3)	Conventions: Appositives and Appositive Phrases (L.7.1.a)	Speaking and Listening: Collaborative Discussion (SL.7.1, a–d)
		Research: Digital Multimedia Presentation (W.7.6; W.7.7; W.7.8; SL.7.2; SL.7.5)
		Present an Explanatory Essay (W.7.2; SL.7.1; SL.7.2; SL.7.4; SL.7.5; SL.7.6)
Independent Learning provides students with the opportunity to analyze a selection independently. To facilitate students' independence, no skills have been assigned.		Share Your Independent Learning (SL.7.1)
		Writing to Sources: Explanatory Essay (W.7.2, a–b) Speaking and Listening: Oral Presentation (SL.7.4)
		Reflect on the Unit

Jump Start

Ask students to think about moving to a new city or town. What are some steps they could take to feel more at home and make new friends? Have students share ideas and experiences and discuss how taking such steps affects the "turning point" of moving to a new place.

Turning Points

Ask students what the phrase *turning point* suggests to them. Point out that as they work through this unit, they will read about turning points in people's lives.

Video

Project the introduction video in class or ask students to open the video in their interactive textbooks.

Discuss It If you want to make this a digital activity, go online and navigate to the Discussion Board. Alternatively, students can share their responses in a class discussion.

Block Scheduling

Each day in this Pacing Plan represents a 40- to 50-minute class period. Teachers using block scheduling may combine days to reflect their class schedule. In addition, teachers may revise pacing to differentiate and support core instruction by integrating components and resources as students require.

UNIT 3

Turning Points

Life is filled with little moments and big moments. Most of the time they just pass by, but sometimes an event or experience can change someone's life in an instant.

A Transformation

Discuss It What sorts of turning points occur in nature and in the human experience?

Write your response before sharing your ideas.

224

Pacing Plan

Introduce Whole-Class Learning

Unit Introduction

A Christmas Carol: Scrooge and Marley, Act I

A Christmas Carol: Scrooge and Marley, Act II

Media: *from* Scrooge

Performance Task

1 2 3 4 5 6 7 8 9 10 11 12 13 14 15 16 17 18

DIGITAL PERSPECTIVES — Audio | Video | Document | Annotation Highlights | EL Highlights | Online Assessment

UNIT 3

UNIT INTRODUCTION

ESSENTIAL QUESTION: What can cause a sudden change in someone's life?

LAUNCH TEXT EXPLANATORY ESSAY MODEL
At the Crossroads

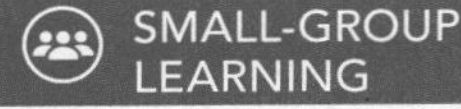

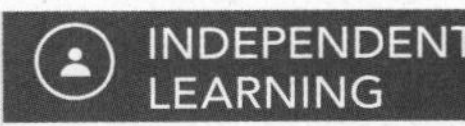

WHOLE-CLASS LEARNING

COMPARE

ANCHOR TEXT: DRAMA
A Christmas Carol: Scrooge and Marley, Act I
Israel Horovitz

ANCHOR TEXT: DRAMA
A Christmas Carol: Scrooge and Marley, Act II
Israel Horovitz

MEDIA: FILM
from Scrooge
directed by Henry Edwards

PERFORMANCE TASK
WRITING FOCUS:
Write an Explanatory Essay

SMALL-GROUP LEARNING

SHORT STORY
Thank You, M'am
Langston Hughes

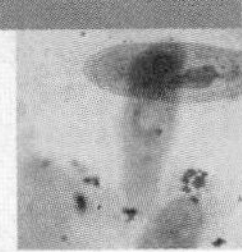

MEMOIR
from An American Childhood
Annie Dillard

MEDIA: PHOTO GALLERY
Urban Farming Is Growing a Greener Future
Hillary Schwei

PERFORMANCE TASK
SPEAKING AND LISTENING FOCUS:
Present an Explanatory Essay

INDEPENDENT LEARNING

REFLECTIVE ESSAY
Little Things Are Big
Jesús Colón

NEWS ARTICLE
Profile: Malala Yousafzai
BBC

BIOGRAPHY
Noor Inayat Khan
from Women Heroes of WWII
Kathryn J. Atwood

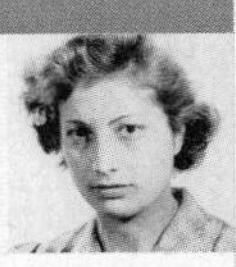

SHORT STORY
A Retrieved Reformation
O. Henry

PERFORMANCE-BASED ASSESSMENT PREP
Review Evidence for an Explanatory Essay

PERFORMANCE-BASED ASSESSMENT

Explanatory Text: Essay and Oral Presentation

PROMPT:
What can cause a significant change in someone's life?

225

What can cause a sudden change in someone's life?

Introduce the Essential Question and point out that students will respond to related prompts.

- **Whole-Class Learning** *How does Scrooge's character transform over the course of the play?*
- **Small-Group Learning** *How are the turning points in the selections similar to and different from each other?*
- **Performance-Based Assessment** *What can cause a significant change in someone's life?*

Using Trade Books with Turning Points

Refer to the Teaching with Trade Books section for suggestions on how to incorporate the following thematically-related titles into this unit:

- *The Outsiders* by S. E. Hinton
- *Hush* by Jacqueline Woodson
- *The Cay* by Theodore Taylor

Current Perspectives

To increase student engagement, search online for stories about turning points in people's lives, and invite your students to recommend stories they find. Always preview content before sharing it with your class.

- **Article: How Hurricane Katrina Led One Teen to Howard University and Beyond *(Essence)*** How one teenager's experiences after Hurricane Katrina shaped her future.
- **Video: High-Tech, Low-Cost Robotic Hand Changes Girl's Life *(CBS)*** Faith Lennox, a seven-year-old girl, receives a 3D-printed prosthetic hand that costs about $50.

Introduce Small-Group Learning

Day 19 | Thank You, M'am: 20 21 22 23 24 | *from* An American Childhood: 25 26 27 28 | Media: Urban Farming Is Growing a Greener Future: 29 30 | Performance Task: 31 32 | Introduce Independent Learning: 33 | Independent Learning: 34 | Performance-Based Assessment: 35 36

INTRODUCTION

About the Unit Goals

These unit goals were backward designed from the Performance-Based Assessment at the end of the unit and the Whole-Class and Small-Group Performance Tasks. Students will practice and become proficient in many more standards over the course of this unit.

Unit Goals

Review the goals with students and explain that as they read and discuss the selections in this unit, they will improve their skills in reading, writing, research, language, and speaking and listening.

- Have students watch the video on Goal Setting.
- A video on this topic is available online in the Professional Development Center.

Reading Goals Tell students they will read and evaluate explanatory texts. They will also read fiction, drama, a news article, a biography, and a memoir to better understand the ways writers express ideas.

Writing and Research Goals Tell students that they will learn the elements of writing an explanatory essay. They will also write their own explanatory essay. Students will also conduct research to clarify and explore ideas.

Language Goal Tell students that they will develop a deeper understanding of choosing language that expresses ideas precisely and concisely.

Speaking and Listening Explain to students that they will work together to build on one another's ideas, develop consensus, and communicate with one another. They will also learn to incorporate audio, visuals, and text in presentations.

HOME Connection

A Home Connection letter to students' parents or guardians is available in the Interactive Teacher's Edition. The letter explains what students will be learning in this unit and how they will be assessed.

UNIT 3 INTRODUCTION

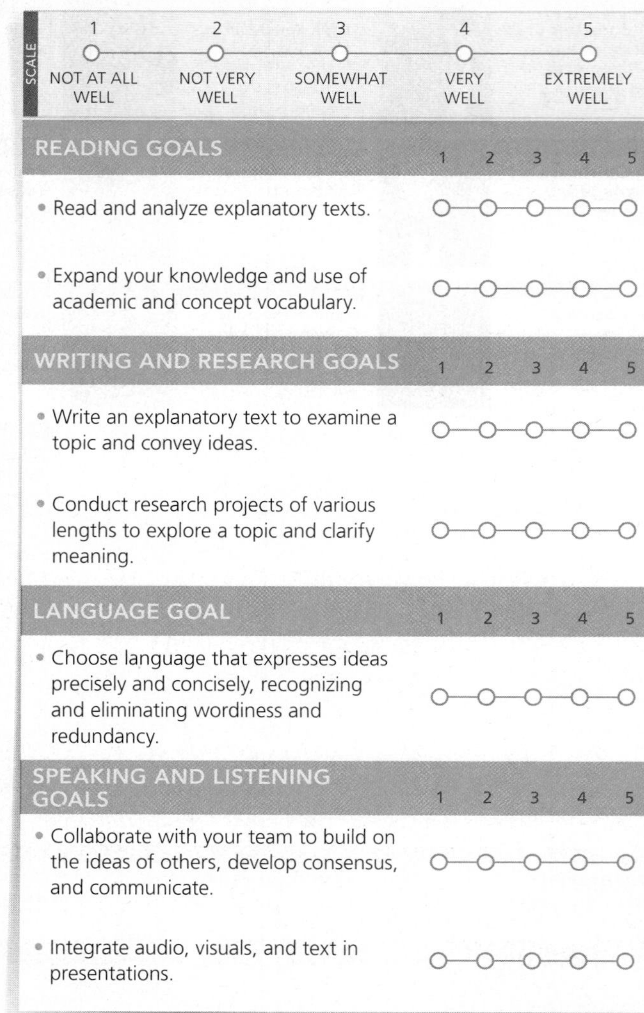

Unit Goals

Throughout this unit you will deepen your perspective about turning points in people's lives by reading, writing, speaking, listening, and presenting. These goals will help you succeed on the Unit Performance-Based Assessment.

Rate how well you meet these goals right now. You will revisit your ratings later when you reflect on your growth during this unit.

SCALE

1	2	3	4	5
NOT AT ALL WELL	NOT VERY WELL	SOMEWHAT WELL	VERY WELL	EXTREMELY WELL

READING GOALS	1	2	3	4	5
• Read and analyze explanatory texts.	O	O	O	O	O
• Expand your knowledge and use of academic and concept vocabulary.	O	O	O	O	O
WRITING AND RESEARCH GOALS	**1**	**2**	**3**	**4**	**5**
• Write an explanatory text to examine a topic and convey ideas.	O	O	O	O	O
• Conduct research projects of various lengths to explore a topic and clarify meaning.	O	O	O	O	O
LANGUAGE GOAL	**1**	**2**	**3**	**4**	**5**
• Choose language that expresses ideas precisely and concisely, recognizing and eliminating wordiness and redundancy.	O	O	O	O	O
SPEAKING AND LISTENING GOALS	**1**	**2**	**3**	**4**	**5**
• Collaborate with your team to build on the ideas of others, develop consensus, and communicate.	O	O	O	O	O
• Integrate audio, visuals, and text in presentations.	O	O	O	O	O

STANDARDS

Language
Acquire and use accurately grade appropriate general academic and domain-specific words and phrases; gather vocabulary knowledge when considering a word or phrase important to comprehension or expression.

AUTHOR'S PERSPECTIVE: Ernest Morrell, Ph.D.

Goals and Identity Setting and meeting goals is closely linked to our sense of self, so it is important to help students learn to think of themselves as powerful readers, writers, and speakers. Introduce the importance of goal setting by comparing it to the actions of outstanding high school athletes. How do these athletes excel and make it to the college or professional level? They continue to improve by establishing and working to reach challenging new goals.

Then ask students: "What goals do you need to set in order to continue to develop as a powerful reader? As a skilled writer? As an effective speaker?" Have students decide on their own

Academic Vocabulary: Explanatory Text

Academic terms appear in all subjects and can help you read, write, and discuss with more precision. Explanatory writing relies on facts to inform or explain. Here are five academic words that will be useful to you in this unit as you analyze and write explanatory texts.

Complete the chart.

1. Review each word, its root, and mentor sentences.
2. Use the information and your own knowledge to predict the meaning of each word.
3. For each word, list at least two related words.
4. Refer to the dictionary or other resources if needed.

TIP

FOLLOW THROUGH
Study the words in this chart, and mark them or their forms wherever they appear in the unit.

WORD	MENTOR SENTENCES	PREDICT MEANING	RELATED WORDS
contribute ROOT: **-trib-** *"give"*	1. Jennifer likes to *contribute* to the discussion when she has something meaningful to add. 2. Julio wants to *contribute* a short story to the school literary magazine.		tribute; attribute
consistent ROOT: **-sist-** *"stand"*	1. Keeping *consistent* pressure on a wound helps stop bleeding. 2. The runner kept a *consistent* routine to prepare for the race.		
maintain ROOT: **-tain-** *"hold"*	1. The disabled train struggled to *maintain* speed. 2. The veterinarian *maintained* her belief that dogs need grooming.		
observation ROOT: **-serv-** *"watch over"*	1. Watching the rat every day, the scientist learned about it through *observation*. 2. *Observation* of the moon was impossible because it was a cloudy night.		
sufficient ROOT: **-fic-** *"make do"*	1. In order to prove your point, you must provide *sufficient* evidence. 2. I don't have *sufficient* money to buy that shirt.		

DIGITAL PERSPECTIVES

Academic Vocabulary: Explanatory Text

Introduce the blue academic vocabulary words in the chart on the student page. Point out that the root of each word provides a clue to its meaning. Discuss the mentor sentences to ensure students understand each word's usage. Students should also use the mentor sentences as context to help them predict the meaning of each word. Check that students are able to fill the chart in correctly. Complete pronunciations, parts of speech, and definitions are provided for you. Students are only expected to provide the definition.

Possible responses:

contribute *v.* (kuhn TRIHB yoot)
Meaning: to give to a cause, event, project, etc.
Related words: tribute, attribute
Additional words related to the root *-trib-*: contributor, contribution

consistent *adj.* (kuhn SIS tuhnt)
Meaning: agreeing; in accord with; constantly following the same course
Related words: constant, consistency, inconsistent, inconsistency
Additional words related to the root *-sist-*: assist, assistance, desist, insist, persist, resist

maintain *v.* (mayn TAYN)
Meaning: to keep in good condition; to keep in existence or to preserve
Related words: maintaining, maintenance
Additional words related to the root *-tain-*: retain, retainer, contain, container

observation *n.* (ob zuhr VAY shuhn)
Meaning: the act of noticing; something observed
Related words: observe, observatory
Additional words related to the root *-serv-*: observer, observable, conserve, reserve, preserve

sufficient *adj.* (suh FIHSH uhnt)
Meaning: enough; the right amount as needed
Related words: insufficient, sufficiency
Additional words related to the root *-fic-*: sufficiently, suffice

goals and write them down. As they work through this unit, direct students to refer back to their goals to assess how successfully they have achieved them. Guide students to develop reasonable benchmarks for assessment. Possibilities include increased reading fluency, greater comprehension, improved grades on essays, and more comfort speaking up in groups, for instance. Then have students set goals for developing these skills as they finish high school and prepare to enter college and the workplace.

PERSONALIZE FOR LEARNING

English Language Support

Cognates Many of the academic words have Spanish cognates. Use these cognates with students whose home language is Spanish.
ALL LEVELS

contribute—contribuir
consistent—consistente
observation—observación
sufficient—suficiente

Purpose of the Launch Text

The Launch Text provides students with a common starting point to address the unit topic. After reading the Launch Text, all students will be able to participate in discussions about turning points.

Lexile: 930 The easier reading level of this selection makes it perfect to assign for homework. Students will need little or no support to understand it.

Additionally, "At the Crossroads" provides a writing model for the Performance-Based Assessment students complete at the end of the unit.

Launch Text: Explanatory Essay Model

Remind students to determine the main idea of the text as well as other ideas the author develops along the way. Have students pay attention to the structure of the text. They should note that the author doesn't state a position on whether Nick Kleckner was "right" or "wrong" to do what he did. Rather, the author simply tells Nick's story. The author also makes clear the cause-and-effect relationships among the events in the story.

Encourage students to read this text on their own and annotate unfamiliar words and sections of text they think are particularly important.

AUDIO SUMMARIES

Audio summaries of "At the Crossroads" are available in both English and Spanish in the Interactive Teacher's Edition or Unit Resources. Assigning these summaries before students read the Launch Text may help them build additional background knowledge and set a context for their reading.

LAUNCH TEXT | EXPLANATORY ESSAY MODEL

This selection is an example of an **explanatory text,** a type of writing in which the author shares detailed information about a topic or process. This is the type of writing you will develop in the Performance-Based Assessment at the end of the unit.

As you read, notice that the author presents facts without offering opinions or arguments.

At the Crossroads

NOTES

1 In April of 2012, 25-year-old Nick Kleckner was working as an electrician and cabdriver in northern California. And then, suddenly, he found himself at a crossroads. He left it all—his job, his family, his friends—and bought a one-way plane ticket to Jacksonville, Florida. He had a bold plan in mind. He was going to walk to California with virtually nothing on his back. He hoped the journey would change his life, but he had no idea how!

2 Nick, who was not exactly prepared, had nothing in the way of survival skills, so he planned to survive on the goodness of the people he met on the road.

3 Using the handle "Hobo Nick," Nick began his journey on April 5, leaving Jacksonville with a backpack, a sleeping bag, and a travel kit. He also had an iPod and the ability to receive Internet service. Throughout the journey, he would document his experience in minute detail and send daily updates to his mother, who'd post them on his blog.

4 The question is: Why? What would make someone take off like that? Nick had a comfortable life. He had a good income, a house, a new car, and a new motorcycle. He was moving forward with his life. By society's standards he should have been happy—but he wasn't.

5 Nick was in a rut. His life felt repetitive and boring. It lacked a higher purpose. He felt he wasn't growing as a person. He had "things" but didn't appreciate them. "It got to the point where I couldn't deal with everything anymore," Nick said later. "I felt a lot of pressure, stress, and anxiety and decided to get out."

6 As Hobo Nick, he trekked across miles of scorched desert and endured nights of pounding rain. In the towns and cities, he

PERSONALIZE FOR LEARNING

English Language Support

Idioms Help students understand the idioms *take off, in a rut,* and *deal with.* Explain that in the article, *take off* (paragraph 4) means "to go away, often suddenly." (Surprised by the bear on his hiking trail, Roger decided to take off as fast as he could.) *In a rut* (paragraph 5) means "trapped in monotonous routine." (Mindy felt she was in a rut because she did the exact same thing day after day.) *Deal with* (paragraph 5) means "to take action with regard to someone or something." (I am going to have to deal with this problem.) **ALL LEVELS**

AUTHOR'S PERSPECTIVE Elfrieda Hiebert, Ph.D.

Word Networks Vary by Word Type Concept maps or nets—the graphic organizers that gather the essential attributes of a word's meaning—vary depending on the type of word they help capture. For example, concept maps for physical phenomena can differ from those that describe people and social situations.

- In concept maps related to physical phenomenon, the words are typically not synonyms; rather, they are connected by topic. For example, for the topic *travel necessities,* the words slept on the street, where he knew that there were people to help him out.

7 Even with help, it was a hard journey. Nick would sometimes go days without food, or search dumpsters for things to eat. But whenever he felt that he had more than he needed, he decided to "pay it forward" by giving to other folks he encountered on his way. Paying it forward was one of Nick's goals on his journey—giving more than he received. If he was offered money or a gift card he didn't need, he gave it away to people who did. He was surprised at people's generosity along the way. There was a time in Mississippi when the cars actually pulled over to the side of the road to check on him and give him money. The experience taught him a valuable lesson: if you share what you have, and help others as much as possible, you will never be stranded.

8 In his blog, Nick chronicled the important changes brought about by his selfless lifestyle and rejection of material things. He has learned to live in the moment and to be thankful for everything he has.

9 On September 29, after an epic 2,500-mile walk across the North American continent, Nick managed to make it all the way to Huntington Beach, California. More than a hundred family members, friends and well-wishers were waiting for him. During the six months of his journey, he destroyed five pairs of shoes and lost about 55 pounds.

10 In the future, Nick plans to do another cross-country trip. "The point is always to give more than you take," he says, adding that "the biggest takeaway from this experience is to have realized that mankind is better than I ever dreamed." ❧

NOTES

WORD NETWORK FOR TURNING POINTS

Vocabulary A Word Network is a collection of words related to a topic. As you read the selections in this unit, identify interesting words related to the idea of turning points and add them to your Word Network. For example, you might begin by adding words from the Launch Text, such as *purpose, journey,* and *experience*. Continue to add words as you complete this unit.

TURNING POINTS

purpose

journey

experience

Tool Kit
Word Network Model

DIGITAL 
PERSPECTIVES

Word Network for Turning Points

Tell students that they can fill in the Word Network as they read the texts in the unit, or they can jot down the words elsewhere and add them later. Point out to students that people may have personal associations with some words. A word that one student thinks is related to the concept of turning points might not be a word another student would pick. However, students should feel free to add any relevant words to their Word Network. Each person's Word Network will be unique. If you choose to print the Word Network, distribute it to students at this point so they can use it throughout the rest of the unit.

backpack, shoes, money, and *iPod* all have different meanings, but each could be used in a word network.

- Concept maps about people and social situations contain words that have subtle differences in meaning and cannot necessarily be substituted for one another. For example, for a network built around the word *generosity, kindness, help,* and *sharing* carry similar meanings but are not interchangeable.

To help students build their word knowledge, reinforce the power of word networks. Often, common words reveal the concepts represented by rare words, especially in narratives. In describing traits of characters or plot and setting details, an author will use different words rather than repeating the same word. For example, *journey, pilgrimage,* and *voyage* are all less common words for *trip*.

Summary

Have students read the introductory paragraph. Provide them with tips for writing a summary:

- Write in the present tense.
- Make sure to include the title of the work.
- Be concise: a summary should not be equal in length to the original text.
- If you need to quote the words of the author, use quotation marks.
- Don't put your own opinions, ideas, or interpretations into the summary. The purpose of writing a summary is to accurately represent what the author says, not to provide a critique.

See possible Summary on student page.

Launch Activity

Explain to students that as they work on this unit, they will have many opportunities to discuss the topic of turning points. Remind them that there is no right or wrong position, but they should be able to support their positions with evidence from the material they've viewed, read, and analyzed as well as their prior knowledge.

Encourage students to keep open minds and really listen to their classmates.

Summary

Write a summary of "At the Crossroads." A **summary** is a concise, complete, and accurate overview of a text. It should not include a statement of your opinion or an analysis.

Possible response: In the explanatory text "At the Crossroads,"we learn about a young man named Nick Kleckner who decided to walk across the country. He felt like he was going nowhere in life and hoped that the journey would change his life. Nick was unprepared, and the journey was difficult. But he got a lot of help along the way – and he gave others all that he had but didn't need. Nick's opinion of people improved during his journey. He concluded that if you share what you have and help others as much as you can, everything will work out well.

Launch Activity

Thumbs Up/Thumbs Down Consider this statement: **A person's life can change in an instant.**

- Record your position on the statement and explain your thinking.

  ☐ Strongly Agree ☐ Agree ☐ Disagree ☐ Strongly Disagree

- Form a group with like-minded students in one corner of the classroom.
- Discuss questions such as "What examples from the text or your own prior knowledge led you to take this position?"
- After your discussion, have a representative from each group present a brief two- or three-minute summary of the group's position.
- After all the groups have presented their views, move into the four corners again. If you change your corner, be ready to explain why.

WriteNow Express and Reflect

Personal Reflection Have students write one or two paragraphs about whether they would like to go on a journey such as the one Nick took. Why or why not? What challenges did Nick face that seem especially difficult to them? What parts of Nick's journey do they think they might like?

DIGITAL PERSPECTIVES  

QuickWrite

Consider class discussions, presentations, the video, and the Launch Text as you think about the prompt. Record your first thoughts here.

PROMPT: **What can cause a significant change in someone's life?**

Possible response: I think the biggest changes in people's lives happen when they do something completely new. We all have some things that we want to do, or have wanted to do for a long time, but have never tried. A couple of months ago I started taking a martial arts class. I'd wanted to do that for a long time, but was scared. I'm not very tough; I wanted to take this class because I *want* to be tough. It's been really hard. It's even harder than I thought it would be. But it's absolutely worth it. I'm happier taking the class than I have been in years.

EVIDENCE LOG FOR TURNING POINTS

Review your QuickWrite. Summarize your point of view in one sentence to record in your Evidence Log. Then, record evidence from "At the Crossroads" that supports your point of view.

After each selection, you will continue to use your Evidence Log to record the evidence you gather and the connections you make. This graphic shows what your Evidence Log looks like.

Tool Kit
Evidence Log Model

Title of Text: ______ Date: ______

CONNECTION TO PROMPT	TEXT EVIDENCE/DETAILS	ADDITIONAL NOTES/IDEAS

How does this text change or add to my thinking? Date: ______

QuickWrite

In this QuickWrite, students should present their own answer to the question based on the material in the Unit Opener. This initial response will help inform their work when they complete the Performance-Based Assessment at the end of the unit. Students should make sure they answer the question clearly and support their response with relevant evidence and logical reasoning.

See possible QuickWrite on student page.

Evidence Log for Turning Points

Students should record their initial response in their Evidence Logs. Then, they should record evidence from "At the Crossroads" that supports their initial response.

If you choose to print the Evidence Log, distribute it to students at this point so they can use it throughout the rest of the unit.

Performance-Based Assessment: Refining Your Thinking

- Have students watch the video on Refining Your Thinking.
- A video on this topic is available online in the Professional Development Center.

OVERVIEW

WHOLE-CLASS LEARNING

Essential Question

Everyone faces a crossroad, or a turning point, at some time in his or her life. For many, these turning points can be life-changing events. Fortunately, they often change lives for the better, bringing about a positive outcome. During Whole-Class Learning, students will read selections about people who experience turning points in their lives and how they are changed by them.

Whole-Class Learning Strategies

Review the Learning Strategies with students and explain that as they work through Whole-Class Learning they will develop strategies to work in large-group environments.

- Have students watch the video on Whole-Class Learning Strategies.
- A video on this topic is available online in the Professional Development Center.

You may wish to discuss some action items to add to the chart as a class before students complete it on their own. For example, for "Clarify by asking questions," you might solicit the following from students:

- Ask a follow-up question to another student's question if you are still unsure.
- If you still need more information, ask the person speaking to elaborate.

Block Scheduling

Each day in this Pacing Plan represents a 40–50 minute class period. Teachers using block scheduling may combine days to reflect their class schedule. In addition, teachers may revise pacing to differentiate and support core instruction by integrating components and resources as students require.

OVERVIEW: WHOLE-CLASS LEARNING

ESSENTIAL QUESTION:

What can cause a sudden change in someone's life?

People change a little bit every day as they learn and enjoy new experiences, but is it possible for a person to change in an instant? You will work with your whole class to explore the concept of turning points. The selections you are going to read provide some interesting insights.

Whole-Class Learning Strategies

Throughout your life, in school, in your community, and in your career, you will continue to learn and work in large-group environments.

Review these strategies and the actions you can take to practice them as you work with your whole class. Add ideas of your own for each category for each step. Get ready to use these strategies during Whole-Class Learning.

STRATEGY	ACTION PLAN
Listen actively	• Eliminate distractions. For example, put your cellphone away. • Keep your eyes on the speaker. •
Clarify by asking questions	• If you're confused, other people probably are, too. Ask a question to help your whole class. • If you see that you are guessing, ask a question instead. •
Monitor understanding	• Notice what information you already know and be ready to build on it. • Ask for help if you are struggling. •
Interact and share ideas	• Share your ideas and answer questions, even if you are unsure. • Build on the ideas of others by adding details or making a connection. •

Pacing Plan

Unit Introduction: 1, 2

Introduce Whole-Class Learning: 3

A Christmas Carol: Scrooge and Marley, Act I: 4, 5, 6, 7, 8, 9

A Christmas Carol: Scrooge and Marley, Act II: 10, 11, 12

Media: *from* Scrooge: 13, 14, 15

Performance Task: 16, 17, 18

WHOLE-CLASS LEARNING

CONTENTS

DIGITAL PERSPECTIVES

Contents

Anchor Texts Preview the anchor texts with students to generate interest. Encourage students to discuss other texts they may have read or movies or television shows they may have seen that deal with the issues of turning points and life-changing experiences.

You may wish to conduct a poll to determine which selection students think looks more interesting and discuss the reasons for their preference. Students can return to this poll after they have read the selections to see if their preference changed.

Performance Task

Write an Explanatory Essay Explain to students that after they have finished reading the selections, they will write an explanatory essay. To help them prepare, encourage students to think about the topic as they progress through the selections and as they participate in the Whole-Class Learning experience.

Introduce Small-Group Learning

Thank You, M'am

from An American Childhood

Media: Urban Farming Is Growing a Greener Future

Performance Task

Introduce Independent Learning

Independent Learning

Performance-Based Assessment

19 20 21 22 23 24 25 26 27 28 29 30 31 32 33 34 35 36

A Christmas Carol: Scrooge and Marley, Act I

AUDIO SUMMARIES
Audio summaries of *A Christmas Carol: Scrooge and Marley,* Act I, are available online in both English and Spanish in the Interactive Teacher's Edition or Unit Resources. Assigning these summaries prior to reading the selection may help students build additional background knowledge and set a context for their first read.

Summary

This is the first act of the drama *A Christmas Carol: Scrooge and Marley*, by Israel Horovitz. The play is based on Charles Dickens's novella. It focuses on a stingy man named Ebenezer Scrooge. The ghost of Scrooge's business partner, Jacob Marley, aims to make Scrooge kinder. It is Christmas Eve; Scrooge has no love for the season and is reluctant to give his employee Bob Cratchit any time off at all. Marley's ghost appears to Scrooge, followed by the Ghost of Christmas Past, who shows Scrooge moments from Scrooge's youth, in efforts to save Scrooge from the doom his unkindly ways will bring down upon him.

Insight

In the scene with the Ghost of Christmas Past, we see how disappointing moments in Scrooge's life led him to withdraw from close relationships, becoming selfish and cold. Act I begins to teach the drama's overarching lesson of the value of having friendship, family, and a kind spirit.

ESSENTIAL QUESTION:
What can cause a sudden change in someone's life?

Connection to Essential Question

While you will probably never be visited by a series of holiday ghosts, reflecting on how you live your life—and whether you really want to live that way—can change your life for the better.

WHOLE-CLASS LEARNING PERFORMANCE TASK
How does Scrooge's character transform over the course of the play?

UNIT PERFORMANCE-BASED ASSESSMENT
What can cause a significant change in someone's life?

Connection to Performance Tasks

Whole-Class Learning Performance Task In Act I, Scrooge remains fairly cynical, but he is filled with regret when the Ghost of Christmas Past reminds Scrooge what he gave up for wealth.

Unit Performance-Based Assessment Marley's ghost gives Scrooge evidence that Scrooge's life will lead to the same kind of torment that Marley finds himself in. Seeing that the path you're on leads somewhere you don't want to go can motivate you to change.

DIGITAL PERSPECTIVES

 Audio  Video  Document | Annotation Highlights | Online Assessment

LESSON RESOURCES

	Making Meaning	Language Development
Lesson	**First Read** **Close Read** **Analyze the Text** **Analyze Craft and Structure**	**Concept Vocabulary** **Word Study** **Conventions**
Instructional Standards	**RL.7.10** By the end of the year, read and comprehend literature . . . **RL.7.3** Analyze how particular elements of a story or drama interact. **RL.7.5** Analyze how a drama's or poem's form or structure . . .	**L.7.4** Determine or clarify the meaning of unknown and multiple-meaning words and phrases . . . **L.7.4.b** Use common, grade-appropriate Greek or Latin affixes and roots . . . **L.7.4.c** Consult general and specialized reference materials . . . **L.7.1** Demonstrate command of the conventions . . .
STUDENT RESOURCES		
Available online in the Interactive Student Edition or Unit Resources	Selection Audio First-Read Guide: Fiction Close-Read Guide: Fiction	Word Network Evidence Log
TEACHER RESOURCES		
Selection Resources Available online in the Interactive Teacher's Edition or Unit Resources	Audio Summaries: English and Spanish Annotation Highlights Accessible Leveled Text First Read Extension Questions Analyze Craft and Structure: Dialogue in Drama	Concept Vocabulary and Word Study Conventions: Subject-Verb Agreement
Reteach/Practice (RP) Available online in the Interactive Teacher's Edition or Unit Resources	Analyze Craft and Structure: Dialogue in Drama (RP)	Word Study: Latin Prefix *mal-* (RP) Conventions: Subject-Verb Agreement (RP)
Assessment Available online in Assessments	Selection Test: English Selection Test: Spanish Extension Selection Test	
My Resources	A Unit 3 Answer Key is available online and in the Interactive Teacher's Edition.	

Reading Support

Text Complexity Rubric: *A Christmas Carol: Scrooge and Marley*, Act 1	
Quantitative Measures	
Lexile: NP **Text Length:** 7,319 words	
Qualitative Measures	
Knowledge Demands ①—②—❸—④—⑤	Students will not be familiar with the situation that is central to the selection. The selection references many aspects of life in London during the nineteenth century that will be challenging for students.
Structure ①—②—③—❹—⑤	The selection is a play adapted from a novella. Students may find stage directions and dialogue difficult to follow.
Language Conventionality and Clarity ①—②—③—❹—⑤	The selection contains numerous long sentences with embedded phrases and clauses and challenging vocabulary.
Levels of Meaning/Purpose ①—②—❸—④—⑤	The concept is straightforward (a miser learns generosity and kindness), but sophisticated language and structure may make it difficult for some to grasp.

DECIDE AND PLAN

English Language Support

Provide English Learners with support for structure and language as they read the selection.

Structure Students may be confused by the stage directions. Explain that on stage, a director uses music and other sounds to help set a mood and convey meaning. Readers must rely on stage directions to help them understand what an audience would hear. Have students preview the selection and note that the stage directions are in brackets and italics.

Language Students will likely have difficulty with the numerous complex sentences and above-level vocabulary. Instead of trying to understand every word, encourage students to scan for events in each section that they understand. Ask them to write sentences restating the information they understood.

Strategic Support

Provide students with strategic support to ensure that they can successfully read the text.

Structure Make sure students understand that in Act I, a man revisits four key episodes from his past and learns something important from each scene. Have students divide a sheet of paper into four parts and take notes as they read each scene.

Language For students who may have difficulty with complex sentences, encourage them to break the sentences down into smaller chunks or identify the meaning of unfamiliar words or phrases. Then have them reread the whole sentences.

Challenge

Provide students who need to be challenged with ideas for how they can go beyond a simple interpretation of the text.

Text Analysis Remind students that in drama, authors use dialogue as one method of revealing the traits, moods, or changes in a character. Have students reread Act I, Scene 5 and describe Scrooge's feelings at this point. What details in the dialogue reveal Scrooge's emotions? Why would he want to see all of the place at once?

Written Response Challenge students to read part of the original novella by Charles Dickens. Ask students to write an essay discussing the similarities and differences between the original and the adaptation, including whether the adaptation captures the mood of the novella and is true to its characters and action.

TEACH

Read and Respond

Have students do their first read of the selection. Then have them complete their close read. Finally, work with them on the Making Meaning and Language Development activities.

Standards Support Through Teaching and Learning Cycle

IDENTIFY NEEDS

Analyze results of the Beginning-of-Year Assessment, focusing on the items relating to Unit 3. Also take into consideration student performance to this point and your observations of where particular students struggle.

DECIDE AND PLAN

- If students have performed poorly on items matching these standards, then provide selection scaffolds before assigning them the on-level lesson provided in the Student Edition.
- If students have done well on the Beginning-of-Year Assessment, then challenge them to keep progressing and learning by giving them opportunities to practice the skills in depth.
- Use the Selection Resources listed on the Planning pages for *A Christmas Carol: Scrooge and Marley,* Act I, to help students continually improve their ability to master the standards.

Instructional Standards: *A Christmas Carol: Scrooge and Marley*, Act I

	Catching Up	This Year	Looking Forward
Reading	You may wish to administer the **Analyze Craft and Structure: Dialogue in Drama (RP)** worksheet to help students analyze dialogue.	**RL.3** Analyze how particular elements of a story or drama interact.	Have students think of other stories, plays, and movies they have read or seen and discuss how dialogue is utilized effectively.
Language	Review the **Word Study: Latin Prefix *mal-* (RP)** worksheet with students to ensure they understand the meaning of the prefix. You may wish to administer the **Conventions: Subject-Verb Agreement (RP)** worksheet to ensure students understand how to make subjects and verbs agree in number.	**L.4.b** Use common, grade-appropriate Greek or Latin affixes and roots as clues to the meaning of a word. **L.1** Demonstrate command of the conventions of standard English grammar and usage when writing or speaking.	Have students identify words in the selection that use other prefixes they may recognize. Have students find sentences in the play that demonstrate proper subject-verb agreement so they can understand how this convention works.

ANALYZE AND REVISE

- Analyze student work for evidence of student learning.
- Identify whether or not students have met the expectations in the standards.
- Identify implications for future instruction.

TEACH

Implement the planned lesson, and gather evidence of student learning.

Jump Start

FIRST READ Prior to students' first read, engage them in a discussion about what kind of things make people change—and why.

A Christmas Carol: Scrooge and Marley, Act I

Why might people resist change? Do experiences that cause people to change have to be "real" according to the laws of science? Why or why not? Modeling questions such as these will help students connect to *A Christmas Carol: Scrooge and Marley*, Act I, and to the Performance Task assignment. Selection audio and print capability for the selection are available in the Interactive Teacher's Edition.

Concept Vocabulary

Support students as they rank the words. Ask if they've ever heard, read, or used them. Reassure them that the definitions for these words are listed in the selection.

FIRST READ

Students should perform the steps of the first read independently.

NOTICE: You may want to encourage students to notice how and why Scrooge changes as the play goes on.

ANNOTATE: Remind students to mark text that includes both direct (clearly stated) and indirect (implied) characterization. Also remind students to pay attention to and mark stage directions as well as dialogue.

CONNECT: Encourage students to make connections beyond the text. If they cannot make connections to their own lives or other texts, have them consider movies and TV shows.

RESPOND: Students will answer questions and write a summary to demonstrate understanding.

Point out to students that while they will always complete the Respond step at the end of the first read, the other steps will probably happen somewhat concurrently. You may wish to print copies of the **First-Read Guide: Fiction** for students to use.

Remind students that during their first read, they should not answer the close-read questions that appear in the selection.

MAKING MEANING

About the Playwright

As a teenager, **Israel Horovitz** (1939–2020) did not like books by Charles Dickens. As he got older, however, he came to appreciate Dickens's style and stories. Horovitz referred to Dickens as "a masterful storyteller." He imagined that, if Dickens were still alive, he would be "our greatest television writer, or perhaps screenwriter." As Horovitz adapted Dickens's novella into a play, he thought about which character was his favorite. Surprisingly, it was Scrooge, who reminded Horovitz of his own father.

A Christmas Carol: Scrooge and Marley, Act I

Concept Vocabulary

You will encounter the following words as you read *A Christmas Carol: Scrooge and Marley,* Act I. Before reading, note how familiar you are with each word. Then, rank the words in order from most familiar (1) to least familiar (6).

WORD	YOUR RANKING
covetous	
morose	
resolute	
impossible	
malcontent	
miser	

After completing the first read, come back to the concept vocabulary and review your rankings. Mark changes to your original rankings as needed.

First Read DRAMA

Apply these strategies as you conduct your first read. You will have an opportunity to complete the close-read notes after your first read.

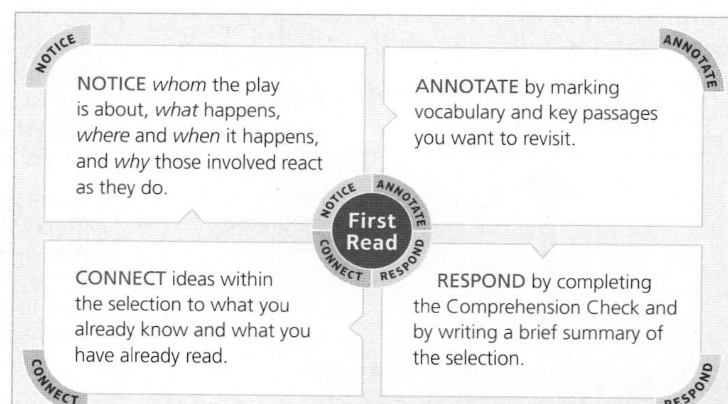

Tool Kit
First-Read Guide and Model Annotation

STANDARDS
Reading Literature
By the end of the year, read and comprehend literature, including stories, dramas, and poems, in the grades 6–8 text complexity band proficiently, with scaffolding as needed at the high end of the range.

CROSS-CURRICULAR PERSPECTIVES

Social Studies Have students research and write short reports on Victorian England. They should include information about the social structure of the society, the economy, and the industrialization that was taking place during this time. Have students share their information with the class, and encourage students to notice how these elements are reflected in the play.

ANCHOR TEXT | DRAMA

A Christmas Carol: Scrooge and Marley

Act I

Israel Horovitz

BACKGROUND

Charles Dickens's novella, *A Christmas Carol,* from which this play was adapted, shows sympathy for the struggles of the poor. The story is set in England during the nineteenth century, a time of rapid industrial growth. In this booming economy, the wealthy lived in luxury, but the poor and the working class suffered.

CHARACTERS

Jacob Marley, a specter
Ebenezer Scrooge, not yet dead, which is to say still alive
Bob Cratchit, Scrooge's clerk
Fred, Scrooge's nephew
Thin Do-Gooder
Portly Do-Gooder
Specters (Various), carrying money-boxes
The Ghost of Christmas Past
Four Jocund Travelers
A Band of Singers
A Band of Dancers
Little Boy Scrooge
Young Man Scrooge
Fan, Scrooge's little sister
The Schoolmaster
Schoolmates
Fezziwig, a fine and fair employer
Dick, young Scrooge's co-worker
Young Scrooge
A Fiddler
More Dancers
Scrooge's Lost Love
Scrooge's Lost Love's Daughter
Scrooge's Lost Love's Husband
The Ghost of Christmas Present
Some Bakers
Mrs. Cratchit, Bob Crachit's wife
Belinda Cratchit, a daughter
Martha Cratchit, another daughter
Peter Cratchit, a son
Tiny Tim Cratchit, another son
Scrooge's Niece, Fred's wife
The Ghost of Christmas Future, a mute Phantom
Three Men of Business
Drunks, Scoundrels, Women of the Streets
A Charwoman
Mrs. Dilber
Joe, an old second-hand goods dealer
A Corpse, very like Scrooge
An Indebted Family
Adam, a young boy
A Poulterer
A Gentlewoman
Some More Men of Business

AUTHOR'S PERSPECTIVE **Kelly Gallagher, M.Ed.**

The Value of Rereading To get the most out of a text, it is important for students to move beyond surface-level comprehension into deeper, inferential meaning that yields insights and understanding. Give students re-reading strategies such as having them ask themselves the following four questions, in order, as they read:

1. What does it say?
2. What does it mean?
3. How is it said?
4. Why does it matter?

Question 1 taps literal comprehension, which readers must do before they can move on to uncovering deeper meaning in a text. Question 2 requires students to return to the text to provide strong evidence of their interpretation by citing specific details and passages. Question 3 asks students to think about the author's technique. Question 4 gives students the opportunity to think deeply about the issues that will affect their lives. After all, asking "Why does it matter?" is the reason why we read and teach great literature in the first place.

CLOSE READ 

Remind students that adjectives describe something or someone. You may wish to model the close read using the following think-aloud format. Possible responses to questions on the student page are included. You may also want to print copies of the **Close-Read Guide: Fiction** for students to use.

ANNOTATE: As I read paragraph 4, I look for and highlight words that describe something or someone.

QUESTION: I think the playwright chose these words to paint a picture of Scrooge. These adjectives describe someone who views money as the most important thing in the world and wants nothing to do with people.

CONCLUDE: The playwright's strong word choice gives readers a picture of Scrooge as a miserable, angry, and probably lonely man.

Additional **English Language Support** is available in the Interactive Teacher's Edition.

NOTES

THE PLACE OF THE PLAY Various locations in and around the City of London, including Scrooge's Chambers and Offices; the Cratchit Home; Fred's Home; Scrooge's School; Fezziwig's Offices; Old Joe's Hide-a-Way.

THE TIME OF THE PLAY The entire action of the play takes place on Christmas Eve, Christmas Day, and the morning after Christmas, 1843.

Scene 1

1 [*Ghostly music in auditorium. A single spotlight on* Jacob Marley, D.C. *He is ancient; awful, dead-eyed. He speaks straight out to auditorium.*]

2 **Marley.** [*Cackle-voiced*] My name is Jacob Marley and I am dead. [*He laughs.*] Oh, no, there's no doubt that I am dead. The register of my burial was signed by the clergyman, the clerk, the undertaker . . . and by my chief mourner . . . Ebenezer Scrooge . . . [*Pause; remembers*] I am dead as a doornail.

3 [*A spotlight fades up, Stage Right, on* Scrooge, *in his counting-house*[1] *counting. Lettering on the window behind* Scrooge *reads: "Scrooge and Marley, Ltd." The spotlight is tight on* Scrooge's *head and shoulders. We shall not yet see into the offices and setting. Ghostly music continues, under.* Marley *looks across at* Scrooge; *pitifully. After a moment's pause*]

4 I present him to you: Ebenezer Scrooge . . . England's most tightfisted hand at the grindstone, Scrooge! a squeezing, wrenching, grasping, scraping, clutching, **covetous**, old sinner! secret, and self-contained, and solitary as an oyster. The cold within him freezes his old features, nips his pointed nose, shrivels his cheek, stiffens his gait; makes his eyes red, his thin lips blue; and speaks out shrewdly in his grating voice. Look at him. Look at him . . .

5 [Scrooge *counts and mumbles.*]

6 **Scrooge.** They owe me money and I will collect. I will have them jailed, if I have to. They owe me money and I will collect what is due me.

7 [Marley *moves towards* Scrooge; *two steps. The spotlight stays with him.*]

1. **counting-house** *n.* office for keeping financial records and writing business letters.

covetous (KUHV uh tuhs) *adj.* greedy and jealous

CLOSE READ

ANNOTATE: Mark the use of descriptive words in paragraph 4.

QUESTION: Why might the playwright have chosen these words?

CONCLUDE: How does the playwright's word choice affect the reader's understanding of Scrooge's character?

PERSONALIZE FOR LEARNING

Challenge

Description Have students think about the description of Scrooge in paragraph 4. Prompt students to create a character of their own. Students should consider what the character thinks and feels, and what motivates him or her. Ask them to write a vivid description of the character they create.

8 **Marley.** [*Disgusted*] He and I were partners for I don't know how many years. Scrooge was my sole executor, my sole administrator, my sole assign, my sole residuary legatee,[2] my sole friend and my sole mourner. But Scrooge was not so cut up by the sad event of my death, but that he was an excellent man of business on the very day of my funeral, and solemnized[3] it with an undoubted bargain. [*Pauses again in disgust*] He never painted out my name from the window. There it stands, on the window and above the warehouse door: Scrooge and Marley. Sometimes people new to our business call him Scrooge and sometimes they call him Marley. He answers to both names. It's all the same to him. And it's cheaper than painting in a new sign, isn't it? [*Pauses; moves closer to* Scrooge] Nobody has ever stopped him in the street to say, with gladsome looks, "My dear Scrooge, how are you? When will you come to see me?" No beggars implored him to bestow a trifle, no children ever ask him what it is o'clock, no man or woman now, or ever in his life, not once, inquire the way to such and such a place. [Marley *stands next to* Scrooge *now. They share, so it seems, a spotlight.*] But what does Scrooge care of any of this? It is the very thing he likes! To edge his way along the crowded paths of life, warning all human sympathy to keep its distance.

9 [*A ghostly bell rings in the distance.* Marley *moves away from* Scrooge, *now, heading* D. *again. As he does, he "takes" the light:* Scrooge *has disappeared into the black void beyond.* Marley *walks* D.C., *talking directly to the audience. Pauses*]

10 The bell tolls and I must take my leave. You must stay a while with Scrooge and watch him play out his scroogey life. It is now the story: the once-upon-a-time. Scrooge is busy in his counting-house. Where else? Christmas eve and Scrooge is busy in his counting-house. It is cold, bleak, biting weather outside: foggy withal: and, if you listen closely, you can hear the people in the court go wheezing up and down, beating their hands upon their breasts, and stamping their feet upon the pavement stones to warm them . . .

11 [*The clocks outside strike three.*]

12 Only three! and quite dark outside already: it has not been light all day this day.

13 [*This ghostly bell rings in the distance again.* Marley *looks about him. Music in.* Marley *flies away.*]

14 [*N.B.* Marley's *comings and goings should, from time to time, induce the explosion of the odd flash-pot,* I.H.]

NOTES

2. **sole residuary legatee** *n.* legal term for a person who inherits someone's home after he or she dies.

3. **solemnized** *v.* honored or remembered. Marley is being sarcastic.

PERSONALIZE FOR LEARNING

English Language Support

Multiple-Meaning Words Explain to students that the word *sole* in paragraph 8 has several meanings. As it is used in the play, it is an adjective that means "the only one." *Sole* can also be a noun that means "the bottom of a shoe or foot" or "a type of fish." **ALL LEVELS**

TEACHING

Remind students that sarcasm is a form of expression in which a person's words mean one thing but the person really means something else. A person can use sarcasm to be funny, irritating, or even insulting. You may wish to model the close read using the following think-aloud format. Possible responses to questions on the student page are included.

ANNOTATE: As I read lines in paragraph 10, I look for dialogue in which Scrooge says one thing but really means something else.

QUESTION: Scrooge thinks people who celebrate Christmas are fools. He expresses this to his nephew in a sarcastic way.

CONCLUDE: This attitude tells me that Scrooge is a nasty person who is clearly unhappy.

NOTES

Scene 2

1 [*Christmas music in, sung by a live chorus, full. At conclusion of song, sound fades under and into the distance. Lights up in set: offices of Scrooge and Marley, Ltd.* Scrooge *sits at his desk, at work. Near him is a tiny fire. His door is open and in his line of vision, we see* Scrooge's *clerk,* Bob Cratchit, *who sits in a dismal tank of a cubicle, copying letters. Near* Cratchit *is a fire so tiny as to barely cast a light: perhaps it is one pitifully glowing coal?* Cratchit *rubs his hands together, puts on a white comforter*[4] *and tries to heat his hands around his candle.* Scrooge's Nephew *enters, unseen.*]

2 **Scrooge.** What are you doing, Cratchit? Acting cold, are you? Next, you'll be asking to replenish your coal from my coal-box, won't you? Well, save your breath, Cratchit! Unless you're prepared to find employ elsewhere!

3 **Nephew.** [*Cheerfully; surprising* Scrooge] A merry Christmas to you, Uncle! God save you!

4 **Scrooge.** Bah! Humbug![5]

5 **Nephew.** Christmas a "humbug," Uncle? I'm sure you don't mean that.

6 **Scrooge.** I do! Merry Christmas? What right do you have to be merry? What reason have you to be merry? You're poor enough!

7 **Nephew.** Come, then. What right have you to be dismal? What reason have you to be **morose**? You're rich enough.

8 **Scrooge.** Bah! Humbug!

9 **Nephew.** Don't be cross, Uncle.

10 **Scrooge.** What else can I be? Eh? When I live in a world of fools such as this? Merry Christmas? What's Christmastime to you but a time of paying bills without any money; a time for finding yourself a year older, but not an hour richer. If I could work my will, every idiot who goes about with "Merry Christmas" on his lips, should be boiled with his own pudding, and buried with a stake of holly through his heart. He should!

11 **Nephew.** Uncle!

12 **Scrooge.** Nephew! You keep Christmas in your own way and let me keep it in mine.

13 **Nephew.** Keep it! But you don't keep it, Uncle.

14 **Scrooge.** Let me leave it alone, then. Much good it has ever done you!

4. **comforter** *n.* long, woolen scarf.

5. **Humbug** *interj.* nonsense.

morose *adj.* (muh ROHS) gloomy; ill-tempered

CLOSE READ

ANNOTATE: Mark words in paragraph 10 that show Scrooge's attitude toward Christmas.

QUESTION: What does Scrooge think of people, such as his nephew, that celebrate Christmas?

CONCLUDE: What does this attitude reveal about Scrooge's character?

DIGITAL PERSPECTIVES

15 **Nephew.** There are many things from which I have derived good, by which I have not profited, I daresay. Christmas among the rest. But I am sure that I always thought of Christmas time, when it has come round—as a good time: the only time I know of, when men and women seem to open their shut-up hearts freely, and to think of people below them as if they really were fellow-passengers to the grave, and not another race of creatures bound on other journeys. And therefore, Uncle, though it has never put a scrap of gold or silver in my pocket, I believe that it *has* done me good, and that it *will* do me good; and I say, God bless it!

16 [*The Clerk in the tank applauds, looks at the furious* Scrooge *and pokes out his tiny fire, as if in exchange for the moment of impropriety.* Scrooge *yells at him.*]

17 **Scrooge.** [*To the clerk*] Let me hear another sound from *you* and you'll keep your Christmas by losing your situation. [*To the nephew*] You're quite a powerful speaker, sir. I wonder you don't go into Parliament.[6]

18 **Nephew.** Don't be angry, Uncle. Come! Dine with us tomorrow.

19 **Scrooge.** I'd rather see myself dead than see myself with your family!

20 **Nephew.** But, why? Why?

21 **Scrooge.** Why did you get married?

22 **Nephew.** Because I fell in love.

23 **Scrooge.** That, sir, is the only thing that you have said to me in your entire lifetime which is even more ridiculous than "Merry Christmas!" [*Turns from* Nephew] Good afternoon.

24 **Nephew.** Nay, Uncle, you never came to see me before I married either. Why give it as a reason for not coming now?

25 **Scrooge.** Good afternoon, Nephew!

26 **Nephew.** I want nothing from you; I ask nothing of you; why cannot we be friends?

27 **Scrooge.** Good afternoon!

28 **Nephew.** I am sorry with all my heart, to find you so **resolute**. But I have made the trial in homage to Christmas, and I'll keep my Christmas humor to the last. So A Merry Christmas, Uncle!

29 **Scrooge.** Good afternoon!

30 **Nephew.** And a Happy New Year!

31 **Scrooge.** Good afternoon!

NOTES

6. **Parliament** national legislative body of Great Britain, in some ways like the U.S. Congress.

resolute (REHZ uh loot) *adj.* determined

PERSONALIZE FOR LEARNING

Challenge

Speculate Review paragraphs 18–23, which reveal, without saying it directly, why Scrooge has cut himself off from his nephew (his nephew married a poor woman "simply" because he fell in love). Have students write a brief scene in which Scrooge's nephew first comes to Scrooge and tells him he's going to marry. What does the nephew say to Scrooge? How does Scrooge respond? How does the scene end?

NOTES

32 **Nephew.** [*He stands facing* Scrooge.] Uncle, you are the most . . . [*Pauses*] No, I shan't. My Christmas humor is intact . . . [*Pause*] God bless you, Uncle . . . [Nephew *turns and starts for the door; he stops at* Cratchit's *cage*.] Merry Christmas, Bob Cratchit . . .

33 **Cratchit.** Merry Christmas to you sir, and a very, very happy New Year . . .

34 **Scrooge.** [*Calling across to them*] Oh, fine, a perfection, just fine . . . to see the perfect pair of you; husbands, with wives and children to support . . . my clerk there earning fifteen shillings a week . . . and the perfect pair of you, talking about a Merry Christmas! [*Pauses*] I'll retire to Bedlam![7]

35 **Nephew.** [*To* Cratchit] He's **impossible**!

36 **Cratchit.** Oh, mind him not, sir. He's getting on in years, and he's alone. He's noticed your visit. I'll wager your visit has warmed him.

37 **Nephew.** Him? Uncle Ebenezer Scrooge? *Warmed?* You are a better Christian than I am, sir.

38 **Cratchit.** [*Opening the door for* Nephew; *two* Do-Gooders *will enter, as* Nephew *exits*] Good day to you, sir, and God bless.

39 **Nephew.** God bless . . . [*One man who enters is portly, the other is thin. Both are pleasant.*]

40 **Cratchit.** Can I help you, gentlemen?

41 **Thin Man.** [*Carrying papers and books; looks around* Cratchit *to* Scrooge] Scrooge and Marley's, I believe. Have I the pleasure of addressing Mr. Scrooge, or Mr. Marley?

42 **Scrooge.** Mr. Marley has been dead these seven years. He died seven years ago this very night.

43 **Portly Man.** We have no doubt his liberality[8] is well represented by his surviving partner . . . [*Offers his calling card*]

44 **Scrooge.** [*Handing back the card; unlooked at*] . . . Good afternoon.

45 **Thin Man.** This will take but a moment, sir . . .

46 **Portly Man.** At this festive season of the year, Mr. Scrooge, it is more than usually desirable that we should make some slight provision for the poor and destitute, who suffer greatly at the present time. Many thousands are in want of common necessities; hundreds of thousands are in want of common comforts, sir.

47 **Scrooge.** Are there no prisons?

7. **Bedlam** *n.* hospital in London for the mentally ill.

impossible (ihm POS uh buhl) *adj.* disagreeable; unreasonable

8. **liberality** *n.* generosity.

PERSONALIZE FOR LEARNING

English Language Support

Informal Language Explain to students that the word *impossible* in paragraph 35 literally means "not capable of being or happening," but as it is used here it has another meaning. The use of the word *impossible* here is an informal use of the word that describes someone who is very unreasonable. For example, If you have a friend who always argues with you no matter what you say, you might get frustrated and say, "You're impossible!" **ALL LEVELS**

DIGITAL PERSPECTIVES

48 **Portly Man.** Plenty of prisons.

49 **Scrooge.** And aren't the Union workhouses still in operation?

50 **Thin Man.** They are. Still, I wish that I could say that they are not.

51 **Scrooge.** The Treadmill[9] and the Poor Law[10] are in full vigor, then?

52 **Thin Man.** Both very busy, sir.

53 **Scrooge.** Ohhh, I see. I was afraid, from what you said at first, that something had occurred to stop them from their useful course. [*Pauses*] I'm glad to hear it.

54 **Portly Man.** Under the impression that they scarcely furnish Christian cheer of mind or body to the multitude, a few of us are endeavoring to raise a fund to buy the Poor some meat and drink, and means of warmth. We choose this time, because it is a time, of all others, when Want is keenly felt, and Abundance rejoices. [*Pen in hand; as well as notepad*] What shall I put you down for, sir?

55 **Scrooge.** Nothing!

56 **Portly Man.** You wish to be left anonymous?

57 **Scrooge.** I wish to be left alone! [*Pauses; turns away; turns back to them*] Since you ask me what I wish, gentlemen, that is my answer. I help to support the establishments that I have mentioned: they cost enough: and those who are badly off must go there.

58 **Thin Man.** Many can't go there; and many would rather die.

59 **Scrooge.** If they would rather die, they had better do it, and decrease the surplus population. Besides—excuse me—I don't know that.

60 **Thin Man.** But you might know it!

61 **Scrooge.** It's not my business. It's enough for a man to understand his own business, and not to interfere with other people's. Mine occupies me constantly. Good afternoon, gentlemen!

62 [Scrooge *turns his back on the gentlemen and returns to his desk.*]

63 **Portly Man.** But, sir, Mr. Scrooge . . . think of the poor.

64 **Scrooge.** [*Turns suddenly to them. Pauses*] Take your leave of my offices, sirs, while I am still smiling.

65 [*The* Thin Man *looks at the* Portly Man. *They are undone. They shrug. They move to the door.* Cratchit *hops up to open it for them.*]

NOTES

9. **the Treadmill** kind of mill wheel turned by the weight of people treading steps arranged around it, this device is used to punish prisoners.

10. **Poor Law** the original 16th-century Poor Laws called for overseers of the poor in each neighborhood to provide relief for the needy. The New Poor Law of 1834 made the workhouses in which the poor sometimes lived and worked extremely harsh and unattractive places.

CLOSE READ

ANNOTATE: Mark the words in paragraph 54 that describe the Portly Man's reasons for asking for help.

QUESTION: What do these details reveal about the setting?

CONCLUDE: How does this information affect your understanding of the drama?

CLOSE READ

Remind students that formal language is different from the kind of language we usually use with our friends and family. It is often wordier and "stiffer." You may wish to model the close read using the following think-aloud format. Possible responses to questions on the student page are included.

ANNOTATE: As I read paragraph 54, I look for words that Portly Man uses to tell Scrooge why he is asking for funds to help the poor.

QUESTION: That Portly Man is asking for donations for the poor tells me that during the 1800s in London there was a serious divide between the wealthy and the poor, and the poor didn't have basic comforts.

CONCLUDE: I understand what a terrible person Scrooge is in this play, that he is able but unwilling to help poor people who desperately need things as simple as food and a warm place to stay.

CROSS-CURRICULAR PERSPECTIVES

Social Studies Review paragraphs 49–51 and have students research the institutions Scrooge talks about in this scene (the Union workhouses; the Treadmill; the Poor Law) and write short reports on these topics. What were these institutions? Why where they created? What were they like for the people affected by them? What finally happened to these institutions? Guide the class to discuss how this information affects their understanding of both the scene and Scrooge's character.

TEACHING

CLOSE READE

Remind students to focus on Cratchit's attitude toward Scrooge as they read paragraphs 78–95. Tell students they should look for words in the dialogue that reveal Cratchit's attitude. You may wish to model the close read using the following think aloud format. Possible responses to questions on the student page are included.

ANNOTATE: As I read paragraphs 78–95, I notice details about how Cratchit behaves politely and calmly toward Scrooge in spite of Scrooge's bad attitude.

QUESTION: I think the playwright included this exchange to emphasize how Cratchit is tolerant and also a happy person who has a family to go home to. Cratchit doesn't let Scrooge's behavior get to him.

CONCLUDE: The conversation reveals that Cratchit is a good man and a hard worker and still wishes his ill-tempered boss a Merry Christmas after barely getting time off to be with his family.

NOTES

66 **Thin Man.** Good day, sir . . . [*To* Cratchit] A merry Christmas to you, sir . . .

67 **Cratchit.** Yes. A Merry Christmas to both of you . . .

68 **Portly Man.** Merry Christmas . . .

69 [Cratchit *silently squeezes something into the hand of the* Thin Man.]

70 **Thin Man.** What's this?

71 **Cratchit.** Shhhh . . .

72 [Cratchit *opens the door; wind and snow whistle into the room.*]

73 **Thin Man.** Thank you, sir, thank you.

74 [Cratchit *closes the door and returns to his workplace.* Scrooge *is at his own counting table. He talks to* Cratchit *without looking up.*]

75 **Scrooge.** It's less of a time of year for being merry, and more a time of year for being loony . . . if you ask me.

76 **Cratchit.** Well, I don't know, sir . . . [*The clock's bell strikes six o'clock.*] Well, there it is, eh, six?

77 **Scrooge.** Saved by six bells, are you?

CLOSE READ

ANNOTATE: Mark details in paragraphs 78–95 that show Cratchit's attitude toward Scrooge.

QUESTION: Why might the playwright have included this exchange between Cratchit and Scrooge?

CONCLUDE: What does this conversation reveal about Cratchit's character?

78 **Cratchit.** I must be going home . . . [*He snuffs out his candle and puts on his hat.*] I hope you have a . . . very very lovely day tomorrow, sir . . .

79 **Scrooge.** Hmmm. Oh, you'll be wanting the whole day tomorrow, I suppose?

80 **Cratchit.** If quite convenient, sir.

81 **Scrooge.** It's not convenient, and it's not fair. If I was to stop half-a-crown for it, you'd think yourself ill-used, I'll be bound?

82 [Cratchit *smiles faintly.*]

83 **Cratchit.** I don't know, sir . . .

84 **Scrooge.** And yet, you don't think me ill-used when I pay a day's wages for no work . . .

85 **Cratchit.** It's only but once a year . . .

86 **Scrooge.** A poor excuse for picking a man's pocket every 25th of December! But I suppose you must have the whole day. Be here all the earlier the next morning!

87 **Cratchit.** Oh, I will, sir. I will. I promise you. And, sir . . .

88 **Scrooge.** Don't say it, Cratchit.

89 **Cratchit.** But let me wish you a . . .

90 **Scrooge.** Don't say it, Cratchit. I warn you . . .

91 **Cratchit.** Sir!

PERSONALIZE FOR LEARNING

Strategic Support

Stage Directions Explain to students that stage directions, such as those in paragraph 74, are notes included in a play to describe how the work is meant to be performed or staged. They might describe sets, costumes, lighting, or sound effects, as well as the appearance and physical actions of characters. Stage directions can be used to reveal things about a character that the dialogue doesn't. For example, a character whose feelings are hurt might look like he is about to cry, then walk off the stage without saying a word. Remind students that when they read a play they should pay as much attention to the stage directions as they do to the dialogue.

DIGITAL PERSPECTIVES

92 **Scrooge.** Cratchit!

93 [Cratchit *opens the door.*]

94 **Cratchit.** All right, then, sir . . . well . . . [*Suddenly*] Merry Christmas, Mr. Scrooge!

95 [*And he runs out the door, shutting same behind him.* Scrooge *moves to his desk; gathering his coat, hat, etc. A* Boy *appears at his window . . . .*]

96 **Boy.** [*Singing*] "Away in a manger . . ."

97 [Scrooge *seizes his ruler and whacks at the image of the* Boy *outside. The* Boy *leaves.*]

98 **Scrooge.** Bah! Humbug! Christmas! Bah! Humbug! [*He shuts out the light.*]

99 *A note on the crossover, following Scene 2:*

100 [Scrooge *will walk alone to his rooms from his offices. As he makes a long slow cross of the stage, the scenery should change. Christmas music will be heard, various people will cross by* Scrooge, *often smiling happily.*

NOTES

NOTES

11. **misanthrope** (MIHS uhn throhp) *n.* a person who hates or distrusts everyone.

malcontent (MAL kuhn tehnt) *n.* a person who is always unhappy

miser (MY zuhr) *n.* greedy person who keeps and refuses to spend money, even at the expense of his or her own comfort

12. **specter** *n.* ghost.

13. **deliquesce** (dehl ih KWEHS) *v.* melt away.

14. **gruel on the hob** thin broth warming on a ledge at the back or side of the fireplace.

101 *There will be occasional pleasant greetings tossed at him.*

102 Scrooge, *in contrast to all, will grump and mumble. He will snap at passing boys, as might a horrid old hound.*

103 *In short,* Scrooge's *sounds and movements will define him in contrast from all other people who cross the stage: he is the misanthrope,*[11] *the* **malcontent**, *the* **miser**. *He is* Scrooge.

104 *This statement of* Scrooge's *character, by contrast to all other characters, should seem comical to the audience.*

105 *During* Scrooge's *crossover to his rooms, snow should begin to fall. All passers-by will hold their faces to the sky, smiling, allowing snow to shower them lightly.* Scrooge, *by contrast, will bat at the flakes with his walking-stick, as might an insomniac swat at a sleep-stopping, middle-of-the-night swarm of mosquitoes. He will comment on the blackness of the night, and, finally, reach his rooms and his encounter with the magical specter:*[12] Marley, *his eternal mate.*]

Scene 3

1 **Scrooge.** No light at all . . . no moon . . . *that* is what is at the center of Christmas Eve: dead black: void . . .

2 [Scrooge *puts his key in the door's keyhole. He has reached his rooms now. The door knocker changes and is now* Marley's *face. A musical sound: quickly: ghostly.* Marley's *image is not at all angry, but looks at* Scrooge *as did the old* Marley *look at* Scrooge. *The hair is curiously stirred; eyes wide open, dead: absent of focus.* Scrooge *stares wordlessly here. The face, before his very eyes, does deliquesce.*[13] *It is a knocker again.* Scrooge *opens the door and checks the back of same, probably for* Marley's *pigtail. Seeing nothing but screws and nuts,* Scrooge *refuses the memory.*]

3 Pooh, pooh!

4 [*The sound of the door closing resounds throughout the house as thunder. Every room echoes the sound.* Scrooge *fastens the door and walks across the hall to the stairs, trimming his candle as he goes; and then he goes slowly up the staircase. He checks each room: sitting room, bedrooms, lumber-room. He looks under the sofa, under the table: nobody there. He fixes his evening gruel on the hob,*[14] *changes his jacket.* Scrooge *sits near the tiny low-flamed fire, sipping his gruel. There are various pictures on the walls: all of them now show likenesses of* Marley. Scrooge *blinks his eyes.*]

5 Bah! Humbug!

6 [Scrooge *walks in a circle about the room. The pictures change back into their natural images. He sits down at the table in front of the*

VOCABULARY DEVELOPMENT

Dictionary Use Point out that the word *misanthrope* in paragraph 103 begins with the prefix *mis-*. Review the prefix *mis-*, which means "badly" (*misjudge*); "unfavorably, in a suspicious manner" (*misdoubt*); and "lack of" (*mistrust*). Have students find other words with this prefix in the text, or have them think of other words they are familiar with that begin with *mis-*. Then, have students try to define the words and use a dictionary to confirm their answers.

fire. A bell hangs overhead. It begins to ring, of its own accord. Slowly, surely, begins the ringing of every bell in the house. They continue ringing for nearly half a minute. Scrooge *is stunned by the phenomenon. The bells cease their ringing all at once. Deep below* Scrooge, *in the basement of the house, there is the sound of clanking, of some enormous chain being dragged across the floors; and now up the stairs. We hear doors flying open.*]

NOTES

7 Bah still! Humbug still! This is not happening! I won't believe it!

8 [Marley's Ghost *enters the room. He is horrible to look at: pigtail, vest, suit as usual, but he drags an enormous chain now, to which is fastened cash-boxes, keys, padlocks, ledgers, deeds, and heavy purses fashioned of steel. He is transparent.* Marley *stands opposite the stricken* Scrooge.]

9 How now! What do you want of me?

10 **Marley.** Much!

11 **Scrooge.** Who are you?

12 **Marley.** Ask me who I was.

13 **Scrooge** Who were you then?

14 **Marley.** In life, I was your business partner: Jacob Marley.

15 **Scrooge.** I see . . . can you sit down?

16 **Marley.** I can.

17 **Scrooge.** Do it then.

18 **Marley.** I shall. [Marley *sits opposite* Scrooge, *in the chair across the table, at the front of the fireplace.*] You don't believe in me.

19 **Scrooge.** I don't.

20 **Marley.** Why do you doubt your senses?

21 **Scrooge.** Because every little thing affects them. A slight disorder of the stomach makes them cheat. You may be an undigested bit of beef, a blot of mustard, a crumb of cheese, a fragment of an underdone potato. There's more of gravy than of grave about you, whatever you are!

22 [*There is a silence between them.* Scrooge *is made nervous by it. He picks up a toothpick.*]

23 Humbug! I tell you: humbug!

24 [Marley *opens his mouth and screams a ghostly, fearful scream. The scream echoes about each room of the house. Bats fly, cats screech, lightning flashes.* Scrooge *stands and walks backwards against the wall.* Marley *stands and screams again. This time, he takes his head and lifts it from his shoulders. His head continues to*

PERSONALIZE FOR LEARNING

Strategic Support

Word Choice Use paragraph 21 to review the importance of precise word choice. Discuss how the author's choice of precise and strong words adds to the power of Scrooge's dialogue. To illustrate this, quickly paraphrase Scrooge's speech for students: "My stomach is sensitive. You're probably just a bad dream caused by something I ate at dinner." Guide students to identify how the speech changed without using the playwright's precise language.

NOTES

15. **apparition** *n.* ghost.

scream. Marley's *face again appears on every picture in the room: all screaming.* Scrooge, *on his knees before* Marley.]

25 Mercy! Dreadful apparition,[15] mercy! Why, O! why do you trouble me so?

26 **Marley.** Man of the worldly mind, do you believe in me, or not?

27 **Scrooge.** I do. I must. But why do spirits such as you walk the earth? And why do they come to me?

28 **Marley.** It is required of every man that the spirit within him should walk abroad among his fellow-men, and travel far and wide; and if that spirit goes not forth in life, it is condemned to do so after death. [Marley *screams again; a tragic scream; from his ghostly bones.*] I wear the chain I forged in life. I made it link by link, and yard by yard. Is its pattern strange to *you*? Or would you know, you, Scrooge, the weight and length of the strong coil you bear yourself? It was full as

246 UNIT 3 • TURNING POINTS

heavy and long as this, seven Christmas Eves ago. You have labored on it, since. It is a ponderous chain.

29 [*Terrified that a chain will appear about his body,* Scrooge *spins and waves the unwanted chain away. None, of course, appears. Sees* Marley *watching him dance about the room.* Marley *watches* Scrooge; *silently.*]

30 **Scrooge.** Jacob. Old Jacob Marley, tell me more. Speak comfort to me, Jacob . . .

31 **Marley.** I have none to give. Comfort comes from other regions, Ebenezer Scrooge, and is conveyed by other ministers, to other kinds of men. A very little more, is all that is permitted to me. I cannot rest, I cannot stay, I cannot linger anywhere . . . [*He moans again.*] My spirit never walked beyond our counting-house—mark me!—in life my spirit never roved beyond the narrow limits of our money-changing hole; and weary journeys lie before me!

32 **Scrooge.** But you were always a good man of business, Jacob.

33 **Marley.** [*Screams word "business"; a flash-pot explodes with him.*] *BUSINESS!!!* Mankind was my business. The common welfare was my business; charity, mercy, forbearance, benevolence, were, all, my business. [Scrooge *is quaking.*] Hear me, Ebenezer Scrooge! My time is nearly gone.

34 **Scrooge.** I will, but don't be hard upon me. And don't be flowery, Jacob! Pray!

35 **Marley.** How is it that I appear before you in a shape that you can see, I may not tell. I have sat invisible beside you many and many a day. That is no light part of my penance. I am here tonight to warn you that you have yet a chance and hope of escaping my fate. A chance and hope of my procuring, Ebenezer.

36 **Scrooge.** You were always a good friend to me. Thank'ee!

37 **Marley.** You will be haunted by Three Spirits.

38 **Scrooge.** Would that be the chance and hope you mentioned, Jacob?

39 **Marley.** It is.

40 **Scrooge.** I think I'd rather not.

41 **Marley.** Without their visits, you cannot hope to shun the path I tread. Expect the first one tomorrow, when the bell tolls one.

42 **Scrooge.** Couldn't I take 'em all at once, and get it over, Jacob?

NOTES

CLOSE READ

ANNOTATE: Mark the words in paragraphs 30–34 that show Scrooge's reaction to Marley.

QUESTION: What do these words reveal about Scrooge at this point in the play?

CONCLUDE: What does Scrooge's reaction in these paragraphs suggest about his character?

DIGITAL PERSPECTIVES 

CLOSE READ

Remind students to focus on the playwright's word choices as they focus on paragraphs 30–34 and to think about what word choice tells them about Scrooge. You may wish to model the close read using the following think-aloud format. Possible responses to questions on the student page are included.

ANNOTATE: As I read paragraphs 30–34, I look for words that tell me how Scrooge reacts to Marley now that Marley has appeared as a ghost.

QUESTION: The words Scrooge speaks to Marley in these paragraphs reveal that Scrooge is scared of Marley's ghost and is trying to be nice and also complimentary toward Marley.

CONCLUDE: Scrooge's reaction tells me that he is starting to think about the way he treated Marley when the two of them were business partners. Scrooge is starting to feel regret for the way he used to behave.

PERSONALIZE FOR LEARNING

Strategic Support

Irony Review irony as something that does not match up with what is expected, such as the ironic fate of Marley shown in paragraph 31. Point out that another example of irony in the play is that Scrooge once worked for Fezziwig, who treated his employees very well. Yet Scrooge now treats Cratchit horribly. Challenge students to find other examples of irony in the play.

NOTES

43 **Marley.** Expect the second on the next night at the same hour. The third upon the next night when the last stroke of twelve has ceased to vibrate. Look to see me no more. Others may, but you may not. And look that, for your own sake, you remember what has passed between us!

44 [Marley *places his head back upon his shoulders. He approaches the window and beckons to* Scrooge *to watch. Outside the window, specters fly by, carrying money-boxes and chains. They make a confused sound of lamentation.* Marley, *after listening a moment, joins into their mournful dirge. He leans to the window and floats out into the bleak, dark night. He is gone.*]

45 **Scrooge.** [*Rushing to the window*] Jacob! No, Jacob! Don't leave me! I'm frightened! [*He sees that* Marley *has gone. He looks outside. He pulls the shutter closed, so that the scene is blocked from his view. All sound stops. After a pause, he re-opens the shutter and all is quiet, as it should be on Christmas Eve. Carolers carol out of doors, in the distance.* Scrooge *closes the shutter and walks down the stairs. He examines the door by which* Marley *first entered.*] No one here at all! Did I imagine all that? Humbug! [*He looks about the room.*] I did imagine it. It only happened in my foulest dream-mind, didn't it? An undigested bit of . . . [*Thunder and lightning in the room; suddenly*] Sorry! Sorry!

46 [*There is silence again. The lights fade out.*]

Scene 4

1 [*Christmas music, choral, "Hark the Herald Angels Sing," sung by an onstage choir of children, spotlighted,* D.C. *Above,* Scrooge *in his bed, dead to the world, asleep, in his darkened room. It should appear that the choir is singing somewhere outside of the house, of course, and a use of scrim*[16] *is thus suggested. When the singing is ended, the choir should fade out of view and* Marley *should fade into view, in their place.*]

2 **Marley.** [*Directly to audience*] From this point forth . . . I shall be quite visible to you, but invisible to him. [*Smiles*] He will feel my presence, nevertheless, for, unless my senses fail me completely, we are—you and I—witness to the changing of a miser: that one, my partner in life, in business, and in eternity: that one: Scrooge. [*Moves to staircase, below* Scrooge] See him now. He endeavors to pierce the darkness with his ferret eyes.[17] [*To audience*] See him, now. He listens for the hour.

16. **scrim** *n.* see-through fabric backdrop used to create special effects in the theater.

17. **ferret eyes** A ferret is a small, weasel-like animal used for hunting rabbits. This expression means to stare continuously, the way a ferret hunts.

DIGITAL PERSPECTIVES

Illuminating the Text To help students understand the impact of Scrooge's encounter with Marley's ghost, use the search term "a Christmas Carol 1951" to find video footage of the 1951 film. (Note: Be sure to preview any video before showing it to students.) Have students view 11:00–21:10, then have them discuss how seeing this scene from the film helps illuminate the play. **(Research to Clarify)**

248 UNIT 3 • TURNING POINTS

DIGITAL PERSPECTIVES

3 [*The bells toll.* Scrooge *is awakened and quakes as the hour approaches one o'clock, but the bells stop their sound at the hour of twelve.*]

4 **Scrooge.** [*Astonished*] Midnight! Why this isn't possible. It was past two when I went to bed. An icicle must have gotten into the clock's works! I couldn't have slept through the whole day and far into another night. It isn't possible that anything has happened to the sun, and this is twelve at noon! [*He runs to window; unshutters same; it is night.*] Night, still. Quiet, normal for the season, cold. It is certainly not noon. I cannot in any way afford to lose my days. Securities come due, promissory notes,[18] interest on investments: these are things that happen in the daylight! [*He returns to his bed.*] Was this a dream?

5 [Marley *appears in his room. He speaks to the audience.*]

6 **Marley.** You see? He does not, with faith, believe in me fully, even still! Whatever will it take to turn the faith of a miser from money to men?

7 **Scrooge.** Another quarter and it'll be one and Marley's ghostly friends will come. [*Pauses; listens*] Where's the chime for one? [*Ding, dong*] A quarter past [*Repeats*] Half-past! [*Repeats*] A quarter to it! But where's the heavy bell of the hour one? This is a game in which I lose my senses! Perhaps, if I allowed myself another short doze . . .

8 **Marley.** . . . Doze, Ebenezer, doze.

9 [*A heavy bell thuds its one ring; dull and definitely one o'clock. There is a flash of light.* Scrooge *sits up, in a sudden. A hand draws back the curtains by his bed. He sees it.*]

10 **Scrooge.** A hand! Who owns it! Hello!

11 [*Ghostly music again, but of a new nature to the play. A strange figure stands before* Scrooge*—like a child, yet at the same time like an old man: white hair, but unwrinkled skin, long, muscular arms, but delicate legs and feet. Wears white tunic; lustrous belt cinches waist. Branch of fresh green holly in its hand, but has its dress trimmed with fresh summer flowers. Clear jets of light spring from the crown of its head. Holds cap in hand. The Spirit is called* Past.]

12 Are you the Spirit, sir, whose coming was foretold to me?

13 **Past.** I am.

14 **Marley.** Does he take this to be a vision of his green grocer?

NOTES

CLOSE READ

ANNOTATE: Mark details in paragraph 4 that describe the setting.

QUESTION: Why might the playwright have included these details?

CONCLUDE: How do these details work together to increase the tension?

18. **promissory notes** *n.* written promises to pay someone a certain sum of money.

CLOSE READ

Remind students that they will be looking for details in paragraph 4 that describe the setting. You may wish to model the close read using the following think-aloud format. Possible responses to questions on the student page are included.

ANNOTATE: As I read paragraph 4, I notice and mark details that tell me about the setting.

QUESTION: I wonder why the playwright chose to emphasize the darkness in Scrooge's room and his confusion with the time of day.

CONCLUDE: The details about the darkness of midnight when Scrooge expects it to be daytime work together to create a tense feeling at Scrooge's confused state. Scrooge is disoriented, making me feel as if something eerie is about to happen.

NOTES

15 **Scrooge.** Who, and what are you?

16 **Past.** I am the Ghost of Christmas Past.

17 **Scrooge.** Long past?

18 **Past.** Your past.

19 **Scrooge.** May I ask, please, sir, what business you have here with me?

20 **Past.** Your welfare.

21 **Scrooge.** Not to sound ungrateful, sir, and really, please do understand that I am plenty obliged for your concern, but, really, kind spirit, it would have done all the better for my welfare to have been left alone altogether, to have slept peacefully through this night.

22 **Past.** Your reclamation, then. Take heed!

23 **Scrooge.** My what?

24 **Past.** [*Motioning to* Scrooge *and taking his arm*] Rise! Fly with me! [*He leads* Scrooge *to the window.*]

25 **Scrooge.** [*Panicked*] Fly, but I am a mortal and cannot fly!

26 **Past.** [*Pointing to his heart*] Bear but a touch of my hand here and you shall be upheld in more than this!

27 [Scrooge *touches the spirit's heart and the lights dissolve into sparkly flickers. Lovely crystals of music are heard. The scene dissolves into another. Christmas music again*]

Scene 5

1 [Scrooge *and the* Ghost of Christmas Past *walk together across an open stage. In the background, we see a field that is open; covered by a soft, downy snow: a country road.*]

2 **Scrooge.** Good Heaven! I was bred in this place. I was a boy here!

3 [Scrooge *freezes, staring at the field beyond.* Marley's *ghost appears beside him; takes* Scrooge's *face in his hands, and turns his face to the audience.*]

4 **Marley.** You see this Scrooge: stricken by feeling. Conscious of a thousand odors floating in the air, each one connected with a thousand thoughts, and hopes, and joys, and care long, long forgotten. [*Pause*] This one—this Scrooge—before your very eyes, returns to life, among the living. [*To audience, sternly*] You'd best pay your most careful attention. I would suggest rapt.[19]

19. **rapt** *adj.* giving complete attention; totally carried away by something.

VOCABULARY DEVELOPMENT

Multiple Meanings Point out the word *mortal* (paragraph 25) and explain to students that as it is used here it is a noun that means "a human being." Explain that *mortal* can also be an adjective that means "causing or having caused death" (a mortal injury); "subject to death" (a mortal man); "marked by unrelenting hostility" (a mortal enemy); and "marked by great intensity or severity" (mortal fear). Point out that all of these meanings relate to being alive or dying.

5 [*There is a small flash and puff of smoke and* Marley *is gone again.*]

6 **Past.** Your lip is trembling, Mr. Scrooge. And what is that upon your cheek?

7 **Scrooge.** Upon my cheek? Nothing . . . a blemish on the skin from the eating of overmuch grease . . . nothing . . . [*Suddenly*] Kind Spirit of Christmas Past, lead me where you will, but quickly! To be stagnant in this place is, for me, unbearable!

8 **Past.** You recollect the way?

9 **Scrooge.** Remember it! I would know it blindfolded! My bridge, my church, my winding river! [*Staggers about, trying to see it all at once. He weeps again.*]

10 **Past.** These are but shadows of things that have been. They have no consciousness of us.

11 [*Four jocund travelers enter, singing a Christmas song in four-part harmony—"God Rest Ye Merry Gentlemen."*]

12 **Scrooge.** Listen! I know these men! I remember the beauty of their song!

13 **Past.** But, why do you remember it so happily? It is Merry Christmas that they say to one another! What is Merry Christmas to you, Mr. Scrooge? Out upon Merry Christmas, right? What good has Merry Christmas ever done you, Mr. Scrooge? . . .

14 **Scrooge.** [*After a long pause*] None. No good. None . . . [*He bows his head.*]

15 **Past.** Look, you, sir, a school ahead. The schoolroom is not quite deserted. A solitary child, neglected by his friends, is left there still.

16 [Scrooge *falls to the ground; sobbing as he sees, and we see, a small boy, the young* Scrooge, *sitting and weeping, bravely, alone at his desk: alone in a vast space, a void.*]

17 **Scrooge.** I cannot look on him!

18 **Past.** You must, Mr. Scrooge, you must.

19 **Scrooge.** It's me. [*Pauses; weeps*] Poor boy. He lived inside his head . . . alone . . . [*Pauses; weeps*] poor boy. [*Pauses; stops his weeping*] I wish . . . [*Dries his eyes on his cuff*] ah! it's too late!

20 **Past.** What is the matter?

21 **Scrooge.** There was a boy singing a Christmas Carol outside my door last night. I should like to have given him something: that's all.

NOTES

CLOSE READ

ANNOTATE: Mark words in paragraphs 15–19 that describe Scrooge's emotions and behavior.

QUESTION: What does the playwright reveal through these words?

CONCLUDE: What can you conclude about the Ghost of Christmas Past's effect on Scrooge based on this description?

DIGITAL PERSPECTIVES

CLOSE READ

Remind students to focus on words in paragraphs 15–19 that show Scrooge's emotions or behavior. You may wish to model the close read using the following think-aloud format. Possible responses to questions on the student page are included.

ANNOTATE: As I read paragraphs 15–19, I notice and mark words that tell me about how Scrooge is feeling and behaving.

QUESTION: The playwright's use of words like *solitary, neglected, sobbing, alone,* and *poor boy* reveals that Scrooge feels sad looking back on his life as a lonely schoolboy.

CONCLUDE: The Ghost of Christmas Past made Scrooge feel regret and sadness in looking back at his life and is probably feeling that he should have been kinder as an adult.

PERSONALIZE FOR LEARNING

English Language Support

Ellipses in Dialogue Tell students that when an ellipsis is used in dialogue (paragraph 19) it indicates a pause. The pause can reveal something about a character. Perhaps the words are difficult for the character to get out because the character is emotional, or the character is searching for words.

Discuss the difference in these two lines of dialogue: "I always thought you were a wonderful person." "I always thought you were a . . . wonderful person." What might the ellipsis in the second sentence suggest? **ALL LEVELS**

CLOSER LOOK

Analyze Character

Students may have marked paragraph 28 during their first read. Use this dialogue to help students understand Scrooge's character. Encourage students to talk about the annotations that they marked. You may want to model a close read with the class based on the highlights shown in the text.

ANNOTATE: Have students mark details in paragraph 28 that reveal how Scrooge became the person he is, or have students participate while you highlight them.

QUESTION: Guide students to consider what these details might tell them. Ask what a reader can infer from these details and accept student responses.

Possible response: Because Fan says "Father is so much kinder than he ever used to be," we can infer that in the past, their father was not kind. This allows us to also infer that Scrooge had a difficult childhood.

CONCLUDE: Help students to formulate conclusions about the importance of these details in the text. Ask students what this suggests.

Possible response: It suggests that Scrooge might be the way he is because of how his father treated him when he was young.

Explain that authors usually don't reveal everything about a **character** at once. Rather, they choose when to reveal important details about their characters. In this case, we learn something about Scrooge's life before the play began. This is called **backstory**. Most characters have a backstory because they were "alive" before the story we're reading began. The backstory has shaped the character we are reading about.

NOTES

22 **Past.** [*Smiles; waves his hand to* Scrooge] Come. Let us see another Christmas.

23 [*Lights out on a little boy. A flash of light. A puff of smoke. Lights up on older boy*]

24 **Scrooge.** Look! Me, again! Older now! [*Realizes*] Oh, yes . . . still alone.

25 [*The boy—a slightly older* Scrooge*—sits alone in a chair, reading. The door to the room opens and a young girl enters. She is much, much younger than this slightly older* Scrooge. *She is, say, six, and he is, say, twelve. Elder* Scrooge *and the* Ghost of Christmas Past *stand watching the scene, unseen.*]

26 **Fan.** Dear, dear brother, I have come to bring you home.

27 **Boy.** Home, little Fan?

28 **Fan.** Yes! Home, for good and all! Father is so much kinder than he ever used to be, and home's like heaven! He spoke so gently to me one dear night when I was going to bed that I was not afraid to ask him once more if you might come home; and he said "yes" . . . you should; and sent me in a coach to bring you. And you're to be a man and are never to come back here, but first, we're to be together all the Christmas long, and have the merriest time in the world.

29 **Boy.** You are quite a woman, little Fan!

30 [*Laughing; she drags at boy, causing him to stumble to the door with her. Suddenly we hear a mean and terrible voice in the hallway. Off. It is the* Schoolmaster.]

31 **Schoolmaster.** Bring down Master Scrooge's travel box at once! He is to travel!

32 **Fan.** Who is that, Ebenezer?

33 **Boy.** O! Quiet, Fan. It is the Schoolmaster, himself!

34 [*The door bursts open and into the room bursts with it the* Schoolmaster.]

35 **Schoolmaster.** Master Scrooge?

36 **Boy.** Oh, Schoolmaster, I'd like you to meet my little sister, Fan, sir . . .

37 [*Two boys struggle on with* Scrooge's *trunk.*]

38 **Fan.** Pleased, sir . . . [*She curtsies.*]

39 **Schoolmaster.** You are to travel, Master Scrooge.

40 **Scrooge.** Yes, sir, I know sir . . .

PERSONALIZE FOR LEARNING

English Language Support

Multiple-Meaning Words Discuss the word *coach* in paragraph 28, pointing out that it has several meanings. As it is used here, it is a noun meaning "a horse-drawn carriage." It can also mean "a railroad passenger car," "a bus," or "a class of passenger air transportation." A coach is also someone who helps or trains others (e.g., an acting coach; a soccer coach). As a verb, *coach* means "to instruct or help" (e.g., to coach baseball or coach a team). **ALL LEVELS**

DIGITAL PERSPECTIVES

NOTES

41 [*All start to exit, but* Fan *grabs the coattail of the mean old* Schoolmaster.]

42 **Boy.** Fan!

43 **Schoolmaster.** What's this?

44 **Fan.** Pardon, sir, but I believe that you've forgotten to say your goodbye to my brother, Ebenezer, who stands still now awaiting it . . . [*She smiles, curtsies, lowers her eyes.*] pardon, sir.

45 **Schoolmaster.** [*Amazed*] I . . . uh . . . harumph . . . uhh . . . well, then . . . [*Outstretches hand*] Goodbye, Scrooge.

46 **Boy.** Uh, well, goodbye, Schoolmaster . . .

47 [*Lights fade out on all but* Boy *looking at* Fan; *and* Scrooge *and* Past *looking at them.*]

48 **Scrooge.** Oh, my dear, dear little sister, Fan . . . how I loved her.

NOTES

20. **apprenticed** (uh PREHN tihst) *v.* received instruction in a trade as well as food and housing or wages in return for work.

49 **Past.** Always a delicate creature, whom a breath might have withered, but she had a large heart . . .

50 **Scrooge.** So she had.

51 **Past.** She died a woman, and had, as I think, children.

52 **Scrooge.** One child.

53 **Past.** True. Your nephew.

54 **Scrooge.** Yes.

55 **Past.** Fine, then. We move on, Mr. Scrooge. That warehouse, there? Do you know it?

56 **Scrooge.** Know it? Wasn't I apprenticed[20] there?

57 **Past.** We'll have a look.

58 [*They enter the warehouse. The lights crossfade with them, coming up on an old man in Welsh wig:* Fezziwig.]

59 **Scrooge.** Why, it's old Fezziwig! Bless his heart; it's Fezziwig, alive again!

60 [Fezziwig *sits behind a large, high desk, counting. He lays down his pen; looks at the clock: seven bells sound.*]

61 Quittin' time . . .

62 **Fezziwig.** Quittin' time . . . [*He takes off his waistcoat and laughs: calls off*] Yo ho, Ebenezer! Dick!

63 [Dick Wilkins *and* Ebenezer Scrooge—*a young man version—enter the room.* Dick *and* Ebenezer *are* Fezziwig's *apprentices.*]

64 **Scrooge.** Dick Wilkins, to be sure! My fellow-'prentice! Bless my soul, yes. There he is. He was very much attached to me, was Dick. Poor Dick! Dear, dear!

65 **Fezziwig.** Yo ho, my boys. No more work tonight. Christmas Eve, Dick. Christmas, Ebenezer!

66 [*They stand at attention in front of* Fezziwig; *laughing*]

67 Hilli-ho! Clear away, and let's have lots of room here! Hilli-ho, Dick! Chirrup, Ebenezer!

68 [*The young men clear the room, sweep the floor, straighten the pictures, trim the lamps, etc. The space is clear now. A fiddler enters, fiddling.*]

69 Hi-ho, Matthew! Fiddle away . . . where are my daughters?

70 [*The fiddler plays. Three young daughters of* Fezziwig *enter followed by six young adult male suitors. They are dancing to the music. All employees come in: workers, clerks, housemaids, cousins, the baker, etc. All dance. Full number wanted here. Throughout the*

PERSONALIZE FOR LEARNING

English Language Support

Slang Explain that the slang in paragraph 67 is informal, nonstandard vocabulary that is often unique to a particular group of people or a culture. Point out that every language has slang words. Examples of American slang are: "I had a ball at the party last night." "Don't worry about that. It's no biggie." Explain what these expressions mean. Then, ask students to write or say an example of slang from their native language and explain what it means.
ALL LEVELS

dance, food is brought into the feast. It is "eaten" in dance, by the dancers. Ebenezer *dances with all three of the daughters, as does* Dick. *They compete for the daughters, happily, in the dance.* Fezziwig *dances with his daughters.* Fezziwig *dances with* Dick *and* Ebenezer. *The music changes:* Mrs. Fezziwig *enters. She lovingly scolds her husband. They dance. She dances with* Ebenezer, *lifting him and throwing him about. She is enormously fat. When the dance is ended, they all dance off, floating away, as does the music.* Scrooge *and the* Ghost of Christmas Past *stand alone now. The music is gone.*]

71 **Past.** It was a small matter, that Fezziwig made those silly folks so full of gratitude.

72 **Scrooge.** Small!

73 **Past.** Shhh!

74 [*Lights up on* Dick *and* Ebenezer]

75 **Dick.** We are blessed, Ebenezer, truly, to have such a master as Mr. Fezziwig!

76 **Young Scrooge.** He is the best, best, the very and absolute best! If ever I own a firm of my own, I shall treat my apprentices with the same dignity and the same grace. We have learned a wonderful lesson from the master, Dick!

77 **Dick.** Ah, that's a fact, Ebenezer. That's a fact!

78 **Past.** Was it not a small matter, really? He spent but a few pounds[21] of his mortal money on your small party. Three or four pounds, perhaps. Is that so much that he deserves such praise as you and Dick so lavish now?

79 **Scrooge.** It isn't that! It isn't that, Spirit. Fezziwig had the power to make us happy or unhappy; to make our service light or burdensome; a pleasure or a toil. The happiness he gave is quite as great as if it cost him a fortune.

80 **Past.** What is the matter?

81 **Scrooge.** Nothing particular.

82 **Past.** Something, I think.

83 **Scrooge.** No, no. I should like to be able to say a word or two to my clerk just now! That's all!

84 [Ebenezer *enters the room and shuts down all the lamps. He stretches and yawns.* The Ghost of Christmas Past *turns to* Scrooge *all of a sudden.*]

85 **Past.** My time grows short! Quick!

86 [*In a flash of light,* Ebenezer *is gone, and in his place stands an* Older Scrooge, *this one a man in the prime of his life. Beside him*

NOTES

CLOSE READ

ANNOTATE: Mark details in paragraphs 70–76 that describe young Scrooge's behavior and personality.

QUESTION: Why might the playwright have included these descriptions?

CONCLUDE: How do these details deepen your understanding of Scrooge?

21. **pounds** *n.* common type of money used in Great Britain.

Have students focus on words in paragraphs 70–76 that reflect on young Scrooge. You may wish to model the close read using the following think-aloud format. Possible responses to questions on the student page are included.

ANNOTATE: As I read paragraphs 70–76, I notice and mark details that tell me what young Scrooge was like.

QUESTION: I wonder if the playwright chose to describe the mood of the dance to show that Scrooge was happier when he was a young man.

CONCLUDE: The descriptions of the dance and the dialogue between young Scrooge and Dick tell me that at one time Scrooge was a good person and had learned a lesson about treating people well. The details make me feel a little more sympathetic toward Scrooge as an older man.

NOTES

stands a young woman in a mourning dress. She is crying. She speaks to the man, with hostility.]

87 **Woman.** It matters little . . . to you, very little. Another idol has displaced me.

88 **Man.** What idol has displaced you?

89 **Woman.** A golden one.

90 **Man.** This is an even-handed dealing of the world. There is nothing on which it is so hard as poverty; and there is nothing it professes to condemn with such severity as the pursuit of wealth!

91 **Woman.** You fear the world too much. Have I not seen your nobler aspirations fall off one by one, until the master-passion, Gain, engrosses you? Have I not?

92 **Scrooge.** No!

93 **Man.** What then? Even if I have grown so much wiser, what then? Have I changed towards you?

94 **Woman.** No . . .

95 **Man.** Am I?

96 **Woman.** Our contract is an old one. It was made when we were both poor and content to be so. You are changed. When it was made, you were another man.

97 **Man.** I was not another man: I was a boy.

98 **Woman.** Your own feeling tells you that you were not what you are. I am. That which promised happiness when we were one in heart is fraught with misery now that we are two . . .

99 **Scrooge.** No!

100 **Woman.** How often and how keenly I have thought of this, I will not say. It is enough that I have thought of it, and can release you . . .

101 **Scrooge.** [*Quietly*] Don't release me, madame . . .

102 **Man.** Have I ever sought release?

103 **Woman.** In words. No. Never.

104 **Man.** In what then?

105 **Woman.** In a changed nature: in an altered spirit. In everything that made my love of any worth or value in your sight. If this has never been between us, tell me, would you seek me out and try to win me now? Ah, no!

106 **Scrooge.** Ah, yes!

107 **Man.** You think not?

PERSONALIZE FOR LEARNING

Strategic Support

Symbolism Draw students' attention to paragraphs 87–89. Review symbolism: the use of an object, person, animal, place, or image to represent something else. A symbol has its own meaning, but also stands for something larger than itself, usually an abstract idea. Authors use symbolism to express a concept without talking about it directly and to make a story more interesting. In paragraphs 87–89, as Scrooge and the woman talk about what he now loves, rather than say "You now love money more than you love me," the woman says: "Another idol has displaced me. . . . A golden one." The idol is a symbol for what Scrooge loves (once the woman, now wealth) and "golden" is a symbol for wealth. Encourage students to identify other examples of symbolism they might notice in the play.

108 **Woman.** I would gladly think otherwise if I could, heaven knows! But if you were free today, tomorrow, yesterday, can even I believe that you would choose a dowerless girl[22]—you who in your very confidence with her weigh everything by Gain; or, choosing her, do I not know that your repentance and regret would surely follow? I do; and I release you. With a full heart, for the love of him you once were.

109 **Scrooge.** Please, I . . . I . . .

110 **Man.** Please, I . . . I . . .

111 **Woman.** Please. You may—the memory of what is past half makes me hope you will—have pain in this. A very, very brief time, and you will dismiss the memory of it, as an unprofitable dream, from which it happened well that you awoke. May you be happy in the life that you have chosen for yourself . . .

112 **Scrooge.** No!

113 **Woman.** Yourself . . . alone . . .

114 **Scrooge.** No!

115 **Woman.** Goodbye, Ebenezer . . .

116 **Scrooge.** Don't let her go!

117 **Man.** Goodbye.

118 **Scrooge.** No!

119 [*She exits.* Scrooge *goes to younger man: himself.*]

120 You fool! Mindless loon! You fool!

121 **Man.** [*To exited woman*] Fool. Mindless loon. Fool . . .

122 **Scrooge.** Don't say that! Spirit, remove me from this place.

123 **Past.** I have told you these were shadows of the things that have been. They are what they are. Do not blame me, Mr. Scrooge.

124 **Scrooge.** Remove me! I cannot bear it!

125 [*The faces of all who appeared in this scene are now projected for a moment around the stage: enormous, flimsy, silent.*]

126 Leave me! Take me back! Haunt me no longer!

127 [*There is a sudden flash of light: a flare.* The Ghost of Christmas Past *is gone.* Scrooge *is, for the moment, alone onstage. His bed is turned down, across the stage. A small candle burns now in* Scrooge's *hand. There is a child's cap in his other hand. He slowly crosses the stage to his bed, to sleep.* Marley *appears behind* Scrooge, *who continues his long, elderly cross to bed.* Marley *speaks directly to the audience.*]

NOTES

22. **a dowerless girl** girl without a dowry, the property or wealth a woman brought to her husband in marriage.

CLOSE READ

ANNOTATE: In paragraphs 111–122, mark Scrooge's words to his younger self.

QUESTION: What do these words reveal about the ways in which Scrooge's feelings have changed?

CONCLUDE: How does this change deepen the reader's understanding of Scrooge's personality?

DIGITAL PERSPECTIVES

CLOSE READ

As students read paragraphs 111–122, remind them to focus on the words Scrooge is saying to his younger self. You may wish to model the Close Read using the following think-aloud format. Possible responses to the questions on the student page are included.

ANNOTATE: As I read paragraphs 111–122, I notice and mark words Scrooge speaks to his younger self.

QUESTION: I think these words show that Scrooge realizes how awful he had behaved toward other people. He is feeling panic and calling himself a fool for his mistakes.

CONCLUDE: This change shows the reader that Scrooge actually does have feelings and that he feels regret and sadness for his past actions.

CLOSER LOOK

Analyze Character

Students may have marked lines in paragraph 128 during their first read. Use this dialogue to help students understand how Scrooge is changing. Encourage students to talk about the annotations that they marked. You may want to model a close read with the class based on the highlights shown in the text.

ANNOTATE: Have students mark details in paragraph 128 that indicate Scrooge is changing, or have students participate while you highlight them.

QUESTION: Guide students to consider what these details might tell them. Ask what a reader can infer from these details, and accept student responses.

Possible response: Marley is telling the reader or viewer what Scrooge is doing on stage. Scrooge regrets how he has behaved in the past.

CONCLUDE: Help students to formulate conclusions about the importance of these details in the text. Ask students what this suggests.

Possible response: Though Scrooge initially indicated he had no interest in changing, he is beginning to change as a result of his experience with the Ghost of Christmas Past.

Point out that this is an example of **indirect characterization**. Scrooge is not saying he is changing. But his action—taking off his boyhood cap with regret—suggests that he is changing (by showing regret) as thinks about his past.

NOTES

128 **Marley.** Scrooge must sleep now. He must surrender to the irresistible drowsiness caused by the recognition of what was. [*Pauses*] The cap he carries is from ten lives past: his boyhood cap . . . donned atop a hopeful hairy head . . . askew, perhaps, or at a rakish angle. Doffed now in honor of regret.[23] Perhaps even too heavy to carry in his present state of weak remorse . . .

129 [Scrooge *drops the cap. He lies atop his bed. He sleeps. To audience*]

130 He sleeps. For him, there's even more trouble ahead. [*Smiles*] For you? The play house tells me there's hot cider, as should be your anticipation for the specter Christmas Present and Future, for I promise you both. [*Smiles again*] So, I pray you hurry back to your seats refreshed and ready for a miser—to turn his coat of gray into a blazen Christmas holly-red. [*A flash of lightning. A clap of thunder. Bats fly. Ghosty music.* Marley *is gone.*] ❧

23. **donned . . . regret** To *don* and *doff* a hat means to put it on and take it off, *askew* means "crooked," and *at a rakish angle* means "having a dashing or jaunty look."

DIGITAL PERSPECTIVES

Illuminating the Text To help students understand the impact of Scrooge's ending his relationship with the woman he was going to marry and cutting himself off from people, use the search term "a Christmas Carol 1951" to find video of the 1951 film. (Note: Be sure to preview any video before showing it to students.) Have students view this scene, then have them discuss how seeing it in the film helps illuminate the play. **(Research to Clarify)**

DIGITAL PERSPECTIVES

Comprehension Check

Complete the following items after you finish your first read.

1. When Marley was alive, what relationship did he have with Scrooge?

2. In what year and city is the play set?

3. What does Scrooge say to those who wish him a "Merry Christmas"?

4. **Notebook** Write a brief summary of *A Christmas Carol: Scrooge and Marley,* Act I.

RESEARCH

Research to Clarify Choose at least one unfamiliar detail from the text. Briefly research that detail. In what way does the information you learned shed light on an aspect of the play?

Comprehension Check

Possible responses:

1. They were business partners.
2. The play is set in 1843 in London.
3. Scrooge says, "Humbug!" or "Bah! Humbug!"
4. Summaries will vary; however, students should include: Ebenezer Scrooge is a miserable miser who hates Christmas; one Christmas Eve, the ghost of his dead business partner, Jacob Marley, appears in Scrooge's home; Marley drags an enormous chain because he did not help others while he was alive; he says Scrooge will suffer the same fate, but Marley has arranged for Scrooge to be saved; Scrooge will be visited by three spirits; the first spirit, the Ghost of Christmas Past, takes Scrooge on a journey through scenes from his past; Scrooge sees his school, his sister Fan, the business where he was an apprentice, and the end of his relationship with a woman he once loved; these are painful experiences for Scrooge, and afterward he falls into a deep sleep.

Research

Research to Clarify If students struggle to identify an unfamiliar detail, have them skim the play looking for new and interesting topics, such as the Poor Law, workhouses, or counting-houses in Victorian London.

PERSONALIZE FOR LEARNING

Challenge

Extend Ask students to write a paragraph predicting what they think will happen in Act II. Remind them there is no right or wrong answer, but their responses should be based on what they've read. If needed, guide them to consider the path Scrooge seems to be on now: he started out bitter and hateful and has now experienced regret. What might he feel next?

Jump Start

CLOSE READ Have students close read the title, *A Christmas Carol: Scrooge and Marley,* Act I. Point out that the play is based on a novel titled *A Christmas Carol.* Ask students to suggest why the playwright chose this title. What does the title suggest about the playwright's intention in writing this play?

Close Read the Text

Walk students through the annotation model on the student page. Encourage them to complete items 2 and 3 on their own. Review and discuss the sections students have marked. If needed, continue to model close reading by using the Annotation Highlights in the Interactive Teacher's Edition.

Analyze the Text

Possible responses:

1. Marley's ghost drags the chain as punishment for the life he lived. When he was alive, he cared only about business and did nothing to help others. **DOK 2**
2. (a) Scrooge's past experiences made him a bitter, lonely miser who is unpleasant to everyone he encounters. **DOK 2** (b) Yes, I do think that Scrooge should be excused, mostly because he looks back with sadness on his life and feels regret about how he has treated people. **DOK 1**
3. Responses will vary. Students may conclude that revisiting events from the past can cause a sudden change in someone's life. **DOK 4**

FORMATIVE ASSESSMENT

Analyze the Text

- **If** students fail to cite evidence, **then** remind them to support their ideas with specific information from the text.
- **If** students fail to identify key cause-and-effect relationships or important events in the play, **then** have them review the relevant sections of the play.

MAKING MEANING

A CHRISTMAS CAROL: SCROOGE AND MARLEY, ACT I

Close Read the Text

1. This model, from Scene 5, paragraph 4, shows two sample annotations, along with questions and conclusions. Close read the passage, and find another detail to annotate. Then, write a question and conclusion.

ANNOTATE: I notice that the playwright has used lots of *s*'s in this dialogue.

QUESTION: Why might the writer have made this choice?

CONCLUDE: The repeated s sound makes it seem as if Marley were hissing or whispering, creating an eerie mood.

Marley. You see this Scrooge: stricken by feeling. Conscious of a thousand odors floating in the air, each one connected with a thousand thoughts, and hopes, and joys, and care long, long forgotten. [*Pause*] This one—this Scrooge—before your very eyes, returns to life, among the living. [*To audience, sternly*] You'd best pay your most careful attention. I would suggest rapt.

ANNOTATE: After a series of long, hypnotic statements, these are short and formal.

QUESTION: What effect does this change in word choice and sentence structure create?

CONCLUDE: Marley is unpredictable and used to being obeyed.

Tool Kit
Close-Read Guide and Model Annotation

2. For more practice, go back into the text and complete the close-read notes.
3. Revisit a section of the text you found important during your first read. Read this section closely and **annotate** what you notice. Ask yourself **questions** such as "Why did the author make this choice?" What can you **conclude**?

Analyze the Text

CITE TEXTUAL EVIDENCE to support your answers.

Notebook Respond to these questions.

1. **Connect** Why does Marley's ghost drag a chain fastened to cash-boxes, keys, padlocks, ledgers, deeds, and heavy steel purses?
2. (a) **Deduce** What effects have Scrooge's past experiences had on the person he has become? (b) **Evaluate** Based on Scrooge's past experiences, do you think he should be excused for his current attitudes and behavior? Explain.
3. **Essential Question:** ***What can cause a sudden change in someone's life?*** What have you learned about what can cause a sudden change in someone's life by reading Act I of this play?

STANDARDS
Reading Literature
- Analyze how particular elements of a story or drama interact.
- Analyze how a drama's or poem's form or structure contributes to its meaning.

260 UNIT 3 • TURNING POINTS

PERSONALIZE FOR LEARNING

English Language Support

Understanding Stage Directions Have students reread Scene 1, paragraphs 2–8. Have students identify the stage directions in these lines. Ask them how they recognize that these are stage directions. **EMERGING**

Ask students to identify one stage direction that gives information about a character's action, and another one that gives information about the setting or the scene. **EXPANDING**

Ask students to write a stage direction explaining what happens in Scene 2. **BRIDGING**

Analyze Craft and Structure

Text Structure: Dialogue in Drama **Dialogue** is a conversation between characters. In a play, dialogue serves several key functions.

- When a play is performed, dialogue helps the audience understand what characters feel and think.
- Characters' words and speech patterns give clues to their personalities.
- Dialogue advances the plot and develops the **conflict,** or struggle between opposing forces.
- In a dramatic script, a character's name appears before the lines he or she speaks. For example:

Mrs. Perez. Come on, kids! We're leaving.

Jen. Wait for me! *Please* wait for me!

Practice

CITE TEXTUAL EVIDENCE to support your answers.

Use the chart below to identify and analyze examples of dialogue in Act I of *A Christmas Carol: Scrooge and Marley*.

EXAMPLE OF DIALOGUE	WHAT DOES IT SAY?	WHAT DOES IT MEAN?	WHAT DOES IT SHOW ABOUT THE CHARACTER?
How now! What do you want of me?... Humbug! I tell you: humbug! (Scene 3, paragraphs 9–23)	a. See possible responses in Teacher's Edition.	b.	c.
Marley. [Directly to audience] *From this point . . . for the hour.* (Scene 4, paragraph 2)	d.	e.	f.

DIGITAL PERSPECTIVES

Analyze Craft and Structure

Point out that dialogue is critical in a play. In a novel or short story, the author can include information and explanations. However, in a play, there are usually no opportunities to offer explanations. Dialogue alone must move the story forward and show what characters are feeling and thinking. For more support, see **Analyze Craft and Structure: Dialogue in Drama.**

MAKE IT INTERACTIVE

Have students write a short scene in which two characters have an interaction that is expressed solely through dialogue.

Practice

Possible responses:

a. Scrooge argues with Marley's ghost and asks who he is. He says the apparation may be just a result of indigestion.

b. Scrooge doubts the ghost's existence.

c. Scrooge is closed to the idea that Marley might have a message for him.

d. Marley explains that he will become invisible to Scrooge, but not to the audience.

e. He is explaining the structure of the scene.

f. Marley is interested in Scrooge's reactions to what he sees.

FORMATIVE ASSESSMENT

Analyze Craft and Structure

- **If** students have difficulty identifying dialogue in the play, **then** show them pages from the text and point out the dialogue and how it is formatted.
- **If** students have difficulty understanding how dialogue reveals character, **then** review particularly revealing lines of dialogue and discuss what they say about the character. For Reteach and Practice, see **Analyze Craft and Structure: Dialogue in Drama (RP).**

WriteNow Inform and Explain

Describe Have students imagine they are making a movie version of *A Christmas Carol: Scrooge and Marley*. What actors, or what kinds of actors, would they cast in the roles of the characters in the play? Why? Have students write 1–3 paragraphs identifying their choices and explaining their reasons for these choices.

Concept Vocabulary

Why These Words?

Possible responses:

1. The concept vocabulary helps the reader understand Scrooge's character and personality because they are strong words that vividly describe a certain kind of person.
2. *dismal, rich, cross*

Practice

Possible responses:

1. A *covetous* person might try to accumulate as many possessions or as much money as he or she could.
2. A *morose* person might be gloomy or ill-tempered, not enjoying life and not getting along with people.
3. Someone might be *resolute* if he or she were determined to reach a particular goal.
4. Someone might be described as being *impossible* if he or she argued about every little thing.
5. At a party, a *malcontent* would sit in a corner, never smile, and refuse to talk to anyone or disagree with anything anyone said.
6. A *miser* would not be expected to do anything generous or share money, but would be expected to be greedy and refuse to help anyone who is in need.

Word Network

Possible words: *regret, reclamation, comfort, penance*

Word Study

For more support, see **Concept Vocabulary and Word Study.**

Possible responses:

1. Everyone on the committee felt that Wendy was a *malcontent* because she said every idea we had was bad and never offered a good idea of her own.
2. Words, definitions, and sentences will vary.

FORMATIVE ASSESSMENT

Concept Vocabulary

If students fail to see the connection among the words, **then** have them use each word in a sentence and consider how the sentences are similar.

Word Study

If students have trouble finding appropriate words, **then** review using a dictionary to find words. For Reteach and Practice, see **Word Study: Latin Prefix *mal-* (RP).**

LANGUAGE DEVELOPMENT

A CHRISTMAS CAROL: SCROOGE AND MARLEY, ACT I

Concept Vocabulary

covetous	resolute	malcontent
morose	impossible	miser

Why These Words? The concept vocabulary words relate to Scrooge's character and personality in Act I of the play. For example, Scrooge shows he is a *miser* by refusing to share his coal with Cratchit, and demonstrates he is a *malcontent* when he walks through the street, unhappy about the Christmas activities going on around him.

1. How does the concept vocabulary sharpen the reader's understanding of Scrooge?
2. What other words in the selection describe Scrooge's character and personality?

WORD NETWORK

Add interesting words related to turning points from the text to your Word Network.

Practice

Notebook The concept vocabulary words appear in *A Christmas Carol.* Respond to the prompts, using the vocabulary words to show your understanding.

1. What might someone do if he or she were *covetous*?
2. How might a person behave if he or she were *morose*?
3. Describe a situation in which someone might be *resolute*.
4. What character traits might cause a person to be viewed as *impossible?*
5. How would a *malcontent* behave at a party?
6. What actions and behaviors might be expected of a *miser?*

Word Study

Latin Prefix: *mal-* The Latin prefix *mal-* means "bad." As an adjective, the word *malcontent* means "dissatisfied with current conditions or circumstances." As a noun, *malcontent* means "a discontented, or unhappy, person."

1. Write your own sentence that correctly uses the word *malcontent*, either as a noun or an adjective.
2. Using a dictionary or thesaurus, find three other words that have the prefix *mal-*. Record a definition for each word and write a sentence that correctly uses it.

STANDARDS

Language

Determine or clarify the meaning of unknown and multiple-meaning words and phrases based on *grade 7 reading and content*, choosing flexibly from a range of strategies.

b. Use common, grade-appropriate Greek or Latin affixes and roots as clues to the meaning of a word.

c. Consult general and specialized reference materials, both print and digital, to find the pronunciation of a word or determine or clarify its precise meaning or its part of speech.

AUTHOR'S PERSPECTIVE Elfrieda Hiebert, Ph.D.

Frequency of Concepts in Narrative Texts In describing character traits or problems, skilled authors rarely repeat the same word, other than to achieve unity through repetition. Instead, authors use different words to create an interesting style. For instance, authors use a variety of words to describe setting, such as *lagoon, swales, bog*. Specifically, in *The Wizard of Oz,* L. Frank Baum describes what Dorothy and her companions see on arriving in the Emerald City with these words: *brilliance, dazzled, glittering*. Word variety also helps authors build characterization in jobs (*actor, lawyer, expert*) and roles (*adult/relative, female, male*). Especially in

Conventions

Subject-Verb Agreement Writers need to maintain **subject-verb agreement**, which means that subjects and their verbs must agree in number.

- To check subject-verb agreement, determine whether a subject is singular or plural, and then make sure its verb matches.

SUBJECT	EXAMPLE
Singular subject and verb	**Jake writes** a new poem every day.
Plural subject and verb	**Books take** us to new places.

- A **compound subject** consists of two subjects joined by a conjunction such as *and, or,* or *nor.* When the subjects joined are plural, they take a plural verb. When the subjects joined are singular or when they differ in number, refer to the rules in the chart below.

AGREEMENT RULES	EXAMPLE
Two or more singular subjects joined by *and* take a plural verb.	English **and** math **are** my favorite subjects.
Singular subjects joined by *or* or *nor* take a singular verb.	Painting **or** drawing **is** a creative activity. Neither Lucy **nor** Carmen **takes** this class.
When a singular subject and a plural subject are joined by *or* or *nor*, the verb agrees with the closer subject.	Neither the bear nor the **tigers are** happy in that enclosure. Flowers or a **tree is** what this yard needs.

Read It

Underline the subject-verb agreement in these sentences from the selection.

1. These are but shadows of things that have been.
2. The young men clear the room, sweep the floor, straighten the pictures, trim the lamps, etc.
3. He is the best, best, the very and absolute best!

Write It

Respond to these items.

1. Rewrite the following sentences to correct the subject-verb agreement.
   - **a.** Mexico and Canada is part of North America.
   - **b.** Wood or stone are a good material for this house.
   - **c.** A truck or several cars is what we need for this trip.
2. **Notebook** Write a four-sentence paragraph in which at least two sentences have compound subjects. Make sure that all the sentences have correct subject-verb agreement.

EVIDENCE LOG

Before moving on to a new selection, go to your Evidence Log and record what you've learned from Act I of *A Christmas Carol: Scrooge and Marley.*

STANDARDS

Language
Demonstrate command of the conventions of standard English grammar and usage when writing or speaking.

stories, the concepts represented by rare words are often known by common words that most students understand, such as *down* and *blah* for the rare words *lethargic, listless, slothful,* and *sluggish*. However, the more complex the text, the rarer the words that describe a particular concept will be. For instance, in a complex text, rather than describing a character as *calm*, the author might use *phlegmatic*. However, be sure that students understand that words such as these in a concept network have subtle differences in meaning and cannot necessarily be substituted for one another.

DIGITAL PERSPECTIVES 

Conventions

Subject-Verb Agreement Review subject-verb agreement with students, focusing on singular subjects and compound subjects. Also remind them that when singular and plural subjects are joined by *or* or *nor*, the verb must agree with the closer subject. (Ten grapes or an apple is what I'd like for a snack.) For more support, see **Conventions: Subject-Verb Agreement.**

MAKE IT INTERACTIVE

Have students fill in the correct verb for each sentence:
Baseball and soccer _____ two of my favorite games. (are)
Blue or red _____ the best color for this sign. (is)
Neither ducks nor swans _____ seen here anymore. (are)
Neither desks nor a chair _____ necessary in this room. (is)

Read It

1. These are but shadows of things that have been.
2. The young men clear the room, sweep the floor, straighten the pictures, trim the lamps, etc.
3. He is the best, best, the very and absolute best!

Write It

Possible responses:

1. (a) Mexico and Canada *are* part of North America. (b) Wood or stone *is* a good material for this house. (c) A truck or several cars *are* what we need for this trip.
2. Paragraphs will vary.

Evidence Log Support students in completing their Evidence Log. This paced activity will help prepare them for the Performance-Based Assessment at the end of the unit.

An **English Language Support Lesson** on Subject-Verb Agreement is available in the Interactive Teacher's Edition.

FORMATIVE ASSESSMENT

Conventions

- **If** students have trouble with subject-verb agreement, **then** show them how to identify singular and plural subjects, and singular and plural verbs.
- **If** students have trouble identifying identify singular and plural subjects, **then** review subjects, and what makes a subject singular or plural. For Reteach and Practice, see **Conventions: Subject-Verb Agreement (RP).**

Selection Test

Administer the "A Christmas Carol: Scrooge and Marley, Act II (*with an excerpt from* Scrooge)" Selection Test, which is available in both print and digital formats online in Assessments.

A Christmas Carol: Scrooge and Marley, Act II

AUDIO SUMMARIES
Audio summaries of *A Christmas Carol: Scrooge and Marley*, Act II, are available online in both English and Spanish in the Interactive Teacher's Edition or Unit Resources. Assigning these summaries prior to reading the selection may help students build additional background knowledge and set a context for their first read.

Summary

This is the second act of the drama A *Christmas Carol: Scrooge and Marley* by Israel Horovitz. Scrooge receives visits from the ghosts of Christmas Present and Future. They show him the results of his actions today, and what will happen years from now if he fails to change. He sees that he is causing misery and will leave no good legacy behind if he stays on his present course. Repenting for his misdeeds, Scrooge immediately begins to change his ways.

Insight

This story suggests that even someone who has been doing something wrong for most of his or her life can, with the right evidence, be jarred into changing his or her ways. It is ultimately strongly positive and shows how a person can greatly help others if he or she chooses.

ESSENTIAL QUESTION:
What can cause a sudden change in someone's life?

Connection to Essential Question

Scrooge realizes the harm he is causing, and he sees that things will get much worse both for others and for him if he does not reach out to help other people.

WHOLE-CLASS LEARNING PERFORMANCE TASK
How does Scrooge's character transform over the course of the play?

UNIT PERFORMANCE-BASED ASSESSMENT
What can cause a significant change in someone's life?

Connection to Performance Tasks

Whole-Class Learning Performance Task Scrooge changes greatly, becoming much more generous and hopeful.

Unit Performance-Based Assessment Coming to grips with the results of your actions, and understanding what will happen if you stay on your present course, can greatly change you.

DIGITAL PERSPECTIVES

Audio

Video

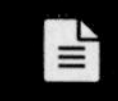
Document

Annotation Highlights

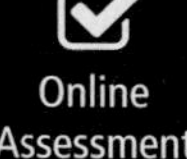
Online Assessment

LESSON RESOURCES

	Making Meaning	Language Development	Effective Expression
Lesson	**First Read** **Close Read** **Analyze the Text** **Analyze Craft and Structure**	**Concept Vocabulary** **Word Study** **Conventions**	**Writing to Sources** **Speaking and Listening**
Instructional Standards	**RL.7.10** By the end of the year, read and comprehend literature . . . **RL.7.1** Cite several pieces of textual evidence . . . **RL.7.3** Analyze how particular elements of a story or drama interact. **RL.7.5** Analyze how a drama's or poem's form . . .	**L.7.4** Determine or clarify the meaning of unknown and multiple-meaning words and phrases . . . **L.7.4.b** Use common, grade-appropriate Greek or Latin affixes and roots . . . **L.7.4.c** Consult general and specialized reference materials . . . **L.7.4.d** Verify the preliminary determination of the meaning . . . **L.7.5** Demonstrate understanding of figurative language . . . **L.7.5.b** Use the relationship between particular words . . . **L.7.1.b** Choose among simple, compound, complex . . .	**W.7.2** Write informative/explanatory texts . . . **W.7.2.a** Introduce a topic clearly . . . **W.7.2.d** Develop the topic . . . **W.7.2.d** Use precise language . . . **W.7.2.e** Establish and maintain . . . **W.7.2.f** Provide a concluding statement . . . **W.7.9** Draw evidence from literary . . . **W.7.9.a** Apply *grade 7 Reading standards* . . . **W.7.7** Conduct short research projects . . . **SL.7.4** Present claims and findings . . . **SL.7.5** Include multimedia components . . .
STUDENT RESOURCES			
Available online in the Interactive Student Edition or Unit Resources	Selection Audio First-Read Guide: Fiction Close-Read Guide: Fiction	Word Network	Evidence Log
TEACHER RESOURCES			
Selection Resources Available online in the Interactive Teacher's Edition or Unit Resources	Audio Summaries: English and Spanish Annotation Highlights Accessible Leveled Text First Read Extension Questions Analyze Craft and Structure: Stage Directions	Concept Vocabulary and Word Study Conventions: Sentence Structures	Writing to Sources: Explanatory Essay Speaking and Listening: Costume Plan
Reteach/Practice (RP) Available online in the Interactive Teacher's Edition or Unit Resources	Analyze Craft and Structure: Stage Directions (RP)	Word Study: Greek Prefix *para-* (RP) Conventions: Sentence Structures (RP)	Writing to Sources: Explanatory Essay (RP) Speaking and Listening: Costume Plan (RP)
Assessment Available online in Assessments	Selection Test: English Selection Test: Spanish		Extension Selection Test
My Resources	A Unit 3 Answer Key is available online and in the Interactive Teacher's Edition.		

Reading Support

Text Complexity Rubric: *A Christmas Carol: Scrooge and Marley, Act II*	
Quantitative Measures	
Lexile: NP Text Length: 8,289 words	
Qualitative Measures	
Knowledge Demands ①—②—❸—④—⑤	Students will not be familiar with the situation that is central to the selection. The selection references many aspects of life in London during the nineteenth century that will be challenging for students.
Structure ①—②—③—❹—⑤	This selection is a play adapted from a novella. Students may find stage directions and dialogue difficult to follow.
Language Conventionality and Clarity ①—②—③—❹—⑤	The selection contains numerous long sentences with embedded phrases and clauses, and challenging vocabulary.
Levels of Meaning/Purpose ①—②—❸—④—⑤	The concept is straightforward (a miser learns generosity and kindness), but sophisticated language and structure may make it difficult for some to grasp.

DECIDE AND PLAN

English Language Support

Provide English Learners with support for structure and language as they read the selection.

Structure Discuss with students why reading a play is such a unique experience. Point out that a play is presented almost entirely as dialogue. Guide students to discuss the components of the play.

Meaning Make certain students are following the action by discussing the events and time changes as they read. Encourage students to keep notes or a timeline to help them understand the events as they unfold.

Strategic Support

Provide students with strategic support to ensure that they can successfully read the text.

Knowledge Demands Have students summarize what is happening in the play at this point. What have they learned about Scrooge so far? What hope is there for him to escape his fate?

Language / Clarity Have students note punctuation that influences how the lines will be spoken. Then have them read aloud some of the lines with a partner.

Challenge

Provide students who need to be challenged with ideas for how they can go beyond a simple interpretation of the text.

Text Analysis Remind students that stage directions and dialogue are the main tools a playwright uses to achieve a purpose. Have students analyze the stage directions and dialogue in Act II, Scene 3. What mood is the writer creating? What is Scrooge's demeanor?

Written Response Arrange students in groups of four and assign the roles of Scrooge, Cratchit, and the two men seeking money for charity. Have students conduct a dramatic reading of the dialogue. After students practice in their groups, have students present their dialogues to the class.

TEACH

Read and Respond

Have students do their first read of the selection. Then have them complete their close read. Finally, work with them on the Making Meaning, Language Development, and Effective Expression activities.

Standards Support Through Teaching and Learning Cycle

IDENTIFY NEEDS

Analyze results of the Beginning-of-Year Assessment, focusing on the items relating to Unit 3. Also take into consideration student performance to this point and your observations of where particular students struggle.

DECIDE AND PLAN

- If students have performed poorly on items matching these standards, then provide selection scaffolds before assigning them the on-level lesson provided in the Student Edition.
- If students have done well on the Beginning-of-Year Assessment, then challenge them to keep progressing and learning by giving them opportunities to practice the skills in depth.
- Use the Selection Resources listed on the Planning pages for *A Christmas Carol: Scrooge and Marley,* Act II to help students continually improve their ability to master the standards.

Instructional Standards: *A Christmas Carol: Scrooge and Marley,* Act II

	Catching Up	This Year	Looking Forward
Reading	You may wish to administer the **Analyze Craft and Structure: Stage Directions (RP)** worksheet to help students better understand stage directions.	**RL.3** Analyze how particular elements of a story or drama interact.	Have students think of other plays and movies they have read or seen and discuss how stage directions are essential to a script.
Writing	You may wish to administer the **Writing to Sources: Explanatory Essay (RP)** worksheet to help students better understand explanatory essays.	**W.2** Write informative/explanatory texts to examine a topic and convey ideas, concepts, and information through the selection, organization, and analysis of relevant content.	Have students write short "un-explanatory" essays, in which they intentionally do poor jobs of explaining something, so they can appreciate when something is explained well.
Speaking and Listening	You may wish to administer the **Speaking and Listening: Costume Plan (RP)** worksheet to help students better understand how to make a costume plan.	**SL.5** Include multimedia components and visual displays in presentations to clarify claims and findings and emphasize salient points.	Challenge students to research the costume designers of famous stage plays or films to better appreciate the art form.
Language	Review the **Word Study: Greek Prefix *para-* (RP)** worksheet with students to ensure they understand the meaning of the prefix. You may wish to administer the **Conventions: Sentence Structures (RP)** worksheet to help students better understand the four types of sentences.	**L.4.b** Use common, grade-appropriate Greek or Latin affixes and roots as clues to the meaning of a word. **L.1.b** Choose among simple, compound, complex, and compound-complex sentences to signal differing relationships among ideas.	Have students identify words in the selection that use other prefixes they may recognize. Have students use a piece of writing from another source and identify all four types of sentences within that text.

ANALYZE AND REVISE

- Analyze student work for evidence of student learning.
- Identify whether or not students have met the expectations in the standards.
- Identify implications for future instruction.

TEACH

Implement the planned lesson, and gather evidence of student learning.

Jump Start

FIRST READ Prior to students' first read, engage them in a discussion about whether revisiting the past is helpful or not. This will help them make connections between the text and their own ideas and experiences.

A Christmas Carol: Scrooge and Marley, Act II

Will Scrooge be able to become a different person? Is it too late for him to change? Modeling questions such as these will help students connect to *A Christmas Carol: Scrooge and Marley*, Act II, and to the Performance Task assignment. Selection audio and print capability for the selection are available in the Interactive Teacher's Edition.

Concept Vocabulary

Support students as they rank the words. Ask if they've ever heard, read, or used them. Reassure them that the definitions for these words are listed in the selection.

FIRST READ

Students should perform the steps of the first read independently.

NOTICE: Encourage students to continue to notice how and why Scrooge changes as the story goes on.

ANNOTATE: Remind students to mark dialogue that includes characterization, and important or revealing stage directions.

CONNECT: Encourage students to make connections beyond the text. If they cannot make connections to their own lives or other texts, have them consider movies and TV shows.

RESPOND: Students will answer questions and write a summary to demonstrate understanding.

Point out to students that while they will always complete the Respond step at the end of the first read, the other steps will probably happen somewhat concurrently. You may wish to print copies of the **First-Read Guide: Fiction** for students to use.

Remind students that during their first read, they should not answer the close-read questions that appear in the selection.

MAKING MEANING

Playwright

Israel Horovitz

A Christmas Carol: Scrooge and Marley, Act II

Concept Vocabulary

You will encounter the following words as you read *A Christmas Carol: Scrooge and Marley,* Act II. Before reading, note how familiar you are with each word. Then, rank the words in order from most familiar (1) to least familiar (6).

WORD	YOUR RANKING
parallel	
altered	
strive	
dispelled	
earnest	
infinitely	

After completing the first read, come back to the concept vocabulary and review your rankings. Mark changes to your original rankings as needed.

First Read DRAMA

Apply these strategies as you conduct your first read. You will have an opportunity to complete the close-read notes after your first read.

STANDARDS
Reading Literature
By the end of the year, read and comprehend literature, including stories, dramas, and poems, in the grades 6–8 text complexity band proficiently, with scaffolding as needed at the high end of the range.

CROSS-CURRICULAR PERSPECTIVES

Social Studies Victorian society was made up of several social and economic classes. Have students research these different classes and write short reports on this aspect of Victorian society. Where does Scrooge fit in? Where does Bob Cratchit fit in? How does the play reflect this society?

ANCHOR TEXT | DRAMA

A Christmas Carol: Scrooge and Marley

Act II

Israel Horovitz

BACKGROUND

In mid-nineteenth century England, millions of peasants moved to the cities. There, they lived in overcrowded slums. Adults and many children worked up to 12 hours a day, 6 days a week. In contrast, factory owners and professionals lived in grand houses with at least one—and often many—servants. These differences in social conditions play a part in *A Christmas Carol.*

Scene 1

1 [*Lights. Choral music is sung. Curtain.* Scrooge, *in bed, sleeping, in spotlight. We cannot yet see the interior of his room.* Marley, *opposite, in spotlight equal to* Scrooge's. Marley *laughs. He tosses his hand in the air and a flame shoots from it, magically, into the air. There is a thunder clap, and then another; a lightning flash, and then another. Ghostly music plays under. Colors change.* Marley's *spotlight has gone out and now reappears, with* Marley *in it, standing next to the bed and the sleeping* Scrooge. Marley *addresses the audience directly.*]

2 **Marley.** Hear this snoring Scrooge! Sleeping to escape the nightmare that is his waking day. What shall I bring to him now? I'm afraid nothing would astonish old Scrooge now. Not after what he's seen. Not a baby boy, not a rhinoceros, nor anything in between would astonish Ebenezer Scrooge

NOTES

NOTES

just now. I can think of nothing . . . [*Suddenly*] that's it! Nothing! [*He speaks confidentially.*] I'll have the clock strike one and, when he awakes expecting my second messenger, there will be no one . . . nothing. Then I'll have the bell strike twelve. And then one again . . . and then nothing. Nothing . . . [*Laughs*] nothing will . . . astonish him. I think it will work.

3 [*The bell tolls one.* Scrooge *leaps awake.*]

4 **Scrooge.** One! One! This is it; time! [*Looks about the room*] Nothing!

5 [*The bell tolls midnight.*]

6 Midnight! How can this be? I'm sleeping backwards.

7 [*One again*]

8 Good heavens! One again! I'm sleeping back and forth! [*A pause.* Scrooge *looks about.*] Nothing! Absolutely nothing!

9 [*Suddenly, thunder and lightning.* Marley *laughs and disappears. The room shakes and glows. There is suddenly springlike music.* Scrooge *makes a run for the door.*]

10 **Marley.** Scrooge!

11 **Scrooge.** What?

12 **Marley.** Stay you put!

13 **Scrooge.** Just checking to see if anyone is in here.

14 [*Lights and thunder again: more music.* Marley *is of a sudden gone. In his place sits the* Ghost of Christmas Present*—to be called in the stage directions of the play,* Present*—center of room. Heaped up on the floor, to form a kind of throne, are turkeys, geese, game, poultry, brawn, great joints of meat, suckling pigs, long wreaths of sausages, mince-pies, plum puddings, barrels of oysters, red hot chestnuts, cherry-cheeked apples, juicy oranges, luscious pears, immense twelfth cakes, and seething bowls of punch, that make the chamber dim with their delicious steam. Upon this throne sits* Present, *glorious to see. He bears a torch, shaped as a Horn of Plenty.*[1] Scrooge *hops out of the door, and then peeks back again into his bedroom.* Present *calls to* Scrooge.]

15 **Present.** Ebenezer Scrooge. Come in, come in! Come in and know me better!

16 **Scrooge.** Hello. How should I call you?

17 **Present.** I am the Ghost of Christmas Present. Look upon me.

18 [Present *is wearing a simple green robe. The walls around the room are now covered in greenery, as well. The room seems to be a perfect grove now: leaves of holly, mistletoe and ivy reflect the stage lights.*

1. **Horn of Plenty** horn overflowing with fruits, flowers, and grain, representing wealth and abundance.

PERSONALIZE FOR LEARNING

English Language Support

Multiple-Meaning Words Explain to students that the word *strike* in paragraph 2 has several meanings. As it's used in this part of the play, it's a verb that means "to indicate by sounding." The kind of clocks used during this period indicated the time by striking a bell with a little hammer. When a clock "strikes one," a bell sounds indicating the time is one o'clock. *Strike* can also mean: "to hit" (Ron tried to strike Steve.); "to arrive with detrimental effect" (A disaster will strike.); "to pierce or penetrate" (The wind seemed to strike through our clothes.); and "to make a military attack" (The army will strike at dawn.) **ALL LEVELS**

Suddenly, there is a mighty roar of flame in the fireplace and now the hearth burns with a lavish, warming fire. There is an ancient scabbard girdling the Ghost's *middle, but without sword. The sheath is gone to rust.*]

19 You have never seen the like of me before?

20 **Scrooge.** Never.

21 **Present.** You have never walked forth with younger members of my family: my elder brothers born on Christmases past.

22 **Scrooge.** I don't think I have. I'm afraid I've not. Have you had many brothers, Spirit?

23 **Present.** More than eighteen hundred.

24 **Scrooge.** A tremendous family to provide for! [Present *stands*] Spirit, conduct me where you will. I went forth last night on compulsion, and learnt a lesson which is working now. Tonight, if you have aught to teach me, let me profit by it.

25 **Present.** Touch my robe.

26 [Scrooge *walks cautiously to* Present *and touches his robe. When he does, lightning flashes, thunder claps, music plays. Blackout*]

Scene 2

1 [*PROLOGUE*: Marley *stands spotlit,* L. *He speaks directly to the audience.*]

2 **Marley.** My ghostly friend now leads my living partner through the city's streets.

3 [*Lights up on* Scrooge *and* Present]

4 See them there and hear the music people make when the weather is severe, as it is now.

5 [*Winter music. Choral group behind scrim, sings. When the song is done and the stage is re-set, the lights will fade up on a row of shops, behind the singers. The choral group will hum the song they have just completed now and mill about the streets,*[2] *carrying their dinners to the bakers' shops and restaurants. They will, perhaps, sing about being poor at Christmastime, whatever.*]

6 **Present.** These revelers, Mr. Scrooge, carry their own dinners to their jobs, where they will work to bake the meals the rich men and women of this city will eat as their Christmas dinners. Generous people these . . . to care for the others, so . . .

NOTES

CLOSE READ

ANNOTATE: Mark the details in paragraphs 5–6 that describe the setting.

QUESTION: Why might the playwright have chosen to begin the scene with these details?

CONCLUDE: How does this information help you to better understand the play?

2. **mill about the streets** walk around aimlessly.

DIGITAL  PERSPECTIVES  

CLOSE READ

Remind students that they will be looking for details in paragraphs 5–6 that describe the setting. You may wish to model the close read using the following think-aloud format. Possible responses to questions on the student page are included. You may also want to print copies of the **Close-Read Guide: Fiction** for students to use.

ANNOTATE: As I read paragraphs 5–6, I notice and highlight words and phrases that describe the scene's setting.

QUESTION: I think the playwright chose these details to show Scrooge how the poor people are working hard, even at Christmastime, and are singing instead of complaining.

CONCLUDE: This information helps me understand that all of the characters who are much less fortunate than Scrooge accept their circumstances, whereas Scrooge himself has so much but has done nothing but act miserly and nasty to other people.

NOTES

3. **incense** (IHN sehns) *n.* any of various substances that produce a pleasant odor when burned.

7 [Present *walks among the choral group and a sparkling incense*[3] *falls from his torch on to their baskets, as he pulls the covers off of the baskets. Some of the choral group become angry with each other.*]

8 **Man #1.** Hey, you, watch where you're going.

9 **Man #2.** Watch it yourself, mate!

10 [Present *sprinkles them directly, they change.*]

11 **Man #1.** I pray go in ahead of me. It's Christmas. You be first!

12 **Man #2.** No, no. I must insist that YOU be first!

13 **Man #1.** All right, I shall be, and gratefully so.

14 **Man #2.** The pleasure is equally mine, for being able to watch you pass, smiling.

15 **Man #1.** I would find it a shame to quarrel on Christmas Day . . .

16 **Man #2.** As would I.

17 **Man #1.** Merry Christmas then, friend!

18 **Man #2.** And a Merry Christmas straight back to you!

19 [*Church bells toll. The choral group enter the buildings: the shops and restaurants; they exit the stage, shutting their doors closed behind them. All sound stops.* Scrooge *and* Present *are alone again.*]

20 **Scrooge.** What is it you sprinkle from your torch?

21 **Present.** Kindness.

22 **Scrooge.** Do you sprinkle your kindness on any particular people or on all people?

23 **Present.** To any person kindly given. And to the very poor most of all.

24 **Scrooge.** Why to the very poor most?

25 **Present.** Because the very poor need it most. Touch my heart . . . here, Mr. Scrooge. We have another journey.

26 [Scrooge *touches the* Ghost's *heart and music plays, lights change color, lightning flashes, thunder claps. A choral group appears on the street, singing Christmas carols.*]

Scene 3

1 [Marley *stands spotlit in front of a scrim on which is painted the exterior of* Cratchit's *four-roomed house. There is a flash and a clap and* Marley *is gone. The lights shift color again, the scrim flies away, and we are in the interior of the* Cratchit *family home.*

268 UNIT 3 • TURNING POINTS

Scrooge *is there, with the spirit* (Present), *watching* Mrs. Cratchit *set the table, with the help of* Belinda Cratchit *and* Peter Cratchit, *a baby, pokes a fork into the mashed potatoes on his highchair's tray. He also chews on his shirt collar.*]

2 **Scrooge.** What is this place, Spirit?

3 **Present.** This is the home of your employee, Mr. Scrooge. Don't you know it?

4 **Scrooge.** Do you mean Cratchit, Spirit? Do you mean this is Cratchit's home?

5 **Present.** None other.

6 **Scrooge.** These children are his?

7 **Present.** There are more to come presently.

8 **Scrooge.** On his meager earnings! What foolishness!

9 **Present.** Foolishness, is it?

10 **Scrooge.** Wouldn't you say so? Fifteen shillings[4] a week's what he gets!

11 **Present.** I would say that he gets the pleasure of his family, fifteen times a week times the number of hours a day! Wait, Mr. Scrooge. Wait, listen and watch. You might actually learn something . . .

12 **Mrs. Cratchit.** What has ever got your precious father then? And your brother, Tiny Tim? And Martha warn't as late last Christmas by half an hour!

13 [Martha *opens the door, speaking to her mother as she does.*]

14 **Martha.** Here's Martha, now, Mother! [*She laughs. The* Cratchit Children *squeal with delight.*]

15 **Belinda.** It's Martha, Mother! Here's Martha!

16 **Peter.** Marthmama, Marthmama! Hullo!

17 **Belinda.** Hurrah! Martha! Martha! There's such an enormous goose for us, Martha!

18 **Mrs. Cratchit.** Why, bless your heart alive, my dear, how late you are!

19 **Martha.** We'd a great deal of work to finish up last night, and had to clear away this morning, Mother.

20 **Mrs. Cratchit.** Well, never mind so long as you are come. Sit ye down before the fire, my dear, and have a warm, Lord bless ye!

21 **Belinda.** No, no! There's Father coming. Hide, Martha, hide!

22 [Martha *giggles and hides herself.*]

NOTES

4. **fifteen shillings** small amount of money for a week's work.

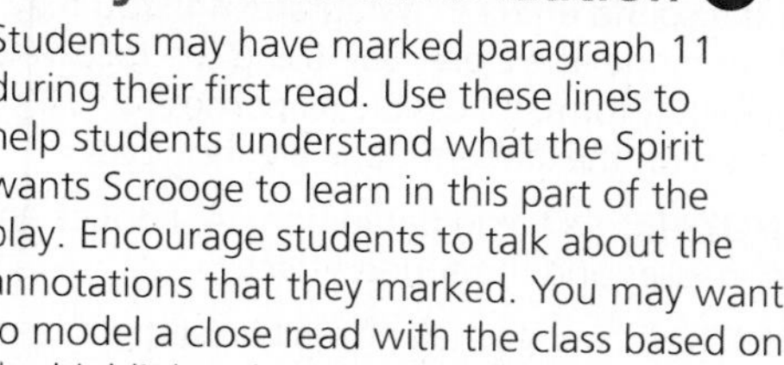

CLOSER LOOK

Analyze Characterization

Students may have marked paragraph 11 during their first read. Use these lines to help students understand what the Spirit wants Scrooge to learn in this part of the play. Encourage students to talk about the annotations that they marked. You may want to model a close read with the class based on the highlights shown in the text.

ANNOTATE: Have students mark details in these lines that suggest what the Spirit wants Scrooge to learn, or have students participate while you highlight them.

QUESTION: Guide students to consider what these details might tell them. Ask what a reader can infer from these details, and accept student responses.

Possible response: The Spirit wants Scrooge to learn that people can be happy even if they don't have money.

CONCLUDE: Help students to formulate conclusions about the importance of these details in the text. Ask students why the author might have included these details.

Possible response: The Spirit will show Scrooge other examples of people being happy without money in hopes that Scrooge will learn that money isn't the most important thing in the world.

Point out that the Spirit has not directly said this. It is suggested by what the Spirit says after Scrooge is amazed that Cratchit has such a large family even though he earns so little money.

Remind students that authors don't always express ideas directly. Sometimes they suggest, or imply, them. Explain that this is one way that they reveal **characterization**, or what the characters are like. When an author implies something about a character, it is called **indirect characterization**. Draw students' attention to paragraph 6 (Scrooge: These children are his?). What does this suggest? (Scrooge knows nothing about Cratchit's personal life.)

PERSONALIZE FOR LEARNING

Challenge

Minimum Wage Laws In paragraph 10, readers learn that Scrooge pays Cratchit a very low wage. Have students research minimum wage laws—what they are, who they help, why they were created, and when they were established—in England and in the United States. You might also have students use their research to form the basis of a brief writing activity in which they define what they think makes for fair labor standards, including pay, hours of employment, workplace safety, time off, and so on.

CLOSE READ

Remind students that they will focus on pauses and the sound effect in paragraph 44. You may wish to model the close read using the following think-aloud format. Possible responses to question on the student page are included.

ANNOTATE: As I read paragraph 44, I notice and mark pauses and the sound effect.

QUESTION: Pauses make Cratchit seem more thoughtful, creating a somber mood. The sound effect helps the audience understand Cratchit's final words, "one would never know," meaning that Tim is growing weaker, not stronger.

CONCLUDE: Cratchit is worried and doubtful about Tim's condition for the future.

NOTES

23 **Martha.** Where? Here?

24 **Peter.** Hide, hide!

25 **Belinda.** Not there! *THERE!*

26 [Martha *is hidden.* Bob Cratchit *enters, carrying* Tiny Tim *atop his shoulder. He wears a threadbare and fringeless comforter hanging down in front of him.* Tiny Tim *carries small crutches and his small legs are bound in an iron frame brace.*]

27 **Bob and Tiny Tim.** Merry Christmas.

28 **Bob.** Merry Christmas my love, Merry Christmas Peter, Merry Christmas Belinda. Why, where is Martha?

29 **Mrs. Cratchit.** Not coming.

30 **Bob.** Not coming: Not coming upon Christmas Day?

31 **Martha.** [*Pokes head out*] Ohhh, poor Father. Don't be disappointed.

32 **Bob.** What's this?

33 **Martha.** 'Tis I!

34 **Bob.** Martha! [*They embrace.*]

35 **Tiny Tim.** Martha! Martha!

36 **Martha.** Tiny Tim!

37 [Tiny Tim *is placed in* Martha's *arms.* Belinda *and* Peter *rush him offstage.*]

38 **Belinda.** Come, brother! You must come hear the pudding singing in the copper.

39 **Tiny Tim.** The pudding? What flavor have we?

40 **Peter.** Plum! Plum!

41 **Tiny Tim.** Oh, Mother! I love plum!

42 [*The children exit the stage giggling.*]

43 **Mrs. Cratchit.** And how did little Tim behave?

44 **Bob.** As good as gold, and even better. Somehow he gets thoughtful sitting by himself so much, and thinks the strangest things you ever heard. He told me, coming home, that he hoped people saw him in the church, because he was a cripple, and it might be pleasant to them to remember upon Christmas Day, who made lame beggars walk and blind men see. [*Pauses*] He has the oddest ideas sometimes, but he seems all the while to be growing stronger and more hearty . . . one would never know. [*Hears* Tim's *crutch on floor outside door*]

45 **Peter.** The goose has arrived to be eaten!

46 **Belinda.** Oh, mama, mama, it's beautiful.

CLOSE READ

ANNOTATE: Mark the pauses and the sound effect in paragraph 44.

QUESTION: Why might the playwright have included the pauses and sound effects in the dialogue?

CONCLUDE: What can you conclude about Bob Cratchit's state of mind as a result of these details?

CROSS-CURRICULAR PERSPECTIVES

Social Studies Review paragraph 38. Explain to students that in Victorian times, families such as the Cratchits had a large copper vat that was used to heat water for cooking, washing, and laundry. Mrs. Cratchit is now using the vat to cook the Christmas pudding, which is steaming in the vat on a small stove. The vat has a spout, and when the steam comes out it makes a whistling sound, like singing. So the pudding "singing in the copper" means it's steaming in the copper vat.

47 **Martha.** It's a perfect goose, Mother!

48 **Tiny Tim.** To this Christmas goose, Mother and Father I say . . . [*Yells*] Hurrah! Hurrah!

49 **Other Children.** [*Copying* Tim] Hurrah! Hurrah!

50 [*The family sits round the table.* Bob and Mrs. Cratchit *serve the trimmings, quickly. All sit; all bow heads; all pray.*]

51 **Bob.** Thank you, dear Lord, for your many gifts . . . our dear children; our wonderful meal; our love for one another; and the warmth of our small fire—[*Looks up at all*] A merry Christmas to us, my dear. God bless us!

52 **All.** [*Except* Tim] Merry Christmas! God bless us!

53 **Tiny Tim.** [*In a short silence*] God bless us every one.

54 [*All freeze. Spotlight on* Present *and* Scrooge]

55 **Scrooge.** Spirit, tell me if Tiny Tim will live.

56 **Present.** I see a vacant seat . . . in the poor chimney corner, and a crutch without an owner, carefully preserved. If these shadows remain unaltered by the future, the child will die.

NOTES

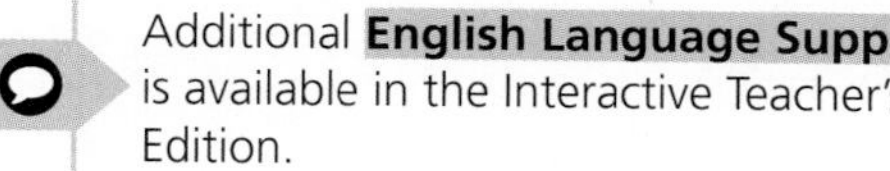

Additional **English Language Support** is available in the Interactive Teacher's Edition.

PERSONALIZE FOR LEARNING

English Language Support

Multiple-Meaning Words Explain to students that the word *trimmings* in paragraph 50 has several meanings. As it's used in this part of the play, it's a noun that means "additional foods that are served with a main dish" (We had turkey and all the trimmings.). Explain to students that they might also encounter this word without the *s*. Trimming is a verb that can mean "decorating" (We will be trimming our Christmas tree tonight.) or "cutting or clipping" (Today, I am trimming the bushes in front of the house.). **ALL LEVELS**

CLOSE READ

Remind students that as they read paragraphs 62–71, they should focus on how Mrs. Cratchit's attitude toward Scrooge is different from Bob Cratchit's. You may wish to model the close read using the following think-aloud format. Possible responses to questions on the student page are included.

ANNOTATE: As I read paragraphs 62–71, I notice and mark words that show differences in how Mrs. Cratchit and Bob Cratchit each feel about Scrooge.

QUESTION: I think the playwright chose to show this contrast because some people are not as forgiving as others, and Scrooge's past actions are not easily forgiveable.

CONCLUDE: For me, the contrast reveals that Bob Cratchit is probably so surprised to see a caring side of Scrooge that he is willing to treat him with extra kindness. Mrs. Cratchit, on the other hand, knows her husband has been treated poorly for so long that she does not share his enthusiasm for toasting Scrooge.

NOTES

CLOSE READ

ANNOTATE: In paragraphs 62–71, mark words and phrases that highlight the differences between Mrs. Cratchit's and Bob Cratchit's attitudes toward Scrooge.

QUESTION: Why might the playwright have chosen to show this contrast in their attitudes through their dialogue?

CONCLUDE: What does the contrast reveal about the personality of each character?

57 **Scrooge.** No, no, kind Spirit! Say he will be spared!

58 **Present.** If these shadows remain unaltered by the future, none other of my race will find him here. What then? If he be like to die, he had better do it, and decrease the surplus population.

59 [Scrooge *bows his head. We hear* Bob's *voice speak* Scrooge's *name.*]

60 **Bob.** Mr. Scrooge . . .

61 **Scrooge.** Huh? What's that? Who calls?

62 **Bob.** [*His glass raised in a toast*] I'll give you Mr. Scrooge, the Founder of the Feast!

63 **Scrooge.** Me, Bob? You toast *me*?

64 **Present.** Save your breath, Mr. Scrooge. You can't be seen or heard.

65 **Mrs. Cratchit.** The Founder of the Feast, indeed! I wish I had him here, that miser Scrooge. I'd give him a piece of my mind to feast upon, and I hope he'd have a good appetite for it!

66 **Bob.** My dear! Christmas Day!

67 **Mrs. Cratchit.** It should be Christmas Day, I am sure, on which one drinks the health of such an odious, stingy, unfeeling man as Mr. Scrooge . . .

68 **Scrooge.** Oh. Spirit, must I? . . .

69 **Mrs. Cratchit.** You know he is, Robert! Nobody knows it better than you do, poor fellow!

70 **Bob.** This is Christmas Day, and I should like to drink to the health of the man who employs me and allows me to earn my living and our support and that man is Ebenezer Scrooge . . .

71 **Mrs. Cratchit.** I'll drink to his health for your sake and the day's, but not for his sake . . . a Merry Christmas and a Happy New Year to you, Mr. Scrooge, wherever you may be this day!

72 **Scrooge.** Just here, kind madam . . . out of sight, out of sight . . .

73 **Bob.** Thank you, my dear. Thank you.

74 **Scrooge.** Thank you, Bob . . . and Mrs. Cratchit, too. No one else is toasting me, . . . not now . . . not ever. Of that I am sure . . .

75 **Bob.** Children . . .

76 **All.** Merry Christmas to Mr. Scrooge.

77 **Bob.** I'll pay you sixpence, Tim, for my favorite song.

VOCABULARY DEVELOPMENT

Word Analysis Discuss the meanings of the adjectives Mrs. Cratchit uses in paragraph 67 to describe Scrooge: *odious* ("arousing or deserving hatred or disgust"); *stingy* ("not generous; unwilling to spend money or share things"); *unfeeling* ("lacking kindness or sympathy"). Then, have students find two synonyms for each of these words. Discuss the synonyms and their shades of meaning in relation to each of Mrs. Cratchit's words.

NOTES

78 **Tiny Tim.** Oh, Father, I'd so love to sing it, but not for pay. This Christmas goose—this feast—you and Mother, my brother and sisters close with me: that's my pay—

79 **Bob.** Martha, will you play the notes on the lute, for Tiny Tim's song.

80 **Belinda.** May I sing, too, Father?

81 **Bob.** We'll all sing.

82 [*They sing a song about a tiny child lost in the snow—probably from Wordsworth's poem.* Tim *sings the lead vocal; all chime in for the chorus. Their song fades under, as the* Ghost of Christmas Present *speaks.*]

83 **Present.** Mark my words, Ebenezer Scrooge. I do not present the Cratchits to you because they are a handsome, or brilliant family. They are not handsome. They are not brilliant. They are not well-dressed, or tasteful to the times. Their shoes are not even waterproofed by virtue of money or cleverness spent. So when the pavement is wet, so are the insides of their shoes and the tops of their toes. These are the Cratchits, Mr. Scrooge. They are not highly special. They are happy, grateful, pleased with one another, contented with the time and how it passes. They don't sing very well, do they? But, nonetheless, they do sing . . . [*Pauses*] think of that, Scrooge. Fifteen shillings a week and they do sing . . . hear their song until its end.

84 **Scrooge.** I am listening. [*The chorus sings full volume now, until . . . the song ends here.*] Spirit, it must be time for us to take our leave. I feel in my heart that it is . . . that I must think on that which I have seen here . . .

85 **Present.** Touch my robe again . . .

86 [Scrooge *touches* Present's *robe. The lights fade out on the* Cratchits, *who sit, frozen, at the table.* Scrooge *and* Present *in a spotlight now. Thunder, lightning, smoke. They are gone.*]

Scene 4

1 [Marley *appears* D.L. *in single spotlight. A storm brews. Thunder and lightning.* Scrooge *and* Present *"fly" past,* U. *The storm continues, furiously, and, now and again,* Scrooge *and* Present *will zip past in their travels.* Marley *will speak straight out to the audience.*]

2 **Marley.** The Ghost of Christmas Present, my co-worker in this attempt to turn a miser, flies about now with that very miser, Scrooge, from street to street, and he points out

PERSONALIZE FOR LEARNING

English Language Support

Idioms Explain the idiom *mark my words* in paragraph 83 to students. *Mark my words* means "Pay attention to what I say." (When used in this way, *mark* means "to take notice of.") Ask students the following question: When might someone use the expression *mark my words*? **ALL LEVELS**

NOTES

partygoers on their way to Christmas parties. If one were to judge from the numbers of people on their way to friendly gatherings, one might think that no one was left at home to give anyone welcome . . . but that's not the case, is it? Every home is expecting company and . . . [*He laughs.*] Scrooge is amazed.

3 [Scrooge *and* Present *zip past again. The lights fade up around them. We are in the* Nephew's *home, in the living room.* Present *and* Scrooge *stand watching the* Nephew: Fred *and his wife, fixing the fire.*]

4 **Scrooge.** What is this place? We've moved from the mines!

5 **Present.** You do not recognize them?

6 **Scrooge.** It is my nephew! . . . and the one he married . . .

7 [Marley *waves his hand and there is a lightning flash. He disappears.*]

8 **Fred.** It strikes me as sooooo funny, to think of what he said . . . that Christmas was a humbug, as I live! He believed it!

9 **Wife.** More shame for him, Fred!

10 **Fred.** Well, he's a comical old fellow, that's the truth.

11 **Wife.** I have no patience with him.

12 **Fred.** Oh, I have! I am sorry for him; I couldn't be angry with him if I tried. Who suffers by his ill whims? Himself, always . . .

13 **Scrooge.** It's me they talk of, isn't it, Spirit?

14 **Fred.** Here, wife, consider this. Uncle Scrooge takes it into his head to dislike us, and he won't come and dine with us. What's the consequence?

15 **Wife.** Oh . . . you're sweet to say what I think you're about to say, too, Fred . . .

16 **Fred.** What's the consequence? He don't lose much of a dinner by it, I can tell you that!

17 **Wife.** Ooooooo, Fred! Indeed, I think he loses a very good dinner . . . ask my sisters, or your bachelor friend, Topper . . . ask any of them. They'll tell you what old Scrooge, your uncle, missed: a dandy meal!

18 **Fred.** Well, that's something of a relief, wife. Glad to hear it! [*He hugs his wife. They laugh. They kiss.*] The truth is, he misses much yet. I mean to give him the same chance every year, whether he likes it or not, for I pity him. Nay, he is my only uncle and I feel for the old miser . . . but, I tell you, wife: I see

PERSONALIZE FOR LEARNING

English Language Support

Multiple-Meaning Words Explain to students that the word *company* in paragraph 2 has several meanings. As it's used in this part of the play, it's a noun that means "visitors; guests" (We are having company for dinner tonight.). *Company* can also mean: "association with another" (I enjoy Judy's company.); "a group of performing artists" (Tyrel just joined a theater company.); "a firefighting unit" (My uncle is a firefighter in Company B.); and "a business" (Sandy just got a job with an international company.). **ALL LEVELS**

my dear and perfect mother's face on his own wizened cheeks and brow: brother and sister they were, and I cannot erase that from each view of him I take . . .

19 **Wife.** I understand what you say, Fred, and I am with you in your yearly asking. But he never will accept, you know. He never will.

20 **Fred.** Well, true, wife. Uncle may rail at Christmas till he dies. I think I shook him some with my visit yesterday . . . [*Laughing*] I refused to grow angry . . . no matter how nasty he became . . . [*Whoops*] It was HE who grew angry, wife! [*They both laugh now.*]

21 **Scrooge.** What he says is true, Spirit . . .

22 **Fred and Wife.** Bah, humbug!

23 **Fred.** [*Embracing his wife*] There is much laughter in our marriage, wife. It pleases me. You please me . . .

24 **Wife.** And you please me, Fred. You are a good man . . . [*They embrace.*] Come now. We must have a look at the meal . . . our guests will soon arrive . . . my sisters, Topper . . .

25 **Fred.** A toast first . . . [*He hands her a glass*] A toast to Uncle Scrooge . . . [*Fills their glasses*]

26 **Wife.** A toast to him?

27 **Fred.** Uncle Scrooge has given us plenty of merriment, I am sure, and it would be ungrateful not to drink to his health. And I say . . . *Uncle Scrooge!*

28 **Wife.** [*Laughing*] You're a proper loon,[5] Fred . . . and I'm a proper wife to you . . . [*She raises her glass.*] Uncle Scrooge! [*They drink. They embrace. They kiss.*]

29 **Scrooge.** Spirit, please, make me visible! Make me audible! I want to talk with my nephew and my niece!

30 [*Calls out to them. The lights that light the room and* Fred *and wife fade out.* Scrooge *and* Present *are alone, spotlit.*]

31 **Present.** These shadows are gone to you now, Mr. Scrooge. You may return to them later tonight in your dreams. [*Pauses*] My time grows short, Ebenezer Scrooge. Look you on me! Do you see how I've aged?

32 **Scrooge.** Your hair has gone gray! Your skin, wrinkled! Are spirits' lives so short?

33 **Present.** My stay upon this globe is very brief. It ends tonight.

34 **Scrooge.** Tonight?

35 **Present.** At midnight. The time is drawing near!

NOTES

5. **a proper loon** silly person.

NOTES

36 [*Clock strikes 11:45.*]

37 Hear those chimes? In a quarter hour, my life will have been spent! Look, Scrooge, man. Look you here.

38 [*Two gnarled baby dolls are taken from* Present's *skirts.*]

39 **Scrooge.** Who are they?

40 **Present.** They are Man's children, and they cling to me, appealing from their fathers. The boy is Ignorance; the girl is Want. Beware them both, and all of their degree, but most of all beware this boy, for I see that written on his brow which is doom, unless the writing be erased.

41 [*He stretches out his arm. His voice is now amplified: loudly and oddly.*]

42 **Scrooge.** Have they no refuge or resource?

43 **Present.** Are there no prisons? Are there no workhouses? [*Twelve chimes*] Are there no prisons? Are there no workhouses?

44 [*A* Phantom, *hooded, appears in dim light,* D., *opposite.*]

45 Are there no prisons? Are there no workhouses?

PERSONALIZE FOR LEARNING

Strategic Support

Analyze Theme Review paragraph 40 and help students analyze the text. Use these questions to prompt discussion: *What does the Spirit mean in paragraph 40 when he says that the boy and girl clinging to his feet are "Man's children"? Why should we beware of them both? Why should we "most of all" beware of the boy? Why is "doom" written on the boy's brow? What is the playwright's message in this part of the play?*

46 [Present *begins to deliquesce.* Scrooge *calls after him.*]

47 **Scrooge.** Spirit, I'm frightened! Don't leave me! Spirit!

48 **Present.** Prisons? Workhouses? Prisons? Workhouses . . .

49 [*He is gone.* Scrooge *is alone now with the* Phantom, *who is, of course, the* Ghost of Christmas Future. *The* Phantom *is shrouded in black. Only its outstretched hand is visible from under his ghostly garment.*]

50 **Scrooge.** Who are you, Phantom? Oh, yes. I think I know you! You are, are you not, the Spirit of Christmas Yet to Come? [*No reply*] And you are about to show me the shadows of the things that have not yet happened, but will happen in time before us. Is that not so, Spirit? [*The* Phantom *allows* Scrooge *a look at his face. No other reply wanted here. A nervous giggle here.*] Oh, Ghost of the Future, I fear you more than any Specter I have seen! But, as I know that your purpose is to do me good and as I hope to live to be another man from what I was, I am prepared to bear you company. [Future *does not reply, but for a stiff arm, hand and finger set, pointing forward.*] Lead on, then, lead on. The night is waning fast, and it is precious time to me. Lead on, Spirit!

51 [Future *moves away from* Scrooge *in the same rhythm and motion employed at its arrival.* Scrooge *falls into the same pattern, a considerable space apart from the* Spirit. *In the space between them,* Marley *appears. He looks to* Future *and then to* Scrooge. *He claps his hands. Thunder and lightning. Three* Businessmen *appear, spotlighted singularly: One is* D.L.; *one is* D.R.; *one is* U.C. *Thus, six points of the stage should now be spotted in light.* Marley *will watch this scene from his position,* C. Scrooge *and* Future *are* R. *and* L. *of* C.]

52 **First Businessman.** Oh, no, I don't know much about it either way, I only know he's dead.

53 **Second Businessman.** When did he die?

54 **First Businessman.** Last night, I believe.

55 **Second Businessman.** Why, what was the matter with him? I thought he'd never die, really . . .

56 **First Businessman.** [*Yawning*] Goodness knows, goodness knows . . .

57 **Third Businessman.** What has he done with his money?

58 **Second Businessman.** I haven't heard. Have you?

59 **First Businessman.** Left it to his Company, perhaps. Money to money; you know the expression . . .

NOTES

CLOSE READ

ANNOTATE: Mark the words and phrases that the Ghost of Christmas Present repeats in paragraphs 43–48.

QUESTION: Why might the playwright have chosen to have the Ghost of Christmas Present repeat these words and phrases upon departing?

CONCLUDE: What effect does this repetition have on the reader?

DIGITAL PERSPECTIVES

Remind students to focus on repeated words and phrases as they read paragraphs 43–48. You may wish to model the close read using the following think-aloud format. Possible responses to questions on the student page are included.

ANNOTATE: As I read paragraphs 43–48, I notice and mark words and phrases repeated by the Ghost of Christmas Present.

QUESTION: I think that the Ghost of Christmas Present repeats these words and phrases over and over to remind Scrooge of how he suggested the poor go to prisons or workhouses instead of helping find warmth and shelter on Christmas.

CONCLUDE: To me, this repetition has a strong effect of making Scrooge feel scared and probably guilty of his earlier disregard for the poor. Scrooge tries to talk to the Spirit and the only reply he receives is the repeated words.

PERSONALIZE FOR LEARNING

Challenge

Analyze Review paragraph 50 and call student attention to the stage directions. Conduct this discussion with the students: The Ghost of Christmas Future occasionally gestures but doesn't speak in paragraph 50. Why? Is this a good choice on the part of the author? Why or why not? Then, have students imagine that this Spirit does speak, and write a paragraph of dialogue that he might say to Scrooge when they first meet. Remind them there is no right or wrong response, but their dialogue should be based on what they've read.

NOTES

60 **Third Businessman.** He hasn't left it to *me*. That's all I know . . .

61 **First Businessman.** [*Laughing*] Nor to me . . . [*Looks at* Second Businessman] You, then? You got his money???

62 **First Businessman.** [*Laughing*] Me, me, his money? Nooooo!

63 [*They all laugh.*]

64 **Third Businessman.** It's likely to be a cheap funeral, for upon my life, I don't know of a living soul who'd care to venture to it. Suppose we make up a party and volunteer?

65 **Second Businessman.** I don't mind going if a lunch is provided, but I must be fed, if I make one.

66 **First Businessman.** Well, I am the most disinterested among you, for I never wear black gloves, and I never eat lunch. But I'll offer to go, if anybody else will. When I come to think of it, I'm not all sure that I wasn't his most particular friend: for we used to stop and speak whenever we met. Well, then . . . bye, bye!

67 **Second Businessman.** Bye, bye . . .

68 **Third Businessman.** Bye, bye . . .

69 [*They glide offstage in three separate directions. Their lights follow them.*]

70 **Scrooge.** Spirit, why did you show me this? Why do you show me businessmen from my streets as they take the death of Jacob Marley? That is a thing past. You are *future!*

71 [Jacob Marley *laughs a long, deep laugh. There is a thunder clap and lightning flash, and he is gone.* Scrooge *faces* Future, *alone on stage now.* Future *wordlessly stretches out his arm-hand-and-finger-set, pointing into the distance,* U. *There, above them, scoundrels "fly" by, half-dressed and slovenly. When this scene has passed, a woman enters the playing area. She is almost at once followed by a second woman; and then a man in faded black; and then, suddenly, an old man, who smokes a pipe. The old man scares the other three. They laugh, anxious.*]

72 **First Woman.** Look here, old Joe, here's a chance! If we haven't all three met here without meaning it!

73 **Old Joe.** You couldn't have met in a better place. Come into the parlor. You were made free of it long ago, you know; and the other two ain't strangers [*He stands; shuts a door. Shrieking*] We're all suitable to our calling. We're well matched. Come into the parlor. Come into the parlor . . . [*They follow him* D. Scrooge *and* Future *are now in their midst, watching; silent. A truck comes in on which is set a small wall with*

fireplace and a screen of rags, etc. All props for the scene.] Let me just rake this fire over a bit . . .

74 [*He does. He trims his lamp with the stem of his pipe. The* First Woman *throws a large bundle on to the floor. She sits beside it, crosslegged, defiantly*.]

75 **First Woman.** What odds then? What odds, Mrs. Dilber? Every person has a right to take care of themselves. HE always did!

76 **Mrs. Dilber.** That's true indeed! No man more so!

77 **First Woman.** Why, then, don't stand staring as if you was afraid, woman! Who's the wiser? We're not going to pick holes in each other's coats, I suppose?

78 **Mrs. Dilber.** No, indeed! We should hope not!

79 **First Woman.** Very well, then! That's enough. Who's the worse for the loss of a few things like these? Not a dead man, I suppose?

80 **Mrs. Dilber.** [*Laughing*] No, indeed!

81 **First Woman.** If he wanted to keep 'em after he was dead, the wicked old screw, why wasn't he natural in his lifetime? If he had been, he'd have had somebody to look after him when he was struck with Death, instead of lying gasping out his last there, alone by himself.

82 **Mrs. Dilber.** It's the truest word that was ever spoke. It's a judgment on him.

83 **First Woman.** I wish it were a heavier one, and it should have been, you may depend on it, if I could have laid my hands on anything else. Open that bundle, old Joe, and let me know the value of it. Speak out plain. I'm not afraid to be the first, nor afraid for them to see it. We knew pretty well that we were helping ourselves, before we met here, I believe. It's no sin. Open the bundle, Joe.

84 **First Man.** No, no, my dear! I won't think of letting you being the first to show what you've . . . earned . . . earned from this. I throw in mine.

85 [*He takes a bundle from his shoulder, turns it upside down, and empties its contents out on to the floor*.]

86 It's not very extensive, see . . . seals . . . a pencil case . . . sleeve buttons . . .

87 **First Woman.** Nice sleeve buttons, though . . .

88 **First Man.** Not bad, not bad . . . a brooch there . . .

89 **Old Joe.** Not really valuable, I'm afraid . . .

NOTES

CLOSE READ

ANNOTATE: In paragraph 75, mark the word that is emphasized.

QUESTION: Why did the playwright choose to emphasize this word?

CONCLUDE: How does emphasizing this word reveal the First Woman's attitude toward the man of whom she speaks?

DIGITAL PERSPECTIVES 

CLOSE READ

Remind students that words can be emphasized by how they're printed on the page. You may wish to model the close read using the following think-aloud format. Possible responses to questions on the student page are included.

ANNOTATE: As I read lines paragraph 75, I see a word printed differently from the others.

QUESTION: I think the playwright chose to emphasize this word to capture the way the woman is speaking at the moment. They all know who "he" refers to, and emphasizing this word suggests that the woman has certain feelings about him.

CONCLUDE: I think the emphasis on this word adds a note of emotion to what the woman is saying. Emphasizing this word reveals that the First Woman's attitude is not positive. I think the woman didn't like "him" very much.

HOW LANGUAGE WORKS

Adding Emphasis to Words Review paragraph 75 and explain that there are four ways to emphasize words when we write: capital letters (such as paragraph 75), italics, boldface, and underlining. The close-read question refers to using capital letters. This sentence could also be written using italics (*He* always did!), boldface (**He** always did!), or underlining (<u>He</u> always did!). In print, it's common to use capital letters, italics, or boldface. When we write by hand, it's easier to use capital letters or underlining.

NOTES

90 **First Man.** How much, old Joe?

91 **Old Joe.** [*Writing on the wall with chalk*] A pitiful lot, really. Ten and six and not a sixpence more!

92 **First Man.** You're not serious!

93 **Old Joe.** That's your account and I wouldn't give another sixpence if I was to be boiled for not doing it. Who's next?

94 **Mrs. Dilber.** Me! [*Dumps out contents of her bundle*] Sheets, towels, silver spoons, silver sugar-tongs . . . some boots . . .

95 **Old Joe.** [*Writing on wall*] I always give too much to the ladies. It's a weakness of mine and that's the way I ruin myself. Here's your total comin' up . . . two pounds-ten . . . if you asked me for another penny, and made it an open question, I'd repent of being so liberal and knock off half-a-crown.

96 **First Woman.** And now do MY bundle, Joe.

97 **Old Joe.** [*Kneeling to open knots on her bundle*] So many knots, madam . . . [*He drags out large curtains; dark*] What do you call this? Bed curtains!

98 **First Woman.** [*Laughing*] Ah, yes, bed curtains!

99 **Old Joe.** You don't mean to say you took 'em down, rings and all, with him lying there?

100 **First Woman.** Yes, I did, why not?

101 **Old Joe.** You were born to make your fortune and you'll certainly do it.

102 **First Woman.** I certainly shan't hold my hand, when I can get anything in it by reaching it out, for the sake of such a man as he was. I promise you, Joe. Don't drop that lamp oil on those blankets, now!

103 **Old Joe.** His blankets?

104 **First Woman.** Whose else's do you think? He isn't likely to catch cold without 'em, I daresay.

105 **Old Joe.** I hope that he didn't die of anything catching? Eh?

106 **First Woman.** Don't you be afraid of that. I ain't so fond of his company that I'd loiter about him for such things if he did. Ah! You may look through that shirt till your eyes ache, but you won't find a hole in it, nor a threadbare place. It's the best he had, and a fine one, too. They'd have wasted it, if it hadn't been for me.

107 **Old Joe.** What do you mean "They'd have wasted it"?

108 **First Woman.** Putting it on him to be buried in, to be sure. Somebody was fool enough to do it, but I took it off again . . .

109 [*She laughs, as do they all, nervously.*]

PERSONALIZE FOR LEARNING

Strategic Support

Historical Context Review paragraph 94 and explain Scrooge's bed curtains to students. Scrooge slept in a bed with bedposts, around which hung curtains that could be drawn shut when he went to sleep. (These can be seen in the 1951 film at 20:50–21:03.) Immediately after Scrooge died, this woman took down the curtains (and the rings from which they hung) while Scrooge was still lying in the bed. Now she is selling them.

110 If calico[6] ain't good enough for such a purpose, it isn't good enough then for anything. It's quite as becoming to the body. He can't look uglier than he did in that one!

111 **Scrooge.** [*A low-pitched moan emits from his mouth; from the bones.*] *OOOOOOOooooOOOOOoooooOOOOOOOO oooooOOOOOOooooooOO!*

112 **Old Joe.** One pound six for the lot. [*He produces a small flannel bag filled with money. He divvies it out. He continues to pass around the money as he speaks. All are laughing.*] That's the end of it, you see! He frightened every one away from him when he was alive, to profit us when he was dead! Hah ha ha!

113 **All.** HAHAHAHAhahahahahahah!

114 **Scrooge.** *OOoooOOoooOOOoooOOOoooOOoooOOoooOOOooo!* [*He screams at them.*] Obscene demons! Why not market the corpse itself, as sell its trimming??? [*Suddenly*] Oh, Spirit, I see it, I see it! This unhappy man—this stripped-bare corpse . . . could very well be my own. My life holds **parallel**! My life ends that way now!

115 [Scrooge *backs into something in the dark behind his spotlight.* Scrooge *looks at* Future, *who points to the corpse.* Scrooge *pulls back the blanket. The corpse is, of course,* Scrooge, *who screams. He falls aside the bed; weeping.*]

116 Spirit, this is a fearful place. In leaving it, I shall not leave its lesson, trust me. Let us go!

117 [Future *points to the corpse.*]

118 Spirit, let me see some tenderness connected with a death, or that dark chamber, which we just left now, Spirit, will be forever present to me.

119 [Future *spreads his robes again. Thunder and lightning. Lights up, U., in the* Cratchit *home setting.* Mrs. Cratchit *and her daughters, sewing*]

120 **Tiny Tim's Voice.** [*Off*] And He took a child and set him in the midst of them.

121 **Scrooge.** [*Looking about the room; to* Future] Huh? Who spoke? Who said that?

122 **Mrs. Cratchit.** [*Puts down her sewing*] The color hurts my eyes. [Rubs her eyes] That's better. My eyes grow weak sewing by candlelight. I shouldn't want to show your father weak eyes when he comes home . . . not for the world! It must be near his time . . .

NOTES

6. **calico** (KAL ih koh) *n.* coarse and inexpensive cotton cloth.

CLOSE READ

ANNOTATE: Mark the sounds and sound effects in paragraphs 111–114.

QUESTION: Why do you think the author chose to include these details?

CONCLUDE: What effect does this choice have on the reader?

parallel (PAR uh lehl) *adj.* having the same direction or nature; similar

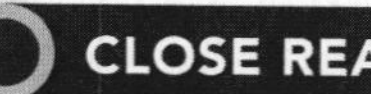 

CLOSE READ

Remind students that they're looking for sounds. You may wish to model the close read using the following think-aloud format. Possible responses to questions on the student page are included.

ANNOTATE: As I read paragraphs 111–114, I see text that I recognize as sounds.

QUESTION: I think the author chose to use sounds to show how upset Scrooge is in this part of the play.

CONCLUDE: I think these sounds have an emotional effect. Scrooge is so upset that he can't express himself in words. Instead, he resorts to a loud moan that conveys how unsettled he is by what he's seeing here.

PERSONALIZE FOR LEARNING

Strategic Support

Dramatic Structure Review paragraph 118 and explain to students that there are two reasons the Spirit takes Scrooge to Cratchit's house. One reason is that the Spirit of Christmas Present took Scrooge there. Now this Spirit is showing Scrooge what will happen to the Cratchits in the future. But first the Spirit takes Scrooge to his own future corpse, which prompts Scrooge to say, "Spirit, let me see some tenderness connected with a death..." in paragraph 118. The Spirit then shows tenderness in the Cratchit family's mourning for Tiny Tim.

CLOSE READ

Remind students that as they read paragraphs 123–136, they should focus on conversation between the characters and the words they use to identify each other. You may wish to model the following close read using the following think-aloud format. Possible responses to questions on the student page are included.

ANNOTATE: As I read paragraphs 123–136, I notice terms the characters use when talking about or speaking to each other.

QUESTION: I think the playwright chose to use "he" in place of Tiny Tim only once, maybe because the family is so sad they can't say his name. Mrs. Cratchit says "his father" instead of "your father" to her children probably because she is thinking so much about Tiny Tim. That Bob Cratchit calls his family "wife" and "children" makes it seem that he is distant from them, and exclaims "My little, little child!" in referring to Tiny Tim.

CONCLUDE: These terms help the reader to understand that Tiny Tim is the focus of the conversation between Bob Cratchit and his family.

NOTES

CLOSE READ

ANNOTATE: In paragraphs 123–136, mark the terms the characters use to identify each other in the dialogue.

QUESTION: Why might the playwright have included these terms in the dialogue?

CONCLUDE: How do these terms help the reader to better understand the conversation?

123 **Peter.** [*In corner, reading. Looks up from book*] Past it, rather. But I think he's been walking a bit slower than usual these last few evenings, Mother.

124 **Mrs. Cratchit.** I have known him walk with . . . [*Pauses*] I have known him walk with Tiny Tim upon his shoulder and very fast indeed.

125 **Peter.** So have I, Mother! Often!

126 **Daughter.** So have I.

127 **Mrs. Cratchit.** But he was very light to carry and his father loved him so, that it was not trouble—no trouble. [Bob, *at door*]

128 And there is your father at the door.

129 [Bob Cratchit *enters. He wears a comforter. He is cold, forlorn.*]

130 **Peter.** Father!

131 **Bob.** Hello, wife, children . . .

132 [*The daughter weeps; turns away from* Cratchit.]

133 Children! How good to see you all! And you, wife. And look at this sewing! I've no doubt, with all your industry, we'll have a quilt to set down upon our knees in church on Sunday!

134 **Mrs. Cratchit.** You made the arrangements today, then, Robert, for the . . . service . . . to be on Sunday.

135 **Bob.** The funeral. Oh, well, yes, yes, I did. I wish you could have gone. It would have done you good to see how green a place it is. But you'll see it often. I promised him that I would walk there on Sunday, after the service. [*Suddenly*] My little, little child! My little child!

136 **All Children.** [*Hugging him*] Oh, Father . . .

137 **Bob.** [*He stands*] Forgive me. I saw Mr. Scrooge's nephew, who you know I'd just met once before, and he was so wonderful to me, wife . . . he is the most pleasant-spoken gentleman I've ever met . . . he said "I am heartily sorry for it and heartily sorry for your good wife. If I can be of service to you in any way, here's where I live." And he gave me this card.

138 **Peter.** Let me see it!

139 **Bob.** And he looked me straight in the eye, wife, and said, meaningfully, "I pray you'll come to me, Mr. Cratchit, if you need some help. I pray you do." Now it wasn't for the sake of anything that he might be able to do for us, so much as for his kind way. It seemed as if he had known our Tiny Tim and felt with us.

PERSONALIZE FOR LEARNING

English Language Support

Multiple-Meaning Words Explain to students that the word *light* in paragraph 127 has several meanings. As it's used in this part of the play, it's an adjective that means "having little weight." As an adjective, *light* can also mean: "not abundant" (A light rain was falling.); "easily disturbed" (David is a light sleeper.); and "gentle" (I felt a light touch on my arm.). *Light* can also be a noun that means "something that makes vision possible" (Turn on the light.) and "daylight" (At this time of year, it gets light at 5 A.M.). **ALL LEVELS**

140 **Mrs. Cratchit.** I'm sure that he's a good soul.

141 **Bob.** You would be surer of it, my dear, if you saw and spoke to him. I shouldn't be at all surprised, if he got Peter a situation.

142 **Mrs. Cratchit.** Only hear that, Peter!

143 **Martha.** And then, Peter will be keeping company with someone and setting up for himself!

144 **Peter.** Get along with you!

145 **Bob.** It's just as likely as not, one of these days, though there's plenty of time for that, my dear. But however and whenever we part from one another, I am sure we shall none of us forget poor Tiny Tim—shall we?—or this first parting that was among us?

146 **All Children.** Never, Father, never!

147 **Bob.** And when we recollect how patient and mild he was, we shall not quarrel easily among ourselves, and forget poor Tiny Tim in doing it.

148 **All Children.** No, Father, never!

149 **Little Bob.** I am very happy, I am. I am. I am very happy.

150 [Bob *kisses his little son, as does* Mrs. Cratchit, *as do the other children. The family is set now in one sculptural embrace. The lighting fades to a gentle pool of light, tight on them.*]

151 **Scrooge.** Specter, something informs me that our parting moment is at hand. I know it, but I know not how I know it.

152 [Future *points to the other side of the stage. Lights out on* Cratchits. Future *moves slowing, gliding.* Scrooge *follows.* Future *points opposite.* Future *leads* Scrooge *to a wall and a tombstone. He points to the stone.*]

153 Am I that man those ghoulish parasites[7] so gloated over? [*Pauses*] Before I draw nearer to that stone to which you point, answer me one question. Are these the shadows of things that will be, or the shadows of things that MAY be, only?

154 [Future *points to the gravestone.* Marley *appears in light well* U. *He points to grave as well. Gravestone turns front and grows to ten feet high. Words upon it:* Ebenezer Scrooge: *Much smoke billows now from the grave. Choral music here.* Scrooge *stands looking up at gravestone.* Future d*oes not at all reply in mortals' words, but points once more to the gravestone. The stone undulates and glows. Music plays, beckoning* Scrooge. Scrooge *reeling in terror*]

155 Oh, no. Spirit! Oh, no, no!

156 [Future's *finger still pointing*]

NOTES

7. **ghoulish parasites** (GOOL ish PAR uh syts) referring to the men and women who stole and divided Scrooge's goods after he died.

WriteNow Analyze and Interpret

Explanation Call student attention to the stage directions in paragraph 154. Before Scrooge looks at the gravestone, he asks the Spirit, "Are these the shadows of things that will be, or the shadows of things that MAY be, only?" Have students write a paragraph explaining what Scrooge means by this and why he is asking the question. Ask volunteers to share their responses with the class.

NOTES

altered (AWL tuhrd) *adj.* changed

strive (STRYV) *v.* make a great effort; try very hard

157 Spirit! Hear me! I am not the man I was. I will not be the man I would have been but for this intercourse. Why show me this, if I am past all hope?

158 [Future *considers* Scrooge's *logic. His hand wavers.*]

159 Oh. Good Spirit, I see by your wavering hand that your good nature intercedes for me and pities me. Assure me that I yet may change these shadows that you have shown me by an **altered** life!

160 [Future's *hand trembles; pointing has stopped.*]

161 I will honor Christmas in my heart and try to keep it all the year. I will live in the Past, the Present, and the Future. The Spirits of all Three shall **strive** within me. I will not shut out the lessons that they teach. Oh, tell me that I may sponge away the writing that is upon this stone!

162 [Scrooge *makes a desperate stab at grabbing* Future's *hand. He holds firm for a moment, but* Future, *stronger than* Scrooge, *pulls away.* Scrooge *is on his knees, praying.*]

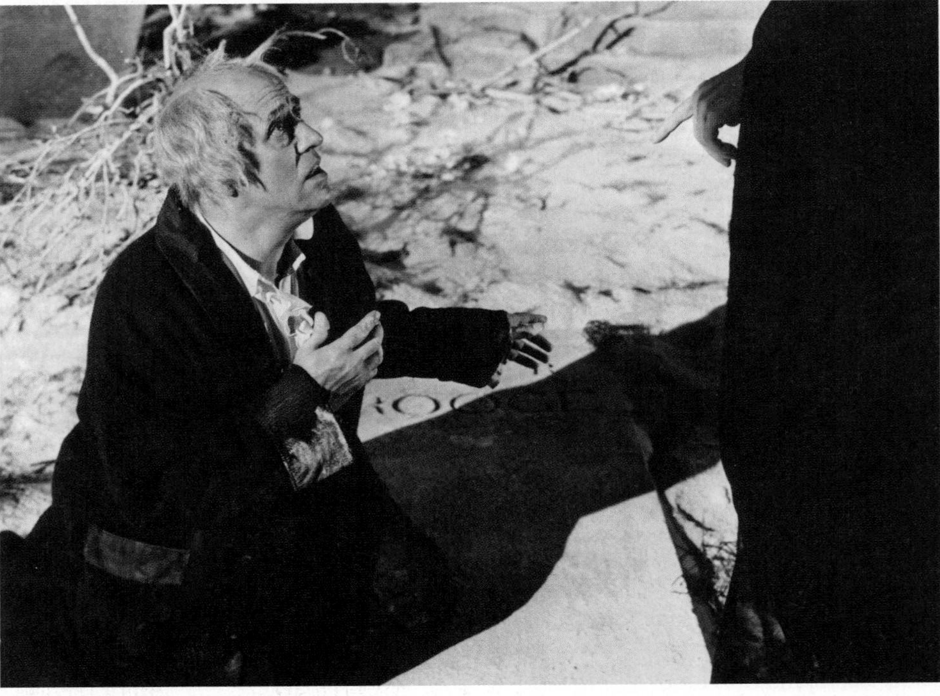

DIGITAL PERSPECTIVES

Illuminating the Text Review paragraph 161. To help students understand the impact of Scrooge's final moments with the Ghost of Christmas Future, use the search term "a Christmas Carol 1951" to find video footage online showing the 1951 film. Be sure to preview any video before showing it to students. Have students view 1:11:35–1:13:30, then have students discuss how seeing this scene from the film helps illuminate the play.

163 Spirit, dear Spirit, I am praying before you. Give me a sign that all is possible. Give me a sign that all hope for me is not lost. Oh, Spirit, kind Spirit, I beseech thee: give me a sign . . .

164 [Future *deliquesces, slowly, gently.* The Phantom's *hood and robe drop gracefully to the ground in a small heap. Music in. There is nothing in them. They are mortal cloth. The* Spirit *is elsewhere.* Scrooge *has his sign.* Scrooge *is alone. Tableau. The light fades to black.*]

Scene 5

1 [*The end of it.* Marley, *spotlighted, opposite* Scrooge, *in his bed, spotlighted.* Marley *speaks to audience, directly.*]

2 **Marley.** [*He smiles at* Scrooge.] The firm of Scrooge and Marley is doubly blessed; two misers turned; one, alas, in Death, too late; but the other miser turned in Time's penultimate nick.[8] Look you on my friend, Ebenezer Scrooge . . .

3 **Scrooge.** [*Scrambling out of bed; reeling in delight*] I will live in the Past, in the Present, and in the Future! The Spirits of all Three shall strive within me!

4 **Marley.** [*He points and moves closer to Scrooge's bed.*] Yes, Ebenezer, the bedpost is your own. Believe it! Yes, Ebenezer, the room is your own. Believe it!

5 **Scrooge.** Oh, Jacob Marley! Wherever you are, Jacob, know ye that I praise you for this! I praise you . . . and heaven . . . and Christmastime! [*Kneels facing away from* Marley] I say it to you on my knees, old Jacob, on my knees! [*He touches his bed curtains.*] Not torn down. My bed curtains are not at all torn down! Rings and all, here they are! They are here: I am here: the shadows of things that would have been, may now be **dispelled**. They will be, Jacob! I know they will be!

6 [*He chooses clothing for the day. He tries different pieces of clothing and settles, perhaps, on a dress suit, plus a cape of the bed clothing: something of color.*]

7 I am light as a feather, I am happy as an angel. I am as merry as a schoolboy. [*Yells out window and then out to audience*] Merry Christmas to everybody! Merry Christmas to everybody! A Happy New Year to all the world! Hallo here! Whoop! Whoop! Hallo! Hallo! I don't know what day of the month it is! I don't care! I don't know anything! I'm quite a baby! I don't care! I don't care a fig! I'd much rather be a baby

NOTES

8. **in Time's penultimate nick** just at the last moment.

dispelled (dihs PEHLD) *v.* driven away; scattered

DIGITAL PERSPECTIVES

CLOSER LOOK

Analyze Characterization

Students may have marked lines in paragraph 5 during their first read. Use these lines to help students understand the changes taking place in Scrooge. Encourage students to talk about the annotations that they marked. You may want to model a close read with the class based on the highlights shown in the text.

ANNOTATE: Have students mark details in paragraph 5 that indicate how Scrooge has been affected by his experience with the Spirits, or have students participate while you highlight them.

QUESTION: Guide students to consider what these details might tell them. Ask what a reader can infer from these details and accept student responses.

Possible response: Scrooge intends to act differently from now on.

CONCLUDE: Help students to formulate conclusions about the importance of these details in the text. Ask students why the playwright might have included these details.

Possible response: These details indicate that Scrooge intends to be different. When Scrooge was with the Ghost of Christmas Future, it was suggested that he could change future events if he became a better person. Here he is saying that those shadows can now be dispelled (driven away, or changed), indicating that he will behave differently to make that happen. Point out that this is not directly stated but it is strongly suggested. The playwright could have had Scrooge say "I will change," but saying it this way is more subtle and adds texture to the play.

One rule of good fiction writing is "Show don't tell," which means show characterization rather than just saying it. Here, the playwright is showing us that Scrooge intends to change rather than directly saying it.

DIGITAL PERSPECTIVES

Illuminating the Text Review paragraphs 1–7 and call student attention to Scrooge's attitude. To help students understand the how elated Scrooge is when he wakes up in his bed, use the search term "a Christmas Carol 1951" to find video footage online showing the 1951 film. Be sure to preview any video before showing it to students.

Have students view 1:13:31–1:16:30, then have students discuss how seeing this scene from the film helps illuminate the play.

CLOSE READ

Remind students that as they read paragraphs 12–22, they should look for details that show Scrooge's attitude and behavior toward Adam. You may wish to model the following close read using the following think-aloud format. Possible responses to questions on the student page are included.

ANNOTATE: As I read paragraphs 12–22, I notice and mark words that show how Scrooge feels about Adam and how Scrooge treats Adam.

QUESTION: These words show that Scrooge is very kind and encouraging toward Adam and also trusts Adam to go buy the turkey.

CONCLUDE: I think that Scrooge is starting to realize how happy he feels when he is kind and generous toward others. He even shows a little bit of humor when he tells Adam how much money he'll receive if he's quick to bring back the turkey.

NOTES

CLOSE READ

ANNOTATE: In paragraphs 12–22, mark words that show Scrooge's attitude and behavior toward Adam.

QUESTION: What do these word choices reveal about Scrooge?

CONCLUDE: How does Scrooge's attitude and behavior toward Adam reveal a transformation in his character?

than be an old wreck like me or Marley! (Sorry, Jacob. wherever ye be!) Hallo! Hallo there!

8 [*Church bells chime in Christmas Day. A small boy, named* Adam, *is seen now* D.R., *as a light fades up on him.*] Hey, you boy! What's today? What day of the year is it?

9 **Adam.** Today, sir? Why, it's Christmas Day!

10 **Scrooge.** It's Christmas Day, is it? Whoop! Well, I haven't missed it after all, have I? The Spirits did all they did in one night. They can do anything they like, right? Of course they can! Of course they can!

11 **Adam.** Excuse me, sir?

12 **Scrooge.** Huh? Oh, yes, of course. What's your name, lad?

13 [Scrooge *and* Adam *will play their scene from their own spotlights.*]

14 **Adam.** Adam, sir.

15 **Scrooge.** Adam! What a fine, strong name! Do you know the poulterer's[9] in the next street but one, at the corner?

16 **Adam.** I certainly should hope I know him, sir!

17 **Scrooge.** A remarkable boy! An intelligent boy! Do you know whether the poulterer's have sold the prize turkey that was hanging up there? I don't mean the little prize turkey, Adam. I mean the big one!

18 **Adam.** What, do you mean the one they've got that's as big as me?

19 **Scrooge.** I mean, the turkey the size of Adam: that's the bird!

20 **Adam.** It's hanging there now, sir.

21 **Scrooge.** It is? Go and buy it! No, no. I am absolutely in **earnest**. Go and buy it and tell 'em to bring it here, so that I may give them the directions to where I want it delivered, as a gift. Come back here with the man, Adam, and I'll give you a shilling. Come back here with him in less than five minutes, and I'll give you half-a-crown!

22 **Adam.** Oh, my sir! Don't let my brother in on this.

23 [Adam *runs offstage.* Marley *smiles.*]

24 **Marley.** An act of kindness is like the first green grape of summer: one leads to another and another and another. It would take a queer man indeed to not follow an act of kindness with an act of kindness. One simply whets the tongue for more . . . the taste of kindness is too too sweet. Gifts—goods—are lifeless. But the gift of goodness one feels in the giving is full of life. It . . . is . . . a . . . wonder.

9. **poulterer's** (POHL tuhr uhrz) *n.* British term for a person or a store that sells poultry.

earnest (UR nihst) *adj.* serious and heartfelt; not joking

HOW LANGUAGE WORKS

Sentence Structures Call student attention to sentence structure in paragraphs 20 and 21. Review simple, compound, complex, and compound-complex sentences. Have students identify the sentence types in the following lines from the play and explain why they chose each sentence type.

1. It's hanging there now, sir. (Paragraph 20) (simple)
2. Go and buy it and tell 'em to bring it here, so that I may give them the directions to where I want it delivered, as a gift. (paragraph 21) (complex)
3. Come back here with him in less than five minutes, and I'll give you half-a-crown. (paragraph 21) (compound)

NOTES

25 [*Pauses; moves closer to* Scrooge, *who is totally occupied with his dressing and arranging of his room and his day. He is making lists, etc.* Marley *reaches out to* Scrooge.]

26 **Adam.** [Calling, off] I'm here! I'm here!

27 [Adam *runs on with a man, who carries an enormous turkey.*]

28 Here I am, sir. Three minutes flat! A world record! I've got the poultryman and he's got the poultry! [*He pants, out of breath.*] I have earned my prize, sir, if I live . . .

29 [*He holds his heart, playacting.* Scrooge *goes to him and embraces him.*]

30 **Scrooge.** You are truly a champion, Adam . . .

31 **Man.** Here's the bird you ordered, sir . . .

32 **Scrooge.** *Oh, my, MY!!!* Look at the size of that turkey, will you! He never could have stood upon his legs, that bird! He would have snapped them off in a minute, like sticks of

PERSONALIZE FOR LEARNING

English Language Support

Idioms Explain to students that the phrase *three minutes flat* (paragraph 28) is a way of saying "in exactly three minutes." As it's used here, *flat* is an adjective that means "exact." Point out that *flat* can have other meanings. It can also mean: "lying at full length or spread out on the ground" (He was flat on his back.); "having a smooth or even surface" (The ocean was flat.); and "lacking bubbles or sparkle" (The soda was flat.). **ALL LEVELS**

CLOSE READ

Remind students that as they read paragraphs 49–56, they should look for details that show the Portly Man's reaction to Scrooge.

ANNOTATE: As I read paragraphs 49–56, I notice and mark the Portly Man's reaction to Scrooge after Scrooge addresses him kindly.

QUESTION: I think the playwright included these details to show the Portly Man's surprise at Scrooge's kind words and offer of repayment and to show the Portly Man's excited and happy reaction during their conversation.

CONCLUDE: The Portly Man's reaction shows that Scrooge's character has changed a lot for the better. It seems that Scrooge is starting to get used to being kind and that he might actually be a changed man. He is enjoying making people happy.

NOTES

sealingwax! Why you'll never be able to carry that bird to Camden-Town, I'll give you money for a cab . . .

33 **Man.** Camden-Town's where it's goin', sir?

34 **Scrooge.** Oh, I didn't tell you? Yes, I've written the precise address down just here on this . . . [*Hands paper to him*] Bob Cratchit's house. Now he's not to know who sends him this. Do you understand me? Not a word . . . [*Handing out money and chuckling*]

35 **Man.** I understand, sir, not a word.

36 **Scrooge.** Good. There you go then . . . this is for the turkey . . . [*Chuckle*] . . . and this is for the taxi. [*Chuckle*] . . . and this is for your world-record run, Adam . . .

37 **Adam.** But I don't have change for that, sir.

38 **Scrooge.** Then keep it, my lad. It's Christmas!

39 **Adam.** [*He kisses* Scrooge's *cheek, quickly.*] Thank you, sir. Merry, Merry Christmas! [*He runs off.*]

40 **Man.** And you've given me a bit overmuch here, too, sir . . .

41 **Scrooge.** Of course I have, sir. It's Christmas!

42 **Man.** Oh, well, thanking you, sir. I'll have this bird to Mr. Cratchit and his family in no time, sir. Don't you worry none about that. Merry Christmas to you, sir, and a very happy New Year, too . . .

43 [*The man exits.* Scrooge *walks in a large circle about the stage, which is now gently lit. A chorus sings Christmas music far in the distance. Bells chime as well, far in the distance. A gentlewoman enters and passes.* Scrooge *is on the streets now.*]

44 **Scrooge.** Merry Christmas, madam . . .

45 **Woman.** Merry Christmas, sir . . .

46 [*The portly businessman from the first act enters.*]

47 **Scrooge.** Merry Christmas, sir.

48 **Portly Man.** Merry Christmas, sir.

49 **Scrooge.** Oh, you! My dear sir! How do you do? I do hope that you succeeded yesterday! It was very kind of you. A Merry Christmas.

50 **Portly Man.** Mr. Scrooge?

51 **Scrooge.** Yes, Scrooge is my name though I'm afraid you may not find it very pleasant. Allow me to ask your pardon. And will you have the goodness to—[*He whispers into the man's ear.*]

CLOSE READ

ANNOTATE: In paragraphs 49–56, mark words and phrases that indicate the Portly Man's reaction to Scrooge.

QUESTION: Why might the playwright have included these details?

CONCLUDE: What does the Portly Man's reaction show about Scrooge's character at this point in the play?

52 **Portly Man.** Lord bless me! My dear Mr. Scrooge, are you *serious!?!*

53 **Scrooge.** If you please. Not a farthing[10] less. A great many back payments are included in it, I assure you. Will you do me that favor?

54 **Portly Man.** My dear sir, I don't know what to say to such munifi—

55 **Scrooge.** [*Cutting him off*] Don't say anything, please. Come and see me. Will you?

56 **Portly Man.** I will! I will! Oh I will, Mr. Scrooge! It will be my pleasure!

57 **Scrooge.** Thank'ee, I am much obliged to you. I thank you fifty times. Bless you!

58 [Portly Man *passes offstage, perhaps by moving backwards.* Scrooge *now comes to the room of his* Nephew *and* Niece. *He stops at the door, begins to knock on it, loses his courage, tries again, loses his courage again, tries again, fails again, and then backs off and runs at the door, causing a tremendous bump against it. The* Nephew *and* Niece *are startled.* Scrooge, *poking head into room*]

59 Fred!

60 **Nephew.** Why, bless my soul! Who's that?

61 **Nephew and Niece.** [*Together*] How now? Who goes?

62 **Scrooge.** It's I. Your Uncle Scrooge.

63 **Niece.** Dear heart alive!

64 **Scrooge.** I have come to dinner. May I come in, Fred?

65 **Nephew.** *May you come in???!!!* With such pleasure for me you may, Uncle!!! What a treat!

66 **Niece.** What a treat, Uncle Scrooge! Come in, come in!

67 [*They embrace a shocked and delighted* Scrooge: Fred *calls into the other room.*]

68 **Nephew.** Come in here, everybody, and meet my Uncle Scrooge! He's come for our Christmas party!

69 [*Music in. Lighting here indicates that day has gone to night and gone to day again. It is early, early morning.* Scrooge *walks alone from the party, exhausted, to his offices, opposite side of the stage. He opens his offices. The offices are as they were at the start of the play.* Scrooge *seats himself with his door wide open so he can see into the tank, as he awaits* Cratchit, *who enters, head down, full of guilt.* Cratchit, *starts writing almost before he sits.*]

NOTES

10. **farthing** (FAHR thihng) *n.* small British coin.

CLOSER LOOK

Analyze Conflict

Students may have marked lines in paragraph 78 during their first read. Use these lines to help students understand the extent of Scrooge's transformation. Encourage them to talk about the annotations that they marked. You may want to model a close read with the class based on the highlights shown in the text.

ANNOTATE: Have students mark details in paragraph 78 that indicate Scrooge's transformation is going beyond him being a nicer employer, or have students participate while you highlight them.

QUESTION: Guide students to consider what these details might tell them. Ask what a reader can infer from these details, and accept student responses.

Possible response: Scrooge is determined to do everything he can to lead a better life.

CONCLUDE: Help students to formulate conclusions about the importance of these details in the text. Ask students why the author might have included these details.

Possible response: These details show how much Scrooge has changed and indicates the kind of person he plans to be from now on.

Remind students that **conflict** is the struggle between opposing forces. There are two kinds of conflicts: internal and external. In an **external conflict**, a character struggles against another character, nature, or society. In an **internal conflict**, like Scrooge's, the character struggles against his or her own feelings. Note that earlier in the play, Scrooge knew nothing about Bob Cratchit's personal life, not even that he had many children. As a "new man," Scrooge clearly intends to be much more personally involved with Cratchit. Scrooge is no longer going to cut himself off from other people. His internal struggle is over.

NOTES

70 **Scrooge.** What do you mean by coming in here at this time of day, a full eighteen minutes late, Mr. Cratchit? Hallo, sir? Do you hear me?

71 **Bob.** I am very sorry, sir. I *am* behind my time.

72 **Scrooge.** You are? Yes, I certainly think you are. Step this way, sir, if you please . . .

73 **Bob.** It's only but once a year, sir . . . It shall not be repeated. I was making rather merry yesterday and into the night . . .

74 **Scrooge.** Now, I'll tell you what, Cratchit. I am not going to stand this sort of thing any longer. And therefore . . .

75 [*He stands and pokes his finger into* Bob's *chest.*]

76 I am . . . about . . . to . . . raise . . . your salary.

77 **Bob.** Oh, no, sir. I . . . [*Realizes*] what did you say, sir?

78 **Scrooge.** A Merry Christmas, Bob . . . [*He claps* Bob's *back.*] A merrier Christmas, Bob, my good fellow! than I have given you for many a year. I'll raise your salary and endeavor to assist your struggling family and we will discuss your affairs this very afternoon over a bowl of smoking bishop.[11] Bob! Make up the fires and buy another coal scuttle before you dot another i, Bob. It's too cold in this place! We need warmth and cheer, Bob Cratchit! Do you hear me? DO . . . YOU . . . HEAR . . . ME?

79 [Bob Cratchit *stands, smiles at* Scrooge*:* Bob Cratchit *faints. Blackout. As the main lights black out, a spotlight appears on* Scrooge*:* C. *Another on* Marley*: He talks directly to the audience.*]

80 **Marley.** Scrooge was better than his word. He did it all and **infinitely** more; and to Tiny Tim, who did NOT die, he was a second father. He became as good a friend, as good a master, as good a man, as the good old city knew, or any other good old city, town, or borough in the good old world. And it was always said of him that he knew how to keep Christmas well, if any man alive possessed the knowledge. [*Pauses*] May that be truly said of us, and all of us. And so, as Tiny Tim observed . . .

81 **Tiny Tim.** [*Atop* Scrooge's *shoulder*] God Bless Us, Every One . . .

82 [*Lights up on chorus, singing final Christmas Song.* Scrooge *and* Marley *and all spirits and other characters of the play join in. When the song is over, the lights fade to black.*] ❧

11. smoking bishop a type of mulled wine or punch that was especially popular in Victorian England at Christmas time.

infinitely (IHN fuh niht lee) *adv.* enormously; remarkably

Comprehension Check

Complete the following items after you finish your first read.

1. Who is the second spirit that Scrooge encounters?

2. What does the Ghost of Christmas Present sprinkle on people in the street?

3. Who is the third spirit that Scrooge encounters?

4. What is the last thing the Ghost of Christmas Future shows Scrooge?

5. **Notebook** Write a brief summary of *A Christmas Carol: Scrooge and Marley*, Act II.

RESEARCH

Research to Clarify Choose at least one unfamiliar detail from the text. Briefly research that detail. In what way does the information you learned shed light on an aspect of the play?

DIGITAL PERSPECTIVES

Comprehension Check

Possible responses:

1. The Ghost of Christmas Present; Present
2. Kindness
3. The Ghost of Christmas Future; the Spirit of Christmas Yet to Come; Future
4. Scrooge's gravestone
5. Summaries will vary; however, students should include: Scrooge is visited by the second spirt—the Ghost of Christmas Present; the spirit takes Scrooge to Bob Cratchit's house, and Scrooge sees that the family is happy even though they are poor; the spirit tells Scrooge that unless the shadows he sees are altered, Cratchit's young son, Tiny Tim, will die; the spirit takes Scrooge to his nephew's house; Scrooge sees that, though Fred and his wife do not have money, they are very happy together; Scrooge next encounters the Ghost of Christmas Future, who shows Scrooge businessmen talking about a funeral no one wants to attend, three people who have been with a dying man whose possessions they took after the man died and are now selling, and, finally, Scrooge's gravestone; terrified, Scrooge swears he has changed; he wakes up in his bed on Christmas day; he embraces Christmas and is immediately nice to people; he sends a huge turkey to Bob Cratchit's house and goes to Fred's home, where he receives a warm welcome; the next day, he tells Cratchit he's going to raise his salary and help him with his family. Scrooge has completely transformed.

Research

Research to Clarify If students struggle to identify an unfamiliar detail, have them reread the play and notice an idea or concept that might be new to them, such as Victorian terms or customs.

PERSONALIZE FOR LEARNING

Challenge

Extend Ask students to consider what they think will happen next Christmas. Have them write 1–2 paragraphs describing Scrooge's Christmas one year after the story ends. How will he behave? What will he do and say? Remind them there is no right or wrong answer, but their responses should be based on what they've read.

Jump Start

CLOSE READ Have students consider the structure of this drama. Point out that this is Act II of the play. Ask students to suggest why the author of the play chose to end Act I where he did. What does this suggest about the author's intention in writing this play?

Close Read the Text

Walk students through the annotation model on the student page. Encourage them to complete items 2 and 3 on their own. Review and discuss the sections students have marked. If needed, continue to model close reading by using the Annotation Highlights in the Interactive Teacher's Edition.

Analyze the Text

Possible responses:

1. (a) Scrooge is happy at the end of the play because he realizes what it feels like to be kind to others and receive kindness in return. (b) I think Scrooge will live up to his promise very well. He was transformed into a new person by the end of the play. (c) Marley talks about Scrooge at the end of the play and explains how Scrooge became a good man and acted on his word. **DOK 2**
2. Yes, I think they do the right thing by forgiving Scrooge immediately. They are setting an example by being good people and also showing trust that some people can truly change for the better when given the chance. **DOK 1**
3. Responses will vary. Students may conclude that learning to face an unpleasant future can cause a sudden change in someone's life. **DOK 4**

FORMATIVE ASSESSMENT

Analyze the Text

- **If** students fail to cite evidence, **then** remind them to support their ideas with specific information from the text.
- **If** students fail to grasp key ideas or events in the play, **then** have them discuss the plot, and illustrate with examples.

MAKING MEANING

A CHRISTMAS CAROL: SCROOGE AND MARLEY, ACT II

Close Read the Text

1. This model, from Scene 1, paragraph 18, shows two sample annotations, along with questions and conclusions. Close read the passage, and find another detail to annotate. Then, write a question and conclusion.

ANNOTATE: The words *flame, fireplace, burns, warming,* and *fire* appear in one sentence.

QUESTION: What effect is created with this word choice?

CONCLUDE: The Ghost of Christmas Present has brought warmth and comfort into Scrooge's home.

Present is wearing a simple green robe.... Suddenly, there is a mighty roar of flame in the fireplace and now the hearth burns with a lavish, warming fire. There is an ancient scabbard girdling the Ghost's middle, but without sword. The sheath is gone to rust.

ANNOTATE: The Ghost of Christmas Present wears a rusty scabbard and there is no sword in it.

QUESTION: What idea is being conveyed by these details?

CONCLUDE: The Ghost of Christmas Present represents peace.

Tool Kit
Close-Read Guide and Model Annotation

2. For more practice, go back into the text and complete the close read notes.
3. Revisit a section of the text you found important during your first read. Read this section closely and **annotate** what you notice. Ask yourself **questions** such as "Why did the author make this choice?" What can you **conclude**?

Analyze the Text

CITE TEXTUAL EVIDENCE to support your answers.

Notebook Respond to these questions.

1. (a) **Analyze** Why is Scrooge happy at the end of the play? (b) **Predict** How well do you think Scrooge will live up to his promise to learn his "lessons"? (c) **Support** What details in Act II support your prediction?
2. **Take a Position** Do you think Cratchit and Scrooge's nephew do the right thing by forgiving Scrooge immediately? Explain.
3. **Essential Question** *What can cause a sudden change in someone's life?* What have you learned about what can cause a sudden change in someone's life by reading Act II of this play?

STANDARDS
Reading Literature
- Cite several pieces of textual evidence to support analysis of what the text says explicitly as well as inferences drawn from the text.
- Analyze how particular elements of a story or drama interact.
- Analyze how a drama's or poem's form or structure contributes to its meaning.

292 UNIT 3 • TURNING POINTS

PERSONALIZE FOR LEARNING

Strategic Support

Extend Review "Man's children" (Ignorance and Want) clinging to the Spirit of Christmas Present. What does this symbolize? Have students identify some of Man's other "children" that might cling to this Spirit. Why does Man have so many of these "children"?

Analyze Craft and Structure

Text Structure: Stage Directions The written text of a play is called a **script.** The two main parts of a script are **dialogue,** or conversations between characters, and stage directions. **Stage directions** instruct actors on how to move and speak, or they describe what the stage should look and sound like. If you are reading a play instead of watching a performance, you get certain information *only* from the stage directions. Stage directions are usually written in italic type and set off by brackets or parentheses.

Stage directions are the playwright's instructions to the director and actors to guide them in performing and interpreting the script. Through stage directions, playwrights convey important information about:

- the setting and the context
- the scenery, lighting, and sound effects
- the behavior and actions of the actors
- the ways in which actors should deliver lines

Practice

CITE TEXTUAL EVIDENCE to support your answers.

Use the chart to analyze the playwright's use of stage directions in Act II of *A Christmas Carol: Scrooge and Marley*. In the center column, identify key details that are important to understanding the stage direction; for example, the actors involved or the types of sound effects. In the right column, summarize what you learn from the stage direction; for example, how the characters feel or move.

STAGE DIRECTION	KEY DETAILS	WHAT YOU LEARN FROM IT
[Lights. Choral music is sung….the audience directly.] (Scene 1, paragraph 1)	a. See possible responses in the Teacher's Edition.	b.
[Church bells toll….are alone again.] (Scene 2, paragraph 19)	c.	d.
[Jacob Marley laughs…They laugh, anxious.] (Scene 4, paragraph 71)	e.	f.

PERSONALIZE FOR LEARNING

English Language Support

Understanding Stage Directions Have students reread Act II, Scene 2, lines 1–15.

Have students identify the stage directions in these lines. Ask them how they recognize that these are stage directions. **EMERGING**

Ask students to identify one stage direction that gives information about a character's action, and another one that gives information about the setting or the scene. **EXPANDING**

Ask students to write a stage direction explaining what happens in Scene II. **BRIDGING**

An expanded **English Language Support Lesson** on Stage Directions is available in the Interactive Teacher's Edition.

DIGITAL PERSPECTIVES 

Analyze Craft and Structure

Review and reinforce the importance of stage directions in a play. Point out that stage directions are an opportunity for a playwright to show instead of tell. For example, instead of having a character say "I'm angry," the playwright can write a stage direction having that character silently slamming his fist on a table. For more support, see **Analyze Craft and Structure: Stage Directions.**

MAKE IT INTERACTIVE

Have students write a short scene in which two characters have an interaction that is expressed mainly through stage directions.

Possible responses:

[Lee is seated at a table, studying. Laura enters.]

Lee: Sorry about yesterday. Still angry?

Laura: No. [*She deliberately drops her heavy book on the table.*]

Lee: Are you sure?

Laura: Yes. [*She opens her book, then slams it shut.*]

Lee: Still friends?

Laura: Sure. [*She scoops up her books and strides out.*]

Practice

Possible responses:

a. Scrooge is in bed. Marley shoots fire from his hand. Marley appears in one place and then, instantly, in another.

b. Marley has magical powers. He is about to interact with Scrooge.

c. Chorus is on stage, church bells ring, and shop doors close. They disappear, leaving Scrooge and Marley on stage.

d. Stores are closing for the holiday.

e. Marley disappears. Future shows Scrooge scoundrels and then a group rushes on stage, frightened by an old man.

f. Scrooge faces his future alone, and it is scary.

FORMATIVE ASSESSMENT

Analyze Craft and Structure

- **If** students have difficulty identifying stage directions in the play, **then** show them pages from the text and point out the stage directions and how they are formatted.
- **If** students have difficulty understanding how stage directions reveal character, **then** review particularly revealing stage directions and discuss what they say about the character they relate to.

For Reteach and Practice, see **Analyze Craft and Structure: Stage Directions (RP).**

Concept Vocabulary

Why These Words?

Possible responses:

1. The concept vocabulary helps sharpen the reader's understanding of how Scrooge changes because these words express ways that people can change and the effects of people changing.
2. *lesson* (Scene 1, paragraph 24; Scene 4, paragraphs 116 and 161); *profit* (Scene 1, paragraph 24)

Practice

Possible responses:

1. Two people on *parallel* paths in their lives are a doctor and a veterinarian.; People who experience an unexpected act of kindness might be *altered* and decide to do something they've never previously done.; I would like to *strive* to tease my brother less.; A fear of dogs might be *dispelled* by getting to know one dog really well.; An *earnest* person is serious about what he or she says. An insincere person is not.; Someone who is *infinitely* generous would always help others.
2. Two people on *similar* paths in their lives are a doctor and a veterinarian.; People who experience an unexpected act of kindness might be *transformed* and decide to do something they've never previously done.; I would like to *try* to tease my brother less.; A fear of dogs might be *eliminated* by getting to know one dog really well.; A *sincere* person is serious about what he or she says. An insincere person is not.; Someone who is always generous would *always* help others. The replacement words do not change the sentences that much and might have only a slightly different meaning.

Word Network

Possible words: *astonish, compulsion, fearful, hope*

Word Study

For more support, see **Concept Vocabulary and Word Study**.

Possible responses:

1. One common example of *parallel* lines is railroad tracks.
2. *paraprofessional*: a trained aide who assists a professional person (as a teacher or doctor) Many law firms hire *paraprofessionals* with legal training to help the lawyers on staff. *paramedical*: concerned with supplementing the work of highly trained medical professionals. A person with *paramedical* training can be of great help to injured people during a disaster.

LANGUAGE DEVELOPMENT

A CHRISTMAS CAROL: SCROOGE AND MARLEY, ACT II

Concept Vocabulary

parallel	strive	earnest
altered	dispelled	infinitely

Why These Words? The concept vocabulary words relate to Scrooge's transforming character and personality. For example, after the Spirits' visits he is an *altered* man who is *infinitely* more pleasant and willing to help other people.

1. How does the concept vocabulary sharpen the reader's understanding of how Scrooge changes?
2. What other words in the selection describe Scrooge's change in character and personality?

Practice

Notebook Confirm the definitions for the six concept vocabulary words. Consult a dictionary as necessary to verify the meanings. Then, complete the activities.

1. Use each concept vocabulary word in a sentence that demonstrates its meaning.
2. Rewrite each sentence using a **synonym,** or word with a similar meaning, for the concept vocabulary word. How does the replacement change the meaning of the sentence?

WORD NETWORK

Add interesting words related to turning points from the text to your Word Network.

Word Study

Greek Prefix: *para-* The Greek prefix *para-* means "beside." In the word *parallel*, the prefix is combined with a Greek root that means "of one another." So, *parallel* means "beside one another." Two lines that are *parallel* extend in the same direction beside one another and are always the same distance apart.

1. Write your own sentence that correctly uses the word *parallel*.
2. Using a dictionary or thesaurus, find two other words or phrases that contain the Greek prefix *para-*. Record a definition for each word or phrase, and write a sentence that correctly uses it.

STANDARDS

Language

- Determine or clarify the meaning of unknown and multiple-meaning words and phrases based on *grade 7 reading and content,* choosing flexibly from a range of strategies.
  - b. Use common, grade-appropriate Greek or Latin affixes and roots as clues to the meaning of a word.
  - c. Consult general and specialized reference materials, both print and digital, to find the pronunciation of a word or determine or clarify its precise meaning or its part of speech.
  - d. Verify the preliminary determination of the meaning of a word or phrase.
- Demonstrate understanding of figurative language, word relationships, and nuances in word meanings.
  - b. Use the relationship between particular words to better understand each of the words.

FORMATIVE ASSESSMENT

Concept Vocabulary

If students fail to see the connection among the words, **then** have them use each word in a sentence and consider how the sentences are similar.

Word Study

If students have trouble finding appropriate words, **then** review using a dictionary to find words. For Reteach and Practice, see **Word Study: Greek Prefix *para-* (RP).**

Conventions

Sentence Structures In English, there are four types of sentence structure.

- A **simple sentence** consists of one independent clause—a group of words that has a subject and a verb and that can stand by itself as a complete thought.

  EXAMPLE: My cousin Tyrone and I are close friends.

- A **compound sentence** consists of two or more independent clauses linked by a conjunction such as *and, but,* or *or.*

  EXAMPLE: I like spending time with Tyrone, **and** we like doing the same things.

- A **complex sentence** contains one **independent clause** and one or more dependent clauses. A dependent clause is a group of words that has a subject and verb but is not a complete thought.

  EXAMPLE **Tyrone lives in my neighborhood,** although his house is not very close to mine.

- A **compound-complex sentence** consists of two or more **independent clauses** and one or more dependent clauses.

  EXAMPLE: **We often go to the park,** and, if we have all afternoon, **we might go to a movie.**

Read It

Reread these sentences from the selection. Identify each sentence structure, and then underline and label the clauses as independent or dependent.

1. He has the oddest ideas sometimes, but he seems all the while to be growing stronger and more hearty.
2. Tonight, if you have aught to teach me, let me profit by it.
3. The lights shift color again, the scrim flies away, and we are in the interior of the Cratchit family home.
4. I'll have the clock strike one and, when he awakes expecting my second messenger, there will be no one.

Write It

Notebook Write an example of each sentence type.

1. simple
2. compound
3. complex
4. compound-complex

STANDARDS

Language
Choose among simple, compound, complex, and compound-complex sentences to signal differing relationships among ideas.

PERSONALIZE FOR LEARNING

English Language Support

Subjects and Verbs Review with students that subjects perform the action in a sentence and verbs express the action that is performed. Show students simple sentences and have them identify the subject and verb in each. **ALL LEVELS**

DIGITAL PERSPECTIVES

Conventions

Sentence Structures Review simple, compound, complex, and compound-complex sentences. Also review independent and dependent clauses. For more support, see **Conventions: Sentence Structures.**

MAKE IT INTERACTIVE

Have students write an example of each type of sentence:

simple (It might rain today.)

compound (I am going to bed early because I am very tired.)

complex (Before crossing the street, Jason always looks both ways.)

compound-complex (After seeing the film, Renee told all her friends about it because she was sure they would enjoy it as much as she did.)

Read It

1. compound – He has the oddest ideas sometimes (independent), but he seems all the while to be growing stronger and more hearty (independent).
2. complex – Tonight, if you have aught to teach me (dependent), let me profit by it (dependent).
3. compound – The lights shift color again (independent), the scrim flies away (independent), and we are in the interior of the Cratchit family home (independent).
4. compound-complex – I'll have the clock strike one (independent) and, when he awakes expecting my second messenger (dependent), there will be no one (dependent).

Write It

Possible responses:

1. simple: Karen was surprised by the high number of people at the drama club auditions.
2. compound: People went on stage to audition one at a time and everyone was given five minutes.
3. complex: Russell wanted the lead part, which he was convinced he could do well.
4. compound-complex: Janet had rehearsed for days and, wanting to show her range of talent, she had chosen a scene in which she played two characters.

FORMATIVE ASSESSMENT

Conventions

- **If** students have trouble with sentence structures, **then** review each type of sentence and discuss how it is formed.
- **If** students have trouble identifying identify compound, complex, or compound-complex sentences, **then** review independent and dependent clauses.

For Reteach and Practice, see **Conventions: Sentence Structures (RP).**

Writing to Sources

Review the role of stage directions with students. Explain what role they have in a play. Stage directions can help readers understand the characters and actions in a play. Remind students to begin their essay by stating the central idea, and to support their central idea in each paragraph of the essay. Students should be sure to include details and examples from the play and remember to end their essay with a strong conclusion. For more support, see **Writing to Sources: Explanatory Essay**.

Vocabulary and Conventions Connection
Remind students that when they write their explanatory essay, they should try to include concept vocabulary words as well as a variety of vivid descriptive words.

Reflect on Your Writing

1. Responses will vary. Encourage students to be specific in their responses and to give a reason or reasons why it was easy or hard to find appropriate stage directions.
2. Responses will vary. Encourage students to be specific in their responses and to give a reason or reasons why their ideas about stage directions did or didn't change.
3. **Why These Words?** Responses will vary. Have students list specific words they chose that make their essay vivid.

FORMATIVE ASSESSMENT
Writing to Sources

If students have trouble writing about how the stage directions affected their understanding and enjoyment of the play, **then** ask them to tell you their response and give you reasons why they feel as they do. Then, have students write their ideas in paired sentences (how they feel/reason). For Reteach and Practice, see **Writing to Sources: Explanatory Essay (RP).**

EFFECTIVE EXPRESSION

A CHRISTMAS CAROL: SCROOGE AND MARLEY, ACT II

Writing to Sources

An **explanatory essay** defines, explains, or interprets ideas, events, or processes in an organized, logical way.

Assignment
Write an **explanatory essay** in which you analyze how the stage directions in *A Christmas Carol: Scrooge and Marley* enhance your understanding and enjoyment of the play. Be sure to provide details and specific examples from the play to support your ideas.

- Begin with an introductory paragraph in which you state the central idea of your essay.
- Organize your essay so that each paragraph or section clearly supports your central idea.
- Support your analysis with details, quotations, and examples from the play.
- Maintain a formal style in your writing, and use precise words and phrases that help your audience understand your ideas.
- Provide a conclusion that reinforces the explanation you present in your essay.

Vocabulary and Conventions Connection Consider including several of the concept vocabulary words in your essay. Also, remember to use a variety of sentence structures to make your writing more interesting.

parallel	strive	earnest
altered	dispelled	infinitely

Reflect on Your Writing

After you have written your essay, answer these questions.

1. Was it easy or difficult to find stage directions that helped you enjoy or understand the play?
2. Have your ideas about stage directions changed after writing this essay? Why, or why not?
3. **Why These Words?** The words you choose make a difference in your writing. Which words did you specifically choose to make your ideas clear?

STANDARDS
Writing
• Write informative/explanatory texts to examine a topic and convey ideas, concepts, and information through the selection, organization, and analysis of relevant content.
a. Introduce a topic clearly, previewing what is to follow; organize ideas, concepts, and information, using strategies such as definition, classification, comparison/contrast, and cause/effect; include formatting, graphics, and multimedia when useful to aiding comprehension.
b. Develop the topic with relevant facts, definitions, concrete details, quotations, or other information and examples.
d. Use precise language and domain-specific vocabulary to inform about or explain the topic.
e. Establish and maintain a formal style.
f. Provide a concluding statement or section that follows from and supports the information or explanation presented.
• Draw evidence from literary or informational texts to support analysis, reflection, and research.
a. Apply *grade 7 Reading standards* to literature.

PERSONALIZE FOR LEARNING

Challenge
Speculate Ask students to imagine a play that has no stage directions and to write a paragraph addressing the following questions. How would a lack of stage directions affect the reader? Would it make it easier or harder to understand or appreciate the play and its characters? Why?

Speaking and Listening

Costume plans provide descriptions and sketches or images of the clothing that actors will wear on stage during the performance of a drama. Costume plans should reflect the drama's setting as well as the vision of the playwright who created the characters.

Assignment

Work with a partner to conduct research on the clothing that was worn in Victorian-era England. Then, create and present **costume plans** for two different characters from *A Christmas Carol: Scrooge and Marley*.

1. **Analyze the Characters** Work with your partner to review the play and analyze the characters. Select two characters on which to focus. Take notes on the following details:
   - the social positions of the characters
   - how the season would influence the characters' clothing
2. **Conduct Research** Use the Internet and library resources to find information and visuals to accurately develop realistic costume plans for both characters. You will need to know:
   - the types of clothing the characters would have worn based on their social position
   - the types of clothing that were typically popular during the season
   - fabrics and materials that were available during the time period
3. **Develop Your Costume Plans** Use the information from your analysis and your research to create costume plans. In your plans, show and describe the types of clothing, including the colors and fabrics. Include pictures and sketches to illustrate your descriptions.
4. **Deliver Your Presentation**
   - Explain why you chose each costume.
   - Ask classmates for feedback about whether your costumes reflect what they imagined as they read the play.

PRESENTATION EVALUATION GUIDE

Rate each statement on a scale of 1 (not demonstrated) to 5 (demonstrated).

- ☐ The costume plans were creative and original.
- ☐ The costume plans accurately reflected both the characters and the time period.
- ☐ The speakers clearly explained the decisions behind each costume.
- ☐ The presentation was illustrated with pictures and sketches.

EVIDENCE LOG

Before moving on to a new selection, go to your Evidence Log and record what you've learned from *A Christmas Carol: Scrooge and Marley*, Act II.

STANDARDS

Writing

Conduct short research projects to answer a question, drawing on several sources and generating additional related, focused questions for further research and investigation.

Speaking and Listening

- Present claims and findings, emphasizing salient points in a focused, coherent manner with pertinent descriptions, facts, details, and examples; use appropriate eye contact, adequate volume, and clear pronunciation.
- Include multimedia components and visual displays in presentations to clarify claims and findings and emphasize salient points.

PERSONALIZE FOR LEARNING

Challenge

Speculate Ask students to imagine this play set in modern times and write 1–2 paragraphs revising their costume plan. How would the clothing they pick for the actors change? Why would they make these choices?

DIGITAL PERSPECTIVES

Speaking and Listening

1. **Analyze the Characters** Remind students that partners should focus on only two characters from the play. Remind them to pay attention to those characters' social positions and what they might wear during the Christmas season at that time.
2. **Conduct Research** Encourage students to use library resources as well as online research for information and images for their costume plans. You may wish to guide students by suggesting search terms for finding clothing styles, types, fabrics, etc., during the time period.
3. **Develop Your Costume Plans** Remind students to include detailed and informative visuals in their costume plans. Tell students that the more descriptive their information and visuals are, the more effective and interesting their costume plans will be.
4. **Deliver Your Presentation** Remind students to take their time when they give their presentations. They should also make sure everyone can clearly see any images they have. For more support, see **Speaking and Listening: Costume Plan**.

Evidence Log Support students in completing their Evidence Log. This paced activity will help prepare them for the Performance-Based Assessment at the end of the unit.

FORMATIVE ASSESSMENT

Speaking and Listening

- **If** students have trouble finding information, **then** suggest sources they can use.
- **If** students have trouble choosing two characters to focus on, **then** suggest to partners that they can decide on similar characters, contrasting characters, or characters of different gender or age.

For Reteach and Practice, see **Speaking and Listening: Costume Plan (RP).**

Selection Test

Administer the "A Christmas Carol: Scrooge and Marley, Act II (*with an excerpt from* Scrooge)" Selection Test, which is available in both print and digital formats online in Assessments.

from Scrooge

AUDIO SUMMARIES
Audio summaries of "Scrooge" are available online in both English and Spanish in the Interactive Teacher's Edition or Unit Resources. Assigning these summaries prior to reading the selection may help students build additional background knowledge and set a context for their first read.

Summary

This video is from an adaptation of *A Christmas Carol* called *Scrooge* (1935). In this section, the Ghost of Christmas Present takes Scrooge to see how his employee Bob Cratchit is celebrating Christmas with his family. Bob brings Tiny Tim home from church with him. The family jokes and laughs with each other. The goose they had bought for dinner arrives, and the family eats together. Scrooge is delighted to watch him. But the Ghost of Christmas Present tells him Tiny Tim will die. When Scrooge asks the spirit to spare Tiny Tim, the spirit quotes Scrooge's own words to him about how the deaths of poor people will help decrease the population. Scrooge seems ashamed of his words and sorry for the Cratchits. Mrs. Cratchit dislikes Scrooge, but Bob insists that the family drink to Scrooge's health; the family is very compassionate.

Insight

Scrooge comes to understand the consequences of his callousness. Reflecting on his earlier words, and the kindness of this family, helps him see the error of his ways.

ESSENTIAL QUESTION:
What can cause a sudden change in someone's life?

Connection to Essential Question

When the Ghost of Christmas Present tells Scrooge that Tiny Tim will not survive without help, it causes Scrooge to begin to feel sympathy. Scrooge's lack of feeling starts to disappear as he learns more about his own life.

WHOLE-CLASS LEARNING PERFORMANCE TASK
How does Scrooge's character transform over the course of the play?

UNIT PERFORMANCE-BASED ASSESSMENT
What can cause a significant change in someone's life?

Connection to Performance Tasks

Whole-Class Learning Performance Task Scrooge changes from cold and uncaring to kind.

Unit Performance-Based Assessment Understanding the circumstances, fears, joys, and hardships that other people face has made Scrooge less focused on himself and his wealth. He begins to care for others once he is shown how his actions affect them.

DIGITAL PERSPECTIVES

Audio

Video

Document

Annotation Highlights
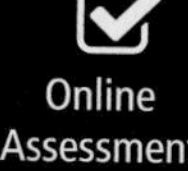
Online Assessment

LESSON RESOURCES

	Making Meaning	Language Development	Effective Expression
Lesson	**First Review and Close Review** **Analyze the Media**	**Media Vocabulary**	**Writing to Compare**
Instructional Standards	**RL.7.10** By the end of the year, read and comprehend literature . . . **L.7.6** Acquire and use accurately grade-appropriate general academic and domain-specific words and phrases . . . **RL.7.1** Cite several pieces of textual evidence . . .	**L.7.6** Acquire and use accurately grade-appropriate general academic and domain-specific words and phrases . . .	**RL.7.7** Compare and contrast a written story . . . **W.7.2** Write informative/explanatory texts . . . **W.7.2.b** Develop the topic . . . **W.7.2.d** Use precise language . . . **W.7.2.f** Provide a concluding statement . . . **W.7.9** Draw evidence from literary . . . **W.7.9.a** Apply *grade 7 Reading standards* to literature . . . **SL.7.2** Analyze the main ideas and supporting details . . . **W.7.4** Produce clear and coherent writing . . .
STUDENT RESOURCES			
Available online in the Interactive Student Edition or Unit Resources	Selection Audio First-Review and Close-Review Guide: Media: Video		Evidence Log
TEACHER RESOURCES			
Selection Resources Available online in the Interactive Teacher's Edition or Unit Resources	Audio Summaries: English and Spanish First Review Extension Questions	Media Vocabulary	Writing to Compare: Essay
My Resources	A Unit 3 Answer Key is available online and in the Interactive Teacher's Edition.		

Media Complexity Rubric: *from* Scrooge

Quantitative Measures	
Format and Length: Approximately 9 minute movie clip	
Qualitative Measures	
Knowledge Demands ① ② ❸ ④ ⑤	To fully understand the movie clip, prior knowledge is needed about the novella, *A Christmas Carol*.
Structure ① ❷ ③ ④ ⑤	The movie clip closely follows the novella's narrative in which the Ghost of Christmas Present takes Scrooge to the Cratchit home during their Christmas dinner.
Language Conventionality and Clarity ① ② ③ ❹ ⑤	The dialogue in the movie clip contains sophisticated language and challenging vocabulary with antiquated, British dialect.
Levels of Meaning/Purpose ① ② ❸ ④ ⑤	Meaning and concepts are allegorical, but easy to grasp.

TEACHING

Jump Start

FIRST REVIEW In *A Christmas Carol: Scrooge and Marley*, students read about a character who reaches a major turning point in his life. Now they're going to watch a scene from a film version of the same story. Engage students in a discussion about how seeing a movie version of a story might be different from reading the story.

Scrooge

What advantages might there be for telling a story through film? What are the disadvantages? How are the film and the play different? Modeling questions such as these will help students connect the scene from *Scrooge* to the Whole-Class Performance Task assignment. Selection audio is available in the Interactive Teacher's Edition.

Project the video in class or ask students to open the video in their interactive textbooks.

Media Vocabulary

Encourage students to discuss the media vocabulary. Have they seen or used these terms or concepts before? Do they use any of them in their speech or writing? Encourage students to explain how film might be an to advantage when telling a story.

FIRST REVIEW

Have students perform the steps of the first review independently.

WATCH: Students should pay attention to how the screenplay, the actors' performances, and editing are used to bring the story to life.

NOTE: Students should note the time stamp of any scenes or moments they find especially powerful or important.

CONNECT: Encourage students to increase their understanding by connecting the film, its performances, and editing to other media they have seen or heard.

RESPOND: Students will answer questions to demonstrate understanding.

Point out to students that while they will complete the Respond step at the end of the first review, the other steps will probably happen somewhat concurrently. You may wish to print copies of the **First-Review Guide: Media: Video** for students to use.

MAKING MEANING

A CHRISTMAS CAROL: SCROOGE AND MARLEY

Comparing Text to Media

In this lesson, you will watch a clip from the film *Scrooge*. You will then compare the film clip to the written dramatic adaptation of *A Christmas Carol: Scrooge and Marley.* While watching the film clip, note the differences in how each medium—text and film—tells the story.

from SCROOGE

from Scrooge

Media Vocabulary

The following words or concepts will be useful to you as you analyze, discuss, and write about media.

screenplay: the written script of a film, including acting instructions and scene directions	All films begin with a screenplay, including those based on other works.
director: the creative artist responsible for interpreting the screenplay	The director is responsible for the film's visual and dramatic effect on an audience.
performance: an actor's portrayal of a character	An actor's performance affects how the audience responds to a character.
editing: how separate shots filmed during production are arranged to tell a story, add suspense, and set pacing	An editor combines, rearranges, and cuts film and adds things, such as music and special effects.

First Review MEDIA: VIDEO

Apply these strategies as you watch the video. Be sure to note time codes so you can revisit specific sections later.

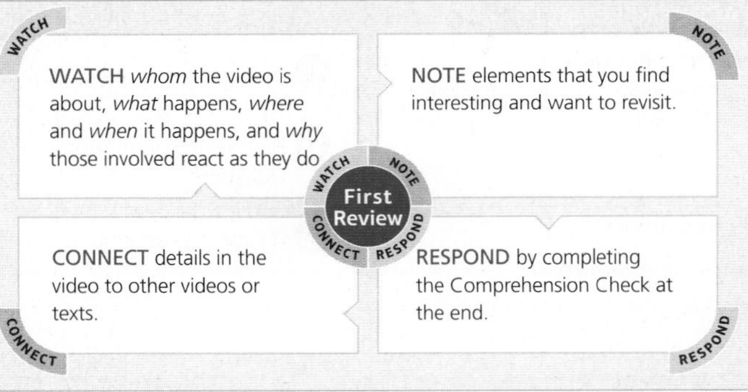

STANDARDS

Reading Literature
By the end of the year, read and comprehend literature, including stories, dramas, and poems, in the grades 6–8 text complexity band proficiently, with scaffolding as needed at the high end of the range.

Language
Acquire and use accurately grade-appropriate general academic and domain-specific words and phrases; gather vocabulary knowledge when considering a word or phrase important to comprehension or expression.

MEDIA | FILM

from Scrooge

Directed by Henry Edwards

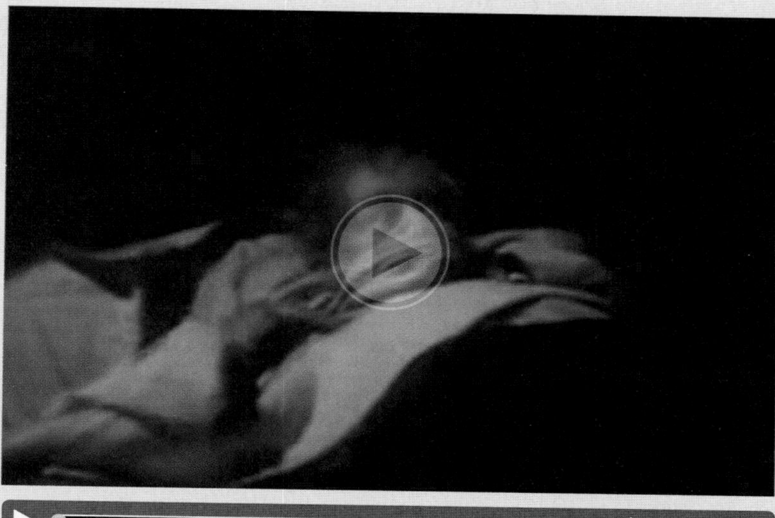

BACKGROUND

Charles Dickens first published *A Christmas Carol* in 1843. The novella was an instant success and has become a holiday classic. *A Christmas Carol* has inspired many television and film adaptations, including this 1935 British film *Scrooge*. The title role of Ebenezer Scrooge is played by Seymour Hicks, a British actor, playwright, and producer.

NOTES

DIGITAL PERSPECTIVES

Enriching the Selection To help students better understand how movies are made, use the search term "filmmaking" to find video footage online showing the process. (Note: Be sure to preview any video before showing it to students.) Have students discuss what they see and hear in the video and how this helps them understand and appreciate the film *Scrooge*. Then, have students write a paragraph summarizing their ideas about how the video about filmmaking in general related to *A Christmas Carol*.

Comprehension Check

Possible responses:

1. The clip shows the moment in the play when Scrooge wakes up to find he is in the presence of the ghost of Christmas Present. The ghost takes him to observe Bob Cratchit and his family enjoying their Christmas meal.
2. Martha hides and the family tells Bob Cratchit that Martha won't be joining them for Christmas dinner. Then Martha surprises her father and Tiny Tim by coming out from her hiding place.
3. Cratchit says Tiny Tim is growing stronger. Although Mrs Cratchit says that she wishes she could believe him, she doesn't.
4. I think the actor who plays Bob Cratchit gives the most engaging performance. He is so happy to be with his family and have a Christmas dinner with everyone around him and shows his excitement by his movements and the tone of his voice.

Research

Research to Clarify If students struggle to choose one of the three elements, have them rewatch the scene and notice an idea or concept that might be new to them, such as the characters' tones of voice, camera angles, or how clips are arranged.

Comprehension Check

Complete the following items after you finish your first review.

1. What part of the story does the film clip show?

2. What joke does the Cratchit family play on Bob Cratchit when he returns home?

3. What hopeful statement does Cratchit make about Tiny Tim? Does Mrs. Cratchit agree with him?

4. **Notebook** Write a few sentences in which you explain which actor you think gives the most engaging performance in the film clip.

RESEARCH

Research to Clarify Choose one element of the film, such as the direction, performance, or editing. Briefly research that element. In what way does the information you learned shed light on the experience of watching the film?

300 UNIT 3 • TURNING POINTS

PERSONALIZE FOR LEARNING

Challenge

Research Encourage students to conduct research on a different element of the film than the one they chose for the "Research to Clarify" activity and write a brief report on this aspect of filmmaking. In their report, students should answer the following questions: Does knowing about this additional element of filmmaking increase your understanding of or appreciation for the selection? In what way?

Close Review

Watch the excerpt from *Scrooge* again. Write any new observations that seem important. What **questions** do you have? What can you **conclude**?

from SCROOGE

Analyze the Media

CITE TEXTUAL EVIDENCE to support your answers.

Notebook Complete the activities.

1. (a) **Interpret** What do you think the Ghost of Christmas Present means when he says Scrooge may be "more worthless than millions"? (b) **Make Inferences** Based on the details in the clip, do you think Scrooge understands and appreciates the Ghost's meaning? Why or why not?
2. **Essential Question:** ***What can cause a sudden change in someone's life?*** What have you learned about what can cause a sudden change in someone's life by watching *Scrooge*?

LANGUAGE DEVELOPMENT

Media Vocabulary

screenplay	director
performance	editing

Use the vocabulary words in your responses to the questions.

1. Identify something that a film can allow viewers to see or experience that a text version of the same story would not.
2. How did the film portray the Cratchit family?
3. How did the film clip capture the experience of both Scrooge and the Cratchit family?
4. Do you think the film clip portrayed the story accurately and realistically? Why or why not?

STANDARDS

Reading Literature
Cite several pieces of textual evidence to support analysis of what the text says explicitly as well as inferences drawn from the text.

Language
Acquire and use accurately grade-appropriate general academic and domain-specific words and phrases; gather vocabulary knowledge when considering a word or phrase important to comprehension or expression.

DIGITAL PERSPECTIVES

Jump Start

CLOSE REVIEW Ask students to identify their favorite part of the film excerpt and explain why they liked it. How does the scene or moment in the film compare with the scene or moment in the play?

Close Review

If needed, model close reviewing by using the Closer Review notes in the Interactive Teacher's Edition.

Remind students to use Accountable Talk in their discussions and to support one another as they complete the close review. You may wish to print copies of the **Close-Review Guide: Media: Video** for students to use.

Analyze the Media

1. (a) I think that the Ghost of Christmas Present means to remind Scrooge of all the times he said the poor weren't worth anything, even though he didn't know them. "More worthless than millions" I think means Scrooge is less deserving to live than all of these other people are because he has been a terrible person. (b) Yes, I think Scrooge understands and appreciates the Ghost's meaning because he realizes how terrible it was to suggest the poor people weren't worth anything.
2. Responses will vary.

Media Vocabulary

For more support, see **Media Vocabulary.**

Possible responses:

1. A film can show the expressions of the characters and how they interact.
2. The film portrayed the Cratchit family as close, loving, kind, and caring to each other.
3. The film was effective in showing how the Cratchit family was able to remain as happy as it could be, even with Tiny Tim being in poor health. The film captured Scrooge's experience by thoughtfully showing his emotions while he was looking at and reflecting on his life.
4. Yes, I think the film clip portrayed the story accurately and realistically, as far as the real people were concerned. The film stayed true to the story.

FORMATIVE ASSESSMENT

Analyze the Media

If students struggle to close review the film, **then** provide the Analyze the Media questions available online in the Interactive Teacher's Edition or Unit Resources. Answers and DOK levels are also available.

Media Vocabulary

If students struggle to answer the media vocabulary questions, **then** review relevant parts of the film and point out how the film demonstrates or relates to the terms and concepts in the media vocabulary.

TEACHING

Writing to Compare

As students prepare to compare the play *A Christmas Carol: Scrooge and Marley* with the excerpt from the film Scrooge, remind them to think about how each version presents the same story and how the written play and film version are similar and different.

Planning and Prewriting

Compare Play and Film Techniques Ask students to refer to the chart as they analyze characters, setting, and mood in the play and in the film. Have them consider the questions in the chart in order to compare techniques used fro the same story in each medium.

Possible responses:

1. I think the play allows the reader's imagination to fill in details, because readers will have their own ideas about how the characters look, what the places look like, and what the mood of each scene is based on stage directions.
2. The film version for me is more effective because I can see the characters' facial expressions, see how the characters interact with one another, and have a better picture of life as it was at that time. I also think that the emotions Scrooge experiences have more impact in the film than in the play.

EFFECTIVE EXPRESSION

A CHRISTMAS CAROL: SCROOGE AND MARLEY

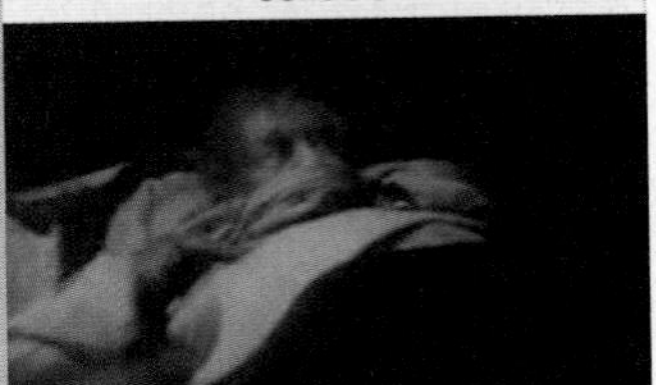
from SCROOGE

Writing to Compare

Both the drama *A Christmas Carol: Scrooge and Marley* and the film *Scrooge* tell the same story, but they reflect the use of different techniques that are unique to each medium. To compare reading the play with watching the film, look for similarities and differences in how the two mediums present the same subject.

Assignment

Write a **comparison-and-contrast essay** in which you analyze the similarities and differences between the two versions of Charles Dickens's famous novel. Describe the techniques unique to each medium, and conclude your essay by explaining which adaptation you think is more effective.

Planning and Prewriting

Compare Play and Film Techniques Discuss the techniques used in the play and in the film to tell the same story. Use the chart below to guide your analysis of the two mediums. Identify the similarities and differences in the ways the play and the film develop characters, setting, and mood.

	PLAY	FILM
Characters	How are characters described and developed?	How do actors' performances develop the characters?
Setting	How do stage directions convey the setting?	What setting details have the greatest impact on the viewer?
Mood	How does the playwright create the mood, or atmosphere, in different scenes?	How do lighting, editing, directing, and sound effects create the mood in different scenes?

Notebook Respond to these questions.

1. Which medium, written drama or film, gives the audience's imagination more room to fill in details? Explain.
2. Which version of this story is more effective? Why?

STANDARDS

Reading Literature
Compare and contrast a written story, drama, or poem to its audio, filmed, staged, or multimedia version, analyzing the effects of techniques unique to each medium.

Writing
- Write informative/explanatory texts to examine a topic and convey ideas, concepts, and information through the selection, organization, and analysis of relevant content.
  b. Develop the topic with relevant facts, definitions, concrete details, quotations, or other information and examples.
- Draw evidence from literary or informational texts to support analysis, reflection, and research.
  a. Apply grade 7 *Reading standards* to literature.

Speaking and Listening
Analyze the main ideas and supporting details presented in diverse media and formats and explain how the ideas clarify a topic, text, or issue under study.

PERSONALIZE FOR LEARNING

English Language Support

Comparison Help students better understand how to compare two things by reviewing the uses and meanings of appropriate words and phrases: better; more; less; not as good as; didn't do as good a job; more effective; less effective; much better, much less effective; superior; inferior. **ALL LEVELS**

Drafting

Create an Outline There are two main ways to organize a comparison-and-contrast essay: the block method and the point-by-point method. If you choose the block method of comparison, you will write about each medium separately. If you choose the point-by-point method, each paragraph will analyze one feature as it is developed in both the play and the film. Create an outline, using one of the following models as a guide.

Block Method of Comparison

I. **Introduction** Present the topic and identify the two sources you will compare and contrast.
II. ***A Christmas Carol: Scrooge and Marley***
   A. Techniques used in the written play
   B. Strengths of the medium
   C. Limitations of the medium
III. **from *Scrooge***
   A. Techniques used in the film
   B. Strengths of the medium
   C. Limitations of the medium
IV. **Conclusion** Explain which version you think is more effective and why.

Point-by-Point Method of Comparison

I. **Introduction** Present the topic and identify the two sources you will compare and contrast.
II. **Characters**
   A. *A Christmas Carol: Scrooge and Marley*
   B. from *Scrooge*
III. **Setting**
   A. *A Christmas Carol: Scrooge and Marley*
   B. from *Scrooge*
IV. **Mood**
   A. *A Christmas Carol: Scrooge and Marley*
   B. from *Scrooge*
V. **Conclusion** Explain which version you think is more effective and why.

Use Precise Language When comparing a written play and a film, using precise language and technical vocabulary will enable you to accurately discuss your subjects. For example, when discussing the sounds in a film, you might use technical terms such as *soundtrack, dialogue,* and *sound effects.*

Support Your Conclusion In the final paragraph of your essay, present an evaluation in which you explain which medium tells the story more effectively. Support your evaluation with evidence.

Review, Revise, and Edit

Review the assignment to make sure your essay fulfills the requirements. Ask yourself:

- Does my essay have a clear organization that highlights the points of comparison?
- Are my ideas supported by relevant evidence?
- Does my conclusion state and support my evaluation as to which medium is more effective?
- Is my essay free from errors in spelling, punctuation, and grammar?

EVIDENCE LOG

Before moving on to a new selection, go to your Evidence Log and record what you've learned from the film clip from *Scrooge*.

STANDARDS

Reading Literature
Compare and contrast a written story, drama, or poem to its audio, filmed, staged, or multimedia version, analyzing the effects of techniques unique to each medium.

Writing
- Write informative/explanatory texts to examine a topic and convey ideas, concepts, and information through the selection, organization, and analysis of relevant content.
  d. Use precise language and domain-specific vocabulary to inform about or explain the topic.
  f. Provide a concluding statement or section that follows from and supports the information or explanation presented.
- Produce clear and coherent writing in which the development, organization, and style are appropriate to task, purpose, and audience.

DIGITAL PERSPECTIVES

Drafting

Create an Outline Refer students to the outline models on the student page and have them consider each method. Remind students that the block method has a separate analysis of each medium, while the point-by-point method analyzes both mediums feature-by-feature.

Also remind students that they need to include an evaluation in the final paragraph of their essay that explains whether they think the play or the film tells the story more effectively. Tell students to make sure that they have included evidence from both the play and the film to support their evaluation.

Use Precise Language Encourage students to think about the words and terms they will use in their analysis of the play and the film. Remind students that their writing will be more effective if they use technical terms specific to the film and precise language that is more specific to the play.

For more support, see **Writing to Compare: Comparison-and-Contrast Essay.**

Evidence Log Support students in completing their Evidence Log. This paced activity will help prepare them for the Performance-Based Assessment at the end of the unit.

FORMATIVE ASSESSMENT

Writing to Compare

If students are unable to find points of comparison or cite specific evidence, **then** have students skim *A Christmas Carol: Scrooge and Marley* and rewatch the film excerpt from *Scrooge* for ideas.

PERSONALIZE FOR LEARNING

Strategic Support

Characterization Help students understand characterization by discussing how the play and the film reveal and develop Scrooge's character. Are there aspects of his character revealed or developed in the play that are not revealed or developed in the film? Does the film show his character differently, or reveal aspects of his character that the play does not? Why might the play or the film do this differently?

Jump Start

Work with students to develop and articulate their ideas about turning points and the selections they read. Guide them with questions such as "Is change itself good or bad?" "How much does it matter what brings about a change?" "Can a turning point change someone without that person making an effort?" "What can happen to a person as a result of experiencing a turning point in life?" As students share, ask them to cite specific examples from the play or film to support their ideas.

Write an Explanatory Essay

Make sure students understand what they are being asked to do in the Assignment. Explain that they are being asked to write an explanatory cause-and-effect essay that discusses how Scrooge's character transforms over the course of the play and the film.

Students should complete the assignment using word processing software to take advantage of editing tools and features.

Elements of a Cause-and-Effect Essay

Remind students that a cause-and-effect essay, like any other explanatory text, must be well organized. Help them decide whether they will describe the cause first and effect second, start with an effect and explain its cause(s), or use some other organizational method. Point out that giving definitions for terms and explaining conditions can help introduce a topic and aid comprehension. Transitions such as *because, thus, first, next, as a result,* and *therefore* can help clarify the relationships between ideas and concepts within the essay.

MAKE IT INTERACTIVE

Project "At the Crossroads" from the Interactive Teacher's Edition and have students identify the elements of a cause-and-effect essay, such as introduction, cause, effect, evidence, examples, transition words and phrases, and concluding statement.

Academic Vocabulary

Ask students to describe how incorporating academic vocabulary words will help them explain the transformation of Scrooge's character.

PERFORMANCE TASK: WRITING FOCUS

WRITING TO SOURCES

- A CHRISTMAS CAROL: SCROOGE AND MARLEY
- *from* SCROOGE

Write an Explanatory Essay

You have just read and watched selections that relate to someone experiencing a turning point in life. In *A Christmas Carol: Scrooge and Marley* and in the clip from the film *Scrooge*, we meet Ebenezer Scrooge, a bitter miser who undergoes a transformation when he is visited by three spirits.

Assignment

Review the selections in this section, and analyze the ways in which specific events and experiences contribute to Scrooge's transformation. Then, write a **cause-and-effect essay** in which you address the following prompt:

> How does Scrooge's character transform over the course of the play?

ACADEMIC VOCABULARY

As you craft your essay, consider using some of the academic vocabulary you learned in the beginning of the unit.

contribute
consistent
maintain
observation
sufficient

Tool Kit

Student Model of an Informative/Explanatory Essay

Elements of a Cause-and-Effect Essay

A **cause-and-effect essay** explains why something happens or what happens as a result of something else. A successful cause-and-effect essay includes the following elements:

- an introduction that grabs readers' interest and a strong, insightful conclusion
- a well-defined central idea that is supported by textual evidence
- detailed analysis and factual explanations of events or experiences and the relationships among them
- a clear, logical organization with effective transitions that show causes and effects
- precise language and specific vocabulary that is appropriate to the topic and audience
- a formal style and an objective tone

Model Essay For a model of a well-crafted cause-and-effect essay, see the Launch Text, "At the Crossroads."

Challenge yourself to find all of the elements of a cause-and-effect essay in the text. You will have an opportunity to review these elements as you prepare to write your own essay.

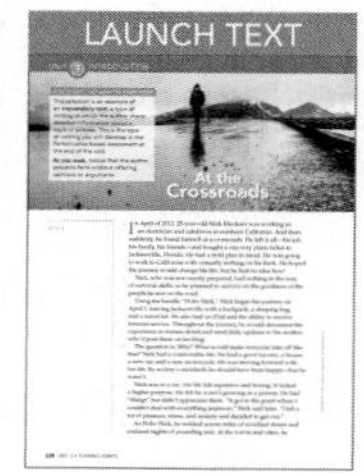

STANDARDS

Writing

- Write informative/explanatory texts to examine a topic and convey ideas, concepts, and information through the selection, organization, and analysis of relevant content.
- Write routinely over extended time frames and shorter time frames for a range of discipline-specific tasks, purposes, and audiences.

AUTHOR'S PERSPECTIVE **Kelly Gallagher, M.Ed.**

Revision E.B. White once said, "The best writing is rewriting." Unfortunately, many students come to us with the "I wrote it once; I'm done" philosophy. Demonstrate the importance of *revision* – making writing better by looking at it again – through teacher modeling. First, write with the class for eight minutes on a specific topic. Then, complete the activity with the class.

1. Display your first draft on the screen. Use think alouds as you use RADAR strategies for revision: REPLACE; ADD; DELETE; and REORDER. For each change you implement, mark the type of change you made.
2. Have students use the same process on their first drafts. Remind students that they will work on making their papers *correct* later; for now,

Prewriting / Planning

Develop Your Ideas To develop ideas for your essay, consider the various causes for and effects of the transformation in Scrooge's character over the course of the play. Review the play, and identify three key events or experiences that you think are most significant in bringing about this transformation. The topic web shown provides an example of causes and effects in the Launch Text. To develop your ideas, create a topic web for each key event and experience you will discuss in your essay.

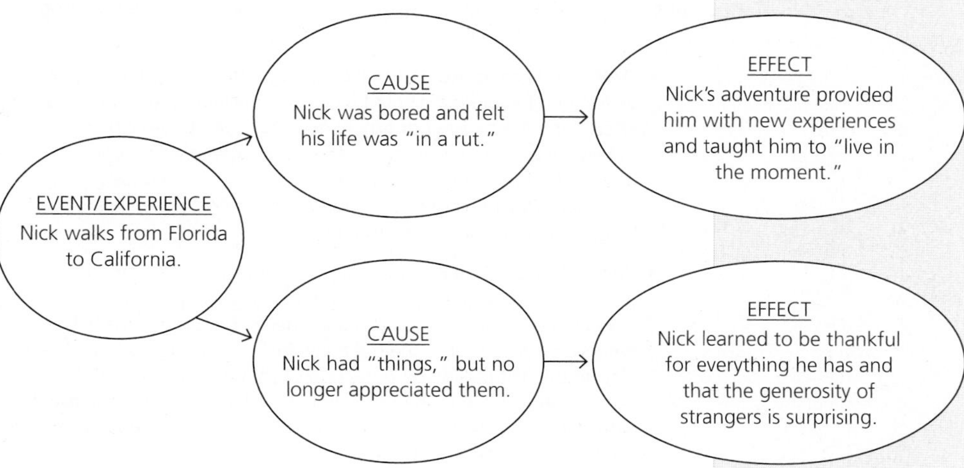

Connect Across Texts In order to effectively support the analysis you present, you will need relevant details, quotations, and examples from the selections. Review the texts that you have read so far in this unit, using your topic webs as a guide, and take notes on passages that strongly support the causes and effects on which you are focusing. Try to vary the ways in which you incorporate support. For example, you can use **direct quotations,** or the playwright's exact words, when these words are important to making your point. Alternatively, you can **paraphrase,** or restate in your own words, a complex idea or a broad example to make its importance clear to your audience.

EVIDENCE LOG

Review your Evidence Log and identify key details you may want to include in your essay.

STANDARDS

Writing

Write informative/explanatory texts to examine a topic and convey ideas, concepts, and information through the selection, organization, and analysis of relevant content.

a. Introduce a topic clearly, previewing what is to follow; organize ideas, concepts, and information, using strategies such as definition, classification, comparison/contrast, and cause/effect; include formatting, graphics, and multimedia when useful to aiding comprehension.

b. Develop the topic with relevant facts, definitions, concrete details, quotations, or other information and examples.

DIGITAL PERSPECTIVES

Prewriting/Planning

Develop Your Ideas Have students review the play, keeping in mind Scrooge's transformation and events that caused him to change so much. Have students refer to the example topic web as they begin to organize their ideas about the causes and effects of Scrooge's transformation.

See possible responses in the chart on the student page.

Connect Across Texts Remind students that they should always correctly and thoroughly attribute the source of text evidence. Quotations and paraphrases should be linked with the title of the work. When referring to something that takes place in both the drama and the film, the writer must make note of that fact.

they are to revise with the goal of being able to point out places where their second draft is better than their first.

Last, have students hold their two drafts side-by-side as you modeled, and indicate which RADaR strategies they used to revise their first drafts.

Drafting

Develop Your Introduction Remind students of the importance of a good introduction. It makes people want to read what comes next. Encourage students to include an engaging opening sentence to grab their readers' attention.

Organize Logically Remind students that they should decide how they are going to organize their explanation before they start writing. Tell students that they can organize causes and effects by order of importance or in chronological order. Once they have decided on an organizational structure, remind students that they should make sure to follow that structure throughout their draft.

Use Transitions Tell students that using transitions to show causes and effects in their writing will make their essays flow smoothly. Have them refer to the chart while writing about both causes and effects as they are drafting.

PERFORMANCE TASK: WRITING FOCUS

Drafting

Develop Your Introduction To introduce your topic and show why it is interesting, begin your essay with an engaging opening sentence. For example, you might begin with a rhetorical question or an interesting quotation. You should then provide a clear statement of your central idea as well as background information to establish context for your readers.

Organize Logically To help readers follow your explanation for the transformation of Scrooge's character, you must logically organize your ideas and information so that readers can easily follow the causes and effects of key events and experiences. To do so, use one of the following structures:

- **Order of Importance:** In this type of organization, each paragraph or section of your essay should focus on explaining the causes and effects of one key event or experience. You may choose either to begin with the most important event or experience in order to capture your readers' attention, or to arouse their curiosity by beginning with your least important event or experience and building toward your most important one.
- **Chronological Order:** This organizational structure is especially useful if your key events and experiences build on each other as a result of a sequence of causes and effects. First, sequence the events or experiences in the order in which they occurred in the play. In the first paragraph or section of your essay, explain the causes that resulted in the first event as well as the effects the event had—these effects serve as the cause for the event or experience you will discuss next, and so on.

Use Transitions Transition words and phrases will help you to explain the links between causes and effects and clarify the analysis on which your explanation is based. Incorporate transitions, such as the ones shown, to help your audience to follow your train of thought.

TO SHOW A CAUSE	*if, when, because of, since, due to, until, in order to, provided that*
TO SHOW AN EFFECT	*then, as a result, consequently, therefore, after, eventually*

STANDARDS

Writing

Write informative/explanatory texts to examine a topic and convey ideas, concepts, and information through the selection, organization, and analysis of relevant content.

a. Introduce a topic clearly, previewing what is to follow; organize ideas, concepts, and information, using strategies such as definition, classification, comparison/contrast, and cause/effect; include formatting, graphics, and multimedia when useful to aiding comprehension.

c. Use appropriate transitions to create cohesion and clarify the relationships among ideas and concepts.

AUTHOR'S PERSPECTIVE: **Jim Cummins, Ph.D.**

The Importance of Frequent Writing Writing on a daily basis for varied audiences is especially important for second language learners because it enables them to express their ideas and also brings home to them and their teachers what aspects of language they need assistance with. Frequent writing can be accomplished through a combination of low-stakes (informal, ungraded) and high stakes (formal, revised, graded) writing. Using this approach allows the teacher to nurture writing without needing to grade everything. Here are some suggestions for fostering regular writing:

- Do Quickwrites daily to review lessons and learning.
- Assign public writing, aimed at real audiences.
- Include personal writing, such as journals and diaries.
- Have students write reactions in response to their readings. Students can upload their reviews to class or school webpages.
- Have students write across genres. Try each one, having students pay attention to the conventions of each genre, such as stage directions in drama and dialogue in fiction. All genres have value; for example, poetry is powerful and likely easier for ESL students because of its condensed vocabulary. These assignments can be linked to word networks, too.

LANGUAGE DEVELOPMENT: CONVENTIONS

Revise Sentences to Heighten Interest

Playwrights, such as Israel Horovitz, typically use a variety of sentence structures in their writing to create interesting dialogue and effective stage directions. Use the following strategies to revise your sentences to create variety:

- Combine short, choppy sentences.
- Combine sentences that repeat ideas.
- Combine sentences to clarify the connections among ideas.

As you apply these strategies, use a variety of sentence structures.

Read It

These sentences from the Launch Text show how the author revised sentences to create variety by using the strategies listed.

PROBLEM	BEFORE REVISION	SOLUTION AND REVISION
short, choppy sentences	He had a good income. He had a house. He had a new car. He had a new motorcycle.	Combine ideas into one simple sentence by using a conjunction: ***He had a good income, a house, a new car, and a new motorcycle.***
two sentences that repeat an idea	By society's standards he should have been happy. He wasn't happy.	Use a compound sentence to combine sentences: ***By society's standards he should have been happy—but he wasn't.***
two sentences that lack a clear connection between ideas	In the towns and cities, he slept on the street. He knew people would help him out.	Use a complex sentence to clarify connections: ***In the towns and cities, he slept on the street, where he knew that there were people to help him out.***

Write It

As you draft your essay, use a variety of sentence structures to heighten readers' interest. Revise sentences, using the chart as a reference.

TIP

PUNCTUATION

Use dashes to indicate a quick break in thought and a return to that thought. *(I know—and I'm sure I'm right—who the culprit is.)*

STANDARDS

Writing

Write informative/explanatory texts to examine a topic and convey ideas, concepts, and information through the selection, organization, and analysis of relevant content.

d. Use precise language and domain-specific vocabulary to inform about or explain the topic.

Language

- Demonstrate command of the conventions of standard English grammar and usage when writing or speaking.
  b. Choose among simple, compound, complex, and compound-complex sentences to signal differing relationships among ideas.
- Use knowledge of language and its conventions when writing, speaking, reading, or listening.
  a. Choose language that expresses ideas precisely and concisely, recognizing and eliminating wordiness and redundancy.

DIGITAL PERSPECTIVES

Revise Sentences to Heighten Interest

Read It

Point out that one reason the Launch Text is interesting to read is the author's use of different sentence types. There are places in the Launch Text where the writer uses several short simple sentences in a row. However, the author does this to create a bouncy, engaging rhythm. Good writers are careful to use varied sentence structures to achieve specific effects. Remind students that readers will be more engaged by a variety of sentence types than a repetition of the same types of sentences. This is especially true if short, choppy sentences are repeated many times.

MAKE IT INTERACTIVE

Project these sentences from "At the Crossroads" from the Interactive Teacher's Edition and ask students to identify each sentence type.

He was going to walk to California with virtually nothing on his back. (simple)

He hoped the journey would change his life, but he had no idea how! (compound)

If he was offered money or a gift card he didn't need, he gave it away to people who did. (complex)

Nick, who was not exactly prepared, had nothing in the way of survival skills, so he planned to survive on the goodness of the people he met on the road. (compound-complex)

Write It

As students revise their draft, they should check to make sure they don't have too many of the same types of sentences. They should also revise short, choppy sentences by combining them.

PERSONALIZE FOR LEARNING

English Language Support

Revising Sentences Review with students how to combine short, choppy sentences. Provide the following sentences and have students revise them.

Janet likes her new skates. She uses them all the time.

It is raining today. We will have our picnic next Sunday.

I will study tonight. There will be an important test tomorrow.

I've already seen that film. I'm willing to see it again. **ALL LEVELS**

TEACHING

Revising

Evaluating Your Draft

Remind students that self-evaluation is an important step in the writing process. They should use the chart to determine what revision their draft requires in addition to the suggestions given here.

Revising for Focus and Organization

Review Your Conclusion Encourage students to read their conclusion to a partner or classmate to see if it adequately summarizes the writing and leaves a lasting impression. Also encourage students to ask the listener how the conclusion might be strengthened.

Use Domain-Specific Vocabulary Remind students to use signal words from the chart to make sure they are expressing their ideas about causes and effects clearly. Remind them that signal words and phrases can show how causes and effects relate, so they should choose their words carefully.

PERFORMANCE TASK: WRITING FOCUS

Revising

Evaluating Your Draft

Use the following checklist to evaluate your first draft. Then, use your evaluation and the instruction on this page to guide your revision.

FOCUS AND ORGANIZATION	EVIDENCE AND ELABORATION	CONVENTIONS
☐ Provides an engaging introduction and an insightful conclusion.	☐ Provides detailed analysis and factual explanations of events and experiences.	☐ Attends to the norms and conventions of the discipline, especially the correct use of a variety of sentence structures.
☐ Contains a clear statement of the central idea as well as the context surrounding it.	☐ Supports analysis and explanations with a variety of evidence.	☐ Establishes and maintains a formal style and objective tone.
☐ Uses a clear organization with effective transitions that show causes and effects.	☐ Uses precise language that is appropriate to audience and purpose.	

WORD NETWORK

Include interesting words from your Word Network in your essay.

STANDARDS

Writing

Write informative/explanatory texts to examine a topic and convey ideas, concepts, and information through the selection, organization, and analysis of relevant content.

d. Use precise language and domain-specific vocabulary to inform about or explain the topic.

f. Provide a concluding statement or section that follows from and supports the information or explanation presented.

Revising for Focus and Organization

Review Your Conclusion In a cause-and-effect essay, an effective conclusion not only summarizes the central idea, but it also provides new insight into the relationship between the causes and effects. The concluding section should suggest to readers how the ideas in your essay might deepen their understanding of the topic. Review your conclusion to be sure that it addresses the prompt, summarizes your central idea, and provides new insight into the subject matter.

Use Domain-Specific Vocabulary To express your thoughts as precisely as possible in your writing, it is important to choose the right words. You can use signal words and phrases to indicate your certainty of the validity of a particular cause or effect, or to show how important specific causes and effects are in relation to each other. Use signal words, such as the ones shown, to make your explanation clear and precise.

SIGNAL WORDS	
DEGREES OF CERTAINTY	*may, certainly, probably, necessarily, perhaps, definitely, without a doubt, conclusively, possibly, in some way*
LEVELS OF IMPORTANCE	*primarily, most important, equally relevant, fundamentally, of greater concern, meaningless, insignificant, secondary, lesser*

HOW LANGUAGE WORKS

Revising Sentences Review the four sentence types.

- Simple sentence – consists of one independent clause.
- Compound sentence – two or more independent clauses linked by a word such as *and, but,* or *or.*
- Complex sentence – one independent clause and one or more dependent clauses.
- Compound-complex – two or more independent clauses and one or more dependent clauses.

Have students identify the following sentences:

- Although he could appreciate the classical paintings, Robert decided he liked the modern ones most. (complex)
- Robert went to the museum on Saturday. (simple)
- Before he looked at the American paintings, Robert went to the sculpture garden, and he ate lunch there. (compound-complex)
- Robert enjoyed a pleasant lunch outdoors, and he was eager to see more art. (compound)

PEER REVIEW

Exchange essays with a classmate. Use the checklist to evaluate your classmate's essay and provide supportive feedback.

1. Is there an engaging introduction and an insightful conclusion?
   ☐ yes ☐ no If no, suggest that the writer add these elements.
2. Is there support from the selections for the writer's analysis and explanation?
   ☐ yes ☐ no If no, point out where the writer should provide support.
3. Is the essay logically organized so that the relationships between causes and effects are clear?
   ☐ yes ☐ no If no, point out where the writer should make these connections clearer.
4. What is the strongest part of your classmate's essay? Why?

____

____

Editing and Proofreading

Edit for Conventions Reread your draft for accuracy and consistency. Correct errors in grammar and word usage. Be sure you have maintained a formal style and an objective tone in your writing by identifying and replacing any slang terms, abbreviations, and casual expressions. Your essay should use academic language and vocabulary that conveys knowledge and credibility.

Proofread for Accuracy Read your draft carefully, looking for errors in spelling and punctuation. Pay careful attention to the punctuation, indentation, and capitalization of quotations. Use quotation marks to set off short quotations. Longer quotations of four or more lines should begin on a new line, be indented, and appear without quotation marks.

Publishing and Presenting

Create a final version of your essay and share it with your class by posting it on a class or school Web site. Then, review several classmates' essays, and respond online by leaving comments and suggestions. Remember to be respectful and polite when offering feedback.

Reflecting

Reflect on what you learned as you wrote your essay. How did writing about the events and experiences that caused Scrooge's transformation help to deepen your understanding of what defines a turning point in a person's life?

STANDARDS

Writing

- Write informative/explanatory texts to examine a topic and convey ideas, concepts, and information through the selection, organization, and analysis of relevant content.
  - e. Establish and maintain a formal style.
- With some guidance and support from peers and adults, develop and strengthen writing as needed by planning, revising, editing, rewriting, or trying a new approach, focusing on how well purpose and audience have been addressed.
- Use technology, including the Internet, to produce and publish writing and link to and cite sources as well as to interact and collaborate with others, including linking to and citing sources.

DIGITAL PERSPECTIVES

Peer Review

Before students begin their peer review, remind them that they are reviewing for clarity and completeness, not whether they agree or disagree with the writer's ideas. They should not comment on whether their classmate is "right" or "wrong." They should make helpful suggestions if they see something in the essay that could be better.

Editing and Proofreading

As students proofread, they should check for grammar, spelling, and punctuation errors. Remind them to check that all causes lead to logical, relevant effects, and all effects are linked to logical, relevant causes. Also remind students to check for a variety of sentence types.

Publishing and Presenting

Before students review their classmates' essays, remind them to:

- Be honest, but maintain a respectful tone in their comments.
- Use formal rather than informal language.
- Move the discussion forward by building on the ideas of others.
- Disagree respectfully. Different opinions are fine, but they should be expressed politely.
- Support their position with evidence if they disagree.

Reflecting

Encourage students to reflect not only on their essay and the process of writing it, but also on the comments they received.

PERSONALIZE FOR LEARNING

Challenge

Speculate Ask students to speculate on whether any other character in the play or film changes during or after the story. Have them write a paragraph identifying a character other than Scrooge who they think changes or will change. They should discuss why they think this character changes as well as how and when he or she changes.

OVERVIEW

SMALL-GROUP LEARNING

Essential Question

Explain that a sudden turning point may change how a person chooses to live from that moment forward. For example, the person may make choices about what to study and where to spend time that he or she would not have made before. During Small-Group Learning, students will read selections that reveal and describe personal turning points in people's lives and how their lives were changed forever.

Small-Group Learning Strategies

Review the Learning Strategies with students and explain that as they work through Small-Group Learning they will develop strategies to work in small-group environments.

- Have students watch the video on Small-Group Learning Strategies.
- A video on this topic is available online in the Professional Development Center.

You may wish to discuss some action items to add to the chart as a class before students complete it on their own. For example, for "Prepare," you might solicit the following action from students:

- Put away books, papers, and belongings that could distract you from group discussions.

Block Scheduling

Each day in this Pacing Plan represents a 40–50 minute class period. Teachers using block scheduling may combine days to reflect their class schedule. In addition, teachers may revise pacing to differentiate and support core instruction by integrating components and resources as students require.

OVERVIEW: SMALL-GROUP LEARNING

ESSENTIAL QUESTION:

What can cause a sudden change in someone's life?

Can someone's life change in the course of a day or even an hour or even a minute? Is it possible to wake up the next day and be a different person? You will read selections that talk about changes, both big and small. You will work in a group to continue your exploration of turning points.

Small-Group Learning Strategies

Throughout your life, in school, in your community, and in your career, you will continue to learn and work with others.

Look at these strategies and the actions you can take to practice them as you work in teams. Add ideas of your own for each step. Use these strategies during Small-Group Learning.

STRATEGY	ACTION PLAN
Prepare	• Complete your assignments so that you are prepared for group work. • Organize your thinking so you can contribute to your group's discussion. •
Participate fully	• Make eye contact to signal that you are listening and taking in what is being said. • Use text evidence when making a point. •
Support others	• Build off ideas from others in your group. • Invite others who have not yet spoken to do so. •
Clarify	• Paraphrase the ideas of others to ensure that your understanding is correct. • Ask follow-up questions. •

Pacing Plan

Introduce Whole-Class Learning

Unit Introduction

A *Christmas Carol: Scrooge and Marley*, Act I

A *Christmas Carol: Scrooge and Marley*, Act II

Media: *from* Scrooge

Performance Task

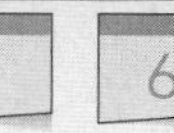

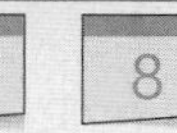
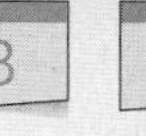

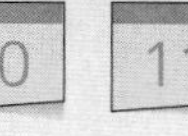

1 2 3 4 5 6 7 8 9 10 11 12 13 14 15 16 17 18

DIGITAL PERSPECTIVES

CONTENTS

SHORT STORY

Thank You, M'am

Langston Hughes

A chance encounter has a powerful impact.

MEMOIR

from An American Childhood

Annie Dillard

Some people suddenly realize that they are ready to grow up.

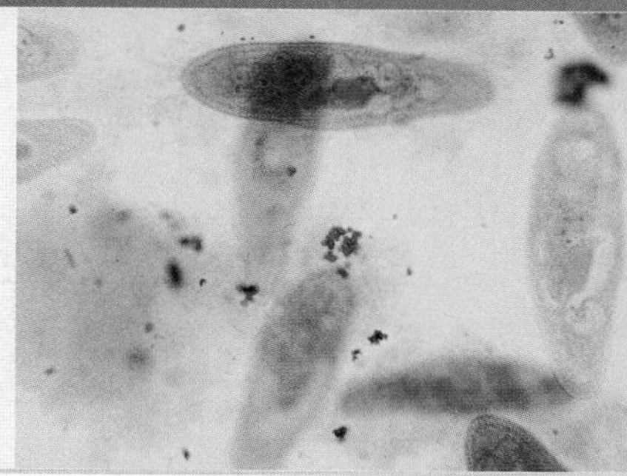

MEDIA: PHOTO GALLERY

Urban Farming Is Growing a Greener Future

Hillary Schwei

How can changes in our surroundings produce changes in ourselves?

PERFORMANCE TASK

SPEAKING AND LISTENING FOCUS

Present an Explanatory Essay

The Small-Group readings feature different turning points that have caused sudden changes—big and small—in people's thinking and their lives in general. After reading the selections, your group will plan and deliver a multimedia presentation about turning points.

Contents

Selections Circulate among groups as they preview the selections. You might encourage groups to discuss any knowledge they already have about any of the selections or the situations and settings shown in the photographs. Students may wish to take a poll within their group to determine which selections look the most interesting.

Remind students that communicating and collaborating in groups is an important skill that they will use throughout their lives—in school, in their careers, and in their community.

Performance Task

Present an Explanatory Essay Give groups time to read about and briefly discuss the multimedia presentation about turning points they will create after reading. Encourage students to do some preliminary thinking about the types of media they may want to use. This may help focus their subsequent reading and group discussion.

Introduce Small-Group Learning

Thank You, M'am

from An American Childhood

Media: Urban Farming Is Growing a Greener Future

Performance Task

Introduce Independent Learning

Independent Learning

Performance-Based Assessment

19 20 21 22 23 24 25 26 27 28 29 30 31 32 33 34 35 36

SMALL-GROUP LEARNING

OVERVIEW

SMALL-GROUP LEARNING

Working as a Team

1. **Take a Position** Remind groups to let all members share their responses. You may wish to set a time limit for this discussion.
2. **List Your Rules** You may want to have groups share their lists of rules and consolidate them into a master list to be displayed and followed by all groups.
3. **Apply the Rules** As you circulate among the groups, ensure that students are staying on task. Consider a short time limit for this step.
4. **Name Your Group** This task can be creative and fun. If students have trouble coming up with a name, suggest that they think of something related to the unit topic. Encourage groups to share their names with the class.
5. **Create a Communication Plan** Encourage groups to include in their plans agreed-upon times during the day to share ideas. They should also devise a method for recording and saving their communications.

Accountable Talk

Remind students that groups should communicate politely. You can post these Accountable Talk suggestions and encourage students to add their own. Students should:

Remember to . . .
Ask clarifying questions.

Which sounds like...
Can you please repeat what you said?
Would you give me an example?
I think you said _____. Did I understand you correctly?

Remember to . . .
Explain your thinking.

Which sounds like . . .
I believe _____ is true because _____.
I feel _____ because _____.

Remember to . . .
Build on the ideas of others.

Which sounds like . . .
When _____ said _____, it made me think of _____.

Working as a Team

1. **Take a Position** In your group, discuss the following question:

   Can people truly change?

   As you take turns sharing your positions, be sure to provide reasons for your choice. After all group members have shared, discuss the personality traits that would be necessary to realize such a genuine change.

2. **List Your Rules** As a group, decide on the rules that you will follow as you work together. Two samples are provided. Add two more of your own. You may add or revise rules based on your experience together.
   - Everyone should participate in group discussions.
   - People should not interrupt.
   - ______________________________
   - ______________________________

3. **Apply the Rules** Share what you have learned about turning points. Make sure each person in the group contributes. Take notes, and be prepared to share with the class one thing that you heard from another member of your group.

4. **Name Your Group** Choose a name that reflects the unit topic.

   Our group's name: ______________________________

5. **Create a Communication Plan** Decide how you want to communicate with one another. For example, you might use online collaboration tools, email, or instant messaging.

   Our group's decision: ______________________________

FACILITATING SMALL-GROUP LEARNING

Forming Groups You may wish to form groups for Small-Group Learning so that each consists of students with different learning abilities. Some students may be adept at organizing information whereas others may have strengths related to generating or synthesizing information. A good mix of abilities can make the experience of Small-Group Learning dynamic and productive.

Making a Schedule

First, find out the due dates for the small-group activities. Then, preview the texts and activities with your group, and make a schedule for completing the tasks.

SELECTION	ACTIVITIES	DUE DATE
Thank You, M'am		
from An American Childhood		
Urban Farming Is Growing a Greener Future		

Working on Group Projects

As your group works together, you'll find it more effective if each person has a specific role. Different projects require different roles. Before beginning a project, discuss the necessary roles and choose one for each group member. Here are some possible roles; add your own ideas.

Project Manager: monitors the schedule and keeps everyone on task
Researcher: organizes research activities
Recorder: takes notes during group meetings

____

____

____

____

____

DIGITAL PERSPECTIVES

Making a Schedule

Encourage groups to preview the reading selections and to consider how long it will take them to complete the activities accompanying each selection. Point out that they can adjust the due dates for particular selections as needed as they work on their small-group projects. However, they must complete all assigned tasks before the group Performance Task is due. Encourage groups to review their schedules when they complete the activities for each selection to make sure they are on track to meet the final due date.

Working on Group Projects

Point out to groups that the roles they assign can also be changed later. Students might have to make changes based on who is best at doing what. Try to make sure that there is no favoritism, cliquishness, or stereotyping by gender or other means in the assignment of roles.

Also, you should review the roles each group assigns to its members. Based on your understanding of students' individual strengths, you might find it necessary to suggest some changes.

AUTHOR'S PERSPECTIVE **Kelly Gallagher, M.Ed.**

The Teacher's Role After the ability to read and write, the skill that employers value most is successful collaboration. Talking with other people can help us all learn more, change our opinions, and make us more thoughtful because we are exposed to ideas that we may not have previously considered. Student collaboration also serves as a useful formative assessment tool. An effective strategy is to ask, "What is worth talking about?" Hearing what students noticed in a selection and what they've missed informs further instruction. Here are some additional strategies for encouraging effective collaboration:

- *Flow in and out of groups* as students work. Model meaningful talk, a lifelong literacy skill.
- *Take notes* on what is being said and what is being implied. See what prior knowledge individuals contribute.
- *Plan pathways for subsequent lessons* based on what you've observed.

Thank You, M'am

AUDIO SUMMARIES
Audio summaries of "Thank You M'am" are available online in both English and Spanish in the Interactive Teacher's Edition or Unit Resources. Assigning these summaries prior to reading the selection may help students build additional background knowledge and set a context for their first read.

Summary

In the short story "Thank You, M'am" by Langston Hughes, a boy named Roger attempts to steal a woman's purse so he can buy blue suede shoes. The woman's purse is so heavy that he can't take it. Instead, the woman, Mrs. Luella Bates Washington Jones, grabs Roger and does not let go. She drags him home with her and insists that he wash his face, then cooks him dinner. Mrs. Jones teaches Roger not to steal—and when he has a chance, he doesn't. She sends him home with money for shoes and on the promise that he will behave better.

Insight

This story shows a moment that seems to turn a boy's life around. Mrs. Jones shows him compassion, but also discipline and a strong sense of right and wrong.

ESSENTIAL QUESTION:
What can cause a sudden change in someone's life?

Connection to Essential Question

Roger's unexpected treatment changes his life. Mrs. Jones doesn't let him off the hook for what he tried to do, but *does* show him kindness he couldn't have expected along with a moral lesson.

SMALL-GROUP LEARNING PERFORMANCE TASK
How are the turning points in the selections similar to and different from each other?

UNIT PERFORMANCE-BASED ASSESSMENT
What can cause a significant change in someone's life?

Connection to Performance Tasks

Small-Group Learning Performance Task These turning points show how someone can get off a destructive, selfish path onto a better one.

Unit Performance-Based Assessment Mrs. Jones greatly changes Roger's life by giving him guidance he has never had.

DIGITAL PERSPECTIVES

 Audio  Video  Document  Annotation Highlights 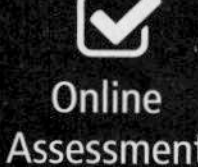 Online Assessment

LESSON RESOURCES

	Making Meaning	Language Development	Effective Expression
Lesson	**First Read** **Close Read** **Analyze the Text** **Analyze Craft and Structure**	**Concept Vocabulary** **Word Study** **Conventions**	**Writing to Sources**
Instructional Standards	**RL.7.10** By the end of the year, read and comprehend literature. . . **L.7.4.a** Use context as a clue . . . **RL.7.1** Cite several pieces of textual evidence to support . . . **RL.7.3** Analyze how particular elements of a story or drama interact.	**L.7.4** Determine or clarify the meaning of unknown and multiple-meaning words . . . **L.7.4.c** Consult general and specialized reference materials . . . **L.7.4.d** Verify the preliminary determination of the meaning . . . **L.7.1** Demonstrate command of the conventions of standard English . . . **L.7.1.a** Explain the function of phrases . . .	**W.7.3** Write narratives . . . **W.7.3.a** Engage and orient the reader . . . **W.7.3.c** Use a variety of transition words . . . **W.7.3.d** Use precise words and phrases . . . **SL.7.1** Engage effectively in a range of collaborative discussions . . . **SL.7.1.b** Follow rules for collegial discussions . . . **SL.7.1.d** Acknowledge new information . . .
STUDENT RESOURCES			
Available online in the Interactive Student Edition or Unit Resources	Selection Audio First-Read Guide: Fiction Close-Read Guide: Fiction	Word Network	Evidence Log
TEACHER RESOURCES			
Selection Resources Available online in the Interactive Teacher's Edition or Unit Resources	Audio Summaries: English and Spanish Annotation Highlights Accessible Leveled Text Spanish Translation Text Questions First Read Extension Questions Analyze Craft and Structure: Plot	Concept Vocabulary and Word Study Conventions: Prepositions and Prepositional Phrases	Writing to Sources: Journal Entry
Reteach/Practice (RP) Available online in the Interactive Teacher's Edition or Unit Resources	Analyze Craft and Structure: Plot (RP)	Word Study: Multiple-Meaning Words (RP) Conventions: Prepositions and Prepositional Phrases (RP)	Writing to Sources: Journal Entry (RP)
Assessment Available online in Assessments	Selection Test: English Selection Test: Spanish Extension Selection Test		
My Resources	A Unit 3 Answer Key is available online and in the Interactive Teacher's Edition.		

Reading Support

Text Complexity Rubric: Thank You, M'am	
Quantitative Measures	
Lexile: 800 Text Length: 1,347 words	
Qualitative Measures	
Knowledge Demands ① ❷ ③ ④ ⑤	The situation may be unfamiliar to some readers (a boy snatches a woman's purse and ends up learning a lesson from her), but the situations and emotions are clearly explained.
Structure ① ❷ ③ ④ ⑤	The selection is a linear narrative with a lot of dialogue.
Language Conventionality and Clarity ① ② ❸ ④ ⑤	This selection contains mostly simple sentence structure with urban dialect, and some slang; contains some ironic or sarcastic statements.
Levels of Meaning/Purpose ① ② ❸ ④ ⑤	Multiple levels of meaning (events are described that also signify the power of love, trust, and dignity); concepts and meanings are mostly explained and easy to grasp.

DECIDE AND PLAN

English Language Support

Provide English Learners with support for language and meaning as they read the selection.

Language Students may get confused reading passages with colloquial language, for example *The large woman simply turned around and kicked him right square in his blue-jeaned sitter.* (paragraph 1); Ask questions to guide students to understand the meaning of colloquial language.

Levels of Meaning/Purpose Help students to rephrase main ideas by pulling sentences from the reading. Write the sentences for reference. For example, *The woman did not watch the boy to see if he was going to run now, nor did she watch her purse which she left behind her on the day-bed.* Guide students to understand the deeper meaning of this gesture.

Strategic Support

Provide students with strategic support to ensure that they can successfully read the text.

Language Remind students that in the story they are about to read, they will find colloquial language and slang. Give an example from the story. Ask students how this language enhances the story and reveals the personality of the characters.

Levels of Meaning/Purpose If students have difficulty understanding the multiple levels of meaning, focus on individual paragraphs. Ask students to first state the events that happen. Then ask them to reread the paragraph to determine what feelings or ideas are conveyed by the actions of Mrs. Jones and Roger. For example, in paragraph 37, what is conveyed when Mrs. Jones leaves her purse where Roger could easily get it? (Trust)

Challenge

Provide students who need to be challenged with ideas for how they can go beyond a simple interpretation of the text.

Text Analysis Ask students to describe the conflict that Roger feels when he gets to Mrs. Jones's home. What are his choices at this point? Why does he choose to stay? How does Mrs. Jones's sharing her personal story about making poor choices when she was younger affect Roger?

Written Response Ask students to speculate on what happened after Roger left Mrs. Jones's home. What effect do they think the interaction between the two had on Roger's life? Have students write an ending to the story.

TEACH

Read and Respond

Have groups do their first read of the selection. Then have them complete their close read. Finally, work with them on the Making Meaning, Language Development, and Effective Expression activities.

Standards Support Through Teaching and Learning Cycle

IDENTIFY NEEDS

Analyze results of the Beginning-of-Year Assessment, focusing on the items relating to Unit 3. Also take into consideration student performance to this point and your observations of where particular students struggle.

DECIDE AND PLAN

- If students have performed poorly on items matching these standards, then provide selection scaffolds before assigning them the on-level lesson provided in the Student Edition.
- If students have done well on the Beginning-of-Year Assessment, then challenge them to keep progressing and learning by giving them opportunities to practice the skills in depth.
- Use the Selection Resources listed on the Planning pages for "Thank You, M'am" to help students continually improve their ability to master the standards.

Instructional Standards: Thank You, M'am

	Catching Up	This Year	Looking Forward
Reading	You may wish to administer the **Analyze Craft and Structure: Plot (RP)** worksheet to ensure students understand the elements of plot.	**RL.3** Analyze how particular elements of a story or drama interact.	Challenge students to draw plot maps for another story they know well.
Writing	You may wish to administer the **Writing to Sources: Journal Entry (RP)** worksheet to help students better understand the form.	**W.3** Write narratives to develop real or imagined experiences or events using effective technique, relevant descriptive details, and well-structured event sequences.	Encourage students to take their journals a step further by drawing plot maps for them.
Language	Review the **Word Study: Multiple-Meaning Words (RP)** worksheet with students to further explore multiple-meaning words. You may wish to administer the **Conventions: Prepositions and Prepositional Phrases (RP)** worksheet to help students better understand prepositional phrases.	**L.4.c** Consult general and specialized reference materials, both print and digital, to find the pronunciation of a word or determine or clarify its precise meaning or its part of speech. **L.1.a** Explain the function of phrases and clauses in general and their function in specific sentences.	Tell students to look up five common words to see if they also have multiple meanings. Challenge students to find sentences within the selection that do not use prepositions to demonstrate how common they are.

ANALYZE AND REVISE

- Analyze student work for evidence of student learning.
- Identify whether or not students have met the expectations in the standards.
- Identify implications for future instruction.

TEACH

Implement the planned lesson, and gather evidence of student learning.

FACILITATING

Jump Start

FIRST READ Why do people want what they want—even to the point of breaking the law? What causes a person's ideas about what is important to change? Engage students in a discussion about desire and change, which sets the context for reading "Thank You, M'am."

Thank You, M'am 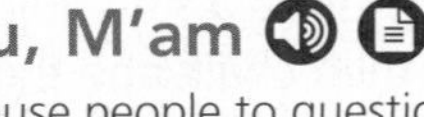

What events cause people to question, or even change, the path they have been on? Can people change in a moment, or only over time? Modeling questions such as these will help students connect to "Thank You, M'am" and to the Small-Group Performance Task assignment. Selection audio and print capability for the selection are available in the Interactive Teacher's Edition.

Concept Vocabulary

Ask groups to look closely at the three types of context clues—synonyms, restatements of ideas, and contrast of ideas and topics—and have group members take turns explaining how the example illustrates the context clue in each case. Encourage groups to think of one other type of context clue that they might encounter in a text. Possibilities include examples, cause-and-effect relationship, and definitions.

FIRST READ

Students should perform the steps of the first read independently.

NOTICE: Encourage students to notice passages that hint at each character's background and help explain each character's motivations.

ANNOTATE: Remind students to mark passages that suggest a turning point or change in one or more of the character's attitudes.

CONNECT: Try to connect each character in the story with someone you know personally or have read about or seen on TV or in movies. These might be young people who seem to be on the wrong path in life, or older people who try to help young people in the community.

RESPOND: Students will answer questions to demonstrate understanding.

Point out to students that while they will always complete the Respond step at the end of the first read, the other steps will probably happen somewhat concurrently. You may wish to print copies of the **First-Read Guide: Fiction** for students to use.

MAKING MEANING

About the Author

Langston Hughes (1902–1967) published his first work just a year after his high school graduation. Though he wrote in many genres, Hughes is best known for his poetry. He was one of the main figures in the Harlem Renaissance, a creative movement among African Americans that took place during the 1920s in Harlem, an area in New York City.

Thank You, M'am

Concept Vocabulary

As you perform your first read of "Thank You, M'am," you will encounter these words.

permit **release** **contact**

Context Clues If these words are unfamiliar to you, try using **context clues** to help you determine their meanings. There are various types of context clues that you may encounter as you read.

Synonyms: The thieves **purloined** the letter and hid it. The police could not find the stolen item for months.

Restatement of an Idea: The woman showed **largesse** when she donated a large sum of money to the charity.

Contrast of Ideas: I did not like the view of the **barren** mountaintop because I am used to being surrounded by lush greenery.

Apply your knowledge of context clues and other vocabulary strategies to determine the meanings of unfamiliar words you encounter during your first read.

First Read FICTION

Apply these strategies as you conduct your first read. You will have an opportunity to complete a close read after your first read.

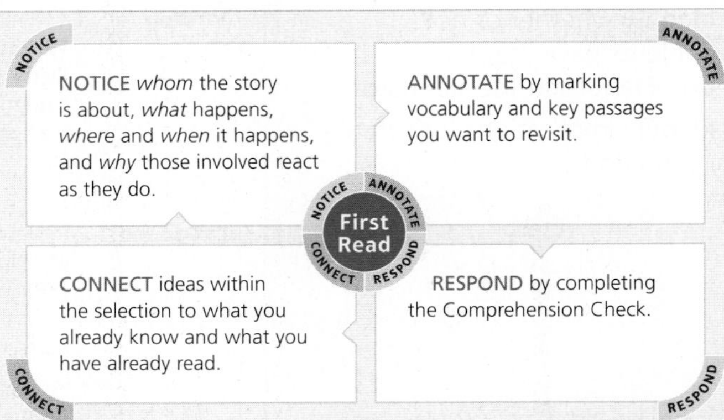

STANDARDS

Reading Literature
By the end of the year, read and comprehend literature, including stories, dramas, and poems, in the grades 6–8 text complexity band proficiently, with scaffolding as needed at the high end of the range.

Language
Use context as a clue to the meaning of a word or phrase.

AUTHOR'S PERSPECTIVE **Jim Cummins, Ph.D.**

Critical Literacies Recent research shows that even early-stage English learners can use higher-order thinking skills and engage with complex social issues with the appropriate instructional support. The following questions illustrate how teachers can support the development of critical thinking:

Step 1: Textual Dimension In order to help students read deeply to understand how the language and multimodal dimensions of the text construct meaning, ask, "When, where, and how did it happen?" and "Who did it? Why?"

Step 2: Personal Dimension Encourage students to reflect critically on the text in relation to their experiences and emotions. Ask, "Have you ever

Thank You, M'am

Langston Hughes

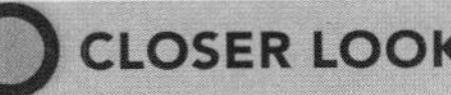

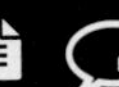

BACKGROUND

In this story, published in 1958, Roger, the protagonist, really wants a pair of blue suede shoes. This particular fashion item became popular after Carl Perkins released his hit song "Blue Suede Shoes" in 1956. Elvis Presley also famously covered the song in the same year.

1 She was a large woman with a large purse that had everything in it but hammer and nails. It had a long strap, and she carried it slung across her shoulder. It was about eleven o'clock at night, dark, and she was walking alone, when a boy ran up behind her and tried to snatch her purse. The strap broke with the sudden single tug the boy gave it from behind. But the boy's weight and the weight of the purse combined caused him to lose his balance. Instead of taking off full blast as he had hoped, the boy fell on his back on the sidewalk and his legs flew up. The large woman simply turned around and kicked him right square in his blue-jeaned sitter. Then she reached down, picked the boy up by his shirt front, and shook him until his teeth rattled.

NOTES

CLOSER LOOK

Analyze Plot

Circulate among groups as students conduct their close read. Suggest that groups close read paragraph 1. Encourage them to talk about the annotations they mark. If needed, provide the following support.

ANNOTATE: Have students mark details in paragraph 1 that establish setting, characters, and basic situation.

QUESTION: Guide students to consider what these details might tell them. Ask what a reader can infer from the expository details, and accept student responses.

Possible responses: Given the situation—a woman alone on the street at night approached by a would-be purse-snatcher—the reader might infer that the woman's purse will be stolen. But the author's description of the woman and her purse suggest that she might not be a helpless victim. The scene actually takes an unexpected turn when the purse turns out to be too heavy for the boy to manage.

CONCLUDE: Help students to formulate conclusions about the importance of these expository details in the text. Ask students why the author might have included these details.

Possible response: The author quickly establishes that this is not going to be a simple story about a petty crime. After the attempted crime in the third sentence, it soon becomes clear that this story is going to be about something else—probably the woman's formidable character or her relationship with the boy.

Remind students that a short story develops a **plot,** or series of events. The plot requires an exposition—the part of plot that establishes setting, characters, and basic situation—in a few swift strokes. By upsetting the reader's expectations about what was going to happen between these two characters, the author has also provided suspense, which will drive the reader to turn the page.

seen, felt, or experienced something like this?" or "Have you ever wanted something similar?"

Step 3: Critical Dimension Engage students in critical analysis of issues in the text by asking questions such as: "Is what this person said valid? Always? Under what conditions? Are there any alternatives to this situation?"

Step 4: Creative/Transformative Dimension Engage students in creative, constructive actions that address the social realities discussed. Ask, "How can the problem or issues be resolved?" and "What role can we play in helping resolve the problem?" Projects can involve drama, role play, art, poetry, stories, and newsletter publication.

Concept Vocabulary

PERMIT If groups are struggling to define the word *permit* in paragraph 3, point out that since the word has multiple meanings, they need to use context clues to determine the correct meaning here. Draw students' attention to the pronunciation guide. Ask whether students know what the word means when the accent is on the first syllable **(possible response:** a license, written permission). Suggest that one meaning may be related to the other. Then draw their attention to the context clue *She still held him. But . . .* Suggest that they try to visualize the scene in which the woman *permits* the boy to bend to reach her purse.

Possible response: In this context, *permit* means "to allow."

RELEASE To help students understand the meaning of *release* in paragraph 11, point out that a clear context clue is provided—the quotation "'Then I won't turn you loose.'" Ask students what kind of context clue this is **(answer:** restatement). Then ask them to define *release*.

Possible response: In this context, *release* means "let go of."

CONTACT If groups are struggling to define the word *contact* in paragraph 21, point out that the word is used twice in the paragraph. Roger put himself "in contact" with the woman first. Now the woman says that contact is "going to last awhile." We know that the boy *snatched* the woman's purse, and now the woman *holds* the boy's shirt. Help students use these clues to define *contact*.

Possible response: In this context, contact means "to touch or connect."

NOTES

Mark context clues or indicate another strategy you used that helped you determine meaning.

permit (puhr MIHT) *v.*

MEANING:

release (rih LEES) *v.*

MEANING:

contact (KON takt) *n.*

MEANING:

2 After that the woman said, "Pick up my pocketbook, boy, and give it here."

3 She still held him tightly. But she bent down enough to **permit** him to stoop and pick up her purse. Then she said, "Now ain't you ashamed of yourself?"

4 Firmly gripped by his shirt front, the boy said, "Yes'm."

5 The woman said, "What did you want to do it for?"

6 The boy said, "I didn't aim to."

7 She said, "You a lie!"

8 By that time two or three people passed, stopped, turned to look, and some stood watching.

9 "If I turn you loose, will you run?" asked the woman.

10 "Yes'm," said the boy.

11 "Then I won't turn you loose," said the woman. She did not **release** him.

12 "Lady, I'm sorry," whispered the boy.

13 "Um-hum! Your face is dirty. I got a great mind to wash your face for you. Ain't you got nobody home to tell you to wash your face?"

14 "No'm," said the boy.

15 "Then it will get washed this evening," said the large woman starting up the street, dragging the frightened boy behind her.

16 He looked as if he were fourteen or fifteen, frail and willow-wild, in tennis shoes and blue jeans.

17 The woman said, "You ought to be my son. I would teach you right from wrong. Least I can do right now is to wash your face. Are you hungry?"

18 "No'm," said the being-dragged boy. "I just want you to turn me loose."

19 "Was I bothering *you* when I turned that corner?" asked the woman.

20 "No'm."

21 "But you put yourself in **contact** with *me*," said the woman. "If you think that that contact is not going to last awhile, you got another thought coming. When I get through with you, sir, you are going to remember Mrs. Luella Bates Washington Jones."

22 Sweat popped out on the boy's face and he began to struggle. Mrs. Jones stopped, jerked him around in front of her, put a half nelson[1] about his neck, and continued to drag him up the street. When she got to her door, she dragged the boy inside, down a hall, and into a large kitchenette-furnished room at the rear of the house. She switched on the light and left the door open. The boy could hear other roomers laughing and talking in the large house. Some of their doors were open, too, so he knew he and the

1. **half nelson** wrestling hold in which an arm is placed under the opponent's armpit from behind with the palm of the hand pressed against the back of the neck.

FACILITATING SMALL-GROUP CLOSE LEARNING

CLOSE READ: Fiction Check in with groups as they read the selection together and offer support as needed.

- Remind the group that when they read a short story, they should be sure to identify the main characters, the conflict, and the plot.
- Ask students to think about whether there is more than one conflict, and whether the conflict(s) are internal or external.
- Challenge students to identify different methods of characterization, such as descriptions of how the characters look, act, and react; what the characters say and what they think. When one group member finds an example, have another group identify what method of characterization is being used, and have a third explain what the example says about the character. Then have members shift these roles right or left.

DIGITAL PERSPECTIVES  

woman were not alone. The woman still had him by the neck in the middle of her room.

23 She said, "What is your name?"

24 "Roger," answered the boy.

25 "Then, Roger, you go to that sink and wash your face," said the woman, whereupon she turned him loose—at last. Roger looked at the door—looked at the woman—looked at the door—*and went to the sink*.

26 "Let the water run until it gets warm," she said. "Here's a clean towel."

27 "You gonna take me to jail?" asked the boy, bending over the sink.

28 "Not with that face, I would not take you nowhere," said the woman. "Here I am trying to get home to cook me a bite to eat and you snatch my pocketbook! Maybe, you ain't been to your supper either, late as it be. Have you?"

29 "There's nobody home at my house," said the boy.

30 "Then we'll eat," said the woman, "I believe you're hungry—or been hungry—to try to snatch my pocketbook."

31 "I wanted a pair of blue suede shoes," said the boy.

32 "Well, you didn't have to snatch *my* pocketbook to get some suede shoes," said Mrs. Luella Bates Washington Jones. "You could of asked me."

33 "M'am?"

34 The water dripping from his face, the boy looked at her. There was a long pause. A very long pause. After he had dried his face and not knowing what else to do dried it again, the boy turned around, wondering what next. The door was open. He could make a dash for it down the hall. He could run, run, run, *run*!

35 The woman was sitting on the day bed. After a while she said, "I were young once and I wanted things I could not get."

36 There was another long pause. The boy's mouth opened. Then he frowned, not knowing he frowned.

37 The woman said, "Um-hum! You thought I was going to say *but*, didn't you? You thought I was going to say, *but I didn't snatch people's pocketbooks*. Well, I wasn't going to say that." Pause. Silence. "I have done things, too, which I would not tell you, son—neither tell God, if He didn't already know. Everybody's got something in common. So you set down while I fix us something to eat. You might run that comb through your hair so you will look presentable."

38 In another corner of the room behind a screen was a gas plate[2] and an icebox. Mrs. Jones got up and went behind the screen. The woman did not watch the boy to see if he was going to run now, nor did she watch her purse, which she left behind her on the day

NOTES

2. **gas plate** hot plate heated by gas that is used for cooking.

CLOSER LOOK

Analyze Character Development

Circulate among groups as students conduct their close read. Suggest that groups close read paragraphs 35–37. Encourage them to talk about the annotations they mark. If needed, provide the following support.

ANNOTATE: Have students mark details that give us a new perspective on Mrs. Jones.

QUESTION: Guide students to consider how these details further develop their ideas about Mrs. Jones. How do these details change their impression of her?

Possible response: Mrs. Jones passes on the chance to say, "I didn't snatch people's pocketbooks." She hints that she has done things that were just as wrong. There is more to Mrs. Jones than righteous anger.

CONCLUDE: Help students to formulate conclusions about the importance of these character details in the text. Ask students why the author might have included these details.

Possible response: The author shows Mrs. Jones as a flawed person. In fact, she may be turning into someone Roger can identify with. She certainly seems to identify with him and recognizes what he needs.

Remind students that a story's **main character** usually changes in the course of the narrative. As they read on, have them think about which character undergoes a bigger change—Roger or Mrs. Jones.

Additional **English Language Support** is available in the Interactive Teacher's Edition.

PERSONALIZE FOR LEARNING

English Language Support

Dialogue Remind students that in dialogue—the character's own words, set between quotation marks—writers often break the rules of language in order to make a character more realistic. Direct students to paragraph 28. Explain that the words "Not with that face, I would not take you nowhere" are spoken by Mrs. Jones. This phrase contains a double negative (*not . . . nowhere*), which is not used in formal English. If the narrator had conveyed Mrs. Jones's speech indirectly, he might have written this: "She said she would not take him anywhere with that face." The difference between these two expressions isn't just the grammar. By letting us hear Mrs. Jones, we get a sense of her character: "not . . . nowhere" has a forceful ring that "not anywhere" lacks.

Ask students to summarize paragraphs 26–34 in their groups, and watch for signs of confusion. **ALL LEVELS**

CLOSER LOOK

Infer Point of View

Circulate among groups as students conduct their close read. Suggest that groups close read paragraphs 38 and 39. Encourage them to talk about the annotations they mark. If needed, provide the following support.

ANNOTATE: Have students mark details that reveal the narrator's point of view. Check in with each group to confirm their understanding of point of view concepts such as third-person limited, in which the narrator reveals the thoughts of one character.

QUESTION: Give students time to consider what these details show. Students may be confused by the double negatives. Ask students to discuss what the line "He did not trust the woman *not* to trust him" means, and accept student responses.

Possible response: The line shows that Roger wants Mrs. Jones to notice him behaving himself; that's why he sits where she can easily see him. He wants Mrs. Jones's trust.

CONCLUDE: Help students to formulate conclusions about why Hughes shows Roger's thought process in these lines. Some discussion-starting questions include, *Was it necessary to include Roger's thoughts here? Has Hughes shown Roger's thoughts in earlier passages?*

Possible response: The author wants to drive home the change in Roger. He doesn't want to be seen as a thief in Mrs. Jones's eyes. We can infer this from Roger's actions alone, but showing his thoughts here emphasizes the importance of the change.

Remind students that other **points of view** include first-person, in which the narrator is one of the characters and uses *I* and *me*; and third-person omniscient, in which the narrator shares all of the characters' inner thoughts and feelings.

NOTES

bed. But the boy took care to sit on the far side of the room, away from her purse, where he thought she could easily see him out of the corner of her eye if she wanted to. He did not trust the woman *not* to trust him. And he did not want to be mistrusted now.

39 "Do you need somebody to go to the store," asked the boy, "maybe to get some milk or something?"

40 "Don't believe I do," said the woman, "unless you just want sweet milk yourself. I was going to make cocoa out of this canned milk I got here."

41 "That will be fine," said the boy.

42 She heated some lima beans and ham she had in the icebox, made the cocoa, and set the table. The woman did not ask the boy anything about where he lived, or his folks, or anything else that would embarrass him. Instead, as they ate, she told him about her job in a hotel beauty-shop that stayed open late, what the work was like, and how all kinds of women came in and out, blondes, redheads, and Spanish. Then she cut him a half of her ten-cent cake.

43 "Eat some more, son," she said.

44 When they were finished eating she got up and said, "Now, here, take this ten dollars and buy yourself some blue suede shoes. And next time, do not make the mistake of latching onto *my* pocketbook *nor nobody else's*—because shoes got by devilish ways will burn your feet. I got to get my rest now. But from here on in, son, I hope you will behave yourself."

45 She led him down the hall to the front door and opened it. "Good night! Behave yourself, boy!" she said, looking out into the street.

46 The boy wanted to say something else other than "Thank you, m'am" to Mrs. Luella Bates Washington Jones, but although his lips moved, he couldn't even say that as he turned at the foot of the barren stoop and looked up at the large woman in the door. Then she shut the door. ❧

CROSS-CURRICULAR PERSPECTIVES

Music Play a recording of "Blue Suede Shoes," either Carl Perkins's or Elvis Presley's version. Explain that both recordings were enormous hits that helped popularize rock and roll. Discuss with students the power of pop music to set trends and turn listeners into consumers. Ask students to discuss in their groups examples of recent or past hit recordings whose lyrics have inspired them to want something or to buy certain products. Then ask them to share whether they or someone they know has ever gone to unusual lengths to acquire something they heard about in a hit recording. Finally, have students talk about how their discussion affects their views about Roger in "Thank You, M'am."

Comprehension Check

Complete the following items after you finish your first read. Review and clarify details with your group.

1. How do Mrs. Jones and Roger meet?

2. What does Roger expect Mrs. Jones to do?

3. What does Mrs. Jones do instead?

4. **Notebook** Confirm your understanding of the story by drawing a storyboard of key events.

RESEARCH

Research to Clarify Research a topic that you think will help you better understand this story. For instance, you might want to learn more about its author, Langston Hughes. In what way does the information you learned shed light on the story? Share your findings with your group.

DIGITAL PERSPECTIVES

Comprehension Check

Possible responses:

1. Roger tries to steal Mrs. Jones's purse.
2. He expects Mrs. Jones to take him to the police.
3. She takes him to her home, tells him to wash his face, feeds him some supper, gives him money to buy blue suede shoes; then she sends him home, warning him to behave.
4. Storyboards will vary but should depict the key events of the story: boy tries to steal woman's purse; she drags him home; she tells him to wash his face; he considers running away but decides to stay; she feeds him and questions him about why he stole her purse; she gives him money for shoes; they say goodbye.

Research

Research to Clarify If groups struggle to narrow their research topic, you may want to suggest that they focus on one of the following aspects of the story or its author: Langston Hughes's life or life in Harlem in the 1950s, Hughes's writing about Harlem, Hughes's writing about working people, Hughes's writing about poverty, or anti-poverty efforts in New York in the 1950s.

PERSONALIZE FOR LEARNING

Challenge

Artist Study Have students illustrate a scene from "Thank You, M'am" using collage, in the style of noted African American artist Romare Bearden (1911–1988). Bearden was born and raised in Harlem; during the 1960s, shortly after the story is set, he began experimenting with collage techniques, using glossy magazine cuttings to tell stories about the civil rights movement. Have students research Bearden's work during this time before they create their collages. **(Research to Explore)**

FACILITATING

Jump Start

CLOSE READ Ask students: *Do you think Roger is going to buy a pair of blue suede shoes with the money Mrs. Jones gave him?* As students discuss in groups, ask them to consider how Roger has changed by the end of the story.

Close Read the Text

If needed, model close reading by using the Annotation Highlights in the Interactive Teacher's Edition. Remind students to use Accountable Talk in their discussions and to support one another as they complete the close read.

Analyze the Text

Possible responses:

1. The woman has been kind and trusted him.
2. Passages will vary.
3. Responses will vary.

Concept Vocabulary

Why These Words? Possible responses: All three words are related to the initial meeting between the two characters. All three words have multiple meanings and can act as both verbs and nouns.

Practice

Possible responses:

1. I don't normally *permit* people to pet my dog, but you may if you are very gentle.
2. We caught fish in the pond but had to *release* the smaller ones.
3. Her sunburn was so sensitive that the slightest *contact* made her flinch.

Word Network

Possible words: *ashamed, sorry, wrong, struggle*

Word Study

For more support, see **Concept Vocabulary and Word Study.**

Possible responses:

In paragraph 2, *permit* means "allow." Other meanings: (v.) formal permission; (n.) a license

In paragraph 10, *release* means "let go of." Other meanings: (n.) the giving up of a right.

In paragraph 20, *contact* means "a meeting or touching of people or things." Other meanings: (v.) to meet or touch

MAKING MEANING

THANK YOU, M'AM

Close Read the Text

With your group, revisit sections of the text you marked during your first read. **Annotate** details that you notice. What **questions** do you have? What can you **conclude**?

Analyze the Text

CITE TEXTUAL EVIDENCE to support your answers.

Complete the activities.

1. **Review and Clarify** With your group, reread paragraph 38 of the story. Why doesn't Roger want to be mistrusted?
2. **Present and Discuss** Now, work with your group to share the passages from the text that you found especially important. Take turns presenting your passages. Discuss what you noticed in the text, the questions you asked, and the conclusions you reached.
3. **Essential Question:** ***What can cause a sudden change in someone's life?*** What has this story taught you about the kinds of events, actions, and people that can cause a change in someone's life? Discuss with your group.

TIP

GROUP DISCUSSION

When you work in your group to answer the Analyze the Text questions, be sure to direct listeners to specific words, sentences, and paragraphs in the story.

LANGUAGE DEVELOPMENT

Concept Vocabulary

permit release contact

Why These Words? The concept vocabulary words from the text are related. With your group, determine what the words have in common. Record your ideas, and add another word that fits the category.

WORD NETWORK

Add interesting words related to turning points from the text to your Word Network.

Practice

Notebook Confirm your understanding of these words by using each word in a sentence. Be sure to use context clues that hint at each word's meaning. Use a dictionary to verify your understanding of each word.

Word Study

Multiple-Meaning Words Many words have more than one meaning. If you are not sure of the meaning of a multiple-meaning word, use context clues to make an educated guess. Then, confirm the word's meaning in a dictionary.

All three concept vocabulary words are multiple-meaning words. First, write the meaning of each word as it is used in the story. Then, use a dictionary to find at least two other meanings for each word.

STANDARDS

Language

Determine or clarify the meaning of unknown and multiple-meaning words and phrases based on *grade 7 reading and content,* choosing flexibly from a range of strategies.

c. Consult general and specialized reference materials, both print and digital, to find the pronunciation of a word or determine or clarify its precise meaning or its part of speech.

d. Verify the preliminary determination of the meaning of a word or phrase.

FORMATIVE ASSESSMENT

Analyze the Text

If students struggle to close read the text, **then** provide the **Thank You, M'am: Text Questions** available online in the Interactive Teacher's Edition or Unit Resources. Answers and DOK levels are also available.

Concept Vocabulary

If students fail to see the connection between the words, **then** have them look at the page where the words appear, or have them try to use each word as a different part of speech.

Word Study

If students have trouble distinguishing between different word meanings, **then** help them find example sentences in the dictionary. For Reteach and Practice, see **Word Study: Multiple-Meaning Words (RP).**

Analyze Craft and Structure

Elements of a Short Story: Plot **Plot** is the related sequence of events in a story. Each event in the plot moves the story forward. A plot has the following elements:

- **Exposition:** introduction of the characters, the setting, and the basic situation
- **Rising Action:** events that introduce a **conflict,** or struggle, and increase the tension; may also include events that explain characters' past actions
- **Climax:** the story's high point, or moment of greatest intensity; often a turning point in the story at which the eventual outcome becomes clear
- **Falling Action:** events that follow the climax
- **Resolution:** the story's final outcome and tying up of loose ends

This diagram will help you to visualize the sequence of plot elements.

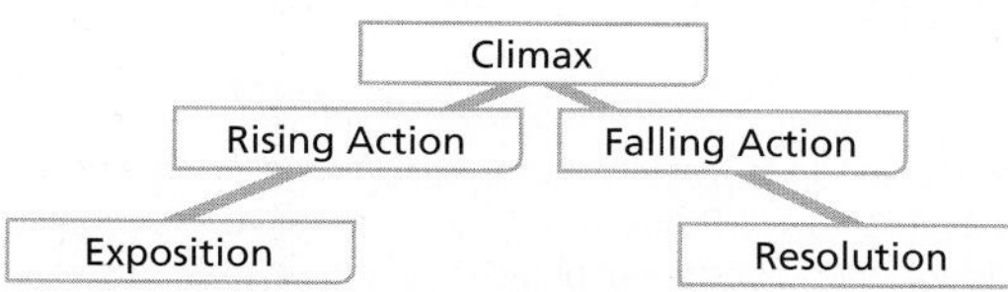

STANDARDS

Reading Literature

- Cite several pieces of textual evidence to support analysis of what the text says explicitly as well as inferences drawn from the text.
- Analyze how particular elements of a story or drama interact.

Practice

CITE TEXTUAL EVIDENCE to support your answers.

Work with your group to fill in this graphic organizer by identifying the elements of plot in "Thank You, M'am."

PLOT ELEMENT	LOCATION IN "THANK YOU, M'AM"
Exposition	Characters: Roger; Mrs. Jones. Setting: a city in the evening. Situation: the boy tries to steal the woman's purse
Rising Action	They struggle; Roger falls down and Mrs. Jones grabs him. She makes Roger come home with her, He wants to run, but listens to her.
Climax	Roger realizes that Mrs. Jones has left her purse alone and he could take it. He chooses not to.
Falling Action	After the climax, Roger eats some food. Mrs. Jones gives him money to buy the shoes and sends him away.
Resolution	Roger leaves Mrs. Jones house. He has been changed by his interaction with Mrs. Jones.

Notebook As a group, respond to the following questions.

1. (a) Identify two plot events that increase the tension between Mrs. Jones and Roger. (b) How does this tension contribute to the rising action in the story?
2. What clues in the story enabled you to identify the climax, or turning point?
3. Do you think the story's resolution provides a sense of satisfaction for the reader? Why or why not?

DIGITAL PERSPECTIVES

Analyze Craft and Structure

Elements of a Short Story: Plot Let students know that there can often be more than one interpretation of where a story's climax takes place, especially when a story contains more than one key character and conflict. The climax is described as both a turning point and the point of greatest emotional tension, and these two things can occur at different points in the story. In "Thank You, M'am," for example, Roger experiences a turning point, but the scene in which Mrs. Jones admits her own flaws may contain more emotional tension. For more support, see **Analyze Craft and Structure: Plot.**

See possible responses in chart on student page.

MAKE IT INTERACTIVE

Project the Interactive Teacher's Edition for "Thank You, M'am" and model identifying the exposition. Then have students return to work in their groups to complete the chart.

Possible responses:

1. (a) After Roger tries to steal Mrs. Jones purse, two more events create tension: Mrs. Jones dragging Roger to her home and later leaving her purse where he could steal it. (b) The first event creates a conflict between Roger and Mrs. Jones; the second event creates a conflict within Roger.
2. Mrs. Jones goes behind the screen and watches Roger out of the corner of her eye to see what he is going to do. Roger wanted her trust, so he decided not to run away.
3. Readers may feel satisfied that Roger learns more about Mrs. Jones and by the change in Roger; they may feel unsatisfied by not knowing what Roger plans to do with the money.

FORMATIVE ASSESSMENT

Analyze Craft and Structure

If students struggle to identify elements of the plot, **then** revisit specific passages to discuss specific dialogue and events contribute to the conflict, climax, and resolution. For Reteach and Practice, see **Analyze Craft and Structure: Plot (RP).**

WriteNow Express and Reflect

Personal Story To reinforce both the theme and the structure topics, have students write brief personal narratives using the structure of a short story. Have students brainstorm times when they experienced a turning point, perhaps focusing on a lesson they learned through a brief interaction with a stranger, with an older person, or both. As they generate details for their writing, encourage them to focus on details that reveal character—both their own and that of the other person in their narrative. Have students organize their events and details in a plot diagram like the one above.

Remind students that they will be the narrators of their personal accounts. However, even though first-person narrators describe themselves directly, they should try to show character details using tools that Hughes uses—action, dialogue, and important details. Point out that Hughes uses figurative language to describe both characters. Mrs. Jones's bag has "everything in it but a hammer and nails"; Roger is "willow-wild." Direct them to use similarly vivid descriptions.

FACILITATING

Conventions

Prepositions and Prepositional Phrases Tell students that several prepositional phrases can be grouped together, and they can appear anywhere in a sentence. Provide the following examples:

- We live in the house / at the bottom / of the hill.
- Under the tree sat a girl reading to her little brother.

Ask students to generate more examples of sentences containing prepositional phrases. For more support, see **Conventions: Prepositions and Prepositional Phrases.**

Read It

MAKE IT INTERACTIVE

Have students work through the activity round-robin style. Student 1 will write down a sentence that contains a preposition; Student 2 will identify the preposition; Student 3 will identify the object of the preposition; and Student 4 will bracket the prepositional phrase. Have students continue rotating through the activity until the chart is complete.

See possible responses in chart on student page.

Write It

Responses will vary. Students' sentences should include prepositional phrases, with each preposition underlined and each object of the preposition circled. Suggest that students use prepositional phrases to provide details about what the subject of their paragraph looks like or how he or she acts.

FORMATIVE ASSESSMENT

Conventions

If students are unable to identify prepositional phrases in the short story, **then** guide them to passages that have a rich selection. Suggest that they first identify individual prepositions and then the phrases that they introduce. For Reteach and Practice, see **Conventions: Prepositions and Prepositional Phrases (RP).**

LANGUAGE DEVELOPMENT

THANK YOU, M'AM

Conventions

Prepositions and Prepositional Phrases A **preposition** relates a noun or a pronoun that follows it to another word in the sentence. Some commonly used prepositions include *at, after, between, for, in, of, on, to, through,* and *with.*

EXAMPLE: The book is on the table.
The preposition *on* relates the noun *table* to another word in the sentence, *book.*

A **prepositional phrase** begins with a preposition and ends with a noun or pronoun—called the **object of the preposition.**

EXAMPLE: The book is on the table.
The prepositional phrase *on the table* begins with the preposition *on* and ends with the noun *table,* which is the object of the preposition.

Read It

Work with your group to identify examples of prepositions and prepositional phrases in "Thank You, M'am." Write your examples in the chart. Mark the prepositional phrases, as shown in Example 1.

EXAMPLE 1	*She was a large woman with a large purse that had everything in it but hammer and nails.*
EXAMPLE 2	The strap broke [with the single tug] the boy gave it [from behind.]
EXAMPLE 3	Firmly gripped [by his shirt front], the boy said, "Yes'm."
EXAMPLE 4	The woman still had him [by the neck][in the middle] [of her room.]

Write It

Notebook Write a paragraph in which you describe someone who has had a positive impact on your life. Correctly use at least three prepositional phrases in your paragraph. Mark the object of the preposition in each phrase.

STANDARDS
Language
Demonstrate command of the conventions of standard English grammar and usage when writing or speaking.
a. Explain the function of phrases and clauses in general and their function in specific sentences.

PERSONALIZE FOR LEARNING

English Language Support

Sentence Frames Emergent and expanding English Language Learners can more fully participate in writing activities when sentence frames guide their responses. To help these students complete the Write It activity, suggest they write about someone who helped them recently. Point out that each sentence starter ends with a preposition.

Direct students to complete the prepositional phrase by adding a noun (or verb *+ing*) with as many other descriptive words as they would like. For example,

- I came here from . . . .
- I met [*helper's name*] in . . . . .

- He/she helped me with . . .
- He/she taught me about . . . .
- I asked him/her for . . . . .
- He/she took me to . . . .
- I am thankful to him/her for . . . .

EMERGING/EXPANDING

EFFECTIVE EXPRESSION

Writing to Sources

In real life, you can often understand a situation better by putting yourself in someone else's shoes. Similarly, when reading a work of fiction, you can often deepen your understanding of the work by considering the points of view of different characters.

Assignment

Use your imagination and details from "Thank You, M'am" to write a **journal entry** about events in the story from the point of view of one of the characters, either Roger or Mrs. Jones. In your journal entry, focus on one of the following:

- ☐ Mrs. Jones's perspective on meeting Roger
- ☐ Roger's perspective on meeting Mrs. Jones

Consider the following questions as you write: What feelings would he or she be likely to express in a journal entry about the experience? What words would he or she use? Refer to details in the story to accurately convey the point of view and personality of the character you chose.

Project Plan Before you begin, decide as a group whether you want to write a journal entry from the point of view of Roger or Mrs. Jones. Make a list of the tasks you will need to complete to fulfill the assignment. Decide how you will organize the work. Then, appoint individual group members to each task.

Clarifying Ideas and Evidence Brainstorm your impressions of Mrs. Jones or Roger. What are they thinking? What are their impressions of each other? What sensory details do you want to include? Use your own imagination and evidence from the text to support your ideas.

Use Transitions Use transitions to show shifts in time or setting in your journal entry. Transition words, phrases, and clauses, such as *meanwhile, while Roger waited, afterwards,* and *all of a sudden*, will help to show the connection between the events you describe as well as the differences between your memories of events and your current reflections on them.

Present After you have completed your journal entry, present your finished work to the class. Make sure all group members have a role to play in the presentation.

Discuss and Reflect Pay close attention and take notes as you listen to the presentations of other groups. When all the groups are done presenting, briefly discuss your thoughts with your group. Are there any ideas that were used by multiple groups? Are there any ideas from other groups' presentations that impressed you? Is there anything you would do differently next time?

EVIDENCE LOG

Before moving on to a new selection, go to your Evidence and record what you learned from "Thank You M'am."

STANDARDS

Writing
Write narratives to develop real or imagined experiences or events using effective technique, relevant descriptive details, and well-structured event sequences.
a. Engage and orient the reader by establishing a context and point of view and introducing a narrator and/or characters; organize an event sequence that unfolds naturally and logically.
c. Use a variety of transition words, phrases, and clauses to convey sequence and signal shifts from one time frame or setting to another.
d. Use precise words and phrases, relevant descriptive details, and sensory language to capture the action and convey experiences and events.

Speaking and Listening
Engage effectively in a range of collaborative discussions with diverse partners on *grade 7 topics, texts, and issues,* building on others' ideas and expressing their own clearly.
b. Follow rules for collegial discussions, track progress toward specific goals and deadlines, and define individual roles as needed.
d. Acknowledge new information expressed by others and, when warranted, modify their own views.

DIGITAL PERSPECTIVES

Writing to Sources

Make sure students understand the difference between the point of view in "Thank You, M'am" and the one they will apply in their journal entries. Hughes's story is written from the third-person limited perspective, in which the narrator sees the world through a single character's eyes.

In this assignment, students will be writing from the first-person point of view. They will use *I* and *me* to refer to the character they choose. They will be able to reveal details about the character's experiences, thoughts, and feelings.

Project Plan Remind groups to consult the schedule for Small-Group Activities as they create their Project Plan. Check to make sure each group has made assignments, and that the work is divided evenly among group members.

Clarifying Ideas and Evidence Check in with students as they generate details for their journal entries to make sure they are consistent with the original narrative's details.

Discuss and Reflect Remind students to engage in active listening while groups are presenting. Have them jot down a few things about the presentations that stood out or that they might ask questions about during the class discussion. For more support, see **Writing to Sources: Journal Entry.**

Evidence Log Support students in completing their Evidence Logs. This paced activity will help prepare them for the Performance-Based Assessment at the end of the unit.

FORMATIVE ASSESSMENT

Writing to Sources

If students are unfamiliar with journal entry format, **then** provide this definition: a journal is a record of a writer's own experiences, thoughts, and observations. Writers often use journal entries to work out their feelings about events. For Reteach and Practice, see **Writing to Sources: Journal Entry (RP).**

Selection Test

Administer the "Thank You, M'am" Selection Test, which is available in both print and digital formats online in Assessments.

PERSONALIZE FOR LEARNING

English Language Support

Journal Entry Point out that students should include words related to the feelings and senses of their chosen character, to make the writing more descriptive. Remind students of the 5 senses: sight, hearing, touch, smell, and taste.

Have students work in pairs to brainstorm for a list of words related to feelings and senses. Ask students to use these words in their journal writing. **EMERGING**

Ask students to work in small groups to generate a list of sensory language. Ask students to think about their character's unique feelings and to use at least two sensory words in their journal entries. **EXPANDING**

As they generate their sensory language, ask them to imagine how the character they have chosen would feel about the other character. Have students include at least 3 sensory details in their writing. **BRIDGING**

An expanded **English Language Support Lesson** on Journal Entry is available in the Interactive Teacher's Edition.

from An American Childhood

AUDIO SUMMARIES
Audio summaries of *from* An American Childhood are available online in both English and Spanish in the Interactive Teacher's Edition or Unit Resources. Assigning these summaries prior to reading the selection may help students build additional background knowledge and set a context for their first read.

Summary

In this excerpt from her memoir *An American Childhood*, Annie Dillard talks about receiving a microscope from her parents and becoming fascinated by the microscopic world. She spent a long winter looking at tiny things, but she saw nothing that fascinated her at first. She wanted to look at living microorganisms, but she couldn't find any. Finally she found an amoeba, and was immensely excited. She wanted to show her parents, but they weren't interested. From this experience, Dillard learned the importance of pursuing one's own interests.

Insight

Dillard writes about how she began to pursue her passions. Her parents would give her supplies and support, but she did what interested her. This narrative will help students understand the significance of intrinsic motivation.

ESSENTIAL QUESTION:
What can cause a sudden change in someone's life?

Connection to Essential Question

Her parents' disinterest seems to give Dillard a sudden epiphany. She realizes that it's okay that they aren't interested in the same things she is and that she should pursue those interests for herself.

SMALL-GROUP LEARNING PERFORMANCE TASK
How are the turning points in the selections similar to and different from each other?

UNIT PERFORMANCE-BASED ASSESSMENT
What can cause a significant change in someone's life?

Connection to Performance Tasks

Small-Group Learning Performance Task In the drama and fiction selections, a character reaches a turning point through interaction with others. In the memoir, the author's turning point comes through discoveries she makes on her own.

Unit Performance-Based Assessment Being unable to interest her parents in her amoeba shifts Dillard's understanding of her relationship to them. She recognizes the importance of having her own life.

DIGITAL PERSPECTIVES

Audio

Video

Document

Annotation Highlights

Online Assessment

LESSON RESOURCES

	Making Meaning	Language Development	Effective Expression
Lesson	**First Read** **Close Read** **Analyze the Text** **Analyze Craft and Structure**	**Concept Vocabulary** **Word Study** **Conventions**	**Speaking and Listening**
Instructional Standards	**RI.7.10** By the end of the year, read and comprehend literary nonfiction . . . **L.7.5.b** Use the relationship between particular words . . . **RI.7.1** Cite several pieces of textual evidence . . . **RI.7.2** Determine two or more central ideas . . . **RI.7.3** Analyze the interactions between . . .	**L.7.4** Determine or clarify the meaning of unknown and multiple-meaning words and phrases . . . **L.7.4.d** Verify the preliminary determination of the meaning . . . **L.7.5** Demonstrate understanding of figurative language . . . **L.7.5.b** Use the relationship between particular words . . . **L.7.1.a** Explain the function of phrases . . . **L.7.2** Demonstrate command of the conventions . . .	**SL.7.1** Engage effectively in a range of collaborative discussions . . . **SL.7.1.a** Come to discussions prepared . . . **SL.7.1.b** Follow rules for collegial discussions . . . **SL.7.1.c** Pose questions . . . **SL.7.1.d** Acknowledge new information . . .
STUDENT RESOURCES			
Available online in the Interactive Student Edition or Unit Resources	Selection Audio First-Read Guide: Nonfiction Close-Read Guide: Nonfiction	Word Network	Evidence Log
TEACHER RESOURCES			
Selection Resources Available online in the Interactive Teacher's Edition or Unit Resources	Audio Summaries: English and Spanish Annotation Highlights Accessible Leveled Text Spanish Translation Text Questions First Read Extension Questions Analyze Craft and Structure: Reflective Writing	Conventions: Appositives and Appositive Phrases Technical Vocabulary and Word Study	Speaking and Listening: Collaborative Discussion English Language Support Lesson: Collaborative Discussion
Reteach/Practice (RP) Available online in the Interactive Teacher's Edition or Unit Resources	Analyze Craft and Structure: Reflective Writing (RP)	Conventions: Appositives and Appositive Phrases (RP) Word Study: The Prefix *en-* (RP)	Speaking and Listening: Collaborative Discussion (RP)
Assessment Available online in Assessments	Selection Test: English Selection Test: Spanish Extension Selection Test		
My Resources	A Unit 3 Answer Key is available online and in the Interactive Teacher's Edition.		

Reading Support

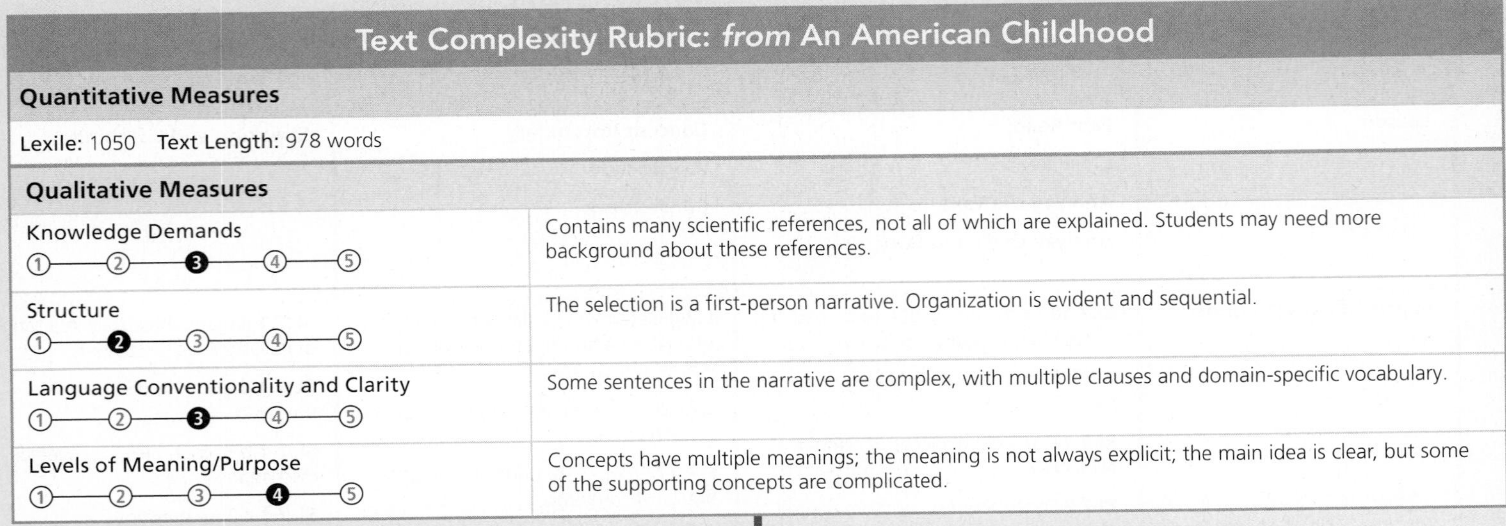

Text Complexity Rubric: *from* An American Childhood	
Quantitative Measures	
Lexile: 1050 **Text Length:** 978 words	
Qualitative Measures	
Knowledge Demands ①—②—❸—④—⑤	Contains many scientific references, not all of which are explained. Students may need more background about these references.
Structure ①—❷—③—④—⑤	The selection is a first-person narrative. Organization is evident and sequential.
Language Conventionality and Clarity ①—②—❸—④—⑤	Some sentences in the narrative are complex, with multiple clauses and domain-specific vocabulary.
Levels of Meaning/Purpose ①—②—③—❹—⑤	Concepts have multiple meanings; the meaning is not always explicit; the main idea is clear, but some of the supporting concepts are complicated.

DECIDE AND PLAN

English Language Support

Provide English learners with support for language and meaning as they read the selection.

Language Students may need help with the language and the vocabulary. For example, in paragraphs 6 and 7 point out that the narrator refers to the *amoeba* as *he*. Ask students to reread the section making this replacement in order to make sure they understand the text.

Levels of Meaning/Purpose Help students to rephrase main ideas by pulling sentences from the reading. Write the sentences for reference. For example, *I sat with my wonderful amoeba, and there he was, rolling his grains more slowly now …* (paragraph 13) Help students understand what the narrator's description of the amoeba tells about her relationship to the natural world.

Strategic Support

Provide students with strategic support to ensure that they can successfully read the text.

Language If students have difficulty with complex sentences, work together to break down sentences into smaller chunks in order to understand their meaning. Ask students to highlight words or phrases that they don't understand. As a group, help to define some of the terms they find difficult.

Levels of Meaning/Purpose If students have difficulty understanding the multiple levels of meaning, focus on individual paragraphs. Ask students to first state the events that happen. Then ask them to reread the paragraph to determine what feelings or ideas are conveyed by the narrator's thoughts and reactions.

Challenge

Provide students who need to be challenged with ideas for how they can go beyond a simple interpretation of the text.

Text Analysis Ask students to consider the lines *I began to understand then, that you do what you do out of your private passion for the thing itself. I had essentially been handed my own life.* (paragraphs 11) Why did the narrator find her parents' reaction to her interests to be so freeing? How might her interests have changed if her parents had reacted differently?

Written Response Ask students to continue their thought process on parental expectations. The narrator clearly felt a freedom in her parents' lack of expectations. She felt her life was her own to fill as she pleased. Have students write an essay that explores ways in which children respond to the expectations of their parents.

TEACH

Read and Respond

Have the groups read the selection and complete the Making Meaning and Language Development activities.

Standards Support Through Teaching and Learning Cycle

IDENTIFY NEEDS

Analyze results of the Beginning-of-Year Assessment, focusing on the items relating to Unit 3. Also take into consideration student performance to this point and your observations of where particular students struggle.

DECIDE AND PLAN

- If students have performed poorly on items matching these standards, then provide selection scaffolds before assigning them the on-level lesson provided in the Student Edition.
- If students have done well on the Beginning-of-Year Assessment, then challenge them to keep progressing and learning by giving them opportunities to practice the skills in depth.
- Use the Selection Resources listed on the Planning pages for the excerpt from *An American Childhood* to help students continually improve their ability to master the standards.

Instructional Standards: *from* An American Childhood

	Catching Up	This Year	Looking Forward
Reading	You may wish to administer the **Analyze Craft and Structure: Reflective Writing (RP)** worksheet to help students better understand the form.	**RI.3** Analyze the interactions between individuals, events, and ideas in a text.	Challenge students to identify other reflective essays they have read to further discuss the form.
Speaking and Listening	You may wish to administer the **Speaking and Listening: Collaborative Discussion (RP)** worksheet to help students better organize their discussions.	**SL.1.b** Follow rules for collegial discussions, track progress toward specific goals and deadlines, and define individual roles as needed.	Have students go beyond discussion by using outside resources to back up their claims.
Language	You may wish to administer the **Word Study: Prefix *en-* (RP)** worksheet to ensure that students will understand the prefix. You may wish to administer the **Conventions: Appositives and Appositive Phrases (RP)** worksheet to help students better understand appositive phrases.	**L.4** Determine or clarify the meaning of unknown and multiple-meaning words and phrases based on *grade 7 reading and content,* choosing flexibly from a range of strategies. **L.1.a** Explain the function of phrases and clauses in general and their function in specific sentences.	Have students find words with other prefixes they recognize in the selection. Have students rewrite sentences without appositives and discuss why they are useful.

ANALYZE AND REVISE

- Analyze student work for evidence of student learning.
- Identify whether or not students have met the expectations in the standards.
- Identify implications for future instruction.

TEACH

Implement the planned lesson, and gather evidence of student learning.

FACILITATING

Jump Start

FIRST READ Engage students in a discussion of transitions and turning points that sets the context for reading the excerpt from *An American Childhood*. Ask: Have you ever really wanted something and then gotten it? What happened next? What did you learn from the experience? Did it change you or the way you saw the world?

from An American Childhood

What experiences have changed you or the way you see the world? What have others said or done that has proved a valuable lesson? Modeling questions such as these will help students connect to the excerpt from *An American Childhood* and to the Small-Group Performance Task assignment. Selection audio and print capability for the selection are available in the Interactive Teacher's Edition.

Technical Vocabulary

Ask groups to look closely at the information about base words and how to use them to determine the meanings of unfamiliar words. Walk students though the strategy using one of the Technical Vocabulary words.

FIRST READ

Students should perform the steps of the first read independently.

NOTICE: You may want to encourage students to notice sensory details the author uses that paint a clear picture of the people, things, places, and events in the narrative.

ANNOTATE: Remind students to mark passages that reveal the author's feelings.

CONNECT: Encourage students to go beyond the text to make connections to times they received a longed-for gift, times they were very fascinated by something, or times they had an important realization about life.

RESPOND: Students will answer questions and write a summary to demonstrate understanding.

Point out to students that while they will always complete the Respond step at the end of the first read, the other steps will probably happen somewhat concurrently. You may wish to print copies of the **First-Read Guide: Nonfiction** for students to use.

MAKING MEANING

About the Author

Annie Dillard (b.1945) published her memoir, *An American Childhood,* in 1987. Dillard's memoir describes her experiences growing up in Pittsburgh, Pennsylvania, during the 1950s. A Pulitzer Prize winner, Dillard received the National Humanities Award from President Barack Obama in 2015.

from An American Childhood

Technical Vocabulary

You will encounter the following words as you read the excerpt from *An American Childhood.*

tissue	enlarged	amoeba

Base Words If these words are unfamiliar to you, analyze each one to see whether it contains a **base word**, or "inside" word, that you know. Then, use your knowledge of the "inside" word, along with context, to determine the meaning of the technical vocabulary word. Here is an example of how to apply the strategy.

Unfamiliar Word: *research*

Familiar "Inside" Word: *search*

Context: The scientist was celebrated for her *research* in microscopic organisms.

Conclusion: Scientists study how things work. Because "search" is in the word *research*, the scientist may have been celebrated for the information she "searched for," or found out, about microscopic organisms.

Apply your knowledge of base words and other vocabulary strategies to determine the meanings of unfamiliar words you encounter during your first read.

First Read NONFICTION

Apply these strategies as you conduct your first read. You will have an opportunity to complete a close read after your first read.

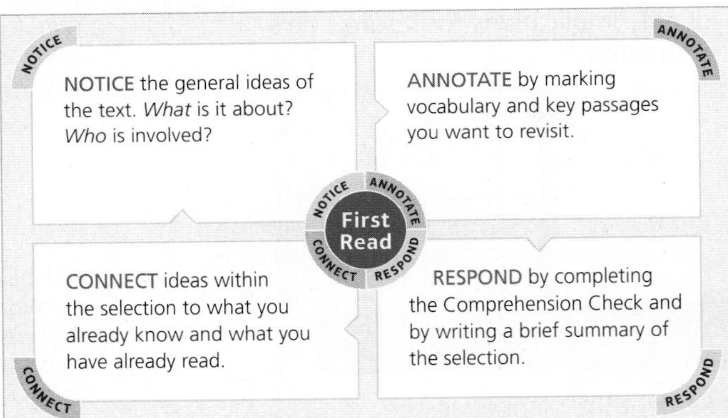

STANDARDS

Reading Informational Text
By the end of the year, read and comprehend literary nonfiction in the grades 6–8 text complexity band proficiently, with scaffolding as needed at the high end of the range.

Language
Use the relationship between particular words to better understand each of the words.

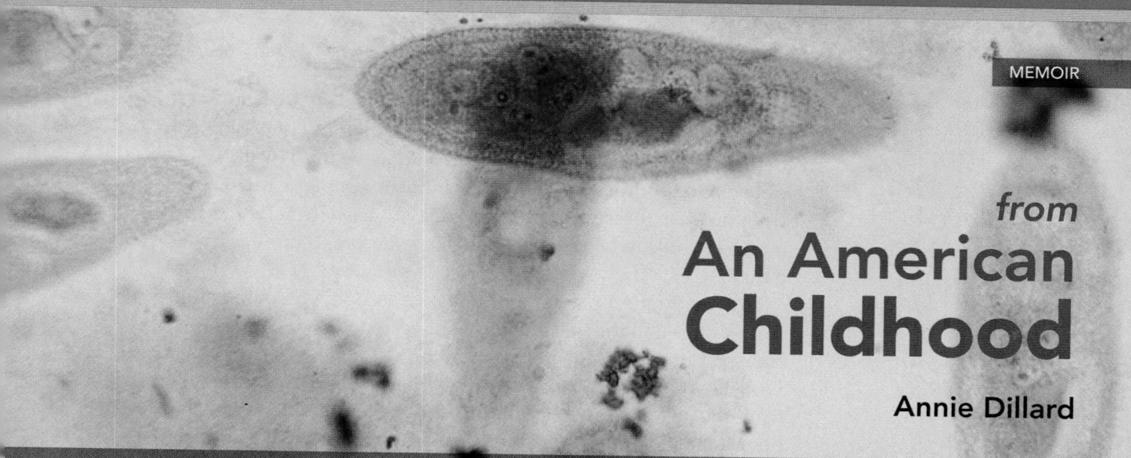

MEMOIR

from An American Childhood

Annie Dillard

BACKGROUND

In the beginning of the excerpt, Annie Dillard mentions *The Field Book of Ponds and Streams*, which sparked her curiosity in microscopes and science. Published in 1930, this text became an important resource for anyone interested in learning about plants and animals in freshwater environments. The book is typically praised for the instructive photographs and drawings it contains, and remains popular today.

1 After I read *The Field Book of Ponds and Streams* several times, I longed for a microscope. Everybody needed a microscope. Detectives used microscopes, both for the FBI and at Scotland Yard. Although usually I had to save my tiny allowance for things I wanted, that year for Christmas my parents gave me a microscope kit.

2 In a dark basement corner, on a white enamel table, I set up the microscope kit. I supplied a chair, a lamp, a batch of jars, a candle, and a pile of library books. The microscope kit supplied a blunt black three-speed microscope, a booklet, a scalpel, a dropper, an ingenious device for cutting thin segments of fragile **tissue**, a pile of clean slides and cover slips, and a dandy array of corked test tubes.

3 One of the test tubes contained "hay infusion." Hay infusion was a wee brown chip of grass blade. You added water to it, and after a week it became a jungle in a drop, full of one-celled animals. This did not work for me. All I saw in the microscope after a week was a wet chip of dried grass, much **enlarged**.

4 Another test tube contained "diatomaceous earth." This was, I believed, an actual pinch of the white cliffs of Dover. On my palm it was an airy, friable[1] chalk. The booklet said it was composed of the silicaceous[2] bodies of diatoms—one-celled creatures that lived in, as it were, small glass jewelry boxes with fitted lids. Diatoms, I read, come in a variety of transparent

NOTES

Mark base words or indicate another strategy you used that helped you determine meaning.

tissue (TIHSH oo) *n.*

MEANING:

enlarged (ehn LAHRJD) *adj.*

MEANING:

1. **friable** (FRY uh buhl) *adj.* easy to crumble.
2. **silicaceous** (sihl ih KAY shee uhs) *adj.* made of silica, like sand.

DIGITAL PERSPECTIVES

Technical Vocabulary

TISSUE If groups are struggling to define the word *tissue* in paragraph 2, point out that if they can't find a base word, they can use context clues or look the word up in a print or online dictionary.

Possible response: In this context, *tissue* means the "material that plants and animals are made of."

ENLARGED If groups are struggling to define the word *enlarged* in paragraph 3, point out that *enlarged* contains the base word *large*. Encourage groups to look at the word as it is used in the selection and use its context, along with knowledge of the base word, to determine the meaning of *enlarged*.

Possible response: *Enlarged* means "made larger."

Technical Vocabulary

AMOEBA If groups are struggling to define the word *amoeba* in paragraph 6, point out that they can use context clues or look the word up in a print or online dictionary.

Possible response: An *amoeba* a "single-celled animal."

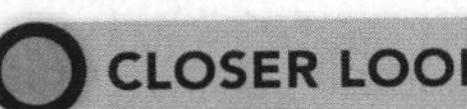

CLOSER LOOK

Analyze Characterization 

Circulate among groups as students conduct their close read. Suggest that groups close read paragraphs 8–11. Encourage them to talk about the annotations they mark. If needed, provide the following support.

ANNOTATE: Have students mark details in these paragraphs that reveal the author's thoughts and feelings, or work with small groups as you highlight them together.

QUESTION: Guide students to consider what these details might tell them. Ask what a reader can infer from the author's thoughts and feelings, and accept student responses.

Possible response: The author's feelings suggest that she is very excited about the amoeba. Her thoughts in paragraph 11 suggest that she is realizing something important.

CONCLUDE: Help students to formulate conclusions about the importance of these details in the text. Ask students why the author might have included these details.

Possible response: These details are leading up to the turning point that the author is describing and they point to the author's message in the selection.

Remind students that **characterization** is the way a writer develops and reveals a character's personality and temperament. Explain that in autobiographical writing and memoir, the author is a character in the narrative and uses the same characterization techniques that an author of fictional writing uses. Writers often reveal a character's traits by showing the character's actions and behavior and by presenting the character's feelings and thoughts. It's up to the reader to make inferences and draw conclusions about a character based on the details the writer provides.

NOTES

Mark base words or indicate another strategy you used that helped you determine meaning.

amoeba (uh MEE buh) *n.*

MEANING:

geometrical shapes. Broken and dead and dug out of geological deposits, they made chalk, and a fine abrasive used in silver polish and toothpaste. What I saw in the microscope must have been the fine abrasive—grit enlarged. It was years before I saw a recognizable, whole diatom. The kit's diatomaceous earth was a bust.

5 All that winter I played with the microscope. I prepared slides from things at hand, as the books suggested. I looked at the transparent membrane inside an onion's skin and saw the cells. I looked at a section of cork and saw the cells, and at scrapings from the inside of my cheek, ditto. I looked at my blood and saw not much; I looked at my urine and saw long iridescent crystals, for the drop had dried.

6 All this was very well, but I wanted to see the wildlife I had read about. I wanted especially to see the famous **amoeba**, who had eluded me. He was supposed to live in the hay infusion, but I hadn't found him there. He lived outside in warm ponds and streams, too, but I lived in Pittsburgh, and it had been a cold winter.

7 Finally late that spring I saw an amoeba. The week before, I had gathered puddle water from Frick Park; it had been festering in a jar in the basement. This June night after dinner I figured I had waited long enough. In the basement at my microscope table I spread a scummy drop of Frick Park puddle water on a slide, peeked in, and lo, there was the famous amoeba. He was as blobby and grainy as his picture; I would have known him anywhere.

8 Before I had watched him at all, I ran upstairs. My parents were still at the table, drinking coffee. They, too, could see the famous amoeba. I told them, bursting, that he was all set up, that they should hurry before his water dried. It was the chance of a lifetime.

9 Father had stretched out his long legs and was tilting back in his chair. Mother sat with her knees crossed, in blue slacks, smoking a Chesterfield. The dessert dishes were still on the table. My sisters were nowhere in evidence. It was a warm evening; the big dining-room windows gave onto blooming rhododendrons.

10 Mother regarded me warmly. She gave me to understand that she was glad I had found what I had been looking for, but that she and Father were happy to sit with their coffee, and would not be coming down.

11 She did not say, but I understood at once, that they had their pursuits (coffee?) and I had mine. She did not say, but I began to understand then, that you do what you do out of your private passion for the thing itself.

12 I had essentially been handed my own life. In subsequent years my parents would praise my drawings and poems, and supply

FACILITATING SMALL-GROUP CLOSE READING

CLOSE READ: Memoir As groups perform the close read, circulate and offer support as needed. Remind groups that when they read a memoir, they should be sure to identify important events in the subject's life and his or her feelings about those events. If the group has difficulty determining which events are important, remind them to think about how events are related to the subject of this unit—turning points.

326 UNIT 3 • TURNING POINTS

me with books, art supplies, and sports equipment, and listen to my troubles and enthusiasms, and supervise my hours, and discuss and inform, but they would not get involved with my detective work, nor hear about my reading, nor inquire about my homework or term papers or exams, nor visit the salamanders I caught, nor listen to me play the piano, nor attend my field hockey games, nor fuss over my insect collection with me, or my poetry collection or stamp collection or rock collection. My days and nights were my own to plan and fill.

13 When I left the dining room that evening and started down the dark basement stairs, I had a life. I sat with my wonderful amoeba, and there he was, rolling his grains more slowly now, extending an arc of his edge for a foot and drawing himself along by that foot, and absorbing it again and rolling on. I gave him some more pond water.

14 I had hit pay dirt. For all I knew, there were paramecia, too, in that pond water, or daphniae, or stentors, or any of the many other creatures I had read about and never seen: volvox, the spherical algal colony; euglena with its one red eye; the elusive, glassy diatom; hydra, rotifers, water bears, worms. Anything was possible. The sky was the limit. ❧

NOTES

Comprehension Check

Complete the following items after you finish your first read. Review and clarify details with your group.

1. What does Dillard most want to see through her microscope?

2. How do Dillard's parents react when she tells them what she discovered when looking through her microscope?

3. **Notebook** Confirm your understanding of the text by writing a summary. Your summary should include Dillard's main points, but it should not include your own opinions of the memoir.

RESEARCH

Research to Clarify Choose at least one unfamiliar scientific detail mentioned in the memoir. Briefly research that detail, and share your findings with your group.

DIGITAL PERSPECTIVES

Comprehension Check

Possible responses:

1. an amoeba
2. Her parents are happy for her but not particularly interested in her discovery.
3. Summaries will vary but should include some of the following elements: The narrator receives a microscope from her parents and begins using it to see many things. However, the thing she most wants to see, an amoeba, eludes her. When she does finally see one and excitedly tries to get her parents to look at it, too, she discovers they are not that interested in it. She learns that her interests and passions belong to her alone and that she can make her own life.

Research

Research to Clarify If groups struggle to choose a detail to research, you may want to suggest they research one of the following topics: the use of microscopes by FBI and Scotland Yard, types of microscopes, diatomaceous earth, diatoms, amoebas, volvox, hydra, rotifers, water bears, and euglena.

PERSONALIZE FOR LEARNING

Challenge

Collage Direct students' attention to paragraph 13. Have them discuss the gift the author received from her parents. Have them consider and discuss these questions: *What is the most important gift you would like to give to your children or to other young people? What do you think is the best way to give this gift?* Challenge each group to create a collage illustrating the gifts that group members would like to pass down to the next generation. Have groups present and display their collages.

Jump Start

CLOSE READ *What events in your life have caused a sudden realization, understanding, or transformation? Was it the event itself or your reaction to the event that caused the change?* As students discuss in their groups, ask them to consider the relationship between things that happen in people's lives and the ways people respond to those events.

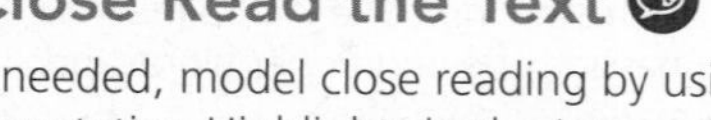

Close Read the Text

If needed, model close reading by using the Annotation Highlights in the Interactive Teacher's Edition.

Remind students to use Accountable Talk in their discussions and to support one another as they complete the close read.

Analyze the Text

1. **Possible response:** The turning point occurs when the narrator excitedly tries to get her parents to look at the amoeba she is so fascinated by and realizes that they do not share her interest. She realizes that her interests and passions belong to her alone and that she can make her own life. This encourages her to follow her passion.
2. **Passages will vary by group.** Remind students to explain why they chose the passage they presented to group members.
3. **Responses will vary.**

Technical Vocabulary

Why These Words? Possible response: The words describe things you might see through a microscope—or how you will see them.

Practice

Possible responses:

When I looked through the microscope, I saw an **amoeba, enlarged** many times. Its **tissue** was strangely fluid.

Word Network

Possible words: *pursuits, passion, subsequent, troubles, enthusiasm*

Word Study

For more support, see **Technical Vocabulary and Word Study**

Possible responses:

enlarge, envelope, encircle, engorge, ensnare

MAKING MEANING

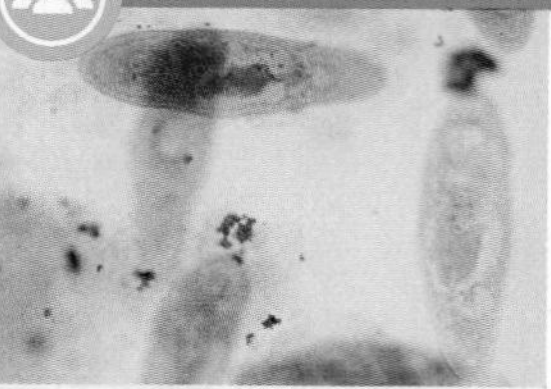

from AN AMERICAN CHILDHOOD

Close Read the Text

With your group, revisit sections of the text you marked during your first read. What do you **notice**? What **questions** do you have? What can you **conclude**?

Analyze the Text

CITE TEXTUAL EVIDENCE to support your answers.

Complete the activities.

1. **Review and Clarify** With your group, reread paragraphs 7–14 of the excerpt. What happens that leads the narrator to a realization about life? What does she realize? How does this realization affect her?
2. **Present and Discuss** Now, work with your group to share the passages from the text that you found especially important.
3. **Essential Question:** ***What can cause a sudden change in someone's life?*** What does the memoir reveal about the ways in which a experience can change someone's life? Discuss.

TIP

GROUP DISCUSSION
When you work in your group to answer the Analyze the Text questions, be sure to support your opinions and ideas with evidence from the text.

LANGUAGE DEVELOPMENT

Technical Vocabulary

tissue	enlarged	amoeba

Why These Words? The technical vocabulary words from the text are related. With your group, determine what the words have in common. Write your ideas, and add another word that fits the category.

Practice

Notebook Confirm your understanding of these words by verifying their meanings in a dictionary. Then, use each word in a sentence. Be sure to include context clues that reveal the words' meanings in your sentences.

WORD NETWORK

Add interesting words related to turning points from the text to your Word Network.

Word Study

Prefix: *en-* The prefix *en-* is often used to turn nouns or adjectives into verbs. In the memoir, Annie Dillard writes about how she used her microscope to see small organisms *enlarged*, or "made larger." The word *large* is an adjective used to describe the size of something. Adding the prefix *en-* to the word *large* creates the verb *enlarge*, which means "to make larger or bigger." For each of the following words, determine how the prefix *en-* turns the base word into a verb, and write a definition for each verb based on your understanding of the meaning of the adjective or noun: *enable, enact, endanger.*

STANDARDS

Language

- Determine or clarify the meaning of unknown and multiple-meaning words and phrases based on *grade 7 reading and content*, choosing flexibly from a range of strategies.
  - d. Verify the preliminary determination of the meaning of a word or phrase.
- Demonstrate understanding of figurative language, word relationships, and nuances in word meanings.
  - b. Use the relationship between particular words to better understand each of the words.

FORMATIVE ASSESSMENT

Analyze the Text

If students struggle to close read the text, then provide the ***from* An American Childhood: Text Questions** available online in the Interactive Teacher's Edition or Unit Resources. Answers and DOK levels are also available.

Concept Vocabulary

If students struggle with the technical vocabulary in this selection, **then** suggest they first look for base words, then examine context clues, and finally check understanding in a dictionary.

Word Study

If students have difficulty identifying words that begin with *en-*, **then** have them consult a dictionary. For Reteach and Practice, see **Word Study: The Prefix *en-* (RP).**

Analyze Craft and Structure

Reflective Writing A **reflective essay** is a short work of nonfiction that expresses an author's thoughts and feelings—or reflections—about an experience or idea. The purpose of reflective writing is to spark readers to respond to the author's ideas with thoughts and feelings of their own.

In a reflective essay, an author typically develops his or her **central ideas**, or most important points, through details about individuals, events, and ideas. Although an author may sometimes state his or her central ideas directly, often the reader must **make inferences**, or educated guesses, based on the details in the text. To do so, notice how the author groups details, and look for sentences or passages that pull these details together.

As you read a reflective essay, think about the thoughts and feelings the author shares and analyze interactions among individuals, events, and ideas. Use the details you notice in your analysis to determine the central ideas.

STANDARDS

Reading Informational Text

- Cite several pieces of textual evidence to support analysis of what the text says explicitly as well as inferences drawn from the text.
- Determine two or more central ideas in a text and analyze their development over the course of the text; provide an objective summary of the text.
- Analyze the interactions between individuals, events, and ideas in a text.

Practice

CITE TEXTUAL EVIDENCE to support your answers.

Notebook Reread the excerpt from *An American Childhood*, and work with your group to analyze the memoir. Use a chart, such as the one shown, to guide your analysis and record your ideas. Then, answer the questions that follow.

PARAGRAPHS	INTERACTIONS	DILLARD'S THOUGHTS AND FEELINGS	MY THOUGHTS AND FEELINGS
1–7	a See possible responses in Teacher's Edition.	b	c
8–11	d	e	f
12–14	g	h	i

1. (a) Based on your analysis, what is one of the central ideas in the excerpt from *An American Childhood*? (b) What might be another central idea Dillard explores in the excerpt? (c) What specific details helped you to identify the central ideas?
2. After analyzing the excerpt, do you feel that Dillard achieved her purpose in writing a reflective piece? Why or why not?

WriteNow Express and Reflect

Rubric Get students thinking about the qualities of good reflective writing by having them create a rubric that includes their own personal criteria for evaluating reflective writing. Qualities in their rubrics might include honesty, universality, and a unique perspective. Have students share their criteria with the class.

DIGITAL PERSPECTIVES

Analyze Craft and Structure

Reflective Writing Explain to students that the interactions in a reflective essay are often a chain of causes and effects. You can analyze and record these interactions by creating a cause-and-effect diagram. You might discover that there are several causes for one effect or that one thing causes several effects. For instance, the gift of the microscope causes other events that eventually lead to the author's realization about her life. For more support, see **Analyze Craft and Structure: Reflective Writing.**

Practice

Possible responses:

a. Narrator interacts with microscope and slides.; b. She is curious and disappointed she doesn't see amoeba.; c. I remember looking through a microscope.; d. Narrator interacts with parents.; e. She is excited to see amoeba and wants to show parents. She realizes her parents aren't interested.; f. My parents are not excited about video games, so I understand.; g. The narrator interacts with microscope and amoeba.; h. She feels free to pursue her own passions.; i. I think her parents could have at least looked at the amoeba.

1. (a) One of the central ideas is how Annie's view of the world is so different from her parents' and that what is mundane to them is so exciting and new for her. (b) Another central idea might be that everyone is unique and is driven by their own passions and interests. (c) The details to this central idea are when Dillard talks about being handed her own life, of her "wonderful amoeba" and how she talks about hitting "pay dirt."
2. I think that Dillard achieved her purpose because she expresses her thoughts and feelings while looking back on her discoveries.

FORMATIVE ASSESSMENT

Analyze Craft and Structure

If students struggle to analyze interactions or to analyze their own thoughts and feelings, **then** guide them in doing so by asking more pointed questions, such as *What does the author think and feel in these paragraphs?* For Reteach and Practice, see **Analyze Craft and Structure: Reflective Writing (RP).**

FACILITATING

Conventions

Appositives and Appositive Phrases As you discuss appositives with students, point out that they often provide helpful context clues. Explain further that students can tell whether or not appositives and appositive phrases need to be set off with commas or dashes by removing the appositive or appositive phrase from the sentence. If the sentence makes sense without it, then commas or dashes are necessary. For more support, see **Conventions: Appositives and Appositive Phrases.**

Read It

See possible responses in chart on student page.

Write It

Possible responses:

Paragraphs will vary, but make sure that students include at least two appositives or appositive phrases and that they punctuate them correctly. Suggest that students use appositives as context clues for their readers to help them determine the meanings of unfamiliar words and technical terms.

FORMATIVE ASSESSMENT

Conventions

If students are unable to identify and use appositives and appositive phrases, then provide sentences with blanks where appositives should go. Have students fill in the appositives. For Reteach and Practice, see **Conventions: Appositives and Appositive Phrases (RP).**

LANGUAGE DEVELOPMENT

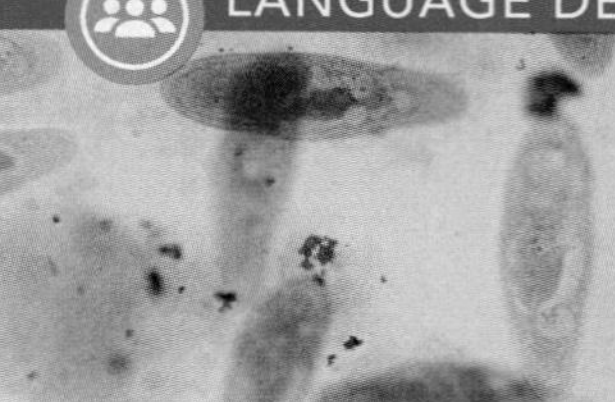

from AN AMERICAN CHILDHOOD

Conventions

Appositives and Appositive Phrases An **appositive** is a noun or pronoun placed next to another noun or pronoun to identify, rename, or explain it.

An **appositive phrase** is an appositive with modifiers, such as adjectives.

APPOSITIVE	APPOSITIVE PHRASE
Our cat, Midnight, likes to sleep on my bed.	Karina—a talented violinist—played a solo.

If the information in an appositive or appositive phrase is essential to understanding the sentence, *do not* set it off with commas or dashes.

EXAMPLE: Have you read the story "Fish Cheeks"?

If the sentence is clear without the information in the appositive or appositive phrase, *do* use commas or dashes to set it off.

EXAMPLE: The author of that story, Amy Tan, is one of my favorites.

Read It

Work with your group to identify examples of appositives and appositive phrases in the selection. Then, discuss Annie Dillard's purpose for including them. Did the appositives and appositive phrases provide useful information to help you understand unfamiliar words or technical terms? Did the information add to your understanding of the excerpt as a whole?

Appositive or Appositive Phrase From the Selection	Noun or Pronoun It Identifies, Renames, or Explains
one-celled creatures	diatoms
grit enlarged	abrasive
the spherical algal colony	volvox

Write It

Notebook Write a paragraph about something in which you are an expert. It could be a type of music, a sport, or a hobby. In your paragraph, use appositives and appositive phrases to help readers understand unfamiliar or technical words, as well as specific references to books or Web sites with which they may be unfamiliar. Use commas or dashes as necessary.

STANDARDS

Language

- Demonstrate command of the conventions of standard English grammar and usage when writing or speaking.
  - a. Explain the function of phrases and clauses in general and their function in specific sentences.
- Demonstrate command of the conventions of standard English capitalization, punctuation, and spelling when writing.

PERSONALIZE FOR LEARNING

English Language Support

Appositives and Appositive Phrases Have students work in pairs to use appositives and appositive phrases to fill in the blanks in the sentences that follow.

1. My brother, ______, loves to cook.
2. My sister, ______, prefers soccer.
3. My mother, ______, is always baking something for a family member or friend.
4. They couldn't even agree about what to name our cat, ______. **ALL LEVELS**

EFFECTIVE EXPRESSION

Speaking and Listening

Assignment

With your group, engage in a **collaborative discussion** in response to one of these questions:

- ☐ What are the advantages and disadvantages of pursuing an interest on your own, without supervision?
- ☐ What are the advantages and disadvantages of sharing hobbies and interests with family or friends?

Project Plan Assign a role to each member of your group. Roles can include a group leader, who keeps the discussion on topic; a timekeeper, who makes sure that the discussion stays within the time alloted by your teacher; and a note taker to record the group's ideas.

Gather Support Work with your group to identify evidence from the excerpt as well as examples from your own experience that support your responses to the question your group chose to discuss. Create a T-chart to list the pros and cons, or advantages and disadvantages, for your topic.

Discuss Here are some things to keep in mind as you hold your group discussion.

- Use the information you noted in the T-chart as well as your own experiences to support your ideas during the discussion.
- Consider the strength of each pro and con. Just because one position has more items does not necessarily mean it is better supported.
- During the discussion, be respectful of others' opinions even if they are different from your own. Express disagreement respectfully by offering **constructive criticism**, or well-reasoned opinions that include both the positive and negative aspects of another group member's contributions. This type of criticism is most likely to persuade another person to adopt your viewpoint, or opinion.
- If a group member provides new information or insights, consider whether this new knowledge changes your views and opinions on the topic.
- Ensure every group member has an opportunity to contribute to the discussion. If you don't fully understand the ideas another group member expresses, ask a question that will help that person elaborate on the ideas he or she expressed.

EVIDENCE LOG

Before moving on to a new selection, go to your Evidence Log and record what you learned from the excerpt from *An American Childhood.*

STANDARDS

Speaking and Listening

Engage effectively in a range of collaborative discussions with diverse partners on *grade 7 topics, texts, and issues,* building on others' ideas and expressing their own clearly.

a. Come to discussions prepared, having read or researched material under study; explicitly draw on that preparation by referring to evidence on the topic, text, or issue to probe and reflect on ideas under discussion.

b. Follow rules for collegial discussions, track progress toward specific goals and deadlines, and define individual roles as needed.

c. Pose questions that elicit elaboration and respond to others' questions and comments with relevant observations and ideas that bring the discussion back on topic as needed.

d. Acknowledge new information expressed by others and, when warranted, modify their own views.

DIGITAL PERSPECTIVES 

Speaking and Listening

Explain to students that a collaborative discussion is like any collaborative project: It involves people working together to achieve a common goal. In this case, the goal is to explore a topic. If groups have difficulty deciding which question to discuss, tell them to choose the one about which people in the group have the most experience. This will make it easier for them to gather support.

Project Plan Encourage students to discuss assignment questions carefully before deciding which to choose. Tell students that they should assign roles based on who is the most comfortable doing each of the tasks.

Gather Support Have students begin by collecting evidence from the selection and then move on to gathering evidence from personal experience. Students should jot down the page and paragraph numbers of any textual evidence so that it can be easily found again.

Discuss Remind students that having an open mind and being flexible enough to change one's opinion based on new information are strengths. For more support, see **Speaking and Listening: Collaborative Discussion.**

Evidence Log Support students in completing their Evidence Log. This paced activity will help prepare them for the Performance-Based Assessment at the end of the unit.

FORMATIVE ASSESSMENT

Speaking and Listening

If groups have difficulty taking turns speaking, **then** give them an object, such as a beanbag, to pass to whoever has the floor. Only the student who has the object may speak. For Reteach and Practice, see **Speaking and Listening: Collaborative Discussion (RP).**

Selection Test

Administer the *from* An American Childhood Selection Test, which is available in both print and digital formats online in Assessments.

PERSONALIZE FOR LEARNING

English Language Support

Preparing for a Collaborative Discussion Have students choose the question from the Assignment section to which they will be responding. Have students prepare a list of ideas and opinions they have about the topic. **EMERGING**

Have students write brief notes about their opinions about the topic and an explanation for each one. **EXPANDING**

Have students prepare an opening statement for the discussion, stating their position on the topic and supporting it with good reasons. **BRIDGING**

An expanded **English Language Support Lesson** on Collaborative Discussion is available in the Interactive Teacher's Edition.

Urban Farming Is Growing a Greener Future

AUDIO SUMMARIES
Audio summaries of "Urban Farming Is Growing a Greener Future" are available online in both English and Spanish in the Interactive Teacher's Edition or Unit Resources. Assigning these summaries prior to reviewing the selection may help students build additional background knowledge and set a context for their first review.

Summary

In this photo gallery by Hillary Schwei, we learn about the phenomenon of urban farming. Growing food locally in cities rather than in the country can have several benefits. The most notable is reducing the cost (and fossil fuel use) that would come from transporting the food over longer distances. Using vacant lots to grow food makes useless bits of land useful and beautiful. It's possible to grow food in surprising places, such as on rooftops, inside brightly lit buildings, and even in the backs of pickup trucks.

Insight

This photo essay introduces students to some basic environmental concepts. It also suggests a way to bring more nature and liveliness to cities.

ESSENTIAL QUESTION:
What can cause a sudden change in someone's life?

Connection to Essential Question

People's lives change when they encounter new possibilities. Urban farming is a surprising idea, one that few people would think of before hearing about it.

SMALL-GROUP LEARNING PERFORMANCE TASK
How are the turning points in the selections similar to and different from each other?

UNIT PERFORMANCE-BASED ASSESSMENT
What can cause a significant change in someone's life?

Connection to Performance Tasks

Small-Group Learning Performance Task The turning points in previous selections demonstrated changes in people's emotional lives and in their relationships with others. This photo essay demonstrates how a turning point in an individual or in an entire society can impact the broader community and the environment.

Unit Performance-Based Assessment This photo essay shows several people who took up urban farming. Doing something completely different from what you're used to—such as farming after a lifetime of doing jobs that are more normal in a city—can change your life.

DIGITAL PERSPECTIVES

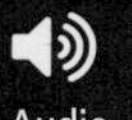
Audio

Video

Document

Annotation Highlights

Online Assessment

LESSON RESOURCES

	Making Meaning	Language Development	Effective Expression
Lesson	**First Review Close Review** / **Analyze the Media**	**Media Vocabulary**	**Research**
Instructional Standards	**RI.7.10** By the end of the year, read and comprehend literary nonfiction . . . **L.7.6** Acquire and use accurately grade-appropriate general academic and domain-specific words and phrases . . .	**L.7.6** Acquire and use accurately grade-appropriate general academic and domain-specific words and phrases . . .	**W.7.6** Use technology, including the Internet . . . **W.7.7** Conduct short research projects . . . **W.7.8** Gather relevant information . . . **SL.7.5** Include multimedia components . . . **SL.7.2** Analyze the main ideas and supporting details . . .
STUDENT RESOURCES			
Available online in the Interactive Student Edition or Unit Resources	Selection Audio First-Review and Close Review Guide: Media: Art and Photography	Word Network	Evidence Log
TEACHER RESOURCES			
Selection Resources Available online in the Interactive Teacher's Edition or Unit Resources	Audio Summaries: English and Spanish Spanish Translation Media Questions First Review Extension Questions	Media Vocabulary	Research: Digital Multimedia Presentation
My Resources	A Unit 3 Answer Key is available online and in the Interactive Teacher's Edition.		

Media Complexity Rubric: Urban Farming Is Growing a Greener Future

Quantitative Measures

Format and Length: 6 photographs with captions

Qualitative Measures	
Knowledge Demands (1–2–**3**–4–5)	To fully understand photographs, prior knowledge is needed about urban farming. Background information introduces the concept to students.
Structure (1–**2**–3–4–5)	Each photograph is labeled with extended caption, making it easy to find information.
Language Conventionality and Clarity (1–2–**3**–4–5)	Background information and captions have some above-level vocabulary and some complex sentences, but context clues will make the text accessible for most students.
Levels of Meaning/Purpose (1–**2**–3–4–5)	Meaning and concepts are straightforward. The main purpose of the selection is to convey the creative ways urban farmers are positively impacting their environments.

Jump Start

FIRST REVIEW Engage students in a discussion of how a photograph can be like a window to the past—or into a distant city. What sorts of things might you discover by looking carefully through such a window? What kinds of details would help you figure out the time and place you're looking at?

Urban Farming Is Growing a Greener Future

How might urban farms change the look and feel of a city? Modeling questions such as this will help students connect to "Urban Farming Is Growing a Greener Future" and to the Small-Group Performance Task assignment. Selection audio and print capability for the selection are available in the Interactive Teacher's Edition.

Concept Vocabulary

Encourage groups to discuss the concept vocabulary. Have they seen the terms in texts before? Do they use any of them in their speech and writing?

Ask groups to look closely at the three terms to discuss what they have in common. Students will notice that two terms are connected: *rural* and *agricultural.*

FIRST REVIEW

Students should perform the steps of the first read independently.

LOOK: Remind students to make a mental note of any details in the photos and captions that raise questions for them.

NOTE: Encourage students should mark any photos with questions they may want revisit during their close review.

CONNECT: Encourage students to make connections beyond the photos themselves. If they cannot make connections to their own lives, have them consider things they have seen or read online or in books or magazines.

RESPOND: Students will answer questions to demonstrate understanding.

Point out to students that while they will always complete the Respond step at the end of the first read, the other steps will probably happen somewhat concurrently. You may wish to print copies of the **First-Review Guide: Media: Art and Photography** for students to use.

MAKING MEANING

About the Author

Hillary Schwei (b. 1980) studied Sustainable Food and Farming at Rutgers University and the University of Montana–Missoula and has worked on various urban gardening and farming programs, both in the United States and abroad. Schwei's belief that sustainable food production reconnects us to our environment and our communities informs her work with urban youth. She strives to educate young people about the benefits that urban, local food production can provide to the communities in which they live.

Urban Farming Is Growing a Greener Future

Concept Vocabulary

These words will be useful to you as you analyze, discuss, and write about the photographs.

rural: characteristic of the country; of or pertaining to agriculture **EXAMPLE:** The family moved from a busy city to a quiet **rural** neighborhood surrounded by farms.
agricultural: related to the science and art of farming **EXAMPLE:** A lot of the **agricultural** land that used to surround the town has been turned from cornfields into houses and stores.
localizing: gathering, collecting, or concentrating in a particular place **EXAMPLE:** **Localizing** food production helps to provide consumers with fresher produce because the produce comes from places near where they live.

First Review MEDIA: ART AND PHOTOGRAPHY

Study the photographs using these strategies.

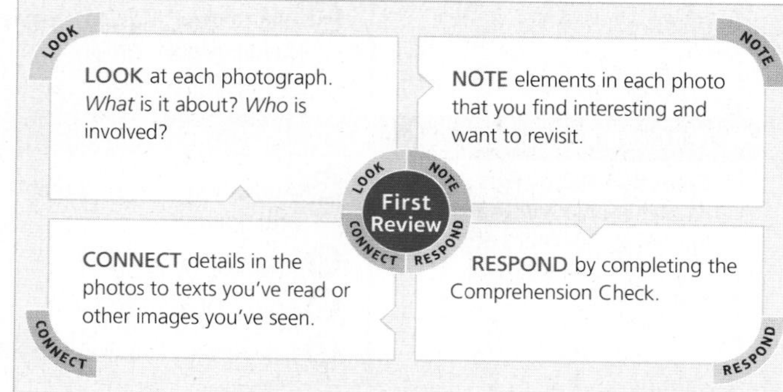

STANDARDS

Reading Informational Text
By the end of the year, read and comprehend literary nonfiction in the grades 6–8 text complexity band proficiently, with scaffolding as needed at the high end of the range.

Language
Acquire and use accurately grade-appropriate general academic and domain-specific words and phrases; gather vocabulary knowledge when considering a word or phrase important to comprehension or expression.

MEDIA | PHOTO GALLERY

Urban Farming Is Growing a Greener Future

Hillary Schwei

BACKGROUND

The year 2008 marked the first time that more people on Earth lived in cities than in **rural** areas. One significant consequence of this turning point is that most people no longer live in the **agricultural** areas that provide them with food.

Some city dwellers are transforming their concrete environments by establishing farms, often in the most unlikely locations. These urban farms create a new landscape that adapts the man-made structures of the city to the purposes of sustainable food production. **Localizing** food production through urban farming provides aesthetic, health, environmental, and economic benefits. Locally grown food not only supplies people with fresh, seasonal produce, but it also strengthens local economies by supporting family farmers and other local businesses. Farming in urban areas reduces the need to transport food over long distances to reach the consumer. The decrease in transportation creates environmental advantages such as lower levels of pollution and decreased fossil fuel use. This photo gallery provides a glimpse at unique and innovative urban farming projects.

PHOTO 1: Urban farms are not a new idea. During both world wars, the government encouraged Americans to plant Victory Gardens where they could grow their own food. Here, in 1943, children work in a garden in New York City.

DIGITAL PERSPECTIVES  

CLOSER REVIEW

Analyze Details 

Circulate among groups as students conduct their first review. Suggest that groups close review Photo 1. Encourage them to talk about the notes they make. If needed, provide the following support.

NOTE: Have students note the details in the photo that reveal things about what the boys are doing and when they did it, or work with small groups to have students participate while you note them together.

QUESTION: Guide students to consider what these details might tell them. Ask what a viewer can infer from the boys' clothing and tools, and accept student responses.

Possible response: The shirts and trousers the boys are wearing look dressier than work clothes today; the scene probably took place a long time ago. They're using garden hoes and rakes.

CONCLUDE: Help students to formulate conclusions about the importance of these details in the photo. Ask students why the photographer might have included these details.

Possible response: The clothes suggest that this photo was taken a long time ago. The tools show that boys are gardening. The sign says that the "Boys of Ludlow Street" are creating something called a "Victory Garden." The photographer likely wanted to show some of the ways that even young citizens were contributing to the war effort by planting gardens in unlikely places.

Remind students that **details** in photographs help establish the setting and the action.

FACILITATING SMALL-GROUP CLOSE REVIEWING

CLOSE REVIEW: Photo Gallery As groups perform the close review, circulate and offer support as needed.

- Remind groups that when looking at photographs, they should first try to identify the subject and setting.
- Point out that each photograph is accompanied by a caption, which gives explanatory details about the photo. Encourage students to review each photo a second time—after they have read the caption.
- Challenge groups to find connections between each photo and the title of the selection. How does the photo support the idea of urban farming's "greener future"?

CLOSER REVIEW

Analyze Contrast

Circulate among groups as students conduct their close review. Suggest that groups close review Photo 2. Encourage them to talk about the notes they make. If needed, provide the following support.

NOTE: Have students note aspects of the photograph that demonstrate the urban setting, or work with small groups to have students participate while you note them together.

QUESTION: Guide students to consider what these details might tell them. Ask what a viewer can infer from the signs of an urban setting, and accept student responses.

Possible response: The skyscrapers in the background and the graffiti on the buildings indicate this is an urban setting.

CONCLUDE: Help students to formulate conclusions about the importance of these details in the photo. Ask students why the photographer might have included these details.

Possible response: The photographer probably wanted to emphasize that this is an unusual farm—it's located right in the middle of a big city.

Remind students that a photographer may choose to convey an idea through **contrast** or difference. By showing details that are opposite, the photographer asks the reader to notice and evaluate the difference.

PHOTO 2: Urban farms can make use of vacant city lots that are often considered **eyesores**, or ugly, unpleasant sights in public places. The farms become not only a source of food and beauty, but provide a location for members of the community to gather. An area of neglected, polluted land next to a railway station in Perth, Australia, has been revived as an organic farm.

NOTES

PHOTO 3: New York City will never completely return to its long-lost agricultural origins, but in 2011, this midtown hotel began growing fruit, vegetables, and herbs on the building's roof to supply the hotel's kitchen. The hotel also keeps honeybees, which roam for miles pollinating city plants.

NOTES

334 UNIT 3 • TURNING POINTS

PHOTO 4: Only 12 percent of Japan's land is suitable for agriculture, but in this company's headquarters in Tokyo, office workers can take time to cultivate produce. One-fifth of the nine-story building is devoted to farming.

NOTES

PHOTO 5: Urban farming, like traditional farming, is a year-round operation. The greenhouses at this farm in Chicago have to be maintained regardless of the season. Each acre of the farm produces 20,000 pounds of produce annually.

NOTES

CROSS-CURRICULAR PERSPECTIVES

Science Call student attention to Photo 5 and its caption. A greenhouse enables plants to be grown all year long. Because occupied school buildings are heated through the cold weather months, plants grown inside a school building can enjoy the same extended growing period that a greenhouse offers. Have interested students conduct research into how to grow plants in a classroom greenhouse environment. Ask them to report on what they learned, giving details about what would be needed to raise plants in the classroom. If you wish to conduct an experiment, obtain the necessary seeds and soil and ask volunteers to carry it out.

CLOSER REVIEW

Analyze Composition 

Circulate among groups as students conduct their close review. Suggest that groups close review Photo 6. Encourage them to talk about the notes they make. If needed, provide the following support.

NOTE: Review with students that a photographer's composition is the way he or she arranges or combines parts of the photograph to form the whole image. Have students note the elements of the photograph's composition, or work with small groups to have students participate while you highlight them together.

QUESTION: Guide students to consider what these details might tell them. Ask what the main elements are in the foreground of the picture and what the main elements are in the background. Accept student responses.

Possible response: The two men and the garden in the truck's bed are in the foreground. A large apartment building is in the background.

CONCLUDE: Help students formulate conclusions about the importance of the details in this photograph. Ask students why the photographer might have chosen to include these details.

Possible response: The composition shows two contrasting elements that the photographer considers important. The men and the garden in the truck show how important gardening is. The large apartment building contrasted with the garden shows that gardening and growing fruits and vegetables is possible anywhere, even in small spaces within a big city.

Remind students that **composition** is the arrangement of items in a photograph. Composition helps viewers see and understand where every element stands in order of importance to the photographer.

PHOTO 6: This 30-year-old pickup truck is a mobile farm and travels around giving students in city schools a chance to experience how food grows. The farmers who own the truck made a film about their exploits and strive to support others who grow produce in creative ways.

NOTES

NOTES

DIGITAL PERSPECTIVES

Enriching the Text Show students the teaser for the video "Truck Farm," available by searching on the Internet. Tell them beforehand to watch carefully as a truck farm is created right before their eyes. Prepare them to take notes on what they see. Can they spot the steps involved?

After students have viewed the video, have small groups discuss and write the steps. Then, as a class, see if everyone noted these steps.

- A mat is laid down in the truck bed.
- Light soil is poured in.
- Another mat is laid down.
- Dark soil is poured in.
- Rows are dug, and seeds are planted.

Point out that the first layer of soil is material that water can circulate through, and the darker layer is growing soil, for the seeds to sprout in.

DIGITAL PERSPECTIVES

Comprehension Check

The selection uses both words and photographs to provide information about urban farming. Use the chart below to note specific details about each photo. Then, describe how each photo relates to the text that accompanies it.

PHOTO	WHAT THE PHOTO SHOWS	HOW THE PHOTO RELATES TO THE TEXT
PHOTO 1	Boys in the 1940s are making their own Victory Garden.	Even back in the 1940s, people raised crops in cities.
PHOTO 2	An urban garden was planted in Perth, Australia.	The people of Perth turned one neglected lot into a garden.
PHOTO 3	A restaurant chef is standing by his own rooftop garden.	It shows how a New York City hotel provides locally grown vegetables for its guests.
PHOTO 4	An officer worker in Japan cultivates produce.	Crops can even be grown in office buildings.
PHOTO 5	A man is working in an urban garden in Chicago.	Urban gardens can provide a significant amount of fresh produce.
PHOTO 6	Two men stand next to a garden in the back of a pickup truck.	Gardens can grow just about anywhere.

Comprehension Check

See possible responses in chart on student page.

PERSONALIZE FOR LEARNING

Challenge

Hydroponic Gardens Have students research "exploring hydroponics" on the Internet. Have them select from the many options available for raising plants without any soil at all, and decide which option would be best for your own classroom. If facilities allow, encourage students to raise some plants of their own. The exercise should drive home the fact that if given water and light, plants can—and will—grow almost anywhere.

FACILITATING

Jump Start

CLOSE REVIEW Ask students to consider the following prompt: If urban gardens keep becoming more popular, what might a city of the future look like? As students discuss the prompt in their groups, have them consider possible developments like gardens and forests on the roofs of office buildings, and greenways instead of streets for pedestrians and cyclists.

Close Review

If needed, model close reviewing by using the Closer Review notes in the Interactive Teacher's Edition.

Remind students to use Accountable Talk in their discussions and to support one another as they complete the close review.

Analyze the Media

Encourage groups to discuss their decisions about the photos using specific reasons for their choices. Was it the way the photo was taken, or was it something in the content?

1. Responses will vary by group. Remind students to review their notes from the first review to get details that support their positions before discussing with the group.
2. Responses will vary by group. Groups should support their explanations with evidence from the photographs.
3. Possible response: The pictures of Perth show how a polluted and empty area was greened up and made useful and even beautiful for people who live in the city. For people in cities like Perth, growing gardens in vacant lots can become a kind of turning point that causes positive changes in people's lives.

Concept Vocabulary

For more support, see **Concept Vocabulary.**

Possible responses:

1. The turning point was in 2008, when for the first time more people lived in cities, or urban areas, than in the countryside—this means most people don't live near the agricultural areas where food is grown.
2. All the images are photos of gardens in some kind of urban area, whether it's in an office building, on a rooftop, or in the back of a truck on a street; they show people localizing produce for people in cities.
3. Some of the benefits are very practical—you can see how close localizing brings the fruits and vegetables being grown to the buildings where urban people live.

MAKING MEANING

URBAN FARMING IS GROWING A GREENER FUTURE

Close Review

With your group, revisit the selection and your first-review notes. Write any new observations that seem important. What **questions** do you have? What can you **conclude**?

Analyze the Media

CITE TEXTUAL EVIDENCE to support your answers.

Notebook Complete the activities.

1. **Present and Discuss** Choose the photo you found most interesting or powerful. Explain what you noticed in the photo, the questions it raised for you, and the conclusions you reached about it.
2. **Review and Synthesize** With your group, review all the photos. In what ways do they increase your understanding of the information communicated in the text?
3. **Essential Question:** ***What can cause a sudden change in someone's life?*** What has this selection taught you about turning points? Discuss with your group.

WORD NETWORK

Add interesting words related to turning points from the text to your Word Network.

STANDARDS

Writing

- Use technology, including the Internet, to produce and publish writing and link to and cite sources as well as to interact and collaborate with others, including linking to and citing sources.
- Conduct short research projects to answer a question, drawing on several sources and generating additional related, focused questions for further research and investigation.
- Gather relevant information from multiple print and digital sources, using search terms effectively; assess the credibility and accuracy of each source; and quote or paraphrase the data and conclusions of others while avoiding plagiarism and following a standard format for citation.

Speaking and Listening

- Analyze the main ideas and supporting details presented in diverse media and formats and explain how the ideas clarify a topic, text, or issue under study.
- Include multimedia components and visual displays in presentations to clarify claims and findings and emphasize salient points.

LANGUAGE DEVELOPMENT

Concept Vocabulary

Use the concept vocabulary words in your responses to the following questions.

rural	agricultural	localizing

1. What turning point is described in the background information for this selection?
2. Identify at least one thing that all of the images have in common.
3. Did the photo gallery change your views on what types of changes can be considered "turning points"? Why or why not? Explain the reasons for your response.

FORMATIVE ASSESSMENT

Analyze the Media

If students struggle to close review the photographs, **then** provide **Urban Farming Is Growing a Greener Future: Media Questions** available online in the Interactive Teacher's Edition or Unit Resources. Answers and DOK levels are also available.

Concept Vocabulary

If students struggle with the concept vocabulary, **then** suggest they look for base words, examine context clues, and finally check understanding in a dictionary.

EFFECTIVE EXPRESSION

Research

Assignment

Work in your group to research and create a **digital multimedia presentation** on one of the following topics:

- ☐ urban farms and community gardens in your area
- ☐ how to start an urban farm or community garden
- ☐ the health and environmental benefits of urban farming
- ☐ where the food used in your school cafeteria comes from and how many "food miles" it travels ("Food miles" is the distance food travels from where it is grown to where it is consumed.)

Focus Your Research Begin by working with your group to formulate a research question to guide and focus your search for sources. A focused research question will also help you avoid sources that are not useful to your topic. Consider the following example:

topic: turning points in modern American literature

vague research question: What are works of American literature that discuss turning points?

revised research question: What new American short stories explore the theme of turning points?

Plan the Project Use the questions in the chart to prepare your presentation. Record your notes in the right column of the chart.

What relevant, reliable print, digital, and multimedia sources can you use in your research? Take notes on the information you obtain from each source. Your final presentation should include a digital Works-Cited list with electronic links to Internet sources.	
What information will be better conveyed by text?	
What information will be better conveyed by images?	
What information will be better conveyed by spoken word, music, or sound?	

TIP

GROUP DISCUSSION

With your group, consider the relationships among your visuals. Should they have a similar look or can they differ? If you decide they should be uniform, how can you achieve that?

EVIDENCE LOG

Before moving on to a new selection, go to your Evidence Log and record what you learned from "Urban Farming Is Growing a Greener Future."

DIGITAL PERSPECTIVES

Research

If groups have trouble deciding how to divide up tasks, encourage them to consider which option plays to their group's strengths the most. For example, if the group has a tech savvy member, he or she may be put in charge of gathering and displaying images. If another student has experience gathering information from the Web or recording links, he or she may be chosen for these tasks.

Focus Your Research Questions Make clear that the coming up with clear, concise questions is half the battle in creating a good presentation. Remind them that choosing a topic everyone can agree on is also important. Explain to students that once the topic is settled, they should discuss the topic and record any questions they have.

Plan the Project Remind students to consult the schedule for the Small-Group activities as they create their project plan. Check to make sure each group has made assignments and that the work is divided evenly among the groups. For more support, see **Research: Digital Multimedia Presentation.**

Evidence Log Support students in completing their Evidence Log. This paced activity will help prepare them for the Performance-Based Assessment at the end of the unit.

PERSONALIZE FOR LEARNING

Strategic Support

Organization Students may require support in separating main ideas from details. Remind them the main, or governing idea, of their presentation must be supported by further information that makes that idea clear—these are the details. Have groups create main idea and details charts, with one box that goes across the top, for the main idea, and as many columns as they need (with a minimum of three) below, for listing the details that support that idea.

FACILITATING

Present an Explanatory Essay

Before groups begin work on their projects, have them clearly differentiate the role each group member will play. Remind groups to consults the schedule for Small-Group Learning to guide their work during the Performance Task.

Students should complete the assignment using presentation software to take advantage of text, graphics, and sound features.

Plan With Your Group

Analyze the Text Remind students that they will need to include evidence from the selections in their explanations. As they fill in the chart to analyze the turning points, they should note page and paragraph numbers of sentences and details they might want to refer to in their presentations. Taking the time to record this information as they plan will save them time when they begin to gather details.

Gather Details and Media Encourage groups to discuss what they should look for as they search for media to include. Point out that students will find many media examples of turning points, so they'll want to choose the ones that best fit their presentations.

Organize Your Ideas Give students a list of transitional words and phrases that they can use to lead the audience from one section of the presentation to the next. For instance, tell students that in addition to words that show sequence, like *first, next,* and *lastly*, they can use words that compare and contrast turning points.

- Compare: *also, like, likewise, similarly*
- Contrast: *but, however, unlike, instead of*

PERFORMANCE TASK: SPEAKING AND LISTENING FOCUS

SOURCES

- THANK YOU, M'AM
- *from* AN AMERICAN CHILDHOOD
- URBAN FARMING IS GROWING A GREENER FUTURE

Present an Explanatory Essay

Assignment

With your group, review the selections you have read in this section, and consider the ways the different turning points are described in the selections. Then, present an **explanatory essay in the form of a multimedia presentation** in response to the following prompt:

How are the turning points in the selections similar to and different from each other?

Use images and other multimedia to emphasize and clarify key points in your presentation.

Plan With Your Group

Analyze the Text With your group, analyze the ways in which the turning points in the selections are similar to and different from each other. Use this chart to organize your ideas about what each text says about turning points and their significance.

SELECTION	What led to the turning point?	Details that describe the turning point	What was the significance of the turning point?
Thank You, M'am			
from An American Childhood			
Urban Farming Is Growing a Greener Future			

Gather Details and Media Each group member should then choose one selection on which he or she will focus for the presentation. Work individually to gather details and information about the turning point in the selection you chose. Next, organize your ideas and draft a brief explanatory essay for your section of the presentation. Your essay should compare and contrast the turning point in the selection you chose to the turning points in the other selections in this section. Then, conduct research to find relevant multimedia to include in your presentation.

Organize Your Ideas As a group, organize the sections of the presentation and decide how you will transition smoothly from one section to the next and one speaker to the next. How will you tie all the information and ideas back together at the end of your presentation?

STANDARDS

Writing

Write informative/explanatory texts to examine a topic and convey ideas, concepts, and information through the selection, organization, and analysis of relevant content.

AUTHOR'S PERSPECTIVE: Ernest Morrell, Ph.D.

Mastering Classroom Talk Complex texts can be intimidating and alien to some students, especially those who have had limited exposure to such texts. However, these same students often show deep critical and analytical skills when considering popular culture. Teachers can use their students' background knowledge of popular culture and their enthusiasm for it to increase motivation and classroom talk, especially debate skills, small-group work, and formal public presentations. Start by incorporating elements of popular culture such as rap and hip-hop, movies, or sports into a traditional unit of study. Place popular culture alongside the other historical/literacy periods covered in the unit so students can use their knowledge of the familiar works as a lens through which to evaluate the new ones. Second, have students evaluate one literary work in the program, such as a poem, alongside a contemporary reference of their choice. This approach helps students gain the understanding and confidence they need to discuss classroom texts and enhance their critical perspectives.

Rehearse With Your Group

Practice With Your Group Before you deliver your presentation, rehearse the presentation as a group. Plan the ways in which you will present your multimedia elements: Will you hold up images or prop them against something, or will you present your information digitally? Practice delivering the presentation using a formal tone, appropriate eye contact, adequate volume, and clear pronunciation.

As you deliver your portion of the presentation, use this checklist to evaluate the effectiveness of your group's rehearsal. Then, use your evaluation and the instruction here to guide your revisions to the presentation.

CONTENT	USE OF MEDIA	PRESENTATION TECHNIQUES
☐ The presentation clearly responds to the prompt. ☐ The presentation includes relevant details from the text. ☐ The presentation effectively compares and contrasts the turning points in the selections.	☐ The presentation includes a variety of multimedia. ☐ The multimedia emphasizes and clarifies key points.	☐ The speaker uses a formal tone and speaks with adequate volume and clear pronunciation. ☐ The speaker maintains eye contact with the audience.

Fine-Tune the Content Put yourself in the position of a person hearing the presentation for the first time. Is there anything he or she might not understand? If so, try restating unclear ideas in several ways to see what way works best.

Improve Your Use of Media Be sure to sequence your multimedia elements in a way that emphasizes your key points. Each piece of multimedia should relate directly to a key point in your presentation and should help your audience to better understand the information.

Brush Up on Your Presentation Techniques Take turns presenting with your group members. Point out places where the speaker may sound flat, be too quiet, or lack clarity.

Present and Evaluate

As you listen to other groups, consider their content, use of media, and presentation techniques. Be ready to ask questions, and discuss the ways in which other groups' presentations helped deepen your understanding of the ways in which turning points impact people's lives.

STANDARDS

Speaking and Listening

- Engage effectively in a range of collaborative discussions with diverse partners on *grade 7 topics, texts, and issues,* building on others' ideas and expressing their own clearly.
- Analyze the main ideas and supporting details presented in diverse media and formats and explain how the ideas clarify a topic, text, or issue under study.
- Present claims and findings, emphasizing salient points in a focused, coherent manner with pertinent descriptions, facts, details, and examples; use appropriate eye contact, adequate volume, and clear pronunciation.
- Include multimedia components and visual displays in presentations to clarify claims and findings and emphasize salient points.
- Adapt speech to a variety of contexts and tasks, demonstrating command of formal English when indicated or appropriate.

DIGITAL PERSPECTIVES

Rehearse With Your Group

Practice With Your Group Suggest that each student practice his or her portion of the presentation several times in front of the group. Afterward, students should ask their practice audience specific questions, such as "Could you hear me?" "Did I speak at the right pace and with a tone appropriate to the subject and purpose?" and "Could you follow my ideas?"

Improve Your Use of Media Remind students that any media they include should directly relate to, clarify, and support their ideas. In addition, media should be suited to purpose and audience. For instance, students should avoid music with offensive lyrics.

Present and Evaluate

Before beginning the presentations, set the expectations for the audience. You may wish to have students consider these questions as groups present.

- What was the presenting group's main idea?
- What were some of their supporting details?
- Which multimedia best illustrated their explanations?
- What presentation skills did this group excel at?

As students provide feedback to the presenting group, remind them that compliments are just as valuable as constructive criticism.

OVERVIEW

INDEPENDENT LEARNING

What can cause a sudden change in someone's life?

Encourage students to think carefully about what they have already learned and what more they want to know about the unit topic of turning points. This is a key first step to previewing and selecting the text or media they will read or review in Independent Learning.

Independent Learning Strategies

Review the Learning Strategies with students and explain that as they work through Independent Learning they will develop strategies to work on their own.

- Have students watch the video on Independent Learning Strategies.
- A video on this topic is available online in the Professional Development Center.

Students should include any favorite strategies that they might have devised on their own during Whole-Class and Small-Group Learning. For example, for the strategy "Create a schedule," students might include:

- Understand the goals and deadlines.
- Make a schedule for what to do each day.

Block Scheduling

Each day in this Pacing Plan represents a 40–50 minute class period. Teachers using block scheduling may combine days to reflect their class schedule. In addition, teachers may revise pacing to differentiate and support core instruction by integrating components and resources as students require.

OVERVIEW: INDEPENDENT LEARNING

ESSENTIAL QUESTION:

What can cause a sudden change in someone's life?

A sudden change in a person's life may come from an inner realization or it may be a result of external forces, such as the actions of others or the environment that surrounds that person. In this section, you will complete your study of turning points by exploring an additional selection related to the topic. You'll then share what you learn with classmates. To choose a text, follow these steps.

Look Back Think about the selections you have already studied. What most interests you about the topic of turning points?

Look Ahead Preview the texts by reading the descriptions. Which one seems most interesting and appealing to you?

Look Inside Take a few minutes to scan through the text you chose. Choose a different one if this text doesn't meet your needs.

Independent Learning Strategies

Throughout your life, in school, in your community, and in your career, you will need to rely on yourself to learn and work on your own. Review these strategies and the actions you can take to practice them during Independent Learning. Add ideas of your own for each category.

STRATEGY	ACTION PLAN
Create a schedule	• Understand your goals and deadlines. • Make a plan for what to do each day. •
Practice what you have learned	• Use first-read and close-read strategies to deepen your understanding. • After you read, evaluate the usefulness of the evidence to help you understand the topic. • Consider the quality and reliability of the source. •
Take notes	• Record important ideas and information. • Review notes before preparing to share with a group. •

Pacing Plan

Introduce Whole-Class Learning

Unit Introduction | A Christmas Carol: Scrooge and Marley, Act I | A Christmas Carol: Scrooge and Marley, Act II | Media: from Scrooge | Performance Task

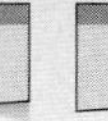
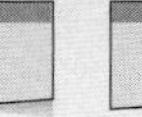

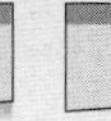

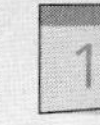
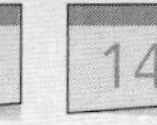

1 2 3 4 5 6 7 8 9 10 11 12 13 14 15 16 17 18

Choose one selection. Selections are available online only.

CONTENTS

Contents

Selections Encourage students to scan and preview the selections before choosing the one they would like to read or review. Suggest that they consider the genre and subject matter of each one before making their decision. You can use the information on the following Planning pages to advise students in making their choice.

Remind students that the selections for Independent Learning are only available in the the Interactive Student Edition. Allow students who do not have digital access at home to preview the selections or review the media selection(s) using classroom or computer lab technology. Then either have students print the selection they choose or provide a printout for them.

Performance Based-Assessment Prep

Review Evidence for an Explanatory Essay Point out to students that collecting evidence during Independent Learning is the last step in completing their Evidence Log. After they finish their independent reading, they will synthesize all the evidence they have compiled in the unit.

The evidence students collect will serve as the primary source of information they will use to complete the writing and oral presentation for the Performance-Based Assessment at the end of the unit.

Little Things Are Big

Summary

"Little Things Are Big" is a reflective essay by Jesus Colon. He recalls one night when he was riding the subway and saw a young woman who was having trouble. She had a baby in one hand, a suitcase in the other, and two young children following her. Colon considered helping her out. But he feared that because she was white and he was Puerto Rican, she would be scared of him and not want his help. Colon regrets his choice and reflects that this is the fruit of prejudice. Prejudice not only harms people directly, it also prevents people from helping others for fear of it.

Insight

This is a thoughtful reflection on how prejudice weakens our social fabric. Students will likely be able to think of other examples, such as how minorities are often afraid to ask the police for help for fear of discrimination.

SELECTION RESOURCES

- First-Read Guide: Nonfiction
- Close-Read Guide: Nonfiction
- Little Things Are Big: Text Questions
- Audio Summaries
- Selection Audio
- Selection Test

Connection to Essential Question

Colon's essay helps readers consider the Essential Question, "What can cause a sudden change in someone's life?" Often, people change when they feel bad about some action or inaction. Students will see that in this essay, guilt lingers, the writer reflects on it and commits to change something they did—or something they failed to do—and wonder why they did it.

Connection to Performance-Based Assessment

The prompt is "What can cause a significant change in someone's life?" Seemingly small events can act like a microcosm, a perfect example of much bigger concerns. The small event that Colon describes helps him change the way he sees the world.

Text Complexity Rubric: Little Things Are Big	
Quantitative Measures	
Lexile: 1150 **Text Length:** 807 words	
Qualitative Measures	
Knowledge Demands (1–2–**3**–4–5)	The central situation involving a man dealing with his awareness of stereotypes may not be familiar to all students, but the concepts and feelings are explained clearly.
Structure (1–**2**–3–4–5)	The selection is a first-person reflective essay told in a straightforward, linear way.
Language Conventionality and Clarity (1–2–3–**4**–5)	The syntax includes many complex sentences that have several subordinate clauses or phrases; the selection has a lot of descriptive sentences with some above-level vocabulary.
Levels of Meaning/Purpose (1–2–**3**–4–5)	The selection has only one level of meaning. The main concept and supporting ideas are clearly stated.

DIGITAL PERSPECTIVES

Audio | Video | Document | Annotation Highlights | EL Highlights | Online Assessment

SELECTION RESOURCES

- First-Read Guide: Nonfiction
- Close-Read Guide: Nonfiction
- Profile: Malala Yousafzai: Text Questions
- Audio Summaries
- Selection Audio
- Selection Test

Profile: Malala Yousafzai

Summary

"Profile: Malala Yousafzai" is a news article about a famous girl who speaks and writes about the importance of education. Malala Yousafzai is from Pakistan, where some people are strongly against allowing girls to seek education. Malala campaigned for education, and militants tried to murder her for it. She survived being shot in the head and has published diaries and an autobiography about her life and work. She has won numerous humanitarian awards, including the Nobel Peace Prize. She is famous worldwide. Malala now goes to school in England. It is safer there than the rural region of Pakistan where she spent her earlier childhood. She still advocates for equal access to education, there and everywhere.

Insight

The way people respond to our actions can change our lives suddenly and drastically. When people try to stop someone from taking action that they deeply care about, often the person they target becomes even more determined to change the world.

Connection to Essential Question

Malala Yousafzai's life experience offers a concrete answer to the Essential Question: "What can cause a sudden change in someone's life?" The violence Malala faced was terrible, and it lead to worldwide fame, allowing her to communicate her message of education to a broader audience.

Connection to Performance-Based Assessment

Students may tap into Malala Yousafzai's experiences to help them address the Peformance-Based Assessment Prompt, "What can cause a significant change in someone's life?" Students may tap into Malala Yousafzai's experiences to help them address the Peformance-Based Assessment Prompt. Facing great opposition can make some people give up; it can give some others more resolve to fight harder than ever.

Text Complexity Rubric: Profile: Malala Yousafzai	
Quantitative Measures	
Lexile: 1330 **Text Length:** 950 words	
Qualitative Measures	
Knowledge Demands ① ② **❸** ④ ⑤	This profile contains references to Taliban, Pakistan, Swat Valley, and militants, not all of which are explained. Students may need more background and historical context about these terms.
Structure ① ② **❸** ④ ⑤	Information in the selection is logically organized, but connections between ideas are not always completely explicit or presented in a predictable sequence. A few headings help with organization.
Language Conventionality and Clarity ① ② ③ **❹** ⑤	The syntax includes many complex sentences that have several subordinate clauses or phrases; selection has a lot of above-level vocabulary.
Levels of Meaning/Purpose ① ② **❸** ④ ⑤	This profile of a young girl combines the struggle to overcome challenges, Malala's cause, and the life events which made her a Nobel Prize winner.

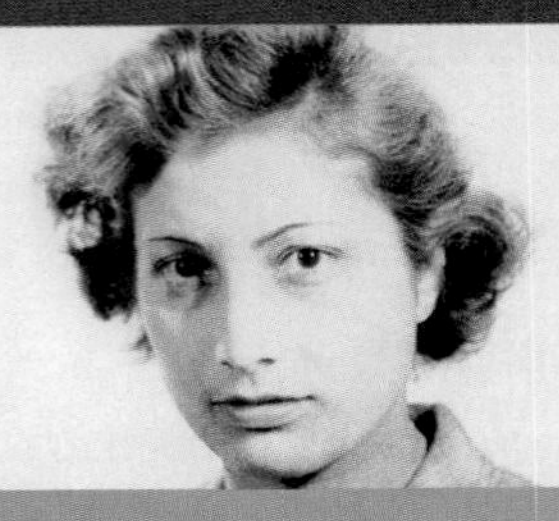

Noor Inayat Khan *from* Women Heroes of WWII

Summary

In this biography of Noor Inayat Khan, Kathryn J. Atwood discusses a hero of World War II. Noor Inayat Khan was born in Russia and grew up in France. After college, she planned to write inspiring stories. Instead, she ended up living one. When Germany began invading continental countries, Noor escaped to England and joined the British Women's Auxiliary Air Force. She became a radio operator for England's air force. But she wasn't satisfied; she wanted to fight the Nazis more directly. She joined the Special Operations Executive, which sent agents into occupied France to fight the Nazis from within. Despite some leaders' doubts that her shy personality would be a poor fit for spy work, Noor was a courageous spy. When the Paris resistance was collapsing, she stayed and passed crucial information back to London. At one point, she was arrested and jailed but found other spies in the prison. Noor was ultimately taken to a death camp with three other British agents. They were killed, and Noor was honored by both Britain and France for her courage.

Insight

World War II was truly international. People from unexpected backgrounds, like this shy South Asian immigrant, made great contributions to defeating the Nazis. Furthermore, the story shows how a shocking problem can greatly change someone's life. It's hard to imagine someone going from writing children's books to being a spy. But when the war came, Noor picked up new skills that led her to make great contributions.

SELECTION RESOURCES

- First-Read Guide: Nonfiction
- Close-Read Guide: Nonfiction
- Noor Inayat Khan *from* Women Heroes of WWII: Text Questions
- Audio Summaries
- Selection Audio
- Selection Test

Connection to Essential Question

The Essential Question is "What can cause a sudden change in someone's life?" Noor changed her whole life—and ultimately gave her life—when it became apparent that the Nazis were an enormous threat.

Connection to Performance-Based Assessment

The prompt is "What can cause a significant change in someone's life?" Many of the changes we've read about in this unit are very personal. But people also change their lives in response to large-scale events that horrify them.

Text Complexity Rubric: Noor Inayat Khan *from* Women Heroes of WWII	
Quantitative Measures	
Lexile: 1170 **Text Length:** 1,782 words	
Qualitative Measures	
Knowledge Demands ①—②—❸—④—⑤	The article contains references to WWII, Hitler, and D-Day, not all of which are explained. Students may need more historical background to understand the selection.
Structure ①—②—❸—④—⑤	Information in the selection is logically organized, but there are several lengthy, descriptive paragraphs.
Language Conventionality and Clarity ①—②—❸—④—⑤	Some complex sentences; many historical references and some above-level vocabulary.
Levels of Meaning/Purpose ①—②—❸—④—⑤	The article presents the story of a WWII hero, emphasizing the contrast between what people expected of her and what she was able to achieve.

DIGITAL PERSPECTIVES
Audio | Video | Document | Annotation Highlights | EL Highlights | Online Assessment

A Retrieved Reformation

Summary

"A Retrieved Reformation" is a short story by O. Henry. In it, a prison inmate named Jimmy Valentine is released. The guards warn him not to go back to breaking into safes when he gets out, but he immediately returns to his life of crime. He is a very skilled criminal, but even so, his way of life is very risky. Because of how good he is at cracking safes, investigators can tell when he's the person who opened one.

One day while planning to rob a bank, Jimmy sees a girl whom he immediately falls in love with. He gives up his life of crime to settle down. He changes his name and opens a store. But shortly before they are to get married, there is a sudden crisis.

Insight

This story provides an optimistic look at how someone can change, and how skills once used to do harm can be turned to good.

SELECTION RESOURCES

- First-Read Guide: Fiction
- Close-Read Guide: Fiction
- A Retrieved Reformation: Text Questions
- Audio Summaries
- Selection Audio
- Selection Test

Connection to Essential Question

This story provides a clear response to the Essential Question: "What can cause a sudden change in someone's life?" In this case, the answer is love at first sight.

Connection to Performance-Based Assessment

The prompt is "What can cause a significant change in someone's life?" Jimmy gives up crime and starts a new life because he doesn't want to put the woman he loves at risk, and he no longer desires to steal the way he once did.

Text Complexity Rubric: A Retrieved Reformation

Quantitative Measures	
Lexile: 850 **Text Length:** 2,794 words	
Qualitative Measures	
Knowledge Demands ①—②—❸—④—⑤	The premise of a criminal who turns his life around may not be familiar to most readers, but the situations and emotions are clearly explained.
Structure ①—②—❸—④—⑤	Linear story; plot elements are mixed with dialogue.
Language Conventionality and Clarity ①—②—③—❹—⑤	The selection has complex and unconventional sentences with embedded clauses and figurative language, and contains some ironic or sarcastic statements; many descriptive passages and above-level vocabulary.
Levels of Meaning/Purpose ①—②—❸—④—⑤	Multiple levels of meaning (including events that signify emotions of transformation and forgiveness); concepts and meanings are mostly explained and easy to grasp.

MY NOTES

DIGITAL PERSPECTIVES

Audio

Video

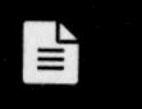
Document

Annotation Highlights

EL Highlights

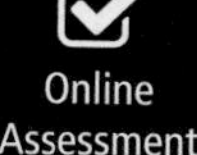
Online Assessment

MY NOTES

ADVISING

You may wish to direct students to use the generic **First-Read** and **Close-Read Guides** in the Print Student Edition. Alternatively, you may wish to print copies of the genre-specific **First-Read** and **Close-Read Guides** for students. These are available online in the Interactive Student Edition or Unit Resources. 

FIRST READ

Students should perform the steps of the first read independently:

NOTICE: Students should focus on the basic elements of the text to ensure they understand what is happening.

ANNOTATE: Students should mark any passages they wish to revisit during their close read.

CONNECT: Students should increase their understanding by connecting what they've read to other texts or personal experiences.

RESPOND: Students will write a summary to demonstrate their understanding.

Point out to students that while they will always complete the Respond step at the end of the first read, the other steps will probably happen somewhat concurrently. Remind students that they will revisit their first-read annotations during the close read.

After students have completed the First-Read Guide, you may wish to assign the Text Questions for the selection that are available in the Interactive Teacher's Edition.

Anchor Standards

In the first two sections of the unit, students worked with the whole class and in small groups to gain topical knowledge and greater understanding of the skills required by the anchor standards. In this section, they are asked to work independently, applying what they have learned and demonstrating increased readiness for college and career.

INDEPENDENT LEARNING

First-Read Guide

Tool Kit
First-Read Guide and Model Annotation

Use this page to record your first-read ideas.

Selection Title: ______________________

NOTICE

NOTICE new information or ideas you learn about the unit topic as you first read this text.

ANNOTATE

ANNOTATE by marking vocabulary and key passages you want to revisit.

NOTICE ANNOTATE First Read CONNECT RESPOND

CONNECT ideas within the selection to other knowledge and the selections you have read.

RESPOND by writing a brief summary of the selection.

CONNECT

RESPOND

STANDARD

Reading Read and comprehend complex literary and informational texts independently and proficiently.

344 UNIT 3 • TURNING POINTS

PERSONALIZE FOR LEARNING

Strategic Support

Text Connections To help students make connections to the text, remind them that ideas in a text may spark memories in readers. Point out that these connections tap into what students already know. They may be connected to personal experiences or something previously read or discovered through media. These associations often help readers better understand what the text means, and can create or maintain reader interest. To pursue and support the text connections approach, ask students to annotate passages that evoke memories and connections for them. Students can organize their ideas in a graphic organizer, such as a T-chart. One column ("Text") should contain passages, enclosed in quotation marks. In the other column ("Connection"), students can use their own words to describe the connection they made to the text. Students can then use this chart to complete the First-Read Guide.

Close-Read Guide

Tool Kit
Close-Read Guide and Model Annotation

Use this page to record your close-read ideas.

Selection Title: ____________________

Close Read the Text

Revisit sections of the text you marked during your first read. Read these sections closely and **annotate** what you notice. Ask yourself **questions** about the text. What can you **conclude**? Write down your ideas.

Analyze the Text

Think about the author's choices of patterns, structure, techniques, and ideas included in the text. Select one, and record your thoughts about what this choice conveys.

QuickWrite

Pick a paragraph from the text that grabbed your interest. Explain the power of this passage.

STANDARD
Reading Read and comprehend complex literary and informational texts independently and proficiently.

DIGITAL PERSPECTIVES

CLOSE READ

Students should begin their close read by revisiting the annotations they made during their first read. Then, students should analyze one of the author's choices regarding the following elements:

- **patterns,** such as repetition or parallelism
- **structure,** such as cause-and-effect or problem-solution
- **techniques,** such as description or dialogue
- **ideas,** such as the author's main idea or claim

MAKE IT INTERACTIVE
Group students according to the selection they have chosen. Then, have students meet to discuss the selection in depth. Their discussions should be guided by their insights and questions.

PERSONALIZE FOR LEARNING

Strategic Support
Analyze the Text Help students complete the Analyze the Text section of the Close-Read Guide. Remind students to study the way that a writer addresses a topic. Suggest that students identify writing-related annotations with these codes:

- **WP:** a writing pattern that is interesting or functional. Remind students to look for word choice, sentence length, or rhythms in the writing.
- **WS:** writing structures that support the genre. For example, students might note the introduction or conclusion, the claims or main ideas, or the key parts of a plot.
- **L:** literary elements or techniques that bring out the art in the writing. Remind students to look for figurative language or other devices that reflect the author's style.
- **I:** Ideas that the author addresses. Ask students to think about the message of the writing.

Once students identify a part of the text, they can then focus on thinking about how that section contributes to the whole.

ADVISING

Share Your Independent Learning

Prepare to Share

Explain to students that sharing what they learned from their Independent Learning selection provides classmates who read a different selection with an opportunity to consider the text as a source of evidence during the Performance-Based Assessment. As students prepare to share, remind them to highlight how their selection contributed to their knowledge of the concept of turning points as well as how the selection connects to the question *What can cause a significant change in someone's life?*

Learn from Your Classmates

As students discuss the Independent Learning selections, direct them to take particular note of how their classmates' chosen selections align with their current position on the Performance-Based Assessment question.

Reflect

Students may want to add their reflection to their Evidence Log, particularly if their insight relates to a specific selection from the unit.

MAKE IT INTERACTIVE

With students, brainstorm a list of ten life experiences that might lead to "turning points" (e.g., moving to a new state or country, starting high school, etc.). Write or project these for everyone to see. Then, ask each student to write down a word or phrase that complements or develops each "turning point." Put all of the word strips in a bag. Have each student come to the front of the class and pick two strips from the bag and affix them next to the life experience "turning point" that they relate to.

Evidence Log Support students in completing their Evidence Log. This paced activity will help prepare them for the Performance-Based Assessment at the end of the unit.

INDEPENDENT LEARNING

EVIDENCE LOG

Go to your Evidence Log and record what you learned from the text you read.

Share Your Independent Learning

Prepare to Share

What can cause a sudden change in someone's life?

Even when you read or learn something independently, your understanding continues to grow when you share what you've learned with others. Reflect on the text you explored independently, and write notes about its connections to the unit topic and Essential Question. In your notes, explain why this text belongs in this unit.

Learn From Your Classmates

Discuss It Share your ideas about the text you explored on your own. As you talk with your classmates, jot down ideas that you learn from them.

Reflect

Review your notes, and underline the most important insight you gained from these writing and discussion activities. Explain how this idea adds to your understanding of the topic of turning points.

AUTHOR'S PERSPECTIVE **Ernest Morrell, Ph.D.**

Preparing Students to Be Powerful Speakers Use these suggestions to help students develop the ability to speak confidently in large discussions or presentations:

1. To help students overcome their fear of public speaking, have them visualize success, practice and get feedback on their speech, and exercise briefly before the speech to release stress.
2. Emphasize the importance of speaking loudly and clearly when presenting to the class. The farther away a listener is, the louder a speaker must talk to be heard clearly. Also have students practice speaking with clarity and articulation, paying special attention to not slurring contractions, reversing sounds, omitting letters, and adding letters.

PERFORMANCE-BASED ASSESSMENT PREP

Review Evidence for an Explanatory Essay

At the beginning of this unit, you expressed your ideas about the following question:

What can cause a significant change in someone's life?

EVIDENCE LOG

Review your Evidence Log and your QuickWrite from the beginning of the unit. Did you learn anything new?

NOTES

Identify three things you learned about that can cause a sudden change in someone's life.

1.

2.

3.

Identify a real-life experience that illustrates one of your ideas about turning points.

____

Develop your thoughts into a topic sentence for an explanatory essay. Complete this sentence starter:

As details in ______________________________
show, significant changes in someone's life can be caused by

____

____

Evaluate Your Evidence Consider your ideas about turning points. How did the texts you read affect your ideas?

STANDARDS

Writing

Write informative/explanatory texts to examine a topic and convey ideas, concepts, and information through the selection, organization, and analysis of relevant content.

a. Introduce a topic clearly, previewing what is to follow; organize ideas, concepts, and information, using strategies such as definition, classification, comparison/contrast, and cause/effect; include formatting, graphics, and multimedia when useful to aiding comprehension.

b. Develop the topic with relevant facts, definitions, concrete details, quotations, or other information and examples.

DIGITAL PERSPECTIVES

Review Evidence for an Explanatory Essay

Evidence Log Students should understand that their viewpoint and perceptions could evolve as they learn more about the subject and are exposed to additional points of view. Point out that just because they started with a particular viewpoint on the question *What can cause a significant change in someone's life?* doesn't mean that their viewpoint can't change after careful consideration of their learning and evidence.

Evaluate Your Evidence

Encourage students to keep in mind that their cause-and-effect essay should include evidence. Their evidence should support the viewpoint and perceptions that they write about. Evidence should be correctly attributed, and come from credible and relevant sources.

3. As students share in whole groups, remind them to listen carefully and fully before responding, take notes while listening so they can respond on point, and speak with courtesy and respect. They may also wish to draft points for a response quickly before speaking.

4. To field questions, tell students to repeat the question before answering it, as this allows a few seconds to think about a response as well as to make sure that everyone hears the question.

Writing to Sources: Explanatory Essay

Students should complete the Performance-Based Assessment independently, with little to no input or feedback during the process. Students should use word processing software to take advantage of editing tools and features.

Prior to beginning the Assessment, ask students to think about what sorts of things they've had to do to change behaviors of their own—was it easy?

Review the Elements of an Effective Explanatory Essay Students can review the work they did earlier in the unit as they complete the Performance-Based Assessment. They may also consult other resources such as:

- the elements of an effective explanatory essay, including information about the subject along with supporting reasons, facts, and examples, available in Whole-Class Learning
- their Evidence Log
- their Word Network

Although students will use evidence from unit selections for their explanatory essay, they may need to collect additional evidence, including facts, anecdotes, quotations from authorities, and examples.

PERFORMANCE-BASED ASSESSMENT

SOURCES

- WHOLE-CLASS SELECTIONS
- SMALL-GROUP SELECTIONS
- INDEPENDENT-LEARNING SELECTION

PART 1

Writing to Sources: Explanatory Essay

In this unit, you read about different examples of turning points. Write an informative essay in which you explain what can cause a significant change in someone's life, how it might have a lasting effect, and what it tells you about someone who has undergone a meaningful change. Develop your topic with relevant facts, details, and information from the texts.

Assignment

Write an **explanatory essay** in response to the following question:

What can cause a significant change in someone's life?

Develop a clear thesis, or controlling idea, in response to the prompt. Then, use sufficient examples and quotations from the selections that you read in this unit to support your response. Your essay should be logically organized and include transitions to show the relationships between ideas. Be sure to maintain a formal style and tone in your writing.

WORD NETWORK

As you write and revise your explanation, use your Word Network to help vary your word choices.

Reread the Assignment Review the assignment to be sure you fully understand it. The assignment may reference some of the academic words presented at the beginning of the unit. Be sure you understand each of the words given below in order to complete the assignment correctly.

Academic Vocabulary

contribute	consistent	maintain
observation	sufficient	

Review the Elements of an Effective Explanatory Essay Before you begin writing, read the Explanatory Essay Rubric. Once you have completed your first draft, check it against the rubric. If one or more of the elements is missing or not as strong as it could be, revise your essay to add or strengthen that component.

STANDARDS

Writing

- Write informative/explanatory texts to examine a topic and convey ideas, concepts, and information through the selection, organization, and analysis of relevant content.
- Produce clear and coherent writing in which the development, organization, and style are appropriate to task, purpose, and audience.
- Draw evidence from literary or informational texts to support analysis, reflection, and research.
- Write routinely over extended time frames and shorter time frames for a range of discipline-specific tasks, purposes, and audiences.

Explanatory Essay Rubric

	Focus and Organization	Evidence and Elaboration	Conventions
4	The introduction is engaging and includes a clear thesis. The thesis is supported by specific details, examples, and quotations from the selections. Ideas are logically organized so that the information is easy to follow. Transitions clearly show the relationships among ideas. The conclusion supports the information in the essay and offers fresh insight into the topic.	Details, examples, and quotations from the selections are specific and relevant. The style and tone are formal and objective. Words are carefully chosen and suited to purpose and audience.	The essay intentionally follows standard English conventions of usage and mechanics.
3	The introduction includes a clear thesis. The thesis is supported by details, examples, and quotations from the selections. Ideas are organized so that the information is easy to follow. Transitions show the relationships among ideas. The conclusion supports the information in the essay.	Details, examples, and quotations are relevant. The style and tone are mostly formal and objective. Words are generally suited to purpose and audience.	The essay follows standard English conventions of usage and mechanics.
2	The introduction states the thesis. The thesis is supported by some details, examples, and quotations from the selections. Ideas are vaguely organized, with a few transitions to orient readers. The conclusion relates to the information in the essay.	Some details and examples are relevant. The style and tone are occasionally formal and objective. Words are somewhat suited to purpose and audience.	The essay sometimes follows standard English conventions of usage and mechanics.
1	The thesis is not clearly stated in the introduction. The thesis is not supported by details, examples, and quotations. Ideas are disorganized and the information is difficult to follow. The conclusion does not include relevant information.	There is little or no relevant support. The style and tone are informal. Words are not appropriate to purpose or audience.	The essay contains many mistakes in standard English conventions of usage and mechanics.

Explanatory Essay Rubric

As you review the Explanatory Essay Rubric with students, remind them that the rubric is a resource that can guide their revisions. Students should pay particular attention to the differences between an essay with a conclusion that restates the thesis (a score of 3) and one with a conclusion that offers a fresh insight into the topic (a score of 4).

PERSONALIZE FOR LEARNING

English Language Support

Syntax Help students who are having difficulty organizing their thoughts work at breaking their ideas down into simple sentences. Remind them that even the simplest sentence has a subject and a verb. Once they've expressed their ideas in the simplest sentences they can write, encourage them to join these sentences together in ways that help make their explanations easier to understand. Point out that when describing cause-and-effect, compound sentences joined with words such as *because* and *therefore* might actually be clearer than a pair of simple sentences. **ALL LEVELS**

Speaking and Listening: Oral Presentation

As students prepare to annotate their essays, remind them to mark points they especially want to emphasize as they speak. They may wish to write instructions for themselves, such as "Pause here" and "Make eye contact here." Also suggest that they make notes about multimedia elements that will appeal to the audience and help get their points across.

Remind students that the effectiveness of an oral explanatory essay relies on how the speaker establishes credibility with his or her audience. If a speaker comes across as confident and authoritative, it will be easier for the audience to give credence to the speaker's presentation.

Review the Rubric As you review the Oral Presentation Rubric with students, remind them that it is a valuable tool that can help them plan their presentation. They should strive to include all of the criteria required to achieve a score of 3. Draw their attention to some of the subtle differences between scores of 2 and 3.

PERFORMANCE-BASED ASSESSMENT

PART 2

Speaking and Listening: Oral Presentation

Assignment

After completing the final draft of your explanatory essay, use it as the foundation for a brief **oral presentation.**

STANDARDS

Speaking and Listening

- Present claims and findings, emphasizing salient points in a focused, coherent manner with pertinent descriptions, facts, details, and examples; use appropriate eye contact, adequate volume, and clear pronunciation.
- Include multimedia components and visual displays in presentations to clarify claims and findings and emphasize salient points.

Do not simply read your essay aloud. Take the following steps to make your presentation lively and engaging.

- Review your explanation and annotate the most important ideas and supporting details.
- Choose multimedia elements that add interest to your presentation.

Review the Rubric Before you deliver your presentation, check your plans against this rubric.

	Content	Organization	Presentation Techniques
3	The introduction is engaging and states the thesis in a compelling way. The presentation includes specific examples, quotations, and multimedia elements to support the thesis. The conclusion offers fresh insight into the topic.	The speaker uses time effectively, spending the right amount on each part. Ideas progress logically, with clear transition among ideas so the information is easy for listeners to follow. The timing of the images matches the timing of the explanation.	The speaker maintains effective eye contact and speaks clearly and with adequate volume.
2	The introduction states a thesis. The presentation includes examples, quotations, and multimedia elements to support the thesis. The conclusion offers some insight and restates important information.	The speaker uses time effectively, spending the right amount of time on most parts. Ideas progress logically with some transitions among ideas. Listeners can mostly follow the speaker's information.	The speaker sometimes maintains effective eye contact and speaks somewhat clearly and with adequate volume.
1	The introduction does not clearly state a thesis. The presentation does not include examples, quotations, or multimedia elements. The conclusion does not restate important information.	The speaker does not use time effectively and focuses too much time on some parts and too little on others. Ideas do not progress logically. Listeners have trouble following the information.	The speaker does not maintain effective eye contact or speak clearly with adequate volume.

DIGITAL PERSPECTIVES

Preparing for the Assignment To help students understand what an effective oral presentation of an essay looks and sounds like, find examples on the Internet of students or adults presenting their own work orally. Project the examples for the class, and have students note the techniques that make each speaker successful (such as gesture, pacing, and tone). Suggest that students record themselves presenting their explanatory essays so they can practice incorporating some of the elements in the examples you showed them.

Reflect on the Unit

Now that you've completed the unit, take a few moments to reflect on your learning.

Reflect on the Unit Goals

Look back at the goals at the beginning of the unit. Use a different colored pen to rate yourself again. Think about readings and activities that contributed the most to the growth of your understanding. Record your thoughts.

Reflect on the Learning Strategies

Discuss It Write a reflection on whether you were able to improve your learning based on your Action Plans. Think about what worked, what didn't, and what you might do to keep working on these strategies. Record your ideas before a class discussion.

Reflect on the Text

Choose a selection that you found challenging and explain what made it difficult.

Explain something that surprised you about a text in the unit.

Which activity taught you the most about turning points? What did you learn?

DIGITAL PERSPECTIVES

Reflect on the Unit

- Have students watch the video on Reflecting on Your Learning
- A video on this topic is available online in the Professional Development Center

Reflect on the Unit Goals Students should re-evaluate how well they met the unit goals now that they have completed the unit. You might ask them to provide a written commentary on the goal they made the most progress with as well as the goal they feel warrants continued focus.

Reflect on the Learning Strategies

Discuss It If you want to make this a digital activity, go online and navigate to the Discussion Board. Alternatively, students can share their learning strategies reflections in a class discussion.

Reflect on the Text Consider having students share their text reflections with one another.

MAKE IT INTERACTIVE

Have students prepare 30-second presentations explaining what they learned about turning points. Explain that that they'll need to summarize their reflections to concisely convey their key insights. Have the class discuss any common themes in student presentations.

Unit Test and Remediation 

After students have completed the Performance-Based Assessment, administer the Unit Test. Based on students' performance on the test, assign the resources as indicated on the Interpretation Guide to remediate. Students who take the test online will be automatically assigned remediation, as warranted by test results.

	Contents	Pacing / # of Days	Genre / Lexile	Vocabulary / Word Study
INTRO	**Unit Introduction**	2*		Academic Vocabulary (L.7.6)
	Launch Text: Rethinking the Wild		Argumentative Text 980L	
WHOLE-CLASS LEARNING	**Whole-Class Learning Introduction**	3		
	HOOK&INSPIRE ***from* Silent Spring** Rachel Carson		Descriptive Nonfiction 1080L	Concept Vocabulary Word Study: Anglo-Saxon Suffix *-ness* (L.7.4)
	COMPARE: **Nobel Speech** Al Gore	5	Speech 1190L	Concept Vocabulary Word Study: Latin Prefix *uni-* (L.7.4.b)
	COMPARE: **Nobel Speech** Al Gore	5	Media: Video NP	Concept Vocabulary
	Performance Task **Writing**	3		
SMALL-GROUP LEARNING	**Small-Group Learning Introduction**	5		
	Turtle Watchers • "Nature" is what We See— • The Sparrow Linda Hogan • Emily Dickinson • Paul Laurence Dunbar		Poetry Collection NP	Concept Vocabulary (L.7.4.c) Word Study: Etymology (L.7.4, b)
	Eagle Tracking at Follensby Pond The Nature Conservancy	3	Media: Photo Gallery NP	Media Vocabulary (L.7.6)
	He—y, Come On Ou—t! Shinichi Hoshi, translated by Stanleigh Jones	4	Short Story 870L	Concept Vocabulary (L.7.4, a) Word Study: Latin Root *-sequ-* (L.7.4.b)
	Performance Task Speaking and Listening	2		
INDEPENDENT LEARNING	**Independent Learning Introduction** Independent Learning Strategies	2		
	***from* My Side of the Mountain** Jean Craighead George		Novel Excerpt 820L	Independent Learning provides students with the opportunity to analyze a selection independently. To facilitate students' independence, no skills have been assigned.
	How Grandmother Spider Stole the Sun Michael J. Caduto and Joseph Bruchac		Myth 850L	
	The Story of Victor d'Aveyron, the Wild Child Eloise Montalban		Expository Nonfiction 980L	
	***from* Of Wolves and Men** Barry Lopez		Essay 1010L	
END OF UNIT	Performance-Based Assessment Writing	2		
	Unit Reflection			
	Unit Test	1		

* Pacing is suggested for a 40- to 50-minute class period. If you use block scheduling, you may combine days to meet your schedule needs.

Analyze Craft and Structure	Conventions / Author's Style	Composition / Research / Speaking and Listening
		Summary (RI.7.2)
Imagery (RI.7.1; RI.7.2; RI.7.4; L.7.5.c)	Conventions: The Subjunctive (L.7.1; L.7.3)	Writing to Sources: Argument (W.7.1, a–d) Speaking and Listening: Multimedia Presentation (SL.7.4; SL.7.5)
Persuasive Speech (RI.7.8)	Conventions: Infinitive Phrases and Gerund Phrases (L.7.1.a)	Writing to Compare: Argument (RI.7.7; W.7.1, a–c; SL.7.3)
		Write an Argument (W.7.1, a–e; W.7.6; W.7.8; W.7.10)
The Speaker in Lyric Poetry (RL.7.5)	Author's Style: Diction and Tone (RL.7.1; RL.7.2; RL.7.4)	Speaking and Listening: Oral Presentation (SL.7.4; SL.7.5; SL.7.6)
		Research: Research Paper (W.7.2, a–b; W.7.7; W.7.8)
Literary Elements: Irony (RL.7.1; RL.7.2; RL.7.3)	Conventions: Punctuation Marks (L.7.2)	Writing to Sources: Alternate Ending (W.7.3, b, d, e; W.7.5)
		Present an Argument (SL.7.1, a–b; SL.7.2; SL.7.3; SL.7.4; SL.7.5; SL.7.6)
Independent Learning provides students with the opportunity to analyze a selection independently. To facilitate students' independence, no skills have been assigned.		Share Your Independent Learning (SL.7.1)
		Writing to Sources: Argument (W.7.1, a–b) Speaking and Listening: Oral Presentation (SL.7.4; SL.7.5; SL.7.6)
		Reflect on the Unit

Jump Start

Use the following prompts to engage students in a discussion about people and the environment.

What is nature?

Do you consider water and air part of nature?

How do people have a positive or negative effect on nature?

Have students write down their answer to each question, then ask volunteers to share their answers to start the discussion.

People and the Planet

Ask students what the phrase *people and the planet* suggests to them. Point out that as they work through this unit, they will read about many examples of humans' relationship with the natural world.

Video

Project the introduction video in class or ask students to open the video in their interactive textbooks.

Discuss It If you want to make this a digital activity, go online and navigate to the Discussion Board. Alternatively, students can share their responses in a class discussion.

Block Scheduling

Each day in this pacing calendar represents a 40–50 minute class period. Teachers using block scheduling may combine days to reflect their class schedule. In addition, teachers may revise pacing to differentiate and support core instruction by integrating components and resources as students require.

UNIT 4

People and the Planet

Many people wonder at the beauty of nature, but do they wonder about the future of our planet?

Arctic Ice

Discuss It In what way are people and animals dependent on our planet?

Write your response before sharing your ideas.

Pacing Plan

Unit Introduction		Introduce Whole-Class Learning	*from* Silent Spring		Nobel Speech					Media: Nobel Speech					Performance Task		
1	2	3	4	5	6	7	8	9	10	11	12	13	14	15	16	17	18

DIGITAL PERSPECTIVES

 Audio  Video  Document Annotation Highlights EL Highlights 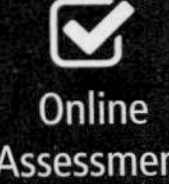 Online Assessment

UNIT 4

UNIT INTRODUCTION

ESSENTIAL QUESTION: What effects do people have on the environment?

LAUNCH TEXT ARGUMENT MODEL
Rethinking the Wild

WHOLE-CLASS LEARNING

ANCHOR TEXT: DESCRIPTIVE NONFICTION
from Silent Spring
Rachel Carson

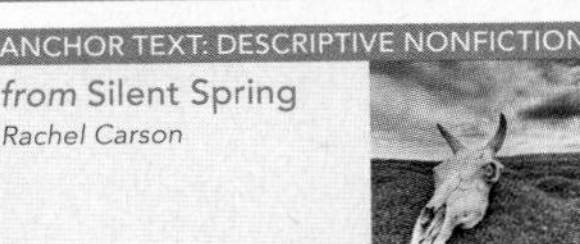

COMPARE

ANCHOR TEXT: SPEECH
Nobel Speech
Al Gore

MEDIA: VIDEO
Nobel Speech
Al Gore

PERFORMANCE TASK
WRITING FOCUS:
Write an Argument

SMALL-GROUP LEARNING

POETRY COLLECTION
Turtle Watchers
Linda Hogan

"Nature" is what We see—
Emily Dickinson

The Sparrow
Paul Laurence Dunbar

MEDIA: PHOTO GALLERY
Eagle Tracking at Follensby Pond
The Nature Conservancy

SHORT STORY
He—y, Come On Ou—t!
Shinichi Hoshi, translated by Stanleigh Jones

PERFORMANCE TASK
SPEAKING AND LISTENING FOCUS:
Present an Argument

INDEPENDENT LEARNING

NOVEL EXCERPT
from My Side of the Mountain
Jean Craighead George

MYTH
How Grandmother Spider Stole the Sun
Michael J. Caduto and Joseph Bruchac

EXPOSITORY NONFICTION
The Story of Victor d'Aveyron, the Wild Child
Eloise Montalban

ESSAY
from Of Wolves and Men
Barry Lopez

PERFORMANCE-BASED ASSESSMENT PREP
Review Evidence for an Argument

PERFORMANCE-BASED ASSESSMENT

Argument: Essay and Oral Presentation

PROMPT:
Are the needs of people ever more important than the needs of animals and the planet?

Unit Introduction 353

What effects do people have on the environment?

Introduce the Essential Question and point out that students will respond to related prompts.

- **Whole-Class Learning** *What is the most significant effect that people have on the environment?*
- **Small-Group Learning** *Do people always have a negative impact on the environment?*
- **Performance-Based Assessment** *Are the needs of people ever more important than the needs of animals and the planet?*

Using Trade Books

Refer to the Teaching with Trade Books section for suggestions on how to incorporate the following thematically-related titles into this unit:

- *Hatchet* by Gary Paulsen
- *My Side of the Mountain* by Jean Craighead George
- *Hoot* by Carl Hiaasen

Current Perspectives

To increase student engagement, search online for stories about people's influence on the environment, and invite your students to recommend stories they find. Always preview content before sharing it with your class.

- **News Story: The Hidden Meltdown of Greenland *(NASA)*** Greenland's glaciers and ice sheets are melting due to human-caused climate change.
- **Video: Weather Versus Climate Change *(National Geographic)*** Astrophysicist Neil deGrasse Tyson explains the difference between weather and climate.

Introduce Small-Group Learning

Day	Activity
19	Introduce Small-Group Learning
20–23	Turtle Watchers • "Nature" is what We See— • The Sparrow
24–26	Media: Eagle Tracking at Follensby Pond
27–30	He—y, Come On Ou—t!
31–32	Performance Task
33	Introduce Independent Learning
34	Independent Learning
35–36	Performance-Based Assessment

About the Unit Goals

These unit goals were backward designed from the Performance-Based Assessment at the end of the unit and the Whole-Class and Small-Group Performance Tasks. Students will practice and become proficient in many more standards over the course of this unit.

Unit Goals

Review the goals with students and explain that as they read and discuss the selections in this unit, they will improve their skills in reading, writing, research, language, and speaking and listening.

- Have students watch the video on Goal Setting.
- A video on this topic is available online in the Professional Development Center.

Reading Goals Tell students they will read and evaluate arguments. They will also read an essay, a speech, and several poems to better understand the ways writers express ideas.

Writing and Research Goals Tell students that they will learn the elements of argumentative writing. They will also write their own argument. Students will write to organize and share ideas; to reflect; and to gather evidence.

Language Goals Tell students that they will develop a deeper understanding of participles and participial phrases.

Speaking and Listening Goals Explain to students that they will work to build on one another's ideas, develop consensus, and communicate.

HOME Connection

A Home Connection letter to students' parents or guardians is available in the Interactive Teacher's Edition. The letter explains what students will be learning in this unit and how they will be assessed.

Unit Goals

Throughout this unit, you will deepen your perspective about space exploration by reading, writing, speaking, listening, and presenting. These goals will help you succeed on the Unit Performance-Based Assessment.

Rate how well you meet these goals right now. You will revisit your ratings later when you reflect on your growth during this unit.

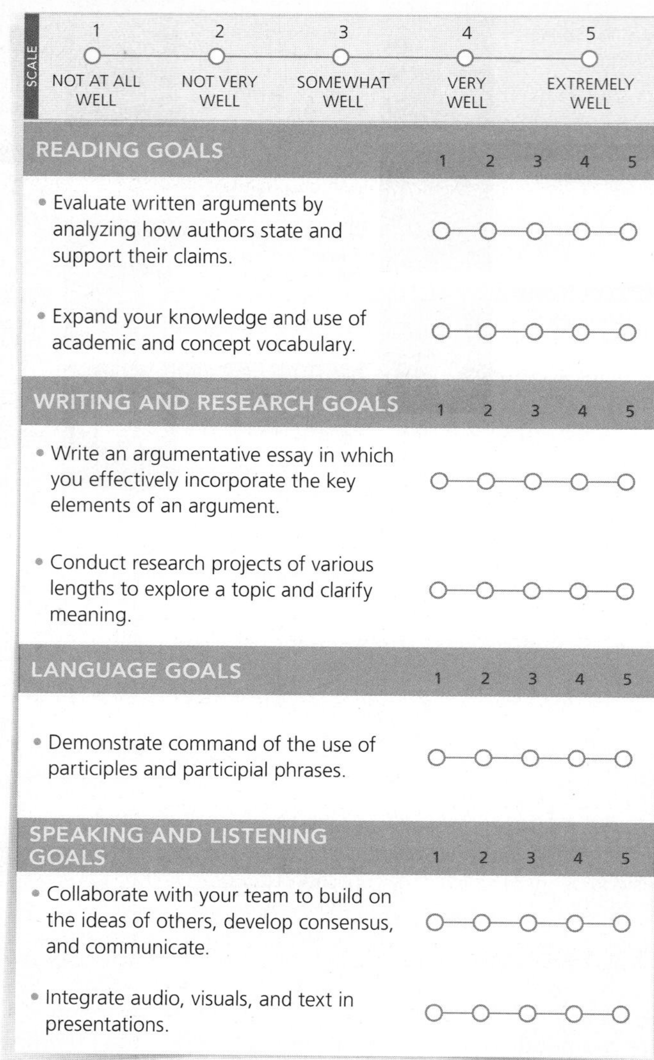

SCALE: 1 NOT AT ALL WELL; 2 NOT VERY WELL; 3 SOMEWHAT WELL; 4 VERY WELL; 5 EXTREMELY WELL

READING GOALS	1	2	3	4	5
• Evaluate written arguments by analyzing how authors state and support their claims.	O	O	O	O	O
• Expand your knowledge and use of academic and concept vocabulary.	O	O	O	O	O

WRITING AND RESEARCH GOALS	1	2	3	4	5
• Write an argumentative essay in which you effectively incorporate the key elements of an argument.	O	O	O	O	O
• Conduct research projects of various lengths to explore a topic and clarify meaning.	O	O	O	O	O

LANGUAGE GOALS	1	2	3	4	5
• Demonstrate command of the use of participles and participial phrases.	O	O	O	O	O

SPEAKING AND LISTENING GOALS	1	2	3	4	5
• Collaborate with your team to build on the ideas of others, develop consensus, and communicate.	O	O	O	O	O
• Integrate audio, visuals, and text in presentations.	O	O	O	O	O

STANDARDS

Language
Acquire and use accurately grade appropriate general academic and domain-specific words and phrases; gather vocabulary knowledge when considering a word or phrase important to comprehension or expression.

AUTHOR'S PERSPECTIVE Ernest Morrell, Ph.D.

Taking Responsibility for Learning Teachers can talk to students about becoming motivated learners. Start by having students reflect on things they are good at outside of class, such as sports, music, and video games. Then have students think about how they take responsibility for their own achievement in these areas, such as having the discipline to practice. Help students further understand the value of becoming independent learners by providing tips on how to do so, such as these:

1. **Be self-motivated and persistent.** Don't be discouraged when faced with minor setbacks.
2. **Develop effective time management skills.** Track assignments and deadlines.
3. **Seek help when necessary.** Don't be afraid to get assistance when you need it.
4. **Set realistic goals.** Then, plan ways to achieve your goals.
5. **Believe in yourself.** Visualize success. Recognize that you have the ability to soar.

Encourage students to add to this list to help them focus on strategies for taking ownership of their learning.

Academic Vocabulary: Argument

Academic terms appear in all subjects and can help you read, write, and discuss with more precision. Here are five academic words that will be useful to you in this unit as you analyze and write arguments.

Complete the chart.

1. Review each word, its root, and mentor sentences.
2. Use the information and your own knowledge to predict the meaning of each word.
3. For each word, list at least two related words.
4. Refer to the dictionary or other resources if needed.

TIP

FOLLOW THROUGH
Study the words in this chart, and mark them or their forms wherever they appear in the unit.

WORD	MENTOR SENTENCES	PREDICT MEANING	RELATED WORDS
ethical ROOT: ***-eth-*** "character" or "custom"	1. The company was praised for its *ethical* business practices. 2. The animal-rights activists argued that it is not *ethical* to experiment on chimpanzees.		ethics; unethical
dissent ROOT: ***-sent-*** "feel"	1. Robin expressed her *dissent* from the opinion that was held by the majority of the class. 2. The king used all of his power to suppress political *dissent* within his country.		
interject ROOT: ***-jec-*** "throw"	1. Every time I tried to express my opinion, Eric would *interject* with his own ideas. 2. As I explain the directions, please feel free to *interject* a question if anything is unclear.		
discord ROOT: ***-cord-*** "heart"	1. Jake acted as a mediator to end the *discord* between his two arguing friends. 2. The two countries signed a peace treaty to end their long history of *discord*.		
accuracy ROOT: ***-cur-*** "care for"	1. He could shoot an arrow with great *accuracy*, almost never missing his target. 2. I was impressed with the *accuracy* of her painting. The portrait looked just like me.		

Academic Vocabulary: Argument

Introduce the blue academic vocabulary words in the chart on the student page. Point out that the root of each word provides a clue to its meaning. Discuss the mentor sentences to ensure students understand each word's usage. Students should also use the mentor sentences as context to help them predict the meaning of each word. Check that students are able to fill the chart in correctly. Complete pronunciations, parts of speech, and definitions are provided for you. Students are only expected to provide the definition.

Possible responses:

ethical ***adj.*** **(EHTH uh kuhl)**
Meaning: related to moral principles

Related words: ethics, unethical

Additional word related to the root *-eth-*: ethos

dissent ***v., n.*** **(dih SEHNT)**
Meaning: to disagree; disagreement

Related words: dissenting, dissentingly

Additional words related to root *-sent-*: sensible, sensation, consent, assent

interject ***v.*** **(ihn tuhr JEHKT)**
Meaning: to throw in between; to interrupt

Related words: interjection, interjecting

Additional words related to root *-ject-*: project, eject, trajectory

discord ***n.*** **(DIHS kawrd)**
Meaning: disagreement; lack of harmony

Related word: discordant

Additional words related to root *-cord-*: accord, concord, cordial

accuracy ***n.*** **(AK yuhr uh see)**
Meaning: being without errors; correctness

Related words: accurate, inaccurate, inaccuracy

Additional words related to root *-cur-*: curator, curious, secure

PERSONALIZE FOR LEARNING

English Language Support
Cognates Some of the academic words have Spanish cognates. Use these cognates with students whose home language is Spanish.

ethical – ético

discord – discordia **ALL LEVELS**

Purpose of the Launch Text

The Launch Text provides students with a common starting point to address the unit topic. After reading the Launch Text, all students will be able to participate in discussions about people and the planet.

Lexile: 980 The easier reading level of this selection makes it perfect to assign for homework. Students will need little or no support to understand it.

Additionally, "Rethinking the Wild" provides a writing model for the Performance-Based Assessment students complete at the end of the unit.

Launch Text: Argument Model

Remind students to determine the main idea of the text as well as other ideas the author develops along the way. Have students pay attention to the structure of the text. They should note that the text's main argument is mentioned in the first paragraph, and then the author develops this idea with a story that demonstrates it. Finally, a conclusion restates the author's position.

Encourage students to read this text on their own and annotate unfamiliar words and sections of text they think are particularly important.

AUDIO SUMMARIES

Audio summaries of "Rethinking the Wild!" are available in both English and Spanish in the Interactive Teacher's Edition or Unit Resources. Assigning these summaries before students read the Launch Text may help them build additional background knowledge and set a context for their reading.

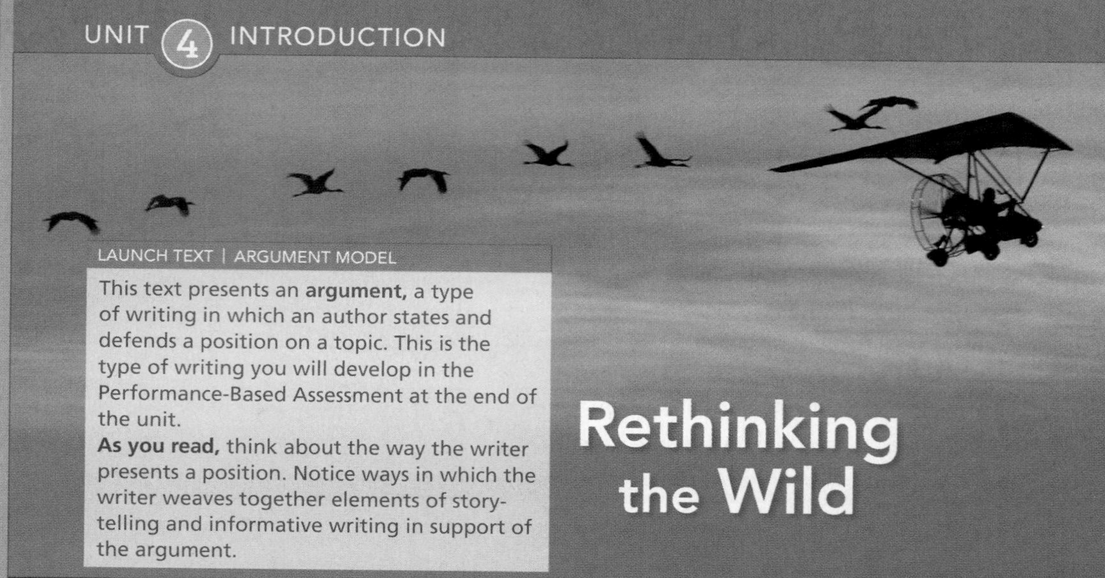

LAUNCH TEXT | ARGUMENT MODEL

This text presents an **argument,** a type of writing in which an author states and defends a position on a topic. This is the type of writing you will develop in the Performance-Based Assessment at the end of the unit.

As you read, think about the way the writer presents a position. Notice ways in which the writer weaves together elements of story-telling and informative writing in support of the argument.

Rethinking the Wild

NOTES

1 There are seven billion people on the planet, and each of us has an impact on the animals and plants we share it with. It's a constant give-and-take, and people have strong opinions. Even though the correct course of action isn't always obvious, sometimes the needs of human beings have to take priority.

2 In Jon Mooallem's book *Wild Ones,* he describes the attempt of one organization to save the whooping crane from extinction. It's a story that may challenge what you thought you knew about the sometimes competing interests of people and animals.

3 The North American whooping crane—one of the few living relics of the Pleistocene era—suffered a huge drop in population in the nineteenth and twentieth centuries. In 1860 there were 1,400 whooping cranes. In 1941 there were just 15, and in 1967 the whooping crane was listed as "endangered."

4 Mooallem explains how Operation Migration planned to save the whooping crane by raising a new flock in Wisconsin. The hard part would come next: getting the birds to migrate to Florida. Here's how they did it: they led the birds there themselves. In a disguised aircraft, that looked and flew like a bird, they flew along with the flock. They avoided talking, and even wore all-white costumes, so that the cranes wouldn't get too comfortable with humans and would remain wild.

5 When the cranes reached Florida, they were put into a "release pen" with no top netting, so the birds could fly away themselves when they were ready. The complex was surrounded by houses. In fact, it was practically in the backyard of a couple named Gibbs. And that's where the second part of the story starts.

CROSS-CURRICULAR PERSPECTIVES

Science Have students research and write short reports on efforts to help birds. As students research, ask them to find the answers to questions like these:

- Who was involved and where?
- What birds were they trying to help?
- What was done?
- Was the effort successful? Why or why not?

Have students share their information with the class, and discuss how this information relates to the Launch text.

6 The Gibbses—an elderly couple who'd lived there for 50 years—loved nothing better than to sit on their back porch, sip tea, and watch the birds as they fed from the two bird feeders they'd set up in the backyard. There were all kinds of birds around—but the Gibbs' favorites were the whooping cranes that had started showing up lately.

7 As far as Operation Migration was concerned, this could destroy their project. Unless something were done about those feeders, the birds would continue to hang around the Gibbs' house. They would no longer be wary of people, and wouldn't be able to survive on their own.

8 After explaining the situation to Mrs. Gibbs, representatives from Operation Migration asked her to remove the feeders from her backyard. She refused! Her husband, it turns out, was dying of Alzheimer's and the only thing that made him happy and brought him into the present was seeing the family of whooping cranes in his own backyard.

9 The scientists were unmoved by Mrs. Gibbs' story. They were thinking of the birds that people had spent 24 hours a day trying to keep wild. They were thinking of all the time and money they had invested in this group of cranes. But in the end they had to back down. How can you ask a woman to choose between her husband and a flock of birds?

10 According to Jon Mooallem, Mrs. Gibbs did what any of us would do. As humans, we're hard-wired to put our particular set of needs above others. We also have a responsibility to be the earth's caretakers, because of the power we have over other species. And sometimes we have to be comfortable balancing our needs with theirs. ❧

NOTES

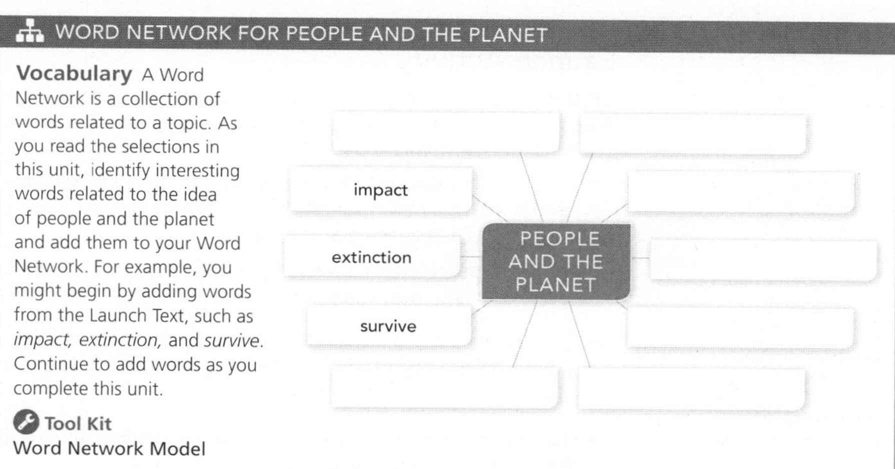

DIGITAL PERSPECTIVES

Word Network for People and the Planet

Tell students that they can fill in the Word Network as they read the texts in the unit, or they can jot down the words elsewhere and add them later. Point out to students that people may have personal associations with some words. A word that one student thinks is related to the concept of people and the planet might not be a word another student would pick. However, students should feel free to add any relevant words to their Word Network. Each person's Word Network will be unique. If you choose to print the Word Network, distribute it to students at this point so they can use it throughout the rest of the unit.

AUTHOR'S PERSPECTIVE **Elfrieda Hiebert, Ph.D.**

Words in Complex Texts Reassure students that complex texts will always have some words that they haven't encountered before. This point needs to be reviewed year after year because the texts always get harder, and with harder texts come more complex words. Share these ideas with students:

- Many words will be familiar, but they may be used in a different way with new topics and meanings.
- Authors choose the more complex words (the rare words) for deliberate effect—not serendipitously—to describe characters and contexts, to develop obstacles or problems, or to show ways of solving problems.

Making and reviewing word networks helps students develop multiple words related to a concept, and the multiple meanings or concept applications for words. Also encourage students to study the words in context. Students may wish to use digital tools as they do so.

INTRODUCTION

Summary

Have students read the introductory paragraph. Provide them with tips for writing a summary:

- Write in the present tense.
- Make sure to include the title of the work.
- Be concise: A summary should not be equal in length to the original text.
- If you need to quote the words of the author, use quotation marks.
- Don't put your own opinions, ideas, or interpretations into the summary. The purpose of writing a summary is to accurately represent what the author says, not to provide a critique.

See a possible summary on the student page.

Launch Activity

Explain to students that as they work on this unit, they will have many opportunities to discuss the topic of people and the planet. Remind them that there is no right or wrong position, but they should be able to support their position with evidence from the material they've read and analyzed as well as their prior knowledge.

Encourage students to keep an open mind and really listen to their classmates.

Summary

Write a summary of "Rethinking the Wild." A **summary** is a concise, complete, and accurate overview of a text. It should not include a statement of your opinion or an analysis.

Possible response: The whooping crane survived mass extinctions that took place during the prehistoric times, but it was facing extinction in the mid-twentieth century. An environmental project raised a new flock of whooping cranes and planned for them to migrate to Florida. It was important that the cranes not get become dependent on humans. However, a local family had a very good reason to want to spend time around them, which presented a challenge to the scientists.

Launch Activity

Let the People Decide Consider this statement: *Mrs. Gibbs was wrong in refusing to remove the bird feeders from her backyard*. Decide your position and explain why you feel this way.

- Prepare a brief statement that expresses your position. Include reasons why you feel as you do. Your statement should be written as a short speech designed to influence people.
- A class discussion will be conducted as if it were a political campaign gathering. When the "campaign" begins, have your statement ready.
- When it's time for you to speak, deliver your statement as if you were giving a political speech. Try to persuade those listening to agree with your position.
- The class will vote on whether Mrs. Gibbs was right or wrong when she refused to remove the bird feeders.

DIGITAL PERSPECTIVES

QuickWrite

Consider class discussions, presentations, the video, your own knowledge, and the Launch Text as you think about the prompt. Record your first thoughts here.

PROMPT: **Are the needs of people ever more important than the needs of animals and the planet?**

Possible response: We still have time to fix much of the damage the environment has sustained. People can be both the cause of the damage and the solution to the problem. If we take away what harms species, they might be able to bounce back. If we take steps to make the environment safer, we can support many different animal and plant types. Many species have already gone extinct. But—though it may take millions of years—new species will evolve to replace them.

EVIDENCE LOG FOR PEOPLE AND THE PLANET

Review your QuickWrite. Summarize your point of view in one sentence to record in your Evidence Log. Then, record evidence from "Rethinking the Wild" that supports your point of view.

After each selection, you will continue to use your Evidence Log to record the evidence you gather and the connections you make. This graphic shows what your Evidence Log looks like.

Tool Kit
Evidence Log Model

Title of Text: ______ Date: ______

CONNECTION TO PROMPT	TEXT EVIDENCE/DETAILS	ADDITIONAL NOTES/IDEAS

How does this text change or add to my thinking? Date: ______

QuickWrite

In this QuickWrite, students should present their own answer to the question based on the material in the Unit Opener. This initial response will help inform their work when they complete the Performance-Based Assessment at the end of the unit. Students should make sure they answer the question with a clearly-stated position and support their position with relevant, logical reasoning.

See a possible QuickWrite on the student page.

Evidence Log for People and the Planet

Students should record their initial response in their Evidence Logs. Then they should record evidence from "Rethinking the Wild" that supports their initial response.

If you choose to print the Evidence Log, distribute it to students at this point so they can use it throughout the rest of the unit.

Performance-Based Assessment: Refining Your Thinking

- Have students watch the video on Refining Your Thinking.
- A video on this topic is available online in the Professional Development Center.

PERSONALIZE FOR LEARNING

English Language Support

Suffix *-tion* Help students understand the suffix *-tion*. Explain that words in which this suffix appears are nouns, and adding this suffix to a verb makes that word a noun. Show students the following words from the Launch Text and discuss the formation and meaning of each:

organization (organize) *extinction (extinct)*
operation (operate) *migration (migrate)*

Ask students to use the noun form of these words in sentences. **ALL LEVELS**

OVERVIEW

WHOLE-CLASS LEARNING

What effects do people have on the environment?

Engage students in a conversation about ways that humans affect the environment. Point out that different societies and cultures relate differently to the environment. There is also an important historical aspect to this relationship. During Whole-Class Learning, students will read and listen to selections about the need to lessen our impact on the environment.

Whole-Class Learning Strategies

Review the Learning Strategies with students and explain that as they work through Whole-Class Learning they will develop strategies to work in large-group environments.

- Have students watch the video on Whole-Class Learning Strategies.
- A video on this topic is available online in the Professional Development Center.

You may wish to discuss some action items to add to the chart as a class before students complete it on their own. For example, for "Interact and share ideas," you might solicit the following from students:

- Encourage others to share their ideas.
- Be respectful of opinions you don't share.

Block Scheduling

Each day in this Pacing Plan represents a 40-50 minute class period. Teachers using block scheduling may combine days to reflect their class schedule. In addition, teachers may revise pacing to differentiate and support core instruction by integrating components and resources as students require.

OVERVIEW: WHOLE-CLASS LEARNING

ESSENTIAL QUESTION:

What effects do people have on the environment?

Our environment provides us with the basic necessities we need to survive—air, water, and soil in which to grow food. However, it's not just a one-way relationship. People's actions also have an impact on the environment. In an era of rapid technological change, we have become very aware of the complex inter-relationship between people and their environment. We depend on the Earth and it depends on us: Getting the balance right is the challenge of our age.

Whole-Class Learning Strategies

Review these strategies and the actions you can take to practice them as you work with your whole class. Add ideas of your own for each strategy.

STRATEGY	ACTION PLAN
Listen actively	• Eliminate distractions. For example, put your cellphone away. • Keep your eyes on the speaker. •
Clarify by asking questions	• If you're confused, other people probably are, too. Ask a question to help your whole class. • If you see that you are guessing, ask a question instead. •
Monitor understanding	• Notice what information you already know and be ready to build on it. • Ask for help if you are struggling. •
Interact and share ideas	• Share your ideas and answer questions, even if you are unsure. • Build on the ideas of others by adding details or making a connection. •

Pacing Plan

Segment	Days
Unit Introduction	1, 2
Introduce Whole-Class Learning	3
from Silent Spring	4, 5
Nobel Speech	6, 7, 8, 9, 10
Media: Nobel Speech	11, 12, 13, 14, 15
Performance Task	16, 17, 18

WHOLE-CLASS LEARNING

CONTENTS

ANCHOR TEXT: DESCRIPTIVE NONFICTION

from Silent Spring

Rachel Carson

An excerpt from the powerful book that inspired a new public awareness about environmental issues.

ANCHOR TEXT: SPEECH

Nobel Speech

Al Gore

A former vice president of the United States calls for the entire human race to unite to save our planet.

MEDIA: VIDEO

Nobel Speech

Al Gore

Watch the former vice president's acceptance speech in Oslo, Norway.

PERFORMANCE TASK

WRITING FOCUS

Write an Argument

There are many ways in which people affect the environment, both positively and negatively. The Whole-Class readings and the video address serious problems with our environment. After reading and viewing, you will write an argument on the topic of the environment.

DIGITAL PERSPECTIVES

Contents

Anchor Texts Preview the anchor texts and media with students to generate interest. Encourage students to discuss other texts they may have read or movies or television shows they may have seen that deal with the issues of people's harmful effects on the environment.

You may wish to conduct a poll to determine which selection students think looks more interesting and discuss the reasons for their preference. Students can return to this poll after they have read the selections to see if their preference changed.

Performance Task

Write an Argument Explain to students that after they have finished reading and listening to the selections, they will write an argument about people's impact on the environment. To help them prepare, encourage students to think about the topic as they progress through the selections and as they participate in the Whole-Class Learning experience.

Introduce Small-Group Learning

Turtle Watchers • "Nature" is what We see— • The Sparrow

Media: Eagle Tracking at Follensby Pond

He—y, Come On Ou—t!

Performance Task

Introduce Independent Learning

Independent Learning

Performance-Based Assessment

19 20 21 22 23 24 25 26 27 28 29 30 31 32 33 34 35 36

from Silent Spring

AUDIO SUMMARIES
Audio summaries of "*from* Silent Spring" are available online in both English and Spanish in the Interactive Teacher's Edition or Unit Resources. Assigning these summaries prior to reading the selection may help students build additional background knowledge and set a context for their first read.

Summary

This excerpt from *Silent Spring* by Rachel Carson is an example of descriptive nonfiction. She describes a town surrounded by nature and farms with a beautiful and healthy ecosystem around it. Plants and animals are abundant and varied. Yet the town and the farms begin to change. Strange diseases become common among the animals, and then the people become sick, too. Some of the deaths are sudden, occurring only hours after people first become sick. Birds are gone, and farm animals no longer give birth to young that can survive. At the end of the excerpt, the author says that no real community has undergone *all* of these disasters—but she warns that every one she lists has happened somewhere, and gone nearly unnoticed.

Insight

Silent Spring was very influential in environmentalism. It brought problems caused by misuse of pesticides to wide attention.

ESSENTIAL QUESTION:
What effects do people have on the environment?

Connection to Essential Question

This selection depicts stark images of the effects DDT and pesticides like it have on once-beautiful parts of nature, offering students a variety of possible responses to the Essential Question.

WHOLE-CLASS LEARNING PERFORMANCE TASK
What is the most significant effect that people have on the environment?

UNIT PERFORMANCE-BASED ASSESSMENT
Are the needs of people ever more important than the needs of animals and the planet?

Connection to Performance Tasks

Whole-Class Learning Performance Task This excerpt from *Silent Spring* connects to the Performance Task. Through its use of descriptive language, the text clearly provides several different examples that showcase the impact of human intervention in the enviroment.

Unit Performance-Based Assessment This selection provides an example for the Performance-Based Assessment to help students understand the long-term effects people can have on the environment. The excerpt ends on the note that while the images Carson has presented have not happened to one specific place, each of these changes has occurred in at least one place, implying it is not too late for people to take action to prevent further destruction of our environment.

DIGITAL PERSPECTIVES

 Audio  Video  Document  Annotation Highlights Online Assessment

LESSON RESOURCES

	Making Meaning	Language Development	Effective Expression
Lesson	**First Read** **Close Read** **Analyze the Text** **Analyze Craft and Structure**	**Concept Vocabulary** **Word Study** **Conventions**	**Writing to Sources** **Speaking and Listening**
Instructional Standards	**RI.7.10** By the end of the year, read and comprehend literary nonfiction. . . **RI.7.1** Cite several pieces of textual evidence . . . **RI.7.2** Determine two or more central ideas in a text . . . **RI.7.4** Determine the meaning of words and phrases . . . **L.7.5.c** Distinguish among the connotations . . .	**L.7.1** Demonstrate command of the conventions of standard English . . . **L.7.3** Use knowledge of language and its conventions . . . **L.7.4** Determine or clarify the meaning of unknown and multiple-meaning words and phrases . . . **L.7.5.b** Use the relationship between particular words . . .	**W.7.1** Write arguments . . . **W.7.1.a** Introduce claim(s) . . . **W.7.1.b** Support claim(s) . . . **W.7.1.c** Use words, phrases, and clauses . . . **W.7.1.d** Establish and maintain a formal style. **W.7.7** Conduct short research projects . . . **W.7.8** Gather relevant information . . . **SL.7.4** Present claims and findings . . . **SL.7.5** Include multimedia components . . .
STUDENT RESOURCES			
Available online in the Interactive Student Edition or Unit Resources	Selection Audio First-Read Guide: Nonfiction Close-Read Guide: Nonfiction	Word Network	Evidence Log
TEACHER RESOURCES			
Selection Resources Available online in the Interactive Teacher's Edition or Unit Resources	Audio Summaries: English and Spanish Annotation Highlights Accessible Leveled Text First Read Extension Questions Analyze Craft and Structure: Imagery	Concept Vocabulary and Word Study Conventions: The Subjunctive	Writing to Sources: Argument Speaking and Listening: Multimedia Presentation
Reteach/Practice (RP) Available online in the Interactive Teacher's Edition or Unit Resources	Analyze Craft and Structure: Imagery (RP)	Word Study: Anglo-Saxon Suffix *-ness* (RP) Conventions: The Subjunctive (RP)	Writing to Sources: Argument (RP) Speaking and Listening: Multimedia Presentation (RP)
Assessment Available online in Assessments	Selection Test: English Selection Test: Spanish Extension Selection Test		
My Resources*	A Unit 4 Answer Key is available online and in the Interactive Teacher's Edition.		

Reading Support

Text Complexity Rubric: *from* Silent Spring	
Quantitative Measures	
Lexile: 1080 **Text Length:** 659 words	
Qualitative Measures	
Knowledge Demands ① ② ③ **❹** ⑤	The central situation described is the impact of chemical use on the environment. Background information to understand what chemicals may have caused the destruction will be necessary for context.
Structure ① **❷** ③ ④ ⑤	The selection is a descriptive excerpt from an environmental science book, broken up into paragraphs that describe different consequences of chemicals.
Language Conventionality and Clarity ① **❷** ③ ④ ⑤	The selection contains many short sentences. Language is used for figurative power and vocabulary is mostly on-level.
Levels of Meaning/Purpose ① ② **❸** ④ ⑤	Selection has only one level of meaning, the devastation of the environment due to chemical misuse.

DECIDE AND PLAN

English Language Support

Provide English Learners with support for context and vocabulary as they read the selection.

Knowledge Demands Tell students that this selection is about the devastating impact of chemical use on the environment. Involve students in a discussion of the topic. Guide students to understand the context of the selection and language related to chemicals, the environment, and preservation.

Meaning Students may find the use of sensory language difficult to grasp. Explain that the author often uses words in a figurative way to create feelings or sensations. Figurative language is language that is used imaginatively rather than literally. Work to support students in analyzing the imagery in the text.

Strategic Support

Provide students with strategic support to ensure that they can successfully read the text.

Knowledge Demands Use the background information to discuss Rachel Carson and her work. Determine students' prior knowledge and experience with chemicals and the environment. Provide additional background if needed.

Levels of Meaning/Purpose As students read, and as they listen, ask them to make notes of the main ideas. If students have trouble finding the main ideas, ask them to read or listen more than once and ask questions to direct them to the main ideas.

Challenge

Provide students who need to be challenged with ideas for how they can go beyond a simple interpretation of the text.

Text Analysis Discuss what it means to use language *figuratively* or *literally*. The selection does both. Ask students to find examples of each type of use in the selection. Then have them discuss their examples in small groups.

Written Response Challenge students to choose a chapter of Carson's book to read and report on. Then have them share their findings with the class.

TEACH

Read and Respond

Have students do their first read of the selection. Then have them complete their close read. Finally, work with them on the Making Meaning, Language Development, and Effective Expression activities.

Standards Support Through Teaching and Learning Cycle

IDENTIFY NEEDS

Analyze results of the Beginning-of-Year Assessment, focusing on the items relating to Unit 4. Also take into consideration student performance to this point and your observations of where particular students struggle.

DECIDE AND PLAN

- If students have performed poorly on items matching these standards, then provide selection scaffolds before assigning them the on-level lesson provided in the Student Edition.
- If students have done well on the Beginning-of-Year Assessment, then challenge them to keep progressing and learning by giving them opportunities to practice the skills in depth.
- Use the Selection Resources listed on the Planning pages for "*from* Silent Spring" to help students continually improve their ability to master the standards.

Instructional Standards: *from* Silent Spring

	Catching Up	This Year	Looking Forward
Reading	You may wish to administer the **Analyze Craft and Structure: Imagery (RP)** worksheet to help students understand how authors use descriptive language to create imagery.	**RI.1** Cite several pieces of textual evidence to support analysis of what the text says explicitly as well as inferences drawn from the text.	Challenge students to rewrite a portion of the selection, striking some of the descriptive language, to show the effect the author's choices made.
Writing	You may wish to administer the **Writing to Sources: Argument (RP)** worksheet to help students better prepare them for their arguments.	**W.1.b** Support claim(s) with logical reasoning and relevant evidence, using accurate, credible sources and demonstrating an understanding of the topic or text.	Challenge students to address counterarguments in their essays.
Speaking and Listening	You may wish to administer the **Speaking and Listening: Multimedia Presentation (RP)** worksheet to help students better prepare for their presentations.	**SL.5** Include multimedia components and visual displays in presentations to clarify claims and findings and emphasize salient points.	Challenge students to locate evidence from official sources, like government agencies.
Language	Review the **Word Study: Anglo-Saxon Suffix *-ness* (RP)** worksheet to help students understand that *-ness* means "the condition or quality of being." Review the **Conventions: The Subjunctive (RP)** worksheet to help students understand that the subjunctive mood is used to express a wish, a hope, or a statement contrary to fact.	**L.4** Determine or clarify the meaning of unknown and multiple-meaning words and phrases based on grade 7 reading and content, choosing flexibly from a range of strategies. **L.1** Demonstrate command of the conventions of standard English grammar and usage when writing or speaking.	Have students locate other suffixes they recognize in the text. Have students practice speaking, switching back and forth from indicative to subjunctive.

TEACH

Implement the planned lesson, and gather evidence of student learning.

ANALYZE AND REVISE

- Analyze student work for evidence of student learning.
- Identify whether or not students have met the expectations in the standards.
- Identify implications for future instruction.

Jump Start

FIRST READ Prior to their first read, engage students in a discussion about environmental damage to help them make connections between the text and their own knowledge.

from Silent Spring 

What causes environmental damage? In what kinds of ways does environmental damage affect people as well as the environment? What have we learned about environmental damage in recent years? Modeling questions such as these will help students connect to this excerpt from *Silent Spring* and to the Performance Task assignment. Selection audio and print capability for the selection are available in the Interactive Teacher's Edition.

Concept Vocabulary

Support students as they rank the words. Ask if they've ever heard, read, or used them. Reassure them that the definitions for these words are listed in the selection.

FIRST READ

As they read, students should perform the steps of the first read:

NOTICE: You may want to encourage students to notice what happens to the town, the area around it, and the people who live there as the selection progresses.

ANNOTATE: Remind students to mark passages they feel are particularly evocative or worthy of analysis in their close read. For example, students may want to focus on Carson's language or on specific changes that affect the town or the people.

CONNECT: Encourage students to make connections beyond the text. If they cannot make connections to their own lives or other texts, have them consider news reports, movies, and TV shows.

RESPOND: Students will answer questions and write a summary to demonstrate understanding. Point out to students that while they will always complete the Respond step at the end of the first read, the other steps will probably happen somewhat concurrently. You may wish to print copies of the **First-Read Guide: Nonfiction** for students to use.

Remind students that during their first read, they should not answer the close-read questions that appear in the selection.

MAKING MEANING

About the Author

Even as a child, **Rachel Carson** (1907–1964) wanted to be a writer. Once in college, she renewed her interest in nature and majored in marine biology. She later earned a master's degree in zoology. Carson had long been worried about the overuse of pesticides and wanted to raise awareness about this problem. Her book *Silent Spring* became one of the most influential environmental texts ever written.

from Silent Spring

Concept Vocabulary

You will encounter the following words as you read the excerpt from *Silent Spring*. Before reading, note how familiar you are with each word. Then, rank the words in order from most familiar (1) to least familiar (6).

WORD	YOUR RANKING
blight	
maladies	
puzzled	
stricken	
stillness	
deserted	

After completing your first read, come back to the concept vocabulary and review your rankings. Mark changes to your original rankings as needed.

Tool Kit
First-Read Guide and Model Annotation

First Read NONFICTION

Apply these strategies as you conduct your first read. You will have an opportunity to complete the close-read notes after your first read.

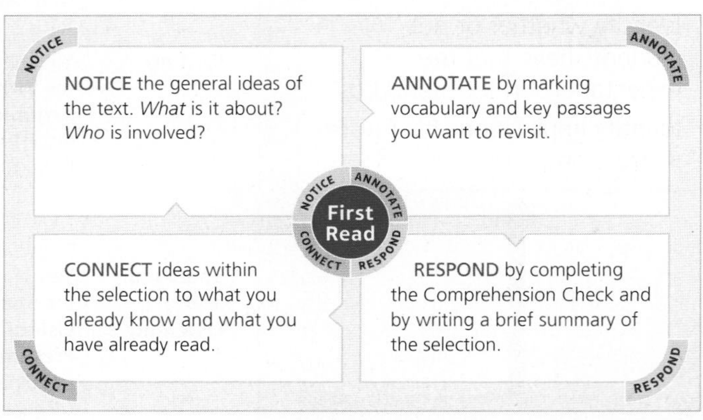

STANDARDS
Reading Informational Text
By the end of the year, read and comprehend literary nonfiction in the grades 6–8 text complexity band proficiently, with scaffolding as needed at the high end of the range.

AUTHOR'S PERSPECTIVE Kelly Gallagher, M.Ed.

Deep Reading *Deep reading* means taking the time to consider more than just what the text says by making inferences, seeing and thinking about information not literally on the page. Teachers can use the following techniques to model how to make inferences:

- **Study Photographs:** Have students study a photo and describe what might have happened in it. Discuss their responses, encouraging students to support their ideas.
- **Complete a Say/Doesn't Say T-Chart:** Draw a T-Chart on the board. On the left, have students write what the passage says (literal comprehension). On the right, have them record what the passage doesn't say. This helps students get at the author's inference.

from Silent Spring

Rachel Carson

BACKGROUND

Pesticides are chemical compounds designed to destroy crop-eating insects. Pesticides can be deadly to many species—including humans—in addition to the insects and other pests they are intended to kill. In 1962, Rachel Carson published *Silent Spring,* which revealed to the public the dangers of DDT, a pesticide in wide use at the time. The awareness raised by *Silent Spring* eventually led the United States to ban DDT entirely in 1972. This excerpt comes from the opening pages of the book.

1 There was once a town in the heart of America where all life seemed to live in harmony with its surroundings. The town lay in the midst of a checkerboard of prosperous farms, with fields of grain and hillsides of orchards where, in spring, white clouds of bloom drifted above the green fields. In autumn, oak and maple and birch set up a blaze of color that flamed and flickered across a backdrop of pines. Then foxes barked in the hills and deer silently crossed the fields, half hidden in the mists of the fall mornings.

2 Along the roads, laurel, viburnum and alder, great ferns and wildflowers delighted the traveler's eye through much of the year. Even in winter the roadsides were places of beauty, where countless birds came to feed on the berries and on the seed heads of the dried weeds rising above the snow. The countryside was, in fact, famous for the abundance and variety of its bird life, and when the flood of migrants was pouring through in spring and fall people traveled from great distances to observe them. Others came to fish the streams, which flowed clear and cold out of the

NOTES

CLOSE READ

ANNOTATE: In paragraph 2, mark details the author uses to describe the rich environment of the town.

QUESTION: Why might the author have used such vivid, descriptive details to describe the town?

CONCLUDE: What can you conclude about the town from these details?

DIGITAL PERSPECTIVES

CLOSE READ

Remind students that they're looking for details that describe a "rich environment." You may wish to model the Close Read using the following think-aloud format. Possible responses to questions on the student page are included. You may also want to print copies of the **Close-Read Guide: Nonfiction** for students to use.

ANNOTATE: As I read paragraph 2, I look for and highlight details that describe the town and the area around it.

QUESTION: I think the author used these details to convey just how rich this area is in wildlife and natural resources, and to reinforce her first sentence, which says the town "seemed to live in harmony with its surroundings." She may be setting up a "before and after" structure.

CONCLUDE: These details tell me that this is an area of great beauty, where wildlife is thriving.

- **Use Positive-Negative Chart:** Have students chart a character's good and bad behavior, positive and negative influence, or the highest and lowest point in a story. This technique is an excellent way to have students track specific literary elements in a novel or a play.
- **Play Literary Dominoes:** Start with the resolution of a narrative and have students work backwards, recording the events that led to it. This creates a chain of key events.

PERSONALIZE FOR LEARNING

English Language Support

Figurative Language Help students understand Carson's figurative language in paragraphs 1 and 2 by discussing and explaining the following images.

- A "checkerboard of . . . farms" is another way of saying the successful farms were set up in a pattern like the squares on a checkerboard.
- "Oak and maple and birch set up a blaze of color" is a way of saying that the red and orange of the leaves made it look as if the trees were on fire.
- "The flood of migrants" refers to the many birds that migrated through the area in the fall and spring. **ALL LEVELS**

CLOSER LOOK

Analyze Author Viewpoint 

Students may have marked text in paragraph 3 during their first read. Use this paragraph to help students understand how Carson introduces the change and why she transitions to it in this way. Encourage students to talk about the annotations that they marked. You may want to model a close read with the class based on the highlights shown in the text.

ANNOTATE: Have students mark text in paragraph 3 that shows how Carson introduces the change, or have students participate while you highlight text.

QUESTION: Guide students to consider what this text might tell them about Carson's intention in this part of the excerpt.

Possible response: By introducing the change suddenly and matter-of-factly, Carson is emphasizing how suddenly and drastically things changed for the town and the people.

CONCLUDE: Help students to formulate conclusions about the importance of this shift and why Carson transitions to it in this way.

Possible response: Carson is giving the reader the same experience as the people in the town: Everything is wonderful until suddenly everything is horrible.

Remind students that the **author's viewpoint** is the perspective a writer uses to share information. Point out that Carson could have led up to the change slowly, preparing readers for how huge and terrible it was going to be. Instead, she chose to suddenly shift from her beautiful descriptions of the area to the "blight" that transformed it. Just as the people in the town didn't see this coming, neither does the reader.

Additional **English Language Support** is available in the Interactive Teacher's Edition.

NOTES

blight (blyt) *n.* something that spoils, prevents growth, or destroys

maladies (MAL uh deez) *n.* illnesses or diseases

puzzled (PUHZ uhld) *adj.* confused and unable to understand something

stricken (STRIHK uhn) *adj.* very badly affected by trouble or illness

stillness (STIHL nihs) *n.* absence of noise or motion

deserted (dih ZUR tihd) *adj.* abandoned; empty

hills and contained shady pools where trout lay. So it had been from the days many years ago when the first settlers raised their houses, sank their wells, and built their barns.

3 Then a strange **blight** crept over the area and everything began to change. Some evil spell had settled on the community: mysterious **maladies** swept the flocks of chickens; the cattle and sheep sickened and died. Everywhere was a shadow of death. The farmers spoke of much illness among their families. In the town the doctors had become more and more **puzzled** by new kinds of sickness appearing among their patients. There had been several sudden and unexplained deaths, not only among adults but even among children, who would be **stricken** suddenly while at play and die within a few hours.

4 There was a strange **stillness**. The birds, for example—where had they gone? Many people spoke of them, puzzled and disturbed. The feeding stations in the backyards were deserted. The few birds seen anywhere were moribund; they trembled violently and could not fly. It was a spring without voices. On the mornings that had once throbbed with the dawn chorus of robins, catbirds, doves, jays, wrens, and scores of other bird voices, there was now no sound; only silence lay over the fields and woods and marsh.

5 On the farms the hens brooded, but no chicks hatched. The farmers complained that they were unable to raise any pigs—the litters were small and the young survived only a few days. The apple trees were coming into bloom but no bees droned among the blossoms, so there was no pollination and there would be no fruit.

6 The roadsides, once so attractive, were now lined with browned and withered vegetation as though swept by fire. These, too, were silent, **deserted** by all living things. Even the streams were now lifeless. Anglers* no longer visited them, for all the fish had died.

7 In the gutters under the eaves and between the shingles of the roofs, a white granular powder still showed a few patches; some weeks before it had fallen like snow upon the roofs and the lawns, the fields and streams.

8 No witchcraft, no enemy action had silenced the rebirth of new life in this stricken world. The people had done it themselves.

9 This town does not actually exist, but it might easily have a thousand counterparts in America or elsewhere in the world. I know of no community that has experienced all the misfortunes I describe. Yet every one of these disasters has actually happened somewhere, and many real communities have already suffered a substantial number of them. A grim specter has crept upon us almost unnoticed, and this imagined tragedy may easily become a stark reality we all shall know. ❧

* **anglers** (ANG gluhrz) *n.* people who fish with a line and hook.

CROSS-CURRICULAR PERSPECTIVES

Science Have students research and write short reports on the effects of environmental damage on people, animals, or plants. Suggest that students narrow their topics by choosing one source of environmental damage, such as the use of pesticides, the burning of fossil fuels, or deforestation. Ask volunteers to share their research with the class, and discuss how this information is reflected in the text. **(Research to Clarify)**

DIGITAL PERSPECTIVES

Comprehension Check

Complete the following items after you finish your first read.

1. What are two animals that attracted visitors to the town?

2. What happened to the animals and the people in the town?

3. What fell on the roofs, lawns, fields, and streams?

4. **Notebook** Write a brief summary of the excerpt from *Silent Spring*.

RESEARCH

Research to Clarify Choose at least one unfamiliar detail from the text. Briefly research that detail. In what way does the information you learned shed light on an aspect of the text?

Comprehension Check

Possible responses:

1. birds and fish
2. Chickens, cattle, and sheep got sick and died; people got sick and there were sudden, unexplained deaths; the wildlife and vegetation died.
3. a white powder
4. There was once an American town of great beauty and abundance that teemed with wildlife and where all life lived in harmony with its surroundings. A strange blight set in and everything changed. Farm animals got sick and died; people got sick and there were unexplained deaths; the wildlife and vegetation died. A white powder had fallen on the town and might have had something to do with these changes. The changes were all caused by people. This town doesn't exist, but there are places that have experienced one or several of these problems. These disasters could become part of everyday life.

Research

Research to Clarify

If students struggle to identify an unfamiliar detail, have them reread the text and notice an idea or concept that might be new to them, such as an animal or plant they don't know, or the impact of chemicals on the environment.

PERSONALIZE FOR LEARNING

Challenge

Research Ask students to research some of the "many real communities" Carson refers to that have experienced the problems she is describing. Have them choose one community that has experienced an environmental problem or disaster and write a paragraph about it. Students may use these questions to start their research: *When and where did this happen? What was the problem? What caused it? Has it been dealt with successfully? Why or why not?* Ask volunteers to share their research with the class and discuss each situation.

TEACHING

Jump Start

CLOSE READ Have students close read the title, *Silent Spring.* Ask students to suggest reasons why Carson picked this particular title. Also ask students to suggest other possible titles. Do they work as well? Why or why not?

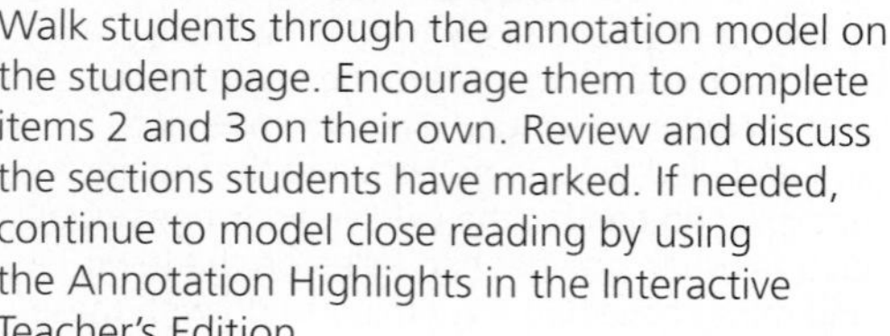

Close Read the Text

Walk students through the annotation model on the student page. Encourage them to complete items 2 and 3 on their own. Review and discuss the sections students have marked. If needed, continue to model close reading by using the Annotation Highlights in the Interactive Teacher's Edition.

Analyze the Text

Possible responses:

1. (a) "Heart of America" suggests a place that is representative of the country and American society. **DOK 2** (b) Carson chose this phrase to convey the idea that this could happen anywhere in the country, and to emphasize how serious this issue is—it could strike us "at our heart." **DOK 3**
2. Carson was writing at a time when the dangers of DDT weren't widely known. For many readers, this was still an issue of the future. **DOK 3**
3. Responses will vary. Students may conclude that people can unknowingly severely damage their local environment.

FORMATIVE ASSESSMENT

Analyze the Text

- **If** students struggle with figurative language, **then** ask volunteers to rephrase the text's figurative language in their own words.
- **If** students struggle with the lack of environmental awareness reflected in the excerpt, **then** remind them that Carson was writing at a time when there was no active environmental movement.

MAKING MEANING

from SILENT SPRING

Close Read the Text

1. This model, from paragraph 3 of the text, shows two sample annotations, along with questions and conclusions. Close read the passage, and find another detail to annotate. Then, write a question and your conclusion.

ANNOTATE: The author uses descriptive details to show the changes in the town.

QUESTION: What kind of mood do these words create?

CONCLUDE: This description creates a sense of destruction and despair.

Then a strange blight crept over the area and everything began to change. Some evil spell had settled on the community: mysterious maladies swept the flocks of chickens; the cattle and sheep sickened and died. Everywhere was a shadow of death. The farmers spoke of much illness among their families.

ANNOTATE: The author uses the words *everything* and *everywhere.*

QUESTION: Why does the author use two words containing the word *every*?

CONCLUDE: The use of these words shows the widespread impact of the blight.

2. For more practice, go back into the text and complete the close-read notes.
3. Revisit a section of the text you found important during your first read. Read this section closely and **annotate** what you notice. Ask yourself **questions** such as "Why did the author make this choice?" What can you **conclude**?

Tool Kit
Close-Read Guide and Model Annotation

Analyze the Text

CITE TEXTUAL EVIDENCE to support your answers.

Notebook Respond to these questions.

1. (a) **Interpret** In paragraph 1, what does the phrase "heart of America" suggest? (b) **Speculate** Why does Carson use this phrase in the first paragraph?
2. **Make Inferences** In the book, the excerpt you read is called "A Fable for Tomorrow." Why does Carson use this title for this section of the book?
3. **Essential Question:** ***What effects do people have on the environment?*** What have you learned about the effects people have on the environment by reading this selection?

STANDARDS

Reading Informational Text
- Cite several pieces of textual evidence to support analysis of what the text says explicitly as well as inferences drawn from the text.
- Determine two or more central ideas in a text and analyze their development over the course of the text; provide an objective summary of the text.
- Determine the meaning of words and phrases as they are used in a text, including figurative, connotative, and technical meanings; analyze the impact of a specific word choice on meaning and tone.

Language
Distinguish among the connotations of words with similar denotations.

Analyze Craft and Structure

Author's Word Choice: Imagery **Imagery** is language that includes **images**—words or phrases that appeal to one or more of the five senses. A writer uses imagery to bring his or her writing to life with vivid descriptions of how the subjects look, sound, feel, taste, or smell. A writer's word choice, or the specific words, phrases, and expressions he or she uses, contributes to memorable imagery. Look at the following examples of imagery, and note the ways in which the individual words help create a realistic image for readers:

- The phrase "sweet, slippery mango slices" appeals to the senses of taste and touch.
- The phrase "glaring lights and wailing sirens" appeals to the senses of sight and hearing.

Writers also create mood through their use of imagery, word choice, and descriptive details. **Mood** is the feeling created in the reader by a piece of writing. The mood of a work may be described with adjectives such as *joyous* or *frightening*. To fully appreciate images and experience the mood of a text, use these strategies:

- determine the specific meanings of unfamiliar words
- consider the **connotations**, or emotional associations, of words, as well as their **figurative**, or nonliteral, **meanings**
- analyze the author's word choice, and make inferences, or educated guesses, as to why the author may have chosen certain words

As you review the excerpt from *Silent Spring,* notice how Carson uses word choice and imagery to create a mood that helps make her central idea more powerful and compelling.

Practice

CITE TEXTUAL EVIDENCE to support your answers.

Notebook Respond to these questions.

1. Review the selection. Then, use a chart like this one to list four images in the text and the sense to which each image appeals.

IMAGE	SENSE
a checkerboard of prosperous farms	sight
streams flowed clear and cold	touch
oak and maple and birch set up a blaze of color	sight
It was a spring without voices.	sound

2. (a) A *specter* is a source of terror or dread. Why might Carson have chosen to use this word in the last sentence of the excerpt? (b) What mood does this word choice create?
3. How does Carson's use of imagery help to develop the central idea of the excerpt? Cite at least two textual examples to support your response.

PERSONALIZE FOR LEARNING

English Language Support

Imagery As students study imagery and connotation, have them list words in the text that have powerful connotations. Have students write a sentence that includes one of the words that they listed. **EMERGING**

Have students write sentences using their words. Remind them that the connotation should be clear from the context of the sentence. **EXPANDING**

Have students write a short paragraph using their words. Then have them trade paragraphs with a partner and point out the connotative words and whether their implied meaning is positive or negative. **BRIDGING**

DIGITAL PERSPECTIVES 

Analyze Craft And Structure

Discuss with students that well-written imagery can make prose read almost like poetry. Also point out that because imagery creates pictures in the reader's mind, different readers might react differently to the same use of imagery. For example, the phrase "the blue blanket of the sky" might suggest warmth and comfort to one reader, while another reader might imagine a vast open space. Encourage students to notice and think about how Carson uses imagery in the excerpt from *Silent Spring*. For more support, see **Analyze Craft and Structure: Imagery.**

MAKE IT INTERACTIVE

Have students write a sentence in which they include imagery. You may wish to provide students with an example as a model, such as the following: *As Allan stood on the beach, he watched the dancing sunlight throw sparkled kisses at the ocean.*

Practice

Possible responses:

1. **See possible responses in the chart on the student page.**
2. (a) Carson may have chosen the word *specter* to emphasize how serious environmental disasters are. (b) This word choice creates a mood of alarm and fear.
3. Carson's use of imagery helps develop the central idea of the excerpt by first creating a sense that everything is fine, and then making readers feel they are facing great danger. Examples: "a town in the heart of America where all life seemed to live in harmony with its surroundings"; "a grim specter has crept upon us almost unnoticed."

FORMATIVE ASSESSMENT

Analyze Craft and Structure

- **If** students have difficulty understanding imagery, **then** review Carson's more accessible images and ask students to say what images they "see" when they read this text.
- **If** students fail to identify images in the excerpt, **then** review two or three examples and discuss how the words create an image.

For Reteach and Practice, see **Analyze Craft and Structure: Imagery (RP).**

TEACHING

Concept Vocabulary

Why These Words

Possible responses:

1. The concept vocabulary gives the reader a sense of what happened when the environmental disaster struck and what it felt like to live in the town afterward.
2. mysterious (paragraph 3); death (paragraph 3); illness (paragraph 3); unexplained (paragraph 3); moribund (paragraph 4); trembled (paragraph 4)

Practice

Possible responses:
1. stillness (quiet/noise); 2. deserted (empty/crowded); 3. puzzled (confused/confident); 4. blight (disease/health); 5. maladies (sicknesses/well-being); 6. stricken (afflicted/cured)

Word Network

Possible words: *spring; countryside; vegetation*

Word Study

For more support, see **Concept Vocabulary and Word Study.**

Possible responses:

1. In the *stillness* of the small room, we could hear our own breathing.
2. The contaminated food caused a great deal of *sickness* among those who had eaten it.

FORMATIVE ASSESSMENT

Concept Vocabulary

If students fail to see the connection among the words, **then** have them use each word in a sentence and think about what is similar about the sentences.

Word Study

If students struggle with understanding the suffix *-ness*, **then** show them several words with this suffix. Review the meaning of each word and discuss how it is formed. For Reteach and Practice, see **Word Study: Anglo-Saxon Suffix *-ness* (RP).**

LANGUAGE DEVELOPMENT

from SILENT SPRING

Concept Vocabulary

blight	puzzled	stillness
maladies	stricken	deserted

Why These Words? The concept vocabulary words from the text are related to unwelcome change—in this case, to a town's landscape. For example, after the town is *stricken* with the mysterious *blight*, there is a strange *stillness* everywhere.

1. How does the concept vocabulary sharpen the reader's understanding of what happens to the town and its people?
2. What other words in the selection are related to this concept?

WORD NETWORK

Add interesting words related to people and the planet from the text to your Word Network.

Practice

Notebook First, correctly complete each sentence using a concept vocabulary word. Then, identify one **synonym**, or word with a similar meaning, and one **antonym**, or word with an opposite meaning, for each vocabulary word.

1. When she returned home from the music festival, the woman found the ________ of her apartment strange in comparison.
2. When the concert hall was ________, you could hear a pin drop from across the room.
3. After carefully following the recipe, Alfredo was _______ when the cake came out of the oven, hard as a rock.
4. The _______ destroyed the potatoes grown in the county.
5. Common ________, such as colds and flus, affect the most people during the winter.
6. Before the return of their lost pet, the family had been ________ with worry and fear.

STANDARDS

Language

- Demonstrate command of the conventions of standard English grammar and usage when writing or speaking.
- Use knowledge of language and its conventions when writing, speaking, reading, or listening.
- Determine or clarify the meaning of unknown and multiple-meaning words and phrases based on *grade 7 reading and content,* choosing flexibly from a range of strategies.
- Use the relationship between particular words to better understand each of the words.

Word Study

Notebook **Anglo-Saxon Suffix: *-ness*** The Anglo-Saxon suffix *-ness* means "the condition or quality of being." It usually indicates that the word in which it appears is a noun. In the text, Carson describes the *stillness* that occurs after the blight as "strange." It is strange because the absence of noise and movement is unusual in the town.

1. Write your own sentence that correctly uses the word *stillness.*
2. Find a word in paragraph 3 of the excerpt that ends with the suffix *-ness*, and write a sentence that shows your understanding of it.

AUTHOR'S PERSPECTIVE **Elfrieda Hiebert, Ph.D.**

Concept Vocabulary Teachers can help students expand their word networks by using morphemes and cognates.

- **Morphemes** are the smallest grammatical unit of a language that cannot be subdivided into further such elements. Tell students that morphemes can be words or parts of words, such as the words *as, the, write,* or the *-ed* in *stayed*. Many new words are members of morphological families of three to five words. For example, words that come from the Anglo-Saxon layer of English use inflected endings (such as *-s/-es, -ed, -ing*) and *-er* and *-est* for comparisons (such as *big, bigger, biggest*).
- **Cognates** are words that are descended from the same language, such as the English word *family,* the Spanish *familia*, the French *famille,* the Italian *famiglia*, and the German *familie*. Explain to students that knowing cognates can help build language by introducing multiple words and ways to decode unfamiliar words.

Conventions

Verb Mood—The Subjunctive Speakers and writers convey their attitudes toward the actions expressed by verbs by using different **moods**. The **indicative mood** is used for statements of fact. By contrast, the **subjunctive mood** expresses one of the following:

- a wish or desire
- a condition that is highly unlikely or contrary to fact
- a request or demand for action

Subjunctive verbs are often found in clauses that begin with *if, as if, as though*, or *that*. This chart shows situations in which a speaker or writer would use the subjunctive mood.

INDICATIVE MOOD	SUBJUNCTIVE MOOD	WHAT SUBJUNCTIVE EXPRESSES
Jill *is coming* with us. She *knows* the answer.	I wish that Jill *were coming* with us. She wishes that she *knew* the answer.	wish
He *will not be* elected.	If he *were* elected, we'd be shocked.	condition that is highly unlikely
I *am* at home. Jake *has* a new car.	If I *were* at home, I'd take a nap. If Jake *had* a new car, he'd be happy.	condition that is contrary to fact
They *are* quiet.	We asked that they *be* quiet.	request
Matt *works* hard.	Kia insisted that Matt *work* hard.	demand or strong suggestion

Avoid using the incorrect verb form to express the subjunctive mood, especially for third-person singular verbs and all forms of the verb *be*.

Incorrect: Blake speaks as if he *was* in charge.

Correct: Blake speaks as if he *were* in charge.

Incorrect: Julia's mother requires that she *gets* home before dinner.

Correct: Julia's mother requires that she *get* home before dinner.

Read It

Identify the mood of each sentence, and tell what it expresses.

1. I wish that the town were filled with birds again.

2. If the town's settlers were present, they would be sad.

Write It

Notebook Identify the incorrect verb form in each sentence. Then, rewrite the sentence correctly.

1. Carson wishes that she was wrong about the fate of the town.
2. The situation Carson relates seems to demand that I am more aware of my effects on the environment.

HOW LANGUAGE WORKS

Subjunctive Mood If students have trouble understanding the subjunctive mood or how or when to use it, give them additional examples. Have students read the following sentences and identify each use of the subjunctive mood.

- I would prefer you were at home instead of here. (expresses a wish)
- If I were able to do this alone, I would not ask you for help. (expresses a condition contrary to fact)
- Rawley insists that he be given time to reply. (expresses a demand)
- I ask that everyone be ready to leave at noon. (expresses a request)

DIGITAL PERSPECTIVES 

Conventions

Verb Mood—The Subjunctive Review the use of the subjunctive mood. Explain that the use of the subjunctive can express things that haven't happened, or that the speaker wishes, hopes, or dreams will happen. Remind students that the subjunctive is often found in a clause beginning with *if* or *that*. For more support, see **Conventions: The Subjunctive.**

MAKE IT INTERACTIVE

Have students write two sentences in the subjunctive mood—one that expresses the speaker's belief that something is contrary to fact, and one that expresses a wish, demand, or request that an action be taken. You may wish to provide students with example sentences as a model, such as the following: *If Spencer were here, he would be laughing constantly. I wish that Darcy were on the swimming team.*

Read It

1. subjunctive; expresses a wish for the return to a healthy state.
2. subjunctive; expresses a situation contrary to fact.

Write It

1. *was*; Carson wishes that she *were* wrong about the fate of the town.
2. *am*; The situation Carson relates seems to demand that I *be* more aware of my effects on the environment.

FORMATIVE ASSESSMENT

Conventions

- **If** students have trouble identifying the subjunctive mood, **then** review what this mood is, when it is used, and how it is formed.
- **If** students have trouble writing in the subjunctive mood, **then** review the sentences in the chart and discuss what each expresses and what verb it requires.

For Reteach and Practice, see **Conventions: The Subjunctive (RP).**

TEACHING

Writing to Sources

Discuss with students the importance of stating a clear position, supporting it with relevant, logical evidence, and including and addressing counterclaims. Also remind students to include details from the excerpt in their argument. For more support, see **Writing to Sources: Argument.**

Reflect on Your Writing

1. Responses will vary. Students should clearly answer the question and give a reason or reasons for their response.
2. Responses will vary. Students should clearly answer the question and give a reason or reasons for their response.
3. **Why These Words?** Responses will vary. Have students list specific examples of words they have chosen that add power to their argument.

FORMATIVE ASSESSMENT

Writing to Sources

- **If** students have trouble articulating a position, **then** ask them to talk with you to verbalize their ideas in one or two sentences. Then have them write their response. For Reteach and Practice, see **Writing to Sources: Argument (RP).**

EFFECTIVE EXPRESSION

from SILENT SPRING

Writing to Sources

Assignment

In *Silent Spring*, Rachel Carson paints a harsh picture of the future. Write an **argument** in which you answer this question: Does Carson's description inspire readers to take action, or does it discourage action because the problem seems so big?

First, decide on your position. Then, review the selection to find specific details that support your position. As you draft, be sure to do the following:

- State your position clearly in the introduction.
- In the body of your argument, support your position with reasons and evidence, including specific details from *Silent Spring*.
- Address alternate, or opposing, positions, and respond with counterarguments that address these views.
- Use transitional words and phrases to connect your ideas and show the relationships among them.
- Establish and maintain a formal style.

Vocabulary and Conventions Connection Think about including several of the concept vocabulary words in your writing. Also, remember to avoid improper shifts in mood in your writing by using verbs in the indicative and subjunctive moods correctly.

blight	puzzled	stillness
maladies	stricken	deserted

Reflect on Your Writing

After you have written your argument, answer these questions.

1. Was it easy or difficult to determine your position?
2. Have your ideas about our ability to solve environmental problems changed after writing this argument? Why or why not?
3. **Why These Words?** The words you choose make a difference in your writing. Which words did you specifically choose to make your argument stronger?

STANDARDS

Writing

Write arguments to support claims with clear reasons and relevant evidence.

a. Introduce claim(s), acknowledge alternate or opposing claims, and organize the reasons and evidence logically.

b. Support claim(s) with logical reasoning and relevant evidence, using accurate, credible sources and demonstrating an understanding of the topic or text.

c. Use words, phrases, and clauses to create cohesion and clarify the relationships among claim(s), reasons, and evidence.

d. Establish and maintain a formal style.

WriteNow Express and Reflect

Brainstorm Have students brainstorm ideas for their argument. Have them ask themselves: *What is my position? Why do I feel this way? What do I think is most important to write about? What evidence can I use to support my position? What counterclaims am I aware of? How will I respond to these counterclaims?* Students can then use their responses to begin writing.

Speaking and Listening

Assignment

Choose one of the following topics, conduct research on the topic, and deliver a **multimedia presentation** of your findings to the class.

- ☐ the importance of *Silent Spring* and the impact it had on the way in which humans view their environment
- ☐ the struggle to ban DDT and the ban's eventual victory
- ☐ the parallels between the current threats to bee populations worldwide and the impacts DDT had on wildlife when Carson wrote *Silent Spring*

1. **Organize Your Presentation**
   - Research the topic you have chosen.
   - Use credible Internet and library resources to gather information and relevant visual aids.
2. **Prepare Your Presentation**
   - Use the information you find to create your presentation.
   - Decide how to sequence textual and visual information so that each emphasizes your main points.
3. **Deliver Your Presentation**
   - Explain why you chose your topic.
   - Maintain eye contact with your audience.
   - Speak at an appropriate volume and with clear pronunciation so as to be heard by the entire class.
4. **Evaluate Presentations** Use a presentation evaluation guide like the one shown to analyze your classmates' presentations.

PRESENTATION EVALUATION GUIDE

Rate each statement on a scale of 1 (Not Demonstrated) to 5 (Demonstrated).

- ☐ The speaker clearly explained the topic and his or her reasons for choosing the topic.
- ☐ The presentation included well-sequenced multimedia that emphasized the main points.
- ☐ The presentation was easy to follow, and the speaker maintained appropriate volume and eye contact.

EVIDENCE LOG

Before moving on to a new selection, go to your log and record what you've learned from *Silent Spring*.

STANDARDS

Writing
- Conduct short research projects to answer a question, drawing on several sources and generating additional related, focused questions for further research and investigation.
- Gather relevant information from multiple print and digital sources, using search terms effectively; assess the credibility and accuracy of each source; and quote or paraphrase the data and conclusions of others while avoiding plagiarism and following a standard format for citation.

Speaking and Listening
- Present claims and findings, emphasizing salient points in a focused, coherent manner with pertinent descriptions, facts, details, and examples; use appropriate eye contact, adequate volume, and clear pronunciation.
- Include multimedia components and visual displays in presentations to clarify claims and findings and emphasize salient points.

DIGITAL PERSPECTIVES

Speaking and Listening

1. **Organize Your Presentation** You may wish to guide students in choosing a topic by having them think about which topic they already know the most about or which one they find most appealing. Then encourage students to confirm that they can find enough information about the topic.
2. **Prepare Your Presentation** As students build their presentation, encourage them to use presentation slides carefully. Remind them that they should not make slides that are hard to read or that have too much text.
3. **Deliver Your Presentation** Encourage students to speak clearly and to try to be comfortable while they present.
4. **Evaluate Presentations** Encourage students to make one supportive comment about each presentation.

For more support, see **Speaking and Listening: Multimedia Presentation.**

Evidence Log Support students in completing their Evidence Log. This paced activity will help prepare them for the Performance-Based Assessment at the end of the unit.

FORMATIVE ASSESSMENT

Speaking and Listening

- **If** students have trouble choosing a topic, **then** suggest the topic you believe best matches each student's interests and abilities.
- **If** students have trouble conducting research, **then** suggest sources they might consult.

For Reteach and Practice, see **Speaking and Listening: Multimedia Presentation (RP).**

Selection Test

Administer the *Silent Spring* Selection Test, which is available in both print and digital formats online in Assessments.

PERSONALIZE FOR LEARNING

Strategic Support

Extend Discuss the beginning and growth of today's environmental movement, and the impact both Rachel Carson and *Silent Spring* had on this movement. Have students research one contemporary environmental group and report on what it does. Also have students consider what the world was like before the modern environmental movement and before environmental awareness became as common as it is today.

Nobel Speech

AUDIO SUMMARIES
Audio summaries of "Nobel Speech" are available online in both English and Spanish in the Interactive Teacher's Edition or Unit Resources. Assigning these summaries prior to reading the selection may help students build additional background knowledge and set a context for their first read.

Summary

In his acceptance speech for the Nobel Peace Prize, Al Gore speaks about the issue of climate change and the effect that it will have on humanity. He says that we face a planetary emergency and that our own survival is at risk. He goes on to state that we have dumped enormous amounts of CO_2 into the atmosphere. This is having negative effects on the environment, some of which we are already seeing. Severe weather events such as droughts and floods have become more common, and these problems will only get worse. The consequences for ignoring the issue are enormous. However, he says, we have a chance to avoid the most severe consequences if we act quickly.

Insight

This speech is a good introduction to global warming. It calls for new and creative solutions to environmental problems, and argues that this provides an opportunity to also address other global problems.

ESSENTIAL QUESTION:
What effects do people have on the environment?

Connection to Essential Question

By burning fossil fuel, people are increasing the amount of CO_2 in the atmosphere, which increases the world's overall temperature.

WHOLE-CLASS LEARNING PERFORMANCE TASK
What is the most significant effect that people have on the environment?

UNIT PERFORMANCE-BASED ASSESSMENT
Are the needs of people ever more important than the needs of animals and the planet?

Connection to Performance Tasks

Whole-Class Learning Performance Task This speech connects to the Performance Task by providing students an example of an argument in which the speaker's viewpoint is made very clear. His intention is to motivate his listeners to act. Gore also includes many anecdotal references and inspiring quotes to support his purpose. Students may use this speech as a framework for their own arguments.

Unit Performance-Based Assessment Gore's speech connects to the Performance-Based Assessment at the end of the unit. The speech cites many useful sources of information that students might want to research for use in their own essays. Equally, because this speech was given in 2007, students will have the opportunity to explore the actions that have been taken, or not taken, to decrease carbon emissions into Earth's atmosphere.

DIGITAL PERSPECTIVES

Audio

Video

Document

Annotation Highlights
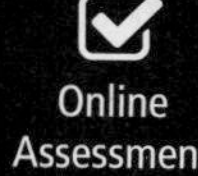
Online Assessment

LESSON RESOURCES

	Making Meaning	Language Development
Lesson	**First Read** **Close Read** **Analyze the Text** **Analyze Craft and Structure**	**Concept Vocabulary** **Word Study** **Conventions**
Instructional Standards	**RI.7.10** By the end of the year, read and comprehend literary nonfiction . . . **RI.7.8** Trace and evaluate the argument and specific claims in a text . . .	**L.7.1** Demonstrate command of the conventions . . . **L.7.1.a** Explain the function of phrases . . . **L.7.4** Determine or clarify the meaning of unknown and multiple-meaning words and phrases . . . **L.7.4.b** Use common, grade-appropriate Greek or Latin affixes and roots . . .
STUDENT RESOURCES		
Available online in the Interactive Student Edition or Unit Resources	Selection Audio First-Read Guide: Nonfiction Close-Read Guide: Nonfiction	
TEACHER RESOURCES		
Selection Resources Available online in the Interactive Teacher's Edition or Unit Resources	Audio Summaries: English and Spanish Annotation Highlights Accessible Leveled Text First Read Extension Questions Analyze Craft and Structure: Persuasive Speech	Concept Vocabulary and Word Study Conventions: Infinitive Phrases and Gerund Phrases English Language Support Lesson: Gerunds
Reteach/Practice (RP) Available online in the Interactive Teacher's Edition or Unit Resources	Analyze Craft and Structure: Persuasive Speech (RP)	Word Study: Latin Prefix *uni-* (RP) Conventions: Infinitive Phrases and Gerund Phrases (RP)
Assessment Available online in Assessments	Selection Test: English Selection Test: Spanish Extension Selection Test	
My Resources	A Unit 4 Answer Key is available online and in the Interactive Teacher's Edition.	

Reading Support

Text Complexity Rubric: Nobel Speech	
Quantitative Measures	
Lexile: 1190 **Text Length:** 2,801 words	
Qualitative Measures	
Knowledge Demands ①—②—❸—④—⑤	Historical and scientific knowledge demands; many historical references throughout the speech, not all of which are explained.
Structure ①—❷—③—④—⑤	The selection is a logically organized speech.
Language Conventionality and Clarity ①—②—❸—④—⑤	Figurative language is used to emphasize important points. The selection contains subject specific vocabulary and many quotes from world leaders and scientists.
Levels of Meaning/Purpose ①—❷—③—④—⑤	Selection has only one level of meaning. The main concept and supporting ideas are clearly stated.

DECIDE AND PLAN

English Language Support

Provide English Learners with support for context and vocabulary as they read the selection.

Knowledge Demands Tell students that this selection is a speech. Make sure students understand the context. Tell students they should expect to see language about the threat of global warming on the planet. Ask students to list words that help convey the warning that Gore delivers. (Students may suggest: emergency, threat, dire, . . .)

Meaning For students who have difficulty understanding figurative language, have them underline or list the phrases that they don't understand. Then have them read those phrases again and work with a partner to try to figure out the comparison the speaker is making.

Strategic Support

Provide students with strategic support to ensure that they can successfully read the text.

Knowledge Demands Use the background information to discuss Al Gore and his work on climate change. Determine students' prior knowledge and experience with global warming. Provide additional background if needed.

Language Students will likely have difficulty with some of the scientific vocabulary. Instead of trying to understand every word, encourage students to scan for ideas in each paragraph that they understand. Ask them to write sentences restating the information they understood.

Challenge

Provide students who need to be challenged with ideas for how they can go beyond a simple interpretation of the text.

Text Analysis Pair students. Have them each take a paragraph and retell it to their partner, using their own descriptions without reading from the text. Encourage them to include details and descriptive language. They may refer to the text as needed to remember details, but should use their own words.

Written Response In paragraph 42, Gore says "We must understand the connections between the climate crisis and the afflictions of poverty, hunger, HIV-AIDS, and other pandemics." Challenge students to choose one of these issues and research the connection between it and climate change. Then ask students to write a short essay about their findings and share their research with the class.

TEACH

Read and Respond

Have the class do their first read of the selection. Then have them complete their close read. Finally, work with them on the Making Meaning and Language Development activities.

Standards Support Through Teaching and Learning Cycle

IDENTIFY NEEDS

Analyze results of the Beginning-of-Year Assessment, focusing on the items relating to Unit 4. Also take into consideration student performance to this point and your observations of where particular students struggle.

DECIDE AND PLAN

- If students have performed poorly on items matching these standards, then provide selection scaffolds before assigning them the on-level lesson provided in the Student Edition.
- If students have done well on the Beginning-of-Year Assessment, then challenge them to keep progressing and learning by giving them opportunities to practice the skills in depth.
- Use the Selection Resources listed on the Planning pages for "Nobel Speech" to help students continually improve their ability to master the standards.

Instructional Standards: Nobel Speech

	Catching Up	This Year	Looking Forward
Reading	You may wish to administer the **Analyze Craft and Structure: Persuasive Speech (RP)** worksheet to help students understand the different appeals a persuasive speech can use.	**RI.8** Trace and evaluate the argument and specific claims in a text, assessing whether the reasoning is sound and the evidence is relevant and sufficient to support the claims.	Challenge students to seek out any irrelevant information in Gore's speech. If there is none, have them discuss how a speech could suffer from unneeded information.
Language	Review the **Word Study: Latin Prefix *uni-* (RP)** worksheet to help students understand that *uni-* means "having or consisting of only one." Review the **Conventions: Infinitive Phrases and Gerund Phrases (RP)** worksheet to help students understand the functions of infinitive and gerund phrases.	**L.4.b** Use common, grade-appropriate Greek or Latin affixes and roots as clues to the meaning of a word. **L.1.a** Explain the function of phrases and clauses in general and their function in specific sentences.	Have students locate other prefixes in the text they recognize. Have students look up the functions of participial phrases to distinguish them from infinitive and gerund phrases.

ANALYZE AND REVISE

- Analyze student work for evidence of student learning.
- Identify whether or not students have met the expectations in the standards.
- Identify implications for future instruction.

TEACH

Implement the planned lesson, and gather evidence of student learning.

Jump Start

FIRST READ Prior to students' first read, engage them in a discussion about global warming and what they already know about it. This will help them make connections between the text and their own ideas and experiences.

Nobel Speech

How serious is climate change? What can we do about it? Modeling questions such as these will help students connect to Al Gore's Nobel Speech and to the Performance Task assignment. Selection audio and print capability for the selection are available in the Interactive Teacher's Edition.

Concept Vocabulary

Support students as they rank the words. Ask if they've ever heard, read, or used them. Reassure them that the definitions for these words are listed in the selection.

FIRST READ

As they read, students should perform the steps of the first read:

NOTICE: Encourage students to notice the general idea of Gore's speech.

ANNOTATE: Remind students to mark text that demonstrates the elements of an effective argument.

CONNECT: Encourage students to make connections beyond the text. If they cannot make connections to their own lives or other texts, have them consider news reports, movies, and TV shows.

RESPOND: Students will answer questions and write a summary to demonstrate understanding.

Point out to students that while they will always complete the Respond step at the end of the first read, the other steps will probably happen somewhat concurrently. You may wish to print copies of the **First-Read Guide: Nonfiction** for students to use.

Remind students that during their first read, they should not answer the close-read questions that appear in the selection.

MAKING MEANING

NOBEL SPEECH (TEXT)

Comparing Text to Media

In this lesson, you will read Al Gore's Nobel Prize acceptance speech and then watch a video of Gore delivering the speech. First, you will complete the first-read and close-read activities for the text of the speech. These activities will help prepare you to compare the speech and the video.

NOBEL SPEECH (VIDEO)

About the Author

Former United States Vice President **Al Gore** (b.1948) was practically born into politics. His father was a senator, and after Gore served a tour of duty in Vietnam, he went on to serve in both houses of Congress before becoming vice president in 1993. As a congressman, Gore became active in environmental issues. He has written several books about the dangers of climate change, and his campaign to educate the public about climate change is the subject of *An Inconvenient Truth*, which won the Academy Award for Best Documentary Feature in 2007.

Tool Kit
First-Read Guide and Model Annotation

STANDARDS
Reading Informational Text
By the end of the year, read and comprehend literary nonfiction in the grades 6–8 text complexity band proficiently, with scaffolding as needed at the high end of the range.

Nobel Speech

Concept Vocabulary

You will encounter the following words as you read the speech. Before reading, note how familiar you are with each word. Then, rank the words in order from most familiar (1) to least familiar (6).

WORD	YOUR RANKING
crisis	
pollution	
urgency	
universal	
illusion	
environment	

After completing your first read, come back to the concept vocabulary and review your rankings. Mark any changes to your original rankings.

First Read NONFICTION

Apply these strategies as you conduct your first read. You will have an opportunity to complete the close-read notes after your first read.

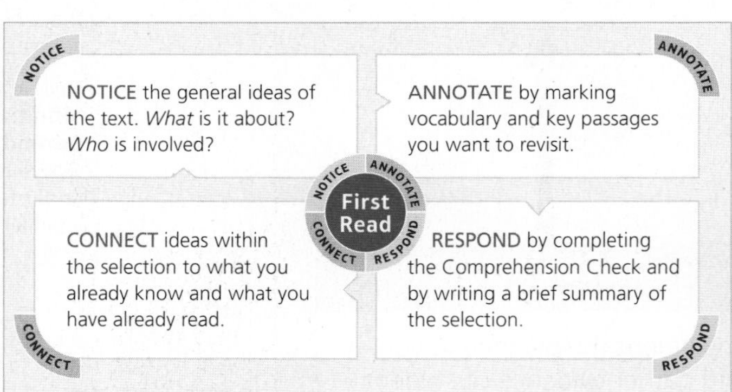

CROSS-CURRICULAR PERSPECTIVES

Science As Al Gore says, global warming and climate change are major issues facing today's world. Have students research this topic and write short reports. What is global warming? What is climate change? What's causing them? What's being done about these problems? Ask volunteers to share their information with the class. **(Research to Clarify)**

372 UNIT 4 • PEOPLE AND THE PLANET

DIGITAL PERSPECTIVES

Nobel Speech

Al Gore

BACKGROUND
The Nobel Peace Prize is a prestigious award granted to those who have done outstanding work to promote peace in the world. The Nobel Prize was established by Alfred Nobel, a Swedish chemist and engineer known for inventing dynamite. The 2007 Nobel Peace Prize was awarded to Al Gore for his efforts to educate people about the threats posed by man-made climate change and to urge people to act against the effects of climate change.

Nobel Lecture, Oslo, December 10, 2007

1 Your Majesties, Your Royal Highnesses, Honorable members of the Norwegian Nobel Committee, Excellencies, Ladies and gentlemen.

2 I have a purpose here today. It is a purpose I have tried to serve for many years. I have prayed that God would show me a way to accomplish it.

3 Sometimes, without warning, the future knocks on our door with a precious and painful vision of what might be. One hundred and nineteen years ago, a wealthy inventor read his own obituary, mistakenly published years before his death. Wrongly believing the inventor had just died, a newspaper printed a harsh judgment of his life's work, unfairly labeling him "The Merchant of Death" because of his invention—dynamite. Shaken by this

NOTES

PERSONALIZE FOR LEARNING

Strategic Support

Alfred Nobel In paragraph 3, Gore tells the story of Alfred Nobel. Help students understand and appreciate the historic context of Gore beginning his speech by referring to Alfred Nobel. Have students research Nobel and write a paragraph about him. Ask volunteers to share their information with the class, and discuss Nobel's life, achievements, and the Nobel Prize.

CLOSE READ 

Remind students that the word *or* is often used to show differences. You may wish to model the Close Read using the following think-aloud format. Possible responses to questions on the student page are included. You may also want to print copies of the **Close-Read Guide: Nonfiction** for students to use.

ANNOTATE: As I read paragraph 7, I notice and highlight words that show two possible futures.

QUESTION: I think that Gore might have chosen the quotation to emphasize how serious this problem is.

CONCLUDE: This makes me think about the importance and urgency of the issue. Gore is saying that this is a matter of life and death.

Additional **English Language Support** is available in the Interactive Teacher's Edition.

NOTES

CLOSE READ

ANNOTATE: Mark words in the quotation in paragraph 7 that show the two different futures to which Gore refers.

QUESTION: Why might Gore have chosen this quotation to show the two different futures facing society?

CONCLUDE: What effect does the inclusion of this quotation have on readers?

crisis (KRY sihs) *n.* time when a situation is very bad or dangerous; turning point at which a change must be made for better or worse

pollution (puh LOO shuhn) *n.* presence or introduction into a space of a substance or thing that has harmful or poisonous effects

condemnation, the inventor made a fateful choice to serve the cause of peace.

4 Seven years later, Alfred Nobel created this prize and the others that bear his name.

5 Seven years ago tomorrow, I read my own political obituary[1] in a judgment that seemed to me harsh and mistaken—if not premature. But that unwelcome verdict also brought a precious if painful gift: an opportunity to search for fresh new ways to serve my purpose.

6 Unexpectedly, that quest has brought me here. Even though I fear my words cannot match this moment, I pray what I am feeling in my heart will be communicated clearly enough that those who hear me will say, "We must act."

7 The distinguished scientists with whom it is the greatest honor of my life to share this award have laid before us a choice between two different futures—a choice that to my ears echoes the words of an ancient prophet: "Life or death, blessings or curses. Therefore, choose life, that both thou and thy seed may live."

8 We, the human species, are confronting a planetary emergency—a threat to the survival of our civilization that is gathering ominous and destructive potential even as we gather here. But there is hopeful news as well: we have the ability to solve this **crisis** and avoid the worst—though not all—of its consequences, if we act boldly, decisively and quickly.

9 However, despite a growing number of honorable exceptions, too many of the world's leaders are still best described in the words Winston Churchill applied to those who ignored Adolf Hitler's threat:[2] "They go on in strange paradox, decided only to be undecided, resolved to be irresolute, adamant for drift, solid for fluidity, all powerful to be impotent."

10 So today, we dumped another 70 million tons of global-warming **pollution** into the thin shell of atmosphere surrounding our planet, as if it were an open sewer. And tomorrow, we will dump a slightly larger amount, with the cumulative concentrations now trapping more and more heat from the sun.

11 As a result, the earth has a fever. And the fever is rising. The experts have told us it is not a passing affliction that will heal by itself. We asked for a second opinion. And a third. And a fourth. And the consistent conclusion, restated with increasing alarm, is that something basic is wrong.

12 We are what is wrong, and we must make it right.

1. **Seven years ago tomorrow . . . obituary** Gore is referring to the highly contested 2000 presidential election, which he lost to George W. Bush.
2. **Winston Churchill . . . threat** Churchill, a British statesman at the time, gave a speech to the House of Commons in 1937 to criticize their failure to respond to the threat of Nazi Germany.

PERSONALIZE FOR LEARNING

English Language Support

Archaic Words Help students understand the words *thou* and *thy* in paragraph 7. Explain that these are archaic, or old, words that are no longer commonly used. *Thou* means "you"; *thy* means "your." Also show students the words *thee* ("you"); *thine* ("your"); and *ye* ("you"). Explain that these words appear in some versions of the Bible and in old texts, but are no longer used today. Ask students why Gore may have chosen to include this quotation. **ALL LEVELS**

DIGITAL PERSPECTIVES

13 Last September 21, as the Northern Hemisphere tilted away from the sun, scientists reported with unprecedented distress that the North Polar ice cap is "falling off a cliff." One study estimated that it could be completely gone during summer in less than 22 years. Another new study, to be presented by U.S. Navy researchers later this week, warns it could happen in as little as 7 years.

14 Seven years from now.

15 In the last few months, it has been harder and harder to misinterpret the signs that our world is spinning out of kilter.[3] Major cities in North and South America, Asia and Australia are nearly out of water due to massive droughts and melting glaciers. Desperate farmers are losing their livelihoods. Peoples in the frozen Arctic and on low-lying Pacific islands are planning evacuations of places they have long called home. Unprecedented wildfires have forced a half million people from their homes in one country and caused a national emergency that almost brought down the government in another. Climate refugees have migrated into areas already inhabited by people with different cultures, religions, and traditions, increasing the potential for conflict. Stronger storms in the Pacific and Atlantic have threatened whole cities. Millions have been displaced by massive flooding in South Asia, Mexico, and 18 countries in Africa. As temperature extremes have increased, tens of thousands have lost their lives. We are recklessly burning and clearing our forests and driving more and more species into extinction. The very web of life on which we depend is being ripped and frayed.

16 We never intended to cause all this destruction, just as Alfred Nobel never intended that dynamite be used for waging war. He had hoped his invention would promote human progress. We shared that same worthy goal when we began burning massive quantities of coal, then oil and methane.

17 Even in Nobel's time, there were a few warnings of the likely consequences. One of the very first winners of the Prize in chemistry worried that, "We are evaporating our coal mines into the air." After performing 10,000 equations by hand, Svante Arrhenius calculated that the earth's average temperature would increase by many degrees if we doubled the amount of CO_2[4] in the atmosphere.

18 Seventy years later, my teacher, Roger Revelle, and his colleague, Dave Keeling, began to precisely document the increasing CO_2 levels day by day.

3. **out of kilter** off balance; not functioning right.
4. **CO_2** carbon dioxide, a naturally occurring gas that is also created through human activities such as burning oil and coal; it is considered a major cause of man-made climate change.

NOTES

CLOSE READ

ANNOTATE: Mark geographic locations in paragraph 15.

QUESTION: Why do you think Gore chooses to include these details?

CONCLUDE: What effect does the inclusion of these locations have on Gore's argument?

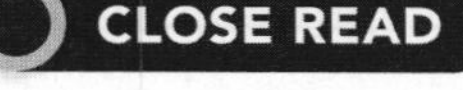

You may wish to model the Close Read using the following think-aloud format. Possible responses to questions on the student page are included.

ANNOTATE: As I read paragraph 15, I notice that Gore has included many geographic locations.

QUESTION: I think that Gore is showing that many areas around the world are affected.

CONCLUDE: He is showing that the effects of climate change are not limited to one region, which makes his argument more powerful.

DIGITAL PERSPECTIVES

Illuminating the Text To help students grasp the magnitude of the kinds of environmental problems and disasters Gore describes in paragraph 15, use search terms such as "environmental disasters" to find video footage online. (Note: Be sure to preview any video before showing it to students.) Have students discuss the video and how it helps them understand the situations Gore describes. Then have students write a paragraph explaining how the video helped them understand or relate to Gore's warning.

CLOSER LOOK

Analyze Word Choice 

Students may have marked paragraphs 23–24 during their first read. Help students appreciate Gore's use of language in this part of the speech. You may want to model a close read with the class based on the highlights shown in the text.

ANNOTATE: Have students mark details in paragraphs 23–24 that demonstrate Gore's use of language and precise word choice to make his argument, or have students participate while you highlight them.

QUESTION: Guide students to consider how Gore is using language to make the speech more powerful and accept student responses.

Possible response: Gore is comparing global warming to nuclear war, and using opposites such as *winter/summer* to make his comparison more vivid. Words like *danger* and *permanent* increase the power of the warning.

CONCLUDE: Help students to formulate conclusions about the importance of these words in the speech. Ask students why this comparison, and this use of language, is so powerful.

Possible response: Comparing global warming to nuclear war is extremely powerful because it implies that global warming would be as devastating as a nuclear war. Making this comparison using these opposite words creates powerful images for the audience and gives the speech an almost poetic quality.

Remind students **word choice** in a speech is critical to conveying a message. Explain that using opposite ideas to create a contrasting effect is a literary technique called **antithesis.** A famous example of this is Neil Armstrong's statement when he landed on the moon: "One small step for man; one giant leap for mankind." Another is the first line of Charles Dickens's *A Tale of Two Cities*: "It was the best of times, it was the worst of times."

NOTES

19 But unlike most other forms of pollution CO_2 is invisible, tasteless, and odorless—which has helped keep the truth about what it is doing to our climate out of sight and out of mind. Moreover, the catastrophe now threatening us is unprecedented—and we often confuse the unprecedented with the improbable.

20 We also find it hard to imagine making the massive changes that are now necessary to solve the crisis. And when large truths are genuinely inconvenient, whole societies can, at least for a time, ignore them. Yet as George Orwell reminds us: "Sooner or later a false belief bumps up against solid reality, usually on a battlefield."

21 In the years since this prize was first awarded, the entire relationship between humankind and the earth has been radically transformed. And still, we have remained largely oblivious to the impact of our cumulative actions.

22 Indeed, without realizing it, we have begun to wage war on the earth itself. Now, we and the earth's climate are locked in a relationship familiar to war planners: "Mutually assured destruction."

23 More than two decades ago, scientists calculated that nuclear war could throw so much debris and smoke into the air that it would block life-giving sunlight from our atmosphere, causing a "nuclear winter." Their eloquent warnings here in Oslo helped galvanize the world's resolve to halt the nuclear arms race.

24 Now science is warning us that if we do not quickly reduce the global warming pollution that is trapping so much of the heat our planet normally radiates back out of the atmosphere, we are in danger of creating a permanent "carbon summer."[5]

25 As the American poet Robert Frost wrote, "Some say the world will end in fire; some say in ice." Either, he notes, "would suffice."

26 But neither need be our fate. It is time to make peace with the planet.

27 We must quickly mobilize our civilization with the **urgency** and resolve that has previously been seen only when nations mobilized for war. These prior struggles for survival were won when leaders found words at the eleventh hour[6] that released a mighty surge of courage, hope and readiness to sacrifice for a protracted and mortal challenge.

urgency (UR juhn see) *n.* state of being very important and needing to be dealt with right away

28 These were not comforting and misleading assurances that the threat was not real or imminent; that it would affect others but not ourselves; that ordinary life might be lived even in the presence of extraordinary threat; that Providence[7] could be trusted to do for us what we would not do for ourselves.

5. **"carbon summer"** a permanent summer caused by too much heat in the atmosphere.
6. **eleventh hour** latest possible moment before it is too late to make a change.
7. **Providence** (PROV uh duhns) *n.* protective care of nature or God.

376 UNIT 4 • PEOPLE AND THE PLANET

29 No, these were calls to come to the defense of the common future. They were calls upon the courage, generosity and strength of entire peoples, citizens of every class and condition who were ready to stand against the threat once asked to do so. Our enemies in those times calculated that free people would not rise to the challenge; they were, of course, catastrophically wrong.

30 Now comes the threat of climate crisis—a threat that is real, rising, imminent, and **universal**. Once again, it is the 11th hour. The penalties for ignoring this challenge are immense and growing, and at some near point would be unsustainable and unrecoverable. For now we still have the power to choose our fate, and the remaining question is only this: Have we the will to act vigorously and in time, or will we remain imprisoned by a dangerous **illusion**?

31 Mahatma Gandhi[8] awakened the largest democracy on earth and forged a shared resolve with what he called "Satyagraha"—or "truth force."

32 In every land, the truth—once known—has the power to set us free.

NOTES

universal (yoo nuh VUR suhl) *adj.* involving everyone in the world or in a particular group; true or appropriate in every situation

illusion (ih LOO zhuhn) *n.* something that appears real but actually is not

8. **Mahatma Gandhi** (1869–1948) Indian activist known for leading the movement against British rule of India and for his doctrine of nonviolent protest.

PERSONALIZE FOR LEARNING

English Language Support

Idioms Help students understand the idioms *11th hour* and *stand against* in paragraphs 29 and 30. Explain that the *11th hour* means "the latest possible time before it is too late." There are 12 hours in the time periods from midnight to noon and from noon to midnight. The 11th hour is the last hour in one of these time cycles, so it has come to mean the latest time something can be done.

Explain that *stand against* means to resist or oppose something. To stand against a threat is to oppose or fight back against that threat. Also point out these idioms: *stand a chance* (to have a chance); *stand for* (to be a symbol for); *stand one's ground* (to maintain one's position); *stand tall* (to exhibit courage, strength, or calm especially in the face of adversity.) **ALL LEVELS**

CLOSE READ

Remind students that quotations are set off by quotation marks. You may wish to model the Close Read using the following think-aloud format. Possible responses to questions on the student page are included.

ANNOTATE: As I read paragraph 38, I look for details that support Gore's claim about people uniting together for an important cause.

QUESTION: I think Gore chose this example because people can agree that fascism was dangerous. The united front against fascism was able to achieve the good things he names.

CONCLUDE: This example might persuade readers because it shows that when people get together to solve a problem, it can benefit the world. Referencing the United Nations and democracy allows Gore to tap into people's belief in freedom.

NOTES

33 Truth also has the power to unite us and bridge the distance between "me" and "we," creating the basis for common effort and shared responsibility.

34 There is an African proverb that says, "If you want to go quickly, go alone. If you want to go far, go together." We need to go far, quickly.

35 We must abandon the conceit that individual, isolated, private actions are the answer. They can and do help. But they will not take us far enough without collective action. At the same time, we must ensure that in mobilizing globally, we do not invite the establishment of ideological conformity and a new lock-step "ism."

36 That means adopting principles, values, laws, and treaties that release creativity and initiative[9] at every level of society in multifold responses originating concurrently and spontaneously.

37 This new consciousness requires expanding the possibilities inherent in all humanity. The innovators who will devise a new way to harness the sun's energy for pennies or invent an engine that's carbon negative may live in Lagos or Mumbai or Montevideo. We must ensure that entrepreneurs and inventors everywhere on the globe have the chance to change the world.

CLOSE READ

ANNOTATE: In paragraph 38, mark the example Gore uses to support his claim.

QUESTION: Why do you think Gore chooses to include this specific example?

CONCLUDE: How does this example help to persuade readers?

38 When we unite for a moral purpose that is manifestly good and true, the spiritual energy unleashed can transform us. The generation that defeated fascism throughout the world in the 1940s found, in rising to meet their awesome challenge, that they had gained the moral authority and long-term vision to launch the Marshall Plan,[10] the United Nations, and a new level of global cooperation and foresight that unified Europe and facilitated the emergence of democracy and prosperity in Germany, Japan, Italy and much of the world. One of their visionary leaders[11] said, "It is time we steered by the stars and not by the lights of every passing ship."

39 In the last year of that war, you gave the Peace Prize to a man from my hometown of 2,000 people, Carthage, Tennessee. Cordell Hull was described by Franklin Roosevelt as the "Father of the United Nations." He was an inspiration and hero to my own father, who followed Hull in the Congress and the U.S. Senate and in his commitment to world peace and global cooperation.

40 My parents spoke often of Hull, always in tones of reverence and admiration. Eight weeks ago, when you announced this prize, the deepest emotion I felt was when I saw the headline in my hometown paper that simply noted I had won the same prize that

9. **initiative** (ih NIHSH uh tihv) *n.* ability to act or take the first step without being urged.
10. **Marshall Plan** United States–financed plan to rebuild Europe after World War II.
11. **One . . . leaders** Omar Bradley (1893–1981), a notable field commander in the United States Army.

PERSONALIZE FOR LEARNING

Challenge

Problem-Solution Suggestion In paragraph 37, Al Gore is saying that new ideas and possible solutions to climate change can come from anyone, anywhere. Have students write one or two paragraphs in which they discuss how an individual might create something or have an idea that will help deal with climate change. Ask students to consider ways that government or the business community could encourage people to find solutions.

Cordell Hull had won. In that moment, I knew what my father and mother would have felt were they alive.

41 Just as Hull's generation found moral authority in rising to solve the world crisis caused by fascism, so too can we find our greatest opportunity in rising to solve the climate crisis. In the Kanji characters used in both Chinese and Japanese, "crisis" is written with two symbols, the first meaning "danger," the second "opportunity." By facing and removing the danger of the climate crisis, we have the opportunity to gain the moral authority and vision to vastly increase our own capacity to solve other crises that have been too long ignored.

42 We must understand the connections between the climate crisis and the afflictions of poverty, hunger, HIV-AIDS and other pandemics. As these problems are linked, so too must be their solutions. We must begin by making the common rescue of the global **environment** the central organizing principle of the world community.

43 Fifteen years ago, I made that case at the "Earth Summit" in Rio de Janeiro. Ten years ago, I presented it in Kyoto. This week, I will urge the delegates in Bali to adopt a bold mandate for a treaty that establishes a universal global cap on emissions and uses the market in emissions trading[12] to efficiently allocate resources to the most effective opportunities for speedy reductions.

44 This treaty should be ratified and brought into effect everywhere in the world by the beginning of 2010—two years sooner than presently contemplated. The pace of our response must be accelerated to match the accelerating pace of the crisis itself.

45 Heads of state should meet early next year to review what was accomplished in Bali and take personal responsibility for addressing this crisis. It is not unreasonable to ask, given the gravity of our circumstances, that these heads of state meet every three months until the treaty is completed.

46 We also need a moratorium[13] on the construction of any new generating facility that burns coal without the capacity to safely trap and store carbon dioxide.

47 And most important of all, we need to put a *price* on carbon—with a CO_2 tax that is then rebated back to the people, progressively, according to the laws of each nation, in ways that shift the burden of taxation from employment to pollution. This is by far the most effective and simplest way to accelerate solutions to this crisis.

NOTES

environment (ehn VY uhrn muhnt) *n.* land, air, and water in which people, animals, and plants live, and all the natural features of these places

12. **universal global cap on emissions . . . market in emissions trading** type of law that uses the market to limit how much pollution factories can emit.
13. **moratorium** (mawr uh TAWR ee uhm) *n.* law to stop or delay something.

HOW LANGUAGE WORKS

Transitions Draw students' attention to Al Gore's use of transitional words and phrases in paragraphs 41–47. Have students look at how Gore begins each paragraph and identify which of these paragraphs starts with a transition. Have students highlight the opening words of each paragraph and analyze how these words help reveal the structure of his argument.

CLOSER LOOK

Analyzing Metaphor

Students may have marked paragraphs 52–54 during their first read. Use these paragraphs to help students see the metaphor Gore is creating. You may want to model a close read with the class based on the highlights shown in the text.

ANNOTATE: Have students highlight language in paragraphs 52–54 that describe a path or a destination.

QUESTION: Guide students to consider what these details might tell them. Ask what a reader can infer from what was marked, and accept student responses.

Possible response: He is explaining that we don't know the way. By referencing shadows and forks in the road, he emphasizes the uncertainty ahead.

CONCLUDE: Help students to formulate conclusions about the importance of the details in the text. Ask students why the author might have included these details.

Possible response: Gore tells the audience that the path is unclear but that we must begin. This allows him to elaborate on the first sentence in paragraph 52: The way ahead is difficult.

Remind students that a **metaphor** is a figure of speech in which one thing is compared to another. In this case, Gore compares the job of finding a solution to climate change to the task of walking somewhere without a path.

NOTES

48 The world needs an alliance—especially of those nations that weigh heaviest in the scales where earth is in the balance. I salute Europe and Japan for the steps they've taken in recent years to meet the challenge, and the new government in Australia, which has made solving the climate crisis its first priority.

49 But the outcome will be decisively influenced by two nations that are now failing to do enough: the United States and China. While India is also growing fast in importance, it should be absolutely clear that it is the two largest CO_2 emitters—most of all, my own country—that will need to make the boldest moves, or stand accountable before history for their failure to act.

50 Both countries should stop using the other's behavior as an excuse for stalemate and instead develop an agenda for mutual survival in a shared global environment.

51 These are the last few years of decision, but they can be the first years of a bright and hopeful future if we do what we must. No one should believe a solution will be found without effort, without cost, without change. Let us acknowledge that if we wish to redeem squandered time and speak again with moral authority, then these are the hard truths:

52 The way ahead is difficult. The outer boundary of what we currently believe is feasible is still far short of what we actually must do. Moreover, between here and there, across the unknown, falls the shadow.

53 That is just another way of saying that we have to expand the boundaries of what is possible. In the words of the Spanish poet, Antonio Machado, "Pathwalker, there is no path. You must make the path as you walk."

54 We are standing at the most fateful fork in that path. So I want to end as I began, with a vision of two futures—each a palpable possibility—and with a prayer that we will see with vivid clarity the necessity of choosing between those two futures, and the urgency of making the right choice now.

55 The great Norwegian playwright, Henrik Ibsen, wrote, "One of these days, the younger generation will come knocking at my door."

56 The future is knocking at our door right now. Make no mistake, the next generation *will* ask us one of two questions. Either they will ask: "What were you thinking; why didn't you act?"

57 Or they will ask instead: "How did you find the moral courage to rise and successfully resolve a crisis that so many said was impossible to solve?" We have everything we need to get started, save perhaps political will, but political will is a renewable resource.

58 So let us renew it, and say together: "We have a purpose. We are many. For this purpose we will rise, and we will act." ❧

WriteNow Express and Reflect

Analysis Review paragraphs 54–58. Have students write a paragraph about whether they think Gore's speech may have convinced or will convince people to act on climate change. Have them explain their ideas and cite specific details from the speech to support their opinion.

DIGITAL PERSPECTIVES

Comprehension Check

Complete the following items after you finish your first read.

1. Why has Al Gore been asked to give this speech?

2. What is the planetary emergency about which Gore is so concerned?

3. According to Gore, how much global-warming pollution was added to the atmosphere on the day he gave the speech?

4. Which American poet does Gore quote in his speech?

5. **Notebook** Write a brief summary of paragraphs 7–21 of the speech.

RESEARCH

Research to Clarify Choose at least one unfamiliar detail from the text. Briefly research that detail. For example, you might want to find out more about Alfred Nobel, the United Nations, or "Earth Summit." In what way does the information you learned shed light on an aspect of the speech?

Comprehension Check

Possible responses:

1. Al Gore was asked to give this speech because he won the Nobel Prize.
2. climate change / global warming
3. 70 million tons
4. Robert Frost
5. Summaries will vary; however, students should include: because of climate change, the human species is facing a planetary emergency; we must act immediately to avoid a terrible fate that could mean the end of our civilization; there are people who don't believe this problem is real, and we continue to put global-warming pollution into the atmosphere; the crisis is getting steadily worse, and might be even worse than people think; we're already seeing the effects of climate change: the North Polar ice cap is melting; cities are running out of water; there are huge wildfires and stronger storms at sea; there is massive flooding; even with all this evidence, some people still refuse to believe global warming is a threat and refuse to try to stop it; one reason is that CO_2, the major cause of global warming, can't be seen or smelled; another reason is that some people prefer to avoid the huge changes necessary to deal with this crisis.

Research

Research to Clarify If students struggle to identify an unfamiliar detail, have them reread the speech and notice an idea or concept that might be new to them, such as CO_2 emissions, Franklin Roosevelt, or Kanji characters.

PERSONALIZE FOR LEARNING

Challenge

Extend Ask students to write a paragraph describing what they think could happen if the problems of global warming and climate change are not addressed. Remind them there is no one answer, but their responses should be based on what they've read. Ask volunteers to share their responses with the class.

Jump Start

CLOSE READ Have students close read paragraphs 3–5. Ask: What vision is Gore talking about? Why is he calling it "precious and painful"? How and why is Gore comparing himself with Alfred Nobel?

Close Read the Text

Walk students through the annotation model on the student page. Encourage them to complete items 2 and 3 on their own. Review and discuss the sections students have marked. If needed, continue to model close reading by using the Annotation Highlights in the Interactive Teacher's Edition.

Analyze the Text

Possible responses:

1. Gore says we never intended to cause so much destruction to the planet, just as Nobel never intended that dynamite be used for waging war. Paragraph 16 **DOK 2**
2. (a) Mutually assured destruction means that people are destroying the planet at the same time as the planet is destroying human life. **DOK 2**
(b) Responses will vary.
3. Responses will vary. Students may conclude that people have caused climate change without intending to.

FORMATIVE ASSESSMENT

Analyze the Text

- **If** students fail to cite evidence, **then** remind them to support their ideas with specific information from the text.
- **If** students fail to identify key ideas or the relationships among key ideas, **then** have them review the relevant sections of the speech.

MAKING MEANING

NOBEL SPEECH

Close Read the Text

1. This model, from paragraph 11 of the text, shows two sample annotations, along with questions and conclusions. Close read the passage and find another detail to annotate. Then, write a question and your conclusion.

Close Read: ANNOTATE · QUESTION · CONCLUDE

ANNOTATE: Gore uses the word *fever* twice.

QUESTION: Why does Gore emphasize this word?

CONCLUDE: Gore is personifying the earth as being vulnerable and feverish—due to global warming.

As a result, the earth has a fever. And the fever is rising. The experts have told us it is not a passing affliction that will heal by itself. We asked for a second opinion. And a third. And a fourth. And the consistent conclusion, restated with increasing alarm, is that something basic is wrong.

ANNOTATE: These short bursts of thought are interesting.

QUESTION: What is the purpose behind this passage?

CONCLUDE: Gore creates a metaphor of earth as a patient and scientists as doctors. The shortness of the passages creates a sense of urgency.

2. For more practice, go back into the text and complete the close-read notes.
3. Revisit a section of the text you found important. Read this section closely and **annotate** what you notice. Ask **questions** such as "Why did the author make this choice?" What can you **conclude**?

Tool Kit
Close-Read Guide and Model Annotation

Analyze the Text

CITE TEXTUAL EVIDENCE to support your answers.

Notebook Respond to these questions.

1. **Compare and Contrast** How does Gore compare Alfred Nobel's intentions and goals with those of modern society?
2. (a) **Interpret** What does Gore mean by "mutually assured destruction"?
(b) **Make a Judgment** Do you think Gore is correct? Explain.
3. **Essential Question** ***What effects do people have on the environment?*** What have you learned about the effects people have on the environment by reading this selection?

STANDARDS
Reading Informational Text
Trace and evaluate the argument and specific claims in a text, assessing whether the reasoning is sound and the evidence is relevant and sufficient to support the claims.

382 UNIT 4 • PEOPLE AND THE PLANET

PERSONALIZE FOR LEARNING

English Language Support

Similar Words As students review the Close-Read Model, help them analyze the word *basic*. Explain to students that as it is used in the speech, the word *basic* (paragraph 11) is an adjective that means "of extreme importance." Gore is saying that something of extreme importance is wrong. Show students the word *basis* and explain that this word is a noun that means "something on which something else is established or based." **ALL LEVELS**

Analyze Craft and Structure

Argument: Persuasive Speech A **persuasive speech** is a work of nonfiction that presents a series of arguments to convince people to think or act in a certain way. When you read or listen to a persuasive speech, be alert to the use of persuasive techniques. Then, decide whether a particular technique provides reasonable and relevant support that persuades you to accept or act on the author's ideas.

- **Appeals to authority** use the statements of experts and well-known people.
- **Appeals to emotion** use words that convey strong feelings.
- **Appeals to reason** use logical arguments backed by facts.

Most arguments will combine these techniques to appeal to their audience on many levels. As you read Gore's speech, analyze his use of persuasive techniques.

Practice

CITE TEXTUAL EVIDENCE to support your answers.

Notebook Respond to these questions.

1. Review the speech. Then, use the chart to identify at least one example of each type of persuasive technique.

PERSUASIVE TECHNIQUE	EXAMPLE
appeal to authority (scientists)	Paragraph 7
appeal to reason (we can solve the crisis if we act fast)	Paragraph 8
appeal to emotions (strong words)	Paragraph 10

2. Analyze the examples of persuasive techniques that you identified in the chart. Determine whether each example is relevant and reasonable support for Gore's argument.
3. (a) What "massive changes" does Gore say must be made to solve the climate crisis? (b) Has Gore persuaded you that these changes are possible? Why or why not?
4. (a) According to Gore, what is "shared responsibility"? (b) Is the support he provides to highlight this idea persuasive and convincing? Why or why not?
5. Write a paragraph in which you briefly summarize Gore's overall argument, and evaluate whether his reasons, evidence, and appeals convinced you of his claims.

PERSONALIZE FOR LEARNING

Strategic Support

Persuasive Techniques Review the three types of persuasive techniques and discuss how and why each one can work. Use these questions to prompt discussion: *Why do people respond to appeals to authority? To appeals to emotion? To appeals to reason? How can an appeal to authority be used dishonestly? In what way can appeals to emotion be used to manipulate an audience? How can an appeal to reason be used to manipulate an audience?*

DIGITAL PERSPECTIVES 

Analyze Craft And Structure

Discuss with students that an effective persuasive speech has more than one type of appeal. The reason this is effective is that a speech with different types of appeals may persuade more people. For example, people who don't respond to an appeal to authority might respond to an appeal to emotion. People who don't respond to an appeal to emotion might respond to an appeal to reason. For more support, see **Analyze Craft and Structure: Persuasive Speech.**

MAKE IT INTERACTIVE

Have students write an appeal to authority, an appeal to emotion, and an appeal to reason. You may wish to provide students with examples as a model, such as the following:

Authority: According to a recent study, air travel is safer than it's ever been.

Emotion: Every patriotic citizen must join this march.

Reason: If we want cleaner parks, we have to be willing to pay taxes.

Practice

1. See possible responses in the chart on the student page.
2. Responses will vary; students should clearly determine whether each example is relevant and reasonable support.
3. (a) We must greatly reduce the amount of CO_2 emissions we're discharging into the atmosphere; we must stop building facilities that burn coal without a way to trap and store carbon dioxide. (b) Responses will vary; students should state a clear position and give a logical reason for their answer.
4. (a) Everyone must be responsible for finding solutions to global warming and everyone should be allowed to contribute to this effort. (b) Responses will vary; students should state a clear position and give a logical reason for their answer.
5. Responses will vary; in addition to a summary, students should state a clear position and give a logical, relevant reason for their answer.

FORMATIVE ASSESSMENT

Analyze Craft and Structure

- **If** students have difficulty understanding persuasive techniques, **then** review each one and provide students with simple examples.
- **If** students have difficulty identifying persuasive techniques in the speech, **then** review relevant parts of the speech and help students study each example.

For Reteach and Practice, see **Analyze Craft and Structure: Persuasive Speech (RP).**

TEACHING

Concept Vocabulary

Why These Words?

Possible responses:

1. Responses will vary. *Crisis* expresses the level that Gore says the problem has reached. *Urgency* expresses his belief in the strength of the need to act.
2. human species (paragraph 8); planetary emergency (paragraph 8); threat (paragraph 8); survival (paragraph 8); civilization (paragraph 8); ominous (paragraph 8); destructive (paragraph 8) consequences (paragraph 8)

Practice

Possible responses:

1. illusion
2. crisis
3. universal
4. urgency
5. environment
6. pollution

Word Network

Possible words: *communities; disasters; misfortunes; caretakers*

Word Study

For more support, see **Concept Vocabulary and Word Study.**

Possible responses:

1. Free education should be a *universal* right for the children of the world.
2. *unicycle*: a vehicle that has a single wheel and is usually propelled by pedals; It takes good balance to ride a unicycle.

   unicellular: having or consisting of a single cell; An amoeba is a unicellular organism.

   unilingual: knowing or using a single language; My younger brother is unilingual—he speaks only English.

FORMATIVE ASSESSMENT

Concept Vocabulary

If students fail to see the connection among the words, **then** have them use each word in a sentence and think about what is similar about the sentences.

Word Study

If students have trouble finding appropriate words, **then** review using a dictionary to find words. For Reteach and Practice, see **Word Study: Latin Prefix *uni-* (RP).**

LANGUAGE DEVELOPMENT

NOBEL SPEECH

Concept Vocabulary

crisis	urgency	illusion
pollution	universal	environment

Why These Words? The concept vocabulary words describe situations or settings. For example, in paragraph 10 of his speech, Gore states that "we dumped another 70 million tons of global-warming *pollution* into the thin shell of atmosphere surrounding our planet, as if it were an open sewer." The word *pollution* describes a poisonous component of a setting—Earth's atmosphere.

1. Select two concept vocabulary words other than *pollution*. Explain how each word describes a setting or a situation.
2. What other words in the selection might describe a setting or a situation?

Practice

Notebook Confirm your understanding of the concept vocabulary words by using them to complete the sentences.

1. Environmental groups work to educate the public and eliminate the __________ that the earth is perfectly healthy.
2. Despite scientific evidence, many world leaders have yet to consider the health of the environment a __________.
3. Water shortages are common across the world, making the problem __________.
4. Leaders such as Gore work with a variety of organizations to create a sense of __________ about environmental issues.
5. Increased instances of wildfires show how the __________ is changing.
6. __________ can affect all parts of our environment, from the water we drink to the air we breathe.

WORD NETWORK

Add interesting words related to people and the planet from the text to your Word Network

Word Study

Latin Prefix: *uni-* The Latin prefix *uni-* means "one." In his speech, Gore defines the climate crisis as *universal* because it affects everyone in the world similarly, as if all people were one entity.

1. Write your own sentence that correctly uses the word *universal*.
2. Using a dictionary, find three other words with the prefix *uni-*. Record a definition for each word and write a sentence using it.

STANDARDS

Language

- Demonstrate command of the conventions of standard English grammar and usage when writing or speaking.
  - a. Explain the function of phrases and clauses in general and their function in specific sentences.
- Determine or clarify the meaning of unknown and multiple-meaning words and phrases based on *grade 7 reading and content*, choosing flexibly from a range of strategies.
  - b. Use common, grade-appropriate Greek or Latin affixes and roots as clues to the meaning of a word.

VOCABULARY DEVELOPMENT

Concept Vocabulary Reinforcement Reinforce students' comprehension with "show-you-know" sentences. The first part of the sentence uses the vocabulary word and the second part clarifies its meaning. Model the strategy with this example: *The storm created a* crisis*; the town had no power or water.* Give students these prompts:

1. After the mud slide, authorities responded with great *urgency*; __________.

   Possible response: they rescued people as fast as they could.
2. The cleanliness of the water was an *illusion*; __________.

   Possible response: it was dangerously polluted.

Conventions

Infinitive Phrases and Gerund Phrases Writers and speakers, such as Al Gore, use various types of phrases to add detail to sentences and to clarify the relationships among ideas. Two types of phrases are infinitive phrases and gerund phrases. An **infinitive** is a verb form that acts as a noun, an adjective, or an adverb. An infinitive usually begins with the word *to*. An **infinitive phrase** is an infinitive plus its own modifiers, objects, or complements.

- **Noun** (functioning as a subject): *To speak Spanish fluently* is my goal.
- **Noun** (functioning as an object): I want *to learn other languages*.
- **Adjective** (modifying *one*): She is the one *to see immediately*,
- **Adverb** (modifying *waited*): Everyone waited *to hear the news*.

A **gerund** is a verb form that ends in *-ing* and acts as a noun. It can function as a subject, an object, a predicate noun, or the object of a preposition. A **gerund phrase** is a gerund plus its own modifiers, objects, or complements.

- **Subject:** *Remodeling the building* was a good idea.
- **Direct Object:** Mischa enjoys *painting with watercolors*.
- **Predicate Noun:** Her favorite sport is *cross-country skiing*.
- **Object of a Preposition:** Nina never tires of *singing holiday songs*.

TIP

CLARIFICATION
In each example, the infinitive or gerund is underlined, and the infinitive phrase or gerund phrase is italicized. Refer to the Grammar Handbook to learn more about these terms.

Read It

1. Reread these sentences from the selection. Mark each infinitive or infinitive phrase and each gerund or gerund phrase. Identify the function each performs in the sentence.
   a. It is a purpose I have tried to serve for many years.
   b. This new consciousness requires expanding the possibilities inherent in all humanity.
   c. It is time to make peace with the planet.
   d. Indeed, without realizing it, we have begun to wage war on the earth itself.

Write It

Notebook Write an example of each sentence named below.

1. A sentence that uses an infinitive as a noun
2. A sentence that uses a gerund as a subject
3. A sentence that uses an infinitive as an adverb
4. A sentence that uses a gerund as an object

PERSONALIZE FOR LEARNING

Challenge

Extend At the end of his speech, Gore says the next generation will ask one of two questions: "What were you thinking; why didn't you act?" or "How did you find the moral courage to rise and successfully resolve a crisis that so many said was impossible to solve?" Ask students to imagine they must answer one of these questions. Have students pick one question and write an answer. Ask volunteers to share their response with the class.

DIGITAL PERSPECTIVES

Conventions

Infinitive Phrases and Gerund Phrases Continue the discussion of infinitive phrases and gerund phrases, focusing on what each one is, how it functions in a sentence, and how to recognize it. For more support, see **Conventions: Infinitive Phrases and Gerund Phrases.**

MAKE IT INTERACTIVE
Write the following sentences on the board. Then have students identify each infinitive phrase and identify its role in the sentence.

We were all excited to see the big game. (to see – adverb modifying *excited*)

Mr. Hadley is the best person to interview for this article. (to interview – adjective modifying *person*)

To visit three national parks is my hope for this vacation. (to visit – noun functioning as subject)

Read It

1. (a) to serve; adverb modifying *tried*
   (b) expanding; direct object
   (c) to make; adjective modifying *time*
   (d) realizing; object of the preposition *without*

Write It

Possible response:

1. To practice until I can play this song perfectly is all I plan to do.
2. Winning tomorrow's game is our focus right now.
3. Jerome scrambled to leave the water when he saw the huge wave.
4. Judy hates knowing the end of a movie she hasn't seen.

An **English Language Support Lesson** on Gerunds is available in the Interactive Teacher's Edition.

FORMATIVE ASSESSMENT

Conventions

- **If** students have trouble identifying or using infinitive phrases, **then** review how they are formed and how they are used.
- **If** students have trouble identifying or using gerund phrases, **then** review how they are formed and how they are used.

For Reteach and Practice, see **Conventions: Infinitive Phrases and Gerund Phrases (RP).**

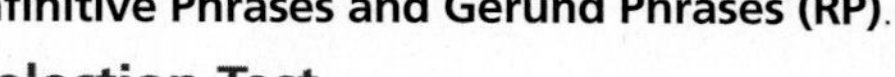

Selection Test

Administer the "Nobel Speech" Selection Test, which is available in both print and digital formats online in Assessments.

Nobel Speech

AUDIO SUMMARIES
Audio summaries of "Nobel Speech" are available online in both English and Spanish in the Interactive Teacher's Edition or Unit Resources. Assigning these summaries prior to watching the selection may help students build additional background knowledge and set a context for their first review.

Summary

This selection is a video of Al Gore's 2007 Nobel Peace Prize acceptance speech. In the speech, former vice president Al Gore speaks to assembled dignitaries and scientists in Oslo, Norway. He begins by talking about how Alfred Nobel was inspired to create the Nobel prize in the first place—by reading his own premature obituary that spoke harshly of his legacy. Similarly, Gore decided to turn full-time to advocating for the environment after reading harsh judgments about his career in politics. His message is ultimately optimistic, calling on listeners to live up to their responsibilities to future generations.

Insight

Hearing a speech gives students a sense of rhetoric that simply reading it cannot. This occurs in much the same way that reading a play provides a different experience than watching that play performed by actors.

ESSENTIAL QUESTION:
What effects do people have on the environment?

Connection to Essential Question

Gore's speech illustrates how civilization has been able to alter the environment, even though these changes are not always apparent. His speech also emphasizes the choices nations can make now to prevent a planetary emergency from occurring.

WHOLE-CLASS LEARNING PERFORMANCE TASK
What is the most significant effect that people have on the environment?

UNIT PERFORMANCE-BASED ASSESSMENT
Are the needs of people ever more important than the needs of animals and the planet?

Connection to Performance Tasks

Whole-Class Learning Performance Task This speech connects to the Performance Task in two ways. First, it provides students an example of an argument in which the speaker's viewpoint is supported by evidence. Second, it provides a wealth of information to help students address the prompt.

Unit Performance-Based Assessment Gore's speech also connects to the Performance-Based Assessment. The speech cites many useful sources of information students can research for use in their own essays. In addition, because this speech was presented in 2007, students will have the opportunity to explore the actions that have been taken, or not taken, to decrease carbon emissions into Earth's atmosphere.

DIGITAL PERSPECTIVES

 Audio  Video  Document  Annotation Highlights 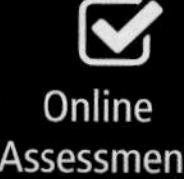 Online Assessment

LESSON RESOURCES

	Making Meaning	Language Development	Effective Expression
Lesson	**First Review** **Close Review** **Analyze the Media**	**Concept Vocabulary**	**Writing to Compare**
Instructional Standards	**RI.7.10** By the end of the year, read and comprehend literary nonfiction. . . **SL.7.3** Delineate a speaker's argument and specific claims . . .	**L.7.4** Determine or clarify the meaning of unknown and multiple-meaning words and phrases . . .	**RI.7.7** Compare and contrast a text . . . **W.7.1** Write arguments . . . **W.7.1.a** Introduce claim(s) . . . **W.7.1.b** Support claim(s) . . . **W.7.1.c** Use words, phrases, and clauses . . . **SL.7.3** Delineate a speaker's argument . . .
STUDENT RESOURCES			
Available online in the Interactive Student Edition or Unit Resources	Selection Audio First-Review Guide: Media-Video Close-Review Guide: Media-Video	Word Network	Evidence Log
TEACHER RESOURCES			
Selection Resources Available online in the Interactive Teacher's Edition or Unit Resources	Audio Summaries: English and Spanish First Review Extension Questions	Concept Vocabulary	Writing to Compare: Argument
Assessment Available online in Assessments	Selection Test: English Selection Test: Spanish Extension Selection Test		
My Resources	A Unit 4 Answer Key is available online and in the Interactive Teacher's Edition.		

Media Complexity Rubric: Nobel Speech

Quantitative Measures	
Format and Length Video; 21 minutes	
Qualitative Measures	
Knowledge Demands ① ② ❸ ④ ⑤	Historical and scientific knowledge demands; many historical references throughout the speech, not all of which are explained.
Structure ① ❷ ③ ④ ⑤	The selection is a formal speech.
Language Conventionality and Clarity ① ② ❸ ④ ⑤	Figurative language is used to emphasize important points. The selection contains subject specific vocabulary and many quotes from world leaders and scientists.
Levels of Meaning/Purpose ① ❷ ③ ④ ⑤	Selection has only one level of meaning. The main concept and supporting ideas are clearly stated.

TEACHING

Jump Start

FIRST REVIEW Assuming that students have read Al Gore's speech, engage them in a discussion about how seeing and hearing Gore deliver the speech might be different from reading the speech.

Nobel Speech

What advantages might there be to seeing and hearing a speech rather than reading it? Is it possible that seeing and hearing a speech could be less effective than reading it? Why? Modeling the questions viewers might ask as they watch Al Gore's Nobel Speech brings the speech alive for students and connects it to the Whole-Class Performance Task assignment. Project the video in class or ask students to open the video in their interactive textbooks.

Concept Vocabulary

Encourage students to discuss the concept vocabulary. Have they seen or used these terms or concepts before? For more support, see **Concept Vocabulary**.

FIRST REVIEW

As they watch, students should perform the steps of the first review:

WATCH: Ask students to note the situation of the speech. How is it being delivered?

NOTE: Students should note the time stamp of any moments they find especially interesting or important.

CONNECT: Encourage students to increase their understanding by connecting the video of the speech to other media they have seen or heard.

RESPOND: Students will answer questions to demonstrate understanding.

Point out to students that while they will complete the Respond step at the end of the first review, the other steps will probably happen somewhat concurrently. You may wish to print copies of the **First-Review Guide: Media: Video** for students to use.

MAKING MEANING

Comparing Text to Media

NOBEL SPEECH (TEXT)

In this lesson, you will watch Al Gore's Nobel Prize acceptance speech. While you watch and listen, think about how the written speech and spoken speech have different effects.

NOBEL SPEECH (VIDEO)

About the Author

Former United States Vice President **Al Gore** (b.1948) continues dedicating his life to environmental issues and is a prominent advocate for solutions to climate change. Since winning a Nobel Prize and donating his portion of the $1.6 million award, Gore has established and runs a nonprofit organization, The Climate Reality Project. He released another book on climate change, *The Future: Six Drivers of Global Change*. Gore also collaborated with NASA, the National Oceanic and Atmospheric Organization (NOAA), and the United States Air Force to launch a satellite into space that would allow anyone to see Earth and track its changes online.

Nobel Speech

Concept Vocabulary

You will encounter the following words as you listen to the speech.

unprecedented (uhn PREHS uh dehn tihd) *adj.* never having happened before; unheard of
recklessly (REHK lihs lee) *adv.* without regard for consequences; carelessly
imminent (IHM uh nuhnt) *adj.* threatening and likely to occur at any moment
unsustainable (uhn suh STAY nuh buhl) *adj.* unable to continue at the same rate or in the same way
emissions (ih MIHSH uhnz) *n.* gas or other substance sent into the air
efficiently (uh FIHSH uhnt lee) *adv.* with the least amount of effort and waste; effectively

First Review MEDIA: VIDEO

Apply these strategies as you conduct your first review. You will have an opportunity to complete a close review after your first review.

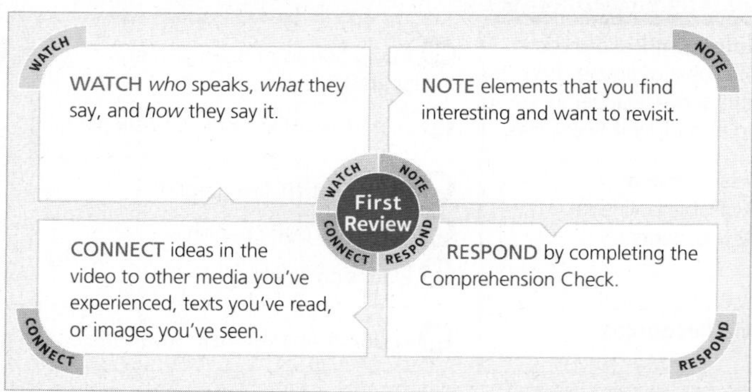

STANDARDS

Reading Informational Text

By the end of the year, read and comprehend literary nonfiction in the grades 6–8 text complexity band proficiently, with scaffolding as needed at the high end of the range.

PERSONALIZE FOR LEARNING

English Language Support

Prefix *un-* Help students better understand the prefix *un-*. Explain that this prefix means "not." Discuss the meaning of each of the following words and how it is formed using this prefix: *unambitious; unskilled; unavailable; unartistic; undesirable; ungraceful; unbelieving; unacceptable*.

Review the two technical vocabulary words that have this prefix: *unprecedented; unsustainable*. Also discuss the suffix *-able* ("capable of, fit for, worthy of being so acted upon"), and discuss the words that have both the prefix and the suffix. **ALL LEVELS**

MEDIA | VIDEO

Nobel Speech

Al Gore

BACKGROUND

Human activities, such as the use of power plants and automobiles, produce large amounts of greenhouse gases such as carbon dioxide. Greenhouse gases trap heat in the atmosphere and are the primary cause of global climate change. Temperature changes that result from global climate change could have disastrous consequences, such as the melting of polar ice caps, extreme weather, and the extinction of many species.

NOTES

DIGITAL PERSPECTIVES

Enriching the Selection To help students understand and appreciate Gore's reference to the North Polar ice cap "falling off a cliff," use the search term "melting polar ice caps" to find video footage online showing melting polar ice. (Note: Be sure to preview any video before showing it to students.) Have students discuss what they see in the video and how this helps them understand and appreciate Gore's concern. Then have students write a paragraph about how the video and Gore's speech are connected. **(Research to Clarify)**

Comprehension Check

Possible responses:

1. Gore is directly addressing those in the audience: the Swedish royal family, the Nobel Committee, and everyone else in the room. He is delivering his message to everyone in the world.
2. One study estimates it could be completely gone during summer in less than 22 years. Another study warns this could happen in 7 years.
3. Cordell Hull won the Nobel Peace Prize in 1945 and was instrumental in establishing the United Nations. He lived in Al Gore's hometown of Carthage, Tennessee.
4. Responses will vary; students should identify specific language in the speech and clearly explain why they chose it.

Research

Research to Clarify If students struggle to choose an element of the video to research, you might suggest that they learn more about who else won the Nobel Prize in 2007.

Comprehension Check

Complete the following items after you finish your first review.

1. Whom is Gore addressing in his speech?

2. What do recent studies say about the North Polar ice cap?

3. Who is Cordell Hull?

4. **Notebook** Choose an example of powerful language in the speech, and explain why this language is so powerful.

RESEARCH

Research to Clarify Choose at least one unfamiliar detail from the text. Briefly research that detail. In what way does the information you learned shed light on an aspect of the speech?

PERSONALIZE FOR LEARNING

Challenge

Research Encourage students to view another speech Gore has given, whether the topic was climate change or something else. They can locate speeches online by using the search term "Al Gore speeches." Then have students write a paragraph comparing the speech they watched with Gore's Nobel Acceptance Speech. Which speech is more effective? Why? Is Gore a good speaker? Why or why not?

DIGITAL PERSPECTIVES

MAKING MEANING

Close Review

Watch the video of Al Gore's Nobel speech again. Write any new observations that seem important. What **questions** do you have? What can you **conclude**?

NOBEL SPEECH (VIDEO)

Analyze the Media

Notebook Complete the activities.

1. Identify a section in the video of Al Gore's speech that you found particularly persuasive. Then, write a short paragraph in which you briefly describe this section, and explain why you chose it.
2. **Essential Question: *What effects do people have on the environment?*** What have you learned about the ways in which people affect the environment from watching the video of Al Gore's speech?

LANGUAGE DEVELOPMENT

Concept Vocabulary

unprecedented	imminent	emissions
recklessly	unsustainable	efficiently

Notebook Demonstrate your understanding of these words in your responses to these questions.

1. Why does Gore most likely use the word *unprecedented* to describe scientists' distress about the North Polar ice cap?
2. Why does Gore most likely use the word *recklessly* to describe the burning and clearing of forests?
3. Why is the word *emissions* important to the speech?
4. According to Gore, what threat to humanity is *imminent*?
5. Why does Gore consider our current approach to climate change *unsustainable*?
6. Name one thing we must do *efficiently* if we are to successfully address global warming.

WORD NETWORK

Add interesting words about people and the planet from the text to your Word Network.

STANDARDS

Speaking and Listening
Delineate a speaker's argument and specific claims, evaluating the soundness of the reasoning and the relevance and sufficiency of the evidence.

Language
Determine or clarify the meaning of unknown and multiple-meaning words and phrases based on *grade 7 reading and content*, choosing flexibly from a range of strategies.

Jump Start

CLOSE REVIEW Engage students in a brief discussion about the differences they noticed between the text of the speech and a video. Ask if watching the video provided any insights that reading the speech did not. Discuss which version of the speech they preferred and why.

CLOSE REVIEW

Remind students to use Accountable Talk in their discussions and to support one another as they complete the close review.

Analyze the Media

1. Responses will vary. Students should describe a specific part of the video and clearly explain why they chose it.
2. Responses will vary. Students might conclude that even when people are told an environmental problem exists, they might choose to deny it or ignore it.

Concept Vocabulary

For more support, see **Concept Vocabulary.**

Possible responses:

1. Gore uses the word *unprecedented* to show that scientists' concern about the North Polar ice cap has never been this great before.
2. Gore uses the word *recklessly* to emphasize the point that people are burning and clearing forests without thought about immediate consequence or any regard for the future.
3. CO_2 *emissions* are a major cause of global warming.
4. Gore believes the threat of climate crisis is *imminent*.
5. Gore considers our current approach to climate change *unsustainable* because we are not doing anything that is effectively stopping it.
6. We need to *efficiently* control emissions to address global warming.

FORMATIVE ASSESSMENT

Analyze the Media

If students struggle to close review the video, **then** encourage them to follow along with the text to anticipate Gore's argument.

Concept Vocabulary

If students struggle to answer the concept vocabulary questions, **then** review relevant parts of the video and discuss how these words are used in the speech.

Writing to Compare

As students prepare to compare the text and a video of Al Gore's Nobel Prize acceptance speech, they will consider the way the delivery impacts the success of the message.

Prewriting

Gather Evidence Encourage students to review each format to consider how each format reveals something they might not have noticed in the other.

a. Text presents the argument. Evidence may be easier to follow because a reader can see the structure.

b. It may be harder to trace the organizational structure in the speech.

c. Text is more effective for allowing readers to review details.

d. Text may feel dense.

e. Spoken word is more musical and more rhythmic.

f. Video is more effective for allowing readers to hear the sounds of the speech. Viewers also see reaction to the speech.

1. Responses may vary. Students may note that the video allows students to hear the way Gore presents the information. Some may say that it sounds like a political campaign speech. The video allows us to hear the rhythm and figurative language in the speech.
2. Students will likely say that Gore's mood comes through in his speech on the video more than it does in the text of the speech. Students may notice themes that they hadn't noticed just in reading the text. For example, they may not have noticed the deep comparison to war that comes through in the speech. They also may notice that for much of the speech, Gore does not speak with the passion the text may suggest. The last section of the speech is very powerful.

EFFECTIVE EXPRESSION

NOBEL SPEECH (TEXT)

NOBEL SPEECH (VIDEO)

Writing to Compare

You have studied the written version and video of Al Gore's Nobel Prize acceptance speech. Now, analyze both versions and consider how the medium in which the message is provided—written or video—affects how persuaded you are by Gore's message.

Assignment

Both the written and video versions of Gore's Nobel speech contain the same message. However, the different modes of delivery, text and speech, may affect how an audience is persuaded by the message.

Write an **argument** in which you state a claim as to which medium more persuasively conveys Gore's argument. Explain how the elements of the video or the written text either strengthen or weaken the argument.

Prewriting

Gather Evidence Review both the text and video. Use a chart like this to gather your notes. In the left column, record key ideas that are conveyed in both the text and video. Then, take note of how effectively that key idea is portrayed in each medium.

KEY IDEA	EFFECTIVENESS IN TEXT	EFFECTIVENESS IN VIDEO
a. See responses in Teacher's Edition	b.	c.
d.	e.	f.

Notebook Respond to these questions.

1. Does the text reveal aspects of the argument that the video does not? Explain.
2. Does the video communicate the author's tone in a way the text does not? Explain.

STANDARDS

Reading Informational Text
Compare and contrast a text to an audio, video, or multimedia version of the text, analyzing each medium's portrayal of the subject.

Writing
Write arguments to support claims with clear reasons and relevant evidence.
b. Support claim(s) with logical reasoning and relevant evidence, using accurate, credible sources and demonstrating an understanding of the topic or text.

Speaking and Listening
Delineate a speaker's argument and specific claims, evaluating the soundness of the reasoning and the relevance and sufficiency of the evidence.

390 UNIT 4 • PEOPLE AND THE PLANET

DIGITAL PERSPECTIVES

Drafting

Craft Your Claim Decide which version of the speech you think is more convincing and write a **claim** in which you state your position. Choose your words carefully so that you state your position in a clear and strong way.

Claim: ______________________________

____

Use Transitions to Connect Ideas Use your notes from the analysis you did earlier to analyze the similarities and differences in the video and the text. Explain the ways in which these differences made one version more persuasive than the other.

To show similarities and differences, use transitions to connect your ideas.

Transitions that show differences

however, unlike, on the other hand, yet, in contrast, but, although

Transitions that show similarities

also, similarly, likewise, too, in addition

Provide Counterarguments To make your argument stronger and more convincing, you must address opposing viewpoints. To do so, summarize the opposing view without offering your opinion about it. Then, use reasons and evidence to offer a counterargument in which you prove why this position is wrong.

Opposing View: ______________________________

____

Counterargument: ______________________________

____

Review, Revise, and Edit

Once you are done drafting, review and revise your essay. Be sure you have provided enough support for your position. Pay close attention to be sure you have used transitions effectively to show the relationships among claims, reasons, and evidence. Identify areas where you can add additional examples to strengthen your argument.

EVIDENCE LOG

Before moving on to a new selection, go to your Evidence Log and record what you've learned from the text and video of Al Gore's Nobel Prize acceptance speech.

STANDARDS

Reading Informational Text
Compare and contrast a text to an audio, video, or multimedia version of the text, analyzing each medium's portrayal of the subject.

Writing
Write arguments to support claims with clear reasons and relevant evidence.

a. Introduce claim(s), acknowledge alternate or opposing claims, and organize the reasons and evidence logically.
b. Support claim(s) with logical reasoning and relevant evidence, using accurate, credible sources and demonstrating an understanding of the topic or text.
c. Use words, phrases, and clauses to create cohesion and clarify the relationships among claim(s), reasons, and evidence.

Drafting

Craft Your Claim Remind students that the claim is the main idea that the argument will develop. Students should decide which format is most effective and then identify the details that help support that claim.

Use Transitions to Connect Ideas If students create an outline, they can identify several ideas that support their claim. You may decide to encourage students to draft their essay first and build in the transitions after. Remind students that the transitions will help readers follow the thoughts.

Provide Counterarguments To help students build a counterargument, ask them to think about the most effective element in the format they have not chosen. Students should write to express the strength of that element, but they should then return to explain why the other format is generally more successful.

Review, Revise, and Edit

As students revise, encourage them to review their draft to be sure they have explained their thinking clearly. Ask them to review their word choice. Finally, remind students to check for grammar, usage, and mechanics. For more support, see **Writing to Compare: Argument.**

Evidence Log Support students in completing their Evidence Log. This paced activity will help prepare them for the Performance-Based Assessment at the end of the unit.

FORMATIVE ASSESSMENT

Writing to Compare

If students are unable to find points of comparison or cite specific evidence, **then** have students skim the speech and rewatch the video.

PERSONALIZE FOR LEARNING

Strategic Support

Comparisons In paragraphs 38 and 41 of the text of the speech, Gore compares the challenge of dealing with climate change to the challenges faced during World War II. Draw students' attention to these paragraphs and discuss why Gore does this. In what way is addressing climate change like fighting a war? What other comparisons to World War II does Gore make? Are these comparisons valid? Why or why not? Do they make the speech stronger? Why or why not?

Jump Start

Ask students to compare Rachel Carson's approach to environmental issues in *Silent Spring* with Al Gore's approach to environmental issues in his Nobel speech. You might guide them with questions such as *"How does each explain the problem?" "Why does this similarity or difference exist?"* As students share, ask them to cite specific examples from the selections to support their ideas.

Write an Argument

Make sure students understand what they are being asked to do in the assignment. Explain that they are being asked to take a position on a question and write an argument supporting their position.

Students should complete the assignment using word processing software to take advantage of editing tools and features.

Elements of an Argument

Remind students that transitional words, phrases, and clauses that show the relationships among claims, reasons, and evidence will greatly help readers follow and understand their argument. Point that it's always better to clearly show the relationships among ideas rather than make the readers make the connection for themselves. Remind students that they'll find the elements of an effective argument in "Rethinking the Wild."

MAKE IT INTERACTIVE

Project "Rethinking the Wild" from the Interactive Teacher's Edition and have students identify the elements of an argument, such as a position on an issue, a context for the issue, evidence that supports the position taken, opposing views, and a clear organizational structure.

Academic Vocabulary

Ask students for examples of how they might use the academic vocabulary in their essays.

PERFORMANCE TASK: WRITING FOCUS

WRITING TO SOURCES

- *from* SILENT SPRING
- NOBEL SPEECH (text)
- NOBEL SPEECH (video)

Tool Kit
Student Model of an Argument

Write an Argument

You have read and watched selections that relate to the effects people have on the environment. In *Silent Spring*, Rachel Carson raised awareness by exposing the negative effects that certain human activities have on the world around them. Decades after *Silent Spring* was published, the public is coming to terms with a new challenge due to the effects of human activity on the environment—climate change. In his Nobel Prize acceptance speech, Al Gore urges society to take action and change its behavior before it is too late.

Assignment

Use the knowledge you gained from the selections in this section as well as from your own experience to write an **argument** in which you take a position on the following question:

What is the most significant effect that people have on the environment?

After you write your argument, turn it into a blog post, and post it to a school or class website. Be sure to include links to your sources.

ACADEMIC VOCABULARY

As you craft your argument, consider using some of the academic vocabulary you learned in the beginning of the unit.

ethical
dissent
interject
discord
accuracy

Elements of an Argument

In an **argument,** the writer states and supports a claim based on factual evidence. An effective argument includes the following elements:

- a clear statement of your claim, or position, on an issue that has more than one side
- the context surrounding the issue
- persuasive evidence and logical reasoning that supports your claim
- statements that acknowledge **counterclaims,** or opposing views, and offer counterarguments to disprove these views
- a clear organizational structure
- words, phrases, and clauses that show the relationships among claims, reasons, and evidence
- a formal style that appeals mainly to the audience's sense of reason

Model Argument For a model of an argument, see the Launch text, "Rethinking the Wild."

Challenge yourself to find the elements of an effective argument in the text. You will have an opportunity to review these elements as you prepare to write your own argument.

STANDARDS

Writing

- Write arguments to support claims with clear reasons and relevant evidence.
- Use technology, including the Internet, to produce and publish writing and link to and cite sources as well as to interact and collaborate with others, including linking to and citing sources.
- Write routinely over extended time frames and shorter time frames for a range of discipline-specific tasks, purposes, and audiences.

392 UNIT 4 • PEOPLE AND THE PLANET

AUTHOR'S PERSPECTIVE **Kelly Gallagher, M.Ed.**

Purposeful Editing Many students resist editing because they don't see its value. Explain that editing, the process of making things correct, adds power to writing. Teachers can model the process by using the Sentence of the Week (SoW) strategy. Before students enter the classroom each Monday, write three sentences with the same structural, grammatical, or style feature on the board. For example:

1. John, 14, is too young to drive.
2. My girlfriend, who is afraid of snakes, refuses to go to the zoo.
3. The player, exhausted from the long game, collapsed.

Students copy the sentences. Below the sentences, write "What do I notice?" Students might write:

- All the sentences have interruptions.
- All have two commas.
- A comma goes before and after the interruption.

Prewriting / Planning

Craft a Claim Review the notes you took on the selections. Craft a one- or two-sentence **thesis statement** that clearly states your claim, or position. Make sure your statement can be supported with several reasons and a variety of relevant evidence.

Address Counterclaims Strong arguments address **counterclaims,** or opposing positions, and explain why these views are flawed. In your argument, address at least one counterclaim and provide a response in which you disprove it, or your counterargument.

Possible counterclaim: ______

Reasons and evidence that support counterclaim: ______

My counterargument: ______

Reasons and evidence that support my counterargument: ______

Gather Evidence Before you begin drafting, gather details that support your claim. Include the strongest and most convincing details to support your claim. In the Launch Text, the writer uses an **anecdote,** a quick story that reinforces a main point, to illustrate how difficult it can be to balance the needs of people and animals.

> *In Jon Mooallem's book,* Wild Ones *he describes the attempt of one organization to save the whooping crane from extinction. It's a story that may challenge what you thought you knew about the sometimes competing interests of people and animals.*

Connect Across Texts To effectively present and support your argument with evidence from the selections, review the texts and note key ideas, examples, and important details. If the exact words are important, use **direct quotations** from the text, or an author's exact words. To simplify a complicated idea and make it easier to understand, **paraphrase** the idea, or restate it in your own words. When using direct quotations, place quotation marks around the exact words of another author. When paraphrasing, be sure your paraphrases correctly reflect the ideas in the original text.

Analyze the ways in which the Launch Text presents and supports an argument. To do so, ask questions such as:

- What important information does the author use to support his or her position? Why might the author have chosen this evidence?
- How does the author's **diction,** or word choice, affect the strength of the argument?

Seeing how an author effectively presents and supports an argument will enable you to better apply these skills to your own writing.

EVIDENCE LOG

Review your Evidence Log and identify key details you may want to include in your argument.

STANDARDS

Writing

- Introduce claim(s), acknowledge alternate or opposing claims, and organize the reasons and evidence logically.
- Support claim(s) with logical reasoning and relevant evidence, using accurate, credible sources and demonstrating an understanding of the topic or text.

DIGITAL PERSPECTIVES

Prewriting/Planning

Craft Encourage students to consider the selections they have read in this unit so far. Remind them to read the prompt and consider the variety of possible topics they might choose. As students draft their claim, they should be able to note a few reasons to support why they believe that their response is the most significant effect that people have on the environment.

Gather Evidence Remind students that when they find online sources they will use for evidence, they should be sure to record the site's name and URL so they can cite their source when they write. The easiest way to capture a URL is to cut and paste the information from their browser into a text document.

Connect Across Texts Remind students to try to connect across both selections: *Silent Spring* and Nobel Speech. Point out that Gore's speech has specific information, and facts and figures, and that the excerpt from *Silent Spring* does not have this level of researchable detail. However, *Silent Spring* has ideas that students can build on.

- If you take out the content between the commas, the sentences still make sense.

Teaching editing skills through sentence study helps students to generate the grammar rules organically.

PERSONALIZE FOR LEARNING

Strategic Support

Finding Trustworthy Sources Remind students that when they conduct online research they should be careful to use only trustworthy sources. These are usually sources with .gov or .edu in their Web address. Point out that sources with .org in their Web address can be trustworthy, but these can also be organizations with an agenda, and the information on those sites might not be objective. Also remind students that anyone can post anything on the Internet — just because something is on the Internet doesn't mean it's true or trustworthy.

TEACHING

Drafting

Organize Your Argument Encourage students to write an outline of their argument, simply listing their position, each reason for taking this position, and each piece of supporting evidence, before writing their first draft. The graphic organizer will be a helpful tool for students to plan their arguments.

Write a First Draft Remind students that their first draft doesn't have to be perfect. In their first draft they should just get their ideas down on paper. They can revise their writing and the order of their ideas when they edit their argument.

Appeal to Your Audience Remind students that in addition to using a formal tone and maintaining standard English, they should not get overly emotional in presenting their argument. Their argument should be strong, but if it's too emotional readers might feel they're not being objective.

PERFORMANCE TASK: WRITING FOCUS

Drafting

Organize Your Argument As you draft, present the supporting evidence you have gathered, starting with your least important points and building to your most important ones. Use transitional words and phrases to unify your writing and show the relationships among your ideas. Use the method shown in the pyramid diagram to outline your argument before you write your first draft.

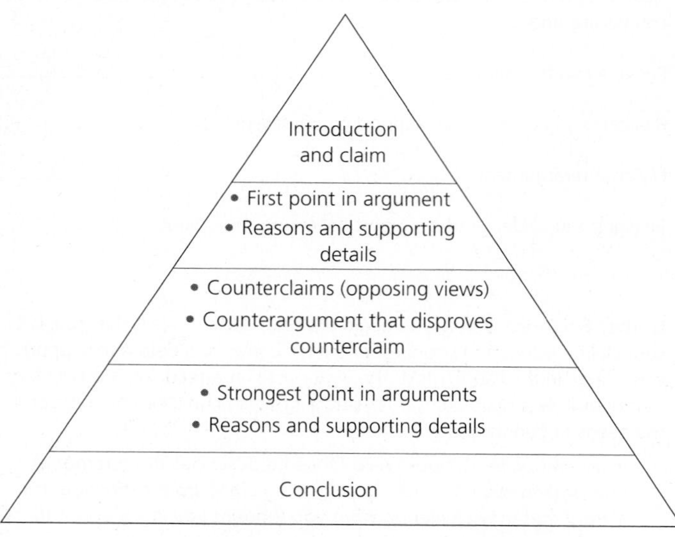

Appeal to Your Audience An **author's style** is the "sound" of his or her writing—it refers to the unique ways an author uses words. Word choice and **tone,** or the author's attitude toward his or her subject, are important elements of style. To keep your audience engaged choose words that add interest. Regardless of your audience, your style should be formal in an argument—never include slang and always maintain standard English.

Address Counterclaims Address counterclaims to your position directly—do not avoid them. To do so, respond to counterclaims with statements that show why these claims are flawed. These statements are your counterargument and should be supported by logical reasons and relevant evidence.

Write a First Draft Review the elements of an effective argument, and write your first draft based on your completed outline and the information you have gathered. Use a variety of sources and different types of evidence for support as you draft your argument.

STANDARDS

Writing

• Write arguments to support claims with clear reasons and relevant evidence.

d. Establish and maintain a formal style.

AUTHOR'S PERSPECTIVE **Jim Cummins, Ph.D.**

Transfer of First Language English learners' home languages are valuable cognitive tools that can be tapped to help them improve the quality of their first drafts. Having students write in their home language often produces higher quality writing than when students write only in English because it helps them capture, express, and organize their ideas. Translation software can be useful as a starting point to help students move from their home language draft to an English draft. Obviously, the machine-translated draft will require editing but this can be done collaboratively with help from the teacher and/or the students' classmates. After students have produced their initial drafts in English, teachers can work with them on the revision process, focusing on such key areas as organization, paragraph formation, and coherence. As students revise with teacher input, teachers should encourage them to pay special attention to cognates and genre rules.

LANGUAGE DEVELOPMENT: CONVENTIONS

Sentence Fluency: Revising Sentences Using Participles

To make your writing flow smoothly, combine sentences using participles and participial phrases. A **participle** is a verb form that acts as an adjective, modifying a noun or pronoun. Present participles end in *-ing*. Past participles usually end in *-ed,* but may have an irregular ending, such as the *-en* in *spoken*.

past participle → noun

She banged her fist against the closed windows.

A **participial phrase** consists of a participle and its modifiers.

A **misplaced modifier** is placed far away from the word it describes.

Misplaced modifier: I heard her voice *listening to the song*.

Revised: *Listening to the song,* I heard her voice.

A **dangling modifier** is not logically connected to any word in the sentence.

Dangling modifier: *Raising the flag,* the wind felt strong.

Revised: *Raising the flag,* the sailors felt the strong wind.

Fixing Choppy Passages Using Participles To fix a choppy passage, identify sentences that can be combined. Then, rewrite the passage using one or more of the following methods:

- **Combine sentences using a present participle.**
  Example: We arranged a tour. We would walk the grounds.
  We arranged a walking tour of the grounds.
- **Combine sentences using a past participle.**
  Example: The food is cooked. It will not spoil.
  The cooked food will not spoil.
- **Combine sentences using a participial phrase.**
  Example: Marisol ate her food quickly. She was running late.
  Running late, Marisol ate her food quickly.

Read It

Review the Launch Text, and identify two sentences that use participles or participial phrases.

Write It

1. Revise each sentence to correct the misplaced or dangling modifier.
   a. Having arrived late for school, a written explanation was needed.
   b. Running swiftly, the audience watched the track star.
2. Choose three paragraphs in your draft. Read the paragraphs aloud, marking any passages that sound choppy. Using one of the methods described, fix the choppy passages by combining sentences.

STANDARDS

Language

- Demonstrate command of the conventions of standard English grammar and usage when writing or speaking.

c. Place phrases and clauses within a sentence, recognizing and correcting misplaced and dangling modifiers.

- Use knowledge of language and its conventions when writing, speaking, reading, or listening.

a. Choose language that expresses ideas precisely and concisely, recognizing and eliminating wordiness and redundancy.

DIGITAL PERSPECTIVES

Sentence Fluency: Revising Sentences Using Participles

Encourage students to combine sentences using participles and participial phrases, but caution them to avoid misplaced modifiers and dangling modifiers. Remind students to look out for and revise these errors when they edit their writing.

Read It

Possible responses: When you buy a recyclable beverage container in California, you pay from four to eight cents per container, depending on the size. (present participle used as an adverb to modify *pay*.)

You have to know what to pull out of your trash, take the tie to sort the recycling from the garbage, and then take the goods to a recycling center. (present participle used as an adjective to modify *center*.)

Write It

1. **Possible responses:** (a) Having arrived late for school, Rory needed a written explanation. (b) The audience watched the track star, who was running swiftly.
2. Responses will vary. Students should effectively revise their draft, correctly using participles or participial phrases to combine choppy sentences.

PERSONALIZE FOR LEARNING

English Language Support

Revising Sentences Review with students how to combine short, choppy sentences using participles or participial phrases. Provide the following sentences for revision.

I was practicing for the concert. I was playing as fast as I could. (Practicing for the concert, I was playing as fast as I could.)

Mary was swimming in the pool. She enjoyed the warm water. (Swimming in the pool, Mary enjoyed the warm water.)

Jose looked around the playground. He saw his friends playing ball. (Looking around the playground, Jose saw his friends playing ball.)

The dog watched the ball sail overhead. The dog started to run after it. (The dog started to run after the ball sailing overhead.) **ALL LEVELS**

TEACHING

Revising

Evaluating Your Draft Remind students to use the chart to evaluate their drafts. This will help them check that it contains all the required elements of a well-constructed and well-organized argument.

Evaluate Your Evidence As students revise to strengthen their evidence, encourage them to add more language that makes the connection between evidence and claims. This will help reinforce their thinking for readers.

Write a Memorable Conclusion Remind students that the conclusion is one of the most important parts of any essay. The conclusion ties the essay together and leaves readers feeling that the essay is complete. In an argument, the conclusion is a chance to restate the position one more time, and to say it in a new way that makes a strong impression on the reader.

PERFORMANCE TASK: WRITING FOCUS

Revising

Evaluating Your Draft

Use the following checklist to evaluate the effectiveness of your first draft. Then, use your evaluation and the instruction on this page to guide your revision.

FOCUS AND ORGANIZATION	EVIDENCE AND ELABORATION	CONVENTIONS
☐ Provides a clearly stated claim and information about the context surrounding the issue.	☐ Supports claims with logical reasoning and persuasive evidence.	☐ Uses a formal style and tone.
☐ Establishes a clear organizational structure that highlights the main points.	☐ Acknowledges opposing claims and offers counterarguments to these views.	☐ Attends to the norms and conventions of the discipline, especially using participles to make writing flow smoothly while avoiding misplaced and dangling modifiers.
☐ Uses words, phrases, and clauses to create cohesion and clarify the relationships among claims, reasons, and evidence.	☐ Word choice reflects consideration of the intended audience.	
☐ Provides a concluding statement that follows from and supports the argument.		

WORD NETWORK

Include interesting words from your Word Network in your essay.

Revising for Focus and Organization

Use Transitions To make the connections between ideas in your argument clear to readers, use transition words and phrases such as *however, nevertheless, even so,* and *in addition*. Consider the relationship between ideas you are trying to express. Then, choose transitional words or phrases that show that relationship.

- to show examples: *for instance, also, in addition*
- to contrast ideas: *however, yet, unlike*
- to show causes and effects: *therefore, since, because, as a result*

Write a Memorable Conclusion Bring your argument to a close by restating your thesis statement and synthesizing, or briefly pulling together, the evidence you presented. End with a memorable statement or section that summarizes your argument in a new way and provides a fresh insight into your claim.

Revising for Evidence and Elaboration

Evaluate Your Evidence To make sure your argument is convincing, evaluate your evidence by asking yourself the following questions.

- Does every piece of evidence support my claim?
- Where can I add evidence to make my argument stronger?
- Have I given proper credit to the source of each piece of evidence I used?

STANDARDS

Writing

- Introduce claim(s), acknowledge alternate or opposing claims, and organize the reasons and evidence logically.
- Use words, phrases, and clauses to create cohesion and clarify the relationships among claim(s), reasons, and evidence.
- Provide a concluding statement or section that follows from and supports the argument presented.

PEER REVIEW

Exchange essays with a classmate. Use the checklist to evaluate your classmate's argument and provide supportive feedback.

1. Is there a clearly stated claim?
   ☐ yes ☐ no If no, suggest ways in which the writer might clarify it.
2. Is there support for the claim based on logical reasoning and relevant evidence from accurate, credible sources?
   ☐ yes ☐ no If no, point out where the writer should provide more support.
3. Are opposing claims acknowledged and effectively addressed with counterarguments?
   ☐ yes ☐ no If no, suggest ways in which the writing can acknowledge and address opposing claims.
4. What is the strongest part of your classmate's essay? Explain.

____

____

Editing and Proofreading

Edit for Conventions Quotations from persuasive sources can make an argument more powerful and convincing. Pay careful attention to the punctuation, indentation, and capitalization of the quotations you include. Use quotation marks to set off short quotations. Longer quotations of four or more lines should begin on a new line, be indented, and appear without quotation marks. Always remember to follow a standard format for citation when using quotations in your writing.

Proofread for Accuracy The syllables in some words are barely heard. Because of this, letters are often left out in spelling. Proofread your argument to make sure you have spelled words with tricky syllables correctly. Double-check the spellings of words such as *different, average,* and *restaurant* in a dictionary. Notice how each word is broken into syllables. Say the word aloud while you look at it, and exaggerate your pronunciation of the sounds and syllables.

Publishing and Presenting

Create a final version of your argument. Then, post it on a class or school website as a blog post. Include links to the sources you used to support your argument.

Reflecting

Reflect on what you learned as you wrote your argument. What was the most challenging part of writing your argument? Did you learn something from transforming your argument into a blog post and posting it on a website?

STANDARDS

Writing
- Use technology, including the Internet, to produce and publish writing and link to and cite sources as well as to interact and collaborate with others, including linking to and citing sources.
- Gather relevant information from multiple print and digital sources, using search terms effectively; assess the credibility and accuracy of each source; and quote or paraphrase the data and conclusions of others while avoiding plagiarism and following a standard format for citation.

Language
- Demonstrate command of the conventions of standard English capitalization, punctuation, and spelling when writing.
  b. Spell correctly.
  c. Consult general and specialized reference materials, both print and digital, to find the pronunciation of a word or determine or clarify its precise meaning or its part of speech.

DIGITAL PERSPECTIVES

Peer Review

Before students begin their peer review, remind them that they are reviewing for clarity and completeness, not whether they agree or disagree with the writer's argument. They should not comment on whether their classmate is "right" or "wrong." They can, however, make helpful suggestions if they see something in the argument that could be better.

Editing and Proofreading

As students proofread, they should check for grammar, spelling, and punctuation errors. Remind them to check that all claims are supported by logical, relevant evidence. Also, remind students to identify sentences that could be revised using participles or participial phrases.

Publishing and Presenting

Before students review their classmates' essays, remind them to:

- Be honest, but maintain a respectful tone in their comments.
- Use formal rather than informal language.
- Move the discussion forward by building on the ideas of others.
- Disagree respectfully. Different opinions are fine, but they should be expressed politely.

Reflecting

Encourage students to reflect not only on their argument and the process of writing it, but also on the comments they received and what it was like to transform their essay into a blog post and put it online.

PERSONALIZE FOR LEARNING

Challenge

Speculate Ask students to speculate on the reasons people continue to do things that negatively impact the environment. Have students write a paragraph describing behavior that has a negative impact on the environment, and speculate on why someone engaging in this behavior would not stop. Ask volunteers to share their responses with the class.

OVERVIEW

SMALL-GROUP LEARNING

What effects do people have on the environment?

Point out to students that although modern society has serious negative impacts on the natural world, some people also work to preserve the environment. Often, their struggle for environmental conservation must overcome the status quo, or "business as usual." During Small-Group Learning, students will read and review selections that show how people appreciate nature and work to protect it.

Small-Group Learning Strategies

Review the Learning Strategies with students and explain that as they work through Small-Group Learning they will develop strategies to work in small-group environments.

- Have students watch the video on Small-Group Learning Strategies.
- A video on this topic is available online in the Professional Development Center.

You may wish to discuss some action items to add to the chart as a class before students complete it on their own. For example, for "Prepare," you might solicit the following from students:

- Discuss the assignments with other students before class.
- Think of key questions you have about the assignments.

Block Scheduling

Each day in this Pacing Plan represents a 40–50 minute class period. Teachers using block scheduling may combine days to reflect their class schedule. In addition, teachers may revise pacing to differentiate and support core instruction by integrating components and resources as students require.

OVERVIEW: SMALL-GROUP LEARNING

ESSENTIAL QUESTION:

What effects do people have on the environment?

Our world is filled with amazing natural wonders. Will our children's children be able to enjoy these wonders as we have? In this section, you will read selections that discuss the relationship between humans and our environment. You will work as a group to continue your exploration of the ways in which people affect the environment.

Small-Group Learning Strategies

Throughout your life, in school, in your community, and in your career, you will continue to learn and work with others.

Look at these strategies and the actions you can take to practice them as you work in teams. Add ideas of your own for each step. Use these strategies during Small Group Learning.

STRATEGY	ACTION PLAN
Prepare	• Complete your assignments so that you are prepared for group work. • Organize your thinking so you can contribute to your group's discussions. •
Participate fully	• Make eye contact to signal that you are listening and taking in what is being said. • Use text evidence when making a point. •
Support others	• Build off ideas from others in your group. • Invite others who have not yet spoken to join the discussion. •
Clarify	• Paraphrase the ideas of others to ensure that your understanding is correct. • Ask follow-up questions. •

Pacing Plan

Unit Introduction — days 1–2
Introduce Whole-Class Learning — day 3
from Silent Spring — days 4–5
Nobel Speech — days 6–10
Media: Nobel Speech — days 11–15
Performance Task — days 16–18

1 2 3 4 5 6 7 8 9 10 11 12 13 14 15 16 17 18

CONTENTS

POETRY COLLECTION

These poets use poetic structure and language to beautifully capture different aspects of the relationship between people and the environment.

MEDIA: PHOTO GALLERY

Follow along as conservationists track the growth of bald eagle populations from Alaska to New York.

SHORT STORY

It might be a bad idea to ignore the obvious.

PERFORMANCE TASK

SPEAKING AND LISTENING FOCUS

Present an Argument

The Small-Group readings present different perspectives on the ways in which humans impact the natural environment. After reading, your group will plan and deliver a multimedia presentation about our relationship to the natural environment.

Overview: Small-Group Learning **399**

DIGITAL PERSPECTIVES

Contents

Selections Circulate among groups as they preview the selections. You might encourage groups to discuss any knowledge they already have about any of the selections or the situations and settings shown in the photographs. Students may wish to take a poll within their group to determine which selections look the most interesting.

Remind students that communicating and collaborating in groups is an important skill that they will use throughout their lives—in school, in their careers, and in their community.

Performance Task

Present an Argument Give groups time to read about and briefly discuss the multimedia presentation they will create after reading. Encourage students to do some preliminary thinking about the types of media they may want to use. This may help focus their subsequent reading and group discussion.

Introduce Small-Group Learning

Turtle Watchers • "Nature" is what We see — • The Sparrow

Media: Eagle Tracking at Follensby Pond

He—y, Come On Ou—t!

Performance Task

Introduce Independent Learning

Independent Learning

Performance-Based Assessment

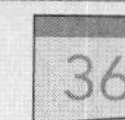

19 20 21 22 23 24 25 26 27 28 29 30 31 32 33 34 35 36

SMALL-GROUP LEARNING

OVERVIEW

SMALL-GROUP LEARNING

Working as a Team

1. **Take a Position** Remind groups to let all members share their responses. You may wish to set a time limit for this discussion.
2. **List Your Rules** You may want to have groups share their lists of rules and consolidate them into a master list to be displayed and followed by all groups.
3. **Apply the Rules** As you circulate among the groups, ensure that students are staying on task. Consider a short time limit for this step.
4. **Name Your Group** This task can be creative and fun. If students have trouble coming up with a name, suggest that they think of something related to the unit topic. Encourage groups to share their names with the class.
5. **Create a Communication Plan** Encourage groups to include in their plans agreed-upon times during the day to share ideas. They should also devise a method for recording and saving their communications.

Accountable Talk

Remind students that groups should communicate politely. You can post these Accountable Talk suggestions and encourage students to add their own. Students should:

Remember to . . .
Ask clarifying questions.

Which sounds like...
Can you please say that again?
Would you give me an example?
I think you said _____. Did I understand you?

Remember to . . .
Explain your thinking.

Which sounds like . . .
I believe _____ is true because _____.
I feel _____ because _____.

Remember to . . .
Build on the ideas of others.

Which sounds like . . .
When _____ said _____, it made me think of _____.
I agree. That makes me think of _______.

OVERVIEW: SMALL-GROUP LEARNING

Working as a Team

1. **Take a Position** In your group, discuss the following question:

   What is our relationship with the natural environment?

   As you take turns sharing your positions, be sure to provide examples for your choice. After all group members have shared, discuss the characteristics of this relationship that are suggested by your responses.

2. **List Your Rules** As a group, decide on the rules that you will follow as you work together. Two samples are provided. Add two more of your own. You may add or revise rules based on your experience together.
   - Come prepared for group discussions.
   - Acknowledge other people's opinions.
   - ______________________________
   - ______________________________

3. **Apply the Rules** Practice working as a group. Share what you have learned about survival. Make sure each person in the group contributes. Take notes and be prepared to share with the class one thing that you heard from another member of your group.

4. **Name Your Group** Choose a name that reflects the unit topic.

   Our group's name: ______________________________

5. **Create a Communication Plan** Decide how you want to communicate with one another. For example, you might use online collaboration tools, email, or instant messaging.

   Our group's decision: ______________________________

FACILITATING SMALL-GROUP LEARNING

Forming Groups You may wish to form groups for Small-Group Learning so that each consists of students with different learning abilities. Some students may be adept at organizing information whereas others may have strengths related to generating or synthesizing information about the environment. A good mix of abilities can make the experience of Small-Group Learning dynamic and productive.

Making a Schedule

First, find out the due dates for the small-group activities. Then, preview the texts and activities with your group and make a schedule for completing the tasks.

SELECTION	ACTIVITIES	DUE DATE
Turtle Watchers "Nature" is what We see— The Sparrow		
Eagle Tracking at Follensby Pond		
He—y, Come On Ou—t!		

Working on Group Projects

Different projects require different roles. As your group works together, you'll find it more effective if each person has a specific role. Before beginning a project, decide among yourselves on each group member's role. Here are some possible roles; add your own ideas.

Project Manager: monitors the schedule and keeps everyone on task

Researcher: organizes research activities

Recorder: takes notes during group meetings

____

____

____

____

____

DIGITAL PERSPECTIVES

Making a Schedule

Encourage groups to preview the reading selections and to consider how long it will take them to complete the activities accompanying each selection. Point out that they can adjust the due dates for particular selections as needed as they work on their small-group projects; however, they must complete all assigned tasks before the group Performance Task is due. Encourage groups to review their schedules upon completing the activities for each selection to make sure they are on track to meet the final due date.

Working on Group Projects

Point out to groups that the roles they assign can also be changed later. Students might have to make changes based on who is best at doing what. Try to make sure that there is no favoritism, cliquishness, or stereotyping by gender or other means in the assignment of roles. Encourage students to think creatively as a group about ways to present the texts and ask for all students' participation.

Also, you should review the roles each group assigns to its members. Based on your understanding of students' individual strengths, you might find it necessary to suggest some changes.

AUTHOR'S PERSPECTIVE **Ernest Morrell, Ph.D.**

Small Group Learning in Higher Education College classrooms are becoming shared discussion spaces, marked by less lecturing and more small groups. That's because college professors increasingly realize that having students work in small groups helps develop higher-level learning and problem-solving skills, increases the success of computer-based instruction, and increases retention rates. As a result, more and more college professors now have small groups lead a portion of class by sharing/presenting what the group has learned. These professors focus on the importance of each group becoming expert at something that they must teach the class. Teachers can point out to students that the project-based small-group learning in colleges is increasingly common in the workplace as well, as collective production is becoming a new norm. Teachers can encourage students to collaborate and develop rubrics to assess how well students are able to work together.

Turtle Watchers • "Nature" is what We see— • The Sparrow

AUDIO SUMMARIES
Audio summaries of these poems are available online in both English and Spanish in the Interactive Teacher's Edition or Unit Resources. Assigning these summaries prior to reading the selection may help students build additional background knowledge and set a context for their first read.

Summary

"Turtle Watchers," "'Nature' is what We see—," and "The Sparrow" are poems about people and their relationship to the natural world.

Linda Hogan's poem "Turtle Watchers" moves between two time periods. In the first, an old woman watches turtles coming in from the sea to lay eggs. In the second, the speaker considers a sea turtle that swam alongside her, and ponders turtles' mystic significance.

"'Nature' is what We see—" is a poem by Emily Dickinson. In the poem, the speaker says that we know nature by what we can see and hear but that nature is something much greater than that.

Paul Laurence Dunbar's poem "The Sparrow" describes a bird that sings at his window. He is too focused on work to pay attention to it, and so it flies away. The speaker says that many good things in life are like that sparrow—we don't realize what we've lost until it's too late.

Insight

All of these poems focus on how nature can be beyond human understanding. In Dickinson's poem, this seems to be unchangeable. In Dunbar's poem, people *could* bond with the "birds of peace and hope and love" but are too distracted. "Turtle Watchers" suggests that we have lost the ability to connect with nature.

ESSENTIAL QUESTION:
What effects do people have on the environment?

Connection to Essential Question

These poems focus not on how people change the environment but on whether people can understand it. Students should consider how easy it is to have unintended effects on something you do not understand.

SMALL-GROUP LEARNING PERFORMANCE TASK
Why do people impact the environment in a harmful way?

UNIT PERFORMANCE-BASED ASSESSMENT
Is it too late to fix the damage that has been done to our environment?

Connection to Performance Tasks

Small-Group Learning Performance Task In this Performance Task, students will develop a multimedia presentation that addresses the impact humans have on the environment. These poems focus on how the natural world is sometimes beyond our understanding. How can that lack of understanding impact the effect we have on nature?

Unit Performance-Based Assessment In Dickinson's poem, nature seems to mean something broader than the parts of our environment that can be damaged. In Hogan's poem, people and wild animals can bond despite the modern world. Dunbar's poem suggests that we are too engrossed in our lives to recognize the world around us.

DIGITAL PERSPECTIVES

 Audio  Video 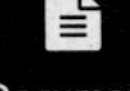 Document  Annotation Highlights 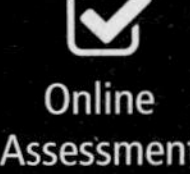 Online Assessment

LESSON RESOURCES

	Making Meaning	Language Development	Effective Expression
Lesson	**First Read** **Close Read** **Analyze the Text** **Analyze Craft and Structure**	**Concept Vocabulary** **Word Study** **Author's Style**	**Speaking and Listening**
Instructional Standards	**RL.7.10** By the end of the year, read and comprehend literature . . . **L.7.4** Determine or clarify the meaning of unknown and multiple-meaning words and phrases . . . **L.7.4.c** Consult general and specialized reference materials . . . **RL.7.5** Analyze how a drama's or poem's form or structure . . .	**L.7.4** Determine or clarify the meaning of unknown and multiple-meaning words and phrases . . . **L.7.4.b** Use common, grade-appropriate Greek or Latin affixes and roots . . . **RL.7.1** Cite several pieces of textual evidence . . . **RL.7.2** Determine a theme or central idea . . . **RL.7.4** Determine the meaning of words and phrases . . .	**SL.7.4** Present claims and findings . . . **SL.7.5** Include multimedia components and visual displays . . . **SL.7.6** Adapt speech to a variety of contexts and tasks . . .
STUDENT RESOURCES			
Available online in the Interactive Student Edition or Unit Resources	Selection Audio First-Read Guide: Poetry Close-Read Guide: Poetry	Word Network	Evidence Log
TEACHER RESOURCES			
Selection Resources Available online in the Interactive Teacher's Edition or Unit Resources	Audio Summaries: English and Spanish Annotation Highlights Text Questions First Read Extension Questions Analyze Craft and Structure: Lyric Poetry	Concept Vocabulary and Word Study Author's Style: Word Choice	Speaking and Listening: Oral Presentation
Reteach/Practice (RP) Available online in the Interactive Teacher's Edition or Unit Resources	Analyze Craft and Structure: Lyric Poetry (RP)	Word Study: Etymology (RP) Author's Style: Word Choice (RP)	Speaking and Listening: Oral Presentation (RP)
Assessment Available online in Assessments	Selection Test: English Selection Test: Spanish Extension Selection Test		
My Resources	A Unit 4 Answer Key is available online and in the Interactive Teacher's Edition.		

Reading Support

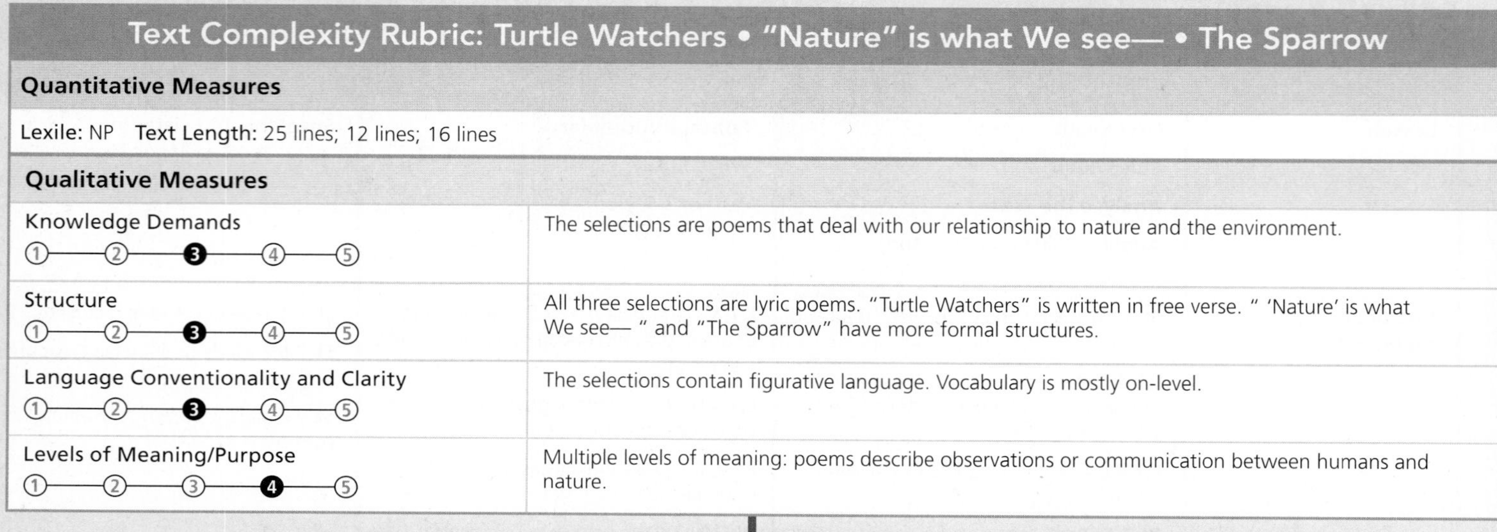

Text Complexity Rubric: Turtle Watchers • "Nature" is what We see— • The Sparrow	
Quantitative Measures	
Lexile: NP **Text Length:** 25 lines; 12 lines; 16 lines	
Qualitative Measures	
Knowledge Demands ①—②—❸—④—⑤	The selections are poems that deal with our relationship to nature and the environment.
Structure ①—②—❸—④—⑤	All three selections are lyric poems. "Turtle Watchers" is written in free verse. " 'Nature' is what We see— " and "The Sparrow" have more formal structures.
Language Conventionality and Clarity ①—②—❸—④—⑤	The selections contain figurative language. Vocabulary is mostly on-level.
Levels of Meaning/Purpose ①—②—③—❹—⑤	Multiple levels of meaning: poems describe observations or communication between humans and nature.

DECIDE AND PLAN

English Language Support

Provide English Learners with support for Knowledge Demands and Meaning as they read the selection.

Knowledge Demands Tell students that these poems deal with the human connection to nature and the environment. They should look for language that describes this relationship and the feelings it evokes.

Meaning Work with students to help them understand the meaning of figurative language by first understanding the literal meaning. For example, discuss the imagery in "Turtle Watchers," in the line *a sea turtle swam beside me both of us watching as if clasped together.*

Strategic Support

Provide students with strategic support to ensure that they can successfully read the text.

Language Remind students that in the poems they are about to read, they will find metaphors and similes. Discuss the difference – similes use the words *like* or *as* to compare, whereas metaphors do not. Give an example from "Turtle Watchers," such as *their eyes streaming water like tears,* and ask students to be on the lookout for other such similes or metaphors.

Meaning For students who have difficulty understanding metaphors and similes, have them underline or list the phrases that they don't understand. Then have them read those phrases again and work with a partner to try to figure out the comparison the poet is making.

Challenge

Provide students who need to be challenged with ideas for how they can go beyond a simple interpretation of the text.

Text Analysis Ask students to make a list of all the metaphors and similes they find in the poems. Pair students and have one say a simile or metaphor. Then have the other describe the image conveyed by these words and tell what they think the poet is trying to describe.

Written Response Encourage students to consider the message of these poems and to write a response poem from the point of view of nature. Ask students to consider how nature might feel about the humans' behavior on the planet.

TEACH

Read and Respond

Have the groups read the selections and complete the Making Meaning, Language Development, and Effective Expression activities.

Standards Support Through Teaching and Learning Cycle

IDENTIFY NEEDS

Analyze results of the Beginning-of-Year Assessment, focusing on the items relating to Unit 4. Also take into consideration student performance to this point and your observations of where particular students struggle.

DECIDE AND PLAN

- If students have performed poorly on items matching these standards, then provide selection scaffolds before assigning them the on-level lesson provided in the Student Edition.
- If students have done well on the Beginning-of-Year Assessment, then challenge them to keep progressing and learning by giving them opportunities to practice the skills in depth.
- Use the Selection Resources listed on the Planning pages for these poems to help students continually improve their ability to master the standards.

Instructional Standards: Turtle Watchers • "Nature" is what We see—" • The Sparrow

	Catching Up	This Year	Looking Forward
Reading	You may wish to administer the **Analyze Craft and Structure: Lyric Poetry (RP)** worksheet to help students understand how lyric poems express the speaker's thoughts and feelings.	**RL.5** Analyze how a drama's or poem's form or structure contributes to its meaning.	Challenge students to seek out other short lyric poems and identify specific examples of word choice that affect meaning or tone.
Speaking and Listening	You may wish to administer the **Speaking and Listening: Oral Presentation (RP)** worksheet to help students understand the different appeals a persuasive speech can use.	**SL.5** Include multimedia components and visual displays in presentations to clarify claims and findings and emphasize salient points.	Challenge students to blend aspects of the poetry slam option with the multimedia presentation.
Language	Review **Author's Style: Word Choice (RP)** to help students understand how an author constructs tone. Review **Word Study Etymology (RP)** to help students understand the origins of words.	**RL.4** Determine the meaning of words and phrases as they are used in a text, including figurative and connotative meanings; analyze the impact of rhymes and other repetitions of sounds on a specific verse or stanza of a poem or section of a story or drama. **L.4** Determine or clarify the meaning of unknown and multiple-meaning words and phrases based on *grade 7 reading and content*, choosing flexibly from a range of strategies.	Have students rewrite one of the poems, changing some of the words for their synonyms, to demonstrate how the meaning and tone changes. Have students look up the etymology of words of their choosing from the selections.

ANALYZE AND REVISE

- Analyze student work for evidence of student learning.
- Identify whether or not students have met the expectations in the standards.
- Identify implications for future instruction.

TEACH

Implement the planned lesson, and gather evidence of student learning.

Jump Start

FIRST READ Engage students in a discussion about the relationship between people and the natural world to set the context for reading the poems. Ask: *Do you think people have had a negative effect on the environment? How? What would you like to change about the relationship? What can you, as an individual, do to live in harmony with nature?*

Concept Vocabulary

Ask groups to look closely at the information about reference materials and how to use them. Walk students through the process of consulting a dictionary. Point out that most dictionaries include keys to pronunciation. Have students consult reference materials for all three Concept Vocabulary words and any unfamiliar words they encounter.

FIRST READ

As they read, students should perform the steps of the first read:

NOTICE: You may want to encourage students to notice sensory details and specific word choices in the poems.

ANNOTATE: Remind students to mark lines they feel are key to each poem's meaning or effect.

CONNECT: Encourage students to go beyond the text to make connections to their own experiences with nature.

RESPOND: Students will answer questions to demonstrate understanding.

Point out to students that while they will always complete the Respond step at the end of the first read, the other steps will probably happen somewhat concurrently. You may wish to print copies of the **First-Read Guide: Poetry** for students to use.

MAKING MEANING

POETRY COLLECTION

Turtle Watchers
"Nature" is what We see—
The Sparrow

Concept Vocabulary

As you perform your first read, you will encounter these words.

ancestors	wisdom	heed

Using a Dictionary To check the meanings of unfamiliar words, consult a print or online dictionary. Dictionaries provide a word's definition, pronunciation, part of speech, variant forms, and etymology, or word origin.

This box shows an example of a dictionary entry for the word *anthology*. Note that the pronunciation is in parentheses, and the etymology is in square brackets.

> **anthology** (an THOL uh jee) *n., pl.* **-gies** [Gr. *anthologia*, a garland, collection of short poems < *anthologos*, gathering flowers < *anthos*, flower + *legein*, to gather] a collection of poems, stories, songs, excerpts, etc., chosen by the compiler.

Apply your knowledge of using a dictionary and other vocabulary strategies to determine the meanings of unfamiliar words you encounter during your first read.

First Read POETRY

Apply these strategies as you conduct your first read. You will have an opportunity to complete a close read after your first read.

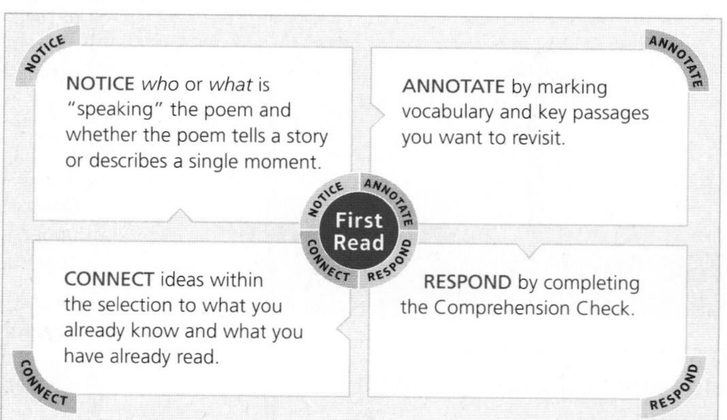

STANDARDS

Reading Literature
By the end of the year, read and comprehend literature, including stories, dramas, and poems, in the grades 6–8 text complexity band proficiently, with scaffolding as needed at the high end of the range.

Language
Determine or clarify the meaning of unknown and multiple-meaning words and phrases based on *grade 7 reading and content*, choosing flexibly from a range of strategies.
c. Consult general and specialized reference materials, both print and digital, to find the pronunciation of a word or determine or clarify its precise meaning or its part of speech.

AUTHOR'S PERSPECTIVE **Jim Cummins, Ph.D.**

How Language Works Briefly explaining the origins of the English language will help demystify the difference between conversational and academic language. Today's English is a hybrid language, formed from a merger of Anglo-Saxon spoken in Britain from about 400–1000 and French brought by the Norman invaders in 1066. Students can see this merger in synonyms of words derived from Anglo-Saxon and Latin/Greek sources: *meet/encounter, ask/inquire, come/arrive.* The Anglo-Saxon words were used by peasants who generally didn't have much education; in contrast, Greek/Latin vocabulary was used by more educated and high-status people and became the language of written text. Today, words with Anglo-Saxon roots are short and commonly used, while words with Greek/Latin roots tend to be low-frequency and long. The most common Anglo-Saxon words in English are determiners (*the, a*); prepositions (*of, to, for,* etc.); pronouns (*he, she, I,* etc.); conjunctions (*and, but,* etc.); common verbs, nouns, and adjectives (*think, little, good,* etc.). Because these words are high-frequency and are used daily, they are generally acquired quickly by English learners.

About the Poets

Linda Hogan (b. 1947) is an award-winning Chickasaw novelist, essayist, poet, and environmentalist. Her writing often addresses topics such as the environment, ecofeminism, and Native American history. An activist and educator, Hogan has spoken at various global conferences and events including the Environmental Literature Conference in Turkey in 2009. She lives in the Colorado mountains and teaches creative writing.

Emily Dickinson (1830–1886) considered books her "strongest friend." Withdrawn and shy, she spent most of her time at home in Amherst, Massachusetts, reading and writing. Most of her 1,775 poems were discovered after her death, including one that begins, "I'm nobody! Who are you?" Today, Dickinson is considered one of the most important American poets.

Paul Laurence Dunbar (1872–1906) was the son of former slaves. Encouraged by his mother, he began writing poetry at an early age. Dunbar was inspired by Harriet Beecher Stowe's novel *Uncle Tom's Cabin,* and in his own work he honored people who fought for the rights of African Americans. Over the course of his life, Dunbar published more than ten volumes of poetry, four novels, and four volumes of short stories.

Backgrounds

Turtle Watchers

Some sea turtles, such as loggerhead sea turtles, travel thousands of miles to lay their eggs on the same beach where they were born. The turtles dig a small nest in the sand, where they lay their eggs, sometimes over a hundred in a single nest. When the eggs hatch, the baby turtles make the dangerous trek back to the ocean to continue the cycle.

"Nature" is what We see—

From ancient Greeks to English romantics to Japanese haiku masters, poets from every period of time have contemplated the beauty of the natural world. The poet William Wordsworth wrote, "Come forth into the light of things, let Nature be your teacher."

The Sparrow

Sparrows are one of the most common birds in the world. They are often seen in North America, but this was not always the case. In the mid-1800s, a man named Nicholas Pike decided to bring several dozen over from England and release them in New York. Since then, these small brown birds have flourished and spread across the continent.

DIGITAL PERSPECTIVES

Turtle Watchers • "Nature" is what We see— • The Sparrow

What is our relationship to the natural world? How does this relationship compare to that of previous generations? What is lost when the environment is damaged? Modeling questions such as these will help students connect to these poems and to the Small-Group Performance Task assignment. Selection audio and print capability for the selection are available in the Interactive Teacher's Edition.

FACILITATING SMALL-GROUP CLOSE READING

CLOSE READ: Poetry Lead a brief discussion of the differences between reading poetry and prose. Remind students that in poetry, sound elements such as rhythm, rhyme, alliteration, and assonance are very important. Briefly review these literary elements. Then suggest that students quietly read aloud the poems in their small groups. A volunteer could read each poem aloud to group members. Students may discuss the sound qualities of the poems in addition to the meaning conveyed.

FACILITATING

Concept Vocabulary

ANCESTORS If groups are struggling to define the word *ancestors* in line 18, guide them in consulting a print or online dictionary. You might direct them also to the word's etymology for a deeper understanding.

Possible response: *Ancestors* means the "people from whom one is descended."

CLOSER LOOK

Analyze Similes

Circulate among groups as students conduct their close read of "Turtle Watchers." Suggest that groups read the entire poem. Encourage them to talk about the annotations they mark. If needed, provide the following support.

ANNOTATE: Have students close read the poem beginning with line 1. Ask students to mark similes— comparisons that use connecting words such as *like* or *as*—or work with small groups as you highlight them together.

QUESTION: Guide students to consider what these comparisons might tell them. Ask what a reader can infer from the similes, and accept student responses.

Possible response: The simile in line 5 suggests that the turtles are crying or sad. The simile in line 7 suggests that old mother sees the turtles as holy and worthy of reverence. The simile in lines 13–14 suggests that the speaker and the turtle are joined together by ancestry. The similes in the last two lines suggest that the speaker feels a connection to the turtles and the ancestors.

CONCLUDE: Help students formulate conclusions about the importance of these similes in the text. Ask students why the author might have included these figures of speech.

Possible response: These similes point to the author's message in the selection: All creatures are connected across time and even species.

Remind students that a **simile** is a figure of speech that uses *like* or *as* to make a comparison between two unlike things or ideas. Point out that poets use similes to create images in the reader's mind.

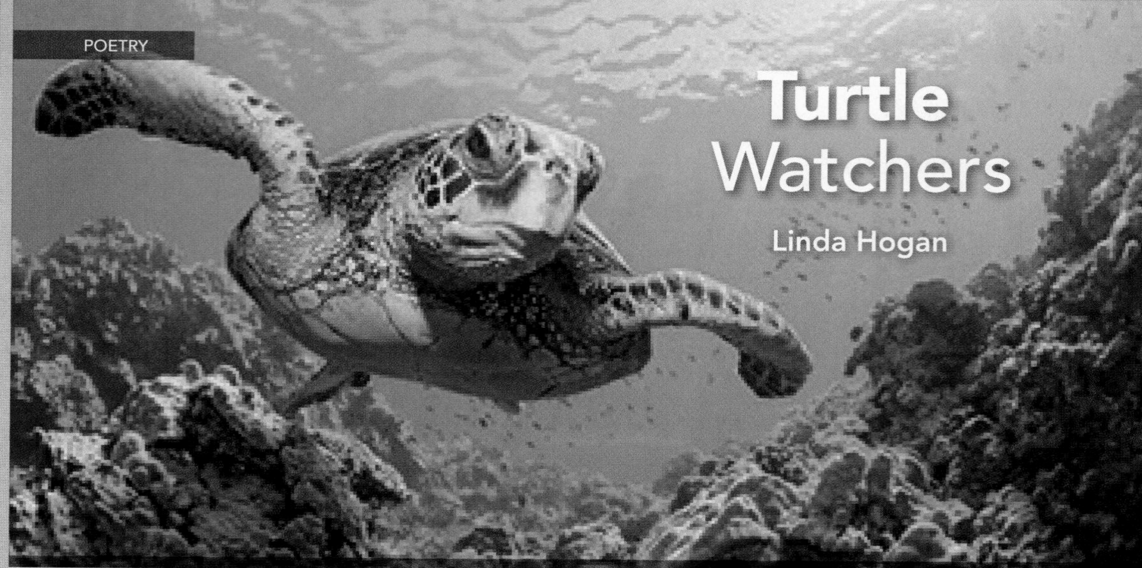

NOTES

Old mother at water's edge
used to bow down to them,
the turtles coming in from the sea,
their many eggs,
their eyes streaming water like tears,
and I'd see it all,
old mother as if in prayer,
the turtles called back to where they were born,
the hungry watchers standing at the edge of trees
hoping for food when darkness gathers.

Years later, swimming in murky waters
a sea turtle swam beside me
both of us watching as if clasped together
in the lineage of the same world
the sweep of the same current,
even rising for a breath of air at the same time
still watching.
My **ancestors** call them
the keepers of doors
and the shore a realm to other worlds,
both ways and
water moves the deep shift of life
back to birth and before
as if there is a path where beings truly meet,
as if I am rounding the human corners.

Use a dictionary or indicate another strategy you used that helped you determine meaning.

ancestors (AN sehs tuhrz) *n.*

MEANING:

404 UNIT 4 • PEOPLE AND THE PLANET

DIGITAL PERSPECTIVES

Illuminating the Text To help students understand the scene described in lines 3–10, show them a video of a sea turtle coming ashore to lay her eggs and the baby sea turtles hatching and scurrying into the water before predators can get them. This will help students understand the "hungry watchers" in lines 9–10. If possible, find a video that explores the ways humans have harmed and helped sea turtle populations around the world.

DIGITAL PERSPECTIVES

Concept Vocabulary

WISDOM If groups are struggling to define the word *wisdom* in line 11, have them consult a print or online dictionary. The speaker's point is that perhaps compared to nature, humans are not so wise after all.

Possible response: *Wisdom* means "understanding, or deep knowledge."

"Nature" is what We see—
The Hill—the Afternoon—
Squirrel—Eclipse—the Bumble bee—
Nay—Nature is Heaven—

"Nature" is what We hear—
The Bobolink[1]—the Sea—
Thunder—the Cricket—
Nay—Nature is Harmony—

"Nature" is what We know—
But have no Art to say—
So impotent our **Wisdom** is
To Her Sincerity—

1. **Bobolink** *n.* small bird.

NOTES

Use a dictionary or indicate another strategy you used that helped you determine meaning.

wisdom (WIHZ duhm) *n.*

MEANING:

HOW LANGUAGE WORKS

Word Choice As students perform their close read, explain that poets choose their words very carefully to establish a particular rhythm and sometimes to rhyme. Remind them that rhyme is the repetition of sounds at the ends of words. Words that rhyme exactly have identical vowel sounds in their final accented syllables. Often poets use end rhymes, or rhymes at the ends of lines. Ask students to begin with line 1 and take note of the last word on each line. Have students identify end rhymes in Dickinson's poem. Then have groups discuss the effect of these end rhymes on the meaning of the poem.

Possible response: The words *see, bee, Sea, Harmony,* and *Sincerity* all end in the same long *e* sound. This rhyming makes the poem fun to read and hear. It also creates a whimsical tone.

FACILITATING

Concept Vocabulary

HEED If groups are struggling to define the word *heed* in line 7, first make sure they see the footnote defining *lay* and understand the rest of lines 5–8. Then guide students in using context clues to figure out the meaning of *heed*. Explain that the word *but* signals contrast, which suggests that *heed* is opposite in meaning to *neglect* in line 8. Tell students to verify the meaning in a print or online dictionary.

Possible response: *Heed* means "to pay attention to."

POETRY

The Sparrow

Paul Laurence Dunbar

NOTES

Use a dictionary or indicate another strategy you used that helped you determine meaning.

heed (heed) *v.*

MEANING:

A little bird, with plumage brown,
Beside my window flutters down,
A moment chirps its little strain,
Ten taps upon my window-pane,
And chirps again, and hops along,
To call my notice to its song;
But I work on, nor **heed** its lay,[1]
Till, in neglect, it flies away.

So birds of peace and hope and love
Come fluttering earthward from above,
To settle on life's window-sills,
And ease our load of earthly ills;
But we, in traffic's rush and din
Too deep engaged to let them in,
With deadened heart and sense plod on,
Nor know our loss till they are gone

1. **lay** *n.* song.

PERSONALIZE FOR LEARNING

English Language Support

Vocabulary of Poems English Learners might have difficulty with some of the language in this poem, beginning with the word *plumage* in line 1. Have groups create personalized glossaries for this selection. Students should note any words that are unfamiliar to anyone in the group and work together to identify their meanings. They can organize their glossaries alphabetically or list the words in the order in which they appear in the selection. Each entry should provide a pronunciation key and a brief definition. **ALL LEVELS**

Comprehension Check

Complete the following items after you finish your first read. Review and clarify details with your group.

TURTLE WATCHERS

1. What are the "hungry watchers" doing?

2. What happens years later?

"NATURE" IS WHAT WE SEE—

1. What does the first stanza say nature is?

2. What does the second stanza say nature is?

3. What does the third stanza say nature is?

THE SPARROW

1. What does the speaker do in response to the bird beside his or her window?

2. According to the speaker, how do we "plod on"?

RESEARCH

Research to Explore Choose one unfamiliar detail mentioned in one of the poems. Briefly research that detail. For instance, you might research the life cycle of the sea turtle. In what way does the information you learned affect your understanding of the poem? Explain.

DIGITAL PERSPECTIVES

Comprehension Check

Possible responses:

Turtle Watchers

1. The hungry watchers are waiting for darkness and hoping to eat.
2. Years later, the speaker swims next to a sea turtle and feels connected to it and to her ancestors.

"Nature" is what We see—

1. The first stanza says nature is what we see.
2. The second stanza says nature is what we hear.
3. The third stanza says nature is what we know.

The Sparrow

1. The speaker is busy and ignores the sparrow.
2. We plod on with a deadened heart and do not see these birds.

Research

Research to Explore If students struggle to choose a detail, have them reread the poems, looking for new concepts or ideas, such as sparrow songs, bobolinks, or turtle nests.

PERSONALIZE FOR LEARNING

Challenge

Punctuation in Poems Direct groups' attention to Dickinson's poem. Have students work together to write an essay responding to this prompt: *What effect does Dickinson's use of dashes and unusual capitalization have in the poem?* Students can research what others have had to say about the poet's use of dashes and unconventional capitalization, but they should write their own response essay, rather than a research report. Challenge each group to use specific details from the poem to support their ideas about Dickinson's use of dashes and unusual capitalization.

FACILITATING

Jump Start

CLOSE READ Ask groups to consider the following prompts: *What effects have you had on the environment? What effects would you like to have on the environment?* As students discuss in their groups, ask them to consider the relationship between people and the environment and the effects that people's choices have on the world around them.

Close Read the Text

If needed, model close reading by using the Annotation Highlights in the Interactive Teacher's Edition. You may want to print copies of the Close-Read Guide: Poetry for students to use as they read.

Remind students to use Accountable Talk in their discussions and to support one another as they complete the close read.

Analyze the Text

Possible responses:

1. "Turtle Watchers" suggests that the connection between humans and the natural world is ancient and essential. " 'Nature' is what We see –" suggests that we are not able to comprehend or describe nature adequately. "The Sparrow" suggests that we are often too busy to appreciate nature until it is too late.
2. Students should support their ideas with evidence from the poems.
3. Responses will vary.

Concept Vocabulary

Why These Words? Possible response: The words all relate to the importance of ancestral knowledge.

Practice

Responses will vary. Encourage students to peer edit their partner's sentences to add context clues if needed.

Word Network

Possible responses: *sea, trees, air, harmony*

Word Study

For more support, see **Concept Vocabulary and Word Study.**

Possible response: Knowing the meaning of ancestors may reinforce the idea of generations and the connection between all humans and nature.

MAKING MEANING

POETRY COLLECTION

TIP

GROUP DISCUSSION

When you work in your group to answer the Analyze the Text questions, be sure to support your opinions and ideas with evidence from the text.

Close Read the Text

With your group, revisit sections of the text you marked during your first read. **Annotate** what you notice. What **questions** do you have? What can you **conclude**?

Analyze the Text

CITE TEXTUAL EVIDENCE to support your answers.

Notebook Complete the activities.

1. **Review and Clarify** With your group, reread the poems. Analyze each poem, and determine the theme about nature that each poem suggests.
2. **Present and Discuss** Now, work with your group to share the lines from the poems that you found especially important. Take turns presenting your lines. Discuss what you noticed in the poems, what questions you asked, and what conclusions you reached.
3. **Essential Question: *What effects do people have on the environment?*** What have these poems taught you about the effects people have on the environment? Discuss with your group.

LANGUAGE DEVELOPMENT

Concept Vocabulary

ancestors	wisdom	heed

Why These Words? The concept vocabulary words from the poems are related. With your group, determine what the words have in common. Write your ideas and add another word that fits the category.

WORD NETWORK

Add interesting words related to people and the planet from the text to your Word Network.

Practice

Notebook Use each concept vocabulary word in a sentence that demonstrates its meaning. Read aloud your sentences to a partner, and discuss any differences in your understandings.

Word Study

Etymology The etymology, or word origin, of the word *ancestors* can help you understand and remember its meaning. *Ancestors* was formed from the Latin prefix *ante-*, meaning "before," and the Latin verb *cedere,* meaning "go." Thus, *ancestors* literally means "those who have gone before us." With your group, discuss "Turtle Watchers." How does understanding the etymology of the word *ancestors* deepen your understanding of the poem?

STANDARDS

Reading Literature

Analyze how a drama's or poem's form or structure contributes to its meaning.

Language

Determine or clarify the meaning of unknown and multiple-meaning words and phrases based on *grade 7 reading and content*, choosing flexibly from a range of strategies.

b. Use common, grade-appropriate Greek or Latin affixes and roots as clues to the meaning of a word.

408 UNIT 4 • PEOPLE AND THE PLANET

FORMATIVE ASSESSMENT

Analyze the Text

If students struggle to close read the text, **then** provide the **Poetry Collection: Text Questions** available online in the Interactive Teacher's Edition or Unit Resources. Answers and DOK levels are also available.

Concept Vocabulary

If students have difficulty seeing the connection among the words, **then** have them use each word in a sentence about the relationship between people and the environment and consider what the sentences have in common.

Word Study

If students have difficulty understanding how the etymology of a word can help them understand its meaning, **then** explain that a word's etymology is its history, or life story. For Reteach and Practice, see **Word Study: Etymology (RP).**

Analyze Craft and Structure

The Speaker in Lyric Poetry When you read a poem you can "hear" a voice speaking to you. That is the voice of the poem's **speaker**. Like the narrator in a story, the speaker in a poem is an imaginary voice created by the poet. The speaker presents a unique view that expresses his or her thoughts, feelings, personality, and attitude toward the subject. Although they sometimes overlap, the speaker's point of view is not necessarily the point of view of the poet.

All three poems in this collection are examples of lyric poetry. A **lyric poem** expresses the thoughts and feelings of a speaker about a setting, a moment, or an idea, such as nature. In this form of poetry, a poet typically uses vivid, musical language to express the speaker's observations, feelings, and insights. As a consequence, the reader's understanding is filtered through and shaped by the speaker's perceptions.

Practice

CITE TEXTUAL EVIDENCE to support your answers.

Work with your group to analyze the poetry in this collection. Answer the questions and use the chart to examine the similarities and differences in approach in each of the poems.

QUESTIONS	Turtle Watchers	"Nature" is what We see—	The Sparrow
What is the poem's subject and the speaker's attitude toward the subject?	The subjects are sea turtles. The speaker's attitude is warm, empathetic, and respectful.	The subject is all of nature. The speaker's attitude is humble, awed, and reverential.	The subject is a sparrow, a type of small songbird. The speaker's attitude is appreciative, regretful, and apologetic.
What vivid words and descriptions are used?	"eyes streaming water like tears"; "old mother as if in prayer"; "clasped together/in the lineage of the same world"	"Eclipse"; "Heaven"; "Thunder"; "So impotent our Wisdom is / To Her Sincerity"	"chirps its little strain, / Ten taps upon my window-pane"; "fluttering earthward from above"; "traffic's rush and din"; "deadened heart"
What is the speaker saying about people's relationship to nature?	The speaker's message is that humans are one with animals.	The speaker's message is that human language is incapable of capturing the full majesty of nature.	The speaker's message is that humans are often too preoccupied to appreciate nature's simple beauties.

PERSONALIZE FOR LEARNING

Strategic Support

Lyric Poetry To help students understand the importance of musicality in lyric poetry, locate a recording of at least one of these poems being read aloud. Have students listen to the recordings in their groups, or individually, using headphones. Then have groups discuss these questions:

How is listening to the poetry different from reading it? What do you notice from listening that you did not notice when you were reading? Did hearing the poem help you to understand it better or to better understand the nature of lyric poetry? Explain.

DIGITAL PERSPECTIVES

Analyze Craft and Structure

Analyze Poetic Form: The Speaker in Lyric Poetry Point out to students that lyric poetry often has a distinctly musical quality. Explain that in ancient Greece, a lyric was originally a song sung to the accompaniment of a stringed instrument called the lyre. Lyric poems, however, achieve their musical effect through *sound devices* like rhythm, rhyme, alliteration, assonance, and onomatopoeia. For more support, see **Analyze Craft and Structure: The Speaker in Lyric Poetry.**

Practice

See possible responses in chart on student page.

FORMATIVE ASSESSMENT

Analyze Craft and Structure

If students struggle to analyze the poems, **then** guide them by asking more pointed questions, such as "What does the image of the turtles' eyes 'streaming water like tears' make you think about and feel?" For Reteach and Practice, see **Analyze Craft and Structure: The Speaker in Lyric Poetry (RP).**

FACILITATING

Author's Style

Word Choice As you discuss word choice with students, guide them in identifying words that contribute to the tone of one of the poems. Then work with groups to identify the tone the words create. For instance, in "Turtle Watchers," the words *bow, prayer, ancestors, realm,* and *beings* create a reverent tone. For more support, see **Author's Style: Word Choice.**

Read It

See possible responses in chart on student page.

Write It

Poems and paragraphs will vary, but should focus on their relationships to the environment. Remind students to think about the tone they want to convey and to choose words that communicate that tone.

FORMATIVE ASSESSMENT

Author's Style

If students are unable to identify the effect of specific word choices, **then** have them generate pairs of words that have similar denotations but very different connotations (such as *home* and *residence; athlete* and *jock; stealthy* and *sneaky*). For Reteach and Practice, see **Author's Style: Word Choice (RP).**

LANGUAGE DEVELOPMENT

POETRY COLLECTION

Author's Style

Diction and Tone An author's word choice, or **diction,** includes not only the specific words but also the phrases and expressions an author uses. In poetry, a poet's word choice plays an important role in creating poetic language, which is specific, imaginative, and rich with emotion. A poet's use of language helps to develop the **tone** of a poem, or the poet's attitude toward his or her subject.

To achieve these effects in a poem, a poet often chooses words not only for their **denotations,** or dictionary definitions, but for the connotations the words evoke in readers. **Connotations** are the ideas and feelings a word brings to mind. Although, two words many have similar denotations, a poet may choose one word over another because of the connotations associated with the word. Consider the following lines of poetry:

- They rolled over the swells until they slid ashore.
- They slammed over the waves until they hit land.

Both examples convey roughly the same information. However, in the first example, the words *rolled, swells,* and *slid* have calming connotations and create a peaceful tone. In the second example, the words *slammed, waves,* and *hit* have harsher connotations and create a dangerous, anxious tone.

A poet's word choice and tone help develop meaning in poem. Analyzing a poet's word choice and tone can help you to **make inferences,** or educated guesses, about the **theme** of a poem, or the insight about life that it suggests.

STANDARDS

Reading Literature

- Cite several pieces of textual evidence to support analysis of what the text says explicitly as well as inferences drawn from the text.
- Determine a theme or central idea of a text and analyze its development over the course of the text; provide an objective summary of the text.
- Determine the meaning of words and phrases as they are used in a text, including figurative and connotative meanings; analyze the impact of rhymes and other repetitions of sounds on a specific verse or stanza of a poem or section of a story or drama.

Read It

Notebook Work with your group to identify specific word choices in each poem, and note how these choices affect meaning and tone. When you have completed the chart, discuss the possible themes your examples suggest.

POEM	WORD OR PHRASE	EFFECT ON MEANING OR TONE
Turtle Watchers	"bow down"	suggests reverence
"Nature" is what We see—	"Bobolink"	suggests specificity, may suggest humor
The Sparrow	"Till, in neglect, it flies away."	suggests formality

Write It

Notebook Using your notes from the chart and your discussion, work individually to write a brief paragraph about the theme of each poem. In each paragraph, support your ideas about the theme with the specific examples you gathered while working with your group. To ensure you describe your thoughts accurately and concisely, consider the connotations of the words you use.

PERSONALIZE FOR LEARNING

English Language Support

Word Choice To help students understand the impact of word choice on meaning and tone, work with groups to paraphrase each line in one of the poems. Then have volunteers read the paraphrase and the original poem. Discuss with students the difference between the two versions. This will help English Learners better understand the poem and the importance of word choice and author's style. **ALL LEVELS**

EFFECTIVE EXPRESSION

Speaking and Listening

Assignment

Using the analysis you have done so far, work with your group to create an **oral presentation** that highlights the theme of one of the poems in the collection. Choose from the following options:

- ☐ a **dramatic reading** in which you use multimedia, such as music, props, and costumes, to convey the meaning and theme of the poem
- ☐ a **digital multimedia presentation** in which you use videos, images, and other digital media to convey the meaning and theme of the poem

Project Plan Assign roles for each member of your group. For groups who have chosen the dramatic reading, roles can include speakers to recite the poem, a sound person, a costume designer, and a person to identify and organize visuals and music. For groups who have chosen the digital multimedia presentation, roles can include a speaker, a multimedia researcher, and a person to organize the information for the presentation.

Plan and Practice Your Delivery To project confidence and a positive attitude, plan and practice your delivery both individually and as a group. As you practice, use the following strategies to refine your presentation techniques:

- **Check equipment.** If your presentation involves use of audio or video, practice your presentation along with the media. Work on the timing of media and how it relates to the rest of the performance.
- **Use your voice well.** Be energetic, but speak clearly and precisely. Enunciate every word. Vary the pitch and speed of your voice to keep listeners engaged. Make sure you are speaking loudly enough to be heard by the entire class.
- **Make eye contact.** Memorize as much of your part of the presentation as possible. Doing so will enable you to make eye contact with your audience more frequently.

Present and Evaluate Once you have rehearsed, present your work to the class. After the presentation, invite comments and feedback from your classmates. Be prepared to answer their questions.

When other groups present their work, listen attentively. Evaluate their performance, and provide feedback to them in a respectful way.

EVIDENCE LOG

Before moving on to a new selection, go to your log and record what you learned from "Turtle Watchers," "'Nature' is what We see—," and "The Sparrow."

STANDARDS

Speaking and Listening

- Present claims and findings, emphasizing salient points in a focused, coherent manner with pertinent descriptions, facts, details, and examples; use appropriate eye contact, adequate volume, and clear pronunciation.
- Include multimedia components and visual displays in presentations to clarify claims and findings and emphasize salient points.
- Adapt speech to a variety of contexts and tasks, demonstrating command of formal English when indicated or appropriate.

PERSONALIZE FOR LEARNING

Strategic Support

Costumes and Props Some groups may need more time to plan their presentations, especially if they have chosen to use costumes and props. Provide additional time and support as needed. For instance, you might ask students in your school's theater classes to provide access to costumes and props.

DIGITAL PERSPECTIVES

Speaking and Listening

Oral Presentation Explain to students that a poem's theme is expressed through word choice, imagery, and tone. Provide students with these questions to help them as they hold their discussions on theme.

1. What is the topic of the poem?
2. What tone, or attitude, does the speaker convey toward the topic?
3. What feelings does the speaker express?
4. How does the poem make readers feel?
5. What theme or big idea about the topic or about life is conveyed by the poem?

Project Plan Remind students that whether they choose a poetry slam or multimedia presentation, they should make sure that their presentation conveys the same tone, or attitude, toward the topic and expresses the same theme as the poem.

Plan and Practice Your Delivery Encourage students to take notes during rehearsal to ensure that they can strengthen their presentations. For more support, see **Speaking and Listening: Oral Presentation.**

An **English Language Support Lesson** on Multimedia Presentation is available in the Interactive Teacher's Edition.

Evidence Log Support students in completing their Evidence Log. This paced activity will help prepare them for the Performance-Based Assessment at the end of the unit.

FORMATIVE ASSESSMENT

Speaking and Listening

If groups have difficulty planning their presentations, **then** assign roles and tasks to group members. For Reteach and Practice, see **Speaking and Listening: Oral Presentation (RP).**

Selection Test

Administer the Poetry Selection Test, which is available in both print and digital formats online in Assessments.

Eagle Tracking at Follensby Pond

AUDIO SUMMARIES
Audio summaries of "Eagle Tracking at Follensby Pond" are available online in both English and Spanish in the Interactive Teacher's Edition or Unit Resources. Assigning these summaries prior to reading the selection may help students build additional background knowledge and set a context for their first read.

Summary

"Eagle Tracking at Follensby Pond" is a photo gallery that was produced by The Nature Conservancy. The gallery documents the eagle reintroduction project at Follensby Pond in the Adirondack Mountains. The bald eagle disappeared from the area in the 1950s, and was reintroduced in the 1980s. Peter Nye, a conservationist with the New York State Department of Environmental Conservation, traveled to Alaska to collect baby eagles to release at Follensby Pond. The eagles thrived and reproduced, and thanks to the reintroduction project, eagles soar once more over the lakes in the Adirondack Mountains.

Insight

This selection shows how reintroduction works, and how it can succeed. An animal may disappear from part of its habitat, but if a healthy population remains somewhere, people can use those animals to reestablish populations elsewhere.

ESSENTIAL QUESTION:
What effects do people have on the environment?

Connection to Essential Question

"Eagle Tracking at Follensby Pond" provides a two-sided connection to the Essential Question, "What effects do people have on the environment?" While people were responsible for the near-extinction of the bald eagle population, people were also responsible for the reintroduction of bald eagles to the Adirondacks.

SMALL-GROUP LEARNING PERFORMANCE TASK
Why do people impact the environment in a harmful way?

UNIT PERFORMANCE-BASED ASSESSMENT
Is it too late to fix the damage that has been done to our environment?

Connection to Performance Tasks

Small-Group Learning Performance Task In this Performance Task, students will develop a multimedia presentation that addresses our impact on the environment. This selection provides students with both positive and negative examples of that impact.

Unit Performance-Based Assessment "Eagle Tracking at Follensby Pond" shows that if we act in a timely manner, it is sometimes possible to repair the damage done to our environment.

DIGITAL PERSPECTIVES

 Audio  Video 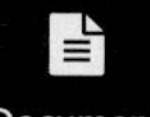 Document  Annotation Highlights 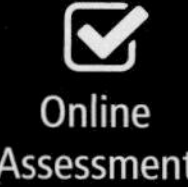 Online Assessment

LESSON RESOURCES

	Making Meaning	Language Development	Effective Expression
Lesson	**First Review** **Close Review** **Analyze the Media**	**Media Vocabulary**	**Research**
Instructional Standards	**RI.7.10** By the end of the year, read and comprehend literary nonfiction . . . **L.7.6** Acquire and use accurately grade-appropriate general academic and domain-specific words . . . **SL.7.2** Analyze the main ideas and supporting details presented in diverse media and formats . . .	**L.7.6** Acquire and use accurately grade-appropriate general academic and domain-specific words . . .	**W.7.2** Write informative/explanatory texts . . . **W.7.2.a** Introduce a topic . . . **W.7.2.b** Develop the topic . . . **W.7.7** Conduct short research . . . **W.7.8** Gather relevant information . . .
STUDENT RESOURCES			
Available online in the Interactive Student Edition or Unit Resources	Selection Audio First-Review Guide: Media Art/ Photography Close-Review Guide: Media Art/ Photography		Evidence Log
TEACHER RESOURCES			
Selection Resources Available online in the Interactive Teacher's Edition or Unit Resources	Audio Summaries: English and Spanish Media Questions First Review Extension Questions	Media Vocabulary	Research: Research Paper
My Resources	A Unit 4 Answer Key is available online and in the Interactive Teacher's Edition.		

Media Complexity Rubric: Eagle Tracking at Follensby Pond

Quantitative Measures	
Format and Length: 6 photos with captions	
Qualitative Measures	
Knowledge Demands ① ❷ ③ ④ ⑤	Introduction, photos, and captions clearly detail the problem and the reintroduction process.
Structure ① ❷ ③ ④ ⑤	The selection consists of 6 photographs with captions.
Language Conventionality and Clarity ① ② ❸ ④ ⑤	The captions in the selection contain conventional syntax and on-level vocabulary.
Levels of Meaning/Purpose ① ❷ ③ ④ ⑤	Meaning and concepts are clear and easy to grasp.

Jump Start

FIRST REVIEW *What role do you think photography might play in preserving an endangered species? Why might images of such an animal be crucial to its ultimate survival?* Engage students in a discussion of what makes people emotional and even passionate about a cause or course of action.

Eagle Tracking at Follensby Pond

What makes the bald eagle so special in the United States? Why is it important to conserve them? Modeling questions such as these will help students connect to "Eagle Tracking at Follensby Pond" and to the Small-Group Performance Task assignment.

Media Vocabulary

Encourage groups to discuss the media vocabulary. Have they seen the terms in texts before?

Ask groups to look closely at the three terms and ask which they think might be technical terms describing the process of making photographs.

FIRST REVIEW

As they review, students should perform the steps of the first review:

LOOK: Remind students to notice what is happening in each photograph.

NOTE: Encourage students to mark any photos with questions they may want to revisit during their close review.

CONNECT: Encourage students to make connections beyond the photos themselves. If they cannot make connections to their own lives, have them consider nature shows they've seen on television or online sites featuring wild animals.

RESPOND: Students will answer questions to demonstrate understanding.

Point out to students that while they will always complete the Respond step at the end of the first read, the other steps will probably happen somewhat concurrently. You may wish to print copies of the **First-Review Guide Media: Art/Photography** for students to use.

About The Nature Conservancy

The Nature Conservancy is a charitable organization that was founded in Virginia in 1951. Its mission is to "conserve the lands and waters on which all life depends." The organization has over one million members and works in 35 countries, as well as all of the 50 states, protecting habitats ranging from grasslands to coral reefs.

Eagle Tracking at Follensby Pond

Media Vocabulary

These words will be useful to you as you view, analyze, and discuss photography.

documentary photography: photographs taken with the main purpose of recording a place, an event, or a person	• Documentary photography aims to portray subjects objectively, or in a way that is based on facts and not influenced by feelings and opinions. • Documentary photos may evoke feelings in viewers based on the subject matter.
vantage point: place where the photographer positions the camera	• A photographer may use a particular vantage point in order to capture the subject in a particular position or in a certain light. • Different vantage points can cause the same subject to be seen differently by the viewer.
monochrome: photos that are black and white	• In early photography, all photographs were monochrome. • Although color photography has existed for decades, photographers still use monochrome to create specific artistic effects.

First Review MEDIA: ART AND PHOTOGRAPHY

Study each photograph and its caption using these strategies.

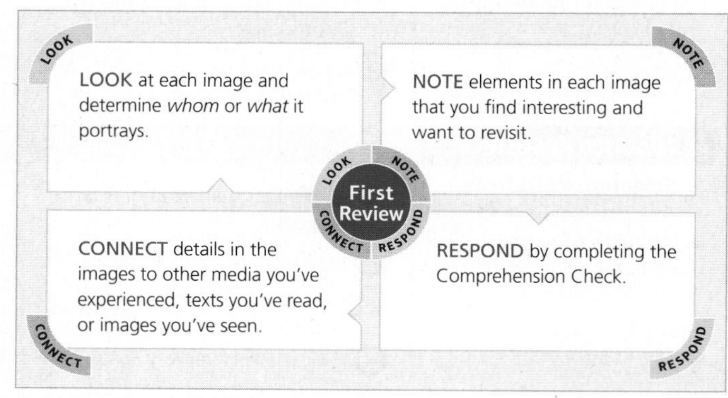

STANDARDS

Reading Informational Text
By the end of the year, read and comprehend literary nonfiction in the grades 6–8 text complexity band proficiently, with scaffolding as needed at the high end of the range.

Language
Acquire and use accurately grade-appropriate general academic and domain-specific words and phrases; gather vocabulary knowledge when considering a word or phrase important to comprehension or expression.

PERSONALIZE FOR LEARNING

English Language Support

Domain-Specific Vocabulary Some students may have difficulty with the word *monochrome*. Tell students that the word *monochrome* is made up of two Greek words, *mono*, meaning "one," and *chrome*, meaning "color." Put together, the words describe something that has one color. Explain that in photography, this usually refers to black and white. Display a newspaper or other source of black-and-white photographs, and have students write a sentence about one of the photos, using the word *monochrome*. **ALL LEVELS**

MEDIA | PHOTO GALLERY

Eagle Tracking
at Follensby Pond

The Nature Conservancy

BACKGROUND

The bald eagle has been a national symbol of the United States since 1782. But by the mid-1900s, decades of habitat destruction, hunting, and the use of pesticides, such as DDT, had brought the bald eagle population within danger of extinction. Since then, social awareness and government protections have helped the bald eagle population make great steps toward recovery.

PHOTO 1: Bald eagles had been absent from Adirondack skies for nearly three decades before they were reintroduced at Follensby Pond in the 1980s.

NOTES

DIGITAL PERSPECTIVES   

CLOSER REVIEW

Analyze Vantage Point 

Circulate among groups as students conduct their close review. Suggest that groups review Photo 1. Encourage them to talk about the notes they make. If needed, provide the following support.

NOTE: Have students note the details in the photo that result from the photographer's close-up vantage point, or work with small groups to have students participate while you note them together.

Possible response: Students may notice the intensity of the bird's eyes, the detail of the beak, or the look of the feathers.

QUESTION: Guide students to consider how the close-up photo makes them respond to the subject. Ask about the emotions it evokes. Accept student responses.

Possible response: The close-up look gives a dramatic, almost surprising sensation; the eyes are striking and the beak is sharp. Students might note that the beak is scratched and scarred and the feathers look soft, almost like fur.

CONCLUDE: Help students to formulate conclusions about the importance of what the close-up photo reveals. Ask students why the photographer might have chosen this vantage point.

Possible response: The photographer probably chose a vantage point that would emphasize an eagle's powerful presence. He or she may also have wanted to indicate certain physical aspects, showing how the eagle's eyes would be good for spotting prey, and its beak would be perfect for killing that prey.

Remind students that the **vantage point** is the place where a photographer sets up a camera. A close-up is a photographic angle that allows artists and journalists to get intimate details of an image. A close-up may be shot with a special lens that allows the photographer to zoom in to get closer to the subject.

FACILITATING SMALL-GROUP CLOSE REVIEWING

CLOSE REVIEW: Photography As groups perform the close review, circulate and offer support as needed.

- Remind groups that when they view photographs, they should identify subject and setting.
- If the group has questions about what they see in a photograph, remind them to read the caption and see what the image is meant to show.
- Challenge students to rewrite the captions that accompany the photographs.

PHOTO 2: In 1981, Endangered Species Unit leader Peter Nye of the New York State Department of Environmental Conservation (NYSDEC) traveled to Alaska to collect eaglets to release at Follensby Pond. At the time, Alaska was one of the few states in the nation with a healthy bald eagle population.

NOTES

PHOTO 3: The eaglets traveled by boat across Alaska's open waters to meet an airplane that was waiting to take them to the continental United States.

NOTES

VOCABULARY DEVELOPMENT

Concept Vocabulary Reinforcement If groups are struggling with the concept of *vantage point*, remind them that the word *vantage* shares the same base as the word *advantage*. Make clear that *advantage* means "a position or circumstance that favors a goal, or objective." Elicit that a good vantage point for seeing great distances would be a high spot with no objects in the way. Then have students use the term *vantage point* in a sentence that demonstrates its meaning, as in "The front row seats gave us a perfect vantage point to see the concert."

PHOTO 4: NYSDEC's Endangered Species Unit rushed the birds to their new home at Follensby Pond.

NOTES

PHOTO 5: Follensby Pond was chosen as the perfect site for this eagle restoration project because of its habitat, abundant food sources, and isolation.

NOTES

DIGITAL  PERSPECTIVES

CLOSER REVIEW

Analyze Documentary Photography 

Circulate among groups as students close review. Suggest that groups review Photo 4. Encourage them to talk about the notes they make. If needed, provide the following support.

NOTE: Have students note details in the photo that show the recovery effort, or work with small groups to have students participate while you note them together.

Possible response: Students may note the number of boxes on the small boat. They may notice the holes in the boxes which allow the birds to breathe.

QUESTION: Guide students to consider what this photo shows. Ask what a viewer can infer from special boxes on the deck of the boat, and accept student responses.

Possible response: Students may suggest that each box contains an eagle. Students may be surprised by the number of boxes, or by the size of the small boat.

CONCLUDE: Help students to formulate conclusions about the function of documentary photography in this image. Ask students why the photographer might have included these details.

Possible response: The people behind the preservation program probably wanted to document the work involved in transferring live eagles from Alaska to New York. Students may also note that this effort to repopulate a region with eagles takes the work of only a few people.

Remind students that **documentary photography** is meant to show viewers a process, an event, or a place. The purpose of these photographs is to show people the steps involved in the restoration project.

CROSS-CURRICULAR PERSPECTIVES

Science As students view Photo 5, they may have more questions about this project. In 1972, when DDT was banned, the eagle population in much of the northeastern United States had been virtually wiped out. By the year 2000, New York State was home to 43 breeding eagles. By 2009 that number had reached 153. The population has continued to increase, but the birds still face challenges. Have students research the history of bald eagles, including their current situation, and write a one-page report.

CLOSER REVIEW

Analyze Vantage Point 

Circulate among groups as students conduct their close review. Suggest that groups review Photo 6. Encourage them to talk about the notes they make. If needed, provide the following support.

NOTE: Have students note details in the photo that show how the vantage point helps make a statement about the subject, or work with small groups to have students participate while you note them together.

Possible response: The photographer took this shot from underneath a bird in flight.

QUESTION: Guide students to consider what these details might tell them. Ask what a viewer can infer from the vantage point, and accept student responses.

Possible response: This vantage point reveals the entire eagle in flight. The wings show a bird that is powerful and flying free.

CONCLUDE: Help students to formulate conclusions about the importance of the photographer's vantage point. Ask students why the photographer might have chosen this view.

Possible response: The photographer probably chose this vantage point to demonstrate the eagle's power and majesty, to show how it looks in flight, and possibly to express how its freedom and independence make it a perfect national symbol.

Remind students that the **vantage point,** or position of the camera, can impact the image captured. For example, if the photographer had shot this image from the same height as the bird, the image might not have revealed the dramatic full wingspan.

PHOTO 6: Today, bald eagles can be seen near many Adirondack lakes as a result of the efforts of NYSDEC's Endangered Species Unit. In 1975, prior to restoration efforts, only one pair of eagles remained in New York. As of 2008, more than 145 pairs of eagles are thriving.

NOTES

NOTES

DIGITAL PERSPECTIVES

Enriching the Text To help students appreciate the power of Photo 6, locate National Public Radio's feature "Retracing Ralph Waldo Emerson's Steps In a Now 'Unchanged Eden,'" and play part or all of it for students. Emphasize that the famous American poet visited Follensby Pond on a visit to New York's Adirondack Mountains in 1858 and wrote about his experience. The radio piece features commentary by environmental activist and writer Bill McKibben and Nature Conservancy guide Mike Carr as they retrace Emerson's path through this pristine wilderness. Have students discuss how the radio feature adds to their understanding of the photo gallery.

DIGITAL PERSPECTIVES

Comprehension Check

Complete the following items after you finish your first review. Review and clarify details with your group.

1. According to the information in the captions, how long were bald eagles missing from the Adirondacks?

2. Where did conservationists collect eaglets for eventual release in New York State?

3. How did the eaglets travel?

4. According to the information in the captions, what is the result of the restoration project?

5. **Notebook** Confirm your understanding of the selection by writing a brief summary of the eagle restoration project at Follensby Pond.

Comprehension Check

Possible responses:

1. Eagles had been missing from the skies of the Adirondacks for nearly three decades before they were brought back in 1981.
2. The conservationists collected the eaglets in Alaska.
3. The eaglets traveled through Alaska over open water by boat, and were flown to the continental United States in a plane.
4. Eagles can now be seen near many Adirondack lakes.
5. Explanations will vary but should note that while eagles could be found in Alaska, they had nearly vanished from the lower 48 states. To get a new eagle population started it was necessary to bring pairs of these birds from the one place that had them in abundance—Alaska.

PERSONALIZE FOR LEARNING

Challenge

Symbolism Every nation chooses symbols to represent its history, culture, and ideals. Have students do some research into the arrow-clutching eagle on the back of a U.S. quarter on quarters minted before 1999. They should discover that the symbol includes 13 arrows, one for each of the original colonies. They should also learn that our own symbol may have its origins in the symbol of the Iroquois (or Haudenosaunee) League in North America, a confederacy of Native groups that used a similar symbol involving a bundle of six arrows—symbolizing the League's six tribes. Some may find that it is also possible that the symbol on the quarter derives from the Dutch Republic in the sixteenth century, whose heraldic emblem involved a lion clutching 17 arrows. The lion stood for courage and independence, the arrows for each of the country's 17 provinces.

Jump Start

Ask students to consider the following prompt: *If you were a photographer tasked with helping an effort to preserve Africa's elephant population, what sort of images would you take and why?* As students discuss the prompt in their groups, have them consider possible image types they might take, such as close-ups to reveal the animal's character, and longer shots that show how herds behave in the wild.

Close Review

If needed, model close reviewing by using the Closer Review notes in the Interactive Teacher's Edition.

Remind students to use Accountable Talk in their discussions and to support one another as they complete the close review.

Analyze the Media

Encourage groups to discuss their decisions about the photos, using specific reasons for their choices.

1. **Responses will vary.** Remind students to defend their selections.
2. **Responses will vary by group.** Groups should discuss the types of information they gleaned from the captions.
3. **Possible response:** Just as human actions can result in the destruction of animals and their habitats, they can also restore and conserve those creatures and their environments.

Media Vocabulary

For more support, see **Media Vocabulary.**

Possible responses:

1. The *documentary photography* shows the steps that the rescuers took to save the eaglets.
2. The *vantage point* of PHOTO 1 is a close up that reveals the features of the eagle's face. PHOTO 2 was taken by a photographer standing in front of a bird. It helps the viewer see size. PHOTO 3 was taken from the vantage point of the ship with the camera aimed forward, revealing the forward motion of the project. PHOTO 4 was taken from a distance showing the size of the lake. PHOTO 5 was taken from the ground with the camera aimed into the trees to set a perspective for the nests. PHOTO 6 was taken from below a flying eagle, making the eagle look majestic.
3. The *monochrome* images seem flatter and less current.

MAKING MEANING

EAGLE TRACKING AT FOLLENSBY POND

Close Review

With your group, revisit the selection and your first-review notes. Jot down any new observations that seem important. What **questions** do you have? What can you **conclude**?

Analyze the Media

Notebook Complete the activities.

1. **Present and Discuss** Choose the photo and caption that you found most interesting or informative. Share your choice with the group, and discuss why you chose it. Explain what you noticed in the photo and caption, what questions it raised for you, and what conclusions you reached about it.
2. **Review and Synthesize** With your group, review the photo gallery. How do the captions add meaning to the photographs? Would the photographs be less effective without the captions? Why or why not?
3. **Notebook** **Essential Question:** ***What effects do people have on the environment?*** How did this photo gallery contribute to your understanding of the ways in which people affect the environment?

LANGUAGE DEVELOPMENT

Media Vocabulary

documentary photography	vantage point	monochrome

Confirm your understanding of the vocabulary words by answering these questions.

1. Do you think the photo gallery effectively conveys information about the eagle restoration project at Follensby Pond?
2. Describe the vantage point of each photograph, and explain how the vantage point affects the subject.
3. How do the monochrome photographs differ from the color photographs?

STANDARDS

Speaking and Listening
Analyze the main ideas and supporting details presented in diverse media and formats and explain how the ideas clarify a topic, text, or issue under study.

Language
Acquire and use accurately grade-appropriate general academic and domain-specific words and phrases; gather vocabulary knowledge when considering a word or phrase important to comprehension or expression.

FORMATIVE ASSESSMENT

Analyze the Text

If students struggle to close review the photography, **then** provide the **Eagle Tracking at Follensby Pond: Media Questions** available online in the Interactive Teacher's Edition or Unit Resources. Answers and DOK levels are also available.

Media Vocabulary

If students struggle to think of good locations for documentary photography, **then** have them consider some of their favorite outdoor parks or wilderness areas.

Research

Assignment

Work in your group to research and write a short **research paper** on one of the following topics:

- ☐ eagle restoration and tracking programs in other states
- ☐ restoration and tracking programs for other endangered species
- ☐ the origins and history of the Endangered Species Act

In your paper, highlight the relationship between the topic you chose to research and the photo gallery, "Eagle Tracking at Follensby Pond."

Formulate a Research Question Work with your group to formulate a research question that will guide your research process. An effective research question should be specific and manageable, and the purpose of your paper will be to answer this question. If you do not limit the scope of your research question, you will find it difficult to address the question fully. Consider the following examples:

Broad Research Question: How do people affect the environment?
Specific Research Question: How does coal mining affect rivers and streams?

Organize Your Information Take notes from each research source to answer your research question. Include only information that is meaningfully related to your topic. Use your notes to organize an outline for your research paper. Consider the following methods of organization:

- **chronological order:** sequencing information about events in the order in which they occur
- **comparison and contrast:** analyzing and explaining the similarities and differences between two or more related subjects
- **cause and effect:** analyzing and explaining reasons or results for something that happens

Notebook Use a chart such as the one shown to organize information for your research paper.

What is our research question?	
What are at least three relevant, reliable print or digital sources we can use?	
What organizational structure will we use to present the information?	

EVIDENCE LOG

Before moving on to a new selection, go to your Evidence Log and record what you learned from "Eagle Tracking at Follensby Pond."

STANDARDS

Writing

- Write informative/explanatory texts to examine a topic and convey ideas, concepts, and information through the selection, organization, and analysis of relevant content.
  a. Introduce a topic clearly, previewing what is to follow; organize ideas, concepts, and information, using strategies such as definition, classification, comparison/ contrast, and cause/ effect; include formatting, graphics, and multimedia when useful to aiding comprehension.
  b. Develop the topic with relevant facts, definitions, concrete details, quotations, or other information and examples.
- Conduct short research projects to answer a question, drawing on several sources and generating additional related, focused questions for further research and investigation.
- Gather relevant information from multiple print and digital sources, using search terms effectively; assess the credibility and accuracy of each source; and quote or paraphrase the data and conclusions of others while avoiding plagiarism and following a standard format for citation.

DIGITAL PERSPECTIVES

Research

Formulate a Research Question Guide students in narrowing their research topics. Using the Broad Research Question example in the student edition, ask students to formulate other Specific Research Questions. For example, students might suggest these ideas: *How does biking help reduce a carbon footprint? What is a carbon footprint? How can carpools help the environment?*

Organize Your Information Remind students that their organizational structure should reflect the type of information that they are presenting and review topics best suited to each type of structure.

If groups have trouble assigning tasks, encourage them to consider each group member's strengths. For example, if one group member has more experience in using search engines to gather information, that student can be chosen to direct research and record links.

For more support, see **Research: Research Paper.**

Evidence Log Support students in completing the Evidence Log. This paced activity will help prepare them for the Performance-Based Assessment at the end of the unit.

FORMATIVE ASSESSMENT

Research

If students have trouble locating reliable sources, **then** encourage them to broaden their search terms to learn more about bird rescue.

PERSONALIZE FOR LEARNING

Strategic Support

Research Students may require support in finding relevant material for their projects. Remind them that using the process of elimination is a good way to narrow down a subject or topic. For instance, if they are looking for eagle restoration programs in different states, they might begin by searching in the browser for "eagle restoration projects by state." They can then examine the list to see which of the possible projects looks like it might yield the most relevant data for their report.

He—y, Come On Ou—t!

AUDIO SUMMARIES
Audio summaries of "H—ey, Come On Ou—t!" are available online in both English and Spanish in the Interactive Teacher's Edition or Unit Resources. Assigning these summaries prior to reading the selection may help students build additional background knowledge and set a context for their first read.

Summary

In "Hey—y, Come On Ou—t!" by Shinichi Hoshi, a village suffers damage from a typhoon and a large hole appears where a shrine had stood. The hole is so deep that it seems bottomless, and the villagers can't decide what to do about it. As news of the hole spreads, people from around the area come to investigate and offer opinions on what to do. Finally, it is decided to give the hole to a businessman in exchange for a new shrine closer to the village. Soon, the hole becomes a dumping ground for everything from nuclear waste and diseased animals to classified documents and personal diaries, and the village seems to have taken care of its trash problems. However, no one is aware of the coming consequences.

Insight

This story is an allegory for pollution. The end of the story implies that everything dumped into the hole is about to pour down from the sky upon the city. Similarly, the things we dump into the environment don't just disappear. There will be future consequences.

ESSENTIAL QUESTION:
What effects do people have on the environment?

Connection to Essential Question

"He—y, Come On Ou—t!" provides an interesting connection to the Essential Question. There are no obvious effects on the environment from human actions in the story. It's not until the end of the story that there are suggestions of long-term consequences.

SMALL-GROUP LEARNING PERFORMANCE TASK
Why do people impact the environment in a harmful way?

UNIT PERFORMANCE-BASED ASSESSMENT
Is it too late to fix the damage that has been done to our environment?

Connection to Performance Tasks

Small-Group Learning Performance Task In this Performance Task, students will develop a multimedia presentation that explores the impact that people have on the environment. This selection provides an example of how what we do in the short term can have consequences in the long term.

Unit Performance-Based Assessment Since the characters in this story are unaware of the environmental damage that they might be creating, students will need to consider the potential impact of their actions on the environment.

DIGITAL PERSPECTIVES

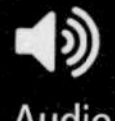 Audio  Video  Document 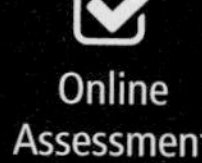 Annotation Highlights Online Assessment

LESSON RESOURCES

	Making Meaning	Language Development	Effective Expression
Lesson	**First Read** **Close Read** **Analyze the Text** **Analyze Craft and Structure**	**Concept Vocabulary** **Word Study** **Conventions**	**Writing to Sources** **Speaking and Listening**
Instructional Standards	**RL.7.10** By the end of the year, read and comprehend literature . . . **L.7.4.a** Use context as a clue . . . **SL.7.1** Engage effectively in a range of collaborative discussions . . . **SL.7.1.d** Acknowledge new information . . . **RL.7.1** Cite several pieces of textual evidence . . . **RL.7.2** Determine a theme or central idea . . . **RL.7.3** Analyze how particular elements . . .	**L.7.4** Determine or clarify the meaning of unknown and multiple-meaning words and phrases . . . **L.7.4.b** Use common, grade-appropriate Greek or Latin affixes and roots . . . **L.7.4.c** Consult general and specialized reference materials . . . **L.7.2** Demonstrate command of the conventions . . .	**W.7.3** Write narratives . . . **W.7.3.b** Use narrative techniques . . . **W.7.3.d** Use precise words and phrases . . . **W.7.3.e** Provide a conclusion . . . **W.7.5** With some guidance and support from peers and adults . . .
STUDENT RESOURCES			
Available online in the Interactive Student Edition or Unit Resources	Selection Audio First-Read Guide: Fiction Close-Read Guide: Fiction	Word Network	Evidence Log
TEACHER RESOURCES			
Selection Resources Available online in the Interactive Teacher's Edition or Unit Resources	Audio Summaries: English and Spanish Annotation Highlights Accessible Leveled Text Spanish Translation Text Questions First Read Extension Questions Analyze Craft and Structure: Elements of a Short Story	Concept Vocabulary and Word Study Conventions: Punctuation Marks	Writing to Sources: Write Your Own Ending
Reteach/Practice (RP) Available online in the Interactive Teacher's Edition or Unit Resources	Analyze Craft and Structure: Elements of a Short Story (RP)	Word Study: Latin Root *-sequ-* (RP) Conventions: Punctuation Marks (RP)	Writing to Sources: Write Your Own Ending (RP)
Assessment Available online in Assessments	Selection Test: English Selection Test: Spanish Extension Selection Test		
My Resources	A Unit 4 Answer Key is available online and in the Interactive Teacher's Edition.		

Reading Support

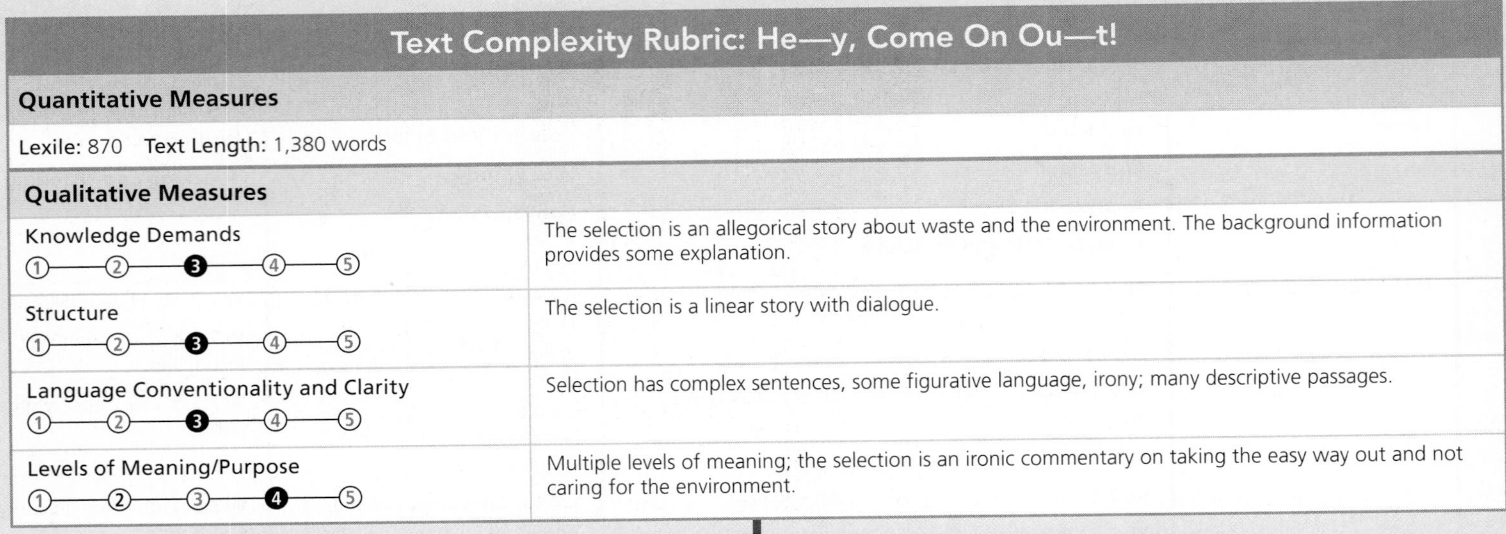

Text Complexity Rubric: He—y, Come On Ou—t!	
Quantitative Measures	
Lexile: 870 Text Length: 1,380 words	
Qualitative Measures	
Knowledge Demands (rating 3 of 5)	The selection is an allegorical story about waste and the environment. The background information provides some explanation.
Structure (rating 3 of 5)	The selection is a linear story with dialogue.
Language Conventionality and Clarity (rating 3 of 5)	Selection has complex sentences, some figurative language, irony; many descriptive passages.
Levels of Meaning/Purpose (rating 4 of 5)	Multiple levels of meaning; the selection is an ironic commentary on taking the easy way out and not caring for the environment.

DECIDE AND PLAN

English Language Support

Provide English Learners with support for Knowledge Demands and Language as they read the selection.

Knowledge Demands Before reading the text, have students summarize the background information. Making notes of what they already know will help them as they read the text.

Language Help students reword long and complex sentences. Using the language from the selection, suggest simpler sentences that convey the same meaning. Ask students to read the new sentences and discuss.

Strategic Support

Provide students with strategic support to ensure that they can successfully read the text.

Knowledge Demands Use the background information to discuss waste and the environment. Determine students' prior knowledge and experience with landfills. Provide additional background if needed.

Levels of Meaning and Purpose If students have difficulty understanding the multiple levels of meaning, focus on individual paragraphs. Ask students to first state the events that happen. Then ask them to reread the paragraph to determine what feelings or ideas are conveyed by the hole and the villagers' reactions to the hole.

Challenge

Provide students who need to be challenged with ideas for how they can go beyond a simple interpretation of the text.

Text Analysis Have students reread paragraphs 18–20 and discuss the role of the scientist in the story. Why can't he admit he doesn't have an answer for the hole? What is the result? What point might the author be making?

Written Response Challenge students to write an essay about what the hole symbolizes in the story. Have students use evidence from the text to support their ideas.

TEACH

Read and Respond

Have the groups read the selection and complete the Making Meaning, Language Development, and Effective Expression activities.

Standards Support Through Teaching and Learning Cycle

IDENTIFY NEEDS

Analyze results of the Beginning-of-Year Assessment, focusing on the items relating to Unit 4. Also take into consideration student performance to this point and your observations of where particular students struggle.

DECIDE AND PLAN

- If students have performed poorly on items matching these standards, then provide selection scaffolds before assigning them the on-level lesson provided in the Student Edition.
- If students have done well on the Beginning-of-Year Assessment, then challenge them to keep progressing and learning by giving them opportunities to practice the skills in depth.
- Use the Selection Resources listed on the Planning pages for "He—y, Come On Ou—t!" to help students continually improve their ability to master the standards.

Instructional Standards: He—y, Come On Ou—t!

	Catching Up	This Year	Looking Forward
Reading	You may wish to administer the **Analyze Craft and Structure: Elements of a Story (RP)** worksheet to help students understand the types of irony used in literature.	**RL.3** Analyze how particular elements of a story or drama interact.	Have students identify these types of irony in other works they are familiar with. Have them cite evidence to support what they find.
Writing	You may wish to administer the **Writing to Sources: Write Your Own Ending (RP)** worksheet to better prepare students to write their endings.	**W.3.e** Provide a conclusion that follows from and reflects on the narrated experiences or events.	Challenge students to write not just an ending, but an epilogue or a sequel to the story.
Language	Review the **Conventions: Punctuation Marks (RP)** worksheet to help students understand how authors use punctuation. Review the **Word Study: Latin Root *-sequ-* (RP)** worksheet to better familiarize students with words that have more than one meaning.	**L.2** Demonstrate command of the conventions of standard English capitalization, punctuation, and spelling when writing. **L.4** Determine or clarify the meaning of unknown and multiple-meaning words and phrases based on *grade 7 reading and content*, choosing flexibly from a range of strategies.	Challenge students to rewrite parts of the selection using different punctuation. Have them analyze how this changes the effect. Have students list words they believe have only one meaning, and then look them up to see if there are multiple meanings.

ANALYZE AND REVISE

- Analyze student work for evidence of student learning.
- Identify whether or not students have met the expectations in the standards.
- Identify implications for future instruction.

TEACH

Implement the planned lesson, and gather evidence of student learning.

FACILITATING

Jump Start

FIRST READ *What do we know about the destination of the stuff we put in our garbage cans? Can we really make the waste we create disappear?* Engage students in a discussion about our relationship with garbage that sets the context for reading the short story "He—y, Come On Ou—t!"

He—y, Come On Ou—t! 

Do we create too much waste? Is it possible to dispose of all waste without harming the environment? Modeling questions such as these will help students connect to "He—y, Come On Ou—t!" and to the Small-Group Performance Task assignment. Selection audio and print capability for the selection are available in the Interactive Teacher's Edition.

Concept Vocabulary

Have groups discuss the different types of context clues illustrated on the student page. For each word used in the examples (*throng, gawked, composure*), encourage groups to come up with a definition based on the clues provided. Ask group members if they can think of any other types of context clues. Possibilities include antonyms, cause and effect, and agent-object.

FIRST READ

As they read, students should perform the steps of the first read:

NOTICE: You may want to encourage students to notice the kinds of people who react to the hole as the story develops.

ANNOTATE: Remind students to mark contrasts, such as contrasts between old and new, that occur throughout the story.

CONNECT: Encourage students to connect specific portions of text with items they have read or heard about in the news, seen on TV or in movies, or experienced firsthand.

RESPOND: Students will answer questions and develop a storyboard to demonstrate understanding.

Point out to students that while they will always complete the Respond step at the end of the first read, the other steps will probably happen somewhat concurrently. You may wish to print copies of the **First-Read Guide: Fiction** for students to use.

MAKING MEANING

About the Author

Shinichi Hoshi (1926–1997), a Japanese writer, is best known for his "short-short stories," in which he makes observations about human nature and society. Hoshi wrote more than a thousand short-short stories, as well as longer fantasy stories, detective stories, biographies, and travel articles. In addition, he was one of the first Japanese science-fiction writers. Hoshi's stories have been translated into many languages, and devoted readers enjoy their unexpected plot turns.

He—y, Come On Ou—t!

Concept Vocabulary

As you perform your first read of "He—y, Come On Ou—t!" you will encounter these words.

disposal	consequences	resolved

Context Clues If these words are unfamiliar to you, try using **context clues**—or words and phrases that appear nearby in the text—to help you determine their meanings. There are various types of context clues that you may encounter as you read.

Synonyms: A **throng** gathered around the hole, so the village built a fence to keep the crowd from getting too close.

Restatement of an Idea: People traveled to the village to see the hole, and when they arrived, they were so impressed by its depth that they **gawked** at it.

Contrast of Ideas: The scientist was able to keep his **composure** despite the fact that he was scared of the deep hole.

Apply your knowledge of context clues and other vocabulary strategies to determine the meanings of unfamiliar words you encounter during your first read.

First Read FICTION

Apply these strategies as you conduct your first read. You will have an opportunity to complete a close read after your first read.

NOTICE *whom* the story is about, *what* happens, *where* and *when* it happens, and *why* those involved react as they do.

ANNOTATE by marking vocabulary and key passages you want to revisit.

First Read: NOTICE, ANNOTATE, CONNECT, RESPOND

CONNECT ideas within the selection to what you already know and what you have already read.

RESPOND by completing the Comprehension Check.

STANDARDS

Reading Literature
By the end of the year, read and comprehend literature, including stories, dramas, and poems, in the grades 6–8 text complexity band proficiently, with scaffolding as needed at the high end of the range.

Language
Determine or clarify the meaning of unknown and multiple-meaning words and phrases based on *grade 7 reading and content*, choosing flexibly from a range of strategies.
a. Use context as a clue to the meaning of a word or phrase.

FACILITATING SMALL-GROUP CLOSE READING

CLOSE READ: Narrative Check in with each group as they perform the close read, offering support as needed.

- Remind students that when they read a narrative, they should identify the main characters and the plot elements. Emphasize, however, that not all narratives neatly fit this pattern. Therefore, students should decide which elements *are* reflected in the story they are reading.
- If the group is confused about certain aspects of the story, suggest that they think about the culture represented in the story, or that of the author.
- Challenge groups to identify the narrative's theme and the specific details that reinforce it.

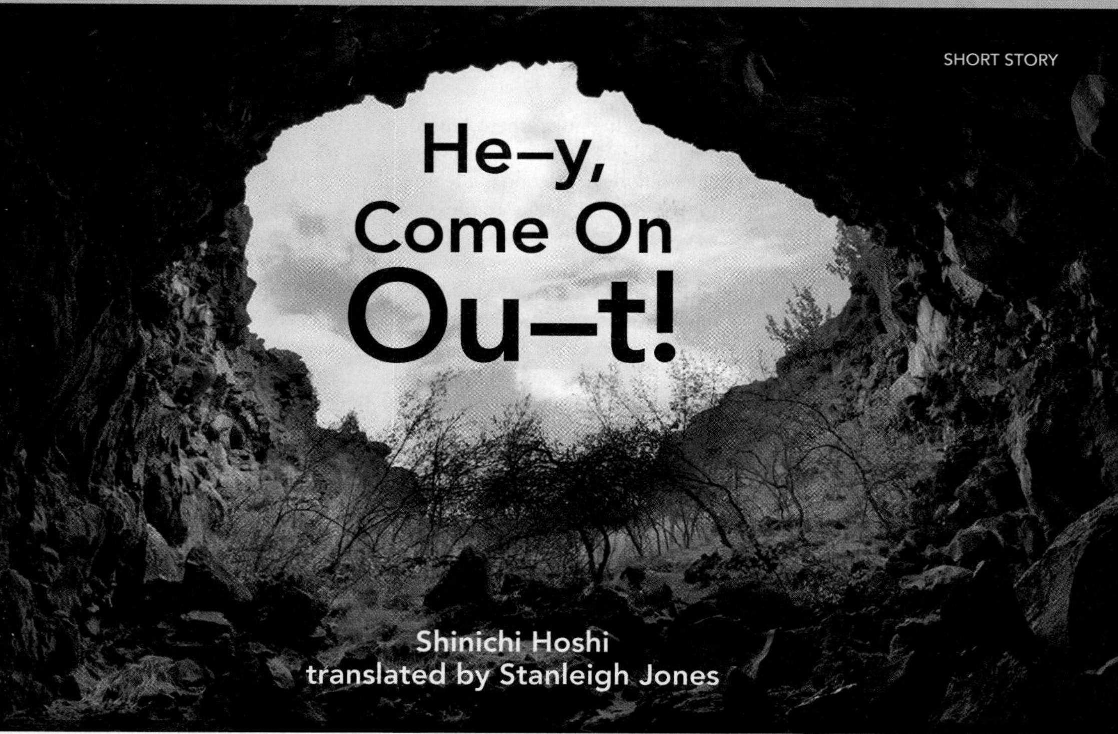

SHORT STORY

He–y, Come On Ou–t!

Shinichi Hoshi
translated by Stanleigh Jones

BACKGROUND
Each year, the world generates billions of tons of waste. Much of that waste is disposed of in landfills, where heavy metals and toxins can leak into the environment. The oceans have also been polluted with vast amounts of trash because, for many decades, it was common practice to get rid of chemicals, garbage, and even nuclear waste by dumping them directly into the ocean.

1 The typhoon had passed and the sky was a gorgeous blue. Even a certain village not far from the city had suffered damage. A little distance from the village and near the mountains, a small shrine had been swept away by a landslide.

2 "I wonder how long that shrine's been here."

3 "Well, in any case, it must have been here since an awfully long time ago."

4 "We've got to rebuild it right away."

5 While the villagers exchanged views, several more of their number came over.

6 "It sure was wrecked."

7 "I think it used to be right here."

8 "No, looks like it was a little more over there."

9 Just then one of them raised his voice. "Hey what in the world is this hole?"

NOTES

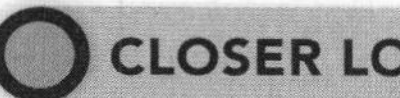

Analyze Setting

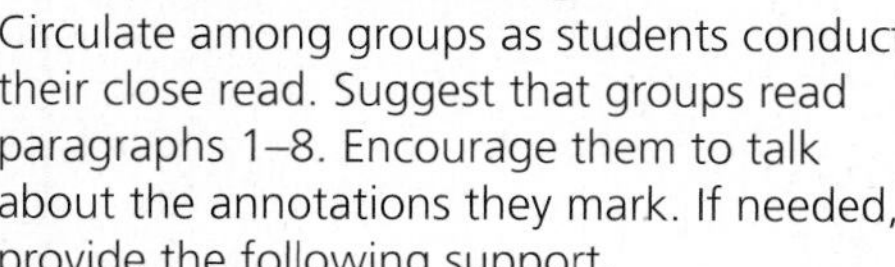

Circulate among groups as students conduct their close read. Suggest that groups read paragraphs 1–8. Encourage them to talk about the annotations they mark. If needed, provide the following support.

ANNOTATE: Have students mark details in paragraphs 1–8 that establish the setting, or work with small groups as you highlight them together.

QUESTION: Guide students to consider what these details might tell them. Ask what a reader can infer from these details about setting, and accept student responses.

Possible response: The story is set in a nameless village near a nameless city. Outside the village was a small shrine that was destroyed by a typhoon. No one is sure how old the shrine was or exactly where it lay.

CONCLUDE: Help students formulate conclusions about the importance of these details in the text. Ask students why the author might have included these details.

Possible response: The author is vague about the setting, as if it could be any rural village in Asia. The shrine suggests that villagers were once religious; but since they can't remember when it was built or where it stood, they seem less religious now.

Remind students that the **setting** is the time and place in which a story takes place. The setting of the village and shrine introduced in the first page of the story is so generic that they could represent any village and any religion—in fact, they could symbolize something else.

VOCABULARY DEVELOPMENT

Word Analysis To practice the vocabulary skill for this lesson, have students use context to define *typhoon* and *landslide* in paragraph 1. Remind students that one type of context clue is the cause-and-effect clue. Provide this sentence to model how cause and effect can reveal meaning: *Because the* undergrowth *between the forest trees was so thick, we used* machetes *to make a path through it.*

In this case, the *undergrowth* is the cause of using *machetes*, which in turn cut a path. Students can infer that *undergrowth* is low-growing vegetation between the taller trees of a forest, and that *machetes* are tools for cutting.

Have students analyze the causes and effects described in paragraph 1 to determine the meaning of *typhoon* and *landslide*. Then create a sentence showing how they are related by cause and effect. (Possible response: *Typhoon:* big storm; *landslide:* the downward flow of earth on a hill. "The heavy rains brought by the *typhoon* soaked the hillside, leading to a *landslide* that brought down trees and houses.")

NOTES

10 Where they had all gathered there was a hole about a meter in diameter. They peered in, but it was so dark nothing could be seen. However, it gave one the feeling that it was so deep it went clear through to the center of the earth.

11 There was even one person who said, "I wonder if it's a fox's hole."

12 "He—y, come on ou—t!" shouted a young man into the hole. There was no echo from the bottom. Next he picked up a pebble and was about to throw it in.

13 "You might bring down a curse on us. Lay off," warned an old man, but the younger one energetically threw the pebble in. As before, however, there was no answering response from the bottom. The villagers cut down some trees, tied them with rope and made a fence which they put around the hole. Then they repaired to the village.

14 "What do you suppose we ought to do?"

15 "Shouldn't we build the shrine up just as it was over the hole?"

16 A day passed with no agreement. The news traveled fast, and a car from the newspaper company rushed over. In no time a scientist came out, and with an all-knowing expression on his face he went over to the hole. Next, a bunch of gawking curiosity seekers showed up; one could also pick out here and there men of shifty glances who appeared to be concessionaires.[1] Concerned that someone might fall into the hole, a policeman from the local substation kept a careful watch.

17 One newspaper reporter tied a weight to the end of a long cord and lowered it into the hole. A long way down it went. The cord ran out, however, and he tried to pull it out, but it would not come back up. Two or three people helped out but when they all pulled too hard, the cord parted at the edge of the hole. Another reporter, a camera in hand, who had been watching all of this, quietly untied a stout rope that had been wound around his waist.

18 The scientist contacted people at his laboratory and had them bring out a high-powered bull horn, with which he was going to check out the echo from the hole's bottom. He tried switching through various sounds, but there was no echo. The scientist was puzzled, but he could not very well give up with everyone watching him so intently. He put the bull horn right up to the hole, turned it to its highest volume, and let it sound continuously for a long time. It was a noise that would have carried several dozen kilometers above ground. But the hole just calmly swallowed up the sound.

19 In his own mind the scientist was at a loss, but with a look of apparent composure he cut off the sound and, in a manner

1. **concessionaires** (kuhn sehsh uh NAIRZ) *n.* businesspersons.

PERSONALIZE FOR LEARNING

English Language Support

Cohesion Review paragraph 10 with students. English Learners may struggle with cohesive devices, which refer to some of the methods writers use to express their ideas smoothly and succinctly. These methods include the use of references (such as pronouns referring to things before or after them) or elliptical constructions (where certain words inside phrases or clauses are left out). For example, the first sentence in paragraph 10 provides an example of the elliptical type of cohesion: "Where they had all gathered there was a hole about a meter in diameter." The word *Where* substitutes for "The place where."

Challenge students to "translate" the following example from paragraph 16.

Concerned that someone might fall into the hole, a policeman from the local substation kept a careful watch.

Knowing the types of constructions that can cause confusion for English Language Learners, you can offer more targeted help when they have trouble comprehending specific sentences. **ALL LEVELS**

suggesting that the whole thing had a perfectly plausible explanation, said simply, "Fill it in."

20 Safer to get rid of something one didn't understand.

21 The onlookers, disappointed that this was all that was going to happen, prepared to disperse. Just then one of the concessionaires, having broken through the throng and come forward, made a proposal.

22 "Let me have that hole. I'll fill it in for you."

23 "We'd be grateful to you for filling it in," replied the mayor of the village, "but we can't very well give you the hole. We have to build a shrine there."

24 "If it's a shrine you want, I'll build you a fine one later. Shall I make it with an attached meeting hall?"

25 Before the mayor could answer, the people of the village all shouted out.

26 "Really? Well, in that case, we ought to have it closer to the village."

27 "It's just an old hole. We'll give it to you!"

28 So it was settled. And the mayor, of course, had no objection.

29 The concessionaire was true to his promise. It was small, but closer to the village he did build for them a shrine with an attached meeting hall.

30 About the time the autumn festival was held at the new shrine, the hole-filling company established by the concessionaire hung out its small shingle at a shack near the hole.

31 The concessionaire had his cohorts mount a loud campaign in the city. "We've got a fabulously deep hole! Scientists say it's at least five thousand meters deep! Perfect for the **disposal** of such things as waste from nuclear reactors."

32 Government authorities granted permission. Nuclear power plants fought for contracts. The people of the village were a bit worried about this, but they consented when it was explained that there would be absolutely no above-ground contamination[2] for several thousand years and that they would share in the profits. Into the bargain, very shortly a magnificent road was built from the city to the village.

33 Trucks rolled in over the road, transporting lead boxes. Above the hole the lids were opened, and the wastes from nuclear reactors tumbled away into the hole.

34 From the Foreign Ministry and the Defense Agency boxes of unnecessary classified documents were brought for disposal. Officials who came to supervise the disposal held discussions on golf. The lesser functionaries, as they threw in the papers, chatted about pinball.

NOTES

Use context clues or indicate another strategy you used that helped you determine meaning.

disposal (dihs POH zuhl) *n.*

MEANING:

2. **contamination** (kuhn tam uh NAY shuhn) *n.* pollution by poison or another dangerous substance.

DIGITAL PERSPECTIVES

Concept Vocabulary

DISPOSAL If groups are struggling to define the word *disposal* in paragraph 31, point out that the word has multiple meanings, so they should use context to determine the correct meaning here. Draw students' attention to the phrase *such things as waste from nuclear reactors*. Point out that this is an "example" context clue, because it gives an example of the types of things that require *disposal*.

Possible response: In this context, *disposal* means "getting rid of."

CROSS-CURRICULAR CONNECTIONS

Science In paragraph 31, the concessionaire declares the hole "perfect for the disposal of such things as waste from nuclear reactors." In fact, disposing of nuclear waste remains a challenge in nations that have nuclear reactors. Have students research the various methods that have been used for this purpose.

Offer these questions to guide their research and organize their findings.

- Why is nuclear waste treated differently from other chemical waste?
- What happened to the nuclear waste from the first nuclear fission experiments conducted by the United States?
- How is nuclear waste disposed of in the U.S. today?
- What problems has Japan had with nuclear waste in the 21st century?

Ask volunteers to share their research with the class.

Concept Vocabulary

CONSEQUENCES If groups are struggling to define the word *consequences* in paragraph 37, suggest that they focus on these context clues: *junk dealers* and *these problems*. Point out that these clues are "example" types of context clues; *junk dealers* and *these problems* both seem to be examples of the *consequences* of over-production. In other words, they are examples of the ______ of over-production.

Possible response: In this context, *consequences* means "results."

RESOLVED If groups struggle to define the word *resolved* in paragraph 37, point out that the word has multiple meanings, so they need to use context to determine the correct meaning here. Draw students' attention to these surrounding words: *it was thought, these problems,* and *eventually*. Ask students, *What do people tend to* think*—or hope—will* eventually *happen to* problems*?*

Possible response: In this context, *resolved* means "settled."

Additional **English Language Support** is available in the Interactive Teacher's Edition.

NOTES

Use context clues or indicate another strategy you used that helped you determine meaning.

consequences (KON suh kwehns ihz) *n.*

MEANING:

resolved (rih ZOLVD) *v.*

MEANING:

35 The hole showed no signs of filling up. It was awfully deep, thought some; or else it might be very spacious at the bottom. Little by little the hole-filling company expanded its business.

36 Bodies of animals used in contagious disease experiments at the universities were brought out and to these were added the unclaimed corpses of vagrants. Better than dumping all of its garbage in the ocean, went the thinking in the city, and plans were made for a long pipe to carry it to the hole.

37 The hole gave peace of mind to the dwellers of the city. They concentrated solely on producing one thing after another. Everyone disliked thinking about the eventual **consequences**. People wanted only to work for production companies and sales corporations; they had no interest in becoming junk dealers. But, it was thought, these problems too would gradually be **resolved** by the hole.

38 Young girls whose betrothals[3] had been arranged discarded old diaries in the hole. There were also those who were inaugurating new love affairs and threw into the hole old photographs of themselves taken with former sweethearts. The police felt comforted as they used the hole to get rid of accumulations of expertly done counterfeit bills. Criminals breathed easier after throwing material evidence into the hole.

39 Whatever one wished to discard, the hole accepted it all. The hole cleansed the city of its filth; the sea and sky seemed to have become a bit clearer than before.

40 Aiming at the heavens, new buildings went on being constructed one after another.

41 One day, atop the high steel frame of a new building under construction, a workman was taking a break. Above his head he heard a voice shout:

42 "He—y, come on ou—t!"

43 But, in the sky to which he lifted his gaze there was nothing at all. A clear blue sky merely spread over all. He thought it must be his imagination. Then, as he resumed his former position, from the direction where the voice had come, a small pebble skimmed by him and fell on past.

44 The man, however, was gazing in idle reverie[4] at the city's skyline growing ever more beautiful, and he failed to notice. ❧

3. **betrothals** (bih TRO<u>TH</u> uhlz) *n.* promises of marriage.
4. **idle reverie** (Y duhl REHV uh ree) daydreaming.

WriteNow Express and Reflect

Poem Have students reread paragraph 39. Ask volunteers to identify the personification used in this passage. ("The hole <u>accepted</u>; the hole <u>cleansed</u> the city. . . .") Ask students to write poems from the point of view of the hole. Have them work in their groups to generate ideas, imagining what else the hole might do, how it might it feel, what it knows of the world above, and so on.

Suggest they choose from following structures:

- Japanese haiku (17 syllables, in 3 lines of 5/7/5 syllables)
- Japanese tanka (31 syllables, in 5 lines of 5/7/5/7/7 syllables, respectively)
- A ballad
- A sonnet
- A free-verse poem
- A concrete poem, in which the words of the poem are arranged to form a shape.

The speaker in the poem should reflect an understanding of the hole as represented in "He—y, Come on Ou—t!" Have student volunteers share their poems with the class.

Comprehension Check

Complete the following items after you finish your first read. Review and clarify details with your group.

1. What does the young man shout into the hole at the beginning of the story?

2. Why do the villagers tell the young man not to throw the pebble into the hole?

3. How is the hole used?

4. What does the workman hear at the end of the story?

5. **Notebook** Confirm your understanding of the story by drawing a storyboard of key events.

RESEARCH

Research to Clarify Briefly research an unfamiliar detail in the story. For instance, you might want to learn more about sinkholes or the disposal of waste from nuclear power plants. How does the information you learned deepen your understanding of the story? Share your findings with your small group.

DIGITAL PERSPECTIVES

Comprehension Check

Possible responses:

1. He shouts, "He—y, come on ou—t!"
2. They are afraid it will bring a curse on them.
3. It is used to dispose of poisonous, toxic, and unwanted things: nuclear, experimental, and construction waste; counterfeit money; old love letters; incriminating evidence; the bodies of dead vagrants; and so on.
4. He hears a voice shout, "He—y, come on ou—t!" A pebble skims by him.
5. Storyboards should depict the key events of the story: Villagers examine site of shrine destroyed after a storm and find a deep hole; against advice of elders a boy shouts and throws a pebble down hole; news of deep hole spreads and people come to gawk and study it; concessionaire offers to buy it and then charges people to dispose of waste; hole becomes receptacle of every kind of waste imaginable as the nearby city explodes with development; worker hears a call from the sky as a pebble whizzes past.

Research

Research to Clarify If groups struggle to narrow their research topic, suggest they research an aspect of sinkholes, such as: What causes sinkholes to form? Are more sinkholes forming today than in the past? What are some consequences of sinkholes around human settlements?

PERSONALIZE FOR LEARNING

Challenge

Connecting Across Genres Have students study a Japanese genre that deals with concerns about the environment: Gojira movies (Gojira is known in the United States as Godzilla). Have students do online research, suggesting one of the following research prompts:

- Trace the references to radioactive waste and nuclear weapons in some of the early films.
- Show how changing attitudes about technology in Japanese culture have mirrored Godzilla's changing character.
- Explain why such films have been popular in Japan since the middle of the last century.

Ask volunteers to share their research with the class.

Jump Start

CLOSE READ Ask students to consider this prompt: *Your community can choose between great productivity with high levels of pollution or less productivity within a cleaner environment. Which would you choose, and why?*

Close Read the Text

If needed, model close reading by using the Annotation Highlights in the Interactive Teacher's Edition.

Remind students to use Accountable Talk in their discussions and to support one another as they complete the close read.

Analyze the Text

Possible responses:

1. The long list of items reinforces how much garbage the people have.
2. Passages will vary by group. Remind students to explain why they chose the passage they presented to group members.
3. Responses will vary by group.

Concept Vocabulary

Why These Words? Possible response: All three words relate to the outcome of a process. They help readers understand the effects of the characters' actions.

Practice

Possible response: One way to reduce the negative *consequences* of waste is to reduce its production. For example, some cities have *resolved* the problem of plastic-bag *disposal* by preventing stores from handing them out.

Word Network

Possible words: *village, mountains, trees, contamination, disposal*

Word Study

For more support, see **Concept Vocabulary and Word Study.**

Possible responses:

1. Responses will vary.
2. *sequel,* a story that follows an existing one. *subsequent:* following, later. *sequence:* an order or pattern.

MAKING MEANING

HE—Y, COME ON OU—T

TIP

GROUP DISCUSSION
As you complete the Analyze the Text section with your group, consider other members' responses. Did the responses of your classmates change your original ideas or thoughts on the story? Why or why not?

WORD NETWORK
Add interesting words related to people and the planet from the text to your Word Network.

STANDARDS

Speaking and Listening
• Engage effectively in a range of collaborative discussions with diverse partners on *grade 7 topics, texts, and issues,* building on others' ideas and expressing their own clearly.
d. Acknowledge new information expressed by others and, when warranted, modify their own views.

Language
Determine or clarify the meaning of unknown and multiple-meaning words and phrases based on *grade 7 reading and content,* choosing flexibly from a range of strategies.
b. Use common, grade-appropriate Greek or Latin affixes and roots as clues to the meaning of a word.
c. Consult general and specialized reference materials, both print and digital, to find the pronunciation of a word or determine or clarify its precise meaning or its part of speech.

Close Read the Text

With your group, revisit sections of the text you marked during your first read. **Annotate** what you notice. What **questions** do you have? What can you **conclude**?

Analyze the Text

CITE TEXTUAL EVIDENCE to support your answers.

Notebook Complete the activities.

1. **Review and Clarify** Review the short story with your group. Why do you think the author includes so many details about what people put into the hole? What effect do these details have on the reader?
2. **Present and Discuss** Now, work with your group to share the passages from the text that you found especially important. Take turns presenting your passages.
3. **Essential Question:** ***What effects do people have on the environment?*** What has this story taught you about the effects that people have on the environment? Discuss with your group.

LANGUAGE DEVELOPMENT

Concept Vocabulary

consequences resolved disposal

Why These Words? The concept vocabulary words from the text are related. With your group, determine what the words have in common. Write your ideas and add another word that fits the category.

Practice

Notebook Confirm your understanding of these words by using them to write a response to this question: *How should we dispose of the toxic and polluting byproducts of human activity?*

Word Study

Latin Root: *-sequ-* The Latin root *-sequ-* means "to follow." In the story, the author writes that people disliked thinking of the *consequences* of dumping things in the hole because people did not want to think of the things that might *follow* as a result of their actions.

1. Write your own sentence that correctly uses the word *consequences*.
2. Use a dictionary to find three other words that contain the root *-sequ-*. Write each word's definition in your own words and write an example sentence for each.

426 UNIT 4 • PEOPLE AND THE PLANET

FORMATIVE ASSESSMENT

Analyze the Text

If students struggle to close read the text, **then** provide the **He—y, Come On Ou—t!: Text Questions** available online in the Interactive Teacher's Edition or Unit Resources. Answers and DOK levels are also available.

Concept Vocabulary

If students fail to see the connection among the vocabulary words, **then** have them use the words to describe a cause and effect and think about where the words fit into the explanation.

Word Study

If students struggle to find words with the Latin root *-sequ-*, **then** have them use an online resource to find related words.

For Reteach and Practice, see **Word Study: Latin Root *-sequ-* (RP).**

Analyze Craft and Structure

Literary Elements: Irony **Irony** is a literary element that involves a contradiction or contrast of some kind. In literature, authors often use irony to entertain and to convey a **theme,** or message. There are several types of irony.

TYPE OF IRONY	DEFINITION	EXAMPLE	PURPOSE
DRAMATIC IRONY	a contrast between what the reader knows and what the character knows	an unaware character approaching a door that only the audience can see is actually a trap set by another character	to create excitement, suspense, or tragedy or to keep the readers' interest
SITUATIONAL IRONY	a contrast between what a reader or character expects and what actually happens	expecting a big, strong man to be the hero of a story and finding out that a young girl actually saves the day	to create humor or tragedy
VERBAL IRONY	a contrast between what a narrator or character says and what he or she means	a character saying "I love cleaning up other peoples' messes" when the character actually hates cleaning up after others	to create humor or build suspense

Depending on how an author chooses to use a certain type of irony, all types of irony can help the author to develop the theme of a story.

Practice

CITE TEXTUAL EVIDENCE to support your answers.

Notebook Work with your group to respond to these questions.

1. (a) What type of irony is used in the story? (b) What details in the story enabled you to identify this type of irony?
2. (a) What theme is conveyed through Hoshi's use of irony? (b) What details in the story enabled you to identify this theme?
3. (a) What does the irony tell you about the characters? (b) What details from the story support this inference?
4. What comment do you think the author may be making about the relationship between people and the environment?

STANDARDS

Reading Literature

- Cite several pieces of textual evidence to support analysis of what the text says explicitly as well as inferences drawn from the text.
- Determine a theme or central idea of a text and analyze its development over the course of the text; provide an objective summary of the text.
- Analyze how particular elements of a story or drama interact.

DIGITAL PERSPECTIVES  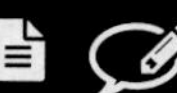

Analyze Craft and Structure

Analyze Elements of a Short Story While students have no trouble understanding verbal irony, situational irony can be more difficult to identify in a text. Sometimes readers confuse situational irony with coincidence. Explain that both coincidences and situational irony are jarring. Something is ironic when you expect a different outcome. In contrast, coincidence—such as the discovery of a shared experience or the chance occurrence of two events at the same time—is jarring because it can seem improbable, but its significance ends there. We often find situational irony in a twist at the end of a story. For more support, see **Analyze Craft and Structure: Elements of a Short Story.**

Practice

Possible responses:

1. (a) The story is an example of situational irony. (b) The villagers believe that the hole has a bottom, and they use it as a garbage collection site. They do not expect it to lead to another city.
2. (a) Hoshi's story develops the theme that people don't explore the consequences of their actions, and this ignorance can lead to bad outcomes. (b) Details include the fact that animals used in contagious disease experiments and the unclaimed corpses are thrown away without worry.
3. (a) The characters do not think about their actions. (b) Details include the fact that the people are always producing new things and throwing away old things.
4. The author may be saying that the people pay no attention to the environment.

FORMATIVE ASSESSMENT

Analyze Craft and Structure

If students have difficulty locating situational irony, **then** ask them what they expected to happen immediately before the ending of the story. Have them compare that with what actually occurred. For Reteach and Practice, see **Analyze Craft and Structure: Elements of a Short Story (RP).**

PERSONALIZE FOR LEARNING

English Language Support

Irony vs. Coincidence Many English Learners confuse the concepts of irony and coincidence. They may see anything unexpected as irony, when it may be simple coincidence. To make sure English Learners understand the difference, provide these examples, and encourage students to explain their responses.

1. *Two students meet for the first time in the cafeteria. After chatting for a while, they figure out that they have the same dentist.* Irony or coincidence? (Coincidence—two people unexpectedly discovered something in common.)
2. *The dentist, it turns out, has terrible teeth.* Irony or coincidence? (Irony—there is a strong expectation that dentists will have healthy teeth.)

When writers use irony, it is often to support the story's theme. Ask students to discuss the ending of the story. After the shock of it, it may seem fitting. In "He—y, Come on Ou—t!," it is ironic but also fitting that all the trash is coming back to the people who thought they were rid of it, even if that result was unexpected. **ALL LEVELS**

FACILITATING

Conventions

Punctuation Marks As you review the explanations and examples of the various types of punctuation with students, consider providing additional examples for clarification.

For more support, see **Conventions: Punctuation Marks.**

Read It

See possible responses in chart on student page.

Write It

Responses will vary. Student paragraphs should meet the following criteria:

- describe a place in nature
- use sensory details
- use at least three of the types of punctuation from the chart

FORMATIVE ASSESSMENT

Conventions

If students are unclear about choosing between a semicolon and a colon, **then** point out that a semicolon separates elements of equal importance, such as main clauses. A colon introduces elements of unequal importance. For Reteach and Practice, see **Conventions: Punctuation Marks (RP).**

LANGUAGE DEVELOPMENT

Conventions

Punctuation Marks Writers use **punctuation marks** to make their meaning clearer. Each punctuation mark serves a specific purpose, as shown in this chart.

PUNCTUATION/USAGE	EXAMPLE
A **colon (:)** introduces information that defines, explains, or provides a list of what came before the colon.	Huck likes to fetch various things: sticks, balls, toys, and old shoes.
A **semicolon (;)** joins related independent clauses to form compound sentences.	We hiked in the woods in the morning; in the afternoon, we swam in the lake.
A **hyphen (-)** joins two or more separate words into a single word.	Maria was the front-runner in the election.
A **dash (—)** sets off information that interrupts a thought.	I could hear music—what's the name of that song?—floating through the open window.
Brackets ([ ]) add clarifying information within a quotation.	Arjun said, "That was the year [2015] that we won the championship game."
Parentheses (( )) enclose extra information in a sentence without changing its meaning.	Can you explain that term to me (linear equations)?

Read It

Work with your group to identify examples of uses of punctuation marks in "He—y, Come On Ou—t!" Write your examples in the chart, identifying the punctuation marks.

EXAMPLE	PUNCTUATION MARK
The hole cleansed the city of its filth; the sea and sky seemed to have become a bit clearer than before. (paragraph 39)	semicolon
Above his head he heard a voice shout: "He—y, come on ou—t!" (paragraphs 41–42)	colon; dash
Little by little, the hole-filling company expanded its business. (paragraph 35)	hyphen

STANDARDS

Language
Demonstrate command of the conventions of standard English capitalization, punctuation, and spelling when writing.

Write It

Notebook Write a paragraph describing a place you go to enjoy nature. Your place might be a balcony, park, beach, or garden. Use specific sensory details to help readers see and feel the place you are describing. Practice using punctuation marks by including three of the punctuation marks you learned.

PERSONALIZE FOR LEARNING

English Language Support

Using Colons and Semicolons Have students write their opinion about the selection. Tell them to use colons and semicolons in their writing.

Ask students to write two or three sentences and then share them with a partner. **EMERGING**

Have students write a paragraph and then share it with the class. Ask students to point out where they used colons and semicolons and explain why they were used. **EXPANDING**

Ask students to write a speech expressing their opinion and then deliver the speech for the class. Ask students to point out where they used colons and semicolons and explain why they were used. **BRIDGING**

An expanded **English Language Support Lesson** on Punctuation is available in the Interactive Teacher's Edition.

EFFECTIVE EXPRESSION

Writing to Sources

You can often understand a situation better by thinking about what might happen next. The same thing is true of a fictional story. By imagining what happens after the story ends, you can deepen your understanding of the story itself.

Assignment

Use your imagination to write an **alternate ending** in which you explore what might happen after the story ends. Write at least three paragraphs that narrate what happens after the pebble skims past the man at the end of "He—y, Come On Ou—t!"

Discuss Purpose Based on what you know from the story, what do you think might happen next? In your group, decide the kind of ending you want to create. Do you want your ending to be funny, sad, ironic, or hopeful?

Brainstorm Consider several ideas for alternative endings. For each idea, list which characters will be involved and jot down what they say and do. Consider the effect the ending will have on the reader. Track ideas in a chart like this one.

IDEA	CHARACTERS	ACTIONS THAT HAPPEN	EFFECT

Capture the Action and Experiences To create a vivid engaging picture for your readers, use narrative techniques, descriptive details, and sensory language to capture the action and convey experiences and events. Consider the following strategies:

- **Develop Characters Through Dialogue:** Bring your characters to life by using dialogue—what the characters say to each other. Do not report everything a character says. Instead, create conversations that vividly show characters' feelings, gestures, and expressions as he or she reacts to events and experiences.
- **Develop Description Through Sensory Language:** When describing the setting, context, characters, and events, use sensory language to enhance your descriptions. Try to incorporate precise and colorful nouns, adjectives, verbs, and adverbs into your writing to engage readers.

Review and Revise After you have completed your alternate ending, each group member should review it individually, and note suggestions for revisions. Then, meet as a group to discuss members' suggestions, and come to a consensus, or agreement, on how to revise the first draft of your narrative.

EVIDENCE LOG

Before moving on to a new selection, go to your log and record what you learned from "He—y, Come On Ou—t!"

STANDARDS

Writing

Write narratives to develop real or imagined experiences or events using effective technique, relevant descriptive details, and well-structured event sequences.

b. Use narrative techniques, such as dialogue, pacing, and description, to develop experiences, events, and/or characters.

d. Use precise words and phrases, relevant descriptive details, and sensory language to capture the action and convey experiences and events.

e. Provide a conclusion that follows from and reflects on the narrated experiences or events.

- With some guidance and support from peers and adults, develop and strengthen writing as needed by planning, revising, editing, rewriting, or trying a new approach, focusing on how well purpose and audience have been addressed.

PERSONALIZE FOR LEARNING

Strategic Support

Collaborative Writing Once groups have settled on a genre, brainstormed ideas, and roughly outlined their endings, suggest that they tag-team the writing. Have one group member start off the agreed-upon plot, writing one or two sentences. Then have the next student pick up the writing from there, adding one or two more sentences, and so on.

When groups have finished drafting, have a group member read it aloud while the others read along, each making notes to request revisions or corrections. Finally, have group members create a final draft before presenting their endings to the class.

DIGITAL PERSPECTIVES

Writing to Sources

Discuss Purpose As they plan their ending, suggest that students work together to decide the mood they want their ending to convey.

Brainstorm Once students have identified the type of ending they will build, encourage them to spend time working out a plan for the story. Remind students to make sure that everyone in the group is participating.

Capture the Action and Experiences Encourage students to think about the tone they want to convey, whether one of panic, cooperation, surprise, or humor. Once they know this, students can gather details that will help to develop the tone they have selected.

Review and Review As students revise their new endings, remind them to work together to improve the text. Groups may assign each student a revision focus, such as transitions, descriptive language, or cohesion of plot.

For more support, see **Writing to Sources: Write Your Own Ending.**

Evidence Log Support students in completing their Evidence Log. This paced activity will help prepare them for the Performance-Based Assessment at the end of the unit.

FORMATIVE ASSESSMENT

Writing to Sources

If students are unable to write an ending that follows logically from the short story details, **then** have them map out the original story's plot using a plot diagram, and suggest that they think of the climax of the original story as just having begun when the story ends. For Reteach and Practice, see **Writing to Sources: Write Your Own Ending (RP).**

Selection Test

Administer the "He—y, Come on Ou—t!" Selection Test, which is available in both print and digital formats online in Assessments.

FACILITATING

Present an Argument

Assignment Before groups begin work on their projects, have them clearly differentiate the role each group member will play. Remind groups to consult the schedule for Small-Group Learning to guide their work during the Performance Task.

Students should complete the assignment using presentation software to take advantage of text, graphics, and sound features.

Plan With Your Group

Analyze the Text Remind students that they will need to include evidence from the selections in their arguments. As they fill in the chart, groups should note page and paragraph numbers of sentences and details they might want to refer to or include in their presentations. Taking the time to record this information as they plan will save them time when they begin to gather evidence.

Gather Evidence and Media Examples Discuss with students how they can use media examples to support their arguments. Remind students to consider using media to address counterclaims. For instance, if students are arguing that people have a negative impact on the environment, they should also address the point that some conservationists have worked hard to help the environment. Students may be able to locate images or video to develop this counterclaim.

PERFORMANCE TASK: SPEAKING AND LISTENING FOCUS

SOURCES

- TURTLE WATCHERS
- "NATURE" IS WHAT WE SEE—
- THE SPARROW
- EAGLE TRACKING AT FOLLENSBY POND
- HE—Y, COME ON OU—T!

Present an Argument

Assignment

You have read different perspectives on the relationship between human beings and the natural environment. With your group, develop and deliver a **multimedia presentation** in which you respond to the following question:

Do people always have a negative impact on the environment?

Plan With Your Group

Analyze the Texts With your group, review the selections you have read in Small-Group Learning. What message does each selection send about the relationship between people and nature? Consider changes in the environment and ways people's actions contribute to the changes. Discuss as a group, and write your ideas in the chart. Then, come to a consensus, or agreement, on the claim you will make in your presentation.

SELECTION	What does the selection suggest about people's impact on the environment?
Turtle Watchers "Nature" is what We see— The Sparrow	
Eagle Tracking at Follensby Pond	
He—y, Come On Ou—t!	

Gather Evidence and Media Examples Determine which group members will work to identify examples from the texts that support your claim, and which members will work on gathering multimedia. Then, brainstorm ideas for your multimedia presentation. Identify photos, illustrations, audio, and video that illustrate the examples you will use to support your claim.

STANDARDS

Speaking and Listening

- Engage effectively in a range of collaborative discussions with diverse partners on *grade 7 topics, texts, and issues,* building on others' ideas and expressing their own clearly.
  - a. Come to discussions prepared, having read or researched material under study; explicitly draw on that preparation by referring to evidence on the topic, text, or issue to probe and reflect on ideas under discussion.
  - b. Follow rules for collegial discussions, track progress toward specific goals and deadlines, and define individual roles as needed.
- Analyze the main ideas and supporting details presented in diverse media and formats and explain how the ideas clarify a topic, text, or issue under study.

AUTHOR'S PERSPECTIVE **Ernest Morrell, Ph.D.**

Active Classroom Listening Teachers can help students participate in class more effectively by discussing how to ask critical questions in classroom conversations. Teachers can guide students to determine which questions are most important and will yield good answers by modeling questions that synthesizing multiple viewpoints and tap critical thinking skills. Here are some samples to use:

- What are the implications of…?
- What is the difference between …and …?
- What is the counterargument for …?
- What are the strengths and weaknesses of…?
- What is another way to look at…?

Remind students to avoid yes/no questions because they cut off discussion. Teachers can also teach students to use *critical listening*—weighing what has been said to decide if they agree with it or not. Critical listening can help students identify the salient parts of each question and integrate these parts to formulate an idea or an opinion.

Organize Your Presentation Decide the order of your multimedia presentation and the role each group member will play. Choose your words carefully to make your claim clear. Select multimedia that best illustrate your ideas and will make the most impact on your audience. Then, write a script for your presentation that details what each speaker will say to audience during the presentation. Your script is where you can add important details, and explain the relationship between your multimedia and the point that it highlights.

MULTIMEDIA PRESENTATION SCRIPT		
	Slide	Script
Speaker 1		
Speaker 2		
Speaker 3		

Rehearse With Your Group

Practice With Your Group As you run through rehearsals, use this checklist to evaluate the effectiveness of your multimedia presentation.

CONTENT	USE OF MEDIA	PRESENTATION TECHNIQUES
☐ The presentation includes a clearly stated claim. ☐ The evidence from the texts supports the claim. ☐ The presentation is logically organized.	☐ Multimedia elements support and elaborate on the claim. ☐ Multimedia elements add to and strengthen the presentation.	☐ Transitions between speakers' sections are smooth. ☐ Each speaker speaks clearly.

Fine-Tune the Content To strengthen your multimedia presentation, review each speaker's section to make sure it clearly expresses and supports the group's claim about whether or not people always negatively impact the environment.

Improve Your Use of Media Review all multimedia in your presentation. Make sure each piece adds something interesting to the presentation and contributes toward your overall claim.

Present and Evaluate

When you present as a group, be sure that each member has taken into account each of the checklist items. As you watch other groups, evaluate how well their presentations meet the checklist requirements.

STANDARDS

Speaking and Listening

- Delineate a speaker's argument and specific claims, evaluating the soundness of the reasoning and the relevance and sufficiency of the evidence.
- Present claims and findings, emphasizing salient points in a focused, coherent manner with pertinent descriptions, facts, details, and examples; use appropriate eye contact, adequate volume, and clear pronunciation.
- Include multimedia components and visual displays in presentations to clarify claims and findings and emphasize salient points.
- Adapt speech to a variety of contexts and tasks, demonstrating command of formal English when indicated or appropriate.

DIGITAL PERSPECTIVES

Organize Your Ideas Discuss with students some strategies for organizing an argument. For instance, students might consider organizing ideas according to the selections. That is, after their introduction, they could present all their evidence and media related to one selection, and then all the evidence and media related to the next selection, and so on. Alternatively, students might choose a cause-effect, comparison-contrast, or problem-solution organizational structure.

Practice With Your Group Suggest that students practice using any multimedia equipment they will need to use in the presentation. They should make sure they know how to use the equipment and that it is working correctly.

Improve Your Use of Media Remind students that any media they include should directly clarify and support their ideas. In addition, media should be suited to purpose and audience. For instance, students should avoid music that conveys the wrong tone for their presentation.

Present and Evaluate

Before beginning the presentations, set the expectations for the audience. You may wish to have students consider these questions as groups present.

- What was the presenting group's claim?
- What was some of their supporting evidence?
- Which multimedia best supported the claim?
- What presentation skills did this group excel at?

As students provide feedback to the presenting group, remind them that compliments are just as valuable as constructive criticism.

PERSONALIZE FOR LEARNING

Strategic Support

Checklist Provide students with multiple copies of the practice checklist. Students can use these checklists to evaluate their own and others' presentations. Students with dysgraphia will especially benefit from using a checklist like this one when evaluating presentations. Some students may benefit from focusing on one column during their evaluations, and varying the column over the course of several presentations.

OVERVIEW

INDEPENDENT LEARNING

What effects do people have on the environment?

Encourage students to think carefully about what they have already learned and what more they want to know about the unit topic of people and the planet. This is a key first step to previewing and selecting the text or media they will read or review in Independent Learning.

Independent Learning Strategies

Review the Learning Strategies with students and explain that as they work through Independent Learning they will develop strategies to work on their own.

- Have students watch the video on Independent Learning Strategies.
- A video on this topic is available online in the Professional Development Center.

Students should include any favorite strategies that they might have devised on their own during Whole-Class and Small-Group Learning. For example, for the strategy "Create a schedule" students might include:

- Anticipate other responsibilities.
- Leave extra time for problems or unexpected issues.

Block Scheduling

Each day in this Pacing Plan represents a 40–50 minute class period. Teachers using block scheduling may combine days to reflect their class schedule. In addition, teachers may revise pacing to differentiate and support core instruction by integrating components and resources as students require.

OVERVIEW: INDEPENDENT LEARNING

ESSENTIAL QUESTION:

What effects do people have on the environment?

Our natural environment has an impact on everybody and everything on the planet. In this section, you will complete your study of people and the planet by exploring an additional selection related to the topic. You'll then share what you learn with classmates. To choose a text, follow these steps.

Look Back Think about the selections you have already studied. What more do you want to know about the environment?

Look Ahead Preview the texts by reading the descriptions. Which one seems most interesting and appealing to you?

Look Inside Take a few minutes to scan through the text you chose. Choose a different one if this text doesn't meet your needs.

Independent Learning Strategies

Throughout your life, in school, in your community, and in your career, you will need to rely on yourself to learn and work on your own. Review these strategies and the actions you can take to practice them during Independent Learning. Add ideas of your own for each category.

STRATEGY	ACTION PLAN
Create a schedule	• Understand your goals and deadlines. • Make a plan for what to do each day. •
Practice what you have learned	• Use first-read and close-read strategies to deepen your understanding. • After you read, evaluate the usefulness of the evidence to help you understand the topic. • Consider the quality and reliability of the source. •
Take notes	• Record important ideas and information. • Review your notes before preparing to share with a group. •

Pacing Plan

Unit Introduction: 1, 2
Introduce Whole-Class Learning: 3
from Silent Spring: 4, 5
Nobel Speech: 6, 7, 8, 9, 10
Media: Nobel Speech: 11, 12, 13, 14, 15
Performance Task: 16, 17, 18

Choose one selection. Selections are available online only.

CONTENTS

NOVEL EXCERPT

from My Side of the Mountain
Jean Craighead George

Can you imagine living in a tree?

MYTH

How Grandmother Spider Stole the Sun
Michael J. Caduto and Joseph Bruchac

A Native American myth explains the origin of the sun.

EXPOSITORY NONFICTION

The Story of Victor d'Aveyron, the Wild Child
Eloise Montalban

Does Victor hold the key to defining what is human?

ESSAY

from Of Wolves and Men
Barry Lopez

How do our imagination and humanity influence our ideas about the nature of animals?

PERFORMANCE-BASED ASSESSMENT PREP

Review Evidence for an Argument

Complete your Evidence Log for the unit by evaluating what you've learned and synthesizing the information you have recorded.

Contents

Selections Encourage students to scan and preview the selections before choosing the one they would like to read or review. Suggest that they consider the genre and subject matter of each one before making their decision. You can use the information on the following Planning pages to advise students in making their choice.

Remind students that the selections for Independent Learning are only available in the Interactive Student Edition. Allow students who do not have digital access at home to preview the selections or review the media selection(s) using classroom or computer lab technology. Then either have students print the selection they choose or provide a printout for them.

Performance Based-Assessment Prep

Review Evidence for an Argument Point out to students that collecting evidence during Independent Learning is the last step in completing their Evidence Log. After they finish their independent reading, they will synthesize all the evidence they have compiled in the unit.

The evidence students collect will serve as the primary source of information they will use to complete the writing and oral presentation for the Performance-Based Assessment at the end of the unit.

Introduce Small-Group Learning

Turtle Watchers • "Nature" is what We see— • The Sparrow

Media: Eagle Tracking at Follensby Pond

He—y, Come On Ou—t!

Performance Task

Introduce Independent Learning

Independent Learning

Performance-Based Assessment

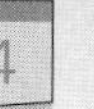
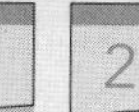
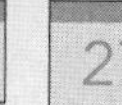

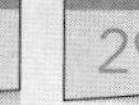

19 20 21 22 23 24 25 26 27 28 29 30 31 32 33 34 35 36

INDEPENDENT LEARNING

from My Side of the Mountain

Summary

"The Old, Old Tree" is an excerpt from the novel *My Side of the Mountain* by Jean Craighead George. The narrator looks at a large old tree, and thinks about how to make it into a home. He realizes that part of it is rotten, and hollows it out. He is exhausted and hungry, but manages to take care of himself and find some edible plants. Later, he sees a crow sneaking around. He follows it back to its nest to collect eggs. He makes a fire to cook his food, and then figures out more ways to make his life easier, using fire and water.

Insight

This selection illustrates how familiarity with nature can help keep someone alive. It also shows someone taking food directly from nature as a way to live.

SELECTION RESOURCES

- First-Read Guide: Fiction
- Close-Read Guide: Fiction
- *from* My Side of the Mountain: Text Questions
- Audio Summaries
- Selection Audio
- Selection Test

Connection to Essential Question

This text shows a direct relationship between the narrator and nature, and provides an angle on the Essential Question, "What effects do people have on the environment?" The young man relies on nature and his knowledge of it to help him plan to survive in the woods.

Connection to Performance-Based Assessment

The prompt is "Is it too late to fix the damage that has been done to our environment?" Students may decide that this text shows a safe relationship between the narrator and his environment. He is working on living off the land, and without significant tools or machines, his use or abuse of nature is very limited.

Text Complexity Rubric: *from* My Side of the Mountain

Quantitative Measures	
Lexile: 820 **Text Length:** 1,487 words	
Qualitative Measures	
Knowledge Demands ① ② **❸** ④ ⑤	Students may not have direct experience with the narrator's challenges of survival in the wilderness, but the concepts are explained clearly.
Structure ① **❷** ③ ④ ⑤	The first-person narrative is told in a straightforward, linear way; conversational language and dialogue make it easy to follow.
Language Conventionality and Clarity ① ② **❸** ④ ⑤	The selection contains figurative language. Syntax and vocabulary are on-level.
Levels of Meaning/Purpose ① ② **❸** ④ ⑤	The selection has only one level of meaning. The main concept and supporting ideas are clearly stated.

DIGITAL PERSPECTIVES 

Audio | Video | Document | Annotation Highlights | EL Highlights | Online Assessment

SELECTION RESOURCES

- First-Read Guide: Fiction
- Close-Read Guide: Fiction
- How Grandmother Spider Stole the Sun: Text Questions
- Audio Summaries
- Selection Audio
- Selection Test

How Grandmother Spider Stole the Sun

Summary

Michael J. Kaduto and Joseph Bruchac have retold this Muskogee myth, "How Grandmother Spider Stole the Sun." At first, there was no light on one side of the world. Life was dark and difficult for the animals until one of them told the others about the Sun. He had heard about the Sun on the other side of the world. The animals decided to steal part of the Sun to bring home. The first animals who tried were burned and their injuries changed they way they looked forever. Finally, Grandmother Spider and the Buzzard found a way to bring the Sun to the sky.

Insight

This story is partly about the interdependence of nature, and partly about the importance of animals that humans usually don't like. The spider and the buzzard, not the most photogenic of animals, play key roles in bringing light to everyone else. This is analogous to their important roles in the ecosystem.

Connection to Essential Question

The Essential Question is "What effects do people have on the environment?" This creation myth explains parts of the world as the Muskogee Indians knew it. The animals play a role in changing nature for the benefit of animals and people. Some of the animals were hurt by their interference.

Connection to Performance-Based Assessment

As a creation myth, the story tells about the beginning of the relationship between man and nature. The prompt is "Is it too late to fix the damage that has been done to our environment?" In this story, touching the Sun forever changes the animals that touch it, and this may set up the power that nature has over other living things.

Text Complexity Rubric: How Grandmother Spider Stole the Sun

Quantitative Measures	
Lexile: 850 **Text Length:** 665 words	
Qualitative Measures	
Knowledge Demands (1 **2** 3 4 5)	The selection is a fantastical Native American origin myth.
Structure (1 **2** 3 4 5)	The selection is a simple, linear story.
Language Conventionality and Clarity (1 **2** 3 4 5)	The selection contains simple sentence structure and vocabulary.
Levels of Meaning/Purpose (1 2 **3** 4 5)	The myth explains how Earth was created and how various animals earned their characteristics.

The Story of Victor d'Aveyron, the Wild Child

Summary

"The Story of Victor d'Aveyron, the Wild Child" is a piece of expository nonfiction that reports on a child who grew up in the wilderness in France around 200 years ago. When he was discovered, he was about twelve years old, could not speak, and seemed to have been living in the woods for a long time. Scientists were eager to study him, especially so they could understand whether he could learn to speak, because many thought that language and empathy were traits that only humans had. Ultimately, Victor did learn to understand and read a few words, but never could speak.

Insight

This selection covers an unusual case that probes the boundaries between human and animal, wild and civilized.

SELECTION RESOURCES

- First-Read Guide: Nonfiction
- Close-Read Guide: Nonfiction
- The Story of Victor d'Aveyron, the Wild Child: Text Questions
- Audio Summaries
- Selection Audio
- Selection Test

Connection to Essential Question

This text looks at the Essential Question from a different angle. The Essential Question is "What effects do people have on the environment?" The text asks students what effects the environment—and a lack of human interaction—might have on a person.

Connection to Performance-Based Assessment

The prompt is "Is it too late to fix the damage that has been done to our environment?" Researchers have found "developmental windows" or critical periods of development. Without human interaction, this wild child might have lost opportunities for growth. Students might consider whether nature might be the same way, whether opportunities for new growth are being irretrievably lost.

Text Complexity Rubric: The Story of Victor d'Aveyron, the Wild Child	
Quantitative Measures	
Lexile: 980 **Text Length:** 733 words	
Qualitative Measures	
Knowledge Demands ① ❷ ③ ④ ⑤	The situation of a boy raised in the wild and later studied by scientists may be unfamiliar to readers, but the situation is clearly explained.
Structure ① ❷ ③ ④ ⑤	The selection is structured in a straightforward, logical way.
Language Conventionality and Clarity ① ❷ ③ ④ ⑤	The selection contains simple sentence structure and on-level vocabulary.
Levels of Meaning/Purpose ① ② ❸ ④ ⑤	The selection raises some questions about why the boy was alone in the woods.

DIGITAL PERSPECTIVES

Audio | Video | Document | Annotation Highlights | EL Highlights | Online Assessment

from Of Wolves and Men

Summary

In this excerpt from *Of Wolves and Men*, Barry Lopez writes from the Alaskan woods. He provides his perspective on what little is known about wolves. He begins by telling the story of the wolves in Alaska who ate dogs during the very cold winter. Different groups offered different explanations for why the wolves began eating dogs that winter. Wolves provoke strong emotions, especially when we find them dangerous. We know little about wolves, and Lopez says that some claims that most people think are true are not. Wolves show a lot of variety, like people do, and we do not fully understand them. In the end, he says, it is difficult to pin down the truth.

Insight

This selection emphasizes the mismatch between imagination and reality. But it does not seek to replace a set of myths with new facts; it simply emphasizes what we do not know. Even a part of nature as heavily studied as wolves are can remain mysterious.

SELECTION RESOURCES

- First-Read Guide: Nonfiction
- Close-Read Guide: Nonfiction
- *from* Of Wolves and Men: Text Questions
- Audio Summaries
- Selection Audio
- Selection Test

Connection to Essential Question

The Essential Question is "What effects do people have on the environment?" In this essay, Lopez shows how animals can use human civilization as a source of food and how people fight back against such animals.

Connection to Performance-Based Assessment

This essay includes an interesting perspective on the prompt "Is it too late to fix the damage that has been done to our environment?" This selection portrays nature as mysterious and resilient. It makes only passing reference to the ease with which people have killed large numbers of wolves. Lopez's essay suggests that people and wolves can live together, but that humans do not fully understand nature.

Text Complexity Rubric: *from* Of Wolves and Men	
Quantitative Measures	
Lexile: 1010 **Text Length:** 1,578 words	
Qualitative Measures	
Knowledge Demands (1 **2** 3 4 5) — 2	The topic of wolf behavior and the study of wolves may be unfamiliar to students.
Structure (1 2 **3** 4 5) — 3	Information in the selection is logically organized, but connections between ideas are not always completely explicit or in a predictable sequence.
Language Conventionality and Clarity (1 2 **3** 4 5) — 3	The selection contains some above-level vocabulary and complex sentences. Language is sometimes used for figurative power.
Levels of Meaning/Purpose (1 2 3 **4** 5) — 4	The main idea is clear, but some of the supporting concepts are complicated. The writing suggests that human knowledge of wolves is limited and may be based on what people want to believe.

MY NOTES

MY NOTES

ADVISING

You may wish to direct students to use the generic **First-Read** and **Close-Read Guides** in the Print Student Edition. Alternatively, you may wish to print copies of the genre-specific **First-Read** and **Close-Read Guides** for students. These are available online in the Interactive Student Edition or Unit Resources.

FIRST READ

Students should perform the steps of the first read independently.

NOTICE: Students should focus on the basic elements of the text to ensure they understand what is happening.

ANNOTATE: Students should mark any passages they wish to revisit during their close read.

CONNECT: Students should increase their understanding by connecting what they've read to other texts or personal experiences.

RESPOND: Students will write a summary to demonstrate their understanding.

Point out to students that while they will always complete the Respond step at the end of the first read, the other steps will probably happen somewhat concurrently. Remind students that they will revisit their first-read annotations during the close read. You may wish to print copies of the First-Read Guide for students to use.

After students have completed the First-Read Guide, you may wish to assign the Text Questions for the selection that are available in the Interactive Teacher's Edition.

Anchor Standards

In the first two sections of the unit, students worked with the whole class and in small groups to gain topical knowledge and greater understanding of the skills required by the anchor standards. In this section, they are asked to work independently, applying what they have learned and demonstrating increased readiness for college and career.

INDEPENDENT LEARNING

First-Read Guide

Tool Kit
First-Read Guide and Model Annotation

Use this page to record your first-read ideas.

Selection Title: ____________________________________

NOTICE new information or ideas you learn about the unit topic as you first read this text.

ANNOTATE by marking vocabulary and key passages you want to revisit.

First Read

CONNECT ideas within the selection to other knowledge and the selections you have read.

RESPOND by writing a brief summary of the selection.

STANDARD
Reading Read and comprehend complex literary and informational texts independently and proficiently.

434 UNIT 4 • PEOPLE AND THE PLANET

PERSONALIZE FOR LEARNING

Strategic Support

Writing a Summary Students may struggle with writing a summary for the Respond section of the First-Read Guide. Discuss the components of a successful summary, and have students create a checklist to help them review and revise their First-Read Guide entry.

- Explain that a summary should be short and should identify the title and author of a selection.
- For a nonfiction text, students should remember to include important details and facts that help them with the main idea. For a fiction text, remind students to focus on plot, characters, setting, and the problem or conflict in the selection.
- Students should use their own words to summarize a selection. If they include exact words from the text, those words should be enclosed in quotation marks.

Close-Read Guide

Use this page to record your first-read ideas.

Tool Kit
Close-Read Guide and Model Annotation

Selection Title: ____________________

Close Read the Text

Revisit sections of the text you marked during your first read. Read these sections closely and **annotate** what you notice. Ask yourself **questions** about the text. What can you **conclude**? Write down your ideas.

Analyze the Text

Think about the author's choices of patterns, structure, techniques, and ideas included in the text. Select one and record your thoughts about what this choice conveys.

QuickWrite

Pick a paragraph from the text that grabbed your interest. Explain the power of this passage.

STANDARD
Reading Read and comprehend complex literary and informational texts independently and proficiently.

CLOSE READ

Students should begin their close read by revisiting the annotations they made during their first read. Then students should analyze one of the author's choices regarding the following elements:

- **patterns,** such as repetition or parallelism
- **structure,** such as cause-and-effect or problem-solution
- **techniques,** such as description or dialogue
- **ideas,** such as the author's main idea or claim

MAKE IT INTERACTIVE
Group students according to the selection they have chosen. Then have students meet to discuss the selection in depth. Their discussions should be guided by their insights and questions.

PERSONALIZE FOR LEARNING

Strategic Support
QuickWrite To scaffold support for the QuickWrite, help students organize and develop their ideas about a specific paragraph in the text. Have them read aloud to a partner the paragraph they chose, summarize the main idea and supporting details, and point out specific examples in the writing that captured their interest. Students may point to specific vocabulary, direct quotations, dialogue, descriptions, imagery, or visuals and/or captions related to the paragraph they chose. Students should also talk with their partner about something more they would like to know. For example, they might have questions about the main idea or details in the paragraph, or they might want to know more about how the writer decided to craft the paragraph.

ADVISING

Share Your Independent Learning

Prepare to Share

Explain to students that sharing what they learned from their Independent Learning selection provides classmates who read a different selection with an opportunity to consider the text as a source of evidence during the Performance-Based Assessment. As students prepare to share, remind them to highlight how their selection contributed to their knowledge of the concept of people and the planet as well as how the selection connects to the question *What effects do people have on the environment?*

Learn From Your Classmates

As students discuss the Independent Learning selections, direct them to take particular note of how their classmates' chosen selections align with their current position on the Performance-Based Assessment question.

Reflect

Students may want to add their reflection to their Evidence Log, particularly if their insight relates to a specific selection from the unit.

MAKE IT INTERACTIVE

Have the class take part in a friendly, impromptu debate. Divide the class into two teams and assign one of the following positions to each team.

- People have mainly negative impacts on the environment.
- People have mainly positive impacts on the environment.

Give teams time to prepare. Then have members of each team alternate, giving short arguments for their team's position.

Evidence Log Support students in completing their Evidence Log. This paced activity will help prepare them for the Performance-Based Assessment at the end of the unit.

INDEPENDENT LEARNING

EVIDENCE LOG

Go to your Evidence Log and record what you learned from the text you read.

Share Your Independent Learning

Prepare to Share

What effects do people have on the environment?

Even when you read something independently, your understanding continues to grow when you share what you've learned with others. Reflect on the text you explored independently and write notes about its connection to the unit. In your notes, consider why this text belongs in this unit.

Learn From Your Classmates

Discuss It Share your ideas about the text you explored on your own. As you talk with your classmates, jot down ideas that you learn from them.

Reflect

Mark the most important insight you gained from these writing and discussion activities. Explain how this idea adds to your understanding of the topic of our environment.

STANDARDS

Speaking and Listening
Engage effectively in a range of collaborative discussions with diverse partners on *grade 7 topics, texts, and issues,* building on others' ideas and expressing their own clearly.

AUTHOR'S PERSPECTIVE **Ernest Morrell, Ph.D.**

Self-facing Notes Some students may not believe that they need to take notes because they'll remember what the teacher and their classmates said. However, taking notes can provide more than a memory jog. To reinforce the importance of taking good notes, teachers should remind students that they will need notes to learn effectively from their peers. In addition, self-facing notes may help students in discussion because these notes will help them prepare the key points they want to share. Point out that the Share Your Independent Learning activity will help students in these ways:

- **Provide Feedback:** Making self-facing notes will help students give classmates useful comments about their independent reading, which will result in deeper learning.
- **Share Key Ideas:** Model how to jot down information that is essential to understanding. Focus on identifying the main ideas and critical details. Students can use these notes to help them make valuable discussion contributions.
- **Expand on Others' Ideas:** Explain to students that effective notes help them cut to the heart of the matter and so provide a scaffolding for what others may have noticed in the reading.

PERFORMANCE-BASED ASSESSMENT PREP

Review Evidence for an Argument

At the beginning of this unit, you took a position on the following question:

Are the needs of people ever more important than the needs of animals and the planet? Explain your position.

EVIDENCE LOG

Review your Evidence Log and your QuickWrite from the beginning of the unit. Has your position changed?

☐ YES	☐ NO
Identify at least three pieces of evidence that convinced you to change your mind.	Identify at least three pieces of evidence that reinforced your initial position.
1.	1.
2.	2.
3.	3.

State your position: ______

Identify a possible counterclaim: ______

Evaluate the Strength of Your Evidence

Do you have enough evidence to support your argument? Do you have enough evidence to refute a counterclaim? If not, make a plan.

☐ Do more research. ☐ Talk with my classmates.

☐ Reread a selection. ☐ Ask an expert.

☐ Other: ______

STANDARDS

Writing

Write arguments to support claims with clear reasons and relevant evidence.

a. Introduce claim(s), acknowledge alternate or opposing claims, and organize the reasons and evidence logically.

b. Support claim(s) with logical reasoning and relevant evidence, using accurate, credible sources and demonstrating an understanding of the topic or text.

DIGITAL PERSPECTIVES

Review Evidence for an Argument

Evidence Log Students should understand that their position on an issue could evolve as they learn more about the subject and are exposed to additional points of view. Point out that just because they took an initial position on the question *Is it too late to fix the damage that has been done to our environment?* doesn't mean that their position can't change after careful consideration of their learning and evidence.

Evaluate the Strength of Your Evidence

Remind students that they can use different types of evidence to support their argument, including:

- facts
- statistics
- quotations from reliable authorities
- examples
- details

Students should also evaluate the reliability of their evidence. Discuss the characteristics of reliable, or credible evidence:

- reliable sources, including government, educational, and professional organizations
- experts and scientists
- confirmation provided by other sources

Writing to Sources: Argument

Students should complete the Performance-Based Assessment independently, with little to no input or feedback during the process. Students should use word processing software to take advantage of editing tools and features.

Prior to beginning the assessment, ask students to think about what they already know about the role of human actions in creating environmental damage—like habitat loss or climate change—and what more they would like to know about slowing or reversing the process.

Review the Elements of Effective Argument Students can review the work they did earlier in the unit as they complete the Performance-Based Assessment. They may also consult other resources such as:

- the elements of an effective argument, including a clear statement of the claim, persuasive evidence and logical reasoning that support the claim, and a clear organizational structure, available in Whole-Class Learning
- their Evidence Log
- their Word Network

Although students will use evidence from unit selections for their argument, they may need to collect additional evidence, including facts, statistics, anecdotes, quotations from authorities, or examples.

SOURCES

- WHOLE-CLASS SELECTIONS
- SMALL-GROUP SELECTIONS
- INDEPENDENT-LEARNING SELECTION

PART 1

Writing to Sources: Argument

In this unit, you read about the effect that people have on the environment. You read selections, both fiction and nonfiction, that express different perspectives on the relationship between people and the environment.

Write an Argument

Write an **argument** in which you state and defend a claim in response to the following question:

Are the needs of people ever more important than the needs of animals and the planet?

State your claim with accuracy and support it with logical reasoning and specific, relevant evidence from the selections in this unit. Organize your ideas effectively, and use transitions to create cohesion and show the relationships between your claim, reasons, and evidence. Provide a conclusion that supports your argument and offers new insight into the topic. Remember to maintain a formal style and tone in your writing.

WORD NETWORK

As you write and revise your argument, use your Word Network to help vary your word choices.

Reread the Assignment Review the assignment to be sure you fully understand it. The assignment may reference some of the academic vocabulary words presented at the beginning of the unit. Be sure you understand each of these words in order to complete the assignment correctly.

ethical	dissent	interject
discord	accuracy	

Review the Elements of Effective Argument Before you begin writing, review the Argument Rubric. Once you have completed your first draft, check it against the rubric. If one or more of the elements is missing or not as strong as it could be, revise your essay to add or strengthen that component.

STANDARDS

Writing

- Write arguments to support claims with clear reasons and relevant evidence.
- Produce clear and coherent writing in which the development, organization, and style are appropriate to task, purpose, and audience.
- Write routinely over extended time frames and shorter time frames for a range of discipline-specific tasks, purposes, and audiences.

Argument Rubric

	Focus and Organization	Evidence and Elaboration	Language Conventions
4	The introduction is engaging and states the claim in a persuasive way. The claim is supported by logical reasons and relevant evidence, and opposing claims are addressed. Reasons and evidence are logically organized so that the argument is easy to follow. Transitions clearly show the relationships between the claim, reasons, and evidence. The conclusion supports the argument and offers a new insight into the topic.	Details, examples, and quotations from the selections are specific and relevant. The style and tone of the argument are formal and objective. Words are carefully chosen and suited to purpose and audience.	The argument intentionally follows standard English conventions of usage and mechanics.
3	The introduction is somewhat engaging and states the claim clearly. The claim is supported by reasons and evidence, and opposing claims are acknowledged. Reasons and evidence are organized so that the argument is easy to follow. Transitions show the relationships between the claim, reasons, and evidence. The conclusion supports the argument.	Details, examples, and quotations from the selections are relevant. The style and tone of the argument are mostly formal and objective. Words are generally suited to purpose and audience.	The argument demonstrates accuracy in standard English conventions of usage and mechanics.
2	The introduction states the claim. The claim is supported by some reasons and evidence, and opposing claims may be briefly acknowledged. Reasons and evidence are vaguely organized with a few transitions to orient readers. The conclusion relates to the argument.	Some details and examples from the selections are relevant. The style and tone of the argument are occasionally formal and objective. Words are somewhat suited to purpose and audience.	The argument demonstrates some accuracy in standard English conventions of usage and mechanics.
1	The claim is not clearly stated. The claim is not supported by reasons and evidence, and opposing claims are not acknowledged. Reasons and evidence are disorganized and the argument is difficult to follow. The conclusion does not include relevant information.	There is little or no relevant support. The style and tone are informal. Words are not appropriate to purpose or audience.	The argument contains mistakes in standard English conventions of usage and mechanics.

DIGITAL PERSPECTIVES

Argument Rubric

As you review the Argument Rubric with students, remind them that the rubric is a resource that can guide their revisions. Students should pay particular attention to the differences between an argument that contains all of the required elements (a score of 3) and one that is comprehensive, engaging, and progresses in a logical and thoughtful manner (a score of 4).

PERSONALIZE FOR LEARNING

English Language Support

Syntax If students are having difficulty organizing their argument, have them break their argument down into simple sentences. Remind them that even the simplest sentence has a subject and a verb, but that is all it needs. Once they've expressed their ideas in the simplest sentences they can write, encourage them to join these sentences together in ways that help make their arguments clearer and more effective. Point out that when making an argument, complex sentences joined with words like "because" or "although" can actually be clearer than a pair of simple sentences. **ALL LEVELS**

ASSESSING

Speaking and Listening: Oral Presentation

Students should annotate their written argument in preparation for the oral presentation, marking the important elements (claim, reasons, evidence, and counterclaims) as well as critical anecdotes or facts.

Remind students that the effectiveness of an oral argument relies on how the speaker establishes credibility with his or her audience. If a speaker comes across as confident and authoritative, it will be easier for the audience to give credence to the speaker's claim.

Review the Oral Presentation Rubric As you review the Oral Presentation Rubric with students, remind them that it is a valuable tool that can help them plan their presentation. They should strive to include all of the criteria required to achieve a score of 3. Draw their attention to some of the subtle differences between scores of 2 and 3.

PERFORMANCE-BASED ASSESSMENT

PART 2

Speaking and Listening: Oral Presentation

Assignment

After completing the final draft of your argument, use it as the foundation for a three- to five-minute **oral presentation.**

STANDARDS

Speaking and Listening

- Present claims and findings, emphasizing salient points in a focused, coherent manner with pertinent descriptions, facts, details, and examples; use appropriate eye contact, adequate volume, and clear pronunciation.
- Include multimedia components and visual displays in presentations to clarify claims and findings and emphasize salient points.
- Adapt speech to a variety of contexts and tasks, demonstrating command of formal English when indicated or appropriate.

Do not simply read your argument aloud. Take these steps to make your presentation engaging.

- Review your argument, and mark reasons and evidence that best support your claim.
- Choose multimedia components to add interest to your presentation.
- Deliver your argument with confidence, and remember to use a formal tone.

Review the Rubric Before you deliver your presentation, rehearse it with a peer and check your plans against this rubric.

	Content	Organization	Presentation Techniques
3	The introduction is engaging and establishes the claim in a persuasive way. The presentation includes strong, valid reasons and evidence to support the claim and answers counterclaims. The conclusion supports the argument and offers fresh insight into the topic.	The speaker uses time effectively, spending the right amount on each part. Ideas progress logically, with clear transitions among ideas. The sequence of the multimedia matches the timing of the speaker.	The speaker maintains eye contact and speaks clearly. The speaker presents the argument with confidence and uses a formal tone.
2	The introduction establishes a claim. The presentation includes valid reasons and evidence to support the claim. The conclusion supports the argument.	The speaker uses time effectively, spending the right amount of time on most parts. Ideas progress logically with some transitions among ideas. The sequence of multimedia sometimes matches the timing of the speaker.	The speaker sometimes maintains eye contact and speaks somewhat clearly. The speaker uses a formal tone when presenting the argument.
1	The introduction does not state a claim. The presentation does not include reasons or evidence to support the claim. The conclusion does not relate to the argument presented.	The speaker does not use time effectively and focuses too much time on some parts. Ideas do not progress logically. Listeners have trouble following the argument. The sequence of multimedia does not match the timing of the speaker.	The speaker does not maintain eye contact or speak clearly. The speaker uses an informal tone and presents the argument in a way that lacks confidence.

DIGITAL PERSPECTIVES

Preparing for the Assignment To help students understand what an effective oral presentation of an argument looks and sounds like, find online examples of students or adults presenting arguments. Project the examples for the class, and have students note the techniques that make each speaker successful (that is gesture, pacing, tone, and so on). Suggest that students record themselves presenting their arguments so they can practice incorporating some of the elements in the examples you showed them.

Reflect on the Unit

Now that you've completed the unit, take a few moments to reflect on your learning.

Reflect on the Unit Goals

Review the goals at the beginning of the unit. Use a different colored pen to rate yourself again. Think about readings and activities that contributed the most to the growth of your understanding. Record your thoughts.

Reflect on the Learning Strategies

Discuss It Write a reflection on whether you were able to improve your learning based on your Action Plans. Think about what worked, what didn't, and what you might do to keep working on these strategies. Record your ideas before a class discussion.

Reflect on the Text

Choose a selection that you found challenging and explain what made it difficult.

Explain something that surprised you about a text in the unit.

Which activity taught you the most about the environment? What did you learn?

DIGITAL PERSPECTIVES

Reflect on the Unit

- Have students watch the video on Reflecting on Your Learning.
- A video on this topic is available online in the Professional Development Center.

Reflect on the Unit Goals

Students should reevaluate how well they met the unit goals now that they have completed the unit. You might ask them to provide a written commentary on the goal they made the most progress with as well as the goal they feel warrants continued focus.

Reflect on the Learning Strategies

Discuss It If you want to make this a digital activity, go online and navigate to the Discussion Board. Alternatively, students can share their learning strategies reflections in a class discussion.

Reflect on the Text

Consider having students share their text reflections with one another.

MAKE IT INTERACTIVE

Have students prepare one slide using presentation software that summarizes their reflection.

Collate student slides into a presentation that can be viewed by the class. Students should be prepared to give a 30-second oral summary for their slide.

Unit Test and Remediation 

After students have completed the Performance-Based Assessment, administer the Unit Test. Based on students' performance on the test, assign the resources as indicated on the Interpretation Guide to remediate. Students who take the test online will be automatically assigned remediation, as warranted by test results.

UNIT 5 AT A GLANCE

	Contents		Pacing / # of Days	Genre / Lexile	Vocabulary / Word Study
INTRO	**Unit Introduction**		2*		Academic Vocabulary (L.7.6)
	Launch Text: Against the Odds			Informative Text 800L	
WHOLE-CLASS LEARNING	**Whole-Class Learning Introduction**		3		
	The Dust Bowl CriticalPast	COMPARE		Media: Video NP	Media Vocabulary (L.7.6)
	***from* The Grapes of Wrath** John Steinbeck	COMPARE	4	Novel Excerpt 600L	Concept Vocabulary Word Study: Old English Suffix *-less* (L.7.4)
	The Circuit HOOK&INSPIRE Francisco Jiménez		6	Short Story 730L	Concept Vocabulary Word Study: Old English Suffix: *-ly* (L.7.4)
	Performance Task **Writing**		3		
SMALL-GROUP LEARNING	**Small-Group Learning Introduction**		5		
	A Work in Progress Aimee Mullins			Personal Narrative 930L	Concept Vocabulary (L.7.4.a) Word Study: Latin Prefix *extra-* (L.7.4.b)
	***from* The Story of My Life** Helen Keller	COMPARE	2	Autobiography Excerpt 970L	Concept Vocabulary (L.7.4.a) Word Study: Greek Root *-myst-* (L.7.4.b)
	How Helen Keller Learned to Talk Helen Keller, with Anne Sullivan	COMPARE	2	Media: Interview NP	Media Vocabulary (L.7.6)
	A Young Tinkerer Builds a Windmill, Electrifying a Nation Sarah Childress		3	News Article 1020L	Concept Vocabulary (L.7.4.a) Word Study: Etymology (L.7.4, b)
	Performance Task Speaking and Listening		2		
INDEPENDENT LEARNING	**Independent Learning Introduction**		2		Independent Learning provides students with the opportunity to analyze a selection independently. To facilitate students' independence, no skills have been assigned.
	The Girl Who Fell from the Sky Juliane Koepcke			Personal Narrative 790L	
	Four Skinny Trees ***from* The House on Mango Street** Sandra Cisneros			Novel Excerpt 690L	
	Rikki-tikki-tavi Rudyard Kipling			Short Story 1010L	
	***from* Facing the Lion: Growing Up Maasai on the African Savanna** Joseph Lemasolai Lekuton			Memoir 800L	
END OF UNIT	Performance-Based Assessment Writing		2		
	Unit Reflection				
	Unit Test		1		

* Pacing is suggested for a 40- to 50-minute class period. If you use block scheduling, you may combine days to meet your schedule needs.

Analyze Craft and Structure	Conventions / Author's Style	Composition / Research / Speaking and Listening
		Summary (RI.7.2)
Theme (RL.7.2; RL.7.3)	Author's Style: Description (L.7.6)	Writing to Compare: Argumentative Essay (RL.7.9; W.7.1, a–c; W.7.9, a)
Theme (RL.7.1; RL.7.2)	Conventions: Commas (L.7.2, a)	Writing to Sources: Explanation (RL.7.2; W.7.2, b; W.7.9, a) Speaking and Listening: Role-Play Interview (SL.7.1, a, c; SL.7.4; W.7.7)
		Write an Informative Essay (W.7.2, a–f; W.7.10; L.7.2, a–b)
Word Choice and Humor (RI.7.3; RI.7.4; RI.7.6)	Conventions: Informal Grammar (L.7.1; L.7.2)	Speaking and Listening: Group Discussion (SL.7.1, a–c)
Autobiographical Writing (RI.7.6)	Conventions: Types of Dependent Clauses (L.7.1.c)	Writing to Compare: Multimedia Presentation (RI.7.7; W.7.2, a–b; W.7.9.b; SL.7.1.b; SL.7.2; SL.7.5)
Biographical Writing (RI.7.1; RI.7.3; RI.7.5)	Conventions: Capitalization (L.7.2)	Writing to Sources: How-to-Essay (W.7.2.a; W.7.2.b; W.7.7; W.7.8)
		Present Multimedia Profiles (W.7.2; W.7.9; SL.1, a; SL.7.4; SL.7.5)
Independent Learning provides students with the opportunity to analyze a selection independently. To facilitate students' independence, no skills have been assigned.		Share Your Independent Learning (SL.7.1)
		Writing to Sources: Informative Essay (W.7.2, a–b; W.7.4; W.7.9; W.7.10) Speaking and Listening: Oral Presentation (W.7.6; SL.7.4; SL.7.5)
		Reflect on the Unit

INTRODUCTION

Jump Start

Ask students whether they have ever encountered an obstacle that stood in the way of something that they wanted to do. Were they able to overcome the obstacle? How?

Facing Adversity

Ask students what the phrase *facing adversity* suggests to them. Point out that as they work through this unit, they will read many examples about people who have faced adversity and overcome obstacles.

Video

Project the introduction video in class or ask students to open the video in their interactive textbooks.

Discuss It If you want to make this a digital activity, go online and navigate to the Discussion Board. Alternatively, students can share their responses in a class discussion.

Block Scheduling

Each day in this pacing calendar represents a 40–50 minute class period. Teachers using block scheduling may combine days to reflect their class schedule. In addition, teachers may revise pacing to differentiate and support core instruction by integrating components and resources as students require.

UNIT 5

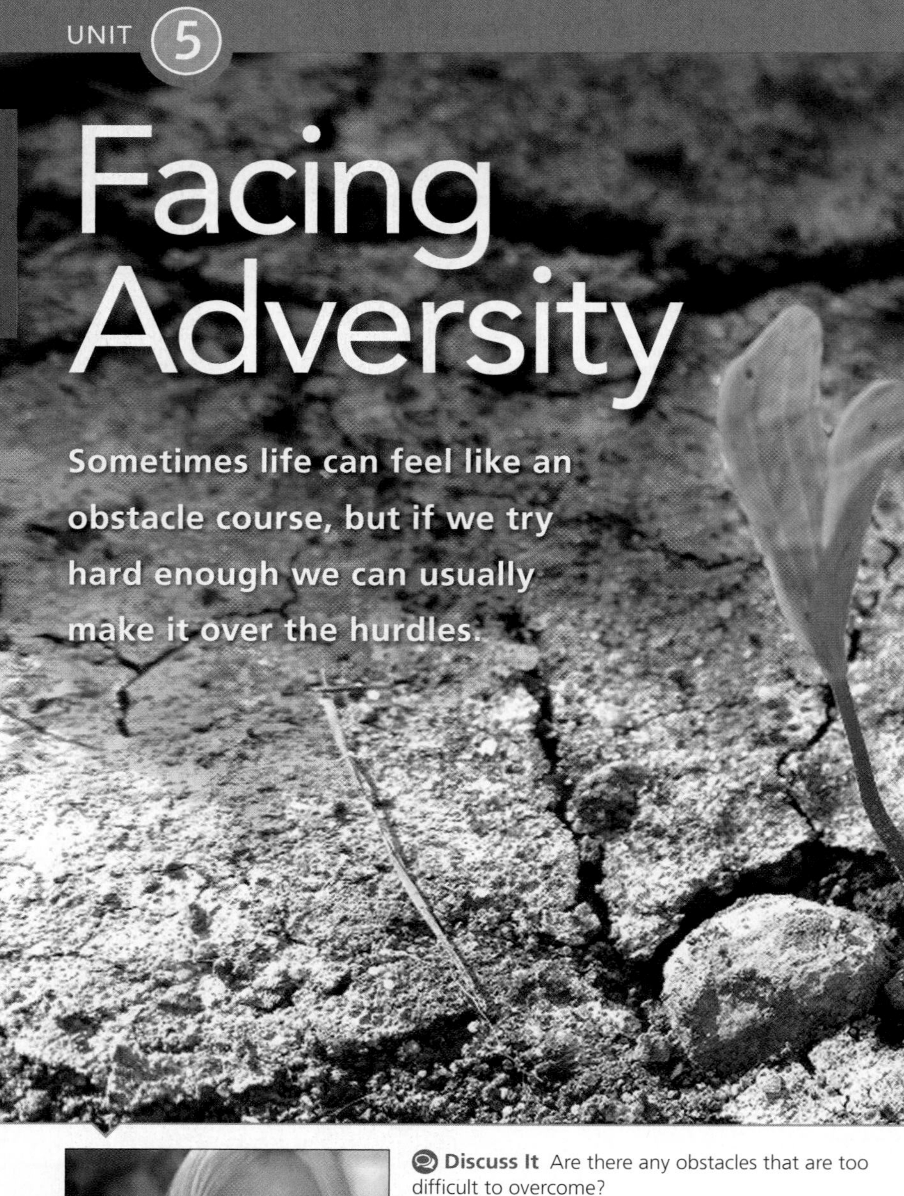

Facing Adversity

Sometimes life can feel like an obstacle course, but if we try hard enough we can usually make it over the hurdles.

Exclusive: Bethany Hamilton

Discuss It Are there any obstacles that are too difficult to overcome?

Write your response before sharing your ideas.

442

Pacing Plan

Days	Activity
1–2	Unit Introduction
3	Introduce Whole-Class Learning
4–5	Media: The Dust Bowl
6–9	*from* The Grapes of Wrath
10–15	The Circuit
16–18	Performance Task

DIGITAL PERSPECTIVES

 Audio  Video 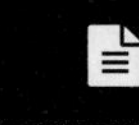 Document | Annotation Highlights | EL Highlights 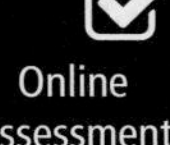 Online Assessment

UNIT 5

UNIT INTRODUCTION

ESSENTIAL QUESTION:

How do we overcome obstacles?

LAUNCH TEXT INFORMATIVE MODEL
Against the Odds

WHOLE-CLASS LEARNING	SMALL-GROUP LEARNING	INDEPENDENT LEARNING
MEDIA: VIDEO The Dust Bowl *CriticalPast*	PERSONAL NARRATIVE A Work in Progress *Aimee Mullins*	PERSONAL NARRATIVE The Girl Who Fell from the Sky *Juliane Koepcke*
ANCHOR TEXT: NOVEL EXCERPT *from* The Grapes of Wrath *John Steinbeck*	AUTOBIOGRAPHY EXCERPT *from* The Story of My Life *Helen Keller*	NOVEL EXCERPT Four Skinny Trees *from* The House on Mango Street *Sandra Cisneros*
ANCHOR TEXT: SHORT STORY The Circuit *Francisco Jiménez*	MEDIA: INTERVIEW How Helen Keller Learned to Talk *Helen Keller, with Anne Sullivan*	SHORT STORY Rikki-tikki-tavi *Rudyard Kipling*
	NEWS ARTICLE A Young Tinkerer Builds a Windmill, Electrifying a Nation *Sarah Childress*	MEMOIR *from* Facing the Lion: Growing Up Maasai on the African Savanna *Joseph Lemasolai Lekuton*
PERFORMANCE TASK WRITING FOCUS: Write an Informative Essay	PERFORMANCE TASK SPEAKING AND LISTENING FOCUS: Present Multimedia Profiles	PERFORMANCE-BASED ASSESSMENT PREP Review Evidence for an Informative Essay

(COMPARE: The Dust Bowl / The Grapes of Wrath; COMPARE: The Story of My Life / How Helen Keller Learned to Talk)

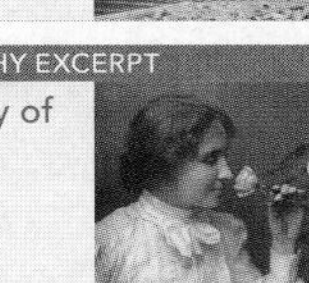

PERFORMANCE-BASED ASSESSMENT

Informative Text: Essay and Oral Presentation

PROMPT:

How can people overcome adversity in the face of overwhelming obstacles?

443

How do we overcome obstacles?

Introduce the Essential Question and point out that students will respond to related prompts.

- **Whole-Class Learning** How did the characters cope with the obstacles they faced?
- **Small-Group Learning** How do people face challenges in order to overcome adversity?
- **Performance-Based Assessment** How can people overcome adversity in the face of overwhelming obstacles?

Using Trade Books

Refer to the Teaching with Trade Books section in this book or online in *my*Perspectives+ for suggestions on how to incorporate the following thematically-related titles into this unit:

- *Letters From Rifka* by Karen Hesse
- *No Promises in the Wind* by Irene Hunt
- *The Clay Marble* by Minfong Ho

Current Perspectives

To increase student engagement, search online for stories about facing adversity and overcoming obstacles, and invite your students to recommend stories they find. Always preview content before sharing it with your class.

- **News Story: USC considers ways to get blind football player into a game (AP, 9/23/15)** An article by Dan Greenspan about Jake Olson, a blind football player for USC, and his coach's efforts to get him into a game
- **Video: The 'inspirational' teen singer with Down's syndrome (BBC, 2/4/15)** A video of Amy Purdy, three-time Paralympic champion sharing her experiences in facing adversity

Introduce Small-Group Learning

A Work in Progress

from The Story of My Life

Media: How Helen Keller Learned to Talk

A Young Tinkerer Builds a Windmill, Electrifying a Nation

Performance Task

Introduce Independent Learning

Independent Learning

Performance-Based Assessment

19 20 21 22 23 24 25 26 27 28 29 30 31 32 33 34 35 36

About the Unit Goals

These unit goals were backward designed from the Performance-Based Assessment at the end of the unit and the Whole-Class and Small-Group Performance Tasks. Students will practice and become proficient in many more standards over the course of this unit.

Unit Goals

Review the goals with students and explain that as they read and discuss the selections in this unit, they will improve their skills in reading, writing, research, language, and speaking and listening.

Reading Goals Tell students they will read and analyze informative texts. They will also read a novel excerpt, news articles, and short stories to better understand the ways writers express ideas.

Writing and Research Goals Tell students that they will learn the elements of writing an informative text. They will also write their own informative text. Students will write for a number of reasons, including organizing and sharing ideas, reflecting on experiences, and gathering evidence. They will conduct research to clarify and explore ideas.

Language Goal Tell students that they will develop a deeper understanding of using coordinate adjectives. They will then practice using coordinate adjectives here in their own writing.

Speaking and Listening Goals Explain to students that they will work together to build on one another's ideas, develop consensus, and communicate with one another. They will also learn to incorporate audio, visuals, and text in presentations.

HOME Connection

A Home Connection letter to students' parents or guardians is available in *my*Perspectives+. The letter explains what students will be learning in this unit and how they will be assessed.

Unit Goals

Throughout this unit you will deepen your perspective about facing adversity by reading, writing, speaking, listening, and presenting. These goals will help you succeed on the Unit Performance-Based Assessment.

Rate how well you meet these goals right now. You will revisit your ratings later when you reflect on your growth during this unit.

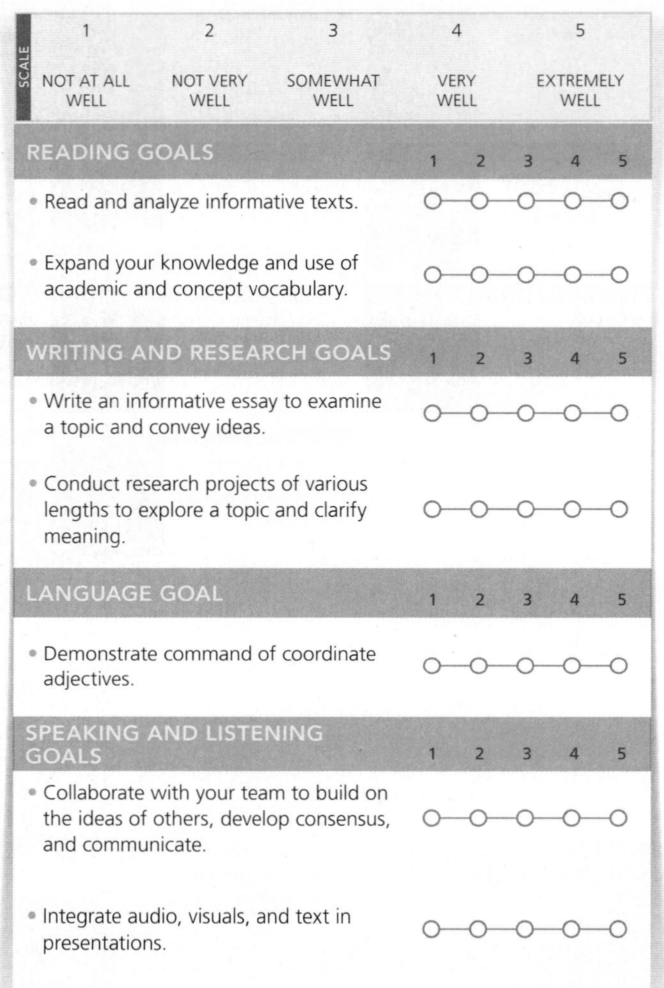

SCALE	1	2	3	4	5
	NOT AT ALL WELL	NOT VERY WELL	SOMEWHAT WELL	VERY WELL	EXTREMELY WELL

READING GOALS	1	2	3	4	5
• Read and analyze informative texts.	O	O	O	O	O
• Expand your knowledge and use of academic and concept vocabulary.	O	O	O	O	O

WRITING AND RESEARCH GOALS	1	2	3	4	5
• Write an informative essay to examine a topic and convey ideas.	O	O	O	O	O
• Conduct research projects of various lengths to explore a topic and clarify meaning.	O	O	O	O	O

LANGUAGE GOAL	1	2	3	4	5
• Demonstrate command of coordinate adjectives.	O	O	O	O	O

SPEAKING AND LISTENING GOALS	1	2	3	4	5
• Collaborate with your team to build on the ideas of others, develop consensus, and communicate.	O	O	O	O	O
• Integrate audio, visuals, and text in presentations.	O	O	O	O	O

STANDARDS

Language

Acquire and use accurately grade appropriate general academic and domain-specific words and phrases; gather vocabulary knowledge when considering a word or phrase important to comprehension or expression.

AUTHOR'S PERSPECTIVE Ernest Morrell, Ph.D.

How to Support Kids When They Have Trouble When setting goals with students, have them consider these questions:

1. What are the opportunities open to me if I achieve this goal?
2. What are the biggest challenges that I will face in attempting to achieve this goal?
3. What support will I need from others in order to achieve this goal and how will I ensure that I get that support?

The first question helps students see that setting goals helps them take control of their life and focus on the issues that matter to them. As a result, they are likely to make good decisions. The second question helps students understand that achieving goals takes hard work, resilience, and determination. The third question reassures students that help is available and shows them the importance of seeking—and accepting—help when necessary.

DIGITAL PERSPECTIVES

Academic Vocabulary: Informative Text

Academic terms appear in all subjects and can help you read, write, and discuss with more precision. Informative writing relies on facts to inform or explain. Here are five academic words that will be useful to you in this unit as you analyze and write informative texts.

Complete the chart.

1. Review each word, its root, and the mentor sentences.
2. Use the information and your own knowledge to predict the meaning of each word.
3. For each word, list at least two related words.
4. Refer to the dictionary or other resources if needed.

TIP

FOLLOW THROUGH
Study the words in this chart, and mark them or their forms wherever they appear in the unit.

WORD	MENTOR SENTENCES	PREDICT MEANING	RELATED WORDS
deviate ROOT: **-via-** "way"	1. Don't *deviate* from the route I gave you or you'll get lost! 2. She was making an important point, but she allowed herself to *deviate* into side issues.		viable; viaduct
persevere ROOT: **-sever-** *"strict; serious"*	1. Despite the difficulties Claudine had finding time to study, she *persevered* and received a degree. 2. Though the soccer team was losing in the first half, they were able to *persevere* and win the game.		
determination ROOT: **-term-** "end"	1. Because of his *determination* to do well on the test, Robert studied for many hours. 2. Despite the heavy rain, Jenny's *determination* allowed her to complete her first marathon.		
diversity ROOT: **-ver-** "turn"	1. There is cultural *diversity* in the United States because people come from many different places. 2. The oceans are filled with a *diversity* of marine life.		
tradition ROOT: **-tra-/-tran-** "across"	1. My grandfather passed along many family *traditions* that had been practiced for generations. 2. Many people follow *tradition* and serve turkey on Thanksgiving.		

Academic Vocabulary: Informative Text

Introduce the blue academic vocabulary words in the chart on the student page. Point out that the root of each word provides a clue to its meaning. Discuss the mentor sentences to ensure students understand each word's usage. Students should also use the mentor sentences as context to help them predict the meaning of each word. Check that students are able to fill the chart in correctly. Complete pronunciations, parts of speech, and definitions are provided for you. Students are only expected to provide the definition.

Possible responses:

deviate *v.* (DEE vee ayt)
Meaning: depart from an established plan
Related words: deviation, deviating
Additional words related to root *-via-*: viaduct, trivial, obvious, devious

persevere *v.* (pur suh VIHR)
Meaning: to continue despite difficulty
Related words: persevering, severe
Additional words related to root *-sever-*: severance, persist

determination *n.* (dih tur muh NAY shuhn)
Meaning: conclusion; firm decision
Related words: deter, determine, determining
Additional words related to root *-term-*: determined, terminal

diversity *n.* (duh VUR suh tee)
Meaning: variety; differences within a group
Related words: divergent, diversified, diversify
Additional words related to root *-ver-*: diverse, inverse converse, reverse

tradition *n.* (truh DIHSH uhn)
Meaning: long-established custom or practice
Related words: traditionalist, traditionally, untraditional
Additional words related to root *-tra/tran-*: traditional, transfer

PERSONALIZE FOR LEARNING

English Language Support

Cognates Many of the academic words have Spanish cognates. Use these cognates with students whose home language is Spanish.
ALL LEVELS

thesis – tesis
persevere – perseverar
determination – determinación
diversity – diversidad
tradition – tradición

Purpose of the Launch Text

The Launch Text provides students with a common starting point to address the unit topic. After reading the Launch Text, all students will be able to participate in discussions about facing adversity.

Lexile: 800 The easier reading level of this selection makes it perfect to assign for homework. Students will need little or no support to understand it.

Additionally, "Against the Odds" provides a writing model for the Performance-Based Assessment students complete at the end of the unit.

Launch Text: Informative Model

Remind students to pay attention to how the author structures the essay and develops ideas, and in particular to note how the author shows cause-and-effect relationships among ideas in the essay.

Encourage students to read this text on their own and annotate unfamiliar words and sections of text they think are particularly important.

AUDIO SUMMARIES

Audio summaries of "Against the Odds" are available in both English and Spanish in the Interactive Teacher's Edition or Unit Resources. Assigning these summaries before students read the Launch Text may help them build additional background knowledge and set a context for their reading.

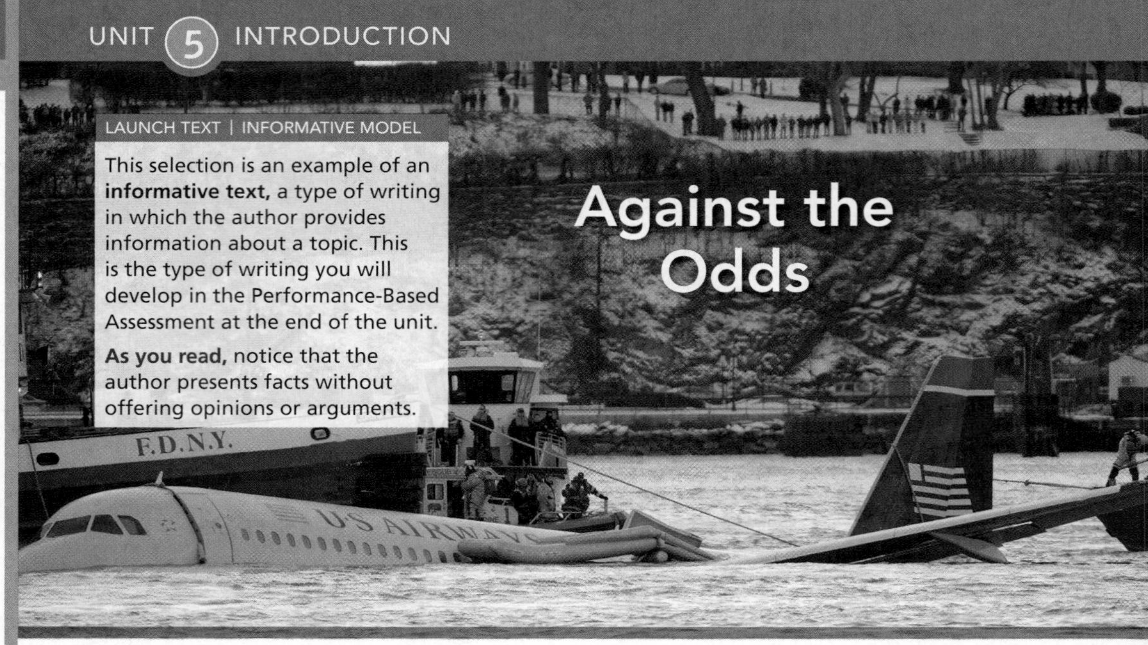

LAUNCH TEXT | INFORMATIVE MODEL

This selection is an example of an **informative text,** a type of writing in which the author provides information about a topic. This is the type of writing you will develop in the Performance-Based Assessment at the end of the unit.

As you read, notice that the author presents facts without offering opinions or arguments.

Against the Odds

NOTES

1 "If you have to ditch a commercial aircraft in the Hudson River," the news anchor joked, "this is the guy you want."

2 The "guy" was US Airways pilot Chesley "Sully" Sullenberger III, a 57-year-old former Air Force fighter pilot and a 29-year veteran of US Airways.

3 On January 15, 2009, Sullenberger was the pilot on US Airways Flight 1549 from New York's LaGuardia Airport to Charlotte, North Carolina.

4 Flight 1549 left the tarmac at 3:25 P.M. Sullenberger thought he was in for an average flight—a routine, everyday trip.

5 The flight was unremarkable for the first 90 seconds. Then something caught the eye of copilot Jeff Skiles. At 3,000 feet, he saw a flock of Canada geese headed toward the plane. Moments later the geese struck the fuselage, wings, and engine.

6 The 150 passengers felt a powerful thud against the airplane, followed by severe vibrations from the engine. One passenger said it sounded like sneakers thumping around in a dryer. There was a loud explosion. The cabin filled up with smoke. There was a horrible smell and then an eerie quiet: both engines were disabled.

7 Sullenberger made a Mayday radio call to air traffic control and calmly explained the situation. They discussed the options: The plane could either return to LaGuardia or land at Teterboro Airport in New Jersey.

8 Sullenberger knew the situation was too dire for the plane to stay in the air long enough for either plan to be successful. He had about 30 seconds to find an alternative. The pilot decided on a

DIGITAL PERSPECTIVES

Illuminating the Text To help students appreciate the events described in the Launch Text, use the search term "Flight 1549" (paragraph 3) to find video footage of the plane in the Hudson, the rescue of its passengers, and interviews with Sully Sullenberger. (Note: Be sure to preview any video before showing it to students.)

Have students discuss what they see and how this helps them understand "Against the Odds." Then, have students write a paragraph discussing whether the video affected their response to the Launch Text. Did it change their ideas about what they read? Why or why not? If their ideas changed, in what way did they change?

radical move: He'd ditch the plane in the Hudson River—despite the fact that passenger jets are not built to land on water.

9 "Brace for impact!" came the captain's voice over the intercom. A hush fell over the passengers. They thought they were going to die.

10 Sullenberger lowered the plane's nose in a gradual glide toward the river. The plane managed to clear the George Washington Bridge and, against the odds, land safely on the surface of the Hudson. It skidded across the water at 145 mph and finally slowed to a stop.

11 "He was thinking in nanoseconds," said a former airline pilot, speaking of Sullenberger. "He made all the right choices at all the right times. He might have been staring at the instruments, but he was feeling that airplane in his hands. He picked his landing spot and went for it."

12 Now Sullenberger's job was to get the people off the plane, which was quickly filling up with water.

13 Witnesses were convinced that everyone on Flight 1549 was dead. What they couldn't see was that passengers were already exiting the plane. With water seeping into the plane, Sullenberger and Skiles walked the length of the cabin twice, calling "Is anyone there?" The water was so cold they had to walk on top of the seats. But they would not leave the plane until they were sure everyone was out.

14 "He's the man," said one of the rescued passengers. "If you want to talk to a hero, get a hold of him."

15 After all the thanking was over, Sullenberger was humble. "You're welcome," he said simply. Like most heroes, he didn't want the label. According to him, he was just doing his job.

16 But 154 men, women, and children owed their lives to a modest man who faced adversity with cool competence on one of the most remarkable days in aviation history. ❧

NOTES

WORD NETWORK FOR FACING ADVERSITY

Vocabulary A Word Network is a collection of words related to a topic. As you read the selections in this unit, identify interesting words related to the idea of overcoming obstacles and add them to your Word Network. For example, you might begin by adding words from the Launch Text, such as *dire*, *humble*, and *competence*. Continue to add words as you complete this unit.

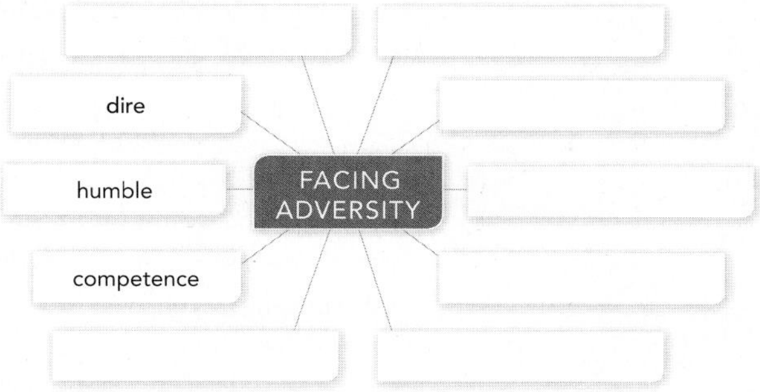

FACING ADVERSITY

dire

humble

competence

Tool Kit
Word Network Model

DIGITAL PERSPECTIVES

Word Network for Facing Adversity

Tell students that they can fill in the Word Network as they read the texts in the unit, or they can jot down the words elsewhere and add them later. Point out to students that people may have personal associations with some words. A word that one student thinks is related to the concept of facing adversity might not be a word another student would pick. However, students should feel free to add any relevant words to their Word Network. Each person's Word Network will be unique. If you choose to print the Word Network, distribute it to students at this point so they can use it throughout the rest of the unit.

AUTHOR'S PERSPECTIVE **Elfrieda Hiebert, Ph.D.**

Rare Words Increasing reading comprehension relies on a connection between fluency and vocabulary. **Rare words** are less frequently used words that represent what might be a common idea. Instead of calling a character *nervous,* an author might use *disconcerted* or *flustered.* In reading/language arts, where many rare unknown words pertain to known concepts, teachers should emphasize semantic connections across words. This can be achieved effectively with concept maps or word networks that help students understand the essential characteristics of a word's meaning. Here's an example for *sluggish:*

heavy	blah	indolent	inactive
comatose	inert	off	sullen

Digital tools, including online dictionaries, often have features to help demonstrate the increasing complexity of the spectrum of these words by filtering out levels of complexity.

INTRODUCTION

Summary

Have students read the introductory paragraph. Provide them with tips for writing a summary:

- Write in the present tense.
- Make sure to include the title of the work.
- Be concise: a summary should not be equal in length to the original text.
- If you need to quote the words of the author, use quotation marks.
- Don't put your own opinions, ideas, or interpretations into the summary. The purpose of writing a summary is to accurately represent what the author says, not to provide a critique.

See possible summary on student page.

Launch Activity

Explain to students that as they work on this unit, they will have many opportunities to discuss the topic of facing adversity. Remind them that there is no right or wrong position, but they should be able to support their position with evidence from the material they've read as well as their prior knowledge.

Encourage students to keep an open mind and really listen to their classmates

Summary

Write a summary of "Against the Odds." A **summary** is a concise, complete, and accurate overview of a text. It should not include a statement of your opinion or an analysis.

Possible response: The informative text "Against the Odds" describes the actions of Chesley "Sully" Sullenberger, a veteran airline pilot whose skill saved many lives. In early 2009, he was flying a plane full of passengers out of New York City. Less than two minutes into the flight, a flock of geese collided with the plane. The impact disabled the plane's engines. Sullenberger knew that the plane could not stay in the air long enough to get safely back to the airport. Instead, he landed in the Hudson River. With quick thinking and skilled piloting, he saved all the passengers.

Launch Activity

Let the People Decide Consider this statement: Chesley Sullenberger wasn't really a hero because, as he himself said, facing adversity was part of his job.

- Record your position on the statement and explain your thinking.

☐ Strongly Agree ☐ Agree ☐ Disagree ☐ Strongly Disagree

- As a class, discuss what makes someone a hero.
- After the discussion, determine whether you have changed your mind.
- Those who changed their mind will be given a chance to read a new statement.

QuickWrite

Consider class discussions, presentations, the video, and the Launch Text as you think about the prompt. Record your first thoughts here.

PROMPT: **How can people overcome adversity in the face of overwhelming obstacles?**

Possible response: It's hard to think fast in an unfamiliar situation that's unfolding very quickly. The best way to be able to overcome adversity is practice. You don't have to practice *exactly* the thing you want to prepare for; there are too many possibilities for that. It's not like Sullenberger had ever landed a plane in the Hudson River before, but he knew what to do because he had spent so much time flying planes. So he could immediately tell the best course of action. I spend some of my free time practicing math problems beyond homework. A test never has exactly the same questions as my practice, but my practice is close enough that I can think quickly no matter how hard the test is.

EVIDENCE LOG FOR FACING ADVERSITY

Review your QuickWrite and summarize your point of view in one sentence to record in your Evidence Log. Then, record evidence from "Against the Odds" that supports your point of view.

Prepare for the Performance-Based Assessment at the end of the unit by completing the Evidence Log after each selection.

Tool Kit
Evidence Log Model

Title of Text: ______ Date: ______

CONNECTION TO PROMPT	TEXT EVIDENCE/DETAILS	ADDITIONAL NOTES/IDEAS

How does this text change or add to my thinking? Date: ______

DIGITAL PERSPECTIVES

QuickWrite

In this QuickWrite, students should present their own answer to the question based on the material in the Unit Opener. This initial response will help inform their work when they complete the Performance-Based Assessment at the end of the unit. Students should make sure they answer the question with a clearly stated position and support their position with relevant, logical reasoning.

See possible QuickWrite on student page.

Evidence Log for Facing Adversity

Students should record their initial response in their Evidence Logs. Then, they should record evidence from "Against the Odds" that supports their initial response.

If you choose to print the Evidence Log, distribute it to students at this point so they can use it throughout the rest of the unit.

Performance-Based Assessment: Refining Your Thinking

- Have students watch the video on Refining Your Thinking.
- A video on this topic is available online in the Professional Development Center.

PERSONALIZE FOR LEARNING

English Language Support

Idioms Help students understand the idioms *against the odds* (title) and *ditch* (paragraph 1). Explain that against the odds means "there's little chance of success." When you manage to achieve something *against the odds,* you succeed even though there are many things that can stop you. A variation on this expression is "against all odds." That's what Sullenberger did when he realized he could not get back to the airport. To *ditch* something means to get rid of it. In the text, *ditch* has a bit of a different meaning. To *ditch* a plane means to make a forced landing on water. **ALL LEVELS**

WHOLE-CLASS LEARNING

How do we overcome obstacles?

Facing obstacles may be a part of life for everyone at one time or another. But sometimes, adversity can be so extreme that it seems impossible to overcome. During Whole-Class Learning, students will read selections about people who faced adversity and accomplished more than they ever dreamed they could.

Whole-Class Learning Strategies

Review the Learning Strategies with students and explain that as they work through Whole-Class Learning they will develop strategies to work in large-group environments.

- Have students watch the video on Whole-Class Learning Strategies.
- A video on this topic is available online in the Professional Development Center.

You may wish to discuss some action items to add to the chart as a class before students complete it on their own. For example, for "Monitor understanding," you might solicit the following from students:

- Review all of the notes you have taken so far to see whether you need more information or detail for clarification.

Block Scheduling

Each day in this Pacing Plan represents a 40–50-minute class period. Teachers using block scheduling may combine days to reflect their class schedule. In addition, teachers may revise pacing to differentiate and support core instruction by integrating components and resources as students require.

OVERVIEW: WHOLE-CLASS LEARNING

ESSENTIAL QUESTION:

How do we overcome obstacles?

Everyone has a bad day now and then. Most of the time we take a deep breath and keep going, but what happens when we meet an obstacle we don't think we can overcome? You will work with your whole class to explore the concept of facing adversity. The selections you are going to read present different examples of obstacles that had to be overcome.

Whole-Class Learning Strategies

Throughout your life, in school, in your community, and in your career, you will continue to learn and work in large-group environments.

Review these strategies and the actions you can take to practice them as you work with your whole class. Add ideas of your own for each step. Get ready to use these strategies during Whole-Class Learning.

STRATEGY	ACTION PLAN
Listen actively	• Eliminate distractions. For example, put your cellphone away. • Keep your eyes on the speaker. •
Clarify by asking questions	• If you're confused, other people probably are, too. Ask a question to help your whole class. • If you see that you are guessing, ask a question instead. •
Monitor understanding	• Notice what information you already know and be ready to build on it. • Ask for help if you are struggling. •
Interact and share ideas	• Share your ideas and answer questions, even if you are unsure. • Build on the ideas of others by adding details or making a connection. •

Pacing Plan

Unit Introduction: 1, 2

Introduce Whole-Class Learning: 3

Media: The Dust Bowl: 4, 5

from The Grapes of Wrath: 6, 7, 8, 9

The Circuit: 10, 11, 12, 13, 14, 15

Performance Task: 16, 17, 18

WHOLE-CLASS LEARNING (3–18)

CONTENTS

COMPARE

DIGITAL PERSPECTIVES

Contents

Anchor Texts Preview the anchor texts and media with students to generate interest. Encourage students to discuss other texts they may have read or movies or television shows they may have seen that deal with the issues of facing adversity and overcoming obstacles.

You may wish to conduct a poll to determine which selection students think looks more interesting and discuss the reasons for their preference. Students can return to this poll after they have read the selections to see if their preference changed.

Performance Task

Write an Informative Essay Explain to students that after they have finished reading the selections, they will write an informative essay about people facing adversity and overcoming obstacles. To help them prepare, encourage students to think about the topic as they progress through the selections and as they participate in the Whole-Class Learning experience.

Introduce Small-Group Learning — 19

A Work in Progress — 20 21 22 23

from The Story of My Life — 24 25

Media: How Helen Keller Learned to Talk — 26 27

A Young Tinkerer Builds a Windmill, Electrifying a Nation — 28 29 30

Performance Task — 31 32

Introduce Independent Learning — 33

Independent Learning — 34

Performance-Based Assessment — 35 36

The Dust Bowl

AUDIO SUMMARIES
Audio summaries of "The Dust Bowl" are available online in both English and Spanish in the Interactive Teacher's Edition or Unit Resources. Assigning these summaries prior to watching the video may help students build additional background knowledge and set a context for their first review.

Summary

The film "The Dust Bowl" discusses the natural and human causes of a great disaster. By 1930, much of the southern plains had been overplowed and overfarmed. A long drought that began in 1931 dried up the overplowed soil. Then winds blew across the flatlands, stirring up the dried soil, creating enormous dust storms. These dust storms continued for ten years and were devastating to many of those who endured them. In this video selection, some of the people who lived through the Dust Bowl years tell personal stories of this terrible time.

Insight

This selection uses photographs, interviews, and historical film footage to create a disturbing picture of what came to be called the Dust Bowl. Students will see the real hardship a climate disaster can cause and how people got through it.

ESSENTIAL QUESTION:
How do we overcome obstacles?

Connection to Essential Question

"The Dust Bowl" connects clearly and directly to the Essential Question, *How do we overcome obstacles?* The obstacles that Dust Bowl farm families had to overcome went beyond the huge storms of black dust to dealing with the economic devastation that followed.

WHOLE-CLASS LEARNING PERFORMANCE TASK
How did the individuals in the selections cope with the obstacles they faced?

UNIT PERFORMANCE-BASED ASSESSMENT
How can people overcome adversity in the face of overwhelming obstacles?

Connection to Performance Tasks

Whole-Class Learning Performance Task In this Performance Task, students will present an informative essay about how the people and characters in these selections coped with the obstacles they faced. This selection presents students with evidence about what people do when their choices are extremely limited.

Unit Performance-Based Assessment The Performance-Based Assessment for this unit asks students to write an informative essay in response to the question: *How can people overcome adversity in the face of overwhelming obstacles?* The selections will provide students with stories of characters, both real and imaginary, who have faced hardships.

DIGITAL PERSPECTIVES

Audio

Video

Document

Annotation Highlights

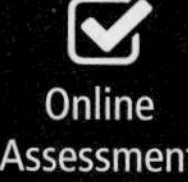
Online Assessment

LESSON RESOURCES

	Making Meaning	Language Development
Lesson	**First Review** **Close Review** **Analyze the Media**	**Media Vocabulary**
Instructional Standards	**RI.7.10** By the end of the year, read and comprehend literary nonfiction . . .	**L.7.6** Acquire and use accurately grade-appropriate general academic and domain-specific words and phrases . . .
STUDENT RESOURCES		
Available online in the Interactive Student Edition or Unit Resources	Selection Audio First-Review Guide: Media: Video Close-Review Guide: Media: Video	
TEACHER RESOURCES		
Selection Resources Available online in the Interactive Teacher's Edition or Unit Resources	Audio Summaries: English and Spanish First Review Extension Questions	Media Vocabulary
My Resources	A Unit 5 Answer Key is available online and in the Interactive Teacher's Edition.	

Media Complexity Rubric: The Dust Bowl

Quantitative Measures	
Format and Length: Approximately 10.5 minute video excerpt	
Qualitative Measures	
Knowledge Demands ①—②—❸—④—⑤	Prior knowledge of the Dust Bowl era, the Depression, and labor migrations in America are required in order to understand the film clip. Try to make clear the differences between the Great Depression and the dust storms of the Dirty Thirties, which are two discrete events that happened to occur in the same decade.
Structure ①—❷—③—④—⑤	The excerpt illuminates this period in American history with narration, images and film clips from the time period, and interviews with those who experienced the Dust Bowl firsthand.
Language Conventionality and Clarity ①—❷—③—④—⑤	The interviews contain colloquialisms, accents, and lingo but are not on the whole difficult to grasp. The narration is heavily informative.
Levels of Meaning/Purpose ①—②—❸—④—⑤	Concepts are historical but not difficult to understand.

Jump Start

FIRST REVIEW Engage students in a discussion about the Dust Bowl. If students are unfamiliar with the Dust Bowl, ask them to speculate on why something might have this name. What comes to mind when they hear the term "Dust Bowl"?

The Dust Bowl

Why might people have to struggle to survive a "dust bowl"? Just how difficult was it to survive the Dust Bowl? Modeling questions such as these will help students connect to "The Dust Bowl" and to the Whole-Class Performance Task assignment. Selection audio for the selection is available in the Interactive Teacher's Edition.

Project the video in class or ask students to open the video in their interactive textbooks.

Media Vocabulary

Encourage students to discuss the media vocabulary. Have they seen or used these terms or concepts before?

FIRST REVIEW

Have students perform the steps of the first review independently.

WATCH: Students should pay attention to the causes and effects of the Dust Bowl and consider how it affected the lives of the people in the video.

NOTE: Students should note the time stamp of any facts they find interesting or important, or moments they find especially powerful.

CONNECT: Encourage students to increase their understanding by connecting the video to other media or news reports they have seen or heard, or other stories they've read.

RESPOND: Students will answer questions to demonstrate understanding. Point out to students that while they will complete the Respond step at the end of the first review, the other steps will probably happen somewhat concurrently. You may wish to print copies of the **First-Review Guide: Media: Video** for students to use.

MAKING MEANING

THE DUST BOWL

Comparing Media to Text

You will now watch a video about the Dust Bowl. First, complete the first-review and close-review activities. In the next lesson, you will read an excerpt from *The Grapes of Wrath* and then compare the depiction of historical events in the video and the novel excerpt.

from THE GRAPES OF WRATH

The Dust Bowl

Media Vocabulary

These words will be useful as you analyze, discuss, and write about the video.

panoramic shot: film shot showing a wide, unbroken view	• The panoramic shot of the Grand Canyon was breathtaking. • Directors often use panoramic shots in the beginning of films to establish the setting.
voiceover: voice commenting or narrating off-camera	• The voiceover helps the audience to follow a narrative. • If there is a break in the sequence of events, a voiceover can re-orient the audience.
transition: in media, changes from one scene or shot to another	• One example of a transition is when a scene changes to another location. • Another example of a transition is when a director signals the end of a scene by using a "fade to black."

First Review MEDIA: VIDEO

Study the video and take notes as you watch.

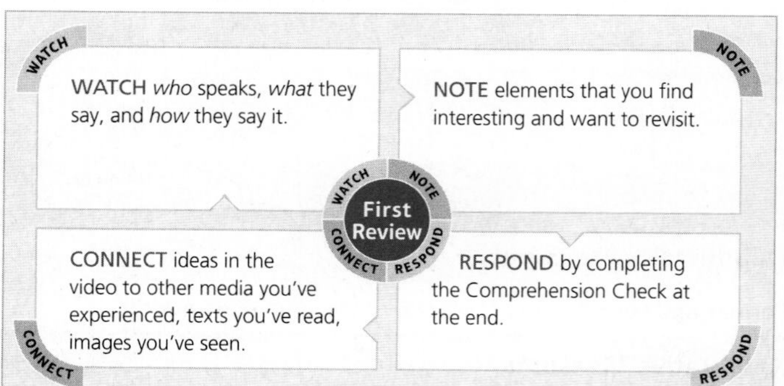

STANDARDS
Reading Informational Text
By the end of the year, read and comprehend literary nonfiction in the grades 6–8 text complexity band proficiently, with scaffolding as needed at the high end of the range.

DIGITAL PERSPECTIVES

MEDIA | VIDEO

The Dust Bowl

CriticalPast

BACKGROUND

One of the most devastating events in U.S. history was the formation of the Dust Bowl. After a period of over-farming in the 1920s, a severe drought struck the region around the Oklahoma panhandle in the early 1930s. The extended drought caused the topsoil to dry up, and without a strong root system of grasses to hold it in place, the soil was blown by winds. These dust storms blackened the sky and were sometimes referred to as black blizzards.

NOTES

CLOSER REVIEW

Analyze Cinematic Technique

Circulate among students as they conduct their close review. Have students review the video beginning at 6:40 and ending at 6:47. Encourage students to share their insights about this segment and provide the following support.

NOTE: Have students note details in the video that show the setting of a dust storm.

QUESTION: Guide students to consider what these details might tell them. Ask what a viewer can infer from the fact that the farm house and other human structures are very small compared to the giant dust, and accept student responses.

Possible response: The viewer can see that the farm is tiny compared to the giant dust cloud. The farm and the people on it will be overtaken by the destruction of the dust storm.

CONCLUDE: Help students to formulate conclusions about the importance of these details in the video. Ask students why the director might have included these details.

Possible responses: It's a dramatic shot that gives the viewer a sense of the scale of the disaster. You can't see any crops in the fields, just dirt. You get the sense that the farm is doomed, and its own empty fields are fueling the storm.

Remind students that a panoramic shot is a **cinematic technique** in which the camera shows a wide view of open landscape. Often directors use panoramic shots to establish the greatness, beauty, or breadth, of a location. However, panoramic shots can also show large-scale devastation.

CROSS-CURRICULAR PERSPECTIVES

Social Studies Have students research and write short reports on the Dust Bowl to find information that is not in the video or that elaborates on information in the video. Have students share their findings with the class, and discuss how this information relates to the video or deepens their understanding of the video.

Comprehension Check

Possible responses:

1. (a) They allowed their cattle to overgraze, heavily damaging the soil. (b) Then the farmers came and removed the top cover of soil, which weakened the land.
2. They came to make their living off the land by farming and ranching.
3. (a) The climate began to change in the early 1930s. (b) The hot, dry weather caused a drought, which contributed to difficult conditions for farmers and ranchers.
4. People used farming techniques that worked well in other places but were not appropriate for the plains; people used machines like tractors that plowed enormous tracts of land; people plowed land that had never been plowed before; people plowed more land than should have been plowed.

Research

Research to Clarify If students struggle to identify an unfamiliar detail, have them rewatch the video and notice an idea or concept that might be new to them, such as things related to farming, farm equipment, or dust storms.

Comprehension Check

Complete the following items after you finish your first review.

1. (a) According to the video, what did the cattlemen do? (b) What group followed the cattlemen to the area, and what did they do?

2. Why did so many people move to the area that eventually became known as the Dust Bowl?

3. (a) When did the climate first start to change? (b) What effects did the change have?

4. **Notebook** How did human activity contribute to creating the Dust Bowl?

RESEARCH

Research to Clarify Choose at least one unfamiliar detail from the video. Briefly research that detail. In what way does the information you learned shed light on an aspect of the story told in this video?

PERSONALIZE FOR LEARNING

Challenge

Research Encourage students to research the settlement patterns in the late-1800s Great Plains, briefly described at the beginning of the film (0:45–1:40). Direct students to learn more about how ranchers and farmers used the land in this period and how this background information helps them understand the causes of the Dust Bowl of the 1930s.

MAKING MEANING

Close Review

Watch "The Dust Bowl" again. Write any new observations that seem important. What **questions** do you have? What can you **conclude**?

THE DUST BOWL

Analyze the Media

Notebook Complete the activities.

1. **Evaluate** What moment, image, or detail in "The Dust Bowl" did you find particularly powerful? Why?
2. **Analyze** (a) What sort of information do you learn from the first-person accounts in the video? (b) What sort of information do you learn from voiceover narration? (c) Do you find these types of information to be of equal value? Explain why or why not.
3. **Essential Question:** *How do we overcome obstacles?* What have you learned about how people deal with obstacles by seeing "The Dust Bowl"? Explain.

LANGUAGE DEVELOPMENT

Media Vocabulary

panoramic shot **voiceover** **transition**

Use the media vocabulary words in your responses to these questions.

1. How does the *panoramic shot* at the beginning of the video help you understand what follows?
2. How does the *voiceover* contribute to the images in "Surviving the Dust Bowl"?
3. Which *transition* in the video creates the most powerful dramatic effect? Explain.

EVIDENCE LOG

Before moving on to a new selection, go to your Evidence Log and record what you've learned from the video "The Dust Bowl."

STANDARDS

Language
Acquire and use accurately grade-appropriate general academic and domain-specific words and phrases; gather vocabulary knowledge when considering a word or phrase important to comprehension or expression.

DIGITAL PERSPECTIVES

Close Review

If needed, model close reviewing by using the Closer Review notes in the Interactive Teacher's Edition.

Remind students to use Accountable Talk in their discussions and to support one another as they complete the close review.

Analyze the Media

1. Responses will vary. Students should (a) identify a specific part of the video, and (b) clearly explain why they chose it.
2. Responses will vary. Students should differentiate between the content related by interview subjects and by the narrator.
3. Responses will vary. Students might conclude that people can cooperate with one another so they don't make a bad situation worse.

Media Vocabulary

For more support, see **Media Vocabulary.**

Possible responses:

1. The panoramic shot provides an introduction to region.
2. "The Dust Bowl" uses *voiceover* to provide background and historical information while the viewer sees images on the screen. Fictional films and TV shows use voiceover. This technique was effective in these instances because it helped me understand the stories.
3. Answers will vary. Students should demonstrate understanding of what a transition is in film, as well as the effect a specific transition has in telling the story of the Dust Bowl.

Evidence Log Support students in completing their Evidence Log. This paced activity will help prepare them for the Performance-Based Assessment at the end of the unit.

VOCABULARY DEVELOPMENT

Media Vocabulary Reinforcement Students will benefit from additional practice with the media vocabulary. Reinforce their comprehension with "show-you-know" sentences. The first part of the sentence uses the vocabulary word in context. The second part clarifies the first. Model the strategy with this example for *panoramic shot*:

This film has a great *panoramic shot*; it shows a huge dust storm approaching a farm.

Then, give students this sentence prompt, and coach them in creating the clarification part:

The use of *voiceover* in this movie made the story clear; _________.

Possible response: the narrator explained why the main character left his native country.

FORMATIVE ASSESSMENT

Media Vocabulary

- **If** students struggle to answer the media vocabulary questions, **then** review relevant parts of the video and discuss how these techniques are used in the video.

from The Grapes of Wrath

AUDIO SUMMARIES
Audio summaries of "*from* The Grapes of Wrath" are available online in both English and Spanish in the Interactive Teacher's Edition or Unit Resources. Assigning these summaries prior to reading the selection may help students build additional background knowledge and set a context for their first read.

Summary

In this moving excerpt from the novel *The Grapes of Wrath*, author John Steinbeck describes the heartbreaking preparations of families getting ready to leave their farms in Oklahoma, devastated by drought and dust storms, to try to make new lives in California. Everything they take will have to fit in a pickup truck, so they try to sell the possessions they have lived with and treasured for so long. But the Dust Bowl and the Great Depression have left thousands of farm families in desperate poverty. Everyone is selling, and few are buying. The prices are weak, but the desperation and bitterness are strong.

Insight

This selection offers insight into how this terrible period of American history affected the lives of ordinary people. The excerpt is about more than the loss of a family's possessions. It reveals how deep the pain of an economic disaster can go.

ESSENTIAL QUESTION:
How do we overcome obstacles?

Connection to Essential Question

The excerpt from *The Grapes of Wrath* connects clearly and directly to the Essential Question. The obstacles Dust Bowl farm families had to overcome required huge sacrifices, which are symbolized by the loss of tools, farm animals, and "roses red under glass."

WHOLE-CLASS LEARNING PERFORMANCE TASK
How did the individuals in the selections cope with the obstacles they faced?

UNIT PERFORMANCE-BASED ASSESSMENT
How can people overcome adversity in the face of overwhelming obstacles?

Connection to Performance Tasks

Whole-Class Learning Performance Task In this Performance Task, students will present an informative essay about how the characters in these selections coped with the obstacles they faced. This selection presents students with evidence about what people do when their choices are extremely limited.

Unit Performance-Based Assessment The tenant farmers Steinbeck describes in this excerpt from *The Grapes of Wrath* faced insurmountable obstacles to keeping their land. The topsoil was depleted by unsustainable farming, and then it was swept away by drought and high winds over the flat plains. After years of unprofitable farming, in the midst of the Great Depression, banks foreclosed. The landlords lost the farms, and the tenant farmers were thrown off. The families had no savings, and there were no jobs. This selection gives insight into what people do when they can do nothing else. They move on.

DIGITAL PERSPECTIVES

Audio

Video

Document

Annotation Highlights

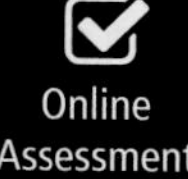
Online Assessment

LESSON RESOURCES

	Making Meaning	Language Development	Effective Expression
Lesson	**First Read** **Close Read** **Analyze the Text** **Analyze Craft and Structure**	**Concept Vocabulary** **Word Study** **Author's Style**	**Writing to Compare**
Instructional Standards	**RL.7.10** By the end of the year, read and comprehend literature . . . **RL.7.2** Determine a theme or central idea of a text . . . **RL.7.3** Analyze how particular elements of a story or drama interact.	**L.7.4** Determine or clarify the meaning of unknown and multiple-meaning words and phrases . . . **L.7.4.b** Use common, grade-appropriate Greek or Latin affixes and roots . . . **L.7.6** Acquire and use accurately grade-appropriate general academic and domain-specific words and phrases . . .	**RL.7.9** Compare and contrast a fictional portrayal . . . **W.7.1** Write arguments . . . **W.7.1.a** Introduce claim(s) . . . **W.7.1.b** Support claim(s) with logical reasoning . . . **W.7.1.c** Use words, phrases, and clauses to create cohesion . . . **W.7.9** Draw evidence from literary or informational texts . . . **W.7.9.a** Apply *grade 7 Reading standards* to literature . . .
STUDENT RESOURCES			
Available online in the Interactive Student Edition or Unit Resources	Selection Audio First-Read Guide: Fiction Close-Read Guide: Fiction	Word Network	Evidence Log
TEACHER RESOURCES			
Selection Resources Available online in the Interactive Teacher's Edition or Unit Resources	Audio Summaries: English and Spanish Annotation Highlights Accessible Leveled Text First Read Extension Questions Analyze Craft and Structure: Theme	Concept Vocabulary and Word Study Author's Style: Description	Writing to Compare: Essay
Reteach/Practice (RP) Available online in the Interactive Teacher's Edition or Unit Resources	Analyze Craft and Structure: Theme (RP)	Word Study: Suffix *–less* (RP) Author's Style: Description (RP)	
Assessment Available online in Assessments	Selection Test: English Selection Test: Spanish Extension Selection Test		
My Resources	A Unit 5 Answer Key is available online and in the Interactive Teacher's Edition.		

Reading Support

Text Complexity Rubric: *from* The Grapes of Wrath	
Quantitative Measures	
Lexile: 600 **Text Length:** 1,403 words	
Qualitative Measures	
Knowledge Demands ①—❷—③—④—⑤	A good background on American labor, the Depression, and the Dust Bowl will help students understand Steinbeck's excerpt. Some discussion of Modernist-style writing may also be warranted.
Structure ①—②—③—❹—⑤	The structure is ostensibly simple, but the form it takes is intuitive and somewhat hard to follow for a young reader. Rereading may be required.
Language Conventionality and Clarity ①—②—③—❹—⑤	Some difficult above-level vocabulary rendered in a modernist style. Complex sentence structures and unique syntax.
Levels of Meaning/Purpose ①—②—③—❹—⑤	The excerpt touches on sorrow and loss, the extent to which migrant laborers in the Dust Bowl were participants in their own debasement, and how the demands of the economy stripped whole generations and families of their humanity.

DECIDE AND PLAN

English Language Support

Provide English Learners with support for language and meaning as they read the selection.

Language Encourage students to explore Steinbeck's unique language and to take note of interesting inconsistencies, like the switch from third-person, to second-person, to first-person plural. Discuss with students Steinbeck's intent in writing this way, and what other modernists might have influenced him.

Meaning Though the items in the excerpt are often described as "old" or "rank," there is still a strong sense of attachment to them. Ask the students to discuss why the people are sorting through them, and why in the end they choose to burn them all instead of sell them.

Strategic Support

Provide students with strategic support to ensure that they can successfully read the text.

Language Ask students to analyze the language and decide whether the text is a monologue from a single character. If so, who is the character speaking, and who is he or she speaking to? Discuss with students how the fluid use of colloquial speech helps to create a feeling of being there with the person.

Meaning Remind students that it's more important to get the general idea from a text like this than it is to know each individual word. Discuss strategies for getting through a text, such as rereading, note-taking, or discussion.

Challenge

Provide students who need to be challenged with ideas for how they can go beyond a simple interpretation of the text.

Text Analysis Challenge students to put themselves in the place of migrant workers in the Dust Bowl. Ask why they may have spoken with such stark urgency and despair. Discuss the economic forces that drove people to abandon, or burn, their possessions.

Written Response If some students would like to look deeper into the era, have them do research. Encourage them to go to the library or to interview their own family members. Have students write a short report and provide a conclusion as to whether they believe Steinbeck's portrayal of life then was accurate.

TEACH

Read and Respond

Have students do their first read of the selection. Then have them complete their close read. Finally, work with them on the Making Meaning, Language Development, and Effective Expression activities.

Standards Support Through Teaching and Learning Cycle

IDENTIFY NEEDS

Analyze results of the Beginning-of-Year Assessment, focusing on the items relating to Unit 5. Also take into consideration student performance to this point and your observations of where particular students struggle.

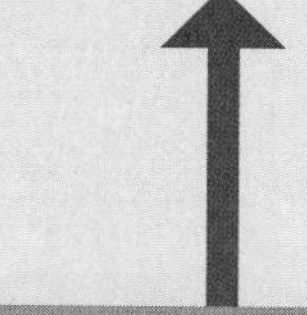

DECIDE AND PLAN

- If students have performed poorly on items matching these standards, then provide selection scaffolds before assigning them the on-level lesson provided in the Student Edition.
- If students have done well on the Beginning-of-Year Assessment, then challenge them to keep progressing and learning by giving them opportunities to practice the skills in depth.
- Use the Selection Resources listed on the Planning pages for "*from* The Grapes of Wrath" to help students continually improve their ability to master the standards.

Instructional Standards: *from* The Grapes of Wrath

	Catching Up	This Year	Looking Forward
Reading	You may wish to administer the **Analyze Craft and Structure: Setting and Cultural Context (RP)** worksheet to help students understand how to determine the setting and cultural context of a written work.	**RL.3** Analyze how particular elements of a story or drama interact.	Have students discuss how the dialogue from the selection informs on the plot and themes.
Language	Review the **Author's Style: Description (RP)** worksheet to help students understand how authors create images with words. Review the **Word Study: Suffix *–less* (RP)** worksheet to help students understand the meanings of the suffixes *–ness* and *–less*.	**L.6** Acquire and use accurately grade-appropriate general academic and domain-specific words and phrases; gather vocabulary knowledge when considering a word or phrase important to comprehension or expression. **L.4.b** Use common, grade-appropriate Greek or Latin affixes and roots as clues to the meaning of a word.	Discuss instances of active and passive voice within the selection. Have students locate any other suffixes they recognize in the text.

ANALYZE AND REVISE

- Analyze student work for evidence of student learning.
- Identify whether or not students have met the expectations in the standards.
- Identify implications for future instruction.

TEACH

Implement the planned lesson, and gather evidence of student learning.

TEACHING

Jump Start

FIRST READ Engage students in a discussion about what kind of hardship or misfortune might cause their families to leave their homes and start over in another place. Then review the extent of damage to the farms of the southern plains, as seen in "The Dust Bowl."

from The Grapes of Wrath

What is it like to leave one place and start your life over someplace else? What might be the hardest part of leaving your life behind and starting over? Is this experience the same or different for adults and children? Why? Modeling questions such as these will help students connect to "*from* The Grapes of Wrath" and to the Performance Task assignment. Selection audio and print capability for the selection are available in the Interactive Teacher's Edition.

Concept Vocabulary

Support students as they rank the words. Ask if they've ever heard, read, or used them. Reassure them that the definitions for these words are listed in the selection.

FIRST READ

As they read, students should perform the steps of the first read:

NOTICE: You may want to encourage students to notice how Steinbeck tells the story and how he reveals what the characters are feeling.

ANNOTATE: Remind students to mark text that includes both direct (clearly stated) and indirect (implied) characterization.

CONNECT: Encourage students to make connections beyond the text. If they cannot make connections to their own lives or other texts, have them consider movies and TV shows.

RESPOND: Students will answer questions and write a summary to demonstrate understanding. Point out to students that while they will always complete the Respond step at the end of the first read, the other steps will probably happen somewhat concurrently. You may wish to print copies of the **First-Read Guide: Fiction** for students to use.

Remind students that during their first read, they should not answer the close-read questions that appear in the selection.

MAKING MEANING

THE DUST BOWL

Comparing Media to Text

You will now read an excerpt from *The Grapes of Wrath*. Complete the first-read and close-read activities. Then, compare the depiction of historical events in the video with that in the novel excerpt.

from THE GRAPES OF WRATH

About the Author

Few writers portray more vividly than **John Steinbeck** (1902–1968) what it was like to live through the Great Depression of the 1930s. His stories and novels capture the poverty, desperation, and social injustice experienced by many working-class Americans during this bleak period. While many of his characters suffer tragic fates, they almost always exhibit bravery and dignity in their struggles.

Tool Kit
First-Read Guide and Model Annotation

STANDARDS

Reading Literature
By the end of the year, read and comprehend literature, including stories, dramas, and poems, in the grades 6–8 text complexity band proficiently, with scaffolding as needed at the high end of the range.

from The Grapes of Wrath

Concept Vocabulary

You will encounter the following words as you read an excerpt from *The Grapes of Wrath*. Before reading, note how familiar you are with each word. Then, rank the words in order from most familiar (1) to least familiar (6).

WORD	YOUR RANKING
ruthless	
bitterness	
toil	
sorrow	
doomed	
frantically	

After completing your first read, come back to the concept vocabulary and review your rankings. Mark any changes to your original rankings.

First Read FICTION

Apply these strategies as you conduct your first read. You will have an opportunity to complete the close-read notes after your first read.

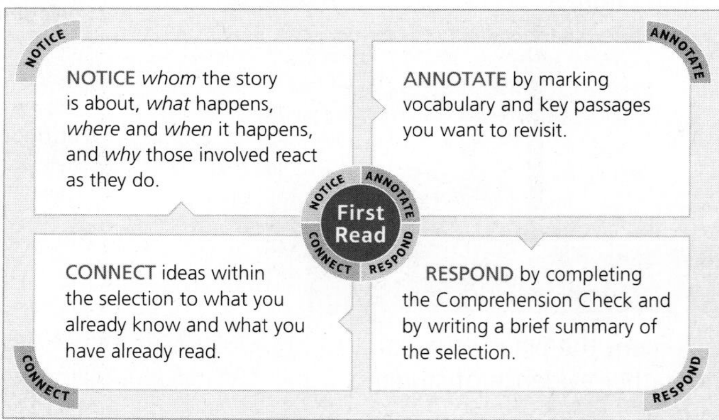

PERSONALIZE FOR LEARNING

English Language Support

Similar Words Help students understand the differences between *toil*, *toll*, and *tool*. Explain that as it's used in the text, *toil* is a verb that means "do long, difficult, tiring work." (It is not easy to toil in the hot sun picking fruit.) *Toll* is a noun that means "a tax or fee." (We had to pay a toll to drive over the bridge.) *Tool* is a noun that typically means "a handheld device that aids in accomplishing a task." (A hammer is a tool that's used to drive nails into wood.)

ANCHOR TEXT | NOVEL EXCERPT

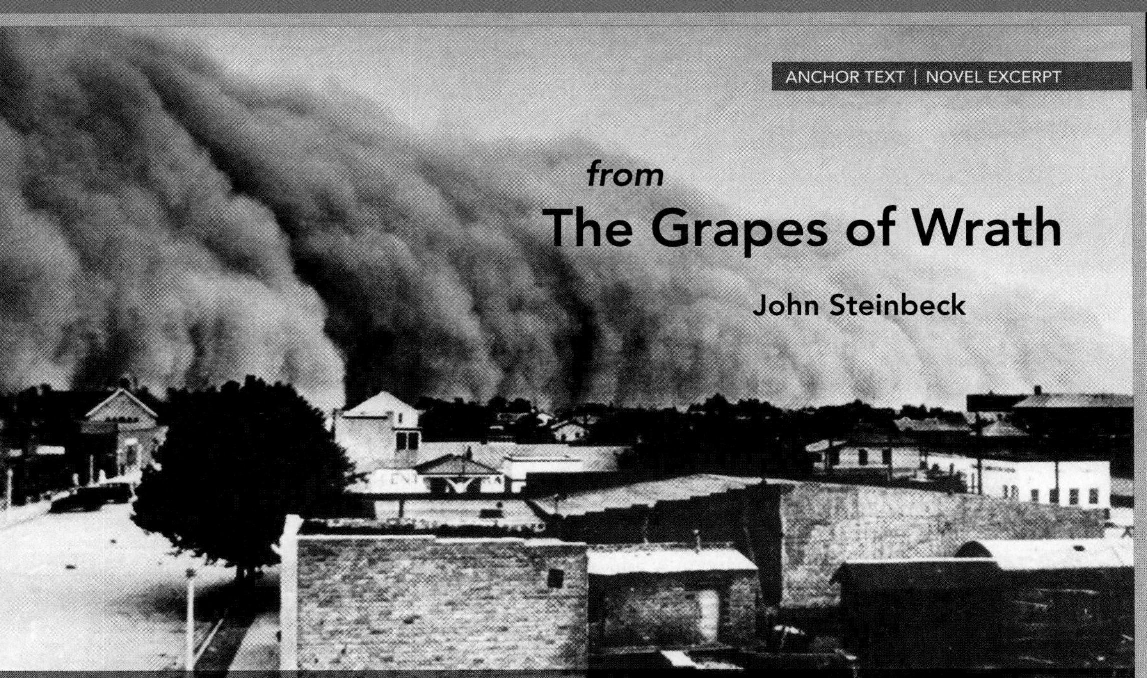

from The Grapes of Wrath

John Steinbeck

BACKGROUND

During the Great Depression, a severe drought in Oklahoma caused massive dust storms that blew away topsoil and destroyed farmland. Devastated farming families had no choice but to sell all their belongings and leave. This is the situation faced by the Joad family in John Steinbeck's novel *The Grapes of Wrath*. In this excerpt, the narrator describes the aftermath of the devastating drought.

1 In the little houses the tenant people sifted their belongings and the belongings of their fathers and of their grandfathers. Picked over their possessions for the journey to the west. The men were **ruthless** because the past had been spoiled, but the women knew how the past would cry to them in the coming days. The men went into the barns and the sheds.

2 That plow, that harrow, remember in the war we planted mustard? Remember a fella wanted us to put in that rubber bush they call guayule?[1] Get rich, he said. Bring out those tools—get a few dollars for them. Eighteen dollars for that plow, plus freight—Sears Roebuck.[2]

NOTES

ruthless (ROOTH lihs) *adj.* having no compassion or pity

1. **guayule** (gwy YOO lee) a desert shrub containing rubber, native to Mexico and Texas. During the Great Depression, it was thought that guayule could be profitably processed for rubber.
2. **Sears Roebuck** company that sold clothes, farm equipment, and other goods by mail order, which supplied much of rural America.

CROSS-CURRICULAR PERSPECTIVES

Social Studies

Farming Review paragraphs 2 and 3 and call student attention to the farm equipment described. Have students research and write a short report about one of the farming tools or pieces of equipment mentioned in paragraphs 2–3: plow, harrow, harness, carts, seeders, hoes. They should include information about what the tool is and what it is used for, as well as an image for each. Remind students that this story takes place in the 1930s, so their images should reflect what this equipment looked like at that time. Have volunteers share their research with the class, and discuss how the information and images help students understand the story.

Additional **English Language Support** is available in the Interactive Teacher's Edition.

NOTES

bitterness (BIHT uhr nihs) *n.* quality of having a sharp, unpleasant taste; condition causing pain or sorrow

toil (TOYL) *v.* work hard and with difficulty

sorrow (SOR oh) *n.* great sadness; suffering

3 Harness, carts, seeders, little bundles of hoes. Bring 'em out. Pile 'em up. Load 'em in the wagon. Take 'em to town. Sell 'em for what you can get. Sell the team and the wagon, too. No more use for anything.

4 Fifty cents isn't enough to get for a good plow. That seeder cost thirty-eight dollars. Two dollars isn't enough. Can't haul it all back—Well, take it, and a **bitterness** with it. Take the well pump and the harness. Take halters, collars, hames, and tugs.[3] Take the little glass brow-band jewels, roses red under glass. Got those for the bay gelding.[4] 'Member how he lifted his feet when he trotted?

5 Junk piled up in a yard.

6 Can't sell a hand plow any more. Fifty cents for the weight of the metal. Disks and tractors, that's the stuff now.

7 Well, take it—all junk—and give me five dollars. You're not buying only junk, you're buying junked lives. And more—you'll see—you're buying bitterness. Buying a plow to plow your own children under, buying the arms and spirits that might have saved you. Five dollars, not four. I can't haul 'em back—Well, take 'em for four. But I warn you, you're buying what will plow your own children under. And you won't see. You can't see. Take 'em for four. Now, what'll you give for the team and wagon? Those fine bays, matched they are, matched in color, matched the way they walk, stride to stride. In the stiff pull-straining hams[5] and buttocks, split-second timed together. And in the morning, the light on them, bay light. They look over the fence sniffing for us, and the stiff ears swivel to hear us, and the black forelocks! I've got a girl. She likes to braid the manes and forelocks, puts little red bows on them. Likes to do it. Not any more. I could tell you a funny story about that girl and that off bay. Would make you laugh. Off horse is eight, near is ten, but might of been twin colts the way they work together. See? The teeth. Sound all over. Deep lungs. Feet fair and clean. How much? Ten dollars? For both? And the wagon—I'd shoot 'em for dog feed first. Oh, take 'em! Take 'em quick, mister. You're buying a little girl plaiting the forelocks, taking off her hair ribbon to make bows, standing back, head cocked, rubbing the soft noses with her cheek. You're buying years of work, **toil** in the sun; you're buying a **sorrow** that can't talk. But watch it, mister. There's a premium goes with this pile of junk and the bay horses—so beautiful—a packet of bitterness to grow in your house and to flower, some day. We could have saved you, but you cut us down, and soon you will be cut down and there'll be none of us to save you.

3. **halters, collars, hames, and tugs** parts of the harnesses used to attach horses to horse-drawn plows.
4. **bay gelding** reddish-brown male horse.
5. **hams** back of a horse's knee.

PERSONALIZE FOR LEARNING

Strategic Support

Author's Style Discuss the writing technique Steinbeck uses to tell the story in paragraphs 4–7. We experience the men selling their possessions through the speech of one unnamed character as he argues with the junk dealer. Steinbeck doesn't include the junk dealer's side of this conversation, though we know he is talking to the man because the man is responding to what the dealer is saying. Steinbeck could have chosen to tell this part of the story by revealing both sides of the conversation but chose to do it this way. A likely reason is that it's more dramatic this way. We learn the thoughts and feelings of the man selling his possessions as they spill out in one long nonstop rush, which makes this entire episode much more emotional.

DIGITAL PERSPECTIVES

8 And the tenant men came walking back, hands in their pockets, hats pulled down. Some bought a pint and drank it fast to make the impact hard and stunning. But they didn't laugh and they didn't dance. They didn't sing or pick the guitars. They walked back to the farms, hands in pockets and heads down, shoes kicking the red dust up.

9 Maybe we can start again, in the new rich land—in California, where the fruit grows. We'll start over.

10 But you can't start. Only a baby can start. You and me—why, we're all that's been. The anger of a moment, the thousand pictures, that's us. This land, this red land, is us; and the flood years and the dust years and the drought years are us. We can't start again. The bitterness we sold to the junk man—he got it all right, but we have it still. And when the owner men told us to go, that's us; and when the tractor hit the house, that's us until we're dead. To California or any place—every one a drum major leading a parade of hurts, marching with our bitterness. And some day—the armies of bitterness will all be going the same way. And they'll all walk together, and there'll be a dead terror from it.

11 The tenant men scuffed home to the farms through the red dust.

12 When everything that could be sold was sold, stoves and bedsteads, chairs and tables, little corner cupboards, tubs and tanks, still there were piles of possessions; and the women sat among them, turning them over and looking off beyond and back, pictures, square glasses, and here's a vase.

13 Now you know well what we can take and what we can't take. We'll be camping out—a few pots to cook and wash in, and mattresses and comforts, lantern and buckets, and a piece of canvas. Use that for a tent. This kerosene can. Know what that is? That's the stove. And clothes—take all the clothes. And—the rifle? Wouldn't go out naked of a rifle. When shoes and clothes and food, when even hope is gone, we'll have the rifle. When grampa came—did I tell you?—he had pepper and salt and a rifle. Nothing else. That goes. And a bottle for water. That just about fills us. Right up the sides of the trailer, and the kids can set in the trailer, and granma on a mattress. Tools, a shovel and saw and wrench and pliers. An ax, too. We had that ax forty years. Look how she's wore down. And ropes, of course. The rest? Leave it—or burn it up.

14 And the children came.

15 If Mary takes that doll, that dirty rag doll, I got to take my Indian bow. I got to. An' this roun' stick—big as me. I might need this stick. I had this stick so long—a month, or maybe a year. I got to take it. And what's it like in California?

16 The women sat among the **doomed** things, turning them over and looking past them and back. This book. My father had it. He

NOTES

CLOSE READ

ANNOTATE: Mark examples of repetition of words and phrases in paragraph 10.

QUESTION: What ideas are being emphasized through repetition? Why does the narrator keep using the pronouns "us" and "we"?

CONCLUDE: What can you conclude about the narrator by the words he uses and ideas he conveys?

doomed (doomd) *adj.* destined to a bad outcome

CLOSE READ

You may wish to model the Close Read using the following think-aloud format. Possible responses to questions on the student page are included. You may also want to print copies of the **Close-Read Guide: Fiction** for students to use.

ANNOTATE: As I read paragraph 10, I see that Steinbeck doesn't just repeat the word *years*, but each time he uses it he adds something to this word.

QUESTION: I think Steinbeck repeats the word *years* to emphasize how long these people have been farming this land together.

CONCLUDE: I can conclude that the narrator sympathizes with the people he is describing. He is one of them.

HOW LANGUAGE WORKS

Repetition Use paragraph 10 to discuss the value of well-crafted repetition. Point out that Steinbeck could have written the text this way: "the flood, dust, and drought years." But he repeats not only *years*, but also *and* and *the*, giving the reader a sense of the ongoing trials and challenges these people faced, and creating a rhythm that emphasizes how long and how often these people faced these difficulties. Show students the following two sentences: Caleb wished until he had no more wishes left. Caleb wished and wished and wished until he had no more wishes left. Which is a stronger sentence? Why?

CLOSE READ

You may wish to model the Close Read using the following think-aloud format. Possible responses to questions on the student page are included.

ANNOTATE: As I read paragraphs 17–18, I highlight the punctuation.

QUESTION: I notice that in each paragraph there are several consecutive questions followed by several statements ending in periods. The dashes indicate the narrator is inserting additional thoughts or emphasis.

CONCLUDE: I think the effect created by the punctuation helps give the narrator an urgency by asking a number of difficult questions and then providing equally difficult answers. The narrator is digging deep into his emotions to describe the plight of these people, and the phrases within dashes help emphasize this tone.

NOTES

CLOSE READ

ANNOTATE: Mark the punctuation in paragraphs 17 and 18.

QUESTION: What patterns are created by the questions and statements? What do the dashes indicate?

CONCLUDE: What effect do the patterns and use of dashes create? How do they bring to life this unnamed narrator?

frantically (FRAN tuh klee) *adv.* acting wildly with anger, worry, or pain

liked a book. *Pilgrim's Progress.*[6] Used to read it. Got his name in it. And his pipe—still smells rank. And this picture—an angel. I looked at that before the fust three come—didn't seem to do much good. Think we could get this china dog in? Aunt Sadie brought it from the St. Louis Fair.[7] See? Wrote right on it. No, I guess not. Here's a letter my brother wrote the day before he died. Here's an old-time hat. These feathers—never got to use them. No, there isn't room.

17 How can we live without our lives? How will we know it's us without our past? No. Leave it. Burn it.

18 They sat and looked at it and burned it into their memories. How'll it be not to know what land's outside the door? How if you wake up in the night and know—and *know* the willow tree's not there? Can you live without the willow tree? Well, no, you can't. The willow tree is you. The pain on that mattress there—that dreadful pain—that's you.

19 And the children—if Sam takes his Indian bow an' his long roun' stick, I get to take two things. I choose the fluffy pilla. That's mine.

20 Suddenly they were nervous. Got to get out quick now. Can't wait. We can't wait. And they piled up the goods in the yards and set fire to them. They stood and watched them burning, and then **frantically** they loaded up the cars and drove away, drove in the dust. The dust hung in the air for a long time after the loaded cars had passed. ❧

6. ***Pilgrim's Progress*** Christian story by John Bunyan about living virtuously.
7. **St. Louis Fair:** The World's Fair of 1904, celebrating a hundred years of American ownership of lands west of the Mississippi River.

VOCABULARY DEVELOPMENT

Multiple Meanings Call students' attention to the word *rank* in paragraph 16. Explain to students that the word has several meanings. As used in the text, it's an adjective that means "offensive in odor or flavor." (That rotten food has a rank smell.) Explain to students that they will probably more often encounter this word as a noun or a verb. As a noun it can mean "a grade of official standing in a hierarchy." (After years of service, Smith held the rank of general.); "line of soldiers ranged side by side in close order" (The soldiers stood at attention in the ranks.); "the body of enlisted personnel" (Jane rose quickly through the ranks.). As a verb it can mean "to determine the relative position of; to rate" (Ken ranked his favorite books from one to ten.); "to take or have a position in relation to others" (Melinda ranks first in her class.).

Comprehension Check

Complete the following items after you finish your first read.

1. What big change is taking place in the lives of these characters?

2. What are the men doing in paragraph 7?

3. What happens after the people burn their belongings?

4. **Notebook** Write a brief summary of this excerpt from *The Grapes of Wrath.*

RESEARCH

Research to Clarify Choose at least one unfamiliar detail from the text. Briefly research that detail. In what way does the information you learned shed light on an aspect of the story?

DIGITAL PERSPECTIVES

Comprehension Check

Possible responses:

1. They are leaving their farms.
2. They are selling their possessions.
3. They leave as fast as they can.
4. Summaries will vary, but students should include: people who are being forced to leave their farms look through their belongings, deciding what to keep and what to leave behind; the men take farm equipment to the junk dealer to sell but are disappointed and angry when they are paid much less than they believe these possessions are worth; returning with the money they raised, they decide to burn whatever they don't take before leaving for California; they worry about starting over and leaving their past behind, but they have no choice—they must leave; they set fire to what they can't take, watch it burn, then drive away over a dust-covered road.

Research

Research to Clarify If students struggle to identify an unfamiliar detail, have them reread the text and notice words or details that might be new to them, such as farm equipment or words in dialect.

PERSONALIZE FOR LEARNING

Challenge

Interpret Ask students to consider a particularly moving passage or two from the story—for example, this passage from paragraph 18:

> How'll it be not to know what land's outside the door? How if you wake up in the night and know—and *know* the willow tree's not there? Can you live without the willow tree? Well, no, you can't. The willow tree is you. The pain on that mattress there—that dreadful pain—that's you.

Have students rewrite the passage(s), expressing the ideas in their own words. Ask volunteers to share their rewrites with the class.

Jump Start

CLOSE READ Have students close read the title, *The Grapes of Wrath.* Have students discuss the meaning of *wrath* (strong, vengeful anger or indignation; punishment for an offense or a crime). Discuss how wrath and punishment are reflected in the excerpt. What does this suggest about Steinbeck's intention in writing this story?

Close Read the Text

Walk students through the annotation model on the student page. Encourage them to complete items 2 and 3 on their own. Review and discuss the sections students have marked. If needed, continue to model close reading by using the Annotation Highlights in the Interactive Teacher's Edition.

Analyze the Text

Possible responses:

1. Details include the names of farming tools and farm equipment among the men's possessions. The men also discuss details about planting crops. (Paragraphs 2–3) **DOK 2**
2. The general attitude of the characters is anger and bitterness. You can tell because of what they say to the junk dealer when they sell their possessions. (Paragraph 7) **DOK 3**
3. They burn their possessions because they know they are never coming back and they're angry they're being forced to leave. Also, burning their possessions symbolizes the end of the lives they've led until now. **DOK 3**
4. Responses will vary. Students may conclude that one way some people deal with obstacles is moving to a new place and starting over. **DOK 3**

FORMATIVE ASSESSMENT

Analyze the Text

- **If** students fail to cite evidence, **then** remind them to support their ideas with specific information from the text.
- **If** students fail to grasp key ideas in the text, **then** have them review the relevant sections of the excerpt.

from THE GRAPES OF WRATH

Close Read the Text

1. This model, from paragraph 1, shows two sample annotations, along with questions and conclusions. Close read the passage, and find another detail to annotate. Then, write a question and your conclusion.

ANNOTATE • QUESTION • Close Read • CONCLUDE

ANNOTATE: There is repetition here, of words and ideas.

QUESTION: What ideas are being emphasized through repetition?

CONCLUDE: The tenants are sorting through generations of memories and belongings.

In the little houses the tenant people sifted their belongings and the belongings of their fathers and of their grandfathers. Picked over their possessions for the journey to the west. The men were ruthless because the past had been spoiled, but the women knew how the past would cry to them in the coming days.

ANNOTATE: The author personifies the past by saying it "would cry to them in the coming days."

QUESTION: Why did the author make this choice?

CONCLUDE: The women understand how much they will miss the past.

2. For more practice, go back into the text and complete the close-read notes.
3. Revisit a section of the text you found important during your first read. Read this section closely and **annotate** what you notice. Ask yourself **questions** such as "Why did the author make this choice?" What can you **conclude**?

Tool Kit
Close-Read Guide and Model Annotation

Analyze the Text

CITE TEXTUAL EVIDENCE to support your answers.

Notebook Respond to these questions.

1. **Classify** What story details reveal that these characters are farm people?
2. **Interpret** What is the general attitude of the characters? How can you tell?
3. **Analyze** Why do the characters burn their belongings at the end of the excerpt?
4. **Essential Question:** ***How do we overcome obstacles?*** What have you learned about how people deal with obstacles by reading this selection?

STANDARDS
Reading Literature
- Determine a theme or central idea of a text and analyze its development over the course of the text; provide an objective summary of the text.
- Analyze how particular elements of a story or drama interact.

Analyze Craft and Structure

Theme Every successful literary work develops at least one **theme**, or central message. Themes can be expressed as general truths about people or life. Writers develop themes through careful selection of significant story details, including the following elements:

- **Setting** is the time and place in which a story occurs.
- **Cultural and historical context** is the social, cultural, and historical environment of the characters, including major events that affect them.
- Characters' actions and reactions to situations can reveal **themes**, or insights about human nature.

In *The Grapes of Wrath*, Steinbeck uses the setting of Oklahoma during the Great Depression to develop themes about how people respond to great hardships, such as drought. The cultural and historical context of the novel includes the ongoing drought and the disappearance of usable farmland, the resulting conditions of poverty, and the different roles that men and women traditionally follow in that time and place.

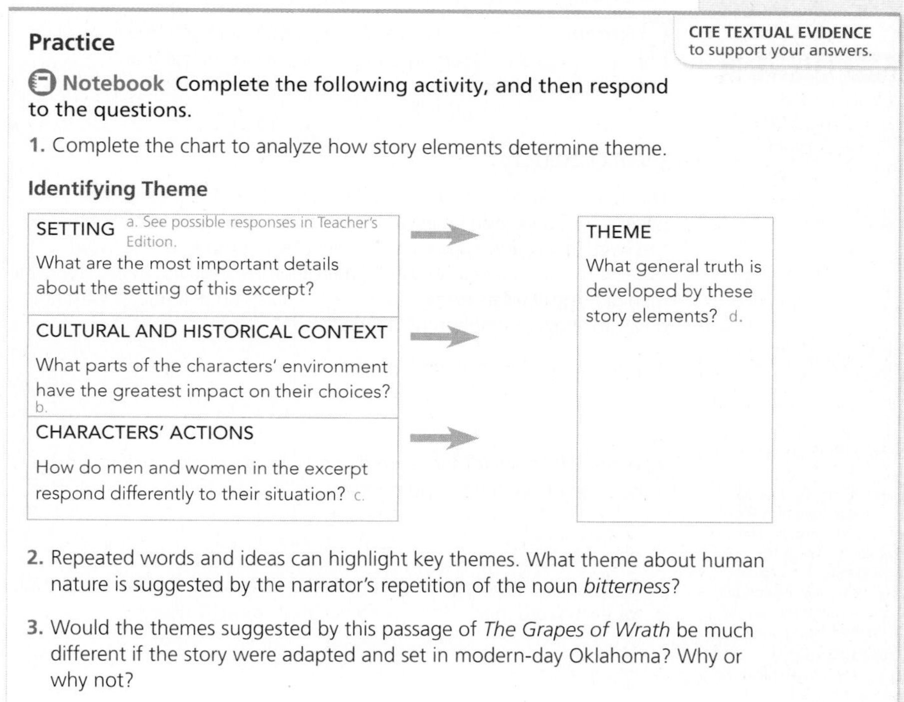

Practice

CITE TEXTUAL EVIDENCE to support your answers.

Notebook Complete the following activity, and then respond to the questions.

1. Complete the chart to analyze how story elements determine theme.

Identifying Theme

SETTING a. See possible responses in Teacher's Edition. What are the most important details about the setting of this excerpt?	→	THEME What general truth is developed by these story elements? d.
CULTURAL AND HISTORICAL CONTEXT What parts of the characters' environment have the greatest impact on their choices? b.	→	
CHARACTERS' ACTIONS How do men and women in the excerpt respond differently to their situation? c.	→	

2. Repeated words and ideas can highlight key themes. What theme about human nature is suggested by the narrator's repetition of the noun *bitterness*?
3. Would the themes suggested by this passage of *The Grapes of Wrath* be much different if the story were adapted and set in modern-day Oklahoma? Why or why not?

PERSONALIZE FOR LEARNING

English Language Support

Finding the Theme Have students read a short story and determine the theme. After their activity, have students persuade a partner about their opinion regarding the theme.

Have students create a poster that illustrates the theme of the story. **EMERGING**

Have students write a few sentences describing the theme and how the characters and story events point to it. Also have them explain how the theme is universal. **EXPANDING**

Ask students to write a paragraph stating the theme of the story. Tell them to include text evidence and explain how the evidence directly or indirectly supports their theme. **BRIDGING**

An expanded **English Language Support Lesson** on Theme is available in the Interactive Teacher's Edition.

Analyze Craft and Structure

Setting, Cultural Context, and Theme Point out that Steinbeck doesn't directly set the scene in this excerpt—he doesn't say this part of the story takes place on farms. Instead, he reveals the setting through details such as the people owning farming tools and equipment. Similarly, he establishes the cultural context through the words the characters speak. Draw students' attention to the following text: "That just about fills us. Right up the sides of the trailer, and the kids can set in the trailer, and granma on a mattress." (paragraph 13) Discuss what these words reveal about these people and the world they live in. For more support, see **Analyze Craft and Structure: Setting and Cultural Context.**

Practice

Possible responses:

1. a. dust of the farmlands, abandoned tools and possessions.
   b. They cannot survive as farmers due to drought and the failing economy. They have to sell off and even burn any equipment and possessions they cannot take to California.
   c. Men are ruthless; women are regretful.
   d. Driven into poverty by both natural and economic disaster, people will make heartbreaking and seemingly heartless decisions in order to follow any path toward hope and survival.
2. The hardship of their experience has made the people tremendously bitter. Their bitterness leads them to discard valuable farm tools and family heirlooms that hold sentimental value. All that matters is their ability to survive, and there seems to be no room for sentiment in their lives.
3. Answers will vary. Students should address the themes of the story and not just the specific conditions of the time as modern-day conditions might create a different outcome.

FORMATIVE ASSESSMENT

Analyze Craft and Structure

- **If** students have difficulty identifying elements of setting, **then** show them setting-related details in the text and discuss what they reveal about where the story takes place.
- **If** students have difficulty understanding cultural context, **then** review appropriate parts of the text and discuss what they reveal about the world in which these characters live.

For Reteach and Practice, see **Analyze Craft and Structure: Setting and Cultural Context (RP).**

Concept Vocabulary

Why These Words?

Possible responses:

1. The concept vocabulary sharpens the reader's understanding because the words describe how the characters feel as they leave their farms and start over.
2. spoiled (paragraph 1); stunning (paragraph 8); anger (paragraph 10); drought (paragraph 10); dust (paragraph 10); flood (paragraph 10)

Practice

Possible responses:

A *ruthless* person might go after whatever he or she wants in spite of who might be hurt. A person might feel *sorrow* after losing something of value that cannot be replaced. A person might express *bitterness* toward someone by insulting them. Shoveling snow is a form of *toil*. If something is *doomed*, it is sure to be destroyed or ruined. Someone might behave *frantically* if they believe they are late in getting to a very important event.

Word Network

Possible words: *journey; past; coming days; remember; burn it; hope*

Word Study

For more support, see **Concept Vocabulary and Word Study**

Possible responses:

1. The *ruthless* politician won the election but made many enemies along the way.
2. heartless: without kindness or caring; pitiless: without sympathy; purposeless: aimless, having no direction or goal
3. Answers will vary.

FORMATIVE ASSESSMENT

Word Study

If students have trouble finding appropriate words, **then** review using a dictionary to find different word forms. For Reteach and Practice, see **Word Study: Suffix *-less* (RP).**

LANGUAGE DEVELOPMENT

from THE GRAPES OF WRATH

Concept Vocabulary

ruthless	toil	doomed
bitterness	sorrow	frantically

Why These Words? The concept vocabulary words describe extreme emotions or conditions that people experience. For example, the men feel much *bitterness* as they sell their belongings, the women feel great *sorrow* as they say good-bye to their homes, and the characters *frantically* load their cars and leave their homes behind.

1. How does the concept vocabulary sharpen the reader's understanding of the story's characters and setting?

2. What other words in the selection describe or relate to the difficult conditions these characters face?

Practice

Notebook The concept vocabulary words appear in the excerpt from *The Grapes of Wrath*. Use each word in a sentence that demonstrates your understanding of the word's meaning.

WORD NETWORK

Add interesting words from the text about facing adversity to your Word Network.

Word Study

Old English Suffix: *-less* The Old English suffix *-less* means "not having" or "unable to be acted on or to act." It usually indicates that the word in which it appears is an adjective. For example, the word *ruthless* means "having no pity," "merciless," or "cruel." In the story, the men are described as *ruthless* as they pick through belongings with no outward show of emotion or feeling.

1. Write your own sentence that correctly uses the word *ruthless*.

2. Write definitions for these words, consulting a dictionary if you need help: *heartless, pitiless, purposeless*.

3. Think of two other words that have the suffix *-less*. Record a definition for each word, and write a sentence that correctly uses it.

STANDARDS

Language

- Determine or clarify the meaning of unknown and multiple-meaning words and phrases based on *grade 7 reading and content*, choosing flexibly from a range of strategies.
  - b. Use common, grade-appropriate Greek or Latin affixes and roots as clues to the meaning of a word.
- Acquire and use accurately grade-appropriate general academic and domain-specific words and phrases; gather vocabulary knowledge when considering a word or phrase important to comprehension or expression.

AUTHOR'S PERSPECTIVE **Elfrieda Hiebert, Ph.D.**

Digital Tools As students develop and expand their word networks, remind them of the digital tools available and of their value. Explain what digital tools offer—pronunciation; audio; word families; definitions; links to synonyms and antonyms; interactive levels of complexity of synonyms and antonyms; words in context sentences, and so much more. Experiment with these digital tools:

- Lexipedia, for example, is a visual thesaurus. Users type in any word and Lexipedia displays that word with others in the word network, color-coded by parts of speech and relationships. Hover over the word for a full definition.
- Snappy Words is similar, providing words arranged in networks.

Author's Style

Description Descriptions of people, places, and things are shaped by **word choice**, the specific language an author uses to create a strong impression.

Word choice also helps a writer create **imagery** —descriptive language that appeals to one or more of the five senses.

	EXAMPLES FROM THE TEXT	NOTES
Precise words	That plow, that harrow, remember in the war we planted mustard?	Plow, harrow, mustard are all simple, precise words.
	The tenant men scuffed home to the farms through the red dust.	The verb *scuffed* is much more precise than a verb such as *walked* or *went*.
Imagery	Take the little glass brow-band jewels, roses red under glass.	These words appeal to the sense of sight.
	And his pipe—still smells rank.	These words appeal to the sense of smell.
	I choose the fluffy pilla.	These words appeal to the sense of touch.

Practice

CITE TEXTUAL EVIDENCE to support your answers.

Complete the activity, and then respond to the questions.

1. Reread paragraph 7 of "*The Grapes of Wrath*." Use the chart below to show three examples of Steinbeck's word choice to describe the horses.

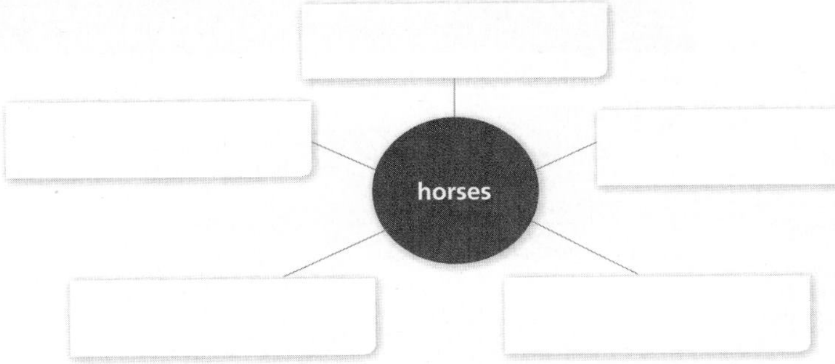

2. **Evaluate** (a) Which words from the graphic organizer enable you to imagine the horses most clearly? Explain your choices. (b) To which senses do the words you chose appeal?

3. **Interpret** (a) To what sense do the images in paragraph 13 mostly appeal? (b) What mood or atmosphere does the use of these images create?

- Lingro turns a website into a clickable dictionary, providing a variety of definitions. For example, clicking on the word "writing" on the website provides six different definitions.
- Shahi, another visual dictionary, melds Wiktionary content with Flickr images and more.

DIGITAL  PERSPECTIVES

Author's Style

Description Discuss choosing words that appeal to the five senses. What type of words appeal to sight? Sound? Taste? Smell? Feel? Also, remind students that similes and metaphors are tools they can use to write effective descriptions and create imagery. (Jason looked like he was about to explode. / Suddenly, Jason exploded.) For more support, see **Author's Style: Description.**

MAKE IT INTERACTIVE

Have students write a detailed, vivid sentence describing something in the room without actually mentioning the object. When they read the description to the class, can other students guess what they're describing?

Practice

Possible responses:

1. matched in color; stiff pull-straining hams and buttocks; they look over the fence sniffing for us; stiff ears swivel to hear us; deep lungs; feet fair and clean
2. Answers will vary.
3. (a) visual (b) The images create a mood of resignation and desperation as the narrator lists the few necessities they will bring.

FORMATIVE ASSESSMENT

Author's Style

- **If** students struggle with description, **then** review easily-accessible descriptions in the text and discuss why each is an effective description.
- **If** students have trouble understanding or interpreting imagery, **then** review images in the text and discuss the picture each creates for the reader.

For Reteach and Practice, see **Author's Style: Description (RP).**

TEACHING

Writing to Compare

As students prepare to compare the documentary video "The Dust Bowl" with the excerpt from the novel *The Grapes of Wrath,* they will analyze how the sources convey historical information about farmers.

Prewriting

Analyze Perspectives Encourage students to focus on the points of view of the rancher in the video and the farmers in the novel excerpt. Have them consider how these points of view differ.

Possible responses in chart on student page:

a. Some farmers misused the land and contributed to the erosion of the soil. A long drought made the situation much worse for farmers.

b. Tenant farmers could not find work in the Dust Bowl region. Many sold their possessions and headed west to California.

c. The images of barren farmland and dead livestock make a powerful impression.

d. The information about farmers selling their most cherished possessions for little money is dismaying.

Possible responses to Notebook questions:

1. The video focuses on wheat farmers, claiming they were only interested in monetary gain and did not take good care of the land; background music heightens the effect. The literary text focuses on tenant farmers' attitudes toward their desperate economic situation and their efforts to deal with it.
2. The video is more persuasive because it provides broader historical information about the causes and results of the Dust Bowl.

EFFECTIVE EXPRESSION

THE DUST BOWL

from THE GRAPES OF WRATH

Writing to Compare

The documentary video you watched provides in-depth information about the Dust Bowl, the historical event that is an essential part of the setting of John Steinbeck's novel *The Grapes of Wrath*. Now, deepen your understanding of the topic by analyzing what you have learned and expressing your ideas in writing.

Assignment

The video "The Dust Bowl" and the novel *The Grapes of Wrath* present very different perspectives, or points of view, about the role of farmers in the 1930s drought and its aftermath. Were farmers innocent victims of a natural disaster, or were they guilty of creating the disaster due to poor land management?

Write an **argumentative essay** in which you state and support an argument about the role of farmers in the Dust Bowl. Use details from Steinbeck's novel and the documentary video as evidence to support your claim. Strengthen your support by addressing one counterclaim.

Prewriting

Analyze Perspectives Review both sources to understand how the video and the novel present different perspectives on farmers during the Dust Bowl. Complete the chart to summarize how each source depicts the role of farmers. Then, include details from each source that produce a strong impression or impact.

	HISTORICAL VIDEO: "THE DUST BOWL"	LITERARY TEXT: from *THE GRAPES OF WRATH*
Role of Farmers in the Dust Bowl	a. See answers in Teacher's Edition.	b.
Strong Impressions	c.	d.

Notebook Respond to these questions.

1. How do the video and the novel use different techniques to influence an audience's response?
2. Which perspective on the role of farmers in the Dust Bowl is more persuasive? Why?

STANDARDS

Reading Literature
Compare and contrast a fictional portrayal of a time, place, or character and a historical account of the same period as a means of understanding how authors of fiction use or alter history.

Writing
- Write arguments to support claims with clear reasons and relevant evidence.
  - a. Introduce claim(s), acknowledge alternate or opposing claims, and organize the reasons and evidence logically.
  - b. Support claim(s) with logical reasoning and relevant evidence, using accurate, credible sources and demonstrating an understanding of the topic or text.

PERSONALIZE FOR LEARNING

Challenge

Spoken Language Have students rewatch the video "The Dust Bowl" and focus on the personal stories told by people who lived through the Dust Bowl. Ask students to write a paragraph discussing how the everyday speech of the people in the video compares with how characters speak in *The Grapes of Wrath*. How are they different? How are they similar?

Drafting

Outline Your Essay Complete the outline to plan and draft your argumentative essay. Adjust the outline as needed.

I. **Introduction** Begin with a strong opening that clearly states the claim you are making about how much responsibility farmers should bear for the Dust Bowl.

Opening Claim: ______________________

____

____

II. **Body**

A. **Provide Evidence from Sources** Choose evidence from the sources that supports your argument. Consider whether you will begin with your strongest evidence, or present your strongest evidence last.

Evidence: ______________________

____

Evidence: ______________________

____

Evidence: ______________________

____

B. **Address a Counterclaim** Introduce the counterclaim, or opposite position, presented in the video or novel. Then, explain why you think this argument is weak or incomplete.

Counterclaim: ______________________

____

Your Response: ______________________

____

III. **Conclusion** End your essay by summarizing your claim and leaving your readers with an important idea or perspective on the subject.

Closing Idea: ______________________

____

____

Reviewing, Revising, and Editing

Once you have written a complete draft, revise it for clarity and effectiveness. Is your claim clear and strong? Do you provide enough evidence to support your argument? Do you describe the counterclaim fairly and explain why you think your claim is stronger?

Swap drafts with a partner to review and proofread one another's work. Make changes and correct errors to prepare a final draft.

EVIDENCE LOG

Before moving on to a new selection, go to your Evidence Log and record what you've learned from this excerpt from *The Grapes of Wrath*.

STANDARDS

Reading Literature
Compare and contrast a fictional portrayal of a time, place, or character and a historical account of the same period as a means of understanding how authors of fiction use or alter history.

Writing
Write arguments to support claims with clear reasons and relevant evidence.

a. Support claim(s) with logical reasoning and relevant evidence, using accurate, credible sources and demonstrating an understanding of the topic or text.
c. Use words, phrases, and clauses to create cohesion and clarify the relationships among claim(s), reasons, and evidence.

- Draw evidence from literary or informational texts to support analysis, reflection, and research.
  a. Apply grade 7 Reading standards to literature.

DIGITAL PERSPECTIVES

Drafting

Outline Your Essay Remind students that as they compare the video and the text, they should keep in mind that one is nonfiction and the other is fiction; they should address any impact this has on their comparison between the two.

Regardless of which organizational structure students choose, encourage them to use transitional words to link the ideas that appear in the body of their essay.

Reviewing, Revising, and Editing

Remind students to check that they've included specific details from both the video and the text to support their claims. Ask them to review their word choice. Finally, remind students to check for grammar, usage, and mechanics. For more support, see **Writing to Compare: Argumentative Essay.**

Evidence Log Support students in completing their Evidence Log. This paced activity will help prepare them for the Performance-Based Assessment at the end of the unit.

FORMATIVE ASSESSMENT

Writing to Compare

If students are unable to provide specific examples and details, **then** have them skim the excerpt from *The Grapes of Wrath* and rewatch "The Dust Bowl" for ideas.

Selection Test

Administer the "*from* The Grapes of Wrath (*with* The Dust Bowl)" Selection Test, which is available in both print and digital formats online in Assessments.

PERSONALIZE FOR LEARNING

Strategic Support

Organization Review point-by-point comparison as an organizational structure for this kind of essay. Explain that with this kind of structure, writers focus on one idea at a time and discuss how it relates to the things being compared. For example, if the first idea is land management, the writer would discuss land management as it relates to the video and then discuss land management as it relates to the text, pointing out similarities and differences between the two. After discussing land management, the writer would move on to the next idea, which might be weather. Remind students that when using this kind of structure they should still end their essay with a concluding paragraph.

The Circuit

AUDIO SUMMARIES
Audio summaries of "The Circuit" are available online in both English and Spanish in the Interactive Teacher's Edition or Unit Resources. Assigning these summaries prior to reading the selection may help students build additional background knowledge and set a context for their first read.

Summary

"The Circuit" is one of author Francisco Jiménez's best-known stories. The narrator, a young Latino boy, comes back from a day of picking strawberries to find all the family's belongings packed. With strawberry picking season over, the family has to move on. In the next place, he and his brother pick grapes with their father and hide from school authorities. But after the grape season, the narrator finally gets to join other students in the sixth grade, where he has a great teacher. Things are looking up.

Insight

This selection reveals what life can be like when supporting a family means that even children have to work. Although the narrator must move again just as the teacher, Mr. Lema, begins to show him real opportunities, the story helps students understand what a difference one adult can make in a child's life.

ESSENTIAL QUESTION:
How do we overcome obstacles?

Connection to Essential Question

"The Circuit" connects to the Essential Question by showing that one of the ways we may be able to overcome obstacles is through the help of someone else.

WHOLE-CLASS LEARNING PERFORMANCE TASK
How did the individuals in the selections cope with the obstacles they faced?

UNIT PERFORMANCE-BASED ASSESSMENT
How can people overcome adversity in the face of overwhelming obstacles?

Connection to Performance Tasks

Whole-Class Learning Performance Task In this Performance Task, students will write an informative essay about coping with obstacles. This selection shows a boy turning to a supportive adult for help in coping with the obstacles he faces.

Unit Performance-Based Assessment For the narrator of "The Circuit," one of the biggest obstacles he faces is the difficulty of getting an education. Students should consider that his family is constantly moving from one crop to another to find work, leaving him unable to stay in the same school for any length of time. And much of the year he has to work in the fields. In this situation, what does Mr. Lema offer him that would help him overcome adversity?

DIGITAL PERSPECTIVES

 Audio  Video 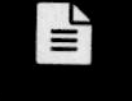 Document  Annotation Highlights 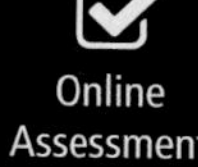 Online Assessment

LESSON RESOURCES

	Making Meaning	Language Development	Effective Expression
Lesson	**First Read** **Close Read** **Analyze the Text** **Analyze Craft and Structure**	**Concept Vocabulary** **Word Study** **Conventions**	**Writing to Sources** **Speaking and Listening**
Instructional Standards	**RL.7.10** By the end of the year, read and comprehend literature . . . **RL.7.1** Cite several pieces of textual evidence . . . **RL.7.2** Determine a theme or central idea of a text . . .	**L.7.4** Determine or clarify the meaning of unknown and multiple-meaning words and phrases . . . **L.7.4.a** Use context as a clue . . . **L.7.4.b** Use common, grade-appropriate Greek or Latin affixes and roots . . . **L.7.2** Demonstrate command of the conventions of standard English . . . **L.7.2.a** Use a comma to separate coordinate adjectives.	**RL.7.2** Determine a theme or central idea . . . **W.7.2** Write informative/explanatory texts . . . **W.7.2.b** Develop the topic . . . **W.7.9.a** Apply grade 7 Reading standards to literature . . . **SL.7.1** Engage effectively in a range of collaborative discussions . . . **SL.7.4** Present claims and findings . . . **W.7.7** Conduct short research projects . . .
STUDENT RESOURCES			
Available online in the Interactive Student Edition or Unit Resources	Selection Audio First-Read Guide: Fiction Close-Read Guide: Fiction	Word Network	Evidence Log
TEACHER RESOURCES			
Selection Resources Available online in the Interactive Teacher's Edition or Unit Resources	Audio Summaries: English and Spanish Annotation Highlights Accessible Leveled Text First Read Extension Questions Analyze Craft and Structure: Theme	Concept Vocabulary and Word Study Word Study: Old English Suffix *-ly* Conventions: Commas	Writing to Sources: Explanation Speaking and Listening: Role-Play Interview
Reteach/Practice (RP) Available online in the Interactive Teacher's Edition or Unit Resources	Analyze Craft and Structure: Theme (RP)	Word Study: Old English Suffix *-ly* (RP) Conventions: Commas (RP)	Writing to Sources: Explanation (RP) Speaking and Listening: Role-Play Interview (RP)
Assessment Available online in Assessments	Selection Test: English Selection Test: Spanish Extension Selection Test		
My Resources	A Unit 5 Answer Key is available online and in the Interactive Teacher's Edition.		

Reading Support

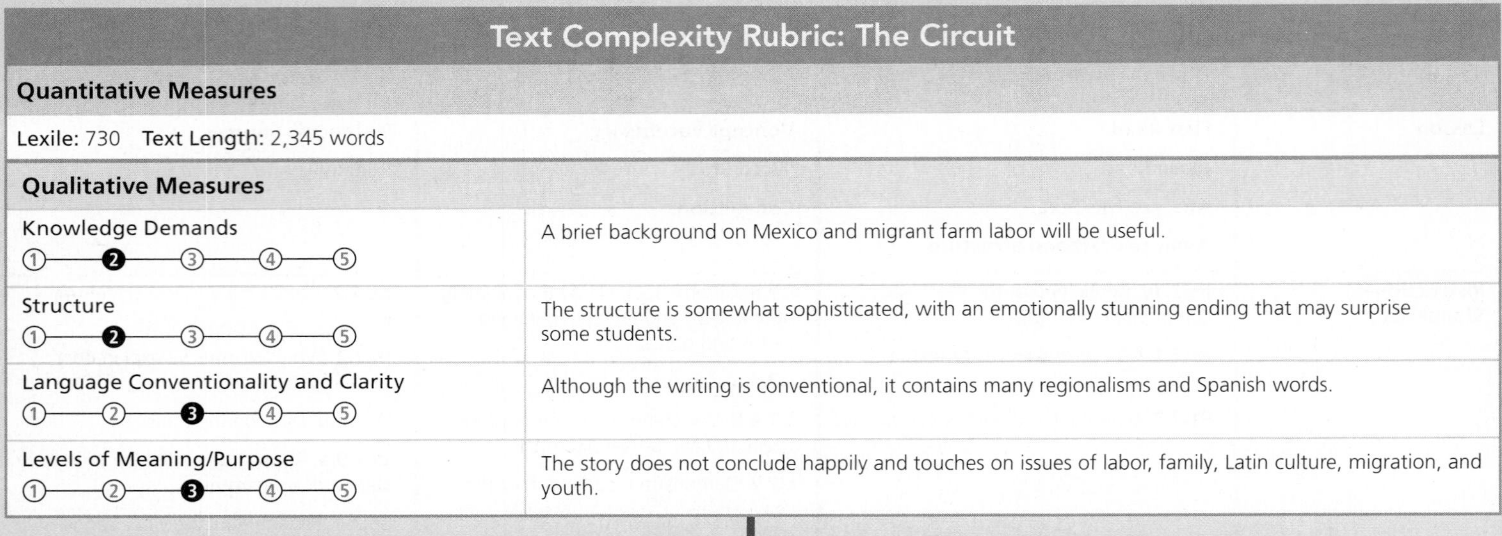

Text Complexity Rubric: The Circuit	
Quantitative Measures	
Lexile: 730 **Text Length:** 2,345 words	
Qualitative Measures	
Knowledge Demands ① ❷ ③ ④ ⑤	A brief background on Mexico and migrant farm labor will be useful.
Structure ① ❷ ③ ④ ⑤	The structure is somewhat sophisticated, with an emotionally stunning ending that may surprise some students.
Language Conventionality and Clarity ① ② ❸ ④ ⑤	Although the writing is conventional, it contains many regionalisms and Spanish words.
Levels of Meaning/Purpose ① ② ❸ ④ ⑤	The story does not conclude happily and touches on issues of labor, family, Latin culture, migration, and youth.

DECIDE AND PLAN

English Language Support

Provide English learners with support for language and structure as they read the selection.

Language Ask students to think about why Jiménez may have included words in Spanish, and then to think about what it means that the boy's new teacher speaks to him in English. Encourage them to think about what an author is trying to do when he writes in two languages at the same time and not just one.

Structure Toward the end, readers are made to feel some relief for the poor narrator, who now has a good school to attend and a teacher who wants to teach him the trumpet. The sudden reversal is devastating, though not unexpected. Talk about why Jiménez composed the story in this way, instead of just showing the family moving on to the next farm.

Strategic Support

Provide students with strategic support to ensure that they can successfully read the text.

Language Ask students to read the story and use context to figure out the meaning of unknown words, such as *sharecropper, Caranchita,* and *carne con chile.* Later, look them up together.

Structure Ask students if they understand what really happened in the story's ending. Talk about whether it is accurate to think the boy will return to the school and one day learn the trumpet. Encourage them to think about how the manner in which the story was constructed supports their conclusion.

Challenge

Provide students who need to be challenged with ideas for how they can go beyond a simple interpretation of the text.

Text Analysis Ask students to make note of where in the text, before the ending, the author prepared the reader for the turn of events as they played out. Ask them to consider whether there was any way they could have predicted that the boy would be taken out of school so suddenly. Have them discuss with each other how this story benefitted from such a stunning conclusion.

Written Response Challenge students to come up with their own ending for "The Circuit." Tell them to imagine, in just a few paragraphs, that they are the narrator who had these experiences, and to use their imaginations to create a new conclusion.

TEACH

Read and Respond

Have students do their first read of the selection. Then have them complete their close read. Finally, work with them on the Making Meaning, Language Development, and Effective Expression activities.

Standards Support Through Teaching and Learning Cycle

IDENTIFY NEEDS

Analyze results of the Beginning-of-Year Assessment, focusing on the items relating to Unit 5. Also take into consideration student performance to this point and your observations of where particular students struggle.

DECIDE AND PLAN

- If students have performed poorly on items matching these standards, then provide selection scaffolds before assigning them the on-level lesson provided in the Student Edition.
- If students have done well on the Beginning-of-Year Assessment, then challenge them to keep progressing and learning by giving them opportunities to practice the skills in depth.
- Use the Selection Resources listed on the Planning pages for "The Circuit" to help students continually improve their ability to master the standards.

Instructional Standards: The Circuit

	Catching Up	This Year	Looking Forward
Reading	You may wish to administer the **Analyze Craft and Structure: Theme (RP)** worksheet to help students understand how to determine a work's theme.	**RL.2** Determine a theme or central idea of a text and analyze its development over the course of the text; provide an objective summary of the text.	Challenge students to discuss how characters, plot, and setting help inform the themes.
Writing	You may wish to administer the **Writing to Sources: Explanation (RP)** worksheet to help students understand how to write an informative essay.	**W.2** Write informative/ explanatory texts to examine a topic and convey ideas, concepts, and information through the selection, organization, and analysis of relevant content.	Challenge students to incorporate outside research into their essays.
Speaking and Listening	You may wish to administer the **Speaking and Listening: Role-Play Interview (RP)** worksheet to help students prepare for their role playing.	**SL.1.c** Pose questions that elicit elaboration and respond to others' questions and comments with relevant observations and ideas that bring the discussion back on topic as needed.	Challenge students to improvise portions of their role plays; i.e., allow the class to ask questions.
Language	You may wish to administer the **Conventions: Commas (RP)** worksheet to help students understand how commas signal a brief pause in a sentence. You may wish to administer the **Word Study: Old English Suffix *-ly* (RP)** worksheet to help students understand how *-ly* changes words into adverbs.	**L.2** Demonstrate command of the conventions of standard English capitalization, punctuation, and spelling when writing. **L.4.b** Use common, grade-appropriate Greek or Latin affixes and roots as clues to the meaning of a word.	Introduce students to dashes and ellipses. Have students practice adding *-ly* to the end of words.

TEACH

Implement the planned lesson, and gather evidence of student learning.

ANALYZE AND REVISE

- Analyze student work for evidence of student learning.
- Identify whether students have met the expectations in the standards.
- Identify implications for future instruction.

Jump Start

FIRST READ Prior to students' first read, remind them that this unit's theme is facing adversity. Briefly explain that migrant workers move from place to place picking different crops, and engage students in a discussion about what kinds of adversity people living such lives might face.

The Circuit

What is it like to be constantly moving from place to place? What obstacles might people who constantly move face that other people might not have to deal with? Modeling questions such as these will help students connect to "The Circuit" and to the Performance Task assignment. Selection audio and print capability for the selection are available in the Interactive Teacher's Edition.

Concept Vocabulary

Support students as they rank the words. Ask if they've ever heard, read, or used any of them. Reassure them that the definitions for these words are listed in the selection.

FIRST READ

As they read, students should perform the steps of the first read:

NOTICE: You may want to encourage students to notice how the family's moving about affects the narrator of the story.

ANNOTATE: Remind students to mark text that reveals obstacles and issues the characters in the story have to deal with.

CONNECT: Encourage students to make connections beyond the text. If they cannot make connections to their own lives or other texts, have them consider movies, TV shows, and news reports.

RESPOND: Students will answer questions and write a summary to demonstrate understanding.

Point out to students that while they will always complete the Respond step at the end of the first read, the other steps will probably happen somewhat concurrently. You may wish to print copies of the **First-Read Guide: Fiction** for students to use.

Remind students that during their first read, they should not answer the close-read questions that appear in the selection.

MAKING MEANING

About the Author

Francisco Jiménez (b. 1943) was born in Mexico and came to the United States with his family when he was four years old. The family settled in California and became migrant workers. Although he could not go to school before the harvest ended, Jiménez studied in the fields. His hard work paid off as he went on to become an outstanding teacher and award-winning writer.

The Circuit

Concept Vocabulary

You will encounter the following words as you read "The Circuit." Before reading, note how familiar you are with each word. Then, rank the words in order from most familiar (1) to least familiar (6).

WORD	YOUR RANKING
thoroughly	
wearily	
instinctively	
enthusiastically	
hesitantly	
understandingly	

After completing your first read, come back to the concept vocabulary and review your rankings. Mark any changes to your original rankings.

Tool Kit
First-Read Guide and Model Annotation

First Read FICTION

Apply these strategies as you conduct your first read. You will have an opportunity to complete the close-read notes after your first read.

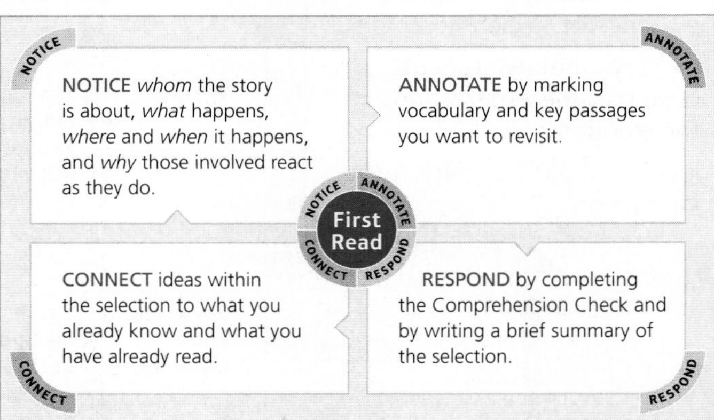

STANDARDS
Reading Literature
By the end of the year, read and comprehend literature, including stories, dramas, and poems, in the grades 6–8 text complexity band proficiently, with scaffolding as needed at the high end of the range.

CROSS-CURRICULAR PERSPECTIVES

Social Studies Have students research and list the crops grown in the United States that must be picked by hand and the regions in which the crops are grown. Tell students to note when the crops are harvested. Ask volunteers to share their information with the class, and encourage students to notice how it is reflected in the story.

The Circuit

Francisco Jiménez

BACKGROUND

This selection is from *The Circuit: Stories from the Life of a Migrant Child,* a collection of autobiographical short stories by Francisco Jiménez. In this story, the narrator, Panchito, tells of his difficult early years as part of a family of migrant farm workers. To him, life consisted of constant moving and work, with school wedged in around harvesting jobs. The "circuit" in the title refers to the path migrant workers take every year to find jobs.

NOTES

1 It was that time of year again. Ito, the strawberry sharecropper,[1] did not smile. It was natural. The peak of the strawberry season was over and the last few days the workers, most of them braceros,[2] were not picking as many boxes as they had during the months of June and July.

2 As the last days of August disappeared, so did the number of braceros. Sunday, only one—the best picker—came to work. I liked him. Sometimes we talked during our half-hour lunch break. That is how I found out he was from Jalisco, the same state in Mexico my family was from. That Sunday was the last time I saw him.

3 When the sun had tired and sunk behind the mountains, Ito signaled us that it was time to go home. "*Ya esora*,"[3] he yelled in his broken Spanish. Those were the words I waited for twelve hours a day, every day, seven days a week, week after week. And the thought of not hearing them again saddened me.

1. **sharecropper** (SHAIR krop uhr) *n.* one who works for a share of a crop; tenant farmer.
2. **braceros** (bruh SAIR ohs) *n.* migrant Mexican farm laborers who harvest crops.
3. ***Ya esora*** (yah ehs AW rah) Spanish for "It's time." *(Ya es hora.)*

DIGITAL PERSPECTIVES

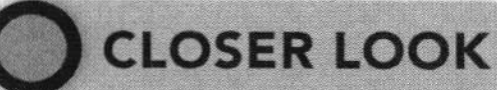

CLOSER LOOK

Analyze Cultural Context

Students may have marked text in paragraph 2 during their first read. Use this paragraph to help students understand the cultural context of the story. Encourage them to talk about the annotations that they marked. You may want to model a close read with the class based on the highlights shown in the text.

ANNOTATE: Have students mark details in paragraph 2 that reveal the cultural context of the story, or have students participate while you highlight them.

QUESTION: Guide students to consider what these details tell them.

Possible response: The narrator is from Mexico. People disappear from his life.

CONCLUDE: Help students to formulate conclusions about the importance of these details. Ask what these details reveal about the narrator's life.

Possible response: It is probably hard for the narrator to make or keep friends because people often suddenly disappear from his life.

Remind students that **cultural context** is the historical background and values that influence a writer. Point out that the author directly states the narrator is from Mexico, but indirectly establishes that people disappear from his life. This may happen often because we know that, as migrant workers, the narrator's family moves frequently. All this movement—and the loss of potential friendships—is part of the author's cultural context.

PERSONALIZE FOR LEARNING

English Language Support

Multiple-Meaning Words Call student attention to the word *peak* in paragraph 1. Explain that the word has several meanings. As it's used in this part of the text, it's a noun that means "the highest level, or greatest degree." (The peak of the strawberry season is the time when there are the most strawberries to be picked. After this time, there will be fewer and fewer strawberries.) Explain that as a noun, *peak* can also mean "a pointed part of a garment" (Leroy saluted, touching the peak of his cap.) or "the top of a hill or mountain" (We climbed for two hours and finally reached the mountain peak.). *Peak* can also be an adjective that means "being at or reaching the maximum" (peak levels; peak output) and "relating to, or being a period of maximum activity" (peak business hours). **ALL LEVELS**

NOTES

4 As we drove home Papá did not say a word. With both hands on the wheel, he stared at the dirt road. My older brother, Roberto, was also silent. He leaned his head back and closed his eyes. Once in a while he cleared from his throat the dust that blew in from outside.

5 Yes, it was that time of year. When I opened the front door to the shack, I stopped. Everything we owned was neatly packed in cardboard boxes. Suddenly I felt even more the weight of hours, days, weeks, and months of work. I sat down on a box. The thought of having to move to Fresno[4] and knowing what was in store for me there brought tears to my eyes.

6 That night I could not sleep. I lay in bed thinking about how much I hated this move.

7 A little before five o'clock in the morning, Papá woke everyone up. A few minutes later, the yelling and screaming of my little brothers and sisters, for whom the move was a great adventure, broke the silence of dawn. Shortly, the barking of the dogs accompanied them.

8 While we packed the breakfast dishes, Papá went outside to start the "Carcanchita."[5] That was the name Papá gave his old '38 black Plymouth. He bought it in a used-car lot in Santa Rosa in the Winter of 1949. Papá was very proud of his little jalopy. He had a right to be proud of it. He spent a lot of time looking at other cars before buying this one. When he finally chose the Carcanchita, he checked it **thoroughly** before driving it out of the car lot. He examined every inch of the car. He listened to the motor, tilting his head from side to side like a parrot, trying to detect any noises that spelled car trouble. After being satisfied with the looks and sounds of the car, Papá then insisted on knowing who the original owner was. He never did find out from the car salesman, but he bought the car anyway. Papá figured the original owner must have been an important man because behind the rear seat of the car he found a blue necktie.

thoroughly (THUR oh lee) *adv.* completely; entirely

9 Papá parked the car out in front and left the motor running. "*Listo*,"[6] he yelled. Without saying a word Roberto and I began to carry the boxes out to the car. Roberto carried the two big boxes and I carried the two smaller ones. Papá then threw the mattress on top of the car roof and tied it with ropes to the front and rear bumpers.

10 Everything was packed except Mamá's pot. It was an old large galvanized[7] pot she had picked up at an army surplus store in Santa Maria. The pot had many dents and nicks, and the

4. **Fresno** (FREHZ noh) *n.* city in central California.
5. **Carcanchita** (kahr kahn CHEE tah) affectionate name for the car.
6. ***Listo*** (LEES toh) Spanish for "Ready."
7. **galvanized** (GAL vuh nyzd) *adj.* coated with zinc to prevent rusting.

PERSONALIZE FOR LEARNING

Strategic Support

Author's Style Discuss the point of view from which Jiménez tells the story (first-person point of view of the narrator). This means readers will know only what the narrator knows. For example, in paragraph 4 we get a sense of how Papá and Roberto feel because of what the narrator observes, but we don't learn their feelings directly from them because they don't tell the narrator. Remind students that in *The Grapes of Wrath*, John Steinbeck alternated between the third person (when the narrator told the story) and the first person (when an individual character was telling the story). Encourage students to consider how the point of view affects a story.

more dents and nicks it acquired the more Mamá liked it. "*Mi olla,*"[8] she used to say proudly.

11 I held the front door open as Mamá carefully carried out her pot by both handles, making sure not to spill the cooked beans. When she got to the car, Papá reached out to help her with it. Roberto opened the rear car door and Papá gently placed it on the floor behind the front seat. All of us then climbed in. Papá sighed, wiped the sweat from his forehead with his sleeve, and said **wearily**: "*Es todo.*"[9]

12 As we drove away, I felt a lump in my throat. I turned around and looked at our little shack for the last time.

13 At sunset we drove into a labor camp near Fresno. Since Papá did not speak English, Mamá asked the camp foreman if he needed any more workers. "We don't need no more," said the foreman, scratching his head. "Check with Sullivan down the road. Can't miss him. He lives in a big white house with a fence around it."

14 When we got there, Mamá walked up to the house. She went through a white gate, past a row of rose bushes, up the stairs to the front door. She rang the doorbell. The porch light went on and a tall husky man came out. They exchanged a few words. After the man went in, Mamá clasped her hands and hurried back to the car. "We have work! Mr. Sullivan said we can stay there the whole season," she said, gasping and pointing to an old garage near the stables.

15 The garage was worn out by the years. It had no windows. The walls, eaten by termites, strained to support the roof full of holes. The dirt floor, populated by earth worms, looked like a gray road map.

16 That night, by the light of a kerosene lamp, we unpacked and cleaned our new home. Roberto swept away the loose dirt, leaving the hard ground. Papá plugged the holes in the walls with old newspapers and tin can tops. Mamá fed my little brothers and sisters. Papá and Roberto then brought in the mattress and placed it on the far corner of the garage. "Mamá, you and the little ones sleep on the mattress. Roberto, Panchito, and I will sleep outside under the trees," Papá said.

17 Early next morning Mr. Sullivan showed us where his crop was, and after breakfast, Papá, Roberto, and I headed for the vineyard to pick.

18 Around nine o'clock the temperature had risen to almost one hundred degrees. I was completely soaked in sweat and my mouth felt as if I had been chewing on a handkerchief. I walked over to the end of the row, picked up the jug of water we had

8. ***Mi olla*** (mee OH yah) Spanish for "My pot."
9. ***Es todo*** (ehs TOH thoh) Spanish for "That's everything."

NOTES

wearily (WIHR uh lee) *adv.* in a tired manner

CLOSE READ

ANNOTATE: Mark the words and phrases in paragraph 15 that the describe the garage.

QUESTION: What effect do these words create?

CONCLUDE: What can you conclude about the lives of migrant workers from this passage?

DIGITAL PERSPECTIVES  

CLOSE READ

You may wish to model the close read using the following think-aloud format. Possible responses to questions on the student page are included. You may also want to print copies of the **Close-Read Guide: Fiction** for students to use.

ANNOTATE: As I read paragraph 15, I see descriptive language used to describe the garage.

QUESTION: The effect is one of great pity for the people who must live in such a place.

CONCLUDE: I can make conclusions about how grim and depressing the family's living quarters are. The additional detail comparing the floor to a road map may imply the nature of their lives—they frequently move from one place to another.

PERSONALIZE FOR LEARNING

English Language Support

Idioms Review paragraphs 12 and 17. Help students understand the idioms "lump in my throat" (paragraph 12) and "head for" (paragraph 17). The expression "have a lump in your throat" means "feeling like you're about to cry." It's used to describe someone who is feeling a lot of emotion and might start crying. "Head for" means "to go toward." When the narrator says he *headed for* the vineyard, he means that he went toward the vineyard to pick grapes. **ALL LEVELS**

CLOSE READ 

You may wish to model the close read using the following think-aloud format. Possible responses to questions on the student page are included.

ANNOTATE: As I read paragraph 20, I look for verbs that describe the actions of the sun, mountains and valley, and the vines.

QUESTION: The author instills a sense that nature is powerful and has a will. This emphasizes the idea that the workers' lives are controlled more by nature than their own free will.

CONCLUDE: The text would not have been as effective if the author had simply said that the sun was setting behind the mountains.

NOTES

instinctively (ihn STIHNGK tihv lee) *adv.* done automatically, without thinking

CLOSE READ

ANNOTATE: Mark the verbs in paragraph 20 that describe the actions of the sun, mountains and valley, and vines.

QUESTION: Why has the author chosen verbs that make nonhuman things seem human?

CONCLUDE: Would the text be as effective if the author had made different choices?

brought, and began drinking. "Don't drink too much; you'll get sick," Roberto shouted. No sooner had he said that than I felt sick to my stomach. I dropped to my knees and let the jug roll off my hands. I remained motionless with my eyes glued on the hot sandy ground. All I could hear was the drone of insects. Slowly I began to recover. I poured water over my face and neck and watched the dirty water run down my arms to the ground.

19 I still felt dizzy when we took a break to eat lunch. It was past two o'clock and we sat underneath a large walnut tree that was on the side of the road. While we ate, Papá jotted down the number of boxes we had picked. Roberto drew designs on the ground with a stick. Suddenly I noticed Papá's face turn pale as he looked down the road. "Here comes the school bus," he whispered loudly in alarm. **Instinctively**, Roberto and I ran and hid in the vineyards. We did not want to get in trouble for not going to school. The neatly dressed boys about my age got off. They carried books under their arms. After they crossed the street, the bus drove away. Roberto and I came out from hiding and joined Papá. "*Tienen que tener cuidado*,"[10] he warned us.

20 After lunch we went back to work. The sun kept beating down. The buzzing insects, the wet sweat, and the hot dry dust made the afternoon seem to last forever. Finally the mountains around the valley reached out and swallowed the sun. Within an hour it was too dark to continue picking. The vines blanketed the grapes, making it difficult to see the bunches. "*Vamonos*,"[11] said Papá, signaling to us that it was time to quit work. Papá then took out a pencil and began to figure out how much we had earned our first day. He wrote down numbers, crossed some out, wrote down some more. "*Quince*,"[12] he murmured.

21 When we arrived home, we took a cold shower underneath a water hose. We then sat down to eat dinner around some wooden crates that served as a table. Mamá had cooked a special meal for us. We had rice and tortillas with "*carne con chile*,"[13] my favorite dish.

22 The next morning I could hardly move. My body ached all over. I felt little control over my arms and legs. This feeling went on every morning for days until my muscles finally got used to the work.

23 It was Monday, the first week of November. The grape season was over and I could now go to school. I woke up early that morning and lay in bed, looking at the stars and savoring the

10. ***Tienen que tener cuidado*** (tee EHN ehn kay tehn EHR kwee THAH thoh) Spanish for "You have to be careful."
11. ***Vámonos*** (VAH moh nohs) Spanish for "Let's go."
12. ***Quince*** (KEEN say) Spanish for "Fifteen."
13. **"*carne con chile*"** (KAHR nay kuhn CHIHL ay) dish of ground meat, hot peppers, beans, and tomatoes.

thought of not going to work and of starting sixth grade for the first time that year. Since I could not sleep, I decided to get up and join Papá and Roberto at breakfast. I sat at the table across from Roberto, but I kept my head down. I did not want to look up and face him. I knew he was sad. He was not going to school today. He was not going tomorrow, or next week, or next month. He would not go until the cotton season was over, and that was sometime in February. I rubbed my hands together and watched the dry, acid stained skin fall to the floor in little rolls.

NOTES

24 When Papá and Roberto left for work, I felt relief. I walked to the top of a small grade next to the shack and watched the Carcanchita disappear in the distance in a cloud of dust. Two hours later, around eight o'clock, I stood by the side of the road waiting for school bus number twenty. When it arrived I climbed in. Everyone was busy either talking or yelling. I sat in an empty seat in the back.

"Finally, after struggling for English words, I managed to tell her that I wanted to enroll in the sixth grade."

25 When the bus stopped in front of the school, I felt very nervous. I looked out the bus window and saw boys and girls carrying books under their arms. I put my hands in my pant pockets and walked to the principal's office. When I entered I heard a woman's voice say: "May I help you?" I was startled. I had not heard English for months. For a few seconds I remained speechless. I looked at the lady who waited for an answer. My first instinct was to answer her in Spanish, but I held back. Finally, after struggling for English words, I managed to tell her that I wanted to enroll in the sixth grade. After answering many questions, I was led to the classroom.

26 Mr. Lema, the sixth grade teacher, greeted me and assigned me a desk. He then introduced me to the class. I was so nervous and scared at that moment when everyone's eyes were on me that I wished I were with Papá and Roberto picking cotton. After taking roll, Mr. Lema gave the class the assignment for the first hour. "The first thing we have to do this morning is finish reading the story we began yesterday," he said **enthusiastically**. He walked up to me, handed me an English book, and asked me to read. "We are on page 125," he said politely. When I heard this, I felt my blood rush to my head; I felt dizzy. "Would you like to read?" he asked **hesitantly**. I opened the book to page 125. My mouth was dry. My eyes began to water. I could not begin. "You can read later," Mr. Lema said **understandingly**.

27 For the rest of the reading period I kept getting angrier and angrier at myself. I should have read, I thought to myself.

enthusiastically (ehn thoo zee AS tihk lee) *adv.* with eager interest

hesitantly (HEHZ uh tuhnt lee) *adv.* in an unsure or cautious way

understandingly (uhn duhr STAN dihng lee) *adv.* in a knowing way; kindly

VOCABULARY DEVELOPMENT

Concept Vocabulary Reinforcement Reinforce students' understanding of both the story and the three concept vocabulary words in paragraph 26. Ask: Why is Mr. Lema speaking *enthusiastically*? What does this tell you about him? Why does he speak *hesitantly* when he asks the narrator to read? What causes him to be hesitant? Why does he speak *understandingly* when he tells the narrator he can read later? What does Mr. Lema understand about the narrator?

CLOSER LOOK

Analyze Author's Choices 

Students may have marked text in paragraph 31 during their first read. Use this paragraph to help students understand what the end of the story signifies. Encourage them to talk about the annotations that they marked. You may want to model a close read with the class based on the highlights shown in the text.

ANNOTATE: Have students mark details in paragraph 31 that bring the story to a close, or have students participate while you highlight them.

QUESTION: Guide students to consider what these details tell them.

Possible response: The family is going to move again.

CONCLUDE: Help students to formulate conclusions about the importance of these details. Ask how this reveals what the narrator's life is like.

Possible response: Every time the narrator begins to feel at home someplace, he's uprooted by his family moving yet again.

Remind students that **author's choices** direct the timing of information in a text. Point out that, as important as this moment is to the story, Jiménez doesn't directly say the family is moving again. He doesn't have to, because in the beginning of the story he clearly established the significance of the packed boxes. Nor does Jiménez have to say that this will keep happening to the narrator. That, too, is clearly established. Explain that sometimes an important idea in a story is stronger or more dramatic if it isn't said directly because readers fill in "missing" information using their imaginations.

NOTES

28 During recess I went into the rest room and opened my English book to page 125. I began to read in a low voice, pretending I was in class. There were many words I did not know. I closed the book and headed back to the classroom.

29 Mr. Lema was sitting at his desk correcting papers. When I entered he looked up at me and smiled. I felt better. I walked up to him and asked if he could help me with the new words. "Gladly," he said.

30 The rest of the month I spent my lunch hours working on English with Mr. Lema, my best friend at school.

31 One Friday during lunch hour Mr. Lema asked me to take a walk with him to the music room. "Do you like music?" he asked me as we entered the building. "Yes, I like *corridos*,"[14] I answered. He then picked up a trumpet, blew on it, and handed it to me. The sound gave me goose bumps. I knew that sound. I had heard it in many corridos. "How would you like to learn how to play it?" he asked. He must have read my face because before I could answer, he added: "I'll teach you how to play it during our lunch hours."

32 That day I could hardly wait to tell Papá and Mamá the great news. As I got off the bus, my little brothers and sisters ran up to meet me. They were yelling and screaming. I thought they were happy to see me, but when I opened the door to our shack, I saw that everything we owned was neatly packed in cardboard boxes. ❧

14. ***corridos*** (koh REE thohs) *n.* ballads.

DIGITAL PERSPECTIVES

Enriching the Text To help students understand and appreciate what the narrator's life is like, use the search term "U.S. migrant workers" to find video footage online showing the world of migrant workers in the United States. (Note: Be sure to preview any video before showing it to students.) Have students discuss the video and how it helps them understand the text. Also discuss how the video adds to their understanding of the reports on migrant workers they wrote and listened to earlier. Then, have students write a paragraph about how the video and "The Circuit" are connected. **(Research to Clarify)**

Comprehension Check

Complete the following items after you finish your first read.

1. What kind of work does Panchito's family do?

2. Why does the family move at the beginning of the story?

3. Why does Papá warn his sons that the school bus is coming when they are picking grapes?

4. Who befriends Panchito at school?

5. **Notebook** Write a brief summary of "The Circuit" to confirm your understanding of the story.

RESEARCH

Research to Clarify Choose at least one unfamiliar detail from the text. Briefly research that detail. In what way does the information you learned shed light on an aspect of the story?

DIGITAL PERSPECTIVES

Comprehension Check

Possible responses:

1. They are migrant farm workers.
2. They have been picking strawberries, but strawberry season is over, so they must find other work.
3. The boys should be in school, but they are working instead.
4. His teacher, Mr. Lema, befriends him.
5. Summaries will vary; however, students should include: The narrator is a boy from Mexico whose family finds jobs as migrant farm workers; when the strawberry seasons ends, the family moves to Fresno, where they get jobs picking grapes. When the grape season ends, the narrator goes to school, starting sixth grade. He is scared and nervous—he has no friends and he hasn't spoken English in months. His teacher, Mr. Lema, is a friendly, understanding man who helps him with his English. When Mr. Lema offers to teach him to play the trumpet, it looks like the narrator will begin to truly enjoy school. He rushes home to tell his family the good news, only to learn they are moving again.

Research

Research to Clarify If students struggle to identify an unfamiliar detail, have them reread the text and notice details or words that might be new to them, such as the names of places or Spanish words.

PERSONALIZE FOR LEARNING

Challenge

Extend Ask students to consider what will happen next to the narrator of "The Circuit." Have them write one or two paragraphs from the narrator's point of view, briefly describing what happens to him in the next place his family moves to. Ask volunteers to share their responses with the class.

Jump Start

CLOSE READ Have students close read the title, "The Circuit." Point out that the story has only two stops on this "circuit," yet it reflects a much bigger path. Ask students how Jiménez conveys the idea of a circuit in the story. Is this a good title for the story? Why or why not?

Close Read the Text

Walk students through the annotation model on the student page. Encourage them to complete items 2 and 3 on their own. Review and discuss the sections students have marked. If needed, continue to model close reading by using the Annotation Highlights in the Interactive Teacher's Edition.

Analyze the Text

Possible responses:

1. (a) He is sad and about to cry. (paragraph 12) **DOK 2** (b) He would like to stay in one place. **DOK 3**
2. (a) Mr. Lema offers to give him music lessons. **DOK 2** (b) He will never be able to take music lessons because his family is moving. **DOK 3**
3. He probably feels disappointed and frustrated because he was just starting to really like school and he wanted to learn to play the trumpet. (paragraph 31) **DOK 3**
4. Responses will vary. Students may conclude that one way to face adversity is to accept what happens and do the best you can. **DOK 3**

FORMATIVE ASSESSMENT

Analyze the Text

- **If** students fail to cite evidence, **then** remind them to support their ideas with specific information from the text.
- **If** students fail to grasp key ideas in the text, **then** have them review the relevant sections of the story.

MAKING MEANING

THE CIRCUIT

Close Read the Text

1. This model, from paragraph 3, shows two sample annotations, along with questions and conclusions. Close read the passage, and find another detail to annotate. Then, write a question and your conclusion.

Close Read: ANNOTATE · QUESTION · CONCLUDE

ANNOTATE: The author describes the sun as being "tired."

QUESTION: Why did the author choose to describe the sun in this way?

CONCLUDE: The author personifies the sun as "tired" to suggest the fatigue of the workers.

When the sun had tired and sunk behind the mountains, Ito signaled us that it was time to go home. "*Ya esora,*" he yelled in his broken Spanish. Those were the words I waited for twelve hours a day, every day, seven days a week, week after week. And the thought of not hearing them again saddened me.

ANNOTATE: This sentence has a repetitive structure.

QUESTION: What effect is created by the repetition?

CONCLUDE: The structure of this sentence mirrors the long, repetitive working days in the fields.

2. For more practice, go back into the text and complete the close-read notes.
3. Revisit a section of the text you found important during your first read. Read this section closely and **annotate** what you notice. Ask yourself **questions** such as "Why did the author make this choice?" What can you **conclude**?

Tool Kit
Close-Read Guide and Model Annotation

Analyze the Text

CITE TEXTUAL EVIDENCE to support your answers.

Notebook Respond to these questions.

1. (a) **Interpret** How does Panchito feel as his family drives away from the "little shack"? (b) **Make Inferences** What does this detail suggest about him?
2. (a) What is the best thing that happens to Panchito on the last day of school? (b) **Make Inferences** What is the worst thing?
3. **Draw Conclusions** How does Panchito most likely feel when he sees the packed boxes at the end of the story? Why?
4. **Essential Question** *How do we overcome obstacles?* What have you learned about facing adversity by reading this selection?

STANDARDS
Reading Literature
• Cite several pieces of textual evidence to support analysis of what the text says explicitly as well as inferences drawn from the text.
• Determine a theme or central idea of a text and analyze its development over the course of the text; provide an objective summary of the text.

PERSONALIZE FOR LEARNING

English Language Support

New Words In paragraphs 28–31, the narrator talks about asking Mr. Lema to help him with English words he doesn't know. Ask students to identify two or three new words in the text that they don't know and would like help with. Help students use context clues to define each word, discuss the word, and ask students to use it in a sentence. **ALL LEVELS**

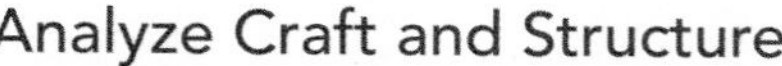

Analyze Craft and Structure

Theme The **theme**, or central idea of a story, is an insight about life that the story conveys. Although the themes of a work are sometimes directly stated, more often they are hinted at or suggested.

- **Stated themes** are expressed directly within a text. Classic fables, like *The Fox and the Grapes*, have stated themes provided at the story's end.
- **Implied themes** are suggested by the author by story details and are not directly expressed. Most narratives, like "The Circuit," have implied themes. It's important to note that there is no single "correct" theme for a work: You must infer, or make educated guesses, about themes based on story clues.

To infer a theme—

- Identify the main conflict of the story and its outcome.
- Examine characters' responses to conflicts, and identify any lessons learned.
- Look for repeated ideas expressed by story characters.
- Analyze the story's title to see if it hints at or reveals an important aspect of the story.

Practice

CITE TEXTUAL EVIDENCE to support your answers.

Notebook **Complete the activity, and then respond to the questions.**

1. To begin inferring theme, complete this chart with clues from the text. Then, in the final row of the chart, write your ideas about theme, based on your analysis of the clues you gathered.

MAIN CONFLICT	CHARACTERS' RESPONSES	REPEATED IDEAS	STORY'S TITLE
Panchito longs to be like other kids but his family is continually uprooted for work.	Pachito fights back tears. Papá records of how much they earn. Pachito can't go to school regularly.	People leave suddenly. Daily routines are described many times. Pachito often nearly cries.	A circuit is a repeated cycle. The story discusses many cycles: days, weeks, seasons, harvests, moving.
Theme(s) A boy's desires to maintain his pride and to belong in society are challenged by his family's need to move repeatedly as they seek seasonal farm work.			

2. (a) Why do you think Francisco Jiménez titled this story "The Circuit"? (b) What clues to theme might the title reveal?

3. If you were to adapt this story and provide a stated theme, what would be the theme, how would it be revealed, and by whom?

DIGITAL PERSPECTIVES

Analyze Craft and Structure

Theme Remind students that at the beginning of the story, the narrator mentions liking one of the other workers, a man he never sees again after that day (paragraph 2). Ask students to imagine a story in which this is the central event. What might be the theme of that story? (Appreciate your friends, for you never know when you might lose them.) For more support, see **Analyze Craft and Structure: Theme.**

MAKE IT INTERACTIVE

Have students write one-sentence themes for stories. It can be the theme of a story they've read or a movie they've seen. Have students share their themes and discuss what the story would tell.

Possible response:

In *The Wizard of Oz*, Dorothy wants to find the perfect place to live, and finally learns it's her own home. Theme: Be thankful for what you have.

Practice

Possible responses:

1. See possible responses in chart on student page.
2. (a) The title reinforces that being uprooted and starting over is a cycle that happens to Panchito again and again. (b) A circuit is a cycle that is difficult to break, and Panchito's family seems stuck in a cycle of being uprooted.
3. Answers will vary.

FORMATIVE ASSESSMENT

Analyze Craft and Structure

- **If** students have difficulty understanding theme, **then** relate one or two simple stories (like "The Three Little Pigs" or "The Tortoise and the Hare") and discuss the message in each story.
- **If** students have difficulty identifying theme in the text, **then** review theme-related parts of the text and discuss what message the author is trying to communicate in that part of the story.

For Reteach and Practice, see **Analyze Craft and Structure: Theme (RP).**

PERSONALIZE FOR LEARNING

Strategic Support

Theme Help students further understand identifying themes of magazine articles or TV shows. (They might also identify the theme of the Launch Text, "Against the Odds.") Ask students to explain how they determined the themes. Is the theme directly or indirectly stated in the article or show? What parts of the article or show help them understand the theme? Can a text or show have more than one theme? Why or why not?

TEACHING

Concept Vocabulary

Why These Words?

Possible responses:

1. The concept vocabulary sharpens the reader's understanding of "The Circuit" by describing characters' feeling or actions. The narrator is in many different situations and feels many different things. These words help describe what he's feeling and how he's acting at different times in the story.
2. smile (paragraph 1); disappeared (paragraph 2); signaled (paragraph 3); saddened (paragraph 3); silent (paragraph 4); yelling (paragraph 7); screaming (paragraph 7)

Practice

Possible responses:

1. One should *thoroughly* check that everyone is wearing a seat belt before driving anywhere in a car.
2. A person might behave *wearily* when he or she is coming home from a day of hard work.
3. Someone might *instinctively* react to danger by running away or by hiding his or her face.
4. People responding *enthusiastically* might leap to their feet, clap their hands loudly, and cheer.
5. Someone asking a question *hesitantly* might speak quietly and sound unsure.
6. Someone listening to a friend *understandingly* might smile and nod often.

Word Network

Possible words: *tired, saddened, silent, move, sick, careful, good news*

Word Study

For more support, see **Concept Vocabulary and Word Study.**

Possible responses:

1. When Lee saw Tanya begin to stumble, she *instinctively* reached out to help her.
2. Sample answers provided. *Quickly:* "with speed." After waking up late, I dressed *quickly* in order to catch the bus. *Quietly:* "without noise." Gina shut the door *quietly* so she wouldn't wake Grandpa from his nap. *Gladly:* "with joy or cheer." After struggling to start the lawn mower, Mona *gladly* accepted her neighbor's help.

FORMATIVE ASSESSMENT

Word Study

If students have trouble finding appropriate words, **then** review using a dictionary to find words. For Reteach and Practice, see **Word Study: Old English Suffix *-ly* (RP).**

LANGUAGE DEVELOPMENT

THE CIRCUIT

Concept Vocabulary

thoroughly	instinctively	hesitantly
wearily	enthusiastically	understandingly

Why These Words? The concept vocabulary words from the text describe ways in which characters act or respond. For example, after Papá works hard to load the car, he wipes his forehead *wearily*; when the narrator and his brother are told the school bus is coming, they run away *instinctively* (done automatically without thinking).

1. How does the concept vocabulary sharpen the reader's understanding of characters in "The Circuit"?

2. What other words in the selection are used to describe feelings or actions?

Practice

Notebook The concept vocabulary words appear in "The Circuit." Respond to these questions, based on your knowledge of each word.

1. What is a task that should be done *thoroughly*?
2. When might someone behave *wearily*?
3. How might someone *instinctively* react to danger?
4. How might people behave if they were responding *enthusiastically*?
5. How might someone sound when asking a question *hesitantly*?
6. What might someone do when listening to a friend *understandingly*?

WORD NETWORK

Add interesting words from the text about facing adversity to your Word Network.

Word Study

Old English Suffix: *-ly* When added to the ends of adjectives, the Old English suffix *-ly* creates an adverb that describes how something was done. For example, when *-ly* is added to the adjective *thorough*, it creates an adverb, *thoroughly*, which means "in a thorough way or manner."

1. Write your own sentence that correctly uses the word *instinctively*.

2. Think of three other words that contain the suffix *-ly*. Record a definition and write a context sentence for each word.

STANDARDS

Language

Determine or clarify the meaning of unknown and multiple-meaning words and phrases based on *grade 7 reading and content*, choosing flexibly from a range of strategies.

a. Use context as a clue to the meaning of a word or phrase.

b. Use common, grade-appropriate Greek or Latin affixes and roots as clues to the meaning of a word.

WriteNow Express and Reflect

Concept Vocabulary QuickWrite Have students write a paragraph in which they use all the concept vocabulary words. Tell students their writing can be fiction or nonfiction, but point out that fiction will give them more flexibility. Make it clear that they should not simply write six unrelated sentences—they should write a coherent essay, article (nonfiction), or story (fiction) that makes sense and has a beginning, middle, and end.

Conventions

Commas Commas are essential tools for writers. **Commas (,)** signal a brief pause; they enable readers to absorb information in meaningful, accurate chunks.

Use the chart to review the functions of commas.

USING COMMAS	EXAMPLE
Use a comma before a conjunction that joins independent clauses—groups of words that can stand on their own in sentences.	Julia started laughing, and she could not stop.
Use a comma after an introductory word, phrase, or clause.	If it rains, will you still be able to start the project?
Use commas to separate three or more words, phrases, or clauses in a series.	The salad consisted of lettuce, carrots, cucumber, and olives.
Use a comma to separate coordinate adjectives. These are consecutive adjectives that modify the same noun and whose order can be reversed. Coordinate adjectives can be linked together smoothly with the word *and*.	John wrote a funny, insightful play. John wrote an insightful, funny play. [John wrote a funny *and* insightful play.]

Read It

1. Reread these sentences from "The Circuit." Identify the function of the comma or commas in each sentence.
   - **a.** As the last days of August disappeared, so did the number of braceros.
   - **b.** Suddenly I felt even more the weight of hours, days, weeks, and months of work.
   - **c.** I sat at the table across from Roberto, but I kept my head down.
   - **d.** After the man went in, Mamá clasped her hands and hurried back to the car.

Write It

Notebook

1. Write a sentence using two coordinate adjectives to describe a house.
2. Write a sentence using three coordinate adjectives to describe a person.
3. Write a sentence correctly using commas to separate three or more words in a series.
4. Write a compound sentence correctly using a comma to separate independent clauses.

STANDARDS

Language

- Demonstrate command of the conventions of standard English capitalization, punctuation, and spelling when writing.
- Use a comma to separate coordinate adjectives..

DIGITAL PERSPECTIVES

Conventions

Commas Tell students that a good way to figure out where to place commas is to read sentences aloud. Where you naturally pause while reading, place a comma. Point out that the pause may be short or subtle. Remind students that commas should never be used in place of a period. See possible responses in the chart on the student page. For more support, see **Conventions: Commas.**

MAKE IT INTERACTIVE

Have students write sentences with commas and then read them aloud. Can other students tell where to place the comma?

Read It

Possible responses:

1. (a) after an introductory word, phrase, or clause
   (b) to separate three or more words, phrases, or clauses in a series
   (c) before a conjunction that joins independent clauses in a compound sentence
   (d) after an introductory word, phrase, or clause

Write It

Possible responses:

1. The tall, brown house blended in with the trees around it.
2. Everyone liked Miranda because she was friendly, smart, and polite.
3. The buffalo bellowed, snorted, and roared as they thundered across the plains.
4. We can go to the flower show, or we can see a photography exhibition.

FORMATIVE ASSESSMENT

Conventions

- **If** students have trouble understanding commas, **then** review what commas do and when to use them.
- **If** students have trouble using commas correctly, **then** show them several sentences with commas and discuss comma use in each.

For Reteach and Practice, see **Conventions: Commas (RP).**

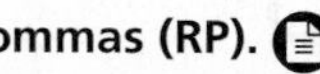

HOW LANGUAGE WORKS

Commas Use "The Circuit" to reinforce students' understanding of commas. Choose sentences from the text that have commas, and have students identify what each comma does in each sentence. If students demonstrate solid, consistent understanding of commas, you may wish to discuss two other uses of commas: to offset parenthetical information ("Ito, the strawberry sharecropper, did not smile." / "My older brother, Roberto, was also silent.") and punctuate quotations ("Gladly," he said. / "You can read later," Mr. Lema said understandingly.).

TEACHING

Writing to Sources

Discuss with students the importance of stating their ideas clearly so readers know exactly what they are explaining in their explanation. Also remind students that it's important they explain why they believe the theme they've identified is the theme of the story. If they use ideas the author states directly, they should quote or paraphrase the appropriate text. If they use ideas the author states indirectly, they should explain how they arrived at their conclusion about this text. For more support, see **Writing to Sources: Explanation.**

Vocabulary and Conventions Connection Remind students that they should try to use concept vocabulary words in their explanation. They should also use commas to show relationships among parts of sentences.

Reflect on Your Writing

Possible responses:

1. Responses will vary. Encourage students to be specific in their responses and to give a reason (or reasons) why it was easy or difficult to determine the theme.
2. Responses will vary. If students need support, help them revisit their decision-making process.
3. Responses will vary. Have students list specific words they chose that describe the effect of patterns on the story's meaning.

FORMATIVE ASSESSMENT

Writing to Sources

If students have trouble determining the theme, **then** ask them to tell you, in one sentence, what message they think the author is trying to convey in the story. For Reteach and Practice, see **Writing to Sources: Explanation (RP).**

EFFECTIVE EXPRESSION

THE CIRCUIT

Writing to Sources

Assignment

In "The Circuit," the narrator's life follows a pattern as his family moves from workplace to workplace. Write a short **explanation** of additional patterns you find in the story (related to characters' behavior, actions, seasons, and so on). Conclude your explanation with observations about how these patterns give meaning to the story.

When you write your explanation:

- Analyze evidence from the text to determine the main idea you want to convey.
- Include details from the text to support your ideas.
- Organize your explanation in a clear, logical way.
- Conclude by restating your main idea and providing an additional thought or idea.

Vocabulary and Conventions Connection Think about including several of the concept vocabulary words in your writing. Also, remember to correctly use commas in your sentences.

thoroughly	instinctively	hesitantly
wearily	enthusiastically	understandingly

Reflect on Your Writing

After you have written your explanation, answer these questions.

1. Was it easy or difficult to identify and analyze patterns in the story? Why?
2. (a) What decisions did you make about organizing your ideas? (b) What did you end up liking or disliking about those decisions?
3. **Why These Words?** The words you choose make a difference in your writing. Which words did you choose to describe the effect of patterns on the story's meaning?

STANDARDS

Reading Literature
Determine a theme or central idea of a text and analyze its development over the course of the text; provide an objective summary of the text.

Writing
- Write informative/explanatory texts to examine a topic and convey ideas, concepts, and information through the selection, organization, and analysis of relevant content.
  - b. Develop the topic with relevant facts, definitions, concrete details, quotations, or other information and examples.
- Draw evidence from literary or informational texts to support analysis, reflection, and research.
  - a. Apply *grade 7 Reading standards* to literature.

PERSONALIZE FOR LEARNING

English Language Support

Writing Informative Essays Have students choose a topic for an Informative essay, such as how "The Circuit" is affected by its setting. Encourage students to use adverbs and adjectives in their writing.

Ask students to write a topic sentence for an essay on their topic. **EMERGING**

Ask students to write an Informative paragraph on their topic. Remind students to introduce their topic, support it with details, and write a solid conclusion. **EXPANDING**

Ask students to write an Informative essay comparing and contrasting a quality of two different stories, such as the setting of "The Circuit" and the setting of another story they have read recently. **BRIDGING**

An expanded **English Language Support Lesson** on Writing Informative Essays is available in the Interactive Teacher's Edition.

Speaking and Listening

Assignment
Work with a partner to research what life was like for migrant farm workers and their families in the time period of "The Circuit" (from about the 1940s to the 1960s, mainly in California—but also in other parts of the United States). Come up with questions such as:

- Where did families travel to harvest grapes, strawberries, and cotton?
- How did the children of migrant farm workers attend school?

Then, work with your partner to answer the questions, drawing on information from the story and research. Then, **role-play** an interview between a reporter and a farm worker to present your information.

1. **Plan Your Presentation**
   - Research and discuss the topic and questions.
   - Use the Internet and library resources to gather information.
2. **Rehearse Your Presentation**
   - Decide who will role-play the reporter and who will role-play the farm worker.
   - Practice what each of you will say during your role-play.
3. **Deliver Your Presentation**
   - Once you begin, stay in character until the role-play is finished.
   - Speak as if you were the person you are role-playing.
   - Maintain appropriate eye contact with each other.
4. **Evaluate Presentations** Use a presentation evaluation guide like the one shown to analyze your own as well as your classmates' presentations.

PRESENTATION EVALUATION GUIDE

Rate each statement on a scale of 1 (not demonstrated) to 5 (demonstrated).

☐ The role-play presented important, relevant information.
☐ The role-play was realistic.
☐ The people role-playing stayed in character.
☐ The role-players maintained eye contact with each other.
☐ The role-players spoke loudly enough to hear them.

EVIDENCE LOG

Before moving on to a new selection, go to your Evidence Log and record what you've learned from "The Circuit."

STANDARDS

Speaking and Listening
- Engage effectively in a range of collaborative discussions (one-on-one, in groups, and teacher-led) with diverse partners on *grade 7 topics, texts, and issues,* building on others' ideas and expressing their own clearly.
  a. Come to discussions prepared, having read or researched material under study; explicitly draw on that preparation by referring to evidence on the topic, text, or issue to probe and reflect on ideas under discussion.
  c. Pose questions that elicit elaboration and respond to others' questions and comments with relevant observations and ideas that bring the discussion back on topic as needed.
- Present claims and findings, emphasizing salient points in a focused, coherent manner with pertinent descriptions, facts, details, and examples; use appropriate eye contact, adequate volume, and clear pronunciation.

Writing
- Conduct short research projects to answer a question, drawing on several sources and generating additional related, focused questions for further research and investigation.

PERSONALIZE FOR LEARNING

Strategic Support

Extend Discuss with students that other people, besides migrant workers, have jobs in which they face adversity and obstacles as part of their daily life. Ask: *Who are some other people that face adversity on an ongoing basis as part of their jobs?* (police, firefighters, soldiers) *In what ways are the lives of these people, and the adversity they face, similar to the lives of migrant workers? In what ways are their lives, and the adversity they face, different from the lives of migrant workers?*

DIGITAL PERSPECTIVES

Speaking and Listening

1. **Plan Your Presentation** You may wish to help students choose their sources of information. Remind them that there are a variety of sources on this topic, from objective news reports to first-hand accounts written by migrant workers.
2. **Rehearse Your Presentation** Remind students to take each other's preference into account when deciding which role each partner will play. If both people want to play the same role, partners should find a fair way to decide who gets it.
3. **Deliver Your Presentation** Remind students to speak clearly and to take their time when they give their presentations. There's no need to rush.
4. **Evaluate Presentations** Encourage students to make one supportive comment about each presentation.

For more support, see **Speaking and Listening: Role-Play Interview.**

Evidence Log Support students in completing their Evidence Log. This paced activity will help prepare them for the Performance-Based Assessment at the end of the unit.

FORMATIVE ASSESSMENT

Speaking and Listening

- **If** students have trouble finding information, **then** suggest sources they can use.
- **If** students have trouble delivering their presentation to the class as role-play, **then** have them present their information as monologues, with each person speaking one at a time.

For Reteach and Practice, see **Speaking and Listening: Role-Play Interview (RP).**

Selection Test

Administer the "The Circuit" Selection Test, which is available in both print and digital formats online in Assessments.

Jump Start

Ask students to write one or two additional things they have learned about facing adversity in life as a result of seeing "The Dust Bowl" and reading the excerpt from "The Grapes of Wrath" and "The Circuit." You might guide them with questions such as these:, "What were some of the most difficult obstacles the characters faced?" "What do you think might help people to overcome obstacles and endure hardships?" "What good might come from having to face adversity?" As students share, ask them to cite specific examples from the selections to support their ideas.

Write an Informative Essay

Make sure students understand what they are being asked to do in the assignment. Explain that they are being asked to write an informative essay that describes how the characters in the selections coped with the obstacles they faced.

Students should complete the assignment using word processing software to take advantage of editing tools and features.

Elements of an Informative Essay

Remind students that informative essays contain vivid details and sensory images that engage the reader and that support the writer's ideas. Students should choose interesting and accurate descriptive words.

MAKE IT INTERACTIVE

Project "Against the Odds" from the Interactive Teacher's Edition and have students identify examples of descriptive language and vivid imagery ("powerful thud"; "severe vibrations"; "sounded like sneakers thumping around in a dryer").

Academic Vocabulary

Ask students for examples of how they might use the academic vocabulary in their essays.

PERFORMANCE TASK: WRITING FOCUS

WRITING TO SOURCES

- THE DUST BOWL
- *from* THE GRAPES OF WRATH
- THE CIRCUIT

Write an Informative Essay

You have just read and watched selections that relate to how people deal with obstacles. "The Dust Bowl" shows the devastating effects of a drought. The excerpt from *The Grapes of Wrath* depicts farmers who lost their land and had to leave their homes. "The Circuit" portrays farm workers who don't have permanent homes.

Assignment

Write an **informative essay** in which you answer this question:

> How did the individuals in the selections cope with the obstacles they faced?

Describe the hardships faced by the people or characters in the selections, and inform the reader about how they dealt with those obstacles. Use details from the selections to support your ideas.

ACADEMIC VOCABULARY

As you craft your essay, consider using some of the academic vocabulary you learned in the beginning of the unit.

deviate
persevere
determination
diversity
tradition

Elements of an Informative Essay

An **informative essay** presents information about a topic. Ideas are supported with precise, factual details.

An effective informative essay contains these elements:

- an introduction in which the topic and thesis are revealed
- supporting factual details that support the writer's ideas
- clear, consistent organization
- a conclusion in which the writer's thesis is restated and additional insights are provided
- a formal, objective tone

Tool Kit
Student Model of an Informative Essay

Model Informative Essay For a model of an informative essay, see the Launch text, "Against the Odds."

Challenge yourself to find all of the elements of an informative essay in the text. You will have an opportunity to review these elements as you prepare to write your own essay.

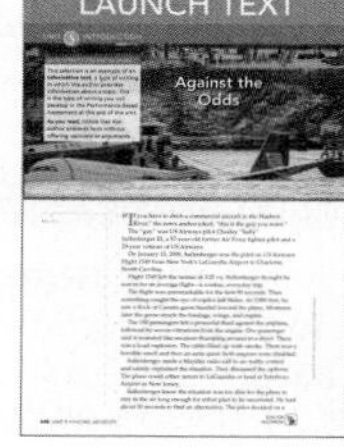

STANDARDS

Writing

- Write informative/explanatory texts to examine a topic and convey ideas, concepts, and information through the selection, organization, and analysis of relevant content.
- Write routinely over extended time frames and shorter time frames for a range of discipline-specific tasks, purposes, and audiences.

AUTHOR'S PERSPECTIVE **Kelly Gallagher, M.Ed.**

Read, Analyze, Emulate Teachers can use scaffolding to help students grow as writers by studying good writing with them. When students recognize the qualities of good writing, they begin producing it.

Step 1: Read Provide students with excellent narratives from the text and direct them to "read like a writer" by paying attention to ideas, style, voice, and organization. Encourage students to look for the moves the writer made to elicit a response in readers.

Step 2: Analyze Focus on the ideas by asking students questions such as "What is the writer's theme? How did the writer develop it?" Then turn to style and voice, asking, "How did the writer develop the characters?" "What effect did

Prewriting / Planning

Gather Details Revisit the selections to gather specific details that provide information you will share in your essay. Complete this chart as you identify obstacles and coping strategies, or methods of handling or overcoming challenges. In some sources, different people may exhibit methods of dealing with problems.

	OBSTACLE	COPING STRATEGIES
The Grapes of Wrath		
"The Dust Bowl"		
"The Circuit"		

Formulate a Thesis A strong thesis statement will give your essay a sharp focus, indicating both your subject and the central message you want to share with readers. An effective thesis statement should:

- State one key idea clearly and directly.
- Use precise, formal language.
- Avoid overgeneralizations and vague or unnecessary words.

Notice how one of the following statements would be a much stronger stronger thesis statement for an informative essay.

Overgeneralization and informal language: Everybody's afraid of something, and that's just how it is no matter who you are.

Sharply focused thesis: Many literary works show that facing one's greatest fear is a difficult but worthwhile challenge that can build character and solve problems.

Review the details you gathered and look for a single idea about obstacles and coping strategies that connects them. Use your analysis to formulate a thesis statement below.

My thesis about how individuals cope with obstacles: ______________________

____

EVIDENCE LOG

Review your Evidence Log and identify key details you may want to include in your essay.

STANDARDS

Writing

- Write informative/explanatory texts to examine a topic and convey ideas, concepts, and information through the selection, organization, and analysis of relevant content.
  a. Introduce a topic clearly, previewing what is to follow; organize ideas, concepts, and information, using strategies such as definition, classification, comparison/contrast, and cause/effect; include formatting, graphics, and multimedia when useful to aiding comprehension.
  b. Develop the topic with relevant facts, definitions, concrete details, quotations, or other information and examples.
  c. Use appropriate transitions to create cohesion and clarify the relationships among ideas and concepts.

DIGITAL PERSPECTIVES

Prewriting/Planning

Gather Details Encourage students to focus on one selection at a time. Help them understand that the obstacles may be different in the selections, based on differences in medium, writing style, language, etc. Remind them that coping strategies will likely be different for different obstacles.

Formulate a Thesis Guide students to understand that a thesis statement may need to evolve. Have them try writing a thesis statement and then go through a process of checking how well the thesis statement aligns with each selection. When they encounter details or ideas that challenge the thesis statement, they should consider ways in which the thesis statement may need to be revised.

the dialogue have?" "What sensory details did the writer use?" and "Where do you hear the author's distinctive voice?" Finally, ask questions about organization, such as "How did the writer pace events?" "What do you notice about the writer's paragraphing decisions?"

Step 3: Emulate Select one or two or the writer's moves to practice. Guide students to follow the models they studied as they write.

TEACHING

Organize Details Remind students to challenge their own thesis statements as they put details and evidence in order. They should not simply discard important details that do not agree with their thesis; they should use these challenges to strengthen the validity of their thesis.

Drafting

Write a First Draft Remind students that a strong introduction will not only help readers but will help them as well because writing a good introduction will help them focus on what they want to communicate in their essay.

Remind students to utilize strong transitions as they move from point to point in their draft. Choosing strong transitions at the drafting stage is one way students can double-check that they are following a logical and clear sequence of ideas to support their thesis.

Point out that a strong conclusion is just as important as a strong introduction. Students are writing about three selections, each with its own characters and events, so they'll be presenting many different ideas. A strong conclusion will help to tie everything together for the reader.

PERFORMANCE TASK: WRITING FOCUS

Organize Details Your informative essay will explain specific coping strategies presented in three selections. Before you draft, decide the order in which you will discuss the works. For example, you might begin by discussing the work that contains the strongest support for your thesis statement. On the other hand, you might decide to build up to your strongest ideas.

Complete this outline to plan the details and ideas you will include in the body of your essay.

First Selection: **Details and Analysis:**

Second Selection: **Details and Analysis:**

Third Selection: **Details and Analysis:**

STANDARDS

Writing

Write informative/explanatory texts to examine a topic and convey ideas, concepts, and information through the selection, organization, and analysis of relevant content.

a. Introduce a topic clearly, previewing what is to follow; organize ideas, concepts, and information, using strategies such as definition, classification, comparison/contrast, and cause/effect; include formatting, graphics, and multimedia when useful to aiding comprehension.

b. Develop the topic with relevant facts, definitions, concrete details, quotations, or other information and examples.

f. Provide a concluding statement or section that follows from and supports the information or explanation presented.

Drafting

Write a First Draft As you draft, focus on writing down your ideas without worrying about word choice and grammar. You will have a chance to revise and edit your work once your draft is finished.

Follow these steps to create your draft:

- Begin with a strong introduction that presents your thesis statement and clearly identifies the selections you will discuss.
- Follow the organization you planned in the body of your essay, using transitions, such as *similarly, in contrast,* or *however,* to make comparisons, move from one topic to another, or emphasize key ideas.
- End your draft with a conclusion that connects ideas from the body to your thesis statement and leaves readers with a single, powerful message.

AUTHOR'S PERSPECTIVE **Jim Cummins, Ph.D.**

Working in Pairs There is an important sense in which the development of academic expertise on the part of English learners is a process of socialization rather than simply instruction. As a result, English writing development will be enhanced when students can work in pairs to create texts to share with others. That's because the process of collaboration and communication entails social interaction, which fosters language development.

- First, teachers can partner students to read, discuss, and react to a reading in the unit. Select a text, such as a nonfiction article, poem, or narrative.
- Have partners discuss the text, make notes about their ideas, and together write a response that highlights what they found important, or responds to a prompt teachers provide. Encourage students to include specific details from the text in their drafts.
- Then, teachers can invite partners to share their writing with the whole class. Guide students to explain how working together helped them express their ideas more effectively than working alone.

LANGUAGE DEVELOPMENT: CONVENTIONS

The Use of Commas

Revise Incorrect Use of Commas The correct use of commas will help to ensure that your informative essay is clear to readers. Knowing when not to use commas is just as important as knowing when to use them. Here are some guidelines and examples taken from the Launch Text:

	INCORRECTLY PUNCTUATED SENTENCE	CORRECTLY PUNCTUATED SENTENCE
Separate **coordinate adjectives** with a comma, but do not separate the adjectives from the noun they modify.	Sullenberger thought he was in for an average flight—a routine, everyday, trip.	Sullenberger thought he was in for an average flight—a routine, everyday trip.
Do not separate **compound subjects** with a comma.	With water seeping into the plane, Sullenberger, and Skiles, walked the length of the cabin twice, calling "Is anyone there?"	With water seeping into the plane, Sullenberger and Skiles walked the length of the cabin twice, calling "Is anyone there?"
Do not separate **compound verbs** with a comma.	Sullenberger made a Mayday radio call to air traffic control, and calmly explained the situation.	Sullenberger made a Mayday radio call to air traffic control and calmly explained the situation.

TIP

COORDINATE ADJECTIVES

You can recognize coordinate adjectives because they can be separated by the word *and*. (He was a rich, famous writer = He was a rich and famous writer.)

Read It

Read this paragraph and identify the coordinate adjectives, compound subjects, and compound verbs.

Commas and other punctuation marks are critical to clear writing. Be sure to review and revise any incorrect uses of commas and punctuation in your writing. Strive to create clear, understandable sentences.

Write It

As you draft your essay, remember to use commas properly. Copy the faulty sentences and re-punctuate them, either adding or removing commas.

FAULTY SENTENCE	MY REVISION
We inched across the rickety, swaying, bridge.	We inched across the rickety, swaying bridge.
Studying together, Glenda, and Jasmine, helped each other earn better grades.	Studying together, Glenda and Jasmine helped each other earn better grades.
At summer camp we learned archery, and knots.	At summer camp, we learned archery and knots.
The actor bowed, and smiled.	The actor bowed and smiled.

STANDARDS

Language

- Demonstrate command of the conventions of standard English capitalization, punctuation, and spelling when writing.
  a. Use a comma to separate coordinate adjectives.

DIGITAL PERSPECTIVES

The Use of Commas

Remind students that reading what they've written out loud is an excellent way to identify incorrect use of commas. When we read our writing out loud, we tend to automatically pause where there should be a comma. If they find themselves pausing and there is no comma, or they don't naturally pause and there is a comma, they should consider revising that part of the sentence.

Read It

Coordinate adjectives: clear, understandable

Compound subjects: Commas … punctuation marks

Compound verbs: be sure; strive to

MAKE IT INTERACTIVE

Project these sentences from "Against the Odds" from the Interactive Teacher's Edition and ask students to identify the compound subject or compound verb in each. Point out that there is no comma separating the parts of the compound subject or compound verb.

Paragraph 10: It skidded across the water at 145 mph and finally slowed to a stop. (skidded/slowed)

Paragraph 11: He picked his landing spot and he went for it. (picked/went)

Paragraph 13: With water seeping into the plane, Sullenberger and Skiles walked the length of the cabin twice, calling "Is anyone there? Come forward!" (Sullenberger and Skiles)

Write It

Review the chart on this page, pointing out the specific use of commas to revise the sentences.

PERSONALIZE FOR LEARNING

English Language Support

Commas Review with students how to revise sentences that have an incorrect use of commas. Provide the following sentences and have students revise them.

The huge graceful airplane landed safely at the airport.
(The huge, graceful airplane landed safely at the airport.)

Anne, and Leo will meet us at the park.
(Anne and Leo will meet us at the park.)

I read books, and magazines.
(I read books and magazines.)

Marco swims, and jogs for exercise.
(Marco swims and jogs for exercise.)

TEACHING

Revising

Evaluating Your Draft

Remind students to use the chart to evaluate their draft to make sure it contains all the required elements of a well-constructed, well-organized, informative essay, and to be sure it addresses both parts of the assignment.

Revising for Focus and Organization

Provide a Clear Conclusion Encourage students to use highlighting to track the details and evidence from the selections they are using in their essays. When they're finished, they can review and make sure each paragraph utilizes details and evidence and that the details are from all three selections.

Revising for Evidence and Elaboration

Support Ideas With Relevant Evidence Advise students that in the revision stage, they may need to make difficult decisions about deleting examples and evidence. Some evidence that was present in the essay's original outline may now be superfluous, and some of a writer's "favorite" examples may lead to tangents.

Maintain a Formal Tone Remind students that maintaining a formal tone is essential to an effective essay. Ask them to pay attention to the words they are using and to avoid any language that would be used for informal communication.

PERFORMANCE TASK: WRITING FOCUS

Revising

Evaluating Your Draft

Use the checklist to evaluate the effectiveness of your draft. Then, use your evaluation and instruction on this page to guide your revision.

FOCUS AND ORGANIZATION	EVIDENCE AND ELABORATION	CONVENTIONS
☐ Provides an introduction that reveals the topic and thesis.	☐ Clearly shows relationships among ideas.	☐ Uses words, phrases, and clauses that create cohesion and clarify the relationships among ideas.
☐ Is organized clearly and logically.	☐ Supports ideas with relevant evidence and details from the selections.	☐ Attends to the norms and conventions of the discipline, especially correct use of commas.
☐ Provides a concluding statement that brings the essay to a satisfying close.	☐ Maintains a formal tone.	

WORD NETWORK

Include interesting words from your Word Network in your essay.

STANDARDS

Writing

• Write informative/explanatory texts to examine a topic and convey ideas, concepts, and information through the selection, organization, and analysis of relevant content.

a. Introduce a topic clearly, previewing what is to follow; organize ideas, concepts, and information, using strategies such as definition, classification, comparison/contrast, and cause/effect; include formatting (e.g., headings), graphics (e.g., charts, tables), and multimedia when useful to aiding comprehension.

b. Develop the topic with relevant facts, definitions, concrete details, quotations, or other information and examples.

d. Use precise language and domain-specific vocabulary to inform about or explain the topic.

e. Establish and maintain a formal style.

Revising for Focus and Organization

Provide a Clear Conclusion Review the conclusion you have drafted, and check to be sure that it follows logically from your thesis and body paragraphs. Strive to keep your conclusion brief but engaging. You might consider ending your conclusion with a question or with a powerful quotation from a text you read.

Revising for Evidence and Elaboration

Support Ideas With Relevant Evidence Evaluate with a critical eye the details you have used to support ideas. First mark the ideas or claims you make. Then, mark support you have given. Add details as needed, and delete unneeded or irrelevant information.

Maintain a Formal Tone A writer's tone is his or her attitude toward the audience or subject. Apply the following steps to revise for a formal tone in your essay:

- Identify any informal language or any slang expressions in your essay. Change them to formal, academic language appropriate for an essay.
- Underline any **clichés** (overused expressions, such as "what goes around comes around") or **idioms** (figurative expressions, such as "a chip on your shoulder"). Replace clichés and slang with fresh, original language that better suits your audience.

HOW LANGUAGE WORKS

Incorrect Use of Commas Review the rules for revising sentences for incorrect use of commas:

1. Separate coordinate adjectives but do not separate the adjectives from the noun.

   Incorrect: The large red, balloon floated across the sky.

   Revision: The large, red balloon floated across the sky.

2. Do not separate parts of a compound subject or object.

   Incorrect: Lenore, and Ellie are teaching me archery.

   Revision: Lenore and Ellie are teaching me archery.

   Incorrect: In the distance we could see whales, and dolphins.

   Revision: In the distance we could see whales and dolphins.

3. Do not separate the parts of a compound verb.

   Incorrect: The waves pounded, and crashed against the cliffs.

   Revision: The waves pounded and crashed against the cliffs.

PEER REVIEW

Exchange essays with a classmate. Use the checklist to evaluate your classmate's essay and provide supportive feedback.

1. Is there an effective introduction?
   ☐ yes ☐ no If no, suggest a better way the writer could introduce the topic.
2. Are the writer's ideas supported by details and support from the selections?
   ☐ yes ☐ no If no, point out where the writer should provide support.
3. Are there clear connections among ideas?
   ☐ yes ☐ no If no, point out where the writer should use transitions to make these connections clearer.
4. What is the strongest part of your classmate's essay?

Editing and Proofreading

Edit for Conventions Reread your draft for accuracy and consistency. Correct errors in grammar and word usage. Review your use of commas to ensure that you have followed punctuation rules.

Proofread for Accuracy Read your draft carefully, looking for errors in spelling and punctuation. Also, check your spelling of homonyms—words that sound the same but are spelled differently and have different meanings: for example, *their, they're,* and *there*.

Publishing and Presenting

Create a final version of your essay. Share it with your class or with a small group of classmates, so you can get constructive feedback. In turn, review and comment on your classmates' work. As a group, discuss what your essays have in common and the ways in which they are different.

Reflecting

Reflect on what you learned as you wrote your essay. How did writing the essay heighten your understanding of how people deal with obstacles? What did you learn from peer review that might help you with future writing assignments?

STANDARDS

Language

Demonstrate command of the conventions of standard English capitalization, punctuation, and spelling when writing.

a. Use a comma to separate coordinate adjectives.

b. Spell correctly.

DIGITAL PERSPECTIVES

Peer Review

Before students begin their peer review, remind them that they are reviewing for clarity and completeness, not whether they agree or disagree with the writer's ideas. They should not comment on whether their classmate is "right" or "wrong." They can, however, make helpful suggestions if they see something in the essay that could be better.

Editing and Proofreading

As students proofread, they should check for grammar, spelling, and punctuation errors. Remind them to check that all causes lead to logical, relevant effects, all effects are linked to logical, relevant causes, and all three selections are discussed. Also remind students to check for the correct use of commas.

Publishing and Presenting

Before students review their classmates' essays, remind them to:

- Be honest, but maintain a respectful tone in their comments.
- Use formal rather than informal language.
- Move the discussion forward by building on the ideas of others.
- Disagree respectfully. Different opinions are fine, but they should be expressed politely.
- If you disagree, support your position with evidence.

Reflecting

Encourage students to reflect not only on their essay, the process of writing it, and any new understanding of how people deal with obstacles they may have gained from writing this essay, but also on what they may have learned from reviewing others' work and the comments they received on their essays.

PERSONALIZE FOR LEARNING

Challenge

Extend Remind students that dealing with adversity and obstacles can either defeat people or make them stronger, depending on the situation and how people deal with the challenges they're facing. Have students write two paragraphs, one describing someone who is defeated by adversity, and one describing someone who overcomes obstacles and is made stronger because of the experience. Ask volunteers to share their responses with the class.

OVERVIEW

SMALL-GROUP LEARNING

How do we overcome obstacles?

Explain that overcoming obstacles often requires people to have a great deal of resilience, and that facing adversity can be life-changing or even inspiring at times. During Small-Group Learning, students will read selections that show how people's lives changed because they faced adversity and overcame obstacles.

Small-Group Learning Strategies

Review the Learning Strategies with students and explain that as they work through Small-Group Learning they will develop strategies to work in small-group environments.

- Have students watch the video on Small-Group Learning Strategies.
- A video on this topic is available online in the Professional Development Center.

You may wish to discuss some action items to add to the chart as a class before students complete it on their own. For example, for "Clarify," you might solicit the following from students:

- Write down specific points you might want explained during discussions.
- Ask others to elaborate on any ideas you think are unclear.

Block Scheduling

Each day in this Pacing Plan represents a 40–50 minute class period. Teachers using block scheduling may combine days to reflect their class schedule. In addition, teachers may revise pacing to differentiate and support core instruction by integrating components and resources as students require.

OVERVIEW: SMALL-GROUP LEARNING

ESSENTIAL QUESTION:

How do we overcome obstacles?

You've hit a bump in the road. Now what should you do? You will read selections that describe obstacles that people have faced and how they were able to overcome them. You will work in a group to continue your exploration of the topic of facing adversity.

Small-Group Learning Strategies

Throughout your life, in school, in your community, and in your career, you will continue to learn and work with others.

Look at these strategies and the actions you can take to practice them as you work in teams. Add ideas of your own for each step. Use these strategies during Small-Group Learning.

STRATEGY	ACTION PLAN
Prepare	• Complete your assignments so that you are prepared for group work. • Organize your thinking so you can contribute to your group's discussions. •
Participate fully	• Make eye contact to signal that you are listening and taking in what is being said. • Use text evidence when making a point. •
Support others	• Build off ideas from others in your group. • Invite others who have not yet spoken to do so. •
Clarify	• Paraphrase the ideas of others to ensure that your understanding is correct. • Ask follow-up questions. •

488 UNIT 5 • FACING ADVERSITY

Pacing Plan

Unit Introduction		Introduce Whole-Class Learning	Media: The Dust Bowl		from The Grapes of Wrath				The Circuit						Performance Task		
1	2	3	4	5	6	7	8	9	10	11	12	13	14	15	16	17	18

CONTENTS

Contents

Selections Circulate among groups as they preview the selections. You might encourage groups to discuss any knowledge they already have about any of the selections or the situations and settings shown in the photographs. Students may wish to take a poll within their group to determine which selections look the most interesting.

Remind students that communicating and collaborating in groups is an important skill that they will use throughout their lives—in school, in their careers, and in their community.

Performance Task

Present Multimedia Profiles Give groups time to read about and briefly discuss the multimedia presentation they will create after reading. Encourage students to do some preliminary thinking about the types of media they may want to use. This may help focus their subsequent reading and group discussion.

Introduce Small-Group Learning

A Work in Progress

from The Story of My Life

Media: How Helen Keller Learned to Talk

A Young Tinkerer Builds a Windmill, Electrifying a Nation

Performance Task

Introduce Independent Learning

Independent Learning

Performance-Based Assessment

19 20 21 22 23 24 25 26 27 28 29 30 31 32 33 34 35 36

SMALL-GROUP LEARNING

OVERVIEW

SMALL-GROUP LEARNING

Working as a Team

1. **Take a Position** Remind groups to let all members share their responses. You may wish to set a time limit for this discussion.
2. **List Your Rules** You may want to have groups share their lists of rules and consolidate them into a master list to be displayed and followed by all groups.
3. **Apply the Rules** As you circulate among the groups, ensure that students are staying on task. Consider a short time limit for this step.
4. **Name Your Group** This task can be creative and fun. If students have trouble coming up with a name, suggest that they think of something related to the unit topic. Encourage groups to share their names with the class.
5. **Create a Communication Plan** Encourage groups to include in their plans agreed-upon times during the day to share ideas. They should also devise a method for recording and saving their communications.

Accountable Talk

Offer students these Accountable Talk suggestions:

Remember to . . .
Ask clarifying questions.

Which sounds like...
Can you please repeat what you said?
Would you give me an example?
I think you said _____. Did I understand you?

Remember to . . .
Explain your thinking.

Which sounds like . . .
I believe _____ is true because _____.

Remember to . . .
Build on the ideas of others.

Which sounds like . . .
When _____ said _____, it made me think of _____.

OVERVIEW: SMALL-GROUP LEARNING

Working as a Team

1. **Take a Position** In your group, discuss the following question:

   Are any challenges impossible to overcome?

   As you take turns sharing your ideas, be sure to provide examples to make your response clear. After all group members have shared, discuss your responses. Were other group members' responses similar to yours? Did other group members share challenges that you had not thought of, but could relate to?

2. **List Your Rules** As a group, decide on the rules that you will follow as you work together. Samples are provided; add two more of your own. You may add or revise rules based on your experience together.
   - Everyone should participate in group discussions.
   - People should not interrupt.
   - ______________________________
   - ______________________________

3. **Apply the Rules** Practice working as a group. Share what you have learned about overcoming obstacles. Make sure each person in the group contributes. Take notes and be prepared to share with the class one thing that you heard from another member of your group.

4. **Name Your Group** Choose a name that reflects the unit topic.

   Our group's name: ______________________________

5. **Create a Communication Plan** Decide how you want to communicate with one another. For example, you might use online collaboration tools, email, or instant messaging.

   Our group's decision: ______________________________

AUTHOR'S PERSPECTIVE **Kelly Gallagher, M.Ed.**

Accountability in Group Work The teacher's role during group work is to serve as the facilitator rather than as the leader. This means that the teacher should support the thinking and discussion but not provide the answers or content direction. Problems can arise if a group is unfocused, if the task is not meaningful, or if there is no accountability. To help groups work together well, achieve their goals, and ensure accountability, teachers can follow these three steps:

1. First, define and clarify the task. Explain why it is valuable, and make sure students know what they are expected to do.
2. Let each group know that one student will be selected randomly to share the group's thinking. This randomness builds in accountability.
3. Pull the whole class back together to share back information and to check learning.

If groups struggle, teachers can prod them with questions that support how they will get to the answer. For example, if they are unable to find the main point of the essay, ask them: "In this type of text, where might a reader look to find the main idea?"

Making a Schedule

First, find out the due dates for the Small-Group activities. Then, preview the texts and activities with your group, and make a schedule for completing the tasks.

SELECTION	ACTIVITIES	DUE DATE
A Work in Progress		
from The Story of My Life		
How Helen Keller Learned to Talk		
A Young Tinkerer Builds a Windmill, Electrifying a Nation		

Working on Group Projects

As your group works together, you'll find it more effective if each person has a specific role. Different projects require different roles. Before beginning a project, discuss the necessary roles and choose one for each group member. Here are some possible roles; add your own ideas.

Project Manager: monitors the schedule and keeps everyone on task
Researcher: organizes research activities
Recorder: takes notes during group meetings

____
____
____
____
____

DIGITAL PERSPECTIVES

Making a Schedule

Encourage groups to preview the reading selections and to consider how long it will take them to complete the activities accompanying each selection. Point out that they can adjust the due dates for particular selections as needed as they work on their small-group projects, however, they must complete all assigned tasks before the group Performance Task is due. Encourage groups to review their schedules upon completing the activities for each selection to make sure they are on track to meet the final due date.

Working on Group Projects

Point out to groups that the roles they assign can also be changed later. Students might have to make changes based on who is best at doing what. Try to make sure that there is no favoritism, cliquishness, or stereotyping by gender or other means in the assignment of roles.

Also, you should review the roles each group assigns to its members. Based on your understanding of students' individual strengths, you might find it necessary to suggest some changes.

FACILITATING SMALL-GROUP LEARNING

Forming Groups You may wish to form groups for Small-Group Learning so that each consists of students with different learning abilities. Some students may be adept at organizing information whereas other may have strengths related to generating or synthesizing information. A good mix of abilities can make the experience of Small-Group Learning dynamic and productive.

A Work in Progress

AUDIO SUMMARIES
Audio summaries of "A Work in Progress" are available online in both English and Spanish in the Interactive Teacher's Edition or Unit Resources. Assigning these summaries prior to reading the selection may help students build additional background knowledge and set a context for their first read.

Summary

Shortly after Aimee Mullins was born, she reports in "A Work in Progress," doctors amputated both her legs below the knee. But that is not the beginning to a sad story. Aimee's life is a story of adventure, excitement, and achievement. At every turn, people try to put her into a mold—the stereotype of a disabled person who should work as hard as possible to seem normal. But Aimee is not normal. She is remarkable. Refusing to allow anyone to limit her, she becomes a world-record-setting athlete and fashion model.

Insight

This intriguing memoir is a loud affirmation of the need to be oneself. Mullins deals with her physical problems, her prosthetics, and the authority figures in her life with humor and irreverence as she moves from athlete to fashion model to international celebrity.

ESSENTIAL QUESTION:
How do we overcome obstacles?

Connection to Essential Question

The connection of "A Work in Progress" to the essential question is clear and strong. Aimee Mullins faces powerful physical and social obstacles, but she seems to see them all as challenges and opportunities.

SMALL-GROUP LEARNING PERFORMANCE TASK
How do people overcome enormous challenges?

UNIT PERFORMANCE-BASED ASSESSMENT
How can people overcome adversity in the face of overwhelming obstacles?

Connection to Performance Tasks

Small-Group Learning Performance Task In this Performance Task, students will present an informative essay about how people face challenges to overcome adversity. This selection provides students with the insight that being yourself is the surest path to the kind of success you value.

Unit Performance-Based Assessment Aimee Mullins is an excellent example of a person who has the confidence and drive to use whatever life gives her to build an extraordinary life. For Aimee, obstacles are seen as opportunities. This is an important insight that students can use in responding to the assessment.

DIGITAL PERSPECTIVES  Audio  Video Document  Annotation Highlights  Online Assessment

LESSON RESOURCES

	Making Meaning	Language Development	Effective Expression
Lesson	**First Read** **Close Read** **Analyze the Text** **Analyze Craft and Structure**	**Concept Vocabulary** **Word Study** **Conventions**	**Speaking and Listening**
Instructional Standards	**RI.7.10** By the end of the year, read and comprehend literary nonfiction . . . **L.7.4** Determine or clarify the meaning of unknown and multiple-meaning words and phrases . . . **L.7.4.a** Use context as a clue . . . **RI.7.3** Analyze the interactions between . . . **RI.7.4** Determine the meaning of words and phrases . . . **RI.7.6** Determine an author's point of view or purpose . . .	**L.7.4** Determine or clarify the meaning of unknown and multiple-meaning words and phrases . . . **L.7.4.b** Use common, grade-appropriate Greek or Latin affixes and roots . . . **L.7.1** Demonstrate command of the conventions of standard English . . . **L.7.2** Demonstrate command of the conventions of standard English . . .	**SL.7.1** Engage effectively in a range of collaborative discussions . . . **SL.7.1.a** Come to discussions prepared . . . **SL.7.1.b** Follow rules for collegial discussions . . . **SL.7.1.c** Pose questions . . .
STUDENT RESOURCES			
Available online in the Interactive Student Edition or Unit Resources	Selection Audio First-Read Guide: Nonfiction Close-Read Guide: Nonfiction	Word Network	Evidence Log
TEACHER RESOURCES			
Selection Resources Available online in the Interactive Teacher's Edition or Unit Resources	Audio Summaries: English and Spanish Annotation Highlights Accessible Leveled Text Spanish Translation Text Questions First Read Extension Questions Analyze Craft and Structure: Word Choice and Humor	Concept Vocabulary and Word Study Conventions: Informal Grammar	Speaking and Listening: Group Discussion
Reteach/Practice (RP) Available online in the Interactive Teacher's Edition or Unit Resources	Analyze Craft and Structure: Word Choice and Humor (RP)	Word Study: Latin Prefix *extra-* (RP) Conventions: Informal Grammar (RP)	Speaking and Listening: Group Discussion (RP)
Assessment Available online in Assessments	Selection Test: English Selection Test: Spanish Extension Selection Test		
My Resources	A Unit 5 Answer Key is available online and in the Interactive Teacher's Edition.		

Reading Support

Text Complexity Rubric: A Work in Progress	
Quantitative Measures	
Lexile: 930 **Text Length:** 1,973 words	
Qualitative Measures	
Knowledge Demands ①—❷—③—④—⑤	This is a personal story told by an accomplished athlete.
Structure ①—②—❸—④—⑤	"A Work in Progress" is the transcription of a speech given by Aimee Mullins for *The Moth Radio Hour* storytelling series. The structure is conventional.
Language Conventionality and Clarity ①—②—❸—④—⑤	The language is simple, conventional, and clear with most vocabulary on-level, aside from a few difficult technical terms.
Levels of Meaning/Purpose ①—②—❸—④—⑤	Straightforward meaning and purpose.

DECIDE AND PLAN

English Language Support

Provide English Learners with support for language and meaning as they read the selection.

Language Discuss with students the narrative form and style of Mullins' piece, which will seem somewhat different from others they've read. Discuss how the fact that it was a speech delivered in public changes the tone and the language used.

Meaning Ask students to talk with each other about what they learned about disability and prosthetics, and whether they knew that it was possible for a person without her lower legs to become a professional athlete. Encourage them to think about what they may have to do to overcome their own obstacles.

Strategic Support

Provide students with strategic support to ensure that they can successfully read the text.

Language Have students go through the text and think about what makes it a unique story. Discuss "voice" in writing and talk about how much work it can take to sound familiar. To understand the effect achieved, they can make a list of familiar phrases and words and contrast them with the more difficult words, such as "prosthetic" or "polypropylene."

Meaning Discuss the idea that when we "truly own what it is that makes us different, we're able to find the source of our greatest creative power." Ask students if they think this is true, and then discuss it. Discuss how society views the unconventional.

Challenge

Provide students who need to be challenged with ideas for how they can go beyond a simple interpretation of the text.

Text Analysis Ask students to reread the text and locate clues that indicate that Mullins' story is a speech. Make a short list for them of "colloquialisms." Discuss what makes a colloquialism. Talk about why more formal written work would not include phrases such as, "I was like, 'What?'"

Written Response Challenge students to write their own inspirational story for *The Moth Radio Hour*. Tell them they can take something from their own life, or an inspirational idea from a friend or family member outside of school. Tell them that the focus for this speech will be the crafting of a strong voice to tell a good story in under eight minutes.

TEACH

Read and Respond

Have groups read the selection and complete the Making Meaning, Language Development, and Effective Expression activities.

Standards Support Through Teaching and Learning Cycle

IDENTIFY NEEDS

Analyze results of the Beginning-of-Year Assessment, focusing on the items relating to Unit 5. Also take into consideration student performance to this point and your observations of where particular students struggle.

DECIDE AND PLAN

- If students have performed poorly on items matching these standards, then provide selection scaffolds before assigning them the on-level lesson provided in the Student Edition.
- If students have done well on the Beginning-of-Year Assessment, then challenge them to keep progressing and learning by giving them opportunities to practice the skills in depth.
- Use the Selection Resources listed on the Planning pages for "A Work in Progress" to help students continually improve their ability to master the standards.

Instructional Standards: A Work in Progress

	Catching Up	This Year	Looking Forward
Reading	You may wish to administer the **Analyze Craft and Structure: Humor (RP)** worksheet to help students understand how an author can construct point of view through humor.	**RI.6** Determine an author's point of view or purpose in a text and analyze how the author distinguishes his or her position from that of others.	Work with students to discuss how the humor of the selection helps the reader to see from narrator's point of view.
Speaking and Listening	You may wish to administer the **Speaking and Listening: Group Discussion (RP)** worksheet to help students prepare for their discussion.	**SL.1** Engage effectively in a range of collaborative discussions with diverse partners on *grade 7 topics, texts, and issues*, building on others' ideas and expressing their own clearly.	Challenge students to have a debate rather than a discussion.
Language	You may wish to administer the **Conventions: Informal Grammar (RP)** worksheet to help students understand the difference between direct and indirect objects. You may wish to administer the **Word Study Latin Prefix *extra-* (RP)** worksheet to help students understand that *extra-* means "beyond the scope of."	**L.1,2** Demonstrate command of the conventions of standard English grammar and usage when writing or speaking. **L.4.b** Use common, grade-appropriate Greek or Latin affixes and roots as clues to the meaning of a word.	Have students incorporate commas into their sentences to add direct and indirect objects. Have students find other examples of Latin prefixes.

ANALYZE AND REVISE

- Analyze student work for evidence of student learning.
- Identify whether students have met the expectations in the standards.
- Identify implications for future instruction.

TEACH

Implement the planned lesson, and gather evidence of student learning.

FACILITATING

Jump Start

FIRST READ To establish a context for reading the selection, engage students in a discussion of the different challenges people face in their lives. Ask: *What challenges have you faced? What challenges have other people you know faced? What enables people to overcome such challenges?*

A Work in Progress

What enables some people to face huge challenges with humor and grace? How can humor help people face adversity? What other qualities and attitudes can help people face adversity? Modeling the questions readers might ask as they read "A Work in Progress" brings the text alive for students and connects it to the Small-Group Performance Task question. Selection audio and print capability for the selection are available in the Interactive Teacher's Edition.

Concept Vocabulary

Ask groups to look closely at the information on context clues and how to use them. Walk students though the process of using each type of context clue. Explain that while context clues sometimes appear in the same sentence as an unfamiliar word, they can also appear in surrounding sentences.

FIRST READ

Have students perform the steps of the first read independently:

NOTICE: You may want to encourage students to notice details and specific word choices that add humor in the selection.

ANNOTATE: Remind students to mark vocabulary and key passages.

CONNECT: Encourage students to go beyond the text to make connections to their own experiences with adversity.

RESPOND: Students will answer questions and write a summary to demonstrate understanding.

Point out to students that while they will always complete the Respond step at the end of the first read, the other steps will probably happen somewhat concurrently. You may wish to print copies of the **First-Read Guide: Nonfiction** for students to use.

MAKING MEANING

About the Author

Aimee Mullins (b. 1976) is an athlete, model, and actor. At the age of one, she needed to have both of her legs amputated below the knee. Mullins learned how to walk and run with prosthetics, enabling her to participate in the 1996 Paralympic Games, where she set three world records in running and jumping events.

A Work in Progress

Concept Vocabulary

As you perform your first read of "A Work in Progress," you will encounter these words.

accomplishments extraordinary celebrate

Context Clues If these words are unfamiliar to you, try using **context clues** to help you determine their meanings. To do so, look for clues given by other words in the text that surround the unfamiliar words. There are various types of context clues that you may encounter as you read.

Synonyms: His **aberrant** behavior was unexpected. It is strange for him to be impolite.

Restatement of an idea: Because of a rare bone disease, her bones are **delicate** and more likely to break.

Contrast of ideas and topics: James will not eat foods made with **artificial** ingredients; he shops only at organic food stores.

Apply your knowledge of context clues and other vocabulary strategies to determine the meanings of other unfamiliar words you encounter during your first read.

First Read NONFICTION

Apply these strategies as you conduct your first read. You will have an opportunity to complete a close read after your first read.

NOTICE the general ideas of the text. *What* is it about? *Who* is involved?

ANNOTATE by marking vocabulary and key passages you want to revisit.

CONNECT ideas within the selection to what you already know and what you have already read.

RESPOND by completing the Comprehension Check and by writing a brief summary of the selection.

First Read

STANDARDS

Reading Informational Text

By the end of the year, read and comprehend literary nonfiction in the grades 6–8 text complexity band proficiently, with scaffolding as needed at the high end of the range.

Language

Determine or clarify the meaning of unknown and multiple-meaning words and phrases based on *grade 7 reading and content*, choosing flexibly from a range of strategies.

a. Use context as a clue to the meaning of a word or phrase.

AUTHOR'S PERSPECTIVE **Jim Cummins, Ph.D.**

Language Awareness Vocabulary knowledge is an extremely robust predictor of students' reading comprehension. The Frayer model is an effective tool for enabling students to extend their vocabulary knowledge in a systematic way. The tool aims to deepen students' knowledge of words and concepts by focusing their attention not only on simple definitions but also on characteristics of the concept and examples and nonexamples of it.

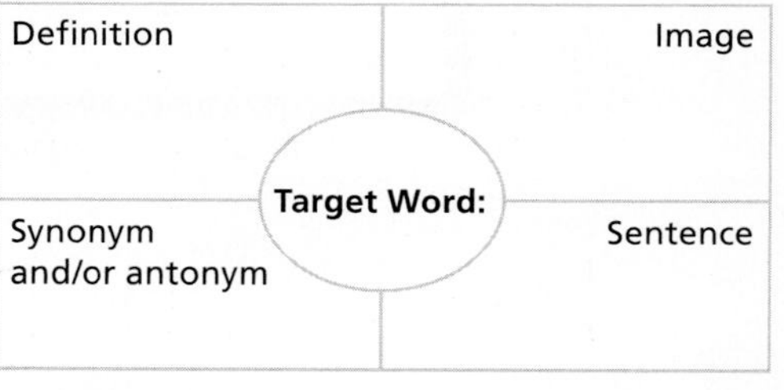

DIGITAL PERSPECTIVES

PERSONAL NARRATIVE

A Work in Progress

Aimee Mullins

BACKGROUND

A prosthetic is an artificial substitute for a missing body part. Over the past few decades, prosthetic technology has advanced greatly. Modern prosthetics can often fully replace the function of a missing limb due to the invention of lighter materials and more sophisticated designs.

1 So two weeks ago I was a bridesmaid, and the reception was actually here at the New York Public Library, and I will never forget this wedding. Yes, it was very beautiful. But more importantly, I survived the slick marble floors that are all over this building. Tile and marble floors are public enemy number one to a stiletto-loving girl like me. And I had five-inch heels on that night.

2 Most people learn to walk in very high heels. They bend their ankle so that the ball of the foot touches the ground first; you have more stability.

NOTES

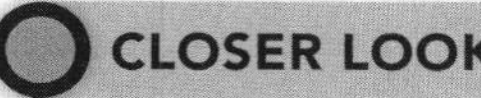

CLOSER LOOK

Hyperbole

Circulate among groups as students conduct their close read. Suggest that groups close read paragraph 1. Encourage them to talk about the annotations they mark. If needed, provide the following support.

ANNOTATE: Have students mark words and phrases that are examples of hyperbole, or using exaggerations for comic effect.

QUESTION: Guide students to consider what these word choices might tell them. Ask what a reader can infer from the exaggerations, and accept student responses.

Possible response: The hyperbole adds humor and sets the tone for the selection. The reader understands that the author has a good sense of humor and uses it to face challenges in her life and to entertain others.

CONCLUDE: Help students formulate conclusions about the importance of humor in the text. Ask students why the author might have taken a humorous tone toward her subject.

Possible response: The humor sets readers at ease, helps them identify with the author, and entertains them.

Reminds students that **hyperbole** is a deliberate overstatement or exaggeration used for comic effect.

Create an electronic template and have students work in groups of "language detectives" to enter new and interesting words onto the group's template. If time allows, encourage students to complete two to five words each day. Where multiple home languages are represented in a group, students could take turns entering words in their home language, and all members of the group could learn that word. At the end of each week, the teacher could compile the words into a class quiz.

PERSONALIZE FOR LEARNING

English Language Support

Exaggeration Review paragraph 1 with students. Exaggeration is often based on idiomatic expressions, such as "public enemy number one." To help students understand the exaggeration in this selection, have them listen to the audio recording of Aimee Mullins reading her work for *The Moth Radio Hour* (available for free download). Hearing the author's inflections as they follow along in the text will help students make inferences about when Mullins is exaggerating and will help them understand the humor in the selection. **ALL LEVELS**

CLOSER LOOK

Analyze Tone

Circulate among groups as students conduct their close read. Suggest that groups read paragraphs 3 and 4. Encourage them to talk about the annotations they mark. If needed, provide the following support.

ANNOTATE: Have students mark words and phrases that show the author's tone, or her attitude toward the subject and the audience.

QUESTION: Guide students to consider what these word choices might tell them. Ask what a reader can infer from the author's tone, and accept student responses.

Possible response: The author's tone is informal and funny. Readers can infer that she is self-confident enough to joke about herself and her challenges.

CONCLUDE: Help students formulate conclusions about tone and author's purpose in the text. Ask students to identify what her tone suggests about her purpose.

Possible response: The author's tone suggests her purpose is not only to inform but also to entertain.

Remind students that **tone** is an author's attitude toward his or her audience or subject. Tone can often be described by a single adjective, such as formal, serious, playful, or ironic. In prose, word choice, sentence structure, and repetition can contribute to tone.

NOTES

3 I don't have ankles, so I hit each step on the stiletto, which makes the possibility of the banana peel wipeout very likely. But given the choice between practicality and theatricality, I say, "Go big or go home, man. Go down in flames if you're gonna go."

4 I guess I'm a bit of a daredevil. I think that the nurses at DuPont Institute would agree. I spent a lot of time there as a child. Doctors amputated[1] both of my legs below the knee when I was an infant, and then when I was five, I had a major surgery to correct the wonky direction in which my tibia was growing. So I had two metal pins to hold that—full plaster casts on both legs. I had to use a wheelchair because I couldn't wear prosthetics.

5 One of the best things about getting out of the hospital is the anticipation of the day you return to school—I had missed so much class, I just couldn't wait to get back and see all my friends. But my teacher had a different idea about that. She tried to prevent me from returning to class, because she said that in the condition I was in, I was "inappropriate," and that I would be a distraction to the other students (which of course I was, but not because of the casts and the wheelchair).

6 Clearly she needed to make my difference invisible because she wanted to control her environment and make it fit into her idea of what "normal" looked like.

7 And it would've been a lot easier for me to fit into what "normal" looked like. I know I wanted that back then. But instead I had these wooden legs with a rubber foot that the toes broke off of, and they were held on with a big bolt that rusted out because I swam in the wooden legs.

8 You're not supposed to swim in the wooden legs, because, you know, the wood rots out.

9 So there I was in second grade music class, doing the twist, and mid-twist I hear this [*makes loud cracking sound*]. And I'm on the floor, and the lower half of my left leg is in splinters across the room. The teacher faints on the piano, and the kids are screaming. And all I'm thinking is, *My parents are gonna kill me. I broke my leg!*

10 It's a mess.

11 But then a few years later, my prosthetist[2] tells me, "Aimee, we got waterproof legs for you. No more rusty bolts!"

12 This is a revelation, right? This is gonna change my life. I was so excited to get these legs . . . until I saw them.

1. **amputated** (AM pyoo tayt ihd) *v.* removed surgically.
2. **prosthetist** (PROS thuh tihst) *n.* professional who fits and designs prosthetic limbs.

FACILITATING SMALL-GROUP Close Reading

CLOSE READ: Autobiographical Narratives As groups perform the close read, circulate and offer support as needed.

- Remind groups that when they are reading an autobiographical narrative, they are reading a story that the author is telling about his or her own life.
- Explain that in most autobiographical narratives, the author's voice and tone are very important to understanding the theme, or big idea, of the selection.
- Point out that voice and tone are determined by word choice, sentence structure, and choice of details.
- Challenge groups to imagine the author's voice as they read and to identify her tone in their own words.

494 UNIT 5 • FACING ADVERSITY

DIGITAL PERSPECTIVES

13 They were made of polypropylene, which is that white plastic "milk jug" material. And when I say "white," I'm not talking about skin color; I'm talking about *the color white.* The "skin color" was the rubber foam foot painted "Caucasian," which is the nastiest shade of nuclear peach that you've ever seen in your life. It has nothing to do with any human skin tone on the planet. And these legs were so good at being waterproof that they were *buoyant*. So when I'd go off the high dive, I'd go down and come straight back up feet first. They were the bane of my existence.

14 But then we're at the Jersey Shore one summer. By the time we get there, there's three hundred yards of towels between me and the sea. And I know this is where I first honed my ability to run really fast. I was the white flash. I didn't wanna feel hundreds of pairs of eyes staring at me. And so I'd get myself into the ocean, and I was a good swimmer, but no amount of swimming technique can control buoyant legs.

15 So at some point I get caught in a rip current, and I'm migrating from my vantage point of where I could see my parents' towel. And I'm taking in water, and I'm fighting, fighting, fighting. And all I could think to do was pop off these legs and put one under each armpit, with the peach feet sticking up, and just bob, thinking, *Someone's gotta find me.*

16 And a lifeguard did. And I'm sure he will collect for therapy bills. You know? Like, they don't show that on *Baywatch*.[3]

17 But they saved my life, those legs.

18 And then when I was fourteen it was Easter Sunday, and I was gonna be wearing a dress that I had purchased with my own money—the first thing I ever bought that wasn't on sale.

19 Momentous event; you never forget it. I'd had a paper route since I was twelve, and I went to The Limited, and I bought this dress that I thought was the height of sophistication—sleeveless safari dress, belted, hits at the knee.

20 Coming downstairs into the living room, I see my father waiting to take us to church. He takes one look at me, and he says, "That doesn't look right. Go upstairs and change."

21 I was like, "What? My super-classy dress? What are you talking about? It's the best thing I own."

NOTES

3. ***Baywatch*** popular television show from the late 1990s about the lives of fictional lifeguards.

HOW LANGUAGE WORKS

Italics Call student attention to the italics in paragraphs 13–16. Explain that italics are used to distinguish letters, words, and phrases from the rest of the sentence. For instance, italics are used for titles and also for words used as words and foreign words. Explain that italics may also be used for emphasis and to distinguish a character's or writer's thoughts. Have students work in their groups to decide why each of the following is italicized in the selection: *the color white* (paragraph 13), *buoyant* (paragraph 13), *Someone's gotta find me* (paragraph 15), and *Baywatch* (paragraph 16).

NOTES

22 He said, "No, you can see the knee joint when you walk. It doesn't look right. It's inappropriate to go out like that. Go change."

23 And I think something snapped in me. I refused to change. And it was the first time I defied my father. I refused to hide something about myself that was true, and I refused to be embarrassed about something so that other people could feel more comfortable.

24 I was grounded for that defiance.

25 So after church the extended family convenes at my grandmother's house, and everybody's complimenting me on how nice I look in this dress, and I'm like, "Really? You think I look nice? Because my parents think I look inappropriate."

26 I outed them (kinda mean, really).

27 But I think the public utterance of this idea that I should somehow hide myself was so shocking to hear that it changed their mind about why they were doing it.

28 And I had always managed to get through life with somewhat of a positive attitude, but I think this was the start of me being able to accept myself. You know, okay, I'm not normal. I have strengths. I've got weaknesses. It is what it is.

29 And I had always been athletic, but it wasn't until college that I started this adventure in Track and Field. I had gone through a lifetime of being given legs that just barely got me by. And I thought, *Well, maybe I'm just having the wrong conversations with the wrong people. Maybe I need to go find people who say, "Yes, we can create* anything *for you in the space between where your leg ends and the ground."*

30 And so I started working with engineers, fashion designers, sculptors, Hollywood prosthetic makeup artists, wax museum designers to build legs for me.

31 I decided I wanted to be the fastest woman in the world on artificial legs, and I was lucky enough to arrive in track at just the right time to be the first person to get these radical sprinting legs modeled after the hind leg of a cheetah, the fastest thing that runs—woven carbon fiber.[4] I was able to set three world records with those legs. And they made no attempt at approximating humanness.

32 Then I get these incredibly lifelike silicon legs—hand-painted, capillaries, veins. And, hey, I can be as tall as I wanna be, so I get different legs for different heights. I don't have to shave. I can wear open-toed shoes in the winter. And most importantly,

4. **carbon fiber** (KAHR buhn FY buhr) *n.* very strong, lightweight material.

DIGITAL PERSPECTIVES

Enriching the Text To help students understand how the carbon fiber sprinting legs work, show them a video of a sprinter using them. You might also consider showing students the TED video from 1998 in which Mullins talks about her career as a runner and her experience in the Paralympics. **(Research to Clarify)**

496 UNIT 5 • FACING ADVERSITY

I can opt out of the cankles[5] I most certainly would've inherited genetically.

33 And then I get these legs made for me by the late, great Alexander McQueen, and they were hand-carved of solid ash with grapevines and magnolias all over them and a six-inch heel. And I was able to walk the runways of the world with supermodels. I was suddenly in this whirlwind of adventure and excitement. I was being invited to go around the world and speak about these adventures, and how I had legs that looked like glass, legs covered in feathers, porcelain legs, jellyfish legs—all wearable sculpture.

34 And I get this call from a guy who had seen me speak years ago, when I was at the beginning of my track career, and he says, "We loved it. We want you to come back." And it was clear to me he didn't know all these amazing things that had happened to me since my sports career.

35 So as I'm telling him, he says, "Whoa, whoa, whoa. Hold on, Aimee. The reason everybody liked you all those years ago was because you were this sweet, vulnerable, naïve girl, and if you walk onstage today, and you are this polished young woman with too many **accomplishments**, I'm afraid they won't like you."

36 For real, he said that. Wow.

37 He apparently didn't think I was vulnerable enough now. He was asking me to be *less than*, a little more downtrodden. He was asking me to disable myself for him and his audience.

38 And what was so shocking to me about that was that I realized I had moved past mere acceptance of my difference. I was having *fun* with my difference. Thank *God* I'm not normal. I get to be ***extraordinary***. And I'll decide what is a weakness and what is a strength.

39 And so I refused his request.

40 And a few days later, I'm walking in downtown Manhattan at a street fair, and I get this tug on my shirt, and I look down. It's this little girl I met a year earlier when she was at a pivotal moment in her life. She had been born with a brittle bone disease that resulted in her left leg being seven centimeters shorter than her right. She wore a brace and orthopedic[6] shoes and they got her by, but she wanted to do more.

5. **cankles** (KANG kuhlz) *n.* informal term for thick ankles.
6. **orthopedic** (awr thuh PEE dihk) *adj.* designed to treat a muscular or skeletal problem.

NOTES

Mark context clues or indicate another strategy you used that helped you determine meaning.

accomplishments (uh KOM plihsh muhnts) *n.*

MEANING:

extraordinary (ehk STRAWR duh nehr ee) *adj.*

MEANING:

DIGITAL PERSPECTIVES

Concept Vocabulary

ACCOMPLISHMENTS If groups are struggling to define the word *accomplishments* in paragraph 35, direct their attention to context clues in paragraphs 34 and 35. For example, the author is telling the man with whom she's speaking about the "amazing things that had happened" to her, and he then describes her as "polished." Have students infer the meaning of the word *accomplishments* based on these clues.

Possible response: Based on the context clues, the word *accomplishments* must mean "noteworthy or impressive achievements."

EXTRAORDINARY If groups are struggling to understand the meaning of *extraordinary* in paragraph 38, guide them through the process of using a contrast context clue to understand it. Point out that the author contrasts being extraordinary with being normal, so *extraordinary* must be the opposite of *normal*. Point out that context also suggests the author is thankful to be extraordinary, so it must be a positive thing. Tell students to verify the meaning in a print or online dictionary.

Possible response: *Extraordinary* means "very special."

VOCABULARY DEVELOPMENT

Concept Vocabulary Reinforcement To increase familiarity with the concept vocabulary words, ask students to use each of the words in a sentence about their own accomplishments. Encourage students to use each type of context clue—synonym, restatement, and contrast—in the sentences. Have students share their sentences in their small groups and identify the context clues used by group members.

Concept Vocabulary

CELEBRATE If groups are struggling to find context clues for the word *celebrate* in paragraph 44, direct their attention to paragraph 43. Ask: What details describe the girl's new leg? What do these details suggest about the girl's feelings about the leg? Is the leg merely functional, or something more? What does this tell you about the meaning of the word *celebrate*? Tell students to verify the meaning in a print or online dictionary.

Possible responses: *Celebrate* means "enjoy and publicly acknowledge."

NOTES

Mark context clues or indicate another strategy you used that helped you determine meaning.

celebrate (SEHL uh brayt) *v.*

MEANING:

41 And like all Internet-savvy kindergarteners, she gets on the computer and Googles "new leg," and she comes up with dozens of images of prosthetics, many of them mine. And she prints them out, goes to school, does show-and-tell on it, comes home, and makes a startling pronouncement to her parents:

42 "I wanna get rid of my bad leg," she says. "When can I get a new leg?"

43 And ultimately that was the decision her parents and doctors made for her. So here she was, six months after the amputation, and right there in the middle of the street fair she hikes up her jeans leg to show me her cool new leg. And it's pink, and it's tattooed with the characters of *High School Musical 3*, replete with red, sequined Mary Janes on her feet.

44 And she was proud of it. She was proud of herself. And the marvelous thing was that this six-year-old understood something that it took me twenty-something years to get, but that we both did discover—that when we can **celebrate** and truly own what it is that makes us different, we're able to find the source of our greatest creative power. ❧

PERSONALIZE FOR LEARNING

Strategic Support

Distinctiveness Review paragraph 44 and discuss the writer's attitude about prosthetic legs. Have students quick write about something that sets them apart from others and that they might see as a disadvantage. Tell them to identify this difference and then discuss how they might celebrate this difference and use it as a source for creative power and strength. Give students the option to share their responses in their small groups, but do not require it.

Comprehension Check

Complete the following items after you finish your first read. Review and clarify details with your group.

1. Why does the author, Aimee Mullins, have difficulty walking across the marble floor of the library?

2. What happened between Mullins and her father that caused her to be grounded?

3. What does Mullins do to become more involved with the quality of her limbs?

4. According to the author, what is the source of the "greatest creative power"?

5. **Notebook** Confirm your understanding of the selection by briefly summarizing key events.

RESEARCH

Research to Clarify Choose at least one unfamiliar detail from the text. Briefly research that detail. In what way does the information you learned shed light on the selection? Share your findings with your small group.

Research to Explore Choose something from the text that interested you. For instance, you might want to learn more about the newest kinds of prosthetic limbs. How does this information deepen your understanding of the personal narrative? Share your findings with your small group.

DIGITAL PERSPECTIVES

Comprehension Check

Possible responses:

1. because she likes to wear high heels but does not have ankles to help her balance in them
2. She refused to change out of a dress that showed her knees.
3. She worked with designers and manufacturers to make sure they were made to meet her needs and her taste.
4. According to the author, we can find the greatest source of our creative power "when we can celebrate and truly own what it is that makes us different."
5. The author's legs are amputated when she is five, and she is equipped with wooden legs. However, the bolts in these legs get rusty when she swims and the legs tend to break. Eventually, she realizes she can ask for better legs. She is equipped with legs that help her run so fast that she breaks world records and other legs that are works of art. Subsequently, she discovers that her difference from others is her greatest strength.

Research

Research to Clarify Remind groups to adequately narrow their topics and search terms for research. For instance, "prosthetic legs" is too broad a topic and would probably yield an overwhelming amount of information, but narrowing the topic to "carbon fiber sprinting legs" would be more effective. Have groups present the findings of their research to the class.

Research to Explore Tell students that the topic suggested here is just one possibility. They should choose the topic for further research that most interests them. Here are some additional ideas: the Americans with Disabilities Act, the Paralympics, cheetahs, silicon legs, and wearable sculpture.

PERSONALIZE FOR LEARNING

Challenge

Narrative The author of "A Work in Progress" describes how she overcame the physical challenges associated with having had both of her legs amputated beneath the knee. This is a serious topic, but the author presents her story in a positive way and writes with a sense of humor that reflects her personality and brings her words to life.

Have students write a short autobiographical narrative about a challenge they've faced. Encourage them to incorporate exaggeration, comic diction, and other humorous elements in a manner similar to that employed by author Aimee Mullins. Point out that students need not write about anything they feel is too personal—a challenge might simply be studying for and passing a tough test, working hard to make a sports team, learning to play an instrument, and so on.

Jump Start

CLOSE READ Ask groups to consider the following prompt: *What challenges are you currently facing? How can you overcome these challenges?* As students discuss in their groups, remind them to listen respectfully to the challenges faced by group members.

Close Read the Text

If needed, model close reading by using the Annotation Highlights in the Interactive Teacher's Edition. Remind students to use Accountable Talk in their discussions and to support one another as they complete the close read. You may want to print copies of the **Close Read Guide: Nonfiction** for students to use.

Analyze the Text

1. **Possible response:** The teacher said she was "inappropriate." The real reason might be she is afraid of people who are different or that she is unsure how to act.
2. Passages will vary. Students should discuss why they think the passages are important.
3. Responses will vary. Students should support their ideas with details from the selection.

Concept Vocabulary

Why These Words? Possible response: The words all relate to overcoming obstacles.

Practice

Responses will vary, but student discussions should demonstrate an understanding of each word.

Word Network

Possible words: *progress, bane, hone, vulnerable*

Word Study

For more support, see **Concept Vocabulary and Word Study.**

Possible response: words include *extracurricular, extrasensory, extraterrestrial*

MAKING MEANING

A WORK IN PROGRESS

TIP

GROUP DISCUSSION

When you work with your group, be sure to cite textual details to support your ideas.

WORD NETWORK

Add interesting words related to facing adversity from the text to your Word Network.

STANDARDS

Reading Informational Text

- Analyze the interactions between individuals, events, and ideas in a text.
- Determine the meaning of words and phrases as they are used in a text, including figurative, connotative, and technical meanings; analyze the impact of a specific word choice on meaning and tone.
- Determine an author's point of view or purpose in a text and analyze how the author distinguishes his or her position from that of others.

Language

Determine or clarify the meaning of unknown and multiple-meaning words and phrases based on *grade 7 reading and content*, choosing flexibly from a range of strategies.

b. Use common, grade-appropriate Greek or Latin affixes and roots as clues to the meaning of a word.

Close Read the Text

With your group, revisit sections of the text you marked during your first read. What do you **notice**? What **questions** do you have? What can you **conclude**?

Analyze the Text

CITE TEXTUAL EVIDENCE to support your answers.

Notebook Complete the activities.

1. **Review and Clarify** With your group, reread paragraphs 5–6. What reason did the narrator's teacher give for not wanting her to return to class? What do you think might have been the real reason?
2. **Present and Discuss** Now, work with your group to share the passages from the text that you found especially important. Take turns presenting your passages. Discuss what you noticed in the text, the questions you asked, and the conclusions you reached.
3. **Essential Question:** ***How do we overcome obstacles?*** What has this selection taught you about facing adversity? Discuss with your group.

LANGUAGE DEVELOPMENT

Concept Vocabulary

accomplishments	extraordinary	celebrate

Why These Words? The concept vocabulary words from the text are related. With your group, determine what the words have in common. Write down your ideas, and add another word that fits the category.

Practice

Confirm your understanding of the concept vocabulary words by using them in a discussion with your group in which you address the following question: *What makes a person extraordinary?*

Word Study

Latin Prefix *extra-* The Latin prefix *extra-* means "beyond the scope of" or "in addition to what is usual or expected." At the end of the selection, the author realizes that what makes her different also makes her *extraordinary*, or beyond what is ordinary or expected. With your group, identify and define two other words you know that include this prefix.

FORMATIVE ASSESSMENT

Analyze the Text

If students struggle to close read the text, **then** provide the **A Work in Progress: Text Questions** available online in the Interactive Teacher's Edition or Unit Resources. Answers and DOK levels are also available.

Concept Vocabulary

If students have difficulty identifying the connection among the words, **then** have them use each word in a sentence about facing adversity and consider what the sentences have in common.

Word Study

If students have difficulty identifying words that begin with the prefix *extra-*, **then** guide them in adding *extra-* to the beginnings of various adjectives. For Reteach and Practice, see **Word Study: Latin Prefix *extra-* (RP).**

Analyze Craft and Structure

Author's Purpose: Word Choice and Humor The main purpose of humorous writing is to entertain readers. Authors may incorporate elements of humorous writing into more serious writing in order to express the lighter, human side of otherwise difficult situations. Some literary techniques that authors use to create humor are:

LITERARY TECHNIQUE	DEFINITION	EXAMPLE
HYPERBOLE	intentional, sometimes outrageous, exaggeration for effect	describing a small patch of ice as a "vast, frozen lake"
COMIC DICTION	words chosen to make the reader laugh; these word choices often include slang and other informal language	"Letting the cat out of the bag is a lot easier than putting it back in."
INCONGRUITY	when something is out of place or inappropriate for a situation or setting	wearing bunny ears instead of a veil with a bridal outfit

Practice

CITE TEXTUAL EVIDENCE to support your answers.

Reread "A Work in Progress." Then, work with your group to analyze the narrative. Use the chart to record your ideas. The first two rows have identified humorous passages for you to analyze. In the last two rows, identify the humorous passages on your own.

PARAGRAPHS	HUMOROUS ELEMENT	PURPOSE AND EFFECT
1: "But more importantly, I survived the slick marble floors that are all over this building."	Comic diction in the choice of the word "survived"	We would ordinarily say we "walk" across a floor. By stating she "survived the . . . floors" the author makes us sympathetic to her everyday challenges.
3: "I don't have ankles, so I hit each step on the stiletto, which makes the possibility of a banana peel wipeout very likely."	Hyperbole in the image of a "banana peel wipeout"	The author gives us a mental image of an exaggerated accident such as a cartoon-character slipping, flipping in the air, and falling down.
4–21 ". . . the nastiest shade of nuclear peach that you've ever seen . . ."	Comic diction in using "nuclear" with "peach"	The author chooses an extreme term, "nuclear," to exaggerate the intensity of the peach tone of the prosthetic foot.
22–44 "And like all Internet-savvy kindergarteners . . ."	Hyperbole in exaggerating the intelligence most of us assume in young children	The author explodes the idea that five-year-old children are completely innocent and unaware of the larger world.

PERSONALIZE FOR LEARNING

English Language Support

Using Hyperbole Have students think of a person that they know or that they know of that they can describe using hyperbole. For example, *Marco eats 42 bowls of cereal for breakfast.*

Have students write two sentences describing the person. **EMERGING**

Ask students to write a paragraph about the person. **EXPANDING**

Ask students to write a brief biography in which they use hyperbole to describe what the character looks like and what he or she can do. **BRIDGING**

An expanded **English Language Support Lesson** on Hyperbole is available in the Interactive Teacher's Edition.

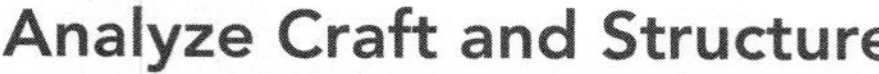

DIGITAL PERSPECTIVES

Analyze Craft and Structure

Author's Purpose: Word Choice and Humor When authors use humor in their writing, they aren't necessarily trying to get their readers to laugh aloud—but they are trying to entertain them in some way. Writers can convey a serious theme while incorporating humor, as Aimee Mullins does in "A Work in Progress."

Satire, limericks, farce, and humorous essays such as "A Work in Progress" are examples of humorous writing. For more support, see **Analyze Craft and Structure: Humor.**

See possible responses in the chart on the student page.

Practice

Responses will vary. Students should identify the humorous parts of the passage they chose, add humor to it, and then replace humorous wording with non-humorous wording.

FORMATIVE ASSESSMENT

Analyze Craft and Structure

If students struggle to analyze the humor, **then** guide them in doing so by directing their attention to a specific passage and asking questions about it. For instance, you might direct students' attention to paragraph 9 and ask: "What effect does the information in brackets have on the reader? What happens that is unexpected or incongruous? What is ironic or unexpected about the author's thoughts in the last sentence of the paragraph?" For Reteach and Practice, see **Analyze Craft and Structure: Humor (RP).**

FACILITATING

Conventions

Informal Grammar As you discuss Mullins's use of informal grammar with students, guide them to understand the situations in which formal and informal grammar are considered appropriate. Discuss why most scholarly, legal, business, news and other professional informative writing uses formal grammar and how the effectiveness of informative writing might be altered if writers use more informal grammar. For more support, see **Conventions: Informal Grammar.**

Read It

1. See possible responses in the chart on the student page.
2. Answers will vary. Students should identify examples of how listeners' connection with the speaker is greater if the speaker uses informal grammar.

Write It

Paragraphs will vary but should be cogent and understandable while using colloquial diction.

FORMATIVE ASSESSMENT

Conventions

If students are having difficulty differentiating between formal and informal grammar, **then** have them observe peers' casual conversation and write down example sentences, word for word. Then have them mark the sentences by circling any grammar they believe would need to be changed if it were written for an essay. For Reteach and Practice, see **Conventions: Informal Grammar (RP).**

LANGUAGE DEVELOPMENT

A WORK IN PROGRESS

Conventions

Informal Grammar "A Work in Progress" is transcribed, or copied, from a speech that Aimee Mullins gave at the New York Public Library. While speaking, Mullins chose **informal grammar,** or casual language rules, to connect with her audience. Some features of her spoken language include:

- **Colloquial Contractions** Words such as *gonna* (going to), *wanna* (want to) and *kinda* (kind of) combine two words in a way that imitates casual conversation.
- **Informal Transitions** People often add casual words and phrases such as *man, I'm like, so there I was,* and *you know* when they speak to link ideas or create emphasis.
- **Introductory Conjunctions** Starting sentences with the conjunctions *and, but,* or *so* can smooth the transition from one sentence into another in informal speech, even though they are discouraged in more formal writing.

Read It

1. Work with your group to find two more examples of informal grammar in "A Work in Progress." Then, rewrite each example of informal grammar to follow standard English grammar rules.

INFORMAL GRAMMAR FROM TEXT	STANDARD GRAMMAR
And all I'm thinking is, *My parents are gonna kill me.*	The only thought in my mind is, *My parents are going to be extremely angry with me.*
This is a revelation, right? This is gonna change my life.	This revelation is going to change my life.
And a lifeguard did. And I'm sure he will collect for therapy bills. You know? Like, they don't show that on *Baywatch*.	A lifeguard did find me, and I'm sure he will need therapy to recover from the shock. This was not likely part of his training.
For real, he said that. Wow. I outed them (kinda mean, really).	He actually said that, even though it's hard to believe I exposed them, and when I think about it, I realize I was fairly mean.

2. Compare the impact of Mullins's original words and the versions that follow standard grammar rules. What are the advantages of Mullins's original language choices?

Write It

Notebook Write a paragraph that uses informal language to tell about a funny incident that happened to you or someone you know. Imagine that you are sharing this story aloud with an audience, and writing down what you say as you are speaking. Use colloquial contractions, informal transitions, and introductory conjunctions to create a feeling of lively, spoken language.

STANDARDS

Speaking and Listening
Engage effectively in a range of collaborative discussions with diverse partners on *grade 7 topics, texts, and issues*, building on others' ideas and expressing their own clearly.
a. Come to discussions prepared, having read or researched material under study; explicitly draw on that preparation by referring to evidence on the topic, text, or issue to probe and reflect on ideas under discussion.
b. Follow rules for collegial discussions, track progress toward specific goals and deadlines, and define individual roles as needed.
c. Pose questions that elicit elaboration and respond to others' questions and comments with relevant observations and ideas that bring the discussion back on topic as needed.

Language
- Demonstrate command of the conventions of standard English grammar and usage when writing or speaking.
- Demonstrate command of the conventions of standard English capitalization, punctuation, and spelling when writing.

EFFECTIVE EXPRESSION

Speaking and Listening

Assignment

With your group, conduct a **discussion** in which you analyze one of the following quotations from the selection.

- ☐ "And I had always been athletic, but it wasn't until college that I started this adventure in Track and Field. I had gone through a lifetime of being given legs that just barely got me by. And I thought, *Well, maybe I'm just having the wrong conversations with the wrong people. Maybe I need to go find people who say, 'Yes, we can create* anything *for you in the space between where your leg ends and the ground.'*" (paragraph 29)
- ☐ "And the marvelous thing was that this six-year-old understood something that it took me twenty-something years to get, but that we both did discover—that when we can celebrate and truly own what it is that makes us different, we're able to find the source of our greatest creative power." (paragraph 44)

Organize Your Discussion Assign roles for each member of your group. Roles can include a group leader, who keeps the discussion on topic; a timekeeper, who makes sure that the discussion takes no longer than 15 minutes; and a note-taker to record the group's ideas. Once you have chosen a quotation, use these questions to guide your group's discussion. Use a chart like this one to record ideas from your discussion.

Here are some things to keep in mind as you hold your group discussion.

- Draw on the selection to explore and support ideas. Support viewpoints with examples and details from the selection.
- Take turns speaking. Listen to other students' ideas, and respond with relevant observations and questions that prompt them to elaborate on their thoughts.

DISCUSSION QUESTIONS	RESPONSES
1. What does the quotation mean? How could you paraphrase it, or restate the ideas in your own words?	
2. What happens that causes the author to express these ideas? What caused her to reach this understanding?	
3. Do you think it would help society if more people felt as this author feels? Why or why not?	

EVIDENCE LOG

Before moving on to a new selection, go to your Evidence Log and record what you learned from "A Work in Progress."

DIGITAL PERSPECTIVES

Speaking and Listening

Explain that students will be discussing the quotation's significance in the selection, as well as what it means to them personally.

Organize Your Discussion Have groups record answers to all three discussion questions in the chart. Then, have them formulate at least one more question of their own and add rows to the chart as necessary. Remind students to support their ideas with details from the text and from their own experience. For more support, see **Speaking and Listening: Group Discussion.**

Evidence Log Support students in completing their Evidence Log. This paced activity will help prepare them for the Performance-Based Assessment at the end of the unit.

FORMATIVE ASSESSMENT

Speaking and Listening

If groups have difficulty organizing their discussions, **then** assign roles and tasks to group members. For Reteach and Practice, see **Speaking and Listening: Group Discussion (RP).**

Selection Test

Administer the "A Work in Progress" Selection Test, which is available in both print and digital formats online in Assessments.

PERSONALIZE FOR LEARNING

Strategic Support

Discussion Sensitivity The topic of the essay may be an emotional one for some students. Provide an outlet for expressing feelings that students might have in response to the essay or to the quotations called out in the group discussion assignment. Some students might be better able to complete the discussion assignment with a partner rather than in a group.

from The Story of My Life

AUDIO SUMMARIES
Audio summaries of the excerpt from *The Story of My Life* are available online in both English and Spanish in the Interactive Teacher's Edition or Unit Resources. Assigning these summaries prior to reading the selection may help students build additional background knowledge and set a context for their first read.

Summary

In this excerpt from Helen Keller's autobiography, *The Story of My Life*, Keller describes a moment that changed her life forever. At the age of seven, unable to see, hear, or speak, a new teacher, Annie Sullivan, works with Helen to connect words and language by signing words into the palm of Helen's hand. It is a slow process until one day, Helen makes the connection between the word being spelled in her hand, "water," and the cool liquid she feels. It's at this point that a new world opens up for Helen Keller.

Insight

This selection helps students understand that apparently hopeless challenges can be met with intelligence, courage, and compassion.

ESSENTIAL QUESTION:
How do we overcome obstacles?

Connection to Essential Question

The Story of My Life provides a strong connection to the Essential Question, "How do we overcome obstacles?" Helen Keller faced enormous obstacles due to her inability to see, hear, or speak. However, with the help of her teacher, she learned to overcome these obstacles and live a remarkable life.

SMALL-GROUP LEARNING PERFORMANCE TASK
How do people face challenges in order to overcome adversity?

UNIT PERFORMANCE-BASED ASSESSMENT
How can people overcome adversity in the face of overwhelming obstacles?

Connection to Performance Tasks

Small-Group Learning Performance Task In this Performance Task, students will present an informative essay about how people face challenges to overcome adversity. This selection provides students with examples of courage and compassion.

Unit Performance-Based Assessment As students work on the assessment, they will need to support their response to the prompt with evidence about facing challenges. From the moment of her revelation at the water pump, Keller faces a stunning challenge with eagerness and courage.

DIGITAL PERSPECTIVES

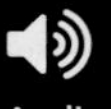 Audio
 Video
 Document
 Annotation Highlights
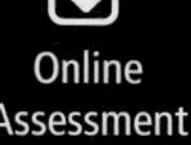 Online Assessment

LESSON RESOURCES

	Making Meaning	Language Development
Lesson	**First Read** **Close Read** **Analyze the Text** **Analyze Craft and Structure**	**Concept Vocabulary** **Word Study** **Conventions**
Instructional Standards	**RI.7.10** By the end of the year, read and comprehend literary nonfiction . . . **L.7.4** Determine or clarify the meaning of unknown and multiple-meaning words and phrases . . . **L.7.4.a** Use context as a clue . . . **RI.7.4** Determine the meaning of words and phrases as they are used in a text . . . **RI.7.6** Determine an author's point of view or purpose . . .	**L.7.4** Determine or clarify the meaning of unknown and multiple-meaning words and phrases . . . **L.7.4.b** Use common, grade-appropriate Greek or Latin affixes and roots . . . **L.7.1.c** Place phrases and clauses within a sentence . . .
STUDENT RESOURCES		
Available online in the Interactive Student Edition or Unit Resources	Selection Audio First-Read Guide: Nonfiction Close-Read Guide: Nonfiction	Word Network
TEACHER RESOURCES		
Selection Resources Available online in the Interactive Teacher's Edition or Unit Resources	Audio Summaries: English and Spanish Annotation Highlights Accessible Leveled Text Spanish Translation Text Questions First Read Extension Questions Analyze Craft and Structure: Autobiographical Writing	Concept Vocabulary and Word Study Conventions: Types of Dependent Clauses
Reteach/Practice (RP) Available online in the Interactive Teacher's Edition or Unit Resources	Analyze Craft and Structure: Autobiographical Writing (RP)	Word Study: Greek Root *-myst-* (RP) Conventions: Types of Dependent Clauses (RP)
Assessment Available online in Assessments	Selection Test: English Selection Test: Spanish Extension Selection Test	
My Resources	A Unit 5 Answer Key is available online and in the Interactive Teacher's Edition.	

Reading Support

Text Complexity Rubric: *from* The Story of My Life	
Quantitative Measures	
Lexile: 970 Text Length: 733 words	
Qualitative Measures	
Knowledge Demands ①—②—❸—④—⑤	Background knowledge on Helen Keller's life will help with understanding.
Structure ①—❷—③—④—⑤	The structure is simple and the excerpt is short.
Language Conventionality and Clarity ①—②—❸—④—⑤	Conventional language and on-level vocabulary.
Levels of Meaning/Purpose ①—②—❸—④—⑤	The story discusses education, learning, and disability, as well as Keller's struggle to overcome a unique obstacle to her own ability to learn.

DECIDE AND PLAN

English Language Support

Provide English learners with support for knowledge and language as they read the selection.

Knowledge Discuss with students the era in which Helen Keller lived. There were no institutional mechanisms in place to help people who were deaf, mute, and blind. Talk about how she went on to write a book, the one they read an excerpt from, and to achieve many things while earning the admiration of people across America.

Language Ask students if they know how Miss Sullivan is "spelling" words like "d-o-l-l" to Helen Keller. If any student has a deaf family member, or knows about American Sign Language, have them talk about it in class. Discuss the severe challenges of understanding the most basic elements of language, starting from a point, like Helen Keller, of absolute deafness and blindness.

Strategic Support

Provide students with strategic support to ensure that they can successfully read the text.

Knowledge Tell students to discuss the epiphany Helen Keller had as a "misty consciousness" came over her and she began to understand the "mystery of language." Tell them to consider how Keller's words in this excerpt help us to understand what it's really like to learn language for a person who cannot see or hear.

Language Ask students what they think of Helen Keller's writing style. How do they think she "writes" so well if she cannot see or hear? Use this discussion to segue into the idea that there are no obstacles to learning to write well. Although we are all different, ultimately it is possible to achieve clarity and beauty in writing.

Challenge

Provide students who need to be challenged with ideas for how they can go beyond a simple interpretation of the text.

Text Analysis Challenge students to investigate Helen Keller's ability to learn new things. Ask them whether, based on their reading of the text, they believe that a person who is deaf, mute, and blind has the same access to all knowledge as one who is just deaf, or just blind. Then have them reread the text and think about what the greatest obstacles were that Keller faced.

Written Response Suggest that students take the role of Miss Sullivan, from Helen Keller's excerpt. Ask them how they might go about teaching a young deaf or blind girl or boy, and what their tactics might be to get messages across to them. Have them write this up and ask that they include modern technology and conveniences that might help.

TEACH

Read and Respond

Have the groups read the selection and complete the Making Meaning and Language Development activities.

Standards Support Through Teaching and Learning Cycle

IDENTIFY NEEDS

Analyze results of the Beginning-of-Year Assessment, focusing on the items relating to Unit 5. Also take into consideration student performance to this point and your observations of where particular students struggle.

DECIDE AND PLAN

- If students have performed poorly on items matching these standards, then provide selection scaffolds before assigning them the on-level lesson provided in the Student Edition.
- If students have done well on the Beginning-of-Year Assessment, then challenge them to keep progressing and learning by giving them opportunities to practice the skills in depth.
- Use the Selection Resources listed on the Planning pages "*from* The Story of My Life" to help students continually improve their ability to master the standards.

Instructional Standards: *from* The Story of My Life

	Catching Up	This Year	Looking Forward
Reading	You may wish to administer the **Analyze Craft and Structure: Autobiographical Writing (RP)** worksheet to help students understand the tenets of autobiography.	**RI.6** Determine an author's point of view or purpose in a text and analyze how the author distinguishes his or her position from that of others.	Challenge students to discuss what purpose an autobiography may have other than to entertain.
Language	You may wish to administer the **Conventions: Types of Dependent Clauses (RP)** worksheet to help students understand adverb, relative and noun-dependent clauses. You may wish to administer the **Word Study: Greek Root *-myst* -(RP)** worksheet to help students understand that the root *-myst-* means "secret."	**L.1.a** Explain the function of phrases and clauses in general and their function in specific sentences. **L.4.b** Use common, grade-appropriate Greek or Latin affixes and roots as clues to the meaning of a word.	Have students locate gerund, participial, and infinitive phrases in the selection. Have students find other examples of Greek root words.

ANALYZE AND REVISE

- Analyze student work for evidence of student learning.
- Identify whether students have met the expectations in the standards.
- Identify implications for future instruction.

TEACH

Implement the planned lesson, and gather evidence of student learning.

Jump Start

FIRST READ Can you imagine not having the ability to see, hear, or speak, or even knowing that language exists? Engage students in a discussion about the importance of language that sets the context for reading the excerpt from *The Story of My Life*. As students share their thoughts, guide them to identify specific factors that affected their responses.

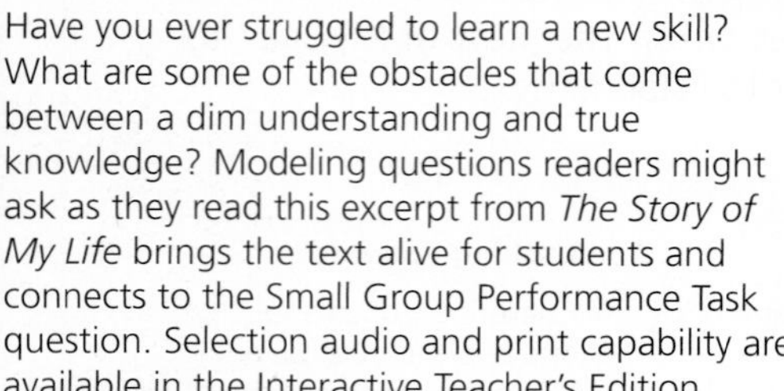

from The Story of My Life

Have you ever struggled to learn a new skill? What are some of the obstacles that come between a dim understanding and true knowledge? Modeling questions readers might ask as they read this excerpt from *The Story of My Life* brings the text alive for students and connects to the Small Group Performance Task question. Selection audio and print capability are available in the Interactive Teacher's Edition.

Concept Vocabulary

Have groups discuss the different types of context clues illustrated on the student page. For each word used in the examples (*comprehend, obstacles*), encourage groups to come up with a definition based on the clues provided. Ask group members if they can think of any other types of context clues.

FIRST READ

Have students perform the steps of the first read independently.

NOTICE: Encourage students to notice each instance of Miss Sullivan attempting to teach Helen Keller something.

ANNOTATE: Remind students to mark passages showing Helen's reaction to the obstacles she faces in trying to understand what Miss Sullivan is teaching her.

CONNECT: Have students compare Helen's struggle to understand language with their own struggles to learn new skills—or with the struggles of other people with physical disabilities about whom students have read or heard.

RESPOND: Students will answer questions and write a summary to demonstrate understanding.

Point out to students that while they will always complete the Respond step at the end of the first read, the other steps will probably happen somewhat concurrently. You may wish to print copies of the **First-Read Guide: Nonfiction** for students to use.

MAKING MEANING

Comparing Text to Media

from THE STORY OF MY LIFE

In this lesson, you will compare a passage from Helen Keller's autobiography with a scene from "How Helen Keller Learned to Talk." First, complete the first-read and close-read activities for the excerpt from *The Story of My Life*. The work you do with your group will help prepare you to compare the excerpt and the video.

HOW HELEN KELLER LEARNED TO TALK

About the Author

A serious illness left **Helen Keller** (1880–1968) blind and deaf before she was two years old. When Keller was nearly seven, her family hired Anne Sullivan, a teacher from the Perkins School for the Blind, to help her learn to communicate. Keller and Sullivan developed a remarkable teacher-student relationship as well as a unique friendship.

from The Story of My Life

Concept Vocabulary

As you perform your first read of the excerpt from *The Story of My Life*, you will encounter these words.

imitate　　mystery　　barriers

Context Clues If these words are unfamiliar to you, try using **context clues** to help you determine their meanings. There are various types of context clues that you may encounter as you read.

Synonyms: With the help of her teacher, she was able to **comprehend** or understand new ideas.

Restatement of an idea: There were many **obstacles** on her path, but she would not let them block her progress.

Apply your knowledge of context clues and other vocabulary strategies to determine the meanings of other unfamiliar words you encounter during your first read.

First Read NONFICTION

Apply these strategies as you conduct your first read. You will have an opportunity to complete a close read after your first read.

NOTICE the general ideas of the text. *What* is it about? *Who* is involved?

ANNOTATE by marking vocabulary and key passages you want to revisit.

CONNECT ideas within the selection to what you already know and what you have already read.

RESPOND by completing the Comprehension Check and by writing a brief summary of the selection.

STANDARDS

Reading Informational Text
By the end of the year, read and comprehend literary nonfiction in the grades 6–8 text complexity band proficiently, with scaffolding as needed at the high end of the range.

Language
Determine or clarify the meaning of unknown and multiple-meaning words and phrases based on *grade 7 reading and content*, choosing flexibly from a range of strategies.

a. Use context as a clue to the meaning of a word or phrase.

FACILITATING SMALL-GROUP CLOSE READING

CLOSE READ: Autobiography Circulate among groups as they perform their close read, offering support as needed.

- Remind students that when reading an autobiography, they should look for traditional narrative elements such as characters, setting, and key events.
- Written from the first-person point of view, autobiographical writing includes the author's thoughts and feelings about events as they happen. However, autobiography also includes the author's reflections, as an older person, on the significance of the events.
- As they read, suggest that students try to distinguish between the thoughts and feelings Helen recalls having about events at the time they took place and her reflections on those events as a mature adult.

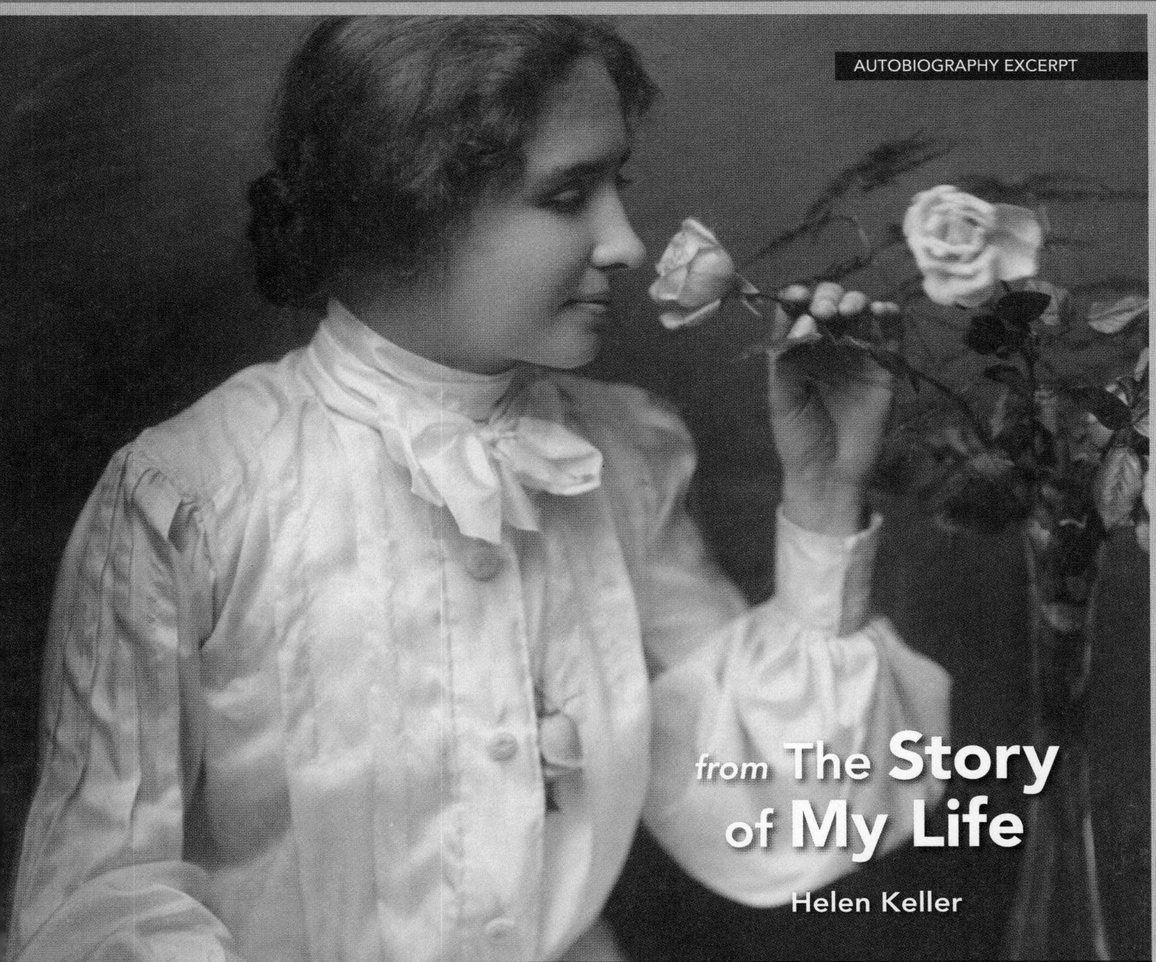

BACKGROUND

In this excerpt from her autobiography, Helen Keller describes her first experience with language at the age of six. *The Story of My Life* was published in 1903, when Keller was 23 years old.

1 The morning after my teacher came she led me into her room and gave me a doll. The little blind children at the Perkins Institution[1] had sent it and Laura Bridgman had dressed it; but I did not know this until afterward.

2 When I had played with it a little while, Miss Sullivan slowly spelled into my hand the word "d-o-l-l." I was at once interested in this finger play and tried to **imitate** it. When I finally succeeded in making the letters correctly I was flushed with childish pleasure

NOTES

Mark context clues or indicate another strategy you used that helped you determine meaning.

imitate (IHM uh tayt) *v.*

MEANING:

1. **Perkins Institution** The Perkins School for the Blind, founded in 1829 in Boston.

VOCABULARY DEVELOPMENT

Word Forms Have students find another form of the word *imitate* in paragraph 2. Then model other forms of the words *imitate* and *mystery* in sentences. Challenge students to identify the part of speech and definition of each form.

Kathryn learned the dance step by *imitating* her big sister. (Possible response: present participle meaning "following the model of or copying")

There is no comparison between *imitation* chocolate and the real thing. (Possible response: noun meaning "artificial or manufactured")

The *mysterious* valentine was signed "an admirer." (Possible response: adjective meaning "causing curiosity while difficult to identify")

Gabriel only smiled *mysteriously* when I asked where he had been. (Possible response: adverb meaning "in a way that is difficult to understand or interpret")

Concept Vocabulary

IMITATE If groups are struggling to define the word *imitate* (paragraph 2), point out that they can use context clues to infer the meaning. Draw their attention to the context clue *succeeded in making . . . correctly*. Point out that this is a context clue that restates an idea. Have students use this context clue to define the word.

Possible response: In this context, *imitate* means "to follow as a model" or "to copy."

MYSTERY If groups need help defining the word *mystery* (paragraph 4), point out that they can use context clues to infer the meaning. Draw their attention to the context clue *revealed*. Point out that this is a cause-and-effect context clue because it relates the target word (*mystery*) to its result (*revealed*). Have students use this context clue to define the word.

Possible response: In this context, *mystery* means "something hidden" or "something difficult to know."

BARRIERS To help groups struggling to define *barriers* (paragraph 4), draw their attention to the context clue *set [my soul] free. There were* barriers *still, it is true . . .* Have students restate the second part of this clue (possible response: *Although there were still* barriers) to more clearly show the contrast it draws to the first part of the clue (*set [my soul] free*). Help students see that a barrier must be something that contrasts with or prevents something from being free.

Possible response: In this context, *barriers* means "obstacles." You may want to point out that a *barrier* can also mean fence, but in this case the word is used more generally, to refer to Helen's disabilities.

Additional **English Language Support** is available in the Interactive Teacher's Edition.

NOTES

and pride. Running downstairs to my mother I held up my hand and made the letters for *doll*. I did not know that I was spelling a word or even that words existed; I was simply making my fingers go in monkey-like imitation. In the days that followed I learned to spell in this uncomprehending way a great many words, among them *pin, hat, cup,* and a few verbs like *sit, stand,* and *walk*. But my teacher had been with me several weeks before I understood that everything has a name.

3 One day, while I was playing with my new doll, Miss Sullivan put my big rag doll into my lap also, spelled "d-o-l-l" and tried to make me understand that "d-o-l-l" applied to both. Earlier in the day we had had a tussle over the words "m-u-g" and "w-a-t-e-r." Miss Sullivan had tried to impress it upon me that "m-u-g" is *mug* and that "w-a-t-e-r" is *water*, but I persisted in confounding the two. In despair she had dropped the subject for the time, only to renew it at the first opportunity. I became impatient at her repeated attempts and, seizing the new doll, I dashed it upon the floor. I was keenly delighted when I felt the fragments of the broken doll at my feet. Neither sorrow nor regret followed my passionate outburst. I had not loved the doll. In the still, dark world in which I lived there was no strong sentiment or tenderness. I felt my teacher sweep the fragments to one side of the hearth, and I had a sense of satisfaction that the cause of my discomfort was removed. She brought me my hat, and I knew I was going out into the warm sunshine. This thought, if a wordless sensation may be called a thought, made me hop and skip with pleasure.

4 We walked down the path to the well-house,[2] attracted by the fragrance of the honeysuckle with which it was covered. Someone was drawing water and my teacher placed my hand under the spout. As the cool stream gushed over one hand she spelled into the other the word *water*, first slowly, then rapidly. I stood still, my whole attention fixed upon the motions of her fingers. Suddenly I felt a misty consciousness as of something forgotten—a thrill of returning thought; and somehow the **mystery** of language was revealed to me. I knew then that "w-a-t-e-r" meant the wonderful cool something that was flowing over my hand. That living word awakened my soul, gave it light, hope, joy, set it free! There were **barriers** still, it is true, but barriers that could in time be swept away.

5 I left the well-house eager to learn. Everything had a name, and each name gave birth to a new thought. As we returned to the house every object which I touched seemed to quiver with life.

Mark context clues or indicate another strategy you used that helped you determine meaning.

mystery (MIHS tuh ree) *n.*

MEANING:

barriers (BAR ee uhrz) *n.*

MEANING:

2. **well-house** small building containing a well.

PERSONALIZE FOR LEARNING

English Language Support

Understanding Verb Tense Help students analyze the sequence of events in paragraph 1 in order to better understand the role that verb-tense shifts play in narrative writing. Have students create a timeline of the events described on this page. Help students understand that some events occurred before the incident being described. These earlier events are expressed in the past perfect tense, which is formed with *had* + past participle of the verb. The past perfect tense expresses events that occurred before a specific time in the past, which appear in the past tense.

Suggest that students begin by identifying the specific events being described.

Possible response: Perkins students sent a doll. / Laura Bridgeman dressed it. / Helen's teacher came. / Miss Sullivan led Helen to her room. / She gave Helen a doll. / Later Helen learned where it came from. **EMERGENT**

That was because I saw everything with the strange, new sight that had come to me. On entering the door I remembered the doll I had broken. I felt my way to the hearth and picked up the pieces. I tried vainly to put them together. Then my eyes filled with tears; for I realized what I had done, and for the first time I felt repentance and sorrow.

6 I learned a great many new words that day. I do not remember what they all were; but I do know that *mother, father, sister, teacher* were among them—words that were to make the world blossom for me, "like Aaron's rod, with flowers."[3] It would have been difficult to find a happier child than I was as I lay in my crib at the close of that eventful day and lived over the joys it had brought me, and for the first time longed for a new day to come. ❧

3. **"like Aaron's rod, with flowers"** in the Old Testament of the Bible, the staff of Aaron miraculously gives forth buds and flowers.

NOTES

CLOSER LOOK

Analyzing Figurative Language

Circulate among groups as students conduct their close read. Suggest that groups read paragraph 5. Encourage them to talk about the annotations they mark. If needed, provide the following support.

ANNOTATE: Have groups mark details in paragraph 5 that Keller uses to describe her reaction to what she learned in paragraph 4; then have them highlight phrases within these details where she uses words in an unusual, non-literal way. Groups may work independently, or you may work with small groups as you highlight them together.

QUESTION: Ask, "What effect does the author create with these expressions?" Accept student responses.

Possible response: "Gave birth" and "quiver with life" both suggest a new world that has opened up for Helen Keller now that she has an understanding of language.

CONCLUDE: Help students to formulate conclusions about the importance of these figures of speech in the text. Ask students why the author might have included these details.

Possible response: Keller wants the reader to understand how this new understanding is opening up a world for her of which she was previously unaware.

Remind students that writers use **figurative language** to make unusual comparisons. The figures of speech Keller uses here include the following:

- **personification**, in which inanimate objects are given human characteristics ("each name gave birth to a new thought"; "every object . . . seemed to quiver with life")
- **metaphor**, in which the author states or implies that two dissimilar things are alike. (When Keller says "I saw . . . with a strange, new sight" she compares her new understanding to seeing.)

FACILITATING

Comprehension Check

Possible responses:

1. The smell of honeysuckle
2. The sense of touch
3. She felt a desire to learn the name of everything she came into contact with.
4. Helen's teacher gives her a doll and then writes "d-o-l-l" in Helen's hand. Helen is able to copy this and other words spelled into her hand, but she does not understand how these sensations relate to the things they name. Helen and her teacher walk to the well-house, where someone is pumping water. Helen's teacher holds Helen's hand under the water, while spelling the word water in the other hand. Helen realizes that the word represents the things she feels on her hand. This helps her to understand language and brings her great joy and hope.

Research

Research to Clarify If groups struggle to narrow their research topic, suggest the following narrower research topics: early life, experience at the Perkins School for the Blind, or experience working with Helen Keller. Whichever topic students choose, encourage them to use reliable research sources and explain how what they learned sheds light on the excerpt from *The Story of My Life*.

Research to Explore Suggest that students focus on Helen's life after the moment described in the excerpt. If students have trouble narrowing their topics, suggest they explore her continued work with Annie Sullivan, her formal education, or her work on behalf of people with disabilities. Remind students to connect their research with the excerpt.

Comprehension Check

Complete the following items after you finish your first read. Review and clarify details with your group.

1. What attracts Keller and her teacher toward the well-house?

2. Through which sense does Keller experience the water?

3. Once Helen Keller learns the word for water, what is she eager to do next?

4. **Notebook** Confirm your understanding of the excerpt by writing a brief summary of it.

RESEARCH

Research to Clarify Research an unfamiliar detail in the excerpt. For example, you might want to learn more about Helen Keller's teacher, Anne Sullivan. In what way does the information you learned shed light on the excerpt? Share your findings with your group.

Research to Explore Choose something from the text that interested you. For example, you might want to learn more about how blind people learn to read. How does this information deepen your understanding of the text? Share your findings with your group.

PERSONALIZE FOR LEARNING

Challenge

Research Why did Annie Sullivan write into Helen's hand? Did she invent this method or did she learn it? Was she writing out alphabet letters as we know them? Did Sullivan and Helen Keller change the way people like Helen are educated? Have students look for the answers to one or more of these questions as they research methods for teaching people with profound vision and hearing loss. Suggest that they present their information chronologically, to show how methods have changed over time. Ask students to share their findings with the class.

MAKING MEANING

Close Read the Text

With your group, revisit sections of the text you marked during your first read. **Annotate** details that you notice. What **questions** do you have? What can you **conclude**?

from THE STORY OF MY LIFE

Analyze the Text

CITE TEXTUAL EVIDENCE to support your answers.

Notebook Complete the activities.

1. **Review and Clarify** With your group, reread the excerpt. How does the author use **imagery,** or words and phrases that appeal to the five senses? How does her use of imagery affect the reader?
2. **Present and Discuss** Now work with your group to share the passages from the text that you found especially important. Take turns presenting your passages. Discuss what you noticed in the text, the questions you asked, and the conclusions you reached.
3. **Essential Question: *How do we overcome obstacles?*** What has this excerpt taught you about how people overcome obstacles? Discuss with your group.

GROUP DISCUSSION
When you work in your group to answer the Analyze the Text questions, be sure to direct listeners to specific words, sentences, and paragraphs in the selection.

LANGUAGE DEVELOPMENT

Concept Vocabulary

imitate mystery barriers

Why These Words? The concept vocabulary words from the text are related. With your group, determine what the words have in common. Write your ideas and add another word that fits the category.

Practice

Notebook Confirm your understanding of these words from the text by using them in sentences. Be sure to use context clues that demonstrate your understand of the meaning of each word.

Word Study

Greek Root: *-myst-* The Greek root *-myst-* means "secret." In the selection, Helen Keller describes how the *mystery*, or "secret," of language was revealed to her through her experience with water at the well-house. Identify another word you know with the Greek root *-myst-*, and use it in a sentence that shows your understanding of the word's meaning.

WORD NETWORK
Add interesting words related to facing adversity from the text to your Word Network.

STANDARDS
Reading Informational Text
Determine the meaning of words and phrases as they are used in a text, including figurative, connotative, and technical meanings; analyze the impact of a specific word choice on meaning and tone.
Language
Determine or clarify the meaning of unknown and multiple-meaning words and phrases based on *grade 7 reading and content*, choosing flexibly from a range of strategies.
b. Use common, grade-appropriate Greek or Latin affixes and roots as clues to the meaning of a word.

DIGITAL PERSPECTIVES

Jump Start

CLOSE READ Ask students to consider the following prompt: *How would you teach someone who cannot see or hear to communicate?* As students discuss the prompt in their groups, have them consider what obstacles they and their student would face.

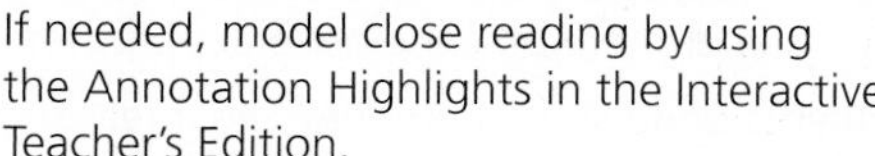

Close Read the Text

If needed, model close reading by using the Annotation Highlights in the Interactive Teacher's Edition.

Remind students to use Accountable Talk in their discussions and to support one another as they complete the close read.

Analyze the Text

1. Possible response: Keller appeals to the senses of smell ("fragrance of the honeysuckle") and touch ("cool stream"). She expresses joy and hope.
2. Passages will vary by group. Remind students to explain why they chose the passage they presented to group members.
3. Responses will vary by group.

Concept Vocabulary

Why These Words? Possible response: In this selection, all three words relate to overcoming hardship, especially the struggle to understand something.

Practice

Possible response: Helen learned to *imitate* writing by making the same symbols in her hand that Miss Sullivan had. Even though Helen could copy the letters in her hand, their meaning remained a *mystery*. When Helen finally understood that the letters were names for things, she overcame a huge *barrier* to communication.

Word Network

Possible responses: *succeeded, uncomprehending, tussle, confounding, attempts, vainly*

Word Study

For more support, see **Concept Vocabulary and Word Study.**

Possible response:

mystical: having a spiritual meaning that can't be understood by senses or thought (Visiting the shrine of my ancestors was an almost mystical experience.)

FORMATIVE ASSESSMENT

Analyze the Text

If students struggle to close read the text, **then** provide ***from* The Story of My Life: Text Questions** available online in the Interactive Teacher's Edition or Unit Resources. Answers and DOK levels are also available.

Concept Vocabulary

If students fail to see the connection among the vocabulary words, **then** create a concept map graphic organizer with each word radiating from a circle in the middle, to be filled in with the thematic connection of the words. Help students see that the common theme is overcoming adversity or struggling to learn. For Reteach and Practice, see **Word Study: Greek Root *-myst-* (RP).**

FACILITATING

Analyze Craft and Structure

Author's Purpose: Autobiographical Writing Remind students that in addition to writing to entertain or inform, there are other important purposes for writing. One is to persuade; argument, like that found in newspapers' editorial pages, is an example of this type of writing. Another purpose writers may have is to express themselves—for example, to explore their feelings or express an emotion. Journal writing, much poetry, and many forms of personal writing have an expressive purpose. Make sure students understand that much writing combines two or more of these general purposes.

Help students understand how they can infer purpose from word choice and tone. In the first sample response provided, for example, draw students' attention to the word *monkey-like*: This **word** reveals the author's **tone**, or attitude toward her younger self (frank and unsparing), and it helps her **to explain** each step in the long road to understanding. For more support, see **Analyze Craft and Structure: Autobiographical Writing.**

Practice See possible responses in the chart on the student page.

FORMATIVE ASSESSMENT

Analyze Craft and Structure

If students have difficulty determining the author's purpose through the passages they identified, **then** have them look for a striking word or phrase within those passages and then ask themselves, What is the author's tone here? Provide students with some possible tone descriptors, such as *awed, frank, frustrated, determined, sentimental, unsentimental.* For what purpose is this tone best suited? To entertain, express a feeling, explain, or persuade? For Reteach and Practice, see **Analyze Craft and Structure: Autobiographical Writing (RP).**

LANGUAGE DEVELOPMENT

from THE STORY OF MY LIFE

STANDARDS

Reading Informational Text

- Determine the meaning of words and phrases as they are used in a text, including figurative, connotative, and technical meanings; analyze the impact of a specific word choice on meaning and tone.
- Determine an author's point of view or purpose in a text and analyze how the author distinguishes his or her position from that of others.

Analyze Craft and Structure

Author's Purpose: Autobiographical Writing Autobiographical writing is a form of nonfiction narrative writing in which the author provides true accounts of events which he or she directly experienced. Autobiographical writing relates the author's thoughts, feelings, and reflections on the events he or she describes in the narrative. In autobiographical writing, the author is the narrator and uses the **first-person point of view** because he or she takes part in the events described.

In an autobiographical work, an author may have many purposes, or reasons for writing. For example, a comedian might write an autobiography to both entertain readers with humor and to inform them about the events surrounding his or her experiences. You can determine an author's purpose by analyzing the author's word choice and the author's **tone,** or his or her attitude toward the subject and audience.

Practice

CITE TEXTUAL EVIDENCE to support your answers.

Reread the excerpt from *The Story of My Life.*

Notebook Use the chart to identify specific sentences or passages from the selection that contribute to the author's purpose. Make inferences, or educated guesses, about the ways in which the author's tone and word choice in these sections suggest her purpose for writing.

SELECTION DETAIL	POSSIBLE PURPOSE
"I did not know that I was spelling a word or even that words existed; I was simply making my fingers go in a monkey-like imitation." (paragraph 2)	To explain (what Helen did and did not understand at that time)
"Neither sorrow nor regret followed my passionate outburst. I had not loved the doll. In the still, dark world in which I lived, there was no strong sentiment or tenderness."(paragraph 3)	To explain (in frank words what Helen's inner world was like), to express (the young Helen's feelings)
"I stood still, my whole attention fixed upon the motion of her fingers. Suddenly I felt a misty consciousness as of something forgotten—a thrill of returning thought, and somehow the mystery of language was revealed to me." (paragraph 4)	To explain (how Helen came to understand language); to express (how that gradual recognition felt, and the mystery of the moment her understanding "clicked")

When you have finished, share your ideas with your small group. Work together to determine Helen Keller's purpose or purposes for writing. List several details from the excerpt that support your inferences about Keller's purpose. Then, answer the following question: *How does Helen Keller use autobiographical writing to effectively express her purpose and unique point of view?*

PERSONALIZE FOR LEARNING

English Language Support

Connotations Connotations can relate to an author's purpose by suggesting emotions associated with a word. Draw students' attention to the word *tussle* (paragraph). *Tussle* means "a physical contest or intense struggle." Describe the associations the word has: here, it suggests strength and stubbornness. Connect this tone to a possible purpose: the tone suggests the writer wants to express what it felt like before she had language. **ALL LEVELS**

LANGUAGE DEVELOPMENT

Conventions

Types of Dependent Clauses Good writers use a variety of clauses to enliven their writing and to provide detail.

A **clause** is a group of words with its own subject and verb. An **independent clause,** or **main clause,** can stand alone as a complete sentence. A **dependent**, or **subordinate, clause** also has a subject and a verb, but it cannot stand alone as a complete sentence.

Dependent clauses are classified according to how they function in a sentence.

- An **adverb clause** acts as an adverb in a sentence. It begins with a subordinating conjunction, such as *although, if, when,* or *because.*
- A **relative**, or **adjective**, **clause** acts as an adjective. It usually begins with a relative pronoun, such as *who, whom, whose, which,* or *that.*
- A **noun clause** acts as a noun. It begins with a word such as *what, whatever, when, where, how,* or *why.*

In the examples in this chart, each type of dependent clause is underlined.

TYPE OF CLAUSE	EXAMPLE
Adverb Clause	Because Keller could not see or hear, she struggled to understand language. (acts as an adverb, modifying the verb *struggled*)
Relative Clause	Anne Sullivan, who was her teacher, helped Keller break through the barriers that challenged her. (acts as an adjective, modifying *Anne Sullivan*)
Noun Clause	Keller made the connection between the feel of the water and what Sullivan was writing on her hand. (acts as a noun, the object of the preposition *between*)

Read It

Work with your group to identify examples of dependent clauses in the excerpt. Write your examples in the chart, and label the type of dependent clause shown in each example.

EXAMPLE FROM THE TEXT	TYPE OF DEPENDENT CLAUSE
a. See possible responses in Teacher's Edition	b.
c.	d.
e.	f.

Write It

Notebook Write a paragraph describing a time you overcame a barrier to learning. Use specific sensory details to help readers see, hear, smell, and feel the experience. In your paragraph, correctly use at least one adverb clause, one relative clause, and one noun clause.

DIGITAL PERSPECTIVES

Conventions

Types of Dependent Clauses In order to complete the Read It and Write It activities, students may need additional explanation of dependent clauses. As necessary, provide the following instruction:

- Some adjective clauses begin with relative adverbs, such as *when* or *where* (e.g., "the village where I grew up). Any adjective clause, whether it begins with a relative pronoun or a relative adverb, answers the question what kind, which one, or how many about a noun or pronoun in another clause.
- Sometimes the word introducing a relative clause or a noun clause is not expressed but is understood.

  Examples: The pants [that] I like best have pleats. I know [that] you can hear me.

For more support, see **Conventions: Types of Dependent Clauses.**

Read It

Possible responses:

a. There were barriers still, it is true, but barriers that could in time be swept away.
b. adjective clause modifying *barriers*
c. When I had played with it a little while, Miss Sullivan slowly spelled into my hand the word "d-o-l-l."
d. adverb clause modifying *spelled*
e. I did not know that I was spelling a word or even that words existed; I was simply making my fingers go in a monkey-like imitation.
f. noun clauses acting as the compound object of the verb *know*

PERSONALIZE FOR LEARNING

English Language Support

Using Adverb and Adjective Clauses Have students research additional information about a part of Helen Keller's life and then ask them to write about what they learned using adverb and adjective clauses.

Ask students to write three sentences about what they learned from their research. **EMERGING**

Ask students to write a paragraph about what they learned. **EXPANDING**

Ask students to write a few paragraphs about what they learned from their research and if they were surprised by what they learned. **BRIDGING**

An expanded **English Language Support Lesson** on Adverb and Adjective Clauses is available in the Interactive Teacher's Edition. 

FORMATIVE ASSESSMENT

Conventions

If students have difficulty distinguishing between dependent clauses and phrases in a sentence, **then** make sure they understand that any clause must contain both a subject and its predicate, or verb. Make sure students understand that *-ing* forms of verbs are verbals, and not verbs themselves. For Reteach and Practice, see **Conventions: Types of Dependent Clauses (RP).**

How Helen Keller Learned to Talk

AUDIO SUMMARIES
Audio summaries of "How Helen Keller Learned to Talk" are available online in both English and Spanish in the Interactive Teacher's Edition or Unit Resources. Assigning these summaries prior to reviewing the video may help students build additional background knowledge and set a context for their first review.

Summary

In the video "How Helen Keller Learned to Talk," Anne Sullivan describes the process she used to teach Helen Keller how to speak. While Sullivan talks, Keller demonstrates the same actions Sullivan is describing. First, Sullivan describes that when they first met, Keller had almost no means of communicating. The two women then demonstrate that when Keller placed her hand on Sullivan's face in a particular position, she could feel the different types of vibrations of human speech. After much teaching and practice, Helen learned to say her first word, "it," and later her first sentence.

Insight

This selection helps students understand that challenges that may seem hopeless can be met with intelligence, courage, and perseverance.

ESSENTIAL QUESTION:
How do we overcome obstacles?

Connection to Essential Question

Helen Keller faced great obstacles in her life. Students may see that until she can grasp the concept of language, the rest of the world remains out of her reach. Anne Sullivan's actions and dedication model one response to the Essential Question.

SMALL-GROUP LEARNING PERFORMANCE TASK
How do people face challenges in order to overcome adversity?

UNIT PERFORMANCE-BASED ASSESSMENT
How can people overcome adversity in the face of overwhelming obstacles?

Connection to Performance Tasks

Small-Group Learning Performance Task In this Performance Task, students will present an informative essay to show the steps and actions people take to overcome adversity. This video provides students with a vivid demonstration of the steps Helen Keller and Anne Sullivan took together to overcome adversity.

Unit Performance-Based Assessment As students work on the assessment, they will need to support their response to the prompt with support about facing challenges. From this video, students can easily infer the countless hours of work Helen Keller endured to overcome the obstacles she faced.

DIGITAL PERSPECTIVES

 Audio  Video 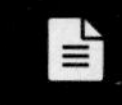 Document  Annotation Highlights 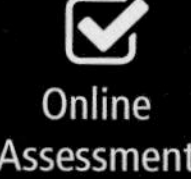 Online Assessment

LESSON RESOURCES

	Making Meaning	Language Development	Effective Expression
Lesson	**First Review** **Close Review** **Analyze the Media**	**Media Vocabulary**	**Writing to Compare**
Instructional Standards	**RI.7.10** By the end of the year, read and comprehend literary nonfiction . . . **L.7.6** Acquire and use accurately grade-appropriate general academic and domain-specific words and phrases . . .	**L.7.6** Acquire and use accurately grade-appropriate general academic and domain-specific words and phrases . . .	**RI.7.7** Compare and contrast a text . . . **W.7.2** Write informative/explanatory texts . . . **W.7.2.a** Introduce a topic clearly . . . **W.7.2.b** Develop the topic . . . **W.7.9.b** Apply *grade 7 Reading standards* to literary nonfiction . . . **SL.7.1.b** Follow rules for collegial discussions . . . **SL.7.2** Analyze the main ideas . . . **SL.7.5** Include multimedia components . . .
STUDENT RESOURCES			
Available online in the Interactive Student Edition or Unit Resources	Selection Audio First-Review Guide: Media: Video Close-Review Guide: Media: Video		Evidence Log
TEACHER RESOURCES			
Selection Resources Available online in the Interactive Teacher's Edition or Unit Resources	Audio Summaries: English and Spanish Spanish Translation Media Questions First Review Extension Questions	Media Vocabulary	Writing to Compare: Multimedia Presentation
My Resources	A Unit 5 Answer Key is available online and in the Interactive Teacher's Edition.		

Media Complexity Rubric: How Helen Keller Learned to Talk

Quantitative Measures	
Format and Length: video of 3 minutes, 4 seconds	
Qualitative Measures	
Knowledge Demands ① ② **❸** ④ ⑤	Prior knowledge of Helen Keller and Anne Sullivan will be required to understand the clip.
Structure ① ② **❸** ④ ⑤	The clip's structure is simple, as Anne narrates and Helen demonstrates their process.
Language Conventionality and Clarity ① **❷** ③ ④ ⑤	Anne Sullivan's language is clear and easily accessible.
Levels of Meaning/Purpose ① ② **❸** ④ ⑤	The concepts of education and disability and are not hard to grasp.

FACILITATING

Jump Start

FIRST REVIEW Use the following prompt to start a discussion in groups: *How might a dramatic story like Helen Keller's lend itself to both text and film?* As students discuss, urge them to also share moments in books and movies that have moved them deeply—and why.

How Helen Keller Learned to Talk

What would it be like to touch a person's face and feel vocal vibrations for the first time? Modeling a question like this will help students connect to "How Helen Keller Learned to Talk" and to the Small-Group Performance Task.

Project the video in class or ask students to open the video in their interactive textbooks.

Media Vocabulary

Encourage groups to discuss the media vocabulary. Have they seen the terms in texts before? Do they use any of them in their speech and writing?

Ask groups to look closely at the three terms and ask how they might relate to scenes they have scene in movies and on television. For more support, see **Media Vocabulary.**

FIRST REVIEW

Have students perform the steps of the first review independently:

WATCH: Remind students to pay close attention to how the two women interact with each other.

NOTE: Encourage students to note any parts they may want to revisit during their close review.

CONNECT: Encourage students to make connections beyond the video. If they cannot make connections to their own lives, have them consider people they know or have read about who faced extraordinary challenges.

RESPOND: Students will answer questions and write a summary to demonstrate understanding.

Point out to students that while they will always complete the Respond step at the end of the first review, the other steps will probably happen somewhat concurrently. You may wish to print copies of the **First-Review Guide: Media: Video** for students to use.

MAKING MEANING

from THE STORY OF MY LIFE

Comparing Text to Media

You will now watch "How Helen Keller Learned to Talk," an interview that shows Keller with her teacher, Anne Sullivan. As you watch the video, consider the differences in how Helen Keller's experience is portrayed in her autobiography and in the interview.

HOW HELEN KELLER LEARNED TO TALK

About Anne Sullivan

This video shows Helen Keller with her teacher, **Anne Sullivan** (1866–1936). Sullivan herself was visually impaired, and in her early years she lived in a home for the poor following the death of her mother. She rose from these conditions to become a legendary teacher. Her first step was finding an opening as a student at the Perkins School for the Blind when she was 14. At age 21, she became Helen Keller's teacher.

How Helen Keller Learned to Talk

Media Vocabulary

These words will be useful to you as you analyze, discuss, and write about the video.

long shot: camera shot in which the entire subject is visible as well as some of the background around the subject	• Long shots are often used to show something happening in the background behind the subject. • Filmmakers will sometimes use a long shot to establish the setting of a scene.
medium shot: camera shot in which the subject is seen from a medium distance, usually from the waist up	• A medium shot is useful for showing two characters engaging in dialogue. • Medium shots are often used in the transition between a long shot and close-up shot.
close-up shot: camera shot in which the subject is shown at close range; typically the subject's head and shoulders are shown, with no background visible	• A close-up shot is often used to show the facial expression of a character. • Close-up shots can also be used to show a detail on a prop or what characters are doing with their hands.

First Review MEDIA: VIDEO

Study the video and take notes as you watch.

WATCH *who* speaks, *what* they say, and *how* they say it.

NOTE elements that you find interesting and want to revisit.

First Review

CONNECT ideas in the video to other media you've experienced, texts you've read, or images you've seen.

RESPOND by completing the Comprehension Check at the end.

STANDARDS

Reading Informational Texts
By the end of the year, read and comprehend literary nonfiction in the grades 6–8 text complexity band proficiently, with scaffolding as needed at the high end of the range.

Language
Acquire and use accurately grade-appropriate general academic and domain-specific words and phrases; gather vocabulary knowledge when considering a word or phrase important to comprehension or expression.

DIGITAL 
PERSPECTIVES

MEDIA | INTERVIEW

How Helen Keller Learned to Talk

Helen Keller, with Anne Sullivan

BACKGROUND

This video interview with Helen Keller and Anne Sullivan was made in 1928. In the interview, Sullivan demonstrates and explains how Keller learned to talk by feeling the vibrations that are made in a person's mouth and throat when he or she is speaking.

NOTES

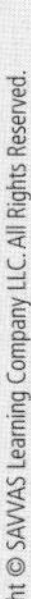

CLOSER REVIEW

Analyze Close-Up Shots

Circulate among groups as students conduct their close review. Suggest that groups close review 1:19–1:37 and 2:47–3:04 in the film. Encourage them to talk about what they note. If needed, provide the following support.

NOTE: Have students note details in the film that show the effect of the close-up shots, or work with small groups to have students participate while you note them together.

QUESTION: Guide students to consider what these details might tell them. Ask what a viewer can better understand and infer from these close-up shots, and accept student responses.

Possible response: The close-up shots show the people's faces in greater detail. The viewer can see the exact position of Helen's fingers on Anne's face. The viewer can infer that it took a great deal of work for them to succeed. In the close-up of Helen, the viewer sees a big change as she speaks—an expression of joy comes across her face.

CONCLUDE: Help students to formulate conclusions about the importance of these details in the video. Ask students why the director might have included these details.

Possible response: Because Helen learned to speak by close physical contact with Anne's face, the director wanted viewers to see the faces clearly. Using close-up shots allows viewers to gain a vivid understanding of her achievement.

Remind students that **close-up shots** are just one of many techniques film directors use in both documentary (nonfiction) and fictional films to help viewers better understand the story.

FACILITATING SMALL-GROUP LEARNING

CLOSE REVIEW: Film As groups perform the close review of this video, circulate and offer support as needed.

- Remind groups that this is a documentary, or nonfiction, film and that the people in the scene are the actual Helen Keller and Anne Sullivan, not actors portraying them.
- If the group is confused by the process described by Anne Sullivan, suggest that they feel the vibrations on themselves as they speak by holding a finger to their throat, lips, and nose.
- Challenge groups to come up with their own paraphrase of what happened in the scene.

FACILITATING

Comprehension Check

Possible responses:

1. Helen was six years and eight months old.
2. Helen placed her thumb on her larnyx (throat), one finger on her lips, and one finger on the side of her nose.
3. "I am not dumb now."

MAKING MEANING

Comprehension Check

Complete the following items after you finish your first review.

1. How old was Helen Keller when Anne Sullivan first met her?

2. In what position on her teacher's face did Keller have to place her hand in order to feel the vibrations of the spoken word?

3. What does Keller say at the end of the interview?

MAKING MEANING

Close Review

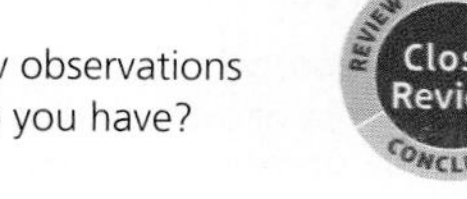

Watch the film clip again. Record any new observations that seem important. What **questions** do you have? What can you **conclude**?

HOW HELEN KELLER LEARNED TO TALK

Analyze the Media

Notebook Complete the activities.

1. **Present and Discuss** Choose the section of the video you find most interesting or powerful. Share your choice with the group, and discuss why you chose it. Explain what you noticed in the section, the questions it raised for you, and the conclusions you reached about it.
2. **Review and Synthesize** With your group, review the video interview. How does the video deepen your understanding of the challenges Helen Keller faced? How does it highlight her triumphs? Explain.
3. Notebook **Essential Question: *How do we overcome obstacles?*** What have you learned about overcoming obstacles and facing adversity from the interview?

LANGUAGE DEVELOPMENT

Media Vocabulary

Use the vocabulary words in your responses to the items.

long shot | medium shot | close-up shot

1. What type of shot is used at the very beginning of the video? Why do you think the director used that shot?
2. What type of shot is used as Anne Sullivan is introducing Helen Keller at the beginning of the video?
3. What type of shot is used when Sullivan is demonstrating how Keller placed her hand on Sullivan's face? What does the shot enable the director of the video to show?

STANDARDS

Language

Acquire and use accurately grade-appropriate general academic and domain-specific words and phrases; gather vocabulary knowledge when considering a word or phrase important to comprehension or expression.

DIGITAL PERSPECTIVES

Jump Start

CLOSE REVIEW Ask students to consider the following prompt: *If you were a filmmaker trying to show this interview from Helen's point of view, how would you go about it?* As students discuss the prompt in their groups, have them consider possible approaches—such as using some combination of camera angles and sound to convey Helen's perspective.

Close Review

If needed, model close reviewing by using the Closer Review note in the Interactive Teacher's Edition.

Remind students to use Accountable Talk in their discussions and to support one another as they complete the close review.

Analyze the Media

Encourage groups to discuss their decisions about the scene using specific reasons for their choices.

1. Responses will vary by group. Remind students to review their notes from the first review to get details that support their assertions before discussing with the group.
2. Responses will vary by group. Groups should provide details and evidence to enhance their descriptions.
3. Responses will vary. Students should cite how Helen Keller's traumatic struggle and eventual success suggests both the difficulty and the possibility of overcoming obstacles.

Media Vocabulary

For more support, see **Media Vocabulary.** 

Possible responses:

1. medium shot
2. a long shot
3. a close-up

FORMATIVE ASSESSMENT

Analyze the Media

If students struggle to close review the film clip, **then** provide the **How Helen Keller Learned to Talk: Media Questions** available online in the Interactive Teacher's Edition or Unit Resources. Answers and DOK levels are also available.

Media Vocabulary

If students struggle to identify the kind of shot at the beginning of the film clip, **then** have them review the definitions of the three shots.

FACILITATING

Writing to Compare

Planning and Prewriting

Compare the Text and Video If groups have trouble making these comparisons, urge them to define and clarify what is relevant in the two selections—the filmed interview and the autobiography. For example, have them compare who tells the story in each selection and how the medium helps determine that aspect. Also urge them to consider what elements must be included for the basic message of the selections to be expressed, whether in print or on film.

Possible responses:

1. The description of coming to understand language by feeling water flowing shows that Keller was curious and eager to learn. The video shows one ingenious way that Keller was able to learn something with Sullivan's help.
2. The text explains how Keller came to understand the concept of language; the video explains one way she learned to use it.
3. The text depicts Keller in her own words but is limited to written expression. The video shows how Keller could learn things despite her disabilities, but it is limited to the perspective of Sullivan.

See possible responses in chart on student page.

FORMATIVE ASSESSMENT

Prepare to Compare

If students are unable to compare the film scene with the text, **then** have them write a brief summary of what happens in each.

EFFECTIVE EXPRESSION

from THE STORY OF MY LIFE

HOW HELEN KELLER LEARNED TO TALK

Writing to Compare

Both the *The Story of My Life* and "How Helen Keller Learned to Talk" show the sense of triumph that Keller experiences from overcoming challenges with language through the help of her teacher, Anne Sullivan.

Assignment

Create a **multimedia presentation** about Keller's life and education in which you compare and contrast the text and the video. In your presentation, explain how the written account and the video portray the subject, Helen Keller, in different ways. Choose from these options:

- ☐ an **instructional booklet** illustrating Sullivan's lessons to Keller
- ☐ an **informational Web site** about Keller and her education
- ☐ a **museum guide** for an exhibit about Keller and her education

Planning and Prewriting

Compare the Text and Video Using a chart, such as the one shown, work with your group to analyze the ways in which the text and video portray the subjects of Keller and Sullivan as well as Keller's educational process.

PORTRAYAL	AUTOBIOGRAPHY EXCERPT	VIDEO INTERVIEW	SIMILARITIES AND DIFFERENCES
Keller	Keller is an articulate writer who describes scenese and show the reader her inner struggles and accomplishments.	Keller is silent but then speaks, first only sounds and words. Finally, she triumphantly speaks an entire sentence.	In the text, Keller's thoughts are evident. The film can't show thought. Her personality comes through in both.
Sullivan	Sullivan's thoughts are less prominent. The reader gets a sense of her perseverance.	Sullivan describes the work of breaking through. Her facial expressions convey her feelings.	The text is told from Keller's perspective. The video gives more information about Sullivan.
Educational Process	The reader gains an understanding of Keller's first, emerging sensations of sound, words, and meanings.	The viewer witnesses how Keller learned an amazing technique that allowed her to use language.	The video shows Keller's learning achievements far after the event in the text.

Notebook Respond to the following items.

1. What details in the text help readers to understand Keller's thoughts and experiences? Does the video enable viewers to gain the same understanding of Keller's personality?
2. How does the portrayal of Sullivan and Keller in the video expand your understanding of them from the text?
3. Briefly summarize the strengths and weaknesses of each medium's portrayal of Keller.

STANDARDS

Reading Informational Text
Compare and contrast a text to an audio, video, or multimedia version of the text, analyzing each medium's portrayal of the subject.

PERSONALIZE FOR LEARNING

Strategic Support

Support for Making Comparisons Students may require support in locating relevant information for making comparisons between the text and the video. Suggest to students that they compare and contrast the content of each selection—what Helen is shown learning in the book excerpt and in the video. Explain that because film is a visual medium, students should look at the key visual elements in the clip, particularly how the body is used, and compare them to descriptions of the body and physical sensations in the book excerpts. Students can also compare the voice of the selections' subject, Helen Keller—her narrator's voice in the text and her speaking voice in the video.

Assign Tasks Make a list of tasks you will have to accomplish in order to finish your presentation. Assign the tasks to individual group members. Adapt this list to suit the needs of your group.

TASK LIST

Research the Topic: Decide whether you need more background information on Keller and Sullivan. If you do, research and gather the information.

Assigned To: ______________________

Locate Media: Find multimedia elements—audio, video, and images—that will highlight the information in your presentation and engage your audience.

Assigned To: ______________________

Gather Quotes and Details: Identify details from both selections that support and clarify your central ideas. Note direct quotations that will strengthen the support for your main points.

Assigned To: ______________________

Make a Rough Outline: Organize a sequence for your content so that the text and multimedia elements complement each other. You can change the sequence as you develop your presentation.

Assigned To: ______________________

Drafting

Determine Your Central Idea Write a one-sentence thesis in which you state your central idea.

Thesis: ______________________

Work with your group to incorporate the media so that it supports your central idea.

Include Comparisons of Text to Video Use your notes from the analysis you did earlier to create a script that explains how the text and the video contribute in different ways to your understanding of Helen Keller and her education.

Reviewing, Revising, and Editing

Before presenting your finished work to the class, check to be sure that all the media and text you have chosen to include add value to the presentation. If necessary, revise the arrangement of content so that the text and multimedia elements transition more smoothly.

EVIDENCE LOG

Before moving on to a new selection, go to your Evidence Log and record what you've learned from the text excerpt from *The Story of My Life* and the video "How Helen Keller Learned to Talk."

STANDARDS

Writing

- Write informative/explanatory texts to examine a topic and convey ideas, concepts, and information through the selection, organization, and analysis of relevant content.
  - a. Introduce a topic clearly, previewing what is to follow; organize ideas, concepts, and information, using strategies such as definition, classification, comparison/ contrast, and cause/ effect; include formatting, graphics, and multimedia when useful to aiding comprehension.
  - b. Develop the topic with relevant facts, definitions, concrete details, quotations, or other information and examples.
- Draw evidence from literary or informational texts to support analysis, reflection, and research.
  - b. Apply *grade 7 Reading standards* to literary nonfiction.

Speaking and Listening

- Engage effectively in a range of collaborative discussions with diverse partners on *grade 7 topics, texts, and issues,* building on others' ideas and expressing their own clearly.
  - b. Follow rules for collegial discussions, track progress toward specific goals and deadlines, and define individual roles as needed.
- Analyze the main ideas and supporting details presented in diverse media and formats and explain how the ideas clarify a topic, text, or issue under study.
- Include multimedia components and visual displays in presentations to clarify claims and findings and emphasize salient points.

DIGITAL PERSPECTIVES

Assign Tasks

Guide groups to work cooperatively in assigning tasks to individual group members. Make sure all group members are active and engaged.

Drafting

Determine Your Central Idea Remind students that their thesis statement should clearly state their point of comparison between the treatment of the content in the two media, text and video. In the drafting phase, students should be flexible to possible changes in the central idea they decide at the outset of the project.

Include Comparisons of Text to Video Remind students to provide examples and evidence from both text and the video sources when describing their comparisons. Examples should be concise; text and dialogue should be quoted directly or be accurately paraphrased.

Reviewing, Revising, and Editing

Guide students to include attributions to title and author for all sources of content in their presentations. As a new source is introduced it can be easily attributed in transitional language. Subsequent references to sources do not need to be fully attributed but do need to be clearly identified to avoid audience confusion. For more support see: **Writing to Compare: Multimedia Presentation**

Evidence Log Support students in completing their Evidence Log. This paced activity will help prepare them for the Performance-Based Assessment at the end of the unit.

FORMATIVE ASSESSMENT

Writing to Compare

If students are unable to find an observation for each medium in each category in the chart, **then** have them fill in only the sections they feel confident about.

DIGITAL PERSPECTIVES

Enriching the Text To give students a different perspective on the same content, locate online clips from the 1962 film version and the 1979 and 2000 TV movie versions of *The Miracle Worker,* and show the water pump scene that corresponds to the autobiography excerpt. Because filmed versions are based on Helen Keller's autobiography but are adapted for a dramatic retelling, students can compare and contrast Keller's own account of the scene in her autobiography to filmmakers' dramatized adaptations of the same events. To extend this activity, students can also locate the script to the stage play *The Miracle Worker* for an additional point of comparison.

A Young Tinkerer Builds a Windmill, Electrifying a Nation

AUDIO SUMMARIES
Audio summaries of "A Young Tinkerer Builds a Windmill, Electrifying a Nation" are available online in both English and Spanish in the Interactive Teacher's Edition or Unit Resources. Assigning these summaries prior to reading the selection may help students build additional background knowledge and set a context for their first read.

Summary

Sarah Childress's news article "A Young Tinkerer Builds a Windmill, Electrifying a Nation," tells the story of an African teenager who had a big impact on his family and his country. William Kamkwamba was just a teenager whose family couldn't afford the $80 a year it cost in Malawi to keep him in school. So he helped out on the family farm and read the books donated to the local library. In one of them he saw a windmill, and that was the beginning of a remarkable story. William began to build his own windmill and, even though it looked silly and was noisy, it gave his family electricity for the first time. Soon, the outside world learned about the windmill in the small village of Masitala, and William's life started to change.

Insight

The inspiring story of William Kamkwamba shows how determination and ingenuity can not only build a windmill but change a life.

ESSENTIAL QUESTION:
How do we overcome obstacles?

Connection to Essential Question

The challenge in William Kamkwamba's life is how to get an education and help his family. He begins the process of educating himself by reading, and that leads him to an endeavor that improves his family's life. His innovation and persistence were noticed by people who paid for him to continue his education, and his TED talks brought his story to a wider audience.

SMALL-GROUP LEARNING PERFORMANCE TASK
How do people face challenges in order to overcome adversity?

UNIT PERFORMANCE-BASED ASSESSMENT
How can people overcome adversity in the face of overwhelming obstacles?

Connection to Performance Tasks

Small-Group Learning Performance Task In this Performance Task, students will present an informative essay about how people face challenges to overcome adversity. This selection provides students with examples of ingenuity and determination.

Unit Performance-Based Assessment William Kamkwamba is a young man with a desire for education, but his family cannot afford to pay for it. Students should consider that, while Kamkwamba had some remarkable luck later in his story, he begins with actively pursuing knowledge by reading books from the local library. One of those books presented him with the idea that changed the course of his life and the knowledge to pursue it.

DIGITAL PERSPECTIVES

Audio

Video

Document

Annotation Highlights

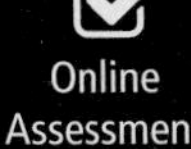
Online Assessment

LESSON RESOURCES

	Making Meaning	Language Development	Effective Expression
Lesson	**First Read** **Close Read** **Analyze the Text** **Analyze Craft and Structure**	**Concept Vocabulary** **Word Study** **Conventions**	**Writing to Sources**
Instructional Standards	**RI.7.10** By the end of the year, read and comprehend literary nonfiction . . . **L.7.4** Determine or clarify the meaning of unknown and multiple-meaning words . . . **L.7.4.a** Use context as a clue . . . **RI.7.1** Cite several pieces of textual evidence . . . **RI.7.3** Analyze the interactions between . . . **RI.7.5** Analyze the structure an author uses . . .	**L.7.4** Determine or clarify the meaning of unknown and multiple-meaning words and phrases . . . **L.7.4.b** Use common, grade-appropriate Greek or Latin affixes and roots . . . **L.7.2** Demonstrate command of the conventions of standard English . . .	**W.7.2.a** Introduce a topic clearly . . . **W.7.2.b** Develop the topic . . . **W.7.7** Conduct short research projects . . . **W.7.8** Gather relevant information from multiple print and digital sources . . .
STUDENT RESOURCES			
Available online in the Interactive Student Edition or Unit Resources	Selection Audio First-Read Guide: Nonfiction Close-Read Guide: Nonfiction	Word Network	Evidence Log
TEACHER RESOURCES			
Selection Resources Available online in the Interactive Teacher's Edition or Unit Resources	Audio Summaries: English and Spanish Annotation Highlights Accessible Leveled Text Spanish Translation Text Questions First Read Extension Questions Analyze Craft and Structure: Biographical Writing	Concept Vocabulary and Word Study Conventions: Capitalization	Writing to Sources: How-to-Essay
Reteach/Practice (RP) Available online in the Interactive Teacher's Edition or Unit Resources	Analyze Craft and Structure: Biographical Writing (RP)	Word Study: Etymology (RP) Conventions: Capitalization (RP)	Writing to Sources: How-to-Essay (RP)
Assessment Available online in Assessments	Selection Test: English Selection Test: Spanish Extension Selection Test		
My Resources	A Unit 5 Answer Key is available online and in the Interactive Teacher's Edition.		

Reading Support

Text Complexity Rubric: A Young Tinkerer Builds a Windmill, Electrifying a Nation	
Quantitative Measures	
Lexile: 1020 **Text Length:** 1,077 words	
Qualitative Measures	
Knowledge Demands (1) **2** (3) (4) (5)	Students may need an introduction to African issues, culture, and economic struggles, but otherwise the story is straightforward.
Structure **1** (2) (3) (4) (5)	The story is a short journalistic piece with a conventional structure.
Language Conventionality and Clarity (1) **2** (3) (4) (5)	The language is simple and conventional, very clear, and easy to read.
Levels of Meaning/Purpose (1) **2** (3) (4) (5)	The true story works as an inspirational piece and as a kind of short primer on Africa, development, and entrepreneurialism.

DECIDE AND PLAN

English Language Support

Provide English Learners with support for knowledge and meaning as they read the selection.

Knowledge Ask students to think about what they learned from the short article by Sarah Childress. Ask language learners to consider the facts and interesting ideas they took from the piece, and then have them discuss with each other how the article challenged them to think differently about Africa and its people.

Meaning Discuss with students the different lessons they can take from the article. Talk about what might happen in their own communities if they built an electricity-producing windmill today. Would the community use or appreciate it? The topic of jealousy in the article is very interesting. Encourage students to think about why it came up as an issue for William Kamkwamba.

Strategic Support

Provide students with strategic support to ensure that they can successfully read the text.

Knowledge Ask students to reread the text and make a list of interesting topics, ideas, and words in Sarah Childress's article. Then have them point out Malawi on a world map and discuss the climate and the countries surrounding it. In doing this, they can understand that learning comes not just from reading an article, but also from reading *around* a topic, in other books and resources.

Meaning Encourage students to consider how this article perhaps challenges certain stereotypes that Americans may have about African cultures. Ask them how the article made them think differently about life in a country like Malawi.

Challenge

Provide students who need to be challenged with ideas for how they can go beyond a simple interpretation of the text.

Text Analysis Ask students to take this information and write their own one-page article with it. Challenge them to use William Kamkwamba's story and frame it, like a journalist would, in their own way. Then, discuss the differences in perspective between their work and the work of other classmates.

Written Response Ask students to consider what their own community, school, or family needs and to write a proposal for making it happen. If it requires research, encourage them to visit a library or to go online to study what they would have to do in their own communities to achieve the kind of thing William Kamkwamba has.

TEACH

Read and Respond

Have the class do their first read of the selection. Then, have them complete their close read. Finally, work with them on the Making Meaning, Language Development, and Effective Expression activities.

Standards Support Through Teaching and Learning Cycle

IDENTIFY NEEDS

Analyze results of the Beginning-of-Year Assessment, focusing on the items relating to Unit 5. Also take into consideration student performance to this point and your observations of where particular students struggle.

DECIDE AND PLAN

- If students have performed poorly on items matching these standards, then provide selection scaffolds before assigning them the on-level lesson provided in the Student Edition.
- If students have done well on the Beginning-of-Year Assessment, then challenge them to keep progressing and learning by giving them opportunities to practice the skills in depth.
- Use the Selection Resources listed on the Planning pages for "A Young Tinkerer Builds a Windmill, Electrifying a Nation" to help students continually improve their ability to master the standards.

Instructional Standards: A Young Tinkerer Builds a Windmill, Electrifying a Nation

	Catching Up	This Year	Looking Forward
Reading	You may wish to administer the **Analyze Craft and Structure: Biographical Writing (RP)** worksheet to help students understand the elements of biographical writing.	**RI.5** Analyze the structure an author uses to organize a text, including how the major sections contribute to the whole and to the development of the ideas.	Challenge students to consider other ways an author might structure a biography.
Writing	You may wish to administer the **Writing to Sources: How-to Essay (RP)** worksheet to help students understand the tenets of autobiography.	**W.2.b** Develop the topic with relevant facts, definitions, concrete details, quotations, or other information and examples.	Take the assignment to the next level by challenging students to make their own "How-To" videos.
Language	You may wish to administer the **Conventions: Capitalization (RP)** worksheet to help students understand that capital letters signal the beginning of a sentence or quotation and identify proper nouns and proper adjectives. You may wish to administer the **Word Study: Transitions (RP)** worksheet to help students understand that both single words (such as "because" and "since") and phrases (such as "for that reason") can be transitions.	**L.2** Demonstrate command of the conventions of standard English capitalization, punctuation, and spelling when writing. **L.4** Determine or clarify the meaning of unknown and multiple-meaning words and phrases based on *grade 7 reading and content,* choosing flexibly from a range of strategies.	Have students locate capital letters in the selection. Have students find other suffixes they recognize in the text.

ANALYZE AND REVISE

- Analyze student work for evidence of student learning.
- Identify whether students have met the expectations in the standards.
- Identify implications for future instruction.

TEACH

Implement the planned lesson, and gather evidence of student learning.

FACILITATING

Jump Start

FIRST READ Use the following prompt to start a group discussion: *Have you ever taught yourself a difficult skill?* Engage students in a discussion about the potential and limitations of self-teaching that sets the context for reading "A Young Tinkerer Builds a Windmill, Electrifying a Nation." As students share their thoughts, guide them to identify specific factors that affected their responses.

A Young Tinkerer Builds a Windmill, Electrifying a Nation

Can a self-taught child help a nation develop? Modeling questions that readers might ask as they read "A Young Tinkerer Builds a Windmill, Electrifying a Nation" brings the text alive for students and connects to the Small Group Performance Task question. Selection audio and print capability are available in the Interactive Teacher's Edition.

Concept Vocabulary

Ask groups to look closely at the three types of context clues—synonym, restatement of an idea, and contrast of ideas and topics—and have group members take turns explaining how the example illustrates the context clue in each case.

FIRST READ

Have students perform the steps of the first read independently:

NOTICE: Encourage students to notice details about William Kamkwamba and the people in his life—family members, villagers, teacher.

ANNOTATE: Remind students to mark passages showing William's thoughts and actions and the reactions of the people around him.

CONNECT: Compare William's activities to those of other inventors or innovators you know, have read about, or have seen in the media.

RESPOND: Students will answer questions and write a summary to demonstrate understanding.

Point out to students that while they will always complete the Respond step at the end of the first read, the other steps will probably happen somewhat concurrently. You may wish to print copies of the **First-Read Guide: Nonfiction** for students to use.

MAKING MEANING

About the Author

Sarah Childress (b. 1980) is a Senior Reporter at *Frontline,* PBS's investigative journalism series. Childress has also written articles for *Newsweek* and *The Wall Street Journal.*

A Young Tinkerer Builds a Windmill, Electrifying a Nation

Concept Vocabulary

As you perform your first read of "A Young Tinkerer Builds a Windmill, Electrifying a Nation," you will encounter these words.

scarcity   desire   attempts

Context Clues If these words are unfamiliar to you, try using **context clues** to help you determine their meanings. There are various types of context clues that you may encounter as you read.

Synonyms: Due to the **insufficiency**, or lack, of electricity, he was inspired to come up with a solution to power his home.

Restatement of an Idea: More power supplies are needed for the expansion of the electrical grid, which will lead to the **proliferation** of the home use of electric appliances.

Contrast of Ideas and Topics: He **strived** to make his invention work, but he eventually had to quit.

Apply your knowledge of context clues and other vocabulary strategies to determine the meaning of other unfamiliar words you encounter during your first read.

First Read NONFICTION

Apply these strategies as you conduct your first read. You will have an opportunity to complete a close read after your first read.

NOTICE the general ideas of the text. *What* is it about? *Who* is involved?

ANNOTATE by marking vocabulary and key passages you want to revisit.

CONNECT ideas within the selection to what you already know and what you have already read.

RESPOND by completing the Comprehension Check and by writing a brief summary of the selection.

STANDARDS

Reading Informational Text
By the end of the year, read and comprehend literary nonfiction in the grades 6–8 text complexity band proficiently, with scaffolding as needed at the high end of the range.

Language
Determine or clarify the meaning of unknown and multiple-meaning words and phrases based on *grade 7 reading and content,* choosing flexibly from a range of strategies.
a. Use context as a clue to the meaning of a word or phrase.

FACILITATING SMALL-GROUP CLOSE LEARNING

CLOSE READ: News Article Circulate among groups as they perform their close read, offering support as needed.

- Remind students that when reading a newspaper article, they should expect to find answers to the 5*W-how?* questions in the early paragraphs.
- Point out that since this story focuses on a particular person, it has features of a biography, a narrative form. Remind students to look for narrative techniques, like characterization.
- Remind students to look for hallmarks of informative texts as well, such as main ideas and supporting evidence—facts, examples, and anecdotes.

A Young Tinkerer Builds a Windmill, Electrifying a Nation

Sarah Childress

BACKGROUND
Malawi is a landlocked country in southeastern Africa, one-fifth of which is taken up by the enormous Lake Malawi. Malawi's economy is mostly farming-based, and most of its citizens live in rural areas. Only a small number of the almost seventeen million Malawians have access to electricity, which is typically limited to large cities.

1 Masitala, Malawi—On a continent woefully short of electricity, 20-year-old William Kamkwamba has a dream: to power up his country one windmill at a time.

2 So far, he has built three windmills in his yard here, using blue-gum trees and bicycle parts. His tallest, at 39 feet, towers over this windswept village, clattering away as it powers his family's few electrical appliances: 10 six-watt light bulbs, a TV set, and a radio. The machine draws in visitors from miles around.

3 Self-taught, Mr. Kamkwamba took up windmill building after seeing a picture of one in an old textbook. He's currently working on a design for a windmill powerful enough to pump water from wells and provide lighting for Masitala, a cluster of buildings where about 60 families live.

4 Then, he wants to build more windmills for other villages across the country. Betting he can do it, a group of investors are putting him through school.

NOTES

DIGITAL PERSPECTIVES   

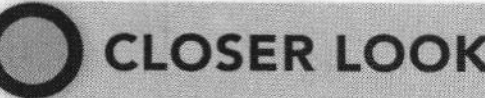

CLOSER LOOK

Analyzing Description

Circulate among groups as students conduct their close read. Suggest that groups close read paragraph 2. Encourage them to talk about the annotations they mark. If needed, provide the following support.

ANNOTATE: Have groups mark descriptions of the tallest windmill and people's reaction to it in paragraph 2.

QUESTION: Ask, "What does this description help the reader to understand?" Accept student responses.

Possible response: 39 feet is very tall—taller than a telephone pole, I think. The house Mr. Kamkwamba lives in doesn't have many appliances compared to what I am used to—in fact, I wouldn't even consider lightbulbs appliances!

CONCLUDE: Help students to formulate conclusions about the importance of these details in the text. Ask students why the author might have included these details.

Possible response: The windmill must have been tricky for one person to build, especially using trees and spare parts. Mr. Kamkwamba must be quite resourceful. Apparently it takes a very tall windmill to power just a few appliances. And yet this tall windmill is a local attraction, so it must be unusual in this area to have any power at all. Mr. Kamkwamba's village must be very poor, very remote, or both.

Remind students that **description** in a newspaper article includes facts, examples, statistics, quotations from interviews with people involved, and direct observations. Journalists try to present these facts objectively, without judgment or bias.

DIGITAL PERSPECTIVES

Illuminating the Text Before or after their first reading of the text, ask each group to create a *K-W-L* chart about windmills, and then have them fill out the first two columns (*I **K**now; I **W**ant to Know*). Show a brief video or other concise online resource explaining how windmills work. After reviewing sources, have students complete the final column (*I **L**earned*). Then have groups share what they learned, and as a class try to resolve any unanswered questions from the middle column. Be sure to preview the online resource before sharing it with the class. **(Research to Clarify)**

Concept Vocabulary

SCARCITY If groups are struggling to define the word *scarcity* in paragraph 8, point out that they can use context clues to infer the meaning. Draw their attention to the context clue *energy poverty,* which is defined in the text as "the scarcity of modern fuels and electrical supplies in poor parts of the world." Have students use this context clue to define the word.

Possible response: In this context, *scarcity* means "lack" or "shortage."

Additional **English Language Support** is available in the Interactive Teacher's Edition.

NOTES

Mark context clues or indicate another strategy you used that helped you determine meaning.

scarcity (SKAYR suh tee) *n.*

MEANING:

5 "I was thinking about electricity," says Mr. Kamkwamba, explaining how he got hooked on wind. "I was thinking about what I'd like to have at home, and I was thinking, 'What can I do?'"

6 To meet his family's growing power needs, he recently hammered in a shiny store-bought windmill next to the big one at his home and installed solar panels. He has another windmill still in its box that he'll put up at a house 70 miles away in the capital, Lilongwe, where he now goes to school.

7 A few years ago, he built a windmill for the primary school in Masitala. He used it to teach an informal windmill-building course. Lately, he has offered to help the village handyman down the road build his own machine.

8 "Energy poverty"—the **scarcity** of modern fuels and electrical supplies in poor parts of the world—is a subject of great interest to development economists. The windmill at the Kamkwamba family compound, a few brick buildings perched on a hill overlooking the village, has turned it into a stop for the curious: People trekking across Malawi's arid plains drop by. Villagers now regularly make the dusty walk up the hill to charge their cellphones.

9 The contraption causing all the fuss is a tower made from lashed-together blue-gum tree trunks. From a distance, it resembles an old oil derrick.[1] For blades, Mr. Kamkwamba used flattened plastic pipes. He built a turbine from spare bicycle parts. When the wind kicks up, the blades spin so fast they rock the tower violently back and forth.

10 Mr. Kamkwamba's wind obsession started six years ago. He wasn't going to school anymore because his family couldn't afford the $80-a-year tuition.

11 When he wasn't helping his family farm groundnuts and soybeans, he was reading. He stumbled onto a photograph of a windmill in a text donated to the local library and started to build one himself. The project seemed a waste of time to his parents and the rest of Masitala.

12 "At first, we were laughing at him," says Agnes Kamkwamba, his mother. "We thought he was doing something useless."

13 The laughter ended when he hooked up his windmill to a thin copper wire, a car battery, and a light bulb for each room of the family's main house.

14 The family soon started enjoying the trappings of modern life: a radio and, more recently, a TV. They no longer have to buy paraffin for lantern light. Two of Mr. Kamkwamba's six sisters stay up late studying for school.

1. **derrick** (DER ik) *n.* metal framework used in oil drilling.

HOW LANGUAGE WORKS

Transitions Call student attention to the shift in time between paragraphs 6 and 7. Some students may be confused by the way this article jumps around in time. Although biographies often proceed chronologically, the newspaper format of this article demands that the author put the most important ideas, rather than the earliest events, first. Draw students' attention to transitions

that appear in this article, such as *so far* (paragraph 2), *then* (paragraph 4), *recently* (paragraph 6), and *years ago* (paragraph 7). Then, ask students to use transitions in the text to help them place the following events in time order:

(a) William Kamkwamba built windmills for his home. (b) William saw a picture of a windmill in a book. (c) William is working on a windmill to light and pump water for Masitala. (d) William built a windmill for a primary school in Masitala. (e) William stopped going to school.

Possible response: e, b, a, d, c

NOTES

15 "Our lives are much happier now," Mrs. Kamkwamba says.

16 The new power also attracted a swarm of admirers. Last November, Hartford Mchazime, a Malawian educator, heard about the windmill and drove out to the Kamkwamba house with some reporters. After the news hit the blogosphere, a group of entrepreneurs scouting for ideas in Africa located Mr. Kamkwamba. Called TED, the group, which invites the likes of Al Gore and Bono to share ideas at conferences, invited him to a brainstorming session earlier this year.

17 In June, Mr. Kamkwamba was onstage at a TED conference in Tanzania. (TED stands for Technology Entertainment Design.) "I got information about a windmill, and I try and I made it," he said in halting English to a big ovation. After the conference, a group of entrepreneurs, African bloggers, and venture capitalists[2]—some teary-eyed at the speech—pledged to finance his education.

18 His backers have also showered him with new gadgets, including a cellphone with a hip-hop ringtone, a laptop, and an iPod. (Kelly Clarkson's "Breakaway" is his current favorite tune.) They rewired his family's house, replacing the homemade switches he made out of flip-flop parts.

19 They're paying for him to attend an expensive international academy in the capital, Lilongwe, for children of expatriate missionaries and aid workers. But his teacher, Lorilee MacLean, sometimes worries about his one-track mind and about all the attention he's getting.

20 "I don't want him to be seen as William the windmill maker," said Mrs. MacLean one day recently. While Mr. Kamkwamba quietly plowed through homework, his classmates were busy gossiping and checking their Facebook profiles.

21 Mr. Kamkwamba has taught his family to maintain the windmill when he's away at school. His sister Dolice and cousin Geoffrey can quickly scamper up the tower, as it sways and clatters in the wind, to make repairs.

22 A steady stream of curiosity seekers make the trip to the Kamkwamba compound—mostly unannounced. The visits are unsettling for the reserved family.

23 One afternoon, a pair of Malawian health workers came by to get a closer look and meet Mr. Kamkwamba. The family scattered, leaving the pair—dressed in shirts and ties for the occasion—standing awkwardly in the yard.

24 "We have heard about this windmill, and so we wanted to see it for ourselves," one finally spoke up. Mr. Kamkwamba

2. **venture capitalists** *n.* people who provide money to small companies in exchange for partial ownership of those companies. If the companies grow, venture capitalists make money.

PERSONALIZE FOR LEARNING

English Language Support

Cultural Concepts Call students' attention to the description of TED in paragraph 16. TED is a nonprofit group founded in 1984 to spread innovative ideas through short, powerful talks. Its popularity has exploded along with the growth of the Internet, and hundreds of millions of people worldwide have viewed "TED Talks" on the organization's website. The *T* in TED stands for "technology," which is the topic for most of the speakers on the TED stage today. English-language learners may find inspiration in viewing William Kamkwamba's first and second talks and witnessing his growth as a public speaker. The first talk, filmed in 2007, is about 4 minutes long and accessible through TED's website. The second talk, from 2009, is about the same length. **ALL LEVELS**

Concept Vocabulary

DESIRE If groups are struggling to define the word *desire* in paragraph 26, point out that they can use contrasting context clues to infer the meaning. Draw their attention to *causing some tensions* in the sentence before *admire*, and to *desire* in the following sentence. Have students contrast the meanings of *causing tension* and *admire*. Have students use these clues to define the word.

Possible responses: In this context, *desire* is a verb meaning "to want something they admire or think is good."

ATTEMPTS If groups are struggling to define the word *attempts* in paragraph 27, point out that they can use context clues to infer the meaning. Draw their attention to the context clues *started building his own* and *help him rebuild,* which appear before and after the word in the same paragraph. Have students use these clues to define the word.

Possible responses: In this context, *attempts* is a noun meaning "tries, or efforts; steps taken to get something done."

NOTES

Mark context clues or indicate another strategy you used that helped you determine meaning.

desire (dih ZY uhr) *v.*

MEANING:

attempts (uh TEMPTS) *n.*

MEANING:

came around to shake hands, then quickly moved away to show another visitor around.

25 Jealousy is a social taboo in these parts, but Fred Mwale, an educator who works in Wimbe, the area that includes Masitala, says the family's new prosperity is causing some tensions.

26 "People do **desire** what is happening here. They come, and admire," he says. "They think that they might get the same support if they build a windmill."

27 Down the hill, the village handyman started building his own windmill after secretly studying Mr. Kamkwamba's. A gust of wind blew the blades off the man's first few **attempts**. Mr. Kamkwamba offered to help him rebuild, but got no reply.

28 "I'm waiting to see if he's serious," Mr. Kamkwamba says. ❧

VOCABULARY DEVELOPMENT

Multiple Meanings Review paragraph 28. Tell students that the word *serious* has multiple meanings. Have students reread the last sentence in the article and discuss the following sentences.

1. The congregation grew *serious* when the minister asked them to reflect on the past year. (thoughtful, solemn)
2. She only reads *serious* novels. (requiring great effort to create or understand)
3. People who are *serious* about acting should audition. (feeling sincere, wholehearted, or committed)
4. Chocolate can cause *serious* health problems for dogs. (significant because of risk or danger)

Guide students to identify which meaning is used in the sentence from the text. Discuss how to use context clues to define a word with multiple meanings.

Comprehension Check

Complete the following items after you finish your first read. Review and clarify details with your group.

1. What inspired William Kamkwamba to build a windmill?

2. What materials did Kamkwamba use to build his first windmill?

3. What is "energy poverty"?

4. **Notebook** Confirm your understanding of the article by writing a brief summary of it.

RESEARCH

Research to Clarify Research an unfamiliar detail in the article. In what way does the information you learned shed light on the article? Share your findings with your small group.

Research to Explore Research other ways that energy poverty is being addressed in poor parts of the world. Share your findings with your group.

DIGITAL PERSPECTIVES

Comprehension Check

Possible responses:

1. He was thinking about electricity and what he'd like to have at home. He saw a photo of a windmill in a library book.
2. blue gum trees, bicycle parts, plastic pipes
3. the scarcity, or lack, or modern fuels and electrical supplies in the developing world
4. A young, self-taught man from Malawi named William Kamkwamba built windmills to power his home. His windmills were discovered and reported on and he attracted many admirers, including the TED group and other powerful supporters. Kamkwamba, who is now receiving an education at a private school in Malawi's capital, has other windmill projects underway in other parts of his village as well as in the capital. He has inspired others to build windmills to help improve access to energy in the region.

Research

Research to Clarify If students have difficulty choosing a detail to investigate further, suggest that they look more deeply into windmills, focusing either on how a windmill can be rigged to generate electricity or how they were used originally in the various cultures where they emerged. Remind students to explain how their findings shed light on the text.

Research to Explore Suggest that students interested in looking into renewable energy projects look at the websites of international aid and development groups like the Center for Global Development, or groups focusing on energy development like the International Energy Agency. Students may want to investigate the state of Africa's power grids—the systems of wires, switches, and substations that connect energy producers to consumers.

PERSONALIZE FOR LEARNING

Challenge

Research Groups researching energy poverty in Africa may want to investigate how climate change could be affected as African nations continue to develop their electrical grids. For example, students may want to pursue these lines of investigation:

- Which renewable energy sources are being developed in Africa?
- How might the development of African nations affect climate change?
- What is the relationship between the amount of fossil fuels extracted from African nations and people's access to energy in those nations?

Ask groups to share their findings with the class.

FACILITATING

Jump Start

CLOSE READ Ask students to consider the following prompt: *Can one young person drive a nationwide change? Do you dream of changing your community, and how would you do it?* As students discuss the prompt in their groups, have them consider what obstacles they might face.

Close Read the Text

If needed, model close reading by using the Annotation Highlights in the Interactive Teacher's Edition.

Remind students to use Accountable Talk in their discussions and to support one another as they complete the close read.

Analyze the Text

1. **Possible response:** Because his family had no electricity, Kamkwamba figured out how to make a windmill, which changed his life and perhaps the lives of many other people.
2. Passages will vary by group.
3. Responses will vary by group.

Concept Vocabulary

Why These Words? Possible response: In this selection, all three words relate to poverty, limited technology, and efforts to relieve it.

Practice

Possible responses:

- Kamkwamba has responded to the *scarcity* of power by building windmills to produce electricity.
- Kamkwama's success created a *desire* for more windmills in the region.
- Kamkwamba's neighbor's first *attempts* at building his own windmill failed.

Word Network

Possible words: *self-taught, poverty, jealousy, taboo, tensions, rebuild*

Word Study

For more support, see **Concept Vocabulary and Word Study.**
Responses will vary, but students should explain how knowing the words' etymologies influences their understanding of the words' meanings.

MAKING MEANING

A YOUNG TINKERER BUILDS A WINDMILL, ELECTRIFYING A NATION

GROUP DISCUSSION
When you work in your group to answer the Analyze the Text questions, be sure to direct listeners to specific words, sentences, and paragraphs in the story.

WORD NETWORK
Add interesting words related to facing adversity from the text to your Word Network.

STANDARDS
Reading Informational Text
• Cite several pieces of textual evidence to support analysis of what the text says explicitly as well as inferences drawn from the text.
• Analyze the interactions between individuals, events, and ideas in a text.
• Analyze the structure an author uses to organize a text, including how the major sections contribute to the whole and to the development of the ideas.
Language
Determine or clarify the meaning of unknown and multiple-meaning words and phrases based on *grade 7 reading and content*, choosing flexibly from a range of strategies.
b. Use common, grade-appropriate Greek or Latin affixes and roots as clues to the meaning of a word.

Close Read the Text

With your group, revisit sections of the text you marked during your first read. What do you **notice**? What **questions** do you have? What can you **conclude**?

Analyze the Text

CITE TEXTUAL EVIDENCE to support your answers.

Notebook Complete the activities.

1. **Review and Clarify** Review the selection with your group. How did the lack of modern conveniences inspire William Kamkwamba to be innovative? What were the results of his innovations?
2. **Present and Discuss** Now, work with your group to share the passages from the text that you found especially important. Take turns presenting your passages. Discuss what you noticed in the text, the questions you asked, and the conclusions you reached.
3. **Essential Question: *How do we overcome obstacles?*** What has this selection taught you about how people overcome obstacles?

LANGUAGE DEVELOPMENT

Concept Vocabulary

scarcity desire attempts

Why These Words? The concept vocabulary words from the text are related. With your group, determine what the words have in common. Record your ideas, and add another word that fits the category.

Practice

Notebook Confirm your understanding of these words by using them in sentences containing context clues.

Word Study

Etymology The **etymology** of a word is its origin. Etymologies show how words enter the English language and how they change over time. Check a dictionary for a guide to the symbols and abbreviations used in etymologies. *Desire* comes from Middle English *desiren* < Old French *desirer* < Latin *desiderare*, which means "from the stars." Knowing this, you can gain a better understanding of the meaning of *desire* ("to wish for").

With your group, look up the etymology of at least three other words in the selection. Describe how knowing each etymology helps you better understand the words.

FORMATIVE ASSESSMENT

Analyze the Text

If students struggle to close read the text, **then** provide the **A Young Tinkerer Builds a Windmill: Text Questions** available online in the Interactive Teacher's Edition or Unit Resources.

Concept Vocabulary

If students fail to see the connection between the vocabulary words, **then** have them revisit the context in which the words were used in the article.

Word Study

If students are unable to use other transitions while describing a process, **then** have them think of synonyms to transitions on the student page.

For Reteach and Practice, see **Word Study: Etymology (RP).**

Analyze Craft and Structure

Text Structure: Biographical Writing When a nonfiction text tells a story, it is a work of **narrative nonfiction**. **Biographical writing** is a type of narrative nonfiction in which the author tells about events in another person's life. The elements of biographical writing include:

- a real-life person who is the subject of the biography
- factual information about the setting and context
- details and descriptions that help develop the subject's character
- **direct quotations**, a person's exact words, from the subject and other people that have a relationship with or significant knowledge of the subject, such as a close friend or a historian
- the use of **narrative pacing**, which is the way an author shapes the flow of information in a text—how much information readers receive in a given section of text and the order in which they receive it

Practice

CITE TEXTUAL EVIDENCE to support your answers.

Work with your group to analyze the elements of biographical writing in the article and the ways the author structures information to effectively develop her ideas. Model your analysis on the example in the chart, using the blank rows to capture the information you find.

PARAGRAPH	ELEMENTS OF BIOGRAPHICAL WRITING	CONTRIBUTION TO DEVELOPMENT OF IDEAS
8	• relevant facts • information about the setting • descriptive details	• The definition of "energy poverty" and the facts about the setting show why the windmill is important. • The descriptive details enable the reader to picture the setting.

DIGITAL PERSPECTIVES 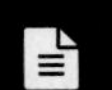  

Analyze Craft and Structure

Biographical Writing To help students grasp the concept, have them think of how they could apply the elements of biographical writing to someone they know very well. For instance, a student might think of his or her best friend and ask and answer questions to work through the elements of biographical writing: *What's his or her name?* (the subject of the biography), *Where does he or she live?* (factual information about the setting), and so on. You might wish to provide an example to model the process and apply the elements of biography. For more support, see **Analyze Craft and Structure: Biographical Writing.**

Student responses will vary but should show how authors structure information to develop ideas.

FORMATIVE ASSESSMENT

Analyze Craft and Structure

If groups have difficulty identifying and analyzing elements of biographical writing, **then** have them refer to the T-chart created in the teaching note above, or instruct them to create a similar chart. The chart will help them see the relationship between each element and its contribution to the text's development. For Reteach and Practice, see **Analyze Craft and Structure: Biographical Writing (RP).**

PERSONALIZE FOR LEARNING

English Language Support

Writing Interview Questions Have students write a list of people that they would like to interview to find out more about Mr. Kamkwamba.

Have pairs of students write two open-ended questions for one of the people on their list. **EMERGING**

Have students write three open-ended questions and one closed question for one of the people on their list and then have them explain why they want to ask them. **EXPANDING**

Have students write two closed questions and three open-ended questions for a person on their list. Have students explain the kinds of information they would want to gather from their questions. **BRIDGING**

An expanded **English Language Support Lesson** on Personal Interviews is available in the Interactive Teacher's Edition.

FACILITATING

Conventions

Capitalization Remind students of some of the important instances when capitalization is needed: names, titles, days of the week and months of the year, countries, cities, and so on. For more support, see **Conventions: Capitalization.**

Read It

Answers will vary.

Write It

Possible responses:

1. William Kamkwamba [proper noun: name of person] is only twenty years old [not proper adjective or noun], but he has built a windmill [not a proper noun] to provide electricity to his family in Malawi [proper noun: name of country].
2. William's [first word of sentence, proper noun: name of person] windmill [not a proper noun] has brought a lot of attention to the small [not a proper adjective] village [not a proper noun] of Masitala where the Kamkwamba [proper adjective] family [not a proper noun] lives.

Possible Response: Students' paragraphs will vary, but they should use at least three proper nouns, one proper adjective, and one quotation.

FORMATIVE ASSESSMENT

Conventions

If students have difficulty identifying words that should NOT be capitalized in the Write It activity, **then** remind them that most nouns and adjectives are common because they do not name *particular* things. For Reteach and Practice, see **Conventions: Capitalization (RP).**

LANGUAGE DEVELOPMENT

A YOUNG TINKERER BUILDS A WINDMILL, ELECTRIFYING A NATION

Conventions

Capitalization **Capital letters** signal the beginning of a sentence or quotation and identify proper nouns and proper adjectives. Learning to use correct capitalization will ensure that your writing looks professional and authoritative.

Proper nouns include the names of people, geographic locations, specific events and time periods, organizations, languages, historical events and documents, and religions. **Proper adjectives** are derived from proper nouns, as in *French* (from *France*) and *Canadian* (from *Canada*). Here are some examples taken from the selection you have just read:

Sentence beginning: The contraption causing all the fuss . . .

Quotation: ". . . I was thinking, 'What can I do?"

Proper nouns: His sister Dolice and cousin Geoffrey . . .

Proper adjectives: One afternoon, a pair of Malawian health workers . . .

Read It

Work with your group to identify examples of correct capitalization in the selection. Find two examples in the selection for each of the following items.

1. a sentence beginning
2. a proper adjective
3. a person's name
4. a quotation

Write It

Identify the errors in capitalization in each sentence, and note the reason each word should or should not begin with a capital letter. Then, revise each sentence to correct the capitalization.

1. William kamkwamba is only Twenty Years Old, but he has built a Windmill to provide electricity to his family in malawi.

2. william's Windmill has brought a lot of attention to the Small Village of Masitala, where his kamkwamba Family lives.

Notebook Finally, write a biographical paragraph in which you briefly describe a person you admire. In your paragraph, use at least three proper nouns, one proper adjective, and a quotation. Reread your paragraph to confirm that you have used correct capitalization.

STANDARDS

Language

Demonstrate command of the conventions of standard English capitalization, punctuation, and spelling when writing.

PERSONALIZE FOR LEARNING

English Language Support

Capitalization English language learners may need to be reminded that capitalization rules are different for different languages. In Spanish, for example, the first-person pronoun, *yo*; months of the year; days of the week; languages; and nationalities (*inglés, español*) are NOT capitalized. Marking capitalization errors in the following sentences will benefit all of your students, particularly those whose home language is Spanish. (To show the correct responses, letters whose cases are incorrect appear in boldface.)

1. **w**hen **i** read the article about William **k**amkwamba, **i** was inspired.
2. Many **a**frican nations struggle with **E**nergy **P**overty.
3. **i**n Malawi, the main language is **c**hichewa.

ALL LEVELS

Writing to Sources

A **how-to essay** is a written, step-by-step explanation of how to make or do something.

Assignment

Work with your group to write a **how-to essay** in which you address one of the following topics:

- ☐ How to make a windmill. What do you need to make a windmill? What steps should you take? How can it be designed and connected to make it a source of electric power?
- ☐ Where is Masitala, Malawi? Is it close to the capital of Malawi? What directions would you give someone who wants to travel from Malawi's capital to Masitala?

Conduct Research Work with your group to find the information you will need to write your essay. Consult multiple print and digital sources, and evaluate the credibility of each source you use. Take notes on each source so that you can cite your sources accurately in a **Works-Cited list,** or **bibliography,** at the end of your essay.

Organize Your Essay Use **chronological organization**, or step-by-step organization, when you write your how-to essay. A reader needs clear, well-organized directions in order to complete a task successfully. If the steps are out of order, or if they are unclear, he or she will have a difficult time following your directions.

Use Clarifying Transitions Be sure to use transitions that indicate time and sequence as you write your essay. Transitions, such as *first, next, until,* and *meanwhile* will help you to organize and clarify the steps in your essay.

Format Your Essay To help readers follow your directions include headings, illustrations, and graphics in your essay. Place headings before each section of your essay, and place graphics and illustrations in the section of your essay that describes the step the image shows.

EVIDENCE LOG

Before moving on to a new selection, go to your Evidence Log and record what you learned from "A Young Tinkerer Builds a Windmill, Electrifying a Nation."

STANDARDS

Writing

- Introduce a topic clearly, previewing what is to follow; organize ideas, concepts, and information, using strategies such as definition, classification, comparison/contrast, and cause/effect; include formatting, graphics, and multimedia when useful to aiding comprehension.
- Develop the topic with relevant facts, definitions, concrete details, quotations, or other information and examples.
- Conduct short research projects to answer a question, drawing on several sources and generating additional related, focused questions for further research and investigation.
- Gather relevant information from multiple print and digital sources, using search terms effectively; assess the credibility and accuracy of each source; and quote or paraphrase the data and conclusions of others while avoiding plagiarism and following a standard format for citation.

PERSONALIZE FOR LEARNING

Strategic Support

Graphic Organizers As they plan their how-to essays, students may benefit from organizing their steps in a flow chart, especially if they have branching options for completing the process. Some word-processing programs provide flow charts that users can type into directly, and flow charts can be arranged horizontally or vertically. Students may add as many boxes to their charts as needed.

DIGITAL PERSPECTIVES

Writing to Sources

Conduct Research Direct students to keep a record of all the sources they use to find information.

Windmill: Suggest that students watch any of many do-it-yourself windmill-building videos on channels like YouTube. Advise students to refer to printed articles as well, however, so they can quickly refer to the process in general, the order of steps, and the technical vocabulary.

Travel: Suggest that students writing directions to Matisala include landmarks that would help travelers find this remote location, such as river crossings. Many online satellite maps will let users switch between satellite view and street-map views. Suggest students review travel websites to find various travel options—rental car, bus, hired car, etc.—and the costs and benefits of each.

Organize Your Essay Suggest students devote a half-page to each numbered step. Then, as they continue to gather information, they will have room to add notes and sketches to the appropriate step.

Use Clarifying Transitions Remind students that not all transitions in a how-to essay must emphasize chronological order. There are instances when transitions will be needed to demonstrate clarification, comparison, causes and effects, and to signal summary and conclusion.

Format Your Essay Provide students with examples of appropriate styles for headings that are noticeable and not distracting. Guide them on the wording of headings so they help readers with navigation of the text and are not too lengthy. For more support, see **Writing to Sources: How-to Essay.**

Evidence Log Support students in completing their Evidence Log. This paced activity will help prepare them for the Performance-Based Assessment at the end of the unit.

FORMATIVE ASSESSMENT

Writing to Sources

If students have trouble explaining a particular step, **then** suggest that they break it down into a series of smaller steps. Encourage students to exchange their papers with partners in their groups to check the clarity of their how-to processes. For Reteach and Practice, see **Writing to Sources: How-to Essay (RP).**

Selection Test

Administer the Selection Test for "A Young Tinkerer Builds a Windmill, Electrifying a Nation," which is available in both print and digital formats online in Assessments.

Present Multimedia Profiles

Before groups begin work on their projects, have them clearly differentiate the role each group member will play. Remind groups to consult the schedule for Small-Group Learning to guide their work during the Performance Task.

Students should complete the assignment using presentation software to take advantage of text, graphics, and sound features.

Plan With Your Group

Analyze the Text Remind students that they will need to include specific details and quotations from the selections in their explanations. As they fill in the chart to analyze what the selections say about how people overcome challenges, groups should note paragraph numbers of quotations and details they might want to refer to or include in their presentations. Taking the time to record this information as they plan will save them time when they begin to gather evidence.

Gather Details and Media Discuss how students can use multimedia to support their explanations. Remind students they might want to use audio clips from "A Work in Progress" and film clips or stills from "How Helen Keller Learned to Talk." An Internet search will yield photographs and other visual aids to accompany "A Young Tinkerer Builds a Windmill, Electrifying a Nation."

SOURCES

- A WORK IN PROGRESS
- *from* THE STORY OF MY LIFE
- HOW HELEN KELLER LEARNED TO TALK
- A YOUNG TINKERER BUILDS A WINDMILL, ELECTRIFYING A NATION

Present Multimedia Profiles

Assignment

Review the selections you have just read and viewed. Work in your small group to present a series of multimedia profiles, in which you address this question:

How do people overcome enormous challenges?

Plan with Your Group

Analyze the Text With your group, review the selections you have read in this section. Discuss the people, the challenges they faced, and the strengths and qualities that enabled them to overcome these obstacles. Use this chart to organize your ideas.

SELECTION	PERSON	CHALLENGE(S) FACED	STRENGTHS OR QUALITIES POSSESSED BY THE PERSON	OUTCOME
A Work in Progress				
from The Story of My Life				
How Helen Keller Learned to Talk				
A Young Tinkerer Builds a Windmill, Electrifying a Nation				

STANDARDS

Writing

- Write informative/explanatory texts to examine a topic and convey ideas, concepts, and information through the selection, organization, and analysis of relevant content.
- Draw evidence from literary or informational texts to support analysis, reflection, and research.

Gather Details and Media Each member should draft a brief informative profile about one of the people described in one of the selections. The profile should be able to stand alone as a section of the group presentation. Then, find relevant multimedia to include in your report. Be sure to sequence the multimedia elements so that they clarify and emphasize your important points.

Organize Your Ideas As a group, decide how you will transition from one section to the next and from one speaker to the next.

AUTHOR'S PERSPECTIVE **Ernest Morrell, Ph.D.**

Digital Speech Since "a picture is worth a thousand words," help students find and use effective images for oral presentations. Remind students to give full credit to visual sources, as they would for print ones. Teachers can guide students to create rhetorically powerful digital presentations such as slideshows, blogs, and online forums using these suggestions:

- **Keep It Simple:** Choose one striking image rather than several smaller ones. Position the visual carefully, allowing "white space" to make the image stand out.
- **Go for Quality:** Choose clear, high-quality images or take high-resolution photos.
- **Limit Bullet Points and Text:** The most effective slideshows have limited text. Suggest that slides should have no more than six words across and six lines down of text.
- **Choose Color and Font Carefully:** Cool colors (blues, greens) work best for backgrounds; warm colors (orange, red) work best for objects in the foreground. Use a simple, standard font such as Arial or Helvetica.

Last, teachers can help students create a rubric to assess presentations.

Rehearse with Your Group

Practice with Your Group Before your presentation, rehearse as a group. Plan the ways in which you will present your multimedia elements, and prepare to begin any necessary equipment. Ensure that each member uses a formal tone, appropriate eye contact, adequate volume, and clear pronunciation.

As you deliver your portion of the presentation, use this checklist to evaluate the effectiveness of your group's rehearsal. Then, use your evaluation and the instruction that follows to guide your revisions to the presentation.

CONTENT	USE OF MEDIA	PRESENTATION TECHNIQUES
☐ The presentation clearly responds to the prompt. ☐ The presentation includes relevant details from the texts. ☐ The sections of the presentation are logically organized.	☐ The presentation includes a variety of multimedia. ☐ The multimedia emphasizes and clarifies key points. ☐ Equipment functions properly.	☐ Presenters speak loudly and clearly. ☐ Presenters maintain eye contact.

Fine-Tune the Content To make your presentation stronger, you may need to go back into the texts to find more details to support your main ideas. Work with your group to identify key points that are not clear to listeners. Find another way to word these ideas.

Improve Your Use of Media Be sure to sequence your multimedia so that each piece relates directly to a key point in your presentation and helps your audience to better understand the information.

Brush Up on Your Presentation Techniques Practice delivering your presentation several times as a group so you are comfortable. Give one another feedback and encouragement to improve and polish your presentation.

Present and Evaluate

Remember that you must work as a team to make your presentation effective. Give all classmates your full attention when they are presenting. As you listen to other groups, consider their content, use of media, and presentation techniques. Ask questions to clarify your understanding of the information presented in other classmates' presentations.

STANDARDS

Speaking and Listening

Engage effectively in a range of collaborative discussions with diverse partners on *grade 7 topics, texts, and issues,* building on others' ideas and expressing their own clearly.

a. Come to discussions prepared, having read or researched material under study; explicitly draw on that preparation by referring to evidence on the topic, text, or issue to probe and reflect on ideas under discussion.

- Present claims and findings, emphasizing salient points in a focused, coherent manner with pertinent descriptions, facts, details, and examples; use appropriate eye contact, adequate volume, and clear pronunciation.
- Include multimedia components and visual displays in presentations to clarify claims and findings and emphasize salient points.

DIGITAL PERSPECTIVES

Rehearse With Your Group

Practice With Your Group Suggest that students practice using any multimedia equipment they will need to use in the presentation. They should make sure they know how to use the equipment and that it is working correctly.

Improve Your Use of Media Remind students that any media they include should directly relate to, clarify, and support their ideas. In addition, media should be suited to the purpose and audience. For instance, students should avoid music that conveys the wrong tone for their presentation.

Brush Up on Your Presentation Techniques Remind groups to make sure that all members know the order in which they are presenting. Practicing the transition from one speaker to the next will ensure the presentation flows smoothly.

Present and Evaluate

Before beginning the presentations, set the expectations for the audience. You may wish to have students consider these questions as groups present:

- What was the presenting group's main idea about each selection?
- Which supporting details were most effective?
- Which multimedia best supported the explanation?
- In which presentation skills did this group excel?

As students provide feedback to the presenting group, remind them that compliments are just as valuable as constructive criticism.

PERSONALIZE FOR LEARNING

Strategic Support

Check-In As groups finalize their presentations, circulate among them and check in to ensure that each group member has a role in the presentation and is prepared for his or her part. You may also wish to review the media students plan to use, determining whether it is appropriate for the classroom setting, is reliable and will function as intended when it needs to, and is practical (or could be replaced with a simpler method of presentation that might be more effective). Remind groups that they should have an idea of how long their presentation will take to deliver so that it doesn't seem too short or run too long.

OVERVIEW

INDEPENDENT LEARNING

How do we overcome obstacles?

Encourage students to think carefully about what they have already learned and what more they want to know about the unit topic of facing adversity and overcoming obstacles. This is a key first step to previewing and selecting the text they will read in Independent Learning.

Independent Learning Strategies

Review the Learning Strategies with students and explain that as they work through Independent Learning they will develop strategies to work on their own.

- Have students watch the video on Independent Learning Strategies.
- A video on this topic is available online in the Professional Development Center.

Students should include any favorite strategies that they might have devised on their own during Whole-Class and Small-Group Learning. For example, for the strategy "Create a schedule," students might include:

- Understand the goals and deadlines.
- Make a schedule for what to do each day.

Block Scheduling

Each day in this Pacing Plan represents a 40–50-minute class period. Teachers using block scheduling may combine days to reflect their class schedule. In addition, teachers may revise pacing to differentiate and support core instruction by integrating components and resources as students require.

OVERVIEW: INDEPENDENT LEARNING

ESSENTIAL QUESTION:

How do we overcome obstacles?

Sometimes people feel overwhelmed by life's problems. The selections you read are about people who faced big problems and managed to overcome them. In this section, you will complete your study of facing adversity by exploring an additional selection related to the topic. You'll then share what you learn with classmates. To choose a text, follow these steps.

Look Back Think about the selections you have already studied. What more do you want to know about facing adversity?

Look Ahead Preview the selections by reading the descriptions. Which one seems the most interesting and appealing to you?

Look Inside Take a few minutes to scan through the text you chose. Choose a different one if this text doesn't meet your needs.

Independent Learning Strategies

Throughout your life, in school, in your community, and in your career, you will need to rely on yourself to learn and work on your own. Review these strategies and the actions you can take to practice them during Independent Learning. Add ideas of your own for each category.

STRATEGY	ACTION PLAN
Create a schedule	• Understand your goals and deadlines. • Make a plan for what to do each day. •
Practice what you have learned	• Use first-read and close-read strategies to deepen your understanding. • After you read, evaluate the usefulness of the evidence to help you understand the topic. • Consider the quality and reliability of the source. •
Take notes	• Record important ideas and information. • Review your notes before preparing to share with a group. •

Pacing Plan

Introduce Whole-Class Learning

Unit Introduction: 1 2 3

Media: The Dust Bowl: 4 5

from The Grapes of Wrath: 6 7 8 9

The Circuit: 10 11 12 13 14 15

Performance Task: 16 17 18

Choose one selection. Selections are available online only.

CONTENTS

PERSONAL NARRATIVE

The Girl Who Fell from the Sky

Juliane Koepcke

Can a teenage girl survive in the rain forest all by herself?

NOVEL EXCERPT

Four Skinny Trees

from The House on Mango Street

Sandra Cisneros

A young girl finds inner strength in an unexpected place.

SHORT STORY

Rikki-tikki-tavi

Rudyard Kipling

Can one little mongoose protect the people and animals around him from two deadly cobras?

MEMOIR

from Facing the Lion: Growing Up Maasai on the African Savanna

Joseph Lemasolai Lekuton

Sometimes life forces a person to step *way* outside of "the comfort zone."

PERFORMANCE-BASED ASSESSMENT PREP

Review Evidence for an Informative Essay

Complete your Evidence Log for the unit by evaluating what you have learned and synthesizing the information you have recorded.

DIGITAL PERSPECTIVES

Contents

Selections Encourage students to scan and preview the selections before choosing the one they would like to read. Suggest that they consider the genre and subject matter of each one before making their decision. You can use the information on the following Planning pages to advise students in making their choice.

Remind students that the selections for Independent Learning are only available in the Interactive Student Edition. Allow students who do not have digital access at home to preview the selections or review the media selection(s) using classroom or computer lab technology. Then either have students print the selection they choose or provide a printout for them.

Performance Based-Assessment Prep

Review Evidence for an Informative Essay Point out to students that collecting evidence during Independent Learning is the last step in completing their Evidence Log. After they finish their independent reading, they will synthesize all the evidence they have compiled in the unit.

The evidence students collect will serve as the primary source of information they will use to complete the writing and oral presentation for the Performance-Based Assessment at the end of the unit.

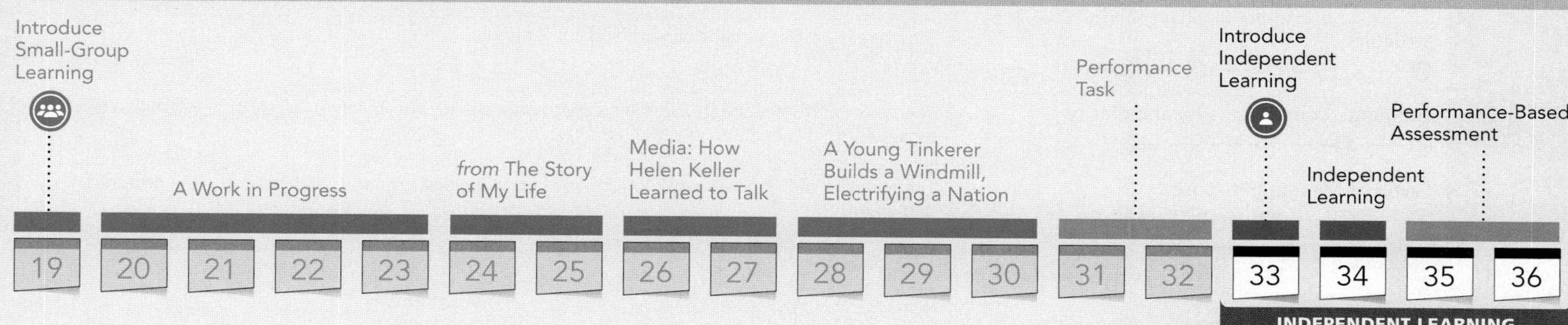

SELECTION RESOURCES

- First-Read Guide: Nonfiction
- Close-Read Guide: Nonfiction
- The Girl Who Fell from the Sky: Text Questions
- Audio Summaries
- Selection Audio
- Selection Test

The Girl Who Fell from the Sky

Summary

In "The Girl Who Fell from the Sky," Juliane Koepcke tells her amazing story of survival. As a teenager, Juliane lives for two years with her parents at the research station they run in the Peruvian rainforest. Then she moves back to Lima to finish high school. She and her mother board a plane to fly back to visit her father and the plane crashes. Juliane, still strapped into her seat, falls 10,000 feet to the ground and survives. This narrative describes how she stays alive, finds a tiny river and follows it, and finally finds people many days after the crash.

Insight

From this selection, students can learn that some knowledge and a mighty will to live can be enough to save a life. Juliane spends 11 days in the jungle before reaching a shelter from which she is rescued. She is the only survivor of LANSA Flight 508.

Connection to Essential Question

This selection connects directly to the Essential Question—*How do we overcome obstacles?*—by showing a young woman who overcomes almost unimaginable adversity.

Connection to Performance-Based Assessment

In this assessment, students will be called upon to write an informative essay responding to this question: "How can people overcome adversity in the face of overwhelming obstacles?" The story of Juliane Koepcke's survival will help them discuss the personal qualities adversity can evoke in a person.

Text Complexity Rubric: The Girl Who Fell from the Sky

Quantitative Measures	
Lexile: 790 **Text Length:** 2,128 words	
Qualitative Measures	
Knowledge Demands (1 ❷ 3 4 5)	Mostly familiar situations. The story is exciting, true, and somewhat exotic, but no prior knowledge is absolutely necessary.
Structure (❶ 2 3 4 5)	Structure is simple, straightforward, and conventional.
Language Conventionality and Clarity (1 ❷ 3 4 5)	The syntax and sentence structure are easy to understand. Vocabulary is largely on-level, with a few regionalisms included.
Levels of Meaning/Purpose (1 2 ❸ 4 5)	The meaning of Koepcke's work touches on family, biology, courage, wilderness survival, fortune, and youth.

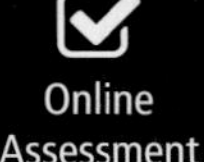

DIGITAL PERSPECTIVES

Audio | Video | Document | Annotation Highlights | EL Highlights | Online Assessment

SELECTION RESOURCES

- First-Read Guide: Fiction
- Close-Read Guide: Fiction
- Four Skinny Trees: Text Questions
- Audio Summaries
- Selection Audio
- Selection Test

Four Skinny Trees

Summary

The speaker in Sandra Cisneros's "Four Skinny Trees" describes four skinny trees, surviving in the city. The trees seem to have an inner strength. They just keep on going and reaching into the sky, no matter what. The speaker says when she needs help and strength, she turns to them for inspiration.

Insight

From this selection, students can learn that there are sources of inspiration in unlikely places.

Connection to Essential Question

This selection connects directly to the essential question *How do we overcome obstacles?* by talking about finding comfort and inspiration in our environment.

Connection to Performance-Based Assessment

In this assessment, students will write an informative essay responding to this question: "How can people overcome adversity in the face of overwhelming obstacles?" This poem provides students with one element that can be used in answering that question.

Text Complexity Rubric: Four Skinny Trees	
Quantitative Measures	
Lexile: 690 **Text Length:** 196 words	
Qualitative Measures	
Knowledge Demands 1 (of 5)	Beyond the idea of trees growing in urban settings, this prose does not require previous knowledge.
Structure 1 (of 5)	Structure is simple, straightforward, and conventional.
Language Conventionality and Clarity 3 (of 5)	The syntax and sentence structure are easy to understand. Vocabulary is on-level.
Levels of Meaning/Purpose 3 (of 5)	The meaning of Cisneros's work is very personal and impressionistic. Most readers will see the metaphor of the trees and their strength.

SELECTION RESOURCES

- First-Read Guide: Fiction
- Close-Read Guide: Fiction
- Rikki-tikki-tavi: Text Questions
- Audio Summaries
- Selection Audio
- Selection Test

Rikki-tikki-tavi

Summary

Rudyard Kipling's short story "Rikki-tikki-tavi" describes the adventures of a young mongoose in India. He adopts a family and becomes their guardian. In the family's garden, he meets Darzee, a tailorbird who has lost a baby bird to Nag, a cobra in the garden. The cobra has also frightened the family's son, Teddy. Nag terrorizes the other animals and threatens the family's safety. Rikki-tikki-tavi resolves to get rid of the five-foot-long poisonous snake.

Insight

This selection explores how determination, cleverness, and agility can overcome enemies with great power.

Connection to Essential Question

This selection connects directly to the essential question *How do we overcome obstacles?* by showing an example of a small animal that does just that.

Connection to Performance-Based Assessment

In this assessment, students will write an informative essay responding to this question: "How can people overcome adversity in the face of overwhelming obstacles?" They will be able to use examples of the little mongoose's determination and intelligence in his battle against Nag.

Text Complexity Rubric: Rikki-tikki-tavi

Quantitative Measures	
Lexile: 1010 **Text Length:** 5,699 words	
Qualitative Measures	
Knowledge Demands ①—❷—③—④—⑤	"Rikki-tikki-tavi" is a familiar children's story. Some knowledge of cobras and mongeese is helpful.
Structure ①—②—❸—④—⑤	Structure is conventional and straightforward.
Language Conventionality and Clarity ①—②—❸—④—⑤	The syntax and sentence structure are not difficult, though the register is somewhat elevated and some vocabulary is above-level.
Levels of Meaning/Purpose ①—❷—③—④—⑤	This is an exciting story for children with a straightforward conclusion.

DIGITAL PERSPECTIVES

Audio | Video | Document | Annotation Highlights | EL Highlights | Online Assessment

from Facing the Lion: Growing Up Maasai on the African Savanna

Summary

In this excerpt from *Facing the Lion: Growing Up Maasai on the African Savanna,* Kenyan leader Joseph Lemasolai Lekuton describes the hardships he faced to get an education. His family had a farm with cows and they had sold several of the cows to allow him to go to an elite boarding school. As a very poor boy among wealthy students, he felt out of place and often did not know how to act. He studied very hard and was determined to succeed. But the hardest part of his school days was actually the trip back home on holidays.

Insight

This selection helps students understand that even great poverty can be overcome with courage and persistence.

SELECTION RESOURCES

- First-Read Guide: Nonfiction
- Close-Read Guide: Nonfiction
- Facing the Lion: Growing Up Maasai on the African Savanna: Text Questions
- Audio Summaries
- Selection Audio
- Selection Test

Connection to Essential Question

In this selection, Joseph Lekuton gives one answer to the essential question *How do people overcome obstacles?* He relied on himself and worked diligently to keep his grades up.

Connection to Performance-Based Assessment

When students write an informative essay in response to the question, "How can people overcome adversity in the face of overwhelming obstacles?" they can refer to the difficulties faced by Joseph Lekuton. His memoir describes fighting the feelings that he was an outsider, focusing on studying and learning, and navigating difficulties just to get to and from school during school vacations.

Text Complexity Rubric: *from* Facing the Lion: Growing Up Maasai on the African Savanna

Quantitative Measures	
Lexile: 800 **Text Length:** 1,971 words	
Qualitative Measures	
Knowledge Demands (3 of 5)	Students will need background information on Africa, Kenya, and nomadic life. Students may need background on boarding schools.
Structure (2 of 5)	Structure is a conventional story told in a memoir style.
Language Conventionality and Clarity (3 of 5)	The syntax and vocabulary are easy to understand, but there are a few regionalisms.
Levels of Meaning/Purpose (3 of 5)	The real-life story touches on the nature of education, poverty, and cultural marginalization in an African setting.

ADVISING

You may wish to direct students to use the generic **First-Read** and **Close-Read Guides** in the Print Student Edition. Alternatively, you may wish to print copies of the genre-specific **First-Read** and **Close-Read Guides** for students. These are available online in the Interactive Student Edition or Unit Resources.

FIRST READ

Students should perform the steps of the first read independently.

NOTICE: Students should focus on the basic elements of the text to ensure they understand what is happening.

ANNOTATE: Students should mark any passages they wish to revisit during their close read.

CONNECT: Students should increase their understanding by connecting what they've read to other texts or personal experiences.

RESPOND: Students will write a summary to demonstrate their understanding.

Point out to students that while they will always complete the Respond step at the end of the first read, the other steps will probably happen somewhat concurrently. Remind students that they will revisit their first-read annotations during the close read.

After students have completed the First-Read Guide, you may wish to assign the Text Questions for the selection that are available in the Interactive Teacher's Edition.

Anchor Standards

In the first two sections of the unit, students worked with the whole class and in small groups to gain topical knowledge and greater understanding of the skills required by the anchor standards. In this section, they are asked to work independently, applying what they have learned and demonstrating increased readiness for college and career.

INDEPENDENT LEARNING

First-Read Guide

Tool Kit
First-Read Guide and Model Annotation

Use this page to record your first-read ideas.

Selection Title: ____________________

NOTICE new information or ideas you learn about the unit topic as you first read this text.

ANNOTATE by marking vocabulary and key passages you want to revisit.

CONNECT ideas within the selection to other knowledge and the selections you have read.

RESPOND by writing a brief summary of the selection.

STANDARD
Reading Read and comprehend complex literary and informational texts independently and proficiently.

532 UNIT 5 • FACING ADVERSITY

PERSONALIZE FOR LEARNING

Challenge

Additional Questions To help students reflect on their first read and prepare for the close read, encourage them to think about what more they would like to know about a text. Ask students to write two to three questions they have about the text. Then, students can meet in small groups with others who have read the same text. Each group can share First-Read Guides and their additional questions before proceeding to the close read.

Close-Read Guide

Tool Kit
Close-Read Guide and Model Annotation

Use this page to record your close-read ideas.

Selection Title: ______________________________

Close Read the Text

Revisit sections of the text you marked during your first read. Read these sections closely and **annotate** what you notice. Ask yourself **questions** about the text. What can you **conclude?** Write down your ideas.

Analyze the Text

Think about the author's choices of patterns, structure, techniques, and ideas included in the text. Select one, and record your thoughts about what this choice conveys.

QuickWrite

Pick a paragraph from the text that grabbed your interest. Explain the power of this passage.

STANDARD
Reading Read and comprehend complex literary and informational texts independently and proficiently.

DIGITAL PERSPECTIVES

CLOSE READ

Students should begin their close read by revisiting the annotations they made during their first read. Then, students should analyze one of the author's choices regarding the following elements:

- **patterns,** such as repetition or parallelism
- **structure,** such as cause-and-effect or problem-solution
- **techniques,** such as description or dialogue
- **ideas,** such as the author's main idea or claim

MAKE IT INTERACTIVE
Group students according to the selection they have chosen. Then, have students meet to discuss the selection in-depth. Their discussions should be guided by their insights and questions.

PERSONALIZE FOR LEARNING

Challenge

Group Review Have students who have read the same text collaborate to write a group review of the entire text. The review should include a summary and excerpts from each group member's Close-Read Guide. Group members should agree on contributions, the order in which the excerpts will appear, and how the excerpts will fit into paragraphs within the review. Together, group members should revise and edit the writing for coverage of the entire text, and make sure ideas are logically organized and expressed clearly. They can use signal words and transitions to connect the ideas and writing of all the contributors. After editing and proofreading, the completed reviews may be posted in a blog or printed and distributed to the class.

ADVISING

Share Your Independent Learning

Prepare to Share

Explain to students that sharing what they learned from their Independent Learning selection provides classmates who read a different selection with an opportunity to consider the text as a source of evidence during the Performance-Based Assessment. As students prepare to share, remind them to highlight how their selection contributed to their knowledge of the concept of facing adversity as well as how the selection connects to the question *How do we overcome obstacles?*

Learn From Your Classmates

As students discuss the Independent Learning selections, direct them to take particular note of how their classmates' chosen selections align with their current position on the Performance-Based Assessment question.

Reflect

Students may want to add their reflection to their Evidence Log, particularly if their insight relates to a specific selection from the unit.

MAKE IT INTERACTIVE

With students, create a game of "Concentration" by naming obstacles that people face in life and how the obstacles can be overcome. Make up fifteen 3-by-5-inch index cards with an obstacle or a way to overcome an obstacle written on each card. Then, make a matching set of cards. (You will have 30 cards altogether.) Shuffle all of the cards. Place the cards face down in five rows of 6 each. Each person then takes one turn, turning over two cards. If they match, the cards remain right side up. If they do not match, they are placed face down again, and the next person takes a turn. The game continues until all of the cards are matched and face up.

Evidence Log Support students in completing their Evidence Log. This paced activity will help prepare them for the Performance-Based Assessment at the end of the unit.

INDEPENDENT LEARNING

EVIDENCE LOG

Go to your Evidence Log and record what you learned from the text you read.

Share Your Independent Learning

Prepare to Share

How do we overcome obstacles?

Even when you read something independently, your understanding continues to grow when you share what you have learned with others. Reflect on the text you explored independently and write notes about its connection to the unit. In your notes, consider why this text belongs in this unit.

Learn From Your Classmates

Discuss It Share your ideas about the text you explored on your own. As you talk with your classmates, jot down ideas that you learn from them.

Reflect

Review your notes, and mark the most important insight you gained from these writing and discussion activities. Explain how this idea adds to your understanding of the topic of facing adversity.

STANDARDS

Speaking and Listening

Engage effectively in a range of collaborative discussions with diverse partners on *grade 7 topics, texts, and issues,* building on others' ideas and expressing their own clearly.

AUTHOR'S PERSPECTIVE **Ernest Morrell, Ph.D.**

Powerful Speaking in Small Groups

Explain to students that learning how to speak with confidence, without over-compensating, will help them make and/or defend an argument and point of view in a small group. Point out that their goal is to be convincing, but not argumentative. To help build this skill, provide students with the following guidelines:

1. Earn credibility. Speakers who are prepared with evidence tailored to their audience's needs will sway their audience with the power of their proof. As a result, these speakers will have no need to try to harass or intimidate their listeners.

2. Choose words carefully. Effective speakers use the exact words they need, words that convey their precise meaning. Further, effective speakers avoid "loaded words" that attempt to sway an audience by appealing to stereotypes.

3. Be audible, not loud. Speakers who avoid shouting convey their point with greater confidence than those who do raise their voices

PERFORMANCE-BASED ASSESSMENT PREP

Review Evidence for an Informative Essay

At the beginning of this unit, you expressed your ideas about the following question:

How can people overcome adversity in the face of overwhelming obstacles?

EVIDENCE LOG

Review your Evidence Log and your QuickWrite from the beginning of the unit. Did you learn anything new?

NOTES

Identify at least three things that you learned about how we overcome obstacles.

1.

2.

3.

Identify a real-life experience that illustrates one of your ideas about how we overcome obstacles. ______________________________
____
____

Develop your thoughts into a topic sentence for an informative essay. Complete this sentence starter:

As events and details in ______________________________

show, people can overcome obstacles by ______________________________

____

Evaluate the Strength of Your Evidence Consider your ideas about overcoming obstacles. How did the texts you read affect your ideas? Identify relevant details in the texts that deepened your understanding of the ways in which people overcome obstacles. Also, note specific passages in the texts that gave you key insights or changed your ideas about facing adversity.

STANDARDS

Writing

Write informative/explanatory texts to examine a topic and convey ideas, concepts, and information through the selection, organization, and analysis of relevant content.

a. Introduce a topic clearly, previewing what is to follow; organize ideas, concepts, and information, using strategies such as definition, classification, comparison/contrast, and cause/effect; include formatting, graphics, and multimedia when useful to aiding comprehension.

b. Develop the topic with relevant facts, definitions, concrete details, quotations, or other information and examples.

DIGITAL PERSPECTIVES

Review Evidence for an Informative Essay

Evidence Log Students should understand that their informative essay can evolve as they learn more about the subject and are exposed to additional points of view. Point out that just because students identified three things about how we overcome obstacles for the question *How can people overcome adversity in the face of overwhelming obstacles?* doesn't mean that those three things can't change after careful consideration of their learning and evidence.

Evaluate the Strength of Your Evidence Encourage students to keep in mind that their informative essay should include evidence. Their evidence should support the viewpoint and perceptions that they write about. Evidence may include facts such as statistics, physical details, anecdotes (personal experience of the student or others), and expert opinion. The evidence that they provide in their essay should support and strengthen their viewpoint.

Writing to Sources: Informative Essay

Students should complete the Performance-Based Assessment independently, with little to no input or feedback during the process. Students should use word processing software to take advantage of editing tools and features.

Prior to beginning the assessment, ask students to think about obstacles they have faced and overcome, and how they did it.

Review the Elements of an Effective Informative Essay Students can review the work they did earlier in the unit as they complete the Performance-Based Assessment. They may also consult other resources such as:

- the elements of an informative essay, including relevant facts, descriptions, and examples that illustrate causes and effects, and detailed explanations that show cause-and-effect relationships, available in Whole-Class Learning
- their Evidence Log
- their Word Network

Although students will use evidence from unit selections for their informative essays, they may need to collect additional evidence, including relevant facts, details, and quotations from the text.

SOURCES

- WHOLE-CLASS SELECTIONS
- SMALL-GROUP SELECTIONS
- INDEPENDENT-LEARNING SELECTION

WORD NETWORK

As you write and revise your essay, use your Word Network to help vary your word choices.

STANDARDS

Writing

- Write informative/explanatory texts to examine a topic and convey ideas, concepts, and information through the selection, organization, and analysis of relevant content.
- Produce clear and coherent writing in which the development, organization, and style are appropriate to task, purpose, and audience.
- Draw evidence from literary or informational texts to support analysis, reflection, and research.
- Write routinely over extended time frames and shorter time frames for a range of discipline-specific tasks, purposes, and audiences.

PART 1

Writing to Sources: Informative Essay

In this unit, you read about people who overcame various obstacles. You will now write an informative essay in which you explore the topic of facing adversity as illustrated by the selections in this unit.

Assignment

Write an **informative essay** in response to the following question:

How can people overcome adversity in the face of overwhelming obstacles?

Develop a clear thesis in response to the prompt. Your thesis for this informative essay should make a generalization about ways in which people persevere as they struggle to overcome adversity.

Then, use specific examples and quotations from the selections to support your response. Your ideas should be logically organized, and your essay should include transitions to show the relationships between ideas. Use precise vocabulary and a formal tone in your writing. Be sure to include a conclusion that follows from and supports the information in your essay.

Reread the Assignment Review the assignment to be sure you fully understand it. The assignment may reference some of the academic words presented at the beginning of the unit. Be sure you understand each of the words given below in order to complete the assignment correctly.

Academic Vocabulary

deviate	determination	tradition
persevere	diversity	

Review the Elements of an Effective Informative Essay Before you begin writing, read the Informative Essay Rubric. Once you have completed your first draft, check it against the rubric. If one or more of the elements is missing or not as strong as it could be, revise your essay to add or strengthen that component.

Informative Essay Rubric

	Focus and Organization	Evidence and Elaboration	Conventions
4	The introduction is engaging and includes a clear thesis. The thesis is supported by specific details, examples, and quotations from the selections. Ideas are logically organized so that the explanation is easy to follow. Transitions clearly show the relationships among ideas. The conclusion supports the information in the essay and offers fresh insight into the topic.	Details, examples, and quotations from the selections are specific and relevant. The style and tone is formal and objective. Words are carefully chosen and suited to purpose and audience.	The essay consistently adheres to standard English conventions of usage and mechanics.
3	The introduction includes a clear thesis. The thesis is supported by details, examples, and quotations from the selections. Ideas are organized so that the information is easy to follow. Transitions show the relationships among ideas. The conclusion supports the information in the essay.	Details, examples, and quotations from the selections are relevant. The style and tone is mostly formal and objective. Words are generally suited to purpose and audience.	The essay mostly adheres to standard English conventions of usage and mechanics.
2	The introduction states the thesis. The thesis is supported by some details, examples, and quotations from the selections. Ideas are vaguely organized, with a few transitions to orient readers. The conclusion relates to the information in the essay.	Some details and examples from the selection are relevant. The style and tone is occasionally formal and objective. Words are somewhat suited to purpose and audience.	The essay contains some mistakes in standard English conventions of usage and mechanics.
1	The thesis is not clearly stated. The thesis is not supported by details, examples, and quotations from the selections. Ideas are disorganized and the explanation is difficult to follow. The conclusion does not include relevant information.	There is little or no relevant support. The style and tone is informal. Words are not appropriate to purpose or audience.	The essay contains many mistakes in standard English conventions of usage and mechanics.

DIGITAL PERSPECTIVES

Informative Essay Rubric

As you review the Informative Rubric with students, remind them that the rubric is a resource that can guide their revisions. Students should pay particular attention to the differences between an essay that includes transitions that show the relationships among ideas (a score of 3) and transitions that *clearly* show the relationships among ideas (a score of 4).

Speaking and Listening: Oral Presentation

Students should annotate their written informative essay in preparation for the oral presentation, marking the important elements (thesis, quotations drawn from text) as well as any supporting facts or statistics.

Remind students that the effectiveness of an oral informative essay relies on how the speaker establishes credibility with his or her audience. If a speaker comes across as confident and authoritative, it will be easier for the audience to give credence to the speaker's presentation.

Review the Oral Presentation Rubric As you review the Oral Presentation Rubric with students, remind them that it is a valuable tool that can help them plan their presentation. They should strive to include all of the criteria required to achieve a score of 3. Draw their attention to some of the subtle differences between scores of 2 and 3.

PERFORMANCE-BASED ASSESSMENT

STANDARDS

Writing

Use technology, including the Internet, to produce and publish writing and link to and cite sources as well as to interact and collaborate with others, including linking to and citing sources.

Speaking and Listening

- Present claims and findings, emphasizing salient points in a focused, coherent manner with pertinent descriptions, facts, details, and examples; use appropriate eye contact, adequate volume, and clear pronunciation.
- Include multimedia components and visual displays in presentations to clarify claims and findings and emphasize salient points.

PART 2

Speaking and Listening: Oral Presentation

Assignment

After completing your informative essay, use it as the foundation for a brief **multimedia presentation.** Record your presentation and post it on a class or school Web site so you can watch the presentations outside of class and respond and interact digitally.

Use these tips to make your presentation engaging:

- Review your essay, and mark the most important ideas and supporting details from your introduction, body paragraphs, and conclusion.
- Use appropriate eye contact, and speak with clear pronunciation and adequate volume.
- Include well-sequenced multimedia that emphasizes key points.

Review the Oral Presentation Rubric Before you deliver your presentation, check your plans against this rubric.

	Content	Organization	Presentation Techniques
3	The introduction states the thesis in a compelling way. The presentation includes specific examples, quotations, and multimedia elements. The conclusion offers fresh insight into the topic.	The speaker uses time effectively. Ideas progress logically, with clear transition among ideas. The timing of the images matches the timing of the explanation.	The speaker maintains effective eye contact and speaks clearly and with adequate volume.
2	The introduction states a thesis. The presentation includes examples, quotations, and multimedia elements. The conclusion offers some insight into the topic.	The speaker uses time effectively, spending the right amount of time on most parts. Ideas progress logically with some transitions among ideas. Listeners can mostly follow the speaker's explanation.	The speaker sometimes maintains effective eye contact and speaks somewhat clearly and with adequate volume.
1	The introduction does not clearly state a thesis. The presentation does not include examples, quotations, or multimedia elements. The conclusion does not restate important information.	The speaker does not use time effectively. Ideas do not progress logically.	The speaker does not maintain effective eye contact or speak clearly with adequate volume.

DIGITAL PERSPECTIVES

Preparing for the Assignment To help students understand what an effective oral presentation of an essay looks and sounds like, find examples on the Internet of students or adults reading from their own work. Project the examples for the class, and have students note the techniques that make each speaker successful (gesture, pacing, tone, and so on). Suggest that students record themselves presenting their informative essays so they can practice incorporating some of the elements in the examples you showed them.

Reflect on the Unit

Now that you've completed the unit, take a few moments to reflect on your learning.

Reflect on the Unit Goals

Look back at the goals at the beginning of the unit. Use a different colored pen to rate yourself again. Think about readings and activities that contributed the most to the growth of your understanding. Record your thoughts.

Reflect on the Learning Strategies

Discuss It Write a reflection on whether you were able to improve your learning based on your Action Plans. Think about what worked, what didn't, and what you might do to keep working on these strategies. Record your ideas before a class discussion.

Reflect on the Text

Choose a selection that you found challenging and explain what made it difficult.

Describe something that surprised you about a text in the unit.

Which activity taught you the most about facing adversity and overcoming obstacles? What did you learn?

DIGITAL PERSPECTIVES   

Reflect on the Unit

- Have students watch the video on Reflecting on Your Learning.
- A video on this topic is available online in the Professional Development Center.

Reflect on the Unit Goals

Students should re-evaluate how well they met the unit goals now that they have completed the unit. You might ask them to provide a written commentary on the goal they made the most progress with as well as the goal they feel warrants continued focus.

Reflect on the Learning Strategies

Discuss It If you want to make this a digital activity, go online and navigate to the Discussion Board. Alternatively, students can share their learning strategies reflections in a class discussion.

Reflect on the Text

Consider having students share their text reflections with one another.

MAKE IT INTERACTIVE

Have students prepare one slide using presentation software that summarizes their reflection.

Collate student slides into a presentation that can be viewed by the class. Students should be prepared to give a 30-second oral summary for their slide.

Unit Test and Remediation 

After students have completed the Performance-Based Assessment, administer the Unit Test. Based on students' performance on the test, assign the resources as indicated on the Interpretation Guide to remediate. Students who take the test online will be automatically assigned remediation, as warranted by test results.

RESOURCES

CONTENTS

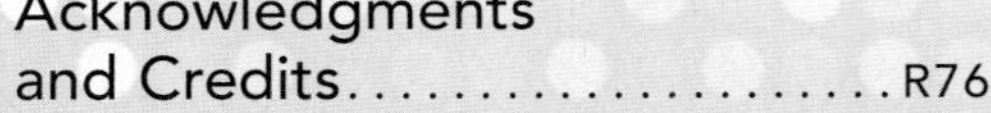

Marking the Text: Strategies and Tips for Annotation

When you close read a text, you read for comprehension and then reread to unlock layers of meaning and to analyze a writer's style and techniques. Marking a text as you read it enables you to participate more fully in the close-reading process.

Following are some strategies for text mark-ups, along with samples of how the strategies can be applied. These mark-ups are suggestions; you and your teacher may want to use other mark-up strategies.

*	Key Idea
!	I love it!
?	I have questions
◯	Unfamiliar or important word
----	Context Clues

Suggested Mark-Up Notations

WHAT I NOTICE	HOW TO MARK UP	QUESTIONS TO ASK
Key Ideas and Details	• Highlight key ideas or claims. • Underline supporting details or evidence.	• What does the text say? What does it leave unsaid? • What inferences do you need to make? • What details lead you to make your inferences?
Word Choice	• Circle unfamiliar words. • Put a dotted line under context clues, if any exist. • Put an exclamation point beside especially rich or poetic passages.	• What inferences about word meaning can you make? • What tone and mood are created by word choice? • What alternate word choices might the author have made?
Text Structure	• Highlight passages that show key details supporting the main idea. • Use arrows to indicate how sentences and paragraphs work together to build ideas. • Use a right-facing arrow to indicate foreshadowing. • Use a left-facing arrow to indicate flashback.	• Is the text logically structured? • What emotional impact do the structural choices create?
Author's Craft	• Circle or highlight instances of repetition, either of words, phrases, consonants, or vowel sounds. • Mark rhythmic beats in poetry using checkmarks and slashes. • Underline instances of symbolism or figurative language.	• Does the author's style enrich or detract from the reading experience? • What levels of meaning are created by the author's techniques?

* Key Idea
! I love it!
? I have questions
◯ Unfamiliar or important word
---- Context Clues

NOTES

In a first read, work to get a sense of the main idea of a text. Look for key details and ideas that help you understand what the author conveys to you. Mark passages which prompt a strong response from you.

Here is how one reader marked up this text.

MODEL

INFORMATIONAL TEXT

from Classifying the Stars

Cecilia H. Payne

1 Sunlight and starlight are composed of waves of various lengths, which the eye, even aided by a telescope, is unable to separate. We must use more than a telescope. In order to sort out the component colors, the light must be dispersed by a prism, or split up by some other means. For instance, sunbeams passing through rain drops are transformed into the myriad-tinted rainbow. The familiar rainbow spanning the sky is Nature's most glorious demonstration that light is composed of many colors.

2 The very beginning of our knowledge of the nature of a star dates back to 1672, when Isaac Newton gave to the world the results of his experiments on passing sunlight through a prism. To describe the beautiful band of rainbow tints, produced when sunlight was dispersed by his three-cornered piece of glass, he took from the Latin the word *spectrum*, meaning an appearance. The rainbow is the spectrum of the Sun. . . .

3 In 1814, more than a century after Newton, the spectrum of the Sun was obtained in such purity that an amazing detail was seen and studied by the German optician, Fraunhofer. He saw that the multiple spectral tints, ranging from delicate violet to deep red, were crossed by hundreds of fine dark lines. In other words, there were narrow gaps in the spectrum where certain shades were wholly blotted out. We must remember that the word spectrum is applied not only to sunlight, but also to the light of any glowing substance when its rays are sorted out by a prism or a grating.

MODEL

First-Read Guide

You may want to use a guide like this to organize your thoughts after you read. Here is how a reader completed a First-Read Guide.

Use this page to record your first-read ideas.

Selection Title: Classifying the Stars

NOTICE new information or ideas you learned about the unit topic as you first read this text.

Light = different waves of colors. (Spectrum)

Newton - the first person to observe these waves using a prism.

Faunhofer saw gaps in the spectrum.

ANNOTATE by marking vocabulary and key passages you want to revisit.

Vocabulary
- myriad
- grating
- component colors

Different light types = different lengths

Isaac Newton also worked theories of gravity.

Multiple spectral tints? "colors of various appearance"

Key Passage:
Paragraph 3 shows that Fraunhofer discovered more about the nature of light spectrums: he saw the spaces in between the tints.

NOTICE ANNOTATE First Read CONNECT RESPOND

CONNECT ideas within the selection to other knowledge and the selections you have read.

I remember learning about prisms in science class.

Double rainbows! My favorite. How are they made?

RESPOND by writing a brief summary of the selection.

Science allows us to see things not visible to the naked eye. What we see as sunlight is really a spectrum of colors. By using tools, such as prisms, we can see the components of sunlight and other light. They appear as single colors or as multiple colors separated by gaps of no color. White light contains a rainbow of colors.

CLOSE READING

* Key Idea
! I love it!
? I have questions
Unfamiliar or important word
---- Context Clues

In a close read, go back into the text to study it in greater detail. Take the time to analyze not only the author's ideas but the way that those ideas are conveyed. Consider the genre of the text, the author's word choice, the writer's unique style, and the message of the text.

Here is how one reader close read this text.

MODEL

INFORMATIONAL TEXT

from Classifying the Stars

Cecilia H. Payne

NOTES

explanation of sunlight and starlight

What is light and where do the colors come from?

This paragraph is about Newton and the prism.

What discoveries helped us understand light?

Fraunhofer and gaps in spectrum

1 Sunlight and starlight are composed of waves of various lengths, which the eye, even aided by a telescope, is unable to separate. We must use more than a telescope. In order to sort out the component colors, the light must be dispersed by a prism, or split up by some other means. For instance, sunbeams passing through rain drops are transformed into the myriad-tinted rainbow. The familiar rainbow spanning the sky is Nature's most glorious demonstration that light is composed of many colors.

2 The very beginning of our knowledge of the nature of a star dates back to 1672, when Isaac Newton gave to the world the results of his experiments on passing sunlight through a prism. To describe the beautiful band of rainbow tints, produced when sunlight was dispersed by his three-cornered piece of glass, he took from the Latin the word *spectrum*, meaning an appearance. The rainbow is the spectrum of the Sun. . . .

3 In 1814, more than a century after Newton, the spectrum of the Sun was obtained in such purity that an amazing detail was seen and studied by the German optician, Fraunhofer. He saw that the multiple spectral tints, ranging from delicate violet to deep red, were crossed by hundreds of fine dark lines. In other words, there were narrow gaps in the spectrum where certain shades were wholly blotted out. We must remember that the word spectrum is applied not only to sunlight, but also to the light of any glowing substance when its rays are sorted out by a prism or a grating.

MODEL

Close-Read Guide

Use this page to record your close-read ideas.

> You can use the Close-Read Guide to help you dig deeper into the text. Here is how a reader completed a Close-Read Guide.

Selection Title: Classifying the Stars

Close Read the Text

Revisit sections of the text you marked during your first read. Read these sections closely and **annotate** what you notice. Ask yourself **questions** about the text. What can you **conclude?** Write down your ideas.

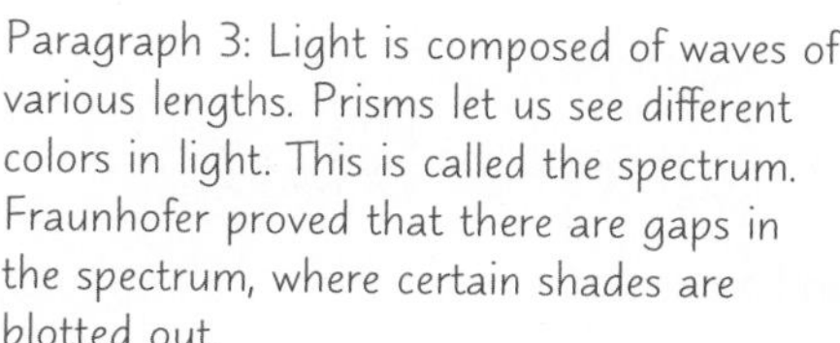

Paragraph 3: Light is composed of waves of various lengths. Prisms let us see different colors in light. This is called the spectrum. Fraunhofer proved that there are gaps in the spectrum, where certain shades are blotted out.

More than one researcher studied this and each built off the ideas that were already discovered.

Analyze the Text

Think about the author's choices of patterns, structure, techniques, and ideas included in the text. Select one, and record your thoughts about what this choice conveys.

The author showed the development of human knowledge of the spectrum chronologically. Helped me see how ideas were built upon earlier understandings. Used dates and "more than a century after Newton" to show time.

QuickWrite

Pick a paragraph from the text that grabbed your interest. Explain the power of this passage.

The first paragraph grabbed my attention, specifically the sentence "The familiar rainbow spanning the sky is Nature's most glorious demonstration that light is composed of many colors." The paragraph began as a straightforward scientific explanation. When I read the word "glorious," I had to stop and deeply consider what was being said. It is a word loaded with personal feelings. With that one word, the author let the reader know what was important to her.

TOOL KIT: CLOSE READING

WRITING

Argument

When you think of the word *argument,* you might think of a disagreement between two people, but the word has another meaning, too. An argument is a logical way of presenting a belief, conclusion, or stance. A good argument is supported with reasoning and evidence.

Argument writing can be used for many purposes, such as changing a reader's opinion or bringing about an action or a response from a reader.

Elements of an Argumentative Text

An **argument** sets forth a belief or stand on an issue. A well-written argument may convince the reader, change the reader's mind, or motivate the reader to take a certain action.

An effective argument contains these elements:

- a precise claim
- consideration of alternate claims, or opposing positions, and a discussion of their strengths and weaknesses
- logical organization that makes clear connections among claim, reasons, and evidence
- valid reasoning and evidence
- a concluding statement or section that follows from and supports the argument
- formal and objective language and tone
- error-free grammar, including accurate use of transitions

MODEL

ARGUMENT: SCORE 1

Celebrities Should Try to Be Better Role Models

A lot of Celebrities are singers or actors or actresses or athletes. Kids spend tons of time watching Celebrities on TV. They listen to their songs. They read about them. They watch them play and perform. No matter weather the Celebrities are good people or bad people. Kids still spend time watching them. The kids will try to imitate what they do. Some of them have parents or brothers and sisters who are famous also.

Celebrities don't seem to watch out what they do and how they live. Some say, *"Why do I care? It's none of you're business"!* Well, that's true. But it's bad on them if they do all kinds of stupid things. Because this is bad for the kids who look up to them.

Sometimes celebrity's say they wish they are not role models. *"I'm just an actor!" "I'm just a singer"!* they say. But the choice is not really up to them. If their on TV all the time, then kids' will look up to them, no matter what. It's stupid when Celebrities mess up and then nothing bad happens to them. That gives kids a bad lesson. Kids will think that you can do stupid things and be fine. That is not being a good role model.

Some Celebrities give money to charity. That's a good way to be a good role model. But sometimes it seems like Celebrities are just totally messed up. It's hard always being in the spotlight. That can drive Celebrities kind of crazy. Then they act out.

It is a good idea to support charities when you are rich and famous. You can do a lot of good. For a lot of people. Some Celebrities give out cars or houses or free scholarships. You can even give away your dresses and people can have an auction to see who will pay the most money for them. This can help for example the Humane Society. Or whatever charity or cause the celebrity wants to support.

Celebrities are fun to watch and follow, even when they mess up. I think they don't realize that when they do bad things, they give teens wrong ideas about how to live. They should try to keep that under control. So many teens look up to them and copy them, no matter what.

The claim is not clearly stated in the introduction or elsewhere.

Some of the ideas in the essay do not relate to the stated position or focus on the issue.

The word choice in the essay is not effective and lends it an informal tone.

The progression of ideas is not logical or well-controlled.

Errors in spelling, capitalization, punctuation, grammar, usage, and sentence boundaries are frequent. The fluency of the writing and effectiveness of the essay are affected by these errors.

The conclusion does not clearly restate the claim.

WRITING

MODEL

ARGUMENT: SCORE 2

Celebrities Should Try to Be Better Role Models

Most kids spend tons of time watching celebrities on TV, listening to their songs, and reading about them. No matter how celebrities behave—whether they do good things or bad—they are role models for kids. They often do really dumb things, and that is not good considering they are role models.

> The introduction does not state the argument claim clearly enough.

Sometimes celebrity's say they wish they were not role models. *"I'm just an actor!"* or, *"I'm just a singer!"* they say. But the choice is not really up to them. If they are on TV all the time, then kids' will look up to them. No matter what. It's really bad when celebrities mess up and then nothing bad happens to them. That gives kids a false lesson because in reality there are bad things when you mess up. That's why celebrities should think more about what they are doing and what lessons they are giving to kids.

> Errors in spelling, grammar, and sentence boundaries decrease the effectiveness of the essay.

Some celebrities might say, *"Why do I care? Why should I be bothered?"* Well, they don't have to. But it's bad on them if they do all kinds of stupid things and don't think about how this affects the kids who look up to them. Plus, they get tons of money, much more even than inventors or scientists or other important people. Being a good role model should be part of what they have to do to get so much money.

> The word choice in the essay contributes to an informal tone.

When you are famous it is a good idea to support charities. Some celebrities give out cars, or houses, or free scholarships. They even sometimes give away their dresses and people have an auction to see who will pay the most money for them. This can help for example the Humane Society, or whatever charity or cause the celebrity wants to support.

> The writer does not make use of transitions and sentence connections.

Sometimes it seems like celebrities are more messed up than anyone else. That's in their personal lives. Imagine if people wanted to take pictures of you wherever you went, and you could never get away. That can drive celebrities kind of crazy, and then they act out.

> Some of the ideas in the essay do not relate to the stated position or focus on the issue.

Celebrities can do good things and they can do bad things. They don't realize that when they do bad things, they give teens wrong ideas about how to live. So many teens look up to them and copy them, no matter what. They should make an effort to be better role models.

> The essay has a clear conclusion.

TOOL KIT: WRITING

MODEL

ARGUMENT: SCORE 3

Celebrities Should Try to Be Better Role Models

Kids look up to the celebrities they see on TV and want to be like them. Parents may not *want* celebrities to be role models for their children, but they are anyway. Therefore, celebrities should think about what they say and do and live lives that are worth copying. Celebrities should think about how they act because they are role models.

"I'm just an actor!" or, *"I'm just a singer!"* celebrities sometimes say. *"Their parents and teachers are the ones who should be the role models!"* But it would be foolish to misjudge the impact that celebrities have on youth. Kids spend hours every day digitally hanging with their favorite stars. Children learn by imitation, so, for better or worse, celebrities are role models. That's why celebrities should start modeling good decision-making and good citizenship.

With all that they are given by society, celebrities owe a lot back to their communities and the world. Celebrities get a lot of attention, time, and money. Often they get all that for doing not very much: acting, singing, or playing a sport. It's true; some of them work very hard. But even if they work very hard, do they deserve to be in the news all the time and earn 100 or even 1000 times more than equally hard-working teachers, scientists, or nurses? I don't think so. After receiving all that, it seems only fair that celebrities take on the important job of being good role models for the young people who look up to them.

Celebrities can serve as good role models is by giving back. Quite a few use their fame and fortune to do just that. They give scholarships, or even build and run schools; they help veterans; they visit hospitals; they support important causes such as conservation, and women's rights. They donate not just money but their time and talents too. This is a great way to be a role model.

Celebrities should recognize that as role models, they have a responsibility to try to make good decisions and be honest. Celebrities should step up so they can be a force for good in people's lives and in the world.

The writer's word choice is good but could be better.

The introduction mostly states the claim.

The ideas relate to the stated position and focus on the issue.

The sentences are varied and well controlled and enhance the effectiveness of the essay.

The progression of ideas is logical, but there could be better transitions and sentence connections to show how ideas are related.

The conclusion mostly follows from the claim.

WRITING

MODEL

ARGUMENT: SCORE 4

Celebrities Should Try to Be Better Role Models

Like it or not, kids look up to the celebrities they see on TV and want to be like them. Parents may not *want* celebrities to be role models for their children, but the fact is that they are. With such an oversized influence on young people, celebrities have a responsibility to think about what they say and do and to live lives that are worth emulating. In short, they should make an effort to be better role models.

Sometimes celebrities say they don't want to be role models. "I'm just an actor!" or "I'm just a singer!" they protest. "Their parents and teachers are the ones who should be guiding them and showing them the right way to live!" That is all very well, but it would be foolish to underestimate the impact that celebrities have on children. Kids spend hours every day digitally hanging out with their favorite stars. Children learn by imitation, so for better or worse, celebrities act as role models.

Celebrities are given a lot of attention, time, and money. They get all that for doing very little: acting, singing, or playing a sport very well. It's true some of them work very hard. But even if they work hard, do they deserve to be in the news all the time and earn 100 or even 1,000 times more than equally hardworking teachers, scientists, or nurses? I don't think so.

With all that they are given, celebrities owe a lot to their communities and the world. One way they can serve as good role models is by giving back, and quite a few celebrities use their fame and fortune to do just that. They give scholarships or even build and run schools; they help veterans; they entertain kids who are sick; they support important causes such as conservation and women's rights. They donate not just money but their time and talents too.

Celebrities don't have to be perfect. They are people too and make mistakes. But they should recognize that as role models for youth, they have a responsibility to try to make good decisions and be honest about their struggles. Celebrities should step up so they can be a force for good in people's lives.

The writer has chosen words that contribute to the clarity of the essay.

The writer clearly states the claim of the argument in the introduction.

The essay is engaging and varied.

There are no errors to distract the reader from the fluency of the writing and effectiveness of the essay.

The writer uses transitions and sentence connections to show how ideas are related.

The writer clearly restates the claim and the most powerful idea presented in the essay.

Argument Rubric

	Focus and Organization	Development	Language/Conventions
4	The introduction is effective and states the claim in a relevant way. The claim is supported by clear reasons and relevant evidence. Reasons and evidence are clear and logically organized so that the argument is cohesive and easy to follow. The conclusion is clear and effective.	Sources are credible and accurate, and effectively support the claim. The argument demonstrates an understanding of the thesis by providing strong evidence and effectively addressing counterclaims.	The argument consistently uses precise language and standard English. The argument demonstrates sophisticated sentence structures and varied word choice. The tone of the argument is formal and objective.
3	The introduction is effective and states the claim. The claim is mostly supported by logical reasons and evidence. Reasons and evidence are organized so that the argument is mostly easy to follow. The conclusion is mostly clear and effective.	Sources are mostly credible and accurate and support the claim. The argument mostly demonstrates an understanding of the thesis by providing adequate evidence and addressing counterclaims.	The argument mostly demonstrates use of precise language and accuracy in standard English. The argument demonstrates varied sentence structures and word choice. The tone of the argument is mostly formal and objective.
2	The introduction is limited, and the stated argument is weak. The claim is supported by some reasons and evidence but is sometimes difficult to follow. Reasons and evidence are organized somewhat logically with occasional lapses. The conclusion somewhat relates to the claim.	Some sources are relevant and support the claim. The argument demonstrates some understanding of the thesis by providing some evidence and an attempt to address counterclaims.	The argument demonstrates inconsistent command of precise language and accuracy in standard English. The argument uses basic or repetitive sentence structures and word choice. The tone of the argument is somewhat formal and objective.
1	The claim is not clearly stated. The claim is not supported by reasons and evidence. Reasons and evidence are disorganized and the argument is difficult to follow. The conclusion does not exist or does not include relevant information.	There is little or no reliable, relevant evidence The argument does not demonstrate an understanding of the thesis and does not provide examples.	The argument contains mistakes in standard English. The argument demonstrate little or no variety in sentence structures or word choice. The tone of the argument is informal.

Informative/Explanatory Texts

Informative and explanatory writing should rely on facts to inform or explain. Informative writing serves several purposes: to increase readers' knowledge of a subject, to help readers better understand a procedure or process, or to provide readers with an enhanced comprehension of a concept. It should also feature a clear introduction, body, and conclusion.

Information/explanatory texts present facts, details, data, and other kinds of evidence to give information about a topic. Readers turn to informational and explanatory texts when they wish to learn about a specific idea, concept, or subject area, or if they want to learn how to do something.

An effective informational/explanatory text contains these elements:

- a topic sentence or thesis statement that introduces the concept or subject
- relevant facts, examples, and details that expand upon a topic
- definitions, quotations, and/or graphics that support the information given
- headings (if desired) to separate sections of the essay
- a structure that presents information in a direct, clear manner
- clear transitions that link sections of the essay
- precise words and technical vocabulary where appropriate
- formal and objective language and tone
- a conclusion that supports the information given and provides fresh insights

MODEL

INFORMATIVE: SCORE 1

Kids, School, and Exercise: Problems and Solutions

In the past, children ran around and even did hard physical labor. Today most kid's just sit most of the time. They don't know the old Outdoor Games. Like tether ball. and they don't have hard chores to do. Like milking the cows. But children should be Physically Active quite a bit every day. That doesn't happen very much any more. Not as much as it should anyway.

Even at home when kid's have a chance to run around, they choose to sit and play video games, for example. Some schools understand that it's a problem when students don't get enough exercise. Even though they have had to cut Physical Education classes. Some also had to make recess shorter.

But lots of schools are working hard to find ways to get kid's moving around again. Like they used to long ago.

Schools use volunteers to teach kid's old-fashioned games. Old-fashioned games are an awesome way to get kid's moving around like crazy people.

Some schools have before school activities. Such as games in the gym. Other schools have after school activities. Such as bike riding or outdoor games. They can't count on kid's to be active. Not even on their own or at home. So they do the activities all together. Kids enjoy doing stuff with their friends. So that works out really well.

If you don't exercise you get overweight. You can end up with high blood pressure and too much colesterol. Of course its also a problem if you eat too much junk food all the time. But not getting enough exercise is part of the problem too. That's why schools need to try to be part of the solution.

A break during class to move around helps. Good teachers know how to use exercise during classes. There are all kinds of ways to move in the classroom that don't mean you have to change your clothes. Classes don't have to be just about math and science.

Schools are doing what they can to get kids moving, doing exercise, being active. Getting enough exercise also helps kid's do better in school. Being active also helps kids get strong.

There are extensive errors in spelling, capitalization, punctuation, grammar, usage, and sentence boundaries.

Many of the ideas in the essay do not focus on the topic.

The word choice shows the writer's lack of awareness of the essay's purpose and tone.

The essay's sentences are not purposeful, varied, or well-controlled. The writer's sentences decrease the effectiveness of the essay.

The essay is not well organized. Its structure does not support its purpose or respond well to the demands of the prompt.

The essay is not particularly thoughtful or engaging.

MODEL

INFORMATIVE: SCORE 2

Kids, School, and Exercise: Problems and Solutions

In the past, children ran around a lot and did chores and other physical work. Today most kid's sit by a TV or computer screen or play with their phones. But children should be active for at least 60 minutes a day. Sadly, most don't get nearly that much exercise. And that's a big problem.

Some schools understand that it's a problem when students don't get enough exercise. Even though they have had to cut Physical Education classes due to budget cuts. Some also had to make recess shorter because there isn't enough time in the schedule. But they are working hard to find creative ways that don't cost too much or take up too much time to get kid's moving. Because there's only so much money in the budget, and only so much time in the day, and preparing to take tests takes lots of time.

Schools can use parent volunteers to teach kid's old-fashioned games such as kick-the-can, hopscotch, foursquare, tetherball, or jump rope. Kid's nowadays often don't know these games! Old-fashioned games are a great way to get kid's moving. Some schools have before school activities, such as games in the gym. Other schools have after school activities, such as bike riding or outdoor games. They can't count on kid's to be active on their own or at home.

A break during class can help students concentrate when they go back to work. There are all kinds of ways to move in the classroom. And you don't have to change your clothes or anything. Wiggling, stretching, and playing a short active game are all good ideas. Good teachers know how to squeeze in time during academic classes like math and language arts.

Not getting enough exercise is linked to many problems. For example, unhealthy wait, and high blood pressure and colesterol. When students don't' get enough exercise, they end up overweight.

Physical activity also helps kid's do better in school. Kids who exercise have better attendance rates. They have increased attention span. They act out less. They have less stress and learn more. Being active also helps muscles and bones. It increases strength and stamina.

Schools today are doing what they can to find a solution by being creative and making time for physical activity before, during, and after school. They understand that it is a problem when kid's don't get enough exercise.

Not all the ideas in the essay focus on the topic.

The writer uses some transitions and sentence connections.

Some of the ideas in the essay are reasonably well developed. Some details and examples add substance to the essay.

Some ideas are well developed. Some examples and details are well chosen and specific and add substance to the essay.

Some details are specific and well chosen.

There are errors in spelling, punctuation, grammar, usage, and sentence boundaries that decrease the effectiveness of the essay.

The essay is not well organized. Its organizing structure does not support its purpose well or respond well to the demands of the prompt.

MODEL

INFORMATIVE: SCORE 3

Kids, School, and Exercise: Problems and Solutions

A 2008 report said school-age children should be physically active for at least 60 minutes a day. Sadly, most children don't get nearly that much exercise. Lots of schools have cut Physical Education classes because of money and time pressures. And there's less recess than there used to be. Even at home when kids have a chance to run around, many choose screen time instead. No wonder so many of us are turning into chubby couch potatoes!

Not getting exercise is linked to many problems, for example unhealthy weight, and high blood pressure and cholesterol. Studies show physical activity also helps students do better in school: it means better attendance rates, increased attention span, fewer behavioral problems, less stress, and more learning. Being active helps develop strong muscles and bones. It increases strength and stamina.

Many schools around the country get that there are problems when students are inactive. They are working hard to find creative solutions that don't cost too much or take up precious time in the school schedule.

Some schools are using parent volunteers to teach kids active games such as kick-the-can, hopscotch, foursquare, tetherball, or jump rope. These games are more likely to get kids moving than just sitting gossiping with your friends or staring at your phone. Some schools have before school activities such as run-around games in the gym. Other schools have after school activities such as bike riding or outdoor games. They can't count on kids to be active on their own.

There are all kinds of fun and healthy ways to move in the classroom, without changing clothes. An active break during class can help students concentrate when they go back to work. Creative teachers know how to squeeze in active time even during academic classes. Wiggling, stretching, and playing a short active game are all good ideas.

Schools today understand that it is a problem when kids don't get enough exercise. They are doing what they can to find a solution by being creative and making time for physical activity before, during, and after school.

The essay is fairly thoughtful and engaging.

Almost all the ideas focus on the topic.

The ideas in the essay are well developed, with well-chosen and specific details and examples.

The writer uses transitions and connections, such as *"Not getting exercise is linked…"* *"Many schools …"* *"Some schools…"* *"Other schools…"*

Ideas in the essay are mostly well developed.

Words are chosen carefully and contribute to the clarity of the essay.

WRITING

MODEL

INFORMATIVE: SCORE 4

Kids, School, and Exercise: Problems and Solutions

In 2008, the U.S. Department of Health and Human Services published a report stating that all school-age children need to be physically active for at least 60 minutes a day. Sadly, most children don't get nearly the recommended amount of exercise. Due to budget cuts and time pressure, many schools have cut Physical Education classes. Even recess is being squeezed to make room for more tests and test preparation.

> The writer explains the problem and its causes.

Lack of exercise can lead to many problems, such as unhealthy weight, high blood pressure, and high cholesterol. Physical activity helps develop strong muscles and bones, and it increases strength and stamina. Studies show physical activity leads to better attendance rates, increased attention span, fewer behavioral problems, less stress, and more learning. When kids don't get enough physical activity, a lot is at stake!

> The writer clearly lays out the effects of the problem.

Many schools around the country are stepping up to find innovative solutions—even when they don't have time or money to spare. Some have started before-school activities such as active games in the gym. Others have after-school activities such as bike riding or outdoor games. Just a few extra minutes a day can make a big difference!

> The writer turns to the solution. The essay's organizing structure supports its purpose and responds to the demands of the prompt.

Some schools try to make the most of recess by using parent volunteers to teach kids active games such as kick-the-can, hopscotch, foursquare, tetherball, or jump rope. Volunteers can also organize races or tournaments—anything to get the kids going! At the end of recess, everyone should be a little bit out of breath.

> The writer includes specific examples and well-chosen details.

Creative educators squeeze in active time even during academic classes. It could be a quick "brain break" to stretch in the middle of class, imaginary jump rope, or a game of rock-paper-scissors with legs instead of fingers. There are all kinds of imaginative ways to move in the classroom, without moving furniture or changing clothes. And research shows that an active break during class can help students focus when they go back to work.

> The progression of ideas is logical and well controlled.

> Details and examples add substance to the essay.

Schools today understand the problems that can arise when kids don't have enough physical activity in their lives. They are meeting the challenge by finding opportunities for exercise before, during, and after school. After all, if students do well on tests but end up unhealthy and unhappy, what is the point?

> The essay is thoughtful and engaging.

TOOL KIT: WRITING

Informational/Explanatory Rubric

	Focus and Organization	Development	Language/Conventions
4	The introduction is effective and sets forth the topic in a relevant way. The ideas progress logically. A variety of transitions are included to show the relationship among ideas and create cohesion. The conclusion is relevant and effective and follows from the rest of the essay.	The topic is developed with relevant facts, definitions, details, quotations, and examples. The writing demonstrates an insightful understanding of the topic by explaining clearly and elaborating on information provided.	The essay uses standard English conventions of usage and mechanics. Word choice is precise and relevant to the task. Sentences are varied and interesting. The tone of the writing is formal and objective.
3	The introduction is somewhat relevant and effective. The ideas progress somewhat logically. Some transitions are included with occasional gaps in cohesion. The conclusion is relevant and mostly follows from the rest of the essay.	The topic is developed with some relevant facts, definitions, details, quotations, and other examples. The writing demonstrates an understanding of the topic by explaining adequately and elaborating on information provided.	The essay demonstrates general accuracy in standard English. Word choice is often precise and generally appropriate to the task. Sentences are mostly varied and interesting. The tone of the writing is mostly formal and objective.
2	The introduction sets forth the topic. More than one idea is presented. A few transitions are included, but ideas may be hard to follow. The conclusion does not completely follow from the rest of the essay.	The topic is developed with a few relevant facts, definitions, details, quotations, or other examples. The writing demonstrates some understanding of the topic but supporting information is not complete or is sometimes inaccurate.	The essay demonstrates some accuracy in standard English. Word choice is somewhat appropriate to the task. There is little sentence variation. The tone is inconsistently formal and objective.
1	The topic is not clearly stated. Ideas do not follow a logical progression. Transitions are not included. The conclusion is missing or does not follow from the rest of the essay.	The topic is not developed with reliable or relevant evidence. The writing demonstrates little or no understanding of the topic.	The essay contains mistakes in standard English. Word choice is imprecise. There is little or no sentence variation. The tone is neither formal nor objective.

WRITING

Narrative

Narrative writing conveys an experience, either real or imaginary, and uses time order to provide structure. Usually its purpose is to entertain, but it can also instruct, persuade, or inform. Whenever writers tell a story, they are using narrative writing. Most types of narrative writing share certain elements, such as characters, setting, a sequence of events, and, often, a theme.

Elements of a Narrative Text

A **narrative** is any type of writing that tells a story, whether it is fiction, nonfiction, poetry, or drama.

An effective nonfiction narrative contains these elements:

- an engaging beginning in which characters and setting are established
- characters who participate in the story events
- a well-structured, logical sequence of events
- details that show time and place
- effective story elements such as dialogue, description, and reflection
- a narrator who relates the events from a particular point of view
- use of language that brings the characters and setting to life

An effective fictional narrative usually contains these elements:

- an engaging beginning in which characters, setting, or a main conflict is introduced
- a main character and supporting characters who participate in the story events
- a narrator who relates the events of the plot from a particular point of view
- details that show time and place
- narrative techniques such as dialogue, description, and suspense
- use of language that vividly brings to life characters and events

MODEL

NARRATIVE: SCORE 1

Mind Scissors

There's a bike race. Right away people start losing. But me and Thad were winning. Thad is the kid who always wins is who is also popular. I don't like Thad. I pumped pumping hard at my pedals, I knew the end was coming. I looked ahead and all I could see was Thad, and the woods.

I pedaled harder and then I was up to Thad. That was swinging at me, I swerved, I kept looking at him, I was worried!

That's stick had untied my shoelace and it was wrapped around my pedal! But I didn't know it yet.

We were out of the woods. I still wanted to win, I pedaled even faster. than my pedals stopped!

I saw with my mind the shoelace was caught in my pedal. No worries, I have the superpower of mind scissors. That's when my mind looked down and I used my mind scissors. I used the mind scissors to cut the shoelace my right foot was free.

That's how I became a superhero. I save people with my mind scissors now.

The story's beginning is not clear or engaging.

The narrative does not include sensory language and precise words to convey experiences and to develop characters.

Events do not progress logically. The ideas seem disconnected, and the sentences do not include transitions.

The narrative contains mistakes in standard English conventions of usage and mechanics.

The conclusion does not connect to the narrative.

WRITING

MODEL

NARRATIVE: SCORE 2

Mind-Scissors

When I was a baby I wound up with a tiny pair of scissors in my head. What the doctors couldn't have predicted is the uncanny ability they would give me. This past summer that was when I discovered what I could do with my mind-scissors.

Every summer there's a bike race. The kid who always wins is Thad who is popular.

The race starts. Right away racers start losing. After a long time pumping hard at my pedals, I knew the end was coming. I looked ahead and all I could see was Thad, and the woods.

I pedaled harder than ever. I was up to Thad. I turned my head to look at him. He was swinging a stick at me, I swerved, I kept looking at him, boy was I worried.

We were now out of the woods. Still hopeful I could win, I pedaled even faster. Suddenly, my pedals stopped!

Oh no! Thad's stick had untied my shoelace and it was wrapped around my pedal!

I was going to crash my bike. That's when my mind looked down. That's when I knew I could use my mind-scissors. I used the mind scissors to cut the shoelace my right foot was free.

That's how I won the race.

The story's beginning introduces the main character.

Events in the narrative progress somewhat logically, and the writer use some transition words.

The writer uses some description in the narrative.

The narrative demonstrates some accuracy in standard English conventions of usage and mechanics.

The words vary between vague and precise. The writer uses some sensory language.

The conclusion is weak and adds very little to the narrative.

MODEL

NARRATIVE: SCORE 3

Mind-Scissors

When I was a baby I wound up with a tiny pair of scissors in my head. Lots of people live with pieces of metal in their heads. We just have to be careful. What the doctors couldn't have predicted is the uncanny ability they would give me.

Every summer there's a bike race that ends at the lake. The kid who always wins is Thad Thomas the Third, who is popular. This past summer that was about to change. It's also when I discovered what I could do with my mind-scissors.

The race starts. Right away racers start falling behind. After what seemed an eternity pumping hard at my pedals, I knew the end had to be in sight. I looked ahead and all I could see was Thad, and the opening to the woods—the last leg of the race.

I felt like steam was coming off my legs. I could see Thad's helmet. I turned my head to flash him a look. Only, Thad was the one who was gloating! And then I saw it—he was holding a stick he had pulled off a low-hanging branch.

He jabbed it toward me. I swerved out of the way. I kept pedaling, shifting my eyes to the right, to see what he was going to do.

But I waited too long. Then Thad made a slashing motion. Then he tossed the stick aside, yelled, "Yes!" and zoomed forward.

What happened? I felt nothing. We were now out of the woods and into the clearing before the finish line. Still hopeful I could win, I pedaled even faster. Suddenly, there was a jerk. My pedals had stopped!

I looked down. Oh no! My shoelace was wrapped around my pedal! Thad's stick had untied it!

I looked for a place to crash. That's when my head started tingling. I looked down at the shoelace. I concentrated really hard. I could see the scissors in my mind, floating just beside the pedal. Snip! The shoelace broke and my foot was free.

Thad was too busy listening to his fans cheer him on as I rode past him. Thanks to the mind-scissors, I won.

The story's beginning is engaging and clearly introduces the main character and situation.

Events in the narrative progress logically, and the writer uses transition words frequently.

The writer uses precise words and some sensory language to convey the experiences in the narrative and to describe the characters and scenes.

The writer uses some description and dialogue to add interest to the narrative and develop experiences and events.

The narrative demonstrates accuracy in standard English conventions of usage and mechanics.

The conclusion follows from the rest of the narrative.

WRITING

MODEL

NARRATIVE: SCORE 4

Mind-Scissors

As long as I wear my bike helmet, they say I'll be okay. Lots of people live with pieces of metal in their heads. We just have to be careful. When I was a baby I wound up with a tiny pair of scissors in mine. What the doctors couldn't have predicted is the uncanny ability they would give me.

Every summer there's a bike race that ends at the lake. The kid who always wins is Thad Thomas the Third, who is popular, but if you ask me, it's because he knows how to sweet-talk everyone. This past summer that was about to change. It's also when I discovered what I could do with my mind-scissors.

The race starts. Right away, racers start falling behind. After what seemed an eternity pumping hard at my pedals, I knew the end had to be in sight. I looked ahead and all I could see was Thad and the opening to the woods—the last leg of the race.

I put my stamina to the test—pedaling harder than ever, I felt like steam was coming off my legs. Thad's red helmet came into view. As I could sense I was going to overtake him any second, I turned my head to flash him a look. Only, to my befuddlement, Thad was the one who was gloating! And then I saw it—he was holding a stick he had pulled off a low-hanging branch.

He jabbed it toward me. I swerved out of the way. Was he trying to poke me with it? I kept pedaling, shifting my eyes to the right, to see what he was going to do.

But I waited too long. Thad made a slashing motion. Then he tossed the stick aside, yelled, "Yes!" and zoomed forward.

What happened? I felt nothing. We were now out of the woods and into the clearing before the finish line. Still hopeful I could win, I pedaled even faster. Suddenly, there was a jerk. My pedals had stopped!

I looked down. Oh no! My shoelace was wrapped around my pedal! Thad's stick had untied the shoelace!

I coasted as I looked for a place to crash. That's when my head started tingling. I got this funny notion to try something. I looked down. I had the tangled shoelace in my sights. I concentrated really hard. I could see the scissors in my mind, floating just beside the pedal. Snip! The shoelace broke and my right foot was free.

Thad was busy motioning his fans to cheer him on as I made my greatest effort to pedal back up to speed. Guess who made it to the finish line first?

The story's beginning is engaging and introduces the main character and situation in a way that appeals to a reader.

The writer uses techniques such as dialogue and description to add interest to the narrative and to develop the characters and events.

Events in the narrative progress in logical order and are linked by clear transitions.

Writer uses vivid description and sensory language to convey the experiences in the narrative and to help the reader imagine the characters and scenes.

The writer uses standard English conventions of usage and mechanics.

Writer's conclusion follows from the events in the narrative.

Narrative Rubric

	Focus and Organization	Development of Ideas/ Elaboration	Conventions
4	The introduction is engaging and introduces the characters and situation in a way that appeals to readers. Events in the narrative progress in logical order and are linked by clear transitions. The conclusion effectively follows from and reflects on the narrated experiences or events.	The narrative effectively includes techniques such as dialogue and description to add interest and to develop the characters and events. The narrative effectively includes precise words and phrases, relevant descriptive details, and sensory language to convey experiences and events. The narrative effectively establishes voice through word choice, sentence structure, and tone.	The narrative intentionally uses standard English conventions of usage and mechanics. The narrative effectively varies sentence patterns for meaning, reader interest, and style.
3	The introduction is somewhat engaging and clearly introduces the characters and situation. Events in the narrative progress logically and are often linked by transition words. The conclusion mostly follows from and reflects on the narrated experiences or events.	The narrative includes adequate dialogue and description to add interest and develop experiences and events. The narrative includes some precise words and sensory language to convey experiences and events. The narrative adequately establishes voice through word choice, sentence structure, and tone.	The narrative mostly demonstrates accuracy in standard English conventions of usage and mechanics. The narrative mostly varies sentence patterns for meaning, reader interest, and style.
2	The introduction occasionally introduces characters. Events in the narrative progress somewhat logically and are sometimes linked by transition words. The conclusion adds very little to the narrated experiences or events.	The narrative includes some dialogue and descriptions. The words in the narrative vary between vague and precise, and some sensory language is included. The narrative occasionally establishes voice through word choice, sentence structure, and tone.	The narrative demonstrates some accuracy in standard English conventions of usage and mechanics. The narrative occasionally varies sentence patterns for meaning, reader interest, and style.
1	The introduction does not introduce characters and an experience or there is no clear introduction. The events in the narrative do not progress logically. The ideas seem disconnected and the sentences are not linked by transitions. The conclusion does not connect to the narrative or there is no conclusion.	Dialogue and descriptions are not included in the narrative. The narrative does not incorporate sensory language or precise words to convey experiences or to develop characters. The narrative does not establish voice through word choice, sentence structure, and tone.	The narrative contains mistakes in standard English conventions of usage and mechanics. The narrative does not vary sentence patterns for meaning, reader interest, and style.

RESEARCH

Conducting Research

You can conduct research to gain more knowledge about a topic. Sources such as articles, books, interviews, or the Internet have the facts and explanations that you need. Not all of the information that you find, however, will be useful—or reliable. Strong research skills will help you find accurate information about your topic.

Narrowing or Broadening a Topic

The first step in any research is finding your topic. Choose a topic that is narrow enough to cover completely. If you can name your topic in just one or two words, it is probably too broad. Topics such as mythology, hip hop music, or Italy are too broad to cover in a single report. Narrow a broad topic into smaller subcategories.

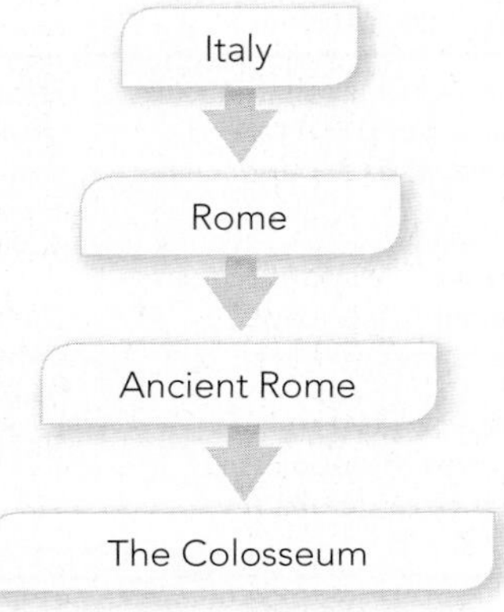

When you begin to research, pay attention to the amount of information available. If there is way too much information on your topic, you may need to narrow your topic further.

You might also need to broaden a topic if there is not enough information for your purpose. A topic is too narrow when it can be thoroughly presented in less space than the required size of your assignment. It might also be too narrow if you can find little or no information in library and media sources. Broaden your topic by including other related ideas.

Generating Research Questions

Use research questions to focus your research. Specific questions can help you avoid wasting time. For example, instead of simply hunting for information about Peter Pan, you might ask, "What inspired J. M. Barrie to write the story of Peter Pan?" or "How have different artists shown Peter Pan?"

A research question may also lead you to find your topic sentence. The question can also help you focus your research plan. Write your question down and keep it in mind while you hunt for facts. Your question can prevent you from gathering unnecessary details. As you learn more about your topic, you can always rewrite your original question.

Consulting Print and Digital Sources

An effective research project combines information from multiple sources. It is important not to rely too heavily on a single source. The creativity and originality of your research depends on how you combine ideas from many places. Plan to include a variety of these resources:

- **Primary and Secondary Sources:** Use both primary sources (firsthand or original accounts, such as interview transcripts and newspaper articles) and secondary sources (accounts that are not created at the time of an event, such as encyclopedia entries).
- **Print and Digital Resources:** The Internet allows fast access to data, but print resources are often edited more carefully. Plan to include both print and digital resources in order to guarantee that your work is accurate.
- **Media Resources:** You can find valuable information in media resources such as documentaries, television programs, podcasts, and museum exhibitions.
- **Original Research:** Depending on your topic, you may wish to conduct original research to include among your sources. For example, you might interview experts or eyewitnesses or conduct a survey of people in your community.

Using Online Encyclopedias

Online encyclopedias are often written by anonymous contributors who are not required to fact-check information. These sites can be very useful as a launching point for research, but should not be considered accurate. Look for footnotes, endnotes, or hyperlinks that support facts with reliable sources that have been carefully checked by editors.

Evaluating Sources It is important to evaluate the credibility and accuracy of any information you find. Ask yourself questions such as these to evaluate other sources:

- **Authority:** Is the author well known? What are the author's credentials? Does the source include references to other reliable sources? Does the author's tone win your confidence? Why or why not?
- **Bias:** Does the author have any obvious biases? What is the author's purpose for writing? Who is the target audience?
- **Currency:** When was the work created? Has it been revised? Is there more current information available?

RESEARCH

Using Search Terms

Finding information on the Internet is easy, but it can be a challenge to find facts that are useful and trustworthy. If you type a word or phrase into a search engine, you will probably get hundreds—or thousands—of results. However, those results are not guaranteed to be relevant or accurate.

These strategies can help you find information from the Internet:

- Create a list of topic keywords before you begin using a search engine. Use a thesaurus to expand your list.
- Enter six to eight keywords.
- Choose unique nouns. Most search engines ignore articles and prepositions. Verbs may lead to sources that are not useful. Use modifiers, such as adjectives, when necessary to specify a category. For example, you might enter "ancient Rome" instead of "Rome."
- Use quotation marks to focus a search. Place a phrase in quotation marks to find pages that include exactly that phrase. Add several phrases in quotation marks to narrow your results.
- Spell carefully. Many search engines correct spelling automatically, but they cannot catch every spelling error.
- Scan search results before you click them. The first result isn't always the most useful. Read the text and notice the domain before make a choice.
- Consult more than one search engine.

Evaluating Internet Domains

Not everything you read on the Internet is true, so you have to evaluate sources carefully. The last three letters of an Internet URL identify the site's domain, which can help you evaluate the information of the site.

- **.gov**—Government sites are sponsored by a branch of the United States federal government and are considered reliable.
- **.edu**—Information from an educational research center or department is likely to be carefully checked, but may include student pages that are not edited or monitored.
- **.org**—Organizations are nonprofit groups and usually maintain a high level of credibility but may still reflect strong biases.
- **.com** and **.net**—Commercial sites exist to make a profit. Information might be biased to show a product or service in a good light.

R26

Taking Notes

Use different strategies to take notes:

- Use index cards to create notecards and source cards. On each source card, record information about each source you use—author, title, publisher, date of publication, and relevant page numbers. On each notecard, record information to use in your writing. Use quotation marks when you copy exact words, and indicate the page number(s) on which the information appears.
- Photocopy articles and copyright pages. Then, highlight relevant information. Remember to include the Web addresses of printouts from online sources.
- Print articles from the Internet or copy them directly into a "notes" folder.

You will use these notes to help you write original text.

Source Card

[A]
Papp, Joseph,
and Elizabeth Kirkland

Shakespeare Alive!

Bantam Books, 1988

Notecard

Only the upper classes could read.

Most of the common people in
Shakespeare's time could not read.
Source Card: A, p. 5.

Quote Accurately Responsible research begins with the first note you take. Be sure to quote and paraphrase your sources accurately so you can identify these sources later. In your notes, circle all quotations and paraphrases to distinguish them from your own comments. When photocopying from a source, include the copyright information. Include the Web addresses of printouts from online sources.

RESEARCH

Reviewing Research Findings

You will need to review your findings to be sure that you have collected enough accurate and appropriate information.

Considering Audience and Purpose

Always keep your audience in mind as you gather information. Different audiences may have very different needs. For example, if you are writing a report for your class about a topic you have studied together, you will not need to provide background information in your writing. However, if you are writing about the topic for a national student magazine, you cannot assume that all of your readers have the same information. You will need to provide background facts from reliable sources to help inform those readers about your subject. When thinking about your research and your audience, ask yourself:

- Who am I writing for?
- Have I collected enough information to explain my topic to this audience?
- Do I need to conduct more research to explain my topic clearly?
- Are there details in my research that I can leave out because they are already familiar to my audience?

Your purpose for writing will also affect your research review. If you are researching to satisfy your own curiosity, you can stop researching when you feel you understand the answer completely. If you are writing a research report that will be graded, you need to think about your assignment. When thinking about whether or not you have enough information, ask yourself:

- What is my purpose for writing?
- Will the information I have gathered be enough to achieve my purpose?
- If I need more information, where might I find it?

Synthesizing Sources

Effective research writing is more than just a list of facts and details. Good research synthesizes—gathers, orders, and interprets—those elements. These strategies will help you synthesize effectively:

- Review your notes. Look for connections and patterns among the details you have collected.
- Organize notes or notecards to help you plan how you will combine details.
- Pay close attention to details that emphasize the same main idea.
- Also look for details that challenge each other. For many topics, there is no single correct opinion. You might decide to conduct additional research to help you decide which side of the issue has more support.

Types of Evidence

When reviewing your research, also think about the kinds of evidence you have collected. The strongest writing combines a variety of evidence. This chart describes three of the most common types of evidence.

TYPE OF EVIDENCE	DESCRIPTION	EXAMPLE
Statistical evidence includes facts and other numerical data used to support a claim or explain a topic.	Statistical evidence are facts about a topic, such as historical dates, descriptions about size and number, and poll results.	Jane Goodall began to study chimpanzees when she was 26 years old.
Testimonial evidence includes any ideas or opinions presented by others. Testimonies might be from experts or people with special knowledge about a topic.	Firsthand testimonies present ideas from eyewitnesses to events or subjects being discussed.	Goodall's view of chimps has changed: "When I first started at Gombe, I thought the chimps were nicer than we are. But time has revealed that they are not. They can be just as awful."
	Secondary testimonies include commentaries on events by people who were not directly involved.	Science writer David Quammen points out that Goodall "set a new standard, a very high standard, for behavioral study of apes in the wild."
Anecdotal evidence presents one person's view of the world, often by describing specific events or incidents.	An anecdote is a story about something that happened. Personal stories can be part of effective research, but they should not be the only kind of evidence presented. Anecdotes are particularly useful for proving that broad generalizations are not accurate.	It is not fair to say that it is impossible for dogs to use tools. One researcher reports the story of a dog that learned to use a large bone as a back scratcher.

R29

RESEARCH

Incorporating Research into Writing

Avoiding Plagiarism

Whether you are presenting a formal research paper or an opinion paper on a current event, you must be careful to give credit for any ideas or opinions that are not your own. Presenting someone else's ideas, research, or opinion as your own—even if you have phrased it in different words—is *plagiarism*, the equivalent of academic stealing, or fraud.

Do not use the ideas or research of others in place of your own. Read from several sources to draw your own conclusions and form your own opinions. Incorporate the ideas and research of others to support your points. Credit the source of the following types of support:

- Statistics
- Direct quotations
- Indirectly quoted statements of opinions
- Conclusions presented by an expert
- Facts available in only one or two sources

When you are drafting and revising, circle any words or ideas that are not your own. Follow the instructions on pages R32 and R33 to correctly cite those passages.

Reviewing for Plagiarism Take time to review your writing for accidental plagiarism. Read what you have written and take note of any ideas that do not have your personal writing voice. Compare those passages with your resource materials. You might have copied them without remembering the exact source. Add a correct citation to give credit to the original author. If you cannot find the questionable phrase in your notes, think about revising your word choices. You want to be sure that your final writing reflects your own thinking and not someone else's work.

Quoting and Paraphrasing

When including ideas from research into your writing, you will decide to quote directly or paraphrase.

Direct Quotation Use the author's exact words when they are interesting or persuasive. You might decide to include direct quotations in these situations:

- to share a strong statement
- to reference a historically significant passage
- to show that an expert agrees with your position
- to present an argument to which you will respond

Include complete quotations, without deleting or changing words. If you need to leave out words for space or clarity, use ellipsis points to show where you removed words. Enclose direct quotations in quotation marks.

Paraphrase A paraphrase restates an author's ideas in your own words. Be careful to paraphrase accurately. Beware of making sweeping generalizations in a paraphrase that were not made by the original author. You may use some words from the original source, but a good paraphrase does more than simply rearrange an author's phrases, or replace a few words with synonyms.

Original Text	"Some teens doing homework while listening to music and juggling tweets and texts may actually work better that way, according to an intriguing new study performed by two high-school seniors." *Sumathi Reddy, "Teen Researchers Defend Media Multitasking"*
Patchwork Plagiarism phrases from the original are rearranged, but they too closely follow the original text.	An intriguing new study conducted by two high-school seniors suggests that teens work better when they are listening to music and juggling texts and tweets.
Good Paraphrase	Two high-school students studied homework habits. They concluded that some people do better work while multitasking, such as studying and listening to music or checking text messages at the same time.

Maintaining the Flow of Ideas

Effective research writing is much more that just a list of facts. Maintain the flow of ideas by connecting research information to your own ideas. Instead of simply stating a piece of evidence, use transitions to connect information you found from outside resources and your own thinking. The transitions in the box on the page can be used to introduce, compare, contrast, and clarify.

Choosing an effective organizational strategy for your writing will help you create a logical flow of ideas. Once you have chosen a clear organization, add research in appropriate places to provide evidence and support.

Useful Transitions

When providing examples:

for example   for instance   to illustrate   in [name of resource], [author]

When comparing and contrasting ideas or information:

in the same way   similarly   however   on the other hand

When clarifying ideas or opinions:

in other words   that is   to explain   to put it another way

RESEARCH

ORGANIZATIONAL STRUCTURE	USES
Chronological order presents information in the sequence in which it happens.	historical topics; science experiments; analysis of narratives
Part-to-whole order examines how several categories affect a larger subject.	analysis of social issues; historical topics
Order of importance presents information in order of increasing or decreasing importance.	persuasive arguments; supporting a bold or challenging thesis
Comparison-and-contrast organization presents similarities and differences.	addressing two or more subjects

Formats for Citing Sources

When you cite a source, you acknowledge where you found your information and you give your readers the details necessary for locating the source themselves. Within the body of a paper, you provide a short citation, a footnote number linked to a footnote, or an endnote number linked to an endnote reference. These brief references show the page numbers on which you found the information. Prepare a reference list at the end of a research report to provide full bibliographic information on your sources. These are two common types of reference lists:

- A bibliography provides a listing of all the resources you consulted during your research.
- A works-cited list indicates the works your have referenced in your writing.

The chart on the next page shows the Modern Language Association format for crediting sources. This is the most common format for papers written in the content areas in middle school and high school. Unless instructed otherwise by your teacher, use this format for crediting sources.

Focus on Citations When you revise your writing, check that you cite the sources for quotations, factual information, and ideas that are not your own. Most word-processing programs have features that allow you to create footnotes and endnotes.

Identifying Missing Citations These strategies can help you find facts and details that should be cited in your writing:

- Look for facts that are not general knowledge. If a fact was unique to one source, it needs a citation.
- Read your report aloud. Listen for words and phrases that do not sound like your writing style. You might have picked them up from a source. If so, use you notes to find the source, place the words in quotation marks, and give credit.
- Review your notes. Look for ideas that you used in your writing but did not cite.

MLA (8th Edition) Style for Listing Sources

Book with one author	Pyles, Thomas. *The Origins and Development of the English Language.* 2nd ed., Harcourt Brace Jovanovich, 1971. [Indicate the edition or version number when relevant.]
Book with two authors	Pyles, Thomas, and John Algeo. *The Origins and Development of the English Language.* 5th ed., Cengage Learning, 2004.
Book with three or more authors	Donald, Robert B., et al. *Writing Clear Essays.* Prentice Hall, 1983.
Book with an editor	Truth, Sojourner. *Narrative of Sojourner Truth.* Edited by Margaret Washington, Vintage Books, 1993.
Introduction to a work in a published edition	Washington, Margaret. Introduction. *Narrative of Sojourner Truth,* by Sojourner Truth, edited by Washington, Vintage Books, 1993, pp. v–xi.
Single work in an anthology	Hawthorne, Nathaniel. "Young Goodman Brown." *Literature: An Introduction to Reading and Writing,* edited by Edgar V. Roberts and Henry E. Jacobs, 5th ed., Prentice Hall, 1998, pp. 376–385. [Indicate pages for the entire selection.]
Signed article from an encyclopedia	Askeland, Donald R. "Welding." *World Book Encyclopedia,* vol. 21, World Book, 1991, p. 58.
Signed article in a weekly magazine	Wallace, Charles. "A Vodacious Deal." *Time,* 14 Feb. 2000, p. 63.
Signed article in a monthly magazine	Gustaitis, Joseph. "The Sticky History of Chewing Gum." *American History,* Oct. 1998, pp. 30–38.
Newspaper article	Thurow, Roger. "South Africans Who Fought for Sanctions Now Scrap for Investors." *Wall Street Journal,* 11 Feb. 2000, pp. A1+. [For a multipage article that does not appear on consecutive pages, write only the first page number on which it appears, followed by the plus sign.]
Unsigned editorial or story	"Selective Silence." Editorial. *Wall Street Journal,* 11 Feb. 2000, p. A14. [If the editorial or story is signed, begin with the author's name.]
Signed pamphlet or brochure	[Treat the pamphlet as though it were a book.]
Work from a library subscription service	Ertman, Earl L. "Nefertiti's Eyes." *Archaeology,* Mar.–Apr. 2008, pp. 28–32. *Kids Search,* EBSCO, New York Public Library. Accessed 7 Jan. 2017. [Indicating the date you accessed the information is optional but recommended.]
Filmstrips, slide programs, videocassettes, DVDs, and other audiovisual media	*The Diary of Anne Frank.* 1959. Directed by George Stevens, performances by Millie Perkins, Shelley Winters, Joseph Schildkraut, Lou Jacobi, and Richard Beymer, Twentieth Century Fox, 2004. [Indicating the original release date after the title is optional but recommended.]
CD-ROM (with multiple publishers)	Simms, James, editor. *Romeo and Juliet.* By William Shakespeare, Attica Cybernetics / BBC Education / Harper, 1995.
Radio or television program transcript	"Washington's Crossing of the Delaware." *Weekend Edition Sunday,* National Public Radio, 23 Dec. 2013. Transcript.
Web page	"Fun Facts About Gum." ICGA, 2005–2017, www.gumassociation.org/index.cfm/facts-figures/fun-facts-about-gum. Accessed 19 Feb. 2017. [Indicating the date you accessed the information is optional but recommended.]
Personal interview	Smith, Jane. Personal interview, 10 Feb. 2017.

All examples follow the style given in the MLA Handbook, 8th edition, published in 2016.

MODEL

Evidence Log

Unit Title: Discovery

Perfomance-Based Assessment Prompt:
Do all discoveries benefit humanity?

My initial thoughts:
Yes - all knowledge moves us forward.

As you read multiple texts about a topic, your thinking may change. Use an Evidence Log like this one to record your thoughts, to track details you might use in later writing or discussion, and to make further connections.

Here is a sample to show how one reader's ideas deepened as she read two texts.

Title of Text: Classifying the Stars   Date: Sept. 17

CONNECTION TO THE PROMPT	TEXT EVIDENCE/DETAILS	ADDITIONAL NOTES/IDEAS
Newton shared his discoveries and then other scientists built on his discoveries.	Paragraph 2: "Isaac Newton gave to the world the results of his experiments on passing sunlight through a prism." Paragraph 3: "In 1814 . . . the German optician, Fraunhofer . . . saw that the multiple spectral tints . . . were crossed by hundreds of fine dark lines."	It's not always clear how a discovery might benefit humanity in the future.

How does this text change or add to my thinking? This confirms what I think.   Date: Sept. 20

Title of Text: Cell Phone Mania   Date: Sept. 21

CONNECTION TO THE PROMPT	TEXT EVIDENCE/DETAILS	ADDITIONAL NOTES/IDEAS
Cell phones have made some forms of communication easier, but people don't talk to each other as much as they did in the past.	Paragraph 7: "Over 80% of young adults state that texting is their primary method of communicating with friends. This contrasts with older adults who state that they prefer a phone call."	Is it good that we don't talk to each other as much? Look for article about social media to learn more about this question.

How does this text change or add to my thinking?   Date: Sept. 25
Maybe there are some downsides to discoveries. I still think that knowledge moves us forward, but sometimes there are negative effects.

MODEL

Word Network

A word network is a collection of words related to a topic. As you read the selections in a unit, identify interesting theme-related words and build your vocabulary by adding them to your Word Network.

Use your Word Network as a resource for your discussions and writings. Here is an example:

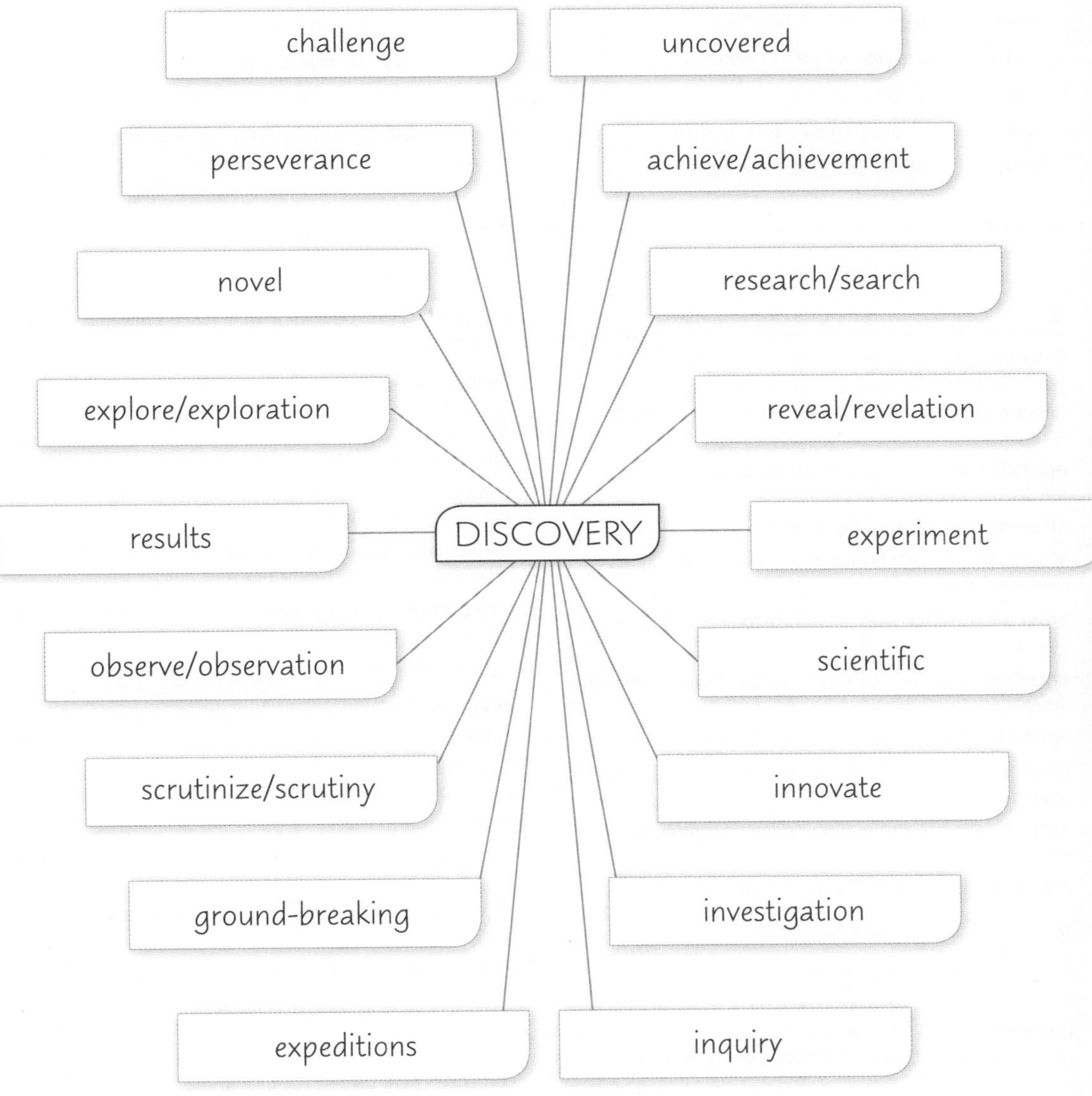

TOOL KIT: PROGRAM RESOURCES

ACADEMIC / CONCEPT VOCABULARY

Academic vocabulary appears in **blue type.**

Pronunciation Key

Symbol	Sample Words	Symbol	Sample Words
a	***at, catapult, Alabama***	oo	***boot, soup, crucial***
ah	***father, charms, argue***	ow	***now, stout, flounder***
ai	***care, various, hair***	oy	***boy, toil, oyster***
aw	***law, maraud, caution***	s	***say, nice, press***
awr	***pour, organism, forewarn***	sh	***she, abolition, motion***
ay	***ape, sails, implication***	u	***full, put, book***
ee	***even, teeth, really***	uh	***ago, focus, contemplation***
eh	***ten, repel, elephant***	ur	***bird, urgent, perforation***
ehr	***merry, verify, terribly***	y	***by, delight, identify***
ih	***it, pin, hymn***	yoo	***music, confuse, few***
o	***shot, hopscotch, condo***	zh	***pleasure, treasure, vision***
oh	***own, parole, rowboat***		

A

accomplishments (uh KOM plihsh muhnts) *n.* goals reached; achievements; tasks done skillfully

accuracy (AK yuhr uh see) *n.* being without errors; correctness

agricultural (ag ruh KUHL chuhr uhl) *adj.* related to the science and art of farming

altered (AWL tuhrd) *adj.* changed

alternative (awl TUR nuh tihv) *adj.* representing a different option

amoeba (uh MEE buh) *n.* microscopic, single-celled animal

ancestors (AN sehs tuhrz) *n.* people from whom one is descended; forefathers

aptitude (AP tuh tood) *n.* natural ability or talent

assumption (uh SUHMP shuhn) *n.* something taken for granted

atmosphere (AT muhs fihr) *n.* the gas surrounding the earth; the air

attempts (uh TEHMPTS) *n.* tries; attacks

B

barriers (BAR ee uhrz) *n.* obstructions; things that block passage

bitterness (BIHT uhr nihs) *n.* quality of having a sharp, unpleasant taste; condition causing pain or sorrow

blight (blyt) *n.* something that spoils, prevents growth, or destroys

bond (bond) *n.* uniting connection; link

C

calculus (KAL kyuh luhs) *n.* math used to study change

canals (kuh NALZ) *n.* artificial waterways for transportation or irrigation

capitalistic (kap uh tuh LIHS tihk) *adj.* characteristic of an economic system that is privately owned

catapulted (KA tuh puhl tihd) *v.* launched forward with machine-like force

catastrophic (kat uh STROF ihk) *adj.* disastrous

cede (seed) *v.* formally give up rights

celebrate (SEHL uh brayt) *v.* mark a happy occasion by engaging in a pleasurable activity

certainty (SUR tuhn tee) *n.* sure fact; freedom from doubt

charitable (CHAR ih tuh buhl) *adj.* kind and forgiving; lenient

chronic (KRON ihk) *adj.* lasting a long time or recurring often

close-up shot (KLOHS uhp) (shot) *n.* camera shot in which the subject is shown at close range; typically, the subject's head and shoulders are shown, with no visible background

colonize (KOL uh nyz) *v.* establish a new home far away

composition (kom puh ZIHSH uhn) *n.* arrangement of elements in a drawing

connects (kuh NEHKTS) *v.* joins together

consequence (KON suh kwehns) *n.* result; outcome; effect

consequences (KON suh kwehns ihz) *n.* results of an action or actions

consistent (kuhn SIHS tuhnt) *n.* keeping to the same principles; reliable

contact (KON takt) *n.* connection; communication; *v.* get in touch with; communicate with

contradict (kon truh DIHKT) *v.* dispute or disagree with

contribute (kuhn TRIHB yoot) *v.* give to a cause, event, project, etc.

covetous (KUHV uh tuhs) *adj.* greedy and jealous

crisis (KRY sihs) *n.* time when a situation is very bad or dangerous; turning point at which a change must be made for better or worse

D

deserted (dih ZUR tihd) *adj.* abandoned; empty

desire (dih ZYR) *v.* want; long for

determination (dih tuhr muh NAY shuhn) *n.* conclusion; firm decision

devastated (DEH vuh stay tihd) *v.* destroyed; completely upset

deviate (DEE vee ayt) *v.* depart from an established plan

dialogue (DY uh log) *n.* conversation; words spoken by characters in a story, drama, etc.

director (duh REHK tuhr) *n.* creative artist responsible for interpreting a screenplay

discord (DIHS kawrd) *n.* disagreement; lack of harmony

discordant (dihs KAWRD uhnt) *adj.* lacking harmony

discredit (dihs KREHD iht) *v.* disbelieve; cast doubt on *n.* loss of trust or faith; disbelief

dispelled (dihs PEHLD) *v.* driven away; scattered

disposal (dihs POH zuhl) *n.* act of getting rid of somehting

dissent (dih SEHNT) *v.* disagree; *n.* disagreement

diversity (dy VUR suh tee) *n.* variety; differences within a group

documentary photography (dok yuh MEHN tuhr ee) (fuh TOG ruh fee) *n.* photographs taken with the main purpose of recording a place, an event, or a person

doomed (doomd) *adj.* destined to a bad outcome

E

earnest (UR nihst) *adj.* serious and heartfelt; not joking

editing (EHD ih tihng) *n.* how separate shots filmed during production are arranged to tell a story, add suspense, and set pacing

efficiently (ih FIHSH uhnt lee) *adv.* with the least amount of effort and waste; effectively

emissions (ih MIHSH uhnz) *n.* gas or other substance sent into the air

encouraged (ehn KUR ihjd) *v.* inspired; offered support to

enlarged (ehn LAHRJD) *v.* made bigger; increased in size

enterprise (EHN tuhr pryz) *n.* business venture or company

enthusiastically (ehn thoo zee AS tuh klee) *adv.* with eager interest

environment (ehn VY ruhn muhnt) *n.* land, air, and water in which people, animals, and plants live, and all the natural features of these places

ethical (EHTH uh kuhl) *adj.* conforming to moral standards

excruciatingly (ehk SKROO shee ay tihng lee) *adv.* painfully; miserably

extinct (ehk STIHNGKT) *adj.* no longer in existence

extraordinary (ehk STRAWR duh nehr ee) *adj.* better than ordinary; exceptional

F

flung (fluhng) *v.* threw with force

forlorn (fawr LAWRN) *adj.* abandoned or deserted

frantically (FRAN tuh klee) *adv.* acting wildly with anger, worry, or pain

frustrated (FRUHS trayt ihd) *adj.* prevented from accomplishing

G

generosity (jehn uhr OS uh tee) *n.* willingness to give or share

H

heed (heed) *v.* pay close attention to

hesitantly (HEHZ uh tuhnt lee) *adv.* in an unsure or cautious way

human voice (HYOO muhn) (voys) *n.* central conveyer of events and interactions in a radio play

I

illusion (ih LOO zhuhn) *n.* something that appears real but actually is not

imitate (IHM uh tayt) *v.* act the same as; copy

immense (ih MEHNS) *adj.* very large

imminent (IHM uh nuhnt) *adj.* threatening and likely to occur at any moment

impairments (ihm PAIR muhnts) *n.* injury; damage

impossible (ihm POS uh buhl) *adj.* disagreeable; unreasonable

indignity (ihn DIHG nuh tee) *n.* feeling that one has been disrespected

infinitely (IHN fuh niht lee) *adv.* enormously; remarkably

influence (IHN floo uhns) *v.* affect someone in an important way

instinctively (ihn STIHNGK tihv lee) *adv.* done automatically, without thinking

interject (ihn tuhr JEHKT) *v.* throw in between; interrupt

interstellar (ihn tuhr STEHL uhr) *adj.* between or among stars in space

J

justify (JUHS tuh fy) *v.* give good reason for an action

L

lamented (luh MEHNT ihd) *v.* expressed regret

light/shadow (lyt) / (SHAD oh) *n.* techniques that add depth to a drawing and make it more realistic

localizing (LOH kuh lyz ihng) *v.* gathering, collecting, or concentrating in a particular place

long shot (lawng) (shot) *n.* camera shot in which the entire subject is visible as well as some of the background around the subject

lurched (lurcht) *v.* staggered; moved unsteadily

M

maintain (mayn TAYN) *v.* keep up; declare to be true

maladies (MAL uh deez) *n.* illnesses or diseases

malcontent (MAL kuhn tehnt) *n.* person who is always unhappy

medium shot (MEE dee uhm) (shot) *n.* camera shot in which the subject is seen from a medium distance, usually from the waist up

miser (MY zuhr) *n.* greedy person who keeps and refuses to spend money, even at the expense of his or her own comfort

mission control (MIHSH uhn) (kuhn TROHL) *n.* command center for the control, monitoring, and support of activities connected with manned space flight

monochrome (MON uh krohm) *n.* photos that are black and white

monotony (muh NOT uh nee) *n.* sameness; boredom

morose (muh ROHS) *adj.* gloomy; ill-tempered

mosaic (moh ZAY ihk) *adj.* made of many small pieces of colored glass or stone

mutation (myoo TAY shuhn) *n.* change in form, nature, or qualities

mystery (MIHS tuh ree) *n.* quality of being unexplained or kept secret

N

notable (NOH tuh buhl) *adj.* important; remarkable

O

observation (ob zuhr VAY shuhn) *n.* act of watching or noticing; something observed

P

panoramic shot (pan uh RAM ihk) (shot) *n.* film shot showing a wide, unbroken view

parallel (PAR uh lehl) *adj.* having the same direction or nature; similar

performance (puhr FAWR muhns) *n.* actor's portrayal of a character

permit (puhr MIHT) *v.* allow

perseverance (puhr suh VIHR uhns) *n.* continued, patient effort

persevere (puhr suh VIHR) *v.* continue despite difficulty

perspective (puhr SPEHK tihv) *n.* particular way of looking at something; point of view

perspective (puhr SPEHK tihv) *n.* technique used to create the illusion of a three-dimensional world on a two-dimensional surface, such as a piece of paper

philanthropist (fih LAN thruh pihst) *n.* wealthy person who donates to charities

planetary (PLAN uh tehr ee) *adj.* having to do with planets

pollution (puh LOO shuhn) *n.* presence or introduction into a space of a substance or thing that has harmful or poisonous effects

puzzled (PUHZ uhld) *adj.* confused and unable to understand something

Q

questions (KWEHS chuhnz) *n.* what the interviewer chooses to ask an interviewee to elicit specific information

R

recklessly (REHK lihs lee) *adv.* without regard for consequences; carelessly

release (rih LEES) *n.* act of letting go; *v.* let go; set free

reproach (rih PROHCH) *n.* criticism or disapproval

resilience (rih ZIHL yuhns) *n.* ability to recover quickly

resolute (REHZ uh loot) *adj.* determined

resolved (rih ZOLVD) *v.* offered a solution for; solved

rural (RUR uhl) *adj.* characteristic of the country; of or pertaining to agriculture

ruthless (ROOTH lihs) *adj.* having no compassion or pity

S

scarcity (SKAIR suh tee) *n.* quality of being hard to find; rarity

screenplay (SKREEN play) *n.* written script of a film, including acting instructions and scene directions

set (seht) *n.* where the interview takes place

silence (SY luhns) *n.* absence of sound

sorrow (SAWR oh) *n.* great sadness; suffering

sound effects (sownd) (uh FEHKTS) *n.* sounds produced artificially for a radio production

squabbling (SKWOB lihng) *v.* fighting noisily over small matters

stillness (STIHL nihs) *n.* absence of noise or motion

stimulus (STIHM yuh luhs) *n.* something that causes action or reaction

stricken (STRIHK uhn) *adj.* very badly affected by trouble or illness

strive (stryv) *v.* make a great effort; try very hard

struggling (STRUHG lihng) *v.* trying to do with difficulty

subconciously (suhb KON shuhs lee) *adv.* occuring in the mind without one's full awareness

submerged (suhb MURJD) *adj.* completely covered with a liquid

sufficient (suh FIHSH uhnt) *adj.* enough; the right amount as needed

supervision (soo puhr VIH zhuhn) *n.* act of watching over someone

T

thoroughly (THUR oh lee) *adv.* completely; entirely

threatening (THREHT uhn ihng) *adj.* dangerous

tissue (TIHSH oo) *n.* masses of cells forming parts of animals or plants

toil (toyl) *v.* work hard and with difficulty

tone (tohn) *n.* attitude of an interviewer or interviewee toward the subject matter or audience

tradition (truh DIHSH uhn) *n.* long-established custom or practice

transition (tran ZIHSH uhn) *n.* in media, change from one scene or shot to another

U

understandingly (uhn duhr STAN dihng lee) *adv.* in a knowing way; kindly

universal (yoo nuh VUR suhl) *adj.* involving everyone in the world or in a particular group; true or appropriate in every situation

unprecedented (uhn PREHS uh dehn tihd) *adj.* never having happened before; unheard of

unsustainable (uhn suh STAY nuh buhl) *adj.* unable to continue at the same rate or in the same way

urgency (UR juhn see) *n.* state of being very important and needing to be dealt with right away

V

vantage point (VAN tihj) (poynt) *n.* place where the photographer positions the camera

voiceover (VOYS oh vuhr) *n.* voice commenting or narrating off-camera

W

wearily (WIHR uh lee) *adv.* in a tired manner

wisdom (WIHZ duhm) *n.* knowledge; the quality of being wise

VOCABULARIO ACADÉMICO/ VOCABULARIO DE CONCEPTOS

El vocabulario académico está en **letra azul**.

GLOSARIO: VOCABULARIO ACADÉMICO / VOCABULARIO DE CONCEPTOS

A

accomplishments / logros *s.* objetivos alcanzados; hazañas; tareas realizadas hábilmente

accuracy / exactitud *s.* sin errores; corrección

agricultural / agrícola *adj.* relativo a la ciencia o al arte del cultivo y la labranza de la tierra

altered / alteró *v.* cambió

alternate / alterno *adj.* cada dos, uno sí y otro no; *s.* suplente

alternative / alternativa *s.* una opción entre dos o más cosas

amoeba / ameba *s.* / animal microscópico unicelular

ancestors / ancestros *s.* personas de las cuales alguien desciende; antepasados

animation / animación *s.* técnica cinematográfica por medio de la cual se crea la ilusión de movimiento

aptitude / aptitud *s.* habilidad natural o talento

assumption / suposición *s.* algo que se da por hecho

atmosphere / atmósfera *s.* el gas que envuelve la Tierra; el aire

attempts / intentos / atentados *s.* tentativas; ataques

B

barriers / barreras *s.* obstáculos; cosas que bloquean el paso

bitterness / amargura *s.* cualidad de sabor intenso y desagradable; condición que causa dolor o tristeza

blight / plaga *s.* algo que se echa a perder, impide el crecimiento o destruye

bond / vínculo *s.* una conexión que une; lazo

C

calculus / cálculo *s.* cuenta que se usa en matemáticas para estudiar el cambio

canals / canales *s.* cauces de agua artificial para el transporte o el riego

capitalistic / capitalista *adj.* relativo a un sistema económico basado en la propiedad privada

catapulted / catapultó *v.* lanzó con la fuerza de una máquina

catastrophic / catastrófico *adj.* con una consecuencia desastrosa

cede / ceder *v.* dar derechos formalmente a otros

celebrate / celebrar *v.* ensalzar una ocasión especial realizando una actividad placentera

certainty / certeza *s.* conocimiento de que algo es cierto; libre de toda duda

charitable / comprensivo *adj.* benévolo y flexible; indulgente

chronic / crónico *adj.* que dura mucho tiempo o se repite con frecuencia

climate / clima *s.* condiciones atmosféricas de un lugar durante un período de tiempo

close-up shot / primer plano *s.* toma de cámara en la que se muestra al muy de cerca

colonize / colonizar *v.* establecerse en otro territorio lejos de casa

composition / composición *s.* distribución o arreglo de las partes de un cuadro o una escultura

connects / conecta *v.* junta dos cosas

consequence / consecuencia *s.* la relación del efecto a la causa

consequences / consecuencias *s.* resultados de una acción o acciones

consistent / congruente *adj.* que mantiene los mismos principios; coherente

contact / contacto *s.* trato, comunicación; *v.* to get in touch with / contactar, comunicarse

context / contexto *s.* entorno más próximo; entorno de una palabra que influye en su significado

contradict / contradecir *v.* discutir o estar en desacuerdo con alguien o algo

contribute / contribuir *v.* participar en una causa, un evento, un proyecto, etc.

cookies / cookies *s.* pequeños archivos de datos que los sitios webs guardan en las computadoras

covetous / codicioso *adj.* envidioso, avaricioso

crisis / crisis *s.* momento en el que una situación es mala o peligrosa; punto de inflexión en el cual se debe cambiar para bien o para mal

D

deserted / abandonado *adj.* que está desatendido; vacío

desire / deseo *s.* anhelo por algo; petición

determination / determinación *s.* conclusión; decisión firme

devastated / devastó *v.* destruyó; apenó profundamente

development / desarrollo *s.* etapa o aspecto en crecimiento

dialogue / diálogo *s.* conversación

dilemma / dilema *s.* situación en la que se tiene que tomar una decisión difícil

direction / dirección *s.* el plan que tiene el director para una producción o sus instrucciones a los actores y al resto del equipo

discord / discordia *s.* desacuerdo: falta de armonía

discordant / discordante *adj.* sin armonía

discredit / no creer *v.* descreer; *s.* descrédito; pérdida o falta de fe, desprestigio

dispelled / disipó *v.* desvaneció; esparció

disposal / desecho *s.* acción de deshacerse de algo

dissent / disentir *v.* estar en desacuerdo; *s.* disconformidad

diversity / diversidad *s.* variedad; diferencias dentro de un grupo

documentary photography / fotografía documental *s.* fotografías que documentan y retratan un evento

doomed / estaba condenado *v.* estaba destinado a un final desgraciado

E

earnest / serio *adj.* que no bromea

editing / editar *v.* organizar las distintas tomas que se hicieron en la filmación para contar una historia, añadir suspenso y marcar el ritmo de la película

efficiently / eficientemente *adv.* con la mínima cantidad de esfuerzo y gasto; eficazmente

emissions / emisiones *s.* gases y otras sustancias expulsadas en el aire

encouraged / animó *v.* inspiró; ofreció respaldo o apoyo

enlarged / se amplió *v.* se hizo más grande; aumentó de tamaño

enterprise / empresa *s.* iniciativa de negocio o compañía

enthusiastically / con estusiasmo *adv.* con interés y ganas

environment / medio ambiente *s.* la tierra, aire y agua en los que las personas, animales y plantas habitan, así como los rasgos distintivos de esos lugares

ethical / ético *adj.* conforme a unos estándares morales

excruciatingly / terriblemente *adv.* penosamente; miserablemente

extinct / extinto *adj.* que ya no existe

F

flung / lanzado *v.* arrojado con fuerza

forlorn / abandonado *adj.* que lo han dejado o está desierto

fragment / fragmentar *v.* romper o dividir en partes pequeñas; *s.* fragmento; parte pequeña dividida o rota

frantically / frenéticamente *adv.* actuar atacadamente, con enojo, preocupación o dolor

frustrated / frustró *v.* impidió lograr algo

G

generosity / generosidad *s.* voluntad de dar o de compartir

H

heed / prestar atención *v.* mantener plena concentración en algo o alguien

hesitantly / con vacilación *adv.* de manera reacia

I

icon / icono *s.* imagen o símbolo en una computadora

illusion / ilusión *s.* algo que parece real pero no lo es

imitate / imitar *v.* actuar igual a como lo hace alguien; copiar

immense / inmenso *adj.* enorme

imminent / inminente *adj.* amenazador, que puede ocurrir en cualquier momento

impairments / discapacidades *s.* lesiones; daños

impossible / imposible *adj.* incapaz de existir u ocurrir

indignity / indignidad *s.* cualidad de no sentirse digno o respetado

infinitely / infinitamente *adv.* que no se puede; sin límites

influence / influencia *s.* acción de influir en alguien considerablemente

instinctively / instintivamente *adv.* hecho de manera automática, sin pensar

interject / interrumpir *v.* interponer; cortar la continuidad de algo

interstellar / interestelar *adj.* que está en una zona del espacio entre dos o más estrellas

J

justify / justificar *v.* dar buenas razones para llevar a cabo una acción

L

lamented / lamentó *v.* expresó arrepentimiento

light / shadow / claroscuro *s.* técnica que se usa para dar volumen a una imagen

localizing / localizar *v.* juntar, reunir o concentrar en un lugar particular

long shot / plano general *s.* toma de cámara en la que se ve todo el sujeto y parte del fondo

lurched / se tambaleó *v.* dio tumbos, se movió a trompicones

GLOSARIO: VOCABULARIO ACADÉMICO / VOCABULARIO DE CONCEPTOS

M

maintain / sostener *v.* mantener; afirmar que algo es verdad

maladies / enfermedades *s.* dolencias

malcontent / insatisfecho *s.* persona que está siempre descontenta

manual / manual *s.* instrucciones o información en forma de libro

medium shot / plano medio *s.* toma de cámara en la que se ve al sujeto desde una distancia media

miser / avaro *adj.* avaricioso, tacaño

Mission control / centro de control *s.* centro de mando para vuelos al espacio tripulados

monochrome / monocromático *adj.* fotografías en blanco y negro

monotony / monotonía *s.* falta de variedad; aburrimiento

morose / hosco / taciturno *adj.* malhumorado; melancólico

mosaic / mosaico *s.* obra hecha con muchas piezas pequeñas de vidrio o piedras de colores

mutation / mutación *s.* cambio de forma, naturaleza o atributos

mystery / misterio *s.* cualidad de ser inexplicable o un secreto

N

narration / narración *s.* acción de contar una historia

notable / notable *adj.* extraordinario; destacado

O

observation / observación *s.* acción de contemplar; algo que se observa

P

panoramic shot / plano panorámico *s.* plano cinematográfico que muestra una vista completa y amplia

parallel / paralelo *adj.* que va en la misma dirección o tiene la misma naturaleza; similar

performance / representación *s.* actuación o presentación formal delante de una audiencia; espectáculo

permit / permitir *v.* dar permiso, autorizar

perseverance / perseverancia *s.* esfuerzo constante y paciente

persevere / perseverar *v.* seguir pese a las dificultades

perspective / perspectiva *s.* ilusión de profundidad en el arte

philanthropist / filantrópo *s.* persona rica que hace donativos a causas benéficas

planetary / planetario *adj.* relativo a los planetas

pollution / contaminación *s.* la presencia o introducción a un espacio de sustancias perjudiciales o de cosas que tienen efectos dañinos o venenosos

proportion / proporción *s.* relación del tamaño de los elementos en el arte

puzzled / perplejo *adj.* confundido y sin poder entender algo

Q

questioning / interrogatorio *s.* lo que el entrevistador ha elegido como preguntas

R

recklessly / imprudentemente *adv.* sin dar importancia a las consecuencias; descuidadamente

release / liberar *v.* acción de dejar ir; soltar

reproach / reproche *s.* desaprobación; crítica

resilience / resiliencia *s.* capacidad de recuperarse rápidamente

resolute / resuelto *adj.* firme y con un propósito claro

retain / contratar *v.* emplear; fichar

retain / retener *v.* conservar o recordar

rural / rural *adj.* relativo al campo; perteneciente a la agricultura

ruthless / despiadado *adj.* sin compasión piedad

S

scarcity / escasez *s.* cualidad de ser difícil de encontrar; rareza

screenplay / guión *s.* el texto que se usa en la producción de una película

setting / set *s.* donde tiene lugar la entrevista

solid drawing / dibujo sólido *s.* técnica para hacer que una imagen parezca tridimensional

sorrow / pena *s.* tristeza profunda; sufrimiento

sound effect / efecto de sonido *s.* sonidos producidos artificialmente para acompañar al guión radiofónico y cinematográfico, una obra teatral o una producción

squabbling / reñir *v.* pelearse en voz muy alta sobre asuntos de poca importancia

staging / puesta en escena *s.* la representación de una idea para que quede clara

stillness / quietud *s.* ausencia de ruido o movimiento

stimulus / estímulo *s.* algo que lleva a la acción o la reacción

stricken / afligido *adj.* muy afectado por problemas o por una enfermedad

strive / esforzarse *v.* hacer un gran esfuerzo; luchar

struggling / en apuros *adj.* en aprietos; intentando salir adelante con dificultad

subconciously / subconscientemente *adv.* que ocurre en la mente sin ser consciente de ello

submerged / sumergido *adj.* cubierto completamente

sufficient / suficiente *adj.* bastante; que tiene la cantidad exacta que se necesita

supervision / supervisión *s.* acción de vigilar a alguien

T

thesis / tesis *s.* trabajo formal de investigación; opinión apoyada con argumentos

throroughly / completamente *adv.* totalmente, plenamente

threatening / amenazador *adj.* peligroso

timing / duración *s.* número de fotogramas que se usan para una acción

tissue / tejido *s.* estructuras de células que forman partes de animales o plantas

together / juntos *s.* el uno con el otro

toil / esforzarse *v.* trabajar arduamente

tone / tono *s.* la actitud que adopta el hablante hacia un tema o su audiencia

tradition / tradición *s.* costumbre o práctica establecida desde hace mucho tiempo

transition / transición *s.* cambio de una condición, un lugar o una actividad a otros diferentes

U

understandingly / con comprensión *adv.* compasivamente

universal / universal *adj.* que incluye a todo el mundo o a todo un grupo; certero y adecuado en todas las situaciones

unprecedented / sin precedentes *adj.* que nunca ha pasado antes; inaudito

unsustainable / insostenible *adj.* que no puede continuar con el mismo ritmo o de la misma manera

urgency / urgencia *s.* estado o situación que necesita atención inmediata por su importancia

V

vantage point / punto de vista *s.* posición de la cámara

voiceover / voz en off *s.* voz que comenta o narra detrás de la cámara

W

wearily / con cansancio *adv.* con poca energía

wisdom / sabiduría *s.* conocimiento; cualidad de ser sabio

LITERARY TERMS HANDBOOK

ANALOGY An ***analogy*** makes a comparison between two or more things that are similar in some ways but otherwise unalike.

ANECDOTE An ***anecdote*** is a brief nonfiction story about an interesting, amusing, or strange event. Writers tell anecdotes to entertain or to make a point.

ARGUMENT In an ***argument***, the writer states and supports a claim, or opinion, based on factual evidence and logical reasoning. Most arguments are composed of an ***introduction***, in which a claim is stated; the ***body***, in which the claim is supported by evidence; and the ***conclusion***, in which the claim is summarized or restated.

AUTHOR'S POINT OF VIEW The attitude toward a topic an author reveals in a piece of nonfiction writing shows the ***author's point of view***.

AUTHOR'S PURPOSE An ***author's purpose*** is his or her main reason for writing. For example, an author may want to entertain, inform, or persuade the reader. Sometimes an author is trying to teach a moral lesson or reflect on an experience. An author may have more than one purpose for writing.

AUTOBIOGRAPHY An ***autobiography*** is the story of the writer's own life, told by the writer. Autobiographical writing may tell about the person's whole life or only a part of it.

Because autobiographies are about real people and events, they are a form of nonfiction. Most autobiographies are written in the ***first-person point of view***.

BIOGRAPHY A ***biography*** is a form of nonfiction in which a writer tells the life story of another person. Most biographies are written about famous or admirable people. Although biographies are nonfiction, the most effective ones share the qualities of good narrative writing.

BLOG A ***blog post*** is a piece of online writing added to an online journal, called a ***blog***. Writers of blogs provide information or express thoughts on various subjects.

CAUSE AND EFFECT ***A cause-and effect essay*** examines the relationship between events. Effective essays contain clearly stated events and outcomes, using examples, evidence and logic.

CHARACTER A ***character*** is a person or an animal that takes part in the action of a literary work. The main, or ***major,*** character is the most important character in a story, poem, or play. A ***minor*** character is one who takes part in the action but is not the focus of attention.

Characters are sometimes classified as flat or round. A ***flat character*** is one-sided and often stereotypical. A ***round character,*** on the other hand, is fully developed and exhibits many traits—often both faults and virtues. Characters can also be classified as dynamic or static. A ***dynamic character*** is one who changes or grows during the course of the work. A ***static character*** is one who does not change.

CHARACTER TRAITS ***Character traits*** are the individual qualities that make each character unique.

CHARACTERIZATION ***Characterization*** is the act of creating and developing a character. Authors use two major methods of characterization—***direct*** and ***indirect.*** When using direct characterization, a writer states the ***characters' traits,*** or characteristics.

When describing a character indirectly, a writer depends on the reader to draw conclusions about the character's traits. Sometimes the writer tells what other participants in the story say and think about the character.

CHRONOLOGICAL ORDER Writers often sequence events in narratives using ***chronological order***, so that one event proceeds to the next in the order in which they actually happened.

CLIMAX The ***climax,*** also called the turning point, is the high point in the action of the plot. It is the moment of greatest tension, when the outcome of the plot hangs in the balance. See ***Plot.***

COLLABORATIVE DISCUSSION The exploration of a topic in a group setting in which all individuals participate is called a ***collaborative discussion.***

COMEDY A ***comedy*** is a literary work, especially a play, which is light, often humorous or satirical, and ends happily. Comedies frequently depict ordinary characters faced with temporary difficulties and conflicts. Types of comedy include ***romantic comedy,*** which involves problems between lovers, and the ***comedy of manners,*** which satirically challenges social customs of a society.

COMPARISON-AND-CONTRAST ESSAY An essay in which an author lays out the differences and similarities between two subjects is called a ***comparison-and-contrast essay***.

Comparison-and-contrast essays can be organized using ***point-by-point organization*** in which one aspect of both subjects is discussed, then another aspect, and so on. ***Block method organization*** presents all the details of one subject, then all details about the next subject.

CONFLICT A ***conflict*** is a struggle between opposing forces. Conflict is one of the most important elements of stories, novels, and plays because it causes the action. There are two kinds of conflict: external and internal. An ***external conflict*** is one in which a character struggles against some outside force, such as another person. Another kind of external conflict may occur between a character and some force in nature.

R44

An ***internal conflict*** takes place within the mind of a character. The character struggles to make a decision, take an action, or overcome a feeling.

CONNOTATIONS The ***connotation*** of a word is the set of ideas associated with it in addition to its explicit meaning. The connotation of a word can be personal, based on individual experiences. More often, cultural connotations—those recognizable by most people in a group—determine a writer's word choices.

COUNTERCLAIM Opposing views to the main claim of an argument are called ***counterclaims***.

CONSTRUCTIVE CRITCISM Respectful disagreements and critiques, meant to improve an outcome, are referred to as ***constructive criticism***.

CULTURAL CONTEXT The ***cultural context*** of a literary work is the economic, social, and historical environment of the characters. This includes the attitudes and customs of that culture and historical period.

DENOTATION The ***denotation*** of a word is its dictionary meaning, independent of other associations, that the word may have. The denotation of the word ***lake,*** for example, is "an inland body of water." "Vacation spot" and "place where the fishing is good" are connotations of the word ***lake.***

DESCRIPTION A ***description*** is a portrait, in words, of a person, place, or object. Descriptive writing uses images that appeal to the five senses—sight, hearing, touch, taste, and smell.

DIALECT ***Dialect*** is the form of a language spoken by people in a particular region or group. Dialects differ in pronunciation, grammar, and word choice. The English language is divided into many dialects. British English differs from American English.

DIALOGUE A ***dialogue*** is a conversation between characters. In poems, novels, and short stories, dialogue is usually set off by quotation marks to indicate a speaker's exact words.

In a play, dialogue follows the names of the characters, and no quotation marks are used.

DICTION ***Diction*** is a writer's word choice and the way the writer puts those words together. Diction is part of a writer's style and may be described as formal or informal, plain or fancy, ordinary or technical, sophisticated or down-to-earth, old-fashioned or modern.

DIRECT QUOTATIONS Quotations that show a person's exact words in quotation marks are ***direct quotations. Personal interviews*** are a research method often used by authors as a source of direct quotations.

DRAMA A ***drama*** is a story written to be performed by actors. Although a drama is meant to be performed, one can also read the script, or written version, and imagine the action. The ***script*** of a drama is made up of dialogue and stage directions. The ***dialogue*** is the words spoken by the actors. The ***stage directions,*** usually printed in italics, tell how the actors should look, move, and speak. They also describe the setting, sound effects, and lighting.

Dramas are often divided into parts called ***acts.*** The acts are often divided into smaller parts called ***scenes.***

EDITORIAL An ***editorial*** is a type of argument that typically appears in a newspaper and takes a position on a specific topic.

ESSAY An ***essay*** is a short nonfiction work about a particular subject. Most essays have a single major focus and a clear introduction, body, and conclusion.

There are many types of essays. An ***informal essay*** uses casual, conversational language. A ***historical essay*** gives facts, explanations, and insights about historical events. An ***expository essay*** explains an idea by breaking it down. A ***narrative essay*** tells a story about a real-life experience. An ***informational essay*** explains a process. A ***persuasive essay*** offers an opinion and supports it. A ***humorous essay*** uses humor to achieve the author's purpose. A ***descriptive essay*** creates an engaging picture of a subject, by using vivid, sensory details. A ***how-to essay*** is a step-by-step explanation of how to make or do something. An ***explanatory essay*** is a short piece of nonfiction in which the author explains, defines, or interprets ideas, events, or processes. A ***reflective essay*** is a brief prose work in which an author presents his or her thoughts or feelings—or reflections—about an experience or an idea.

EXAMPLE An ***example*** is a fact, idea or event that supports an idea or insight.

EXPOSITION In the plot of a story or a drama, the ***exposition,*** or introduction, is the part of the work that introduces the characters, setting, and basic situation.

EXPOSITORY WRITING ***Expository writing*** is writing that explains or informs.

FANTASY A ***fantasy*** is highly imaginative writing that contains elements not found in real life. Examples of fantasy include stories that involve supernatural elements, stories that resemble fairy tales, stories that deal with imaginary places and creatures, and science-fiction stories.

FICTION ***Fiction*** is prose writing that tells about imaginary characters and events. Short stories and novels are works of fiction. Some writers base their fiction on actual events and people, adding invented characters, dialogue, settings, and plots. Other writers rely on imagination alone.

FIGURATIVE LANGUAGE ***Figurative language*** is writing or speech that is not meant to be taken literally. The many types of figurative language are known as ***figures of speech.*** Common figures of speech include metaphor, personification, and simile. Writers use figurative language to state ideas in vivid and imaginative ways.

R45

GLOSSARY: LITERARY TERMS HANDBOOK

FRAME STORY A ***frame story*** is a story that brackets—or frames—another story or group of stories. This framing device creates a story-within-a-story narrative structure.

FREE VERSE ***Free verse*** is poetry not written with a ***formal structure***, or in a regular, rhythmical pattern, or meter. The poet is free to write lines of any length or with any number of stresses, or beats. Free verse is therefore less constraining than ***metrical verse,*** in which every line must have a certain length and a certain number of stresses.

GENRE A ***genre*** is a division or type of literature. Literature is commonly divided into three major genres: poetry, prose, and drama. Each major genre is, in turn, divided into lesser genres, as follows:

1. ***Poetry:*** lyric poetry, concrete poetry, dramatic poetry, narrative poetry, epic poetry
2. ***Prose:*** fiction (novels and short stories) and nonfiction (biography, autobiography, letters, essays, and reports)
3. ***Drama:*** serious drama and tragedy, comic drama, melodrama, and farce

HISTORICAL CONTEXT The ***historical context*** of a literary work includes the actual political and social events and trends of the time. When a work takes place in the past, knowledge about that historical time period can help the reader understand its setting, background, culture, and message, as well as the attitudes and actions of its characters. A reader must also take into account the historical context in which the writer was creating the work, which may be different from the time period of the work's setting.

HUMOR ***Humor*** is writing intended to evoke laughter. While most humorists try to entertain, humor can also be used to convey a serious theme.

HYPERBOLE ***Hyperbole*** is a form of figurative language that uses exaggeration for effect.

IDIOM An ***idiom*** is an expression that has a meaning particular to a language or region.

IMAGERY ***Imagery*** is a technique of writing with images.

IMAGES ***Images*** are words or phrases that appeal to one or more of the five senses. Writers use images to describe how their subjects look, sound, feel, taste, and smell. Poets often paint images, or word pictures, that appeal to the senses. These pictures help you to experience the poem fully.

INFERENCES An ***inference*** is a guess based on clues. Very often in literature, authors leave some details unstated; it is up to readers to "fill in the blanks" and infer details about characters, events, and setting.

IRONY ***Irony*** is a contradiction between what happens and what is expected. There are three main types of irony. ***Situational irony*** occurs when something happens that directly contradicts the expectations of the characters or the audience. ***Verbal irony*** is created when words are used to suggest the opposite of their meaning. In ***dramatic irony,*** the audience is aware of something that the character or speaker is not aware of. The result is suspense or humor.

JOURNAL A ***journal*** is a daily or periodic account of events and the writer's thoughts and feelings about those events. Personal journals are not normally written for publication, but sometimes they do get published later with permission from the author or the author's family.

LETTERS A ***letter*** is a written communication from one person to another. In personal letters, the writer shares information and his or her thoughts and feelings with one other person or group. Although letters are not normally written for publication, they sometimes do get published later with the permission of the author or the author's family.

LYRIC POEM A ***lyric poem*** is a highly musical verse that expresses the observations and feelings of a single speaker. It creates a single, unified impression.

MAIN IDEA The ***main idea*** is the ***central idea*** or most important point in a text.

MEDIA Stories and information are shared using different forms of ***media***. Books and magazines are a type of media. Film, video, and digital are other forms of media. A ***multimedia presentation*** is created from combination of words, images, sounds, and video.

MEDIA ACCOUNTS ***Media accounts*** are reports, explanations, opinions, or descriptions written for television, radio, newspapers, and magazines. While some media accounts report only facts, others include the writer's thoughts and reflections.

METAPHOR A ***metaphor*** is a figure of speech in which something is described as though it were something else. A metaphor, like a simile, works by pointing out a similarity between two unlike things.

MONOLOGUE A ***monologue*** is a dramatic speech presented by a single character in a play. The character speaks from the first-person point of view and relates his or her thoughts and feelings.

MOOD The ***mood*** is the feeling created in a reader by a piece of writing. Writers create mood by using imagery, word choice and descriptive details.

MOTIVE A ***motive*** is a reason that explains or partially explains a character's thoughts, feelings, actions, or speech. Writers try to make their characters' motives, or motivations, as clear as possible. If the motives of a main character are not clear, then the character will not be believable.

Characters are often motivated by needs, such as food and shelter. They are also motivated by feelings, such as fear, love, and pride. Motives may be obvious or hidden.

NARRATION ***Narration*** is writing that tells a story. The act of telling a story is also called narration. Any story told in fiction, nonfiction, poetry, or even drama is called a narrative.

Writers of narratives employ many techniques to bring their stories to life. For example, most narratives contain a plot, setting, characters, and theme. The readers' experience can be enhanced by varied **narrative pacing**, in which the writer speeds up or slows down the plot events to create effects such as suspense.

NARRATIVE A ***narrative*** is a story. Novels and short stories are types of fictional narratives. Biographies and autobiographies are nonfiction narratives.

NARRATIVE POEM A ***narrative poem*** is a story told in verse. Narrative poems often have all the elements of short stories, including characters, conflict, and plot.

NARRATOR A ***narrator*** is a speaker or a character who tells a story. The narrator's perspective is the way he or she sees things. A ***third-person narrator*** is one who stands outside the action and speaks about it. A ***first-person narrator*** is one who tells a story and participates in its action.

NONFICTION ***Nonfiction*** is prose writing that presents and explains ideas or that tells about real people, places, objects, or events. Autobiographies, biographies, essays, reports, letters, memos, and newspaper articles are all types of nonfiction.

NOVEL A ***novel*** is a long work of fiction. Novels contain such elements as characters, plot, conflict, and setting. The writer of novels, or novelist, develops these elements. In addition to its main plot, a novel may contain one or more subplots, or independent, related stories. A novel may also have several themes.

See ***Fiction*** and ***Short Story.***

ONOMATOPOEIA ***Onomatopoeia*** is the use of words that imitate sounds. ***Crash, buzz, screech, hiss, neigh, jingle,*** and ***cluck*** are examples of onomatopoeia. ***Chickadee, towhee,*** and ***whippoorwill*** are onomatopoeic names of birds.

ORGANIZATION The structure of a text or media presentation is referred to as its **organization**. Common organizational structures are cause-and-effect, comparison-and contrast, order of importance, and chronological order. Writers choose organizational structures that best suit their topic and purpose.

OXYMORON An ***oxymoron*** (pl. ***oxymora***) is a figure of speech that links two opposite or contradictory words in order to point out an idea or situation that seems contradictory or inconsistent but on closer inspection turns out to be somehow true.

PARAPHRASE When you ***paraphrase***, you restate a text using your own words.

PERSONIFICATION ***Personification*** is a type of figurative language in which a nonhuman subject is given human characteristics.

PERSUASION ***Persuasion*** is used in writing or speech that attempts to convince the reader or listener to adopt a particular opinion or course of action. Newspaper editorials and letters to the editor use persuasion. So do advertisements and campaign speeches given by political candidates.

Writers use a combination of persuasive techniques to argue their point of view. ***Appeals to authority*** use the statements of experts. ***Appeals to emotion*** use words that convey strong feelings. ***Appeals to reason*** use logical arguments backed by facts.

PLAYWRIGHT A ***playwright*** is a person who writes plays. William Shakespeare is regarded as the greatest playwright in English literature.

PLOT ***Plot*** is the sequence of events in which each event results from a previous one and causes the next. In most novels, dramas, short stories, and narrative poems, the plot involves both characters and a central conflict. The plot usually begins with an ***exposition*** that introduces the setting, the characters, and the basic situation. This is followed by the ***inciting incident,*** which introduces the central conflict. The conflict then increases during the ***development*** until it reaches a high point of interest or suspense, the ***climax.*** The climax is followed by the ***falling action,*** or end, of the central conflict. Any events that occur during the ***falling action*** make up the ***resolution*** or ***denouement.***

Some plots do not have all of these parts. Some stories begin with the inciting incident and end with the resolution. See ***Conflict.***

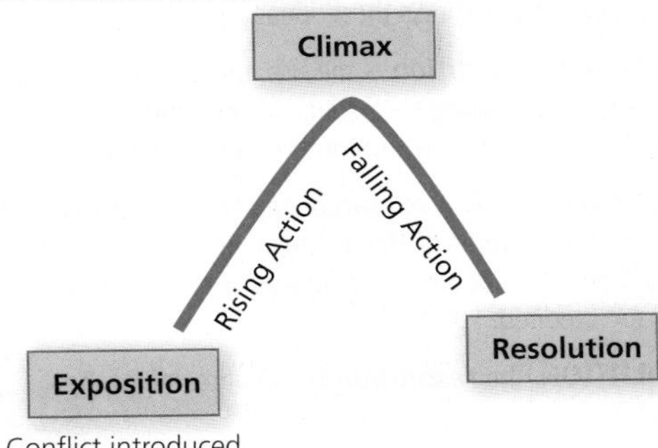

POETRY ***Poetry*** is one of the three major types of literature, the others being prose and drama. Most poems make use of highly concise, musical, and emotionally charged language. Many also make use of imagery, figurative language, and special devices of sound such as rhyme. Major types of poetry include ***lyric poetry, narrative poetry,*** and ***concrete poetry.***

POINT OF VIEW ***Point of view*** is the perspective, or vantage point, from which a story is told. It is either a

R47

narrator outside the story or a character in the story. ***First-person point of view*** is told by a character who uses the first-person pronoun "I."

The two kinds of ***third-person point of view,*** limited and omniscient, are called "third person" because the narrator uses third-person pronouns such as he and she to refer to the characters. There is no "I" telling the story.

In stories told from the ***omniscient third-person point of view,*** the narrator knows and tells about what each character feels and thinks.

In stories told from the ***limited third-person point of view,*** the narrator relates the inner thoughts and feelings of only one character, and everything is viewed from this character's perspective.

PRESENTATION A presentation is the act of showing or demonstrating something to an audience. ***Oral presentations***, spoken aloud to a live audience, may include other ***visual presentation*** forms, such as charts, diagrams, illustrations, and photos. Video clips and slide shows often are key parts of ***digital presentations***, which are created partly or entirely on a computer.

PROSE ***Prose*** is the ordinary form of written language. Most writing that is not poetry, drama, or song is considered prose. Prose is one of the major genres of literature and occurs in fiction and nonfiction.

QUOTATION ***Quotations*** are groups of words that are taken from a text, a speech, or from an interview and are used or repeated by someone other than the original author or speaker. Quotations must be attributed to the original writer or speaker.

READ CLOSELY To ***read closely*** involves careful analysis of a text, its ideas, and the ways in which the author chooses to express those ideas.

REPETITION ***Repetition*** is the use, more than once, of any element of language—a sound, word, phrase, clause, or sentence. Repetition is used in both prose and poetry.

RESEARCH PAPER A ***research paper*** provides detailed information on a topic or thesis. Effective research papers are built on information from a variety of credible sources, which are credited.

RESOLUTION The ***resolution*** is the outcome of the conflict in a plot.

RETELLING A ***retelling*** of a story can be either written or oral and should include a clear sequence of events and narrative techniques such as dialogue and description.

RHYME ***Rhyme*** is the repetition of sounds at the ends of words. Poets use rhyme to lend a songlike quality to their verses and to emphasize certain words and ideas. Many traditional poems contain ***end rhymes,*** or rhyming words at the ends of lines.

Another common device is the use of ***internal rhymes,*** or rhyming words within lines. Internal rhyme also emphasizes the flowing nature of a poem.

RHYTHM ***Rhythm*** is the pattern of stressed and unstressed syllables in spoken or written language.

SCAN To ***scan*** is to run your eyes over the text to find answers to questions, to clarify, or to find supporting details.

SCENE A ***scene*** is a section of uninterrupted action in the act of a drama.

SCIENCE FICTION ***Science fiction*** combines elements of fiction and fantasy with scientific fact. Many science-fiction stories are set in the future.

SCRIPT A ***script*** is the written version of a play or film. It includes ***dialogue*** and ***stage directions***.

SENSORY LANGUAGE ***Sensory language*** is writing or speech that appeals to one or more of the five senses.

SETTING The ***setting*** of a literary work is the time and place of the action. The setting includes all the details of a place and time—the year, the time of day, even the weather. The place may be a specific country, state, region, community, neighborhood, building, institution, or home. Details such as dialects, clothing, customs, and modes of transportation are often used to establish setting. In most stories, the setting serves as a backdrop—a context in which the characters interact. Setting can also help to create a feeling, or atmosphere.

SHORT STORY A ***short story*** is a brief work of fiction. Like a novel, a short story presents a sequence of events, or plot. The plot usually deals with a central conflict faced by a main character, or protagonist. The events in a short story usually communicate a message about life or human nature. This message, or central idea, is the story's theme.

SIMILE A ***simile*** is a figure of speech that uses ***like*** or ***as*** to make a direct comparison between two unlike ideas. Everyday speech often contains similes, such as "pale as a ghost," "good as gold," "spread like wildfire," and "clever as a fox."

SKIM To ***skim*** is to look over the text quickly, to get a sense of important ideas before reading.

SOUND DEVICES ***Sound devices*** are techniques used by writers to give musical effects to their writing. Some of these include ***onomatopoeia, alliteration, rhyme, meter,*** and ***repetition.***

SPEAKER The ***speaker*** is the imaginary voice a poet uses when writing a poem. The speaker is the character who tells the poem. This character, or voice, often is not identified by name. There can be important differences between the poet and the poem's speaker.

SPEECH A ***speech*** is a work that is delivered orally to an audience. There are many kinds of speeches suiting almost every kind of public gathering. Types of speeches include ***dramatic, persuasive,*** and ***informative.***

STAGE DIRECTIONS ***Stage directions*** are notes included in a drama to describe how the work is to be performed or staged. Stage directions are usually printed in italics and enclosed within parentheses or brackets. Some stage directions describe the movements, costumes, emotional states, and ways of speaking of the characters.

STAGING ***Staging*** includes the setting, lighting, costumes, special effects, and music that go into a stage performance of a drama.

SUMMARY A ***summary*** is a short, clear description of the main ideas of something, such as a text, a film, or a presentation. Effective summaries are objective—free from bias or evaluation.

SYMBOL A ***symbol*** is anything that stands for or represents something else. Symbols are common in everyday life. A dove with an olive branch in its beak is a symbol of peace. A blindfolded woman holding a balanced scale is a symbol of justice. A crown is a symbol of a king's status and authority.

SYMBOLISM ***Symbolism*** is the use of symbols. Symbolism plays an important role in many different types of literature. It can highlight certain elements the author wishes to emphasize and also add levels of meaning.

THEME A ***theme*** is a central message in a literary work that can usually be expressed in a general statement about human beings or about life. The theme of a work is not a summary of its plot.

Although a theme may be stated directly in the text, it is more often presented indirectly. When the theme is stated indirectly, or implied, the reader must figure out what the theme is by looking at what the work reveals about people or life.

TONE The ***tone*** of a literary work is the writer's attitude toward his or her audience and subject. The tone can often be described by a single adjective, such as ***formal*** or ***informal, serious*** or ***playful, bitter*** or ***ironic.*** Factors that contribute to the tone are word choice, sentence structure, line length, rhyme, rhythm, and repetition.

UNIVERSAL THEME A ***universal theme*** is a message about life that is expressed regularly in many different cultures and time periods. Folk tales, epics, and romances often address universal themes like the importance of courage, the power of love, or the danger of greed.

WEIGHTED WORDS Words that have strong emotional associations beyond their basic meanings are ***weighted words.***

WORD CHOICE A writer's ***word choice*** is the way the writer puts those words together. Diction is part of a writer's style and may be described as formal or informal, plain or fancy, ordinary or technical, sophisticated or down-to-earth, old-fashioned or modern.

MANUAL DE TÉRMINOS LITERARIOS

ANALOGY / ANALOGÍA Una ***analogía*** establece una comparación entre dos o varias cosas que comparten similitudes, pero son distintas en todo lo demás.

ANECDOTE / ANÉCDOTA Una ***anécdota*** es un relato corto de no ficción sobre un acontecimiento extraño, interesante o divertido. Los escritores cuentan anécdotas para entretener o explicar algo importante.

ARGUMENT / ARGUMENTO En un ***argumento*** los escritores exponen y defienden una afirmación o una opinión, para lo cual se basan en hechos probados o razonamientos lógicos. Casi todos los argumentos tienen una ***introducción***, en la que se expone una afirmación; un ***desarrollo***, en el que se respalda la afirmación con evidencia; y una ***conclusión***, en la que se resume o replantea la afirmación.

AUTHOR'S POINT OF VIEW / PUNTO DE VISTA DEL AUTOR La postura hacia el tema que revela el autor de un texto de no ficción muestra el ***punto de vista del autor***.

AUTHOR'S PURPOSE / PROPÓSITO DEL AUTOR El ***propósito del autor*** es la razón principal por la que este autor o autora escribe. Por ejemplo, un autor puede buscar entretener, informar o persuadir al lector. En ocasiones un autor intenta enseñarnos una lección moral o reflexionar sobre una experiencia. Un autor puede tener más de un propósito por los que escribir.

AUTOBIOGRAPHY / AUTOBIOGRAFÍA Una ***autobiografía*** es la historia de la vida del propio autor. Los textos autobiográficos pueden hablar de la vida completa del autor o solo de una parte.

Como las autobiografías tratan sobre gente y acontecimientos reales, son consideradas como no ficción. La mayoría de las autobiografías están escritas en narrador en primera persona.

BIOGRAPHY / BIOGRAFÍA Una ***biografía*** es un tipo de texto de no ficción donde el escritor explica la historia de la vida de otra persona. La mayoría de las biografías son sobre gente famosa y admirable. Aunque las biografías están consideradas libros de no ficción, las de mayor calidad suelen compartir cualidades con los buenos textos narrativos.

BLOG / BLOG Una ***entrada de blog*** es un texto en línea que se aporta a un diario en línea llamado ***blog***. Los autores de blogs ofrecen información o expresan su opinión sobre distintos temas.

CAUSE AND EFFECT / CAUSA Y EFECTO Un ***ensayo de causa y efecto*** estudia la relación que hay entre los sucesos. Los ensayos eficaces exponen claramente los sucesos y sus resultados. Para ello utilizan ejemplos, evidencia y lógica.

CHARACTER / PERSONAJE Un ***personaje*** es una persona o un animal que participa en la acción de una obra literaria. El personaje ***principal*** o protagonista es el más importante de una historia, poema u obra teatral. El personaje ***secundario*** participa también en la acción pero no es el centro de atención.

A menudo se clasifican los personajes como planos o redondos.

Un ***personaje plano*** es unilateral y a menudo estereotipado.

Un ***personaje redondo***, por el contrario, está desarrollado completamente y presenta muchos rasgos (a menudo tanto defectos como virtudes). También se pueden clasificar a los personajes como dinámicos o estáticos. Un ***personaje dinámico*** es aquel que cambia o evoluciona a lo largo de la obra. Un ***personaje estático*** es aquel que no cambia.

RASGOS DEL PERSONAJE Los ***rasgos del personaje*** son las características particulares que hacen que cada personaje sea único.

CHARACTERIZATION / CARACTERIZACIÓN La ***caracterización*** es la acción de crear y desarrollar un personaje. Los autores utilizan dos métodos principales de caracterización: ***directa*** e ***indirecta.*** Cuando se utiliza la caracterización directa, el escritor describe los ***rasgos del personaje*** o sus características.

En cambio, cuando se describe a un personaje indirectamente, el escritor depende del lector para que pueda extraer conclusiones sobre los rasgos del personaje. A veces el escritor cuenta lo que otros personajes que participan en la historia dicen o piensan sobre el personaje en cuestión.

CHRONOLOGICAL ORDER / ORDEN CRONOLÓGICO Los escritores suelen enumerar los sucesos de la narración en ***orden cronológico***, de manera que un suceso lleva al siguiente en el orden en el que tuvieron lugar.

CLIMAX / CLÍMAX El ***clímax,*** también llamado momento culminante, es el punto más elevado de la acción de una trama. Es el momento de mayor tensión, es decir, cuando el desenlace de la trama pende de un hilo. Ver ***Trama.***

COLLABORATIVE DISCUSSION / DISCUSIÓN COLABORATIVA Se conoce como ***discusión colaborativa*** a la exploración de un tema en grupo, con la participación de todos los miembros del grupo.

COMEDY / COMEDIA Una ***comedia*** es una obra literaria, especialmente una obra de teatro, que es ligera, a menudo cómica o satírica y tiene un final feliz. Las comedias describen a personajes normales que se enfrentan a dificultades y conflictos temporales. Algunos tipos de comedia incluyen la ***comedia romántica***, que contiene problemas entre amantes, y la ***comedia de costumbres,*** que cuestiona satíricamente las costumbres sociales de un sector de la sociedad.

COMPARISON-AND-CONTRAST ESSAY / ENSAYO DE COMPARACIÓN Y CONTRASTE Se conoce como ***ensayo de comparación y contraste*** al ensayo en el que el autor expone las diferencias y similitudes entre dos asuntos.

Los ensayos de comparación y contraste pueden utilizar una ***organización de punto por punto*** en la que primero se trata un aspecto de los dos asuntos, después otro y así sucesivamente. También se puede emplear una ***organización de método de bloques*** en la que primero se presentan todos los detalles de uno de los asuntos, seguidos por los detalles del otro asunto.

CONFLICT / CONFLICTO Un ***conflicto*** es una lucha entre fuerzas opuestas. El conflicto es uno de los elementos más importantes de los cuentos, novelas y obras de teatro porque provoca la acción. Hay dos tipos de conflictos: externos e internos.

Un ***conflicto externo*** se da cuando un personaje lucha contra una fuerza ajena a él, como por ejemplo otra persona. Otro tipo de conflicto externo puedo ocurrir entre un personaje y una fuerza de la naturaleza.

Un ***conflicto interno*** tiene lugar en la mente de un personaje. El personaje lucha por tomar una decisión, llevar a cabo una acción o frenar un sentimiento.

CONNOTATIONS / CONNOTACIONES La ***connotación*** de una palabra es el conjunto de ideas que se asocian con esta, más allá de su significado explícito. La connotación de una palabra puede ser personal, basada en una experiencia individual. Con frecuencia son las connotaciones culturales, aquellas que son reconocibles por la mayoría de las personas de un grupo, las que determinan la elección de un autor.

COUNTERCLAIM / CONTRAARGUMENTO Se conoce como ***contraargumento*** a la opinión contraria a la expresada en un argumento anterior.

CONSTRUCTIVE CRITICISM / CRÍTICA CONSTRUCTIVA Se conoce como ***crítica constructiva*** a las diferencias de opinión que se exponen de manera respetuosa y que tienen como fin mejorar un resultado.

CULTURAL CONTEXT / CONTEXTO CULTURAL El ***contexto cultural*** de una obra literaria es el entorno económico, social e histórico de los personajes. Este incluye los comportamientos y costumbres de dicho período cultural e histórico.

DENOTATION / DENOTACIÓN La ***denotación*** de una palabra es su significado del diccionario, independientemente de otras asociaciones que se le puedan otorgar. La denotación de la palabra *lago* sería "una masa de agua que se acumula en un terreno". "Un lugar de vacaciones" o "un lugar adonde se puede ir de pesca" son connotaciones de la palabra *lago.*

DESCRIPTION / DESCRIPCIÓN Una ***descripción*** es un retrato en palabras de una persona, lugar u objeto. Los textos descriptivos utilizan imágenes que se relacionan con los cinco sentidos: vista, oído, tacto, gusto y olfato.

DIALECT / DIALECTO Un ***dialecto*** es la variedad de una lengua que habla un grupo o una región particular. Los dialectos se diferencian en la pronunciación, gramática y elección de las palabras utilizadas. La lengua inglesa está dividida en muchos dialectos. Por ejemplo, el inglés británico es distinto del inglés americano.

DIALOGUE / DIÁLOGO Un ***diálogo*** es una conversación entre personajes. En los poemas, novelas y cuentos en inglés, los diálogos se indican normalmente entre comillas para señalar que estas son las palabras exactas que dice un personaje.

En una obra de teatro, los diálogos se colocan detrás de los nombres de los personajes y no se utilizan comillas.

DICTION / DICCIÓN La ***dicción*** es tanto la elección de las palabras que hace un escritor como la manera de combinarlas. La dicción forma parte del estilo de un escritor y puede ser descrita como formal o informal, sencilla o elegante, corriente o técnica, sofisticada o sobria, anticuada o moderna.

DIRECT QUOTATIONS / CITAS DIRECTAS Las ***citas directas*** presentan las palabras exactas que dijo alguien y se ponen entre comillas. Las ***entrevistas personales*** son uno de los métodos de investigación que utilizan los autores como fuente de citas directas.

DRAMA / DRAMA Un ***drama*** es una historia escrita para ser representada por actores. Aunque está destinada a ser representada, también se puede, únicamente, leer su texto e imaginar la acción. El ***texto dramático***, o guión, está compuesto de diálogos y acotaciones. Los ***diálogos*** son palabras que dicen los personajes. Las ***acotaciones*** aparecen normalmente en cursiva e indican cómo deben verse, moverse o hablar los personajes. También describen el decorado, los efectos de sonido y la iluminación.

Los dramas suelen estar divididos en distintas partes denominadas ***actos.*** Los actos aparecen a menudo divididos en partes más pequeñas denominadas ***escenas.***

EDITORIAL / EDITORIAL Un ***editorial*** es un tipo de argumento que suele aparecer en los periódicos y que adopta una postura en un asunto determinado.

ESSAY / ENSAYO Un ***ensayo*** es un texto de no ficción corto sobre un tema particular. La mayoría de los ensayos se concentran en un único aspeco fundamental y tienen una introducción clara, un desarrollo y una conclusión.

Hay muchos tipos de ensayos. Un ***ensayo informal*** emplea lenguaje coloquial y conversacional. Un ***ensayo histórico*** nos presenta hechos, explicaciones y conocimientos sobre acontecimientos históricos.

R51

Un ***ensayo expositivo*** expone una idea desglosándola. Un ***ensayo narrativo*** cuenta una historia sobre una experiencia real. Un ***ensayo informativo*** explica un proceso. Un ***ensayo argumentativo*** ofrece una opinión y la argumenta. Un ***ensayo humorístico*** utiliza el humor para lograr el propósito del autor. Un ***ensayo explicativo*** aclara, define e interpreta ideas, acontecimientos o procesos. En un ***ensayo reflexivo*** el autor presenta sus pensamientos y sentimientos o reflexiones sobre una experiencia o idea.

EXAMPLE / EJEMPLO Un ***ejemplo*** es un dato, idea o suceso que respalda un concepto o una visión de las cosas.

EXPOSITION / PLANTEAMIENTO En el argumento de una historia o drama, el ***planteamiento*** o introducción es la parte de la obra que presenta a los personajes, escenarios y situación básica.

EXPOSITORY WRITING / TEXTO EXPOSITIVO Un ***texto expositivo*** es un texto que explica e informa.

FANTASY / LITERATURA FANTÁSTICA La ***literatura fantástica*** son textos con elementos muy imaginativos que no pueden encontrarse en la vida real. Algunos ejemplos de literatura fantástica incluyen historias que contienen elementos supernaturales, historias que recuerdan a los cuentos de hadas, historias que tratan de lugares y criaturas imaginarias e historias de ciencia ficción.

FICTION / FICCIÓN La ***ficción*** son obras en prosa que hablan de sucesos y personajes imaginarios. Los relatos y las novelas son obras de ficción. Algunos escritores se inspiran para sus obras de ficción en sucesos y personas reales, a los que añaden también personajes, diálogos, escenarios y tramas inventados. Otros escritores se sirven únicamente de la imaginación.

FIGURATIVE LANGUAGE / LENGUAJE FIGURADO El ***lenguaje figurado*** es un texto o diálogo que no se debe interpretar literalmente. A los numerosos tipos de lenguaje figurado se los llama ***figuras retóricas.*** Algunas de las más comunes son las metáforas, las personificaciones y los símiles. Los escritores utilizan el lenguaje figurado para expresar ideas de una manera imaginativa y vívida.

FRAME STORY / NARRACIÓN ENMARCADA Una ***narración enmarcada*** es una historia que pone entre paréntesis o enmarca otra historia o grupo de historias. Este recurso literario crea la estructura narrativa de una historia dentro de otra historia.

FREE VERSE / VERSO LIBRE El ***verso libre*** es poesía que no tiene una ***estructura formal***; es decir, que no sigue un patrón rítmico ni métrico normal. El poeta es libre de escribir versos de la extensión que prefiera y con un número libre de acentos. Por consiguiente, el verso libre es menos restrictivo que el ***verso métrico***, en el que cada verso debe contener acentos y un número concreto de sílabas.

GENRE / GÉNERO Un ***género*** es una clase o tipo de literatura. La literatura se divide normalmente en tres géneros principales: poesía, prosa y drama. Cada uno de estos géneros está, a su vez, dividido en otros géneros menores:

1. ***Poesía:*** poesía lírica, poesía concreta, poesía dramática, poesía narrativa, poesía épica
2. ***Prosa:*** ficción (novelas y cuentos cortos) y no ficción (biografías, autobiografías, cartas, ensayos y reportajes)
3. ***Drama:*** drama serio y tragedia, comedia, melodrama y farsa

HISTORICAL CONTEXT / CONTEXTO HISTÓRICO El ***contexto histórico*** de una obra literaria lo constituyen los verdaderos acontecimientos y tendencias político-sociales de la época. Cuando una obra tiene lugar en el pasado, el conocimiento previo sobre ese período histórico puede ayudar al lector a comprender la ambientación, trasfondo, cultura y mensaje, así como las actitudes y acciones de sus personajes. Un lector también debe tener en cuenta el contexto histórico en el que el escritor creó su obra, ya que puede ser distinto del contexto real en el que se desarrolla la obra.

HUMOR / HUMOR El ***humor*** es una forma de escribir que incita a la risa. Si bien es cierto que la mayoría de los humoristas tratan de entretener, también se puede utilizar el humor para transmitir un tema serio.

HYPERBOLE / HIPÉRBOLE La ***hipérbole*** es un tipo de figura retórica que utiliza la exageración para provocar un efecto en el lector.

IDIOM / MODISMOS Los ***modismos*** son expresiones idiomáticas que tienen un significado particular en una lengua o región.

IMAGERY / IMAGINERÍA La ***imaginería*** es la técnica de escribir con imágenes.

IMAGES / IMÁGENES La ***imágenes*** son palabras o frases que se relacionan con uno o varios de los cinco sentidos. Los escritores utilizan imágenes para describir qué apariencia tienen, cómo suenan, sienten, saben y huelen las personas u objetos descritos. Los poetas suelen dibujar imágenes o hacer una descripción visual que se vincula con los sentidos. Estas descripciones visuales nos ayudan a experimentar el poema en su totalidad.

INFERENCES / INFERENCIAS Una inferencia es una suposición que se basa en pistas. Es frecuente en la literatura que los autores no lo expliquen todo; les corresponde a los lectores "llenar los espacios en blanco" e inferir detalles sobre los personajes, sucesos y ambiente.

IRONY / IRONÍA Una ***ironía*** es una contradicción entre lo que ocurre realmente y lo que se espera que pase. Hay tres tipos principales de ironía. La ***ironía situacional*** que se da cuando ocurre algo que se contradice directamente con aquello que los personajes o la audiencia espera. La ***ironía verbal*** que se crea cuando se usan las palabras para insinuar algo distinto a su significado literal. La ***ironía dramática,*** en la que audiencia conoce algo que el personaje o la persona que habla no sabe. El resultado es el suspenso o el humor.

JOURNAL / DIARIO Un ***diario*** es un relato periódico o diario de acontecimientos y reflexiones u opiniones que el escritor tiene sobre esos acontecimientos. Los diarios personales no se escriben normalmente para ser publicados, pero en ocasiones se publican más tarde con el permiso del autor o de la familia del autor.

LETTERS / CARTAS Una ***carta*** es una comunicación escrita de una persona a otra. En las cartas personales, los escritores comparten información, así como sus opiniones y sentimientos sobre otra persona o grupo. Aunque las cartas no se escriben normalmente para ser publicadas, a veces se publican más tarde con el permiso del autor o de la familia del autor.

LYRIC POEM / POEMA LÍRICO Un ***poema lírico*** es un verso con mucha musicalidad que expresa las observaciones y sentimientos de una sola persona. Crea una impresión única y unificada.

MAIN IDEA / IDEA PRINCIPAL La ***idea principal*** es la ***idea central*** o lo más importante de un texto.

MEDIA ACCOUNTS / REPORTAJES PERIODÍSTICOS Los ***reportajes periodísticos*** son relatos, explicaciones, opiniones o descripciones escritas para televisión, radio, periódicos o revistas. Si bien algunos reportajes periodísticos solo relatan hechos, otros incluyen también las opiniones y reflexiones del autor.

METAPHOR / METÁFORA Una ***metáfora*** es una figura retórica que se utiliza para identificar una cosa con algo distinto. Una metáfora, al igual que un símil, se obtiene analizando las similitudes que comparten dos cosas distintas.

MONOLOGUE / MONÓLOGO Un ***monólogo*** en una obra de teatro es un parlamento por parte de un personaje. El personaje habla desde el punto de vista de primera persona y comparte sus pensamientos y sentimientos.

MOOD / ATMÓSFERA La ***atmósfera*** es la sensación que un texto produce en el lector. Los escritores crean la atmósfera mediante el uso de imaginería, su elección de palabras y los detalles descriptivos.

MOTIVE / MOTIVACIÓN Una ***motivación*** es una razón que explica total o parcialmente las opiniones, sentimientos, acciones o diálogos de los personajes. El escritor intenta exponer las motivaciones o motivos de la manera más clara posible. Si las motivaciones de un personaje principal no están claras, el personaje no será creíble.

Las motivaciones que mueven con frecuencia a los personajes son necesidades tales como encontrar comida o un refugio. Además les pueden motivar también sentimientos como el miedo, el amor y el orgullo. Las motivaciones pueden ser claras u ocultas.

NARRATION / NARRACIÓN Una ***narración*** es un texto que cuenta una historia. También se denomina narración a la acción de contar una historia. Una historia contada en ficción, no ficción, poesía o incluso en drama es conocida como narración.

Los escritores emplean distintas técnicas para darles vida a sus historias. Por ejemplo, las narraciones suelen tener una trama, un escenario, varios personajes y un tema. La experiencia de los lectores se enriquece con el uso de distintos ***ritmos narrativos***, mediante los que el escritor acelera o desacelera los sucesos de la narración para crear una variedad de efectos como el suspenso.

NARRATIVE / TEXTO NARRATIVO Un ***texto narrativo*** es una historia. Las novelas y los cuentos son tipos de textos narrativos de ficción. Las biografías y las autobiografías son textos narrativos de no ficción.

NARRATIVE POEM / POEMA NARRATIVO Un ***poema narrativo*** es una historia contada en verso. Un poema narrativo cuenta a menudo con todos los elementos de los cuentos; incluye personajes, conflicto y trama.

NARRATOR / NARRADOR Un ***narrador*** es la persona o personaje que cuenta una historia. El punto de vista del narrador es la manera en la que él o ella ve las cosas. Un ***narrador en tercera persona*** es aquel que solo habla de la acción sin implicarse en ella. Un ***narrador en primera persona*** es aquel que cuenta una historia y además participa en su acción.

NONFICTION / NO FICCIÓN Una ***no ficción*** es un texto en prosa que presenta y explica ideas, o que trata de personas, lugares, objetos o acontecimientos de la vida real. Las autobiografías, biografías, ensayos, reportajes, cartas, memorandos y artículos periodísticos son todos diferentes tipos de no ficción.

NOVEL / NOVELA Una ***novela*** es una obra larga de ficción. Las novelas contienen elementos tales como los personajes, la trama, el conflicto y los escenarios. Los escritores de novelas o novelistas desarrollan estos elementos. Aparte de tu trama principal, una novela puede contener una o varias subtramas, o narraciones independientes o relacionadas con la trama principal. Una novela puede contener también diversos temas. Ver ***Ficción*** y ***Cuento.***

ONOMATOPOEIA / ONOMATOPEYA Una ***onomatopeya*** es el uso de las palabras que imitan sonidos. ***Cataplam, zzzzzz, zas, din don, glu glu glu, achís*** y ***crag*** son ejemplos de onomatopeyas El ***cuco,*** la ***urraca*** y el ***pitirre*** son nombres onomatopéyicos de aves.

ORGANIZATION / ORGANIZACIÓN La estructura de un texto o de una presentación audiovisual es lo que se conoce como su ***organización***. Algunas estructuras organizativas comunes son: causa y efecto, comparación y contraste, orden de importancia y orden cronológico. Los escritores eligen la organización que mejor se adapte al tema y propósito de su texto.

OXYMORON / OXÍMORON Un ***oxímoron*** (pl. ***oxímoron***) es una figura retórica que vincula dos palabras contrarias u opuestas con el fin de indicar que una idea o situación, que parece contradictoria o incoherente a simple vista, encierra algo de verdad cuando la analizamos detenidamente.

PARAPHRASE / PARÁFRASIS Una ***paráfrasis*** es cuando explicamos un texto con nuestras propias palabras.

PERSONIFICATION / PERSONIFICACIÓN La ***personificación*** es una figura retórica con la que se atribuyen características humanas a un animal o una cosa.

PERSUASION / PERSUASIÓN La ***persuasión*** se utiliza cuando escribimos o hablamos para convencer a nuestro lector o interlocutor de que debe adoptar una opinión concreta o tomar un rumbo en sus decisiones. Los editoriales periodísticos y las cartas del editor emplean la persuasión. Asimismo, la publicidad y los discursos electorales que los políticos pronuncian en campaña también la utilizan.

Los escritores emplean distintas técnicas persuasivas para defender sus opiniones. Las ***apelaciones a la autoridad*** usan lo que han dicho diversos expertos. Las ***apelaciones a las emociones*** usan palabras que transmiten sentimientos profundos. Las ***apelaciones a la razón*** utilizan argumentos lógicos fundamentados con datos.

PLAYWRIGHT / DRAMATURGO Un ***dramaturgo*** es una persona que escribe obras de teatro. A William Shakespeare se le considera el mejor dramaturgo de la literatura inglesa.

PLOT / TRAMA Una ***trama*** es la secuencia de acontecimientos en la cual cada uno de estos acontecimientos es el resultado de otro acontecimiento anterior y la causa de uno nuevo que lo sigue. En la mayoría de novelas, dramas, relatos y poemas narrativos, la trama contiene personajes y un conflicto central. La trama suele comenzar con un ***planteamiento*** o introducción que presenta el escenario, los personajes y la situación básica. A esto le sigue el ***suceso desencadenante***, que presenta el conflicto central. El conflico va aumentando durante el ***desarrollo*** hasta que alcanza el punto más elevado de interés o suspenso, el ***clímax.*** El clímax va seguido de una ***acción descendente*** del conflicto central. Todos los acontecimientos que ocurren durante la ***acción descendente*** forman el ***desenlace***.

Algunas tramas no tienen todas estas partes. Algunas historias comienzan con el suceso desencadenante y acaban con un desenlace. Ver ***Conflicto.***

POETRY / POESÍA La ***poesía*** es uno de los tres géneros más importantes de la literatura junto con la prosa y el drama. La mayoría de los poemas utilizan lenguaje muy conciso, musical y cargado de emoción. Muchos también emplean imágenes, lenguaje figurado y recursos sonoros especiales como la rima. Los tipos de poesía más importante son: la ***poesía lírica,*** la ***poesía narrativa*** y la ***poesía concreta.***

POINT OF VIEW / PUNTO DE VISTA El ***punto de vista*** es la perspectiva, o el punto de observación, desde la que se cuenta una historia. Puede tratarse de un narrador situado fuera de la historia o un personaje dentro de ella. El ***punto de vista en primera persona*** corresponde a un personaje que utiliza el pronombre "yo" o la conjugación de los verbos en primera persona de singular. Los dos tipos de ***punto de vista en tercera persona***, limitado y omnisciente, son conocidos como "tercera persona" porque el narrador utiliza los pronombres de tercera persona como "él" y "ella" y la conjugación de los verbos en tercera persona para referirse a los personajes. Por el contrario, no se utiliza el pronombre "yo".

En las historias contadas desde el ***punto de vista en tercera persona omnisciente***, el narrador sabe y cuenta todo lo que sienten y piensan los personajes.

En las historia contadas desde el ***punto de vista en tercera pesona limitado***, el narrador relata los pensamientos y sentimientos de solo un personaje, y se cuenta todo desde la perspectiva de ese personaje.

PRESENTATION / PRESENTACIÓN Una ***presentación*** es el acto de mostrar o enseñar algo a una audiencia. Las ***presentaciones orales***, que se comunican a una audiencia en vivo, pueden incluir ***presentaciones visuales*** como tablas, diagramas, ilustraciones y fotografías. Los videoclips y las diapositivas suelen ser parte de las ***presentaciones digitales***, que se crean parcial o totalmente en computadora.

PROSE / PROSA La ***prosa*** es la forma más corriente del lenguaje escrito. La mayoría de los textos escritos que no se consideran poesía, drama o canción son textos en prosa.

La prosa es uno de los géneros más importantes de la literatura y puede ser de ficción o de no ficción.

QUOTATION / CITA Las ***citas*** son grupos de palabras que se toman de un texto, de un discurso o de una entrevista y que alguien distinto al autor original las usa o repite. Siempre se debe informar quién es el autor original de la cita.

READ CLOSELY / LEER CON ATENCIÓN ***Leer con atención*** conlleva un análisis cuidadoso del texto, sus ideas y la manera en la que el autor expresa esas ideas.

REPETITION / REPETICIÓN La ***repetición*** se da cuando se utiliza más de una vez cualquier elemento del lenguaje (un sonido, una palabra, una expresión, un sintagma o una oración). La repetición se emplea tanto en prosa como en poesía.

RETELLING / TRABAJO DE INVESTIGACIÓN Un ***trabajo de investigación*** ofrece información detallada sobre un tema. Los trabajos de investigación eficaces se fundamentan en una variedad de fuentes fiables que se citan.

RESOLUTION / DESENLACE El ***desenlace*** es la resolución del conflicto en una trama.

RETELLING / VOLVER A CONTAR Las historias se pueden ***volver a contar*** de manera escrita u oral. Al volverse a contar una historia, se debe seguir una secuencia clara de los sucesos y utilizar técnicas narrativas como el diálogo y la descripción.

RHYME / RIMA La ***rima*** es la repetición de los sonidos finales de las palabras. Los poetas emplean la rima para revestir de musicalidad sus versos y resaltar ciertas palabras e ideas. Muchos poemas tradicionales contienen ***rimas finales*** o palabras rimadas al final de los versos.

Otro recurso muy común es el uso de ***rimas internas*** o palabras que riman entre ellas en un mismo verso. La rima interna también resalta la fluidez propia de un poema.

RHYTHM / RITMO El ***ritmo*** es el patrón de sílabas acentuadas y no acentuadas en el lenguaje hablado o escrito.

SCAN / OJEAR ***Ojear*** es mirar por encima un texto para buscar la respuesta a una pregunta, clarificar algo o buscar detalles de apoyo.

SCENE / ESCENA Una ***escena*** es una sección de acción ininterrumpida dentro de alguno de los actos de un drama.

SCIENCE FICTION / CIENCIA FICCIÓN La ***ciencia ficción*** combina elementos de ficción y fantásticos con hechos científicos. Muchas historias de cienca ficción están situadas en el futuro.

SCRIPT / GUIÓN Un ***guión*** es la versión escrita de una obra de teatro o de una película. Los guiones se componen de ***diálogos*** y ***acotaciones***.

SENSORY LANGUAGE / LENGUAJE SENSORIAL El ***lenguaje sensorial*** es texto o diálogo que tiene relación con uno o varios de los cinco sentidos.

SETTING / ESCENARIO El ***escenario*** de una obra literaria es el tiempo y lugar en los que ocurre la acción. El escenario incluye todos los detalles sobre el tiempo y el lugar: el año, el momento del día o incluso el tiempo atmosférico. El lugar puede ser un país concreto, un estado, una región, una comunidad, un barrio, un edificio, una institución o el propio hogar. Los detalles como los dialectos, ropa, costumbres y medios de trasporte se emplean con frecuencia para componer el escenario. En la mayoría de historias, los escenarios sirven de telón de fondo, es decir, de contexto en el que los personajes interactúan. El escenario también puede contribuir a crear una determinada sensación o un ambiente.

SHORT STORY / CUENTO Un ***cuento*** es una obra corta de ficción. Al igual que sucede en una novela, los cuentos presentan una secuencia de acontecimientos o trama. La trama suele contener un conflico central al que se enfrenta un personaje principal o protagonista. Los acontecimientos en un cuento normalmente comunican un mensaje sobre la vida o la naturaleza humana. Este mensaje o idea central es el tema de la historia.

SIMILE / SÍMIL Un ***símil*** es una figura retórica que utiliza *como* o *igual que* para establecer una comparación entre dos ideas distintas. Las conversaciones que mantenemos a diario también contienen símiles como, por ejemplo, "pálido como un muerto", "se propaga igual que un incendio" y "listo como un zorro".

SKIM / ECHAR UN VISTAZO ***Echar un vistazo*** a un texto es mirarlo rápidamente para tener una idea de lo más importante antes de comenzar a leerlo.

SOUND DEVICES / RECURSOS SONOROS Los ***recursos sonoros*** o fónicos son técnicas utilizadas por los escritores para dotar de musicalidad a sus textos. Entre ellos se incluyen la ***onomatopeya,*** la ***aliteración,*** la ***rima,*** la ***métrica*** y la ***repetición.***

SPEAKER / YO POÉTICO El ***yo poético*** es la voz imaginaria que emplea un poeta cuando escribe un poema. El yo poético es el personaje que cuenta el poema. Este personaje o voz no suele identificarse con un nombre. Pueden existir notables diferencias entre el poeta y el yo poético.

SPEECH / DISCURSO Un ***discurso*** es una creación que se pronuncia de manera oral ante una audiencia. Hay muchas clases de discursos que se ajustan a diversos tipos de reuniones y actos públicos. Algunos tipos de discursos son el ***dramático,*** el ***persuasivo*** y el ***informativo.***

STAGE DIRECTIONS / ACOTACIONES Las ***acotaciones*** son las notas de un texto dramático y en las que se describe como se debe interpretar o escenificar la obra. Las acotaciones suelen aparecer en cursiva y encerradas entre paréntesis o corchetes. Algunas acotaciones describen los movimientos, el vestuario, los estados de ánimo y el modo en el que deben hablar los personajes.

STAGING / ESCENOGRAFÍA La ***escenografía*** engloba la ambientación, iluminación, vestuario, efectos especiales y música que debe aparecer en el escenario donde se representa un drama.

SUMMARY / RESUMEN Un ***resumen*** es una descripción corta y clara de las ideas principales de algo como un texto, una película o una presentación. Los resúmenes eficaces son objetivos; es decir, son imparciales y no ofrecen valoraciones.

SYMBOL / SÍMBOLO Un ***símbolo*** es algo que representa una cosa diferente. Los símbolos son muy comunes en nuestra vida diaria. Una paloma con una rama de olivo en el pico es un símbolo de la paz. Una mujer con los ojos vendados sujetando una balanza es un símbolo de la justicia. Una corona es un símbolo del poder y la autoridad de un rey.

SYMBOLISM / SIMBOLISMO El ***simbolismo*** es el uso de los símbolos. El simbolismo juega un papel importante en muchos tipos de literatura. Puede ayudar a destacar algunos elementos que el autor quiere subrayar y añadir otros niveles de significado.

THEME / TEMA El ***tema*** es el mensaje central de una obra literaria. Se puede entender como una generalización sobre los seres humanos o la vida. El tema de una obra no es el resumen de su trama.

Aunque el tema puede exponerse directamente en el texto, se suele presentar indirectamente. Cuando se expone el tema indirecta o implícitamente, el lector lo podrá deducir al observar lo que se muestra en la obra sobre la vida y las personas.

TONE / TONO El ***tono*** de una obra literaria es la actitud del escritor hacia sus lectores o hacia aquello sobre lo que escribe. El tono se puede describir con un único adjetivo como, por ejemplo, ***formal*** o ***informal, serio*** o ***jocoso, amargo*** o ***irónico.*** Los factores que contribuyen a crear el tono son la elección de las palabras, la estructura de la oración, el tamaño de un verso, la rima, el ritmo y la repetición.

UNIVERSAL THEME / TEMA UNIVERSAL Un ***tema universal*** es un mensaje sobre la vida que se expresa habitualmente en muchas culturas y períodos históricos diferentes. Los cuentos populares, las epopeyas y los romances suelen abordar temas universales como la importancia de la valentía, el poder del amor o el peligro de la avaricia.

WEIGHTED WORDS / PALABRAS EMOCIONALMENTE CARGADAS Las palabras que producen fuertes asociaciones emocionales son ***palabras emocionalmente cargadas.***

WORD CHOICE / ELECCIÓN DE PALABRAS La ***elección de palabras*** es la forma que tiene un escritor de escoger su lenguaje. La dicción es parte del estilo de un escritor y se describe como formal o informal, llana o elaborada, común o técnica, sofisticada o popular, anticuada o moderna.

PARTS OF SPEECH

Every English word, depending on its meaning and its use in a sentence, can be identified as one of the eight parts of speech. These are nouns, pronouns, verbs, adjectives, adverbs, prepositions, conjunctions, and interjections. Understanding the parts of speech will help you learn the rules of English grammar and usage.

Nouns A **noun** names a person, place, or thing. A **common noun** names any one of a class of persons, places, or things. A **proper noun** names a specific person, place, or thing.

Common Noun	Proper Noun
writer, country, novel	Charles Dickens, Great Britain, *Hard Times*

Pronouns A **pronoun** is a word that stands for one or more nouns. The word to which a pronoun refers (whose place it takes) is the **antecedent** of the pronoun.

A **personal pronoun** refers to the person speaking (first person); the person spoken to (second person); or the person, place, or thing spoken about (third person).

	Singular	Plural
First Person	I, me, my, mine	we, us, our, ours
Second Person	you, your, yours	you, your, yours
Third Person	he, him, his, she, her, hers, it, its	they, them, their, theirs

A **reflexive pronoun** reflects the action of a verb back on its subject. It indicates that the person or thing performing the action also is receiving the action.

I keep *myself* fit by taking a walk every day.

An **intensive pronoun** adds emphasis to a noun or pronoun.

It took the work of the president *himself* to pass the law.

A **demonstrative** pronoun points out a specific person(s), place(s), or thing(s).

this, that, these, those

A **relative pronoun** begins a subordinate clause and connects it to another idea in the sentence.

that, which, who, whom, whose

An **interrogative pronoun** begins a question.

what, which, who, whom, whose

An **indefinite pronoun** refers to a person, place, or thing that may or may not be specifically named.

all, another, any, both, each, everyone, few, most, none, no one, somebody

Verbs A **verb** expresses action or the existence of a state or condition.

An **action verb** tells what action someone or something is performing.

gather, read, work, jump, imagine, analyze, conclude

A **linking verb** connects the subject with another word that identifies or describes the subject. The most common linking verb is *be*.

appear, be, become, feel, look, remain, seem, smell, sound, stay, taste

A **helping verb,** or **auxiliary verb,** is added to a main verb to make a verb phrase.

be, do, have, should, can, could, may, might, must, will, would

Adjectives An **adjective** modifies a noun or pronoun by describing it or giving it a more specific meaning. An adjective answers the questions:

What kind?	*purple* hat, *happy* face, *loud* sound
Which one?	*this* bowl
How many?	*three* cars
How much?	*enough* food

The articles *the, a,* and *an* are adjectives.

A **proper adjective** is an adjective derived from a proper noun.

French, Shakespearean

Adverbs An **adverb** modifies a verb, an adjective, or another adverb by telling *where, when, how,* or *to what extent.*

will answer *soon, extremely* sad, calls *more* often

Prepositions A **preposition** relates a noun or pronoun that appears with it to another word in the sentence.

Dad made a meal *for* us. We talked *till* dusk. Bo missed school *because of* his illness.

Conjunctions A **conjunction** connects words or groups of words. A **coordinating conjunction** joins words or groups of words of equal rank.

bread *and* cheese, brief *but* powerful

Correlative conjunctions are used in pairs to connect words or groups of words of equal importance.

both Luis *and* Rosa, *neither* you *nor I*

PARTS OF SPEECH continued

Subordinating conjunctions indicate the connection between two ideas by placing one below the other in rank or importance. A subordinating conjunction introduces a subordinate, or dependent, clause.

We will miss her *if* she leaves. Hank shrieked *when* he slipped on the ice.

Interjections An **interjection** expresses feeling or emotion. It is not related to other words in the sentence.

ah, hey, ouch, well, yippee

PHRASES AND CLAUSES

Phrases A **phrase** is a group of words that does not have both a subject and a verb and that functions as one part of speech. A phrase expresses an idea but cannot stand alone.

Prepositional Phrases A **prepositional phrase** is a group of words that begins with a preposition and ends with a noun or pronoun that is the **object of the preposition.**

before dawn   as a result of the rain

An **adjective phrase** is a prepositional phrase that modifies a noun or pronoun.

Eliza appreciates the beauty **of a well-crafted poem.**

An **adverb phrase** is a prepositional phrase that modifies a verb, an adjective, or an adverb.

She reads Spenser's sonnets **with great pleasure.**

Appositive Phrases An **appositive** is a noun or pronoun placed next to another noun or pronoun to add information about it. An **appositive phrase** consists of an appositive and its modifiers.

Mr. Roth, **my music teacher**, is sick.

Verbal Phrases A **verbal** is a verb form that functions as a different part of speech (not as a verb) in a sentence. **Participles, gerunds,** and **infinitives** are verbals.

A **verbal phrase** includes a verbal and any modifiers or complements it may have. Verbal phrases may function as nouns, as adjectives, or as adverbs.

A **participle** is a verb form that can act as an adjective. Present participles end in *-ing;* past participles of regular verbs end in *-ed.*

A **participial phrase** consists of a participle and its modifiers or complements. The entire phrase acts as an adjective.

Jenna's backpack, **loaded with equipment,** was heavy.

Barking incessantly, the dogs chased the squirrels out of sight.

A **gerund** is a verb form that ends in *-ing* and is used as a noun.

A **gerund phrase** consists of a gerund with any modifiers or complements, all acting together as a noun.

Taking photographs of wildlife is her main hobby. [acts as subject]

We always enjoy **listening to live music.** [acts as object]

An **infinitive** is a verb form, usually preceded by *to,* that can act as a noun, an adjective, or an adverb.

An **infinitive phrase** consists of an infinitive and its modifiers or complements, and sometimes its subject, all acting together as a single part of speech.

She tries **to get out into the wilderness often.** [acts as a noun; direct object of *tries*]

The Tigers are the team **to beat.** [acts as an adjective; describes *team*]

I drove twenty miles **to witness the event.** [acts as an adverb; tells why I drove]

Clauses A **clause** is a group of words with its own subject and verb.

Independent Clauses An independent clause can stand by itself as a complete sentence.

George Orwell wrote with extraordinary insight.

Subordinate Clauses A subordinate clause cannot stand by itself as a complete sentence. Subordinate clauses always appear connected in some way with one or more independent clauses.

George Orwell, **who wrote with extraordinary insight,** produced many politically relevant works.

An **adjective clause** is a subordinate clause that acts as an adjective. It modifies a noun or a pronoun by telling *what kind* or *which one.* Also called relative clauses, adjective clauses usually begin with a **relative pronoun:** *who, which, that, whom, or whose.*

"The Lamb" is the poem **that I memorized for class.**

An **adverb clause** is a subordinate clause that, like an adverb, modifies a verb, an adjective, or an adverb. An adverb clause tells *where, when, in what way, to what extent, under what condition,* or *why.*

The students will read another poetry collection **if their schedule allows.**

When I recited the poem, Mr. Lopez was impressed.

A **noun clause** is a subordinate clause that acts as a noun.

William Blake survived on **whatever he made as an engraver.**

SENTENCE STRUCTURE

Subject and Predicate

Subject and Predicate A **sentence** is a group of words that expresses a complete thought. A sentence has two main parts: a *subject* and a *predicate*.

A **fragment** is a group of words that does not express a complete thought. It lacks an independent clause.

The **subject** tells *whom* or *what* the sentence is about. The **predicate** tells what the subject of the sentence does or is.

A subject or a predicate can consist of a single word or of many words. All the words in the subject make up the **complete subject.** All the words in the predicate make up the **complete predicate.**

Complete Subject **Complete Predicate**

Both of those girls | have already read *Macbeth*.

The **simple subject** is the essential noun, pronoun, or group of words acting as a noun that cannot be left out of the complete subject. The **simple predicate** is the essential verb or verb phrase that cannot be left out of the complete predicate.

Both of those girls | **have** already **read** *Macbeth*.
[Simple subject: *Both;* simple predicate: *have read*]

A **compound subject** is two or more subjects that have the same verb and are joined by a conjunction.

Neither the horse nor the driver looked tired.

A **compound predicate** is two or more verbs that have the same subject and are joined by a conjunction.

She **sneezed and coughed** throughout the trip.

Complements

Complements A **complement** is a word or word group that completes the meaning of the subject or verb in a sentence. There are four kinds of complements: *direct objects, indirect objects, objective complements,* and *subject complements.*

A **direct object** is a noun, a pronoun, or a group of words acting as a noun that receives the action of a transitive verb.

We watched the **liftoff**.
She drove **Zach** to the launch site.

An **indirect object** is a noun or pronoun that appears with a direct object and names the person or thing to which or for which something is done.

He sold the **family** a mirror. [The direct object is *mirror.*]

An **objective complement** is an adjective or noun that appears with a direct object and describes or renames it.

The decision made her **unhappy**.
[The direct object is *her.*]
Many consider Shakespeare the greatest **playwright.** [The direct object is *Shakespeare.*]

A **subject complement** follows a linking verb and tells something about the subject. There are two kinds: *predicate nominatives* and *predicate adjectives.*

A **predicate nominative** is a noun or pronoun that follows a linking verb and identifies or renames the subject.

"A Modest Proposal" is a **pamphlet.**

A **predicate adjective** is an adjective that follows a linking verb and describes the subject of the sentence.

"A Modest Proposal" is **satirical.**

Classifying Sentences by Structure

Sentences can be classified according to the kind and number of clauses they contain. The four basic sentence structures are *simple, compound, complex,* and *compound-complex.*

A **simple sentence** consists of one independent clause.

Terrence enjoys modern British literature.

A **compound sentence** consists of two or more independent clauses. The clauses are joined by a conjunction or a semicolon.

Terrence enjoys modern British literature, but his brother prefers the classics.

A **complex sentence** consists of one independent clause and one or more subordinate clauses.

Terrence, who reads voraciously, enjoys modern British literature.

A **compound-complex sentence** consists of two or more independent clauses and one or more subordinate clauses.

Terrence, who reads voraciously, enjoys modern British literature, but his brother prefers the classics.

Classifying Sentences by Function

Sentences can be classified according to their function or purpose. The four types are *declarative, interrogative, imperative,* and *exclamatory.*

SENTENCE STRUCTURE continued

A **declarative sentence** states an idea and ends with a period.

An **interrogative sentence** asks a question and ends with a question mark.

An **imperative sentence** gives an order or a direction and ends with either a period or an exclamation mark.

An **exclamatory sentence** conveys a strong emotion and ends with an exclamation mark.

PARAGRAPH STRUCTURE

An effective paragraph is organized around one **main idea,** which is often stated in a **topic sentence.** The other sentences support the main idea. To give the paragraph **unity,** make sure the connection between each sentence and the main idea is clear.

Unnecessary Shift in Person

Do not change needlessly from one grammatical person to another. Keep the person consistent in your sentences.

Max went to the bakery, but **you** can't buy mints there. [shift from third person to second person]

Max went to the bakery, but **he** can't buy mints there. [consistent]

Unnecessary Shift in Voice

Do not change needlessly from active voice to passive voice in your use of verbs.

Elena and I **searched** the trail for evidence, but no clues **were found.** [shift from active voice to passive voice]

Elena and I **searched** the trail for evidence, but we **found** no clues. [consistent]

AGREEMENT

Subject and Verb Agreement

A singular subject must have a singular verb. A plural subject must have a plural verb.

Dr. Boone uses a telescope to view the night sky.

The **students use** a telescope to view the night sky.

A verb always agrees with its subject, not its object.

Incorrect: The best part of the show were the jugglers.

Correct: The best part of the show was the jugglers.

A phrase or clause that comes between a subject and verb does not affect subject-verb agreement.

His **theory**, as well as his claims, **lacks** support.

Two subjects joined by *and* usually take a plural verb.

The **dog** and the **cat are** healthy.

Two singular subjects joined by *or* or *nor* take a singular verb.

The **dog** or the **cat is** hiding.

Two plural subjects joined by *or* or *nor* take a plural verb.

The **dogs** or the **cats are** coming home with us.

When a singular and a plural subject are joined by *or* or *nor,* the verb agrees with the closer subject.

Either the **dogs** or the **cat is** behind the door.

Either the **cat** or the **dogs are** behind the door.

Pronoun and Antecedent Agreement

Pronouns must agree with their antecedents in number and gender. Use singular pronouns with singular antecedents and plural pronouns with plural antecedents.

Doris Lessing uses **her** writing to challenge ideas about women's roles.

Writers often use **their** skills to promote social change.

Use a singular pronoun when the antecedent is a singular indefinite pronoun such as *anybody, each, either, everybody, neither, no one, one, or someone.*

Judge **each** of the articles on **its** merits.

Use a plural pronoun when the antecedent is a plural indefinite pronoun such as *both, few, many,* or *several.*

Both of the articles have **their** flaws.

The indefinite pronouns *all, any, more, most, none,* and *some* can be singular or plural depending on the number of the word to which they refer.

Most of the *books* are in **their** proper places.

Most of the *book* has been torn from **its** binding.

USING VERBS

Principal Parts of Regular and Irregular Verbs

A verb has four principal parts:

Present	Present Participle	Past	Past Participle
learn	learning	learned	learned
discuss	discussing	discussed	discussed
stand	standing	stood	stood
begin	beginning	began	begun

Regular verbs such as *learn* and *discuss* form the past and past participle by adding -*ed* to the present form. **Irregular verbs** such as *stand* and *begin* form the past and past participle in other ways. If you are in doubt about the principal parts of an irregular verb, check a dictionary.

The Tenses of Verbs

The different tenses of verbs indicate the time an action or condition occurs.

The **present tense** expresses an action that happens regularly or states a current condition or general truth.

Tourists **flock** to the site yearly.

Daily exercise **is** good for your heallth.

The **past tense** expresses a completed action or a condition that is no longer true.

The squirrel **dropped** the nut and **ran** up the tree.

I **was** very tired last night by 9:00.

The **future tense** indicates an action that will happen in the future or a condition that will be true.

The Glazers **will visit** us tomorrow.

They **will be** glad to arrive from their long journey.

The **present perfect tense** expresses an action that happened at an indefinite time in the past or an action that began in the past and continues into the present.

Someone **has cleaned** the trash from the park.

The puppy **has been** under the bed all day.

The **past perfect tense** shows an action that was completed before another action in the past.

Gerard **had revised** his essay before he turned it in.

The **future perfect tense** indicates an action that will have been completed before another action takes place.

Mimi **will have painted** the kitchen by the time we finish the shutters.

USING MODIFIERS

Degrees of Comparison

Adjectives and adverbs take different forms to show the three degrees of comparison: the *positive*, the *comparative*, and the *superlative*.

Positive	Comparative	Superlative
fast	faster	fastest
crafty	craftier	craftiest
abruptly	more abruptly	most abruptly
badly	worse	worst

Using Comparative and Superlative Adjectives and Adverbs

Use comparative adjectives and adverbs to compare two things. Use superlative adjectives and adverbs to compare three or more things.

This season's weather was **drier** than last year's.

This season has been one of the **driest** on record.

Jake practices **more often** than Jamal.

Of everyone in the band, Jake practices **most often.**

USING PRONOUNS

Pronoun Case

The **case** of a pronoun is the form it takes to show its function in a sentence. There are three pronoun cases: *nominative, objective,* and *possessive*.

Nominative	Objective	Possessive
I, you, he, she, it, we, you, they	me, you, him, her, it, us, you, them	my, your, yours, his, her, hers, its, our, ours, their, theirs

Use the **nominative case** when a pronoun functions as a *subject* or as a *predicate nominative*.

They are going to the movies. [subject]

The biggest movie fan is **she.** [predicate nominative]

Use the **objective case** for a pronoun acting as a *direct object*, an *indirect object,* or the *object of a preposition.*

The ending of the play surprised **me**. [direct object]

Mary gave **us** two tickets to the play. [indirect object]

The audience cheered for **him.** [object of preposition]

Use the **possessive case** to show ownership.

The red suitcase is **hers.**

COMMONLY CONFUSED WORDS

Diction The words you choose contribute to the overall effectiveness of your writing. **Diction** refers to word choice and to the clearness and correctness of those words. You can improve one aspect of your diction by choosing carefully between commonly confused words, such as the pairs listed below.

accept, except

Accept is a verb that means "to receive" or "to agree to." *Except* is a preposition that means "other than" or "leaving out."

Please **accept** my offer to buy you lunch this weekend.

He is busy every day **except** the weekends.

affect, effect

Affect is normally a verb meaning "to influence" or "to bring about a change in." *Effect* is usually a noun meaning "result."

The distractions outside **affect** Steven's ability to concentrate.

The teacher's remedies had a positive **effect** on Steven's ability to concentrate.

among, between

Among is usually used with three or more items, and it emphasizes collective relationships or indicates distribution. *Between* is generally used with only two items, but it can be used with more than two if the emphasis is on individual (one-to-one) relationships within the group.

I had to choose a snack **among** the various vegetables.

He handed out the booklets **among** the conference participants.

Our school is **between** a park and an old barn.

The tournament included matches **between** France, Spain, Mexico, and the United States.

amount, number

Amount refers to overall quantity and is mainly used with mass nouns (those that can't be counted). *Number* refers to individual items that can be counted.

The **amount** of attention that great writers have paid to Shakespeare is remarkable.

A **number** of important English writers have been fascinated by the legend of King Arthur.

assure, ensure, insure

Assure means "to convince [someone of something]; to guarantee." *Ensure* means "to make certain [that something happens]." *Insure* means "to arrange for payment in case of loss."

The attorney **assured** us we'd win the case.

The rules **ensure** that no one gets treated unfairly.

Many professional musicians **insure** their valuable instruments.

bad, badly

Use the adjective *bad* before a noun or after linking verbs such as *feel, look,* and *seem*. Use *badly* whenever an adverb is required.

The situation may seem **bad**, but it will improve over time.

Though our team played **badly** today, we will focus on practicing for the next match.

beside, besides

Beside means "at the side of" or "close to." *Besides* means "in addition to."

The stapler sits **beside** the pencil sharpener in our classroom.

Besides being very clean, the classroom is also very organized.

can, may

The helping verb *can* generally refers to the ability to do something. The helping verb *may* generally refers to permission to do something.

I **can** run one mile in six minutes.

May we have a race during recess?

complement, compliment

The verb *complement* means "to enhance"; the verb *compliment* means "to praise."

Online exercises **complement** the textbook lessons.

Ms. Lewis **complimented** our team on our excellent debate.

compose, comprise

Compose means "to make up; constitute." *Comprise* means "to include or contain." Remember that the whole comprises its parts or is composed of its parts, and the parts compose the whole.

The assignment **comprises** three different tasks.

The assignment is **composed** of three different tasks.

Three different tasks **compose** the assignment.

different from, different than

Different from is generally preferred over *different than,* but *different than* can be used before a clause. Always use *different from* before a noun or pronoun.

Your point of view is so **different from** mine.

His idea was so **different from** [or **different than**] what we had expected.

farther, further

Use *farther* to refer to distance. Use *further* to mean "to a greater degree or extent" or "additional."

Chiang has traveled **farther** than anybody else in the class.

If I want **further** details about his travels, I can read his blog.

fewer, less

Use *fewer* for things that can be counted. Use *less* for amounts or quantities that cannot be counted. *Fewer* must be followed by a plural noun.

Fewer students drive to school since the weather improved.

There is **less** noise outside in the mornings.

good, well

Use the adjective *good* before a noun or after a linking verb. Use *well* whenever an adverb is required, such as when modifying a verb.

I feel **good** after sleeping for eight hours.

I did **well** on my test, and my soccer team played **well** in that afternoon's game. It was a **good** day!

its, it's

The word *its* with no apostrophe is a possessive pronoun. The word *it's* is a contraction of "it is."

Angelica will try to fix the computer and **its** keyboard.

It's a difficult job, but she can do it.

lay, lie

Lay is a transitive verb meaning "to set or put something down." Its principal parts are *lay, laying, laid, laid. Lie* is an intransitive verb meaning "to recline" or "to exist in a certain place." Its principal parts are *lie, lying, lay, lain.*

Please **lay** that box down and help me with the sofa.

When we are done moving, I am going to **lie** down.

My hometown **lies** sixty miles north of here.

like, as

Like is a preposition that usually means "similar to" and precedes a noun or pronoun. The conjunction *as* means "in the way that" and usually precedes a clause.

Like the other students, I was prepared for a quiz.

As I said yesterday, we expect to finish before noon.

Use **such as,** not **like,** before a series of examples.

Foods **such as** apples, nuts, and pretzels make good snacks.

of, have

Do not use *of* in place of *have* after auxiliary verbs such as *would, could, should, may, might,* or *must.* The contraction of *have* is formed by adding *-ve* after these verbs.

I **would have** stayed after school today, but I had to help cook at home.

Mom **must've** called while I was still in the gym.

principal, principle

Principal can be an adjective meaning "main; most important." It can also be a noun meaning "chief officer of a school." *Principle* is a noun meaning "moral rule" or "fundamental truth."

His strange behavior was the **principal** reason for our concern.

Democratic **principles** form the basis of our country's laws.

raise, rise

Raise is a transitive verb that usually takes a direct object. *Rise* is intransitive and never takes a direct object.

Iliana and Josef **raise** the flag every morning.

They **rise** from their seats and volunteer immediately whenever help is needed.

than, then

The conjunction *than* is used to connect the two parts of a comparison. The adverb *then* usually refers to time.

My backpack is heavier **than** hers.

I will finish my homework and **then** meet my friends at the park.

that, which, who

Use the relative pronoun *that* to refer to things or people. Use *which* only for things and *who* only for people.

That introduces a restrictive phrase or clause, that is, one that is essential to the meaning of the sentence. *Which* introduces a nonrestrictive phrase or clause—one that adds information but could be deleted from the sentence—and is preceded by a comma.

Ben ran to the park **that** just reopened.

The park, **which** just reopened, has many attractions.

The man **who** built the park loves to see people smiling.

when, where, why

Do not use *when, where,* or *why* directly after a linking verb, such as *is*. Reword the sentence.

Incorrect: The morning is when he left for the beach.

Correct: He left for the beach in the morning.

who, whom

In formal writing, use *who* only as a subject in clauses and sentences. Use *whom* only as the object of a verb or of a preposition.

Who paid for the tickets?

Whom should I pay for the tickets?

I can't recall to **whom** I gave the money for the tickets.

your, you're

Your is a possessive pronoun expressing ownership. *You're* is the contraction of "you are."

Have you finished writing **your** informative essay?

You're supposed to turn it in tomorrow. If **you're** late, **your** grade will be affected.

Capitalization

First Words

Capitalize the first word of a sentence.

Stories about knights and their deeds interest me.

Capitalize the first word of direct speech.

Sharon asked, "**D**o you like stories about knights?"

Capitalize the first word of a quotation that is a complete sentence.

Einstein said, "**A**nyone who has never made a mistake has never tried anything new."

Proper Nouns and Proper Adjectives

Capitalize all proper nouns, including geographical names, historical events and periods, and names of organizations.

Thames **R**iver **J**ohn **K**eats the **R**enaissance
United **N**ations **W**orld **W**ar II **S**ierra **N**evada

Capitalize all proper adjectives.

Shakespearean play **B**ritish invaision
American citizen **L**atin **A**merican literature

Academic Course Names

Capitalize course names only if they are language courses, are followed by a number, or are preceded by a proper noun or adjective.

Spanish **H**onors **C**hemistry **H**istory 101
geology **a**lgebra **s**ocial **s**tudies

Titles

Capitalize personal titles when followed by the person's name.

Ms. Hughes **D**r. Perez **K**ing George

Capitalize titles showing family relationships when they are followed by a specific person's name, unless they are preceded by a possessive noun or pronoun.

Uncle Oscar Mangan's **s**ister his **a**unt Tessa

Capitalize the first word and all other key words in the titles of books, stories, songs, and other works of art.

Frankenstein "**S**hooting an **E**lephant"

Punctuation

End Marks

Use a **period** to end a declarative sentence or an imperative sentence.

We are studying the structure of sonnets.
Read the biography of Mary Shelley.

Use periods with initials and abbreviations.

D. H. Lawrence Mrs. Browning
Mt. Everest Maple St.

Use a **question mark** to end an interrogative sentence.

What is Macbeth's fatal flaw?

Use an **exclamation mark** after an exclamatory sentence or a forceful imperative sentence.

That's a beautiful painting! Let me go now!

Commas

Use a **comma** before a coordinating conjunction to separate two independent clauses in a compound sentence.

The game was very close, but we were victorious.

Use commas to separate three or more words, phrases, or clauses in a series.

William Blake was a writer, artist, and printer.

Use commas to separate coordinate adjectives.

It was a witty, amusing novel.

Use a comma after an introductory word, phrase, or clause.

When the novelist finished his book, he celebrated with his family.

Use commas to set off nonessential expressions.

Old English, of course, requires translation.

Use commas with places and dates.

Coventry, England September 1, 1939

Semicolons

Use a **semicolon** to join closely related independent clauses that are not already joined by a conjunction.

Tanya likes to write poetry; Heather prefers prose.

Use semicolons to avoid confusion when items in a series contain commas.

They traveled to London, England; Madrid, Spain; and Rome, Italy.

Colons

Use a **colon** before a list of items following an independent clause.

Notable Victorian poets include the following: Tennyson, Arnold, Housman, and Hopkins.

Use a colon to introduce information that summarizes or explains the independent clause before it.

She just wanted to do one thing: rest.
Malcolm loves volunteering: He reads to sick children every Saturday afternoon.

Quotation Marks

Use **quotation marks** to enclose a direct quotation.

"Short stories," Ms. Hildebrand said, "should have rich, well-developed characters."

An **indirect quotation** does not require quotation marks.

Ms. Hildebrand said that short stories should have well-developed characters.

Use quotation marks around the titles of short written works, episodes in a series, songs, and works mentioned as parts of collections.

"The Lagoon" "Boswell Meets Johnson"

Italics

Italicize the titles of long written works, movies, television and radio shows, lengthy works of music, paintings, and sculptures.

Howards End *60 Minutes* *Guernica*

For handwritten material, you can use underlining instead of italics.

The Princess Bride Mona Lisa

Dashes

Use **dashes** to indicate an abrupt change of thought, a dramatic interrupting idea, or a summary statement.

I read the entire first act of *Macbeth*—you won't believe what happens next.

The director—what's her name again?—attended the movie premiere.

Hyphens

Use a **hyphen** with certain numbers, after certain prefixes, with two or more words used as one word, and with a compound modifier that comes before a noun.

seventy-two
self-esteem
president-elect
five-year contract

Parentheses

Use **parentheses** to set off asides and explanations when the material is not essential or when it consists of one or more sentences. When the sentence in parentheses interrupts the larger sentence, it does not have a capital letter or a period.

He listened intently (it was too dark to see who was speaking) to try to identify the voices.

When a sentence in parentheses falls between two other complete sentences, it should start with a capital letter and end with a period.

The quarterback threw three touchdown passes. (We knew he could do it.) Our team won the game by two points.

Apostrophes

Add an **apostrophe** and an *s* to show the possessive case of most singular nouns and of plural nouns that do not end in *-s* or *-es*.

Blake's poems the mice's whiskers

Names ending in *s* form their possessives in the same way, except for classical and biblical names, which add only an apostrophe to form the possessive.

Dickens's Hercules'

Add an apostrophe to show the possessive case of plural nouns ending in *-s* and *-es*.

the girls' songs the Ortizes' car

Use an apostrophe in a contraction to indicate the position of the missing letter or letters.

She's never read a Coleridge poem she didn't like.

Brackets

Use **brackets** to enclose clarifying information inserted within a quotation.

Columbus's journal entry from October 21, 1492, begins as follows: "At 10 o'clock, we arrived at a cape of the island [San Salvador], and anchored, the other vessels in company."

Ellipses

Use three ellipsis points, also known as an **ellipsis,** to indicate where you have omitted words from quoted material.

Wollestonecraft wrote, "The education of women has of late been more attended to than formerly; yet they are still . . . ridiculed or pitied. . . ."

In the example above, the four dots at the end of the sentence are the three ellipsis points plus the period from the original sentence.

Use an ellipsis to indicate a pause or interruption in speech.

"When he told me the news," said the coach, "I was . . . I was shocked . . . completely shocked."

Spelling

Spelling Rules

Learning the rules of English spelling will help you make **generalizations** about how to spell words.

Word Parts

The three word parts that can combine to form a word are roots, prefixes, and suffixes. Many of these word parts come from the Greek, Latin, and Anglo-Saxon languages.

The **root word** carries a word's basic meaning.

Root and Origin	Meaning	Examples
-leg- (-log-) [Gr.]	to say, speak	*legal, logic*
-pon- (-pos-) [L.]	to put, place	*postpone, deposit*

A **prefix** is one or more syllables added to the beginning of a word that alter the meaning of the root.

Prefix and Origin	Meaning	Example
anti- [Gr.]	against	*antipathy*
inter- [L.]	between	*international*
mis- [A.S.]	wrong	*misplace*

A **suffix** is a letter or group of letters added to the end of a root word that changes the word's meaning or part of speech.

Suffix and Origin	Meaning and Example	Part of Speech
-ful [A.S.]	full of: *scornful*	adjective
-ity [L.]	state of being: *adversity*	noun
-ize (-ise) [Gr.]	to make: *idolize*	verb
-ly [A.S.]	in a manner: *calmly*	adverb

Rules for Adding Suffixes to Root Words

When adding a suffix to a root word ending in *y* preceded by a consonant, change *y* to *i* unless the suffix begins with *i*.

ply + -able = pliable   happy + -ness = happiness
defy + -ing = defying   cry + -ing = crying

For a root word ending in *e*, drop the *e* when adding a suffix beginning with a vowel.

drive + -ing = driving   move + -able = movable
SOME EXCEPTIONS: traceable, seeing, dyeing

For root words ending with a consonant + vowel + consonant in a stressed syllable, double the final consonant when adding a suffix that begins with a vowel.

mud + -y = muddy   submit + -ed = submitted
SOME EXCEPTIONS: mixing, fixed

Rules for Adding Prefixes to Root Words

When a prefix is added to a root word, the spelling of the root remains the same.

un- + certain = uncertain   mis- + spell = misspell

With some prefixes, the spelling of the prefix changes when joined to the root to make the pronunciation easier.

in- + mortal = immortal   ad- + vert = avert

Orthographic Patterns

Certain letter combinations in English make certain sounds. For instance, *ph* sounds like *f*, *eigh* usually makes a long *a* sound, and the *k* before an *n* is often silent.

pharmacy   n**eigh**bor   **k**nowledge

Understanding **orthographic patterns** such as these can help you improve your spelling.

Forming Plurals

The plural form of most nouns is formed by adding *-s* to the singular.

computers   gadgets   Washingtons

For words ending in *s, ss, x, z, sh,* or *ch,* add *-es*.

circus**es**   tax**es**   wish**es**   bench**es**

For words ending in *y* or *o* preceded by a vowel, add *-s*.

key**s**   patio**s**

For words ending in *y* preceded by a consonant, change the *y* to an *i* and add *-es*.

citi**es**   enemi**es**   trophi**es**

For most words ending in *o* preceded by a consonant, add *-es*.

echo**es**   tomato**es**

Some words form the plural in irregular ways.

women   oxen   children   teeth   deer

Foreign Words Used in English

Some words used in English are actually foreign words that have been adopted. Learning to spell these words requires memorization. When in doubt, check a dictionary.

sushi   enchilada   au pair   fiancé
laissez faire   croissant

INDEX OF SKILLS

Analyzing Text

Assessment

Language Conventions

Research

Speaking and Listening

Vocabulary

Writing

R71

INDEX OF AUTHORS AND TITLES

The following authors and titles appear in the print and online versions of Savvas Literature.

ADDITIONAL SELECTIONS: AUTHOR AND TITLE INDEX

The following authors and titles appear in the Online Literature Library.

ACKNOWLEDGMENTS AND CREDITS

Acknowledgments

The following selections appear in Grade 7 of *my*Perspectives. Some selections appear online only.

ABC News—Permissions Dept. Bethany Hamilton video ©ABC News.

Abner Stein. "Two Kinds" from *The Joy Luck Club* by Amy Tan. Used with permission of Abner Stein.

BBC News Online. Profile: Malala Yousafzai ©BBC, December 10, 2014.

BBC Worldwide Americas, Inc. Maya Angelou: Learning to love my mother ©BBC Worldwide Learning.

Best Part Productions. Cyber-Seniors Documentary—Official Trailer ©Best Part Productions.

Bloomsbury Publishing Plc. "Four Skinny Trees" from *The House on Mango Street* by Sandra Cisneros. Copyright ©Sandra Cisneros. Used with permission of Bloomsbury Publishing Plc.

Brilliance Audio. "Packing for Mars" from *Packing for Mars: The Curious Science of Life in the Void* by Mary Roach. Copyright ©2010 by Mary Roach. Used with permission of Brilliance Audio.

C.S. Lewis Company. *Science-Fiction Cradlesong* by C. S. Lewis copyright ©C.S. Lewis Pte. Ltd. Reprinted by permission.

Chicago Review Press. "Noor Inayat Khan," excerpted from *Women Heroes of WWII* by Kathryn J. Atwood. Copyright ©2011 by Kathryn J. Atwood. Reprinted by permission of Chicago Review Press.

Coffee House Press. Linda Hogan, "Turtle Watchers" from *Dark. Sweet.: New & Selected Poems*. Copyright ©2008 by Linda Hogan. Reprinted with the permission of The Permissions Company, Inc., on behalf of Coffee House Press, www.coffeehousepress.org.

Critical Past LLC. "The Dust Bowl" courtesy of CriticalPast.

Curtis Brown, Ltd. (UK). "Chapter 9," from *The Grapes of Wrath* by John Steinbeck, copyright 1939, renewed ©1967 by John Steinbeck.

Don Congdon Associates, Inc. "Dark They Were and Golden-Eyed" by Ray Bradbury, reprinted by permission of Don Congdon Associates, Inc. ©1949 by Standard Magazines, renewed 1976 by Ray Bradbury.

Elaine Markson Literary Agency. "Family" from *Begin Again: Collected Poems* by Grace Paley. Used with permission of Elaine Markson Literary Agency.

Farrar, Straus and Giroux. "Family" from *Begin Again: Collected Poems* by Grace Paley. Copyright ©2000 by Grace Paley. Reprinted by permission Farrar, Straus and Giroux, LLC.; "Thank You, M'am" from *Short Stories* by Langston Hughes. Copyright ©1996 by Ramona Bass and Arnold Rampersad. Reprinted by permission of Hill and Wang, a division of Farrar, Straus and Giroux, LLC. CAUTION: Users are warned that this work is protected under copyright laws and downloading is strictly prohibited. The right to reproduce or transfer the work via any medium must be secured with Farrar, Straus and Giroux, LLC.

Fulcrum Publishing, Inc. "How Grandmother Spider Stole the Sun" from *Keepers of the Earth* by Michael Caduto and Joseph Bruchac. Reprinted by permission of Fulcrum Publishing.

Hachette Book Group USA. "Work in Progress" from *The Moth*, edited by Catherine Burns. Copyright ©2013 by The Moth. Copyright ©2013 by Aimee Mullins. Reprinted by permission of Hachette Books.

Harold Ober Associates. "Thank You, M'am" and "Mother to Son" reprinted by permission of Harold Ober Associates Incorporated. Copyright ©1994 by The Estate of Langston Hughes; "One Friday Morning" and "Thank You, M'am" from *Short Stories* by Langston Hughes. Copyright ©1996 by Ramona Bass and Arnold Rampersad. Reprinted by permission of Harold Ober Associates.

HarperCollins Publishers. Excerpt from pp. 147-9 from *An American Childhood* by Annie Dillard. Copyright ©1987 by Annie Dillard. Reprinted by permission of HarperCollins Publishers.

Houghton Mifflin Harcourt Publishing Co. "Science-Fiction Cradlesong" from *Poems* by C.S. Lewis. Copyright ©1964 by the Executors of the Estate of C.S. Lewis and renewed 1992 by C.S. Lewis Pte Ltd. Reprinted by permission of Houghton Mifflin Harcourt Publishing Company. All rights reserved; "A Fable for Tomorrow" from *Silent Spring* by Rachel Carson. Copyright ©1962 by Rachel L. Carson, renewed 1990 by Roger Christie. Reprinted by permission of Houghton Mifflin Harcourt Publishing Company. All rights reserved.

International Publishers. Adapted from "Little Things Are Big" from *A Puerto Rican in New York and Other Sketches* by Jesus Colon. Copyright ©1982. Used with permission of International Publishers.

Jemison, Mae Carol. Mae Jemison "Starship" courtesy of Dorothy Jemison Foundation for Excellence.

Johnson, Sophie. "'Gotcha Day' Isn't a Cause for Celebration" by Sophie Johnson, from *Huffington Post*, November 3, 2014. Used with permission of the author.

Jones, Stanleigh. "He—y, Come On Ou—t!" from *The Best Japanese Science Fiction Stories* by Shinichi Hoshi, translated by Stanleigh Jones. Reprinted by permission of the translator.

Lerner Publications Company. "Robin Hood: Outlaw of Sherwood Forest" by Paul D. Storrie. Copyright ©2007 by Millbrook Press, Inc. Reprinted with the permission of Graphic Universe, a division of Lerner Publishing group, Inc. All rights reserved. No part of this excerpt may be used or reproduced in any manner whatsoever without the prior written permission of Lerner Publishing Group, Inc.

Little, Brown and Co. (UK). *From Mom & Me & Mom* by Maya Angelou. Copyright ©Maya Angelou. Used with permission of Little, Brown Book Group Ltd.

Malala Fund. "Malala Yousafzai United Nations Speech" reproduced with permission of Curtis Brown Group Ltd, London, on behalf of Malala Yousafzai. Copyright ©Malala Yousafzai, 2013.

McCormick, John. "Bridging the Generational Divide between a Football Father and a Soccer Son" by John McCormick, originally appeared in *Huffington Post*, September 30, 1014. Used with permission of the author. John McCormick has been a contributing blogger to the *Huffington Post* since 2012, writing a month column for the *Post's* Parents page. He is also the author of *Dad, Tell Me a Story: How to Revive the Tradition of Storytelling with Your Children* (Nicasio Press 2013). The book contains 25 stories he created with his own two sons, and provides guidance to parents on how to create a storytelling tradition in their own families.

Minna Murra, Inc. *The Last Dog* by Katherine Paterson. Copyright ©1999 by Minna Murra, Inc. Used by permission of PearlCo Literary Agency, LLC.